SOMETHING ABOUT THE AUTHOR®

Something about
the Author *was named
an "**Outstanding
Reference Source,**"
the highest honor given
by the American
Library Association
Reference and Adult
Services Division.*

ISSN 0276-816X

something ABOUT THE AUTHOR®

**Facts and Pictures about Authors
and Illustrators of Books for Young People**

volume 221

GALE
CENGAGE Learning™

Detroit • New York • San Francisco • New Haven, Conn • Waterville, Maine • London

GALE
CENGAGE Learning

Something about the Author, Volume 221

Project Editor: Lisa Kumar

Editorial: Laura Avery, Pamela Bow, Jim Craddock, Amy Fuller, Andrea Henderson, Margaret Mazurkiewicz, Tracie Moy, Jeff Muhr, Kathy Nemeh, Mary Ruby, Mike Tyrkus

Permissions: Leitha Etheridge-Sims, Tracie Richardson

Imaging and Multimedia: Leitha Etheridge-Sims, Aja Perales

Composition and Electronic Capture: Amy Darga

Manufacturing: Drew Kalasky

Product Manager: Janet Witalec

For product information and technology assistance, contact us at
Gale Customer Support, 1-800-877-4253.
For permission to use material from this text or product,
submit all requests online at **www.cengage.com/permissions.**
Further permissions questions can be emailed to
permissionrequest@cengage.com

Since this page cannot legibly accommodate all copyright notices, the acknowledgments constitute an extension of the copyright notice.

While every effort has been made to ensure the reliability of the information presented in this publication, Gale, a part of Cengage Learning, does not guarantee the accuracy of the data contained herein. Gale accepts no payment for listing; and inclusion in the publication of any organization, agency, institution, publication, service, or individual does not imply endorsement of the editors or publisher. Errors brought to the attention of the publisher and verified to the satisfaction of the publisher will be corrected in future editions.

EDITORIAL DATA PRIVACY POLICY: Does this publication contain information about you as an individual? If so, for more information about our editorial data privacy policies, please see our Privacy Statement at www.gale.cengage.com.

Gale, Cengage Learning
27500 Drake Rd.
Farmington Hills, MI, 48331-3535

LIBRARY OF CONGRESS CATALOG CARD NUMBER 62-52046

ISBN-13: 978-1-4144-6124-3
ISBN-10: 1-4144-6124-0

ISSN 0276-816X

This title is also available as an e-book.
ISBN-13: 978-1-4144-6453-4
ISBN-10: 1-4144-6453-3
Contact your Gale, Cengage Learning sales representative for ordering information.

Printed in Mexico
1 2 3 4 5 6 7 15 14 13 12 11

Contents

Authors in Forthcoming Volumes vii

Introduction ix

SATA Product Advisory Board xi

Illustrations Index 185

Author Index 221

B

Balog, Cyn 1

Beguine, Anna
  See Saintcrow, Lilith 160

Beha, Eileen 3

Beil, Karen Magnuson 1950- 4

Bently, Peter 1960- 8

Berger, Joe 1970- 8

Boie, Kirsten 1950- 10

Borris, Albert 12

Brennan, Sarah Rees 1983- 13

Brown, Paul 1942- 15

Bruno, Elsa Knight 1935-2009 15

Buehner, Mark 1959- 16

C

Caletti, Deb 1963- 21

Cleminson, Katie 25

Cochran, Josh 26

Crelin, Bob 1959(?)- 27

D

Davis, Heather 1970- 30

Deeble, Jason 1979- 32

de Las Casas, Dianne 1970- 32

De Muth, Roger 1948- 34

Doodler, Todd H.
  See Goldman, Todd Harris 50

Dunn, Herb
  See Gutman, Dan 58

Dunstan Muller, Rachel 36

F

Feig, Paul 1962- 38

Feldman, Eve B. 40

Fleming, Sally
  See Walker, Sally M. 173

Ford, John C. 1971- 42

Frazer, Megan 1977- 44

Frazier, Craig 1955- 45

Fucile, Tony 48

G

Goldman, Todd Harris 50

Goodrich, Carter 1959(?)- 51

Greene, Stephanie 1950- 53

Gutman, Dan 1955- 58

H

Haig, Matt 1975- 65

Harbour, Elizabeth 1968- 67

Haseley, Dennis 1950- 69

Hennesy, Carolyn 1962- 75

Himmelman, John 1959- 77

Hoestlandt, Jo 1948- 83

Hoestlandt, Jocelyne
  See Hoestlandt, Jo 83

Holland, Trish 85

Holt, K.A.
  See Roy, Kari Anne 158

I

Ibbotson, Eva 1925-2010 88

J

Jarka, Jeff 94

Jolivet, Joélle 1965- 95

Jordan, Devin 97

K

Kane, Kim 1973(?)- 98

Klise, Kate 1963- 99

Kneen, Maggie 1957- 103

Krenina, Katya 1968- 106

L

Lachenmeyer, Nathaniel 1969- 109

LaFleur, Suzanne 1983- 111

Lang, Glenna 1951- 112

Laroche, Giles 1956- 115

Littman, Sarah Darer 1963- 118

Liu, Cynthea 119

Logsted, Greg 120

London, Jonathan 1947- 121

Lynch, Janet Nichols 1952- 129

M

Mantchev, Lisa 132

Masse, Josée 133

Matthews, Cecily 1945- 135

McDonnell, Patrick 1956- 136

Meyer, L.A. 1942- 139

Meyer, Louis A.
See Meyer, L.A. 139

Mortensen, Lori 1955- 142

Munsinger, Lynn 1951- 145

N

Neff, Henry H. 1973- 153

Nichols, Janet
See Lynch, Janet Nichols 129

O

O'Shaughnessy, Tam 1951- 154

R

Robbins, Jacqui 157

Roy, Kari Anne 1977(?)- 158

S

Saintcrow, Lilith 1976- 160

Schlossberg, Elisabeth 161

Sherwood, Jonathan
See London, Jonathan 121

Sill, Cathryn 1953- 162

Slade, Arthur G. 1967- 164

Slade, Arthur Gregory
See Slade, Arthur G. 164

Slayton, Fran Cannon 168

St. Crow, Lili
See Saintcrow, Lilith 160

T

Taylor, Greg 1951- 171

U

Usher, Mark David
See Usher, M.D. 172

Usher, M.D. 1966- 172

W

Walker, Sally M. 1954- 173

Wang, Lin 1973- 179

Wilson, Karma 179

Authors in Forthcoming Volumes

Below are some of the authors and illustrators that will be featured in upcoming volumes of *SATA*. These include new entries on the swiftly rising stars of the field, as well as completely revised and updated entries (indicated with *) on some of the most notable and best-loved creators of books for children.

*Chitra Banerjee Divakaruni ▮ Divakaruni draws on her own experiences in the portrayals of immigrant Indian women that appear in her award-winning poetry and novels, including *The Palace of Illusions, The Mistress of Spices,* and *One Amazing Thing.* Her middle-grade novels *The Conch Bearer, The Mirror of Fire and Dreaming,* and *Shadowland,* are part Divakaruni's "Brotherhood of the Conch" series and focus on a young teen who finds himself navigating a world of magic infused with Hindu tradition.

*Mordicai Gerstein ▮ Gerstein is the author and illustrator of dozens of books for young readers, among them *Arnold of the Ducks, What Charlie Heard,* and *A Book.* In addition, he has provided the artwork for numerous works by other writers, including popular collaborator Elizabeth Levy. Before he became a writer, Gerstein worked for many years in animation and this experience inspires many of his illustrations. In 2004, he was awarded the prestigious Caldecott Medal for his original picture book *The Man Who Walked between the Towers.*

*G. Brian Karas ▮ Karas has channeled his early interest in art into a successful career as an award-winning illustrator and author of children's books. Karas's distinctive, child-centered illustrations—a blend of pencil, gouache, and pastel—have garnered accolades for their humor, energy, and inventiveness, and have appeared in titles that range from Kobayashi Issa's nostalgic *Today and Today* and Susan Orlean's humorous *Lazy Little Loafers* to Karas's own picture-book take on Greek mythology, *Young Zeus.*

Yossi Leshem ▮ An ornithologist and environmentalist, Leshem used his interest in bird migration to produce a practical result in his native Israel. The Israeli Air Force incurred millions of dollars in damages as well as loss of human life due to bird-aircraft collisions before the scientist found a unique solution, and he outlines his important work in the co-authored picture book *The Man Who Flies with Birds.* A staunch conservationist, Leshem has also worked with Palestine and Jordan to promote the use of birds for agricultural pest control and he has established educational programs focusing on bird migration throughout Israel.

Anna Malaspina ▮ As a lifelong traveler, nonfiction writer Malaspina has visited many interesting places around the world, and she shares her insights in her books *Mahatma Gandhi and India's Independence in World History* and *Tsunamis.* Travel has also inspired her fictional stories *Finding Lincoln* and *Yasmin's Hammer,* the latter a picture book that focuses on a Bangladeshi girl who dreams of going to school while working as a brick chipper to support her family. Brought to life in Doug Chayka's colorful oil paintings, *Yasmin's Hammer* captures the optimism of a young heroine through a free-verse text that reviewers have praised for its realism and sensitivity.

Kaleb Nation ▮ In addition to hosting a radio program, producing YouTube videos, and creating Web logs, Nation also authored his first novel, *The Farfield Curse,* before he reached the age of twenty. Inspired by the popularity of J.K. Rowling's "Harry Potter" novels, *The Farfield Curse* is the first novel in Nation's "Bran Hambric" series and creates a middle-school-friendly mix of magic, adventure, and comeraderie.

Janet Perlman ▮ The short films of Canadian animator and author Perlman have earned her both awards and audience recognition at festivals throughout the world. In addition to directing, designing, and producing animated shorts such as *The Tender Tale of Cinderella Penguin,* and *Invasion of the Space Lobsters,* Perlman also retells several well-known fairy tales with an all-penguin cast in the humorous stories *Cinderella Penguin; or, The Little Glass Flipper, The Penguin and the Pea,* and *The Emperor Penguin's New Clothes.*

*Amy Krouse Rosenthal ▮ A Chicago-based freelance writer, blogger, and commentator, Rosenthal also contributes to National Public Radio, and has co-founded her own T-shirt company. *Little Pea,* the first picture book by this imaginative author, has been followed by numerous other books, among them *The OK Book, Little Oink, Spoon,* and *Cookies: Bite-size Life Lessons.* A collaboration with artist Paul Schmid, *The Wonder Book,* is a verbal concoction that mixes poems and stories, lists and musings, as well as palindromes and entertaining cartoons that capture the ups and downs of childhood.

Katie Van Camp ▮ While she was working as a nanny for the young son of television personality David Letterman, Van Camp was won over by the toddler's love of his beloved stuffed animal, Horsie, as well as by his curiosity. She captures Harry's affectionate spirit in *Harry and Horsie,* which began as a poem and became a picture book with artwork by Canadian illustrator Lincoln Agnew. Another Agnew-Van Camp collaboration, *Cookiebot,* also showcases her whimsical skills as a storyteller.

Dave Whamond ▮ Whamond, the award-winning creator of the "Reality Check" comic strip, has also earned praise for his contributions to the world of children's books. Whamond is the author and illustrator of *My Think-a-Ma-Jink,* a Reuben award winner, and he also creates the humorous illustrations for the popular "Hot Dog and Bob" series of chapter books, which are written by L. Bob Rovetch and include *Hot Dog and Bob and the Particularly Pesky Attack of the Pencil People* and *Hot Dog and Bob and the Surprisingly Slobbery Attack of the Dog-wash Doggies.*

Introduction

Something about the Author (*SATA*) is an ongoing reference series that examines the lives and works of authors and illustrators of books for children. *SATA* includes not only well-known writers and artists but also less prominent individuals whose works are just coming to be recognized. This series is often the only readily available information source on emerging authors and illustrators. You'll find *SATA* informative and entertaining, whether you are a student, a librarian, an English teacher, a parent, or simply an adult who enjoys children's literature.

What's Inside *SATA*

SATA provides detailed information about authors and illustrators who span the full time range of children's literature, from early figures like John Newbery and L. Frank Baum to contemporary figures like Judy Blume and Richard Peck. Authors in the series represent primarily English-speaking countries, particularly the United States, Canada, and the United Kingdom. Also included, however, are authors from around the world whose works are available in English translation. The writings represented in *SATA* include those created intentionally for children and young adults as well as those written for a general audience and known to interest younger readers. These writings cover the entire spectrum of children's literature, including picture books, humor, folk and fairy tales, animal stories, mystery and adventure, science fiction and fantasy, historical fiction, poetry and nonsense verse, drama, biography, and nonfiction. Obituaries are also included in *SATA* and are intended not only as death notices but also as concise overviews of people's lives and work. Additionally, each edition features newly revised and updated entries for a selection of *SATA* listees who remain of interest to today's readers and who have been active enough to require extensive revisions of their earlier biographies.

Autobiography Feature

Beginning with Volume 103, many volumes of *SATA* feature one or more specially commissioned autobiographical essays. These unique essays, averaging about ten thousand words in length and illustrated with an abundance of personal photos, present an entertaining and informative first-person perspective on the lives and careers of prominent authors and illustrators profiled in *SATA*.

Two Convenient Indexes

In response to suggestions from librarians, *SATA* indexes no longer appear in every volume but are included in alternate (odd-numbered) volumes of the series, beginning with Volume 57.

SATA continues to include two indexes that cumulate with each alternate volume: the Illustrations Index, arranged by the name of the illustrator, gives the number of the volume and page where the illustrator's work appears in the current volume as well as all preceding volumes in the series; the Author Index gives the number of the volume in which a person's biographical sketch, autobiographical essay, or obituary appears in the current volume as well as all preceding volumes in the series.

These indexes also include references to authors and illustrators who appear in *Gale's Yesterday's Authors of Books for Children, Children's Literature Review,* and *Something about the Author Autobiography Series*.

Easy-to-Use Entry Format

Whether you're already familiar with the *SATA* series or just getting acquainted, you will want to be aware of the kind of information that an entry provides. In every *SATA* entry the editors attempt to give as complete a picture of the person's life and work as possible. A typical entry in *SATA* includes the following clearly labeled information sections:

PERSONAL: date and place of birth and death, parents' names and occupations, name of spouse, date of marriage, names of children, educational institutions attended, degrees received, religious and political affiliations, hobbies and other interests.

ADDRESSES: complete home, office, electronic mail, and agent addresses, whenever available.

CAREER: name of employer, position, and dates for each career post; art exhibitions; military service; memberships and offices held in professional and civic organizations.

MEMBER: professional, civic, and other association memberships and any official posts held.

AWARDS, HONORS: literary and professional awards received.

WRITINGS: title-by-title chronological bibliography of books written and/or illustrated, listed by genre when known; lists of other notable publications, such as plays, screenplays, and periodical contributions.

ADAPTATIONS: a list of films, television programs, plays, CD-ROMs, recordings, and other media presentations that have been adapted from the author's work.

WORK IN PROGRESS: description of projects in progress.

SIDELIGHTS: a biographical portrait of the author or illustrator's development, either directly from the biographee—and often written specifically for the *SATA* entry—or gathered from diaries, letters, interviews, or other published sources.

BIOGRAPHICAL AND CRITICAL SOURCES: cites sources quoted in "Sidelights" along with references for further reading.

EXTENSIVE ILLUSTRATIONS: photographs, movie stills, book illustrations, and other interesting visual materials supplement the text.

How a *SATA* Entry Is Compiled

SATA editors examine a wide variety of published sources to gather information for an entry. Biographical and bibliographic sources are consulted, as are book reviews, feature articles, published interviews, and material sometimes obtained from the biographee's family, publishers, agent, or other associates. Whenever possible, the author or illustrator is sent a copy of the entry to check for accuracy and completeness.

Entries that have not been verified by the biographees or their representatives are marked with an asterisk (*).

Contact the Editor

We encourage our readers to examine the entire *SATA* series. Please write and tell us if we can make *SATA* even more helpful to you. Give your comments and suggestions to the editor:

Editor
Something about the Author
Gale, Cengage Learning
27500 Drake Rd.
Farmington Hills MI 48331-3535

Toll-free: 800-877-GALE
Fax: 248-699-8070

Something about the Author Product Advisory Board

The editors of *Something about the Author* are dedicated to maintaining a high standard of excellence by publishing comprehensive, accurate, and highly readable entries on a wide array of writers for children and young adults. In addition to the quality of the content, the editors take pride in the graphic design of the series, which is intended to be orderly yet inviting, allowing readers to utilize the pages of *SATA* easily and with efficiency. Despite the longevity of the *SATA* print series, and the success of its format, we are mindful that the vitality of a literary reference product is dependent on its ability to serve its users over time. As literature, and attitudes about literature, constantly evolve, so do the reference needs of students, teachers, scholars, journalists, researchers, and book club members. To be certain that we continue to keep pace with the expectations of our customers, the editors of *SATA* listen carefully to their comments regarding the value, utility, and quality of the series. Librarians, who have firsthand knowledge of the needs of library users, are a valuable resource for us. The *Something about the Author* Product Advisory Board, made up of school, public, and academic librarians, is a forum to promote focused feedback about *SATA* on a regular basis. The nine-member advisory board includes the following individuals, whom the editors wish to thank for sharing their expertise:

Eva M. Davis
Director,
Canton Public Library,
Canton, Michigan

Joan B. Eisenberg
Lower School Librarian,
Milton Academy,
Milton, Massachusetts

Francisca Goldsmith
Teen Services Librarian,
Berkeley Public Library,
Berkeley, California

Susan Dove Lempke
Children's Services Supervisor,
Niles Public Library District,
Niles, Illinois

Robyn Lupa
Head of Children's Services,
Jefferson County Public Library,
Lakewood, Colorado

Victor L. Schill
Assistant Branch Librarian/Children's Librarian,
Harris County Public Library/Fairbanks Branch,
Houston, Texas

Caryn Sipos
Community Librarian,
Three Creeks Community Library,
Vancouver, Washington

Steven Weiner
Director,
Maynard Public Library,
Maynard, Massachusetts

soмeтнiнg
AвоυT тнe
AυThoR

BALOG, Cyn

Personal

Born in Edison, NJ; married; children: two daughters. *Education:* Douglass College of Rutgers University, bachelor's degree (communications).

Addresses

Home—Quakertown, PA. *Agent*—Jim McCarthy, Dystel & Goderich, One Union Square West, Ste. 904, New York, NY 10003. *E-mail*—cyn@cynbalog.com.

Career

Author. Presenter at schools.

Writings

YOUNG-ADULT NOVELS

Fairy Tale, Delacorte Press (New York, NY), 2009.
Sleepless, Delacorte Press (New York, NY), 2010.
Starstruck, Delacorte Press (New York, NY), 2011.
Living Backwards, Delacorte Press (New York, NY), 2012.

Sidelights

After graduating from college with a degree in communications, Cyn Balog worked for a variety of companies before deciding that channeling her storytelling skills

Cyn Balog (Photograph by Christine McDonald. Reproduced by permission.)

Cover of Balog's young-adult novel **Fairy Tale,** *which finds a teen's romance derailed when her boyfriend undergoes an unexpected transformation.* (Delacorte Press 2009. Used by permission of Delcorte Press, an imprint of Random House Children's Books, a division of Random House, Inc.)

into a career was more to her liking. Although her first manuscript did not find a publisher, it did link Balog up with the agent who would ultimately find a publisher interested in her second manuscript. Geared for teen readers, that second manuscript became Balog's debut novel *Fairy Tale.* It has been followed by several more novels, including *Sleepless* and *Starstruck.*

In *Fairy Tale* readers meet Morgan Sparks and Cameron Browne, two high schoolers who seem destined for each other. Not only were they born on the same day, but they have been best friends forever and their feelings are turning romantic. However, just before they both turn sixteen years old, Morgan senses that Cameron has changed. A confrontation with his cousin, Pip, confirms Morgan's feelings, but also leaves her with few options for keeping her football-star boyfriend. In fact, Cameron is a fairy prince who has been called upon to leave human society and rule the fairy people of the Otherworld. Fortunately, Morgan's psychic ability allows her to perceive Cameron's slow transition, which involves growing wings and shrinking down to fairy size, and this ability may serve her well in her efforts to save their relationship. In *School Library Jour-*

nal Megan Honig noted the mix of "pathos" and comedy in *Fairy Tale,* praising the story for "a few choice witticisms and touching moments." "Morgan's flip first-person narration is hilarious," commented Krista Hutley in a *Booklist* review of the same novel, the critic also citing Balog's ability to create a heroine with a "distinctively funny voice."

From fairies Balog turns to another magical creature in *Sleepless.* For Julia, the death of her boyfriend Griffin in a car accident has left her feeling abandoned and alone. Little does she realize that someone—or something—has always been at her side: her Sandman, Eron DeMarchelle. In addition to coaxing Julia to sleep each night, Eron has also fallen in love with the young woman over time. Now, while witnessing her sadness, he also worries that he will be forced to leave as well, for his hundred-year stint as a sandman is about to come to an end. When his replacement turns out to be the newly deceased Griffin, Eron determines to find a way to remain with Julia, even though his efforts put their future relationship at risk. Describing Julia as "a smart heroine" and recommending the alternate narratives of the "star-crossed" lovers, Jessica Miller described *Sleepless* in *School Library Journal* as "an interesting, quick-paced, and compelling paranormal romance."

Biographical and Critical Sources

PERIODICALS

Booklist, May 15, 2009, Krista Hutley, review of *Fairy Tale,* p. 48.
Kirkus Reviews, May 1, 2009, review of *Fairy Tale.*
New York Times Book Review, November 8, 2009, Regina Marler, review of *Fairy Tale,* p. 27.
Publishers Weekly, June 29, 2009, review of *Fairy Tale,* p. 130.
School Library Journal, December, 2009, Megan Honig, review of *Fairy Tale,* p. 106; August, 2010, Jessica Miller, review of *Sleepless,* p. 94.

ONLINE

Cyn Balog Home Page, http://www.cynbalog.com (October 15, 2010).
Cyn Balog Web Log, http://cyn2write.livejournal.com/ (October 15, 2010).
Cynsations Web Log, http://cynthialeitichsmith.blogspot.com/ (October 27, 2009), Cynthia Leitich Smith, interview with Balog.*

*   *   *

BEGUINE, Anna
See SAINTCROW, Lilith

BEHA, Eileen

Personal

Born in WI; married Ralph Beha; children: four. *Education:* Bachelor's degree; Hamline University, M.F.A. (creative writing). *Hobbies and other interests:* Animals.

Addresses

Home—Minneapolis, MN. *E-mail*—tango@eileen beha.com.

Career

Author. Former middle-school principal.

Awards, Honors

Great Stone Face Award nomination, 2011, for *Tango.*

Writings

Tango: The Tale of an Island Dog, Bloomsbury (New York, NY), 2009.

Adaptations

Tango was adapted for audiobook, read by Kimberly Farr, Audio Books, 2009.

Sidelights

In writing *Tango: The Tale of an Island Dog* former middle-school principal Eileen Beha was inspired by her own dog, a Yorkshire terrier. The pup's luck took him from the puppy mill where he was born to a New Hampshire pet store, and from there to the home of Beha's daughter, then living in New York City, before he wound up in the arms of the Wisconsin-based author. *Tango* was also inspired by Beha's love of animals and her memories of summers spent on Canada's Prince Edward Island. The story was sparked by her habit of thinking "What if . . . ?" In this case, what if a small and pampered dog from the big city is transported to a rustic fishing village? Luck plays its part, as readers find out in *Tango.*

Set on Prince Edward Island, *Tango* introduces an engaging Yorkshire terrier who is the spoiled pet of a couple living in New York City. In the tradition of the three pets in Sheila Burnford's *The Incredible Journey,* Tango is separated from his family during a sailing trip, and he washes up on the island's coast, cold, wet, and tangled in a lobster trap. The shivering pup is discovered by a fisherman's widowed wife who takes him in and feeds him. While dealing with all the unfamiliar things in his new rural home, Tango makes enemies of an evil rat named Malachi and a pack of feral cats but befriends a local fox and a preteen runaway named McKenna. Slowly, his dreams of returning to his city home are replaced by a love of these new friends in a novel that weaves "themes of loyalty, courage, and belonging . . . throughout the exciting plot twists," according to *School Library Journal* critic Carol Schene. In *Kirkus Reviews* a contributor commended *Tango* for its "precisely drawn characters," and concluded that Beha's "beguiling, delicately told tale . . . has a heart as big as its hero's."

Biographical and Critical Sources

PERIODICALS

Kirkus Reviews, May 1, 2009, review of *Tango: The Tale of an Island Dog.*
School Library Journal, July, 2009, Carol Schene, review of *Tango,* p. 78.

In Tango *Eileen Beha tells her own version of a little dog's incredible journey.* (Photograph of dog © Jamie Grill/Getty Images. Photograph of harbor © Grant Faint/Getty Images. Jacket design by Donna Mark. Reprinted by permission of Bloomsbury Publishing Inc. All rights reserved.)

ONLINE

Eileen Beha Home Page, http://www.eileenbeha.com (October 15, 2010).*

* * *

BEIL, Karen Magnuson 1950-

Personal

Born February 15, 1950, in Boston, MA; daughter of Victor Berger and Dorothy Magnuson; married James A. Beil (a forester), February 24, 1973; children: Kimberly Erika, Kirsten Annika. *Education:* Attended Upsala College, 1967-68; Syracuse University, B.A. (magazine journalism and English literature; cum laude), 1971.

Addresses

Home—Upstate NY. *E-mail*—KarenBeil@aol.com; info@karenbeil.com.

Career

Author and editor. City News Bureau, Chicago, IL, reporter, 1971-72; New York State Department of Environmental Conservation, Albany, research editor, 1973-75, assistant editor, 1975-76, editor, 1976-78, associate director of information services for *Conservationist* and *New York State Environmental Notice Bulletin,* 1978-81; freelance writer and editor, 1981—. Presenter at schools.

Member

Society of Children's Book Writers and Illustrators, Children's Literary Connection (cofounder, 1998, and vice president, treasurer, and member of executive board of directors), National Audubon Society, Cape Cod Museum of Natural History.

Awards, Honors

Top Nonfiction designation, National Council of Teachers of English, and Quick Pick for Reluctant Readers selection, American Library Association, both 1999, both for *Fire in Their Eyes;* Best Books designation, Bank Street College of Education, 2008, for *Jack's House.*

Writings

FOR CHILDREN

Grandma according to Me, illustrated by Ted Rand, Doubleday (New York, NY), 1992.

A Cake All for Me!, illustrated by Paul Meisel, Holiday House (New York, NY), 1998.

Fire in Their Eyes: Wildfires and the People Who Fight Them, Harcourt Brace (San Diego, CA), 1999.

Mooove Over!: A Book about Counting by Twos, illustrated by Paul Meisel, Holiday House (New York, NY), 2004.

Jack's House, illustrated by Mike Wohnoutka, Holiday House (New York, NY), 2008.

Contributor to periodicals, including *Conservationist.*

Sidelights

Based in upstate New York, Karen Magnuson Beil is a freelance editor and writer who continues to entertain young children with her engaging children's books. In addition to picture books such as *Grandma according to Me, A Cake All for Me!,* and *Jack's House,* Beil also taps her journalism skills and her interest in nature to write *Fire in Their Eyes: Wildfires and the People Who Fight Them,* while *Mooove Over!: A Book about Counting by Twos* presents basic concepts in an entertaining fashion.

Illustrated by Ted Rand, Beil's *Grandma according to Me* portrays how a preschooler views her grandmother. The little girl finds her grandmother beautiful, as the elderly woman has a "comfortable" figure and "story lines" rather than wrinkles. "The childlike text contains several striking images," wrote Joy Fleishhacker in *School Library Journal,* adding that the book conveys a "warmhearted mood." *Booklist* contributor Christie Sylvester observed that *Grandma according to Me* is "lovingly told from the child's point of view."

School Library Journal contributor Pamela K. Bomboy called Beil's *A Cake All for Me!* "a tasty treat." The story features a pig that initially bakes a cake for itself, but later decides to share its treat with visiting friends. Beil uses counting rhyme to tell readers how to make the cake: "One, two, get out the moo./Three, four, open and pour." Illustrator Paul Meisel depicts the happy chef sifting and mixing ingredients and performing other baking-related tasks. A *Publishers Weekly* reviewer commented that the book contains "high spirits and simple pleasures." For hungry readers, *A Cake All for Me!* includes recipes for a cake and frosting.

Beil wrote her nonfiction picture book *Fire in Their Eyes* for slightly older children. The author has a background in environmental conservation and she includes her own photographs in the book. In text and images, she reveals the work of smoke jumpers, brave people who parachute from airplanes to fight forest fires in remote areas of the United States. Dramatic photographs reflect her account and include a tree exploding in flames and a man repairing his parachute. Beil interviewed many smoke jumpers in researching the book, and her text describes their training, methods, and tools. In praise of her efforts, *Booklist* contributor Randy

Meyer wrote that *Fire in Their Eyes* evokes "the drama, excitement, and danger" that characterize the life of these dedicated firefighters.

A cow pushes its way onto a crowded trolley-car in *Mooove Over!*, another picture book by Beil that is illustrated by Meisel. Full of animals of all sorts grouped in even numbers from two to ten, the Countingtown Trolley is ready to roll and all twenty seats are full. When a bossy Bessy in a purple dress attempts to board the trolley, chaos abounds in Beil's animated counting story. In *School Library Journal* Laurie Edwards cited "Meisel's energetic and humorous acrylic illustrations" and concluded that *Mooove Over!* will leave toddlers laughing "as they practice counting by twos."

Brought to life in Mike Wohnoutka's digital cartoon art, *Jack's House* treats readers to what *School Library Journal* critic Susan E. Murray dubbed "a wonderful twist on an age-old rhyme." As readers follow the activities of busy Jack and his construction-savvy team of fellow dogs led by the hardworking Max, they learn how to build a house from the foundation up. When Jack tries to take all the credit for the project, Max plays a trick that "results in a laugh-out-loud moment," according to Murray. With Wohnoutka's colorful pictures of con-

struction machines paired with a text that "chugs along with no surprises," *Jack's House* will entrance fans of "trucks and other big wheels," according to a *Kirkus Reviews* writer.

Beil once told *SATA:* "I grew up in the hills of Connecticut, the only child in a family of story-loving, creative people. My mother was a children's librarian and bird carver (shore birds, not turkeys). My father, ready with a poem, joke, or story for every occasion, brought history to life with stories of his sailing days during the Great Depression of the 1930s. My aunts were children's book illustrators. Books were essential, like food, in my family.

"When I was five, I loved stories and books—their language, their rhythm, their energy. My mother eagerly obliged reading my favorites over and over. But when I was six, Dick, Jane, and their lifeless pets, Spot and Fluff, taught me that reading was dull. I learned to hate to read. Lucky for me, Mother was tenacious. Unlucky for her and probably embarrassing too (she was the librarian in my elementary school), I preferred to do most anything but read. By the time I was nine, she was waging a quiet war, sneaking the latest books into my room, inviting authors to our school: Elizabeth

Karen Magnuson Beil's tale of hungry piggies comes to life in Paul Meisel's art for **A Cake All for Me!** (Holiday House, Inc., 1998. Illustrations copyright © 1998 by Paul Meisel. Reproduced by permission.)

Beil's boy-friendly picture book **Jack's House** *comes to life in Mike Wohnoutka's engaging illustrations.* (Text copyright © 2008 by Karen Magnuson Beil, Illustrations copyright © 2008 by Mike Wohnoutka. Reproduced by permission of Holiday House, Inc.)

George Speare, Oliver Butterworth, and even her old childhood friend Virginia Haviland, folktale collector and children's librarian for the Library of Congress. She was invincible. I didn't stand a chance.

"After school one day my mother asked me to shelve some library books while she went to a meeting. I picked up a biography of Jane Adams, illustrated in black silhouettes. I read the first page and couldn't put it down. This 'Jane' saved people. She never said dumb stuff like 'Look Dick, look. See Spot run.' After I'd read all the biographies in my mother's library, I moved on to historical fiction, nature stories, adventure, and all the rest.

"From then on my favorite trips of summer were our excursions to buy library books at the H.R. Huntting bookbindery in Chicopee, Massachusetts. There, my mother's fried Ben Silberman always let me choose two books to take home—gifts from him to his only school-age customer. Like a mouse searching for the perfect piece of cheese, I would wander the maze of warehouse book stacks all day to make my choices.

"After graduating from college, I searched Chicago for a job. I failed miserably at dreaming up a mattress commercial (it put the boss to sleep). I tried editing a college math textbook (let's just say, math was the only course I managed not to pass in college—I was too

busy reading). I finally landed a job as a news reporter. My first assignment: a five-alarm fire. Gosh, I was a country kid. What's five-alarm? Very spicy chili? What a terrific job that turned out to be. I learned to meet fast deadlines and to interview people—cops, robbers, con artists, judges—to ask the tough questions (and to read upside down).

"When our first daughter turned two, I left my day job as an editor to learn how to make play-dough. While I was practicing my defensive maneuvers to duck flying food, my daughter was learning how easy it was to delay bedtime by sweet-talking me into reading books. And I fell in love all over again with the rhythms and art and beautiful language of children's books.

"I already had a stack of rejected manuscripts before my mother asked me to write a book about wrinkles. *Grandma according to Me* was written for her. Her friends had been talking about their grandkids. One told her grandmother her skin 'didn't fit her face any more.' Another was worried that her grandmother's face had 'cracked.' Try as I might, I couldn't turn an explanation of wrinkles into an exciting book. So I took it from a different angle. How do people see themselves? How does a granddaughter see her grandmother? Is it different from the grandmother's view of herself? As I thought about my mother's relationship with my daughters, the book seemed to write itself. It was a personal tribute to my mother and a celebration of the special relationship between grandmothers and granddaughters. I love that teachers use it to teach point of view. I'm delighted how many people ask me to sign this book for their mothers and grandmothers. Best of all was the first grader who 'loved it because it made (him) feel.'

"I loved working on *Fire in Their Eyes*. It was an adventure right from the start. The idea grabbed me over dinner one night as I listened to my husband and friends talk about fighting forest fires in California. Their stories had everything—adventure, danger, nature, and heroes who were both men and women. I could hardly wait to get home to start making notes. I wanted to write a book that would keep kids on the edges of their seats, just as I'd been. To do this, I needed first-hand experience. So I worked two seasons on a prescribed burn crew. I interviewed firefighters across the country. I photographed new smokejumpers at a tough training camp in Montana. Ten years later, the research and interviews were done. Then the hardest part became deciding which stories to leave out so there'd be room for photos in the sixty-four-page book.

"*A Cake All for Me,* about a hungry pig who bakes a cake all for himself, came from playing with words one morning. A little handmade book sat on my desk that my aunt, Bette Darwin (illustrator of Beverly Cleary's book, *Socks*), had made for me. An old rhyme showed up in my doodles. 'One, two, buckle my shoe' always left me so unsatisfied as a child because it never made sense. 'A big fat hen? Dig and delve? Maids a-court-

ing?' Huh? What? I decided to play with the form to create something fun, something that would make sense, something about counting and measuring.

"Back then my office was in a closet in my kitchen. The kitchen was the place where my daughters got their early starts experimenting in math and science. So I had my setting. And I was hungry, really hungry. So I had my character: me. (The kitchen, by the way, is not a good place to work unless you're a chef.) But when my editor asked later what kind of animal the character was, I had to confess I hadn't thought about it. She wanted an animal. So, who would eat a whole cake? Had to be a PIG! Next Piggy had to have a recipe. My younger daughter and her friends spent the rest of the summer as taste-testers. They were tough critics. Pineapple? No! Coconut? Yuck. Walnuts, lemon, chopped peanuts? No, no, no! Spinach jello? (Just kidding.) Chocolate chips? Yes! It was unanimous. After that, the book was a piece of cake."

Biographical and Critical Sources

PERIODICALS

Booklist, December 1, 1992, Christie Sylvester, review of *Grandma according to Me,* p. 674; May 1, 1999, Randy Meyer, review of *Fire in Their Eyes: Wildfires and the People Who Fight Them,* p. 1588.

Children's Book Review Service, December, 1992, review of *Grandma according to Me,* p. 37.

Children's Book Watch, November, 1992, review of *Grandma according to Me,* p. 4.

Horn Book, spring, 1993, review of *Grandma according to Me,* p. 21; March, 1999, Margaret A. Bush, review of *Fire in Their Eyes,* p. 219.

Kirkus Reviews, September 15, 2004, review of *Mooove Oover!: A Book about Counting by Twos*; August 15, 2008, review of *Jack's House.*

Publishers Weekly, August 17, 1998, review of *A Cake All for Me!,* p. 71.

School Library Journal, February, 1993, Joy Fleishacker, review of *Grandma according to Me,* p. 68; September, 1998, Pamela K. Bomboy, review of *A Cake All for Me!,* p. 164; October, 2004, Laurie Edwards, review of *Mooove Oover!,* p. 109; October, 2008, Susan E. Murray, review of *Jack's House,* p. 101.

Voice of Youth Advocates, August, 2000, review of *Fire in Their Eyes,* p. 163.

ONLINE

Children's Literature Network Web Site, http://www.childrensliteraturenetwork.org/ (October 20, 2010).

Karen Magnuson Beil Home Page, http://www.karenbeil.com (October 20, 2010).*

BENTLY, Peter 1960-

Personal

Born December 29, 1960, in Hampshire, England; married; wife's name Lucy; children: Theo, Tara. *Education:* Oxford University, degree (languages).

Addresses

Home—Totnes, England. *Agent*—Rosemary Canter, United Agents, 12-26 Lexington St., London W1F 0OE, England.

Career

Writer and editor, beginning 1992. Presenter at schools.

Awards, Honors

Roald Dahl Funny Prize shortlist, 2009, for *The Great Dog Bottom Swap;* Red House Children's Book runner up, 2009, for *A Lark in the Ark.*

Writings

(With others) *Chronicle of Aviation,* JL International Pub. (Liberty, MO), 1992.
The Book of Dream Symbols, Chronicle Books (San Francisco, CA), 1995.
A Lark in the Ark (lift-the-flap book), illustrated by Lynn Chapman, Egmont (London, England), 2008.
Shark in the Dark, illustrated by Ben Cort, Walker (New York, NY), 2009.
The Great Dog Bottom Swap, illustrated by Mei Matsuoka, Anderson (London, England), 2009.

General editor of books, including *The Dictionary of World Myth,* Facts on File (New York, NY), 1995, and *The Hutchinson Dictionary of World Myth,* Helicon/ Duncan Baird (Oxford, England), 1996.

"STARCROSS STABLES" READER SERIES

The Storm, Wayland (London, England), 2009.
Showtime, Wayland (London, England), 2009.
Rascal's Heart, Wayland (London, England), 2009.
River Rescue, Wayland (London, England), 2009.

"VAMPIRE SCHOOL" READER SERIES

Casketball Capers, Boxer Books (London, England), 2010.
Ghoul Trip, Boxer Books (London, England), 2010.

Biographical and Critical Sources

PERIODICALS

Kirkus Reviews, May 1, 2009, review of *Shark in the Dark;* May 15, 2009, review of *A Lark in the Ark.*

School Library Journal, October, 2009, Susan Lissim, review of *Shark in the Dark,* p. 86.

ONLINE

United Agents Web site, http://unitedagents.co.uk/ (October 15, 2010), "Peter Bently."*

*   *   *

BERGER, Joe 1970-

Personal

Born 1970, in England; married; children: three.

Addresses

Home—Bristol, England. *E-mail*—berger@easynet.co. uk.

Career

Author, illustrator, cartoonist, and animator.

Awards, Honors

Named UNESCO World Book Day Illustrator for UK/ Ireland, 2010.

Writings

SELF-ILLUSTRATED

Bridget Fitget, Puffin (London, England), 2008, published as *Bridget Fidget and the Most Perfect Pet!,* Dial Books for Young Readers (New York, NY), 2009.
Bridget Fidget: Hold on Tight!, Puffin (London, England), 2010.

Contributor of weekly comic strip to United Kingdom's *Guardian* newspaper.

ILLUSTRATOR

Michael Rosen, editor, *Michael Rosen's A to Z: The Best Children's Poetry from Agard to Zephaniah,* 2009.
Jane Devlin, *Hattie the Bad,* Puffin (London, England), 2009, Dial Books for Young Readers (New York, NY), 2010.
Pascal Wyse, *Wyse Words: A Dictionary for the Bewildered,* Chambers Harrap (Edinburgh, Scotland), 2009.
Jenny Valentine, *Iggy and Me,* HarperCollins (London, England), 2009.
Jenny Valentine, *Iggy and Me and the Happy Birthday,* HarperCollins (London, England), 2010.
Jenny Valentine, *Iggy and Me on Holiday,* HarperCollins (London, England), 2010.

Joe Berger (Reproduced by permission.)

Sally Norton, *101 Things to Do before You're Five,* Viking (London, England), 2010.

Pam Smallcomb, *How I (Almost) Got Rid of My Alien Pen Pal,* Dial Books for Young Readers (New York, NY), 2011.

Work featuring Berger's illustrations have been translated into French and Swedish.

Sidelights

Honored in his native United Kingdom as 2010's World Book Day Illustrator, Joe Berger is an artist and writer whose works range from animated short films to comic strips to book and CD covers. His illustration work includes the original, self-illustrated picture book *Bridget Fidget and the Most Perfect Pet!* and its sequel, *Bridget Fidget, Hold on Tight!* In addition to illustrating his own stories, Berger has also created artwork for other picture books, including Jane Devlin's *Hattie the Bad* and *How I (Almost) Got Rid of My Alien Pen Pal* by Pam Smallcomb. He has also collaborated with Pascal Wyse on *Wyse Words: A Dictionary for the Bewildered,* which is based on a column first published in the weekend edition of London's *Guardian* newspaper. Reviewing Devlin's story, Barbara Elleman wrote in *School Library Journal* that Berger's cartoon "illustrations bring a well-considered pace to the story," while a *Publishers Weekly* critic noted that the "zesty, orange-splashed illustrations" in *Hattie the Bad* "hum with energy and comic hyperbole."

First published in *Bridget Fidget, Bridget Fidget and the Most Perfect Pet!* stars what *School Library Journal*

critic Susan Weitz dubbed a "timeless cartoon poppet" who is "dreaming, dashing, fussing, laughing, [and] dragging her . . . stuffed animal everywhere." In the story, Bridget dreams of having a unicorn named Thunderhooves for her very own. The arrival of a large box gives rise to a hope that is soon dashed as Berger's story weaves to its humorous end. Bridget returns in *Bridget Fidget, Hold on Tight!,* as the girl has another emotional meltdown after she loses her favorite stuffed animal, Captain Cat, during a family shopping trip. In his books, Berger's readers are carried along by illustrations that Weitz described as "so joyfully kinetic that viewers are left breathless."

"Berger's vivacious drawings of the monomaniacal Bridget and her super-chic parents are thoroughly charming," wrote a *Kirkus Reviews* writer, while Patricia Austin noted in *Booklist* that his story "reflect[s] . . . a child's quick mood changes and often optimistic response to life." A *Publishers Weekly* contributor described Bridget as "hyperkinetic and highly imaginative," going on to noted that her creator "has an animator's eye for action." According to *Guardian* contributor Julia Eccleshare, in *Bridget Fidget* "the joy of anticipation and the disappointment that can follow are zippily charted in [Berger's] . . . vigorous story."

Biographical and Critical Sources

PERIODICALS

Booklist, June 1, 2009, Patricia Austin, review of *Bridget Fidget and the Most Perfect Pet!,* p. 62; February 15, 2010, Kara Dean, review of *Hattie the Bad,* p. 80.

Berger pairs a quirky story with his expressive cartoon art in the picture book **Bridget Fidget and the Most Perfect Pet!** (Dial 2009. Reproduced by permission of Penguin Group USA Inc.)

Guardian (London, England), February 14, 2009, Julia Eccleshare, review of *Bridget Fidget,* p. 14.

Kirkus Reviews, May 1, 2009, review of *Bridget Fidget and the Most Perfect Pet!*

Publishers Weekly, June 1, 2009, review of *Bridget Fidget and the Most Perfect Pet!,* p. 46; March 8, 2010, review of *Hattie the Bad,* p. 53.

School Library Journal, June, 2009, Susan Weitz, review of *Bridget Fidget and the Most Perfect Pet!,* p. 79; March, 2010, Barbara Elleman, review of *Hattie the Bad,* p. 117.

ONLINE

Joe Berger Home Page, http://www.joeberger.co.uk (October 15, 2010).

*   *   *

BOIE, Kirsten 1950-

Personal

Born March 19, 1950, in Hamburg, Germany; married; children. *Education:* Attended Southampton University (England); University of Hamburg, graduate degree.

Addresses

Home—Germany. *E-mail*—buero@kirsten-boie.de.

Career

Author. Secondary-school teacher in Germany, 1978-83; writer, beginning 1984.

Awards, Honors

Österreichischen Staatspreise für Kinder-und Jungendliterature, c. 1985, for *Paule ist ein Glücksgriff;* Sonderpreis des Deutschen Jungendliteraturpreises, and Großen Preis der Deutschen Akademie für Kinder-unde Jugendliteratur, both 2008.

Writings

FOR CHILDREN

Paule ist ein Glücksgriff, F. Oetinger (Hamburg, Germany), 1985.

Mit Jakob wurde alles anders, F. Oetinger (Hamburg, Germany), 1986, reprinted, Süddeutsche Zeitung (Munich, Germany), 2006.

Heinzler mögen saure Gurken, F. Oetinger (Hamburg, Germany), 1986.

Opa steht auf rosa Shorts, Mols (Knebel, Germany), 1986.

Mellin die drem Drachen befiehlt, F. Oetinger (Hamburg, Germany), 1987.

Jenny ist meistens schön friedlich, F. Oetinger (Hamburg, Germany), 1988.

King-Kong, das Geheimschwein, illustrated by Silke Brix-Henker, F. Oetinger (Hamburg, Germany), 1989, reprinted, 2010.

Manchmal ist Jonas ein Löwe, illustrated by Philip Waechter, F. Oetinger (Hamburg, Germany), 1989, reprinted, 2006.

King Kong, das Reiseschwein, illustrated by Silke Brix-Henker, F. Oetinger (Hamburg, Germany), 1989.

Entschuldigung, flüsterte der Riese, 1989.

Lisas Geschichte, Jasims Geschichte, F. Oetinger (Hamburg, Germany), 1989, reprinted, 2007.

Alles total geheim, 1990.

Das Augleichskind, F. Oetinger (Hamburg, Germany), 1990.

Mit Kindern redet ja keiner, F. Oetinger (Hamburg, Germany), 1990.

Ein Tiger für Amerika, illustrated by Silke Brix-Henker, F. Oetinger (Hamburg, Germany), 1991.

Geburtstagsrad mit Batman-Klingel, F. Oetinger (Hamburg, Germany), 1991.

Das Ausgleichskind, Fischer Taschenbuch (Germany), 1991.

Moppel wär gerne Romeo, F. Oetinger (Hamburg, Germany), 1991.

Ich ganz cool, F. Oetinger (Hamburg, Germany), 1992, reprinted, 2009.

Schließlich ist letztes Mal auch nichts paßiert, 1992, reprinted, 2006.

Wir werden auch nicht jünger, 1992.

Alles ganz wunderbar weihnachtlich, illustrated by Jutta Bauer, F. Oetinger (Hamburg, Germany), 1992.

Kirsten Boie erzählt vom Angsthaben, 1992.

Der kleine Pirat, illustrated by Silke Brix-Henker, F. Oetinger (Hamburg, Germany), 1992.

Kein Tag für Juli, illustrated by Jutta Bauer, Büchergilde Gutenberg (Frankfurt am Main, Germany), 1992.

King-Kong, das Krimischwein, illustrated by Silke Brix-Henker, F. Oetinger (Hamburg, Germany), 1992.

King-Kong, das Zirkußchwein, illustrated by Silke Brix-Henker, F. Oetinger (Hamburg, Germany), 1992.

Juli, der Finder, illustrated by Jutta Bauer, Beltz & Gelberg (Weinheim, Germany), 1993.

King-Kong, das Liebeßchwein, illustrated by Silke Brix-Henker, F. Oetinger (Hamburg, Germany), 1993.

Lena hat nur Fußball im Kopf, illustrated by Silke Brix-Henker, F. Oetinger (Hamburg, Germany), 1993.

Mittwochs darf ich spielen, illustrated by Philip Waechter, Fischer-Taschenbuch (Frankfurt am Main, Germany), 1993.

Jeder Tag ein Happening, F. Oetinger (Hamburg, Germany), 1993.

Nella-Propella, illustrated by Philip Waechter, F. Oetinger (Hamburg, Germany), 1994, reprinted, 2010.

Vielleicht ist Lena in Lennart verliebt, F. Oetinger (Hamburg, Germany), 1994.

Klar, daß Mama Ole/Anna lieber hat, illustrated by Silke Brix-Henker, F. Oetinger (Hamburg, Germany), 1994.

Mutter, Vater, Kind, illustrated by Peter Knorr, F. Oetinger (Hamburg, Germany), 1994.

Abschiedskuß für Saurus, illustrated by Jutta Bauer, F. Oetinger (Hamburg, Germany), 1994.

Juli tut Gutes, illustrated by Jutta Bauer, Beltz & Gelberg (Weinheim, Germany), 1994.

Erwachsene reden, Marco hat was getan, F. Oetinger (Hamburg, Germany), 1995.

Prinzeßin Rosenblüte, illustrated by Silke Brix, F. Oetinger (Hamburg, Germany), 1995.

Sophies schlimme Briefe, F. Oetinger (Hamburg, Germany), 1995.

Juli und das Monster, illustrated by Jutta Bauer, Beltz & Gelberg (Weinheim, Germany), 1995, reprinted, 2010.

Sehr gefräßig, aber nett, F. Oetinger (Hamburg, Germany), 1995.

King Kong, das Schulschwein, illustrated by Silke Brix-Henker, F. Oetinger (Hamburg, Germany), 1995.

Juli wird erster, illustrated by Jutta Bauer, Beltz & Gelberg (Weinheim, Germany), 1996.

Eine wunderbare Liebe, F. Oetinger (Hamburg, Germany), 1996.

Ein Hund spricht doch nicht mit jedem, illustrated by Silke Brix-Henker, F. Oetinger (Hamburg, Germany), 1996.

Lena zeltet Samstag nacht, F. Oetinger (Hamburg, Germany), 1996.

Lena findet Fan-Sein gut, F. Oetinger (Hamburg, Germany), 1997.

Man darf mit dem Glück nicht drängelig sein, illustrated by Jutta Bauer, F. Oetinger (Hamburg, Germany), 1997.

Mellin, die dem Drachen befiehlt, 1997.

Krippenspiel mit Hund, illustrated by Silke Brix, Omnibus (Munich, Germany), 1997.

Der Prinz und der Bottelknabe oder erzähl mir vom Dow Jones, F. Oetinger (Hamburg, Germany), 1997.

Krisensommer mit UR-Otto, 1998.

Du wirst schon sehen, es wird ganz toll, 1999.

Nicht Chicago. Nicht hier (novel), F. Oetinger (Hamburg, Germany), 1999.

Linnea geht nur ein bißchen verloren, illustrated by Silke Brix-Henker, F. Oetinger (Hamburg, Germany), 1999.

Linnea klaut Magnus die Zauberdose, illustrated by Silke Brix-Henker, F. Oetinger (Hamburg, Germany), 1999.

Linnea will Pflaster, illustrated by Silke Brix-Henker, F. Oetinger (Hamburg, Germany), 1999.

Zum Glück hat Lena die Zahnspange vergeßen, F. Oetinger (Hamburg, Germany), 2000.

Nee! sagte die Fee, 2000.

Linnea rettet schwarzer Wuschel, illustrated by Silke Brix-Henker, F. Oetinger (Hamburg, Germany), 2000.

Linnea findet einen Waisenhund, illustrated by Silke Brix-Henker, F. Oetinger (Hamburg, Germany), 2000.

Wir Kinder aus dem Möwenweg, illustrated by Katrin Engelking, Taschenbuch (Munich, Germany), 2000.

Linnea macht Sperrmüll, illustrated by Silke Brix-Henker, F. Oetinger (Hamburg, Germany), 2001.

Der durch den Spiegel kommt, illustrated by Dorothea Göbel, F. Oetinger (Hamburg, Germany), 2001.

Kerle mieten oder das Leben ändert sich stündlich, Fischer Taschenbuch (Frankfurt am Main, Germany), 2001.

Kann doch jeder sein, wie er will, illustrated by Stefanie Scharnberg, F. Oetinger (Hamburg, Germany), 2002.

Linnea macht Sachen, illustrated by Silke Brix-Henker, F. Oetinger (Hamburg, Germany), 2002.

Sommer im Möwenweg, illustrated by Katrin Engelking, F. Oetinger (Hamburg, Germany), 2002.

Linnea schickt eine Flaschenpost, illustrated by Silke Brix-Henker, F. Oetinger (Hamburg, Germany), 2003.

Verflixt ein Nix, 2003.

Monis Jahr (novel), F. Oetinger (Hamburg, Germany), 2003.

Geburtstag im Möwenweg, illustrated by Katrin Engelking, Taschenbuch (Munich, Germany), 2003.

Die Medlevinger: ein fantastischer Krimi in vier Teilen, illustrations by Volker Fredrich, F. Oetinger (Hamburg, Germany), 2004.

Was war zuerst da?, illustrated by Philip Waechter, Beltz & Gelberg (Weinheim, Germany), 2004.

Skogland, F. Oetinger (Hamburg, Germany), 2005, translated by David Henry Wilson as *The Princess Plot,* Chicken House/Scholastic (New York, NY), 2009.

Weihnachten im Möwenweg, illustrated by Katrin Engelking, Taschenbuch (Munich, Germany), 2005.

Linnea—allerhand und mehr, illustrated by Silke Brix-Henker, F. Oetinger (Hamburg, Germany), 2005.

Lena möchte immer reiten, illustrated by Silke Brix-Henker, F. Oetinger (Hamburg, Germany), 2005.

Albert spielt Verstecken, illustrated by Silke Brix-Henker, F. Oetinger (Hamburg, Germany), 2005.

Josef Schaf will auch einen Menschen, illustrated by Philip Waechter, F. Oetinger (Hamburg, Germany), 2006.

Der kleine Ritter Trenk, illustrated by Barbara Scholz, F. Oetinger (Hamburg, Germany), 2006.

Juli und die Liebe, illustrated by Jutta Bauer, Beltz & Gelberg (Weinheim, Germany), 2006.

Das Ausgleichskind, Fischer-Taschenbuch (Frankfurt am Main, Germany), 2006.

Juli! (collected stories), Beltz & Gelberg (Weinheim, Germany), 2006.

Opa total verliebt, Fischer-Taschenbuch (Frankfurt am Main, Germany), 2006.

Verat in Skogland, F. Oetinger (Hamburg, Germany), 2006, translated by David Henry Wilson as *The Princess Trap,* Chicken House/Scholastic (New York, NY), 2010.

Lena hat eine Tierkümmerbande illustrated by Silke Brix-Henker, Taschenbuch (Munich, Germany), 2006.

Prinzeßin Rosenblüte. Wach geküßt!, 2007.

Alhambra, Büchergilde Gutenberg (Frankfurt am Main, Germany), 2007.

Wieder Nix!, illustrated by Stefanie Scharnberg, F. Oetinger (Hamburg, Germany), 2007.

Mein Bilderbuchschatz, F. Oetinger (Hamburg, Germany), 2007.

Lena Fährt auf Klassenreise, illustrated by Silke Brix-Henker, Taschenbuch (Munich, Germany), 2008.

Ein neues Jahr im Möwenweg, illustrated by Katrin Engelking, F. Oetinger (Hamburg, Germany), 2008.

Prinz und Bottelknabe oder das Tauschgeschäft, Fischer-Taschenbuch (Frankfurt am Main, Germany), 2009.

Seeräubermoses, illustrated by Barbara Scholz, F. Oetinger (Hamburg, Germany), 2009.

24 Geschichten zur Winterzeit: die schönsten Geschichten über die kalte Jahreszeit, illustrated by Tina Nagel, Esslinger (Esslingen, Germany), 2009.

Die schönsten Tiergeschichten zum Vorlesen, illustrated by Dagmar Henze, Ellerman (Hamburg, Germany), 2009.

King-Kong, das Glücksschwein, illustrated by Silke Brix-Henker, F. Oetinger (Hamburg, Germany), 2010.

Paule ist ein Glücksgriff, illustrated by Silke Brix-Henker, F. Oetinger (Hamburg, Germany), 2010.

Jannis und der ziemlich kleine Einbrecher, illustrated by Silke Brix-Henker, F. Oetinger (Hamburg, Germany), 2010.

Geheimnis im Möwenweg, illustrated by Katrin Engelking, F. Oetinger (Hamburg, Germany), 2010.

Ringel, Rangel, Rosen, F. Oetinger (Hamburg, Germany), 2010.

Der durch den Speigel kommt, illustrated by Verena Körting, F. Oetinger (Hamburg, Germany), 2010.

Und dann ist wirklich Weihnachten (story collection), illustrated by Silke Brix-Henker, F. Oetinger (Hamburg, Germany), 2010.

Linnea findet einen Waisenhund, illustrated by Silke Brix-Henker, F. Oetinger (Hamburg, Germany), 2010.

Author's work has been translated into Danish, French, Greek, Japanese, Ukraine, Spanish, Swedish, and Russian.

OTHER

(Under name Kirsten Boie-Grotz) *Brecht, der unbekannte Erzähler: d. Prosa 1913-1934* (dissertation), Klett-Cotta (Stuttgart, Germany), 1978.

Leidenschaft und Disziplin: Kirsten Boies Kinder-und Jugendbücher 1985-2010, illustrated by Birgit Dankert, BibSpider (Berlin, Germany), 2010.

Biographical and Critical Sources

PERIODICALS

Bulletin of the Center for Children's Books, September, 2008, Karen Coats, review of *The Princess Plot,* p. 7.

Kirkus Reviews, May 1, 2009, review of *The Princess Plot.*

Publishers Weekly, May 4, 2009, review of *The Princess Plot,* p. 50.

School Library Journal, October, 2009, Riva Pollard, review of *The Princess Plot,* p. 120.

ONLINE

Kirsten Boie Home Page, http://www.kirsten-boie.de (October 15, 2010).*

*   *   *

BORRIS, Albert

Personal

Married; wife's name Elizabeth; children: Alexandra, Samuel, Jonah. *Education:* Glassboro State College,

B.A. (psychology); Temple University, M.A. (psychology). *Hobbies and other interests:* Running, traveling, outdoor sports.

Addresses

Home—NJ. *Agent*—Andrea Brown, Andrea Brown Literary Agency, andrea@andreabrownlit.com. *E-mail*—afborris@aol.com.

Career

Author and licensed clinical alcohol and drug counselor. Teacher of peer helping; runs teen retreats; works as an adventure educator.

Writings

Crash into Me, Simon Pulse (New York, NY), 2009.

Contributor of poetry to periodicals, including *Painted Bride Journal, Philadelphia Poets,* and *South Street Star.*

Sidelights

Although he has published poetry in several journals, Albert Borris turned to fiction writing as an outgrowth of his work as a counselor to troubled teens and adults. Enthusiastic about the role of nature in building the resilience necessary to face life's challenges without drugs or alcohol, Borris runs retreats for teens and also works as an adventure educator. As he noted on his home page, he wrote his young-adult novel *Crash into Me* "with the intention of telling a good story that might reach a few people and touch a few hearts. . . . I hope this book says a few things to a few people who I'll never meet in person."

For the four teens in *Crash into Me,* a road trip to visit the graves of several famous suicides is scheduled to end in a fitting location: Death Valley, where the teens are planning a joint suicide. Audrey, Owen, Frank, and Jin-Ae have met online, and each of them is dealing with a problem that seems to have no resolution. As they spend the two-week drive together, talking together and building relationships, they begin to rethink their situations and the finality of their solution. As recounted by Owen in his journal, their story plays out in a novel that *School Library Journal* contributor Meredith Robbins described as "compassionate, nonjudgmental, and ultimately hopeful." Borris's "gripping debut . . . gives a spot-on portrayal of depressed and suicidal teens," asserted a *Kirkus Reviews* in appraising *Crash into Me,* and Michael Cart observed in *Booklist* that the author "tackles a formerly off-limits subject . . . with sensitivity and a wide-ranging factual subtext." Citing the teens' interactions as "tense, candid and often tempered with snarky humor," a *Publishers Weekly* contributor praised Borris's "powerful debut" as "a strikingly real account of an improvised family."

Cover of Albert Borris's dramatic young-adult novel Crash into Me, *which follows four troubled teens on a tragic quest.* (Cover photograph by Michael Frost.)

"It's my personal belief that authentic human contact, even in the face of tremendous pain and suffering, makes the difference in our lives," Borris noted on his home page. "I hope that all of my writing . . . speaks to that point." To teens, he advises: "Write. No matter who you are. No matter what you write. Just write. It helps to clarify your thoughts, free you from your own mind, and brings you personal power. The better you can say what it is that you want, the more likely you are to get it."

Biographical and Critical Sources

PERIODICALS

Booklist, May 15, 2009, Michael Cart, review of *Crash into Me,* p. 34.
Bulletin of the Center for Children's Books, January, 2010, Deborah Stevenson, review of *Crash into Me,* p. 187.
Kirkus Reviews, June 1, 2009, review of *Crash into Me.*
Publishers Weekly, July 27, 2009, review of *Crash into Me,* p. 64.
School Library Journal, August, 2009, Meredith Robbins, review of *Crash into Me,* p. 98.

Voice of Youth Advocates, December, 2009, Amanda MacGregor, review of *Crash into Me,* p. 403.

ONLINE

Albert Borris Home Page, http://www.albertborris.com (October 15, 2010).*

*　　*　*　*　*

BRENNAN, Sarah Rees 1983-

Personal

Born September 21, 1983, in Ireland. *Education:* M.A. (creative writing). *Hobbies and other interests:* Reading, swimming, writing.

Addresses

Home—Dublin, Ireland. *E-mail*—sarahreesbrennan@gmail.com.

Career

Author. Worked as a librarian in Surrey, England.

Writings

FANTASY NOVELS

The Demon's Lexicon, Margaret K. McElderry Books (New York, NY), 2009.
The Demon's Covenant, Margaret K. McElderry Books (New York, NY), 2010.
The Demon's Surrender, Margaret K. McElderry Books (New York, NY), 2011.

Contributor of short stories to anthologies, including *Kiss Me Deadly: Thirteen Tales of Paranormal Love,* edited by Trisha Telep, Running Press, 2010.

Author's work has been translated into Russian, French, German, Japanese, and Taiwanese.

Sidelights

In the fantasy novels of young-adult author Sarah Rees Brennan there are no portals to other worlds. In her fiction debut *The Demon's Lexicon,* the first novel in a trilogy, the setting is modern-day England: a modern-day England where school, friends, and household chores share the stage with magic charms, power-hungry magicians, and ruthless demons. "I love writing urban fantasy," Brennan noted on her home page, "because since it's grounded in reality it can make you feel like magic is right around the corner."

Brennand was born in Ireland and also lived in New York City and Surrey, England, where she worked as a librarian while beginning her writing career. A prolific

writer and blogger, she began contributing to Web sites devoted to the "Harry Potter" novels of author J.K. Rowling. She wrote *The Demon Lexicon* during the course of earning a master's degree in creative writing and has quickly completed the remaining two novels in the trilogy: *The Demon's Covenant* and *The Demon's Surrender*.

For sixteen-year-old Nick Ryves and his crippled older brother Alan, every day at their London home presents new dangers, as readers learn in *The Demon's Lexicon*. The boys live under a constant threat of discovery now that their father has been murdered and their mother driven mad by the world's hidden darkness. With Nick's sword and Alan's gun, they have made demon-hunting their cause. Their mother's madness was caused in retaliation for her theft of a powerful charm, and when Alan is injured by a demon and then takes in two teens in need of help, Nick begins to feel the responsibility for everyone's survival resting heavily on his shoulders. To erase the malignant demon mark caused by Alan's injury, Nick must kill the magician responsible; to do nothing will mean Alan's death. However, something does not seem right about the older brother's explana-

Cover of Sarah Rees Brennan's debut novel The Demonl's Lexicon, *featuring artwork by James Porto.* (Illustrated by James Porto. Margaret McElderry Books 2010. Reproduced by permission.)

tions about the family's past, and when Nick searches for the truth he also risks the family's survival.

In reviewing *The Demon's Lexicon* for *Kirkus Reviews,* a writer cited Brennan's "fresh voice," with its "wicked humor and crepuscular sumptuousness," as a strength of a story that "deftly ratchet[s] . . . up the tension and horror to a series of shattering climaxes." Even non-fantasy buffs will enjoy the book's "solid writing" and "fast-paced plot," predicted Leah J. Sparks in a *School Library Journal* review of *The Devil's Lexicon,* and *Horn Book* contributor Lauren Adams praised Brennan's "complex characterization" and her ability to create a "magical England . . . bright with inventive details." In *Voice of Youth Advocates* Bonnie Kunzel recommended *The Demon's Lexicon* to "aficionados of sharp writing, complex characters, fast-paced plots, teen angst, and the struggle between good and evil."

In *The Demon's Covenant* readers once again meet up with Mae and Jamie Crawford, the teens who joined up with the Ryves brothers in *The Demon Lexicon.* For Mae, her hope of returning to a normal life are dashed when she realizes that the magicians of the Obsidian Circle are once again attempting to seduce her brother to join them. Worried that Jamie may be seduced by this evil, she asks Nick and Alan for help, not realizing that Nick may be in as much danger as Jamie from the Circle's powerful and ruthless leader. "Plots thicken, characters deepen, and snark is bantered with witty abandon," noted a *Kirkus Reviews* critic of the second volume in Brennan's urban fantasy series. In *School Library Journal* Anthony C. Doyle wrote that the story's "undercurrent of wit and subtle sarcasm" transforms a tale of "demons, magic, and dysfunctional families into an affecting and fun read," while the *Kirkus Reviews* critic deemed *The Demon's Covenant* a novel that is "not to be missed."

On her home page, Brennan explained why she chooses to write for a teen audience. "Because I think that they're awesome! . . . We're in the midst of a teen revolution: there are huge amounts of teen books out there that are wildly imaginative and just as good (if not better) than the adult ones. Plus the teenage years are really exciting ones: you're discovering love, and yourself, and a whole other world. If you were discovering magic and risking death as well, think about how much more exciting life could be!"

Biographical and Critical Sources

PERIODICALS

Booklist, April 15, 2009, Daniel Kraus, review of *The Demon's Lexicon,* p. 35.
Bulletin of the Center for Children's Books, July-August, 2009, Kate McDowell, review of *The Demon's Lexicon,* p. 436.

Horn Book, September-October, 2009, Lauren Adams, review of *The Demon's Lexicon,* p. 554.

Kirkus Reviews, May 1, 2009, review of *The Demon's Lexicon*; April 15, 2010, review of *The Demon's Covenant.*

School Library Journal, July, 2009, Leah J. Sparks, review of *The Demon's Lexicon,* p. 79; August, 2010, Anthony C. Doyle, review of *The Demon's Covenant,* p. 96.

Voice of Youth Advocates, April, 2010, Bonnie Kunzel, review of *The Demon's Lexicon.*

ONLINE

Sarah Rees Brennan Home Page, http://www.sarahreesbrennan.com (October 15, 2010).

Sarah Rees Brennan Web Log, http://sarahtales.livejournal.com (October 15, 2010).*

*   *   *

BROWN, Paul 1942-

Personal

Born 1942, in Canada. *Education:* College degree.

Addresses

Home—Belleville, Ontario, Canada.

Career

Author and educator. Formerly worked as a teacher; retired.

Awards, Honors

Best Books for Kids and Teens selection, Canadian Children's Book Centre, 2010, for *Wolf Pack of the Winisk River.*

Writings

Wolf Pack of the Winisk River, illustrated by Robert Kakegamic, Lobster Press (Montreal, Quebec, Canada), 2009.

Biographical and Critical Sources

PERIODICALS

Booklist, April 15, 2009, Daniel Kraus, review of *Wolf Pack of the Winisk River,* p. 39.

Canadian Review of Materials, March 20, 2009, Dave Jenkinson, review of *Wolf Pack of the Winisk River.*

Quill & Quire, May, 2009, Robert J. Wiersema, review of *Wolf Pack of the Winisk River.*

Resource Links, June, 2009, review of *Wolf Pack of the Winisk River.*

School Library Journal, December, 2009. Nancy Call, review of *Wolf Pack of the Winisk River,* p. 107.

ONLINE

Lobster Press Web Site, http://www.lobsterpress.com/ (October 20, 2010), "Paul Brown."*

*   *   *

BRUNO, Elsa Knight 1935-2009

Personal

Born January 19, 1935, in Red Bank, NJ; died December 22, 2009, in Toledo, OH, from complications from myeloma; daughter of Robert L. (in banking) and Helga A. Knight; married Dominic M. Bruno, April, 1956; children: Michael, Elsa, Andrew. *Education:* MA. (early childhood education). *Hobbies and other interests:* Tennis, jazz, Italian cooking.

Career

Author and educator. Teacher of kindergarten for twenty-nine years. Presenter at conferences.

Writings

(Reteller) Beatrix Potter, *The Tale of Benjamin Bunny: A Pop-up Book,* Derrydale Books (New York, NY), 1991.

(Reteller) Beatrix Potter, *The Tale of Jemima Puddle-Duck: A Pop-up Book,* Derrydale Books (New York, NY), 1991.

(Reteller) Beatrix Potter, *The Tale of Peter Rabbit,* Derrydale Books (New York, NY), 1991.

(Reteller) Beatrix Potter, *The Tale of Tom Kitten: A Pop-up Book,* Derrydale Books (New York, NY), 1991.

(Reteller) Lewis Carroll, *Alice in Wonderland: Four Pop-up Books,* illustrated by Samantha Smith, Allan, 1992.

Punctuation Celebration, illustrated by Jenny Whitehead, Henry Holt (New York, NY), 2009.

Contributor of poetry, stories, and articles to periodicals, including *Highlights for Children* and *Ladybug.*

Biographical and Critical Sources

PERIODICALS

Booklist, September 1, 2009, Carolyn Phelan, review of *Punctuation Celebration,* p. 95.

Elsa Knight Bruno's picture books included **Punctuation Celebration,** *a work featuring illustrations by Jenny Whitehead.* (Illustrated by Jenny Whitehead. 2009. Reproduced by permission of Henry Holt and Company, LLC.)

Kirkus Reviews, June 1, 2009, review of *Punctuation Celebration.*

School Library Journal, June, 2009, Jayne Damron, review of *Punctuation Celebration,* p. 105.

Toledo Blade, July 25, 2009, Florence Dethy, "Poetry Fuels Ex-Teacher's Punctuation Book."

ONLINE

Macmillan Web Site, http://us.macmillan.com/ (October 15, 2010), "Elsa Knight Bruno."*

*   *   *

BUEHNER, Mark 1959-

Personal

Name pronounced *Bee*-ner; born July 20, 1959, in Salt Lake City, UT; son of Philip H. (a business owner) and Marjorie Buehner; married Caralyn Morris (a writer), 1983; children: Heidi, Grant, Sarah, Samuel, Laura, Jake. *Education:* Attended University of Utah, 1981-82; Utah State University, B.S., 1985. *Religion:* Church of Jesus Christ of Latter-Day Saints (Mormon). *Hobbies and other interests:* Interior and landscape design.

Addresses

Home—Salt Lake City, UT.

Career

Illustrator of children's books. Performs volunteer work with religious organizations and scouting programs.

Awards, Honors

Parent's Choice Award, 1990, for *The Adventures of Taxi Dog* by Debra and Sal Barracca; Children's Choice Award, Children's Book Council (CBC), 1994, and Utah Children's Choice Award, 1997, both for *A Job for Wittilda* by Caralyn Buehner; Gold Medal, National Parenting Best Books, 1994, Oppenheim Toy Portfolio Platinum Award, 1995, American Library Association (ALA) Notable Book designation, Kentucky Bluegrass Award, and Maryland Black-eyed Susan Award, all for *Harvey Potter's Balloon Farm* by Jerdine Nolen; Parent's Choice Award, 1996, ALA Notable Book designation, and *Boston Globe/Horn Book* Honor Award, both 1997, and Society of Illustrators Silver Medal, all for *Fanny's Dream* by Buehner; ALA Notable Book designation, Best Picture Book designation, *Publishers Weekly,* named Cuffies Favorite Picture Book, and Original Art Silver Medal, Society of Illustrators, all 1997, and Children's Choice selection, International Reading Association/CBC, 1998, all for *My Life with the Wave;* by Catherine Cowan.

Illustrator

PICTURE BOOKS

Debra and Sal Barracca, *The Adventures of Taxi Dog,* Dial (New York, NY), 1990.

Debra and Sal Barracca, *Maxi, the Hero,* Dial (New York, NY), 1991.

Caralyn Buehner, *The Escape of Marvin the Ape,* Dial (New York, NY), 1992.

Caralyn Buehner, *A Job for Wittilda,* Dial (New York, NY), 1993.

Jerdine Nolen, *Harvey Potter's Balloon Farm,* Lothrop, Lee & Shepard (New York, NY), 1994.

Caralyn Buehner, *It's a Spoon, Not a Shovel,* Dial (New York, NY), 1995.

Caralyn Buehner, *Fanny's Dream,* Dial (New York, NY), 1996.

Catherine Cowan, *My Life with the Wave,* Lothrop, Lee & Shepard (New York, NY), 1997.

Caralyn Buehner, *I Did It, I'm Sorry,* Dial (New York, NY), 1998.

Alice Shertle, *I Am the Cat,* Lothrop, Lee & Shepard (New York, NY), 1999.

Laura Leuck, *My Monster Mama Loves Me So,* Lothrop, Lee & Shepard (New York, NY), 1999.

Laura Krauss Melmed, *This First Thanksgiving Day: A Counting Story,* HarperCollins (New York, NY), 2001.

Pearl S. Buck, *Christmas Day in the Morning,* HarperCollins (New York, NY), 2002.

Caralyn Buehner, *Snowmen at Night,* Phyllis Fogelman Books (New York, NY), 2002, published in board-book format, Dial (New York, NY), 2004.

Caralyn Buehner, *Superdog: The Heart of a Hero,* Harper-Collins (New York, NY), 2004.

Chuck Wilcoxen, *Niccolini's Lullaby,* Dutton Children's Books (New York, NY), 2004.

Caralyn Buehner, *Snowmen at Christmas,* Dial (New York, NY), 2005.

Caralyn Buehner, *Goldilocks and the Three Bears,* Dial Books for Young Readers (New York, NY), 2007.

Caralyn Buehner, *Snowmen at Night,* Dial Books for Young Readers (New York, NY), 2007.

Caralyn Buehner, *The Escape of Marvin the Ape,* Dial Books for Young Readers (New York, NY), 2007.

Caralyn Buehner, *The Queen of Style,* Dial Books for Young Readers (New York, NY), 2008.

Caralyn Buehner, *Snowmen All Year,* Dial Books For Young Readers (New York, NY), 2010.

Adaptations

The Escape of Marvin the Ape was adapted for CD-ROM.

Sidelights

Highly regarded illustrator Mark Buehner has created artwork for many books written by his wife, Caralyn

Laura Leuck's story in the picture book **My Monster Mama Loves Me So** *features entertaining artwork by Mark Buehner.* (HarperCollins Publishers, 1999. Illustrations copyright © 1999 by Mark Buehner. Used by permission of HarperCollins Children's Books, a division of HarperCollins Publishers.)

Buehner, as well as for stories by other authors such as Debra and Sal Barracca, Catherine Cowan, Chuch Wilcoxen, and Jerdine Nolen. Praised for the gentle humor and vibrant color that distinguishes his oil and acrylic art, Buehner has received a host of honors for his work. Reviewing the Barraccas' *Maxi, the Hero, New York Times Book Review* contributor Michael Anderson noted that Buehner's "panoramic pictures vibrate with detail and activity; so much is happening that the pages seem to be straining to speak aloud." Anderson added that the illustrator draws in large, rounded forms, creating "a reassuringly solid universe, for all of its surprises."

Born and raised in Salt Lake City, Utah, Buehner was the youngest of a family that included seven children. "I've been told that I learned to walk by holding a pencil; maybe that's where this illustrating business got started!," he once commented to *SATA*. He was also inspired by his father, who used to draw pictures to entertain his young son while the family sat through Sunday church services. As a boy, Buehner made "books" by drawing pictures and stapling them together; as he later noted, "I had no idea that what I was doing would eventually become my line of work. Pulling out pencils, paper, and watercolors was just part of my daily routine."

In school, Buehner gained a reputation among his teachers as a good artist, and the praise he received for his drawing skills encouraged him to excel. "I couldn't read as well as the other children," he remembered, "but I remember poring over the illustrations in picture books. I particularly latched onto one small book called *Pierre,* by Maurice Sendak, which I not only read but memorized." By high school, art had become more than just a hobby. Buehner took his first class in oil painting when he was sixteen years old, and, by his own admission, "became a convert"; he still prefers to work in oils.

After graduating from Utah State University in 1985, Buehner and his wife moved to New York City, where they lived for more than four years. New York is home to most of the country's major publishing houses, and Buehner circulated his portfolio. He was given the opportunity to illustrate the Barraccas' *The Adventures of Taxi Dog,* a picture book about a dog named Maxi who accompanies his owner, a cab driver named Jim, on his rounds. The book was praised for containing illustrations that some commentators compared to the work of noted artist/illustrator Chris Van Allsburg: Buehner's oil-over-acrylic technique "gives each scene a subtle, lively play of light and color," according to *School Library Journal* reviewer John Peters.

With the success of *The Adventures of Taxi Dog* and its sequel, *Maxi the Hero,* Buehner soon found other illustration projects coming his way. His work for Nolen's popular *Harvey Potter's Balloon Farm* brought his stylized artwork to the front of bookstore windows. The story of a balloon farmer who teaches his trade to a young African-American girl, *Harvey Potter's Balloon Farm* features "vivid . . . illustrations of balloons with

Buehner teams up with author Laura Krauss Melmed to create the holiday-themed **This First Thanksgiving Day.** (HarperCollins Publishers, 2001. Illustrations copyright © 2001 by Mark Buehner. Used by permission of HarperCollins Children's Books, a division of HarperCollins Publishers.)

expressive faces in every size, color and shape—frogs, demons, elephants, fish, snowmen—and the animals devilishly hidden on every page," according to Ann A. Flowers in *Horn Book.* Reviewing *Harvey Potter's Balloon Farm* for *School Library Journal,* Kathleen Whalin hailed Buehner as "a master character painter" whose "rich, rounded paintings" combine with Nolen's text to create "a most satisfying whole."

In *My Life with the Wave* Buehner brings his artistic talents to bear on Catherine Cowan's retelling of a story by Octavio Paz. The tale of a young boy who grows to love a powerful ocean wave and determines to possess it for himself by bringing it home, *My Life with the Wave* is enlivened by "acrylic and oil paintings that capture the powerful sensuality and surrealism" of Paz's original work, in the opinion of *Horn Book* reviewer Cathryn M. Mercier. Calling the story "a celebration of imagination from beginning to end," *School Library Journal* contributor Wendy Lukehart praised Buehner's technique of "inserting small details with such skill that they do not overpower or detract from the main story."

Buehner contributes art with a holiday flare to both *This First Thanksgiving Day: A Counting Story* and *Christmas Day in the Morning.* With a text by Laura Krauss Melmed, *This First Thanksgiving Day* focuses on the

preparations made for the very first feast celebrating colonists' gratitude, a feast attended both by the Pilgrims and by members of the Wampanoag tribe. Each page contains a numbered item: one napping pilgrim boy, two giggling Wampanoag girls up to twelve tables filled with the various foodstuffs that have been harvested. Each page also contains a picture of a turkey trying to hide from the people preparing the feast; at the end, the bird has managed to avoid capture and watches the celebration from a safe hiding spot. According to a reviewer for *Publishers Weekly,* Buehner "captures the beauty of autumnal skies" in his illustrations, and GraceAnne A. DeCandido felt that the book's "cheer is fairly irrepressible."

Christmas Day in the Morning uses a text drawn from the writing of Nobel laureate Pearl S. Buck. Here Buehner brings "to life for a new generation" a story of a boy's Christmas gift to his father, as Susan Patron explained in her review of the book for *School Library Journal.* In order to show his appreciation to his father, the narrator, Rob, goes out late at night to complete all of the early-morning chores. This way his hard-working father can have Christmas morning to relax. A critic for *Kirkus Reviews* complimented Buehner's "deep-toned, striking illustrations" for Buck's holiday-themed tale.

Buehner often teams up with wife Caralyn Buehner, and the couple has created several popular picture books. In their first project for young children, *The Escape of Marvin the Ape,* a zoo escapee's day-long exploration of New York City—which occurs without so much as a raised eyebrow from passersby—is brought to life with colorful pictures that "are lively enough to need no definition," according to *School Library Journal* contributor Karen James. *A Job for Wittilda* finds a scruffy witch forced away from her cauldron to earn money to feed her forty-plus cats. Lauralyn Persson hailed Buehner's illustrations as "a delight" in her appraisal of the book for *School Library Journal,* and she commended the artist for including "comic touches to discover at every rereading." A *Publishers Weekly* reviewer asserted that "Buehner's sumptuous oil and acrylic paintings exhibit his flair for depicting the play of light and shadow, and for deploying a variety of arresting perspectives."

Stephanie Zvirin, writing in *Booklist,* praised another of the Buehners' collaborative efforts, a variation of the Cinderella story titled *Fanny's Dream.* Zvirin dubbed this work "a truly wonderful mix of storytelling and art from a husband-wife team with a fine sense of humor," and also offered singular accolades to illustrator Buehner for the detail in his "robust, bucolic pictures, which seem almost to jump off the page." *Goldilocks and the Three Bears* also finds the creative couple mining the rich vein of traditional tales. Here Buehner animates his wife's story with an element of absurdity by depicting the spunky Goldilocks in red cowboy boots and including hidden characters that even include a T-rex. "Plenty of fun [is] to be had from this goofy version of the familiar tale," concluded *Booklist* critic Randall Enos,

and in *School Library Journal* Linda M. Kenton dubbed the Buehners' *Goldilocks and the Three Bears* a "warm and pleasing retelling of the classic" tale.

The Buehners focus on the social graces in *It's a Spoon, Not a Shovel* and *I Did It, I'm Sorry,* both of which treat readers to "a handsome combination of humor, puzzles, and lessons in elementary good behavior," according to *Horn Book* reviewer Flowers. The quiz format in *It's a Spoon, Not a Shovel* lets readers choose from among three possible courses of action in a wide variety of social situations, substituting animals for people wondering what to say to the host of a dinner party when showing up late, or how best to react to a disappointing birthday present. In *Booklist* Julie Yates Walton praised the book, noting that *It's a Spoon, Not a Shovel* contains "ample spoonfuls of humor" that make the "medicine go down very easily."

Focusing on ethical questions, *I Did It, I'm Sorry* finds engaging animal characters deciding on the correct course of action in situations where cheating, lying, or ignoring the requests of authority figures would be far easier. "This book brims with the sort of solid values every child should learn: never lie, follow the rules, obey your parents and think of others," noted a *Publishers Weekly* reviewer.

The magical adventures of snowmen are the focus of *Snowmen at Night, Snowmen at Christmas,* and *Snowmen All Year. Snowmen at Night* offers readers an insight into the secret life of snowmen, showing the chilly

Buehner again joins with his wife, author Caralyn Buehner, to create the entertaining **Dex: The Heart of a Hero.** *(Illustrations copyright © 2004 by Mark Buehner. Harper Trophy 2004. Reproduced by permission of Harpercollins Children's Books.)*

fellows busy having snowball fights, sledding, and drinking ice-cold chocolate while human children are asleep. A *Publishers Weekly* reviewer noted that the story's "glee comes through at its most infectious" in Buehner's paintings, and a contributor to *Kirkus Reviews* credited the book's illustrations with being able to "bring this dazzling idea to life."

In *Snowmen at Christmas* the jolly characters gather late at night in the town square to celebrate the holiday by decorating a tree, singing carols, and awaiting a visit from Santa Claus. "Jazzy rhyming verse keeps a buoyant party beat," a critic in *Publishers Weekly* stated. In *Booklist*, Ilene Cooper also praised the book as a "charming" addition to the holiday picture-book genre, adding that "Buehner does magical things with light in his paintings."

Leaving snowmen for superheroes, the Buehners introduce an amazing canine named Dex in *Superdog: The Heart of a Hero.* Teased for his size, the diminutive Dex wants nothing more than to become a hero, so he sets about making himself one. Researching heroes, he starts to work out to build his strength, and ultimately performs an heroic rescues. "Dex cuts a distinctive figure in the illustrations," wrote a critic for *Kirkus Reviews,* while a *Publishers Weekly* reviewer noted that "a few dashes of comic-book-style text blocks and panel art" help to bring out the superhero theme. Ilene Cooper, writing in *Booklist,* praised Buehner for creating "artwork that practically jumps off the page." As in some of his other projects, Buehner also includes hidden pictures in *Superdog;* Grace Oliff pointed out in *School Library Journal* that "he has added to the fun by hiding cats, rabbits, and even a Tyrannosaurus rex in the clouds and shadows."

Buehner again teams up with his wife on *The Queen of Style,* a "quirky fable about empathy and gratitude," according to a *Publishers Weekly* writer. When Queen Sophie grows tired of governing her tiny nation and its quiet, well-behaved citizenry, she decides to add some spice to her life by enrolling in a beauty-school correspondence course. Soon, the queen is summoning her harried subjects to the castle to perfect her hair-cutting and manicuring techniques, and the frequent interruptions eventually causes the populace to revolt. "This is a story that can be enjoyed on many levels time and time again," Mary Jean Smith wrote in *School Library Journal,* and a *Kirkus Reviews* critic predicted that the mix of text and art in *The Queen of Style* "will give readers food for thought as well as a chuckle or two."

Biographical and Critical Sources

PERIODICALS

Booklist, June 1, 1995, Julie Yates Walton, review of *It's a Spoon, Not a Shovel,* p. 1774; April 1, 1999, Stephanie Zvirin, review of *I Am the Cat,* p. 1417; September 1,

2001, GraceAnne A. DeCandido, review of *This First Thanksgiving Day: A Counting Story,* p. 121; October 15, 2002, Ilene Cooper, review of *Snowmen at Night,* p. 409; April 1, 2004, Ilene Cooper, review of *It's a Bird, It's a Plane,* p. 1370; September 1, 2005, Ilene Cooper, review of *Snowmen at Christmas,* p. 142; March 1, 2007, Randall Enos, review of *Goldiocks and the Three Bears,* p. 86.

Five Owls, November-December, 1992, Stephen Fraser, review of *The Escape of Marvin the Ape,* p. 34.

Horn Book, July-August, 1994, Ann A. Flowers, review of *Harvey Potter's Balloon Farm,* p. 442; July-August, 1995, Ann A. Flowers review of *It's a Spoon, Not a Shovel,* p. 476; September-October, 1997, Cathryn M. Mercier, review of *My Life with the Wave,* p. 555; September, 1999, Nancy Vasilakis, review of *I Am the Cat,* p. 621.

Kirkus Reviews, August 15, 2001, review of *This First Thanksgiving Day,* p. 1218; September 15, 2002, review of *Snowmen at Night,* p. 1385; November 1, 2002, review of *Christmas Day in the Morning,* p. 1616; January 15, 2004, review of *Superdog: The Heart of a Hero,* p. 80; November 1, 2005, review of *Snowmen at Christmas,* p. 1190; February 1, 2007, review of *Goldilocks and the Three Bears,* p. 121; July 15, 2008, review of *The Queen of Style.*

New York Times Book Review, January 5, 1992, Michael Anderson, review of *Maxi, the Hero,* p. 23.

Publishers Weekly, June 22, 1992, review of *The Escape of Marvin the Ape,* p. 61; June 28, 1993, review of *A Job for Wittilda,* p. 76; April 13, 1998, review of *I Did It, I'm Sorry,* p. 74; March 15, 1999, review of *I Am the Cat,* p. 59; September 27, 1999, review of *My Monster Mama Loves Me So,* p. 103; August 14, 2000, review of *I Did It, I'm Sorry,* p. 357; September 24, 2001, review of *This First Thanksgiving Day,* p. 44; August 26, 2002, review of *Snowmen at Night,* p. 66; March 1, 2004, review of *Superdog,* p. 69; October 4, 2004, review of *Niccolini's Song,* p. 87; September 26, 2005, review of *Snowmen at Christmas,* p. 88; March 19, 2007, review of *Goldilocks and the Three Bears,* p. 63; August 18, 2008, review of *The Queen of Style,* p. 61.

School Library Journal, January, 1994, Lauralyn Persson, review of *A Job for Wittilda,* p. 87; May, 1994, Kathleen Whalin, review of *Harvey Potter's Balloon Farm,* p. 102; August, 1997, Wendy Lukehart, review of *My Life with the Wave,* p. 129; September, 2001, Pamela K. Bombay, review of *This First Thanksgiving Day,* p. 219; October, 2002, Susan Patron, review of *Christmas Day in the Morning,* p. 57, and Adele Greenlee, review of *Snowmen at Night,* p. 99; September, 2003, Grace Oliff, review of *Fanny's Dream,* p. 83; February, 2004, Grace Oliff, review of *Superdog,* p. 103; April, 2007, Linda M. Kenton, review of *Goldilocks and the Three Bears,* p. 120; September, 2008, Mary Jean Smith, review of *The Queen of Style,* p. 140.

ONLINE

Storyopolis Art Gallery Online, http://www.storyopolis. com/ (April 20, 2005), "Mark Buehner."

Utah Children's Writers and Illustrators Web site, http:// www.ucwi.org/ (July 1, 2004), interview with Caralyn Buehner."*

C

CALETTI, Deb 1963-

Personal

Born June 16, 1963, in San Rafael, CA; daughter of Paul and Evie Caletti; married (divorced, 1999); children: (first marriage) Samantha Bannon, Nicholas Bannon. *Education:* Attended Bellevue (WA) Community College; University of Washington, B.A. (journalism), 1985. *Hobbies and other interests:* Painting, hiking, kayaking, swimming, travel, reading, spending time with family.

Addresses

Home—Seattle, WA. *E-mail*—deb@debcaletti.com.

Career

Writer. Speaker and lecturer.

Member

PEN, Amnesty International.

Awards, Honors

Washington State Arts Commission fellow, 2001; International Reading Association (IRA) Young-Adult Choice designation, and Cooperative Children's Book Council (CCBC) Choice designation, both 2004, both for *The Queen of Everything;* National Book Award finalist, Chicago Public Library Best-of-the-Best designation, and *School Library Journal* Best Books designation, all 2004, IRA Notable Book designation, New York Public Library Book for the Teen Age selection, and PNBA Best Book Award, all 2005, California Young Reader Medal finalist, 2005-06, and PEN USA Literary Award finalist, Washington State Book Award, and YALSA Best Books finalist, all for *Honey, Baby, Sweetheart;* Washington State Book Award finalist, and New York Public Library Book for the Teen Age selection, both 2006, both for *Wild Roses;* New York Public Li-

Deb Caletti (Photograph by Jason Teeples. Reproduced by permission.)

brary Book for the Teen Age selection, American Library Association (ALA) Quick-Picks selection, Cooperative Children's Book Council (CCBC) Choice selection, and South Carolina Young-Adult Book Award nomination, all 2007, all for *The Nature of Jade;* New York Public Library Book for the Teen Age selection,

ALA Best Books for Young Adults designation, and CCBC Choice selection, all 2008, all for *The Fortunes of Indigo Skye;* CCBC Choice selection, 2008, and TAY-SHAS Award, both for *The Secret Life of Prince Charming.*

Writings

YOUNG-ADULT NOVELS

The Queen of Everything, Simon Pulse (New York, NY), 2002.
Honey, Baby, Sweetheart, Simon & Schuster Books for Young Readers (New York, NY), 2004.
Wild Roses, Simon & Schuster (New York, NY), 2005.
The Nature of Jade, Simon & Schuster Books for Young Readers (New York, NY), 2007.
The Fortunes of Indigo Skye, Simon & Schuster Books for Young Readers (New York, NY), 2008.
The Secret Life of Prince Charming, Simon & Schuster Books for Young Readers (New York, NY), 2009.
The Six Rules of Maybe, Simon Pulse (New York, NY), 2010.
Stay, Simon Pulse (New York, NY), 2011.

Cover of Caletti's award-winning young-adult novel, **The Queen of Everything.** (Cover design by Jessica Handelman (NY, 2008). Reprinted with the permission of Simon Pulse, an imprint of Simon & Schuster Children's Publishing Division.)

OTHER

Contributor to anthologies, including *The World of the Golden Compass: The Otherworldly Ride Continues,* edited by Scott Westerfield; *Through the Wardrobe: Your Favorite Authors on C.S. Lewis's Chronicles of Narnia,* edited by Herbie Brennan; *Literary Feast: The Famous Authors Cookbook;* and *First Kiss (Then Tell): A Collection of True Lip-locked Moments,* edited by Cylin Busby.

Adaptations

Caletti's novels were scheduled to be adapted by Vulcan Productions and Infinity Features as the feature-film series *Nine Mile Falls.*

Sidelights

Award-winning author Deb Caletti writes for young adults, and her novels include *The Queen of Everything, Honey, Baby, Sweetheart, The Nature of Jade, The Secret Life of Prince Charming,* and *The Six Rules of Maybe.* Although she loved reading and dreamed of being a writer, Caletti trained as a journalist and finally turned to fiction writing while raising her children. Her determination played a central role in her success: although her first four novel-length manuscripts brought rejections from publishers, she continued to hone her work and persevere. Caletti's fifth novel earned her not only publication but several awards, and her next book, *Honey, Baby, Sweetheart,* was a National Book Award finalist.

Caletti's debut novel, *The Queen of Everything,* is set in the Pacific Northwest, where its author was raised and now makes her home. After her parents' divorce, seventeen-year-old Jordan McKenzie chooses to live with her more "normal" parent, her optometrist father, on an island in Puget Sound, off the coast of Washington State. With this decision Jordan leaves behind her free-spirited mother, who, together with her kinetic artist husband, runs a boarding house populated by an interesting assortment of characters. When Jordon's dad becomes obsessed with the beautiful and married Gayle D'Angelo, however, the teen fears he will do anything to get rid of Gayle's husband. Jordan makes some poor choices, as well, developing a crush on a handsome but cruel classmate at her new high school, while also dealing with the death of a grandparent.

A *Kirkus Reviews* contributor wrote that in *The Queen of Everything* Caletti "expertly succeeds in capturing the way a smart teen can grasp and skewer her world and what passes for everyday normal in a wry tone that never fails to recognize the seriousness of the situation." Miranda Doyle noted in her review of the same novel for *School Library Journal* that "teens will gain insight into how obsessive love can drive even ordinary-seeming individuals to commit terrible acts," while in *Booklist* Debbie Carton predicted that Jordan's "authentic teenage voice . . . will hold readers, as will the emotional issues of sadness and abandonment."

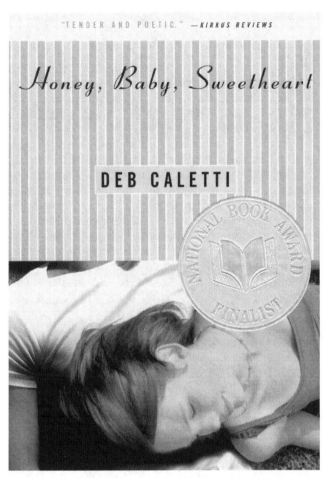

Cover of Caletti's young-adult novel **Honey, Baby, Sweetheart,** *which finds a teen sampling life on the other side of the tracks during a rewarding summer.* (Simon Pulse, 2004. Cover photograph copyright © 2004 by Alain Daussin/Getty Images.)

In *Honey, Baby, Sweetheart* Caletti "fills the pages with wonderful images, sharp dialogue, and memorable characters," according to *Kliatt* critic Claire Rosser. In this novel readers meet Ruby, a high schooler whose life changes during the summer between her junior and senior years. When Ruby falls hard for the handsome Travis, she spends most of the summer riding with him on his motorcycle. After the seemingly jobless Travis gives her a gold chain, however, Ruby learns that he has been breaking into houses and stealing. Although she realizes that being around him could be dangerous, Ruby's feelings for Travis make it difficult for her to break off the relationship. Her librarian mother, Ann, who has been abandoned by Ruby's philandering father many times, knows what her daughter is going through, and the two make a pact to break their dependence on their irresponsible men. A friendship with an elderly woman and a trip down to California to reunite the woman with a caring former lover helps Ruby learn an important lesson about the quality of real love.

Reviewing *Honey, Baby, Sweetheart, Booklist* contributor Gillian Engberg commented that Caletti "writes a compelling, multigenerational story," while Lynn Evarts wrote in *School Library Journal* that "young adults will

see themselves in Ruby and, like her, have some laughs on the road to wisdom." Evarts concluded by noting that *Honey, Baby, Sweetheart* is "full of heart, fun, and energy," and a *Kirkus Reviews* contributor dubbed Ruby's narration "tender and poetic."

Caletti again explores teen emotions and broken homes in *Wild Roses,* a "rich novel" that deals with "themes of passion and recklessness," according to a *Publishers Weekly* contributor. When Cassie Morgan's mom remarries four days after her divorce to Cassie's dad, the seventeen-year-old astronomy buff takes an instant dislike to her new stepfather, Dino Cavalli. A manic-depressive violinist and composer, the volatile and moody Dino proves difficult to live with and level-headed Cassie decides that passion in life, and in people, is a thing to be avoided. Her attraction to Dino's equally passionate student, Ian, presents a problem, therefore, as Cassie attempts to create an emotional balance in her own world.

Caletti "keeps up her funny, smart banter" in *Wild Roses,* according to Rosser, the *Kliatt* critic adding that Cassie's "outrageous family story" is "entertaining without being shallow." The novelist's "perceptions on divorce are crystalline," noted a *Kirkus Reviews* critic, adding that Caletti's tale is "populated with delightfully oddball . . . characters and shot full of genuine wit." *Booklist* critic Jennifer Hubert deemed the novel "a good selection for mother-daughter book clubs," and *School Library Journal* critic Susan Riley concluded that the "profound observations and vivid . . . language" in *Wild Roses* contributes to a "multifaceted and emotionally devastating novel" that will "stick with readers."

A seventeen year old dealing with panic disorder is the focus of *The Nature of Jade.* Now that she has been diagnosed, Jade DeLuna knows that her bouts of dizziness and loss of breath will not kill her. To create a calmer life, the teen takes trips to the Seattle zoo, and she uses the zoo's Webcam as a screen saver on her computer. As she watches the Webcam her interest strays from the elephants to a young man in a red jacket and holding an infant who often visits their pen. Intrigued, Jade meets the boy, Sebastian, and learns that the infant is his son and that they live with Sebastian's grandmother on a houseboat. While falling for Sebastian, Jade is drawn into his life, a life where she can hide from her parents' looming separation, school pressures, and her own fear of death. Through Jade's narration—which combines the teen's fears, worries, and hopes along with her thoughts on Sebastian and accumulated facts about elephants—Caletti expresses what a *School Library Journal* contributor Marie C. Hansen described as "an interesting perspective" that is unique in YA fiction: "that teen parents can form meaningful and loving relationships with their peers." In his *Booklist* review of *The Nature of Jade,* Michael Cart gave the author characteristic praise, writing that Caletti "does a fine job of developing [her] . . . characters" and presents a "captivating" romance.

Cover of Caletti's **The Nature of Jade,** *a story about a teen who puts her own fears in perspective while assisting people facing real challenges.* (Cover design by Lucy Ruth Cummins (NY, 2007). Reprinted with the permission of Simon Pulse, an imprint of Simon & Schuster Children's Publishing Division.)

For the title character in Caletti's YA novel *The Fortunes of Indigo Skye,* life is pretty much perfect. At eighteen, Indigo has a cute boyfriend, a loving family, and a job as a waitress that makes her feel productive and happy. When an anonymous customer leaves Indigo a literal fortune as a tip, the gift proves to be more complex than the teen first thinks. Although friends and family members worry that the fun-loving Indigo will be changed for the worse, she begs to differ. After all, she is sharing the wealth in addition to treating herself to a new car and several other formerly out-of-reach goodies. However, when she realizes that her new-found wealth had caused her to lose touch with the simple values that used to sustain her, Indigo must find a way to change the course of her life in a novel that *School Library Journal* contributor Jessie Spalding described as "filled with rich characters and hilarious interactions." *The Fortunes of Indigo Skye* "encourages thought and examination of what is truly important in life," added Spalding, while *Horn Book* contributor Jennifer M. Brabander predicted that teen readers "will be enthralled by Indigo's personality, her way with words, and how she turns her misfortune back into good fortune." Through Caletti's "infinitely likeable heroine and

richly limned supporting characters," *The Fortunes of Indigo Skye* "makes a fine counterpoint to the ubiquitous rich-girl series books," concluded Bina Williams in *Booklist.*

Although she knows that life is not a fairy tale, Quinn Hunt, the main character in *The Secret Life of Prince Charming,* wants to believe that her efforts to be a good person will be rewarded in love. When she finds out that her boyfriend has another girlfriend on the side, Quinn's optimism begins to erode. But when she is abruptly and unceremoniously dumped, Quinn starts to think that maybe there are no good men after all. Her relationship with her some-time dad only reinforces her growing pessimism: when he fits her into his schedule, the conversation revolves around him, and now it turns out that he has been surreptitiously "collecting" souvenirs from each of the many women in his life. When Quinn and her two sisters decide to return the stolen objects to their rightful owners, they start out on a road trip that leads the young woman to reclaim her upbeat attitude. According to *School Library Journal* contributor Kathleen E. Gruver, *The Secret Life of Prince Charming* "is a thoughtful, funny, and empowering spin on the classic road novel" that will appeal to mature

Cover of Caletti's teen novel **The Secret Life of Prince Charming.** (Reproduced by permission of Simon & Schuster.)

teens pondering "love, relationships, and getting what you need." In *Horn Book* Jennifer M. Brabander called the novel "warmly optimistic and full of humor," adding that Caletti treats romance fans to an "upbeat ending." The author "excels at getting to the heart of her protagonists' mixed-up emotions," concluded a *Kirkus Reviews* writer, the critic adding of *The Secret Life of Prince Charming* that Caletti's "fans will not be disappointed."

In *The Six Rules of Maybe* Caletti focuses on Scarlett Hughes, a thoughtful teen who avoids self-questioning by worrying about those around her. A "fixer", the seventeen year old devotes herself to solving the problems of friends and neighbors, and even her mom, whether they ask for help or not. When her older sister Juliet, a singer, turns up pregnant and married to the baby's father, Hayden, Scarlett involves herself in their marriage, trying to keep Juliet from straying back to an old boyfriend and discounting Hayden's love for her. "Scarlett's adoration of Hayden is both poignant and realistic," noted Cooper in *Booklist,* and a *Publishers Weekly* critic dubbed *The Six Rules of Maybe* "moving." The novel is characteristic Caletti, asserted Brabander, citing its realistic characters and "skillfully crafted sentences that will entice readers racing through to slow down" and enjoy the story. Ultimately, as Suzanne Gordon wrote in *School Library Journal, The Six Rules of Maybe* is "about hope as the fuel of one's dreams and efforts, about the frequent necessity of persistence, and about how to know when to let go."

In her novels, Caletti sometimes uses profane language, and this fact has caused some to criticize her books. Addressing this situation on her home page, the novelist explained her reason for including profanity: "It's simple, really. Some people swear in my books because they are the type of people who would swear. Others don't, because they are the type of people who wouldn't swear. Honesty is the most important thing to me in my work. If I'm not being honest, then I should be fired from my job. It is not my aim to show an idealized world. It is my aim to show the world as it is in all of its beauty and messiness and variety and wackiness and rare moments of perfection."

Biographical and Critical Sources

PERIODICALS

Booklist, November 15, 2002, Debbie Carton, review of *The Queen of Everything,* p. 590; May 15, 2004, Gillian Engberg, review of *Honey, Baby, Sweetheart,* p. 1613; October 1, 2005, Jennifer Hubert, review of *Wild Roses,* p. 47; February 1, 2007, Michael Cart, review of *The Nature of Jade,* p. 41; April 1, 2008, Bina Williams, review of *The Fortunes of Indigo Skye,* p. 40; April 1, 2009, Cindy Dobrez, review of *The Secret Life of Prince Charming,* p. 34; February 15, 2010, Ilene Cooper, review of *The Six Rules of Maybe,* p. 72.

Bulletin of the Center for Children's Books, June, 2004, Deborah Stevenson, review of *Honey, Baby, Sweetheart,* p. 411.

Horn Book, May-June, 2008, Jennifer M. Brabander, review of *The Fortunes of Indigo Skye,* p. 308; July-August, 2009, Jennifer M. Brabander, review of *The Secret Life of Prince Charming,* p. 418; May-June, 2010, Jennifer M. Brabander, review of *The Six Rules of Maybe,* p. 78.

Kirkus Reviews, November 1, 2002, review of *The Queen of Everything,* p. 1610; May 1, 2004, review of *Honey, Baby, Sweetheart,* p. 439; September 15, 2005, review of *Wild Roses,* p. 1023; March 1, 2008, review of *The Fortunes of Indigo Skye*; March 1, 2009, review of *The Secret Life of Prince Charming.*

Kliatt, May, 2004, Claire Rosser, review of *Honey, Baby, Sweetheart,* p. 6; September, 2005, Claire Rosser, review of *Wild Roses,* p. 6; March, 2008, Claire Rosser, review of *The Fortunes of Indigo Skye,* p. 8.

Publishers Weekly, November 18, 2002, review of *The Queen of Everything,* p. 62; June 7, 2004, review of *Honey, Baby, Sweetheart,* p. 51; November 28, 2005, review of *Wild Roses,* p. 52; February 12, 2007, review of *The Nature of Jade,* p. 87; February 11, 2008, review of *The Fortunes of Indigo Skye,* p. 71; January 26, 2009, review of *The Secret Life of Prince Charming,* p. 120; February 22, 2010, review of *The Six Rules of Maybe,* p. 69.

School Library Journal, November, 2002, Miranda Doyle, review of *The Queen of Everything,* p. 158; July, 2004, Lynn Evarts, review of *Honey, Baby, Sweetheart,* p. 102; November, 2005, Susan Riley, review of *Wild Roses,* p. 129; May, 2007, Marie C. Hansen, review of *The Nature of Jade,* p. 129; April, 2008, Jessie Spalding, review of *The Fortunes of Indigo Skye,* p. 139; June, 2009, Kathleen E. Gruver, review of *The Secret Life of Prince Charming,* p. 116; March, 2010, Suzanne Gordon, review of *The Six Rules of Maybe,* p. 154.

Voice of Youth Advocates, February, 2003, review of *The Queen of Everything,* p. 465; August, 2004, Pam Carlson, review of *Honey, Baby, Sweetheart,* p. 208.

ONLINE

Deb Caletti Home Page, http://www.debcaletti.com (October 15, 2010).

Seattle Post-Intelligencer Online, http://seattlepi.nwsource.com/books/ (November 15, 2004), John Marshall, interview with Caletti.

* * *

CLEMINSON, Katie

Personal

Born in England. *Education:* Falmouth College, diploma (art and design); North Wales School of Art, degree (first-class honors), 2007.

Addresses

Home—England.

Career

Author and illustrator.

Awards, Honors

British Booktrust Early Years Award for Best Emerging Illustrator, 2009, for *Box of Tricks*.

Writings

Box of Tricks, Jonathan Cape (London, England), 2009, published as *Magic Box,* Hyperion (New York, NY), 2009.
Wake Up, Red Fox (London, England), 2010.
Cuddle Up, Goodnight, Disney Hyperion Books (New York, NY), 2011.

Sidelights

British writer Katie Cleminson crafts toddler-friendly picture books that mix her engaging, retro-styled ink-and-watercolor art with simple stories featuring likeable young children. Cleminson began her illustration career after studying art and design at Falmouth College and the North Wales School of Art, where she specialized in picture-book art. Her digitally enhanced illustrations, which feature charcoal lines and colored inks, are showcased in picture books that include *Magic Box, Wake Up,* and *Cuddle Up, Goodnight.*

Magic Box, which was published in England as *Box of Tricks,* captures a child's vivid imagination and sense of fun in its story about Eva. The little girl really wants a pet of her very own, and the magic box she receives for her birthday may make her wish come true. With the magic cape and wand that come with the box, Emma conjures up a polar bear named Monty. When the imaginative Eva decides that a party is in order, bunnies and an animal band quickly fill the book's pages. The animals' upbeat music is captured in artwork that moves from charcoal and ink wash to what *School Library Journal* contributor Kathleen Kelly MacMillan characterized as "an explosion of bright colors." Praising Cleminson's "winsome illustrations" in *Magic Box,* a *Kirkus Reviews* writer dubbed the book "a little odd and more than a little engaging." A *Publishers Weekly* critic described Cleminson's debut as "a fantasy about a child who gets to be in charge of everything for a while, and one readers will enter into with pleasure."

Biographical and Critical Sources

PERIODICALS

Kirkus Reviews, May 1, 2009, review of *Magic Box.*
Publishers Weekly, May 11, 2009, review of *Magic Box,* p. 50.
School Library Journal, August, 2009, Kathleen Kelly MacMillan, review of *Magic Box,* p. 72.

ONLINE

Random House Web Site, http://www.randomhouse.co.uk/ (October 20, 2010), "Katie Cleminson."*

* * *

Katie Cleminson illustrates her original story about a jaded young girl and her unusual gift in Magic Box. *(© 2009 by Katie Cleminson. Reprinted by permission of Disney Hyperion, an imprint of Disney Book Group LLC. All rights reserved.)*

COCHRAN, Josh

Personal

Born in Taiwan; married; wife's name Jenny. *Education:* Art Center College of Design, B.F.A. (with honors), 2005. *Hobbies and other interests:* Coffee, good movies, drawing, silk-screening.

Addresses

Home—Brooklyn, NY. *Agent*—Bernstein & Andriulli, 40 W. 40th St., New York, NY 10018. *E-mail*—mail@ joshcochran.net.

Career

Illustrator, animation artist, and educator. Freelance illustrator for editorial, advertising, and Internet clients. Parson's School of Design, New York, NY, instructor. *Exhibitions:* Works exhibited in galleries.

Awards, Honors

Named New Visual Artist, *Print* magazine, 2009; Silver Medal, Society of Illustrators, New York.

Illustrator

"MYSTERIES UNWRAPPED" SERIES

Charles Wetzel, *Haunted U.S.A.,* Sterling (New York, NY), 2008.

Susan Sloate, *The Secrets of Alcatraz,* Sterling Pub. Co. (New York, NY), 2008.

Sudipta Bardhan-Quallen, *The Real Monsters,* Sterling (New York, NY), 2008.

Oliver Ho, *Mutants and Monsters,* Sterling Pub. Co. (New York, NY), 2008.

Sharon Linnéa, *Lost Civilizations,* Sterling Pub. Co. (New York, NY), 2009.

George Edward Stanley, *Medical Marvels,* Sterling (New York, NY), 2009.

OTHER

Contributor to periodicals, including *Atlantic Monthly, Entertainment Weekly, Esquire, Fortune, Gentleman's Quarterly, Good, McSweeney's, Newsweek, New Yorker, New York Times Book Review, New York Times Magazine, Runner's World, Time,* and *Wired.*

Sidelights

Inspired by everything from Japanese wood-block prints to Indie comic books, Josh Cochran is an award-winning illustrator whose sophisticated artwork has appeared in numerous magazines as well as in broadcast media. Known for creating inky line drawings featuring flat, subdued colors and a mid-twentieth-century feel, Cochran's artwork has appeared in several volumes of the "Mysteries Unwrapped," series, among them George Edward Stanley's *Medical Marvels, The Secrets of Alcatraz* by Susan Sloate, and *Mutants and Monsters* by Oliver Ho.

Now living in Brooklyn, New York, Cochran was born in Taiwan and lived in several countries due to his father's career in the U.S. Navy. After graduating with honors from the Art Center College of Design in 2005, he set about looking for clients and impressed an editor at the *New York Times Book Review.* By 2008 Cochran had also attracted the interest of book publishers, and soon picture-book projects were coming his way. In a *School Library Journal* review of Ho's *Mutants and Monsters,* Amy Pickett noted that Cochran's "retro-style line drawings colored with smudgy turquoise, orange, and olive green" contribute to the volume's "splashy, browser-friendly format."

Biographical and Critical Sources

PERIODICALS

Booklist, July 1, 2008, Stephanie Zvirin, review of *Mutants and Monsters,* p. 59; July 1, 2009, Ian Chipman, review of *Lost Civilizations,* p. 59.

Josh Cochran's unique illustrations are a highlight of George E. Stanley's picture book **Medical Marvels.** (Copyright 2009 by George E. Stanley. Illustrations copyright 2009 by Josh Cochran. Used with permission from Sterling Publishing Co, Inc.)

Kirkus Reviews, May 1, 2009, review of *Lost Civilizations.*

School Library Journal, July, 2008, Amy Pickett, review of *Mutants and Monsters,* p. 113; June, 2009, Traci Glass, review of *The Real Monsters,* p. 140.

ONLINE

Illustration Mundo Web Site, http://www.illustrationmundo. com/ (October 15, 2010), "Josh Cochran."

Josh Cochran Home Page, http://www.joshcochran.net (October 15, 2010).*

*　　*　　*

CRELIN, Bob 1959(?)-

Personal

Born c. 1959, in CT; son of Edmund S. Crelin (a university professor); married; has children. *Hobbies and other interests:* Astronomy.

Addresses

Home—Guilford, CT. *E-mail*—suzanne@bobcrelin.com.

Career

Artist, graphic designer, inventor, author, musician, and songwriter. Worked variously as a skateboarder, guitar inlay designer; inventor of Glarebusters outdoor light and Moon Gazers' Wheel. Wandering Star Project, Inc. (nonprofit, astronomy-education organization for children), cofounder. Presenter at schools and conferences.

Member

International Dark-Sky Association.

Awards, Honors

Walter Scott Houston Award, Astronomical League, 2004; *Booklinks* Lasting Connections award, 2009, for *Faces of the Moon.*

Writings

There Once Was a Sky Full of Stars, illustrated by Amie Ziner, Sky Pub. (Cambridge, MA), 2003.
Faces of the Moon, illustrated by Leslie Evans, Charlesbridge (Watertown, MA), 2009.

Bob Crelin shares his enthusiasm for astronomy in his picture book Faces of the Moon, *which features artwork by Leslie Evans.* (Illustrations © 2009 by Leslie Evans. Used with permission by Charlesbridge Publishing, Inc. All rights reserved.)

Contributor of articles to periodicals, including *Sky & Telescope, Home Lighting & Accessories,* and *Branford Review.*

Sidelights

In 1994 Connecticut native and amateur astronomer Bob Crelin sat in the backyard of his suburban home, hoping to show his young daughter the Milky Way. "We couldn't find it," he later recalled in an article for *Sky & Telescope.* "The Milky Way of my boyhood was gone, hidden behind artificial skyglow stretching from horizon to horizon." Interested in why his town's lighting now diffused into the night sky and blotted out the stars, Crelin began researching the subject. As he soon learned, "most light pollution is unnecessary and preventable, much of it merely careless waste from outdoor lighting that's poorly designed, overly bright, or improperly aimed." Now that he had identified the problem, Crelin set about to devise a solution, working with local and state lawmakers to reduce the amount of light pollution in his corner of New England through ordinances and building codes. He also joined with several friends to design the Glarebuster, an outdoor light that curtails light spillover, and cofounded the Wandering Star Project, a nonprofit, astronomy-education organization for children.

Crelin also shares his passion for the night sky in several children's books. *There Once Was a Sky Full of Stars* is a bedtime read-aloud illustrated by Amie Ziner that teaches youngsters why the beautiful night sky is sometimes difficult to see. An interactive book featuring linocut art by Leslie Evans, *Faces of the Moon* presents basic lunar facts, such as why the moon appears to change shape over the course of a month and why it can sometimes be seen during daylight hours. In rhyming verse that encourages memorization, Crelin introduces the name of each lunar phase and discusses the way that light and shadow work to create the illusion of waxing and waning. Die-cut holes allow readers to see the progress of the visible moon across the sky, and Crelin's "simple end note clearly explains this lunar dance of shadow and light," according to a *Kirkus Reviews* writer. Calling *Faces of the Moon* an "appealing ode," Daniel Kraus added in *Booklist* that while "it isn't easy to cram science lessons into graceful poetry, . . . Crelin makes it look effortless." In *Publishers Weekly* a contributor praised Evans' "bright, chunky" block-print illustrations for *Faces of the Moon,* the critic going on to recommend the book's mix of "gentle interactive elements and rhymed verse."

Biographical and Critical Sources

PERIODICALS

Booklist, July 1, 2009, Daniel Kraus, review of *Faces of the Moon,* p. 59.

Children's Bookwatch, July, 2009, review of *Faces of the Moon.*

Kirkus Reviews, June 1, 2009, review of *Faces of the Moon.*

Publishers Weekly, June 15, 2005, review of *Faces of the Moon,* p. 50.

School Library Journal, July, 2009, John Peters, review of *Faces of the Moon,* p. 71.

Science Books and Films, March-April, 2008, Thomas A. Lesser, review of *There Once Was a Sky Full of Stars,* p. 78.

Science World, April 2, 2007, review of *There Once Was a Sky Full of Stars.*

Sky & Telescope, December, 2002, Bob Crelin, "How I Beat Light Pollution in My Hometown," pp. 40-44.

ONLINE

Bob Crelin Home Page, http://bobcrelin.com (October 15, 2010).*

D

DAVIS, Heather 1970-

Personal

Born 1970. *Education:* Bachelor's degree (liberal arts with an emphasis in film).

Addresses

Home—Seattle, WA. *Agent*—Stephen Barbara, Foundry Literary & Media, 33 W. 17th St., New York, NY 10011. *E-mail*—heather@heatherdavisbooks.com.

Career

Writer. Worked as a professional cook and a substitute teacher.

Awards, Honors

Golden Heart Award for best young-adult manuscript, 2006.

Writings

YOUNG-ADULT NOVELS

Never Cry Werewolf, HarperTeen (New York, NY), 2009.
The Clearing, Houghton Mifflin Harcourt (Boston, MA), 2010.
Wherever You Go, Harcourt (Boston, MA), 2011.

Contributor of stories to periodicals, including *Cricket.*

Sidelights

Based in Seattle, Washington, Heather Davis crafts stories for teen readers that include *Never Cry Werewolf* and *The Clearing.* A childhood penchant for storytelling translated into an interest in film by the time Davis en-

Heather Davis (Photograph by Inti St. Clair. Reproduced by permission.)

rolled in college. After graduating, her life took several other twists and turns before her passion for words was rekindled. She had written several unpublished novels for adults, but while working as a substitute teacher at a local elementary school, Davis decided to attempt a novel. She geared her story and characters to appeal to

modern teens and when she showed the first few chapters to one of her bookish sixth-grade students, she was encouraged to forge ahead.

Shelby, the sixteen-year-old heroine in Davis's debut novel, *Never Cry Werewolf,* has annoyed her dad and stepmom beyond the point of toleration, and in response they ship her off to Camp Crescent for the summer. Shelby is unsure about the New Age atmosphere of the camp, which is located in the Pacific Northwest, but things get better when the dishy Austin Bridges III shows up. Not only is Austin the son of a rock-music legend, but he also seems really nice. As Shelby and Austin become friends, he entrusts her with a family secret that is not only dark; it is also about to be revealed by an upcoming full moon in a story that Donna Rosenblum described in *School Library Journal* as "a fast-paced action adventure story with issues of peer pressure, divorce, betrayal, friendship, acceptance, and . . . romance." A *Kirkus Reviews* writer predicted of *Never Cry Werewolf* that "fans of paranormal romance will enjoy this sweet debut," while in *Booklist* Kimberly Garnick wrote that "the direct, first-person narrative" in Davis's novel "makes for a quick read and an easy sell for reluctant readers."

Another sixteen year old living in western Washington is the central figure in *The Clearing,* which a *Publishers Weekly* critic praised for its mix of "old-fashioned romance" and a "time-travel element." Amy escapes from distracted parents and a bad-news boyfriend by moving in with her aunt, who lives in a rural town in the Northern Cascades. While exploring her aunt's farm, she meets Henry, a boy who has been living in an endless summer that began in 1944, when he wished for a miracle. As their friendship strengthens into love, Amy finds the strength to return home and deal with her problems. For Henry, Amy becomes the support he needs to return to his own time, even though this choice may mean danger for his family and the loss of Amy, who he has come to love. In *School Library Journal* Danielle Serra praised the novel's realistic characters, calling Henry "genuine, perceptive, and non-domineering" and Amy "simultaneously vulnerable and strong." Noting the author's ability to craft an unusual teen romance, Melissa Moore added in *Booklist* that *The Clearing* treats readers to "a riveting read that lingers long after the story ends."

Sharing her writing pointers on her joint Web log *Books, Boys, Buzz . . . ,* Davis stressed the importance of revision: rereading for sense, evaluating characters for likeability and motivation, checking mechanics, and getting feedback. "Remember that this is your story," she added. "You are the artist. The things you're trying to tell the world are important and real. Don't ever change your story because of feedback that doesn't resonate or make sense to you. Go with your gut, your heart—and your sixth sense."

Cover of Davis's teen time-travel romance The Clearing. (Reprinted by permission of Houghton Mifflin Harcourt Publishing Company. All rights reserved.)

Biographical and Critical Sources

PERIODICALS

Booklist, July 1, 2009, Kimberly Garnick, review of *Never Cry Werewolf,* p. 55; February 15, 2010, Melissa Moors, review of *The Clearing,* p. 47.

Bulletin of the Center for Children's Books, September, 2009, Kate Quealy-Gainer, review of *Never Cry Werewolf,* p. 14.

Kirkus Reviews, May 1, 2009, review of *Never Cry Werewolf.*

Publishers Weekly, March 22, 2010, review of *The Clearing,* p. 72.

School Library Journal, December, 2009, Donna Rosenblum, review of *Never Cry Werewolf,* p. 112; May, 2010, Danielle Serra, review of *The Clearing,* p. 108.

ONLINE

Books, Boys, Buzz . . . Web Log, http://yawriters.blogspot. com/ (October 15, 2010), Heather Davis, "Writing Tips: Revision."

Heather Davis Home Page, http://www.heatherdavisbooks. com (October 15, 2010).

*   *   *

DEEBLE, Jason 1979-

Personal

Born July 11, 1979, in Wilmington, DE; married; wife's name Danielle; children: one daughter. *Education:* University of Delaware, teaching degree. *Hobbies and other interests:* Art, cartooning.

Addresses

Home—Niantic, CT. *Agent*—Steven Chudney, Chudney Agency, 72 N. State Rd., Ste. 591, Briarcliff Manor, NY 10510.

Career

Educator and writer. Integrated Day Charter School, Norwich, CT, science teacher. Presenter at schools.

Writings

(Self-illustrated) *Sir Ryan's Quest,* Roaring Brook Press (New York, NY), 2009.

Sidelights

Jason Deeble wrote his first picture book, the self-illustrated *Sir Ryan's Quest,* while working as a science teacher at a Connecticut charter school. Born in Wilmington, Delaware, Deeble exhibited a talent for drawing comic characters as a boy. Although he began writing stories in high school, he chose to make teaching his career while attending the University of Delaware. In addition to writing, Deeble now spends his free time drawing comics and enjoying time with his family.

In *Sir Ryan's Quest* an imaginative, pajama-clad boy bypasses the toy box and heads to the kitchen, where a saucepan hat transforms the lad into a valiant knight. A proper knight must have a quest, and for Ryan his quest takes him up mountains (the stairs) and through a jungle (a cluttered closet) on his way to fight a dreaded monster in its lair (the basement). Carrying his wooden sword, the boy knight returns to the kitchen where his doting mother has prepared a congratulatory banquet fit for a hungry monster-slayer. Describing *Sir Ryan's Quest* as "an artful blend of the fantastical and familiar," *Booklist* contributor Shelle Rosenfeld added that Deeble's "charming debut closes with an affectionate, reassuring ending."

Biographical and Critical Sources

PERIODICALS

Booklist, April 1, 2009, Shelle Rosenfeld, review of *Sir Ryan's Quest,* p. 44.

School Library Journal, April, 2009, C.J. Connor, review of *Sir Ryan's Quest,* p. 102.

ONLINE

Jason Deeble Home Page, http://www.jasondeeble.com (October 15, 2010).*

*   *   *

de LAS CASAS, Dianne 1970-

Personal

Born January 15, 1970, in the Philippines; father in the U.S. Navy; married; children: Soleill, Eliana. *Religion:* Roman Catholic. *Hobbies and other interests:* Reading children's literature, writing, listening to music, films and theatre, traveling, meeting new people, spending time with family.

Addresses

Home and office—The Story Connection, P.O. Box 2656, Harvey, LA 70059. *E-mail*—dianne@storyconnection.net.

Career

Storyteller and author. Storyteller affiliated with Southern Artistry, Louisiana State Roster, Louisiana Touring Directory, and Mississippi Arts Education Demonstration Roster. Founder, *Professional Storyteller* (online network). Participant in arts-in-education programs and residencies; performer at schools, libraries, festivals, and museums.

Awards, Honors

iParenting Media Award, Children's Music Web Award, and *Storytelling World* honor designation, all 2003, all for *Jambalaya;* Children's Music Web Award, 2004, for *World Fiesta;* National Parenting Publication Award honor designation, and Children's Music Web Award, both 2006, both for *Jump, Jiggle, and Jam* (audio version); *Storytelling World* Award, 2008, for *The Story Biz Handbook;* iParenting Media Award, 2010, for *Mama's Bayou.*

Writings

FOR CHILDREN

Madame Poulet and Monsieur Roach, illustrated by Marita Gentry, Pelican Pub. (Gretna, LA), 2009.
The Cajun Cornbread Boy: A Well-loved Tale Spiced Up, illustrated by Marita Gentry, Pelican Pub. (Gretna, LA), 2009.

Dianne de Las Casas (Reproduced by permission.)

Mama's Bayou, illustrated by Holly Stone-Barker, Pelican Pub. (Gretna, LA), 2010.

The Gigantic Sweet Potato, illustrated by Marita Gentry, Pelican Pub. (Gretna, LA), 2010.

There's a Dragon in the Library, illustrated by Marita Gentry, Pelican Pub. (Gretna, LA), 2011.

The House That Witchy Built, illustrated by Holly Stone-Barker, Pelican Pub. (Gretna, LA), 2011.

Dinosaur Mardi Gras, illustrated by Marita Gentry, Pelican Pub. (Gretna, LA), 2012.

OTHER

Kamishibai Story Theater: The Art of Picture Telling, illustrated by Philip Chow, Teacher Ideas Press (Westport, CT), 2006.

Story Fest: Crafting Story Theater Scripts, illustrated by Jeanne de la Houssaye, Teacher Ideas Press (Westport, CT), 2006.

Handmade Tales: Stories to Make and Take, illustrated by Philip Chow, Libraries Unlimited (Westport, CT), 2008.

The Story Biz Handbook: How to Manage Your Storytelling Career from the Desk to the Stage, foreword by Margaret Read MacDonald, Libraries Unlimited (Westport, CT), 2008.

Tangram Tales: Story Theater Using the Ancient Chinese Puzzle, illustrated by Philip Chow, Teacher Ideas Press (Westport, CT), 2009.

Scared Silly: Twenty-five Tales to Tickle and Thrill, illustrated by Soleil Lisette, Libraries Unlimited (Santa Barbara, CA), 2009.

Stories on Board!: Creating Board Games from Favorite Tales, illustrated by Soleil Lisette, Libraries Unlimited (Santa Barbara, CA), 2010.

Tell Along Tales: Playing with Participation Stories, Libraries Unlimited (Santa Barbara, CA), 2010.

Tales from the 7,000 Isles: Filipino Folk Stories, Libraries Unlimited (Santa Barbara, CA), 2011.

A Is for Alligator: Draw and Tell Tales from A-Z, illustrated by Marita Gentry, Libraries Unlimited (Santa Barbara, CA), 2012.

Handmade Tales II: More Stories to Make and Take, Libraries Unlimited (Santa Barbara, CA), 2012.

Creator of audio CD's produced by Story Connections, including *Jambalaya: Stories with Louisiana Flavor,* 2003, *World Fiesta: Celebration in Story and Song,* 2004, and *Jump, Jiggle, and Jam: A Rhythmic Romp through Storyland,* 2006.

Sidelights

Dianne de Las Casas is an author and storyteller who draws on her natural vivacity and her vast repertoire of tales and legends from around the world. Performing for children at schools, libraries, and festivals, she captures the essence of her characters using minimal costumes and other props. Instead, de Las Casas creates magic using her voice, hand gestures, body movement, and facial expression. In reviewing de Las Casas's storytelling CD *World Fiesta: Celebration in Story and Song,* Naomi Leithold wrote in *School Library Journal* that the artist's "commanding voice, unique characterizations, emotive vocalizations, and creative methods of reaching out to her audience are most engaging." "I love it when I see the children singing, wiggling and giggling along," de las Casas admitted in discussing her work on her home page. "Not only does it show that they are engaged and using their imaginations. It demonstrates good old-fashioned fun!"

Born in the Philippines, where her father was then serving in the U.S. Navy, de Las Casas also lived in Hawai'i and Spain and traveled throughout Europe and the United States while growing up. She began telling stories to entertain young children while volunteering at the local library on weekends and quickly learned to love it. She has spent years building a repertoire that includes original stories and traditional folk tales from around the world, structuring them to include chants, songs, and other elements of audience participation and salting each with a generous dose of humor. De Las Casas has also adapted several of her stories into illustrated picture books and collections of shorter tales.

In *Mama's Bayou,* illustrated by Holly Stone-Barker, de Las Casas uses a rhyming text to capture the sights and sounds of the Louisiana bayou as dusk comes and animals curl up for sleep. In *School Library Journal* Judith Constantinides predicted that the book's use of repetition and rhythmic animal sounds "will entertain and inform preschoolers." Illustrated by Marita Gentry, *The Cajun Cornbread Boy: A Well-loved Tale Spiced Up* retells "an old story with a Cajun flair," according to the same critic. In de Las Casas's version, an animated

cornbread with long legs runs from a variety of hungry pursuers and credits his speed with the cayenne pepper baked into him. Noting Gentry's "muted, earth-toned" water color-and-pen illustrations, a *Kirkus Reviews* critic added that *The Cajun Cornbread Boy* is "best memorized and shared over some warn cornbread—recipe included."

Other stories by de Las Casas that feature artwork by Gentry include *Madame Poulet and Monsieur Roach, The Gigantic Sweet Potato, There's a Dragon in the Library,* and *Dinosaur Mardi Gras.* Reviewing *The Giant Sweet Potato,* a *Kirkus Reviews* writer predicted that "children will happily join in with the repetitive, cumulative text and enjoy the satisfying end, which naturally features [a recipe for] sweet-potato pie."

In addition to her books for children, de Las Casas also writes story collections and books of storytelling technique that draws on varied cultures. In *Tangram Tales: Story Theatre Using the Ancient Chinese Puzzle* the author structures a classroom-ready program around a seven-piece shape while *Kamishibai Story Theater: The Art of Picture Telling* outlines an informal technique incorporating large decorated pictures that was used by street performance artists in Japan during the early twentieth century. Reviewing *Kamishibai Story Theater* in *School Library Journal,* Mary Jean Smith wrote that de Las Casas's description of three kamishibai techniques and her inclusion of twenty-five tales combine to make "Kamishibai story theater look like fun." For *Teacher Librarian* critic David Loertscher, students' "reading and storytelling" abilities are challenged and encouraged in the "fun and clever technique" introduced in *Tangram Tales.* De Las Casas' most popular professional book to date, *Handmade Tales: Stories to Make and Take,* features innovative ways to jazz up storytelling sessions using common items such as towels, bandanas, napkins, paper, and string.

Biographical and Critical Sources

PERIODICALS

Booklist, April 15, 2005, Naomi Leithold, review of *World Fiesta: Celebration in Story and Song,* p. 1476.
Kirkus Reviews, January 15, 2009, review of *The Cajun Cornbread Boy: A Well-loved Tale Spiced Up*; September 2, 2010, review of *The Giant Sweet Potato.*
Publishers Weekly, March 15, 2004, review of *What's the Story?*, p. 27; September 18, 2006, review of *Jump, Jiggle, and Jam: A Rhythmic Romp through Storyland,* p. 57.
School Library Journal, April, 2004, Stephanie Bange, review of *Jambalaya: Stories with Louisiana Flavor,* p. 81; May, 2005, Beverly Bixler, review of *World Fiesta,* p. 68; April, 2007, review of *Jump, Jiggle, and Jam*; June, 2007, Mary Jean Smith, review of *Kamishibai Story Theater: The Art of Picture Telling,* p. 183;

March, 2009, Judith Constantinides, review of *The Cajun Cornbread Boy,* p. 108; May, 2010, Judith Constantinides, review of *Mama's Bayou,* p. 82.
Teacher Librarian, April, 2009, David Loertscher, review of *Tangram Tales: Story Theatre Using the Ancient Chinese Puzzle,* p. 58.

ONLINE

Dianne de Las Casas Home Page, http://www.storyconnection.net (October 15, 2010).

*   *   *

DE MUTH, Roger 1948-

Personal

Born November 20, 1948, in Passaic, NJ; married; wife's name Naomi; children: Adam, Aaron. *Education:* Rochester Institute of Technology, degree, 1971. *Hobbies and other interests:* Travel, gardening, bookbinding, collecting.

Addresses

Home—Cazenovia, NY. *E-mail*—rdemuth@syr.edu.

Career

Illustrator, author, photographer, toy designer, educator, and landscape designer. De Muth Designs, founder. Rochester Institute of Technology, instructor in illustration, 1978; Syracuse University, Syracuse, NY, associate professor of illustration, beginning 1979. Syracuse Poster Project (arts organization), cofounder, beginning 2001. *Exhibitions:* Works have been exhibited at galleries, including Chameleon Gallery, Cazenovia, NY.

Awards, Honors

Award of merit from Society of Illustrators, New York, and Society of Illustrators, Los Angeles; Oppenheim Toy Portfolio Award, 2008, for *Please Don't Eat Me!*

Writings

SELF-ILLUSTRATED

Please Don't Eat Me!, Blue Apple Books (San Francisco, CA), 2008.
Dinner for Eight, Blue Apple Books (Maplewood, NJ), 2009.

ILLUSTRATOR

Harriet Ziefert, *Messy Bessie: Where's My Homework?,* Blue Apple Books (San Francisco, CA), 2007.

Contributor to periodicals, including *New York Times.*

Sidelights

Roger De Muth is an illustrator, collector, artist, teacher, and overall extremely creative and inventive individual. As a collector, De Muth's interests range widely, from antique pens to vintage art supplies to illustrated ephemera. As a designer, he has focused his talents on everything from garden and furniture design to book construction, enjoying the process of arranging component parts into a cohesive whole. As an illustrator, De Muth works primarily in pen-and ink, highlighting the intricate detail of his ink drawings with loose and light-filled water color. When he travels, he carries unique, home-crafted artist's boxes fit with sketchbooks that he binds himself—his grandfather was a London bookbinder—and covers in decorative pressed leather. His book illustration projects include creating the artwork for Harriet Ziefert's beginning reader *Messy Bessie: Where's My Homework?* as well as for his original self-illustrated stories *Please Don't Eat Me!* and *Dinner for Eight.*

In *Messy Bessie* De Muth brings to life Ziefert's young mouse character, who lives amid a colorful quantity of household clutter. In Ziefert's text, readers are asked to help Messy Bessie find everything from her assignment book to a missing shoe so that she can arrive at school on time. In the colorful cartoon art that fills each die-cut double-page spread, Bessie wades through a sea of objects that reflects De Muth's whimsical sense of humor. "Youngsters who enjoy searching for pictured items will like this book," predicted Lynda Ritterman in her review of *Messy Bessie* for *School Library Journal.*

In the lift-the-flap books *Please Don't Eat Me!* and *Dinner for Eight* De Muth continues to share his quirky humor and detailed cartoon art. *Please Don't Eat Me!* begins as a chubby fish is laid out on a dinner plate, and his plea is directed to the reader, an imagined diner. Also focusing on mealtime, *Dinner for Eight* treats youngsters to an unusual gathering that is hosted by Octopus. Fortunately, eight arms make for light work in the kitchen, and by book's end every guest—from Kal

Roger De Muth invites children into his whimsical world in the pages of his self-illustrated picture book **Dinner for Eight.** (Reproduced by permission of Blue Apple Books.)

Kangaroo to François le Frog—is served with a meal customized for his or her palate. In creating the artwork for his picture books, De Muth creates pencil drawings for each double-page spread. After inking over them and adding detail, he then scans his illustrations into Photoshop where he can add flat expanses of color digitally. Predicting that the interactive aspects of *Dinner for Eight* will "delight . . . young would-be readers," a *Kirkus Reviews* writer added that "De Muth goes the extra mile" in his picture book, placing "humorous surprises under each flap."

Biographical and Critical Sources

PERIODICALS

Kirkus Reviews, May 1, 2009, review of *Dinner for Eight*.
Post-Standard (Syracuse, NY), July 1, 2007, Laura T. Ryan, "Quirks of Art," p. 3.
School Library Journal, October, 2007, Lynda Ritterman, review of *Messy Bessie: Where's My Homework?*, p. 130.

ONLINE

Roger De Muth Home Page, http://www.demuthdesign. com (October 15, 2010).*

*   *   *

DOODLER, Todd H.
See GOLDMAN, Todd Harris

*   *   *

DUNN, Herb
See GUTMAN, Dan

*   *   *

DUNSTAN MULLER, Rachel

Personal
Born in Oakland, CA; immigrated to Canada; married; husband an educator; children: four daughters. *Education:* University of Victoria, degree. *Hobbies and other interests:* Hiking, kayaking.

Addresses
Home—Ladysmith, British Columbia, Canada.

Career
Author, beginning 2001. Presenter at schools.

Member
Writers' Union of Canada.

Writings

Ten Thumb Sam, Orca Book Publishers (Custer, WA), 2007.
When the Curtain Rises, Orca Book Publishers (Custer, WA), 2007.
Squeeze, Orca Book Publishers (Custer, WA), 2010.
The Solstice Cup, Orca Book Publishers (Custer, WA), 2010.

Author of local newspaper columns, including "Penny-Wise."

Author's work has been translated into Swedish and Norwegian.

Sidelights
Rachel Dunstan Muller is a Canadian author who focuses her writing on middle-grade readers. Her novels, which include *Ten Thumb Sam, When the Curtain Rises,*

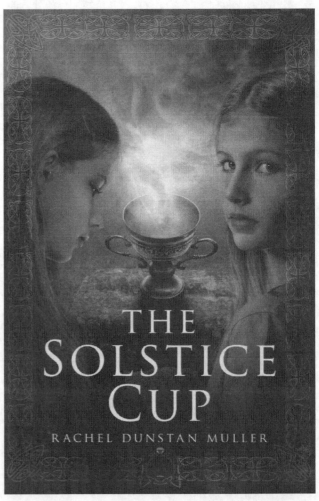

Cover of Rachel Dunstan Muller's **The Solstice Cup,** *an otherworld fantasy about two very different twins.* (Reproduced by permission of Orca Book Publishers.)

Squeeze, and *The Solstice Cup,* are inspired by Dunstan Muller's interests; *Squeeze,* for example, finds four teens encountering danger while on a caving trip and taps into its author's interest in hiking and caving, despite her own fear of confines places. "Writing is a kind of magic," Dunstan Muller explained in an interview posted on the Orca Book Publishers Web site. "I get to create entire worlds—interesting settings, unusual characters—out of thin air. If I do my job properly, I can bring what I'm writing about to life. Then other people can enter my stories as well."

Dubbed "an absolutely delightful book" by *Resource Links* contributor Janey Shabtai, *Ten Thumb Sam* finds ten-year-old Sam Stringbini hoping to clear his name of suspicion when someone sabotages the traveling circus where his parents perform. *When the Curtain Rises* focuses on Chloe, a preteen who decides to solve the mystery surrounding the disappearance of her great grandfather many years ago. Searching the house of Dante Magnus, who was well known as a magician before he vanished, Chloe discovers several secret rooms, one of which holds a strange rosewood box that will either answer the girl's questions or draw her into the same fate that befell her great grandfather. In reviewing *When the Curtain Rises,* Myra Junyk noted in *Resource Links* that Chloe is "a sympathetic character" whose adventure plays out in a story that "will appeal to young teenage readers . . . who love to solve mysteries."

Dunstan Muller turns to fantasy in *The Solstice Cup,* a middle-grade novel set in Northern Ireland in which twin sisters are suddenly transported into the world of the fairie. While thirteen-year-old Breanne finds an ancient gold ring with a purple stone on the day of the winter solstice, she and sister Mackenzie are transported to another world where fairy enchantments lurk every-where, even in food and music. Unlike Mackenzie, Breanne refuses to be cautious and her rash actions culminate in the sisters' capture by an evil fairy princess who hopes to keep the twins trapped forever in the land of fairies. Calling *The Solstice Cup* "a good introduction . . . to the sinister world of pixies," *Booklist* critic Kimberly Garnick added that Dunstan Muller's tale "should enchant and engage readers." In the *Canadian Review of Materials* Mary Thomas cited the author's "nice mix of mythological elements" and her ability to craft a story in which "everyone works through difficulties in a completely believable—if fantastical—way."

Biographical and Critical Sources

PERIODICALS

Booklist, May 15, 2009, Kimberly Gnarlick, review of *The Solstice Cup,* p. 56.
Canadian Review of Materials, February 20, 2009, Mary Thomas, review of *The Solstice Cup.*
Resource Links, April, 2007, Myra Junyk, review of *When the Curtain Rises,* p. 46; April, 2008, Janey Shabtai, review of *Ten Thumb Sam,* p. 11.
School Library Journal, June, 2007, Heather E. Miller, review of *When the Curtain Rises,* p. 154.
Voice of Youth Advocates, April, 2007, Shari Festo, review of *When the Curtain Rises,* p. 53.

ONLINE

Orca Book Publishers Web Site, http://www.orcabook.com/ (October 25, 2010), interview with Muller.

F

FEIG, Paul 1962-

Personal

Born 1962, in Mount Clemens, MI; father a store owner, mother a telephone operator; married c. 1991; wife's name Laurie. *Education:* Attended Wayne State University; University of Southern California Film School, degree.

Addresses

Home—Burbank, CA.

Career

Writer, director, actor, and producer. Worked as a stand-up comedian, studio tour guide, script reader, and script writer. Actor in films and television, including *Dirty Dancing,* 1988, *Good Sports,* 1991, *The Jackie Thomas Show,* 1992, *The Louie Show,* 1996, *Sabrina, the Teenage Witch,* 1996, *Stealing Harvard,* 2002, *Arrested Development,* 2005, and *Walk Hard: The Dewey Cox Story,* 2007. Director of films, including *Unaccompanied Minors,* 2006. Co-executive producer of television series *The Office;* director of episodes of television series, including *Arrested Development, Weeds, The Office, 30 Rock, Mad Men, Bored to Death,* and *Nurse Jackie.*

Awards, Honors

Two Emmy Award nominations, including 2001, for *Freaks and Geeks.*

Writings

FICTION

Superstud; or, How I Became a Twenty-four-Year-Old Virgin, Three Rivers Press (New York, NY), 2005.

(Self-illustrated) *Ignatius MacFarland, Frequenaut!,* Little, Brown (New York, NY), 2008.
Ignatius MacFarland, Frequency Freak-out, illustrated by Shane Hillman, Little, Brown (New York, NY), 2010.

OTHER

(And supervising producer) *Freaks and Geeks* (television series), Apatow Productions/DreamWorks/National Broadcasting Company (NBC), 1999.
Kick Me: Adventures in Adolescence (autobiographical essays), Three Rivers Press (New York, NY), 2002.

Author of screenplay for *The TV Wheel,* 1995, and *I Am David* and *Sick in the Head,* both 2003. Author of scripts for episodes of series television.

Adaptations

Ignatius MacFarland, Frequenaut! was adapted as an audiobook, Brilliance Audio, 2008.

Sidelights

Dubbed "Hollywood's go-to-guy for smart comedies with a warm heart and a nasty sideline in cringes" by London *Guardian* contributor Sam Delaney, American writer Paul Feig worked as an actor and comedian for twenty years before writing and producing the television series *Freaks and Geeks* in the late 1990s. Feig turned penning books in the early 2000s, with the humorous memoir *Kick Me: Adventures in Adolescence* and appeals to younger readers with *Ignatius MacFarland, Frequenaut!*

Born and raised in suburban Detroit, Michigan, Feig got his start in media by taping television commercials for his father's Detroit army-surplus store, and by high school he honed his comedic skills in talent shows. Determined to do stand-up comedy before older audiences, the teen was accompanied by his mother to local nightclubs, when he performed his routine. Feig was also active in local and college theater, and at the end of his

freshman year at Detroit's Wayne State University, he moved to Los Angeles to pursue his dreams. His first job in Hollywood was as a tour guide for Universal Studios.

Feig got the scriptwriting bug after watching the mega-popular film *Raiders of the Lost Ark* and he subsequently enrolled at the University of Southern California's film school. A job as a script reader for Michael Phillips, producer of the films *Taxi Driver* and *The Sting,* came next. Feig missed working in front of a live audience, however. He auditioned to be on the television game show *$25,000 Pyramid* and wound up winning the $29,000 that enabled him to quit his job with Phillips and become a full-time comedian.

Feig honed his craft and became moderately successful. At the same time, he wrote scripts and went to auditions. In 1989, he made the decision to give up touring in order to stay in Los Angeles. Small roles in films and ongoing roles in half-a-dozen television series followed, along with the chance to open for Jay Leno and work with top comedians like Dennis Miller and Bill Maher. Meanwhile, he began developing an idea he had for a television series, the idea that would result in *Freeks and Geeks.*

Freaks and Geeks was based on Feig's experiences during adolescence. "For me," the author admitted on the *Freaks and Geeks* Web site, "high school was about trying to get through the day without getting beaten up or humiliated or having your self-esteem destroyed." Feig's friend, Judd Apatow, brought a proposal for the show to DreamWorks, and a pilot was quickly produced. In the series, which is set in the 1980s, the character of Sam Weir comes closest to representing Feig's own life in episodes that touch on marijuana smoking, cross-dressing, and other daring subjects.

Feig taps the same vein of high-school angst in his first published book, 2002's *Kick Me.* In this collection of essays, the author reveals what it was like to be an underage geek, writing about his sadistic gym teacher, his brief experiment with cross-dressing, and the horrors of dating. According to a *Kirkus Reviews* contributor, Feig is "gifted with a remarkable ability to remember the specific and singular torments of youth," while a *Publishers Weekly* reviewer praised *Kick Me* as an "originally written, imaginatively comic missive." In *Library Journal* Joe Accardi predicted that Feig's comic memoir "is certain to release a rash of memories in all who have finally come to grips with the awkwardness of having grown up," and Kristine Huntley noted in *Booklist* that, "whether he's triumphant or humiliated, Feig is a droll storyteller."

Feig continued to mine what *Library Journal* contributor Barry X. Miller described as "the gnarly, humorous, and heartbreaking nuggets of teen angst" in *Superstud; or, How I Became a Twenty-four-Year-Old Virgin.* He also turns to younger readers in *Ignatius MacFarland,*

Frequenaut!, a self-illustrated novel for middle graders that focuses on a seventh-grade nerd. Since his parents refuse to move the family to another state, Iggy hopes to avoid the taunting of bullying classmates by ejecting himself in to outer space. A homemade rocket constructed of aluminum garbage cans seems to transport the twelve year old to an alien world when he emerges and finds himself surrounded by bizarre vegetation, curious creatures, and Karen, a classmate who Iggy is certain is no longer among the living. Soon Iggy joins Karen in her effort to release everyone trapped in this strange world, which turns out to be an earthly dimension created by a disgruntled English teacher. Although Necia Blundy found that the science-fiction storyline of *Ignatius MacFarland, Frequenaut!* is somewhat confusing, she nonetheless added in *School Library Journal* that Feig's "premise is highly original." In *Kirkus Reviews* a contributor predicted that reluctant readers will enjoy the "gross humor" in the novel, as well as "both a delightfully sarcastic antihero and a bizarre reality for

Paul Feig's humorous children's book Ignatius MacFarland, Frequenaut! *features artwork by Peter Chan.* (Copyright © 2008 by Paul Feig. Reproduced by permission of Little, Brown and Company.)

him to explore." In *Booklist* Ian Chipman dubbed Iggy "an inept adventurer" who "generates a good deal of laughs" in Feig's "goofy, proudly uncool story."

Discussing his approach to writing his brand of droll television comedy with Delaney, Feig explained that "it's important for the people in any comedy to act just like real people act. That means not speaking in a constant stream of pithy one-liners. It means getting into the same sort of horrible, awkward situations we all get into every day. Easily the most funny, fascinating and cringeworthy time in anyone's life is school. It's the only time that you get lumped in with a whole bunch of people without any filter; it's not to do with skills or interests, just age. And you're forced to spend every day with them for years."

Biographical and Critical Sources

BOOKS

Feig, Paul, *Kick Me: Adventures in Adolescence,* Three Rivers Press (New York, NY), 2002.

PERIODICALS

Booklist, September 15, 2002, Kristine Huntley, review of *Kick Me,* p. 184; June 1, 2005, Kristine Huntley, review of *Superstud; or, How I Became a Twenty-four-Year-Old Virgin,* p. 1718; October 15, 2008, Ian Chipman, review of *Ignatius MacFarland, Frequenaut!,* p. 39.

Guardian (London, England), July 4, 2009, Sam Delaney, profile of Feig.

Kirkus Reviews, review of *Kick Me,* p. 1006; August 1, 2008, review of *Ignatius MacFarland, Frequenaut!*

Library Journal, September 1, 2002, Joe Accardi, review of *Kick Me,* p. 175; May 15, 2005, Barry X. Miller, review of *Superstud,* p. 119.

New York Times, January 9, 2000, Eric Schmuckler, review of *Freaks and Geeks,* p. AR39.

New York Times Magazine, September 28, 2008, John Bowe, "The Trouble with Paul Feig," p. 44.

Publishers Weekly, July 1, 2002, review of *Kick Me,* p. 63; May 9, 2005, review of *Superstud,* p. 58.

School Library Journal, December, 2008, Necia Blundy, review of *Ignatius MacFarland, Frequenaut!,* p. 122.

Variety, September 20, 1999, Ray Richmond, "*Freaks and Geeks,*" p. 43.

ONLINE

Film Force Web site, http://www.filmforce.ign.com/ (February 10, 2000), Kenneth Plume, interview with Feig.

Freaks and Geeks Web site, http://www.geocities.com/freaksgeeksweb/ (October 16, 2002), interview with Feig.*

FELDMAN, Eve B.

Personal

Born in New York, NY; married; children: two sons. *Education:* Sarah Lawrence College, B.A.; Harvard University, M.Ed. *Hobbies and other interests:* Reading, writing, cooking, dancing, hula-hooping, enjoying friends and family.

Addresses

Home—Long Island, NY. *E-mail*—eve_feldman@post.harvard.edu.

Career

Teacher and writer. Teaching experience includes middle-grade English as a Second Language, second grade, and remedial reading in more than one language. Presenter at schools; facilitator at workshops.

Member

Author's Guild, Author's League, Society of Children's Book Writers and Illustrators.

Awards, Honors

Best Book designation, Child Study Children's Book Committee, for *Seymour, the Formerly Fearful;* American Booksellers Pick of the List designation, and National Science Teachers Association/Children's Book Council Outstanding Science Trade Book for Children designation, both for *Animals Don't Wear Pajamas;* Florida State Sunshine Award nomination, for *Dog Crazy;* Notable Children's Book designation, National Council of Teachers of English, 2010, for *Billy and Milly, Short and Silly.*

Writings

A Giant Surprise, illustrated by Istvan Banyai, Raintree Publishers (Milwaukee, WI), 1989.

Eek Gob Lope, illustrated by Carl Molno, Raintree Publishers (Milwaukee, WI), 1989.

Get Set and Go, illustrated by Yvette Banek, Raintree Publishers (Milwaukee, WI), 1989.

Mean Aunt Agatha, photographs by Richard Hutchings, Scholastic, Inc. (New York, NY), 1989.

Benjamin Franklin, Scientist and Inventor, F. Watts (New York, NY), 1990.

Seymour, the Formerly Fearful, Four Winds Press (New York, NY), 1990.

The Squire Takes a Wife, illustrated by Bari Weissman, Raintree Publishers (Milwaukee, WI), 1990.

Animals Don't Wear Pajamas: A Book about Sleeping, illustrated by Mary Beth Owens, Henry Holt (New York, NY), 1992.

Dog Crazy, illustrated by Eric Jon Nones, Tambourine Books (New York, NY), 1992.

Eve B. Feldman (Reproduced by permission.)

That Cat!, illustrated by James E. Ransome, Tambourine
    Books (New York, NY), 1994.
Birthdays!: Celebrating Life around the World, BridgeWa-
    ter Books (Mahwah, NJ), 1996.
Billy and Milly, Short and Silly, illustrated by Tuesday
    Mourning, G.P. Putnam's Sons (New York, NY), 2009.

Short fiction included in anthologies *With All My Heart,
with All My Mind,* edited by Sandy Asher, Simon &
Schuster (New York, NY), 1999; and *I Fooled You: Ten
Stories of Tricks, Jokes, and Switcheroos,* edited by Johanna Hurwitz, Candlewick Press (New York, NY),
2010.

Sidelights

While living overseas, New York native Eve B. Feldman channeled her talent for language into a career
teaching English to non-English-speaking children in
both elementary and middle school. Feldman began
writing stories after returning to the United States and
raising her own two children. Her books range from
middle-grade novels such as *Seymour, the Formerly
Fearful,* which focuses on a boy who seems to be afraid
of everything, to nonfiction books such as *Benjamin
Franklin, Scientist and Inventor* and *Animals Don't
Wear Pajamas: A Book about Sleeping.* In the chapter

book *Dog Crazy* Feldman focuses on a young girl who
is determined to have her own dog to love, while *That
Cat!* finds a young child determined to track down her
family cat after the creature escapes its suburban home
and vanishes into the great outdoors. Praising *That Cat!*
for its focus on "everyday happenings," Deborah Abbott added in *Booklist* that "readers will easily share
Molly's feelings and concerns."

In *Animals Don't Wear Pajamas* children are introduced
to sixteen different animals that settle down for sleep in
sometimes-unusual ways. Illustrated in watercolor paintings by Mary Beth Owens that depict anthropomorphic
critters from gorillas to lizards, the book also benefits
from what a *Publishers Weekly* critic described as "the
lulling rhythm of Feldman's repetitive language."

Continuing her focus on young children, Feldman packs
thirteen very short, easy-reading tales into *Billy and
Milly, Short and Silly,* which features engaging art by
Tuesday Mourning. A combination concept book and
beginning reader, the work mixes a handful of well-
selected rhyming words (often one to a page) with
Mourning's illustrations to tell each story, all of which
feature young neighbors Billy and Milly. The artist's
"modern collage illustrations help . . . to connect the
words and encourage readers to guess what's coming
next," noted Robin Smith in her *Horn Book* appraisal of
Billy and Milly, Short and Silly. In *School Library Journal* Julie Roach noted the "clever and slapstick" aspects
of the unique picture book and recommended it as an
aid to children contemplating "rhyme, language, and
story." According to *Bulletin of the Center for Children's Books* contributor Elizabeth Bush, in *Billy and
Milly, Short and Silly* "Feldman turns what could be a
tedious lesson in phonics into an emergent reader fun-
fest," while a *Kirkus Reviews* contributor called Feldman's noun/verb combinations "clever" and dubbed
Billy and Milly, Short and Silly "a wonderfully playful
introduction to language, rhyme and storytelling."

"My love of books goes back as far as I can remember
and remains as strong as ever," Feldman told *SATA.*
"My comparable pleasures are writing, whether exploring character or language, answering some long-
festering questions, or indulging in the never-ending
challenges and joys of research; and spending time with
children while visiting schools or entertaining relatives
and neighbors in my private life!

"I have not outgrown the child in me nor the
comedienne/ actress side of me, and I remain a total fan
of laughter!"

Biographical and Critical Sources

PERIODICALS

Booklist, March 1, 1992, Stephanie Zvirin, review of *Ani-
    mals Don't Wear Pajamas: A Book about Sleeping,* p.

Feldman's engaging story in **Billy and Milly, Short and Silly** *is brought to life in Tuesday Mourning's unique art.* (Putnam 2009. Reproduced by permission of Penguin Putnam, Inc.)

1281; March 15, 1992, review of *Dog Crazy,* p. 1378; October 1, 1994, Deborah Abbott, review of *That Cat!,* p. 326.

Bulletin of the Center for Children's Books, July, 1990, review of *Seymour, the Formerly Fearful,* p. 263; September, 2009, Elizabeth Bush, review of *Billy and Milly, Short and Silly,* p. 17.

Horn Book, May-June, 1992, Elizabeth S. Watson, review of *Animals Don't Wear Pajamas,* p. 360; September-October, 2009, Robin L. Smith, review of *Billy and Milly, Short and Silly,* p. 539.

Kirkus Reviews, May 1, 2009, review of *Billy and Milly, Short and Silly.*

Publishers Weekly, March 9, 1992, review of *Animals Don't Wear Pajamas,* p. 56.

School Library Journal, May, 1990, Todd Morning, review of *Seymour, the Formerly Fearful,* p. 104; April, 1992, Laura Culberg, review of *Dog Crazy,* p. 91; June, 1992, Jacqueline Elsner, review of *Animals Don't Wear Pajamas,* p. 106; September, 1994, Jacqueline Rose, review of *That Cat!,* p. 214; August, 1996, Denise Furgione, review of *Birthdays!: Celebrating Life around the World,* p. 134; July, 2009, Julie Roach, review of *Billy and Milly, Short and Silly,* p. 62.

ONLINE

Eve B. Feldman Home Page, http://www.evebfeldman.com (October 15, 2010).

*   *   *

FLEMING, Sally
See WALKER, Sally M.

*   *   *

FORD, John C. 1971-

Personal

Born 1971, in MI. *Education:* Stanford University, B.A.; University of Michigan, J.D. *Hobbies and other interests:* Swimming.

Addresses

Home—Washington, DC. *Agent*—Sara Crowe, Harvey Klinger, Inc., 300 W. 55th St., Ste. 11V, New York, NY 10019. *E-mail*—John@johncfordbooks.com.

Career

Attorney and author.

Awards, Honors

Agatha Award nomination for Best Children's/Young-Adult Novel, 2009, for *The Morgue and Me*.

Writings

The Morgue and Me, Viking (New York, NY), 2009.

Author's work has been translated into French.

Sidelights

Like Christopher Newell, the fictional protagonist of his debut novel *The Morgue and Me,* John C. Ford was a high-achieving student while growing up in Michigan, and he worked during his last summer at home before heading to his first year of college. Although readers will never know whether Ford shared Christopher's dream of being a spy, that dream inspires the teen to take the unusual summer job that jump-starts the story's action. In the *Journal of Adolescent & Adult Literacy* Lindsey Berry praised Ford's novel, calling *The Morgue and Me* "a captivating story" that weaves together "murder, mystery, criminal investigation, journalism, and photography" while also capturing the "challenges and growth . . . common to anyone who has attended high school."

In *The Morgue and Me* Christopher is eighteen years old and newly graduated from high school. With a scholarship in hand and the promise of attending the same college as his girlfriend Julia, Christopher plans a summer of winding down, enjoying time with friends, and indulging in his hobbies. A summer job at the local morgue seems to be perfect, but then he discovers that a recent death has been prematurely been ruled a suicide; in fact, it is the result of murder. As the teen's curiosity leads him to investigate the unanswered questions surrounding this victim, he links up with the beautiful Tina McIntyre, an ambitious reporter who is looking for a big story to fuel her journalism career. Soon, the trail of evidence leads Christopher and Tina to the doors of city hall, where powerful people are in a position to retaliate in ways that may put the teen's family at risk.

In *The Morgue and Me* Ford draws on the plot twists, arch humor, and red herrings that define many popular whodunits; as a *Publishers Weekly* critic noted, his "dark and stellar debut . . . nicely updates many classic mystery tropes." "Christopher's character is sympathetic and the murder mystery well-constructed," asserted a *Kirkus Reviews* critic, and Terri Clark commented in *School Library Journal* on the novel's "likable, quirky detectives and their crackling chemistry." While noting

that "Ford's unpredictable curveballs and switcheroos never relent," Daniel Kraus added in *Booklist* that *The Morgue and Me* treats readers to "a satisfyingly grim departure from the usual squeaky-clean" mystery. In her *Los Angeles Times* review of Ford's fiction debut, Sarah Weinman predicted that *The Morgue and Me* will appeal to adults as well as to teens and marks "what looks to be a promising career in crime fiction—regardless of bookstore classification."

Biographical and Critical Sources

PERIODICALS

Booklist, May 1, 2009, Daniel Kraus, review of *The Morgue and Me,* p. 39.
Bulletin of the Center for Children's Books, July-August, 2009, Elizabeth Bush, review of *The Morgue and Me,* p. 442.
Journal of Adolescent & Adult Literature, March, 2010, Lindsey Berry, review of *The Morgue and Me,* p. 522.
Kirkus Reviews, May 1, 2009, review of *The Morgue and Me.*

Cover of John C. Ford's debut young-adult novel **The Morgue and Me,** *in which a summer job leads to mystery.* (Viking 2009. Reproduced by permission of Penguin Group USA Inc.)

Los Angeles Times, May 10, 2009, Sarah Weinman, review of *The Morgue and Me.*

Publishers Weekly, June 15, 2009, review of *The Morgue and Me,* p. 51.

School Library Journal, August, 2009, Terri Clark, review of *The Morgue and Me,* p. 102.

Voice of Youth Advocates, August, 2009, Diane P. Tuccillo, review of *The Morgue and Me,* p. 224.

ONLINE

John C. Ford Home Page, http://www.johncfordbooks. com (October 15, 2010).*

* * *

FRAZER, Megan 1977-

Personal

Born 1977; married; children: one son. *Education:* Columbia University, B.A.; Simmons College, M.L.S.

Addresses

Home—Poland, ME. *E-mail*—megan@meganfrazer. com.

Career

Librarian and author. Public librarian in Wakefield, MA; high-school librarian in Boston, MA, and in ME. Presenter at conferences.

Member

American Library Association, Society of Children's Book Writers and Illustrators.

Awards, Honors

New England Children's Book Sellers Advisory Council Top Ten selection, 2009, and Rainbow List inclusion, American Library Association Rainbow Project, and Isinglass award nomination, both 2010, all for *Secrets of Truth and Beauty.*

Writings

Secrets of Truth and Beauty, Hyperion Books (New York, NY), 2009.

Sidelights

Megan Frazer began her debut young-adult novel *Secrets of Truth and Beauty* while living in Boston, Massachusetts, and working as a high-school librarian. She found a lot of support in a local writer's group, and when she relocated to Maine mid-manuscript, Frazer

Megan Frazer (Photograph by Nathan Charles Blakemore. Reproduced by permission.)

decided to join a new online group, called 2009 Debutantes. "The Debs are great because it's a group of other YA and middle-grade authors who are going through the same things I am," she told *Cynsations* online interviewer Cynthia Leitich Smith. "It's wonderful to be able to ask questions, share triumphs, and commiserate over setbacks with people who really get it." Frazer's manuscript eventually found its way into bookstores and attracted the notice of several awards committees.

In *Secrets of Truth and Beauty* readers meet Dara Cohen, a seventeen year old whose current weight problem masks her past as a childhood winner of the Little Miss Maine beauty pageant. When Dara decides to fight back against the prejudices of her classmates by crafting a video project that addresses misconceptions about weight, her already-tense relationship with her parents becomes untenable. Looking for a place to spend the summer, the teen tracks down her older sister, Rachel, who has been estranged from the family ever since she came out as a lesbian. Rachel is living at Jezebel Goat Farm, a farming collective that is run by a group of women who have formed a close-knit community to replace the families that have rejected them due to their sexuality or for other reasons. Over the course of her summer at the farm, Dara learns to see herself through more compassionate eyes and gains the skills to deal with her judgmental mother.

Praising Frazer's novel as "a highly enjoyable read," Kathleen E. Graver added that *Secrets of Truth and Beauty* features "entertaining and appealing" characters. "Pain and sweetness mingle in this enjoyable coming-

of-age tale," asserted a *Kirkus Reviews* writer, the critic citing Frazer's "clean, mellow prose" and her technique of including biracial characters while minimizing race as a criteria for finding difference. In *Publishers Weekly* a reviewer praised Dara as "a likeable, complex heroine" and went on to rank *Secrets of Truth and Beauty* as "a beautifully written coming-of-age story" about "an overweight teen [that] gets her groove back."

Biographical and Critical Sources

PERIODICALS

Kirkus Reviews, June 1, 2009, review of *Secrets of Truth and Beauty.*
Publishers Weekly, June 6, 2009, review of *Secrets of Truth and Beauty,* p. 44.
School Library Journal, August, 2009, Kathleen E. Graver, review of *Secrets of Truth and Beauty,* p. 103.

ONLINE

Megan Frazer Home Page, http://www.meganfrazer.com (October 15, 2010).

Cover of Frazer's young-adult novel **Secrets of Truth and Beauty.** (© 2009 by Megan Frazer. Reproduced by permission of Disney Hyperion, an imprint of Disney Book Group, LLC. All rights reserved.)

Cynsations Web Log, http://cynthialeitichsmith.blogspot.com/ (September 15, 2009), Cynthia Leitich Smith, interview with Frazer.
2009 Debutantes Web log, http://community.livejournal.com/debut2009/ (October 15, 2010), Megan Frazer.

*   *   *

FRAZIER, Craig 1955-

Personal

Born 1955; married; children: two. *Education:* Degree (communication design).

Addresses

Office—Craig Frazier Studio, 90 Throckmorton Ave., Ste. 28, Mill Valley, CA 94941. *E-mail*—studio@craigfrazier.com; Stanley@stanleybooks.com.

Career

Author, illustrator, and graphic designer. Frazier Design, Inc., San Francisco, CA, president and owner, 1978-96; Craig Frazier Studio (illustration), president and owner, 1996—. Designer of trademarks for companies, including LucasArts, of postage stamps for U.S. Postal Service, and of "Critter" font for Adobe. Instructor at California College of Arts and Kent State University summer graduate program. Member of board of advisors, The Portfolio Center, Atlanta, GA, and 2005 Illustrators Conference. *Exhibitions:* Works included in permanent collection at San Francisco Museum of Modern Art.

Awards, Honors

Numerous awards for design.

Writings

SELF-ILLUSTRATED PICTURE BOOKS

Stanley Goes for a Drive, Chronicle Books (San Francisco, CA), 2004.
Stanley Mows the Lawn, Chronicle Books (San Francisco, CA), 2005.
Stanley Goes Fishing, Chronicle Books (San Francisco, CA), 2006.
Hank Finds Inspiration, Roaring Brook Press (New York, NY), 2008.
Lots of Dots, Chronicle Books (San Francisco, CA), 2010.
Bee and Bird, Roaring Brook Press (New York, NY), 2011.

ILLUSTRATOR

George Ella Lyon, *Trucks Roll!,* Atheneum Books for Young Readers (New York, NY), 2007.

Craig Frazier (Photograph by Jock McDonald. Reproduced by permission.)

Tom Corwin, *Mr. Fooster Traveling on a Whim*, Doubleday (New York, NY), 2008.

Contributor of illustrations to periodicals, including *Time, Fortune, Forbes, Business Week, Fast Company, Harvard Business Review, Boston Globe, Reader's Digest, Newsweek, New York Times, Wall Street Journal, Los Angeles Times, Utne Reader*, and *Atlantic Monthly.*

Sidelights

Craig Frazier is an award-winning graphic designer and illustrator who has also ventured into the world of children's literature with picture books such as *Stanley Goes for a Drive, Stanley Goes Fishing, Hank Finds Inspiration*, and *Lots of Dots*. Frazier brings a sense of play and wonder to his surrealistic, digitally enhanced artwork, and he believes that his topsy-turvy vision is best appreciated by youngsters. As he told Kirk Citron in *Graphis*, children "haven't closed down the aperture on the way they see things. They don't know yet that you can't walk on the ceiling, so they just draw it. And they draw it without worrying about how to draw it, yet it communicates." As a *Kirkus Reviews* writer noted, *Lots of Dots* coaxes readers to see the world through artist's eyes as Frazier's lighthearted, rhyming text weaves together his "ebullient illustrations" into a "playful examination into what composes our world and how much is hidden in the everyday."

Frazier published his first self-illustrated children's book, *Stanley Goes for a Drive*, in 2004. The work opens as Stanley takes a ride in his pickup truck on a hot and cloudless summer day. According to a critic in *Publishers Weekly*, the work "soon sheds its initial pragmatism for a dreamlike flight of fancy." While cruising past a herd of cows, Stanley gets an idea: he grabs a bucket, approaches the only black-and-white spotted cow, and begins milking it. As he does, the white spots magically drain off the animal. When Stanley tosses the contents of the bucket into the sky, the milk floats up and forms fluffy clouds that darken and pour rain on the parched landscape. *Stanley Goes for a Drive* received strong praise from reviewers, who paid special attention to the book's hand-drawn, digitally colored illustrations. Frazier's "masterful use of composition surprises readers with large shapes in the foreground that contrast with small, multiple figures in the background to create asymmetric balance and depth," noted Carolyn Janssen in *School Library Journal*. In the words of a *Kirkus Reviews* contributor, "reading this unusual, visually intriguing story is like examining a surrealist painting where something shifts inexplicably as one watches."

In *Stanley Mows the Lawn* "what begins as a routine chore literally takes a turn, with a satisfying and visually creative result," observed a *Kirkus Reviews* critic. When the grass in Stanley's yard grows long enough to cover his feet, he brings out his push mower and begins cutting back and forth in straight, precise rows. A rustling in the grass causes Stanley to halt his work, and he spies Hank the snake slithering through the yard. Abandoning his repetitive pattern of mowing, Stanley begins zigzagging his way through the lawn, making sure to leave patches of tall grass for Hank. In *School Library Journal*, Suzanne Myers Harold remarked that *Stanley Mows the Lawn* "uses subtle humor to convey its theme of seeing the world from another's point of view and finding a mutually agreeable solution."

Stanley returns in *Stanley Goes Fishing* as the kindly gentleman plans to spend a relaxing day with his fishing rod and reel. He launches his boat into a stream and trolls all his favorite spots. Despite his best efforts, however, the only thing he pulls from the water is a soggy old boot. Hoping to change his luck, Stanley casts his line into the sky and starts hauling in one golden fish after another. After catching his fill, a satisfied Stanley returns the fish to the stream. "The crisp, clean illustrations in bright golds, verdant greens, and brilliant blues are a pleasure to behold," wrote *School Library Journal* contributor Maryann H. Owen. Also complimenting Frazier's imaginative artwork, a critic for *Kirkus Reviews* deemed *Stanley Goes Fishing* "a visual conundrum that accentuates the 'art' of looking at the world in different ways."

Stanley is joined by friend Hank the snake in *Hank Finds Inspiration*, which a *Publishers Weekly* contributor dubbed "a perfect union of art and text." In the story, after a subdued Stanley drives to the city in order to find inspiration, Hank hops into a taxicab and follows him, outfitted in a top hat that will help the snake fit in with the high-living urban crowd. Not sure where to find inspiration, Hank asks others for help, traveling from a library to a city park to a flower shop until he slithers into an art gallery and encounters a sculpture that makes his little snake heart soar. Calling the picture

book "inspired," Mary Elam added in _School Library Journal_ that the art work in _Hank Finds Inspiration_ is characteristic Frazier: "crisp graphics" combining "varied perspectives with bold splashes of color" and a striking use of contrasts. "The stylized artwork evokes jazz with its interplay of different shapes and rhythms," according to a _Kirkus Reviews_ writer, while the _Publishers Weekly_ critic maintained that Frazier's "signature high-intensity graphics" in _Hank Finds Inspiration_ "exert their usual force field on readers' attention."

Biographical and Critical Sources

PERIODICALS

Booklist, May 1, 2007, Hazel Rochman, review of _Trucks Roll!,_ p. 99.

Communication Arts, January-February, 1991, Marty Neumeier, "Craig Frazier," p. 32.

Graphis, July-August, 2002, Kirk Citron, "Craig Frazier: Things Are Not What They Seem," pp. 100-111; November-December, 2002, Petual Vrontikis, interview with Frazier.

Horn Book, July-August, 2007, Joanna Rudge Long, review of _Trucks Roll!,_ p. 382.

Kirkus Reviews, July 1, 2004, review of _Stanley Goes for a Drive,_ p. 629; April 1, 2005, review of _Stanley Mows the Lawn,_ p. 416; April 15, 2006, review of _Stanley Goes Fishing,_ p. 405; May 15, 2007, review of _Trucks Roll!;_ August 1, 2008, review of _Hank Finds Inspiration._

Publishers Weekly, September 13, 2004, review of _Stanley Goes for a Drive,_ p. 77; April 28, 2008, review of _Mr. Foster Traveling on a Whim,_ p. 114; July 7, 2008, review of _Mr. Foster Traveling on a Whim,_ p. 44; September 1, 2008, review of _Hank Finds Inspiration,_ p. 54; October 15, 2010, review of _Lots of Dots._

School Library Journal, September, 2004, Carolyn Janssen, review of _Stanley Goes for a Drive,_ p. 160; May, 2005, Suzanne Myers Harold, review of _Stanley Mows the Lawn,_ p. 82; June, 2006, Maryann H. Owen, review of _Stanley Goes Fishing,_ p. 112; September, 2007, Lynn K. Vanca, review of _Trucks Roll!,_ p. 170; September, 2008, Mary Elam, review of _Hank Finds Inspiration,_ p. 146.

ONLINE

Craig Frazier Home Page, http://www.craigfrazier.com (October 20, 2010).

Stanley Books Web site, http://www.stanleybooks.com/ (October 20, 2010).

**Frazier introduces a popular picture-book character in** Stanley Goes Fishing. (© 2003. Used with permission of Chronicle Books, LLC, San Francisco. Visit Chronicle-Books.com.)

FUCILE, Tony

Personal

Born in San Francisco, CA; married; wife's name Stacey; children: Eli, Elinor. *Education:* California Institute of the Arts, degree (animation).

Addresses

Home—CA.

Career

Animator and author and illustrator of children's books. Work for television includes: (animator) *The Bugs Bunny and Tweety Show,* 1986; (principal animator) *Amazing Stories,* 1987; (animator and layout artist) *Christmas in Tattertown* (television film), 1988; and (timing director) *The Ren and Stimpy Show,* 1993. Work in feature films includes: (character animator) *Oliver and Company,* 1988; (character animator) *The Little Mermaid,* 1989; (animation director and character designer) *FernGully: The Last Rainforest,* 1992; (animator) *Aladdin,* 1992; (supervising animator) *The Lion King,* 1994; (supervising animator and character designer) *The Hunchback of Notre Dame,* 1996; (head of animation and character designer) *The Iron Giant,* 1999; (supervising animator and character designer) *The Incredibles,* 2004; and (animator and character designer) *Ratatouille,* 2007.

Writings

(Self-illustrated) *Let's Do Nothing!,* Candlewick Press (Somerville, MA), 2009.

(Illustrator) Kate DiCamillo and Alison McGhee, *Bink and Gollie,* Candlewick Press (Somerville, MA), 2010.

Hallie Durand, *Mitchell's License,* Candlewick Press (Somerville, MA), 2011.

Sidelights

Tony Fucile has a job that may seem enviable to budding comics artists: as a film animator he has worked on popular feature films ranging from *The Lion King* and *The Incredibles* to *Ratatouille.* In *Let's Do Nothing!* Fucile brings to life an amusing story in his unique art, while he takes on the role of illustrator in Kate DiCamillo and Alison McGhee's picture book *Bink and Gollie.* Praising the "delightful digitalized cartoon illustrations" in *Bink and Gollie,* Nancy Menaldi-Scanlan added in *School Library Journal* that Fucile's humorous drawings are "filled with movement" and "successfully portray the . . . changing moods" of the two young friends in DeCamillo and McGhee's beginning reader. "Fucile makes his inklike digital illustrations crackle with energy and sly humor," asserted a *Kirkus Reviews* writer, and in *Booklist* Gillian Engberg praised *Bink and Gollie*

as a "zany hybrid of picture book, graphic novel, and early reader" that comes to life in the artist's "expressive cartoon-style drawings."

Growing up with "Looney Tunes" cartoons and Walt Disney's *Pinocchio,* Fucile eventually discovered Ray Harryhausen's monster movies and the artistry of Warner Brothers animation artist Chuck Jones. After studying animation at Valencia-based California Institute of the Arts, he entered the film industry in the mid-1980s and worked with pencil and paper until the early 1990s, when a job at Pixar studios introduced him to the use of computers for animation and character design. Fucile's decision to branch out into picture-book illustration was inspired by his long-time dream of creating a children's story. His childhood memories of playing with a friend named Steve resulted in *Let's Do Nothing!*

In *Let's Do Nothing!* Fucile uses traditional media such as pencil, ink, and acrylics to create the colorful illustrations that capture the thoughts and antics of two boys with nothing to do. Sal and his younger friend Frankie have read all the comic books, played all their board games, drawn pictures until they could draw no more, and have even tired of home-baked cookies. Bored with everything, Sal and Frankie decide to make a new challenge out of doing nothing—absolutely nothing—for at least ten seconds. No breathing, no blinking, no wiggling, no giggling—nothing. With the turn of each page, readers follow their failed efforts, and Fucile's "pictures

Cover of Tony Fucile's self-illustrated picture book **Let's Do Nothing!,** *which features Fucile's animated cartoon art.* (Copyright © 2009 Tony Fucile. Reproduced by permission of Candlewick Press, Somerville, MA., and Pippin Properties, Inc.)

capture the universality of the moment through the boys' animated body language," according to *School Library Journal* contributor Adrienne Wilson. The author/illustrator's experience in animation "makes itself felt in the [book's] dialogue-based text and exquisite sense of pacing and visual humor," asserted a *Kirkus Reviews* writer, and in *Booklist* John Peters dubbed *Let's Do Nothing!* a story that "should leave plenty of chuckles in its wake."

As an animator, Fucile works from a specific script, so creating the story for *Let's Do Nothing!* was a new experience for him. As he explained in an interview on the Candlewick Web site, "My responsibilities [as an animator] were similar to what an actor gives a director in a live-action film. I was addicted to it, the notion of breathing life into characters with a pencil and paper. Making the art for [*Let's Do Nothing!*] . . . was kind of like animating, but without the in-betweens.

"In an animation shot, we call it the 'storytelling pose'—the single visual idea that must be conveyed to the audience, to connect them with what you're trying to communicate. When you animate, you usually begin with that dominant pose or poses in mind. *Let's Do Nothing!* is really a series of key animation storytelling poses. It scratches that animator itch in me that I'm afraid will never go away."

Biographical and Critical Sources

PERIODICALS

Booklist, July 1, 2009, John Peters, review of *Let's Do Nothing!,* p. 66; September 15, 2010, Gillian Engberg, review of *Bink and Gollie,* p. 68.

Bulletin of the Center for Children's Books, July-August, 2009, Kate Quealy-Gainer, review of *Let's Do Nothing!,* p. 442.

Kirkus Reviews, May 1, 2009, review of *Let's Do Nothing!*

Publishers Weekly, August 9, 2010, review of *Bink and Gollie,* p. 52.

School Library Journal, July, 2009, Adrienne Wilson, review of *Let's Do Nothing!,* p. 63; August, 2010, Nancy Menaldi-Scanlan, review of *Bink and Gollie,* p. 74.

ONLINE

Animation Artist Online, http://www.animationartist.com/ (October 15, 2010), interview with Fucile.

Candlewick Press Web Site, http://www.candlewick.com/ (October 15, 2010), interview with Fucile.*

G

GOLDMAN, Todd Harris
(Todd H. Doodler)

Personal

Male. *Education:* University of Florida, B.S. (accounting), M.A. (accounting).

Addresses

Home—Los Angeles, CA. *E-mail*—todd@davidandgoliathco.com.

Career

Author, pop artist, and entrepreneur. Worked as a certified public accountant for six years; David & Goliath (apparel manufacturer), founder, beginning 1999, and creator of games *Boys Are Stupid* and *Stupidopoly.* Founder of Pop-Factory (art gallery). *Exhibitions:* Work exhibited at the Jack Gallery, Fort Lauderdale, FL; and S2 Art Group and Entertainment Galleries, both Las Vegas, NV.

Writings

SELF-ILLUSTRATED

Goodbye Kitty, Andrews McMeel (Kansas City, MO), 2004.
Boys Are Stupid, Throw Rocks at Them!: And They Make Me Wanna Throw Up!, Workman Publishing (New York, NY), 2005.
Girls Are Weirdos: But They Smell Pretty!, Workman Publishing (New York, NY), 2007.
Work Sucks, Running Press (Philadelphia, PA), 2010.

Author of column "Stupid Stuff by Todd," for *Seventeen* magazine.

Author's work has been translated into Russian.

SELF-ILLUSTRATED CHILDREN'S BOOKS

(Under name Todd H. Doodler) *The Zoo I Drew,* Random House (New York, NY), 2009.
(Under name Todd H. Doodler) *Bear in Underwear,* Blue Apple Books (New York, NY), 2010.
(Under name Todd H. Doodler) *Animal Soup,* Golden Books (New York, NY), 2010.

Sidelights

Todd H. Goldman planned to be an accountant, but after six years working in that field he opted to make a

Cover of Goldman's picture book Boys Are Stupid, Throw Rocks at Them!: And They Make Me Wanna Throw Up!, *which features the author's graphic-style cartoon art.* (Workman, 2005. Reproduced by permission.)

Known for his graphic art, Todd Harris Goldman also creates children's books such as **The Zoo I Drew** *under the name Todd H. Doodler.* (Copyright © 2009 by Todd Harris Goldman. Used by permission of Random House Children's Books, a division of Random House, Inc.)

career switch. Turning to the clothing industry, Goldman founded David & Goliath, a company that licenses product ranging from stuffed animals and key chains to calendars and T-shirts featuring cartoon images and humorous logos. While a staff produces the artwork for his manufacturing ventures, Goldman has become known as a pop artist as well as a children's book author, his single-minded goal to make people laugh, often with irreverent and sometimes tasteless humor.

Published under the pen name Todd H. Doodler, Goldman's books for young children include *The Zoo I Drew, Bear in Underwear,* and *Animal Soup.* Featuring bright, toddler-friendly colors, geometric shapes, and cartoon characters, *The Zoo I Drew* is an alphabet book that mixes animals from A to Z with what *School Library Journal* contributor Mary Elam termed "a smattering of facts about each critter" that "lean . . . toward the whimsical." Although a *Kirkus Reviews* writer noted the clumsiness of the book's rhyming text, *The Zoo I Drew* benefits from "a bright, simple graphic style" that should appeal to children.

With a title that will instantly incite silliness, *Bear in Underwear* finds a bear given the chance to obtain a pair of underwear that is more to his liking than the traditional tighty-whities that he normally wears to school. As Bear models a variety of undies for his friends, others are encouraged to show off their underwear as well, resulting in a board book that "offers candidly silly details on every page," according to a *Publishers Weekly* critic. A range of animals star in *Animal Soup,* an interactive lift-the-flap book in which a succession of differ-

ent creatures are combined by twos into humorously named hybrids that are humorously captured in Goldman's cartoon art.

Biographical and Critical Sources

PERIODICALS

Art Business Review, March, 2006, Joe Jancsurak, "'Stupid Factory' Creator Is 'Post-Pop' Sensation," p. 60.
Bulletin of the Center for Children's Books, September, 2009, Deborah Stevenson, review of *The Zoo I Drew,* p. 15.
Kirkus Reviews, June 1, 2009, review of *The Zoo I Drew.*
Publishers Weekly, March 29, 2010, review of *Bear in Underwear,* p. 58; April 5, 2010, review of *Animal Soup,* p. 62.
School Library Journal, August, 2009, Mary Elam, review of *The Zoo I Drew,* p. 74.

ONLINE

David & Goliath Web Site, http://www.davidandgoliathco.com/ (October 15, 2010).*

*   *   *

GOODRICH, Carter 1959(?)-

Personal

Born c. 1959. *Education:* Rhode Island School of Design, B.F.A.

Addresses

Home—Los Angeles, CA.

Career

Illustrator, character designer, and author of books for children. Film work includes character designer for animated films, including *The Prince of Egypt,* 1998, *Joseph,* 2000, *Sinbad,* 2003, *Open Season,* 2006, *Ratatouille,* 2007, and *Despicable Me,* 2010. Visual development artist for *Monsters Inc.,* 2001, *Finding Nemo,* 2003, *Home on the Range,* 2004, and *Shrek.* Lecturer at schools, including Kapi'olani Community College.

Member

Best Book of the Year selection, Bank Street College of Education, and Cooperative Children's Book Council Choice selection, both 2009, both for *The Hermit Crab.*

Awards, Honors

Two gold medals, Society of Illustrators, New York.

Writings

SELF-ILLUSTRATED

(Adaptor) Clement C. Moore, *A Creature Was Stirring,* Simon & Schuster Books for Young Readers (New York, NY), 2006.

The Hermit Crab, Simon & Schuster Books for Young Readers (New York, NY), 2009.

Say Hello to Zorro!, Simon & Schuster Books for Young Readers (New York, NY), 2010.

ILLUSTRATOR

E.T.A. Hoffmann, *Nutcracker,* translated by Andrea Clark Madden, Ariel Books (New York, NY), 1987.

Charles Dickens, *A Christmas Carol,* afterword by Peter Glassman, Morrow (New York, NY), 1996.

Contributor to periodicals, including *Atlantic Monthly, Forbes, Gentleman's Quarterly, Newsweek,* the *New Yorker, Playboy,* and *Time.*

Sidelights

Well known in the world of film animation, Carter Goodrich has created characters for motion pictures ranging from *The Prince of Egypt* to *Little Nemo,* and

The detailed paintings of Carter Goodrich bring to life a beloved holiday tale in a new edition of Charles Dickens' **A Christmas Carol.**
(Books of Wonder, 1996. Illustrations © 1996 by Carter Goodrich. Used by permission of HarperCollins Publishers.)

his distinctive images have also appeared on covers of the *New Yorker* as well as in the pages of magazines such as *Newsweek* and *Time.* Goodrich began his career in children's publishing as an illustrator, but began to showcase his authorial skills when he adapted and illustrated Clement C. Moore's classic poem "The Night before Christmas" as the picture book *A Creature Was Stirring.* In the years since, Goodrich has created other original, self-illustrated picture books, including *The Hermit Crab* and *Say Hello to Zorro!,* the latter a story about a dog that becomes totally confused when its schedule of sleeping and eating is disrupted.

Goodrich's first illustration project, a version of E.T.A. Hoffmann's popular musical presentation *The Nutcracker,* was followed by another holiday classic: Charles Dickens' *A Christmas Carol.* Reedited as a read-aloud, *A Christmas Carol* features over twenty sepia-toned, watercolor-and-pencil illustrations that *Booklist* critic Hazel Rochman described as "comic and scary but never overwhelming" in their "theatrical" approach.

In *A Creature Was Stirring* Goodrich weaves Moore's poem together with the rhyming narrative of a little boy who is so excited about Santa's arrival that sleep is impossible. As he drifts in and out of restless dreams, the boy imagines the jolly man's visit in a rhyming story that combines with Goodrich's "shadowy" images to "bring readers right into the anticipatory Christmas Eve mood," according to a *Publishers Weekly* critic. The artist creates what a *Kirkus Reviews* writer dubbed "arresting illustrations [that] effectively capture the shadowy blue-and-gray tones of the [boy's] darkened household," while Carolyn Phelan noted in *Booklist* that Goodrich's "rounded forms, soft-textured shading, and expressive characters create an appealing visual interpretation" of the two intertwined poems. In *School Library Journal* Maureen Wade praised *A Creature Was Stirring* for bringing "a delightful new twist to [Moore's] . . . holiday chestnut."

Taking a break from the Christmas season, Goodrich creates an original story that takes readers into the sea in *The Hermit Crab.* A timid hermit crab feels most safe tucked in its shell, and spends its time looking for things to eat. Every once in a while the crab stumbles upon an object that is more beautiful than its current shell, and it is only then that it makes a quick move. One day the crab and its deep-sea friends are gathered around their breakfast when a wooden box drifts down to the ocean floor. When the crab attempts to grasp a tasty bite of food nearby, its newest shell—a hollow toy action figure—shifts the box and releases poor Flounder, which had been trapped underneath. Illustrations in tones of blue and green capture "animated expressions [that] result in humorous interactions among the varied characters," according to *School Library Journal* critic Meg Smith, and a *Publishers Weekly* critic wrote that the book's "visual point of view is . . . strong and reassuringly familiar" to young children. In *Kirkus Reviews*

Another Christmas classic is given the Goodrich touch in **A Creature Was Stirring.** (Adaptation and illustrations copyright © 2006 Carter Goodrich. Reprinted with the permission of Simon & Schuster Books for Young Readers, an imprint of Simon & Schuster Children's Publishing Division.)

a critic dubbed *The Hermit Crab* an "appealing dive into the undersea world" and praised Goodrich for "effectively convey[ing] the perspective of a small creature in a big world."

Biographical and Critical Sources

PERIODICALS

Booklist, September 1, 1996, Hazel Rochman, review of *A Christmas Carol,* p. 134; November 15, 2006, Carolyn Phelan, review of *A Creature Was Stirring,* p. 54.

Kirkus Reviews, November 1, 2006, review of *A Creature Was Stirring,* p. 1129; May 1, 2009, review of *The Hermit Crab.*

Publishers Weekly, September 20, 1996, review of *A Christmas Carol,* p. 92; September 25, 2006, review of *A Creature Was Stirring,* p. 69; June 1, 2009, review of *The Hermit Crab,* p. 47.

School Library Journal, March, 1988, Louise L. Sherman, review of *Nutcracker,* p. 192; October 1996, Jane Marino, review of *A Christmas Carol,* p. 34; October, 2006, Maureen Wade, review of *A Creature Was Stirring,* p. 99; June, 2009, Meg Smith, review of *The Hermit Crab,* p. 88.

Tribune Books (Chicago, IL), December 6, 1987, review of *The Nutcracker,* p. 14.

ONLINE

Simon & Schuster Web Site, http://authors.simonandschuster.com/ (October 21, 2010), "Carter Goodrich."*

*   *   *

GREENE, Stephanie 1950-

Personal

Born September 12, 1950, in New York, NY; daughter of Philip M. (in marketing) and Constance C. (a chil-

dren's book author) Greene; married George A. Radwan (a businessman), May 19, 1976; children: Oliver. *Education:* University of Connecticut, B.A. (French), 1972; attended Université de Rouen, 1970-71; Vermont College, M.F.A. (writing for children and young adults), 2007.

Addresses

Home and office—2320 New Hope Church Rd., Chapel Hill, NC 27514. *E-mail*—scgbooks@aol.com.

Career

The Hour (newspaper), Norwalk, CT, reporter, 1973-75; Ogilvy & Mather, Inc., New York, NY, advertising copywriter, 1976-84; Askey Associates, Keene, NH, co-creative director, 1987-89; Chapel Hill Press, Chapel Hill, NC, editorial director.

Member

Society of Children's Book Writers and Illustrators (regional advisor), Authors Guild, Authors League of America.

Awards, Honors

School Library Journal Best Book designation, and Bank Street College Best Book of the Year designation, both 1991, both for *Owen Foote, Frontiersman;* American Library Association Notable Book designation, 2006, for *Queen Sophie Hartley;* Bank Street College Best Book of the Year designation, c. 2005, for *Moose Crossing;* American Bookseller Pick-of-the-List selection, c. 2001, for *Owen Foote, Money Man;* Notable Book designation, American Library Association, 2005, for *Queen Sophie Hartley.*

Writings

Show and Tell, illustrated by Elaine Clayton, Clarion (New York, NY), 1998.

Not Just Another Moose, illustrated by Andrea Wallace, Marshall Cavendish (New York, NY), 2000.

(Editor with Marshall Brooks) *Fateful Choices: Tales along the Road Taken,* Birch Brook Press (Delhi, NY), 2001.

The Rugrats' First Kwanzaa (based on *Rugrats* television series), Simon & Schuster (New York, NY), 2001.

Betsy Ross and the Silver Thimble, illustrated by Diana Magnuson, Aladdin Paperbacks (New York, NY), 2002.

Falling into Place, Clarion (New York, NY), 2002.

Moose's Big Idea, illustrated by Joe Mathieu, Marshall Cavendish (New York, NY), 2005.

Moose Crossing, illustrated by Joe Mathieu, Marshall Cavendish (New York, NY), 2005.

Pig Pickin', illustrated by Joe Mathieu, Marshall Cavendish (New York, NY), 2006.

Christmas at Stony Creek, illustrated by Chris Sheban, Greenwillow Books (New York, NY), 2007.

The Show-off, illustrated by Joe Mathieu, Marshall Cavendish (New York, NY), 2007.

The Lucky Ones (middle-grade novel), Greenwillow Books (New York, NY), 2008.

Princess Posey and the First-Grade Parade, illustrated by Stéphanie Roth Sisson, G.P. Putnam's (New York, NY), 2010.

Princess Posey and the Perfect Present, illustrated by Stéphanie Roth Sisson, G.P. Putnam's (New York, NY), 2011.

"OWEN FOOTE" CHAPTER-BOOK SERIES

Owen Foote, Second-Grade Strongman, illustrated by Dee De Rosa, Clarion (New York, NY), 1996.

Owen Foote, Soccer Star, illustrated by Martha Weston, Clarion (New York, NY), 1998.

Owen Foote, Frontiersman, illustrated by Martha Weston, Clarion (New York, NY), 1999.

Owen Foote, Money Man, illustrated by Martha Weston, Clarion (New York, NY), 2000.

Owen Foote, Super Spy, illustrated by Martha Weston, Clarion (New York, NY), 2001.

Owen Foote, Mighty Scientist, illustrated by Catherine Bowman Smith, Clarion (New York, NY), 2004.

"SOPHIE HARTLEY" CHAPTER-BOOK SERIES

Queen Sophie Hartley, Clarion (New York, NY), 2005.

Sophie Hartley, on Strike, Clarion (New York, NY), 2006.

Happy Birthday, Sophie Hartley, Clarion Books (Boston, MA), 2010.

Sidelights

The daughter of children's author Constance C. Greene, Stephanie Greene is the author of more than a dozen children's books, among them *Falling into Place, Moose Crossing, Pig Pickin', The Lucky Ones,* and *Christmas at Stony Creek* as well as the "Sophie Hartley" middle-grade novels and the "Owen Foote" beginning chapter-book series. In *Princess Posey and the First-Grade Parade* Greene continues to entertain the early-elementary-grade set in her story about a six year old who has to reinvent herself now that she attends the first grade because she cannot wear the tutu that made her so special and magical at home. Praising the "short sentences" in Greene's "sweet story," a *Kirkus Reviews* writer added that *Princess Posey and the First-Grade Parade* is "just right" for emergent readers.

Born in New York City, Greene studied French at the University of Connecticut, then worked as a journalist and advertising copywriter at several locations around the world. She began writing for children when her son, Oliver, was born and inspired her with his humor and curiosity. Greene's first book, *Owen Foote, Second-Grade Strongman,* was published in 1996 as the first volume in her popular "Owen Foote" series.

In *Owen Foote, Second-Grade Strongman* Owen exhibits the intense concern many younger boys feel when comparing their size and growth to that of their school-aged friends. As the smallest boy in his class, Owen dreads "height-and weight-chart day," especially after being publicly humiliated the year before when the school nurse called him a "pipsqueak." This year the nurse tells Owen's best friend, Joseph, that he is too fat, and now Owen speaks up and asks that she keep her voice down. Although his classmates idolize him for standing up to the thoughtless nurse, parents and teachers are upset and demand Owen's apology. All ends well when the nurse admits that she needs a hearing aid. Writing in *Horn Book,* Nancy Vasilakis called *Owen Foote, Second-Grade Strongman* a believable book in which Greene "appears to have mastered the art of seeing things wholly from a child's perspective."

Owen returns in *Owen Foote, Soccer Star,* where he is now tall enough to play in the town's soccer league. When friend Joseph is bullied by another teammate and ridiculed in front of his fellow players, Owen denies being Joseph's friend, but eventually stands up for his buddy. A reviewer for *Publishers Weekly* noted that Greene's message "about the importance of being a true friend will escape no youngster" reading the story. Kay Weisman, writing in *Booklist,* maintained that, in addition to being an "appealing choice" for beginning chapter-book readers, *Owen Foote, Soccer Star* introduces valuable "issues of sportsmanship, self-esteem, and loyalty."

Owen Foote, Frontiersman finds Owen and Joseph fighting off two older boys who have taken over their tree house, all the while trying to keep Owen's overprotective mother out of the loop. In *Owen Foote, Money Man* the now-eight year old is in dire need of cash, hoping to purchase plastic vomit, whoopee cushions, and other sundry items from a mail-order catalog. He taps his natural entrepreneurial skills and starts a dog-walking business with Joseph and, although his schemes fail, the funds appear, having come from an unexpected source. A reviewer for *Horn Book* lauded *Owen Foote, Frontiersman* for its "good balance of narrative and dialogue," while "kid-friendly humor, good characterization, and a believable and fast-moving plot distinguish" *Owen Foote, Money Man,* according to Jennifer Ralston in a review for *School Library Journal.*

Owen's adventures continue in *Owen Foote, Super Spy* and *Owen Foote, Mighty Scientist,* the latter which finds our hero determined to win his school's science fair with the help of his best friend. Joseph does not share Owen's love for lizards, however, and the collaborative science project soon takes a turn Owen does not like. When the two boys finally pay attention to each other's concerns they learn to work together and produce a good project. Hazel Rochman remarked in *Booklist* that *Owen Foote, Mighty Scientist* is "a great title to spark discussion in science classes" due to the very real way Owen learns from both his scientific successes and fail-

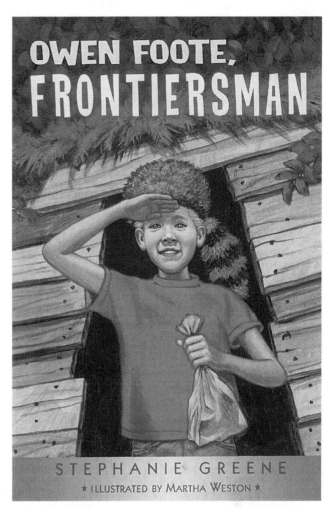

Cover of Stephanie Greene's Owen Foote, Frontiersman, *featuring artwork by John Ward.* (Clarion Books, 1999. Cover illustration copyright © 2002 by John Ward. All rights reserved. Reprinted by permission of Clarion Books, an imprint of Houghton Mifflin Company.)

ures. According to *Horn Book* reviewer Roger Sutton, the boy's "impulsive bossiness is one of his most endearing qualities," while Linda Zeilstra Sawyer concluded in her *School Library Journal* review that Greene's novel "strikes just the right balance of action, humor, and honest emotion."

Geared for middle graders, *Queen Sophie Hartley* introduces another of Greene's likeable child characters. Feeling just plain ordinary, Sophie lists those things she is good at and those she is not, but by comparing herself to her talented older sister her list of "nots" keeps growing. When her mother notes that one of Sophie's strengths is being kind, the girl decides to develop this talent by spending time with her grouchy, wheelchair-bound neighbor and also by befriending the most obnoxious girl in her class at school. "Greene's simple plot, droll dialogue, and strong characters intimately bring the reader into Sophie's world," wrote a *Kirkus Reviews* contributor, while *School Library Journal* reviewer Carol Schene praised Greene's heroine as "likable and resilient." In *Booklist* Carolyn Phelan noted that "Greene conveys Sophie's emotions and thoughts

with ruthless candor," and a *Publishers Weekly* critic wrote that the book's "narrative shines in its depiction of the heartwarming, entirely realistic Hartley family dynamics."

Sophie and her family return in *Sophie Hartley, on Strike* and *Happy Birthday, Sophie Hartley*. Dubbed by *School Library Journal* contributor Michele Shaw as "another winning story" by Greene, *Sophie Hartley, on Strike* finds nine-year-old Sophie upset over the way her mother has distributed the household chores among the four children. Marking her father's recent time on a strike line at work, Sophie and older sister Nora go on strike and refuse to clean and take out the garbage. In *Happy Birthday, Sophie Hartley* the soon-to-be-ten-year-old girl had hoped to get a gorilla for her birthday, until she realizes that her world is expanding with other possibilities because she is growing older. "Readers will empathize with this spunky youngster and her true-to-life problems," predicted Shaw in her review of *Sophie Hartley, on Strike*, while a *Kirkus Reviews* writer noted that "funny family hijinks explode into pure hilarity" on the strength of the story's "lively dialogue and . . . simple plot." "Girls undergoing the same growing-up

Cover of Greene's middle-grade novel Sophie Hartley, on Strike, *featuring artwork by Dan Andreasen.* (Jacket illustration copyright © 2006 by Dan Andreasen. Reprinted by permission of Houghton Mifflin Harcourt Publishing Company. All rights reserved.)

trials will be happy to have Sophie make them laugh," concluded a *Kirkus Reviews* writer, praising the star of *Happy Birthday, Sophie Hartley* as "irrepressible."

As she does in her "Owen Foote" and "Sophie Hartley" series, Greene focuses on issues many children confront in her stand-alone stories for children. *Show and Tell*, for example, finds second-grader Woody learning to adjust to a new teacher in school after being erroneously branded a troublemaker. Eventually, Woody and Mrs. Plunkett resolve their differences, teaching the boy a valuable lesson about relationships and first impressions. Writing in *Booklist*, Lauren Peterson praised *Show and Tell* for its "realistic" dialogue and the author for her ability to handle weighty issues with humor.

Falling into Place introduces eleven-year-old Martha, the oldest child in a blended family. Margaret is just beginning to adjust to her new stepmother and stepsisters when her grandparents move from their house next door to a retirement community because her grandfather, Tad, is sick. Changes keep coming as Margaret's father and stepmother announce that they are going to have a new baby and Tad passes away. Margaret feels overwhelmed and goes to the retirement community to visit her Gran. Hoping to find stability there, she instead learns that Gran is depressed and that Margaret's younger cousin Roy is now staying with the elderly woman. While not wanting to share her grandmother's attention, Margaret includes Roy in a plan to help Gran meet some new friends. As Gran begins coping with the changes in her life, Margaret learns that she must also cope with hers. Jean Gaffney, writing in *School Library Journal*, commented that "the reading is easy, and the plot moves along quickly, naturally, and with some humor." A *Kirkus Reviews* contributor called *Falling into Place* "warm and thoughtful," and noted that the story "investigates the complexities of loss, blended families, and friendship."

Moose and his friend Hildy the Pig are the stars of the chapter books *Moose's Big Idea, Moose Crossing*, and *Pig Pickin'*. In the first title, after Moose loses his antlers, friend Hildy encourages him to look on the bright side. Resigned at first to spending hunting season inside, drawing and reading, Moose gets so bored that he decides to sell coffee to the hunters, and his spirits eventually climb when his antlers start to grow back. In *Moose Crossing*, Moose discovers a sign with his picture on it and concludes that he is famous. Hildy finds her friend's behavior ridiculous when Moose struts around near the sign, preening for his fans. When the humans stopped near Moose's display begin to take photographs, the flash of cameras unnerve the silly moose, and ultimately Hildy comes to his rescue. Laura Scott, in *School Library Journal*, felt that *Moose's Big Idea* provides "lots of laughs," and Kristine M. Casper noted in the same periodical that readers of *Moose Crossing* "will take pleasure in watching Moose realize that being famous is not as much fun as he thought."

Cover of Greene's Falling into Place, *featuring artwork by Mark Elliot.*
(Cover illustration copyright © 2006 by Mark Elliot. All rights reserved. Reprinted by permission of Clarion Books, an imprint of Houghton Mifflin Company.)

Greene turns to the holidays in *Christmas at Stony Creek,* a beginning chapter book illustrated by Chris Sheban. Taking place during a harsh and snowy winter, the story focuses on Pipsqueak the mouse. Although she would rather be out ice-skating with her friends, Pip decides to take it upon herself to help Papa Mouse gather food for the Mouse family's holiday feast. Noting that Sheban's nostalgic pencil drawings "nicely complement the tale," Linda Israelson added in her *School Library Journal* that *Christmas at Stony Creek* benefits from "well-developed" characters, "dialogue [that] flows smoothly," and a storyline that features both "action and suspense."

Published the same year Greene completed her M.F.A. in writing at Vermont College, *The Lucky Ones* is a middle-grade novel that introduces twelve-year-old Cecile. Every year her affluent family spends its summer at Grandfather's estate on Gull Island, in Long Island Sound. While summer has always been a special time, this year is different: Cecile's parents are fighting and her older sister Natalie is morphing into a boy-crazy teen who would rather spend time with a cute neighbor boy. Although Cecile feels rejected as a result

of Natalie's shift into adolescence, the changes that occur in her own life—including buying her first bra and attracting the attention of a handsome local boy—inspire her to retain her compassion for others while attempting to navigate her own teen years. In *School Library Journal* Robyn Zaneski dubbed *The Lucky Ones* a "thoughtful coming-of-age novel" that "introduces a memorable main character." In *Booklist* Carolyn Phelan noted the mid-twentieth-century setting in the novel but added that readers will nonetheless "recognize aspects of themselves in [Greene's] . . . beautifully nuanced story," and a *Publishers Weekly* critic dubbed *The Lucky Ones* a "well-observed" story of adolescence.

Greene once told *SATA:* "Although I've written in one form or another all of my professional life, I wasn't one of those writers who claim they were born with a pencil in hand. In fact, one of my most detested chores as a child was creating the 'Bread and Butter' notes I was required to write as a child every Christmas and birthday. They were enough to put me off writing for life.

"However, I prevailed, and once I had a child of my own and started spending a lot of time both with him and his friends, I remembered how intriguing, how much fun, how humorous, and brave and scary and fascinating children are. I love them best of all human forms, followed closely by the elderly. I like to listen to what children say and watch what they do, and if any book I write can make them laugh or make them think or teach them something or bring them comfort—that's all I ask.

"And, lo and behold! The more I work with wonderful and smart editors—who have made me a better writer with each book—I have come to love the actual work of writing. Word by sometimes painful word, nothing brings me more satisfaction than knowing I have written something good. Except, maybe, talking to my son, taking a walk on a beautiful day, traveling to a place I've never seen before, smelling salt water, listening to sea gulls, feeling the sun on my back, smelling garlic roasting. . . . Okay, so lots of things bring me great satisfaction, but none more than writing—or reading—a great book."

Biographical and Critical Sources

PERIODICALS

Booklist, April 15, 1996, Hazel Rochman, review of *Owen Foote, Second-Grade Strongman,* p. 1438; March 15, 1998, Kay Weisman, review of *Owen Foote, Soccer Star,* p. 1243; November 1, 1998, Lauren Peterson, review of *Show and Tell,* p. 492; September 1, 2000, Kay Weisman, review of *Owen Foote, Money Man,* p. 122; January 1, 2002, Kay Weisman, review of *Owen Foote, Super Spy,* p. 857; October 15, 2002, Diane Foote, review of *Falling into Place,* p. 404; August, 2004, Hazel Rochman, review of *Owen Foote, Mighty Scientist,* p. 1933; April 1, 2005, Carolyn Phelan, re-

view of *Queen Sophie Hartley,* p. 1360; January 1, 2007, Stephanie Zvirin, review of *Sophie Hartley, on Strike,* p. 100; October 1, 2008, Carolyn Phelan, review of *The Lucky Ones,* p. 46; July 1, 2010, Carolyn Phelan, review of *Princess Posey and the First-Grade Parade,* p. 67.

Children's Bookwatch, November, 2004, review of *Owen Foote, Mighty Scientist.*

Horn Book, May-June, 1996, Nancy Vasilakis, review of *Owen Foote, Second-Grade Strongman,* p. 332; May-June, 1998, Roger Sutton, review of *Owen Foote, Soccer Star,* p. 344; September, 1999, review of *Owen Foote, Frontiersman,* p. 610; September, 2000, review of *Owen Foote, Money Man,* p. 569; November-December, 2001, Martha V. Parravano, review of *Owen Foote, Super Spy,* p. 748; September-October, 2004, Roger Sutton, review of *Owen Foote, Mighty Scientist,* p. 583; November-December, 2006, Robin Smith, review of *Sophie Hartley, on Strike,* p. 711.

Kirkus Reviews, October 1, 2001, review of *Owen Foote, Super Spy,* p. 1424; October 1, 2002, review of *Falling into Place,* p. 1470; April 1, 2005, review of *Queen Sophie Hartley,* p. 417; September 15, 2005, review of *Moose Crossing,* p. 1026; September 15, 2006, review of *Pig Pickin';* December 1, 2006, review of *Sophie Hartley, On Strike,* p. 1220; August 1, 2008, review of *The Lucky Ones;* April 15, 2010, review of *Princess Posey and the First-Grade Parade;* May 15, 2010, review of *Happy Birthday, Sophie Hartley.*

Publishers Weekly, February 16, 1998, review of *Owen Foote, Soccer Star,* p. 211; May 2, 2005, review of *Queen Sophie Hartley,* p. 200; August 25, 2008, review of *The Lucky Ones,* p. 75; May 3, 2010, review of *Princess Posey and the First-Grade Parade,* p. 50.

School Library Journal, September, 2000, Jennifer Ralston, review of *Owen Foote, Money Man,* p. 198; October, 2001, Wanda Meyers-Hines, review of *Owen Foote, Super Spy,* p. 118; September, 2002, Jean Gaffney, review of *Falling into Place,* p. 225; October, 2004, Linda Zeilstra Sawyer, review of *Owen Foote, Mighty Scientist,* p. 114; May, 2005, Carol Schene, review of *Queen Sophie Hartley,* p. 83; October, 2005, Laura Scott, review of *Moose's Big Idea,* p. 114; March, 2006, Kristine M. Casper, review of *Moose Crossing,* p. 190; October, 2006, Marilyn Ackerman, review of *Pig Pickin',* p. 112; January, 2007, Michele Shaw, review of *Sophie Hartley, on Strike,* p. 94; October, 2007, Linda Israelson, review of *Christmas at Stony Creek,* p. 98, and Kelly Roth, review of *The Show-off,* p. 116; November, 2008, Robyn Zaneski, review of *The Lucky Ones,* p. 122; June, 2010, Elizabeth Swistock, review of *Princess Posey and the First-Grade Parade,* p. 72; July, 2010, Michele Shaw, review of *Happy Birthday, Sophie Hartley,* p. 60.

ONLINE

Children's Literature Network Web site, http://www.childrensliteraturenetwork.org/ (October 30, 2010), "Stephanie Greene."

Stephanie Greene Home Page, http://stephaniegreenebooks.com (October 30, 2010).*

GUTMAN, Dan 1955-
(Herb Dunn)

Personal

Born October 19, 1955, in New York, NY; son of Sidney J. Gutman (in advertising) and Adeline Berlin (a homemaker); married Nina Wallace (an illustrator), September 25, 1983; children: Sam, Emma. *Education:* Rutgers University, B.A., 1977. *Hobbies and other interests:* Travel, history, technology, sports, pop culture, movies.

Addresses

Office—Haddonfield, NJ.

Career

Video Review Publications, coeditor of *Electronic Fun* magazine, 1982-83; Carnegie Publications, founder and editor-in-chief of *Video Games Player* (later named *Computer Games*) magazine, 1983-84; freelance writer, 1984—.

Member

Society of Children's Book Writers and Illustrators, Society for American Baseball Research.

Awards, Honors

Volunteer State Book Award, Nutmeg Children's Book Award and Sequoyah Book Award, all 2000, Iowa Children's Choice Award and Maud Harte Lovelace Award, both 2001, and California Young Reader Medal, 2003, all for *The Million Dollar Shot;* California Young Reader Medal, 2001, for *Honus and Me;* Keystone to Reading Award, 2000, Black-eyed Susan Book Award, 2002, and Massachusetts Children's Book Award, 2004, all for *Jackie and Me;* Arizona Young Readers Award, and Nutmeg Children's Book Award, both 2003, both for *Babe and Me;* Black-eyed Susan Book Award, 2004, for *The Million Dollar Kick;* Flicker Tale Children's Book Award, 2007, for *Miss Daisy Is Crazy!*

Writings

FOR CHILDREN

Baseball's Biggest Bloopers: The Games That Got Away, Viking (New York, NY), 1993.

Baseball's Greatest Games, Viking (New York, NY), 1994.

World Series Classics, Viking (New York, NY), 1994.

They Came from Centerfield, Scholastic (New York, NY), 1995.

(With Vicki Van Meter) *Taking Flight: My Story,* Viking (New York, NY), 1995.

Ice Skating: From Axels to Zambonis, Viking (New York, NY), 1995, revised as *Ice Skating: An Inside Look at the Stars, the Sport, and the Spectacle,* 1997.

Dan Gutman (Reproduced by permission.)

Gymnastics, Viking (New York, NY), 1996.

The Kid Who Ran for President, Scholastic (New York, NY), 1996.

The Pitcher Who Went Out of His Mind, Scholastic (New York, NY), 1997.

The Catcher Who Shocked the World, Scholastic (New York, NY), 1997.

The Green Monster in Left Field, Scholastic (New York, NY), 1997.

The Shortstop Who Knew Too Much, Scholastic (New York, NY), 1997.

The Million-Dollar Shot, Hyperion (New York, NY), 1997.

(With Keith Bowen) *Katy's Gift,* Running Press (Philadelphia, PA), 1998.

Virtually Perfect, Hyperion (New York, NY), 1998.

(Adaptor) Cal Ripken, Jr., and Mike Bryan, *Cal Ripken, Jr.: My Story,* Dial (New York, NY), 1999.

Funny Boy Meets the Airsick Alien from Andromeda, illustrated by John Dykes, Hyperion (New York, NY), 1999.

The Kid Who Became President, Scholastic (New York, NY), 1999.

Joe DiMaggio, Aladdin (New York, NY), 1999.

(Under pseudonym Herb Dunn) *Jackie Robinson,* Aladdin (New York, NY), 1999.

Funny Boy versus the Bubble-brained Barbers from the Big Bang, illustrated by Mike Dietz, Hyperion (New York, NY), 2000.

Landslide! A Kid's Guide to the U.S. Elections, Simon & Schuster (New York, NY), 2000.

Johnny Hangtime, HarperCollins (New York, NY), 2000.

The Million Dollar Kick, Hyperion (New York, NY), 2001.

Funny Boy Meets the Chit-chatting Cheese from Chattanooga, illustrated by Mike Dietz, Hyperion (New York, NY), 2001.

The Secret Life of Dr. Demented, Pocket Books (New York, NY), 2001.

Qwerty Stevens, Stuck in Time: The Edison Mystery, Simon & Schuster (New York, NY), 2001.

Qwerty Stevens, Stuck in Time with Benjamin Franklin, Simon & Schuster (New York, NY), 2002.

Babe Ruth and the Ice Cream Mess, illustrated by Elaine Garvin, Aladdin Paperbacks (New York, NY), 2003.

Race for the Sky: The Kitty Hawk Diaries of Johnny Moore, Simon & Schuster (New York, NY), 2003.

The Million Dollar Goal, Hyperion (New York, NY), 2003.

The Get Rich Quick Club, HarperCollins (New York, NY), 2004.

The Million Dollar Strike, Hyperion (New York, NY), 2004.

Jackie Robinson and the Big Game, illustrated by Elaine Garvin, Aladdin (New York, NY), 2006.

The Million Dollar Putt, Hyperion (New York, NY), 2006.

The Homework Machine, Simon & Schuster (New York, NY), 2006.

Getting Air, Simon & Schuster (New York, NY), 2007.

Casey Back at Bat (sequel to "Casey at the Bat" by Ernest Lawrence Thayer), illustrated by Steve Johnson and Lou Fancher, HarperCollins (New York, NY), 2007.

Nightmare at the Book Fair, Simon & Schuster (New York, NY), 2008.

Return of the Homework Machine, Simon & Schuster Books for Young Readers (New York, NY), 2009.

The Christmas Genie, illustrated by Dan Santat, Simon & Schuster Books for Young Readers (New York, NY), 2009.

The Talent Show, Simon & Schuster Books for Young Readers (New York, NY), 2010.

Mission Unstoppable, Harper (New York, NY), 2011.

"BASEBALL CARD ADVENTURE" SERIES; FOR CHILDREN

Honus and Me, Avon (New York, NY), 1997.

Jackie and Me, Avon (New York, NY), 1999.

Babe and Me, HarperCollins (New York, NY), 2000.

Shoeless Joe and Me, HarperCollins (New York, NY), 2002.

Mickey and Me, HarperCollins (New York, NY), 2002.

Abner and Me, HarperCollins (New York, NY), 2005.

Satch and Me, HarperCollins (New York, NY), 2006.

Jim and Me, HarperCollins (New York, NY), 2008.

Ray and Me, HarperCollins (New York, NY), 2009.

Roberto and Me, HarperCollins (New York, NY), 2010.

Ted and Me, HarperCollins (New York, NY), 2012.

"MY WEIRD SCHOOL" SERIES; FOR CHILDREN

Miss Daisy Is Crazy!, illustrated by Jim Paillot, HarperCollins (New York, NY), 2004.

Mr. Klutz Is Nuts!, illustrated by Jim Paillot, HarperCollins (New York, NY), 2004.

Mrs. Roopy Is Loopy!, illustrated by Jim Paillot, HarperCollins (New York, NY), 2004.

Miss Hannah Is Bananas!, illustrated by Jim Paillot, HarperCollins (New York, NY), 2005.

Miss Small Is Off the Wall!, illustrated by Jim Paillot, HarperCollins (New York, NY), 2005.

Mr. Hynde Is Out of His Mind!, illustrated by Jim Paillot, HarperCollins (New York, NY), 2005.

Mrs. Cooney Is Loony!, illustrated by Jim Paillot, HarperCollins (New York, NY), 2005.

Miss Lazar Is Bizarre!, illustrated by Jim Paillot, HarperCollins (New York, NY), 2005.

Ms. LaGrange Is Strange!, illustrated by Jim Paillot, HarperCollins (New York, NY), 2005.

Mr. Docker Is Off His Rocker!, illustrated by Jim Paillot, HarperCollins (New York, NY), 2006.

Ms. Kormel Is Not Normal!, illustrated by Jim Paillot, HarperCollins (New York, NY), 2006.

Ms. Todd Is Odd!, illustrated by Jim Paillot, HarperCollins (New York, NY), 2006.

Ms. Patty Is Batty!, illustrated by Jim Paillot, HarperCollins (New York, NY), 2006.

Ms. Holly Is Too Jolly!, illustrated by Jim Paillot, HarperCollins (New York, NY), 2006.

Mr. Macky Is Wacky!, illustrated by Jim Paillot, HarperCollins (New York, NY), 2007.

Ms. Suki Is Kooky!, illustrated by Jim Paillot, HarperCollins (New York, NY), 2007.

Ms. Coco Is Loco!, illustrated by Jim Paillot, HarperCollins (New York, NY), 2007.

Dr. Carbles Is Losing His Marbles!, illustrated by Jim Paillot, HarperCollins (New York, NY), 2007.

Mrs. Yonkers Is Bonkers!, illustrated by Jim Paillot, HarperCollins (New York, NY), 2007.

Mr. Louie Is Screwy!, illustrated by Jim Paillot, HarperCollins (New York, NY), 2007.

My Weird School Daze! (omnibus), HarperCollins (New York, NY), 2007.

Mr. Granite Is from Another Planet!, HarperCollins (New York, NY), 2008.

Mr. Sunny Is Funny!, illustrated by Jim Paillot, HarperCollins (New York, NY), 2008.

Mrs. Dole Is out of Control!, illustrated by Jim Paillot, HarperCollins (New York, NY), 2008.

Ms. Krup Cracks Me Up!, illustrated by Jim Paillot, HarperCollins (New York, NY), 2008.

Coach Hyatt Is a Riot!, illustrated by Jim Paillot, HarperCollins (New York, NY), 2009.

Dr. Brad Has Gone Mad!, illustrated by Jim Paillot, HarperCollins (New York, NY), 2009.

Mrs. Jafee Is Daffy!, illustrated by Jim Paillot, HarperCollins (New York, NY), 2009.

Officer Spence Makes No Sense!, illustrated by Jim Paillot, HarperCollins (New York, NY), 2009.

Miss Laney Is Zany!, illustrated by Jim Paillot, HarperCollins (New York, NY), 2010.

Miss Mary Is Scary!, illustrated by Jim Paillot, HarperCollins (New York, NY), 2010.

Mr. Tony Is Full of Baloney!, illustrated by Jim Paillot, HarperCollins (New York, NY), 2010.

Mrs. Lizzy Is Dizzy!, illustrated by Jim Paillot, HarperCollins (New York, NY), 2010.

Ms. Leakey Is Freaky!, illustrated by Jim Paillot, HarperCollins (New York, NY), 2011.

Miss Child Has Gone Wild!, illustrated by Jim Paillot, HarperCollins (New York, NY), 2011.

Mr. Harrison Is Embarrasin'!, illustrated by Jim Paillot, HarperCollins (New York, NY), 2011.

Mrs. Lilly Is Silly!, illustrated by Jim Paillot, HarperCollins (New York, NY), 2011.

OTHER

The Greatest Games, Compute Books (Greensboro, NC), 1985.

I Didn't Know You Could Do THAT with a Computer!, Compute Books (Greensboro, NC), 1986.

It Ain't Cheatin' If You Don't Get Caught, Penguin (New York, NY), 1990.

(Editor) Douglas J. Hermann, *SuperMemory,* Rodale Press (Emmaus, PA), 1991.

Baseball Babylon: From the Black Sox to Pete Rose; The Real Stories behind the Scandals That Rocked the Game, Penguin (New York, NY), 1992.

Banana Bats and Ding-Dong Balls: A Century of Baseball Invention, Macmillan (New York, NY), 1995.

The Way Baseball Works, Simon & Schuster (New York, NY), 1996.

Recycle This Book: 100 Top Children's Book Authors Tell You How to Go Green, Yearling (New York, NY), 2009.

Also author of self-syndicated column "Computer Report Today," 1983-90, and monthly column in *Success.* Contributor to periodicals, including *Discover, Esquire, Newsweek, Psychology Today, Science Digest, USA Today, Village Voice,* and *Writer's Digest.*

Sidelights

Dan Gutman is a prolific author whose favorite topic—baseball—often appears in the fiction and nonfiction he writes for children. Although he started his career penning nonfiction titles such as *World Series Classics, Baseball's Biggest Bloopers: The Games That Got Away,* and *Baseball Babylon,* Gutman has captured a loyal readership with his humorous middle-grade novels, while his "My Weird School" stories tantalize younger readers with titles such as *Coach Hyatt Is a Riot!* and *Mr. Granite Is from Another Planet!* Other popular books by Gutman include his time-travel "Baseball Card Adventure" books and a sequence of novels that includes *The Million Dollar Shot, The Million Dollar Putt,* and *The Million Dollar Strike.*

Born in New York City, in 1955, Gutman was raised in nearby Newark, New Jersey, and attended Rutgers University, where he earned a bachelor's degree in psychology in 1977. After two years of graduate school, he moved back to New York City, hoping to break into the field of humorous journalism established by writers such as Art Buchwald. Undaunted by the countless rejection letters he received, Gutman persisted, publishing the magazine *Video Games Player* in response to the growing popularity of games like Pac Man and Space

Cover of Gutman's middle-grade novel The Million-Dollar Strike, *featuring artwork by Glinn Dibley.* (Reprinted by permission of Disney Hyperion, an imprint of Disney Group LLC. All rights reserved.)

Invaders. As editor, he was able to establish a healthy track record of published articles, and by the late 1980s he decided to once again submit his work to mainstream magazines. Sports being one of his main interests, Gutman decided that this would be his focus.

Gutman's success at publishing sports articles led him to author several books on baseball, among them *It Ain't Cheatin' If You Don't Get Caught,* which focuses on the unsportsmanlike side of America's favorite pastime. From there, encouragement from his young son inspired Gutman to write for children. *Baseball's Greatest Games* and *Baseball's Biggest Bloopers* were the immediate result of his nonfiction efforts, while his first book of juvenile fiction, *They Came from Centerfield,* deals with baseball while also showcasing Gutman's characteristic humor. With its mix of sports and alien invasion, the story appealed particularly to young boys, and Gutman found himself launched on a new career.

In Gutman's "Baseball Card Adventure" books the author plants interesting historical facts in entertaining stories about some of the greats of the sport. In *Honus and Me* readers meet Joe Stoshak, a preteen baseball fan and player-in-training who supplements his partici-

pation in the sport by collecting baseball cards. While earning money by cleaning out an elderly neighbor's attic, Joe finds an old baseball card that turns out to be the most valuable card in the world. The 1909 "Honus Wagner T-206" is more than just a collector's item, however, as Joe finds out when he is transported back in time to meet the actual baseball player and get a few pointers on his swing. Praising Gutman's "direct, no-frills writing style" and the inclusion of interesting trivia about the early game, a *Publishers Weekly* reviewer added that for readers looking for "a snappy plot along with the play-by-play, this novel hits at least a triple." A *Kirkus Reviews* critic praised *Honus and Me* as "a good fantasy for any baseball fanatic," while in *Booklist* Ilene Cooper maintained that "even readers not into sports will enjoy the fantasy elements."

Gutman continues the "Baseball Card Adventure" series with several more titles involving Joe's time travels to meet famous athletes. In *Jackie and Me* the boy takes a trip back to 1947 and visits with African-American baseball great Jackie Robinson; *Babe and Me* finds Joe and his divorced dad traveling to the year 1932 to take in a famous ball game in which Babe Ruth hits an historic home run; *Shoeless Joe and Me* lands Joe back in 1919, hoping to diffuse the scandal that would destroy the Chicago White Sox and sully the reputation of "Shoeless Joe" Jackson; and *Satch and Me* follows the teen's efforts to clock Negro League pitcher Satchel Paige during the 1942 Negro League World Series. Praising Greene's entire series as "full of action," *School Library Journal* contributor Andrew Medlar predicted that *Jackie and Me* could "spark history discussions and be a good choice for . . . leisure reading." With its "light-hearted" approach, *Satch and Me* nonetheless addresses the racism that permeated both baseball and U.S. society during the World War II era, according to Marilyn Tanaguchi in a review for the same periodical, while a *Kirkus Reviews* writer praised Gutman for creating "a delightful mix of humor, magic and history surrounded by the sheer joy of baseball."

Other "Baseball Card Adventures" books include *Jim and Me, Ray and Me,* and *Roberto and Me.* In *Jim and Me* the year is 1913 and Joe is joined by his middle-school nemesis in an effort to help former Olympic athlete Jim Thorpe the temptations that are destined to destroy his future, while *Ray and Me* finds Joe traveling back to 1920 to keep Cleveland Indians batter Ray Chapman out of the way of a killer fastball. Roberto Clemente is the player at the center of *Roberto and Me,* and here Joe winds up at the 1969 Woodstock music festival while aiming to reach Cincinnati to convince the Pittsburgh Pirate to change planes and avoid a crash that would kill him. Reviewing *Jim and Me* in *Kliatt,* Paula Rohrlick predicted that Gutman's "lively" story "will appeal to middle-school . . . sports fans," while a *Kirkus Reviews* writer cited *Ray and Me* as "deliver[ing] . . . just the right blend of action and information" due to the author's inclusion of environmental themes.

Also focusing on the game of baseball, *Casey Back at Bat,* a picture book featuring artwork by Steve Johnson and Lou Fancher, presents Gutman's sequel to a favorite American poem: "Casey at the Bat" by Ernest Lawrence Thayer. Once more facing the pitcher's mound at Mudville, Casey keeps keeps readers in suspense in a rhyming story that *Horn Book* critic Miriam Lang Budin described as a "clever mock-heroic ballad" which "finds exceptional partnership" in the illustrators' nostalgic-themed collage art.

Gutman moves from the baseball stadium to the political arena in his popular middle-grade novel *The Kid Who Ran for President.* In this story, twelve-year-old Judson Moon decides to test the system and run for the highest office in the land. As his constituency, Judson marshals thousands of U.S. kids who force their parents to pass a constitutional amendment eliminating age restrictions for the office of president by threatening boycotts of household chores, bed-making, and dog-walking. Reviewing the novel for *Booklist,* Carol Phelan dubbed *The Kid Who Ran for President* "an entertaining romp through the political process" that contains "plenty

Gutman's entertaining preteen novel The Homework Machine *features cartoon art by Dan Santat.* (Aladdin Paperbacks, 2007. Cover designed by Michael Nagin and Christopher Grassi (NY, 2006). Reproduced by permission of Simon & Schuster Books for Young Readers, an imprint of Simon & Schuster Children's Publishing Division.)

of humor." In *School Library Journal,* Elisabeth Palmer Abarbanel deemed the book "humorous" as well as an "informative" introduction to the election process, and in *Publishers Weekly* a critic described it as a "snappy, lighthearted farce." In Gutman's sequel, *The Kid Who Became President,* Judson gains elected office and sets a decidedly new tone in Washington, DC.

Other stand-alone novels that capture reader attention without the lure of sports include *Virtually Perfect, The Homework Machine, The Get Rich Quick Club,* and *Getting Air.* In *Virtually Perfect* twelve-year-old Yip, with access to his father's special-effects equipment, creates a "virtual actor" in his computer. Problems arise when the computer-generated, wisecracking teen thespian gains the power to leave the screen and enter reality; Yip has neglected to program the being to know the difference between right and wrong. Praising the novel as a "smoothly diverting "What if?" tale," a contributor for *Publishers Weekly* added that Gutman's "breezy dialogue" and ability to create a fast-paced plot "give this caper the scent of a smartly written sitcom." Noting that Yip's dilemma—whether or not to destroy the creature he has created—provides the story with an intriguing moral center, *School Library Journal* contributor Eunice Weech praised *Virtually Perfect* as "an amusing and thought-provoking novel."

The Homework Machine finds fifth graders Sam, Judy, Brenton, and Kelsey capitalizing on Brenton's computer program, which completes school assignments with no help from humans. Framed as a series of first-person narratives, Gutman's saga includes the perspective of each of the four students, as well as those of their classmates, their teacher, and even the local police chief as the scheme to gain good grades spins out of control. *Return of the Homework Machine* continues the fifth graders' adventures, as Sam, Judy, Brenton, and Kelsey attempt to locate the machine's discarded but still functioning power chip before a school bully can use it to build his own machine. Phelan described *The Homework Machine* as a "fast-paced" and "entertaining" story that also features such serious topics as "ethics and student computer use." In *School Library Journal* Elaine E. Knight praised the same novel, writing that Greene intertwines "a dramatic and thought-provoking story with a strong message about honesty and friendship," while a *Publishers Weekly* critic noted that the author's "over-the-top tale" ends with a compelling plot twist. In her review of *Return of the Homework Machine* Knight was also approving, dubbing the book "an exciting choice" for middle-grade readers that boasts an entertaining plot and an "unconventional and challenging narrative."

Another group of kids teams up in *The Get Rich Quick Club,* as eleven-year-old Gina Turnolo leads four financially savvy schoolmates in a businesslike scheme to sell a story about alien visitors to a tabloid newspaper. Middle-grade readers "will chortle over Gutman's characteristically broad humor," predicted *Booklist* contributor Jennifer Mattson, praising *The Get Rich Quick Club*

Gutman's popular "Baseball Card Adventure" series includes **Abner and Me,** *a book featuring cover art by Steve Chorney.* (Harper Trophy, 2005. Cover art © 2005 by Steve Chorney. All rights reserved. Used by permission of HarperCollins Publishers.)

Geared for older readers, *Getting Air* trades humor for suspense as thirteen-year-old Jimmy and two friends board a plane to a California skateboarding championship, only to find that the flight is hijacked by terrorists. A battle for control of the plane results in a crash landing in the Canadian wilderness where Jimmy, his friends, and three other survivors must now face a new challenge. Calling *Getting Air* "a fast-paced adventure keyed to today's headlines," *Booklist* critic Carolyn Phelan also noted that Gutman's first young-adult novel maintains a slightly unsteady focus due to the author's effort to mix humor with more serious topics. Praising the "can-do attitude" of the young survivors, John Leighton wrote in *School Library Journal* that Gutman's novel features "a true adventure . . . with high-spirited and fundamentally good boys as the central characters."

Gutman once told *SATA:* "As a kid, I was a skinny, nerdy right fielder for the Galante Giants, a little-league team sponsored by the Galante Funeral Home in Newark, New Jersey. I was terrible, but I loved baseball. It's a real thrill to be making a living writing about the game today." One of Gutman's favorite aspects of life as a writer is doing the research: "to dig into old newspapers to research classic ball games, and then re-create them so the readers feel like they're sitting in the stands watching."

Recognizing the popularity his books have among so-called reluctant readers, Gutman views his work as a

Gutman envisions a continuation of a classic American baseball poem in his picture book Casey Back at Bat, *illustrated by Steve Johnson and Lou Fancher.* (Harper Trophy 2007. Illustrations copyright © Lou Fancher & Steve Johnson. Used by permission of HarperCollins Publishers.)

as a "tart, funny" satire of American avarice. In *School Library Journal,* Linda Zeilstra Sawyer noted the story's appeal to reluctant readers, and a *Kirkus Reviews* writer dubbed the book "believable, silly fun."

Another stand-alone novel for the upper elementary grades, *The Christmas Genie* posits an unusual scenario: a small meteorite crashes through the window of Mrs. Walters' classroom and releases a genie who grants one wish to the teacher's amazed fifth-grade students. The students are given forty minutes to choose a wish, as Bob the genie is on a strict timetable after being trapped in a meteorite for millions and millions of light years. The children's decision-making process is detailed by Gutman in what Linda Israelson described in *School Library Journal* as "a lively, thought-provoking, and hilarious discussion" evaluating the proposed wishes. Science, ethics, and history enter into the discussion, as well as running humorous asides from the witty Bob, who admits to a personal friendship with Santa Claus. As narrated by a student named Chase, *The Christmas Genie* "moves chronologically . . . to a surprising climax" that *Booklist* contributor Kathleen Isaacs predicted will keep readers laughing.

contribution to building confidence among these young people. "I know that boys are often reluctant to read (I sure was). My hope is that they'll pick up my books because they like sports and then look up hours later to realize they've been *reading* the whole time. That would give me a lot of satisfaction."

Biographical and Critical Sources

PERIODICALS

Booklist, June 1, 1994, Carolyn Phelan, review of *Baseball's Greatest Games,* p. 1792; September 15, 1994, Chris Sherman, review of *World Series Classics,* p. 134; October 1, 1995, Chris Sherman, review of *Ice Skating: From Axels to Zambonis,* pp. 300-301; May 1, 1996, Chris Sherman, review of *Gymnastics,* p. 1500; July, 1996, Wes Lukowsky, review of *The Way Baseball Works,* p. 1795; November 1, 1996, Carolyn Phelan, review of *The Kid Who Ran for President,* p. 498; April 15, 1997, Ilene Cooper, review of *Honus and Me,* pp. 1428-1429; October 1, 1997, Lauren Peterson, review of *The Million-Dollar Shot,* p. 329; February 1, 1999, Karen Hutt, review of *Jackie and Me,* p. 974; February 1, 2000, Gillian Engberg, review of *Babe and Me,* p. 1023; November 15, 2001, Anne O'Malley, review of *The Million Dollar Kick,* p. 571; January 1, 2002, Carolyn Phelan, review of *Shoeless Joe and Me,* p. 857; September 15, 2002, Carolyn Phelan, review of *Qwerty Stevens, Back in Time with Benjamin Franklin,* p. 235; January 1, 2004, Todd Morning, review of *Race for the Sky: The Kitty Hawk Diaries of Johnny Moore,* p. 856; August, 2004, Jennifer Mattson, review of *The Get Rich Quick Club,* p. 1934; September 1, 2004, John Green, review of *The Million Dollar Strike,* p. 111; March, 1, 2005, Anna Rich, review of *"My Weird School"* series, p. 1218; February 1, 2006, Carolyn Phelan, review of *The Homework Machine,* p. 48; January 1, 2007, GraceAnne A. DeCandido, review of *Casey Back at Bat,* p. 114; July 1, 2007, Carolyn Phelan, review of *Getting Air,* p. 59; April 15, 2009, Carolyn Phelan, review of *Return of the Homework Machine,* p. 38; December 1, 2009, Kathleen Issacs, review of *The Christmas Genie,* p. 41; January 1, 2010, Carolyn Phelan, review of *Roberto and Me,* p. 86.

Family Life, February 1, 2001, Sara Nelson, review of *The Kid Who Became President,* p. 93.

Horn Book, May-June, 2007, Miriam Lang Budin, review of *Casey Back at Bat,* p. 265.

Kirkus Reviews, April 15, 1996, review of *Gymnastics,* p. 202; September 15, 1996, review of *The Kid Who Ran for President,* p. 1400; February 1, 1997, review of *Honus and Me,* p. 223; February 15, 2002, review of *Shoeless Joe and Me,* p. 257; July 1, 2004, review of *The Get Rich Quick Club,* p. 629; January 15, 2006, review of *Satch and Me,* p. 85; February 1, 2006, review of *The Homework Machine,* p. 131; April 15, 2007, review of *Getting Air;* May-June, 2007, Miriam Lang Budin, review of *Casey Back at Bat,* p. 265; June 15, 2008, review of *Nightmare at the Book Fair;*

February 1, 2009, review of *Recycle This Book;* May 1, 2009, review of *Return of the Homework Machine;* September 15, 2009, review of *The Christmas Genie;* February 15, 2010, review of *Roberto and Me.*

Kliatt, March, 2008, Paula Rohrlick, review of *Jim and Me,* p. 14.

Publishers Weekly, November 11, 1996, review of *The Kid Who Ran for President,* p. 76; February 10, 1997, review of *Honus and Me,* p. 84; April 6, 1998, review of *Virtually Perfect,* p. 79; February 1, 1999, review of *Jackie and Me,* p. 87; January 31, 2000, review of *Babe and Me,* p. 108; August 27, 2001, review of *The Million Dollar Kick,* p. 86; March 18, 2002, review of *Babe and Me,* p. 106; January 27, 2003, review of *Honus and Me,* p. 262; September 6, 2004, review of *The Get Rich Quick Club,* p. 63; December 11, 2006, review of *Casey Back at the Bat,* p. 68; July 7, 2008, review of *Nightmare at the Book Fair,* p. 59; October 26, 2009, review of *The Christmas Genie,* p. 57.

School Library Journal, November, 1994, George Delalis, review of *World Series Classics,* pp. 125-126; August, 1996, Janice C. Hayes, review of *Gymnastics,* pp. 155-156; November, 1996, Elisabeth Palmer Abarbanel, review of *The Kid Who Ran for President,* p. 106; December, 1997, Denise E. Agosto, review of *The Million Dollar Shot,* p. 124; August, 1998, Eunice Weech, review of *Virtually Perfect,* p. 163; March, 1999, Andrew Medlar, review of *Jackie and Me,* pp. 209-210; January, 2001, Tim Wadham, review of *Johnny Hangtime,* p. 130; August, 2001, Lisa Prolman, review of *The Edison Mystery,* p. 182; December, 2001, Elaine E. Knight, review of *The Million Dollar Kick,* p. 134; March, 2002, Elaine E. Knight, review of *Shoeless Joe and Me,* p. 231; August, 2002, Doris Losey, review of *Qwerty Stevens, Back in Time with Benjamin Franklin,* p. 188; August, 2004, Linda Zeilstra Sawyer, review of *The Get Rich Quick Club,* p. 87; December, 2004, Taja Alkoriji, review of *The Million Dollar Strike,* p. 146; February, 2006, Marilyn Taniguchi, review of *Satch and Me,* p. 131; April, 2006, Elaine E. Knight, review of *The Homework Machine,* p. 140; January, 2007, Marilyn Taniguchi, review of *Casey Back at Bat,* p. 94; April, 2007, review of *The Million Dollar Putt;* June, 2007, John Leighton, review of *Getting Air,* p. 145; October, 2007, review of *Casey Back at Bat;* September, 2008, Beth Cuddy, review of *Nightmare at the Book Fair,* p. 182; June, 2009, Elaine Lesh Morgan, review of *Coach Hyatt Is a Riot!,* p. 88; July, 2009, Elaine E. Knight, review of *Return of the Homework Machine,* p. 84; October, 2009, Linda Israelson, review of *The Christmas Genie,* p. 80.

Voice of Youth Advocates, February, 1994, Florence H. Munat, review of *Baseball's Biggest Bloopers,* p. 395; April, 1995, Ian B. Lande, review of *World Series Classics,* pp. 45-46; February, 1996, Beth Karpas, review of *Ice Skating,* p. 395; December, 1996, Connie Allerton, review of *Gymnastics,* p. 287.

ONLINE

Dan Gutman Home Page, http://www.dangutman.com (October 20, 2010).

H

HAIG, Matt 1975-

Personal

Born 1975, in Sheffield, England; married; wife's name Andrea; children: Lucas, Pearl. *Education:* Hull University, bachelor's degree; Leeds University, M.A.

Addresses

Home—Leeds, England. *Agent*—Caradoc King, A.P. Watt, 20 John St., London WC1N 2DR, England. *E-mail*—matt@matthaig.com.

Career

Writer. Previously worked in marketing; cofounder of a marketing company.

Awards, Honors

Nestlé Gold Award, and Blue Peter Book of the Year award, both 2009, both for *Shadow Forest.*

Writings

FOR CHILDREN

Shadow Forest, Bodley Head (London, England), 2007, published as *Samuel Blink and the Forbidden Forest,* Putnam (New York, NY), 2007.
Samuel Blink and the Runaway Troll, G.P. Putnam's Sons (New York, NY), 2008.

FOR ADULTS

The Last Family in England (novel), Jonathan Cape (London, England), 2004, published as *The Labrador Pact,* Viking (New York, NY), 2008.
The Dead Fathers Club (novel), Jonathan Cape (London, England), 2006, Viking (New York, NY), 2007.

The Possession of Mr. Cave (novel), Jonathan Cape (London, England), 2008, Viking (New York, NY), 2009.
The Radleys (novel), Free Press (New York, NY), 2010.

Author of nine books on public relations and marketing, including *Brand Failures.* Contributor to periodicals, including *Guardian, Sunday Times, Independent,* and *Sydney Morning Herald.*

Author's work has been translated into Danish, French, German, Icelandic, Italian, Norwegian, Russian, and Spain.

Adaptations

The Dead Father's Club and *The Possession of Mr. Cave* were adapted for film. Alfonso Cuarón was slated to direct a film version of *The Radleys.*

Sidelights

Matt Haig worked in marketing when he first got out of school, and his talent for public relations let him to start his own marketing company and write several well-received books in that field. However, Haig's creative streak eventually held sway over his practical side, and he made the shift to fiction. His fascination with family dynamics led to his first adult novel, *The Last Family in England,* as well as to *The Possession of Mr. Cave,* and *The Radleys,* while the darkly humorous *The Dead Father's Club* finds a boy goaded into committing murder by a ghost bent on revenge. Turning to younger readers, Haig has also produced the award-winning fantasy *Shadow Forest* and its sequel, *The Runaway Troll.*

Haig's first novel, *The Last Family in England,* was released in the United States as *The Labrador Pact.* The story's narrator is Prince, a Labrador retriever whose owner, Adam Hunter, has taken the dog to the veterinarian to be put down. As Prince waits in the veterinarian's office he recounts the events that brought Hunter to the decision to euthanize his pet. Prince admits that he has violated the pact among Labradors to devote their

lives to the protection of their human masters, but explains that the Hunters are a difficult bunch. Adam is conducting a sizzling flirtation with a young aromatherapist; Kate, Adam's wife, has a complicated past that involves the aromatherapist's husband; and the couple's teenagers, Hal and Charlotte, are behaving with typical teen angst and rebellion. As Prince strives to honor his pact, things spiral out of control and dead bodies begin to accumulate. A reviewer for *Publishers Weekly* called *The Labrador Pact* "a little heavy-handed and . . . gimmicky," but predicted that readers will find Prince to be a sympathetic character. A contributor to *Kirkus Reviews* also acknowledged Prince's charm, and *New York Times Book Review* contributor Alison McCulloch dubbed *The Labrador Pact* "dark, comic and quite brilliantly adult."

The plot of *The Dead Fathers Club,* Haig's first novel, was inspired by William Shakespeare's *Hamlet* and shares a parallel story line: young Philip's recently murdered father has returned as a ghost to implore his son to kill the man who murdered him: a man who turns out to be Philip's uncle and the dead man's own brother. Michael Cart described the novel in a review for *Booklist* as "darkly witty and delightfully clever," with a protagonist "whose honesty and innocence, which shine from every sentence, are utterly captivating and heartbreakingly poignant." A *Kirkus Reviews* contributor lauded Haig for "re-imagining a tragic masterpiece with such wit, force and—yes—originality." Joshua Cohen, writing for *Library Journal,* found that Haig "neatly sustains the Hamlet parallel."

In *The Possession of Mr. Cave* a mild-mannered antiques dealer is driven to extremes after the accidental death of his teenage son, Reuben, at the hands of bullies. Years earlier, Reuben's mother was killed by robbers, and Terence Cave illogically blamed Reuben for the tragedy. Now he focuses all his attention on Reuben's twin sister, Bryony, whom he obsessively tries to protect and control even as she begins to assert her independence. In the London *Guardian* John Burnside described Haig's troubled protagonist "neo-Victorian," and noted that he "does not see how grievously he has failed his son until it is too late." "Genuinely repellent from the first," Burnside added, Terence Cave "remains oddly sympathetic" in Haig's "compelling . . . page-turner." According to a *Kirkus Reviews* contributor, in *The Possession of Mr. Cave* Haig "channels Keat's language and Beethoven's harmonies, in a disturbed orchestration of overprotectiveness and paranoia." "Thoroughly capturing a father's desperation, fear, pain, and madness over family fatalities," according to Victor Or in his review for *Library Journal,* the novel shows Haig to be "a good interpreter of the human soul." For London *Independent* contributor James Urquhart, "Cave's grotesque zeal commands the reader's almost voyeuristic attention, and delivers an enthralling addition to the literature of demented protagonists."

Originally commissioned and conceived as a feature script for the UK Film Council Development Fund, *The Radleys* was rewritten as a novel designed to appeal to both older teens and adults. In the novel readers meet Dr. Peter Radley and his wife, Helen, and their teen-aged children, Clara and Rowan. Living in a small English town, they seem to be a typical family, with typical problems and typical joys. However, Peter and Helen are anything but typical, and the secret that they keep from their children—that they are abstaining vampires—is one that they know must eventually out. When Clara is attacked during a date gone wrong and stirred by the violence done her to act on her vampiric urging, Peter and Helen realize that they must divulge the truth if they are going to preserve their quiet life among humans. Citing the "dark humor" in *The Radleys,* Patricia Altner added in *Library Journal* that Haig's "witty novel offers a refreshing take" on a genre that has mushroomed due to the popularity of Stephanie Meyer's "Twilight" novels. *The Radleys* supplies "what jaded fans of the 'Twilight' series need," asserted a *Publishers Weekly* critic: "some fresh blood in the form of a true blue family."

Haig turns to younger readers in his illustrated chapter books *Samuel Blink and the Forbidden Forest* and *Samuel Blink and the Runaway Troll.* Published in the United Kingdom as *Shadow Forest, Samuel Blink and*

Cover of Matt Haig's fantasy themed chapter book Samuel Blink and the Runaway Troll, *featuring artwork by Peter Ferguson.* (Putnam 2008. Reproduced by permission of Penguin Putnam, Inc.)

the Forbidden Forest focuses on Samuel and Martha Blink, recently orphaned siblings who have been sent to live with an aunt in Norway. Despite strict instructions to stay out of the dark and mysterious forest near their aunt's home, the children are drawn into the woods one by one and face both good and evil in their attempts to return home. In a review for *Kidsreads.com,* Norah Piehl described the book as "a sparkling juvenile debut by a writer who understands how children think" and "a superb, briskly plotted fantasy that will appeal both to kids and to his growing numbers of adult readers." Haig's "crisp dialogue, fast-paced action, short chapters, and . . . wry narrative voice bring this tale to life," asserted Steven Engelfried in a *School Library Journal* review.

According to *School Library Journal* reviewer Tasha Saecker, *Samuel Blink and the Runaway Troll* (published as *The Runaway Troll* in Haig's native England) is "just as delightful" as its award-winning precursor. This time around Samuel and Martha are about to start school and must be careful to keep their knowledge of the Shadow Forest a secret. At the same time, they become unexpected hosts to a very worried Troll-son. A friend of Samuel's, Troll-son has run away from the Betterer, an adult troll that coerces the young trolls in his charge to adopt human-like behavior, like bathing more than once a year. While Samuel and Martha hide Troll-son, they must also fend off Mr. Myklebust, a greedy developer who has commercial designs on the Shadow Forest. Saecker admired Haig's blend of fantasy and humor, as well as its quirky characters. A writer for *Kirkus Reviews* offered a similar assessment, describing *Samuel Blink and the Runaway Troll* as an "above-average fantasy," and Toby Clements wrote in the London *Daily Mail* that the author's "jokey, direct style" makes the book "diverting enough for boys." "Well-paced suspense, sympathetic . . . characters and a lovingly described Norwegian setting make this an above-average fantasy," concluded a *Kirkus Reviews* writer in praising Haig's second chapter book.

On his home page, Haig delved into his motivations and inspirations for writing, and also addressed the reason why his adult novels feature teenaged characters. "I suppose it's the age between innocence and experience, and as most fiction deals with character transformation to some extent you're on fertile ground from the start. I think it also helps with observational stuff, to put yourself inside a younger mind, because the world instantly looks a bit newer." Haig is also hopeful that his novels will attract teen readers. "Teenagers are among the best kind of readers," he noted, "because they have the intelligence to understand big ideas, combined with that open-mindedness you tend to shed with age."

Biographical and Critical Sources

PERIODICALS

Booklist, December 1, 2006, Michael Cart, review of *The Dead Fathers Club,* p. 20; February 15, 2009, Michael Cart, review of *The Possession of Mr. Cave,* p. 31.

Daily Telegraph (London, England), February 21, 2009, Toby Clements, review of *The Runaway Troll.*

Guardian (London, England), June 7, 2008, John Burnside, review of *The Possession of Mr. Cave,* p. 11.

Independent (London, England), May 20, 2008, James Urquhart, review of *The Possession of Mr. Cave.*

Kirkus Reviews, November 15, 2006, review of *The Dead Fathers Club,* p. 1147; January 15, 2008, review of *The Labrador Pact;* August 1, 2008, review of *Samuel Blink and the Runaway Troll;* January 1, 2009, review of *The Possession of Mr. Cave.*

Library Journal, December 1, 2006, Joshua Cohen, review of *The Dead Fathers Club,* p. 110; January 1, 2009, Victor Or, review of *The Possession of Mr. Cave,* p. 78; October 1, 2010, Patricia Altner, review of *The Radleys,* p. 67.

New York Times Book Review, April 26, 2009, Victoria Redel, review of *Dangerously Close,* p. 13l; March 23, 2008, Alison McCulloch, review of *The Labrador Pact,* p. 20.

Publishers Weekly, November 19, 2007, review of *The Labrador Pact,* p. 31; November 17, 2008, review of *The Possession of Mr. Cave,* p. 37; October 4, 2010, review of *The Radleys,* p. 27.

School Library Journal, October, 2007, Steven Engelfried, review of *Samuel Blink and the Forbidden Forest,* p. 152; September 1, 2008, Tasha Saecker, review of *Samuel Blink and the Runaway Troll,* p. 182.

Times (London, England), May 17, 2008, Charlotte Stretch, review of *The Possession of Mr. Cave,* p. 13.

USA Today, March 13, 2008, review of *The Labrador Pact,* p. 5.

ONLINE

Kidsreads.com, http://www.kidsreads.com/ (March 20, 2009), Norah Piehl, review of *Samuel Blink and the Forbidden Forest.*

Matt Haig Home Page, http://www.matthaig.com (October 20, 2010).

Monsters and Critics Web site, http://www.monstersandcritics.com/ (March 20, 2009), Angela Youngman, review of *Shadow Forest.**

*   *   *

HARBOUR, Elizabeth 1968-

Personal

Born 1968, in Kent, England; father a surveyor, mother a registered nurse; married; children: two. *Education:* Maidstone Art School, B.A. (illustration; first class; with honours), c. 1990; Royal College of Art, M.A. (illustration), 1992.

Addresses

Home—Kent, England.

Elizabeth Harbour (Reproduced by permission.)

Career

Illustrator, artist, printmaker, and educator. Freelance illustrator and graphic artist. Teacher at art colleges, including Central St. Martins, for three years.

Writings

SELF-ILLUSTRATED

A Gardener's Alphabet, M. Joseph (London, England), 1990.
A First Picture Book of Nursery Rhymes, Viking Penguin (New York, NY), 1995.

ILLUSTRATOR

Susan Purveur, compiler, *Plant That Name!,* Michael Joseph, 1996.
Vivian French, *The Thistle Princess,* Candlewick Press (Cambridge, MA), 1998.
Nettie Lowenstein, reteller, *Anna and the Flowers of Winter,* Puffin (London, England), 2000.
Olivia Warburton, *Our Family: A Keepsake Album,* Lion Hudson (London, England), 2000.
(With Lucy Truman) Alison Mackonochie, *Happy Pregnancy: 100 Tips for a Happy Pregnancy,* MQ Publications, 2004.
Lucy Truman, *Happy Baby: 100 Tips for a Happy Baby,* MQ Publications, 2004.
Gillian Shields, *The Starlight Baby,* Simon & Schuster Books for Young Readers (New York, NY), 2006.
Gillian Shields, *Puppy Love: The Story of Esme and Sam,* Simon & Schuster Children's (London, England), 2008, Simon & Schuster Books for Young Readers (New York, NY), 2009.

Sidelights

Elizabeth Harbour is an illustrator, printmaker, and artist who creates softly tinted images featuring elongated characters and whimsical elements. Working in water

color and gouache, acrylics, India ink line and wash, and etching, Harbour began her illustration career with *A Gardener's Alphabet,* a book that she created during her first year at art school in Maidenstone, England. Harbour's artwork has been featured in picture books by writers that include Gillian Shields and Vivian French. It can also be found on the cover of magazines and books, in advertising, adapted for cards and gift wrap, and gracing the pages of journals and gift books. In a review of *A First Picture Book of Nursery Rhymes, Booklist* contributor Carolyn Phelan remarked on Harbour's use of "soft lines and delicate colors" and added that the "formality" of the artist's images hints at "a gentle humor [that] is pleasing in its own way."

After attending art school, Harbour went on to study illustration at the Royal College of Art, and her work attracted publishers when she solicited illustration projects following graduation. Two early projects, creating artwork for French's *The Thistle Princess* and Nettie Lowenstein's retelling *Anna and the Flowers of Winter,* attracted the interest of critics, a *Publishers Weekly* critic noting of the former book that Harbour's contribution of "elegantly elongated, soft-focus watercolors creates an appropriately bittersweet, romantic mood."

Bringing to life Shields' rhythmic lullaby about a motherless child in *The Starlight Baby,* the artist's "soft-

Harbour's illustration projects include a child's first book of nursery rhymes. (Illustration courtesy of Elizabeth Harbour.)

edged watercolors" boast "sunset-hued" tones that add a reassuring element, according to Jennifer Mattson in *Booklist.* Writing in *School Library Journal,* Linda Staskus agreed, noting that Harbour's pastel-toned "folk-art watercolors lighten the somber tone of this lyrical story." *The Starlight Baby* can be read as "an adoption story," according to a *Kirkus Reviews* writer, the critic adding that Harbour's "dulcet watercolors" feature "meltingly soft pastels and swooping lines."

In *Puppy Love: The Story of Esme and Sam* Shields' humorous story finds a pampered, upper-class poodle named Esme Lamour separated from her rich owners and out on the street. Fortunately, a scrappy, street-smart stray comes to her rescue and leads Esme on a series of adventures which enrich her life and spark romance. In her backdrop to this canine journey through New York City, Harbour creates an urban landscape that "is aglow in soft, gauzy pastels" that give Shields' story "just the right note of sweetness without being overly sentimental," according to a *Kirkus Reviews* writer.

Biographical and Critical Sources

PERIODICALS

Booklist, April 15, 1996, Carolyn Phelan, review of *A First Picture Book of Nursery Rhymes,* p. 1442; February 1, 2006, Jennifer Mattson, review of *The Starlight Baby,* p. 58.

Kirkus Reviews, March 15, 2006, review of *The Starlight Baby*; June 1, 2009, review of *Puppy Love: The Story of Esme and Sam.*

Publishers Weekly, October 19, 1998, review of *The Thistle Princess,* p. 80; June 29, 2009, review of *Puppy Love,* p. 127.

School Library Journal, August, 1996, Dawn Ibey, review of *A First Picture Book of Nursery Rhymes,* p. 136; November 1, 1998, Nancy Menaldi-Scanlon, review of *The Thistle Princess,* p. 84; April, 2006, Linda Staskus, review of *The Starlight Baby,* p. 118; August, 2009, Lisa Egly Lehmuller, review of *Puppy Love,* p. 84.

Times Educational Supplement, December 10, 1999, review of *Anna and the Flowers of Winter,* p. 33.

ONLINE

Elizabeth Harbour Home Page, http://www.danbypress.co.uk (October 15, 2010).

*   *   *

HASELEY, Dennis 1950-

Personal

Surname rhymes with "paisley"; born June 28, 1950, in Cleveland, OH; son of Robert Carl (a sales executive) and Margaret (an account supervisor) Haseley; married

Dennis Haseley (Reproduced by permission.)

Claudia Eleanore Lament (a child psychoanalyst), October 12, 1986; children: Connor McMurray. *Education:* Oberlin College, A.B., 1972; New York University, M.S.W., 1982; New York University Psychoanalytic Institute, degree. *Hobbies and other interests:* Tennis, skiing, running.

Addresses

Home—Brooklyn, NY. *Agent*—c/o Wendy Schmalz Agency, Box 831, Hudson, NY 12534.

Career

Teacher, psychotherapist, and author. Worked variously as a professional fund raiser and community organizer. Jewish Board of Family and Children's Services, New York, NY, therapist, 1982-86; author of books for children, beginning 1982; private practice in psychotherapy and psychoanalysis, beginning 1984. New York University, clinical assistant professor of psychiatry.

Member

Society of Children's Book Writers and Illustrators, Authors Guild.

Awards, Honors

New York Public Library Best Children's Books selection, Child Study Association Children's Books of the Year selection, and Pick of the Lists selection, Ameri-

can Booksellers Association (ABA), all 1983, all for *The Old Banjo*; Parents' Choice Remarkable Book for Literature designation, Parents' Choice Foundation, 1983, for *The Scared One;* Notable Book in the Field of Social Studies selection, National Council for Social Studies, and ABA Pick of the Lists selection, both 1986, and Child Study Association of America Children's Books of the Year selection, 1987, all for *The Kite Flier*; ABA Pick of the Lists selections, and Library of Congress Books of the Year inclusion, both 1991, both for *Shadows*; New York Foundation for the Arts fiction grant, 1994; Best Children's Books selection, Bank Street College of Education, 2008, for *Twenty Heartbeats.*

Writings

FOR CHILDREN

The Sacred One, illustrated by Deborah Howland, Warne (New York, NY), 1983.

The Old Banjo, illustrated by Stephen Gammell, Macmillan (New York, NY), 1983.

The Pirate Who Tried to Capture the Moon, illustrated by Sue Truesdell, Harper (New York, NY), 1984.

The Soap Bandit, illustrated by James Chambless-Rigie, Warne (New York, NY), 1984.

The Kite Flier, illustrated by David Wiesner, Aladdin Books (New York, NY), 1986.

The Cave of Snores, illustrated by Eric Beddows, Harper (New York, NY), 1987.

My Father Doesn't Know about the Woods and Me, illustrated by Michael Hays, Atheneum (New York, NY), 1988.

Ghost Catcher, illustrated by Lloyd Bloom, Harper (New York, NY), 1989.

The Thieves' Market, illustrated by Lisa Desimini, HarperCollins (New York, NY), 1991.

Horses with Wings, illustrated by Lynn Curlee, HarperCollins (New York, NY), 1993.

Crosby, illustrated by Jonathan Green, Harcourt Brace (New York, NY), 1996.

A Story for Bear, illustrated by Jim LaMarche, Silver Whistle Books (New York, NY), 2002.

Photographer Mole, illustrated by Juli Kangas, Dial Books for Young Readers (New York, NY), 2004.

The Invisible Moose, illustrated by Steven Kellogg, Dial Books for Young Readers (New York, NY), 2006.

The Skywriter, illustrated by Dennis Nolan, Roaring Brook Press (New York, NY), 2008.

Twenty Heartbeats, illustrated by Ed Young, Roaring Brook Press (New York, NY), 2008.

YOUNG-ADULT NOVELS

The Counterfeiter, Macmillan (New York, NY), 1987.

Shadows, illustrated by Leslie Bowman, Farrar, Straus (New York, NY), 1991.

Dr. Gravity, Farrar, Straus (New York, NY), 1992.

Getting Him, Farrar, Straus (New York, NY), 1994.

The Amazing Thinking Machine, Dial Books (New York, NY), 2002.

A Trick of the Eye, Dial Books (New York, NY), 2004.

Author's works have been translated into Chinese, French, and Spanish.

Adaptations

The Old Banjo was adapted as a filmstrip with cassette, Random House, 1986; *The Cave of Snores* was included in the video recording *Return to the Magic Library;* a film adaptation of *Norbert, Snorebert* was produced by TVOntario (Chapel Hill, NC).

Sidelights

In addition to his work as a psychotherapist, Dennis Haseley has written extensively for children. His many books include the illustrated read-alouds *The Old Banjo, Horses with Wings, The Kite Flier, The Invisible Moose,* and *The Skywriter,* as well as middle-grade fiction and young-adult novels such as *Getting Him, Shadows,* and

Cover of Haseley's middle-grade novel Getting Him, *featuring cover art by Mark Elliot.* (Farrar, 1994. Jacket art © 1994 by Mark Elliot. Reproduced by permission.)

A Trick of the Eye. Known for their unusual and imaginative subject matter, symbolism, and lyrical prose, Haseley's books have long captured the attention of reviewers.

Haseley grew up in Brecksville, Ohio, where at the age of seven he wrote his first poem. During high school and while a student at Oberlin College, he renewed and developed his talent for writing, working with novelist and screenwriter William Goldman during a semester in New York City. After graduation, Haseley published verse in literary magazines and came to the realization that children's books offered an opportunity for him to showcase his talent. His first book for children, *The Scared One,* is a prose-poem picture book about the rites of passage of a timid Native-American boy who has been nicknamed the Scared One by his playmates. "It is gravely told, and touching" wrote a reviewer in the *Bulletin of the Center for Children's Books,* while a *Publishers Weekly* critic remarked that *The Scared One* "resonates with the cadences of heroic legends."

Many of Haseley's picture books have been praised by reviewers. In *The Old Banjo,* which a *Booklist* reviewer called "a mystical, magical fantasy," a boy living on a Depression-era farm discovers some forgotten musical instruments that magically come alive. Describing the book—illustrated by Stephen Gammell—George A. Woods concluded in the *New York Times Book Review* that "the combo of Mr. Haseley on words and Mr. Gammell on pencil have produced a modest piece that will strike a responsive chord in most readers." Likewise, *School Library Journal* contributor Ellen D. Warwick declared in her review of *The Old Banjo* that "this beautiful book has something important to say about the nature of hope and the persistence of dreams."

My Father Doesn't Know about the Woods and Me takes readers on a walk through the woods with a boy and his father. An imaginative child, the boy empathizes with nature's creatures and feels as though he is successively transformed into each of the animals he sees. This "possibility weaves a magic spell over readers and listeners," wrote David Gale in a *School Library Journal* review of Haseley's tale. Describing *My Father Doesn't Know about the Woods and Me* as a "magical story," a *Booklist* critic likewise remarked that the book "offers possibilities to tweak children's imaginations."

Recommended by *Booklist* contributor Gillian Engberg as "a good choice for winter read-alouds," *The Invisible Moose* once again takes readers into the forest. Featuring illustrations by Steven Kellogg, Haseley's story is set in the northern forests of Canada, where a timid moose worships his true love in secret. When they finally meet, the moose's beloved is cornered by a trapper and trucked off to New York City. With the help of an owl's wizardry, the moose makes his way to the city, where he finds his true love vond helps her return to their forest home by magical means. Kellogg's images "amplify the silliness, magic and sweet romance" in

Cover of Haseley's middle-grade novel **The Amazing Thinking Machine,** *featuring artwork by Kazuhiko Sano.* (Dial Books, 2002. Cover copyright © 2002 by Kazuhiko Sano. Used by permission of Dial Books for Young Readers, A Division of Penguin Young Readers Group, A Member of Penguin Group (USA) Inc., 345 Hudson Street, New York, NY 10014. All rights reserved.)

Haseley's tale, asserted Engberg, while *School Library Journal* critic Wendy Woodfill noted of *The Invisible Moose* that both story and art "are loaded with humorous touches and quirky details that will keep readers entertained." In *Kirkus Reviews* a critic dubbed the same book "unapologetically goofy," adding that Kellogg's "vibrantly colorful illustrations are . . . bursting with tearful and hilarious moments alike."

Another fantasy by Halseley, *The Thieves' Market,* revolves around a group of thieves that opens up a market outside a town where children come at night to choose their dreams. *Booklist* contributor Leone McDermott highly praised the metaphor of the market and the "eerie beauty" of Haseley's text, describing *The Thieves' Market* as "unusual and affecting" and "filled with insight and respect for children's inner lives." This is a story that "may intrigue the curious, the lovers of mystery and magic" predicted Shirley Wilton in a *School Library Journal* review of the book.

Haseley encourages readers to indulge in their own worlds of make-believe in *The Skywriter,* a picture book

illustrated by Dennis Nolan. A dollhouse occupied by the toy figurines of a baker, airplane pilot, and a soldier become the favorite toys of Charles, a young boy, who joins these characters on many vivid imaginary journeys throughout his early childhood. As Charles grows up, he moves on to other activities, leaving the dollhouse and its occupants alone until they are rediscovered while cleaning the playroom for a new baby brother. Although the toys are first discarded, Charles is inspired by his own fond memories to rescue them from the garbage, and ultimately they serve a similar role in fueling the imagination of the boy's younger sibling. In her *School Library Journal* review of *The Skywriter,* Susannah Richards praised the book's "dreamlike images and believable text," while a *Kirkus Reviews* critic noted that Nolan's gentle images and Haseley's "matter-of-fact narration" "combine in an understatement that . . . honors childish imaginations." In *Publishers Weekly* a critic noted the book's underlying theme of how the magic of make believe fades in childhood and concluded that "Haseley's poetic, restrained language pairs well with Nolan's [sepia-toned] representational illustrations."

Many of Haseley's picture books deal with unusual subjects or present readers with allegories. For example, *The Kite Flier* tells the tale of a man who is a stonemason by day and a kite maker by night. When his wife dies after their son is born, the man stops making kites until his son shows an interest in them. As the child grows, the father makes kites that symbolize the boy's development. Years later, when the child has grown into a young man ready to be launched into the world, father and son make a special kite together and then release it. While noting that the book's symbolism might be lost on a young readership, Maria B. Salvadore judged in *School Library Journal* that *The Kite Flier* "may have special appeal to an older audience." Similarly, a *Booklist* critic predicted that Haseley's "quiet story is for the special reader; older children especially will respond to its formal language."

The title of *Twenty Heartbeats* refers to the measure of time that a horse runs to his beckoning master. Captured in Ed Young's collage art, Haseley's story captures the essence of a Chinese proverb as it recounts the master's desire to capture his beloved horse in a painting. He commissions the portrait, but grows angry when the artist does not complete it. Arriving at the artist's studio, the wealthy man learns that the man has a room full of sketches, several years' worth of efforts to capture the horse's most sublime movement. It is only at this moment that the aged artist can wield his brush and, in twenty heartbeats, capture the animal's essence on rice paper. A *Kirkus Reviews* writer noted that *Twenty Heartbeats* may serve as an "allegory about faith," "a reminder to look beyond the obvious," or even as "a treatise on the nature of art," while a *Publishers Weekly* viewed the book as "a confrontation between commerce and art." However one interprets the tale, "Haseley's minimalist text leaves plenty of room for Young's mar-

Haseley's compelling story about the meaning of art comes to life in Ed Young's Asian-inspired illustrations for **Twenty Heartbeats.** (Illustrated by Ed Young. Roaring Book Press 2008. Reproduced by permission of Henry Holt and Company, LLC.)

velous collages to set the scene and develop the characters," asserted Wendy Lukehart in her *School Library Journal* review of *Twenty Heartbeats.* Carolyn Phelan noted in *Booklist* that Young's "handsome artwork evokes every nuance of this memorable story," and the *Publishers Weekly* critic concluded that his "virtuoso illustrations . . . breathe live into the book" with their "elegant brushstrokes and collage design."

Described by *New York Times Book Review* critic Rona Berg as the author's "most ambitious and original work," *Ghost Catcher* presents a parable about "the pull of community and the power of love," according to the critic. Here Haseley tells of a solitary man called Ghost Catcher who has no shadow and so avoids forming relationships with the people of his Hispanic village. Because he has no shadow, he can bring people back from the brink of death. When Ghost Catcher is tempted by curiosity to visit the land of shadows, he is trapped there and must be rescued by the villagers who, through their compassion and efforts, show what it is to depend upon one another. "American children, used to a heavier does of realism or a lighter flight of fantasy, may find this story confusing," maintained Berg, who nonetheless concluded that *Ghost Catcher* can be read and enjoyed on several levels. A *Publishers Weekly* reviewer voiced similar comments, noting that while the book may be too difficult for some children, with its illustrations by Lloyd Bloom, it is still "an intriguing, thoughtful collaboration" and a "highly atmospheric parable."

Haseley's *A Story for Bear* has a fairy-tale quality in its story of a curious bear who watches a young woman reading in a cottage. Over the summer, the bear and the

woman often come together over a book. When she leaves at the end of the summer, she leaves him some books. He keeps them with him as he hibernates, hearing her voice reading to him again. Critics praised the book for its sweet tone and message about words and reading together. In *Booklist,* Julie Cummins commended the artwork and concluded, "This gentle message about the power of words is a tender, wistful celebration of the pleasures of reading." Similarly, a reviewer for *Kirkus Reviews* described the book as a "tender, if unlikely, episode that affirms the value of both the written and the spoken word." In *Publishers Weekly,* a critic found some of the story's inconsistencies to be a weak point, but called *A Story for Bear* "wistful" and added that Jim LaMarche's "artwork conveys the bear and the woman in growing intimacy."

Illustrated by Juli Kangas, *Photographer Mole* tells a lighthearted story of a mole who is the portrait photographer in his village. When he begins to feel that something is missing in his life, Mole leaves town only to return with a wife. In *Publishers Weekly* a reviewer praised the "picturesque, old-fashioned English-village setting evoked in loving detail" by Kangas' old-fashioned art, while in *Kirkus Reviews* a critic noted of the book's atmospheric illustrations that they reflect "an era of cobblestone streets, rolling green hills, red clay-tiled roof cottages, and a menagerie of characters dressed in period clothing." Julie Roach, writing in *School Library Journal,* predicted that *Photographer Mole* will "strike just the right chord with readers," adding that its' charming illustrations "make a nice accompaniment to the sweet and gentle text."

Although Haseley once admitted to *SATA* that, after concentrating on picture books, "it was rather frightening to take on a novel," he has written several longer works for young-adult readers. *The Counterfeiter* and *Dr. Gravity* are humorous treatments, while *Shadows* and *Getting Him* strike a more serious, responsive note. *The Counterfeiter* describes how would-be artist James falls in love with Heather, a cheerleader, and makes counterfeit currency in order to afford to take her on a date. James is a protagonist who "convincingly embodies the peculiar blend of frustration, cynicism and giddy optimism" characteristic of teens, according to a critic for *Publishers Weekly.* Reviewing *The Counterfeiter* for *School Library Journal,* Robert E. Unsworth noted that the book contains "lots of laughs and insight into the perplexities of adolescence."

Haseley's exuberant picture book Crosby *is enlivened by Jonathan Green's colorful paintings.* (Harcourt, 1996. Illustrations © 1996 by Jonathan Green. Reproduced by permission of Houghton Mifflin Harcourt Publishing Company. This material may not be reproduced in any form or by any means without the prior written permission of the publisher.)

With its focus on a man who releases townspeople from
the force of gravity and faces weighty consequences,
Dr. Gravity is a "rambling, old-fashioned novel" and "a
graceful, carefully developed fantasy," according to a
Horn Book contributor. Comparing the work to that of
noted children's author Roald Dahl, Catherine M. Dwyer of *Voice of Youth Advocates* proclaimed that "Haseley has written a wonderful fantasy. *Dr. Gravity* is full
of gentle humor and peopled with well-drawn characters." The *Horn Book* critic also maintained that "there
is much humor in the story," adding that "Haseley's
skilled use of description creates a convincing setting
for fantastic events." As Dwyer concluded, young readers "will love this tale."

Shadows, a short novel written for middle-grade readers, deals with subtle ideas. Young protagonist Jamie
wonders about his absent father and learns about him
through stories his grandfather tells by casting shadows
on a wall. *Shadows* elicited high praise from Liz Rosenberg, who reviewed the book in the *New York Times
Book Review*. Haseley, Rosenberg contended, "possesses

an acute sense of childhood's pathos," putting his talent
to good effect in this "beautifully written novel." Rosenberg added that the novel "combines realism and fantasy," and "is strong and powerfully appealing," a story
"perfect for reluctant readers, as well as all those who
love good books."

Set in a small Ohio town in the late 1950s, *Getting Him*
is a story of revenge against an eccentric sixth grader
named Harold who has accidentally injured the dog of
another boy named Donald. Because precocious Harold,
who is only eight years old, believes in the existence of
extraterrestrials, Donald and several of his friends per-
petrate an elaborate hoax involving "aliens." Citing the
work as a combination science-fiction novel, fantasy,
morality tale, and coming-of-age story, a *Publishers
Weekly* commentator wrote that "Haseley creates a mysterious stark world of preadolescent confusion." In a
School Library Journal review of *Getting Him*, Tim
Rausch noted that while "readers may enjoy the details
of the boys' prank and the mysterious elements of the
plot," the book's characters, except for Harold, "are
flat, stereotypical, and basically unlikable." A *Horn
Book* contributor, on the other hand, described the novel
as "a thoughtful, complex story with an intriguing plot
and rich, believable characters."

Haseley once commented: "I often start a story—
whether for a picture book or a novel—with an image
or metaphor that captures me. For instance, for *Dr.
Gravity,* it was the idea of a town that could float. *Shadows* began when I came upon a reprinted nineteenth-
century book instructing the reader how to make various hand shadows. *Crosby* grew from the images of a
kite's tail made of old socks and scuffed shoes that
looked like turtles. Starting with a key, evocative image, I try to reach in some way into my own experiences and emotions and build a story that becomes for
the reader—and for me—something that's new."

Biographical and Critical Sources

PERIODICALS

Booklist, October 1, 1983, review of *The Old Banjo,* p.
    294; October 1, 1986, review of *The Kite Flier,* p.
    272; January 1, 1989, review of *My Father Doesn't
    Know about the Woods and Me,* p. 788; March 15,
    1991, review of *The Thieves' Market,* p. 1505; No-
    vember 15, 1993, Kay Weisman, review of *Horses
    with Wings,* pp. 630-631; May 1, 2002, review of *A
    Story for Bear,* p. 1533; August, 2004, Terry Glover,
    review of *Trick of the Eye,* p. 1919; February 1, 2006,
    Gillian Engberg, review of *The Invisible Moose,* p.
    55; May 1, 2008, Carolyn Phelan, review of *Twenty
    Heartbeats,* p. 94.
Bulletin of the Center for Children's Books, January, 1984,
    review of *The Scared One,* p. 88.
Five Owls, September-October, 1993, Stephen Fraser, re-
    view of *Horses with Wings,* pp. 10-11.
Globe & Mail (Toronto, Ontario, Canada), May 30, 1987,
    Tim Wynne-Jones, review of *The Cave of Snores.*

Cover of Haseley's young-adult novel **Trick of the Eye,** *in which a
young teen becomes involved in a local theft of famous paintings.* (Dial
Books, 2004. Cover Art copyright the Frick Collection, New York. Used by permission of
Dial Books for Young Readers, A Division of Penguin Young Readers Group, A Member
of Penguin Group (USA) Inc., 345 Hudson Street, New York, NY 10014. All rights reserved.)

Horn Book, March-April, 1993, review of *Dr. Gravity,* pp. 211-212; January-February, 1995, review of *Getting Him,* pp. 59-60.

Kirkus Reviews, February 1, 1983, review of *The Pirate Who Tried to Capture the Moon,* p. 117; September 1, 1993, review of *Horses with Wings,* p. 54; August 1, 1996, review of *Crosby,* p. 1153; March 1, 2002, review of *A Story for Bear,* p. 335; May 1, 2004, review of *Photographer Mole,* p. 442; February 15, 2006, review of *The Invisible Moose,* p. 183; August 15, 2008, review of *The Skywriter;* March 15, 2008, review of *Twenty Heartbeats.*

New York Times Book Review, September 18, 1983, George A. Woods, review of *The Old Banjo,* p. 39; September 9, 1984, Karla Ruskin, review of *The Soap Bandit,* p. 43; October 20, 1991, Liz Rosenberg, review of *Shadows,* p. 53; April 26, 1992, Rona Berg, review of *Ghost Catcher,* p. 25.

Publishers Weekly, September 16, 1983, review of *The Scared One,* p. 125; October 14, 1983, review of *The Old Banjo,* p. 54; June 22, 1984, review of *The Soap Bandit,* p. 99; July 25, 1991, review of *Ghost Catcher,* p. 54; November 7, 1994, review of *Getting Him,* pp. 79-80; September 2, 1996, review of *Crosby,* p. 131; February 18, 2002, review of *A Story for Bear,* p. 96; April 26, 2004, review of *Trick of the Eye,* p. 67; July 5, 2004, review of *Photographer Mole,* p. 55; March 27, 2006, review of *The Invisible Moose,* p. 78; May 5, 2008, review of *Twenty Heartbeats,* p. 61; September 8, 2008, review of *The Skywriter,* p. 50.

School Library Journal, August, 1983, David Gale, review of *The Pirate Who Tried to Capture the Moon,* p. 51; November, 1983, review of *The Old Banjo,* p. 64; November, 1986, Maria B. Salvadore, review of *The Kite Flier,* p. 78; April, 1987, Tim Rausch, review of *The Cave of Snores,* pp. 82-83; October, 1987, Robert E. Unsworth, review of *The Counterfeiter,* pp. 138-139; October, 1988, David Gale, review of *My Father Doesn't Know about the Woods and Me,* p. 121; May, 1991, Shirley Wilton, review of *The Thieves' Market,* p. 78; September, 1996, Judith Constantinides, review of *Crosby,* p. 180; April, 2004, Connie Tyrell Burns, review of *Trick of the Eye,* p. 155; July, 2004, Julie Roach, review of *Photographer Mole,* p. 77; March, 2006, Wendy Woodfill, review of *The Invisible Moose,* p. 192; April, 2008, Wendy Lukehart, review of *Twenty Heartbeats,* p. 110; October, 2008, Susannah Richards, review of *The Skywriter,* p. 110.

Voice of Youth Advocates, December, 1992, Catherine M. Dwyer, review of *Dr. Gravity,* p. 292.

ONLINE

Macmillan Web site, http://us.macmillan.com/ (October 20, 2010), "Dennis Haseley."*

*   *   *

HENNESY, Carolyn 1962-

Personal

Born 1962, in Los Angeles, CA; married Donald Agnelli (an actor), 2007. *Education:* Attended American Conservatory Theater, Royal Academy of Dramatic Art, and California State University at Northridge.

Addresses

Agent—Chris Barrett and Sara Schedeen, Metropolitan Talent Agency, 204 N. Rossmore, Los Angeles, CA 90004. *E-mail*—carolyn@carolynhennesy.com.

Career

Writer, actress, and voice performer. Performed with the Groundlings Sunday Company, Los Angeles, CA. Actor in films, including *I Don't Buy Kisses Anymore,* 1992; *Elite,* 2000; *Global Effect,* 2002; *Engaging Peter,* 2002; *Legally Blonde 2: Red, White, and Blonde,* 2003; *The Second Degree,* 2003; *The Heat Chamber,* 2003; *Wave Babes,* 2003; *Terminator 3: Rise of the Machines,* 2003; *Click,* 2006; *Necessary Evil,* 2008; and *Xander Cohen,* 2010. Actor in television series, including *Big Wave Dave's,* 1993; *Grace under Fire,* 1995; *Night Stand with Dick Dietrick,* 1995; *Arli$$,* 1996; *Party of Five,* 1997; *Jenny,* 1997; *Wings,* 1997; *The Naked Truth,* 1997; *Encore! Encore!,* 1998; *Thanks,* 1999; *It's like, You Know . . .,* 1999; *That '70s Show,* 1999; *Moesha,* 2000; *Strip Mall,* 2000-01; *Dawson's Creek,* 2000-01; *Reba,* 2001; *Judging Amy,* 2002; *Bram and Alice,* 2002; *The Young and the Restless,* 2002; *Any Day Now,* 2002; *The Big O,* 2002—; *What I Like about You,* 2003; *Half & Half,* 2003; *Significant Others,* 2004; *Drake and Josh,* 2006; *General Hospital,* beginning 2007; *Penny Dreadfuls,* 2009; *Cougar Town,* 2009-10; and *Everyone Counts,* 2010. Actor in television films, including *Lightning in a Bottle,* 1993; *Deadly Invasion: The Killer Bee Nightmare,* 1995; *Recipe for Disaster,* 2003; and *Better People,* 2010. Stage actor; voice-over artist for video games.

Awards, Honors

Natalie Schafer Award for Outstanding Comedic Actress, Los Angeles Drama Critics Circle, 2000; Ovation Award, L.A. Stage Alliance, 2006; Daytime Emmy nomination for Best Supporting Actress, 2009, for role in *General Hospital.*

Writings

"PANDORA" YOUNG-ADULT NOVEL SERIES

Pandora Gets Jealous, Bloomsbury Children's Books (New York, NY), 2008.
Pandora Gets Vain, Bloomsbury Children's Books (New York, NY), 2008.
Pandora Gets Lazy, Bloomsbury (New York, NY), 2009.
Pandora Gets Heart, Bloomsbury (New York, NY), 2010.

Sidelights

In addition to her achievements as a performer, Carolyn Hennesy has developed a second career as a writer for "tween" readers. Hennesy's "Pandora" series of novels

for young-adult readers is loosely based on the character from Greek mythology, a young woman whose curiosity compelled her to open a box containing all the mysteries, illnesses, and problems of life and unleashing them on an unsuspecting human world. Hennesy delves into memories of her own teenage years to write the series, focusing on how it felt to have no idea how to succeed in the teenage social world.

Hennesy was born in Los Angeles, California, and is the niece of film and television actress Barbara Rush. She studied acting and performing at the American Conservatory Theatre and the Royal Academy of Dramatic Arts in London, England, and also attended the University of California at Northridge on a drama scholarship. She trained with the prestigious improvisational comedy troupe, the Groundlings, based in Los Angeles, during the 1990s and has appeared on the stage of such illustrious venues as the Mark Taper Forum, Geary Stage, and Arizona Theater Company. She has also appeared in both films and on television and has held recurring roles on a number of television series. In 2000 Hennesy was honored by the Los Angeles Drama Critics Circle with the Natalie Schafer Award for Outstanding Comedic Actress.

Hennesy's novel *Pandora Gets Jealous* sets the stage for the "Pandora" series. Pandora Atheneus Andromaeche Helena—nicknamed Pandy—is a bored thirteen year old with a penchant for getting into trouble. With a big project due at school, Pandy finds a box containing all evil and she decides to take it for her presentation. Unfortunately, the box is accidentally opened and seven great evils are released to roam free in the world. When Zeus hears what she is done, he declares that the impulsive teen must recover the seven evils or face a terrible punishment. As Pandy sets out on her mission, she is joined by her snow-white dog, Dido, and her two best friends, one of whom literally has two left feet. Several gods feel sorry for Pandy and help her in her task, which begins with tracking down Jealousy, which has settled in Delphi.

In a review of *Pandora Gets Jealous,* a contributor to *Kirkus Reviews* noted that Hennesy's fiction debut "starts out light but takes on more serious notes as Pandy sees the widespread catastrophe she's caused." Gillian Engberg, in a review of the novel for *Booklist,* declared that "this imaginative novel will capture fans of light, action-filled, girl-powered adventures." "Harry Potter meets Edith Hamilton in this cheeky rendition of Pandora's famous faux pas," quipped a *Publishers Weekly* critic. "Accurate where it counts," the critic added, "this loosely interpreted myth rarely misses a comic twist."

Pandy continues her search for the evils released onto the world in *Pandora Gets Vain.* Here she, Dido, and her two friends are joined by Homer, a poet who has recently dropped out of gladiator school. The new team sets out after the evil Vanity, which has been spotted in

Alexandria, dealing with setbacks ranging from raging seas to ancient tombs while also encountering magical dolphins and a mystical caravan along the way. In *School Library Journal* Jeff Meyer recommended *Pandora Gets Vain* for reluctant readers because Hennesy's "characters use contemporary teenage idioms," and the author also includes a glossary that will explain any classical references they encounter. Meyer also remarked on the author's ability to keep the action of the novel moving forward, writing that Hennesy's "tongue-in-cheek tone casts a whimsical light upon the overall events."

Hennesy's "Pandora" series continues in *Pandora Gets Lazy* and *Pandora Gets Heart,* as the curious teen continues her quest to recapture the remaining evils she unintentionally released upon the world. In *Pandora Gets Lazy* she is aided by Dionysus but nonetheless runs into difficulties while tracking down Laziness. *Pandora Gets Heart* finds her traveling 1,300 years back in time. Joined by her friends, Pandy heads to Mount Pelion in hopes of tracking down Lust, which is an uninvited guest at the wedding of Thetis, a sea goddess, and King Peleus. Reviewing *Pandora Gets Lazy* for *School Li-*

Carolyn Hennesy introduces teens to the world of myth in **Pandora Gets Lazy,** *a series novel featuring artwork by Wendy Chen.* (Jacket Illustration by Wendy Chen (Jade). Jacket design by Donna Mark. Bloomsbury 2009. Reprinted by permission of Bloomsbury Publishing Inc. All rights reserved.)

brary Journal, Brandy Danner noted that the story draws on many of the characters and events in the first three novels in the series and "Pandora's fans of the series should enjoy it." "Hennesy brings a light, convivial tone to the dialogue and plot" in *Pandora Gets Heart,* according to *School Library Journal* critic Adrienne L. Strock, the critic citing the entire "Pandora" series for its "modern spin."

Biographical and Critical Sources

PERIODICALS

Atlanta Journal-Constitution, April 22, 2009, Richard L. Eldredge, "Actress Turns Scribe between Scenes," p. B2.
Booklist, November 15, 2007, Gillian Engberg, review of *Pandora Gets Jealous,* p. 61.
Bulletin of the Center for Children's Books, March 1, 2008, April Spisak, review of *Pandora Gets Jealous,* p. 294.
Kirkus Reviews, December 1, 2007, review of *Pandora Gets Jealous;* August 1, 2008, review of *Pandora Gets Vain.*
School Library Journal, March 1, 2008, Miriam Lang Budin, review of *Pandora Gets Jealous,* p. 202; January, 2009, Jeff Meyer. review of *Pandora Gets Vain,* p. 104; November, 2009, Brandy Danner, review of *Pandora Gets Lazy,* p. 110; July, 2010, Adrienne L. Strock, review of *Pandora Gets Heart,* p. 90.

ONLINE

Carolyn Hennesy Home Page, http://www.carolynhennesy.com (October 15, 2010).
KidsReads.com, http:// kidsreads.com/ (August 11, 2008), Donna Volkenannt, review of *Pandora Gets Jealous.*
USA Weekend Web log, http://blogs.usaweekend.com/ (August 4, 2008), review of *Pandora Gets Vain.*

*   *   *

HIMMELMAN, John 1959-

Personal

Born October 3, 1959, in Kittery, ME; son of John A. (a manager at the New York Stock Exchange) and Pauline (a receptionist) Himmelman; married Elizabeth Shanahan (an art teacher), September 6, 1982; children: Jeffrey Carl, Elizabeth Ann. *Education:* School of Visual Arts, B.F.A., 1981. *Politics:* "Independent." *Religion:* Christian. *Hobbies and other interests:* Nature photography, martial arts, guitar, travel.

Addresses

Home and office—17 Hunters Ridge Rd., Killingworth, CT 06419. *E-mail*—jhimmel@comcast.net.

John Himmelman (Reproduced by permission.)

Career

Writer and illustrator, 1981—. Teacher of children's book writing and illustration; naturalist and lecturer on nature topics. Muralist for Boston Science Museum, 2001.

Member

Society of Children's Book Writers and Illustrators, Lepidopterists Society, Connecticut Butterfly Association (co-founder), Connecticut Botanical Society, Connecticut Entomological Society, Connecticut Ornithological Society, New Haven Bird Club (past president), Killingworth Land Trust (past president).

Awards, Honors

A Book Can Develop Empathy Award, New York State Humane Association, 1991, for *Ibis, a True Whale Story;* Outstanding Children's Science Trade Book selection, Children's Book Council (CBC), 2000, for *A Pill Bug's Life;* Connecticut Book Award finalist in Best Children's Book Author category, 2003, for *Pipaluk and the Whales;* Connecticut Book Award finalist in nonfiction category, 2003, for *Discovering Moths;* American Bookseller's Association (ABA) "Book Sense" choice, 2006, and Prairie Bud Award, 2009, both for *Chickens to the Rescue;* ABA "Book Sense" choice, 2006, for *Tudley Didn't Know;* CBC and CYBILS Book Award finalist, 2009, for *Katie Loves the Kittens.*

Writings

SELF-ILLUSTRATED

Talester the Lizard, Dial (New York, NY), 1982.

Amanda and the Witch Switch, Viking (New York, NY), 1985.

Amanda and the Magic Garden, Viking (New York, NY), 1986.

The Talking Tree; or, Don't Believe Everything You Hear, Viking (New York, NY), 1986.

Montigue on the High Seas, Viking (New York, NY), 1988.

The Ups and Downs of Simpson Snail, Dutton (New York, NY), 1989.

The Day-off Machine, Silver Burdett (Old Tappan, NJ), 1990.

Ellen and the Goldfish, Harper (New York, NY), 1990.

The Great Leaf Blast-Off, Silver Burdett (Old Tappan, NY), 1990.

Ibis, a True Whale Story, Scholastic (New York, NY), 1990.

The Clover County Carrot Contest, Silver Burdett (Old Tappan, NY), 1991.

A Guest Is a Guest, Dutton (New York, NY), 1991.

The Super Camper Caper, Silver Burdett (Old Tappan, NY), 1991.

Simpson Snail Sings, Dutton (New York, NY), 1992.

Wanted: Perfect Parents, Troll (Mahwah, NJ), 1993.

I'm Not Scared! A Book of Scary Poems, Scholastic (New York, NY), 1994.

Lights Out!, Troll (Mahwah, NJ), 1995.

J.J. versus the Babysitter, Troll (Mahwah, NJ), 1996.

Honest Tulio, Troll (Mahwah, NJ), 1997.

The Animal Rescue Club, HarperCollins (New York, NY), 1998.

Pipaluk and the Whales, National Geographic Society (Washington, DC), 2002.

Discovering Moths: Nighttime Jewels in Your Own Backyard, Down East Books (Camden, ME), 2002.

Frog in a Bog, Charlesbridge (Watertown, MA), 2004.

Mouse in a Meadow, Charlesbridge (Watertown, MA), 2005.

Chickens to the Rescue, Henry Holt (New York, NY), 2006.

Discovering Amphibians: Frogs and Salamanders of the Northeast, Down East Books (Camden, ME), 2006.

Tudley Didn't Know, Sylvan Dell Pub. (Mount Pleasant, SC), 2006.

Katie Loves the Kittens, Henry Holt (New York, NY), 2008.

Who's at the Seashore?: A Roundabout Nature Book, NorthWord Books for Young Readers (Minnetonka, MN), 2008.

Guide to Night-singing Insects of the Northeast (with CD narrated by Kate Davis), additional illustrations by Michael Di Giorgio, Stackpole Books (Mechanicsburg, PA), 2009.

Who's at the Seashore?, NorthWord Books (Lanham, MD), 2009.

Ten Little Hot Dogs, Marshall Cavendish (New York, NY), 2010.

Pigs to the Rescue, Henry Holt (New York, NY), 2010.

Cows to the Rescue, Henry Holt (New York, NY), 2011.

Cricket Radio: Tuning in the Night-singing Insects, Harvard University Press (Cambridge, MA), 2011.

"NATURE UPCLOSE" SERIES; SELF-ILLUSTRATED

A Slug's Life, Children's Press (New York, NY), 1998.

A Salamander's Life, Children's Press (New York, NY), 1998.

A Luna Moth's Life, Children's Press (New York, NY), 1998.

A Ladybug's Life, Children's Press (New York, NY), 1998.

A Dandelion's Life, Children's Press (New York, NY), 1998.

A Wood Frog's Life, Children's Press (New York, NY), 1998.

A Pill Bug's Life, Children's Press (New York, NY), 1999.

A Monarch Butterfly's Life, Children's Press (New York, NY), 1999.

A House Spider's Life, Children's Press (New York, NY), 1999.

A Mouse's Life, Children's Press (New York, NY), 2000.

A Hummingbird's Life, Children's Press (New York, NY), 2000.

An Earthworm's Life, Children's Press (New York, NY), 2000.

A Mealworm's Life, Children's Press (New York, NY), 2001.

ILLUSTRATOR

Barbara Ware Holmes, *Charlotte Cheetham, Master of Disaster,* Harper (New York, NY), 1985.

Marjorie Sharmat, *Go to Sleep, Nicholas Joe,* Harper (New York, NY), 1986.

Michele Stepto, *Snuggle Piggy and the Magic Blanket,* Dutton (New York, NY), 1986.

Barbara Ware Holmes, *Charlotte the Starlet,* HarperCollins (New York, NY), 1988.

Barbara Ware Holmes, *Charlotte Shakespeare and Annie the Great,* HarperCollins (New York, NY), 1989.

Marcia Leonard, *Rainboots for Breakfast,* Silver Burdett (Old Tappan, NY), 1989.

Marcia Leonard, *Shopping for Snowflakes,* Silver Burdett (Old Tappan, NY), 1989.

Julia Hoban, *Buzby,* HarperCollins (New York, NY), 1990.

Marcia Leonard, *What Next?,* Silver Burdett (Old Tappan, NY), 1990.

Eric Carpenter, *Young Christopher Columbus: Discoverer of New Worlds,* Troll (Mahwah, NJ), 1992.

Andrew Woods, *Young George Washington: America's First President,* Troll (Mahwah, NJ), 1992.

Leslie Kimmelman, *Hanukkah Lights, Hanukkah Nights,* HarperCollins (New York, NY), 1992.

Julia Hoban, *Buzby to the Rescue,* HarperCollins (New York, NY), 1993.

Wendy Lewison, *Let's Count,* Joshua Morris, 1995.

Carolyn Graham, *The Story of Myrtle Marie,* Harcourt (New York, NY), 1995.

Graham, *The Story of the Fisherman and the Turtle Princess,* Harcourt (New York, NY), 1995.

Claire Nemes, *Young Thomas Edison: Great Inventor,* Troll (Mahwah, NJ), 1995.

Leslie Kimmelman, *Hooray, It's Passover!,* HarperCollins (New York, NY), 1996.

Leslie Kimmelman, *Uncle Jake Blows the Shofar,* HarperCollins (New York, NY), 1998.

Leslie Kimmelman, *Sound the Shofar!: A Story for Rosh Hashanah and Yom Kippur,* HarperCollins (New York, NY), 1998.

Robert Kraus, *Mort the Sport,* Orchard Books (New York, NY), 2000.

Melissa Stewart, *A Daddy Longlegs Isn't a Spider,* Windward Publishing (Lakeville, MN), 2009.

Also author of *Ben's Birthday Wish* and *Sarah and the Terns,* published by Harcourt; illustrator of *Animal Countdown* and *The Christmas Star,* published by Joshua Morris, and *The Myrtle Marie Chant Book,* published by Harcourt; illustrator of *Ugrashimataro* (animated video), ALC Press. Contributor of articles to *Birdwatcher's Digest* and illustrations to *Wildlife Conservation* magazine.

Adaptations

Katie Loves the Kittens was adapted as a cartoon film by Weston Woods Studios.

Sidelights

Over the course of his career, John Himmelman has written or illustrated numerous books that reflect his love of nature, particularly the interesting plants and creatures to be found in the northeastern United States. In addition to his "Nature Upclose" series, which includes *A Wood Frog's Life, A House Spider's Life,* and

Himmelman takes readers to a topsy-turvy farmyard in **Pigs to the Rescue!,** *featuring illustrations by the author.* (Reproduced by permission of Henry Holt and Company, LLC.)

A Dandelion's Life, he has penned picture-book stories such as *Pipaluk and the Whales, Chickens to the Rescue, Tudley to the Rescue,* and *Katie Loves the Kittens,* the last a story about a rambunctious pup that is excited when several tiny new playmates join her family. *Tudley Didn't Know,* a story about a young painted turtle that trades advice with a host of other wetland creatures, features a creatures that is "full of exuberance and joy at helping his friends," according to *School Library Journal* contributor Susan E. Murray, while in *Booklist* Carolyn Phelan wrote that Himmelman's ink-and-watercolor illustrations "suit the tale's mood and the hero's ingenuous spirit."

Born in Kittery, Maine, Himmelman moved south to Long Island, New York, with his family at age two. "Growing up, my main interests revolved around watching and collecting insects," he once told *SATA,* recalling the bug club he started with friends when he was about ten years old. "In fact, the first book I ever wrote (in third grade) was about this subject. I wanted to be an entomologist and I was eager to learn as much as I could about the little crawly things that surround us. . . . Writing and art were also a very big part of my life. I wrote stories just for the fun of it, and painting and drawing took up a good amount of my spare time."

Because he loved both animals and art, Himmelman had a difficult time deciding which field to study: art or veterinary medicine. "One night, after weeks of deliberation, I went for a walk. I told my parents that I wasn't coming back until I had made a decision. I walked for hours, mulling over my choices. I decided that being a veterinarian would leave me little time for being an artist; however, if I pursued art, there would be other avenues open to me in which I could work with animals, such as wildlife rehabilitation."

Enrolling at the School of Visual Arts in 1977, Himmelman again faced a difficult career decision. He took courses in cartooning, advertising, and creative writing, but recalled that "the prospect of making a living in these fields was frightening! By the last half of my fourth and last year of college, I still had no idea of how I was going to make a living as an artist." On a whim, he took a course in writing and illustrating children's books taught by Dale Payson. Assigned to write and illustrate his own book, Himmelman created a story featuring a lizard named Talester, given to him by his future wife, Betsy; it would eventually become his first published book.

Talester the Lizard tells the story of a pop-eyed green lizard who lives inside a curled-up leaf that hangs over a pond. Every day, he peeks out of his house to see his reflection in the water below, and believes he is looking at another lizard. Although his friend never speaks, Talester finds him a sympathetic listener and enjoys his company. But one day, the pond dries up and his friend disappears. Talester then sets out on a comic adventure

in search of his missing friend, but is unable to find him. He returns home in a rainstorm, and the next morning he is amazed to find that his friend has reappeared. "Pastel pictures, spare in composition, make it clear that Talester sees his reflection," stated Zena Sutherland in the *Bulletin of the Center for Children's Books,* "and children can enjoy the superiority of knowing that." A reviewer for *Publishers Weekly* wrote that *Talester the Lizard* is "sure to please tots and beginning readers."

After earning his bachelor of fine arts degree in 1981, Himmelman used the proceeds from his first book to buy a car and travel across the country. In 1982, he moved to East Haven, Connecticut, married Betsy, and worked a series of odd jobs while building his career as a picture-book author. "It took about six years before I could make a full-time living in children's books," he explained to *SATA.* Meanwhile, he and his wife built a house in a rural area that, as the author recalled, "was surrounded by acres of woods, and I got to pursue my love of nature. In time, birds and insects became my main focus of interest, and they still are." In addition to creating a survey of the number and types of birds that visited bird feeders throughout southern Connecticut, he also helped found the Connecticut Butterfly Association and spent time rehabilitating orphaned and injured wildlife with the Nature Connection. In 1993, Himmelman created an event called the BIG SIT! Taking place in mid-October, the goal of participants is to see how many birds they can list in a twenty-four-hour period (by sight and sound) within a seventeen-foot circle. The BIG SIT! is now an international annual event, with countries from all over the world participating.

Himmelman's "Amanda" books, which include *Amanda and the Witch Switch* and *Amanda and the Magic Garden,* center around a well-meaning witch who encoun-

Himmelman's self-illustrated stories include the humorous and high-energy **Wanted: Perfect Parents.** (Troll Medallion, 1993. Copyright © 1993 John Himmelman. Reproduced by permission.)

ters trouble despite her best efforts. In the first book Amanda walks through the woods using her magic for good things, like making the flowers bloom and teaching the trees to sing. Then she meets a toad and grants his wish to become a witch. However, the toad uses his powers badly, turning Amanda into a toad, transforming rocks into marshmallows, and making a bee become the size of a bear. Finally, after the giant bee attacks the toad-witch, the misguided amphibian begs Amanda to restore him to his old self. In the second book, Amanda plants magic seeds that grow giant vegetables, only to find that any animals eating the vegetables become huge as well. She finally finds another spell that undoes the damage: she grows tiny vegetables that restore the animals to their original size. A reviewer for *Publishers Weekly* called *Amanda and the Witch Switch* "entrancing, graced by witty, almost speaking pictures in brilliant hues." Although Barbara Peklo, reviewing *Amanda and the Magic Garden* for *School Library Journal,* found the story "strained," Denise M. Wilms wrote in *Booklist* that "the changing proportions add a comical element that will appeal to children."

Other picture-book stories by Himmelman include *Wanted: Perfect Parents* and *Mort the Sport*. In the first book Himmelman tells the story of a young boy named Gregory who decides to change households by posting a "help wanted" sign on his bedroom door. When his parents ask him about it, Gregory provides them with a detailed description of the qualities he feels ideal parents should possess: they would never make their children clean their rooms; would allow them to make snowballs out of ice cream, paint all over the walls of the house, and acquire as many pets as they want. Despite such outrageous requirements, Gregory announces the most important quality when he finds that both his mom and dad fit the bill: perfect parents tuck their children into bed, wish them sweet dreams, and check under the bed for monsters. *Mort the Sport* finds a young, sports-loving elephant trying share his free time between the violin lessons his parents want him to take and the baseball games he loves to play. Reviewing *Wanted: Perfect Parents* for *Booklist,* Deborah Abbott stated that "the read-aloud crowd will love the fantasies of this 'perfect' world, made thoroughly enticing by Himmelman's whimsical color drawings." Calling the title character of *Mort the Sport* "an endearingly confused elephant," *School Library Journal* reviewer Judith Constantinides praised the author/illustrator's "brightly colored cartoon illustrations" and noted that the book has "great storytime potential."

In *Frog in a Bog* Himmelman focuses on the web of life in a wetland environment, while his illustrations and simple text for *Mouse in a Meadow* open a window onto the quiet ecosystem in a New England meadow, where readers witness the interaction among spiders, moths, snakes, reptiles, and mammals. Praising *Mouse in a Meadow* for *Kirkus Reviews,* a reviewer noted that the book serves as "an engaging invitation to young naturalist to go outside . . . and look around." In *Pub-*

A love of nature is evident in each of Himmelman's self-illustrated books, including **A Monarch Butterfly's Life.** (Children's Press, 1999. © 1999 by Children's Press, Inc. Reproduced by permission of the author.)

lishers Weekly a critic made special note of Himmelman's "crisp, meticulously detailed watercolors and concise" storyline, adding that the author "skillfully and sympathetically portrays the meadow's circle of life."

Chickens to the Rescue was inspired by a newspaper article Himmelman read and transports readers to Greenstalk Farm, where daily mishaps abound. It is bad enough when the farmer loses his watch, the sheep wander off, and a barnyard duck drives off in the farmer's pickup truck. When cows end up stuck in trees, however, the farm's hens decide that enough is enough, and with the help of eight pigs they clear up, clean up, and otherwise straighten things out so that Sunday can be restful. *Pigs to the Rescue* find the pigs pitching in, giving the poor hens their day of rest by cooking, watering, and tilling, all at the very last minute. Calling Himmelman's story "hilarious," Catherine Callegari had special praise for *Chickens to the Rescue,* noting in *School Library Journal* that "the sheer brilliance of the colored-pencil and watercolor illustrations . . . shine[s] through." "OK, it's a one-joke book," admitted Ilene Cooper in *Booklist,* "but . . . the joke gets funnier each time you turn the page." In *Pigs to the Rescue* "the swine saviors swing into action and seem oblivious to the disasters they leave in their porky wake," according to a *Kirkus Reviews* writer, the critic adding that the book's generous "dose of slapstick" is guaranteed to leave young children nursing the giggles.

In each volume of his "Nature Upclose" series Himmelman focuses reader attention on a single animal or plant, then follows his subject throughout its entire lifetime in a series of detailed paintings he creates to accompany his text. Often, connection with humans threatens the creature, as when a tiny spider is almost sucked into a vacuum cleaner in *A House Spider's Life* or when a dandelion budding in a lawn barely survives a pass of the lawn mower. Noting the variety of subjects covered in "Nature Upclose," *Booklist* contributor Carolyn

Phelan added that series titles serve as "good read-aloud science books for the primary grades," while Anne Chapman wrote in her review of *A Pill Bug's Life* for *School Library Journal* that Himmelman's "large, appealing illustration[s] draw . . . youngsters into the action." Praising the author for creating "vividly illustrated picture stories," *School Library Journal* reviewer Karey Wehner added that the series features a "clearly written and logically organized text, . . . attractive format and cleverly composed illustrations."

Other nature books include *Discovering Moths: Nighttime Jewels in Your Own Backyard, What Can You See at the Seashore?: A Roundabout Nature Book, Guide to Night-singing Insects of the Northeast, Cricket Radio: Tuning in the Sounds of the Nightsinging Insects,* and *Discovering Amphibians: Frogs and Salamanders of the Northeast. Discovering Amphibians* is a field-study book based on Himmelman's research throughout northern New England while *Who's at the Seashore?* takes readers to the region's coastal areas to introduce sandpipers, gulls, and shorebirds as well as snails, sand dollars, and other tide-pool dwellers. The "realistic" large-scale watercolor images [in the latter book] capture the interrelation among shoreline creatures, according to *School Library Journal* critic Patricia Manning, and the author/illustrator's "simple rhyming text" contributes to what Manning dubbed "a pleasing introduction to the . . . ecology of a sandy shore."

Himmelman and his wife now live in rural Killingworth, Connecticut, where Betsy Himmelman provides valuable help with his work. "Not a drawing, painting, or manuscript goes off to an editor or art director without input from . . . Betsy. Being married to an art teacher has helped to ease that uncomfortable feeling of wondering how a piece of art will look to someone else," the author/illustrator explained. Himmelman's son, Jeffrey, is an illustrator who creates fantasy art, while daughter Elizabeth is pursuing an acting career.

In **A Ladybug's Life** *Himmelman's stylized vignettes give young book-bugs much to ponder.* (Children's Press, 1998. © 1998 by Children's Press, Inc. Reproduced by permission.)

While teaching writing to both children and adults as well as "playing" outside as a naturalist occupy much of his non-writing time, Himmelman also enjoys watching and photographing wildlife. "So many natural events," Himmelman concluded, "so many stories to be inspired by them." He is also a martial artist, training in combat Hapkido and Jeet Kune Do.

Biographical and Critical Sources

PERIODICALS

Booklist, March 1, 1987, Denise M. Wilms, review of *Amanda and the Magic Garden,* p. 1013; October 15, 1993, Deborah Abbott, review of *Wanted: Perfect Parents;* February 15, 2004, Ilene Cooper, review of *Frog in a Bog,* p. 1063; March 1, 2005, Karen Hutt, review of *Mouse in a Meadow,* p. 1199; May 15, 2006, Carolyn Phelan, review of *Tudley Didn't Know,* p. 50; November 1, 2006, Ilene Cooper, review of *Chickens to the Rescue,* p. 60; February 1, 2010, Carolyn Phelan, review of *Pigs to the Rescue,* p. 52.

Bulletin of the Center for Children's Books, June, 1982, Zena Sutherland, review of *Talester the Lizard,* p. 188; December 1, 1998, Carolyn Phelan, review of *A Wood Frog's Life,* p. 682; December 1, 1998, Carolyn Phelan, review of *A Dandelion's Life,* p. 682; February 15, 2000, Ellen Mandel, review of *Mort the Sport,* p. 1118.

Christian Science Monitor, August 22, 2006, Joan Russell, "A Writer and Artist by Nature," p. 18.

Kirkus Reviews, January 1, 2004, review of *Frog in a Bog,* p. 37; January 1, 2005, review of *Mouse in a Meadow,* p. 52; September 15, 2006, review of *Chickens to the Rescue,* p. 954; August 15, 2008, review of *Katie Loves the Kittens;* March 1, 2010, review of *Pigs to the Rescue.*

Publishers Weekly, February 5, 1982, review of *Talester the Lizard,* p. 387; June 28, 1985, review of *Amanda and the Witch Switch,* p. 75; February 14, 2005, review of *Mouse in a Meadow,* p. 75; September 22, 2008, review of *Katie Loves the Kittens,* p. 58.

School Library Journal, August, 1987, Barbara Peklo, review of *Amanda and the Magic Garden,* p. 69; March, 2000, Anne Chapman Callaghan, review of *A Pill Bug's Life,* p. 226; March, 2000, Karey Wehner, review of *A Monarch Butterfly's Life,* p. 226; March, 2000, Karey Wehner, review of *A House Spider's Life,* p. 226; April, 2000, Judith Constantinides, review of *Mort the Sport,* p. 107; September, 2002, Sue Sherif, review of *Pipaluk and the Whales,* p. 194; March, 2004, Corrina Austin, review of *Frog in a Bog,* p. 195; May, 2005, Bethany L.W. Hankinson, review of *Mouse in a Meadow,* p. 109; August, 2006, Susan E. Murray, review of *Tudley Didn't Know,* p. 88; October, 2006, Catherine Callegari, review of *Chickens to the Rescue,* p. 112; September, 2008, Jane Marino, review of *Katie Loves the Kittens,* p. 148; December, 2009, Patricia Manning, review of *Who's at the Seashore?,* p. 98; April, 2010, Carolyn Janssen, review of *Pigs to the Rescue,* p. 128.

ONLINE

John Himmelman Home Page, http://www.johnhimmel man.com (October 20, 2010).

John Himmelman Web log, http://allthingsreconsidered again.wordpress.com (October 20, 2010).

* * *

HOESTLANDT, Jo 1948-
(Jocelyne Hoestlandt)

Personal

Born May 13, 1948, in Le Pecq, Yvelines, France; daughter of Daniel (a mushroom producer) and Evelyne (a mushroom producer) Ravary; married Dominique Hoestlandt (an executive vice president), 1970; children: Maud, Bertrand, Olivier. *Education:* Sorbonne, University of Paris, B.A. *Religion:* Roman Catholic.

Addresses

Home—Rueil Malmaison, France.

Career

Educator, author, and illustrator. Teacher in Paris, France, 1969-72; freelance author of children's books. Organizer of reading and writing animations for children in art centers and schools.

Awards, Honors

Sydney Taylor Book Award, Association of Jewish Libraries, Bologna Book Fair Graphics prize, 1994, and Das Rote Tuch award, 1996, all for *Star of Fear, Star of Hope* illustrated by Johanna Kang.

Writings

FOR CHILDREN

Le petit Pousse, Ecole des Loisirs (Paris, France), 1980.

Le moulin a paroles: Abecedaire, illustrated by Frederic Stehr, Ecole des Loisirs (Paris, France), 1980.

La rentrée de mamans, illustrated by Claude and Denise Millet, Bayard Presse (Paris, France), 1990, translated as *Back to School with Mom,* Child's World (Mankato, MN), 1992.

La grande peur sous les étoiles, illustrated by Johanna Kang, Syros (Paris, France), 1993, translated by Mark Polizzotti as *Star of Fear, Star of Hope,* Walker (New York, NY), 1995.

Les amoureue de Leonie, Casterman (Paris, France), 1996.

Une journée pleine de secrets, Syros (Paris, France), 1998.

Les passants de Noël, Syros (Paris, France), 1998.

Peur bleu chez les souris grises, illustrated by Serge Ceccarelli, Actes Sud (Paris, France), 1998.

Jo Hoestlandt (Photograph by Gerard Percicot. Reproduced by permission.)

Mon meilleur ami, illustrated by Christophe Merlin, Casterman (Paris, France), 1998.

Le pouvoir d'Aimé, illustrated by Philippe Mignon, Actes Sud (Paris, France), 1998.

Mémé, t'as du courier, illustrated by Claire Franek, Nathan (Paris, France), 1999, translated by Y. Maudet as *Gran, You've Got Mail!,* illustrated by Aurélie Abolivier, Delacorte Press (New York, NY), 2008.

La Boîte à Bisous, illustrated by Clémentine Collinet, Nathan (Paris, France), 1999.

La Balançoire, illustrated by Christophe Blain, Casterman (Paris, France), 1999.

Et les petites filles dansent Charlotte, la poupée et le chat, illustrated by Frédérick Mansot, Actes Sud (Paris, France), 1999.

Coup de théâtre à l'école, illustrated by Claude and Denis Millet, Bayard Jeunesse (Paris, France), 1999.

Un bonheur de Noël, illustrated by Nathaële Vogel, Actes Sud (Paris, France), 2000.

Oh, les belles lettres, illustrated by Philippe Bertrand, Actes Sud (Paris, France), 2000.

Mon petit papa de rien du tout, illustrated by Johanna Kang, Actes Sud (Paris, France), 2000.

Mes petites étoiles, illustrated by Olivier Laty, Milan (Paris, France), 2000.

Le château fort et le château faible, illustrated by Nathalie Novi, Syros (Paris, France), 2000.

La nuit de la rentrée, illustrated by Martin Berthommier, Bayard Jeunesse (Paris, France), 2000.

Drôle d'endroit pour des vacances, illustrated by Alice Charbin, Nathan (Paris, France), 2000.

La maison de grand-père, illustrated by Henri Fellner, Bayard Jeunesse (Paris, France), 2000.

Réponds-moi quand je t'écris!, illustrated by Olivier Latyk, Casterman (Paris, France), 2001.

Miranda, reine du cirque, illustrated by Pef, Bayard Jeunesse (Paris, France), 2001.

Maîtresse est amoureuse, illustrated by Frédéric Joos, Bayard Jeunesse (Paris, France), 2001.

A pas de louve, illustrated by Marc Daniau, Milan (Paris, France), 2001.

Joyeux Noël les monstres!, illustrated by Philippe Bertrand, Actes Sud (Paris, France), 2001.

Le petit monstre, illustrated by Yves Calarnou, Bayard Jeunesse (Paris, France), 2001.

Le plus beau chien du monde, illustrated by Claude Lapointe, Pocket Jeunesse (Paris, France), 2001.

Portraits en pied des princes, princesses et autres bergères des contes de notre enfance, Album (Paris, France), 2001.

Poings de côté, illustrated by Henri Fellner, Actes Sud (Paris, France), 2002.

Quel stress pour la maîtresse!, illustrated by Eric Gasté, Actes Sud (Paris, France), 2002.

Drôlement mordu, illustrated by Rémi Saillard, Actes Sud (Paris, France), 2003.

L'arche de Zoé, iIllustré par Cyril Hahn, Actes Sud (Paris, France), 2003.

Longue-Epée et Courte-Epée, illustrated by Christophe Merlin, Bayard Jeunesse (Paris, France), 2003.

Maman ne sait pas dire non, illustrated by Jean-François Dumont, Père Castor Flammarion (Paris, France), 2003.

(With Claude Carré) *Par ici, la rentrée!,* illustrated by Béatrice Rodriguez, Actes Sud (Paris, France), 2003.

Un petit kangourou trop doudou!, illustrated by Cyril Hahn, Nathan (Paris, France), 2003.

Les amoureux de Léonie, illustrated by Sophie Toussaint, Casterman (Paris, France), 2003.

Ma petite amoureuse, illustrated by David Merveille, Milan (Paris, France), 2004.

Mimosa et les bonhommes de craie, illustrated by Peter Allen, Nathan (Paris, France), 2004.

Oh, la barbe!, illustrated by Joëlle Passeron, Nathan (Paris, France), 2004.

Parfaite et Rouspète, illustrated by Alex Langlois, Actes Sud (Paris, France), 2004.

Le songe de Constantin, illustrated by Nathalie Novi, Syros (Paris, France), 2005.

Les belles espérances, illustrated by Delphine Grenier, Le Baron Perché, 2005.

Gris-gris et Perlimpinpin, illustrated by Stéphane Sénégas, Père Castor Flammarion (Paris, France), 2005.

(With Claude Carré) *Récré: action!,* illustrated by Béatrice Rodriguez, Actes Sud (Paris, France), 2005.

Tu peux toujours courir!, illustrated by Estelle Meyrand, Nathan (Paris, France), 2005.

Faut pas pousser Mémé, illustrated by Frédéric Rébéna, Nathan (Paris, France), 2006.

L'été où j'ai grandi (film novelization), illustrated by Camille Jourdy, Actes Sud (Paris, France), 2006.

Le moulin à Paroles, illustrated by Olivier Latyk, Bayard Jeunesse (Paris, France), 2006.

Mon p'tit vieux, illustrated by Sandrine Martin, Le Baron Perché, 2006.

L'amour qu'on porte, illustrated by Carmen Segovia, Milan (Paris, France), 2007.

La lettre que j'attends, illustrated by Delphine Grenier, Le Baron Perché, 2007.

Superbricoleur le roi de la clé à molette, illustrated by Barroux, Bayard Jeunesse (Paris, France), 2007.

La cave aux oiseaux, illustrated by Bruno Gibert, Syros (Paris, France), 2008.

Un coeur gros comme ça . . . , illustrated by Frédéric Rébéna, Nathan (Paris, France), 2009.

Quatre histoires complètement givrées, illustrated by Eric Gasté, Hatier (Paris, France), 2009.

Copain!, illustrated by Henri Fellner, Hatier (Paris, France), 2009.

La colonuit de vacances, illustrated by Pronto, Nathan (Paris, France), 2009.

La danse del'éléphante, illustrated by Camille Jourdy, Actes Sud (Paris, France), 2010.

"CHOCOTTES EN PAPIER" SERIES

Simon et la commode pas commode, illustrated by Fanny Talleygas, Actes Sud (Paris, France), 1999.

Marie et les riquiquis du plancher, iIllustrated by Frédérick Mansot, Actes Sud (Paris, France), 1999.

Lucien et les fleurs du balcon, illustrated by Cécile Mordillo, Actes Sud (Paris, France), 1999.

Juliette et les animaux du zoo, illustrated by Nadine Hahn, Actes Sud (Paris, France), 1999.

NOVELS; FOR CHILDREN

Le prince sans rire, Bayard Jeunesse (Paris, France), 2002.

Ma vie, ça n'est pas de la tarte!, Nathan (Paris, France), 2002.

Les frayeurs de la Baby-sitter, Thierry Magnier (Paris, France), 2002.

Cousin contre cousine, Thierry Magnier (Paris, France), 2003.

La demoiselle d'horreru, Thierry Magnier (Paris, France), 2004.

Miriam ou les voix perdues, Syros (Paris, France), 2004.

L'auteur de mes jours, Thierry Magnier (Paris, France), 2006.

Le complexe de l'ornithorynque, Milan (Paris, France), 2007.

Un anniversaire camion, Thierry Magnier (Paris, France), 2007.

Mon p'tit vieux, Syros (Paris, France), 2010.

Sidelights

Jo Hoestlandt is a prolific author of picture books, beginning readers, and middle-grade and young-adult novels. Popular among readers in her native France, Hoestlandt has also gained English-language fans through translation. Winner of the Sydney Taylor Book Award sponsored by the Association of Jewish Libraries, her picture book *Star of Fear, Star of Hope* was described by Maria W. Posner in *School Library Journal* as an "extraordinarily moving picture book" in which the author's "spare prose and appropriately stark illustrations" by Johanna Kang capture the life of a young child living in Nazi-occupied France. "I think words hide secrets, and stories tell secrets more or less hidden by the words," Hoestlandt once told *SATA*.

Star of Fear, Star of Hope was inspired by the experiences of Hoestlandt's family during World War II, experiences that were shared in discussions during her childhood. "None of my family who lived during World War II suffered deportation, though my grandfather was a political prisoner," the author once explained. "When I was very young, however, I understood that many children died just because they were Jewish, and I felt concerned just because I was alive." In *Star of Fear, Star of Hope* the narrative of an elderly woman named Helen takes readers back to Nazi-occupied France in 1942, as she recalls the eve of her ninth birthday. Helen's best friend Lydia, who is Jewish, spends the night at Helen's apartment. During the night, Lydia asks to go home, made frightened by the sound of strangers outside Helen's home. As Lydia leaves, Helen tells her that she is no longer her friend. Helen soon feels bad about her comments, and although she tries to find Lydia the next day, she is too late: Lydia and her family have disappeared. By telling her story to the world, Helen hopes that she and Lydia will meet again one day.

"Fluidly written and centered in events a child can comprehend, [*Star of Fear, Star of Hope*] . . . is an ideal starting point for serious discussions about the Holocaust," noted a reviewer in *Publishers Weekly,* and *Horn Book* commentator Mary M. Burns wrote that Hoestlandt's "poignant account of childhood innocence destroyed" "translates history into a form accessible to young audiences." Kang's artwork drew special praise from *Booklist* contributor Hazel Rochman, who noted that the book's "pastel pictures in sepia tones are understated, with an old-fashioned, almost childlike simplicity."

Gran, You've Got Mail! is a translation of Hoestlandt's 1999 picture book *Mémé, t'as du courier.* Brought to life in illustrations by Aurélie Abolivier, the picture book tells its story in a series of letters between twelve-year-old Annabelle and her great-grandmother, a woman who is attempting to learn how to type on the computer. While Annabelle begins the correspondence as an effort to help Gran tackle modern technology, the book captures the growing relationship between the girl and the elderly woman as they deal with each others' quirks and offer support in times of stress. Noting the "budding camaraderie" that blooms in the pages of *Gran, You've Got Mail!,* Bina Williams added in *Booklist* that Hoestlandt's "charming" story "may inspire some letter writing by readers to elderly relatives." A *Kirkus Reviews* writer praised the translation as "modern" and Hoestlandt's tale as a "believable exploration" of a multigenerational friendship.

"When I was a child, I decided I was a dancer-writer, because I liked to dance and to write," Hoestlandt once recalled to *SATA.* "Later, I understood I have found exactly the same thing in writing and in dancing. I stood on tiptoe, or I was poised at the end of the pen, just as on a leg, light and grave, high and low together, touching earth and sky at the same moment.

"I always try to write unaffectedly, sincerely, with words so simple that they can touch hearts and minds just like sunlight or darkness or dancing snow. People say that all of my books tell love or friend stories. Maybe all that we need to learn during life is actually included in our love and friend stories."

Biographical and Critical Sources

PERIODICALS

Booklist, May 1, 1995, Hazel Rochman, review of *Star of Fear, Star of Hope,* p. 1573; January, 2007, Heidi Estrin, review of *Star of Fear, Star of Hope,* p. 56; November 15, 2008, Bina Williams, review of *Gran, You've Got Mail!,* p. 43.
Bulletin of the Center for Children's Books, June, 1995, review of *Star of Fear, Star of Hope,* p. 347.
Christian Science Monitor, September 28, 1995, Karen Williams, review of *Star of Fear, Star of Hope,* p. B1.
Horn Book, September-October, 1995, Mary M. Burns, review of *Star of Fear, Star of Hope,* pp. 588-589.
Kirkus Reviews, August 1, 2008, review of *Gran, You've Got Mail!*
Publishers Weekly, June 5, 1995, review of *Star of Fear, Star of Hope,* pp. 63-64; October 2, 2000, review of *Star of Fear, Star of Hope,* p. 83.
School Library Journal, August, 1995, Marcia W. Posner, review of *Star of Fear, Star of Hope,* p. 124; September, 2008, Sarah O'Holla, review of *Gran, You've Got Mail!,* p. 184.
Tribune Books (Chicago, IL), September 10, 1995, review of *Star of Fear, Star of Hope,* p. 6.

ONLINE

Thierry Magnier Web site, http://www.editions-thierry-magnier.com/ (October 21, 2010), "Jo Hoestlandt."*

*   *   *

HOESTLANDT, Jocelyne
See HOESTLANDT, Jo

*   *   *

HOLLAND, Trish

Personal

Born in MS; married; children: two. *Education:* B.A. (music therapy); M.S. (public health).

Addresses

Home—Dallas, TX. *E-mail*—trish@trisholland.com.

Career

Freelance writer and author of books for children. Formerly worked in psychiatric hospitals. Presenter at schools.

Member

Society of Children's Book Writers and Illustrators.

Awards, Honors

Parent's Choice award, 2009, for *Ocean's Child.*

Writings

FOR CHILDREN

Lasso the Moon, illustrated by Valeria Petrone, Golden Books (New York, NY), 2005.

(With Christine Ford) *The Soldiers' Night before Christmas,* illustrated by John Manders, Random House (New York, NY), 2006.

Come Back, Zack!, illustrated by Sachiko Yoshikawa, Random House (New York, NY), 2008.

(With Christine Ford) *Ocean's Child,* illustrated by David Diaz, Random House (New York, NY), 2009.

A World of Families, Teaching Strategies (Washington, DC), 2010.

Build It from A to Z, Teaching Strategies (Washington, DC), 2010.

Button, Button, Who's Got the Button?, Teaching Strategies (Washington, DC), 2010.

Neighborhood Song, Teaching Strategies (Washington, DC), 2010.

Trees: Count, Teaching Strategies (Washington, DC), 2010.

Wash and Dry, illustrated by Vinay Kumar, Teaching Strategies (Washington, DC), 2010.

Who Lives in Trees?, Teaching Strategies (Washington, DC), 2010.

Contributor of short fiction to *In Short: How to Teach the Young-Adult Short Story,* by Suzanne I. Barchers, Heinemann, 2005.

Sidelights

Trish Holland grew up in Mississippi and worked in hospitals for many years before beginning her second career as a children's author. Although several of her books have been written for educational publishers, Holland has also worked in collaboration with fellow author Christine Ford to produce the well-received picture books *The Soldiers' Night before Christmas* and *Ocean's Child.* Other books by Holland include *Lasso the Moon,* illustrated by Valeria Petrone, and *Come Back, Zack!,* a story about toddler transportation that is fueled by Sachiko Yoshikawa's colorful digital art. Her educational picture books, which include *A World of Families, Neighborhood Song,* and *Who Lives in Trees?,* are published by Washington, DC-based Teaching Strategies.

A holiday story based on Clement C. Moore's classic poem "The Night before Christmas," *The Soldiers' Night before Christmas,* illustrated by John Manders, takes readers to the Middle East, where homesick soldiers are spending Christmas eve at their barracks. In Holland and Ford's story, this lonely holiday is made more bearable when Sergeant McClaus shows up in a Humvee and distributes gifts to each and every soldier. A *Kirkus Reviews* writer dubbed *The Solders' Night before Christmas* a "witty parody" of the holiday classic, while *School Library Journal* Virginia Walter praised the book as "a lighthearted, even humorous retelling" that will be of special interest to children with parents in the U.S. military. Manders contributes "jazzy illustrations in a cartoon style" that "bring the military characters to life," the *Kirkus Reviews* writer added.

Holland and Ford again team up in *Ocean's Child,* a picture book illustrated by noted artist David Diaz. In this gentle story, an Inuit mother canoes along the Alaskan coast at dusk. Together with her young child, the woman locates sea lions, otters, puffins, polar bears, and other North country creatures, all of which cuddle, hug, and otherwise lovingly care for their young. In *School Library Journal* Susan Scheps noted the the the co-authors end their "brief, descriptive sentences" with a rhythmic refrain. Diaz's "finely crafted, solftly colored graphic style" adds to the gentle tone of *Ocean's Child,* according to Scheps, while *Booklist* critic Linda Perkins

Trish Holland teams up with fellow writer Christine Ford to produce Ocean's Child, *a picture book featuring artwork by David Diaz.* (Golden Books 2009. Used by permission of Golden Books, an imprint of Random House Children's Books, a division of Random House, Inc.)

cited the book's "beautifully stylized animals" and "elegant images." A "simple but melodic bedtime tale," *Ocean's Child* benefits from its "intriguing setting," asserted a *Publishers Weekly* critic, the reviewer adding that "every page" of Holland and Ford's picture book "exudes . . . magic."

Biographical and Critical Sources

PERIODICALS

Booklist, April 1, 2009, Linda Perkins, review of *Ocean's Child,* p. 44.

Kirkus Reviews, November 1, 2006, review of *The Soldiers' Night before Christmas,* p. 1130.

Publishers Weekly, May 4, 2009, review of *Ocean's Child,* p. 47.

School Library Journal, October, 2006, Virginia Walter, review of *The Soldiers' Night before Christmas,* p. 97; July, 2009, Susan Scheps, review of *Ocean's Child,* p. 62.

ONLINE

Trish Holland Home Page, http://www.trisholland.com (October 15, 2010).*

* * *

HOLT, K.A.
See ROY, Kari Anne

I-J

IBBOTSON, Eva 1925-2010

Personal

Born Maria Charlotte Michelle Wiesner, January 21, 1925, in Vienna, Austria; died of a heart attack October 20, 2010, in Newcastle upon Tyne, England; immigrated to Scotland, 1933; daughter of Berthold P. (a physiologist) and Anna (a playwright) Wiesner; married Alan Ibbotson (a university lecturer), June 21, 1948 (deceased, 1998); children: Lalage Ann, Tobias John, Piers David, Justin Paul. *Education:* Bedford College London, B.Sc., 1945; attended Cambridge University, 1946-47; University of Durham, diploma (education), 1965. *Hobbies and other interests:* Ecology and environmental preservation, music, continental literature, history ("My favorite period is 1904!").

Career

Full-time writer. Worked as a research worker. Former university instructor and schoolteacher.

Awards, Honors

Carnegie Medal shortlist, British Library Association, 1979, for *Which Witch?,* and 2001, for *Journey to the River Sea;* Best Romantic Novel of the Year Published in England selection, Romantic Novelists Association, 1983, for *Magic Flutes;* Nestlé Smarties Prize shortlist, 1998, for *The Secret of Platform 13;* London *Guardian* Children's Fiction Award runner-up, Whitbread Children's Book of the Year Award shortlist, and Smarties Children's Gold Award, all 2001, all for *Journey to the River Sea.*

Writings

FOR CHILDREN

The Great Ghost Rescue, illustrated by Simon Stern, Macmillan (London, England), 1975, illustrated by Giulio

Eva Ibbotson (Photograph by Simon Veit-Wilson. Reproduced by permission.)

Maestro, Walck (London, England), 1975, illustrated by Kevin Hawkes, Dutton (New York, NY), 2002.

Which Witch?, illustrated by Annabel Large, Macmillan (London, England), 1979, Scholastic (New York, NY), 1988.

The Worm and the Toffee-nosed Princess, and Other Stories of Monsters (folklore), illustrated by Margaret Chamberlain, Macmillan (London, England), 1983,

illustrated by Russell Ayto, Hodder Children's (London, England), 1997.

The Haunting of Hiram C. Hopgood, Macmillan (London, England), 1987, published as *The Haunting of Granite Falls,* Dutton (New York, NY), 2004.

Not Just a Witch, illustrated by Alice Englander, Macmillan (London, England), 1989, Chivers North America, 1992.

The Secret of Platform 13, illustrated by Sue Porter, Macmillan (London, England), 1994, Dutton (New York, NY), 1998.

Dial-a-Ghost, illustrated by Kirsten Meyer, Macmillan (London, England), 1996, illustrated by Kevin Hawkes, Dutton (New York, NY), 2001.

Monster Mission, illustrated by Teresa Sdralevich, Macmillan (London, England), 1999, published as *Island of the Aunts,* illustrated by Kevin Hawkes, Dutton (New York, NY), 2000.

Journey to the River Sea, illustrated by Kevin Hawkes, Dutton (New York, NY), 2001.

The Star of Kazan, illustrated by Kevin Hawkes, Dutton (New York, NY), 2004.

The Beasts of Clawstone Castle, Macmillan Children's (London, England), 2005, illustrated by Kevin Hawkes, Dutton Children's Books (New York, NY), 2006.

The Dragonfly Pool, illustrated by Kevin Hawkes, Dutton (New York, NY), 2008.

The Ogre of Oglefort, Macmillan Children's London, England), 2010.

ADULT ROMANCE NOVELS

A Countess below Stairs, MacDonald (London, England), 1981, Avon (New York, NY), 1982, reprinted, Speak (New York, NY), 2007, published as *The Secret Countess,* Picador (London, England), 2008.

Magic Flutes, St. Martin's Press (New York, NY), 1982.

A Glove Shop in Vienna, and Other Stories, Century (London, England), 1984, St. Martin's Press (New York, NY), 1992.

A Company of Swans, St. Martin's Press (New York, NY), 1985, reprinted, Speak (New York, NY), 2007.

Madensky Square, St. Martin's Press (New York, NY), 1988.

The Morning Gift, St. Martin's Press (New York, NY), 1993.

A Song for Summer, Arrow (London, England), 1997, St. Martin's Press (New York, NY), 1998.

The Reluctant Heiress, Puffin Books (New York, NY), 2009.

OTHER

Linda Came Today (television drama), ATV, 1965.

Contributor of hundreds of articles and stories to periodicals. Works have been anthologized in books, including *Yearbook of the American Short Story.*

Adaptations

Dial-a-Ghost, The Great Ghost Rescue, The Haunting of Hiram C. Hopgood, Not Just a Witch, The Secret of Platform 13, and *Which Witch?* were all released on audiocassette. *Journey to the River Sea* was adapted for the stage by Carl Miller and produce in Durham, England, 2006. *Countess below Stairs* was adapted as an audiobook, read by Davina Porter, Recorded Books, 2007. *Island of the Aunts, The Great Ghost Rescue,* and *The Haunting of Hiram C. Hopgood* were being adapted for film at the time of Ibbotson's death in 2010.

Sidelights

Vienna-born British writer Eva Ibbotson worked in two markedly different areas of fiction: tongue-in-cheek ghost stories for a young-adult audience and adult romances that were frequently set in her hometown during the early part of the twentieth century. Of this dual career, she herself once commented that, "After years of writing magazine stories and books for children, I am trying hard to break down the barrier between 'romantic novels' and 'serious novels' which are respectfully reviewed." Certainly no one would accuse Ibbotson of being too serious in her ghost stories, which are written in a "spirit" of great fun. As *Horn Book* reviewer Kitty Flynn explained, "Ibbotson's vivid descriptions of the gruesome and grotesque will delight readers, and even the ghastliest of her spectral characters manages to be likable." Still, the smooth, easy flow of her supernatural tales, which won Ibbotson praise from many critics, fit well with the second half of her stated desires as a novelist: "My aim is to produce books that are light, humorous, even a little erudite, but secure in their happy endings. One could call it an attempt to write, in words, a good Viennese waltz!"

Growing up in Austria in a Jewish family, Ibbotson spent time in a church orphanage after her parents separated in 1928. Five years later, she immigrated to Scotland, joining her father in time to avoid the horrors of the Nazi occupation of Europe during World War II. Although she knew no English, she learned her new language while attending Darlinton, a British boarding school. Ibbotson went on to graduate from the University of London, intending to become a physiologist, but the animal experimentation required of this career path caused her to change her mind. Instead, she married academic Alan Ibbotson and embraced the task of running her household and mothering her four children. Ibbotson eventually returned to school in the 1960s and earned a degree in education. She also began writing, and her television play *Linda Came Today* was produced by ATV in 1965. Her first children's book *The Great Ghost Rescue,* was published a decade later, in 1975, marking teh start of a long career in which she would alternate stories for young people with engaging romance novels for adults.

Ibbotson's books for younger readers earned her a large following among both British and American readers who have enjoyed their imaginative plots and clever

Ibbotson's entertaining middle-grade mysteries include **Island of the Ants,** *a story illustrated by Kevin Hawkes.* (Puffin Books, 1999. Illustrations copyright © Kevin Hawkes, 2000. Reproduced by permission of Dutton Children's Books, a division of Penguin Young Readers Group, a member of Penguin Group (USA) Inc., 345 Hudson St., New York, NY 10014. All rights reserved.)

dialogue. Reviewing *The Great Ghost Rescue,* a critic noted in *Growing Point* that the author develops "a gloriously improbable situation with an inexhaustible provision of verbal wit." Noting Ibbotson's penchant for flouting "political correctness," the contributor also wrote that the author pokes fun at "some of the more lumbering conservation-sermons disguised as fiction which are currently being offered to young readers." The novel focuses on Rick Henderson, a serious-minded boarding-school student who is concerned about the environment. Rick sees ghosts as something of an endangered species and he sets about to help them. Humphrey the Horrible, in particular, needs help, because he lacks the ability to frighten the students at Rick's boarding school, and he is joined in seeking Rick's help by family members Headless Aunt Hortensia and George the Screaming Skull, among others. Noting the story's "considerable appeal," *School Library Journal* contributor Steven Engelfried added that *The Great Ghost Rescue* benefits from Ibbotson's "deliciously consistent macabre humor and the entertaining ensemble of ghosts" she conjures up with her pen. According to Ann A. Flowers in *Horn Book,* "the delightfully horrid details and the richly comic assortment of ghosts make [*The Great Ghost Rescue*] an amusing and satisfying story."

Ghosts face the problem of relocation in *The Great Ghost Rescue* and they encounter a similar situation in *The Haunting of Hiram C. Hopgood,* a story published in the United States as *The Haunting of Granite Falls.* Hopgood, a Texas oil magnate, wants to buy an English castle and bring it home with him, and twelve-year-old Alex MacBuff, an orphan who can no longer afford to keep up his ancestral home, is happy to sell one. However, Hopgood demands that the castle arrive in Texas ghost-free, leaving Alex faced with the problem of how to negotiate with resident ancestral spirits that include a Viking warrior, a toothless vampire named Stanislaus, and a hell-hound. Along the way, the preteen has an innocent romance with Hopgood's ten-year-old daughter Helen, whom the ghosts assist when she is kidnaped. Calling *The Haunting of Hiram C. Hopgood* a "combination of farce and fantasy," Elizabeth Finlayson added in *School Librarian* that Ibbotson's novel "has much to offer besides a thoroughly enjoyable story." The tale "gives new meaning to the term 'blended family,'" asserted *Horn Book* contributor Kristi Elle Jemtegaard, the critic also praising the author's "knack for vivid detail" and noting that "the comfort of a happy ending is never in doubt."

Which Witch? is the story of a competition between witches who are eager to become the bride of Arridian, the wicked wizard of the North. A reviewer in *Junior Bookshelf* praised the novel, noting that Ibbotson's writing is so visual and evocative that, "with all respect to [illustrator] Annabel Large," the book's "illustrations are superfluous." *Dial-a-Ghost* finds Ibbotson on similar ground as it relates the activities surrounding a ghost-placement agency. "There are plenty of bloodstains and creepy crawlies," promised a reviewer in *Junior Bookshelf,* "and many rather grotesque humans who help to make the ghosts seem normal."

Not Just a Witch also concerns a competition between witches, but this time the rivalry is between two former friends who have a silly falling out over a hat. Witches Dora and Heckie—short for Hecate—compete with each other to see who can rid a town of the most evil. Employing a classic remedy, Dora turns problem personalities in her town into stone, but Heckie is more imaginative: she transforms her town's evildoers into caged zoo animals. When their private competition is discovered by an entrepreneurial furrier named Lionel Knapsack, the battle between the witches is co-opted: wooing Heckie with chocolate, Lionel hopes to turn a whole prison full of inmates into snow leopards, creatures whose fur is highly marketable. Noting that *Not Just a Witch* deals with the perennial battle between good and evil, a *Publishers Weekly* contributor added that "Ibbotson again blends hilarious social commentary . . . into a potent recipe for fun."

Ibbotson continued to entertain children with her haunted stories in tales such as *The Beasts of Clawstone Castle* and *The Ogre of Oglefort.* In *The Beasts of Clawstone Castle* eleven-year-old Madlyn and younger

brother Rollo go to live with their great-aunt Emily in Scotland, where they find the ancestral home in disrepair and Great-uncle George's finances in equally bad shape. Fortunately, Madlyn has a practical streak: she decides to harness the castle's charm and add some ghostly flair courtesy of Clawstone's resident spectres. To succeed in their plan to draw tourists to their "haunted" castle, Madlyn and Rollo audition several ghosts to find the most frightening, among them a pair of disembodies feet, a woman severed in two by a poorly trained circus magician, and a spook known as the Bloodstained Bride. However, the castle holds other ghosts that may not cooperate with the children, and there is also an earthly power that does not want their plan to succeed. Reviewing *The Beasts of Clawstone Castle* in the London *Guardian,* Adèle Geras wrote that Ibbotson's tale "braid[s] . . . together with delicacy and skill a school story, a war story and a Ruritanian adventure into a funny, moving and uplifting tale which is sparklingly written and full of excitement." Praising the story's cast of "charismatic ghosts," *Booklist* critic Krista Hutley went on to note that Ibbotson's "energetic, diverting read" is "loaded with charm" and "plenty of quirky humor."

In *The Ogre of Oglefort* Ibbotson took readers inside a suburban London boardinghouse managed by a Hag as

In **The Secret of Platform 13** *Ibbotson transports readers into another world, aided by Sue Porter's illustrations.* (Puffin Books, 1994. Reproduced by permission of Puffin Books, a division of Penguin Putnam Books for Young Readers.)

a refuge for witches, wizards, and even trolls who are in between haunts. When residents learn that an evil ogre has captured a beautiful princess, they band together to organize a rescue. However, as Amanda Craig wrote in her London *Times* review, "neither the Ogre nor the princess turn out to be quite as expected" in a novel that is classic Ibbotson. Noting that "the real targets of Ibbotson's wit are what children themselves long to laugh at: bullies, snobbery, vanity and malice," Craig called *The Ogre of Oglefort* "an adventure strewn with misunderstandings, mistakes and magic that will have children and adults laughing aloud."

Although many of Ibbotson's early supernatural tales involved ghosts or witches, *The Secret of Platform 13* marked somewhat of a departure. Next to Platform 13, in an old subway station—or Tube station, as they are called in London—is a gate into a mythic underworld of wizards and fairies. The gate only opens once every nine years, and a spoiled, selfish woman named Larina Trottle takes advantage of one such opening. She kidnaps Raymond, the child prince of the underworld, and takes him to London, hoping to gain a measure of underworld magic in exchange for his return. The denizens of the underworld risk much to come up to the surface and rescue Raymond, aided by Larina's son Ben. Ben, as it turns out, is lovable and kind, whereas Prince Raymond has become a little tyrant under Larina's care. Praising Ibbotson's tale as "fast, fun," and "full of bizarre characters and ideas," a reviewer in *Books for Keeps* dubbed *The Secret of Platform 13* "a real imagination tickler" with a surprise ending.

Described by *School Library Journal* contributor Eva Mitnick as "a rich saga in the tradition of [*A Little Princess* author] Frances Hodgson Burnett," *The Star of Kazan* was written following the death of Ibbotson's husband in 1998. In a contrast from the author's humorous ghostly tales, this novel taps into Ibbotson's past in its focus on Annika, an orphan who lives in Vienna. Although she daydreams about the day her real mother might return to claim her, Annika has a secure and busy life helping her adopted parents in their work as house servants. In addition to developing a talent for cooking, Annika shows a caring nature and makes many good friends. Then her real mother, the wealthy Edeltraut von Tannenberg, arrives and wisks her off to the ancestral family home in Germany, where the girl discovers the dark side of her former day dreams. While she befriends the stable boy, her birth family is aloof and stingy, giving little of food or love. When Annika suspects that something is seriously wrong in the mansion, she finds herself bereft of help. According to Mitnick, *The Star of Kazan* treats Ibbotson fans to "an intensely satisfying read," while *Booklist* critic Gillian Engberg described it as "a galloping historical novel" that serves up "masterful entertainment in the tradition of Joan Aiken's *The Wolves of Willoughby Chase*" and that "will please Harry Potter readers, too."

Ibbotson continued her break with ghostly tales in the children's novels *Journey to the River Sea* and *The*

Dragonfly Pool. Journey to the River Sea takes place in 1910 and focuses on orphaned Maia Fielding. Rather than ghosts, Maia is troubled by her new guardians, the Carters, who bring her to their poorly run rubber plantation in Brazil, where they live while pretending they are back in England. Escaping the confines of the Carter's home, Maia meets new friends and discovers the beauty and mystery of the exotic Amazon rainforest. In addition to becoming enmeshed in the investigations of a pair of British detectives, Maia also discovers her life's calling: to be an explorer. Noting that Ibbotson "does a wonderful job of turning genre themes topsy-turvy," *Booklist* contributor Jean Franklin praised the novel's "plucky" protagonist and "delightfully humorous" prose. *Journey to the River Sea* is "rich in drama, suspense, hints of romance, and a sense of justice," added Jean Gaffney in a review for *School Library Journal,* the critic going on to praise Ibbotson for bringing Brazil's "natural beauty and the time period . . . to life."

Set in 1939, *The Dragonfly Pool* drew on Ibbotson's own memories of England on the verge of World War

Ibbotson's award-winning middle-grade novel **Journey to the River Sea** *marked her shift to more contemplative fiction.* (Puffin Books, 2001. Illustrations copyright © 2001 by Kevin Hawkes. Reproduced by permission of Dutton Children's Books, a division of Penguin Young Readers Group, a member of the Penguin Group (USA) Inc., 345 Hudson St., New York, NY 10014. All rights reserved.)

II. Eleven-year-old Tally is living with her poor but loving father in London when he finds a way to send her to Delderton Hall, a boarding school in rural Devon. In Delderton's progressive environment Tally enjoys an unstructured atmosphere where she can explore her own talents freely. When she and several of her new friends start a folk-dance club, they decide to enter a competition in the tiny European country of Bergania. As nearby Germany gains in power, Bergania valiantly attempts to stand apart, led by its imperiled crown prince Karil. Supportive of the prince, Tally bravely takes her own stand agains the Nazis in a novel that London *Observer* Geraldine Brennan described as a "compassionate" tale about "the power of roots and friendship, the shallowness of status and the burdens of rank." In the London *Times,* Craig also praised *The Dragonfly Pool* as a "delicate and buoyant" tale "blending comedy, history and tragedy with an irresistible wit and verve." Comparing Ibbotson's story to Leonard Wibberly's classic *The Mouse That Roared,* Sarah Ellis added in her *Horn Book* review that every character "is a gem," while "the plottings, near escapes, secret identities revealed, and ethical dilemmas are decorated with the particular wry, confident humor that is Ibbotson's trademark." "Although the battle between good and evil is painted with a broad brush, Ibbotson treats most issues with a wise, subtle, and humorous touch," concluded *School Library Journal* contributor Eva Mitnick, and a *Kirkus Reviews* writer deemed *The Dragonfly Pool* "a romantic tale of friendship, loyalty and heroism."

In contrast to Ibbotson's ghost stories, her adult romance novels, such as *Countess below Stairs, Magic Flutes, Madensky Square, The Reluctant Heiress*, and *The Morning Gift,* are much "quieter" books even though they are nonetheless imbued with the author's good humor and wit. *Madensky Square,* like most of the others, takes place in Vienna—in this case, the Vienna of 1911, which is yet unsullied by World War I. The story of Susanna, a dressmaker whose shop opens onto the quiet square, is told through her diary, in which she reveals a number of surprising details, including an ongoing affair with a nobleman. "This refreshing novel in which the heroine overcomes hardship [and] sticks to her ideals, [is] carried off without sticky sentimentality," wrote a critic in *Publishers Weekly* in a review of *Madensky Square.*

Also published as *The Secret Countess, Countess below Stairs* has remained popular with Ibbotson's readers since it was first published in 1981. The novel is set in the midst of the Russian revolution of 1917, and introduces eighteen-year-old Anna Grazensky. A countess who is watching her world of wealth and privilege fall apart, Anna worries about the safety of everyone in her family as the communists agitate mobs to destroy all vestiges of aristocracy. Unable to preserve their wealth, the Grazenskys flee to England, where Anna studies *A Domestic Servant's Compendium* and then finds work as a maid in a wealthy London neighborhood. Her new employer Rupert, earl of Westerholme, quickly realizes

Cover of Ibbotson's middle-grade novel The Dragonfly Pool, *which once again teams the author with illustrator Kevin Hawkes.* (Reproduced by permission of Penguin Group USA Inc.)

that his new maid is someone special, and his heart begins to wander despite his recently announced engagement to the beautiful Miss Hardwicke.

The Reluctant Heiress is set in the same milieu as *Countess below Stairs,* but in this case Tessa, a young heiress, takes a job as a wardrobe mistress with the Viennese Opera where she hopes to experience real life without anyone learning of her wealth. When an affluent Englishman hires the opera company to perform at his new country estate, love blooms due to a shared interest in music and the arts, despite the man's pending marriage to the beguiling but snobbish Nerine. Noting Ibbotson's ability to bring her Vienna setting to life, Amy Pickett cited *The Reluctant Heiress* for its "vivid details" and rich use of "German phrases and literary allusions."

In addition to humor and a fast-moving story, all of Ibbotson's books were united by their author's ability to create spirited protagonists, many with talents that are overlooked by those around them. "Every kid wants to believe that he or she is special and hopes that someone out there will recognize their hidden talents and unique-

ness, qualities that, too often, adults do fail to see," commented Jeannette Hulick in a profile of the author for the *Bulletin of the Center for Children's Books Online.* "Fortunately," the critic added, "in Ibbotson's worlds, kids do find confirmation that they are, in fact, extraordinary people."

Biographical and Critical Sources

PERIODICALS

Booklist, December 15, 2001, Jean Franklin, review of *Journey to the River Sea,* p. 727; May 1, 2004, Kay Weisman, review of *The Haunting of Granite Falls,* p. 1559; October 15, 2004, Gillian Engberg, review of *The Star of Kazan;* October 1, 2006, Krista Hutley, review of *The Beasts of Clawstone Castle,* p. 54; September 15, 2008, Krista Hutley, review of *The Dragonfly Pool,* p. 50.

Books for Keeps, November, 1995, review of *The Secret of Platform 13,* p. 11.

Growing Point, April, 1975, review of *The Great Ghost Rescue,* p. 2599.

Guardian (London, England), September 13, 2008, Adèle Geras, review of *The Dragonfly Pool,* p. 14.

Horn Book, December, 1975, Ann A. Flowers, review of *The Great Ghost Rescue,* pp. 593-594; January-February, 2002, Christine M. Heppermann, review of *Journey to the River Sea,* p. 78; September-October, 2002, Kitty Flynn, review of *The Great Ghost Rescue,* p. 574; July-August, 2004, Kristi Elle Jemtegaard, review of *The Haunting of Granite Falls,* p. 453; November-December, 2008, Sarah Ellis, review of *The Dragonfly Pool,* p. 706.

Junior Bookshelf, October, 1979, review of *Which Witch?,* p. 279; February, 1990, review of *Not Just a Witch,* p. 27; October, 1996, review of *Dial-a-Ghost,* pp. 202-203.

Kirkus Reviews, June 15, 2003, review of *Not Just a Witch,* p. 859; August 1, 2008, review of *The Dragonfly Pool.*

Observer (London, England), August 3, 2008, Geraldine Brennan, review of *The Dragonfly Pool,* p. 25.

Publishers Weekly, September 2, 1988, review of *Madensky Square,* p. 86; July 21, 2003, review of *Not Just a Witch,* p. 195; November, 2004, review of *The Star of Kazan,* p. 40; July 10, 2006, review of *The Beasts of Clawstone Castle,* p. 82.

School Librarian, February, 1988, Elizabeth Finlayson, review of *The Haunting of Hiram C. Hopgood,* p. 28.

School Library Journal, January, 2002, Jean Gaffney, review of *Journey to the River Sea,* p. 132; August, 2002, Steven Engelfried, review of *The Great Ghost Rescue,* p. 189; October, 2004, Eva Mitnick, review of *The Star of Kazan,* p. 168; November, 2006, Caitlin, review of *The Beasts of Clawstone Castle,* p. 136; November, 2008, Eva Mitnick, review of *The Dragonfly Pool,* p. 124; August, 2009, Amy Pickett, review of *The Reluctant Heiress,* p. 104.

Times (London, England), May 3, 2008, Amanda Craig, review of *The Dragonfly Pool,* p. 15; April 24, 2010, Amanda Craig, review of *The Ogre of Oglefort,* p. 12.

ONLINE

Bulletin of the Center for Children's Books Online, http://www.lis.uiuc.edu/puboff/bccb/ (March 1, 2002), Jeannette Hulick, "Eva Ibbotson."
Penguin Putnam Web site, http://www.penguinputnam.com/ (October 30, 2010).

Obituaries

PERIODICALS

Guardian (London, England), October 22, 2010.
London Telegraph, October 25, 2010.
New York Times, October 27, 2010.*

* * *

JARKA, Jeff

Personal

Born in NY; married; wife's name Theresa; children: one son. *Education:* College degree. *Hobbies and other interests:* Collecting toys.

Addresses

Home—Chicago, IL.

Career

Toy designer and author and illustrator of children's books. Creata Media, Oakbrook Terrace, IL, vice president of creative services, beginning 2001, chief creative officer, 2007—.

Writings

SELF-ILLUSTRATED BOARD BOOKS

Love That Puppy!: The Story of a Boy Who Wanted to Be a Dog, Henry Holt (New York, NY), 2009.
Love That Kitty!: The Story of a Boy Who Wanted to Be a Cat, Henry Holt (New York, NY), 2010.

Sidelights

When Jeff Jarka decided that it was time to fulfill a childhood dream and write and illustrate his own picture book, he took a very methodical approach. As the Chicago-based author explained on his Web log, he scoured "bookstores and libraries and found books I liked that were similar in style or format to what I was looking to create." After researching potential publishers, Jarka narrowed his list down to just over a dozen firms. "Then I made a picture book dummy (rough art

and the words together in a rough book form)," which "took longer than I expected." He sent the dummy to the first publishing house on his list, and when it was returned, rejected, over a month later he submitted it to the next publisher on the list. Sometimes the dummy never came back and Jarka had to create a new one. After a year of this cycle of submission and rejection, he was about to give up on his story. It was then that Jarka was contacted by an editor at Henry Holt and *Love That Puppy!: The Story of a Boy Who Wanted to Be a Dog* was published.

In *Love That Puppy!* readers meet Peter, a little boy who can play fetch as well as any dog. Peter takes the game a bit too far when he decides to BE a dog, curling up in the doghouse, barking at visitors, chasing the mailman, and begging for treats at the dinner table. When his mother decides to play along and put Peter the bad dog in his place, the boy decides to change the rules of his game in a story that *School Library Journal* critic Jayne Damron praised as a "lighthearted" story with "strong boy appeal." A *Kirkus Reviews* writer also noted Jarka's cartoon art, describing Peter's "appropriately broad comic expressions" as "silly and goofy." Recommending Peter's story to young fans of the Cartoon Network, a *Publishers Weekly* critic noted that "Jarka . . . is clearly someone who loves working with both dogs and small children," while the *Kirkus Reviews* writer predicted that readers of *Love That Puppy!* are in for "a howling good time."

Jarka works his magic again in *Love That Kitty!: The Story of a Boy Who Wanted to Be a Cat,* a version of

Jeff Jarka's cartoon art is a feature of his quirky self-illustrated picture book **Love That Puppy!** (Reproduced by permission of Henry Holt and Company, LLC.)

Love That Puppy! for cat fans. When Peter decides that cats have a good life, he pulls on his cat pajamas and begins to purr. While he spends some of his time curled up in the sun, the child/kitty also attracts the attention of his harried mother when he uses upholstered furniture to sharpen his kitty claws, recoils from running water, and even scratches around in the kitty box. Noting the "exaggerated poses and expressions" that add visual humor to the story, Carolyn Phelan added in *Booklist* that *Love That Kitty!* also benefits from Jarka's "deadpan lines of text." "Fans of Peter's first adventure will enjoy this one and look for more to follow," predicted Donna Cardon in her *School Library Journal* review of *Love That Kitty!*

Biographical and Critical Sources

PERIODICALS

Booklist, October 1, 2010, Carolyn Phelan, review of *Love That Kitty!: The Story of a Boy Who Wanted to Be a Cat,* p. 95.
Kirkus Reviews, May 1, 2009, review of *Love That Puppy!: The Story of a Boy Who Wanted to Be a Dog.*
Publishers Weekly, June 1, 2009, review of *Love That Puppy!,* p. 46.
School Library Journal, June, 2009, Jayne Damron, review of *Love That Puppy!,* p. 92; September, 2010, Donna Cardon, review of *Love That Kitty!,* p. 126.

ONLINE

Jeff Jarka Web Site, http://www.lovethatsite.blogspot.com (October 30, 2010).*

* * *

JOLIVET, Joélle 1965-

Personal

Born 1965, in France. *Education:* Arts Appliqués (Paris, France), degree (graphic art); attended Beaux Arts (Paris).

Addresses

Home—Ivry-sur-Seine, France. *E-mail*—jj@joellejolivet.com.

Career

Illustrator and graphic artist.

Awards, Honors

Boston Globe/Horn Book Honor Book designation, Wanda Gag Award Honor Book designation, Premio Andersen, and Premio Nazionale Libro per l'ambiente (Italy), all 2007, and Prix Sorcières, 2008, all for *365 pingouins* by Jean-Luc Fromental; Bourse Goncourt Jeunesse, 2007, for *La trés petite Zébuline* by Véronique Ovaldé; Prix Sorcières, 2008, for *Costumes.*

Writings

SELF-ILLUSTRATED

Léon le cochon, Albin Michel (Paris, France), 1994.
Images et mots, Seuil Jeunesse (France), 1994.
Agathe la vache, Albin Michel (Paris, France), 1995.
(With Valérie Guidoux) *Boîte à lettres,* Seuil Jeunesse (France), 1995.
Tros doudou, Albin Michele Jeunesse (Paris, France), 1995.
Noël le père noël, Albin Michel Jeunesse (Paris, France), 1996.
Tapidou, Seuil Jeunesse (Paris, France), 1999.
Vues d'Ivry, Cornélius (France), 2001.
Zoo logique, Seuil Jeunesse (Paris, France), 2002, translated as *Zoo-ology,* Roaring Brook Press (Brookfield, CT), 2003.
Costumes, Panama (France), 2007, translated as *The Colossal Book of Costumes,* Thames & Hudson (London, England), 2008.
Coloriages, Panama (France), 2008.

ILLUSTRATOR

Christine Brouillet, *Danger, bonbons!,* Souris Noir, Syros (Paris, France), 1989.
Pierre Moessinger, *Ménagerie nocturne,* Nathan (Paris, France), 1990.
Henriette Bichonnier, *Nouse, les mecs,* Nathan (Paris, France), 1991.
F. Krot, *Dans le pétrin,* Souris Noir, Syros (Paris, France), 1991.
J.C. Duluc, *Quest Américain, la fort dévastée,* Albin Michel (Paris, France), 1991.
Emmanuelle Fraisse and Isabelle Jan, *La juistice,* Editions Ouvières Jeunesse, 1991.
Gérard Herzhaft, *Restituta et le coeur-roi,* Casterman (Paris, France), 1991.
Alberto Manzi, *Le village des fous,* Hachette (Paris, France), 1991.
Jean-Loup Craipeau, *Un père,* Souris Noir, Syros (Paris, France), 1992.
M-A. and E. Murail, *Sou manga,* Mango, 1992.
Gerard Herzhaft, *Thorvald, Viking des orcades,* Casterman (Paris, France), 1993.
Babacar Niang, *Sénégal, le retour d'un immigré,* Albin Michel (Paris, France), 1994.
Manfe Obin, *Le rat célibataire et autres contes,* Syros (Paris, France), 1994.
Fables de La Fontaine, Albin Michel Jeunesse (Paris, France), 1994.
Florence Dutruc-Rosset, *L'assassin habite à côté,* Syros (Paris, France), 1995.

Catherine Fogel, *Pas de violon pour les sorcières,* Seuil Jeunesse (Paris, France), 1995.

Bernadète Bidaude, *Le roi des oiseaux et autres contes,* Syros (Paris, France), 1996.

Fiona MacLeod, *Jack et la sorcière de mer et autres contes d'écosse,* Syros (Paris, France), 1997.

Mon livre de chansons, La Martiniére Jeunesse (France), 1997.

101 chansons de toujours, Bayard (Paris, France), 1998.

Les Ateliers des Marmitons, *Petits chefs en cuisine,* Flammarion (Paris, France), 1998.

Faranak Palizban and François Hayward, *Histoires d'Anges,* Seuil Jeunesse (Paris, France), 1998.

Yves Pinguilly, *Contes et legendes de Bretagne,* Nathan (Paris, France), 1998.

Jean-Claude Izzo, *Vivre fatigue,* Librio, 1998.

(With others) *Nos vaches,* Un souriere de toi et j'quitte ma mère (France), 1998.

Le voyage, La Martinire Jeunesse (Paris, France), 1998.

Le plus belles légendes de sorcières, Flammarion (Paris, France), 1998.

Martine Laffon, *La dame qui aimait trop les chevaux,* Seuil Jeunesse (Paris, France), 1999.

Pascal Fauliot, *Issounboshi et autres contes du Japon,* Syros (Paris, France), 1999.

Lilyan Kesteloot, *Soundiata l'enfant-lion,* Casterman (Paris, France), 1999.

Catherine Zarcate, *Le loukoum a la pistache et autres contes d'Orient,* Syros (Paris, France), 2000.

Coline Promeyrat, *Les trois petits pourceaux,* Didier (Paris, France), 2000.

Christian Roche and Jean-Jacques Barrire, *Le bestiaire des philosophes,* Seuil (Paris, France), 2001.

Les plus belles chansons des p'tits lascars, Didier Jeunesse (Paris, France), 2001.

Jean-Luc Fromental, *Monsieur Troublevue et son brochet,* Seuil Jeunesse (Paris, France), 2002.

Bernard Giraudeau, *Les contes d'Humahuaca,* Seuil-Métaillé (France), 2002.

Gudule, *Super-nina au zoo,* Nathan (Paris, France), 2002.

Charles Perrault, *Le petit chaperon rouge,* Albin Michel (Paris. France), 2002.

Thierry Dedieu, *27 poules sur un mur,* Seuil Jeunesse (Paris, France), 2002.

Michel Grimaud, *Cache-cache mortel,* Gallimard Jeunesse (Paris, France), 2003.

Virginie Aladjidi, *Un coeur qui bat,* Thierry Magnier (France), 2004.

(With others) *Color Star,* Un souriere de toi et j'quitte ma mère (France), 2004.

Laura Jaffé, *Presque tout,* Seuil Jeunesse (Paris, France), 2004, translated by Alexis Siegel as *Almost Everything,* Roaring Brook Press (New York, NY), 2005.

Charles and Mary Lamb, *Les contes de Shakespeare,* new edition, Naïve (France), 2005, published as *Tales from Shakespeare,* Harry Abrams (New York, NY), 2007.

(With others) *Le grand livre des lutins, gnomes, elfes . . .* , Albin Michel (Paris, France), 2005.

François David, *Un elephant peut en cacher un autre,* Sarbacane (France), 2005.

Claire Merleau-Ponty and Cécille Mozziconacci, *Histoire des Maori,* Actes Sud Junior (Paris, France), 2006.

Jean-Luc Fromental, *365 pingouins,* Naïve (France), 2006, translated as *365 Penguins,* Abrams Books for Young Readers (New York, NY), 2006.

Véronique Ovaldé, *La trés petite Zébuline,* Actes Sud Junior (Paris, France), 2006.

Jean-Luc Fromental, *24 pingouins avant noël,* paper engineering by Gérard Lo Monaco, Naïve (France), 2007, translated as *24 Penguins before Christmas,* Harry Abrams (New York, NY), 2008.

Fani Marceau, *Vues d'ici,* Naïve (France), 2007, translated as *Panorama: A Foldout Book,* Abrams Books for Young Readers (New York, NY), 2009.

Albna Ivanovitch-Lair and Annie Caldirac, *Le jour de la fin du monde,* Tourbillon (Paris, France), 2009.

Jean Constantin, *Shah Shah Persan,* Editions du Rouergue (France), 2009.

Muriel Bloch, *Le schmat doudou,* Syros (Paris, France), 2009.

Jean-Luc Fromental, *Oops!,* Hélium (Paris, France), 2009, Abrams Books for Young Readers (New York, NY), 2010.

Stéfanie Delestré and Hagar Desanti, *Dictionnaire des personnages populaires de la littérature: XIXe et XXe siécles,* Seuil (Paris, France), 2010.

Jean-Luc Fromental, *Dix p'tits pingouins,* translated as *Ten Little Penguins,* translated by Amanda Katz, Abrams Books for Young Readers (New York, NY), 2010.

Herman Melville, *Moby-Dick,* paper engineering by Gérard Lo Monaco, Gallimard (Paris, France), 2010.

Books featuring author's art have been published in German, Italian, Spanish, Norwegian, Greek, Hebrew, and Portuguese.

ILLUSTRATOR; "ZIGOTOS DE ZOO" SERIES

Yves Hughes, *Faim de loup,* Gallimard Jeunesse (Paris, France), 2004.

Yves Hughes, *Trop bavards,* Gallimard Jeunesse (Paris, France), 2005.

Yves Hughes, *Secret d'elephant,* Gallimard Jeunesse (Paris, France), 2006.

Biographical and Critical Sources

PERIODICALS

Booklist, November 1, 2005, Gillian Engberg, review of *Almost Everything,* p. 50; January 1, 2007, Randall Enos, review of *365 Penguins,* p. 114; March 1, 2009, Daniel Kraus, review of *Panorama: A Foldout Book,* p. 45.

Horn Book, January-February, 2004, Danielle J. Ford, review of *Zoo-ology,* p. 101; January-February, 2008, Anita Silvey, review of *365 Penguins,* p. 20; July-August, 2009, Betty Carter, review of *Panorama,* p. 410.

Kirkus Reviews, October 1, 2005, review of *Almost Everything,* p. 1081; November 15, 2006, review of *365 Penguins,* p. 1173.

Publishers Weekly, November 27, 2006, review of *365 Penguins,* p. 49; April 6, 2009, "Form, Function—and Fun," p. 48; May 17, 2010, review of *Oops!,* p. 49.

School Library Journal, April, 2004, review of *Zoo-ology*; November, 2005, Grace Oliff, review of *Almost Everything,* p. 94; December, 2006, Barbara Auerbach, review of *365 Penguins,* p. 100; April, 2010, Marge Loch-Wouters, review of *Oops!,* p. 124.

ONLINE

Joélle Jolivet Home Page, http://www.joellejolivet.com (October 15, 2010).

Joélle Jolivet Web Log, http://joellejolivet.blogspot.com (October 15, 2010).*

* * *

JORDAN, Devin

Personal

Male. *Education:* Wesleyan University, B.A.; attended Oxford, University.

Addresses

Home—New York, NY.

Career

Author.

Writings

The Dragon's Pearl (based on a story by Virgil Howard and Bill Ryan), Simon & Schuster Books for Young Readers (New York, NY), 2009.

Biographical and Critical Sources

PERIODICALS

Kirkus Reviews, June 1, 2009, review of *The Dragon's Pearl.*

Publishers Weekly, July 6, 2009, review of *The Dragon's Pearl,* p. 52.

School Library Journal, October, 2009, Bethany Issacson, review of *The Dragon's Pearl,* p. 128.

ONLINE

Simon & Schuster Web Site, http://authors.simonandschuster.com/ (October 20, 2010), "Devin Jordan."*

K

KANE, Kim 1973(?)-

Personal

Born c. 1973, in London, England; immigrated to Australia; daughter of Barbara Kane (an art historian). *Education:* Attended law school. *Hobbies and other interests:* Opera, the arts.

Addresses

Home—Melbourne, Victoria, Australia.

Career

Commercial lawyer and author. Writer, beginning 2004.

Awards, Honors

Barbara Ramsden Award for Excellence in Editing (with editor Elise Jones), 2008, and Speech Pathology Australia Book of the Year Award shortlist, and Australian Book Industry Awards Book of the Year for Older Children shortlist, both 2009, all for *Pip: The Story of Olive.*

Writings

Pip: The Story of Olive, Allen & Unwin (Sydney, New South Wales, Australia), 2008, David Fickling Books (New York, NY), 2009.

The Vegetable Ark: A Tale of Two Brothers, illustrated by Sue deGennaro, Allen & Unwin (Sydney, New South Wales, Australia), 2010.

Sidelights

Born in England, Kim Kane practiced law for several years before becoming an author of books for children. Her first novel, *Pip: The Story of Olive,* was first released in Australia, as was her second, the picture book *The Vegetable Ark: A Tale of Two Brothers,* in which Kane retells the story of Noah's ark.

In *Pip* readers meet Olive Garnaut, a twelve-year-old introvert who lives with her busy single attorney mom and has never met her father. Olive has to deal with a lot at her first year at the Joanne d'Arc School for Girls. Small of stature and with a wan complexion that makes her rather invisible among her classmates, the Austra-

Cover of Kim Kane's **Pip: The Story of Olive,** *a novel about a teen's double life that features artwork by Elise Hurst.* (David Fickling Books, 2008. Used by permission of David Fickling Books, an imprint of Random House Children's Books, a division of Random House, Inc.)

lian preteen feels lost when best friend Mathilda becomes a former best friend by linking up with popular but cliquey Ameila. In reaction, Olive finds a new best friend in outgoing alter-ego Pip, a "twin sister" who takes the assertive role in seeking out Olive's missing dad, making new friends, and helping Olive feel like a somebody as she navigates her way through adolescence. Calling Kane's debut novel "original and intelligence," Nicolette Jones added in her London *Times* review that "the story skillfully sustains Pip's double identity for as long as is necessary" to allow readers to be reassured that Olive can stand on her own. In *School Library Journal* D. Maria LaRocca called *Pip* "a charming, empowering, offbeat story of middle-school ups and downs."

Biographical and Critical Sources

PERIODICALS

Kirkus Reviews, May 1, 2009, review of *Pip: The Story of Olive.*
Publishers Weekly, June 1, 2009, review of *Pip,* p. 47.
School Library Journal, July, 2009, D. Maria LaRocco, review of *Pip,* p. 86.
Sunday Times (London, England), July 6, 2008, Nicolette Jones, review of *Pip,* p. 46.

ONLINE

Allen & Unwin Web Site, http://www.allenandunwin.com/ (October 30, 2010), "Kim Kane."*

*   *   *

KLISE, Kate 1963-

Personal

Born 1963, in Peoria, IL; daughter of Thomas S. (a writer and film producer) and Marjorie A. (a business executive) Klise. *Education:* Marquette University, graduate.

Addresses

Home and office—P.O. Box 744, Mountain Grove, MO 65711.

Career

Writer and journalist. Correspondent for *People* magazine.

Awards, Honors

Young Adults' Choice Award, Children's Book Council, 1999, for *Regarding the Fountain,* and 2000, for *Letters from Camp;* Juvenile Fiction Award, Friends of American Writers, 2002, for *Trial by Journal.*

Writings

Letters from Camp, illustrated by sister, M. Sarah Klise, Avon (New York, NY), 1999.
Trial by Journal, illustrated by M. Sarah Klise, HarperCollins (New York, NY), 2001.
Deliver Us from Normal, Scholastic Press (New York, NY), 2005.
Far from Normal, Scholastic Press (New York, NY), 2006.
Grounded, Feiwel & Friends (New York, NY), 2010.
Stand Straight, Ella Kate: The True Story of a Real Giant, illustrated by M. Sarah Klise, Dial Books for Young Readers (New York, NY), 2010.

"GEYSER CREEK MIDDLE SCHOOL" NOVEL SERIES

Regarding the Fountain: A Tale, in Letters, of Liars and Leaks, illustrated by M. Sarah Klise, Avon (New York, NY), 1998.
Regarding the Sink: Where, Oh Where, Did Waters Go?, illustrated by M. Sarah Klise, Harcourt (Orlando, FL), 2004.
Regarding the Trees: A Splintered Saga Rooted in Secrets, illustrated by M. Sarah Klise, Harcourt (Orlando, FL), 2005.
Regarding the Bathrooms: A Privy to the Past, illustrated by M. Sarah Klise, Harcourt (San Diego, CA), 2006.
Regarding the Bees: A Lesson, in Letters, on Honey, Dating, and Other Sticky Subjects, illustrated by M. Sarah Klise, Harcourt (Orlando, FL), 2007.

"LITTLE RABBIT" SERIES

Shall I Knit You a Hat?: A Christmas Yarn, illustrated by M. Sarah Klise, Henry Holt (New York, NY), 2004.
Why Do You Cry?: Not a Sob Story, illustrated by M. Sarah Klise, Henry Holt (New York, NY), 2006.
Imagine Harry, illustrated by M. Sarah Klise, Harcourt (Orlando, FL), 2007.
Little Rabbit and the Night Mare, illustrated by M. Sarah Klise, Harcourt (Orlando, FL), 2008.
Little Rabbit and the Meanest Mother on Earth, illustrated by M. Sarah Klise, Harcourt (Orlando, FL), 2010.

"43 OLD CEMETERY ROAD" SERIES

Dying to Meet You, illustrated by M. Sarah Klise, Harcourt (Boston, MA), 2009.
Over My Dead Body, illustrated by M. Sarah Klise, Harcourt (Boston, MA), 2009.
Till Death Do Us Bark, illustrated by M. Sarah Klise, Harcourt Children's (Boston, MA), 2011.

Sidelights

Kate Klise writes children's books, many of which are designed and illustrated by her sister, M. Sarah Klise. Her "Little Rabbit" series, which include *Shall I Knit You a Hat?: A Christmas Yarn, Imagine Harry,* and *Little Rabbit and the Night Mare,* appeal to very young

children in their stories about a young rabbit. Turning to middle graders, the Klise sisters again team up on the "43 Old Cemetery Road" and "Geyser Creek Middle School" books, which mix letters, memos, newspaper clippings, and e-mails together with numerous graphic elements to chronicle the various adventures of children in and around a specific locale.

Called a "comic epistolary novel" by a critic in the *New York Times Book Review, Regarding the Fountain: A Tale, in Letters, of Liars and Leaks* was the duo's first collaboration as well as their first "Geyser Creek Middle School" story. *Regarding the Fountain* focuses on the need to replace a leaking drinking fountain at the Dry Creek Middle School. When Principal Russ decides to order a replacement from Flowing Waters Fountains, he expects to receive a traditional drinking fountain. To his surprise—and to the delight of the students—Florence Waters turns out to be an artist who creates fountains that are individually sculpted pieces of art. Her ideas for the school fountain include an ice-skating rink, a chocolate-milk dispenser, a natural whirlpool, and a flock of exotic birds. A subplot involves the disappearance of the town's water supply, a mystery resolved with the help of a fifth-grade class working on a history project about the town. Writing in *Kirkus Reviews,* a critic dubbed *Regarding the Fountain* "a tale overflowing with imagination and fun," while Rita Soltan noted in *School Library Journal* that Klise "cleverly establishes character traits and motive" and called the book "fresh, funny, and a delight to read." A *Publishers Weekly* contributor praised the Klise sisters' unique novel as a "good-natured story with an irrepressible main character."

Regarding the Sink: Where, Oh Where, Did Waters Go? finds Flo Waters once again taking center stage as the sixth graders of the now-renamed Geyser Creek Middle School ask her to replace a dilapidated cafeteria sink. The only problem is that Flo has vanished while on a trip to China, and now the middle graders are determined to find her. Meanwhile, to further complicate school life, beans have become a staple of school lunches as the result of slimy Senator Sue Ergass's moneymaking scam (which includes feeding cows nothing but beans so they produce more methane gas). A *Kirkus Reviews* contributor called *Regarding the Sink* "an amusing sequel," while in *Horn Book* Susan P. Bloom commented that "the Klises provide a satisfying denouement to this utter mayhem." In a review for *School Library Journal,* Jean Gaffney called the illustrated novel "a clever, unconventional reading experience."

In *Regarding the Trees: A Splintered Saga Rooted in Secrets* "the puns fall faster than autumn leaves," according to *Horn Book* contributor Susan P. Bloom. Worried over an upcoming school evaluation, Principal Russ asks Flo to assist in trimming the school trees, thereby sparking student protests, a town uprising, and a cooking face-off between two local chefs. All ends well,

Kate Klise collaborates with sister and artist M. Sarah Klise on Regarding the Bathrooms, *one of several books featuring a class of enterprising middle graders.* (Harcourt, Inc. 2006. Illustrations copyright © 2006 by M. Sarah Klise. All rights reserved. Reproduced by permission of Harcourt in North America. This material may not be reproduced in any form or by any means without the prior written permission of the publisher. Reproduced by permission of M. Sarah Klise in the United Kingdom. This material may not be reproduced in any form or by any means without the prior written permission of the publisher.)

however, and romance even blooms. Police reports take their place among letters, newspaper articles, and other communications in *Regarding the Bathrooms: A Privy to the Past* as the principal's hope of renovating a basement bathroom during summer session is stalled when several escaped convicts are found hiding in the school, along with a cache of stolen Roman antiquities. The action moves to seventh grade in *Regarding the Bees,* as budding student romances, stresses over standardized tests, and difficulties surrounding the school mascot's appearance at a regional spelling bee culminate in a flurry of humorous visual communications. Describing *Regarding the Trees* as "filled with humor and whimsical characters," Shelle Rosenfeld added in *Booklist* that "kids will enjoy the peppy, multiformat read." In *School Library Journal* Cheryl Ashton noted that "each page" of the book "is painstakingly laid out in scrapbook form," and a *Kirkus Reviews* writer dubbed *Regarding the Trees* "consistently clever and often hilarious." In *Booklist,* Hazel Rochman added her praise to the Klise

sisters' novels, describing *Regarding the Bees* as a "fast and funny" installment in an "uproarious series."

Part of Klise's "43 Old Cemetery Road" series, *Dying to Meet You* finds curmudgeonly author Ignatius B. Grumply renting an old house in the town of Ghastly while writing the next book in his "Ghost Tamers" series. The home—a creaky old manse—is haunted by a little bookish girl named Olive while an upstairs bedroom is home to Seymour Hope, the eleven-year-old son of the home's owners, who are touring Europe on vacation. True to his name, Grumply does not care for children even though he writes stories for them, and the relationship between the three housemates plays out in the Klise sisters' characteristic mix of story, graphics, and bits of written ephemera. Writing that M. Sarah Klise's cartoon art "add[s] a nice layer" to the story, *Booklist* critic Ian Chipman added that *Dying to Meet You* "delivers an unlikely story with a great deal of likability." In typical Klise fashion, the novel is rich with puns; as a *Publishers Weekly* critic noted, it "is light enough for more tentative readers, with many humorous details to reward those who look closer."

The "43 Old Cemetery Road" series continues in *Over My Dead Body* and *Till Death Do Us Bark*, which also attract reluctant middle-grade readers through their mix of humor and visual energy. In *Over My Dead Body*, Seymour, Olive, and Ignatius continue the authorial collaboration they began in *Dying to Meet You*, at least until Seymour is locked in an orphanage and the conniving activist Dick Tater decides to use the goings on at 43 Old Cemetery Road as an excuse to abolish the holiday of Halloween. "Even the addresses on the letters add to the comedy of this light, diverting romp," according to a *Kirkus Reviews* critic, and Knight wrote that "the short, graphic-heavy text and broad humor" in *Over My Dead Body* "will appeal to middle grade readers."

The first "Little Rabbit" picture book, *Shall I Knit You a Hat?* finds Mother Rabbit knitting a hat for her son to protect him from an oncoming blizzard. Little Rabbit loves his hat and never takes it off, but he is concerned for his other animal friends and suggests that he and his mother make hats for all of them as Christmas gifts. Little Rabbit turns five in *Why Do You Cry?* and creates an imaginary friend in *Imagine Harry*. "The Klises consistently sound notes of tenderness and humor," noted a *Publishers Weekly* contributor of *Shall I Knit You a Hat?*, and *School Library Journal* critic Suzanne Myers Harold cited *Imagine Harry* as a picture book that "strikes a balance between humor and understanding." J.D. Biersdorfer, reviewing *Shall I Knit You a Hat?* for the *New York Times Book Review*, described Klise's story as "a nice change of pace" and noted that "the Klise sisters team up to show that the giving is just as important as the gift."

Worries about an upcoming homework assignment trouble the dreams of Little Rabbit in *Little Rabbit and the Night Mare*, as a grammatical misunderstanding

creates a scary dream character, while running away from home to join the circus seems the best thing to do after Mother Rabbit makes the youngster clean his messy room in *Little Rabbit and the Meanest Mother on Earth*. Praising *Little Rabbit and the Night Mare* as "charming," Susannah Richards added that Klise's "engaging tale about a child's imagination and his strategies to confront his fears is told with gentle humor," and a *Kirkus Reviews* critic dubbed the same book "a worthy introduction to puns." In *Publishers Weekly* a critic dubbed *Little Rabbit and the Meanest Mother on Earth* "charmingly off-kilter," while Catherine Callegari cited the story's two-level approach, writing in *School Library Journal* that "children should relate to [the Klise sisters'] . . . circus tale, and parents will enjoy how the mother saves the day."

In addition to her series fiction, Klise has also written stand-alone novels for preteen readers, among them *Deliver Us from Normal* and *Far from Normal*. In *Deliver Us from Normal* Klise tells the story of twelve-year-old Charlie Harrisong, who lives in Normal, Illinois, but whose poor family is far from the norm. Charlie is teased at school and is embarrassed about his family and their unusual lifestyle. When the Harrisong family

Cover of Klise's middle-grade novel **Deliver Us from Normal,** *featuring artwork by Joe Zeff.* (Cover art image copyright © 2005 by Joe Zeff. Reprinted by permission of Scholastic Inc.)

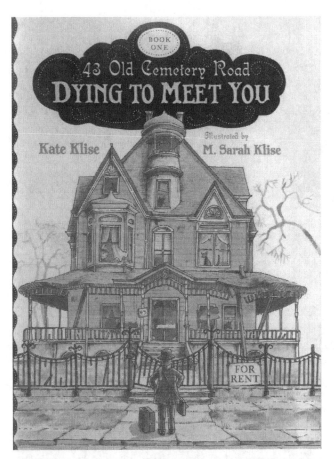

The Klise sisters team up with their characteristic lighthearted approach in **Dying to Meet You,** *a book in their "43 Old Cemetery Road" series.* (Reproduced by permission of Houghton Mifflin Harcourt Publishing Company. This material may not be reproduced in any form or by any means without the prior written permission of the publisher.)

decides to leave town and live on a junky houseboat, Charlie is at first distressed that his life will never, ever be normal, but he eventually learns that not being normal has its benefits. When readers rejoin Charlie in *Far from Normal*, two years have passed and the Harrisong family's circumstances have changed drastically. After Charlie's article about life on the houseboat is published in a national magazine, he and his parents are strong-armed into becoming the spokesfamily for the discount retailer Bargain Bonanza. Although they are set up in an all-expenses-paid luxury apartment with all the Bargain Bonanza merchandise they desire, this glamorous life comes with a cost, and the stress of fame takes its toll on everyone.

In a *Horn Book* review, Susan Dove Lempke wrote that in *Deliver Us from Normal* Klise "shows a gift for getting inside her narrator, [and] delivering his perceptions with immediacy and self-deprecating humor," while *Far from Normal* benefits from a "fast-moving plot" and its author's "grasp of family relationships and her sharp wit." In *Booklist*, Jennifer Hubert compared Klise's humor to that of authors Gordon Korman and David Lubar, noting her arch commentary "on commercialism and the cult of celebrity." Even in the modern world Charlie and his family "remind readers what is

really important—honesty, integrity and the loyalty of family," concluded Janis Flint-Ferguson in her *Kliatt* review of *Far from Normal*.

Another standalone novel by Klise, *Letters from Camp*, also features M. Sarah Klise's unique art. The story focuses on Camp Happy Harmony, where brothers and sisters who cannot get along are sent to learn to love and respect each other. The camp's owners, however, are a group of singers turned con artists who are bent on killing each other and who use the children to do all the work of maintaining the camp, including cleaning septic lines, building fences, and painting, all the while making them wear strange uniforms and sing bizarre songs. Not-so-happy campers are kept in line through drugged food served in the Wysteria Cafeteria. Despite the circumstances, the children learn to cooperate, and brothers and sisters eventually do learn to care for each other as they solve the mysteries of Camp Happy Harmony. A *Publishers Weekly* contributor found the book a "bit less satisfying" than *Regarding the Fountain*, but also noted that "the humor is obvious but kid-friendly, the mystery simple yet fun to solve." Writing in *Booklist*, Debbie Carton commented that the story is "all in all, an entirely satisfying camp adventure that even those who have never been to camp will relish." Other standalone novels by the Kliase sisters include *Trial by Journal*.

In *Stand Straight, Ella Kate: The True Story of a Real Giant* Klise turns to history, recounting the life of Missouri native Ella Kate Ewing in Ella's own words. Born in 1872, Ella now had a glandular condition called gigantism, and by age eighteen she stood over eight feet tall. Having endured a childhood marked by schoolyard taunting, Ella now decided to use her unusual height to her advantage. She worked in Chicago as a museum exhibit and appeared at circuses and county fairs as "The Tallest Lady on Earth," earning enough money to support herself and also aid her parents and the family farm. Reviewing *Stand Straight, Ella Kate* in *Publishers Weekly*, a critic wrote of the acrylic paintings by M. Sarah Klise that they capture "the historical setting" of this "quiet story with unexpected impact."

Biographical and Critical Sources

PERIODICALS

Booklist, August, 1998, Susan Dove Lempke, review of *Regarding the Fountain: A Tale, in Letters, of Liars and Leaks*, p. 2006; September 1, 2001, Shelle Rosenfeld, review of *Trial by Journal*, p. 106; September 1, 2004, Francisca Goldsmith, review of *Regarding the Sink: Where, Oh Where, Did Waters Go?*, p. 124; December 1, 2004, Ilene Cooper, review of *Shall I Knit You a Hat?: A Christmas Yarn*, p. 659; November 1, 2005, Shelle Rosenfeld, review of *Regarding the Trees: A Splintered Saga Rooted in Secrets*, p. 47;

May 1, 2006, Kathleen Odean, review of *Why Do You Cry?: Not a Sob Story,* p. 92; September 1, 2006, Shelle Rosenfeld, review of *Regarding the Bathroom: A Privy to the Past,* p. 129; October 15, 2006, Jennifer Hubert, review of *Far from Normal,* p. 45; August, 2007, Ilene Cooper, review of *Imagine Harry,* p. 69; November 1, 2007, Hazel Rochman, review of *Regarding the Bees: A Lesson in Letters on Honey, Dating, and Other Sticky Subjects,* p. 48; April 1, 2009, Ian Chipman, review of *Dying to Meet You,* p. 36; April 1, 2009, Ian Chipman, review of *Dying to Meet You,* p. 36.

Horn Book, May-June, 1998, Nancy Vasilakis, review of *Regarding the Fountain,* p. 345; May-June, 2001, Susan P. Brabander, review of *Trial by Journal,* p. 328; September-October, 2004, Susan P. Bloom, review of *Regarding the Sink,* p. 588; July-August, 2005, Susan Dove Lempke, review of *Deliver Us from Normal,* p. 471; September-October, 2005, Susan P. Bloom, review of *Regarding the Trees,* p. 582; November-December, 2006, Susan Dove Lempke, review of *Far from Normal,* p. 717; July-August, 2007, Kitty Flynn, review of *Imagine Harry,* p. 380; May-June, 2009, Sarah Ellis, review of *Dying to Meet You,* p. 299.

Kirkus Reviews, July 15, 2004, review of *Regarding the Sink,* p. 688; November 1, 2004, review of *Shall I Knit You a Hat?,* p. 1051; July 15, 2005, review of *Regarding the Trees,* p. 792; May 15, 2006, review of *Why Do You Cry?,* p. 519; July 15, 2006, review of *Regarding the Bathrooms,* p. 725; September 15, 2006, review of *Far from Normal,* p. 958; May 15, 2007, review of *Imagine Harry;* July 1, 2007, review of *Regarding the Bees;* May 1, 2008, review of *Little Rabbit and the Night Mare;* March 1, 2009, review of *Dying to Meet You;* September 1, 2009, review of *Over My Dead Body.*

Kliatt, March, 2005, Nola Theiss, review of *Deliver Us from Normal;* November, 2006, Janis Flint-Ferguson, review of *Far from Normal,* p. 45.

New York Times Book Review, September 20, 1998, review of *Regarding the Fountain,* p. 32; December 19, 2004, J.D. Biersdorfer, review of *Shall I Knit You a Hat?,* p. 26; May 16, 2010, Jerry Griswold, review of *Stand Straight, Ella Kate: The True Story of a Real Giant,* p. 16.

Publishers Weekly, April 30, 2001, review of *Trial by Journal,* p. 78; September 27, 2004, review of *Shall I Knit You a Hat?,* p. 61; May 1, 2006, review of *Why Do You Cry?,* p. 62; July 9, 2007, review of *Imagine Harry,* p. 56; June 16, 2008, review of *Little Rabbit and the Night Mare,* p. 47; April 13, 2009, review of *Dying to Meet You,* p. 49; February 22, 2010, review of *Little Rabbit and the Meanest Mother on Earth,* p. 66; April 26, 2010, review of *Stand Straight, Ella Kate,* p. 107.

School Library Journal, June, 1998, Rita Soltan, review of *Regarding the Fountain,* p. 147; June, 1999, Connie Tyrrell Burns, review of *Letters from Camp,* p. 132; June, 2001, Sharon McNeil, review of *Trial by Journal,* p. 152; October, 2004, Jean Gaffney, review of *Regarding the Sink,* p. 170; November, 2005, Cheryl Ashton, review of *Regarding the Trees,* p. 138; July,

2006, Robin L. Gibson, review of *Why Do You Cry?,* p. 80; August, 2006, Wendy Woodfill, review of *Regarding the Bathrooms,* p. 123; December, 2006, Rebecca Stine, review of *Far from Normal,* p. 148; June, 2007, Suzanne Myers Harold, review of *Imagine Harry,* p. 110; September, 2007, Diana Pierce, review of *Regarding the Bees,* p. 200; August, 2008, Susannah Richards, review of *Little Rabbit and the Night Mare,* p. 96; May, 2009, Michele Shaw, review of *Dying to Meet You,* p. 112; October, 2009, Elaine E. Knight, review of *Over My Dead Body,* p. 129; March, 2010, Catherine Callegari, review of *Little Rabbit and the Meanest Mother on Earth,* p. 122.

Voice of Youth Advocates, April, 2007, Anita Beaman, review of *Far from Normal,* p. 52.

ONLINE

Kate and Sarah Klise Home Page, http://www.kateand sarahklise.com (October 20, 2010).*

*   *   *

KNEEN, Maggie 1957-

Personal

Born 1957, in Liverpool, England. *Education:* Attended Southport Art College; Liverpool Polytechnic, B.A. (illustration); Central School of Art and Design (now St. Martin's School of Art and Design), M.A. (graphic design); attended University College London. *Hobbies and other interests:* Travel, medieval history.

Addresses

Home—Cheshire, England. *Agent*—Eunice McMullen, Low Ibbotsholme Cottage, Off Bridge La., Troutbeck Bridge, Windermere, Cumbria LA23 1HY, England.

Career

Author and illustrator. Worked in advertising for five years, beginning c. 1988; freelance illustrator of children's books, beginning 1989.

Writings

SELF-ILLUSTRATED

Hamlet and the Tales of Sniggery Woods, Henry Holt (New York, NY), 2009.
Chocolate Moose, Dutton Children's Books (New York, NY), 2011.

ILLUSTRATOR

The Twelve Days of Christmas, Harper Collins (London, England), 1992, Dutton Children's Books (New York, NY), 1998.

"Too Many Cooks—", and Other Proverbs, Green Tiger Press (New York, NY), 1992.

The Great Egg Hunt, Templar (Dorking, England), 1993, Chronicle Books (San Francisco, CA), 1994.

A.J. Wood, *Who's Getting Ready for Christmas?,* Chronicle Books (San Francisco, CA), 1993.

Rumer Godden, *Cockcrow to Starlight: A Day Full of Poetry,* Macmillan (London, England), 1996.

When You're Not Looking: A Storytime Counting Book, Simon & Schuster Books for Young Readers (New York, NY), 1996.

Kate Summers, *Milly and Tilly: The Story of a Town Mouse and a Country Mouse,* Dutton Children's Books (New York, NY), 1997.

Dugald Steer, *An Accidental Christmas,* Millbrook Press (Brookfield, CT), 1998.

Kate Summers, *Milly's Wedding,* Orion (London, England), 1998, Dutton Children's Books (New York, NY), 1999.

Tim Preston, *The Lonely Scarecrow,* Dutton Children's Books (New York, NY), 1999.

A.J. Wood, *The Golden Egg,* Chronicle Books (San Francisco, CA), 2000.

Cynthia Rylant, *Thimbleberry Stories,* Harcourt Brace (San Diego, CA), 2000.

Miriam Moss, *The Snow Bear,* Templar (Dorking, England), 2000, Dutton (New York, NY), 2001.

Shirley Menendez, *Allie, the Christmas Spider,* Dutton Children's Books (New York, NY), 2002.

Joanne Ryder, *Mousetail Moon,* Henry Holt (New York, NY), 2002.

Ronne Randall, *The Hanukkah Mice,* Chronicle Books (San Francisco, CA), 2002.

Angela McAllister, *Night-night, Little One,* Random House Children's Books (New York, NY), 2003.

Christine Tagg, *The Perfect Present,* Templar (Dorking, England), 2003, published as *The Very Special Valentine,* Chronicle Books (San Francisco, CA), 2004.

The Halloween Kittens, Chronicle Books (San Francisco, CA), 2004.

Billy Collins, *Daddy's Little Boy,* HarperCollins (New York, NY), 2004.

Bobby Burke, *Daddy's Little Girl,* HarperCollins (New York, NY), 2004.

A.J. Wood, The Christmas Hat, Templar (Dorking, England), 2004.

Anthony Knott, *An Angel Came to Nazareth,* Templar (Dorking, England), 2004, Chronicle Books (San Francisco, CA), 2005.

Dick King-Smith, *Babe: The Gallant Pig*, twentieth-anniversary edition, Knopf (London, England), 2004, Knopf (New York, NY), 2005.

Judy West, *The Lily Pad Ball,* Templar (Dorking, England), 2005.

E.B. White, *Some Pig!: A Charlotte's Web Picture Book,* HarperCollins (New York, NY), 2007.

Joanne Ryder, *Toad by the Road: A Year in the Life of These Amazing Amphibians,* Henry Holt (New York, NY), 2007.

E.B. White, *Wilbur's Adventure: A Charlotte's Web Picture Book,* HarperCollins (New York, NY), 2008.

Emily Hawkins, *Two by Two,* Templar (Dorking, England), 2008.

Emily Hawkins, *Little Fox and the Lost Goose,* Templar (Dorking, England), 2008, published as *Little Snow Goose,* Dutton (New York, NY), 2009.

E.B. White, *No Ordinary Mouse: A Stuart Little Picture Book,* HarperCollins (New York, NY), 2010.

Christine Brodien-Jones, *The Owl Keeper,* Delacorte Press (New York, NY), 2010.

Chocolate Moose, Dutton Children's Books (New York, NY), 2011.

Contributor to periodicals, including *Fighting Fantasy.*

Sidelights

A prolific artist whose detailed, soft-edged images of animal characters also reflect her love of nature, Maggie Kneen has become beloved by many fans of children's books. Beginning with her first illustration project, a 1992 edition of the traditional, holiday-themed song "The Twelve Days of Christmas," Kneen has gone on to bring to life tales by Kate Summers, Tim Preston,

Maggie Kneen's detailed art brings to life Joanne Ryder's nature-themed story in **Mouse Tail Moon.** (Henry Holt and Company, 2002. Illustrations copyright © 2002 by Maggie Kneen. All rights reserved. Reprinted by permission of Henry Holt and Company, LLC.)

Miriam Moss, Cynthia Rylant, Bobbie Burke, and A.J. Wood, among other writers. In 2004 she was also chosen to illustrate the twentieth-anniversary edition of Dick King-Smith's beloved children's story *Babe: The Gallant Pig,* which is considered to be a modern classic. With the beginning chapter book *Hamlet and the Tales of Sniggery Woods* Kneen also marked her debut as a children's author, and she has continued to pair her original stories with her detailed paintings in the humorous picture book *Chocolate Moose.*

"Art was what I did best, so that's what I pursued," Kneen noted on her home page in discussing her career as an illustrator. During her college years, however, her passion lay in the areas of history and archaeology, and while earning her academic credentials in illustration and graphic design at Liverpool Art College and London's Central School of Art and Design, respectively, she also went on archeological digs in both England and Italy. After working for five years as a graphic artist, Kneen recognized that her true calling lay in children's-book illustration and British publishers agreed.

Citing the "lovely, detailed soft-pastel" artwork Kneen creates to pair with Rylant's *Thimbleberry Stories,* Barbara Buckley added in *School Library Journal* that the images "emphasize the rural setting" of Rylant's four animal-centered tales. For a *Publishers Weekly* the same book evoked the work of Beatrix Potter, Kneen's "warm, cheerful illustrations complement[ing] the text with quaint settings." In reviewing *The Lonely Scarecrow,* a story by Tim Preston, a *Publishers Weekly* critic noted that Kneen's "pleasingly plump animals look as snuggly as plush toys." Gay Lynn Van Vleck described Kneen's technique in Moss's *The Snow Bear* as "softened realism," while a *Kirkus Reviews* writer noted of the same book that "gentle illustrations" contribute to Moss's picture-book "tribute to the love of a child for its mother." *Toad by the Road: A Year in the Life of These Amazing Amphibians,* a poetic study of toad life with a text by Joanne Ryder, benefits from what a another *Kirkus Reviews* writer described as Kneen's "gentle illustrations in delicate shades of green and brown" that mix "naturalistic detail and touches of whimsy."

In Kneen's self-illustrated chapter book *Hamlet and the Tales of Sniggery Woods* readers meet a young pig named Hamlet Piggins, whose favorite pastime is making mud pies. When Hamlet inherits Uncle Alf's restaurant at a local market, he expands the menu with his unbridled creativity to the point at which his restaurant is transformed into a traveling school for creative cooks. In the book's three short chapters, Hamlet is aided by his friends, and the author/artist's "old-fashioned watercolor illustrations . . . are well suited to the story," according to *School Library Journal* critic Rebecca Dash. A "warm authorial voice permeates the inviting narrative," wrote a *Kirkus Reviews* writer in discussing *Ham-*

Kneen combines her characteristic soft-edged art with an original story in **Hamlet and the Tales of the Sniggery Woods.** (Reproduced by permission of Henry Holt and Company, LLC.)

let and the Tales of Sniggery Woods, the critic going on to praise the "vivid landscapes and soft vignettes [that] decorate each page of Kneen's "cozy and cheerful" chapter book.

Biographical and Critical Sources

PERIODICALS

Booklist, August, 1997, Ellen Mandel, review of *Milly and Tilly: The Story of a Town Mouse and a Country Mouse,* p. 1997; January 1, 1999, Kathy Broderick, review of *Milly's Wedding,* p. 891; October 1, 1999, GraceAnne A. DeCandido, review of *The Lonely Scarecrow,* p. 363; May 1, 2000, Lauren Peterson, review of *Thimbleberry Stories,* p. 1680; September 15, 2002, Hazel Rochman, review of *Allie, the Christmas Spider,* p. 246; January 1, 2003, Carolyn Phelan, review of *Mouse Tail Moon,* p. 900; April 1, 2007, Carolyn Phelan, review of *Toad by the Road: A Year in the Life of These Amazing Amphibians,* p. 51; November 1, 2009, Hazel Rochman, review of *Little Snow Goose,* p. 52.

Kirkus Reviews, September 1, 2001, review of *The Snow Bear,* p. 1297; October 1, 2002, review of *Mouse Tail Moon,* p. 1479; November 1, 2002, review of *Allie, the Christmas Spider,* p. 1622; February 15, 2003, review of *Night-Night, Little One,* p. 312; November 1, 2005, review of *An Angel Came to Nazareth: A Story of the First Christmas,* p. 1194; October 15, 2006, review of *Some Pig!: A Charlotte Web Picture Book,* p. 1081; March 1, 2007, review of *Toad by the Road,* p. 230; May 1, 2009, review of *Hamlet and the Tales of Sniggery Woods.*

Publishers Weekly, September 7, 1992, Elizabeth Devereaux, review of *The Twelve Days of Christmas,* p. 68; August 5, 1996, review of *When You're Not Looking: A Storytime Counting Book,* p. 440; May 26, 1997, review of *Milly and Tilly,* p. 84; November 30, 1998, review of *Milly's Wedding,* p. 70; August 23, 1999, review of *The Lonely Scarecrow,* p. 56;; April 17, 2000, review of *Thimbleberry Stories,* p. 81; September 3, 2001, review of *The Snow Bear,* p. 86; November 11, 2002, review of *Mouse Tail Moon,* p. 67; December 9, 2002, review of *Night-Night, Little One,* p. 81; September 26, 2005, review of *An Angel Came to Nazareth: A Story of the First Christmas,* p. 87.

School Library Journal, May, 2000, Barbara Buckley, review of *Thimbleberry Stories,* p. 154; October, 2001, review of *The Christmas Surprise,* p. 71, and Gay Lynn Van Vleck, review of *The Snow Bear,* p. 126; October, 2002, Eva Mitnick, review of *Allie, the Chrismas Spider,* p. 61; February, 2003, Dona Ratterree, review of *Mouse Tail Moon,* p. 137; March, 2003, Carolyn Janssen, review of *Night-Night, Little One,* p. 198; May, 2004, Bina Williams, review of *Daddy's Little Girl,* p. 129; June, 2004, Rachel G. Payne, review of *Daddy's Little Boy,* p. 125; April, 2007, Joy Fleishhacker, review of *Toad by the Road,* p. 126; June, 2009, Rebecca Dash, review of *Hamlet and the Tales of Sniggery Woods,* p. 92; October, 2009, Laura Stanfield, review of *Little Snow Goose,* p. 94; May, 2010, Necia Blundy, review of *The Owl Keeper,* p. 106.

ONLINE

Maggie Kneen Home Page, http://www.maggie-kneen.com (October 20, 2010).*

* * *

KRENINA, Katya 1968-

Personal

Born June 15, 1968, in Lviv, Ukraine; daughter of Anatoli (a professor of foreign languages) and Alla (a nurse and skin-care specialist) Olshanetski. *Education:* Lviv Academy of Art, advanced degree (textile and tapestry design; with honors), 1989; Tompkins Cortland Community College, A.A., 1993; Syracuse University, B.F.A. (illustration), 1994, M.F.A. (illustration).

Addresses

Home—P.O. Box 33, Fayetteville, NY 13066. *E-mail*—kren@worldnet.att.net.

Career

Illustrator. Worked in Russia as a graphics designer; Ithaca Refugee Assistance Program, Ithaca, NY, interpreter and case worker, 1992-93; Syracuse Jewish Federation, Syracuse, NY, acculturation coordinator for new Americans, 1993-94; Syracuse Language Systems, Syracuse, designer and illustrator, 1995; freelance illustrator of children's books, beginning 1995.

Member

Society of Children's Book Writers and Illustrators.

Illustrator

Eric A. Kimmel, *The Magic Dreidels: A Hanukkah Story,* Holiday House (New York, NY), 1996.

Charlotte Herman, *How Yussel Caught the Gefilte Fish: A Shabbos Story,* Dutton (New York, NY), 1998.

Marlene Targ Brill, *Tooth Tales from around the World,* Charlesbridge (Watertown, MA), 1998.

Lisa McCourt, *Chicken Soup for Little Souls: A Dog of My Own,* Health Communications (Hollywood, FL), 1998.

J. Patrick Lewis, *The House of Boo,* Atheneum (New York, NY), 1998.

Dee Lillegard, *Balloons, Balloons, Balloons,* Dutton (New York, NY), 1999.

J. Patrick Lewis, *At the Wish of the Fish: A Russian Folktale,* Atheneum Books for Young Readers (New York, NY), 1999.

Eric A. Kimmel, reteller, *The Birds' Gift: A Ukrainian Easter Story,* Holiday House (New York, NY), 1999.

Eric A. Kimmel, reteller, *A Cloak for the Moon,* Holiday House (New York, NY), 2001.

Shutta Crum, *Who Took My Hairy Toe?,* Albert Whitman (Morton Grove, IL), 2001.

Andrew Pelletier, *Sixteen Miles to Spring,* illustrated by Katya Krenina, Albert Whitman (Morton Grove, IL), 2002.

Eric A. Kimmel, reteller, *The Castle of the Cats,* Holiday House (New York, NY), 2004.

Eric A. Kimmel, reteller, *The Mysterious Guests: A Sukkot Story,* Holiday House (New York, NY), 2008.

Eric A. Kimmel, reteller, *The Spider's Gift: A Ukrainian Christmas Story,* Holiday House (New York, NY), 2010.

Sidelights

Born in the Ukraine, Katya Krenina brings an eastern European folk-art element to the illustrations she creates for children's picture books. Krenina designed textiles after studying design at the Lvov Academy of Art, then immigrated to the United States where she worked as a translator and interpreter while completing her master's degree in illustration at Syracuse University. Although she has created art for the stories of a number of writers, many of Krenina's illustrations bring to life

folk-tale retellings by Eric A. Kimmel that include *A Cloak for the Moon, The Castle of the Cats,* and *The Mysterious Guests: A Sukkot Story.*

One of Krenina's earliest illustration projects, Marlene Targ Brill's *Tooth Tales from around the World,* shares the many stories and traditions about human teeth, from the American tooth fairy to the beliefs of ancient cultures. Reviewing the illustrations that shape Brill's text, Ilene Cooper described them in *Booklist* as "eye-catching" and "suffused with whimsy." Other books include *How Yussel Caught the Gefilte Fish: A Shabbos Story* Charlotte Herman's story about a simple-minded boy, *At the Wish of the Fish: A Russian Folktale* by J. Patrick Lewis, and Andrew Pelletier's *Sixteen Miles to Spring,* the last a fable in which two boys travel north and carry warmer weather in their wake. Describing the story as "a playful explanation" for the shift from winter to spring, Ellen Mandel added in her *Booklist* review that *Sixteen Miles to Spring* "is given colorful substance and texture through Krenina's spirited paintings."

Working with Kimmel on the Jewish folktale *A Cloak for the Moon,* Krenina creates gouache paintings surrounded by "intricate borders that echo Chinese and Persian design" in their "exotic richness," according to *Booklist* contributor GraceAnne A. DeCandido. Kim-

mel's story is based on the tale of an eighteenth-century rabbi and focuses on a tailor named Haskel who determines to make the moon a shining cloak so that she will be warmed in the cold night sky. Citing the "graceful details" in Kimmel's text, a *Publishers Weekly* contributor added that in *A Cloak for the Moon* Krenina "effectively depicts the Middle and Far Eastern setting of the tale, as well as its timeless sensibility." "The unusual artwork is the attention getter here," noted Julie Cummins in her *Booklist* review of Kimmel's *The Castle of the Cats,* a story from Krenina's native Ukraine, while in another collaboration, *The Mysterious Guests,* the artist's "dark, rich paintings support the folktale flavor of the original story," according to *School Library Journal* contributor Heidi Estrin.

"Book illustration combines my interest in reading, language, and art," Krenina once told *SATA.* "When I first came to the United States from Ukraine, I worked as a translator and interpreter. Being an illustrator is a lot like being a translator: I am always aware of the written word, my own vision, and my audience when 'translating' a story into art.

"My interest in children's books comes from my childhood and the fact that my parents read to me a lot. I come from a reading culture where books were considered treasures, collected, exchanged between friends, and literally read to pieces. I remember reading a book and feeling a need to draw characters and costumes, to create my own visual world. A book is like the stage of a theater, where all the moods and settings are my creations.

"I work in my studio every day. I approach a new manuscript by reading it many times and taking written notes on all associations and ideas that come to mind. Some illustrators have steps they follow when working on a project (taking reference photographs first, working on composition, and so on). My approach is more intuitive in nature. The only constant in my work is that I put all my love and soul into each book."

Biographical and Critical Sources

PERIODICALS

Booklist, September 1, 1996, Hazel Rochman, review of *The Magic Dreidels: A Hanukkah Story,* p. 137; July, 1998, Ilene Cooper, review of *Tooth Tales from around the World,* p. 1884; September 1, 1998, Carolyn Phelan, review of *The House of Boo,* p. 133; February 1, 1999, Stephanie Zvirin, review of *How Yussel Caught the Gefilte Fish: A Shabbos Story,* p. 979; April 15, 1999, Susan Dove Lempke, review of *The Birds' Gift: A Ukrainian Easter Story,* p. 1533; June 1, 1999, Shelley Townsend-Hudson, review of *At the Wish of the Fish: A Russian Folktale,* p. 1833; July, 2001, GraceAnne A. DeCandido, review of *A Cloak*

Katya Krenina's artwork is paired with Eric A. Kimmel's folktale retelling in The Mysterious Guest, *a Jewish-themed tale.* (Illustrations copyright 2008 by Katya Krenina. Reproduced by permission of Holiday House, Inc.)

for the Moon, p. 2014; August, 2001, John Peters, review of *Who Took My Hairy Toe?,* p. 2124; May 1, 2002, Ellen Mandel, review of *Sixteen Miles to Spring,* p. 1535; October 15, 2004, Julie Cummins, review of *The Castle of the Cats,* p. 410; October 15, 2008, Ian Chipman, review of *The Mysterious Guests: A Sukkot Story,* p. 47.

Bulletin of the Center for Children's Books, September 27, 1996, review of *The Magic Dreidels.*

Kirkus Reviews, February 15, 2002, review of *Sixteen Miles to Spring,* p. 262; October 15, 2004, review of *The Castle of the Cats*; August 1, 2008, review of *The Mysterious Guests.*

Publishers Weekly, September 30, 1996, review of *The Magic Dreidels,* p. 67; February 22, 1999, review of *The Birds' Gift,* p. 94; May 31, 1999, review of *At the Wish of the Fish,* p. 93; February 16, 2001, review of *A Cloak for the Moon,* p. 85; September 15, 2008, review of *The Mysterious Guests,* p. 66.

School Library Journal, May, 2001, Anne Parker, review of *A Cloak for the Moon,* p. 126; October, 2001, DeAnn Tabuchi, review of *Who Took My Hairy Toe?,* p. 137; June, 2002, Wendy S. Carroll, review of *Sixteen Miles to Spring,* p. 107; November, 2004, Grace Oliff, review of *The Castle of Cats,* p. 126; October, 2008, Heidi Estrin, review of *The Mysterious Guests,* p. 114.

ONLINE

Charlesbridge Publishing Web site, http://www.charlesbridge.com/ (October 30, 2010), "Katya Krenina."

Katya Krenina Home Page, http://www.katyakrenina.com (October 30, 2010).*

L

LACHENMEYER, Nathaniel 1969-

Personal

Born 1969; son of Charles (a professor) and Juliana (a psychologist) Lachenmeyer; married; children: one son, one daughter. *Education:* University of Chicago, degree, 1991.

Addresses

Home—GA. *E-mail*—NL@Nathaniellachenmeyer.com.

Career

Author of fiction, nonfiction, and comic books. Advocate and lecturer on mental-health and homelessness issues.

Awards, Honors

Monteiro Lobato award (Brazil), for *Broken Beaks;* Washington State Library Washington Reads selection, 2008, for *Searching for Sasquatch.*

Writings

The Outsider: A Journey into My Father's Struggle with Madness, Broadway Books (New York, NY), 2000.
Broken Beaks, illustrated by Robert Ingpen, [Australia], 2003.
Thirteen: The Story of the World's Most Popular Superstition, Thunder's Mouth Press (New York, NY), 2004.
Searching for Sasquatch, illustrated by Vicki Bradley, Sasquatch Books (Seattle, WA), 2006.
The Decoy, illustrated by Christian Slade, Mitten Press (Ann Arbor, MI), 2007.
The Origami Master, illustrated by Aki Sogabe, Albert Whitman & Company (Morton Grove, IL), 2008.

Author's work has been translated into Portuguese, Chinese, and Korean.

Sidelights

Nathaniel Lachenmeyer is an author whose first book, *The Outsider: A Journey into My Father's Struggle with Madness,* chronicles his attempt to understand the progression of his father's mental illness. *Broken Beaks,* an award-winning picture book that also deals with themes of mental illness and homelessness, marked Lachenmeyer's first work for children, a genre that he has continued to pursue while lecturing and advocating in the area of mental health and wellness.

The Outsider focuses on Lachenmeyer's father, who suffered from schizophrenia, a disease that caused his son to be frightened of him as a child and eventually cut his father out of his life entirely. Charles Lachenmeyer's difficulties began with the loss of his job as a professor of sociology at New York's Hunter College in the mid-1970s, and continued until he left his wife and child in 1981. In 1995, Lachenmeyer was notified that his father had been found in a flophouse in Burlington, Vermont, dead from a heart attack. Father and son had been estranged for more than five years. Struck by the loss, Lachenmeyer took a camera crew and set out to try and trace his father's last few years in an effort to understand what had caused the man's descent into homelessness. He used the return addresses on letters to find the people his father had associated with, including a number of doctors and nurses who could provide more precise information on the man's medical history. Charles had subsisted on government assistance and disability for years before a bureaucratic mix up left him penniless and living on the streets. When Lachenmeyer visited the area in which his father had died, he found that most of the local shopkeepers, as well as their patrons, were familiar with the homeless man.

The Outsider is a compilation of numerous interviews Lachenmeyer conducted over the course of his quest. Gilbert Taylor, in a review for *Booklist,* called Lachenmeyer's effort "a consolingly powerful memoir, especially to readers with a mentally ill parent." A contributor for *Publishers Weekly* remarked that the book is "a

Nathaniel's Lachenmeyer's picture-book story for **The Origami Master** *is brought to life in Aki Sogabe's cut-paper art.* (Reproduced by permission of Albert Whitman & Company.)

heartrending portrait of a man whose emotional illness eventually robbed him of everything, counterbalanced in part by the author's gradual understanding of the plight of homeless people," and a reviewer for *Psychology Today* stated that Lachenmeyer's work "takes us on a spiraling descent into poverty, estrangement and isolation."

Since writing *The Outsider*, Lachenmeyer has channeled his talent for writing into other areas inspired by his curiosity and his interests. In *Thirteen: The Story of the World's Most Popular Superstition* he traces the history of triskaidekaphobia, or the fear of the number thirteen. He discusses several of the suspected origins of this fear, including the most popular origin, which is linked to the number of people in attendance at the biblical Last Supper. A contributor to *Kirkus Reviews* called the book "fast-paced and entertaining," while a reviewer for *Library Bookwatch* remarked that in *Thirteen* Lachenmeyer combines "fine historical insights" and "a fun survey of present-day phobic reactions." "A handy reference source," the book also "offers pleasure reading for the curious," according to Mary Ellen Snodgrass in *Kliatt*, while Richard Morrison dubbed *Thirteen* "an amusing exposé of the Friday the 13th nonsense" in his London *Times* appraisal.

Lachenmeyer turns to younger readers in creating the picture books *Searching for Sasquatch, The Decoy*, and *The Origami Master*. Illustrated by Vicki Bradley, *Searching for Sasquatch* focuses on an amateur cryptozoologist—a man who studies what some consider to

be mythical creatures—who is joined by his son Arlo on a trek through the Pacific Northwest to track down the legendary Sasquatch, or Bigfoot. While father and son enjoy their hikes through the woods even more than they do the search for signs of the giant forest-dwelling man, the boy retains his belief in the possibility that there is such a creature as a Sasquatch, even when his classmates find the idea silly. Calling *Searching for Sasquatch* "a bit quirky," Mary Hazelton added in her *School Library Journal* review that Lachenmeyer's story is enriched by "a thread of sweetness and hope."

Featuring colorful cut-paper images by Washington artist Aki Sogabe, *The Origami Master* transports children to rural Japan, where Shima crafts his intricate origami creations in his mountain home. Outside the man's window, a curious warbler watches as small creatures are crafted out of paper. While Shima sleeps, the bird creates folded-paper creatures of its own, leaving them for the man to find each morning. When Shima hides and discovers the bird at its work, he cages it in the hope that he can capture its wisdom, but the bird proves to be far wiser than the man in the story's memorable ending. Lachenmeyer's "restrained original story will enrich multicultural studies" and inspire reflection in its young audiences, predicted *Booklist* contributor Linda Perkins. In *School Library Journal* Susan Scheps also cited Lachenmeyer's "spare text" as well as Sogabe's "colorful cut paper and watercolor illustrations" among the book's strengths, and a *Kirkus Reviews* writer recommended *The Origami Master* as "a serene lesson about the futility of cages."

Biographical and Critical Sources

PERIODICALS

Booklist, March 1, 2000, Gilbert Taylor, review of *The Outsider: A Journey into My Father's Struggle with Madness,* p. 1183; October 1, 2008, Linda Perkins, review of *The Origami Master,* p. 48.

Contemporary Review, April, 2005, review of *Thirteen: The Story of the World's Most Popular Superstition,* p. 255.

Kirkus Reviews, August 15, 2004, review of *Thirteen,* p. 790; August 1, 2008, review of *The Origami Master.*

Kliatt, November, 2005, Mary Ellen Snodgrass, review of *Thirteen,* p. 32.

Library Bookwatch, February, 2005, review of *Thirteen.*

Library Journal, February 1, 2000, Mary Ann Hughes, review of *The Outsider,* p. 105.

Psychology Today, March-April, 2002, "On Sexuality, Spirituality, Schizophrenia, and More," p. 77.

Publishers Weekly, February 7, 2000, review of *The Outsider,* p. 74.

School Library Journal, October, 2007, Mary Hazelton, review of *Searching for Sasquatch,* p. 120; October, 2008, Susan Scheps, review of *The Origami Master,* p. 114.

Time, April 4, 1997, James Willwerth, "This Is My Father's Life," p. 4.

Times (London, England), December 30, 2004, Richard Morrison, review of *Thirteen,* p. 2.

ONLINE

Nathaniel Lachenmeyer Home Page, http://www.nathaniel lachenmeyer.com (October 20, 2010).*

*   *   *

LaFLEUR, Suzanne 1983-

Personal

Born 1983, in MA. *Education:* Washington & Lee University, B.A. (English and European history; with honors); New School University, M.F.A. (writing for children). *Hobbies and other interests:* Swimming, travel, animated cartoons, sharing stories.

Addresses

Agent—Curtis Brown, Ltd., 10 Astor Pl., New York, NY 10003. *E-mail*—suzlafleur@gmail.com.

Career

Author and educator.

Awards, Honors

Waterstone's Children's Book Prize shortlist, Red House Children's Book Award shortlist, Redbridge Children's Book Award in children's category, and Spellbinding Cumbrian Secondary Schools Book Award in year 7-8 category, all 2010, all for *Love, Aubrey.*

Writings

Love, Aubrey, Wendy Lamb Books (New York, NY), 2009.

Author's work has been translated into German, Korean, Dutch, Swedish, and Indonesian.

Sidelights

Suzanne LaFleur grew up near Boston, Massachusetts, and then attended Washington & Lee University, where she earned honors in her double major: English and European history. She then went to New York City and earned an M.F.A. in writing for children at The New School. While a student, La Fleur wrote the manuscript for her first novel, *Love, Aubrey.*

In *Love, Aubrey* readers meet an eleven year old who is coping with the loss of her father and little sister in a recent car accident. With her mother unable to cope with her own grief and unwilling to care for her remaining daughter, Aubrey is left alone with only her pet fish to comfort her. Fortunately, Gram arrives and takes Aubrey to live with her in northern New England. In Gram's secure home, the girl is able to come to terms with her emotions and also develop close friendships with several children living in her grandmother's neighborhood. When her mother returns and wants to resume parenting, her arrival presents another potential upheaval and Aubrey must decide where her true family resides.

LaFleur's ability to capture the visceral stages of grief in her mix of first-person narrative and unmailed letters is one of the highlights of her debut novel; as Faith Brautigam wrote in *School Library Journal,* in *Love, Aubrey* the author "details the physical responses of the human body to emotional trauma with an immediacy that puts readers inside Aubrey's pain and loss." Aubrey's "detailed progression from denial to acceptance makes her both brave and credible," observed a *Kirkus Reviews* writer, and in *Booklist* Melanie Koss wrote that LaFleur's "heartbreaking and honest" fiction debut "is devastating, humorous, sad, and, most of all,

Cover of Suzanne LaFleur's elementary-grade novel Love, Aubrey, *which finds a young girl learning how to cope with the loss of both parents.* (Wendy Lamb Books, 2009. Used by permission of Wendy Lamb Books, an imprint of Random House Children's Books, a division of Random House, Inc.)

real." Brautigam recommended *Love, Aubrey* as "an excellent choice" for readers grappling with grief, and the *Kirkus Reviews* contributor dubbed the book "honest and realistic portrayal of grief."

On her home page, LaFleur shares writing tips with young writers. "Your story should have a life of its own inside your imagination," she explained. "Make sure you are not worrying too much about what you are writing; instead, listen to your narrator to let the story unfold naturally. You will be very surprised at what you find, and how easy it is to tell the story this way."

Biographical and Critical Sources

PERIODICALS

Booklist, August 1, 2009, Melanie Koss, review of *Love, Aubrey,* p. 67.
Bulletin of the Center for Children's Books, September, 2009, Deborah Stevenson, review of *Love, Aubrey,* p. 27.
Kirkus Reviews, May 1, 2009, review of *Love, Aubrey.*
Publishers Weekly, June 29, 2009, review of *Love, Aubrey,* p. 129.
School Library Journal, September, 2009, Faith Brautigam, review of *Love, Aubrey,* p. 164.

ONLINE

Suzanne LaFleur Home Page, http://www.suzannelafleur. com (October 15, 2010).

*   *   *

LANG, Glenna 1951-

Personal

Born 1951; children. *Education:* University of Chicago, B.A., 1972; Tufts University/School of the Museum of Fine Arts, M.F.A. (printmaking), 1975.

Addresses

Home—Cambridge, MA. *E-mail*—glennalang@earth link.net.

Career

Illustrator and graphic designer. Twocat Graphics (studio), founder. Instructor in printmaking at Art Institute of Boston, Lesley University, and Framingham State College; teacher of illustration and design at School of the Museum of Fine Arts, beginning 1998.

Awards, Honors

American Booksellers Pick-of-the-List selection, 1989, for *My Shadow;* Parent's Guide to Children's Media Award, 1998, for *The Runaway;* Schneider Family Book Award, American Library Association, Dog Writers Association of America Award, Massachusetts Guide Dog Users Association Award, and Young Hoosier Award nomination, all c. 2001, all for *Looking out for Sarah;* (with Marjory Wunsch) *New York Times* Notable Book designation, *Smithsonian* magazine Notable Book designation, and Boston Authors Club award, all 2009, all for *Genius of Common Sense.*

Writings

SELF-ILLUSTRATED

Looking out for Sarah, Charlesbridge (Watertown, MA), 2001.
(With Marjory Wunsch) *Genius of Common Sense: Jane Jacobs and the Story of "The Death and Life of Great American Cities,"* David R. Godine (Boston, MA), 2009.

ILLUSTRATOR

Nancy A. Smith, *Old Furniture: Understanding the Craftsman's Art,* Little, Brown (Boston, MA), 1975.
Robert Louis Stevenson, *My Shadow,* David R. Godine (Boston, MA), 1989.
James Whitcomb Riley, *When the Frost Is on the Punkin,* David R. Godine (Boston, MA), 1991.
Henry Wadsworth Longfellow, *The Children's Hour,* David R. Godine (Boston, MA), 1993.
Robert Frost, *The Runaway,* David R. Godine (Boston, MA), 1998.

Contributor to periodicals, including *American Recorder, Atlantic Monthly, Boston Review,* and *Boston Globe.*

Sidelights

Glenna Lang is an artist and printmaker who lives in Cambridge, Massachusetts, and teaches at Boston's School of the Museum of Fine Arts. In addition to creating editorial illustrations for newspapers and magazines, Lang has also designed book covers, posters, and promotional materials for businesses and various organizations. Beginning in the late 1980s, she began to create art for children's books and in 2001 produced her first original self-illustrated picture book, *Looking out for Sarah.* In addition to illustrating books for children, Lang has also acted on her interest in the urban landscape and the evolution of cities by coauthoring the highly praised nonfiction book *Genius of Common Sense: Jane Jacobs and the Story of "The Death and Life of Great American Cities."*

In Lang's first book-illustration projects her artwork was paired with classic texts by Robert Louis Stevenson, Henry Wadsworth Longfellow, Robert Frost, and

Glenna Lang's detailed graphic illustrations capture the timelessness of James Whitcomb Riley's **When the Frost Is on the Punkin.** (Copyright © 1991 by James Whitcomb Riley, Illustrations by Glenna Lang. Reprinted by permission of David R. Godine, Publisher, Inc.)

James Witcomb Riley. "The Children's Hour," a poem by Longfellow that captures his love for his three daughters, is teamed with well-researched artwork that features images of the poet's New England home and family, images that "gleam with light as they capture the poem's playful spirit," according to a *Publishers Weekly* critic. Reviewing Lang's artwork for Frost's "The Runaway," which captures a foal's experience of winter's first snowfall, *Booklist* critic Carolyn Phelan wrote that her characteristic "flat colors in muted shades" "are simple, pleasing, and accessible to young children," while a *Publishers Weekly* contributor maintained that the artist's "serene illustrations of a New England landscape give Frost's haunting, potentially disturbing poem a happy ending." An ode to autumn, Riley's "When the Frost Is on the Punkin" comes glowingly to life in Lang's "handsome paintings," according to another *Publishers Weekly* critic. As the reviewer added of this work, Lang "adroitly evoke[s] the season's richness" in images that feature "economical detailing and blocks of deep autumnal colors."

The award-winning *Looking out for Sarah,* Lang's first self-illustrated story, was inspired by Sarah Gregory Smith and her guide dog, Perry. Perry is a black Labrador retriever, and his friendly personality and love of treats make him a welcome sight as he guides Sarah along the streets and on and off the commuter rail as she undertakes errands or travels to her job as a musician and teacher. The highlight of Lang's story, which is told from Perry's point of view, is the dog's recollections of the three-hundred-mile walk from Boston to Manhattan that Sarah and Perry undertook as a way to alert the public about the importance of guide dogs. "The spare text and minimal detail in Lang's framed gouache paintings nicely convey the special personal/ professional relationship between dog and owner," wrote a *Horn Book* contributor in reviewing Lang's award-winning picture book. Noting that "the narrative is true to Perry's viewpoint," *Booklist* contributor Hazel Rochman added that Lang's art, "in bold, saturated colors and flat, well-defined shapes, is both childlike and sophisticated." In *Kirkus Reviews* a contributor praised *Looking out for Sarah* as "inspirational," and *School Library Journal* contributor Margaret C. Howell dubbed the work "a charming and informative look at the life of [a] . . . guide dog."

A collaboration with fellow artist Marjory Wunsch, *Genius of Common Sense* introduces young readers to New York City author and activist Jane Jacobs, who in 1961 published a book advocating for the preservation of traditional urban neighborhoods over bulldozing and rebuilding them. Jacobs' opinion was in opposition to advocates of "urban renewal" who believed in tearing down aging areas of cities and replacing them with new, high-rise apartments, shopping malls, and expressways. Illustrating their biography with contemporary and vintage photographs and their own drawings, Lang and Wunsch describe Jacobs' efforts to fight the highway that powerful government official Robert Moses proposed should be run through New York's Washington Square Park. They also evaluate her argument that sterile, modern environments are less conducive to building community than older, informal city neighborhoods. In *Horn Book* Barbara Bader praised the youthful portrait of Jacobs as "an independent-minded, outspoken girl," calling it "a crucial accomplishment" in a book geared for teens. "Lang and Wunsch are to be commended for introducing a fascinating female role model" in *Genius of Common Sense,* according to *School Library Journal* contributor Betty S. Evans, and Rochman predicted that the coauthors' "lively biography of a rebel activist will appeal to teen conservationists wherever they live." Writing in *Alternatives Journal,* Heather MacAndrew wrote that the book illuminates "how [Jacobs'] . . . activism grew from the strength of her convictions and her political savvy. The deliciously subversive but common-sense lessons in this book prod us to trust our own observations, challenge conventional wisdom, and protest with verve and imagination—and to remember to feed the people you're organizing."

"I have found that creating books, especially for young people, is an ideal way to combine my diverse interests," Lang told *SATA*. "All through grade school and high school I loved to write stories and poems. My best friend and I were also thought of as the class artists. So

in high school I edited the literary magazine, illustrated its cover, and designed the layout. In college I developed a special appreciation for architecture (Frank Lloyd Wright's Robie House was outside my dorm-room window), and I discovered printmaking.

"After immersing myself in printmaking for several years at the Museum School in Boston, I had to earn a living. I started freelancing as an illustrator for books, magazines, and newspapers and found gratification in complementing other people's texts with my artwork, either actual prints or 'mock' prints. On the side, I also took on writing and editing jobs. An art director at a publishing house for whom I freelanced suggested I submit a proposal for a children's book based on a classic poem. What a terrific idea, I thought, since I loved poetry *and* I had a two year old as a model and test audience.

"Each of my books derives from a passion. *My Shadow, When the Frost Is on the Punkin, The Children's Hour,* and *The Runaway* are all poems I loved as a child. I wanted young children to enjoy the sound of the words and understand them with the help of a visual narrative.

"As an animal lover and longtime dog owner, I'd always been in awe of guide dogs and wondered how they know what to do. I figured kids must wonder too. If I wrote a book for them, all of us would learn. I interviewed many guide dog owners (and their dogs) and gained so much from each of them. Because of the vi-

sual complexity of having a dog with an intricate harness and his owner in each picture, I needed an actual model. Sarah Smith's walk from Boston to New York gave an extra dimension to the story. She was enthusiastic about the book, had a terrific sense of humor, and was willing to put up with my following her everywhere with my camera. We had a great time working together and visiting schools after *Looking out for Sarah* came out.

"*Genius of Common Sense* grew out of another long-held passion, which I often depicted in my personal artwork: cities, old neighborhoods, and the lively urban mix that Jane Jacobs described in her revolutionary 1961 book, *The Death and Life of Great American Cities. Genius* started out as an illustrated picture book for younger children with fellow illustrator Marjory Wunsch, but my perspicacious publisher, David Godine, saw in the material an empowerment book for young adults. I agreed that Jacobs, with her curiosity, method of observation, independent-thinking, and activism, presented a wonderful role model. It was a thrill to write, research, and find vintage photos about this remarkable heroine who challenged the Establishment and ultimately changed the world by stopping the large-scale bulldozing of urban neighborhoods. And Marjory and I added an unusual touch for a young-adult book: to set the tone in a way that photos could not, we each drew illustrations as chapter openers."

Biographical and Critical Sources

PERIODICALS

Alternatives, July, 2007, Heather MacAndrew, review of *Genius of Common Sense: Jane Jacobs and the Story of "The Death and Life of Great American Cities."*

Booklist, March 1, 1993, Carolyn Phelan, review of *The Runaway,* p. 1216; November 1, 2001, Hazel Rochman, review of *Looking out for Sarah,* p. 483; September 1, 2009, Hazel Rochman, review of *Genius of Common Sense,* p. 79.

Canadian Review of Materials, February 12, 2010, Val Ken Lem, review of *Genius of Common Sense.*

Horn Book, September, 2001, review of *Looking out for Sarah,* p. 575; July-August, 2009, Barbara Bader, review of *Genius of Common Sense,* p. 440.

Kirkus Reviews, August 1, 2001, review of *Looking out for Sarah,* p. 1127.

New York Times Book Review, May 10, 2009, Ruth Conniff, review of *Genius of Common Sense,* p. 14.

Publishers Weekly, December 6, 1991, review of *When The Frost Is on the Punkin,* p. 72; October 11, 1993, review of *The Children's Hour,* p. 87; December 21, 1998, review of *The Runaway,* p. 66; August 27, 2001, review of *Looking out for Sarah,* p. 87.

Resource Links, February, 2010, Alison Edwards, review of *Genius of Common Sense,* p. 38.

Lang collaborates with fellow artist Marjory Wunsch on the biography **Genius of Common Sense.** (Copyright © Author & Illustrator by Glenna Lang and Marjory Wunsch. Reprinted by permission of David R. Godine, Publisher, Inc.)

School Library Journal, September, 2001, Margaret C. Howell, review of *Looking out for Sarah,* p. 193; April, 2009, Betty S. Evans, review of *Genius of Common Sense,* p. 149.

ONLINE

Glenna Lang Home Page, http://www.glennalang.com (October 15, 2010).
School of the Museum of Fine Arts Web site, http://www.smfa.edu/ (October 15, 2010), "Glenna Lang."

*   *   *

LAROCHE, Giles 1956-

Personal

Born July 1, 1956, in Berlin, NH; son of Romeo and Claire Laroche. *Education:* Montserrat College of Art, degree, 1981. *Hobbies and other interests:* Travel, hiking.

Addresses

Home—Salem, MA. *E-mail*—giles@gileslaroche.com.

Career

Artist and illustrator of children's books, with studios in Salem, MA, and Washington, NH. Artist in resident at numerous schools, beginning c. 1990. *Exhibitions:* Paintings, drawings, and illustrations exhibited nationally, including by Society of Illustrators, New York, NY.

Awards, Honors

Notable Book for a Global Society Honor Book designation, International Reading Association, 2001, for *Sacred Places* by Philemon Sturges.

Writings

SELF-ILLUSTRATED

What's Inside?, Houghton Mifflin (Boston, MA), 2009.

ILLUSTRATOR

Lois Lenski, *Sing a Song of People,* Little, Brown (Boston, MA), 1987.
Rachel Field, *General Store,* Little, Brown (Boston, MA), 1988.
Rachel Field, *A Road Might Lead to Anywhere,* Little, Brown (Boston, MA), 1990.
Dayle Ann Dodds, *The Color Box,* Little, Brown (Boston, MA), 1992.

Lee Bennett Hopkins, editor, *Ragged Shadows: Poems of Halloween Night,* Little, Brown (Boston, MA), 1993.
Philemon Sturges, *Bridges Are to Cross,* Putnam's (New York, NY), 1998.
Philemon Sturges, *Sacred Places,* Putnam's (New York, NY), 2000.
Ann Fearrington, *Who Sees the Lighthouse?,* Putnam's (New York, NY), 2002.
Philemon Sturges, *Down to the Sea in Ships,* Putnam's (New York, NY), 2005.
April Jones Prince, *What Do Wheels Do All Day?,* Houghton Mifflin (Boston, MA), 2006.
What's Inside?: Fascinating Structures around the World, Houghton Mifflin (Boston, MA), 2009.

Sidelights

Described by their creator as "paper relief," Giles Laroche's intricate cut-paper-collage illustrations are a feature of his original picture book *What's Inside?: Fascinating Structures around the World* as well as of picture books featuring texts by authors that include Lois Lenski, Dayle Ann Dodds, Philemon Sturges, and Rachel Field. Reviewing April Jones Prince's *What Do Wheels Do All Day?,* a story geared for young boys, *Horn Book* critic Lolly Robinson cited Laroche's "impressive bas-relief cut-paper collages" as among the book's strengths, while Ann Fearrington's *Who Sees the Lighthouse?* was lauded by *Booklist* critic Ilene Cooper as a "celebration of lighthouses" that is also "a wonder of paper craft."

Laroche was inspired to begin his work as an illustrator while working as an assistant at an architectural firm in Cambridge, Massachusetts, as well as by his own explorations with paper in his art studio in Salem, Massachusetts, during the 1980s. His paper-relief technique involves cutting, painting, and gluing up to seven or eight layers of paper within each image, spacing each layer to create the shadows that add a dimensional quality to his work. "I had always enjoyed the collage process," Laroche once told *SATA,* "and I began creating collages depicting scenes of medieval towns and colonial villages. In time my collages became more dimensional, and I found myself hand-coloring my own cut-out collage elements. Then I remembered children's books, and I thought that perhaps my paper reliefs would lend themselves well as book illustrations if they could be lit and photographed in an interesting and dramatic way." Reviewers of Laroche's published illustrations have suggested that the artist's cut-paper collages do indeed work well as illustrations for children's books, especially when a three-dimensional effect is desired.

Allowing children an up-close view of over a dozen of the world's most amazing feats of construction engineering, *What's Inside?* features layered cut-paper images that reproduce buildings both inside and out. As well as depicting structures from the underground tomb of Egypt's King Tutankamun to Sydney, Australia's Op-

era House and the Georgia Aquarium, Laroche includes specific facts about each structure, such as location, date of completion, materials, and special features. Calling *What's Inside?* a "beautiful book," Paula Willey added in *School Library Journal* that Laroche's sculptural images "are depicted with skill and charm" and feature an "intricacy [that] . . . will hold readers spellbound." Featuring a "trademark" style that mixes "drawing, painting, and cut paper," the artwork in *What's Inside?* is enhanced by "minute detail [that] celebrates the awe-inspiring constructions," according to *Booklist* contributor Hazel Rochman.

In Dayle Ann Dodd's *The Color Box* an adventurous monkey crawls into an empty box, only to discover that it is divided into little rooms, each with a hole leading into the next room, and each room being entirely of one color. As a concept book intended to teach little ones about color, Dodd's text may be almost unnecessary, according to *Booklist* reviewer Kay Weisman; instead, "Laroche's appealing cut-paper illustrations will entrance them." The three-dimensionality of Laroche's art is ideal for creating detail in the monochromatic mini-worlds of each two-page spread, reviewers noted. "The layers and shadows effectively distinguish and set off the various shades of the objects," wrote Steven Engelfried in his review of *The Color Box* for *School Library Journal.* The result is "a clever and splashy introduction to colors," concluded Liz Rosenberg in the *New York Times Book Review.*

Alexander the monkey travels through illustrator Giles Laroche's colorful cut-paper landscapes for **The Color Box** *by Dayle Ann Dodds.* (Text copyright © 1992 by Dayle Ann Dodds, Illustrations copyright © 1992 by Giles Laroche. By permission of Little Brown and Company.)

Laroche takes readers through the doors of one of the work's architectural wonders in his intricately crafted picture book **What's Inside?**

Laroche turned his familiarity with the architecture of Salem to advantage in creating the illustrations for Lee Bennett Hopkins' *Ragged Shadows: Poems of Halloween Night.* In this book, fourteen poems by various authors are illustrated with images of four young children in costume trailing through Salem trick-or-treating. The architectural possibilities of Laroche's cut-paper collages are again exploited in two works by Philemon Sturges: *Bridges Are to Cross* and *Sacred Places.* In the first of these collaborations, Sturges selected fifteen bridges, from the high-tech splendor of the Golden Gate Bridge in San Francisco to a 2,000-year-old Spanish aqueduct, thereby displaying a range of styles, technologies, and materials across time. A *Publishers Weekly* critic dubbed *Bridges Are to Cross* one of the best books of the year, and highlighted Laroche's "astonishing 3-D collage illustration." *School Library Journal* reviewer Ronald Jobe was more specific in his praise of the contribution made by Laroche's illustrations, writing of the book that "each bridge . . . has a luminescent quality to it, as if the light is radiating from within. What an effect!"

In *Sacred Places* Sturges offers a brief tour of nearly thirty places across five continents that are considered sacred by some religion. In her review of the work for *School Library Journal,* Patricia Lothrop-Green remarked that Laroche's illustrations offer more information than a photograph of the actual sites could: his "rich and detailed art balances architectural impact with situation, use, and cultural context as a photograph could never do," according to the critic. *Down to the Sea in Ships* marked another collaboration between Sturges and Laroche, and here author and illustrator team up to create what *Booklist* critic Gillian Engberg

described as a "beautifully illustrated" collection of verses honoring boats, from ancient Viking drakars to tall-masted war ships to modern auto ferries. Laroche's "stunning collages" outshine Sturges' text, according to Engberg, while in *School Library Journal* Teresa Pfeifer wrote of *Down to the Sea in Ships* that "author and illustrator work wonders together" in crafting the innovative picture book.

Biographical and Critical Sources

PERIODICALS

Booklist, May 1, 1992, Kay Weisman, review of *The Color Box,* pp. 1606-1607; August, 1993, Kathryn Broderick, review of *Ragged Shadows: Poems of Halloween Night,* p. 2067; October 1, 2000, Ilene Cooper, review

Laroche's detailed cut-paper art captures the dimensional aspect of the architecture in **Who Sees the Lighthouse?**

of *Sacred Places,* p. 360; November 15, 2002, Ilene Cooper, review of *Who Sees the Lighthouse?,* p. 609; May 15, 2005, Gillian Engberg, review of *Down to the Sea in Ships,* p. 1655; April 15, 2006, Carolyn Phelan, review of *What Do Wheels Do All Day?,* p. 50; February 15. 2009, Hazel Rochman, review of *What's Inside?: Fascinating Structures around the World,* p. 78.

Horn Book, May-June, 2006, Lolly Robinson, review of *What Do Wheels Do All Day?,* p. 299.

Kirkus Reviews, June 15, 2002, review of *Who Sees the Lighthouse?,* p. 879; April 15, 2005, review of *Down to the Sea in Ships,* p. 483; May 1, 2006, review of *What Do Wheels Do All Day?,* p. 465.

New York Times Book Review, May 17, 1992, Liz Rosenberg, review of *The Color Box,* p. 34.

Publishers Weekly, September 20, 1993, review of *Ragged Shadows,* p. 30; October 30, 2000, review of *Bridges Are to Cross,* p. 78; June 17, 2002, review of *Who Sees the Lighthouse?,* p. 63.

School Library Journal, June, 1992, Steven Engelfried, review of *The Color Box,* p. 92; December, 1998, Ronald Jobe, review of *Bridges Are to Cross,* p. 116; December, 2000, Patricia Lothrop-Green, review of *Sacred Places,* pp. 136-137; October, 2002, Laurie Von Mehren, review of *Who Sees the Lighthouse?,* p. 105; June, 2005, Teresa Pfeifer, review of *Down to the Sea in Ships,* p. 187; June, 2006, Janet S. Thompson, review of *What Do Wheels Do All Day?,* p. 140; May, 2009, Paula Willey, review of *What's Inside?,* p. 125.

ONLINE

Giles Laroche Home Page, http://www.gileslaroche.com (October 20, 2010).*

* * *

LITTMAN, Sarah Darer 1963-

Personal

Born 1963, in New York, NY; children: two. *Religion:* Jewish. *Hobbies and other interests:* Reading, traveling, playing tennis, swimming, building sand castles, going to hear live music.

Addresses

Home—Cos Cob, CT. *E-mail*—sarahdarerlittman@gmail.com.

Career

Writer and journalist. Worked previously as a financial analyst.

Awards, Honors

Sydney Taylor Award for Older Readers, Association for Jewish Libraries, 2006, for *Confessions of a Closet Catholic;* Best Books of the Year selection, Bank Street College of Education, 2010, for *Purge.*

Writings

Confessions of a Closet Catholic, Dutton Children's Books (New York, NY), 2005.
Purge, Scholastic Press (New York, NY), 2009.
Life, After, Scholastic Press (New York, NY), 2010.
Want to Go Private?, Scholastic Press (New York, NY), 2011.

Columnist for Hearst Newspapers CT and for *CTNews Junkie.com.*

Sidelights

Connecticut author Sarah Darer Littman started writing seriously only after realizing that she spent "too much time trying to please other people instead of following my passion," as she noted on her home page. Her decision to take writing classes eventually encouraged Littman to write her first novel, *Confessions of a Closet Catholic,* winner of the Sydney Taylor Award for Older Readers.

Geared for a young teen readership, *Confessions of a Closet Catholic* utilizes religion and individual identity as its central themes. At the center of the novel is eleven-year-old Justine Silver. Raised in a Jewish family, Justine is undergoing a religious identity crisis. In the spirit of experimentation, she decides to secretly adopt the Roman Catholic faith of her best friend Mac. It is not until her paternal grandmother, Bubbe—who is also a Holocaust survivor—suffers a stroke that Justine begins appreciating the religion of her heritage. A *Publishers Weekly* contributor noted that readers "will find much to savor in the warm, angst-lite tone . . . and will likely relate to the universal conflicts and emotional challenges" of Littman's young protagonist. According to Kimberly Monaghan in *School Library Journal,* "readers can't help but laugh and cry with this winning protagonist," and a *Kirkus Reviews* contributor regarded Littman's characterization of Justine as "both amusing and somber as she negotiates religion, family, and bereavement."

In *Purge* Littman focuses on a more problematic worry: the heath risks associated with bulimia. The topic is close to the author's heart because she suffered from the condition as a young woman. In the novel sixteen-year-old Janie Ryman hopes to beat her cycle of binging and purging by signing herself in to the Golden Slopes residential psychiatric hospital. As the teen becomes enveloped by the surface tensions at the institution—which includes a long-running battle between the "Barfers" and "Starvers"—she begins to go deeper into her own feelings and uncovers memories that, when unmasked, will lead to a healthier view of her self and her world. In *School Library Journal,* Carol A. Edwards noted that "the universality of Janie's blindness to her own behavior is clearly portrayed" in Littman's realistic prose, which mixes conversations, journal entries, and Janie's narration. The "underlying but not heavy-handed

Cover of Sarah Darer Littman's debut young-adult novel Confessions of a Closet Catholic, *featuring artwork by Maria Carluccio.* (Puffin Books, 2005. Cover illustration © 2005 by Maria Carluccio.Reproduced by permission of Puffin Books, a division of Penguin Putnam Books for Young Readers.)

message" in *Purge* "may start a few conversations," in the opinion of a *Kirkus Reviews* writer, while in the *Journal of Adolescent & Adult Literacy* Jennfer Clifton concluded that Littman's novel "uses Janie's honesty and bitter sarcasm to tell a heart-wrenchingly humorous story in a way that lets readers take a close-up look at a difficult topic."

Littman takes readers to Buenos Aires, Argentina, circa 2000 in *Life, After,* where Daniela Bensimon attends private school, courtesy of her attentive and supportive family. When the country becomes unstable due to an economic crisis, Dani and her family move to the United States where the teen must start all over. While dealing with a new school and a new language, the teen also worries over her father, who has become angry and depressed because of the family's downturn in fortunes. When Dani meets Jon, a classmate with Asperger's syndrome, he helps lift her spirits by expanding her world to include new friends and even the possibility of a new romance. Praising *Life, After* as an "empathetic" and "intensely personal" novel, a *Publishers Weekly* critic

added that "the languid pace and wealth of details" in Littman's prose strengthen the novel's "emotionally convincing and absorbing qualities." The "sensitively articulated themes . . . and credible teen banter" in *Life, After* contribute to what John Peter characterized in *Booklist* as "an emotionally complex tale" with special appeal to teens learning English as their second language.

In addition to her work as a published novelist, Littman is also a columnist for several newspapers in Connecticut and she writes op-eds for the news site *CTNews Junkie.com.* As she commented on her columnist Web site, SarahLittman.com, one of the joys she gets from writing editorials "is hearing from people who violently disagree with me." Littman advises aspiring writers to read, "write with a passionate heart, but edit with a cool head."

Biographical and Critical Sources

PERIODICALS

Booklist, August 1, 2010, John Peters, review of *Life, After,* p. 49.
Bulletin of the Center for Children's Books, February, 2005, Elizabeth Bush, review of *Confessions of a Closet Catholic,* p. 257; May, 2009, Deborah Stevenson, review of *Purge,* p. 368.
Journal of Adolescent & Adult Literacy, October, 2009, Jennifer Clifton, review of *Purge,* p. 180.
Kirkus Reviews, January 1, 2005, review of *Confessions of a Closet Catholic,* p. 54; March 1, 2009, review of *Purge.*
Publishers Weekly, February 28, 2005, review of *Confessions of a Closet Catholic,* p. 68; June 28, 2010, review of *Life, After,* p. 129.
School Library Journal, January, 2005, Kimberly Monaghan, review of *Confessions of a Closet Catholic,* p. 132; July, 2009, Carol A. Edwards, review of *Purge,* p. 88.
Voice of Youth Advocates, April, 2005, review of *Confessions of a Closet Catholic,* p. 42; October, 2009, Lucy Schall, review of *Purge,* p. 318.

ONLINE

Greenwich Time Online http://www.greenwichtime.com/ (October 20, 2010), "Sarah Darer Littman."
Sarah Darer Littman Home Page, http://www.sarahdarer littman.com (October 20, 2010).
Sarah Littman Home Page, http://www.sarahlittman.com (October 20, 2010).*

*   *   *

LIU, Cynthea

Personal

Born in OK; married; children: one daughter. *Education:* College degree.

Addresses

Home—Chicago, IL.

Career

Writer and writing coach. Founder of AuthorsNow.com. Presenter at schools and conferences.

Awards, Honors

Oklahoma Book Award finalist, 2009, for *Paris Pan Takes the Dare.*

Writings

Writing for Children and Teens: A Crash Course, Pivotal Pub. (Chicago, IL), 2008.
Paris Pan Takes the Dare, G.P. Putnam's Sons (New York, NY), 2009.
The Great Call of China, Speak (New York, NY), 2009.
What I Didn't Tell You, Putnam (New York, NY), 2010.

Contributor to *The New Writer's Handbook,* edited by Philip Martin.

Biographical and Critical Sources

PERIODICALS

Kirkus Reviews, May 1, 2009, review of *Paris Pan Takes the Dare.*
School Library Journal, August, 2009, Amanda Raklovits, review of *Paris Pan Takes the Dare,* p. 108.

ONLINE

Cynthea Liu Home Page, http://www.cynthealiu.com (October 15, 2010).
Cynthea Liu Web log, http://cynthea.livejournal.com (October 15, 2010).

*   *   *

LOGSTED, Greg

Personal

Born in Amity, NY; married Lauren Baratz (an author); children: Jackie. *Education:* Attended University of Arizona.

Addresses

Home—Danbury, CT.

Career

Author and businessman. Owner of a residential window-cleaning company.

Writings

YOUNG-ADULT NOVELS

Something Happened, Simon Pulse (New York, NY), 2008.
Alibi Junior High, Aladdin (New York, NY), 2009.

"SISTERS 8" CHAPTER-BOOK SERIES

(With Lauren Baratz-Logsted and Jackie Logsted) *Annie's Adventures,* illustrated by Lisa K. Weber, Houghton Mifflin Harcourt (Boston, MA), 2008.
(With Lauren Baratz-Logsted and Jackie Logsted) *Durinda's Dangers,* illustrated by Lisa K. Weber, Houghton Mifflin Harcourt (Boston, MA), 2008.
(With Lauren Baratz-Logsted and Jackie Logsted) *Georgia's Greatness,* illustrated by Lisa K. Weber, Houghton Mifflin Harcourt (Boston, MA), 2009.
(With Lauren Baratz-Logsted and Jackie Logsted) *Jackie's Jokes,* illustrated by Lisa K. Weber, Houghton Mifflin Harcourt (Boston, MA), 2009.
(With Lauren Baratz-Logsted and Jackie Logsted) *Marcia's Madness,* Houghton Mifflin Harcourt (Boston, MA), 2010.
(With Lauren Baratz-Logsted and Jackie Logsted) *Petal's Problems,* Houghton Mifflin Harcourt (Boston, MA), 2010.

Sidelights

In addition to running a local business, Greg Logsted writes fiction for young adults, inspired by his positive memories of his own teen years. Logsted's original novels include *Something Happened* and *Alibi Junior High,* and he has also collaborated with his wife, novelist Lauren Baratz-Logsted, and school-aged daughter Jackie Logsted on the elementary-grade chapter books in the "Sisters 8" series.

Logsted's story in *Something Happened* focuses on a young teen who finds support during a personal loss in a relationship that may be inappropriate. Billy Romero's dad has been killed in an accident, and the thirteen year old now feels lost. Unable to help her son, Billy's mom send him to a psychiatrist, which makes the boy feel discarded. School friends cannot understand how Billy feels, but his eighth-grade English teacher, Miss Gate, is different. Supportive and understanding, Miss Gate first spends after-school time with Billy, but then she begins to inject herself in his personal life. At first enjoying the attention, the young teen soon questions the teacher's motives.Ultimately, he finds himself questioning the fallibility of all the adults in his life in a first-person narrative that is mixed with Billy's letters to his deceased dad. Reviewing Logsted's "disturbing" fiction debut, Hazel Rochman praised *Something Happened* in *Booklist* for its "sensitive, direct story about a teen dealing with adult authority that crosses the line."

Also featuring a young teen, *Alibi Junior High* finds Cody Saron living an exciting life, carried along the career path of his secret-agent dad. Moving from country

to country around the world, where each temporary home base features all the comforts money can buy, the thirteen year old watches his world change dramatically when his dad is forced to go into hiding and Cody is sent to live with his aunt in Connecticut. Instead of living a life on the edge, he now turns his attention to surviving junior high school, where his martial-arts skills, charismatic personality, and intelligence prove to be surprisingly useful. *Alibi Junior High* "balances a suspenseful story with funny scenes" featuring a resourceful teen, according to *Booklist* contributor Todd Morning, while in *School Library Journal* Mairead McInness dubbed Logsted's fictional hero "a regular James Bond" whose story "does a good job of combining crime-fighting action and middle-school angst with current issues." "Funny and fast paced," according to a *Kirkus Reviews* writer, *Alibi Junior High* "fits right in with the beach-read crowd."

Biographical and Critical Sources

PERIODICALS

Booklist, November 15, 2008, Hazel Rochman, review of *Something Happened,* p. 55; August 1, 2009, Todd Morning, review of *Alibi Junior High,* p. 52.
Kirkus Reviews, May 1, 2009, review of *Alibi Junior High.*
Kliatt, September, 2009, Sharon Blumberg, review of *Something Happened,* p. 26.
School Library Journal, March, 2009, Faith Brautigam, review of *Something Happened,* p. 146; June, 2009, Mairead McInnes, review of *Alibi Junior High,* p. 129.
Voice of Youth Advocates, April, 2009, Kristin Anderson, review of *Something Happened,* p. 54.

ONLINE

Greg Logsted Home Page, http://www.greglogsted.com (October 20, 2010).
Houghton Mifflin Web Site, http://www.houghtonmifflin books.com/features/sisters8/ (October 20, 2010), "Sisters 8" series home page.*

*   *   *

LONDON, Jonathan 1947-
(Jonathan Sherwood)

Personal

Born March 11, 1947, in Brooklyn, NY; son of Harry and Anne London; married; wife's name JoAnn (divorced May, 1974); married Maureen Weisenberger (a registered nurse), March 21, 1976; children: (second marriage) Aaron, Sean. *Education:* San Jose State University, B.A., 1969, M.A., 1970; Sonoma State Univer-

Jonathan London (Reproduced by permission.)

sity, teaching certificate for grades K-12, 1985. *Hobbies and other interests:* Hiking, backpacking, kayaking, cross-country skiing.

Addresses

Home and office—P.O. Box 537, Graton, CA 95444. *Agent*—Barbara Kouts, P.O. Box 560, Bellport, NY 11713.

Career

Author of books for children. Worked variously as a freelance laborer, dancer, child counselor, and display installer, beginning 1979; children's writer, beginning 1989. American Booksellers Association, panelist for Children's Book Council, 1993.

Member

Amnesty International, Wilderness Society.

Awards, Honors

Ina Coolbrith Circle Award for Poetry, 1979; Parent-Teacher Association scholarship, 1984; Teachers' Choice selection, International Reading Association

(IRA), 1993, for *Thirteen Moons on Turtle's Back;*
American Booksellers for Children Award, 1993, for
The Eyes of Grey Wolf; Best Book selection, *Child*
magazine, 1995, for *Like Butter on Pancakes,* and 1997,
for *Dream Weaver;* Best Book citation, *Time* magazine,
1996, for *Fireflies, Fireflies, Light My Way;* Parent's
Choice Gold Award, 1997, for *Ali: Child of the Desert;*
Children's Literature Choice selection, Bank Street College
of Education, 1993, for *The Owl Who Became the
Moon,* 1995, for *Where's Home?,* and 1998, for *Ice
Bear and Little Fox;* IRA/Children's Book Council Children's
Choice selection, for "Froggy" series.

Writings

FOR CHILDREN

(With Joseph Bruchac) *Thirteen Moons on Turtle's Back:
A Native American Year of Moons,* illustrated by Thomas
Locker, Philomel Books (New York, NY), 1992.
The Lion Who Had Asthma, illustrated by Nadine Bernard
Westcott, Albert Whitman (Morton Grove, IL), 1992.
Gray Fox, illustrated by Robert Sauber, Viking (New York,
NY), 1993.
(With Lanny Pinola) *Fire Race: A Karuk Coyote Tale,* illustrated
by Sylvia Lang, Chronicle Books (Boston,
MA), 1993.
The Owl Who Became the Moon, illustrated by Ted Rand,
Dutton (New York, NY), 1993.
Into This Night We Are Rising, illustrated by G. Brian
Karas, Viking (New York, NY), 1993.
Voices of the Wild, illustrated by Wayne McCloughlin,
Crown (New York, NY), 1993.
The Eyes of Gray Wolf, illustrated by Jon Van Zyles,
Chronicle Books (Boston, MA), 1993.
Hip Cat (picture book), illustrated by Woodleigh Hubbard,
Chronicle Books (Boston, MA), 1993.
A Koala for Katie: An Adoption Story, illustrated by Cynthia
Jabar, Albert Whitman (Morton Grove, IL), 1993.
Liplap's Wish, illustrated by Sylvia Long, Chronicle Books
(Boston, MA), 1994.
Condor's Egg, illustrated by James Chaffee, Chronicle
Books (Boston, MA), 1994.
Honey Paw and Lightfoot, illustrated by Jon Van Zyles,
Chronicle Books (Boston, MA), 1994.
The Sugaring-off Party, illustrated by Gilles Pelletier, Dutton
(New York, NY), 1995.
Like Butter on Pancakes, illustrated by G. Brian Karas,
Viking (New York, NY), 1995.
Master Elk and the Mountain Lion, illustrated by Wayne
McCloughlin, Crown (New York, NY), 1995.
Where's Home (young-adult novel), Viking (New York,
NY), 1995.
Jackrabbit, illustrated by Deborah Kogan Ray, Crown
(New York, NY), 1996.
The Village Basket Weaver, illustrated by George Crespo,
Dutton (New York, NY), 1996.
Red Wolf Country, illustrated by Daniel San Souci, Dutton
(New York, NY), 1996.

What Newt Could Do for Turtle, illustrated by Louise
Voce, Candlewick Press (Cambridge, MA), 1996.
Fireflies, Fireflies, Light My Way, illustrated by Linda
Messier, Viking (New York, NY), 1996.
Let the Lynx Come In, illustrated by Patrick Benson, Candlewick
Press (Cambridge, MA), 1996.
I See the Moon and the Moon Sees Me, illustrated by Peter
Fiore, Viking (New York, NY), 1996.
Ali, Child of the Desert, illustrated by Ted Lewin, Lothrop,
Lee & Shepard (New York, NY), 1997.
Old Salt, Young Salt, illustrated by Todd L.W. Doney, Lothrop,
Lee & Shepard (New York, NY), 1997.
If I Had a Horse, illustrated by Brooke Scudder, Chronicle
Books (Boston, MA), 1997.
Phantom of the Prairie: Year of the Black-footed Ferret,
illustrated by Barbara Bash, Sierra Club Books for
Children (San Francisco, CA), 1997.
Little Red Monkey, illustrated by Frank Remkiewicz, Dutton
(New York, NY), 1997.
Dream Weaver, illustrated by Rocco Baviera, Silver
Whistle/Harcourt (San Diego, CA), 1997.
Puddles, illustrated by G. Brian Karas, Viking (New York,
NY), 1997.
Moshi Moshi, illustrated by Yoshi Miyake, Millbrook Press
(New York, NY), 1998.
At the Edge of the Forest, illustrated by Barbara Firth,
Candlewick Press (Cambridge, MA), 1998.
Hurricane!, illustrated by Henri Sorensen, Lothrop, Lee &
Shepard (New York, NY), 1998.
Tell Me a Story (autobiography), photographs by Sherry
Shahan, Richard C. Owens (New York, NY), 1998.
The Candystore Man, illustrated by Malcolm Brown, Lothrop,
Lee & Shepard (New York, NY), 1998.
Ice Bear and Little Fox, illustrated by Daniel San Souci,
Dutton (New York, NY), 1998.
Wiggle, Waggle, illustrated by Michael Rex, Silver Whistle/
Harcourt (San Diego, CA), 1999.
Baby Whale's Journey, illustrated by Jon Van Zyles,
Chronicle Books (Boston, MA), 1999.
Shawn and Keeper and the Birthday Party, illustrated by
Renée Williams-Andriani, Dutton (New York, NY),
1999.
What Do You Love?, illustrated by Karen Lee Schmidt,
Harcourt Brace (New York, NY), 2000.
Snuggle Wuggle, illustrated by Michael Rex, Silver Whistle
(San Diego, CA), 2000.
Who Bop, illustrated by Henry Cole, HarperCollins (New
York, NY), 2000.
Shawn and Keeper: Show and Tell, illustrated by Renée
Williams-Andriani, Dutton (New York, NY), 2000.
Panther: Shadow of the Swamp, illustrated by Paul Morin,
Candlewick Press (Cambridge, MA), 2000.
Mustang Canyon, illustrated by Daniel Van Souci, Candlewick
Press (Cambridge, MA), 2000.
(With Aaron London) *White Water,* illustrated by Jill Kastner,
Viking (New York, NY), 2001.
Where the Big Fish Are, illustrated by Adam Gustavson,
Candlewick Press (Cambridge, MA), 2001.
Sun Dance, Water Dance, illustrated by Greg Couch, Dutton
(New York, NY), 2001.

Park Beat: Rhymin' through the Seasons, illustrated by Woodleigh Marx Hubbard, HarperCollins (New York, NY), 2001.

Gone Again Ptarmigan, illustrated by Jon Van Zyle, National Geographic Society (Washington, DC), 2001.

Crocodile: Disappearing Dragon, illustrated by Paul Morin, Candlewick Press (Cambridge, MA), 2001.

Crunch Munch, illustrated by Michael Rex, Red Wagon Books (New York, NY), 2001.

Count the Ways, Little Brown Bear, illustrated by Margie Moore, Dutton (New York, NY), 2002.

Zack at School, illustrated by Jack Medoff, Scholastic (New York, NY), 2002.

What the Animals Were Waiting For, illustrated by Paul Morin, Scholastic (New York, NY), 2002.

Loon Lake, illustrated by Susan Ford, Chronicle Books (San Francisco, CA), 2002.

When the Fireflies Come, illustrated by Terry Widener, Dutton (New York, NY), 2003.

Giving Thanks, illustrated by Gregory Manchess, Candlewick Press (Cambridge, MA), 2003.

"Eat!" Cried Little Pig, illustrated by Delphine Durand, Dutton (New York, NY), 2003.

Zack at the Dentist, illustrated by Jack Medoff, Scholastic (New York, NY), 2004.

Sled Dogs Run, illustrated by Jon Van Zyle, Walker (New York, NY), 2005.

Do Your ABC's, Little Brown Bear, illustrated by Margie Moore, Dutton (New York, NY), 2005.

A Truck Goes Rattley Bumpa, illustrated by Denis Roche, Holt (New York, NY), 2005.

A Train Goes Clickety-clack, illustrated by Denis Roche, Henry Holt (New York, NY), 2007.

My Big Rig, illustrated by Viviana Garofoli, Marshall Cavendish Children (Tarrytown, NY), 2007.

Flamingo Sunset, illustrated by Kristina Rodanas, Marshall Cavendish Children (Tarrytown, NY), 2008.

Little Swan, illustrated by Kristina Rodanas, Marshall Cavendish Children (Tarrytown, NY), 2009.

A Plane Goes Ka-zoom, illustrated by Denis Roche, Henry Holt (New York, NY), 2010.

I'm a Truck Driver, illustrated by David Parkins, Henry Holt (New York, NY), 2010.

Contributor of poems and short stories to periodicals, including *Cricket, Us Kids, Child Life,* and *Short Story International.* Author of other works, including *In a Season of Birds: Poems for Maureen,* sometimes under the pseudonym Jonathan Sherwood.

London's work has been translated into Spanish, German, Greek, Dutch, Danish, French, Japanese, Chinese, and Korean.

"FROGGY" SERIES; FOR CHILDREN

Froggy Gets Dressed, illustrated by Frank Remkiewicz, Viking (New York, NY), 1992.

Let's Go, Froggy!, illustrated by Frank Remkiewicz, Viking (New York, NY), 1994.

Froggy Learns to Swim, illustrated by Frank Remkiewicz, Chronicle Books (Boston, MA), 1995.

Froggy Goes to School, illustrated by Frank Remkiewicz, Viking (New York, NY), 1996.

Froggy's First Kiss, illustrated by Frank Remkiewicz, Viking (New York, NY), 1998.

Froggy Plays Soccer, illustrated by Frank Remkiewicz, Viking (New York, NY), 1999.

Froggy's Halloween, illustrated by Frank Remkiewicz, Viking (New York, NY), 1999.

Froggy Goes to Bed, illustrated by Frank Remkiewicz, Viking (New York, NY), 2000.

Froggy Bakes a Cake, illustrated by Frank Remkiewicz, Grosset & Dunlap (New York, NY) 2000.

Froggy's Best Christmas, illustrated by Frank Remkiewicz, Viking (New York, NY), 2000.

Froggy Eats Out, illustrated by Frank Remkiewicz, Viking (New York, NY), 2001.

Froggy Takes a Bath, illustrated by Frank Remkiewicz, Viking (New York, NY), 2001.

Froggy Plays in the Band, illustrated by Frank Remkiewicz, Viking (New York, NY), 2002.

Froggy Goes to the Doctor, illustrated by Frank Remkiewicz, Viking (New York, NY), 2002.

Froggy's Baby Sister, illustrated by Frank Remkiewicz, Viking (New York, NY), 2003.

Froggy's Day with Dad, illustrated by Frank Remkiewicz, Viking (New York, NY), 2004.

Froggy's Sleepover, illustrated by Frank Remkiewicz, Viking (New York, NY), 2005.

Froggy Rides a Bike, illustrated by Frank Remkiewicz, Viking (New York, NY), 2006.

Froggy Plays T-Ball, illustrated by Frank Remkiewicz, Viking (New York, NY), 2007.

Froggy Goes to Camp, illustrated by Frank Remkiewicz, Viking (New York, NY), 2008.

Froggy's Best Babysitter, illustrated by Frank Remkiewicz, Viking (New York, NY), 2009.

Froggy Goes to Hawai'i, Viking (New York, NY), 2010.

Adaptations

Froggy Gets Dressed and *Honey Paw and Lightfoot* were featured on the PBS television program *Storytime; Hip Cat* and *Thirteen Moons on Turtle's Back* were featured on *Reading Rainbow; What Newt Could Do for Turtle* was adapted for television and broadcast in Great British and Germany.

Sidelights

Jonathan London is a poet-turned-children's author whose picture books reproduce the natural world for young readers. In entertaining stories that include *Gray Fox, Condor's Egg, Crocodile: Disappearing Dragon, Flamingo Sunset,* and many others, London tells fictionalized but unsentimental stories about animals in their natural habitats that reflect the interconnections binding all of nature. In other picture books, especially the "Froggy" series, London's animals take on anthropomorphic and humorous traits. Humans figure in London's storybooks as well, starring in warm family tales

such as *The Sugaring-off Party,* tales of adventure such as *Old Salt, Young Salt* and *Hurricane!,* and rhyming, playful, everyday enjoyments such as *Like Butter on Pancakes, Puddles,* and *I See the Moon and the Moon Sees Me.* London's love of jazzy rhyme and his sense of humor have also led to books that feature the cadences of hip-hop and jazz, such as *Hip Cat* and *The Candystore Man.*

Since embarking on his career as a children's writer in 1989, London has proven himself to be a prolific author, turning out several titles each year. In his first decade as a published writer he penned roughly fifty picture books as well as the juvenile novel *Where's Home?,* and he has shown no signs of slowing. Critics have often praised his poet's eye and ear, lauding London's "spare, lyrical text," as Marianne Saccardi did in a *School Library Journal* review of *The Owl Who Became the Moon.* London's infectious humor has also been noted by many reviewers, particularly in his "Froggy" books, all illustrated by Frank Remkiewicz. The reader "will surely laugh out loud," commented a critic for *Publishers Weekly* in a review of *Froggy Gets Dressed.*

Born in Brooklyn, New York, in 1947, London graduated from California's San Jose State University with an M.A. in 1970. His studies were in the social sci-

London's humorous picture book **Crunch Munch** *is brought to life in Michael Rex's colorful cartoon art.* (Harcourt Inc., 2001. Illustrations copyright © 2001 by Michael Rex. Reproduced by permission of Houghton Mifflin Harcourt Publishing Company. This material may not be reproduced in any for or by any means without the prior written permission of the publisher.)

ences, but it was poetry that captured his imagination. After graduation, London spent several years traveling around the world, encountering other cultures and ways of living. He began writing poetry, meanwhile earning a living in a variety of ways, from a day laborer to dancer and child counselor. With the birth of two sons after his second marriage, London returned to college to earn a teaching certificate, but soon he felt the draw of another creative impulse. Telling stories to his own young sons, London began to wonder if writing children's books might not be a viable option and a way to put his poetic voice to use.

The first children's book London wrote, *The Owl Who Became the Moon,* was actually his fourth book to be published and was inspired by a bedtime fantasy he told his son Sean at age two. This tale about a young boy riding on a train at night who watches and listens to the animals in their wilderness homes was told in verse and announced its author's abiding interest in nature. "With spare elegance, London celebrates both the beauty of nighttime—and the power of the train," noted a reviewer for *Publishers Weekly* in appraising *The Owl Who Became the Moon.*

London's "Froggy" stories had their genesis in the demand of London's other son, Aaron, for a tale. "The image of a frog dressing in winter clothes so he can play in the snow struck my funny bone," the author once told *SATA,* "and my kids' funny bones, too!" In *Froggy Gets Dressed* Froggy wakes up one morning to discover a snow-filled world. Jumping out of bed to go frolic, he is summoned back by his mother and requested to dress in warm clothes. London uses sound effects such as "zoop," "zup," and "zip" for the action of putting on various articles of clothing. Ultimately the poor frog is embarrassed in front of his playmates when his mother yells to tell him he has forgotten his underwear. A reviewer for *Horn Book* noted that the text "has many wonderful sound effects" as well as "plenty of repetition to enhance the silliness of the story."

London serves up more Froggy action in further adventures of the rambunctious amphibian. Froggy and his father go for a bike trip in *Let's Go, Froggy!,* in which "humor, delightful sound effects, and bright, enthusiastic illustrations make the book appealing," according to a *Horn Book* contributor. The frog takes to water in *Froggy Learns to Swim* and overcomes nervousness to finally enjoy his first day of school in *Froggy Goes to School.* In *Booklist* Hazel Rochman concluded that "children will laugh at [Froggy's] innocence and sympathize with his jitters," in this schooldays tale. Froggy becomes the Frog Prince in *Froggy's Halloween,* only to be chased by Princess Frogolina, who wants to plant a kiss on his cheek. Then, in *Froggy's First Kiss,* Valentine's Day provides Froggy and Frogolina the perfect venue for amphibious amours.

Froggy has some trouble preparing for his doctor's visit in *Froggy Goes to the Doctor:* he forgets to put on underwear and also neglects to brush his teeth, much to

Dr. Mugwort's displeasure. The doctor's torments continue when Froggy shouts into her stethoscope and accidentally kicks her in the face when she tests his reflexes. From a visit to the doctor, London lets Froggy go out to play in the picture books *Froggy Plays Soccer, Froggy's Sleepover, Froggy Goes to Camp,* and *Froggy Plays T-Ball. Froggy Goes to Camp* finds the friendly amphibian at Camp Run-a-Muck, where he becomes popular among his fellow campers while tormenting camp counselors. *Froggy Plays T-Ball* captures the frog's love of playing ball, even though he gets confused by all the rules. "As always, London's text is succinct, snappy, and full of fun sound effects," noted Donna Cardon in her *School Library Journal* review of *Froggy Goes to Camp,* and Susan E. Murray added in the same periodical that the hero of *Froggy Plays T-Ball* exudes a "natural exuberance and excitement."

More animals with seemingly human traits appear in *Liplap's Wish, What Newt Could Do for Turtle, Hip Cat,* and *Count the Ways, Little Brown Bear.* The first title is a "wonderful, sensitive story about children's feelings of sadness and loss after the death of a loved one," according to Martha Gordon in *School Library Journal.* London employs a young rabbit named Liplap that has lost its grandmother and finds little solace in busying itself in building a snowman. "This sympathetic book will help comfort generations of grieving children," Gordon concluded. Friendship and sharing are explored in *What Newt Could Do for Turtle,* a "delightful" story, according to a critic in *Kirkus Reviews.*

Count the Ways, Little Brown Bear features a mama and baby bear spending a lazy day together, playing games, reading books, and picking apples. Through it all, the baby bear demands to know how much his mother loves him. She replies with reference to things around them, from the apples on the trees to the stars in the sky, but the little brown bear always declares that it is not enough. Little Brown Bear also appears in *Do Your ABC's, Little Brown Bear,* in which the young cub plays an alphabet game with his father that lasts until bedtime. *Count the Ways, Little Brown Bear* features a "text [that] is sweet and succinct," commented a *Publishers Weekly* contributor, the critic adding that the book also helps young children to learn about counting, addition, and subtraction. Featuring "expressive" artwork by Margie Moore, *Do Your ABC's, Little Brown Bear* will help "youngsters . . . enjoy learning their letters," predicted *School Library Journal* critic Linda L. Walkins.

Animals in their natural habitats are depicted in a bevy of books by London detailing life in the wild. In her *Booklist* review of *Gray Fox,* Emily Melton noted that the "beauty and the cruelty of nature, the dangers posed to wild animals by humans, the invincibility of the animal spirit, and the reassuring cycle of life and death are all part of this book about Gray Fox." A similar title, *The Eyes of Gray Wolf,* brought praise from a reviewer

Margie Moore captures the affectionate relationship between a mother and child in her art for London's picture book **Count the Ways, Little Brown Bear.** (Puffin Books, 2002. Illustration copyright © Margie Moore, 2002. Reproduced by permission of Puffin Books, a division of Penguin Putnam Books for Young Readers.)

for *Publishers Weekly* who noted that "words pour out, as fierce as the arctic cold or as luminous as the yellow moon" in this tale of the leader of a wolf pack who has lost his mate.

In *Voices of the Wild* a dozen different animals describe—in first person—their wariness of a lone kayaker breaching their northern habitat. A *Kirkus Reviews* critic called this a "quietly lyrical book that effectively evokes the experience of observing these wilderness creatures with respect, and without disturbing them." In *Condor's Egg,* London "gives eloquent testament to the first pair of California condors to return to the wild since 1987," according to a *Publishers Weekly* contributor, while Susan Dove Lempke observed in the *Bulletin of the Center for Children's Books* that the author's "text is spare but poetically evokes the lives of the condors in the wild."

London looks at the life cycle of an elk in *Master Elk and the Mountain Lion,* a young calf grows to become a strong bull, defeats the leader or master of the herd, and then defends the herd against an old enemy, the mountain lion. Janice Del Negro noted in a *Booklist* review that the elk's life is "effectively narrated and evocatively described" in London's text. The life of a grizzly bear is narrated in *Honey Paw and Lightfoot,* a "combination of fun and learning" that makes an "eloquent" if "implicit plea for wilderness preservation," according to *Booklist* critic Mary Harris Veeder. Another such plea for preservation comes in *Red Wolf Country,* a "spare and lyrical story" according to Susan S. Verner in the *Bulletin of the Center for Children's Books,* that takes the reader through a year in the life of the red wolf, an endangered species that is native to the southeastern United States.

Mustang Canyon follows a newborn mustang colt that London calls "Little Pinto," as he and his herd of wild horses attempt to survive such challenges as strange stallions, low-flying airplanes, and river rapids. "The words are spare, immediate, and informative," Gillian Engberg wrote in *Booklist,* recommending *Mustang Canyon* as "a must for cowboy wannabes." A *Kirkus Reviews* contributor, commented of the same book that "young readers should not miss the sense of community and family these 'wild' horses must have to survive in their harsh but beautiful land."

London takes readers to southern climes in *Flamingo Sunset,* which details the life cycle of one of the more unusual species of American birds. In his text, London explains flamingo anatomy and nesting behavior, and also notes that hunters and the expansion of human communities have affected the birds' behavior. As Abby Nolan noted in her *Booklist* review of *Flamingo Sunset,* "flamingos no longer nest anywhere in the [United States]." A bird of a different feather is the star of *Little Swan,* which, like *Flamingo Sunset,* also features colored pencil and watercolor artwork by Kristina Rodanas. Here readers follow a baby trumpeter swan, or cygnet, as it hatches, learns to swim and hunt, and prepares for its first migration. Rodanas brings to life this amazing process in images that "lend gentle illumination to the swan family's progress," according to *Booklist* critic Connie Fletcher. In *Kirkus Reviews* a critic dubbed *Little Swan* as "elegantly simple and informative" on the strength of London's "straightforward text" and Rodanas's "splendid" art.

Turning his attention and his lyrical voice to human subjects, London has created a batch of heartwarming and humorous tales for young children that speak of everything from family relations to ethnic differences in tales that teach without being didactic. In *The Sugaring-off Party* he presents the history of a French-Canadian family as condensed in the vital moment of sugaring-off in the maple syrup process. Another family tale, *Giving Thanks,* features artwork by Gregory Manchess that captures the brilliance of the autumn day in which a father and son hike near their home and express their thanks for the wonders of nature. "London's evocative text perfectly re-creates the thrill and excitement of this coming-of-spring ritual," observed Ann W. Moore in her *School Library Journal* review of *The Sugaring-off Party.* In *Publishers Weekly* a critic wrote of *Giving Thanks* that London's "brief text has the lyrical cadence of prayer," and *School Library Journal* critic Maryann H. Owen characterized the author's words as "a simple prayer of appreciation for being alive and at one with nature."

I See the Moon and the Moon Sees Me is a "charmingly adapted nursery favorite," according to a *Kirkus Reviews* writer, while *Like Butter on Pancakes* and *Puddles* both celebrate the simple things in life for a little boy, using onomatopoeic phrasing to tickle little funny bones. "London catalogues a glorious array of the delights of muddy weather," commented *School Library Journal* critic Marcia Hupp in reviewing *Puddles.* More singing rhymes fill the pages of *The Candystore Man,* a be-bop picture book that is reminiscent of London's *Hip Cat.* In this tale, the man behind the soda fountain serves up "ice cream and candy with flair," according to Adele Greenlee in *School Library Journal.*

Narrative tales are recounted in such books as *Ali, Child of the Desert, Hurricane!, At the Edge of the Forest, Moshi Moshi, What the Animals Were Waiting For,* and *The Waterfall.* Saharan cultures are examined in the first title, in which young Ali experiences a rite of passage when a sandstorm separates him from his father on their way to a market. "The theme of a young boy prov-

***London teams up with Daniel San Souci to capture the world of the West's wild horses in* Mustang Canyon.** (Candlewick Press, 2002. Text copyright © 2002 Jonathan London. Illustrations copyright © 2002 by Daniel San Souci. Reproduced by permission of Candlewick Press, Inc., Somerville, MA.)

London's ode to a fascinating bird species is paired with paintings by Kristina Rodanas in **Flamingo Sunset.** (Reproduced by permission of Marshall Cavendish.)

ing himself to his father and achieving manhood is a universal one," noted Janice Del Negro in the *Bulletin of the Center for Children's Books,* "and this strongly plotted title communicates that theme quite successfully." Another storm figures in *Hurricane!,* which recounts an incident from the author's childhood, while *At the Edge of the Forest* tells the story of a sheep farmer's son and a battle with coyotes. "London knows just how to kindle the audience's concern and stoke his drama," commented a reviewer for *Publishers Weekly* on this title. "Author and artist soften a harsh reality without blunting it."

London returns to Africa for *What the Animals Were Waiting For.* A Masai boy named Tepi is waiting, too, although he does not know for what. As he herds his family's livestock, he watches the local wildlife, including giraffes, elephants, and zebras. They all seem to be waiting for something, but every time Tepi asks his grandmother what that something might be, she tells him that he will see eventually. Then a storm comes, ending the dry season—also called the Months of Hunger—and Tepi sees the animals stampede off into the rain and his neighbors go out and dance in celebration. This "poetic telling of how nature's cycle affects animals and humans is well structured and emotionally resonant," Margaret Bush wrote in *School Library Journal. Booklist* critic Carolyn Phelan also commented on

London's poetic voice: "Rhythmic with repeated phrases and studded with sensory details, London's telling is simple yet vivid," she declared.

Sun Dance Water Dance and *When the Fireflies Come* particularly showcase London's background as a poet. Both books celebrate old-fashioned childhood summers, the former with a poem about a trip to go swimming in a river on a hot summer day and the latter with a prose tale about ice cream, baseball, and of course fireflies. Even *When the Fireflies Come* has more than a hint of poetry in it; a *Kirkus Reviews* contributor described London's prose here as "image-rich [and] impressionistic," while a *Publishers Weekly* critic noted that it "appeals to all five senses."

London's novel *Where's Home* marked a change of pace for the author. In his story, a Detroit teenager and his father travel go to San Francisco and there become homeless. Abandoned by a mentally ill mother, young Aaron is left to sort things out when his father takes to the bottle and loses his job. The pair hitchhikes west only to be arrested on charges of vagrancy in San Francisco. Out of jail and in a shelter, Aaron and his father begin to learn lessons from the other people gathered there. Reviewing the novel in *School Library Journal,* Cindy Darling Codell called *Where's Home* "lyrical, yet also spare," and noted that it "threads together incidents of love and loss, fire and friendship, and symbolism."

In all of his books for young children, London blends his poetic voice with concerns about nature and how humans are connected with it. As he once explained to *SATA:* "This act of writing, for me, is a part of my celebration of life, a way to give back a little for all that I have been given."

Biographical and Critical Sources

BOOKS

London, Jonathan, *Tell Me a Story* (autobiography), photographs by Sherry Shahan, Richard C. Owens (New York, NY), 1998.

PERIODICALS

Booklist, March 1, 1992, Karen Hutt, review of *Thirteen Moons on Turtle's Back: A Native American Year of Moons,* p. 1281; January 15, 1993, Kay Weisman, review of *The Owl Who Became the Moon,* and Emily Melton, review of *Gray Fox,* both p. 922; November 1, 1993, Janice Del Negro, review of *Voices of the Wild,* p. 523; March 15, 1995, Mary Harris Veeder, review of *Honey Paw and Lightfoot,* p. 1335; April 1, 1995, Janice Del Negro, review of *Like Butter on Pancakes,* p. 1428; December 15, 1995, Janice Del Negro, review of *Master Elk and the Mountain Lion,*

p. 709; January 1, 1996, Hazel Rochman, review of *Red Wolf Country,* p. 847; June 1, 1996, Hazel Rochman, review of *Froggy Goes to School,* p. 1735; July, 1996, Kay Weisman, review of *Jackrabbit,* p. 1830; November 1, 1998, GraceAnne A. DeCandido, review of *Moshi Moshi;* April 15, 2000, Stephanie Zvirin, review of *Shawn and Keeper Show-and-Tell,* p. 1555; January 1, 2001, Ellen Mandel, review of *Panther: Shadow of the Swamp,* and Carolyn Phelan, review of *Gone Again Ptarmigan,* both p. 963; June 1, 2001, Gillian Engberg, reviews of *White Water* and *Froggy Eats Out,* both p. 1892; December 1, 2001, Carolyn Phelan, review of *Crocodile: Disappearing Dragon,* p. 646; May 15, 2002, Carolyn Phelan, review of *What the Animals Were Waiting For,* p. 1602; August 1, 2002, review of *Mustang Canyon,* p. 1136; December 1, 2002, Gillian Engberg, review of *Mustang Canyon,* p. 675; January 1, 2003, Catherine Andronik, review of *Froggy Goes to the Doctor,* p. 908; February 1, 2004, Carolyn Phelan, review of *Giving Thanks,* p. 980; April 15, 2005, review of *Do Your ABC's, Little Brown Bear,* p. 1460; June 1, 2005, Linda Perkins, review of *Sled Dogs Run,* p. 1822; October 1, 2005, Carolyn Phelan, review of *A Truck Goes Rattley-Bumpa,* p. 64; April 15, 2007, Carolyn Phelan, review of *My Big Rig,* p. 49; April 15, 2008, Abby Nolan, review of *Flamingo Sunset,* p. 47, May 1, 2009, Connie Fletcher, review of *Little Swan,* p. 86; May 1, 2010, Abby Nolan, review of *I'm a Truck Driver,* p. 89.

Bulletin of the Center for Children's Books, February, 1993, review of *The Owl Who Became the Moon,* p. 183; October, 1994, Susan Dove Lempke, review of

Jon Van Zyle's evocative artwork for London's Sled Dogs Run *draws readers into an exotic snowy landscape.* (Illustrations copyright © 2005 by Jon Van Zyle. Reprinted by permission of Walker & Co. All rights reserved.)

Condor's Egg, p. 55; June, 1996, Susan S. Verner, review of *Red Wolf Country,* p. 344; February, 1997, review of *What Newt Could Do for Turtle,* p. 213; June, 1997, Janice Del Negro, review of *Ali, Child of the Desert,* p. 365.

Five Owls, January-February, 1993, review of *Froggy Gets Dressed,* p. 59; September-October, 1994, review of *Liplap's Wish,* p. 10.

Horn Book, spring, 1993, review of *Froggy Gets Dressed,* p. 37; fall, 1994, review of *Let's Go, Froggy!,* p. 280; March-April, 2005, Susan Dove Lempke, review of *Do Your ABC's Little Brown Bear,* p. 191.

Kirkus Reviews, October 1, 1993, review of *Voices of the Wild,* p. 1276; December 1, 1995, review of *I See the Moon and the Moon Sees Me,* p. 1704; November 15, 1996, review of *What Newt Could Do for Turtle,* p. 1671; February 1, 1999, review of *The Waterfall;* November 15, 2001, review of *Count the Ways, Little Brown Bear,* p. 1613; August 1, 2002, review of *Froggy Goes to the Doctor,* p. 1135; May 1, 2003, review of *When the Fireflies Come,* p. 679; January 1, 2005, review of *Froggy's Sleepover;* August 1, 2005, review of *A Truck Goes Rattley-Bumpa,* p. 853; February 15, 2007, review of *My Big Rig;* August 1, 2007, review of *A Train Goes Clickety-clack;* March 1, 2009, review of *Little Swan.*

Publishers Weekly, August 3, 1992, review of *Froggy Gets Dressed,* p. 70; December 28, 1992, review of *The Owl Who Became the Moon;* August 16, 1993, review of *The Eyes of Gray Wolf,* p. 102; October 3, 1994, review of *Condor's Egg,* p. 68; August 16, 1993, review of *Hip Cat,* p. 102; July 20, 1998, review of *The Candystore Man,* p. 219; August 17, 1998, review of *At the Edge of the Forest,* p. 72; November 19, 2001, review of *Count the Ways, Little Brown Bear,* p. 66; June 11, 2001, reviews of *Sun Dance Water Dance* and *White Water,* p. 85; June 24, 2002, review of *Froggy Goes to the Doctor,* p. 59; April 28, 2003, review of *When the Fireflies Come,* p. 69; November 10, 2003, review of *"Eat!" Cried Little Pig,* p. 60; January 5, 2004, review of *Giving Thanks,* p. 60; February 26, 2007, review of *My Big Rig,* p. 88.

Quill & Quire, March, 1995, review of *The Sugaring-off Party,* p. 78; June, 1998, review of *Dream Weaver,* p. 58.

School Library Journal, February, 1993, Marianne Saccardi, review of *The Owl Who Became the Moon,* p. 76; August, 1993, Carolyn Polese, review of *Fire Race: A Karuk Coyote Tale,* p. 159; November, 1994, Martha Gordon, review of *Liplap's Wish,* p. 84; January, 1995, Ann W. Moore, review of *The Sugaring-off Party,* p. 89; August, 1995, Cindy Darling Codell, review of *Where's Home,* pp. 154-155; March, 1996, Joy Fleishhacker, review of *Red Wolf Country,* p. 178; June, 1996, Judith Constantinides, review of *Fireflies, Fireflies Light My Way,* p. 104; May, 1997, Marcia Hupp, review of *Puddles,* p. 104; July, 1998, Margaret Bush, review of *Dream Weaver,* pp. 78-79; October, 1998, Adele Greenlee, review of *The Candystore Man,* p. 107; June, 1999, Gale W. Sherman, review of *Wiggle, Waggle,* p. 100; May, 2000, Susan M. Moore, review of *Snuggle Wuggle,* p. 148; June, 2000, Eliza-

beth O'Brien, review of *Froggy Goes to Bed,* p. 119; September, 2000, Maura Bresnahan, review of *Shawn and Keeper Show-and-Tell,* p. 204; October, 2000, review of *Froggy's Best Christmas,* p. 61; December, 2000, Susan Hepler, review of *What Do You Love?,* p. 114; January, 2001, Arwen Marshall, review of *Panther,* p. 119; April, 2001, Meghan R. Malone, review of *Crunch Munch,* p. 117; May, 2001, Robin L. Gibson, review of *Park Beat: Rhymin' through the Seasons,* and Sue Sherif, review of *Gone Again Ptarmigan,* both p. 128; June, 2001, Diane Olivo-Posner, review of *White Water,* p. 125; July, 2001, Lisa Dennis, review of *Sun Dance Water Dance,* p. 85; November, 2001, Cathie E. Bashaw, review of *Crocodile,* p. 129; April, 2002, Gay Lynn Van Vleck, review of *Count the Ways, Little Brown Bear,* p. 116; May, 2002, Margaret Bush, review of *What the Animals Were Waiting For,* p. 121; September, 2002, Shawn Brommer, review of *Loon Lake,* pp. 199-200; August, 2003, Ruth Semrau, review of *Mustang Canyon,* p. 138; December, 2003, Linda M. Kenton, review of *"Eat!" Cried Little Pig,* and Andrea Tarr, review of *Froggy's Baby Sister,* both p. 119; January, 2004, Maryann H. Owen, review of *Giving Thanks,* p. 100; June, 2004, Holly T. Sneeringer, review of *Froggy's Day with Dad,* p. 114; March, 2005, Linda L. Walkins, review of *Do Your ABC's, Little Brown Bear,* p. 175; September, 2005, Geneviene Gallagher, review of *A Truck Goes Rattley-Bumpa,* p. 177; May, 2007, Susan E. Murray, review of *Froggy Plays T-Ball,* p. 102; October, 2007, Linda Staskus, review of *A Train Goes Clickety-clack,* p. 122; June, 2008, Donna Cardon, review of *Froggy Goes to Camp,* p. 108; July, 2008, Margaret Bush, review of *Flamingo Sunset,* p. 89; April, 2009, Maryann H. Owen, review of *Little Swan,* p. 112.*

*   *   *

LYNCH, Janet Nichols 1952-
(Janet Nichols)

Personal

Born October 3, 1952, in Sacramento, CA; daughter of William R. (a refrigeration engineer) and Lena (a homemaker) Nichols; married Timothy Lynch (a composer and college music instructor); children: Caitlin Grace, Sean Nichols. *Education:* California State University, Sacramento, B.A. (music), 1974; Arizona State University, M.M. (piano), 1976; California State University, Fresno, M.F.A. (creative writing), 2002. *Politics:* Democrat. *Hobbies and other interests:* Bicycling, running, swimming, competing in marathons and triathlons, playing piano and guitar, hiking, skiing, traveling, working for social justice.

Addresses

Home—Visalia, CA. *Agent*—Jodie Rhodes Levine Literary Agency, 8840 Villa La Jolla Dr., Ste. 315, La Jolla, CA 92037. *E-mail*—jnicholslynch@gmail.com.

Janet Nichols Lynch (Photograph by Johanna Coyne. Reproduced by permission.)

Career

Author, educator, and musician. Pianist, beginning 1970; piano teacher, 1972-90; writer, beginning 1979. De Anza College, Cupertino, CA, instructor in music, 1980-90; Skyline College, San Bruno, CA, instructor in music, 1981-90. Divisadero Middle School, Visalia, CA, English teacher, 1999-2005; El Diamante High School, Visalia, English teacher, 2005—. College of the Sequoias, Visalia, instructor in English, 2003-07.

Member

California Association of Teachers of English, Tulare County Peace Coalition, Peace Fresno, Friends of the Tulare County Library.

Awards, Honors

Quick Pick for Reluctant Readers designation, American Library Association, 2009, for *Messed Up.*

Writings

FICTION FOR CHILDREN AND YOUNG ADULTS

(Under name Janet Nichols) *Casey Wooster's Pet Care Service,* Maxwell Macmillan International (New York, NY), 1993.

Peace Is a Four-Letter Word, Heyday Books (Berkeley, CA), 2005.

Messed Up, Holiday House (New York, NY), 2009.

Addicted to Her, Holiday House (New York, NY), 2010.

OTHER

(Under name Janet Nichols) *American Music Makers: An Introduction to American Composers,* Walker & Co. (New York, NY), 1990.

(Under name Janet Nichols) *Women Music Makers: An Introduction to Women Composers,* Walker & Co. (New York, NY), 1992.

Where Words Leave Off Music Begins (short stories), iUniverse, 2005.

Chest Pains (adult novel), Bridge Works Pub. (Lanham, MD), 2009.

Contributor to anthology *Highway 99: A Literary Journey through California's Great Central Valley,* Heyday Books (Berkeley, CA), 2007. Contributor to periodicals, including *Baltimore Review, Bicycling, Bike World, Competetive Cycling, Highlights for Children, New Yorker, San Joaquin Review,* and *Seventeen.*

Sidelights

Trained as a pianist, Janet Nichols Lynch began her writing career with the nonfiction books *American Music Makers: An Introduction to American Composers* and *Women Music Makers: An Introduction to Women Composers,* both published under the name Janet Nichols. She turned to fiction with the middle-grade novel *Casey Wooster's Pet Care Service,* and has since gone on to produce both young-adult novels such as *Peace Is a Four-Letter Word* and *Messed Up* and the adult novel *Chest Pains.* In addition to her writing, Lynch works as an English teacher at a California high school and competes in marathons and triathlons. "I always end up writing about personal relationships, not just between the main characters, but among all the characters in a novel, no matter how minor they are," she once explained.

Set in 1990, during an unusually cold December in California's San Joaquin Valley, *Peace Is a Four-Letter Word* finds Emily Rankin worried less about the future of her farm family's annual orange crop than she is about U.S. involvement in the Persian Gulf, where Iraq has just invaded Kuwait. Inspired by her activist history teacher, Emily joins a local peace demonstration, much to the consternation of family and friends who view the teen's activism as unpatriotic. Lynch creates characters that *Booklist* critic Hazel Rochman characterized as "drawn with real complexity," and Emily's "smart, first-person narrative" reflects a balanced political assessment. Noting that the teen's "new ideology becomes less sure" as the story progresses, "her alienation leads to self-examination and the will to form her own opinions," according to *School Library Journal* contributor Suzanne Gordon.

Lynch focuses on a teen who is forced into adulthood far ahead of schedule in *Messed Up.* Here readers meet R.D., a fifteen-year-old Hispanic from a shattered home whose multiple attempts to graduate from the eighth grade become more challenging when Earl, his long-time guardian, dies. When social workers do not show up to take R.D. into foster care, the boy decides to take advantage of the fact that he has fallen through the welfare cracks. Step by step, in a progression that Daniel Kraus characterized in *Booklist* as "alternately funny and sad," the boy learns to fix his own meals, go shopping, navigate the checking account and pay his bills, and even handle Earl's funeral arrangements. Calling *Messed Up* a "gripping tale," Kraus praised Lynch for her "solid command of a young adult's view on adult life" and *School Library Journal* contributor Adrienne L. Strock predicted that the plight of Lynch's resourceful protagonist "could appeal to reluctant readers."

Another novel for teens that is set in the author's multiethnic San Joaquin Valley community, *Addicted to Her* presents what a *Publishers Weekly* critic described as a "fast paced" and "gripping story" about a high-school junior whose infatuation with a beautiful classmate begins to consume his life. For Rafael Montoya, hard work has made him a success in school, where he has earned a reputation for being a responsible guy. Although he has a crush on Monique, she seems to be out of his league until her boyfriend turns violent and Rafael becomes her rescuer. As their romance grows, Mo-

Cover of Lynch's teen novel Messed Up, *which finds a middle grader trying to make it on his own after his adult caretaker dies.* (Reproduced by permission.)

nique's incessant demands soon compromise Rafael's commitments to his wrestling team and threaten his academic success. Eventually, the young man is forced to reconcile the feelings in his heart with the facts, drawing readers into what the critic praised as a "memorable character study and a powerful account of a consuming teenage relationship."

Lynch once commented: "Ever since I can remember, words have poured out of me. Writing was a part of the way I played as a child. I wrote plays and my schoolmates acted them out. I wrote to pen pals and in my journals. I made up stories and gave some of them to my friends in weekly installments. At eighteen, I wrote all the words and the music for a musical. It wasn't very good. By age twenty-three, I had written 500 poems—enough to know that I would never be a poet. I then began writing articles about bicycle racing for *Competetive Cycling, Bike World,* and *Bicycling* because I was racing bicycles at the time. It actually took me a long time to find my intended genre: not poetry, plays, or nonfiction but fiction. I discovered that the type of books I love to read are also the kind I want to write."

Of her writing process, Lynch told *SATA:* "Everything I know about writing I learned playing the piano. Practice doesn't make perfect, but it certainly improves things. Without studying piano, I never would have understood how very long it takes to develop an art, and I would have been discouraged by rejection letters long ago.

"It's the details that matter in learning a piece of music as well as its whole, and that's true in novel writing also. Pianists practice a small section of a piece over and over, and then step back to see how that little section fits into the whole work, just like a novelist will rework a scene and determine how it relates to the whole novel. Repetition is key in both arts. I have to read a novel I'm writing many times, rework it, and read it some more. My editor offers me suggestions to improve the work, just like a piano teacher critiques a performance. I take her ideas back to my work-in-progress and revise it again.

"I find the processes of learning a piano piece and writing a novel very satisfying. I love the work, or I wouldn't be doing it. In both endeavors, I also have to be self-motivated. No one ever asked me to learn a piano piece or write a novel. I do these things because I'm passionate about them. I live my life absorbed in both music and writing."

Biographical and Critical Sources

PERIODICALS

Booklist, October 1, 2005, Hazel Rochman, review of *Peace Is a Four-Letter Word,* p. 49; April 1, 2009, Daniel Kraus, review of *Messed Up,* p. 33.

Bulletin of the Center for Children's Books, June, 2009, Karen Coats, review of *Messed Up,* p. 409.

Library Journal, October 1, 2008, Patrick Sullivan, review of *Chest Pains,* p. 60.

Publishers Weekly, November 28, 2005, review of *Peace Is a Four-Letter Word,* p. 52; September 8, 2008, review of *Chest Pains,* p. 33; May 10, 2010, review of *Addicted to Her,* p. 46.

School Library Journal, October, 2005, Susanne Gordon, review of *Peace Is a Four-Letter Word,* p. 164; August, 2009, Adrienne L. Strock, review of *Messed Up,* p. 108.

Voice of Youth Advocates, August, 2009, Teresa Copeland, review of *Messed Up,* p. 228.

ONLINE

Janet Nichols Lynch Home Page, http://www.janetnichols lynch.com (October 15, 2010).

M

MANTCHEV, Lisa

Personal

Children: one daughter. *Education:* Attended college. *Hobbies and other interests:* The theatre.

Addresses

Home—Olympic Peninsula, WA. *Agent*—Ashely Grayson Literary Agency, 1324 W. 18th St., San Pedro, CA 90732.

Career

Author and actress.

Writings

"THÉÂTRE ILLUMINATA" SERIES; YOUNG-ADULT NOVELS

Eyes like Stars, Feiwel & Friends (New York, NY), 2009.
Perchance to Dream, Feiwel & Friends (New York, NY), 2010.

Contributor of short fiction to periodicals, including *Abyss, Aeon, Apex, Clarkesworld, Fantasy, Strange Horizons,* and *Weird Tales.*

Adaptations

Eyes like Stars was adapted as an audiobook, read by Cynthia Bishop, Full Cast Audio, 2010.

Sidelights

Fantasy writer Lisa Mantchev draws readers into a magical world in her "Théâtre Illuminata" novel series, which includes *Eyes like Stars* and *Perchance to Dream.* The novels introduce high-spirited seventeen-year-old Beatrice "Bertie" Shakespeare Smith, a foundling who as an infant was discovered abandoned on the doorstep of the Théâtre Illuminata. An assemblage of all the characters from every play ever written, the Théâtre Illuminata operates on rules set forth in a magical book. This stage becomes Bertie's world, a magical place in which best friends are fairies from Shakespeare's *A Midsummer Night's Dream* and nothing is impossible.

Beginning life as a short story titled "All Her World's a Stage," *Eyes like Stars* finds Bertie now old enough to be accountable for her mischievous pranks. According to Théâtre Illuminata rules, she must contribute something to the community; if not, she will be sent out into the real world. But what? As she chronicles Bertie's efforts to hone her talent for improvisation into something that will serve the group, Mantchev also follows a threat to the community that is perpetrated by *Tempest* star Ariel. In *Publishers Weekly* a reviewer described *Eyes like Stars* as "dreamlike," while *Booklist* contributor Gillian Engberg wrote that the text is crafted from chain of "inventive" theatrical vignettes featuring "multiple, even metaphysical narratives filled with delicious banter and familiar characters from the dramatic canon." Engberg also dubbed *Eyes like Stars* a "bravely flamboyant and wholly original romp," while the *Publishers Weekly* critic called the book a "passionate debut" that taps into many teens' love for the theatre. "Readers who have some knowledge of . . . theatrical productions will have the easiest time following the twists and turns of the plot" in *Eyes like Stars,* wrote Cheri Dobbs in *School Library Journal,* the critic adding that Bertie "is a fun character." As a *Kirkus Reviews* writer concluded, "Mantchev seamlessly blends the richly wrought, claustrophobic world of the tradition-bound theater . . . with a decidedly modern sensibility. The result," the critic added, "is electric."

Perchance to Dream, the second novel in Mantchev's series, finds Bertie now charged with the duties of the Teller of Tales. When Nate, a pirate character, is captured by a jealous sea goddess, the teen bravely leaves the Théâtre Illuminata and attempts a rescue, helped by

Ariel and her four wingéd best friends. Reviewing *Perchance to Dream* in *Kirkus Reviews,* a critic described the story as an "exhilarating" tale that is carried along by "Mantchev's fresh, intelligent style." "By turns perilous and comedic, [*Perchance to Dream*] . . . rolls along at breakneck speed," wrote Joyce Adams Burner, the *School Library Journal* critic adding that Mantchev's "fans . . . will cry 'Encore!' as the ending sets up the third in the series."

Biographical and Critical Sources

PERIODICALS

Booklist, May 15, 2009, Gillian Engberg, review of *Eyes like Stars,* p. 48.

Kirkus Reviews, June 1, 2009, review of *Eyes like Stars*; May 1, 2010, review of *Perchance to Dream.*

Publishers Weekly, July 20, 2009, review of *Eyes like Stars,* p. 141.

School Library Journal, August, 2009, Cheri Dobbs, review of *Eyes like Stars,* p. 109; June, 2010, Joyce Adams Burner, review of *Perchance to Dream,* p. 112.

Voice of Youth Advocates, August, 2009, Ann Welton, review of *Eyes like Stars,* p. 240.

ONLINE

Lisa Mantchev Home Page, http://lisamantchev.com (October 15, 2010).*

*   *   *

MASSE, Josée

Personal

Born in Montréal, Québec, Canada; married; children: one daughter. *Education:* Degree, c. 1991.

Addresses

Home—Saint-Jean-sur-Richelieu, Québec, Canada. *Agent*—Lori Nowicki, lori@painted-words.com. *E-mail*—info@joseemasse.com.

Career

Illustrator and graphic artist.

Illustrator

John Wilson, *Les prisonniers du crétcé,* translated from the English by Daniel Charron, Héritage (Saint-Lambert, Québec, Canada), 1997.

André Marois, reteller, *Le chat botté à New York,* Les 400 Coups (Laval, Québec, Canada), 2000.

Carole Tremblay, *Recette de garçon à la sauce pompier,* Les 400 Coups (Laval, Québec, Canada) 2001.

Marilyn Helmer, reteller, *Three Cat and Mouse Tales: Puss-in-Boots, Town Mouse and Country Mouse, Dick Whittington and His Cat,* Kids Can Press (Toronto, Ontario, Canada), 2004.

Johanne Gangé, *Quelle étrange bête chez moi!,* Les 400 Coups (Laval, Québec, Canada), 2004.

Pierrette Dubé, reteller, *Jacques et le haricot magique: un conte classique,* Éditions Imagine (Montréal, Québec, Canada), 2005.

Mireille Levert, *La princesse qui avait presque tout,* Dominique et Cie. (Saint-Lambert, Québec, Canada), 2006, translated as *The Princess Who Had Almost Everything,* Tundra Books (Toronto, Ontario, Canada), 2008.

Gilles Tibo, *La petite princesse et le vent,* Éditions Imagine (Montréal, Québec, Canada), 2006.

Linda Bailey, *Goodnight, Sweet Pig,* Kids Can Press (Toronto, Ontario, Canada), 2007.

Xinran, *Ton histoire d'amour,* Dominique et Cie. (Saint-Lambert, Québec, Canada), 2007.

Bertrand Gauthier, *Oscar n'est pas un braillard,* Éditions du Renouveau Pédagogique (Saint-Lambert, Québec, Canada), 2007.

Xinran, *Motherbridge of Love,* Barefoot Books (Cambridge, MA), 2007.

Gilles Tibo, *La petite princesse et le prince,* Éditions Imagine (Montréal, Québec, Canada), 2008.

Marie-Nicole Marchand, *Parti vert chez les grenouilles,* Bayard Canada Livres (Montréal, Québec, Canada), 2008.

Suzanne Michaud, *Al Zimmer,* Éditions Corne de Brume (Saint-Hubert, Québec, Canada), 2009.

Dori Chaconas, *Mousie Love,* Bloomsbury U.S.A. Children's Books (New York, NY), 2009.

Anna Witte, *Lola's Fandango,* Barefoot Books (Cambridge, MA), 2010.

Gilles Tibo, *La petite princesse et les livres,* Éditions Imagine (Montréal, Québec, Canada), 2010.

Nadine Descheneaux, *Zouzou Cachette,* Éditions du Renouveau Pédagogique (Saint-Lambert, Québec, Canada), 2010.

Marilyn Singer, *Mirror Mirror: A Book of Reversible Verse,* Dutton (New York, NY), 2010.

"JOMUSCH" SERIES; ILLUSTRATOR

Christiane Duchesne, *Jomusch et le troll des cuisines,* Dominique et Cie. (Saint-Lambert, Québec, Canada), 2000.

Christiane Duchesne, *Jomusch et la demoiselle d'en haut,* Dominique et Cie. (Saint-Lambert, Québec, Canada), 2002.

Christiane Duchesne, *Jomusch et les poules de Fred,* Dominique et Cie. (Saint-Lambert, Québec, Canada), 2003.

Christiane Duchesne, *Jomusch et les grands rendez-vous,* Dominique et Cie. (Saint-Lambert, Québec, Canada), 2003.

Christiane Duchesne, *Jomusch et le jumeau mystère,* Dominique et Cie. (Saint-Lambert, Québec, Canada), 2004.

Christiane Duchesne, *Jomusch et le trésor de Mathias,* Dominique et Cie. (Saint-Lambert, Québec, Canada), 2005.

Christiane Duchesne, *Jomusch et le mains de papier,* Dominique et Cie. (Saint-Lambert, Québec, Canada), 2009.

Sidelights

Josée Masse is a Canadian artist and illustrator who lives and works in Montréal. Growing up, she was inspired to begin painting by her father, with whom she spent many hours in his artist's studio. Masse went on to study graphic arts in college and worked as a graphic designer for three years. In the early 1990s, she decided to turn to book illustration and has since gained a reputation for bringing to life picture-book texts featuring sophisticated and often conceptual themes. In addition to collaborating with author Christiane Duchesne on Duchesne's "Jomusch" series, Masse has illustrated stories by both French-and English-language writer, among them Mireille Levert, Linda Bailey, Gilles Tibo, Anna Witte, and Marilyn Singer. Describing her artwork for *Motherbridge of Love,* a book by Chinese activist Xinran that presents a reassuring view of adoption, Deborah Vose wrote in *School Library Journal* that Masse's "soothing paintings . . . are exceptional, and infuse this lyrical poem with a sweet tenderness."

In her illustrations for Mireille Levert's *The Princess Who Had Almost Everything,* Masse brings to life the story of Princess Alicia, a girl who has the best of everything but remains bored and lonely. Linda Kenton noted in *School Library Journal* that the artist's "rich palette" of muted reds and greens combines with her use of "varied perspectives" to reinforce Levert's message: the best things in life are the simple things. Calling *The Princess Who Had Almost Everything* an "enchanting lesson in the importance of simple gifts," a *Kirkus Reviews* writer also credited Masse's "humorous, stylized illustrations" for capturing the story's spoiled young heroine, and in *Booklist* Patricia Austin asserted that the book's "dramatic angular illustrations," rendered in "an earth-tone palette," add "visual interest" to Levert's original fairy tale.

A counting book, Bailey's *Goodnight, Sweet Pig* has been published in both English and French and focuses on a young piglet that is kept from sleep due to constant disruptions in the pig pen. Here Masse's acrylic paintings "are bright and humorous," according to *School Library Journal* critic Donna Atmur, while Tanya Boudreau noted in *Resource Links* that the artist's "technique adds texture" and her paintings "have a worn wooden painted look to them." Masse creates "richly hued" illustrations that "add humor and warmth and wonderful details" to Dori Chaconas's whimsical

picture book *Mousie Love,* according to Linda Kenton in *School Library Journal,* and a *Kirkus Reviews* contributor described the same story as a "fetching little romance" that is complemented by Masse's "bright, cheerful acrylic-and-gel illustrations."

Singer's *Mirror Mirror: A Book of Reversible Verse* was described by *Booklist* critic Patricia Austin as an "ingenious book of reversos," simple free-verse poems that have a different meaning depending whether they are read from top to bottom or from bottom to top. Paired with Singer's intricate verbal puzzles, Masse's "deep-hued paintings create split images" that capture each poem's dual meaning, according to Austin. In *School Library Journal* Joan Kindig described Masse's "vibrant artwork" as "painterly yet unfussy" and deemed *Mirror Mirror* "a marvel to read" and "a must-have for any library."

Biographical and Critical Sources

PERIODICALS

Booklist, October 15, 2008, Patricia Austin, review of *The Princess Who Had Almost Everything,* p. 48; May, 2009, Abby Nolan, review of *Mousie Love,* p. 88; January 1, 2010, Patricia Austin, review of *Mirror Mirror: A Book of Reversible Verse,* p. 81.

Josée Masse's endearing illustrations capture the whimsy in Dori Chaconas's story for **Mousie Love.** (Bloomsbury, 2009. Reprinted by permission of Bloomsbury USA. All rights reserved.)

Bulletin of the Center for Children's Books, April, 2010, Deborah Stevenson, review of *Mirror Mirror,* p. 353.

Globe & Mail (Toronto, Ontario, Canada), November 22, 2008, Susan Perren, review of *The Princess Who Had Almost Everything,* p. D14.

Horn Book, March-April, 2010, Roger Sutton, review of *Mirror Mirror,* p. 79.

Kirkus Reviews, September 15, 2008, review of *The Princess Who Had Almost Everything*; May 1, 2009, review of *Mousie Love.*

Publishers Weekly, September 10, 2007, review of *Motherbridge of Love,* p. 59; June 1, 2009, review of *Mousie Love,* p. 46; February 8, 2010, review of *Poems to Grow On,* p. 48.

Resource Links, April, 2004, Ann Ketcheson, review of *Three Cat and Mouse Tales: Puss-in-Boots, Town Mouse and Country Mouse, Dick Whittington and His Cat,* p. 4; June, 2007, Tanya Boudreau, review of *Goodnight, Sweet Pig,* p. 1; October, 2008, review of *The Princess Who Had Almost Everything,* p. 1.

School Library Journal, July, 2004, Linda M. Kenton, review of *Three Cat and Mouse Tales,* p. 94; June, 2007, Donna Atmur, review of *Goodnight, Sweet Pig,* p. 92; January, 2008, Deborah Vose, review of *Motherbridge of Love,* p. 103; January, 2009, Linda M. Kenton, review of *The Princess Who Had Almost Everything,* p. 78; September, 2009, Linda M. Kenton, review of *Mousie Love,* p. 118; January, 2010, Joan Kindig, review of *Mirror Mirror,* p. 90.

ONLINE

Josée Masse Home Page, http://www.joseemasse.com (October 15, 2010).

Painted Words Web Site, http://www.painted-words.com/ (October 15, 2010), "Josée Masse."*

*   *   *

MATTHEWS, Cecily 1945-

Personal

Born 1945, in St. George, Queensland, Australia; married David Matthews; children: four daughters. *Education:* University of Queensland, diploma (speech therapy). *Hobbies and other interests:* Gardening, quilting, researching family history.

Addresses

Home—Kilcoy, Queensland, Australia. *E-mail*—cecily. matthews@gmail.com.

Career

Writer. Worked in a school library, Ferny Grove, Queensland, Australia.

Cecily Matthews (Reproduced by permission.)

Awards, Honors

Australian Children's Book Council Award shortlist in Early Childhood category, and Australian Family Therapists' Award for younger readers, both 2006, both for *Emily Rapunzel's Hair.*

Writings

Thinking Power, illustrated by Katherine Bradfield, Omnibus (Norwood, South Australia, Australia), 1990.

The Seventh Good Reason, illustrated by Frances Luke, Jam Roll Press (Nundah, Queensland, Australia), 1992.

Captain Orinoco's Onion ("Voyages" reader series), illustrated by Craig Smith, SRA School Group (Santa Rosa, CA), 1994.

Mr. Clutterbus ("Voyages" reader series), illustrated by Lucinda Hunnam, SRA School Group (Santa Rosa, CA), 1994.

My Dog Ben ("Voyages" reader series), illustrated by Ned Culic, SRA School Group (Santa Rosa, CA), 1994.

Why Not? ("Voyages" reader series), illustrated by Ned Culic, SRA School Group (Santa Rosa, CA), 1994.

Monster Magic, illustrated by Caroline Magerl, University of Queensland Press (St. Lucia, Queensland, Australia), 1996.

Emily's Rapunzel Hair, illustrated by Freya Blackwood, ABC Books (Sydney, New South Wales, Australia), 2006.

Omm Pa Pah!, illustrated by Mitch Vane, ABC Books (Sydney, New South Wales, Australia), 2007.

Cock-a-Doodle Doo!, illustrated by Lorette Broekstra, Little Hare Books (Surry Hills, New South Wales, Australia), 2008.

Please Come to My Party!, illustrated by Stuart Billington, Pearson Australia (Sydney, New South Wales, Australia), 2010.

Biographical and Critical Sources

PERIODICALS

Reading Time, Volume 40, number 4, 1996, review of *Monster Magic.*

School Library Journal, October, 2009, Sarah Polace, review of *Cock-a-Doodle-Doo!,* p. 98.

ONLINE

Cecily Matthews Home Page, http://www.cecilymatthews. com (October 15, 2010).

*   *   *

McDONNELL, Patrick 1956-

Personal

Born March 17, 1956, in Elizabeth, NJ; married Karen O'Connell. *Education:* School of Visual Arts, B.F.A., 1978.

Addresses

Home—Edison, NJ.

Career

Cartoonist, animator, and illustrator. Creator of "Mutts" daily syndicated comic strip, 1994—. Creator of animated television commercial for New York Philharmonic, 1993. Guest curator for Charles M. Schulz Museum. Member, Humane Society of the United States Hollywood Office. *Exhibitions:* Works exhibited at Jack Gallery, Los Angeles, CA, 2008.

Member

National Cartoonists Society, Charles M. Schulz Museum, Humane Society of the United States (member of board of directors), Fund for Animals (member of board), Art for Animals, Neighborhood Cats, North Shore Animal League.

Awards, Honors

Adamson Statuette, Swedish Academy of Comic Art, 1997; Ark Trust Genesis Award, 1997, 1999; Harvey Award for best comic strip, 1997, 1999, 2001, 2002, 2003, 2005; Reuben Award, National Cartoonist Society, 1997, for comic strip of the year, and 1999, for car-

toonist of the year; Max and Moritz Award for best international comic strip, 1998; People for the Ethical Treatment of Animals Humanitarian Award, 2001; HSUS Hollywood Genesis Award, 2002, 2005; Harvey Award nomination for Best Syndicated Strip or Panel, 2008, for "Mutts."

Writings

"MUTTS TREASURY" SERIES

Mutts, foreword by Charles M. Schulz, Andrews McMeel (Kansas City, MO), 1996.

Cats and Dogs: Mutts II, Andrews McMeel (Kansas City, MO), 1997.

More Shtuff, Andrews McMeel (Kansas City, MO), 1998.

Yesh!, Andrews McMeel (Kansas City, MO), 1999.

Mutts Sundays, Andrews McMeel (Kansas City, MO), 1999.

Our Mutts, Andrews McMeel (Kansas City, MO), 2000.

A Little Look-See, Andrews McMeel (Kansas City, MO), 2001.

Sunday Mornings, Andrews McMeel (Kansas City, MO), 2001.

What Now?, Andrews McMeel (Kansas City, MO), 2002.

I Want to Be the Kitty!, Andrews McMeel (Kansas City, MO), 2003.

Sunday Afternoons, Andrews McMeel (Kansas City, MO), 2003.

Dog-eared, Andrews McMeel (Kansas City, MO), 2004.

Who Let the Cat Out?, Andrews McMeel (Kansas City, MO), 2005.

Sunday Evenings, Andrews McMeel (Kansas City, MO), 2005.

Cover of Patrick McDonnell's **The Gift of Nothing,** *which features characters from his popular "Mutts" cartoon strip.* (Little, Brown, 2005. Illustration copyright © 2005 by Patrick McDonnell. Mutts © 2005 by Patrick McDonnell, distributed by King Features Syndicate. Reproduced by permission.)

Everyday Mutts, Andrews McMeel (Kansas City, MO), 2006.

Animal Friendly, Andrews McMeel (Kansas City, MO), 2007.

The Best of Mutts, 1994-2004, Andrews McMeel (Kansas City, MO), 2007.

Mutts Shelter Stories: Love, Guaranteed, Andrews Mc-Meel (Kansas City, MO), 2008.

FOR CHILDREN; SELF-ILLUSTRATED

The Gift of Nothing, Little, Brown (New York, NY), 2005.

Just like Heaven, Little, Brown (New York, NY), 2006.

Art, Little, Brown (New York, NY), 2006.

Hug Time, Little, Brown (New York, NY), 2007.

South, Little, Brown (New York, NY), 2008.

Wag!, Little, Brown Books for Young Readers (New York, NY), 2009.

Me—Jane, Little, Brown (New York, NY), 2011.

OTHER

(With wife Karen O'Connell and Georgia Riley de Havenon) *Krazy Kat: The Comic Art of George Herriman,* Harry N. Abrams (New York, NY), 1986.

Bad Baby (comic-strip collection), Fawcett Columbine (New York, NY), 1988.

(Illustrator) *They Said It!: 200 of the Funniest Sports Quips and Quotes,* Oxmoor House (New York, NY), 2000.

Mutts: The Comic Art of Patrick McDonnell, essay by John Carlin, Harry N. Abrams (New York, NY), 2003.

(Illustrator) Eckhart Tolle, *Guardians of Being,* New World Library (Novato, CA), 2009.

Illustrator for Russell Baker's "Observer" column, *New York Times Magazine,* 1978-93; creator of *Jerseyana* cartoon for *New Jersey Monthly,* 1980s; creator of "Bad Baby" monthly strip for *Parents* magazine; illustrator for "Scorecard" column in *Sports Illustrated,* "Bright Ideas" in *Parade,* and "Laughter" in *Reader's Digest.*

Adaptations

Art was adapted as an animated short film, narrated by Bobby McFerrin, released on DVD by Weston Woods, 2008.

Sidelights

Patrick McDonnell is the creator of the popular comic strip "Mutts," which is carried by more than 700 newspapers worldwide and has garnered a host of awards. The humorous, understated cartoon revolves around the adventures of Earl the dog, Mooch the cat, and a cast of eccentric supporting characters. According to George Gene Gustines, writing in the *New York Times,* "Mutts is a throwback. Its daily tales . . . ooze an archaic innocence (and sometimes an anarchic knowingness) that would not have been out of place in a Sunday comics

McDonnell's "Mutts" strip has been collected in several books, among them **Cats and Dogs: Mutts II.** (Andrews McMeel, 1997. Copyright © 1996 by Patrick McDonnell. King Features Syndicate. Reproduced with permission.)

supplement from the 1920's. It's easy to imagine Earl and Mooch rubbing panels with classic strips like George Herriman's 'Krazy Kat' or E.C. Segar's 'Popeye.'"

Born in 1956, McDonnell attended the School of Visual Arts in New York City, and after graduation he began a career as a freelance illustrator. From 1978 to 1993 he drew Russell Baker's "Observer" column in the *New York Times Magazine,* and he also created "Bad Baby," a monthly comic strip that ran in *Parents* magazine for ten years. During this time, McDonnell was also a regular contributor to *Sports Illustrated, Reader's Digest, Parade,* and other national magazines.

Despite his tremendous success, McDonnell decided to pursue his dream of writing and illustrating his own comic strip, and in 1994 he created "Mutts." At its heart is the friendship between Earl, the amiable canine who loves belly rubs, and Mooch, the curious feline who obsesses over little pink socks. According to David Astor, writing in *Editor & Publisher,* "McDonnell is not your typical modern-day cartoonist. While many of his peers produce comics with a hip, cynical edge, McDonnell prefers a kinder, gentler, 'stop-and-smell-the-roses' approach." As Astor continued, "McDonnell also bucks the trend of more topicality in comics by trying to keep the 'real world' from entering" his comic-strip fantasy. The animal cast members of "Mutts" "think about food, sleep, the weather and other basics of life as they get in

*In **South** McDonnell tells a poignant story that introduces a new cast of animal characters.* (Little Brown, 2008. Reproduced by permission of Little Brown.)

and out of all kinds of humorous situations." As Mc-Donnell told *New Jersey Monthly* contributor Anne-marie Conte, "a lot of cartoon animals are people in disguise. I want to keep my animals as animal-like as possible."

In addition to seeing his "Mutts" strip appear in daily syndication, McDonnell has produced a number of "Mutts" anthologies, among them *Mutts Sundays* and *Who Let the Cat Out?* He has also produced several children's books featuring the "Mutts" characters. In *The Gift of Nothing,* for example, McDonnell creates "a perfect meditation on gift giving and friendship," according to a critic in *Kirkus Reviews,* In the book, round-nosed Mooch tries to find the perfect present for Earl on his special day. When readers reunite with Mooch in the pages of *Just like Heaven,* he awakens from a nap just as a fog rolls in and mistakenly believes he has arrived in Heaven. In *South* Mooch helps a lost bird rejoin its flock on its migratory trip south for the winter, while *Wag!* finds the cat joined by frisky Earl as McDonnell's cartoon drawings focus on the mechanism that operates the dog's waggy tail.

"The small, sketchy illustrations hold a great deal of charm," observed *School Library Journal* reviewer Julie Roach in a review of *Just like Heaven,* while a *Kirkus Reviews* critic dubbed *South* a "warm and glowy" picture book in which "McDonnell's sense of just-sweet-enough is exactly right." Also reviewing in *School Library Journal,* Lisa Egly Lehmuller wrote that *Wag!* serves up a "charming story" in which "children will recognize themselves and their pets." A *Kirkus Reviews* writer dubbed the same book "sweet, gentle, [and] delightful," adding that McDonnell's "line drawings and washes . . . show exactly what's needed and no more."

Jules the kitten takes a break from "Mutts" to star in *Hug Time,* which is different from McDonnell's usual restrained cartoon art in its use of warm-toned paper and a range of pastel colors. The loving, red-nosed kitty

decides that it is time to give a hug to every creature on earth. After hugging all his friends and everyone in the park, the cat begins traveling. Jules' final trip, to the North Pole, yields few huggers until a fluffy (and not very hungry) polar bear shares the kitty's affectionate embrace. "McDonnell's carefully mixed gouaches and his able draftsmanship . . . hint at newly revealed talents," noted a *Publishers Weekly*, and in *School Library Journal* Marian Drabkin praised the art in *Hug Time* as "energetic, sketchy," and "dynamic." Citing the book's "environmentally friendly, endangered-species-loving message," a *Kirkus Reviews* critic recommended *Hug Time* as "a fine gift or story-time choice."

Expanding his cast of characters from "Mutts," McDonnell has also created original picture books such as *Art, Wag,* and *South.* In *Art* he crafts a story about a young boy's penchant for creating fanciful doodles, scribbles, and splotches. "The primary-color illustrations are exuberant and joyful and seamlessly match the text," wrote a contributor in *Kirkus Reviews.*

A strong advocate for humane animal welfare, McDonnell serves on the board of directors for the Humane Society of the United States. "People really identify with that special bond we all have with our animal companions," the cartoonist and author remarked on the *King Features* Web site. "Animals have unique personalities all their own. In *Mutts,* I try to express the world from their point of view."

Biographical and Critical Sources

BOOKS

McDonnell, Patrick, *Mutts: The Comic Art of Patrick McDonnell,* essay by John Carlin, Harry N. Abrams (New York, NY), 2003.

PERIODICALS

Booklist, April 1, 2006, Gillian Engberg, review of *Art,* p. 48.

Childhood Education, fall, 2006, May Anne Hannibal, review of *Art,* p. 51.

Editor & Publisher, November 16, 1996, David Astor, "It's Reigning a Cat and Dog in Hit Strip," p. 40; February 1, 2004, Dave Astor, "Syndicates: Art Book Showcases Artistic *Mutts* Strip."

Kirkus Reviews, September 15, 2005, review of *The Gift of Nothing,* p. 1030; March 15, 2006, review of *Art,* p. 296; September 15, 2006, review of *Just like Heaven,* p. 961; October 15, 2007, review of *Hug Time;* August 1, 2008, review of *South;* September 1, 2009, review of *Wag!*

New Jersey Monthly, April, 2006, Annemarie Conte, "His Name Is Earl."

New York Times, September 25, 2005, George Gene Gustines, "Where the Mild Things Are."

Publishers Weekly, November 21, 2005, review of *The Gift of Nothing,* p. 46; August 28, 2006, review of *Just like Heaven,* p. 52; November 19, 2007, review of *Hug Time,* p. 55; July 21, 2008, review of *South,* p. 158.

School Library Journal, January, 2006, Marianne Saccardi, review of *The Gift of Nothing,* p. 108; April, 2006, Marianne Saccardi, review of *Art,* p. 129; November, 2006, Julie Roach review of *Just like Heaven,* p. 105; December, 2007, Marian Drabkin, review of *Hug Time,* p. 94; August, 2008, Wendy Lukehart, review of *South,* p. 98; November, 2009, Lisa Egly Lehmuller, review of *Wag!,* p. 83.

ONLINE

King Features Web site, http://www.kingfeatures.com/ (May 10, 2007), "Patrick McDonnell."

Patrick McDonnell Home Page, http://muttscomics.com (October 30, 2010).*

*   *   *

MEYER, L.A. 1942-
(Louis A. Meyer)

Personal

Born August 22, 1942, in Johnstown, PA; son of Louis, Sr. (an army officer) and Martha (a homemaker) Meyer; married Annetje Lawrence (a retailer), May 28, 1966; children: Matthew, Nathaniel. *Education:* University of Florida, B.A. (English literature), 1964; graduate study at Columbia University, 1970; Boston University, M.F.A. (painting), 1973. *Politics:* "Independent."

Addresses

Home—Corea, ME.

Career

Painter and author. Rockland High School, Rockland, MA, art teacher, 1974-81; Sweetback Graphics (textile design and imprinting firm), Fort Myers Beach, Fl, cofounder, 1981-98; Clair de Loon Gallery (art gallery), Bar Harbor, ME, cofounder beginning 1984; Blue Loon Studio Gallery, Birch Harbor, ME, co-owner. *Military service:* U.S. Navy, 1964-68; became lieutenant.

Writings

FOR CHILDREN

(As Louis A. Meyer) *The Gypsy Bears,* Little, Brown (Boston, MA), 1971.

(As Louis A. Meyer) *The Clean Air and Peaceful Contentment Dirigible Airline,* Little, Brown (Boston, MA), 1972.

L.A. Meyer (Photograph by Annetje Meyer. Reproduced by permission.)

"JACKY FABER" SERIES; YOUNG-ADULT NOVELS

Bloody Jack: Being an Account of the Curious Adventures of Mary "Jacky" Faber, Ship's Boy, Harcourt (San Diego, CA), 2002.

Curse of the Blue Tattoo: Being an Account of the Misadventures of Jacky Faber, Midshipman and Fine Lady, Harcourt (Orlando, FL), 2004.

Under the Jolly Roger: Being an Account of the Further Nautical Adventures of Jacky Faber, Harcourt (Orlando, FL), 2005.

In the Belly of the Bloodhound: Being an Account of a Particularly Peculiar Adventure in the Life of Jacky Faber, Harcourt (Orlando, FL), 2006.

Mississippi Jack: Being an Account of the Further Waterborne Adventures of Jacky Faber, Midshipman, Fine Lady, and the Lily of the West, Harcourt (Orlando, FL), 2007.

My Bonny Light Horseman: Being an Account of the Further Adventures of Jacky Faber, in Love and War, Harcourt (Orlando, FL), 2008.

Rapture of the Deep: Being an Account of the Further Adventures of Jacky Faber, Soldier, Sailor, Mermaid, Spy, Harcourt (Boston, MA), 2009.

The Wake of the Lorelei Lee: Being an Account of the Adventures of Jacky Faber on Her Way to Botany Bay, Harcourt (Boston, MA), 2010.

Adaptations

Meyer's "Bloody Jack" novels were adapted as audiobooks, read by Katherine Kellgren, Listen & Live Audio, 2007.

Sidelights

A painter and author, L.A. Meyer is best known as the creator of the "Jacky Faber" adventure novels for young adults. Under his full name, Louis A. Meyer, he created the children's picture books *The Gypsy Bears* and *The Clean Air and Peaceful Contentment Dirigible Airline* while attending art school in Boston in the early 1970s, but he focused on his painting for many years before returning to writing. Beginning with *Bloody Jack: Being an Account of the Curious Adventures of Mary "Jacky" Faber, Ship's Boy,* Meyer's novels follow the adventures of a young woman who joins the British fleet during the days of high-seas piracy, disguising herself as a young man.

Described by a *Publishers Weekly* critic as "a refreshing and delightful fantasy," Meyer's self-illustrated *The Gypsy Bears* focuses on a family of human-like bears that must leave their home in Romania to escape a famine. Needing to support their two cubs, King Zoltan and Maria find it difficult to make a living by entertaining people with their music because everyone appears to fear them. Eventually trapped and sent to a zoo, the bears escape and make their way to Yellowstone Park, where they are able to resume their nomadic ways without fear. An eccentric inventor builds a flying machine that eventually replaces the airplane and the family car in *The Clean Air and Peaceful Contentment Dirigible Airline,* a picture book by Meyer that Carol Chatfield praised as "bold and brassy" in her *Library Journal* review.

Meyer's "Jacky Faber" books mark a major shift from his earlier works. Geared for an older readership, they feature exciting, fast-paced plots, a resourceful heroine, and an intriguing setting. In a comment to *SATA,* the author once explained the genesis of the series, which occurred while he was busy matting and framing prints to stock his Maine art gallery. "One day in the summer of 2000, I'm framing away in my workshop and listening to British and Celtic folk music on our local community radio station, when the host of the program plays a long string of early nineteenth-century songs that feature young girls dressing up as boys and following their boyfriends out to sea, the most well known of these being 'Jackaroe' and 'Cana-di-i-o.' These generally end up with the girl being found out quickly and happily marrying either the boy or the captain. It occurred to me, however, to wonder what it would be like if the girl, instead of seeking to be with her lover, connives to get on board a British warship in order to just eat regularly and have a place to stay, her being a starving orphan on the streets of late 1700s London. What would she have to do to pull off this deception for a

long period of time? How would she handle the 'necessary' things? What if she goes through the changes of adolescence while on board in the company of 408 rather rough men and boys, and her not having much of a clue as to what is happening to her? What if this ship goes into combat and she has to do her dangerous duty? And, finally, what if she falls in love with one of the boys and can never tell him of her female nature?

"I started making notes and seven months later *Bloody Jack* was done."

Set in turn-of-the-nineteenth-century London, *Bloody Jack* introduces orphaned twelve-year-old Mary, who decides to disguise herself as a boy and sign onto the HMS *Dolphin,* a British warship. Mary must learn the arduous job of a ship's boy, and the opportunities for her to show her mettle are frequent in the face of predatory shipmates, a clash with pirates, and a shipwreck. Throughout, she must maintain her disguise as "Jacky" despite the ongoing changes of puberty and her growing feelings for Jaimy Fletcher, another of the ship's young sailors.

Cover of Meyer's young-adult novel My Bonny Light Horseman, *an installment in his "Bloody Jack Adventures" series.* (Copyright © 2008 by L.A. Meyer. Reproduced by permission of Houghton Mifflin Harcourt Publishing Company. All rights reserved.)

"The action in Jacky's tale will entertain readers with a taste for adventure," contended Carolyn Phelan in a *Booklist* review of *Bloody Jack,* the critic also praising Meyer's effective use of period detail and the strength of Jacky's narrative voice. While not a "rousing, swashbuckling tale of pirates and adventures on the high seas," in the opinion of *School Library Journal* critic Kit Vaughan, *Bloody Jack* serves up "a good story" with a strong, likeable heroine, and a *Publishers Weekly* critic cited the "Dickensian flair" used in depicting the hardships of an orphaned child living on the streets of London. A critic for *Kirkus Reviews* dubbed Meyer's novel "a rousing old-time girl's adventure story" featuring "an outsized heroine who is equal parts gutsy and vulnerable" and recommended *Bloody Jack* as "a first-rate read" for young readers.

Jacky's adventures continue in several more books. *Curse of the Blue Tattoo: Being an Account of the Misadventures of Jacky Faber, Midshipman and Fine Lady* finds Jacky run aground in Boston and enduring life at Mistress Pimm's finishing school in the hopes of gaining some feminine refinement. However, her adventurous nature eventually outs, evicting her from class and involving Jaimy in a murder investigation that requires the teen to navigate the seamy side of the city. "With her propensity for plunging headfirst into trouble, the irrepressible Jacky rolls quickly from one adventure to another," noted Connie Tyrell Burns, in her review of *Curse of the Blue Tattoo* for *School Library Journal.* Although *Horn Book* critic Betty Carter noted that "Jacky develops a social veneer [at school] that reveals itself through her increasingly polished language," the reviewer was quick to assure readers that it "doesn't obliterate her individualism."

Under the Jolly Roger: Being an Account of the Further Nautical Adventures of Jacky Faber finds Jacky fifteen years old and landing in back in London in the hope of finding Jaimy. She returns to the sea unexpectedly, when she is coerced aboard another British ship by a press gang, and ends up involved in a mutiny that leaves the young teen captaining the ship. Another attempt at finishing school plays out following the Battle of Trafalgar in *In the Belly of the Bloodhound: Being an Account of a Particularly Peculiar Adventure in the Life of Jacky Faber*, as Jacky makes her way back to Boston until a short sail to a coastal island leads to abduction on a slave ship bound for Africa. The year is 1806 in *Mississippi Jack: Being an Account of the Further Waterborne Adventures of Jacky Faber, Midshipman, Fine Lady, and the Lily of the West,* as the threat of arrest forces Jacky to travel inland and make her way down the Mississippi as part of a theatrical troupe. Recommending Meyer's series "for fans of historical fiction and pirates," Anna M. Nelson added in her *School Library Journal* review of *Under the Jolly Roger* that "Jacky is a wonderful character, full of high spirits, brains, and heart." For fans, the best part of the "Jacky Faber" series is "watching [Meyer's] . . . cunning, un-

conventional, warmhearted heroine in action," asserted Phelan in *Booklist,* and Claire Rosser agreed in her *Kliatt* review of *Mississippi Jack.* "Jacky is amazing," Rosser asserted, listing the many talents and skills of the worldly wise teen, and "Jacky's adventures are hilarious."

Continuing Meyer's popular nineteenth-century high-seas saga, *My Bonny Light Horseman: Being an Account of the Further Adventures of Jacky Faber, in Love and War* finds Jacky working as a spy with the assignment to monitor the movement of France's deposed emperor Napoleon Bonaparte. In *Rapture of the Deep: Being an Account of the Further Adventures of Jacky Faber, Soldier, Sailor, Mermaid, Spy,* it finally seems to be wedding bells for Jacky and Jaimy, until the bride is snatched from the altar and compelled to help the British Navy track down a treasure lost out at sea. The resilient heroine's adventures continue in *The Wake of the Lorelei Lee: Being an Account of the Adventures of Jacky Faber on Her Way to Botany Bay.* "Amusing nomenclature, historical and cultural in-jokes and colorful locales are strewn . . . throughout [Jacky's] . . . long and tireless narrative," observed a *Kirkus Reviews* writer in appraising *My Bonny Light Horseman,* and Rosser asserted of the same book that "it's Meyer's wit and intelligence that bring the reader along in these totally improbable but entertaining epics."

Biographical and Critical Sources

PERIODICALS

Booklist, November 15, 2002, Carolyn Phelan, review of *Bloody Jack: Being an Account of the Curious Adventures of Mary "Jacky" Faber, Ship's Boy,* p. 595; May 15, 2004, Carolyn Phelan, review of *Curse of the Blue Tattoo: Being an Account of the Misadventures of Jacky Faber, Midshipman and Fine Lady,* p. 1629; August, 2005, Carolyn Phelan, review of *Under the Jolly Roger: Being an Account of the Further Nautical Adventures of Jacky Faber,* p. 2015; November 1, 2006, Carolyn Phelan, review of *In the Belly of the Bloodhound: Being an Account of a Particularly Peculiar Adventure in the Life of Jacky Faber,* p. 50; November 1, 2007, Carolyn Phelan, review of *Mississippi Jack: Being an Account of the Further Waterborne Adventures of Jacky Faber, Midshipman, Fine Lady, and the Lily of the West,* p. 48; September 1, 2009, Carolyn Phelan, review of *Rapture of the Deep: Being an Account of the Further Adventures of Jacky Faber, Soldier, Sailor, Mermaid, Spy,* p. 86.
Kirkus Reviews, March 15, 1972, review of *The Clean Air and Peaceful Contentment Dirigible,* p. 322; August 1, 2002, review of *Bloody Jack,* p. 1137; June 1, 2004, review of *Curse of the Blue Tattoo,* p. 539; July 1, 2005, review of *Under the Jolly Roger,* p. 739; August 1, 2008, review of *My Bonny Light Horseman: Being an Account of the Further Adventures of Jacky Faber, in Love and War.*

Kliatt, May, 2004, Claire Rosser, review of *Curse of the Blue Tattoo,* p. 11; July, 2004, Claire Rosser, review of *In the Belly of the Bloodhound,* p. 22; September, 2007, Claire Rosser, review of *Mississippi Jack,* p. 16; July, 2008, Claire Rosser, review of *In the Belly of the Bloodhound,* p. 19.
Library Journal, May 15, 1971, Muriel Kolb, review of *The Gypsy Bears,* p. 1806; February 15, 1973, Carol Chatfield, review of *The Clean Air and Peaceful Contentment Dirigible,* p. 646.
Publishers Weekly, February 15, 1971, review of *The Gypsy Bears,* p. 79; October 7, 2002, review of *Bloody Jack,* p. 74.
School Library Journal, September, 2002, Kit Vaughan, review of *Bloody Jack,* p. 229; July, 2004, Connie Tyrrell Burns, review of *Curse of the Blue Tattoo,* p. 110; January, 2007, Kristen Oravec, review of *In the Belly of the Bloodhound,* p. 134; November, 2007, review of *Bloody Jack,* p. 70; December, 2007, Kristen Oravec, review of *Mississippi Jack,* p. 136; December, 2009, Kristen Oravec, review of *Rapture of the Deep,* p. 128.

ONLINE

L.A. Meyer Home Page, http://clairdeloon.com (October 15, 2010).*

* * *

MEYER, Louis A.
See MEYER, L.A.

* * *

MORTENSEN, Lori 1955-

Personal

Born 1955, in CA; married (husband an engineer); children: two sons, one daughter. *Education:* Attended California State University—Hayward; Brigham Young University, B.S. (professional dance and art); earned teaching credential (dance education).

Addresses

Home—Northern CA. *Agent*—Kendra Marcus, Book Stop Literary Agency, 67 Meadow View Rd., Orinda, CA 94563. *E-mail*—lori@lorimortensen.com.

Career

Educator and writer. Worked variously as a word processor, sign-language interpreter, substitute high-school teacher, and master canner. Institute of Children's Literature, writing instructor.

Awards, Honors

Best Children's Book of the Year designation, Bank Street College of Education, 2008, for *Harriet Tubman;* National Book of the Year Award, Izaak Walton League

Lori Mortensen (Photograph by Jeanine Mays. Reproduced by permission.)

of America, and Silver Moonbeam Children's Book Award, both 2009, Outstanding Science Book for Students K-12 designation, National Science Teachers Association/Children's Book Council, Mom's Choice Gold Award, and *Skipping Stones* Honor Award, all 2010, and Florida Reading Association Children's Book Award nomination, 2011, all for *In the Trees, Honey Bees.*

Writings

FOR CHILDREN

Leprechauns ("Mysterious Encounters" series), KidHaven Press (Detroit, MI), 2007.

In the Trees, Honey Bees, illustrated by Cris Arbo, Dawn Publications (Nevada City, CA), 2009.

Come See the Earth Turn: The Story of Léon Foucault, illustrated by Raul Allen, Tricycle Press (Berkeley, CA), 2010.

Elephants ("Rocket Animals" series), Marshall Cavendish Benchmark (New York, NY), 2010.

Manners Matter in the Classroom, Capstone Press (Mankato, MN), 2011.

Contributor of short fiction to periodicals, including *Highlights for Children.*

"MONSTERS" NONFICTION SERIES"

Basilisks, KidHaven Press (San Diego, CA), 2006.

Killer Sharks, KidHaven Press (Detroit, MI), 2008.

The Sphinx, KidHaven Press (Detroit, MI), 2008.

"PICTURE-BOOK BIOGRAPHIES" SERIES

Thomas Edison: Inventor, Scientist, and Genius, illustrated by Jeffrey Thompson, Picture Window Books (Minneapolis, MN), 2007.

Harriet Tubman: Hero of the Underground Railroad, illustrated by Frances Moore, Picture Window Books (Minneapolis, MN), 2007.

Amelia Earhart: Female Pioneer in Flight, illustrated by Robert McGuire, Picture Window Books (Minneapolis, MN), 2008.

George Washington Carver: Teacher, Scientist, and Inventor, illustrated by Niamh O'Connor, Picture Window Books (Minneapolis, MN), 2008.

Marie Curie: Prize-winning Scientist, illustrated by Susan Jaekel, Picture Window Books (Minneapolis, MN), 2008.

Thomas Jefferson, a Founding Father of the United States of America, illustrated by Len Ebert, Picture Window Books (Minneapolis, MN), 2008.

"READ-IT READER" SERIES

Bailey's Bike, illustrated by Amy Bailey Muehlenhardt, Picture Window Books (Minneapolis, MN), 2008.

Dirty Gertie, illustrated by Gina Marie Perry, Picture Window Books (Minneapolis, MN), 2009.

Vote for Our Zoo, illustrated by Gina Perry, Picture Window Books (Minneapolis, MN), 2009.

"AMERICAN SYMBOL" NONFICTION SERIES"

Angel Island, illustrated by Matthew Skeens, Picture Window Books (Minneapolis, MN), 2009.

Ellis Island, illustrated by Matthew Skeens, Picture Window Books (Minneapolis, MN), 2009.

The Declaration of Independence, illustrated by Matthew Skeens, Picture Window Books (Minneapolis, MN), 2009.

"INNOVATORS" NONFICTION SERIES"

Doris Taylor: Growing a Beating Heart, KidHaven Press (Detroit, MI), 2009.

Satoshi Tajiri: Pokemon Creator, KidHaven Press (Detroit, MI), 2009.

"MY FIRST GRAPHIC NOVEL" SERIES

The End Zone, illustrated by Mary Sullivan, Stone Arch Books (Mankato, MN), 2009.

Bree's Bike Jump, illustrated by Mary Sullivan, Stone Arch Books (Minneapolis, MN), 2010.

The Cat That Disappeared, illustrated by Rémy Simard, Stone Arch Books (Mankato, MN), 2010.

The Missing Monster Card, illustrated by Rémy Simard, Stone Arch Books (Minneapolis, MN), 2010.

The Lost Lunch, Stone Arch Books (Minneapolis, MN), 2011.

"OUR AMERICAN STORY" SERIES

Paul Revere's Ride, illustrated by Craig Orback, Picture Window Books (Minneapolis, MN), 2010.

The Boston Tea Party, illustrated by Gershom Griffith, Picture Window Books (Minneapolis, MN), 2010.

Writing the U.S. Constitution, illustrated by Siri Weber Feeney, Picture Window Books (Minneapolis, MN), 2010.

"MY COMMUNITY" GRAPHIC PICTURE-BOOK SERIES"

A Day at the Fire Station, Capstone Press (Mankato, MN), 2011.

A Visit to the Vet, Capstone Press (Mankato, MN), 2011.

Going to the Dentist, Capstone Press (Mankato, MN), 2011.

Working on the Farm, Capstone Press (Mankato, MN), 2011.

Sidelights

Based in Northern California, Lori Mortensen is a prolific author who has written beginning readers and graphic novels and contributed to nonfiction book series focusing on everything from U.S. history to biographies to the oddities of the world. In her picture-book biography *Satoshi Tajiri: Pokemon Creator* Mortensen crafts what *School Library Journal* critic Rachel Artley described as a "concise" text that brings to life the man who invented the phenomenally popular PC/trading-card game. Her contributions to the "Our American Story" series, which include *Paul Revere's Ride, The Boston Tea Party,* and *Writing the U.S. Constitution,* were praised by *Booklist* reviewer Ilene Cooper, who asserted that the author presents "lots of information in . . . a compact form." In *Paul Revere's Ride,* for example, Mortensen gives the well-known story of Revere's midnight ride "a thoughtful yet exciting treatment," while illustrations by Craig Orback are "specially appealing."

Mortensen turns from prose nonfiction to dialogue balloons in her books *The End Zone, The Cat That Disappeared,* and *The Missing Monster Card.* Illustrated by Rémy Simard and part of the "My First Graphic Novel" series, the books read like comic books: arranged in multi-panel pages, the stories feature intermittent running texts, sound effects, and animated art. In *The End Zone* Olivia shows that she can be an asset to the boys' touch football team when she is finally invited to substitute for an injured player, while *The Missing Monster Card* follows Ethan as he loses a rare collectible card and then teams up with a friend to locate it. Both sto-

ries "pose a problem with a happy ending," noted *School Library Journal* critic Sandra Welzenbach, the critic adding that the "My First Graphic Novel" books are "good choices for beginning readers." In *Booklist* Kat Kan noted of *The Missing Monster Card* that Mortensen's story is one many readers can relate to, and Simard's "cartoony illustrations add to the appeal for beginning readers." The format of the "My First Graphic Novel" series provides beginning readers with a strong link between words and pictures, allowing them to "easily solve the mystery" in *The Missing Monster Card,* according to *School Library Journal* contributor Kim T. Ha.

Mortensen's multi-award-winning picture book *In the Trees, Honey Bees* focuses on a colony of honey bees living in the wild and helps young children understand the life cycle of these familiar insects. The book is illustrated by Cris Arbo, who modeled her illustrations after a bee hive located in the backyard of her own home. Mortensen uses rhyme, simple vocabulary, and brief phrases in her descriptive text, and she also includes additional facts about honey bees in the book's appendix. In *School Library Journal* Susan Scheps called *In the Trees, Honey Bees* "finely crafted" and "a wonderful choice for sharing aloud," while Arbo's detailed illustrations are "vibrantly colored" and "realistic."

Mortensen's quirky story in **The Cat That Disappeared** *comes to life in Rémy Simard's stylized cartoon art.* (Stone Arch Books, 2010. Reproduced by permission of Capstone Press.)

Biographical and Critical Sources

PERIODICALS

Booklist, March 15, 2010, Kat Kan, review of *The Missing Monster Card,* p. 62, and Ilene Cooper, review of "Our American Story" series, p. 68.

School Library Journal, August, 2007, Sarah O'Holla, review of *Harriet Tubman: Hero of the Underground Railroad,* p. 103; January, 2008, Janet S. Thompson, review of *Leprechauns,* p. 134; August, 2008, Rachel Artley, review of *Satoshi Tajiri: Pokemon Creator,* p. 125, and Tracy H. Chrenka, review of *The Sphinx,* p. 149; January, 2009, Lucinda Snyder Whitehurst, review of *Angel Island,* p. 93; July, 2009, Susan Scheps, review of *In the Trees, Honey Bees,* p. 73; September, 2009, Sandra Welzenbach, review of *The End Zone,* p. 188; May, 2010, Kim T. Ha, review of *The Missing Monster Card,* p. 141.

ONLINE

Lori Mortensen Home Page, http://www.lorimortensen. com (October 15, 2010).

*   *   *

MUNSINGER, Lynn 1951-

Personal

Born December 24, 1951, in Greenfield, MA; daughter of Robert William and Jeanne Munsinger; married Dan Lace (a sales manager), November 27, 1981. *Education:* Tufts University, B.A., 1974; Rhode Island School of Design, B.F.A. (illustration), 1977; additional study in London, England.

Addresses

Home—CT and VT.

Career

Freelance illustrator, 1977—. Has created designs for greeting cards.

Awards, Honors

Volunteer State Award, 1984, for *Howliday Inn* by James Howe; *New York Times* Notable Book selection, 1986, for *Hugh Pine and the Good Place* by Janwillem Van de Wetering; Emphasis on Reading Award (Grades 2-3), 1987-88, for *My Mother Never Listens to Me* by Marjorie Weinman Sharmat; Little Archer Award, 1989, for *Underwear!* by Mary Monsell; Colorado Children's Book Award, 1990, California Young Reader Award (Primary), 1991, and Golden Sower Award (K-3), 1991, all for *Tacky the Penguin* by Helen Lester; Washington Children's Choices Picture Book Award, 2001, for *Hooway for Wodney Wat* by Lester.

Illustrator

Margret Elbow, *The Rootomom Tree,* Houghton Mifflin (Boston, MA), 1978.

William Cole, editor, *An Arkful of Animals: Poems for the Very Young,* Houghton Mifflin (Boston, MA), 1978.

Jane Sutton, *What Should a Hippo Wear,* Houghton Mifflin (Boston, MA), 1979.

Nancy Robison, *The Lizard Hunt,* Lothrop (New York, NY), 1979.

Gloria Skurzynski, *Martin by Himself,* Houghton Mifflin (Boston, MA), 1979.

Elaine M. Willoughby, *Boris and the Monsters,* Houghton Mifflin (Boston, MA), 1980.

Janwillem van de Wetering, *Hugh Pine,* Houghton Mifflin (Boston, MA), 1980.

Karen J. Gounaud, *A Very Mice Joke Book,* Houghton Mifflin (Boston, MA), 1981.

Sandol Stoddard, *Bedtime Mouse,* Houghton Mifflin (Boston, MA), 1981.

James Howe, *Howliday Inn,* Atheneum (New York, NY), 1982.

Judy Delton, *A Pet for Duck and Bear,* edited by Ann Fay, Albert Whitman (Morton Grove, IL), 1982.

Galway Kinnell, *How the Alligator Missed Breakfast,* Houghton Mifflin (Boston, MA), 1982.

Phyllis Rose Eisenberg, *Don't Tell Me a Ghost Story,* Harcourt (New York, NY), 1982.

Helen Lester, *The Wizard, the Fairy, and the Magic Chicken,* Houghton Mifflin (Boston, MA), 1983.

Judy Delton, *Duck Goes Fishing,* Albert Whitman (Morton Grove, IL), 1983.

Joseph Slate, *The Mean, Clean, Giant Canoe Machine,* Crowell, 1983.

Caroline Levine, *Silly School Riddles and Other Classroom Crack-Ups,* Albert Whitman (Morton Grove, IL), 1984.

Judy Delton, *Bear and Duck on the Run,* Albert Whitman (Morton Grove, IL), 1984.

Richard Latta, *This Little Pig Had a Riddle,* Albert Whitman (Morton Grove, IL), 1984.

Ann Tompert, *Nothing Sticks like a Shadow,* Houghton Mifflin (Boston, MA), 1984.

Eve Bunting, *Monkey in the Middle,* Harcourt (New York, NY), 1984.

Marjorie Weinman Sharmat, *My Mother Never Listens to Me,* Albert Whitman (Morton Grove, IL), 1984.

Virginia Mueller, *A Playhouse for Monster,* Albert Whitman (Morton Grove, IL), 1985.

Virginia Mueller, *Monster and the Baby,* Albert Whitman (Morton Grove, IL), 1985.

Seymour Reit and others, *When Small Is Tall, and Other Read-Together Tales,* Random House (New York, NY), 1985.

Helen Lester, *It Wasn't My Fault,* Houghton Mifflin (Boston, MA), 1985.

Judy Delton, *The Elephant in Duck's Garden,* Albert Whitman (Morton Grove, IL), 1985.

Helen Lester, *A Porcupine Named Fluffy,* Houghton Mifflin (Boston, MA), 1986.

Joan Phillips, *My New Boy,* Random House (New York, NY), 1986.

Virginia Mueller, *Monster Can't Sleep,* Albert Whitman (Morton Grove, IL), 1986.

Judy Delton, *Rabbit Goes to Night School,* Albert Whitman (Morton Grove, IL), 1986.

Janwillem van de Wetering, *Hugh Pine and the Good Place,* Houghton Mifflin (Boston, MA), 1986.

William H. Hooks and others, *Read-a-Rebus: Tales and Rhymes in Words and Pictures,* Random House (New York, NY), 1986.

Virginia Mueller, *A Halloween Mask for Monster,* Albert Whitman (Morton Grove, IL), 1986.

Helen Lester, *Pookins Gets Her Way,* Houghton Mifflin (Boston, MA), 1987.

Barbara Bottner, *Zoo Song,* Scholastic (New York, NY), 1987.

Joanna Cole, *Norma Jean, Jumping Bean,* Random House (New York, NY), 1987.

Helen Lester, *Tacky the Penguin,* Houghton Mifflin (Boston, MA), 1988.

Gloria Whelan, *A Week of Raccoons,* Knopf (New York, NY), 1988.

Linda Hayward, *Hello, House!,* Random House (New York, NY), 1988.

Mary Ada Schwartz, *Spiffen, a Tale of a Tidy Pig,* Albert Whitman (Morton Grove, IL), 1988.

Sandol Stoddard, *Bedtime for Bear,* Houghton Mifflin (Boston, MA), 1988.

Mary Elise Monsell, *Underwear!,* Albert Whitman (Morton Grove, IL), 1988.

Susan Heyboer O'Keefe, *One Hungry Monster: A Counting Book in Rhyme,* Little, Brown (Boston, MA), 1989.

Janwillem van de Wetering, *Hugh Pine and Something Else,* Houghton Mifflin (Boston, MA), 1989.

William J. Smith, *Ho for a Hat!,* Little, Brown (Boston, MA), 1989.

Pat Lowery Collins, *Tomorrow, Up and Away,* Houghton Mifflin (Boston, MA), 1990.

Maryann Macdonald, *Hedgehog Bakes a Cake,* Gareth Stevens (Milwaukee, WI), 1990.

Joanna Cole, *Don't Call Me Names,* Random House (New York, NY), 1990.

Helen Lester, *The Revenge of the Magic Chicken,* Houghton Mifflin (Boston, MA), 1990.

Virginia Mueller, *Monster's Birthday Hiccups,* Albert Whitman (Morton Grove, IL), 1991.

Virginia Mueller, *Monster Goes to School,* Albert Whitman (Morton Grove, IL), 1991.

Maryann Macdonald, *Rabbit's Birthday Kite,* Bantam (New York, NY), 1991.

Joanne Oppenheim, *Rooter Remembers: A Bank Street Book about Values,* Viking (New York, NY), 1991.

William Cole, selector, *A Zooful of Animals,* Houghton Mifflin (Boston, MA), 1992.

Helen Lester, *Me First,* Houghton Mifflin (Boston, MA), 1992.

William H. Hooks, *Rough, Tough, Rowdy: A Bank Street Book about Values,* Viking (New York, NY), 1992.

Barbara Brenner, *Group Soup: A Bank Street Book about Values,* Viking (New York, NY), 1992.

Ann Tompert, *Just a Little Bit,* Houghton Mifflin (Boston, MA), 1993.

Valiska Gregory, *Babysitting for Benjamin,* Little, Brown (Boston, MA), 1993.

Helen Lester, *Three Cheers for Tacky,* Houghton Mifflin (Boston, MA), 1994.

William H. Hooks and Betty Boegehold, *The Rainbow Ribbon: A Bank Street Book about Values,* Puffin (New York, NY), 1994.

Abby Levine, *Ollie Knows Everything,* Albert Whitman (Morton Grove, IL), 1994.

Helen Lester, *Lin's Backpack,* Addison-Wesley (New York, NY), 1994.

Sandol Stoddard, *Turtle Time: A Bedtime Story,* Houghton Mifflin (Boston, MA), 1995.

Stephen Krensky, *The Three Blind Mice Mystery,* Dell (New York, NY), 1995.

Ogden Nash, *The Tale of Custard the Dragon,* Little, Brown (Boston, MA), 1995.

Helen Lester, *Listen, Buddy,* Houghton Mifflin (Boston, MA), 1995.

Joanna Cole and Stephanie Calmenson, *Gator Girls,* Morrow (New York, NY), 1995.

Helen Lester, *Princess Penelope's Parrot,* Houghton Mifflin (Boston, MA), 1996.

Ogden Nash, *Custard the Dragon and the Wicked Knight,* Little, Brown (Boston, MA), 1996.

A.M. Monson, *Wanted—Best Friend,* Dial (New York, NY), 1997.

Stephanie Calmenson and Joanna Cole, *Rockin' Reptiles,* Morrow Junior Books (New York, NY), 1997.

Kay Winters, *The Teeny Tiny Ghost,* HarperCollins (New York, NY), 1998.

Helen Lester, *Tacky in Trouble,* Houghton Mifflin (Boston, MA), 1998.

Stephanie Calmenson and Joanna Cole, *Get Well, Gators!,* Morrow Junior Books (New York, NY), 1998.

Jackie French Koller, *One Monkey Too Many,* Harcourt Brace (San Diego, CA), 1999.

Helen Lester, *Hooway for Wodney Wat,* Houghton Mifflin (New York, NY), 1999.

Maryann Macdonald, *Rabbit's Birthday Kite,* Gareth Stevens (Milwaukee, WI), 1999.

Kay Winters, *Whooo's Haunting the Teeny Tiny Ghost?,* HarperCollins (New York, NY), 1999.

Stephanie Calmenson and Joanna Cole, *Gator Halloween,* Morrow Junior Books (New York, NY), 1999.

Carolyn Crimi, *Don't Need Friends,* Doubleday (New York, NY), 1999.

William Wise, *Dinosaurs Forever,* Dial (New York, NY), 2000.

Helen Lester, *Tacky and the Emperor,* Houghton, Mifflin (New York, NY), 2000.

Laura Joffe Numeroff, *What Grandmas Do Best/What Grandpas Do Best,* Little Simon (New York, NY), 2000, published separately, 2001.

Laura Joffe Numeroff, *What Daddies Do Best,* Little Simon (New York, NY), 2001.

Helen Lester, *Score One for the Sloths,* Houghton Mifflin (Boston, MA), 2001.

Patricia Hooper, *A Stormy Ride on Noah's Ark,* Putnam (New York, NY), 2001.

David T. Greenberg, *Skunks!,* Little, Brown (Boston, MA), 2001.

Deborah Lee Rose, *Birthday Zoo,* Albert Whitman (Morton Grove, IL), 2002.

Laura Joffe Numeroff, *What Mommies Do Best,* Little Simon (New York, NY), 2002.

Helen Lester, *Tackylocks and the Three Bears,* Houghton Mifflin (New York, NY), 2002.

Irving Berlin, *God Bless America,* HarperCollins (New York, NY), 2002.

Laura Malone Elliott, *Hunter's Best Friend at School,* HarperCollins (New York, NY), 2002.

My New Boy, Random House (New York, NY), 2003.

Laura Joffe Numeroff, *What Sisters Do Best; What Brothers Do Best,* Little Simon (New York, NY), 2003.

Helen Lester, *Something Might Happen,* Houghton Mifflin (Boston, MA), 2003.

Joanna Cole, *Norma Jean, Jumping Bean,* Random House (New York, NY), 2003.

Kay Winters, *The Teeny Tiny Ghost and the Monster,* HarperCollins (New York, NY), 2004.

Laura Joffe Numeroff, *What Aunts Do Best/What Uncles Do Best,* Simon & Schuster (New York, NY), 2004.

Laura Joffe Numeroff, *Beatrice Doesn't Want To,* Candlewick Press (Cambridge, MA), 2004.

Helen Lester, *Hurty Feelings,* Houghton Mifflin (Boston, MA), 2004.

David T. Greenberg, *Snakes!,* Little, Brown (New York, NY), 2004.

Helen Lester, *Tacky and the Winter Games,* Houghton Mifflin (Boston, MA), 2005.

Jackie French Killer, *Seven Spunky Monkeys,* Harcourt (Orlando, FL), 2005.

Barbara Brenner, William H. Hooks, and Betty Boegehold, *Bunny Tails,* Milk and Cookies Press, 2005.

Laura Malone Elliott, *Hunter and Stripe and the Soccer Showdown,* Katherine Tegen Books (New York, NY), 2005.

William Wise, *Zany Zoo,* Houghton Mifflin (Boston, MA), 2006.

Helen Lester, *Batter up Wombat,* Houghton Mifflin (Boston, MA), 2006.

James Howe, *Howliday Inn,* Aladdin (New York, NY), 2006.

David J. Olson, *The Thunderstruck Stork,* Albert Whitman (Morton Grove, IL), 2007.

Laura Malone Elliott, *Hunter's Big Sister,* Katherine Tegen Books (New York, NY), 2007.

Susan Heyboer O'Keefe, *Hungry Monster ABC,* Little, Brown (New York, NY), 2007.

Helen Lester, *The Sheep in Wolf's Clothing,* Houghton Mifflin (Boston, MA), 2007.

David T. Greenberg, *Crocs!,* Little, Brown (New York, NY), 2008.

Laura Joffe Numeroff and Nate Evans, *The Jellybeans and the Big Dance,* Abrams Books for Young Readers (New York, NY), 2008.

J. Patrick Lewis, *Spot the Plot: A Riddle Book of Book Riddles,* Chronicle Books (San Francisco, CA), 2009.

Helen Lester, *Tacky Goes to Camp,* Houghton Mifflin Books for Children (Boston, MA), 2009.

Tina Casey, *The Underground Gators,* Dutton Children's Books (New York, NY), 2009.

Laura Joffe Numeroff, *What Brothers Do Best: What Sisters Do Best,* Chronicle Books (San Francisco, CA), 2009.

Laura Malone Elliott, *A String of Hearts,* Katherine Tegen Books (New York, NY), 2010.

Virginia Mueller, *Monster Goes to School,* Albert Whitman (Chicago, IL), 2010.

Helen Lester, *Tacky's Christmas,* Houghton Mifflin Harcourt (Boston, MA), 2010.

Laura Joffe Numeroff and Nate Evans, *The Jellybeans and the Big Book Bonanza,* Abrams Books for Young Readers (New York, NY), 2010.

Mary Elise Monsell, *Underwear!,* Albert Whitman (Chicago, IL), 2010.

Laura Joffe Numeroff, *What Puppies Do Best/What Kittens Do Best,* Chronicle Books (San Francisco, CA), 2010.

Laura Joffe Numeroff and Nate Evans, *Ponyella,* Disney/Hyperion Books (New York, NY), 2011.

Laura Joffe Numeroff and Nate Evans, *The Jellybeans and the Big Match,* Abrams Books for Young Readers (New York, NY), 2011.

Illustrator of textbooks. Contributor of illustrations to *Cricket.*

Munsinger's papers are housed at the deGrummond Collection, University of Southern Mississippi.

Sidelights

The whimsical animal characters created by illustrator Lynn Munsinger are familiar to several generations of young readers and decorate the pages of children's books by a wide variety of authors. From Ogden Nash's early-twentieth-century classic *The Tale of Custard the Dragon* to works by such contemporary writers as Joanna Cole, Laura Malone Elliott, Helen Lester, William Wise, Laura Joffe Numeroff, and Virginia Mueller, the illustrator has brought her creative talent and imagination to bear. "It is easy to recognize Munsinger's personable animal characters," wrote Stephanie Zvirin in a *Booklist* review of Elliott's *Hunter's Best Friend at School,* adding that these characters "always seem to sparkle with mischief and good humor." "I . . . feel very fortunate to be an illustrator," the prolific artist once told *SATA.* "I really enjoy my work and cannot conceive of doing anything else."

Born in Greenfield, Massachusetts, in 1951, Munsinger knew she wanted to be an artist from the time she was a young girl. After graduating from high school, she attended Tufts University, moving on to the Rhode Island School of Design after earning her B.A. in 1974, and obtaining her B.F.A. degree three yeas later. She began looking for freelance assignments immediately after graduation, and her first illustration job, Margret El-

A prolific illustrator, Lynn Munsinger has worked with Mary Elise Monsell on the humorous picture book Underwear! (Albert Whitman & Company, 1988. Illustrations © 1988 by Lynn Munsinger. Reproduced by permission.)

bow's *The Rootomom Tree,* was published a year later. Many more book-illustration projects have followed in the years since, earning Munsinger not only legions of young fans but critical praise as well. Of her work for Mary Elise Monsell's *Underwear!,* for instance, a *Booklist* reviewer called the "zany," "perky-colored" illustrations "a perfect foil for the text," while Lori A. Janick maintained in *School Library Journal* that "what could have been an unbelievable moralistic tale . . . is saved by Munsinger's delightful illustrations." Reviewing Judy Delton's *Rabbit Goes to Night School, Booklist* contributor Denise M. Wilms stated that "Munsinger's deft pen-and-ink drawings . . . lend a good deal of personality to the story," while the illustrator's work for *A Stormy Ride on Noah's Ark,* "featuring expressive animal characters and shifting perspectives, capture the balance between the comic and the contemplative achieved in the lilting text" by Patricia Hooper.

While Munsinger has illustrated books for numerous authors, including Delton, Marjorie Weinman Sharmat, Galway Kinnell, and Ann Tompert, she has also developed multi-book working relationships with several popular children's book writers. Dutch-immigrant author Janwillem van de Wetering's three-book series featuring a large, elderly porcupine named Hugh Pine was the first collaboration to benefit from Munsinger's pen-and-ink renderings. In series opener *Hugh Pine,* the wise porcupine learns to walk upright and mimic a small human being in order to avoid being hit by passing cars, and he eventually helps his younger, more inexperienced friends learn to cross busy roads in safety. In *Hugh Pine and the Good Place* the elderly porcupine longs to move out to the deserted island he can see from his home in a tree growing on the Maine coast.

However, following the adage "be careful what you wish for," Pine ultimately changes his mind after a few days of loneliness. In *Hugh Pine and Something Else* Munsinger captures the wise old porcupine as he accompanies his friend, Postman McTosh, to New York City where he meets a host of sophisticated city-dwelling animals before returning to his comfortable woodland home. "Munsinger provides sprightly line drawings with just the right elan to give this porcupine person believability," commented Barbara Elleman in a *Booklist* review of *Hugh Pine and the Good Place.*

The humorous "Monster" stories by Virginia Mueller have also been enhanced by Munsinger's artwork. In full-color illustrations, the illustrator portrays green-furred, toothsome young Monster in a variety of child-like situations and makes the setting particularly monster-like: the Monster family has carnivorous Venus fly-traps instead of regular houseplants, and their anti-macassars are made of spider webs! In *Monster and the Baby* Monster tries to quiet his baby sister with a game of building blocks, but discovers that she is only happy when the buildings crash to the ground. In *A Playhouse for Monster* the young creature thrills to having a place all his own, until he realizes that sharing his new playhouse with friends is far more fun. *A Halloween Mask for Monster* finds the furry green creature donning fear-

Munsinger teams up with William Wise to bring to life an engaging collection of creatures in the picture book Zany Zoo. (Copyright © 2006 by Lynn Munsinger. All rights reserved. Reproduced by permission of Houghton Mifflin Company.)

some masks that look like human children—and scaring everyone in his family—until he decides that the masks are truly *too* scary and his own face will do just fine. A *Publishers Weekly* reviewer praised Mueller's story in *A Halloween Mask for Monster*, noting that it is "made more agreeable because of Munsinger's good-natured pictures." Other "Monster" stories featuring Munsinger art include *Monster Can't Sleep, Monster's Birthday Hiccups,* and *Monster Goes to School.*

Numeroff, author of the popular picture book *If You Give a Mouse a Cookie* and its sequels, teams with Munsinger and coauthor Nate Evans to create several stories featuring the Jellybeans. The Jellybeans are four animal characters—Emily, Nicole, Anna, and Bitsy—who meet each other when they are enrolled in the same beginning ballet class. In *The Jellybeans and the Big Dance* Emily's efforts to inspire the other girls with her passion for dancing result in a successful recital performance. Anna's passion for books and reading is at the center of *The Jellybeans and the Big Book Bonanza,* which finds the four girls helping out at their school's book week, while in *The Jellybeans and the Big Match* Nicole teaches her friends the basic skills they need to know on the soccer field. Other books by Numeroff and Evans include *What Brothers Do Best/ What Sisters Do Best, What Puppies Do Best/What Kittens Do Best,* and *Ponyella.*

Reviewing *The Jellybeans and the Big Dance* in *Booklist,* Gillian Engberg wrote that Munsinger's pastel images "add great depth and emotion" to Numeroff and Evans's story, while a *Publishers Weekly* contributor cited the artist's contribution by noting that her "facility with expressions and body language is as impressive as ever." "It will be hard for young readers to resist this book," predicted Julie R. Ranelli in her *School Library Journal* review of *The Jellybeans and the Big Dance,* because Munsinger's "expressive cartoon animals . . . dance and stumble across the pages in an endearing fashion." Reviewing *The Jellybeans and the Big Book Bonanza* in the same periodical, Sara Lissa Paulson maintained that young readers "will delight in seeing themselves in one of the endearing, fuzzy-looking Jellybean characters," while a *Publishers Weekly* contributor wrote that Munsinger's animal characters "sweetly express friendship dynamics in a group setting."

Munsinger's most prolific working relationship has been with author Helen Lester. Beginning with Lester's 1983 picture book *The Wizard, the Fairy, and the Magic Chicken,* the two have teamed up to create numerous stories filled with a whimsical humor that often borders on zany. Beginning their collaboration with the story of a competition between three sorcerers, Lester and Munsinger produced a sequel, *The Revenge of the Magic Chicken,* which reunites Chicken with his magical friends, a wizard and a fairy. "The text's humor gets the full treatment in Munsinger's raucous art," noted Ilene Cooper, reviewing the appealing picture book for *Booklist.*

Munsinger's many collaborations with writer Helen Lester include the whimsical picture book **Hooway for Wodney Wat.** (Houghton Mifflin, 1999. Illustrations © 1992 by Lynn Munsinger. Reprinted by permission of Houghton Mifflin Harcourt Publishing Company. All rights reserved.)

Several books featuring a penguin named Tacky have also hatched from the creative collaboration between Munsinger and Lester. While most penguins try hard to fit in with their formally attired fellows, in *Tacky the Penguin* readers meet a free spirit. Unlike the properly bow-tied Angel, Goodly, Lovely, and friends, Tacky wears gaudy and rumpled Hawaiian-print shirts, making him a bit of a stand-out around the Arctic Circle. However, when Tacky encounters a band of penguin-snatching hunters, his crazy antics and outrageous garb confound the men so much that they question whether these birds are penguins after all. *Three Cheers for Tacky* finds the nonconformist penguin making a muddle of his team's cheer routine for the Penguin Cheering Contest, although ultimately the out-of-step penguin becomes the highlight of what would otherwise have been a forgettable competition. Athletic training takes a backseat to doughnuts, late-night television, and other lazy habits in *Tacky and the Winter Games,* which finds the penguin taking a less-than-stellar role in the annual penguin games, while the penguin's holiday antics are the focus of *Tacky's Christmas.* In *Tacky Goes to Camp* the penguin's experience at Camp Whoopihaha is highlighted by his off-beat idea of roughing it, an idea that includes pizza, television, roller blades and bunny slippers, and a laid-back attitude.

In *Booklist* reviewer Kathryn Broderick praised Munsinger's "slyly humorous watercolors" in the "Tacky" series and called *Three Cheers for Tacky* "a

funny, funny picture book," while Carolyn Phelan wrote in the same periodical that with *Tacky and the Winter Games* "Lester and Munsinger create a winning combination of action, detail, and understated wit." Calling *Tacky Goes to Camp* the penguin's "funniest [outing] yet," Christine M. Hepperman also cited "Munsinger's always-inviting cartoon art" in her *Horn Book* review. "Somehow, the lovable penguin's goofy, clumsy antics always have a way of saving the day for him and his pals," concluded Gloria Koster in a review of the same book for *School Library Journal*.

Lester and Munsinger have also worked together on several other picture books for young children, many of which feature animal characters. In *A Porcupine Named Fluffy* a prickly young porcupine earns the nickname "Fluffy," despite the fact that his "fluff" consists of sharp, barbed quills. Only after Fluffy meets a young rhinoceros with an equally silly name—Hippo—does he begin to think of his name as a source of fun. In *Me First* portly Pinkerton Pig learn a lesson about being pushy via Munsinger's brightly hued watercolor art, and an opposite dilemma—about a young hippopotamus who takes everything too seriously—is profiled in lighthearted fashion in *Hurty Feelings. Listen, Buddy* features a hare whose mind is wandering in the clouds instead of focusing on what people are telling him, while a rodent with a severe speech impediment stars in the popular picture book *Hooway for Wodney Wat.* And *Batter up, Wombat* finds a rugby-playing Australian

Lester and Munsinger team up again on the humorous farmyard tale **The Sheep in Wolf's Clothing.** (Illustrations copyright © 2007 by Lynn Munsinger. Reprinted by permission of Houghton Mifflin Harcourt Publishing Company. All rights reserved.)

The perennially popular Tacky the Penguin stars in Lester and Munsinger's **Tacky Goes to Camp.** (Illustrations copyright © 2009 by Lynn Munsinger. Reprinted by permission of Houghton Mifflin Harcourt Publishing Company. All rights reserved.)

wombat recruited by a last-placed baseball team in the North American Wildlife League. "Munsinger's expressively drawn pictures . . . wring out every funny nuance," noted Ilene Cooper in a *Booklist* review of *A Porcupine Named Fluffy,* while Julie Roach wrote in *School Library Journal* that the artist's watercolor illustrations for *Hurty Feelings* "bring the tale to life, making Lester's creatures all the more entertaining and enjoyable."

Although animals figure most prominently in Munsinger's drawings, human children take center stage in several books. In Lester's *It Wasn't My Fault,* a young boy is always quick to blame something else for his own actions, while Deborah Lee Rose's *Birthday Zoo* finds a more upbeat fellow enjoying a special party given by the inhabitants of a local zoo. A spoiled girl who utters the foolish wish that she be transformed into a flower is featured in another book by Lester, *Pookins Gets Her Way,* which contains illustrations that are "full of mischief," according to a *Publishers Weekly* critic. *Princess Penelope's Parrot* introduces readers to yet another spoiled child, this time a princess whose nasty words come back to haunt her during her birthday party, when a parrot who refused to speak to her suddenly begins mimicking the girl's mantra—"Gimme, Gimme, Gimme"—in earshot of the wealthy prince Penelope was hoping to impress. The author's "spoiled-brat princess is perfectly embodied in Munsinger's . . . illustra-

tion," asserted Janice M. Del Negro in a review of *Princess Penelope's Parrot* for the *Bulletin of the Center for Children's Books.*

While Munsinger concentrates mainly upon illustrating picture books for young children, she has also done artwork for children's textbooks, designed greeting cards, and contributed illustrations to *Cricket* magazine. Her media of choice continue to be Indian ink applied with crow's-quill pens, to which she often adds washes of water color. "The aspect of illustration that most interests me is development of the characters," Munsinger once explained to *SATA*. "I feel humor and expression add to a character's appeal and aid in telling a story." While Munsinger enjoys drawing all sorts of characters, she admits to a special affection for drawing animals. Fortunately for her, that affection has translated itself into talent. As a *Publishers Weekly* contributor noted in discussing her illustrations for William Wise's poetry collection *Zany Zoo:* "When it comes to imagining anthropomorphized animals, [Munsinger] . . . has few peers. No matter what species she puts her pen to, the result is [both] . . . touching and tickling."

Biographical and Critical Sources

PERIODICALS

Booklist, April 15, 1986, Ilene Cooper, review of *A Porcupine Named Fluffy,* pp. 1223-1224; December 1, 1986, Barbara Elleman, review of *Hugh Pine and the Good Place,* p. 582; February 1, 1987, Denise M. Wilms, review of *Rabbit Goes to Night School,* p. 842; April 1, 1988, review of *Underwear!,* p. 1352; March 1, 1990, Ilene Cooper, review of *The Revenge of the Magic Chicken,* p. 1344; October 1, 1992, Annie Ayres, review of *Me First,* p. 336; February 15, 1994, Kathryn Broderick, review of *Three Cheers for Tacky,* pp. 1092-1093; October 15, 1995, Hazel Rochman, review of *Listen, Buddy,* p. 412; September 1, 1999, Stephanie Zvirin, review of *Gator Halloween,* p. 145; November, 15, 1999, Hazel Rochman, review of *Don't Need Friends,* p. 635; March 15, 2000, review of *Hooway for Wodney Wat,* p. 1346; August, 2002, Hazel Rochman, review of *God Bless America,* p. 1966; September 15, 2002, Cynthia Turnquest, review of *Birthday Zoo,* p. 242; October 1, 2002, Stephanie Zvirin, review of *Hunter's Best Friend at School,* p. 334, and Kathy Broderick, review of *Tackylocks and the Three Bears,* p. 337; September 15, 2003, Gillian Engberg, review of *Something Might Happen,* p. 246; December 1, 2004, Jennifer Mattson, review of *Beatrice Doesn't Want To,* p. 661; September 1, 2005, Shelle Rosenfeld, review of *Hunter and Stripe and the Soccer Showdown,* p. 119, and Carolyn Phelan, review of *Tacky and the Winter Games,* p. 120; April 15, 2006, Jennifer Mattson, review of *Zany Zoo,* p. 55; September 15, 2006, Ilene Cooper, review of *Bat-*

ter up Wombat, p. 68; October 1, 2007, Gillian Engberg, review of *The Sheep in Wolf's Clothing,* p. 66; October 15, 2007, Julie Cummins, review of *The Thunderstruck Stork,* p. 54; April 15, 2008, Gillian Engberg, review of *The Jellybeans and the Big Dance,* p. 48, and Bina Williams, review of *Crocs!,* p. 49; March 15, 2009, Gillian Engberg, review of *The Underground Gators,* p. 68; April 1, 2009, Carolyn Phelan, review of *Tacky Goes to Camp,* p. 46; September 15, 2009, Patricia Austin, review of *What Brothers Do Best/What Sisters Do Best,* p. 64.

Bulletin of the Center for Children's Books, April, 1988, review of *Tacky the Penguin,* p. 159; March, 1990, review of *The Revenge of the Magic Chickens,* pp. 168-169; April, 1996, review of *Custard the Dragon and the Wicked Knight,* p. 273; January, 1997, Janice M. Del Negro, review of *Princess Penelope's Parrot,* p. 179.

Horn Book, March-April, 1987, Karen Jameyson, review of *Hugh Pine and the Good Place,* p. 214; May-June, 1987, Hanna B. Zeiger, review of *Rabbit Goes to Night School,* pp. 328-329; November-December, 1992, Carolyn K. Jenks, review of *Me First,* pp. 716-717; July-August, 1995, review of *Listen, Buddy,* p. 485; September, 2001, review of *Score One for the Sloths,* p. 576; November-December, 2001, review of *A Stormy Ride on Noah's Ark,* p. 736; November-December, 2002, Mary M. Burns, review of *Birthday Zoo,* p. 738; May-June, 2004, Roger Sutton, review of *Snakes!,* p. 313; May-June, 2009, Christine M. Heppermann, review of *Tacky Goes to Camp,* p. 283.

Kirkus Reviews, July 15, 2002, review of *Tackylocks and the Three Bears,* p. 1037; May 1, 2004, review of *Snakes!,* p. 442; July 1, 2004, review of *Hurty Feelings,* p. 632; July 1, 2005, review of *Hunter and Stripe and the Soccer Showdown,* p. 734; August 15, 2005, review of *Seven Spunky Monkeys,* p. 917; October 15, 2005, review of *Tacky and the Winter Games,* p. 1141; May 15, 2007, review of *Hungry Monster ABC;* August 1, 2007, review of *Hunter's Big Sister;* September 1, 2007, reviews of *The Thunderstruck Stork* and *The Sheep in Wolf's Clothing;* February 15, 2008, review of *The Jellybeans and the Big Dance;* April 15, 2008, review of *Crocs!;* March 1, 2009, review of *The Underground Gators;* November, 2009, Stacy Dillon, review of *Spot the Plot: A Riddle Book of Book Riddles,* p. 95.

Publishers Weekly, September 19, 1980, review of *Hugh Pine,* p. 161; May 27, 1983, review of *Duck Goes Fishing,* p. 68; April 25, 1986, review of *A Porcupine Named Fluffy,* p. 73; August 22, 1986, review of *A Halloween Mask for Monster,* p. 93; February 27, 1987, review of *Pookins Gets Her Way,* p. 163; May 8, 1995, review of *The Tale of Custard the Dragon,* p. 295; February 13, 2005, review of *Bunny Tails,* p. 76; February 27, 2006, review of *Zany Zoo,* p. 60; August 6, 2007, review of *The Sheep in Wolf's Clothing,* p. 188; February 11, 2008, review of *The Jellybeans and the Big Dance,* p. 69; May 18, 2009, review of *Tacky Goes to Camp,* p. 54; February 22, 2010, review of *The Jellybeans and the Big Book Bonanza,* p. 66.

School Library Journal, December, 1985, review of *A Playhouse for Monster,* pp. 109-110; August, 1987, re-

view of *Pookins Gets Her Way,* p. 70; March, 1988, Lori A. Janick, review of *Underwear!,* p. 172; April, 1988, Bonnie Wheatley, review of *Tacky the Penguin,* p. 82; October, 1992, George Delalis, review of *Me First,* p. 91; May, 1994, Donna L. Scanlon, review of *Three Cheers for Tacky,* p. 98; November, 2000, Martha Link, review of *Tacky and the Emperor,* p. 126; October, 2001, Robin L. Gibson, review of *Score One for the Sloths,* p. 123; December, 2001, Kathy Piehl, review of *A Stormy Ride on Noah's Ark,* p. 104; September, 2002, Melinda Piehler, review of *Hunter's Best Friend at School,* p. 190; September, 2003, Be Astengo, review of *Something Might Happen,* p. 183; August, 2004, Linda Staskus, review of *The Teeny Tiny Ghost and the Monster,* p. 104; September, 2004, Blair Christolon, review of *Hunter and Stripe and the Soccer Showdown,* p. 169; October, 2004, Julie Roach, review of *Hurty Feelings,* p. 12; November, 2004, Wanda Meyers-Hines, review of *Beatrice Doesn't Want To,* p. 113; September, 2005, Linda Staskus, review of *Seven Spunky Monkeys,* p. 176; August, 2006, Piper L. Nyman, review of *Zany Zoo,* p. 100; October, 2006, Lynn K. Vanca, review of *Batter up Wombat,* p.

116; June, 2007, Kathleen Kelly Macmillian, review of *Hungry Monster ABC,* p. 119; September, 2007, Mary Elam, review of *Hunter's Big Sister,* p. 164, Judy Chichinski, review of *The Sheep in Wolf's Clothing,* p. 169, and Jayne Damron, review of *The Thunderstruck Stork,* p. 173; April, 2008, Teresa Pfeifer, review of *Crocs!,* p. 110; June, 2008, Julie R. Ranelli, review of *The Jellybeans and the Big Dance,* p. 112; April, 2009, Gloria Koster, review of *Tacky Goes to Camp,* p. 110; May, 2009, Lisa Crandall, review of *The Underground Gators,* p. 72; December, 2009, Elaine Lesh Morgan, review of *What Brothers Do Best/What Sisters Do Best,* p. 88; April, 2010, Sara Lissa Paulson, review of *The Jellybeans and the Big Book Bonanza,* p. 136.

ONLINE

Houghton Mifflin Web site, http://www.houghtonmifflin books.com/ (October 15, 2010), "Lynn Munsinger."

N-R

NEFF, Henry H. 1973-

Personal

Born 1973, in MA; son of art historians. *Education:* Cornell University, B.A.

Addresses

Home—San Francisco, CA.

Career

Educator, children's book author, and illustrator. McKinsey & Company, Chicago, IL, management consultant, 1996-2002; high school history and fine-arts teacher in San Francisco, CA, 2002—.

Writings

"TAPESTRY" FANTASY SERIES; SELF-ILLUSTRATED MIDDLE-GRADE NOVELS

The Hound of Rowan, Random House (New York, NY), 2007.
The Second Siege, Random House Children's Books (New York, NY), 2008.
The Fiend and the Forge, Random House Children's Books (New York, NY), 2010.

Sidelights

Henry H. Neff worked in business for several years before making the decision to change careers and also rekindle his childhood passion for writing and drawing. Now a high-school teacher, Neff is also the author of the "Tapestry" series of middle-grade fantasy novels which mix contemporary fantasy, science fiction, and real-world history.

Neff was born in Massachusetts but spent most of his childhood in Chicago, Illinois. His parents were art historians, and he was encouraged to draw and read from

an early age. At Cornell University Neff pursued his interest in art by drawing political cartoons for the *Cornell Daily Sun*. After graduating with a degree in history, he worked as a management consultant for McKinsey & Company in Chicago for six years. Wanting to return to more creative pursuits, he left his job in 2002 to become a high-school history and fine-arts teacher in San Francisco, California. He also began to write and illustrate his own children's books.

Neff's middle-grade novel, *The Hound of Rowan,* includes thirty illustrations by the author. The story focuses on Max McDaniels, a modern preteen who discovers that he has inherited magical abilities. After his magical talents are revealed, Max is invited to attend Rowan Academy, a magic school located in New England. There he encounters hags, bullies, evil shape-changers, and the arch-villain Astaroth. Amanda Raklovitz, writing in *School Library Journal,* stated that *The Hound of Rowan* "is a solid and worthwhile beginning to a new fantasy series," even though it "lacks fully realized secondary characters and relationships." According to a *Kirkus Reviews* critic, "Neff's language is often evocative, incorporating Irish myths like the legend of Cuchulain." Several reviewers noted the novel's similarities to J.K. Rowling's "Harry Potter" series. Harry Williamson, writing for *BookLoons* online, commented that while *The Hound of Rowan* lacks "the same level of imaginative excellence" as Rowling's fiction, "it has its own appeal, with many innovative magical elements."

Neff's "Tapestry" series continues in *The Second Siege* and *The Fiend and the Forge.* In *The Second Siege* Max and friend David are in their second year of school when they are taken into hiding in order to help keep the Book of Thoth safe from Astaroth. As Max goes from place to place, he learns about his family's past and embraces his destiny as an agent for the Red Branch. *The Fiend and the Forge* finds Astaroth able to reshape history with the power of the Book of Origins. Except in Rowan, humans are soon reduced to slavery and lives as peasants, prompting Max to travel the re-

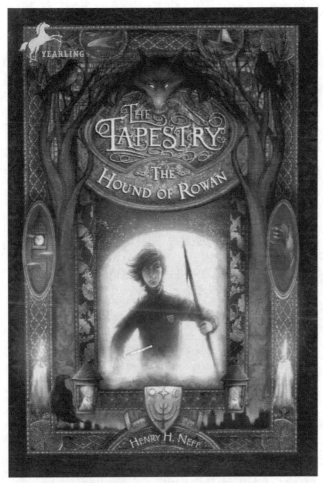

Cover of Henry H. Neff's middle-grade fantasy **The Hound of Rowan,** *featuring artwork by Cory Godbey.* (Used by permission Yearling, an imprint of Random House Children's Books, a division of Random House, Inc.)

configured earth and in search of a way to set things to rights. Writing in *School Library Journal,* Lisa Prolman described *The Second Siege* as "chock-full of magic, myth, and adventure" and added that the novel features "interesting characters and an intense, engaging" storyline. A reviewer in *Kirkus Reviews* found the same novel to be grimmer than *The Hound of Rowan* and also cited Neff's success in creating a surprise ending. "After devouring this title," the reviewer concluded, "young fans will clamor for more."

Biographical and Critical Sources

PERIODICALS

Booklist, September 1, 2007, Diana Tixier Herald, review of *The Hound of Rowan,* p. 105; September 15, 2008, Krista Hurley, review of *The Second Siege,* p. 49.

Bulletin of the Center for Children's Books, November 1, 2007, April Spisak, review of *The Hound of Rowan,* p. 150.

Kirkus Reviews, September 1, 2007, review of *The Hound of Rowan;* August 1, 2008, review of *The Second Siege.*

Magpies, November 1, 2007, Helen Purdie, review of *The Hound of Rowan,* p. 37.

School Library Journal, March 1, 2008, Amanda Raklovitz, review of *The Hound of Rowan,* p. 207; February, 2009, Lisa Prolman, review of *The Second Siege,* p. 106.

ONLINE

Adams Literary Web site, http://www.adamsliterary.com/ (October 20, 2010), "Henry H. Neff."

BookLoons, http://www.bookloons.com/ (September 17, 2008), Hilary Williamson, review of *The Hound of Rowan.*

Henry H. Neff Home Page, http://henryhneff.com (October 20, 2010).*

*   *   *

NICHOLS, Janet
See LYNCH, Janet Nichols

*   *   *

O'SHAUGHNESSY, Tam 1951-

Personal

Born 1951. *Education:* Georgia State University, B.S. (biology), M.S. (biology); University of California at Riverside, Ph.D. (school psychology).

Addresses

Home—CA.

Career

Educator. Worked as a professional tennis player; instructor of biology on the college level; San Diego State University, former professor of school psychology, now emeritus; Sally Ride Science (educational foundation), San Diego, CA, cofounder and currently chief operating officer and executive vice president.

Awards, Honors

(With Sally Ride) Children's Science Writing Award, American Institute of Physics, 1994, for *The Third Planet.*

Writings

(With Sally Ride) *Voyager: An Adventure to the Edge of the Solar System,* Crown (New York, NY), 1992.

(With Sally Ride) *The Third Planet: Exploring the Earth from Space,* Crown (New York, NY), 1994.

(With Sally Ride) *The Mystery of Mars,* Crown (New York, NY), 1999.

(With Kathleen L. Lane and Frank M. Gresham) *Interventions for Children with or at Risk for Emotional and Behavioral Disorders,* Allyn & Bacon (Boston, MA), 2002.

Tam O'Shaughnessy teams up with Sally Ride to write **Misson: Save the Planet,** *a how-to book featuring artwork by Andrew Arnold.* (Flash Point, 2009.

(With Sally Ride) *Exploring Our Solar System,* Crown (New York, NY), 2003.

(With Sally Ride) *Mission: Planet Earth; Our World and Its Climate—and How Humans Are Changing Them,* Roaring Brook Press (New York, NY), 2009.

(With Sally Ride) *Mission: Save the Planet: Things You Can Do to Help Fight Global Warming,* Roaring Brook Press (New York, NY), 2009.

Sidelights

Tam O'Shaughnessy met Sally Ride long before Ride became known for her achievement in becoming the first female U.S. astronaut: they met when both girls were twelve-year-old tennis players. While Ride went on to pursue her dream of going into space, O'Shaughnessy became a professional tennis player, then followed her interest in biology and teaching in college. When Ride began writing for children in the early 1990s, she contacted O'Shaughnessy, who was then a professor of school psychology at the University of California at Riverside. The writing partnership that the two women formed led to O'Shaughnessy's decision to help Ride found Sally Ride Science, an educational foundation dedicated to inspiring young women with an interest in the sciences. In addition to her executive role, O'Shaughnessy helps develop educational materials, such as student texts and teacher guides. Her book-length collaborations with Ride include *Voyager: An Adventure to the Edge of the Solar System, The Third Planet: Exploring the Earth from Space, The Mystery of Mars, Exploring Our Solar System,* and *Mission—Planet Earth; Our World and Its Climate—and How Humans Are Changing Them.*

Part of the "Face-to-Face with Science" series, *Voyager* chronicles NASA's two Voyager missions, which gathered data from Jupiter, Saturn, Neptune, and Uranus. Featuring detailed photographs taken by the unmanned space probe as well as other illustrations, *Voyager* benefits from "a compelling text that makes astronomical facts immediate and accessible," according to a *Publishers Weekly* critic. In *The Mystery of Mars* O'Shaughnessy and Ride present information gained in more-recent NASA expeditions, pairing what *Horn Book* critic Danielle J. Ford described as "gorgeous" high-resolution photographs with a text that "outshines even the remarkable illustrations." In the book the coauthors mix information on Martian history, atmosphere, and environment with a discussion of the space missions to the Red Planet.

Described by *Booklist* critic Gillian Engberg as "a thrilling introduction," *Exploring Our Solar System* combines up-to-the minute facts with numerous visual planetary images. Reviewing this collaboration between Ride and O'Shaughnessy, Ford wrote that *Exploring Our Solar System* is "an uncompromisingly detailed yet age-appropriate survey of the sun, planets, moons, and asteroids" that benefits from its authors' "determination to tackle complex concepts and their talent for explaining them clearly to their audience."

In *The Third Planet* O'Shaughnessy and Ride move closer to home, presenting readers with a view of Earth as it appears from outer space. In addition to discussing the planet's many biomes, the coauthors introduce facts regarding continental drift, glaciation, and seismic activity. With its "dramatic format," *The Third Planet* "demonstrates the sources and the force" of concerns regarding "the planet's continued ability to support life," according to *Booklist* critic Carolyn Phelan.

Ecological themes are also the focus of *Mission—Planet Earth* and *Mission: Save the Planet: Things You Can Do to Help Fight Global Warming,* a pair of books that reflect Ride and O'Shaughnessy's concerns that human activity may be affecting Earth's climate. Bolstered by charts, diagrams, and other visuals, *Mission—Planet Earth* was described by *School Library Journal* critic Lindsay Cesari as an "environmental science primer" that pairs "conceptual thoroughness with ease of comprehension." In *Kirkus Reviews* a critic observed that the tone of the book's text, while "less alarmist" than other books of its kind, "[is] still threaded with lively language . . . and well-stocked with . . . recent scientific findings." More "How to" in its focus, *Mission: Save the Planet* shares ideas for young readers interested in making lifestyle changes that will benefit the biosphere, both at home and in their schools. "The authors' background in science education is evident," noted Cesari, praising the text in *Mission: Save the Planet* as "clear, precise, and kid-friendly."

Biographical and Critical Sources

PERIODICALS

Booklist, July, 1994, Carolyn Phelan, review of *The Third Planet: Exploring the Earth from Space,* p. 1945; January 1, 2000, Gillian Engberg, review of *The Mystery of Mars,* p. 918; December 1, 2003. Gillian Engberg, review of *Exploring Our Solar System,* p. 679.

Horn Book, July-August, 1994, Margaret A. Bush, review of *The Third Planet,* p. 474; March, 2000, Danielle J. Ford, review of *The Mystery of Mars,* p. 216; January-February, 2004, Danielle J. Ford, review of *Exploring Our Solar System,* p. 105.

Publishers Weekly, June 8, 1992, review of *Voyager: An Adventure to the Edge of Our Solar System,* p. 64.

School Library Journal, March, 2000, John Peters, review of *The Mystery of Mars,* p. 261; August, 2009, Lindsay Cesari, reviews of *Mission: Save the Planet: Things You Can Do to Help Fight Global Warming!* and *Mission: Planet Earth; Our World and Its Climate—and How Humans Are Changing Them,* both p. 126.

Sky & Telescope, July, 2000, review of *The Mystery of Mars,* p. 72.

ONLINE

Sally Ride Science Web Site, http://www.sallyridescience.com/ (October 30, 2010), "Tam O'Shaughnessy."*

ROBBINS, Jacqui

Personal

Married; children: two. *Education:* Yale University, B.A. (theatre, anthropology). *Hobbies and other interests:* Baseball.

Addresses

Home—Ann Arbor, MI. *Agent*—Jodi Reamer, Writers House, 21 W. 26th St., New York, NY 10010. *E-mail*—jacqui@jacquirobbins.com.

Career

Educator and author. Worked variously as a drama teacher, SAT tutor, bookstore staffer, and director in residence. Teacher at elementary schools in Chicago, IL, and Philadelphia, PA; currently full-time writer. Penny Seats Theatre Company, Ann Arbor, MI, stage director; volunteer with 826Michigan.

Member

Society of Children's Book Writers and Illustrators.

Writings

The New Girl—and Me, illustrated by Matt Phelan, Atheneum Books for Young Readers (New York, NY), 2006.

Two of a Kind, illustrated by Matt Phelan, Atheneum Books for Young Readers (New York, NY), 2009.

Sidelights

Michigan writer Jacqui Robbins used to be a teacher, and her years in the classroom have provided much of the inspiration for her picture books *The New Girl—and Me* and *Two of a Kind,* the last which a *Kirkus Reviews* writer recommended to "young girls looking for guidance in the ways of friendship." "None of the characters are real students, but they are all situations with which children deal at school," Robbins explained on her home page. "I got frustrated when I was teaching at how easy making friends seemed to be in books. In real life, sometimes people get punched in the head!"

Robbins books *The New Girl—and Me* and *Two of a Kind* are both illustrated by Matt Phelan. In *The New Girl—and Me* narrator Mia is in class the day a new girl named Shakeeta is introduced. When Shakeeta tells the class that she has a pet iguana her new classmates are quick to show interest, but the next day that interest is gone. Quiet and shy, the girl becomes lonely without any friends. However, when Mia and Shakeeta both find themselves excluded from the same soccer game by the class bully, the shared exclusion sparks a discussion of common interests. Noting that the "interracial friendship" between the two girls "is a plus," Jennifer Mattson added in *Booklist* that Phelan's "artwork breathes energy into" the pages of Robbins' picture-

Jacqui Robbins focuses on perennial playground dynamics in her story for **Two of a Kind,** *a picture book featuring illustrations by Matt Phelan.* (Illustrations copyright © 2009 Matt Phelan. Reprinted with the permission of Altheneum Books for Young Readers, an imprint of Simon & Schuster Children's Publishing Division.)

book debut. The two girls "are realistically and sympathetically portrayed," according to *School Library Journal* critic Grace Oliff, and a *Kirkus Reviews* writer concluded that "Robbins's pitch-perfect prose makes . . . [*The New Girl—and Me*] a subtle winner."

In *Two of a Kind* Kayla and Melanie are best friends who are also the envy of the other girls at school because of their athletic prowess and because they have an exclusive friendship in which secrets are told, jokes are shared, and no one else is allowed. Julisa and Anna also have a good friendship, but they are more generous on the playground and allow anyone to join in their games. Anna envies the "cool" Kayla and Melanie, and when she is invited to join them and make their exclusive twosome an exclusive trio the offer is tempting. As readers follow Anna's first-person narrative, she now has to decide what is more important: feeding her ego by joining the playground clique or remaining loyal to best friend Julisa. "Phelan's soft watercolor [and pencil] illustrations . . . add a gentle touch" to *Two of a Kind,* according to *Horn Book* critic Betty Carter, and Robbins' depiction of the elementary-grade girls' "classroom situations are spot-on." In *School Library Journal* Maryann H. Owen wrote that "the book imparts a good lesson that needs reinforcing," while *Booklist* critic Kristen McKulski praised *Two of a Kind* as "a great introduction to early conversations about character, bullying, and peer pressure."

Biographical and Critical Sources

PERIODICALS

Booklist, July 1, 2006, Jennifer Mattson, review of *The New Girl—and Me,* p. 57; September 1, 2009, Kristen McKulski, review of *Two of a Kind,* p. 103.
Bulletin of the Center for Children's Books, September, 2006, Deborah Stevenson, review of *The New Girl—and Me,* p. 29.
Horn Book, September-October, 2009, Betty Carter, review of *Two of a Kind,* p. 545.
Kirkus Reviews, June 1, 2006, review of *The New Girl—and Me,* p. 579; June 1, 2009, review of *Two of a Kind.*
School Library Journal, July, 2006, Grace Oliff and Ann Blanche, review of *The New Girl—and Me,* p. 86; August, 2009, Maryann H. Owen, review of *Two of a Kind,* p. 83.
Tribune Books (Chicago, IL), July 15, 2006, Mary Harris Russell, review of *The New Girl—and Me,* p. 7.

ONLINE

Jacqui Robbins Home Page, http://www.jacquirobbins.com (October 15, 2010).
Jacqui Robbins Web Log, http://jacquirobbins.blogspot.com (October 15, 2010).

ROY, Kari Anne 1977(?)- (K.A. Holt)

Personal

Born c. 1977; married; children: three. *Education:* University of Texas at Austin, B.A. (art history), 1998. *Hobbies and other interests:* Blogging, watching television.

Addresses

Home—Austin, TX. *E-mail*—grashrinker@gmail.com.

Career

Author and poet. Formerly worked in advertising. Presenter at schools and libraries.

Member

Writers' League of Texas.

Writings

FOR CHILDREN

Mike Stellar, Nerves of Steel, Random House (New York, NY), 2009.
Brains for Lunch: A Zombie Novel in Haiku?!, illustrated by Gahan Wilson, Roaring Brook Press (New York, NY), 2010.

OTHER

Haiku Mama, Quirk Books, 2006.
Deadpan: Poems, Main Street Rag Pub. Co. (Charlotte, NC), 2007.

Contributor to periodicals, including Austin, TX, *American-Statesman.*

Sidelights

K.A. Holt is the pen name of Texas-based writer Kari Anne Roy, whose work includes several collections of poetry and articles on technology for a local Austin newspaper. Adopting her Holt pseudonym, Roy also entertains middle-grade readers with *Mike Stellar, Nerves of Steel,* and *Brains for Lunch: A Zombie Novel in Haiku?!,* a collaboration with noted illustrator and cartoonist Gahan Wilson. While embarking on her new career writing for children, Roy decided to actively promote her work, expanding her technical skills into Website design, social networking, and even creating a promotional video featuring a soundtrack created by a local musician. In between writing and raising her three children, Holt also writes haiku and authors the Web log Haikuoftheday.com.

Writing under her pen name K.A. Holt, Kari Anne Roy entertains middle-grade readers with **Mike Stellar, Nerves of Steel,** *a novel featuring artwork by Craig Phillips.* (Yearling, 2009. Used by permission of Yearling, an imprint of Random House Children's Books, a division of Random House, Inc.)

In *Mike Stellar, Nerves of Steel* readers meet an eleven year old whose family is anything but normal. Although Mike has to deal with typical kid-type problems, such as school homework, annoying siblings, and friends that his parents would rather he avoided, there is a

twist. The year is 2174, and Mike's family makes their home near a space ship. So, when the boy's scientist parents announce that the family will be moving soon, they do not mean moving across town. In eight hours, the family will be blasting off for Mars, following the path of an expedition that has seemingly vanished. When his mother's lab assistant, Mr. Shugabert, begins to track Mike's every move and his sister mysteriously disappears, the preteen begins to suspect that something in this hurried trip to Mars is not right. With new friend Larc, Mike turns detective in an effort to figure out why his mom and dad are acting so secretive . . . and may even be spies! *Mike Stellar, Nerves of Steel* features a story that "whizzes by at warp speed," according to a *Publishers Weekly* critic, the reviewer adding that the novel takes readers on "a fun ride with a satisfying resolution." In *Kirkus Reviews* a contributor praised Mike as a likeable young hero who exhibits fine detecting qualities: "savvy sleuthing, sharp observation and courage in the clutch."

Biographical and Critical Sources

PERIODICALS

Kirkus Reviews, May 1, 2009, review of *Mike Stellar, Nerves of Steel.*
Publishers Weekly, June 22, 2009, review of *Mike Stellar, Nerves of Steel,* p. 45.
School Library Journal, November, 2009, Saleena L. Davidson, review of *Mike Stellar, Nerves of Steel,* p. 110.

ONLINE

K.A. Holt Home Page, http://www.kaholt.com (October 15, 2010).
Kari Ann Roy Web Log, http://www.haikuoftheday.com (October 15, 2010).*

S

SAINTCROW, Lilith 1976-
(Anna Beguine, Lili St. Crow)

Personal

Born 1976, in NM; father in the U.S. Air Force; married (divorced); children. *Hobbies and other interests:* Photography.

Addresses

Home—Vancouver, WA. *E-mail*—contact@lilithsaint crow.com.

Career

Novelist and author of short fiction. Volunteer at local bookstore.

Writings

NOVELS

The Society ("Society" series), ImaJinn Books (Cannon City, CO), 2005.
Hunter, Healer ("Society" series), ImaJinn Books (Cannon City, CO), 2005.
(As Anna Beguine) *Smoke* ("Keeper" series), Lulu.com, 2007.
(As Anna Beguine) *Mirror* ("Keeper" series), Lulu.com, 2007.
Steelflower, Samhain Publishing (Macon, GA), 2007.
The Demon's Library, Samhain Publishing (Macon, GA), 2009.

"WATCHER" NOVEL SERIES

Dark Watcher, ImaJinn Books (Cannon City, CO), 2004.
Storm Watcher, ImaJinn Books (Cannon City, CO), 2005.
Fire Watcher, ImaJinn Books (Cannon City, CO), 2006.

Cloud Watcher, ImaJinn Books (Cannon City, CO), 2006.
Mindhealer, ImaJinn Books (Cannon City, CO), 2008.

"DANTE VALENTE" NOVEL SERIES

Working for the Devil, Warner Books (New York, NY), 2005.
Dead Man Rising, Warner Books (New York, NY), 2006.
Saint City Sinners, Orbit (New York, NY), 2007.
The Devil's Right Hand, Orbit (New York, NY), 2007.
To Hell and Back, Orbit (New York, NY), 2008.

"JILL KISMET" NOVEL SERIES

Night Shift, Orbit (New York, NY), 2008.
Hunter's Prayer, Orbit (New York, NY), 2008.
Redemption Alley, Orbit (New York, NY), 2009.
Flesh Circus, Orbit (New York, NY), 2009.
Heaven's Spite, Orbit (New York, NY), 2010.
Angel Town, Orbit (New York, NY), 2011.

"STRANGE ANGELS" YOUNG-ADULT NOVEL SERIES

(As Lili St. Crow) *Strange Angels,* Razorbill (New York, NY), 2009.
(As Lili St. Crow) *Betrayals,* Razorbill (New York, NY), 2009.
(As Lili St. Crow) *Jealousy,* Razorbill (New York, NY), 2010.
(As Lili St. Crow) *Defiance,* Razorbill (New York, NY), 2011.

Biographical and Critical Sources

PERIODICALS

Publishers Weekly, December 12, 2005, review of *Working for the Devil,* p. 43.

School Library Journal, May 26, 2008, review of *Night Shift,* p. 44.

ONLINE

Lilith Saintcrow Home Page, http://www.lilithsaintcrow. com (October 20, 2010).*

*   *   *

SCHLOSSBERG, Elisabeth

Personal

Born in France.

Addresses

Home—Paris, France. *Agent*—Studio Goodwin Sturges, 67 Taber Ave., Providence, RI 02906. *E-mail*—schlossberg.elisabeth@neuf.fr.

Career

Illustrator.

Illustrator

Virginia L. Kroll, *On the Way to Kindergarten,* G.P. Putnam's Sons (New York, NY), 2006.

April Friends, *Valentine Friends,* Scholastic (New York, NY), 2007.

Susan Middleton Elya, *Adiós, Tricycle,* G.P. Putnam's Sons (New York, NY), 2009.

Laura Krauss Melmed, *Eight Winter Nights: A Family Hanukkah Book,* Chronicle Books (San Francisco, CA), 2010.

Also illustrator of books published in France.

Sidelights

Elisabeth Schlossberg is a French artist and illustrator who lives and works in Paris. She specializes in creating engaging art for very young children, often incorporating pastel tones and animal characters. Schlossberg's artwork has appeared in several books published in English, including stories by Virginia L. Kroll, April Friends, Laura Krauss Melmed, and Susan Middleton Elya. Her "soft-edged artwork" for Kroll's read-aloud story in *On the Way to Kindergarten* "conveys a cozy charm," according to *Booklist* critic Julie Cummins, while Martha Topol wrote in *School Library Journal* that the story's "sense of belonging is amplified" in Schlossberg's "friendly, cheerful," oil-pastel paintings.

In *Adiós, Tricycle,* a bilingual story by Elya, the author's "peppy, rhyming text" is paired with soft-toned illustrations by Schlossberg that "capture the mixed emotions" of the story's animal characters, according to *Booklist* critic Shelle Rosenfeld. Praised by the critic as

Elisabeth Schlossberg creates the colorful artwork that greets readers in the pages of Susan Middleton Elya's growing-up-themed picture book **Adiós, Tricycle.** (Putnam, 2009. Reproduced by permission of Penguin Putnam, Inc.)

"a warm, enjoyable choice" for toddler storytimes, *Adiós, Tricycle* helps children learn to part with much-loved but outgrown possessions through the experiences of a young piglet helping out at his family's yard sale. In her "friendly and familiar" images for the picture book, Schlossberg includes what *School Library Journal* critic Susan E. Murray described as "lots of little details for children to pore over."

Biographical and Critical Sources

PERIODICALS

Booklist, February 15, 2006, Julie Cummins, review of *On the Way to Kindergarten*, p. 103; June 1, 2009, Shelle Rosenfeld, review of *Adiós, Tricycle*, p. 60.

Kirkus Reviews, March 1, 2006, review of *On the Way to Kindergarten*, p. 233; June 1, 2009, review of *Adiós, Tricycle*.

School Library Journal, March, 2006, Martha Topol, review of *On the Way to Kindergarten*, p. 195; August, 2009, Susan E. Murray, review of *Adiós, Tricycle*, p. 74.

ONLINE

Elisabeth Schlossberg Home Page, http://elisabeth-schlossberg.com (October 15, 2010).*

* * *

SHERWOOD, Jonathan
See LONDON, Jonathan

* * *

SILL, Cathryn 1953-

Personal

Born February 8, 1953, in Asheville, NC; daughter of Jack Howard (an accountant) and Mary (a homemaker) Powell; married John Sill (an artist and author), March 16, 1975. *Education:* Western Carolina University, B.S. (education), 1975.

Addresses

Home—Franklin, NC.

Career

Educator and author. Macon County Board of Education, Franklin, NC, elementary school teacher, beginning 1976; children's author, beginning 1988.

Writings

ADULT HUMOR

(With husband, John Sill, and brother-in-law Ben Sill) *A Field Guide to Little-known and Seldom-seen Birds of North America*, illustrated by John Sill, Peachtree (Atlanta, GA), 1988.

(With Ben Sill and John Sill) *Another Field Guide to Little-known and Seldom-seen Birds of North America*, illustrated by John Sill, Peachtree (Atlanta, GA), 1990.

(With Ben Sill and John Sill) *Beyond Birdwatching: More than There Is to Know about Birding*, illustrated by John Sill, Peachtree (Atlanta, GA), 1993.

"ABOUT. . ." JUVENILE NONFICTION SERIES

About Birds: A Guide for Children, illustrated by John Sill, Peachtree (Atlanta, GA), 1991.

About Mammals: A Guide for Children, illustrated by John Sill, Peachtree (Atlanta, GA), 1997.

About Reptiles: A Guide for Children, illustrated by John Sill, Peachtree (Atlanta, GA), 1999.

About Amphibians: A Guide for Children, illustrated by John Sill, Peachtree (Atlanta, GA), 2000.

About Insects: A Guide for Children, illustrated by John Sill, Peachtree (Atlanta, GA), 2000.

About Fish: A Guide for Children, illustrated by John Sill, Peachtree (Atlanta, GA), 2002.

About Arachnids: A Guide for Children, illustrated by John Sill, Peachtree (Atlanta, GA), 2003.

About Crustaceans: A Guide for Children, illustrated by John Sill, Peachtree Publishers (Atlanta, GA), 2004.

About Mollusks: A Guide for Children, illustrated by John Sill, Peachtree (Atlanta, GA), 2005.

About Marsupials: A Guide for Children, illustrated by John Sill, Peachtree (Atlanta, GA), 2006.

About Rodents: A Guide for Children, illustrated by John Sill, Peachtree (Atlanta, GA), 2008.

About Penguins: A Guide for Children, illustrated by John Sill, Peachtree Publishers (Atlanta, GA), 2009.

About Raptors: A Guide for Children, illustrated by John Sill, Peachtree Publishers (Atlanta, GA), 2010.

"ABOUT HABITATS" JUVENILE NONFICTION SERIES

Deserts, illustrated by John Sill, Peachtree (Atlanta, GA), 2007.

Wetlands, illustrated by John Sill, Peachtree (Atlanta, GA), 2008.

Mountains, illustrated by John Sill, Peachtree (Atlanta, GA), 2009.

Grasslands, illustrated by John Sill, Peachtree Publishers (Atlanta, GA), 2011.

Sidelights

Based in North Carolina, teacher and author Cathryn Sill joins her husband, artist John Sill, to create nature-themed picture books that team John's detailed water-

color illustrations with Cathryn's simple fact-filled texts. Used by teachers and parents in explaining complex topics to young readers, the Sills' comprehensive "About. . ." series includes titles such as *About Mammals: A Guide for Children* and *About Raptors: A Guide for Children,* as well as the habitat-specific volumes *Deserts, Wetlands, Grasslands,* and *Mountains.* The "About" books have been praised by critics as "inviting, informative, and eye-catching," to quote Patricia Manning in her *School Library Journal* review of *About Amphibians: A Guide for Children.*

Complemented by her husband's water-color paintings and a selection of black-and-white photographs, Sill's simple, direct text presents useful information about anatomy, habitat, life cycle, and other characteristics in each "About. . ." book, and she concludes each volume with an informative afterword. *About Fish: A Guide for Children* is characteristic of the series, and here the author "uses simple words to discuss topics such as how fish move, breathe, and protect themselves from predators," according to *Booklist* critic Carolyn Phelan. As a *Kirkus Reviews* writer predicted, "children will especially enjoy the cooler facts that are included" in *About Crustaceans: A Guide for Children,* and Susan Oliver recommended the same book in *School Library Journal* as "an excellent example of easy nonfiction" that is "perfect for beginning readers or for sharing aloud." According to Phelan, *About Rodents: A Guide for Children* is characteristic of the couples' work: "the elegant simplicity of their writing, illustration, and design" confirms the Sills' "respect" for their young audience of nature lovers.

Capturing the meaning of Sill's text in each of the "About. . ." books are the water-color paintings of John Sill; the images he contributes to *About Arachnids,* for example, were characterized by a *Kirkus Re-*

Cathryn Sill's informative text is paired with her husband's paintings in the nonfiction picture book **About Penguins.** (Reproduced by permission of Peachtree Publishers, Ltd.)

views writer as "meticulously exact close-ups" that "should give casual browsers a delighted shiver or two," and his "nicely composed, precisely delineated, and often beautiful paintings" for *About Penguins* help make that collaborative picture book "a pleasing entry in a dependable series," according to Phelan.

"I enjoy natural history and particularly birds," Sill once told *SATA*. "I am also very fond of teaching. I wanted a simple, informative book about birds to use in my kindergarten classroom. The illustrations needed to be accurate as well as beautiful. Since my husband, John, is an artist and illustrator, we enjoyed working together on [our first "About. . ." book,] *About Birds*.

Biographical and Critical Sources

PERIODICALS

Booklist, June 1, 1997, Carolyn Phelan, review of *About Mammals: A Guide for Children,* p. 1714; June 1, 1999, Carolyn Phelan, review of *About Reptiles: A Guide for Children,* p. 1835; February 1, 2000, Gillian Engberg, review of *About Insects: A Guide for Children,* p. 1026; May 15, 2001, Carolyn Phelan, review of *About Amphibians: A Guide for Children,* p. 1754; March 1, 2002, Carolyn Phelan, review of *About Fish: A Guide for Children,* p. 1138; March 1, 2003, Carolyn Phelan, review of *About Arachnids: A Guide for Children,* p. 1201; May 1, 2004, Carolyn Phelan, review of *About Crustaceans: A Guide for Children,* p. 1561; February 15, 2006, Carolyn Phelan, review of *About Marsupials: A Guide for Children,* p. 100; April 1, 2007, Carolyn Phelan, review of *Deserts,* p. 55; September 15, 2008, Carolyn Phelan, review of *About Rodents: A Guide for Children,* p. 56; September 15, 2009, Carolyn Phelan, review of *About Penguins: A Guide for Children,* p. 61; June 1, 2010, Terrell A. Young and Barbara A. Ward, interview with Cathryn and John Sill, pp. 19-21.

Childhood Education, spring, 2000, Emily A. Johnson, review of *About Reptiles,* p. 172.

Kirkus Reviews, January 15, 2003, review of *About Arachnids,* p. 147; March 1, 2004, review of *About Crustaceans,* p. 229; February 15, 2005, review of *About Mollusks: A Guide for Children,* p. 235; March 1, 2006, review of *About Marsupials,* p. 239; February 15, 2009, review of *Mountains.*

School Library Journal, June, 1997, Susan Oliver, review of *About Mammals,* p. 113; July, 1999, Karey Wehner, review of *About Reptiles,* p. 90; June, 2000, Karey Wehner, review of *About Insects,* p. 98; June, 2001, Patricia Manning, review of *About Amphibians,* p. 141; June, 2002, Jean Pollock, review of *About Fish* p. 126; July, 2003, Karey Wehner, review of *About Arachnids,* p. 119; June, 2004, Susan Oliver, review of *About Crustaceans,* p. 132; April, 2005, Patricia Manning, review of *About Mollusks,* p. 127; May, 2006, Christine Markley, review of *About Marsupials,* p. 117; August, 2007, Joy Fleishhacker, review of

Deserts, p. 106; May, 2008, Kathy Piehl, review of *Wetlands,* p. 118; November, 2008, Kara Schaff Dean, review of *About Rodents,* p. 112; May, 2009, Frances E. Millhouser, review of *Mountains,* p. 98; September, 2009, Karey Wehner, review of *About Penguins,* p. 147.*

*   *   *

SLADE, Arthur G. 1967-
(Arthur Gregory Slade)

Personal

Born July 9, 1967, in Moose Jaw, Saskatchewan, Canada; son of Robert (a farmer) and Anne (a writer) Slade; married Brenda Baker (a singer and writer), August 16, 1997. *Education:* University of Saskatchewan, B.A. (with honors), 1989. *Hobbies and other interests:* Biking, T'ai chi, hockey.

Addresses

Home—Saskatoon, Saskatchewan, Canada. *E-mail*—art@arthurslade.com.

Career

Author and copywriter. Advertising copywriter in Saskatoon, Saskatchewan, Canada, 1990-95; freelance writer, beginning 1995. Has also worked as a hotel night auditor, radio copy writer, and census taker. Teacher of writing at workshops, including at Banff Centre; presenter at schools, libraries, and writer's festivals.

Member

Canadian Society of Children's Authors, Illustrators, and Performers, Writers Union of Canada, Society of Children's Book Writers and Illustrators, Saskatchewan Writers Guild.

Awards, Honors

Governor General's Literacy Award for Children's Literature, 2001, for *Dust;* Saskatoon Book of the Year nomination and Fiction Book of the Year nomination, both 2008, both for *Jolted.*

Writings

FOR CHILDREN

John Diefenbaker: An Appointment with Destiny, XYZ (Montreal, Quebec, Canada), 2001.

Dust, HarperCollins (Toronto, Ontario, Canada), 2001, Wendy Lamb Books (New York, NY), 2003.

Tribes, Wendy Lamb Books (New York, NY), 2002.

Monsterology: The Fabulous Lives of the Creepy, the Revolting, and the Undead, illustrated by Derek Mah, Tundra Books (Toronto, Ontario, Canada), 2005.

Arthur G. Slade (Photograph by Black Box Images. Reproduced by permission.)

Megiddo's Shadow, Wendy Lamb Books (New York, NY), 2006.

Villainology: Fabulous Lives of the Big, the Bad, and the Wicked, illustrated by Derek Mah, Tundra Books (New York, NY), 2007.

Jolted: Newton Starker's Rules for Survival, Wendy Lamb Books (New York, NY), 2009.

The Hunchback Assignments, Wendy Lamb Books (New York, NY), 2009.

The Dark Deeps, Wendy Lamb Books (New York, NY), 2010.

Author of comic-book series "Hallowed Knight" and "Great Scott! Canada's Greatest Scottish Superhero"; author of illustrated short horror-story collection *Shades of Slade.* Author of sound recording *Up There There Are Only Birds,* Shea Publications, 1994.

Author's work has been translated into Chinese, French, and Hungarian.

"NORTHERN FRIGHTS" SERIES

Draugr, illustrated by Ljuba Levstek, Orca Books (Custer, WA), 1997.

The Haunting of Drang Island, Orca Books (Custer, WA), 1998.

The Loki Wolf, Orca Books (Custer, WA), 2000.

"CANADIAN CHILLS" NOVEL SERIES

Return of the Grudstone Ghosts, Coteau Books (Regina, Saskatchewan, Canada), 2002.

Ghost Hotel, Coteau Books (Regina, Saskatchewan, Canada), 2002.

Invasion of the IQ Snatchers, Coteau Books (Regina, Saskatchewan, Canada), 2007.

Sidelights

A fan of the quirky and offbeat, Arthur G. Slade began writing at quite a young age and finished his first novel when he was eighteen years old. Slade has averaged a novel every year since then, among them *Dust, Tribes, Megiddo's Shadow,* and *Jolted: Newton Starker's Rules for Survival,* as well as the books in his "Northern Frights" and "Canadian Chills" series. In the companion volumes *Monsterology: Fabulous Lives of the Creepy, the Revolting, and the Undead* and *Villainology: Fabulous Lives of the Big, the Bad, and the Wicked,* both which feature artwork by Derek Mah, Slade crafts unusual illustrated guide books, chronicling everything from Medusa to Dracula in the first and Attila the Hun to the Phantom of the Opera in the second. The light-hearted approach exhibited in *Monsterology* reflects much of the author's writing; as Susan Perren noted in her Toronto *Globe & Mail* review of the book, "Slade lets fly with vernacular so hip that it might hurt were it not so appropriate for his intended audience." "Slade manages to write about dark matters with the lightest of touches," Tim Wynne-Jones observed in his review of *Jolted,* the *Globe & Mail* critic going on to praise the book's characters as both "believable" and "likeable." "He writes truly imaginative and original stories with deceptive facility," Wynne-Jones added, "navigating the edge of weirdness, never falling in or going too deep," balancing "adventure and humour with thought-provoking material in entertaining fashion."

As a child, Slade was a voracious reader of comic books as well as science-fiction and fantasy novels. He also read every book on Norse mythology that he could get his hands on, and this interest remained through college, where he studied Icelandic literature and Norse mythology. Slade puts this collective knowledge to use in his "Northern Frights" series of middle-grade novels, which are based on Norse myths. "I love putting a new twist on all the old stories that the Vikings used to tell by the firelight," the author once told *SATA.*

Slade took the title for his first book, *Draugr* (pronounced "draw-ger"), from Norse mythology, specifically from the old Icelandic word describing those whose hate prevents them from resting after death. Three young Americans visiting their grandfather in Manitoba are caught in a frightening series of events that involves empty graves, strange disappearances, supernatural connections, and a touch of romance. John

Wilson, writing in *Quill & Quire,* declared of the novel that "*Draugr* sits solidly in the preteen horror genre yet stands above much of its competition in writing and plot development."

The Haunting of Drang Island, a sequel to *Draugr,* is based on the Icelandic legend of the Jormungand, a water-dwelling world-snake. Like *Draugr, The Haunting of Drang Island* features undead creatures, both human and animal, and a heavy dose of suspense. In the novel Canadian teen Michael and his father travel to a remote island off the coast of British Columbia, where Michael's father hopes to finish his book of Norse stories. When the ferry taking them to the island almost capsizes, a horrendous storm pounds the shores, and an ominous message is found, written in blood on the outside of their tent—all during their first twenty-four hours on the island—father and son decide to change their vacation plans. Aiding readers unfamiliar with the Norse myths referenced in Slade's story, Michael's father helpfully explains the ancient tales to his son and Michael's friend Fiona throughout the book. While finding Mi-

Cover illustration of Slade's young-adult novel **Dust,** *which features cover art by Luc Melanson.* (Jacket cover copyright © 2003 by Wendy Lamb Books, an imprint of Random House Children's Books, a division of Random House, Inc.)

chael's father "perhaps a touch pedantic in his exposition of the relevant chunks of mythology" in the midst of "hair-raising situations," Mary Thomas nonetheless admitted in her appraisal of *The Haunting of Drang Island* for *Canadian Review of Materials* that "Slade succeeded admirably in keeping this reader on the edge of her chair."

In *The Loki Wolf*—the third of Slade's "Northern Frights" novels—Angela Laxness starts to have nightmares about being devoured by a larger-than-life wolf. Her parents tell her that they are nothing but dreams, perhaps inspired by the Icelandic tales with which her grandfather has often regaled her. Indeed, there is a shape-shifting Loki Wolf—called an "ulfmadr" in Norse mythology. Ultimately Angela's dreams prove prescient and she and her grandfather meet this supernatural creature while on a family trip to Grandfather's ancestral homeland. "Slade is certainly at his best in *The Loki Wolf,* creating a thoroughly gripping story that will entice readers" into the world of Norse mythology, noted *Quill & Quire* reviewer Jeffrey Canton.

Rather than Norse mythology, *Dust* draws on Canadian folklore and the Bible. Set in the Dust Bowl that transformed the Canadian prairie during the 1930s, this Governor General's Award-winning novel focuses on a small, drought-plagued farming town and the mysterious man called Abram who appears there, promising to bring rain . . . for a price. Although the town's children start disappearing as soon as Abram appears, adults are so distracted by the construction of Abram's rainmaking machine and anticipating the arrival of the promised rain that they do not wonder too much about these disappearances. In fact, it seems as if the only suspicious one is Robert, the older brother of the first child to disappear. Robert perseveres until he discovers Abram's secret: the rain-making machine is powered by the ground-up souls of the vanished children. After Robert finds the bodies of the missing children, their butterfly-shaped souls stored separately in preparation for the upcoming sale, readers witness the final showdown between the boy and Abram, who also harnesses aliens and natural forces. The climax of *Dust* "almost takes one's breath away," wrote *Globe & Mail* critic Susan Perren. A *Publishers Weekly* critic predicted that "readers who like their science fiction on the dark, literary side will be hooked," while in *School Library Journal* Bruce Anne Shook deemed *Dust* an "unusual, well-written story [that] will definitely exercise readers' imaginations."

The central conflict in *Tribes* arises from twelfth-grader Percy Montmount's battle with high-school culture as well as with his own feelings. Percy is the son of an anthropologist, and to distance himself emotionally from the high-school cliques which ostracize him he studies his fellow students as if he were an anthropologist. Percy and his friend Elissa, a misfit from the "Observer" tribe, comment on and record the antics of the Jock Tribe, the Lipstick/Hairspray Tribe, and other competi-

Cover of Slade's fascinating teen sci-fi novel Jolted, *which features artwork by Antonio Javier Caparo.* (Wendy Lamb Books, 2009. Used by permission of Wendy Lamb Books, an imprint of Random House Children's Books, a division of Random house, Inc.)

tive cliques. Percy records his own actions in a similarly detached tone, and through his narration readers slowly learn what Percy is trying to flee: his feelings over the the death of a friend and his emotions resulting from being abandoned by his father. "Slade manages a wide range of weighty topics—Darwin, evolution, the Big Bang, death, suicide, and first love—with a light, humorous touch," maintained a *Kirkus Reviews* contributor. The author also "does an excellent job of drawing readers into Percy's vision of the world, only to have this vision unravel as we, like him, come to a truer understanding," Darren Crovitz wrote in a review of *Tribes* for the *Journal of Adolescent & Adult Literacy.*

With a plot that a *Publishers Weekly* critic predicted "will snag readers immediately," *Jolted* focuses on a fourteen year old boy who is burdened by a tragic family history. Except for his father and his curmudgeonly great-grandmother, everyone in Newton Starker's family has been struck by lightning. And died. The teen is determined to avoid this fate, which hands over his family like a curse. Obsessively, he checks and double-checks weather reports, learns how to read the clouds for potential thunderheads, and takes evasive action

during stormy weather. Although being in the out-of-doors makes Newton the most vulnerable, he bravely travels to Moose Jaw, Saskatchewan, to attend a survival school that will teach him how to break Mother Nature's hold on his life. During his time at Jerry Potts Academy for Survival, he meets several new friends and even a love interest, all of whom are motivated by personal obsessions. Commenting on the mix of e-mails, recipes (Newton is a food fanatic), and compelling storyline in *Jolted*, the *Publishers Weekly* critic added that Slade "offers readers plenty of humor" and a protagonist who "is especially convincing." In *Booklist* Carolyn Phelan described *Jolted* as "an offbeat, likable novel" in which Slade's cast of "quirky characters add spice to the third-person narrative." For *School Library Journal* contributor Connie Tyrrell Burns, the novel has universal teen appeal: "It's message of taking control of one's fate will appeal to every kid," the critic predicted.

The Hunchback Assignments draws on several well-known horror classics of the nineteenth century, among them Victor Hugo's *The Hunchback of Notre Dame,* Mary Shelley's *Frankenstein,* and Robert Louis Stevenson's *The Strange Case of Dr. Jekyll and Mr. Hyde.* In Slade's imaginative tale, which is set in England, the hero is Modo, a fourteen-year-old hunchback who also has the ability to transform his shape at will. Modo's talent has been put to use by Mr. Socrates, a member of the secretive Permanent Association, who has raised the boy since infancy. Joined by fellow agent Octavia Milkweed, Modo is now called to serve the Association in its battle with the power-hungry Clockwork Guild, whose leader, Dr. Hyde, is bent on taking control of the country's industrialized power base for his own benefit. In *The Hunchback Assignments* Slade creates a story that "is more than the straightforward adventure it may appear," according to a *Publishers Weekly* critic, the reviewer adding that the storyline interweaves Modo's battles with "self-loathing and [an] exploration of themes of identity and self." Noting the novel's "steampunk" elements—which include anarchic villains, futuristic, steam-powered technology, and a quasi-Victorian industrialized setting—Francisca Goldsmith concluded in *Booklist* that *The Hunchback Assignments* features "a fantasy element" that sets it "apart." Goldsmith also lauded the novel's "solid story line and well-crafted writing," while a *Kirkus Reviews* contributor remarked that "regular glimpses from the villain's perspective allows readers to fully appreciate Slade's inventive imagination."

Inspired by Slade's grandfather, who served in a British cavalry regiment in Egypt during World War I, *Megiddo's Shadow* marks something of a departure for Slade. As the novel begins, Edward is sixteen years old and living on his parents' Saskatchewan farm, where he has shown a skill in taming wild horses. After his older brother is killed on the European battlefield of the Great War, Edward ignores the protestations of his parents and travels to England, where he enlists in the British cavalry. Soon the teen finds himself in Palestine, where

the British are battling the Turks in a desperate desert campaign. Befriended by loyal friend Buke and inspired by the letters of a young British nurse named Emily, Edward quickly realizes that war is not the noble arm of vengeance, but rather an horrific engine of man's aggression in which his only concern becomes the survival of himself, his horse, and his comrades. In *Horn Book* Sarah Ellis commented on the extensive research that enriches the novel, adding that Slade "puts an original spin on the universals of young men going to war" by weaving historical facts about both the war and cavalry life throughout Edward's story. For Lisa Prolman, reviewing *Megiddo's Shadow* in *School Library Journal,* the novel is "a powerful book that needs to be read," and in *Booklist* Holly Koelling praised Slade's story as one that "skillfully integrates the plot-driven war narrative with the more psychological underpinnings of loss": a loss of innocence, a loss of friends and family, and a loss of one's personal faith in God.

Biographical and Critical Sources

PERIODICALS

Booklist, April 1, 1999, John Peters, review of *The Haunting of Drang Island,* p. 1415; October 15, 2002, Ilene Cooper, review of *Tribes,* p. 402; February 15, 2003, Frances Bradburn, review of *Dust,* p. 1065; December, 2006, Holly Koelling, review of *Megiddo's Shadow,* p. 43; February 15, 2009, Carolyn Phelan, review of *Jolted: Newton Starker's Rules for Survival,* p. 83; August 1, 2009, Francisca Goldsmith, review of *The Hunchback Assignments,* p. 57.
Books in Canada, September-October, 2001, review of *Dust,* pp. 33-34; September, 2002, Gillian Chan, review of *Tribes,* pp. 44-45; October, 2002, interview with Slade, pp. 41-42.
Canadian Children's Literature, annual, 2000, review of *The Haunting of Drang Island,* p. 119; fall, 2001, review of *Dust,* pp. 80-81.
Canadian Literature, summer-autumn, 1999, Gernot R. Wieland, review of *Draugr,* pp. 173-175.
Canadian Review of Materials, November 14, 1997, Mary Thomas, review of *Draugr.*
Globe & Mail (Toronto, Ontario, Canada), August 25, 2001, Susan Perren, review of *Dust;* October 22, 2005, Susan Perren, review of *Monsterology,* p. D22; September 13, 2008, Tim Wynne-Jones, review of *Jolted,* p. D20; September 26, 2009, Tim Wynne-Jones, review of *The Hunchback Assignments,* p. F9.
Horn Book, March-April, 2003, Barbara Scotto, review of *Dust,* pp. 217-219; November-December, 2006, Sarah Ellis, review of *Megiddo's Shadow,* p. 727.
Journal of Adolescent & Adult Literacy, April, 2003, Darren Crovitz, review of *Tribes,* pp. 602-605.
Kirkus Reviews, July 1, 2002, review of *Tribes,* p. 963; April 1, 2003, review of *Dust,* p. 540; October 1, 2006, review of *Megiddo's Shadow,* p. 1025; February 1, 2009, review of *Jolted;* August 1, 2009, review of *The Hunchback Assignments.*
Kliatt, September, 2002, Paula Rohrlick, review of *Tribes,* pp. 13-14; September, 2006, Claire Rosser, review of *Megiddo's Shadow,* p. 18.
Publishers Weekly, September 23, 2002, review of *Tribes,* p. 74; March 31, 2003, review of *Dust,* p. 68; March 9, 2009, review of *Jolted,* p. 48; September 14, 2009, review of *The Hunchback Assignments,* p. 50.
Quill & Quire, January, 1998, John Wilson, review of *Draugr,* p. 38; June, 2000, Jeffrey Canton, review of *The Loki Wolf,* pp. 53-54; August, 2001, Sarah Ellis, review of *Dust,* p. 30.
Resource Links, February, 1998, review of *Draugr,* p. 119; February, 1999, review of *The Haunting of Drang Island,* pp. 27-28; June, 2001, Victoria Pennell, review of *John Diefenbaker: An Appointment with Destiny,* p. 30; April, 2002, K.V. Johansen, review of *Dust,* pp. 41-42; February, 2003, Linda Irvine, review of *Return of the Grudstone Ghosts,* pp. 18-19, and Nadine d'Entremont, review of *Tribes,* pp. 44-45; February, 2006, Maria Forte, review of *Monsterology,* p. 28; June, 2007, Linda Aksomitis, review of *Invasion of the IQ Snatchers,* p. 13; October, 2007, Leslie L. Kennedy, *Villainology: Fabulous Lives of the Big, the Bad, and the Wicked,* p. 46.
School Library Journal, October, 1998, Jinder Johal, review of *Draugr,* pp. 146-147; August, 1999, Linda Greengrass, review of *The Haunting of Drang Island,* p. 164; October, 2002, Todd Morning, review of *Tribes,* pp. 170-171; March, 2003, Bruce Anne Shook, review of *Dust,* p. 240; February, 2006, Michele Capozzella, review of *Monsterology,* p. 137; December, 2006, Lisa Prolman, review of *Megiddo's Shadow,* p. 155; March, 2009, Connie Tyrrell Burns, review of *Jolted,* p. 154; December, 2009, Anthony C. Doyle, review of *The Hunchback Assignments,* p. 132.

ONLINE

Arthur G. Slade Home Page, http://www.arthurslade.com (February 21, 2004).

*   *   *

SLADE, Arthur Gregory
See SLADE, Arthur G.

*   *   *

SLAYTON, Fran Cannon

Personal

Born in VA; married; children: one daughter. *Education:* University of Virginia, B.A. (psychology and religious studies/with distinguished honors), 1989, J.D. *Religion:* Roman Catholic. *Hobbies and other interests:* Sports, volunteering.

Addresses

Home—Charlottesville, VA. *E-mail*—fran@francannonslayton.com.

Career

Attorney and author. Former prosecuting attorney in VA; legal publisher; owner of a title-insurance agency. Vocalist and trumpet player in a rock-and-roll band.

Member

Society of Children's Book Writers and Illustrators (Mid-Atlantic chapter), Phi Beta Kappa.

Writings

When the Whistle Blows, Philomel Books (New York, NY), 2009.

Sidelights

Fran Cannon Slayton worked as a prosecuting attorney in her home state of Virginia for several years before leaving law to pursue another career. When her daughter was born, Slayton decided to stay home, and in the winter of 2004 she began to write, inspired by stories from her close-knit family. Slayton's father grew up in Rowlesburg, West Virginia, during the 1940s and was the son of a railroad foreman. In her short-story collection *When the Whistle Blows* Slayton captures the events in young Jimmy Cannon's life from 1943 to 1949, incorporating the boy's memories of a succession of Halloween seasons within her evocative prose.

In *When the Whistle Blows* readers meet Jimmy Cannon when he is twelve years old. Growing up in a railroad family, Jimmy dreams of joining his father in his job on the B&O railroad, and he is confused when his father discourages these aspirations. Slayton captures the passage of Jimmy's adolescence by focusing on his experiences through seven Halloweens, along with the fall football games and other seasonal adventures the boy shares with his friends and older brothers. As the years pass he gains increasing insights into the life of his somewhat stern father: while the man's participation in a secret society first tantalizes the boy, Jimmy eventually comes to realize that his father's aloofness stems from his knowledge that the age of the steam locomotives which have been the life blood of Rowlesburg is coming to a close. Because of her strong connection to rural Rowlesburg, a former railroad town where both her father and mother were raised, Slayton and her husband purchased a house there, and portions of her book were written on location.

Describing Slayton's interlinking stories as "nostalgia done right," *School Library Journal* contributor Joel Shoemaker added that *When the Whistle Blows* features "telling details and gentle humor" that bring the book's characters to life. Jimmy's coming of age, and his real-

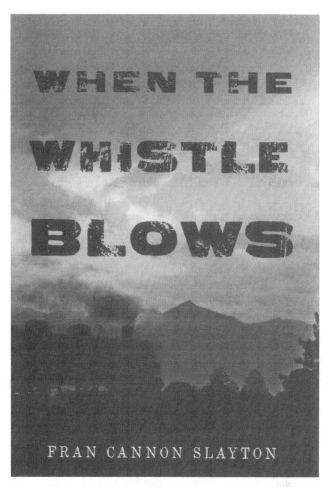

Cover of Fran Cannon Slayton's historical novel When the Whistle Blows, *which brings to life a transformative moment in Slayton's family history.* (Philomel Books, 2009. Reproduced by permission of Penguin Group USA Inc.)

ization that he is embarking on a life very different from that of his forebears, is honed by the author into "a polished paean to a bygone time and place," according to Shoemaker. A *Kirkus Reviews* writer praised Slayton's work as "an unassuming masterpiece" that illustrates the value of "faith, brotherhood and love" in a family tested by technological change. The author's decision to keep the focus on her characters by "exploring actions and sentiments that transcend eras" keeps *When the Whistle Blows* "from becoming too much of a nostalgia piece," wrote *Booklist* critic Ian Chipman, the reviewer praising Slayton's debut as "memorable."

Biographical and Critical Sources

PERIODICALS

Booklist, July 1, 2009, Ian Chipman, review of *When the Whistle Blows,* p. 57.

Bulletin of the Center for Children's Books, October, 2009, Hope Morrison, review of *When the Whistle Blows,* p. 82.

Dominion Post (Morgantown, WV), September 2, 2009, Michelle Wolford, "Author Pens Book about Growing up in Rowlesburg."

Kirkus Reviews, May 1, 2009, review of *When the Whistle Blows.*

School Library Journal, June, 2009, Rick Margolis, review of *When the Whistle Blows,* p. 27.

Voice of Youth Advocates, October, 2009, Jenny Ingram, review of *When the Whistle Blows,* p. 322.

ONLINE

Fran Cannon Slayton Home Page, http://www.francannon slayton.com (October 15, 2010).

Fran Cannon Slayton Web Log, http://franslayton.livejour nal.com (October 15, 2010).*

*   *   *

ST. CROW, Lili
See SAINTCROW, Lilith

T-W

TAYLOR, Greg 1951-

Personal

Born 1951; married; wife's name Joanne; children: Jessica, Ian.

Addresses

Home—Northridge, CA. *Agent*—Scott Miller, Trident Media Group, 41 Madison Ave., Fl. 36, New York, NY 10010.

Career

Screenwriter and novelist.

Awards, Honors

Dorothy Canfield Fisher Award Master List inclusion, 2009, for *Killer Pizza*.

Writings

Killer Pizza, Feiwel & Friends (New York, NY), 2009.

Author of teleplays and of screenplays, including *Prancer*, 1989, *Jumanji*, 1995, and *Harriet the Spy*, 1996.

Sidelights

Greg Taylor lives in California, where he has worked writing scripts for films and television movies since the late 1980s. Inspired by his own two children, Taylor channeled his writing talent into prose, producing the well-received young-adult novel *Killer Pizza*.

In *Killer Pizza* readers meet Toby McGill, a fourteen year old whose dreams of pursuing a career as a professional chef have been fueled by hours spent watching television's Food Network. In order to learn his way around a busy commercial kitchen, Toby gets a job at a local pizza parlor called Killer Pizza. The boy quickly masters the knack for preparing tasty pies and he enjoys working with fellow staffers Strobe and Annabel. However, Toby soon realizes that he has been hired for more than just his ability to spread tomato sauce: he has been hired to train as a monster fighter and the company's pizza delivery service is actually a cover for Killer Pizza's zombie-hunting operation. In *Booklist* Ian Chipman praised Taylor's ability to craft "cinematic and sometimes genuinely scary scenes," and a *Publishers Weekly* contributor described *Killer Pizza* as a "B-movie take-off" that "keeps the action coming at a brisk pace." Taylor's debut novel "delivers some fun, frightful fare," asserted Kimberly Garnick Giarratano, the *School Library Journal* contributor going on to recommend *Killer Pizza* as "a delectable choice for horror fans as well as reluctant readers."

Biographical and Critical Sources

PERIODICALS

Booklist, May 15, 2009, Ian Chipman, review of *Killer Pizza,* p. 55.
Kirkus Reviews, May 1, 2009, review of *Killer Pizza.*
Publishers Weekly, June 15, 2009, review of *Killer Pizza,* p. 50.
School Library Journal, September, 2009, Kimberly Garnick Giarratano, review of *Killer Pizza,* p. 174.

ONLINE

Macmillan Web site, http://us.macmillan.com/ (October 30, 2010), "Greg Taylor."*

*   *   *

USHER, Mark David
See USHER, M.D.

USHER, M.D. 1966-
(Mark David Usher)

Personal

Born February, 1966, in Bad Kreuznach, Germany; immigrated to United States; married October, 1986; wife's name Caroline; children: Isaiah, Estlin, Gawain. *Education:* University of Vermont, B.A. (Greek and Latin; summa cum laude), 1992; University of Chicago, M.A. (classical languages and literatures), 1994, Ph.D. (classical languages and literatures; with distinction), 1997. *Hobbies and other interests:* Carpentry and farming.

Addresses

Home—Shoreham, VT. *E-mail*—musher@uvm.edu.

Career

Educator and author. Willamette University, assistant professor of classics, 1997-2000; University of Vermont, assistant professor, 2000-03, associate professor, beginning 2003, and chair of Classics Department beginning 2005. Works and Days Farm (sheep farm), coowner and operator, beginning 2000. Lecturer; presenter at conventions; participant in seminars and on panels.

Awards, Honors

International Reading Association Children's Book Award, Bank Street College of Education Best Children's Book of the Year designation, 100 Titles for Reading and Sharing selection, New York Public Library, and National Council for the Social Studies/Children's Book Council Notable Trade Book in the Field of Social Studies designation, all c. 2005, all for *Wise Guy.*

Writings

FOR CHILDREN

Wise Guy: The Life and Philosophy of Socrates, illustrated by William Bramhall, Farrar, Straus & Giroux (New York, NY), 2005.
Diogenes, illustrated by Michael Chesworth, Farrar, Straus & Giroux (New York, NY), 2009.
The Golden Ass of Lucius Apuleius, illustrated by T. Motley, David R. Godine (New York, NY), 2011.

OTHER

(As Mark David Usher) *Texts and Their Transformations: Continuity and Change in the Classical Tradition,* University of Chicago Library (Chicago, IL), 1994.
Homeric Stitchings: The Homeric Centos of the Empress Eudocia, Rowman & Littlefield (Lanham, MD), 1998.

M.D. Usher (Photograph by Caroline Usher. Reproduced by permission.)

(Editor as Mark D. Usher) *Homerocentones Eudociae Augustae,* Teubner (Stuttgart, Germany), 1999.
(Author of notes and commentary) *A Student's Seneca: Ten Letters and Selections from De Providentia and De Vita Beata,* revised edition, University of Oklahoma Press (Norman, OK), 2006.

Contributor of poems to periodicals, including *Brown Classical Journal, Burlington Review, Chicago Literary Review,* and *Chrysalis.* Contributor to academic journals and periodicals, including *American Journal of Philology, Amphora, Bryn Mawr Classical Review, Byzantinische Zeitschrift, Classical and Modern Literature, Classical Journal, Classical Philology, Classical Review, Moveable Type,* and *Oral Tradition.* Contributor of translations to periodicals, including *New England Classical Journal.*

Sidelights

An associate professor of the classics at the University of Vermont, M.D. Usher is known among his colleagues for his translations, his journal articles, and his scholarly works. However, Usher is building another school of adherents by sharing his enthusiasm for the teachings of the ancients in the illustrated picture books *Wise Guy: The Life and Philosophy of Socrates, Diogenes,* and *The Golden Ass of Lucius Apuleius,* the last an English-language version of a Latin comic masterpiece.

In *Wise Guy* Usher pairs the life story of Socrates with an overview of the man's teachings, which serve as part of the foundation of Western philosophy. A teacher in

Athens, Socrates addressed issues that are central to humanity, such as right versus wrong, wisdom and justice, and the inspiration for emotions from compassion to courage. Calling Usher's work an "original" and "cheerful picture-book biography," Carolyn Phelan noted in *Booklist* that William Bramhall's "sophisticated ink-and-watercolor" cartoon art has the quality of caricature. Young readers can easily relate to the ancient philosopher presented in *Wise Guy:* as a *Kirkus Reviews* contributor noted, Usher's Socrates "is not only a dedicated seeker of truth but a social gadfly and a hearty partier" as well. In much of his text, the author "distills the essence of Socrates' thinking into approachable terms," according to *School Library Journal* contributor Grace Oliff, and the *Kirkus Reviews* writer called *Wise Guy* "intimate, memorable, [and] outstanding."

Illustrated by Michael Chesworth, *Diogenes* depicts the noted Greek philosopher as an actual dog who values freedom more highly than possessions. For Diogenes (the dog), life in Athens with no home and no job means that his time is his own. He lives on the street, where he begs for food and does what he pleases. Although he is captured by the local dogcatcher, Diogenes is eventually adopted into the household of a wealthy Athenian, where he entertains his host with his musings and leads a comfortable life. A *Kirkus Reviews* writer approved of Usher's decision to cast "a free-ranging mutt" in the place of the cynical Greek, noting that "Diogenes the dog sports the real man's quirks and tricks." The "comical cartoons" that bring to life *Diogenes* "underline the dog's carefree spirit," observed *School Library Journal* contributor Monika Schroeder, the critic predicting that Usher's book will prompt readers to think about the trade-off between riches and happiness and "spark a discussion about humans' desire" for status and material wealth.

Illustrated by T. Motley, *The Golden Ass of Lucius Apuleius* traces the hilarious misadventures of a young man who is a tad too curious about magic for his own good. Hoping to change himself into an owl, he mistakenly turns himself into a donkey instead, and in his new guise he is subsequently sold, stolen, or otherwise shunted from one master to the next. Along the way, he sees the underbelly of the sprawling Roman Empire, with all its saints and villains, its venal merchants and greedy clergy, until he is transformed back into human form through the intervention of the goddess Isis. As Usher explained to *SATA, The Golden Ass of Lucius Apuleius* "is a story of comic redemption and a self-conscious romp in the art of storytelling that has left an indelible mark on subsequent literature: from Chaucer's *Canterbury Tales* to Boccaccio's *Decameron,* from Shakespeare's *A Midsummer Night's Dream* to Carlo Collodi's classic children's tale, *Pinocchio.*"

Biographical and Critical Sources

PERIODICALS

Booklist, January 1, 2006, Carolyn Phelan, review of *Wise Guy: The Life and Philosophy of Socrates,* p. 108.

Kirkus Reviews, November 1, 2005, review of *Wise Guy,* p. 1188; May 1, 2009, review of *Diogenes.*
Publishers Weekly, December 12, 2005, review of *Wise Guy,* p. 66.
School Library Journal, January, 2006, Grace Oliff, review of *Wise Guy,* p. 124; June, 2009, Monika Schroeder, review of *Diogenes,* p. 101.

ONLINE

Macmillan Web Site, http://us.macmillan.com/ (October 15, 2010), "M.D. Usher."
University of Vermont Web Site, http://www.uvm.edu/ (October 15, 2010), "M.D. Usher."

* * *

WALKER, Sally M. 1954-
(Sally Fleming)

Personal

Born October 16, 1954, in East Orange, NJ; daughter of Donald (an insurance agent) and Cleo (an accounting clerk) MacArt; married James Walker (an igneous petrologist), August, 1974; children: one daughter, one son. *Education:* Upsala College, B.A., 1975. *Hobbies and other interests:* Hiking, reading, cooking, gardening.

Addresses

Home—DeKalb, IL. *E-mail*—sallymacwalker@hotmail.com.

Career

Author and literature consultant. Junction Book Store, DeKalb, IL, children's book buyer, 1988-94; Anderson's Bookshops, Naperville, IL, children's book specialist, beginning 1994. Children's literature consultant, beginning 1988; Northern Illinois University, adjunct instructor, 1992-93. Presenter at schools and reading conferences.

Member

International Reading Association, Society of Children's Book Writers and Illustrators.

Awards, Honors

Outstanding Science Trade Book designation, National Science Teachers' Association (NSTA)/Children's Book Council (CBC), 1997, for *Earthquakes,* 2002, for *Fireflies,* 2004, for *Sea Horses;* Children's Choice Award, International Reading Association, 2001, for *Mary Anning, Fossil Hunter;* Best Children's Book of the Year designation, Bank Street College of Education, and Recommended designation, NSTA, both 2002, both for

"Early Bird Physics" series; Robert F. Sibert Informational Book Award, 2006, for *Secrets of a Civil-War Submarine;* Best Children's Book of the Year designation, Bank Street College of Education, 2006, for *Shipwreck Search.*

Writings

NONFICTION; FOR CHILDREN

Born near the Earth's Surface: Sedimentary Rocks ("Earth's Processes" series), Enslow (Hillside, NJ), 1991.

Mary Anning: Fossil Hunter, illustrated by Phyllis V. Saroff, Carolrhoda (Minneapolis, MN), 2001.

(Under pseudonym Sally Fleming) *Ferocious Fangs,* North Word Press, 2001.

(Under pseudonym Sally Fleming) *Fantastic Flyers,* North Word Press, 2001.

(Under pseudonym Sally Fleming) *Rapid Runners,* North Word Press, 2002.

Fossil Fish Found Alive: Discovering the Coelacanth, Carolrhoda (Minneapolis, MN), 2002.

Life in an Estuary ("Ecosystems in Action" series), Lerner (Minneapolis, MN), 2002.

Jackie Robinson (biography), illustrations by Rodney S. Pate, Carolrhoda (Minneapolis, MN), 2003.

Bessie Coleman: Daring to Fly (biography), illustrated by Janice Lee Porter, Carolrhoda Books (Minneapolis, MN), 2003.

Secrets of a Civil War Submarine: Solving the Mysteries of the H.L. Hunley, Carolrhoda Books (Minneapolis, MN), 2005.

Supercroc Found, illustrated by Philip Hood, Millbrook Press (Minneapolis, MN), 2006.

Mystery Fish: Secrets of the Coelacanth, illustrated by Shawn Gould, Millbrook Press (Minneapolis, MN), 2006.

Shipwreck Search: Discovery of the H.L. Hunley, illustrated by Elaine Verstraete, Millbrook Press (Minneapolis, MN), 2006.

The Search for Antarctic Dinosaurs, illustrated by John Bindon, Millbrook Press (Minneapolis, MN), 2008.

(Adaptor) Tim Flannery, *We Are the Weather Makers: The History of Climate Change* (based on *The Weather Makers*), Candlewick Press (Somerville, MA), 2009.

Written in Bone: Buried Lives of Jamestown and Colonial Maryland, Carolrhoda Books (Minneapolis, MN), 2009.

Frozen Secrets: Antarctica Revealed, Carolrhoda Books (Minneapolis, MN), 2010.

"EARTH WATCH" SERIES

Glaciers: Ice on the Move, Carolrhoda (Minneapolis, MN), 1990.

Water Up, Water Down: The Hydrologic Cycle, Carolrhoda (Minneapolis, MN), 1992.

Volcanoes: Earth's Inner Fire, Carolrhoda (Minneapolis, MN), 1994.

Earthquakes, Carolrhoda (Minneapolis, MN), 1996.

"NATURE WATCH" SERIES

Rhinos, photographs by Gerry Ellis, Carolrhoda (Minneapolis, MN), 1996.

Dolphins, Carolrhoda (Minneapolis, MN), 1998.

Hippos, photographs by Gerry Ellis, Carolrhoda (Minneapolis, MN), 1998.

Manatees, Carolrhoda (Minneapolis, MN), 1999.

Sea Horses, Carolrhoda (Minneapolis, MN), 1999.

Rays, Carolrhoda (Minneapolis, MN), 2003.

Crocodiles, Carolrhoda Books (Minneapolis, MN), 2004.

Jaguars, Lerner (Minneapolis, MN), 2009.

"EARLY BIRD NATURE WATCH" SERIES

Fireflies, Lerner (Minneapolis, MN), 2001.

Sea Horses, Lerner (Minneapolis, MN), 2004.

Opossums, Lerner (Minneapolis, MN), 2008.

Mosquitoes, Lerner (Minneapolis, MN), 2009.

"EARLY BIRD PHYSICS" SERIES

(With Roseann Feldman) *Work,* photographs by Andy King, Lerner (Minneapolis, MN), 2002.

(With Roseann Feldman) *Inclined Planes and Wedges,* photographs by Andy King, Lerner (Minneapolis, MN), 2002.

(With Roseann Feldman) *Levers,* photographs by Andy King, Lerner (Minneapolis, MN), 2002.

(With Roseann Feldman) *Pulleys,* photographs by Andy King, Lerner (Minneapolis, MN), 2002.

(With Roseann Feldman) *Screws,* photographs by Andy King, Lerner (Minneapolis, MN), 2002.

(With Roseann Feldman) *Wheels and Axles,* photographs by Andy King, Lerner (Minneapolis, MN), 2002.

"EARLY BIRD ENERGY" SERIES

Sound, photographs by Andy King, Lerner (Minneapolis, MN), 2006.

Electricity, photographs by Andy King, Lerner (Minneapolis, MN), 2006.

Heat, photographs by Andy King, Lerner (Minneapolis, MN), 2006.

Light, photographs by Andy King, Lerner (Minneapolis, MN), 2006.

Magnetism, photographs by Andy King, Lerner (Minneapolis, MN), 2006.

Matter, photographs by Andy King, Lerner (Minneapolis, MN), 2006.

"EARLY BIRD EARTH SCIENCE" SERIES

Fossils, Lerner (Minneapolis, MN), 2007.

Minerals, Lerner (Minneapolis, MN), 2007.

Rocks, Lerner (Minneapolis, MN), 2007.

Soil, Lerner (Minneapolis, MN), 2007.

Caves, Lerner (Minneapolis, MN), 2008.

Earthquakes, Lerner (Minneapolis, MN), 2008.

Glaciers, Lerner (Minneapolis, MN), 2008.

Reefs, Lerner (Minneapolis, MN), 2008.

Volcanoes, Lerner (Minneapolis, MN), 2008.

PICTURE BOOKS

Opossum at Sycamore Road, illustrated by Joel Snyder, Soundprints (Norwalk, CT), 1997.

Seahorse Reef: A Story of the South Pacific, illustrated by Steven James Petruccio, Soundprints (Norwalk, CT), 1997.

The Vowel Family: A Tale of Lost Letters, illustrated by Kevin Luthardt, Carolrhoda Books (Minneapolis, MN), 2008.

Druscilla's Halloween, illustrated by Lee White, Carolrhoda Books (Minneapolis, MN), 2009.

OTHER

The Eighteen-Penny Goose (historical fiction), illustrated by Ellen Beier, HarperCollins (New York, NY), 1998.

(Compiler, with Sandy Whiteley and Kim Summers) *The Teacher's Calendar, 1999-2000,* Contemporary Books (Lincolnwood, IL), 1999.

180 Creative Ideas for Getting Students Involved, Engaged, and Excited, Contemporary Books (Chicago, IL), 2004.

Author's work has been translated into Spanish.

Sidelights

Illinois writer Sally M. Walker has created numerous nonfiction books for young people that brim with questions about nature and the out-of-doors. Titles such as *Glaciers: Ice on the Move* and *Water up, Water Down: The Hydrologic Cycle* attest to the author's personal interest in physical science, while in the books *Hippos, Fireflies,* and *Dolphins* the life cycle and habits of crea-

Sally M. Walker's nonfiction picture books include **Dolphins,** *which pairs her fact-filled text with compelling photographs.* (Fleetham, David B/Visuals Unlimited, photographer. Carolrhoda, 1999. Reproduced by permission.)

tures inhabiting land, sea, and sky are discussed. In addition to her nonfiction works, many of which are divided into series, Walker delves into fiction with the historical story *The Eighteen-Penny Goose* and the humorous *Druscilla's Halloween,* the latter which *Booklist* contributor Carolyn Phelan dubbed a "witty picture book" featuring "a strong main character, imaginative details, and many well-chosen words." She has also written biographies of African-American baseball great Jackie Robinson, early-twentieth-century pilot Bessie Coleman, and nineteenth-century British paleontologist Mary Anning and has adapted Tim Flannery's *The Weather Makers* for younger readers as *We Are the Weather Makers: The History of Climate Change.*

Born in New Jersey, Walker grew up with an interest in nature and she enrolled at Upsala College to study for her B.A. in physical science. As she once told *SATA:* "I first thought about becoming an author when I was a child. At the time, I was worried that the world might run out of horse stories and mysteries. My love of the outdoors led me into the field of geology. Those pursuits melded perfectly with another love: history. In college I took many archeology courses. So when I wasn't looking at rocks I was usually digging in the dirt. Maybe that's why I enjoy gardening now."

As a nonfiction author, Walker has contributed books to several series, among them the "Early Bird Physics" series, with coauthor Roseann Feldman, as well as the "Nature Watch," "Early Bird Earth Science," "Early Bird Energy," and "Earth Watch" series, all published by Carolrhoda. *Rhinos, Hippos, Manatees, Jaguars,* and *Seahorses,* all part of the "Nature Watch" series, contain information about the diet, behavior, life cycle, predators, and habitat of these creatures while also reflecting on each animal's future on a planet threatened by various ecological ills. Dramatic photographs, an index, and a glossary containing key terms all add to the books' usefulness to students. Walker explains in *Hippos* that new DNA evidence has shown that the hippopotamus is a relative of the dolphin and whale rather than the horse or pig—"hippopotamus" means "river horse"—and in *Seahorses* she reveals an intricate ritual greeting shared between courting seahorses. In *Rhinos* readers learn that all but five of one hundred different species of the ancient animal have become extinct, in part due to hunting the creature for its horn. In a review of *Manatees* for *Booklist,* Ellen Mandell cited "Walker's intriguing writing style" and her "lucid, comprehensible explanation" of the physiological mysteries of these sea creatures. Praising *Rhinos,* Susan Oliver noted in *School Library Journal* that the "text . . . is not only appropriately simple, but also rich with information and descriptions that bring the facts to life." In *Appraisal,* Harry Levine called *Hippos* "a concise and thoughtful treatment of an endangered animal species whose habitat, the author points out, is in need of protection."

Walker continues her exploration of the animal kingdom in *Life in an Estuary,* part of the "Ecosystems in Action" series, as well as in *Supercroc Found* and *Fos-*

sil Fish Found Alive: Discovering the Coelacanth. Reviewing *Life in an Estuary* for *School Library Journal,* Kathy Piehl observed that Walker "stresses the dynamic nature of an estuary" as water temperature and the ebb and flow of the ocean's salt water affect it, using "specialized terms" that are defined in the book's thorough glossary. *Fossil Fish Found Alive* makes good on the promise of its sensationalist title in its story about a fish that was thought to be extinct. The Coelacanth was thought to have been an ancient species that died seventy million years ago until one appeared in a fisherman's net in the 1930s. Now known to range from Indonesia to the eastern coast of Africa, the fish is still somewhat of a mystery as none have survived in captivity. Walker reworks this fascinating story for younger readers in *Mystery Fish: Secrets of the Coelacanth.* *Fossil Fish Found Alive* "imbues a still-ongoing scientific treasure hunt with all the suspense and excitement it deserves," noted a *Kirkus Reviews* writer, the critic going on to describe Walker's text as "science-writing at its finest." In *School Library Journal* Ellen Heath praised the same book as "an outstanding history of scientific inquiry" that will entrance "future oceanographers."

Born near the Earth's Surface: Sedimentary Rocks was one of the first books by Walker to focus on Earth science. Written as part of a four-book series titled "Earth's Processes," *Born near the Earth's Surface* covers such things as sinkholes, mudrocks, and erosion and shows how such formations and phenomena provide clues to

Walker takes time out from truth-telling to create a fanciful story in **Druscilla's Halloween,** *a picture book illustrated by Lee White.* (Illustrations copyright © 2009 by Lee White. Reprinted with the permission of Carolrhoda Books, a division of Lerner Publishing Group, Inc. All rights reserved. No part of the excerpt may be used or reproduced in any manner whatsoever without the prior written permission of Lerner Publishing Group, Inc.)

the earth's history. Noting that "everything you always wanted to know about glaciers . . . is covered in this book," an *Appraisal* reviewer explained that Walker's *Glaciers* informs readers about the formation, location, and movement of glaciers and discusses the way that ice has molded the face of the Earth over time. *Earthquakes,* which presents explanations of how earthquakes occur and what to do when one occurs, is a book that *School Library Journal* contributor Eunice Weech hailed as useful for report-writing, "yet readable and visually appealing to browsers." Delving deep into the Earth's core, Walker's *Volcanoes: Earth's Inner Fire* performs an equally important service to young students through its discussion of lava, pyroclastics, magma, plate tectonics, and the location of volcanoes around the planet; the "succinct and intelligible information contained in this book will be an asset" to students, according to an *Appraisal* reviewer.

Walker's award-winning *Secrets of a Civil War Submarine: Solving the Mysteries of the H.L. Hunley* and her companion volume *Shipwreck Search: Discovery of the H.L. Hunley* focus on the search for the *H.L. Hunley,* a Confederate submarine that was lost at sea in 1864 after successfully sinking the steamship USS *Housatonic* during the U.S. Civil War. In 1995 explorers discovered the *H.L. Hunley* off the coast of North Carolina, and in both books Walker follows the efforts of scientists to preserve, raise, and reconstruct the sunken ship. Full of photographs and drawings that chronicle each step of the project, *Secrets of a Civil War Submarine* is geared for upper-elementary students. "The archaeological process is well documented [here] in both words and pictures, and the conclusions are interesting and even surprising," asserted Anna M. Nelson in a review of the book for *School Library Journal,* and Carolyn Phelan wrote in *Booklist* that Walker "really hits her stride . . . in explaining the complex techniques and loving care used in raising the craft." Walker retells the story of the ill-fated submarine in *Shipwreck Search,* treating younger readers to the same fascinating story in "loose sections rather than formal chapters," and creating an "exciting telling [that] will keep the audience interested," according to *Booklist* critic Kathy Broderick.

Walker continues to explore historical mysteries in *Written in Bone: Buried Lives of Jamestown and Colonial Maryland,* which follows the work of forensic anthropologists, archaeologist, historians, and other scientists as they use nine grave sites—including burials of a teenage servant, an African slave, and several colonists of upscale means—to piece together the mode of life in colonial Jamestown and the Chesapeake Bay area. "Readers will be enticed by both the scientific detective work and by the tantalizing mysteries that remain," predicted a *Kirkus Reviews* critic while adding that the photographs of the nine uncovered skeletons will fascinate young readers. Noting that *Written in Bone* "casts a magnifying glass on the hardships and realities of colonial life so often romanticized in American lore," Jeff Meyer added in *School Library Journal* that Walker's

Walker turns to fiction in her historical story **The Eighteen-Penny Goose,** *illustrated by Ellen Beier.* (HarperTrophy, 1999. Illustrations copyright © 1998 by Ellen Beier Curtis. Used by HarperCollins Publishers.)

"text succinctly explains complex forensic concepts" that will be familiar to fans of the popular *CSI* television series. "Few nonfiction authors can infuse history and science with as much suspense as Walker has done" in *Written in Bone,* wrote *Horn Book* contributor Jonathan Hunt, the critic ranking that work with *Fossil Fish Found Alive* and *Secrets of a Civil War Submarine* due to its ability to inspire young readers with the opportunities for working scientists to be "rewarded for their passion and hard work with new insights."

Walker once told *SATA:* "The most rewarding research project I have undertaken recently is solving the mystery of the 'missing pennies' that are mentioned in my book *The Eighteen-Penny Goose.* That search is a story in itself." *The Eighteen-Penny Goose* takes place during the Revolutionary War, when an advance by hostile British troops forces Letty Wright and her family to abandon their home. Worried that her pet goose Solomon might be hurt, the young girl leaves a note asking that he be treated well. When she and her family return, Letty finds her pet alive, but all the rest of the family's geese are gone and the homestead is a mess.

However, the soldiers have been somewhat considerate: in addition to not putting Letty's goose in the cooking pot, they have put around his neck a bag containing a penny for each goose they did have for dinner. Noting that "Walker maintains the inherent suspense of the story throughout," a *Kirkus Reviews* contributor found the conclusion of *The Eighteen-Penny Goose* "rewarding" and the watercolor illustrations by Ellen Beier "realistic." In her review for *Horn Book,* Maeve Visser Knoth added that *The Eighteen-Penny Goose* is one of a "handful of other successful historical easy readers . . . which hold real substance and interest for young readers."

"My husband, Jim, is a geologist," Walker noted in discussing her work as a writer. "He and his colleagues have provided wonderful support (and pictures!) for my many earth science books. My two children—now grown—are my 'reality touchstones,' who remind me that there is a world outside of children's literature. Our two cats let me know when it's time to stop writing and make dinner."

"One of the reasons I write is to learn more about the many subjects that interest me," Walker revealed. "I have so many questions! Writing nonfiction is the perfect solution: I combine the joy of doing research with the satisfaction of finding answers to my questions. The fun afterward is sharing the 'story' of the information I have discovered." "There can never be too many children's books," Walker concluded. "Let's make sure all children are able to read them."

Biographical and Critical Sources

PERIODICALS

Appraisal, autumn, 1990, John D. Stackpole, review of *Glaciers: Ice on the Move,* p. 38; autumn, 1991, Elizabeth C. Schwarzman, review of *Born near the Earth's Surface,* pp. 59-60; winter, 1993, review of *Water up, Water Down: The Hydrologic Cycle,* pp. 54-55; spring, 1995, review of *Volcanoes: Earth's Inner Fire,* pp. 57-58; winter, 1999, Harry Levine, review of *Hippos,* p. 40; autumn, 1999, Thomas Thomasi, review of *Dolphins,* p. 52.

Booklist, January 15, 1993, Carolyn Phelan, review of *Water up, Water Down,* p. 905; December 1, 1996, Julie Corsaro, review of *Rhinos,* p. 660; February 1, 1998, Hazel Rochman, review of *The Eighteen-Penny Goose,* p. 928; May 1, 1998, Stephanie Zvirin, review of *Hippos,* p. 1518; May 1, 1999, Carolyn Phelan, review of *Sea Horses,* p. 1592; September 1, 1999, Carolyn Phelan, review of *Dolphins,* p. 130; December 15, 1999, Ellen Mandel, review of *Manatees,* p. 779; September 15, 2001, Catherine Andronik, review of *Seahorse Reef: A Story of the South Pacific,* p. 229; March 15, 2002, Carolyn Phelan, review of *Fossil Fish Found Alive: Discovering the Coelacanth,* p. 1254; April 15, 2005, Carolyn Phelan, review of *Secrets of a Civil War Submarine: Solving the Mysteries of the H.L. Hunley,* p. 1454; December 1, 2005, Karen Hutt, review of *Electricity,* p. 61; June 1, 2006, Kathy Broderick, review of *Shipwreck Search: Discovery of the H.L. Hunley,* p. 78; September 1, 2006, John Peters, review of *Rocks,* p. 132; February 1, 2009, Carolyn Phelan, review of *Written in Bone: Buried Lives of Jamestown and Colonial Maryland,* p. 41; September 15, 2009, Carolyn Phelan, review of *Druscilla's Halloween,* p. 63; December 1, 2009, Gillian Engberg, review of *We Are the Weather Makers: The History of Climate Change,* p. 55.

Book Report, November-December, 1991, Anne Marie Lilly, review of *Born near the Earth's Surface,* p. 60.

Bulletin of the American Meteorological Society, Lawrence E. Greenleaf, review of *Water up, Water Down,* p. 872.

Bulletin of the Center for Children's Books, September, 1990, review of *Ice,* p. 18.

Childhood Education, spring, 1993, Joan M. Hildebrand, review of *Water up, Water Down,* p. 176.

Horn Book, May, 1998, Maeve Visser Knoth, review of *The Eighteen-Penny Goose,* p. 350; May-June, 2009, Jonathan Hunt, review of *Written in Bone,* p. 328.

Kirkus Reviews, December 1, 1997, review of *The Eighteen-Penny Goose,* p. 1781; April 1, 2002, review of *Fossil Fish Found Alive,* p. 501; February 1, 2009, review of *Written in Bone.*

School Library Journal, August, 1990, Roseanne Cerny, review of *Glaciers,* p. 161; December, 1992, Carolyn Angus, review of *Water up, Water Down,* p. 132; June, 1996, Eunice Weech, review of *Earthquakes,* p. 1996; December, 1996, Susan Oliver, review of *Rhinos,* p. 134; March, 1998, Sharon R. Pearce, review of *The Eighteen-Penny Goose,* p. 189; April, 1998, Michele Snyder, review of *Hippos,* p. 126; November, 1999, Karey Wehner, review of *Sea Horses,* p. 150; July, 2001, Kary Weher, review of *Fireflies,* p. 100; February, 2002, Susan Shaver, reviews of *Wheels and Axles, Pulleys,* and *Inclined Planes and Wedges,* all p. 128; May, 2002, Ellen Heath, review of *Fossil Fish Found Alive,* p. 178; February, 2003, Kathy Piehl, review of *Life in an Estuary,* p. 168; May, 2005, Anna M. Nelson, review of *Secrets of a Civil War Submarine,* p. 161; January, 2007, Michael Giller, reviews of *Fossils* and *Rocks,* both p. 121; February, 2009, Jeff Meyer, review of *Written in Bone,* p. 127; September, 2009, Catherine Callegari, review of *Druscilla's Halloween,* p. 136; December, 2009, Denise Schmidt, review of *We Are the Weather Makers,* p. 138.

Science Books and Films, March, 1993, Doris M. Ellis, review of *Water up, Water Down,* p. 50; June, 1996, Eugene C. Robertson, review of *Earthquakes,* pp. 143-144; July, 2001, Karey Wehner, review of *Fireflies,* p. 100.

Star Tribune (Minneapolis, MN), February 26, 2006, Michael J. Bonafield, review of *Secrets of a Civil War Submarine,* p. F15.

Voice of Youth Advocates, October, 1991, June Muldner, review of *Born near the Earth's Core,* pp. 253-254.

ONLINE

Sally M. Walker Home Page, http://www.sallymwalker. com (October 30, 2010).*

*   *   *

WANG, Lin 1973-

Personal

Born 1973, in China; immigrated to United States. *Education:* Guanghzhou University (Guanghzhou, China), A.B. (commercial art design), 1993; Ghuangzhou Academy of Fine Arts, B.F.A., 1997; Savannah College of Art and Design, M.F.A., 2000.

Addresses

Home—Fremont, CA. *Office*—LinStudio, P.O. Box 1052, Fremont, CA 94538. *E-mail*—linw@linstudio. com.

Career

Artist, graphic designer, and illustrator. Guangzhou Foreign Trade Advertising and Exhibition Corp., illustrator and graphic designer, 1993-95; Saatchi & Saatchi Advertising Co., illustrator, 1996-97; Design Press, staff illustrator, 1998-99; LCG USA, graphic designer and il-

Lin Wang's many illustration projects include a cover of **Greek Mythology.** (Illustration courtesy of Lin Wang.)

lustrator, 1999-2001; freelance artist and illustrator, beginning 1999. LinStudio, art director beginning 1999. *Exhibitions:* Works exhibited in Society of Illustrators Annual Exhibition, 2006.

Awards, Honors

Gold Medal, International Environmental Protection Poster Design Contest (Hong Kong), 1993; Grand Prize for Best Portfolio Representing Illustration for Children's Literature, Society of Children's Book Writers and Illustrators, Los Angeles, 2003.

Illustrator

Mary Cummings, *Three Names of Me,* Albert Whitman (Morton Grove, IL), 2006.

Paula Yoo, *Shining Star: The Anna May Wong Story,* Lee & Low Books (New York, NY), 2009.

Marla Stewart Konrad, *Just like You,* Zonderkidz (Grand Rapids, MI), 2010.

Biographical and Critical Sources

PERIODICALS

Booklist, June 1, 2009, Ilene Cooper, review of *Shining Star: The Anna May Wong Story,* p. 88.

Bulletin of the Center for Children's Books, December, 2006, Deborah Stevenson, review of *Three Names of Me,* p. 165.

Kirkus Reviews, May 1, 2009, review of *Shining Star.*

Publishers Weekly, June 1, 2009, review of *Shining Star,* p. 47.

School Library Journal, October, 2006, Margaret R. Tassia, review of *Three Names of Me,* p. 109; July, 2009, Nancy Menaldi-Scanlan, review of *Shining Star,* p. 74.

ONLINE

Lin Wang Home Page, http://www.linstudio.com (October 15, 2010).*

*   *   *

WILSON, Karma

Personal

Born October 8, in ID; mother an author; married; husband's name Scott; children: Michael, David, Chrissy. *Education:* Attended community college. *Religion:* Christian. *Hobbies and other interests:* Photography, reading, baking, martial arts.

Addresses

Home—Bonner's Ferry, ID. *Agent*—c/o Steven Malk, Writers House, 21 W. 26th St., New York, NY 10010.

Career

Author of books for children. Presenter at schools.

Awards, Honors

Children's Resource Gold Award, and Capitol Choices Noteworthy Book for Children designation, both 2002, Wyoming Buckaroo Book Award nomination, 2002-03, Oppenheim Toy Portfolio Platinum Book Award, American Library Association Notable Book designation, Charlotte Zolotow Highly Commended designation, New Hampshire Ladybug Book Award nomination, and Children's Book of the Year finalist, International Reading Association, all 2003, New York Charlotte Award nomination, Great Lakes Great Books Award nomination, Maryland Children's Book Award nomination, Wisconsin Golden Archers Award nomination, Arizona Young Readers Award nomination, and Virginia Young Readers Award nomination, all 2004, and Washington Children's Choice Picture Award nomination, and Michigan Reader's Association Book Award nomination, both 2005, all for *Bear Snores On;* Texas 2x2 Book Award nomination, 2003, and Missouri Building Block nomination, 2004, both for *Frog in the Bog.*

Writings

FOR CHILDREN

Bear Snores On, illustrated by Jane Chapman, Margaret K. McElderry Books (New York, NY), 2001.

Frog in the Bog, illustrated by Joan Rankin, Margaret K. McElderry Books (New York, NY), 2003.

Cattle Drive, illustrated by Karla Firehammer, Little, Brown (Boston, MA), 2003.

Bear Wants More, illustrated by Jane Chapman, Margaret K. McElderry Books (New York, NY), 2003.

Sweet Briar Goes to School, illustrated by LeUyen Pham, Dial Books for Young Readers (New York, NY), 2003.

Grandmother's Whopper Birthday Cake, Margaret K. McElderry Books (New York, NY), 2003.

Bear Stays up for Christmas, illustrated by Jane Chapman, Margaret K. McElderry Books (New York, NY), 2004.

Dinos on the Go!, illustrated by Laura Radar, Little, Brown (New York, NY), 2004.

Hilda Must Be Dancing, illustrated by Suzanne Watts, Margaret K. McElderry Books (New York, NY), 2004.

Never, Ever Shout in a Zoo, illustrated by Doug Cushman, Little, Brown (New York, NY), 2004.

Mr. Murray and Thumbkin, illustrated by Ard Hoyt, Little, Brown (New York, NY), 2004.

Sweet Briar Goes to Camp, illustrated by LeUyen Pham, Dial Books for Young Readers (New York, NY), 2005.

Dinos in the Snow!, illustrated by Laura Radar, Little, Brown (New York, NY), 2005.

Bear Hugs: Romantically Ridiculous Animal Rhymes, illustrated by Suzanne Watts, Margaret K. McElderry Books (New York, NY), 2005.

Sakes Alive!: A Cattle Drive, illustrated by Karla Firehammer, Little, Brown (New York, NY), 2005.

Mortimer's Christmas Manger, illustrations by Jane Chapman, Margaret K. McElderry Books (New York, NY), 2005.

Mama Always Comes Home, illustrated by Brooke Dyer, HarperCollins (New York, NY), 2005.

Sleepyhead, illustrated by John Segal, Margaret K. McElderry Books (New York, NY), 2006.

Animal Strike at the Zoo, illustrated by Margaret Spengler, HarperCollins (New York, NY), 2006.

Moose Tracks!, illustrated by Jack E. Davis, Margaret K. McElderry Books (New York, NY), 2006.

Bear's New Friend, illustrated by Jane Chapman, Margaret K. McElderry Books (New York, NY), 2006.

How to Bake an American Pie, illustrations by Raul Colon, Margaret K. McElderry Books (New York, NY), 2007.

Bear Feels Sick, illustrated by Jane Chapman, Margaret K. McElderry Books (New York, NY), 2007.

Give Thanks to the Lord: Celebrating Psalm 92, illustrated by Amy Bates, Zonderkidz (Grand Rapids, MI), 2007.

I Will Rejoice!, Zonderkidz (Grand Rapids, MI), 2007.

Hello, Calico!, illustrated by Buket Erdogan, Little Simon (New York, NY), 2007.

Princess Me, illustrated by Christa Unzner, Margaret K. McElderry Books (New York, NY), 2007.

Whopper Cake, Margaret K. McElderry Books (New York, NY), 2007.

Let's Make a Joyful Noise!: A Celebration of Psalm 100, Zonderkidz (Grand Rapids, MI), 2008.

Bear Feels Scared, Margaret K. McElderry Books (New York, NY), 2008.

Friends for Calico!, illustrated by Buket Erdogan, Little Simon (New York, NY), 2008.

Play Nice, Calico!, illustrated by Buket Erdogan, Little Simon (New York, NY), 2008.

Uh-oh, Calico!, illustrated by Buket Erdogan, Little Simon (New York, NY), 2008.

Where Is Home, Little Pip?, illustrated by Jane Chapman, Margaret K. McElderry Books (New York, NY), 2008.

Baby, I Love You, illustrated by Sam Williams, Little Simon (New York, NY), 2009.

Beautiful Babies: A Touch-and-feel Book, Little Simon (New York, NY), 2009.

Don't Be Afraid, Little Pip, illustrated by Jane Chapman, Margaret K. McElderry Books (New York, NY), 2009.

If I Were a Mouse, illustrated by Marsela Hajdinjak-Krec, Zonderkidz (Grand Rapids, MI), 2009.

Mortimer's First Garden, illustrated by Dan Andreasen, Margaret K. McElderry Books (New York, NY), 2009.

Trick or Treat, Calico!, illustrated by Buket Erdogan, Little Simon (New York, NY), 2009.

What's the Weather Inside?: Poems, Margaret K. McElderry Books (New York, NY), 2009.

The Cow Loves Cookies, illustrated by Marcellus Hall, Margaret K. McElderry Books (New York, NY), 2010.

What's in the Egg, Little Pip?, illustrated by Jane Chapman, Margaret K. McElderry Books (New York, NY), 2010.

Bear's Loose Tooth, illustrated by Jane Chapman, Margaret K. McElderry Books (New York, NY), 2011.

Hogwash, illustrated by Jim McMullan, Little, Brown (New York, NY), 2011.

Mama, Why?, Margaret K. McElderry Books (New York, NY), 2011.

Contributor to periodicals.

Sidelights

Karma Wilson made an impressive picture-book debut in 2001 with the publication of *Bear Snores On.* In addition to spawning a series of stories about Bear, *Bear Snores On* won several accolades, including the Oppenheim Toy Portfolio Platinum Book Award, and was signified as an American Library Association notable book. Wilson's signature style involves using rhythmic texts; as the prolific writer noted in an online interview for *Suite 101,* "rhyme gives me this basic set of rules to conform to. I have to think of whatever 'form' I've chosen and there are only so many choices." For Wilson, writing is the easiest aspect of her work: "A good story is the hardest part for me to come up with," she added in her interview.

Born in Idaho, Wilson grew up around a single mom who made her living as a writer. As a child, she read constantly, and she continues to do so in between crafting her own stories. She spent several years writing for magazines, having little luck in attracting the attention of children's-book publishers, until a savvy agent found a home for her manuscript for *Bear Snores On.* "I was about to quit the whole children's-writing business and just focus on magazine writing when I finally said 'to heck with it' and wrote this story about a talking animal that was in rhyme, breaking almost all the rules," she recalled to *Writer* interviewer Jackie Dishner. "For me,

talking animals are . . . a great way to reach kids," Wilson added. "There are no boundaries there. Race, religion, sex—it doesn't matter when it's a bear. That character is available to all children."

Wilson's stories—often humorous and light hearted—are intended primarily to entertain and captivate young readers and listeners. *Bear Snores On,* for example, features the mis-adventures of an anthropomorphized woodland brown bear. In the story, while Bear is fast asleep in its cozy den, safely protected from the cold winter, other forest animals take refuge with it. First Mouse arrives and builds a warm fire. Then Hare appears, bringing pop corn and tea, while Badger offers nuts to the growing gathering. Soon, Bear's cave is filled with numerous forest animals and a party ensues. A contributor to *Kirkus Reviews* acknowledged *Bear Snores On* for its "lyrical text," while *Booklist* reviewer Ellen Mandel cited the "snappy rhythm . . . [that] beckon[s] youngsters into the story."

Bear and friends return in several other stories by Wilson, among them *Bear Wants More, Bear Stays up for Christmas, Bear's New Friend, Bear Feels Sick, Bear Feels Scared,* and *Bear's Loose Tooth,* all which feature illustrations by Jane Chapman. In *Bear Wants More* Bear has just awoken from a long hibernation and immediately begins foraging for food in order to satiate its voracious hunger. Loyal friends bring food, but it is not enough to fill the creature's large tummy. When Bear returns from ransacking the forest, its friends are waiting in its den with a huge feast, but Bear is now too fat to fit through the den's door. In *Bear Stays up for Christmas* Bear is awakened from its winter sleep in time to spend Christmas with its friends, while *Bear*

Karma Wilson's simple picture-book texts have been paired with artwork by illustrators such as Jane Chapman, who collaborated with Wilson on the humorous **Bear Snores On.** (Illustrations copyright © 2002 by Jane Chapman. Reprinted with the permission of Margaret K. McElderry Books, an imprint of Simon & Schuster Children's Publishing Division.)

In **Where Is Home, Little Pip?** *Wilson's Antarctic-bound characters are captured in Jane Chapman's endearing art.* (Illustrations copyright © 2006 Jane Chapman. Reprinted with the permission of Margaret K. McElderry Books, an imprint of Simon & Schuster Children's Publishing Division.)

Feels Scared finds Wilson's loveable brown bear lost in the woods during a stormy day until caring and concerned friends lead the way to its snug cave.

In *Booklist* Connie Fletcher dubbed *Bear Wants More* "an appealing romp about springtime and friendship," while a *Kirkus Reviews* writer concluded that Wilson's "sing-song" rhymes "lend . . . sprightliness to the ebullient tale." Amy Lilien-Harper noted in *School Library Journal* that the story's "rollicking, rhyming text flows smoothly, and the repeated refrain will have youngsters chiming right in." Wilson's use of a "rhyming text and oft-repeated refrain" makes *Bear Feels Sick* "irresistible when read aloud," according to Susan E. Murray in the same periodical. In the view of a *Publishers Weekly* contributor, "Wilson and Chapman . . . tap into the psychology of preschoolers, exploring a common childhood emotion" in *Bear Feels Scared,* while Lilien-Harper wrote of the samw book that the "likeable" Bear "and his animal friends are back in one of their best outings since *Bear Snores On.*"

Frog in the Bog also incorporates Wilson's trademark rhymes and features a hungry frog that counts as it eats: one tick, two fleas, three flies, and so on. As the frog of the title grows bulkier as a result of its large lunch, a nearby alligator takes notice of the greedy amphibian and contemplates a meal of its own. *Frog in the Bog* counts from one up to five, making the book "especially suitable for the youngest beginning counters," according to a *Kirkus Reviews* writer. According to a *Publishers Weekly* critic, Wilson's book successfully melds "early learning concepts, humor and wordplay" into "a jaunty read-aloud," while *School Library Journal* reviewer Linda L. Walkins called *Frog in the Bog* an "imaginative counting book [that] will keep children laughing."

In addition to Chapman, Wilson's stories have come to life through the interpretation of a range of talented illustrators. In *Moose Tracks!,* which a *Publishers Weekly* critic described as a "rhyming, jaunty story [that] brims with eccentric characters," cartoonist Jack E. Davis adds "enough comedy . . . to provide interest for more

than one reading," while Shelle Rosenfeld added in *Booklist* that Davis's "witty, colorful art" pairs with Wilson's "bouncing . . . refrain" to enhance both the mystery and the anticipation" in the tale. *How to Bake an American Pie,* a picture-book history of the United States that weaves cooking metaphors into the story of the nation, features artwork by Raul Colón that adds an element of humor to Wilson's poetic "celebration of our country, its founders, and the immigrants who built it," according to *School Library Journal* critic Barbara Auerbach.

Artist Dan Andreasen contributes detailed paintings to *Mortimer's First Garden,* Wilson's gentle story about a young mouse who decides to grow a sunflower garden, while the author teams up with watercolor artist Marcellus Hall to create an entertaining farmyard rhyme in *The Cow Loves Cookies.* A "lighthearted romp [that] disguises a scary concept" was the way Carol Ann Wilson described *Never, Ever Shout in a Zoo,* a read-aloud story featuring pencil-and-watercolor illustrations by Doug Cushman, and in *Sweet Briar Goes to Camp* Wilson's story about a skunk who befriends a shy porcupine is augmented with reassuring artwork by LeUyen Pham. The amusingly titled *Whopper Cake,* which tells an original tall tale about an elderly gentleman who attempts to bake an enormous cake for his wife's birthday, "is given an industrial-strength boost" by illustrator Will Hillenbrand, whose "jaunty" images are "judiciously sprinkled with patterns," according to a *Kirkus Reviews* writer.

Biographical and Critical Sources

PERIODICALS

Booklist, January 1, 2002, Ellen Mandel, review of *Bear Snores On,* p. 868; April 15, 2003, Connie Fletcher, review of *Bear Wants More,* p. 1479; May 1, 2005, Julie Cummins, review of *Sweet Briar Goes to Camp,* p. 1594; February 15, 2006, Shelle Rosenfeld, review of *Moose Tracks!,* p. 106; April 1, 2007, Ilene Cooper, review of *How to Bake an American Pie,* p. 49; June 1, 2007, Jennifer Mattson, review of *Whopper Cake,* p. 87; November 15, 2007, Carolyn Phelan, review of *Let's Make a Joyful Noise,* p. 45; November 1, 2008, Daniel Kraus, review of *Where Is Home, Little Pip?,* p. 50; February 1, 2009, Carolyn Phelan, review of *Mortimer's First Garden,* p. 47; April 15, 2010, Hazel Rochman, review of *The Cow Loves Cookies,* p. 50.

Kirkus Reviews, November 15, 2001, review of *Bear Snores On,* p. 161; December 1, 2002, review of *Bear Wants More,* p. 1776; November 1, 2004, review of *Bear Stays up for Christmas,* p. 1055; June 15, 2005, review of *Sakes Alive!: A Cattle Drive,* p. 693; October 1, 2005, review of *Dinos in the Snow,* p. 1092; June, 2007, review of *Whopper Cake;* August, 15, 2007, review of *Give Thanks to the Lord;* September 15, 2007, review of *Bear Feels Sick;* February 15, 2009, review of *Mortimer's First Garden.*

Publishers Weekly, October 20, 2003, review of *Frog in the Bog,* p. 52; March 29, 2004, review of *Never, Ever Shout in a Zoo,* p. 61; September 27, 2004, review of *Bear Stays Up for Christmas,* p. 61; October 11, 2004, review of *Dinos on the Go,* p. 78; March 27, 2006, review of *Moose Tracks,* p. 78; November 13, 2006, review of *Sleepy Head,* p. 56; December 18, 2006, review of *I Will Rejoice,* p. 66; October 1, 2007, review of *Princess Me,* p. 55; July 21, 2008, review of *Bear Feels Scared,* p. 158.

Writer's Digest, June, 2008, Jackie Disher, interview with Wilson.

School Library Journal, February, 2003, Amy Lilien-Harper, review of *Bear Wants More,* p. 124; December, 2003, Linda L. Walkins, review of *Frog in the Bog,* p. 130; May, 2004, Carol Ann Wilson, review of *Never, Ever Shout in a Zoo,* p. 127; September, 2004, Tana Elias, review of *Dinos on the Go!,* p. 182; May, 2005, Susan Weitz, review of *Mama Always Comes Home,* p. 105; June, 2005, Kathleen Simonetta, review of *Sweet Briar Goes to Camp,* p. 132; September, 2005, Mary Elam, review of *Sakes Alive!,* p. 188; December, 2005, Lisa Gangemi Kropp, review of *Di-*

Featuring Wilson's characteristic breezy rhyme, Sakes Alive! A Cattle Drive *is illustrated in lighthearted fashion by Karla Firehammer.* (Illustrations copyright © 2005 by Karla Firehammer. By permission of Little, Brown and Company.)

nos in the Snow!, p. 122; October, 2006, Linda Ludke, review of *Sleepyhead,* p. 130; May, 2007, Barbara Auerbach, review of *How to Bake an American Pie,* p. 112; September, 2007, Susan E. Murray, review of *Bear Feels Sick,* p. 178; January, 2008, Linda M. Kenton, review of *Princess Me,* p. 100; April, 2008, Lisa Egly Lehmuller, review of *Let's Make a Joyful Noise: Celebrating Psalm 100,* p. 126; September, 2008, Amy Lilien-Harper, review of *Bear Feels Scared,* and Jane Marino, review of *Where Is Home, Little Pip?,* both p. 161.

ONLINE

Hachette Book Group Web site, http://www.twbookmark. com/ (October 6, 2006).

Karma Wilson Home Page, http://www.bearsnoreson.com (October 30, 2010).

Suite 101 Web site, http://www.suite101.com/ (October 6, 2006), Sue Reichard, "Children's Author Karma Wilson Writes On."*

Illustrations Index

(In the following index, the number of the *volume* in which an illustrator's work appears is given *before* the colon, and the *page number* on which it appears is given *after* the colon. For example, a drawing by Adams, Adrienne appears in Volume 2 on page 6, another drawing by her appears in Volume 3 on page 80, another drawing in Volume 8 on page 1, and so on and so on. . . .)

YABC

Index references to *YABC* refer to listings appearing in the two-volume *Yesterday's Authors of Books for Children,* also published by Gale, Cengage Learning. *YABC* covers prominent authors and illustrators who died prior to 1960.

A

Aas, Ulf *5:* 174
Abbe, S. van
  See van Abbe, S.
Abel, Raymond *6:* 122; *7:* 195; *12:* 3; *21:* 86; *25:* 119
Abelliera, Aldo *71:* 120
Abolafia, Yossi *60:* 2; *93:* 163; *152:* 202
Abrahams, Hilary *26:* 205; *29:* 24, 25; *53:* 61
Abrams, Kathie *36:* 170
Abrams, Lester *49:* 26
Abulafia, Yossi *154:* 67; *177:* 3
Accardo, Anthony *191:* 3, 8
Accornero, Franco *184:* 8
Accorsi, William *11:* 198
Acs, Laszlo *14:* 156; *42:* 22
Acuna, Ed *198:* 79
Adams, Adrienne *2:* 6; *3:* 80; *8:* 1; *15:* 107; *16:* 180; *20:* 65; *22:* 134, 135; *33:* 75; *36:* 103, 112; *39:* 74; *86:* 54; *90:* 2, 3
Adams, Connie J. *129:* 68
Adams, John Wolcott *17:* 162
Adams, Lynn *96:* 44
Adams, Norman *55:* 82
Adams, Pam *112:* 1, 2
Adams, Sarah *98:* 126; *164:* 180
Adams, Steve *209:* 64
Adamson, George *30:* 23, 24; *69:* 64
Addams, Charles *55:* 5
Addison, Kenneth *192:* 173
Addy, Sean *180:* 8
Ade, Rene *76:* 198; *195:* 162
Adinolfi, JoAnn *115:* 42; *176:* 2; *217:* 79
Adkins, Alta *22:* 250
Adkins, Jan *8:* 3; *69:* 4; *144:* 2, 3, 4; *210:* 11, 17, 18, 19
Adler, Kelynn *195:* 47
Adler, Peggy *22:* 6; *29:* 31
Adler, Ruth *29:* 29
Adlerman, Daniel *163:* 2
Adragna, Robert *47:* 145
Agard, Nadema *18:* 1
Agee, Jon *116:* 8, 9, 10; *157:* 4; *196:* 3, 4, 5, 6, 7, 8
Agre, Patricia *47:* 195
Aguirre, Alfredo *152:* 218
Ahl, Anna Maria *32:* 24
Ahlberg, Allan *68:* 6, 7, 9; *165:* 5; *214:* 9
Ahlberg, Janet *68:* 6, 7, 9; *214:* 9

Aicher-Scholl, Inge *63:* 127
Aichinger, Helga *4:* 5, 45
Aitken, Amy *31:* 34
Ajhar, Brian *207:* 126; *220:* 2
Akaba, Suekichi *46:* 23; *53:* 127
Akasaka, Miyoshi *YABC 2:* 261
Akib, Jamel *181:* 13; *182:* 99; *220:* 74
Akino, Fuku *6:* 144
Alain *40:* 41
Alajalov *2:* 226
Albert, Chris *200:* 64
Alborough, Jez *86:* 1, 2, 3; *149:* 3
Albrecht, Jan *37:* 176
Albright, Donn *1:* 91
Alcala, Alfredo *91:* 128
Alcantará, Felipe Ugalde *171:* 186
Alcorn, John *3:* 159; *7:* 165; *31:* 22; *44:* 127; *46:* 23, 170
Alcorn, Stephen *110:* 4; *125:* 106; *128:* 172; *150:* 97; *160:* 188; *165:* 48; *201:* 113; *203:* 39; *207:* 3
Alcott, May *100:* 3
Alda, Arlene *44:* 24; *158:* 2
Alden, Albert *11:* 103
Aldridge, Andy *27:* 131
Aldridge, George *105:* 125
Aldridge, Sheila *192:* 4
Alejandro, Cliff *176:* 75
Alex, Ben *45:* 25, 26
Alexander, Ellen *91:* 3
Alexander, Lloyd *49:* 34
Alexander, Martha *3:* 206; *11:* 103; *13:* 109; *25:* 100; *36:* 131; *70:* 6, 7; *136:* 3, 4, 5; *169:* 120
Alexander, Paul *85:* 57; *90:* 9
Alexeieff, Alexander *14:* 6; *26:* 199
Alfano, Wayne *80:* 69
Aliki
  See Brandenberg, Aliki
Alko, Selina *218:* 2
Allamand, Pascale *12:* 9
Allan, Judith *38:* 166
Alland, Alexandra *16:* 255
Allen, Gertrude *9:* 6
Allen, Graham *31:* 145
Allen, Jonathan *131:* 3, 4; *177:* 8, 9, 10
Allen, Joy *168:* 185; *217:* 6, 7
Allen, Pamela *50:* 25, 26, 27, 28; *81:* 9, 10; *123:* 4, 5
Allen, Raul *207:* 94
Allen, Rowena *47:* 75

Allen, Thomas B. *81:* 101; *82:* 248; *89:* 37; *104:* 9
Allen, Tom *85:* 176
Allender, David *73:* 223
Alley, R.W. *80:* 183; *95:* 187; *156:* 100, 153; *169:* 4, 5; *179:* 17
Allison, Linda *43:* 27
Allon, Jeffrey *119:* 174
Allport, Mike *71:* 55
Almquist, Don *11:* 8; *12:* 128; *17:* 46; *22:* 110
Aloise, Frank *5:* 38; *10:* 133; *30:* 92
Alsenas, Linas *186:* 2
Alter, Ann *206:* 4, 5
Althea
  See Braithwaite, Althea
Altschuler, Franz *11:* 185; *23:* 141; *40:* 48; *45:* 29; *57:* 181
Alvin, John *117:* 5
Ambrus, Victor G. *1:* 6, 7, 194; *3:* 69; *5:* 15; *6:* 44; *7:* 36; *8:* 210; *12:* 227; *14:* 213; *15:* 213; *22:* 209; *24:* 36; *28:* 179; *30:* 178; *32:* 44, 46; *38:* 143; *41:* 25, 26, 27, 28, 29, 30, 31, 32; *42:* 87; *44:* 190; *55:* 172; *62:* 30, 144, 145, 148; *86:* 99, 100, 101; *87:* 66, 137; *89:* 162; *134:* 160
Ames, Lee J. *3:* 12; *9:* 130; *10:* 69; *17:* 214; *22:* 124; *151:* 13
Amini, Mehrdokht *211:* 119
Amon, Aline *9:* 9
Amoss, Berthe *5:* 5
Amstutz, André *152:* 102; *214:* 11, 16
Amundsen, Dick *7:* 77
Amundsen, Richard E. *5:* 10; *24:* 122
Ancona, George *12:* 11; *55:* 144; *145:* 7; *208:* 13
Anderson, Alasdair *18:* 122
Andersen, Bethanne *116:* 167; *162:* 189; *175:* 17; *191:* 4, 5; *218:* 20
Anderson, Bob *139:* 16
Anderson, Brad *33:* 28
Anderson, Brian *211:* 8
Anderson, C.W. *11:* 10
Anderson, Carl *7:* 4
Anderson, Catherine Corley *72:* 2
Anderson, Cecil *127:* 152
Anderson, David Lee *118:* 176
Anderson, Derek *169:* 9; *174:* 180
Anderson, Doug *40:* 111
Anderson, Erica *23:* 65
Anderson, Laurie *12:* 153, 155
Anderson, Lena *99:* 26

Anderson, Peggy Perry *179:* 2
Anderson, Sara *173:* 3
Anderson, Scoular *138:* 13; *201:* 6
Anderson, Susan *90:* 12
Anderson, Tara *188:* 132; *211:* 115
Anderson, Wayne *23:* 119; *41:* 239; *56:* 7; *62:* 26; *147:* 6; *202:* 4, 5
Andreasen, Daniel *86:* 157; *87:* 104; *103:* 201, 202; *159:* 75; *167:* 106, 107; *168:* 184; *180:* 247; *186:* 9; *212:* 101; *220:* 110, 111; *221:* 56
Andrew, Ian *111:* 37; *116:* 12; *166:* 2
Andrew, John *22:* 4
Andrews, Benny *14:* 251; *31:* 24; *57:* 6, 7; *183:* 8
Andrews, Vaughn *166:* 28
Anelay, Henry *57:* 173
Angel, Marie *47:* 22
Angelo, Valenti *14:* 8; *18:* 100; *20:* 232; *32:* 70
Anglund, Joan Walsh *2:* 7, 250, 251; *37:* 198, 199, 200
Anholt, Catherine *74:* 8; *131:* 7; *141:* 5
Anholt, Laurence *141:* 4
Anno, Mitsumasa *5:* 7; *38:* 25, 26, 27, 28, 29, 30, 31, 32; *77:* 3, 4; *157:* 10, 11
Antal, Andrew *1:* 124; *30:* 145
Antram, David *152:* 133
Apostolou, Christy Hale
   See Hale, Christy
Apple, Margot *33:* 25; *35:* 206; *46:* 81; *53:* 8; *61:* 109; *64:* 21, 22, 24, 25, 27; *71:* 176; *77:* 53; *82:* 245; *92:* 39; *94:* 180; *96:* 107; *152:* 4, 5; *162:* 192, 194; *173:* 44; *214:* 21, 22, 23, 24
Appleyard, Dev *2:* 192
Aragones, Sergio *48:* 23, 24, 25, 26, 27
Araneus *40:* 29
Arbo, Cris *103:* 4; *220:* 4, 5
Archambault, Matt *85:* 173; *138:* 19, 20; *143:* 33; *145:* 144; *179:* 103; *187:* 7; *219:* 2
Archer, Janet *16:* 69; *178:* 156
Ardizzone, Edward *1:* 11, 12; *2:* 105; *3:* 258; *4:* 78; *7:* 79; *10:* 100; *15:* 232; *20:* 69,178; *23:* 223; *24:* 125; *28:* 25, 26, 27, 28, 29, 30, 31,33, 34, 35, 36, 37; *31:* 192, 193; *34:* 215, 217; *60:* 173; *64:* 145; *87:* 176; *YABC 2:* 25
Arena, Jill *176:* 49
Arenella, Roy *14:* 9
Argemi, David *197:* 2
Argent, Kerry *103:* 56; *138:* 17; *158:* 134
Arihara, Shino *201:* 98
Arisman, Marshall *162:* 50
Armer, Austin *13:* 3
Armer, Laura Adams *13:* 3
Armer, Sidney *13:* 3
Armitage, David *47:* 23; *99:* 5; *155:* 4
Armitage, Eileen *4:* 16
Armstrong, George *10:* 6; *21:* 72
Armstrong, Shelagh *102:* 114
Armstrong-Ellis, Carey *185:* 196
Arno, Enrico *1:* 217; *2:* 22, 210; *4:* 9; *5:* 43; *6:* 52; *29:* 217, 219; *33:* 152; *35:* 99; *43:* 31, 32, 33; *45:* 212, 213, 214; *72:* 72; *74:* 166; *100:* 169
Arnold, Alli *187:* 40, 41
Arnold, Andrew *219:* 155; *221:* 155
Arnold, Caroline *174:* 5
Arnold, Emily *76:* 7, 9, 10
Arnold, Katya *115:* 11; *168:* 2, 3
Arnold, Tedd *116:* 14; *133:* 152; *160:* 5; *208:* 24, 25, 26, 176
Arnosky, Jim *22:* 20; *70:* 9, 10, 11; *118:* 3, 5; *160:* 8, 10; *189:* 5, 7, 8, 9, 10; *217:* 11, 12, 13, 14
Arnsteen, Katy Keck *105:* 97; *116:* 145
Arsenault, Isabelle *207:* 7
Arrowood, Clinton *12:* 193; *19:* 11; *65:* 210
Artell, Mike *89:* 8
Arting, Fred J. *41:* 63

Artzybasheff, Boris *13:* 143; *14:* 15; *40:* 152, 155
Aruego, Ariane *6:* 4
Aruego, José *4:* 140; *6:* 4; *7:* 64; *33:* 195; *35:* 208; *68:* 16, 17; *75:* 46; *93:* 91, 92; *94:* 197; *109:* 65, 67; *125:* 2, 3, 4, 5; *127:* 188; *143:* 25; *178:* 17, 19, 74; *188:* 166; *202:* 164
Arzoumanian, Alik *177:* 12; *194:* 115
Asare, Meshack *86:* 9; *139:* 19
Ascensios, Natalie *105:* 139
Asch, Frank *5:* 9; *66:* 2, 4, 6, 7, 9, 10; *102:* 18, 19,21; *154:* 12
Ashby, Gail *11:* 135
Ashby, Gil *146:* 4
Ashby, Gwynneth *44:* 26
Ashley, C.W. *19:* 197
Ashmead, Hal *8:* 70
Ashton, Tim *211:* 204
Aska, Warabe *56:* 10
Assel, Steven *44:* 153; *77:* 22, 97
Astrop, John *32:* 56
Atene, Ann *12:* 18
Atherton, Lisa *38:* 198
Atkinson, Allen *60:* 5
Atkinson, J. Priestman *17:* 275
Atkinson, Janet *86:* 147; *103:* 138
Atkinson, Mike *127:* 74
Atkinson, Wayne *40:* 46
Attard, Karl *196:* 22, 23
Attebery, Charles *38:* 170
Atwell, Debby *150:* 6
Atwood, Ann *7:* 9
Aubrey, Meg Kelleher *77:* 159
Auch, Herm *173:* 7, 8
Auch, Mary Jane *173:* 7
Augarde, Steve *25:* 22; *159:* 7; *210:* 43, 44
Austerman, Miriam *23:* 107
Austin, Margot *11:* 16
Austin, Robert *3:* 44
Austin, Virginia *81:* 205; *127:* 221
Auth, Tony *51:* 5; *192:* 18
Avendano, Dolores *158:* 74
Avedon, Richard *57:* 140
Averill, Esther *1:* 17; *28:* 39, 40, 41
Avilés, Martha *218:* 6
Axeman, Lois *2:* 32; *11:* 84; *13:* 165; *22:* 8; *23:* 49; *61:* 116; *101:* 124
Axtel, David *155:* 110
Ayer, Jacqueline *13:* 7
Ayer, Margaret *15:* 12; *50:* 120
Ayers, Alan *91:* 58; *107:* 169
Ayliffe, Alex *95:* 164
Ayto, Russell *111:* 5; *112:* 54; *206:* 7, 8; *213:* 56
Azarian, Mary *112:* 9, 10; *114:* 129; *117:* 171; *137:* 163; *171:* 4, 5; *181:* 161; *188:* 128

B

B.T.B.
   See Blackwell, Basil T.
Baasansuren, Bolormaa *216:* 40
Babbitt, Bradford *33:* 158
Babbitt, Natalie *6:* 6; *8:* 220; *68:* 20; *70:* 242, 243; *194:* 8, 9
Baca, Maria *104:* 5
Bacchus, Andy *94:* 87
Bacha, Andy *109:* 169
Bachelet, Gilles *196:* 18
Bachem, Paul *48:* 180; *67:* 65; *144:* 206
Back, Adam *63:* 125
Back, George *31:* 161
Backes, Nick *190:* 72
Backhouse, Colin *78:* 142
Bacon, Bruce *4:* 74
Bacon, Paul *7:* 155; *8:* 121; *31:* 55; *50:* 42; *56:* 175; *62:* 82, 84
Bacon, Peggy *2:* 11, 228; *46:* 44
Baek, Matthew J. *169:* 95; *202:* 8

Baer, Julie *161:* 2
Baicker-McKee, Carol *177:* 15; *180:* 215
Bailey, Peter *58:* 174; *87:* 221; *194:* 12
Bailey, Sheila *155:* 11
Baker, Alan *22:* 22; *61:* 134; *93:* 11, 12; *146:* 6, 7, 10
Baker, Charlotte *2:* 12
Baker, Garin *89:* 65
Baker, Jeannie *23:* 4; *88:* 18, 19, 20
Baker, Jim *22:* 24
Baker, Joe *82:* 188; *111:* 55; *124:* 70; *197:* 73
Baker, Keith *179:* 6, 7
Baker, Leslie *112:* 214; *132:* 103, 246; *180:* 74, 246
Baldacci, Rudy *184:* 9
Baldridge, Cyrus LeRoy *19:* 69; *44:* 50
Baldus, Jackie *216:* 81
Baldus, Zachary *152:* 231; *187:* 60
Balet, Jan *11:* 22
Balian, Lorna *9:* 16; *91:* 16
Balit, Christina *102:* 24; *159:* 9; *162:* 118, 119; *212:* 2, 3
Ballantyne, R.M. *24:* 34
Ballis, George *14:* 199
Balouch, Kristen *176:* 11
Baltzer, Hans *40:* 30
Banbery, Fred *58:* 15
Bancroft, Bronwyn *216:* 42
Banfill, A. Scott *98:* 7; *112:* 59
Bang, Molly *24:* 37, 38; *69:* 8, 9, 10; *111:* 7,9, 10, 11; *140:* 11; *158:* 37, 38, 39; *195:* 3; *215:* 11, 12, 13, 14
Banik, Yvette Santiago *21:* 136
Banks, Erin Bennett *211:* 12
Banner, Angela
   See Maddison, Angela Mary
Bannerman, Helen *19:* 13, 14
Banning, Greg *202:* 98
Bannon, Laura *6:* 10; *23:* 8
Bantock, Nick *74:* 229; *95:* 6
Banyai, Istvan *185:* 209; *193:* 14, 16; *209:* 155
Baptist, Michael *37:* 208
Baracca, Sal *135:* 206
Baranaski, Marcin *182:* 113
Barasch, Lynne *126:* 16; *186:* 15
Barbarin, Lucien C., Jr. *89:* 88
Barbour, Karen *96:* 5; *74:* 209; *170:* 16
Bare, Arnold Edwin *16:* 31
Bare, Colleen Stanley *32:* 33
Barger, Jan *147:* 11
Bargery, Geoffrey *14:* 258
Barkat, Jonathan *149:* 177; *164:* 254; *181:* 106; *184:* 186; *196:* 11; *198:* 148
Barker, Carol *31:* 27
Barker, Cicely Mary *49:* 50, 51
Barkley, James *4:* 13; *6:* 11; *13:* 112
Barks, Carl *37:* 27, 28, 29, 30, 31, 32, 33, 34
Barling, Joy *62:* 148
Barling, Tom *9:* 23
Barlow, Gillian *62:* 20
Barlow, Perry *35:* 28
Barlowe, Dot *30:* 223
Barlowe, Wayne *37:* 72; *84:* 43; *105:* 5
Barnard, Bryn *88:* 53; *13:* 55; *169:* 13; *193:* 194
Barneda, David *206:* 11
Barner, Bob *29:* 37; *128:* 33; *136:* 19, 20; *177:* 27
Barnes, Hiram P. *20:* 28
Barnes, Tim *137:* 28
Barnes-Murphy, Rowan *88:* 22
Barnett, Charles II *175:* 150
Barnett, Ivan *70:* 14
Barnett, Moneta *16:* 89; *19:* 142; *31:* 102; *33:* 30, 31, 32; *41:* 153; *61:* 94, 97
Barney, Maginel Wright *39:* 32, 33, 34; *YABC 2:* 306
Barnum, Jay Hyde *11:* 224; *20:* 5; *37:* 189, 190
Baron, Alan *80:* 3; *89:* 123
Barr, George *60:* 74; *69:* 64

Barragán, Paula S. *134:* 116; *186:* 158; *216:* 43, 44, 197
Barrall, Tim *115:* 152
Barraud, Martin *189:* 38
Barrauds *33:* 114
Barrer-Russell, Gertrude *9:* 65; *27:* 31
Barret, Robert *85:* 134
Barrett, Angela *40:* 136, 137; *62:* 74; *75:* 10; *76:* 142; *144:* 137; *145:* 14
Barrett, Jennifer *58:* 149
Barrett, John E. *43:* 119
Barrett, Moneta *74:* 10
Barrett, Peter *55:* 169; *86:* 111
Barrett, Robert *62:* 145; *77:* 146; *82:* 35
Barrett, Ron *14:* 24; *26:* 35
Barron, John N. *3:* 261; *5:* 101; *14:* 220
Barrow, Ann *136:* 27
Barrows, Walter *14:* 268
Barry, Ethelred B. *37:* 79; *YABC 1:* 229
Barry, James *14:* 25
Barry, Katharina *2:* 159; *4:* 22
Barry, Robert E. *6:* 12
Barry, Scott *32:* 35
Barshaw, Ruth McNally *203:* 9
Bartenbach, Jean *40:* 31
Barth, Ernest Kurt *2:* 172; *3:* 160; *8:* 26; *10:* 31
Bartholomew, Caty *208:* 153
Bartholomew, Marie *200:* 66
Bartlett, Alison *101:* 88; *165:* 93; *209:* 51
Barton, Byron *8:* 207; *9:* 18; *23:* 66; *80:* 181; *90:* 18, 19, 20, 21; *126:* 29, 30
Barton, Harriett *30:* 71
Barton, Jill *129:* 108; *135:* 120; *145:* 185, 189; *184:* 177
Bartram, Robert *10:* 42
Bartram, Simon *218:* 8
Bartsch, Jochen *8:* 105; *39:* 38
Bascove, Barbara *45:* 73
Base, Graeme *101:* 15, 16, 17, 18; *162:* 8, 10, 12
Baseman, Gary *174:* 12
Bash, Barbara *132:* 9
Baskin, Leonard *30:* 42, 43, 46, 47; *49:* 125, 126, 128, 129,133; *173:* 120
Bass, Saul *49:* 192
Bassett, Jeni *40:* 99; *64:* 30
Basso, Bill *99:* 139; *189:* 134
Batchelor, Joy *29:* 41, 47, 48
Bate, Norman *5:* 16
Bates, Amy June *188:* 170; *189:* 27, 28
Bates, Leo *24:* 35
Batet, Carmen *39:* 134
Batherman, Muriel *31:* 79; *45:* 185
Battaglia, Aurelius *50:* 44
Batten, John D. *25:* 161, 162
Batten, Mary *162:* 14, 15
Battles, Asa *32:* 94, 95
Bauer, Carla *193:* 6
Bauer, Jutta *150:* 32
Bauernschmidt, Marjorie *15:* 15
Baum, Allyn *20:* 10
Baum, Willi *4:* 24, 25; *7:* 173
Bauman, Leslie *61:* 121
Baumann, Jill *34:* 170
Baumhauer, Hans *11:* 218; *15:* 163, 165, 167
Baxter, Glen *57:* 100
Baxter, Leon *59:* 102
Baxter, Robert *87:* 129
Bayer, Herbert *181:* 16
Bayley, Dorothy *37:* 195
Bayley, Nicola *40:* 104; *41:* 34, 35; *69:* 15; *129:* 33, 34, 35
Baylin, Mark *158:* 233
Baynes, Pauline *2:* 244; *3:* 149; *13:* 133, 135,137, 141; *19:* 18, 19, 20; *32:* 208, 213, 214; *36:* 105, 108; *59:* 12, 13, 14, 16, 17, 18, 20; *100:* 158, 159, 243; *133:* 3, 4
Beach, Lou *150:* 150; *207:* 117, 118
Beame, Rona *12:* 40
Bean, Jonathan *196:* 102

Bear's Heart *73:* 215
Beard, Dan *22:* 31, 32
Beard, J.H. *YABC 1:* 158
Bearden, Romare *9:* 7; *22:* 35
Beardshaw, Rosalind *169:* 22; *190:* 22
Beardsley, Aubrey *17:* 14; *23:* 181; *59:* 130, 131
Bearman, Jane *29:* 38
Beaton, Cecil *24:* 208
Beaton, Clare *125:* 28; *208:* 67; *220:* 10, 11, 12
Beauce, J.A. *18:* 103
Beaujard, Sophie *81:* 54
Beccia, Carlyn *189:* 29
Bechtold, Lisze *208:* 29
Beck, Charles *11:* 169; *51:* 173
Beck, Ian *138:* 27; *182:* 150; *190:* 25
Beck, Melinda *203:* 112
Beck, Ruth *13:* 11
Becker, Harriet *12:* 211
Beckerman, Jonathan *208:* 194
Beckett, Sheilah *25:* 5; *33:* 37, 38
Beckhoff, Harry *1:* 78; *5:* 163
Beckhorn, Susan Williams *189:* 32
Beckman, Kaj *45:* 38, 39, 40, 41
Beckman, Per *45:* 42, 43
Beddows, Eric *72:* 70
Bedford, F.D. *20:* 118, 122; *33:* 170; *41:* 220, 221,230, 233
Bee, Joyce *19:* 62
Bee, William *188:* 6
Beeby, Betty *25:* 36
Beech, Carol *9:* 149
Beech, Mark *192:* 122
Beek *25:* 51, 55, 59
Beeke, Tiphanie *177:* 127; *204:* 140; *212:* 178; *218:* 102
Beekman, Doug *125:* 146, 148
Beerbohm, Max *24:* 208
Beeson, Bob *108:* 57
Begin, Mary Jane *82:* 13; *206:* 13
Beha, Philippe *172:* 85
Behr, Joyce *15:* 15; *21:* 132; *23:* 161
Behrens, Hans *5:* 97
Beier, Ellen *135:* 170; *139:* 47; *183:* 164; *221:* 177
Beingessner, Laura *220:* 14
Beinicke, Steve *69:* 18
Beisner, Monika *46:* 128, 131; *112:* 127
Belden, Charles J. *12:* 182
Belina, Renate *39:* 132
Bell, Corydon *3:* 20
Bell, Graham *54:* 48
Bell, Julia *151:* 214
Bell, Julie *159:* 172; *165:* 18
Bell, Thomas P. *76:* 182
Bellamy, Glen *127:* 15
Beltran, Alberto *43:* 37
Bemelmans, Ludwig *15:* 19, 21; *100:* 27
Ben-Ami, Doron *75:* 96; *84:* 107; *108:* 132; *110:* 63; *159:* 157; *197:* 142
Bendall-Brunello, John *150:* 4; *157:* 163; *185:* 3, 4; *203:* 5
Benda, Wladyslaw T. *15:* 256; *30:* 76, 77; *44:* 182
Bender, Robert *77:* 162; *79:* 13; *160:* 23
Bendick, Jeanne *2:* 24; *68:* 27, 28
Benioff, Carol *121:* 42; *175:* 23
Benner, Cheryl *80:* 11
Bennett, Charles H. *64:* 6
Bennett, Erin Susanne *165:* 216
Bennett, F.I. *YABC 1:* 134
Bennett, James *146:* 240
Bennett, Jill *26:* 61; *41:* 38, 39; *45:* 54
Bennett, Rainey *15:* 26; *23:* 53
Bennett, Richard *15:* 45; *21:* 11, 12, 13; *25:* 175
Bennett, Susan *5:* 55
Benny, Mike *142:* 78; *203:* 13, 14; *207:* 85
Benoit, Elise *77:* 74

Benson, Linda *60:* 130; *62:* 91; *75:* 101; *79:* 156; *134:* 129
Benson, Patrick *68:* 162; *147:* 17, 18, 19, 20
Bentley, Carolyn *46:* 153
Bentley, James *149:* 30
Bentley, Roy *30:* 162
Benton, Jim *172:* 22
Benton, Thomas Hart *2:* 99
Berelson, Howard *5:* 20; *16:* 58; *31:* 50
Berenstain, Jan *12:* 47; *64:* 33, 34, 36, 37, 38, 40, 42, 44; *135:* 25, 28, 31, 35
Berenstain, Stan *12:* 47; *64:* 33, 34, 36, 37, 38, 40, 42, 44; *135:* 25, 28, 31, 35
Berenzy, Alix *65:* 13; *73:* 6; *78:* 115
Berg, Joan *1:* 115; *3:* 156; *6:* 26, 58
Berg, Ron *36:* 48, 49; *48:* 37, 38; *67:* 72
Bergen, David *115:* 44; *207:* 34
Berger, Barbara *77:* 14
Berger, Carin *185:* 6
Berger, Joe *221:* 9
Berger, William M. *14:* 143; *YABC 1:* 204
Bergherr, Mary *74:* 170; *151:* 123
Bergin, Mark *114:* 8, 9; *143:* 95; *160:* 26, 27
Bergstreser, Douglas *69:* 76
Bergum, Constance R. *121:* 14, 15; *208:* 31, 32, 33; *209:* 176
Bering, Claus *13:* 14
Berkeley, Jon *139:* 218
Berkowitz, Jeanette *3:* 249
Berman, Paul *66:* 14
Berman, Rachel *217:* 26
Bernal, Richard *154:* 176
Bernadette
    See Watts, Bernadette
Bernard, Gary *216:* 71
Bernardin, James *112:* 24; *167:* 94
Bernasconi, Pablo *183:* 10, 11
Bernath, Stefen *32:* 76
Berner, Rotraut Susanne *214:* 32
Bernhard, Durga *80:* 13
Bernstein, Michel J. *51:* 71
Bernstein, Ted *38:* 183; *50:* 131
Bernstein, Zena *23:* 46
Berridge, Celia *86:* 63
Berrill, Jacquelyn *12:* 50
Berry, Erick
    See Best, Allena
Berry, Holly *205:* 116; *210:* 49, 50
Berry, William D. *14:* 29; *19:* 48
Berry, William A. *6:* 219
Berson, Harold *2:* 17, 18; *4:* 28, 29, 220; *9:* 10; *12:* 19; *17:* 45; *18:* 193; *22:* 85; *34:* 172; *44:* 120; *46:* 42; *80:* 240
Bertholf, Bret *187:* 9; *189:* 32, 33
Berton, Patsy *99:* 16
Bertschmann, Harry *16:* 1
Besco, Don *70:* 99
Beskow, Elsa *20:* 13, 14, 15
Bess, Clayton *63:* 94
Best, Allena *2:* 26; *34:* 76
Betera, Carol *74:* 68
Bethell, Thomas N. *61:* 169
Bethers, Ray *6:* 22
Betteridge, Deirdre *214:* 34
Bettina
    See Ehrlich, Bettina
Betts, Ethel Franklin *17:* 161, 164, 165; *YABC 2:* 47
Betz, Rudolf *59:* 161
Bewick, Thomas *16:* 40, 41, 43, 44, 45, 47; *54:* 150; *YABC 1:* 107
Beyer, Paul J. III *74:* 24
Bezencon, Jacqueline *48:* 40
Biamonte, Daniel *40:* 90
Bianchi, John *91:* 19
Bianco, Pamela *15:* 31; *28:* 44, 45, 46
Bible, Charles *13:* 15
Bice, Clare *22:* 40
Biedrzycki, David *186:* 170; *219:* 7
Bierman, Don *57:* 184
Biggers, John *2:* 123

Biggs, Brian *192:* 38; *196:* 15; *207:* 170
Bikadoroff, Roxanna *201:* 74
Bileck, Marvin *3:* 102; *40:* 36, 37
Bilibin, Ivan *61:* 8, 9, 12, 13, 14, 15, 151, 152, 154, 162
Billington, Patrick *98:* 71
Billout, Guy *144:* 38, 39
Bimen, Levent *5:* 179
Binch, Caroline *81:* 18; *140:* 15, 16; *144:* 115; *211:* 82
Binder, Hannes *169:* 163
Bing, Christopher *126:* 34
Binger, Bill *121:* 46
Binks, Robert *25:* 150
Binzen, Bill *24:* 47
Birch, Reginald *15:* 150; *19:* 33, 34, 35, 36; *37:* 196,197; *44:* 182; *46:* 176; *YABC 1:* 84; *2:* 34, 39
Birchall, Mark *123:* 188
Bird, Esther Brock *1:* 36; *25:* 66
Birdsong, Keith *167:* 85; *219:* 105
Birkett, Georgie *204:* 121
Birkett, Rachel *78:* 206
Birling, Paul *109:* 30
Birmingham, Christian *132:* 243; *143:* 114; *209:* 58; *220:* 20
Birmingham, Lloyd P. *12:* 51; *83:* 13
Biro, Val *1:* 26; *41:* 42; *60:* 178; *67:* 23, 24; *84:* 242, 243
Bischoff, Ilse *44:* 51
Bishop, Don *199:* 133
Bishop, Gavin *97:* 17, 18; *144:* 42, 44; *216:* 52, 55, 56, 57
Bishop, Kathleen Wong *115:* 67
Bishop, Rich *56:* 43
Bite, I. *60:* 14
Bittinger, Ned *93:* 117; *205:* 115
Bjorklund, Lorence *3:* 188, 252; *7:* 100; *9:* 113; *10:* 66; *19:* 178; *33:* 122, 123; *35:* 36, 37, 38, 39,41, 42, 43; *36:* 185; *38:* 93; *47:* 106; *66:* 194; *YABC 1:* 242
Bjorkman, Steve *91:* 199; *160:* 110; *198:* 18; *218:* 188
Blabey, Aaron *214:* 35
Black Sheep *164:* 100
Blackburn, Loren H. *63:* 10
Blackall, Sophie *194:* 140; *209:* 157
Blackford, John *137:* 105; *180:* 36
Blackwell, Basil T. *YABC 1:* 68, 69
Blackwood, Freya *199:* 9
Blackwood, Gary L. *118:* 17
Blades, Ann *16:* 52; *37:* 213; *50:* 41; *69:* 21; *99:* 215
Blair, Jay *45:* 46; *46:* 155
Blaisdell, Elinore *1:* 121; *3:* 134; *35:* 63
Blake, Anne Catharine *189:* 71
Blake, Francis *198:* 4
Blake, Quentin *3:* 170; *10:* 48; *13:* 38; *21:* 180; *26:* 60; *28:* 228; *30:* 29, 31; *40:* 108; *45:* 219; *46:* 165, 168; *48:* 196; *52:* 10, 11, 12,13, 14, 15, 16, 17; *73:* 41, 43; *78:* 84, 86; *80:* 250, 251; *84:* 210, 211, 212; *87:* 177; *96:* 24, 26, 28; *124:* 79; *125:* 32, 34; *181:* 139; *211:* 26, 27
Blake, Robert J. *37:* 90; *53:* 67; *54:* 23; *160:* 28, 29
Blake, William *30:* 54, 56, 57, 58, 59, 60
Blakeslee, Lys *218:* 11, 105
Blanchard, N. Taylor *82:* 140
Blass, Jacqueline *8:* 215
Blazek, Scott R. *91:* 71
Bleck, Cathie *118:* 116
Bleck, Linda *204:* 124
Blegvad, Erik *2:* 59; *3:* 98; *5:* 117; *7:* 131; *11:* 149; *14:* 34, 35; *18:* 237; *32:* 219; *60:* 106; *66:* 16, 17, 18, 19; *70:* 233; *76:* 18; *82:* 106; *87:* 45; *100:* 188; *129:* 125; *132:* 17, 18, 19, 20; *176:* 14; *200:* 140; *YABC 1:* 201
Blessen, Karen *93:* 126
Bliss, Corinne Demas *37:* 38
Bliss, Harry *196:* 27, 28, 29

Blitt, Barry *179:* 199; *187:* 13
Bloch, Lucienne *10:* 12
Blondon, Herve *129:* 48; *183:* 22
Bloom, Lloyd *35:* 180; *36:* 149; *47:* 99; *62:* 117; *68:* 231; *72:* 136; *75:* 185; *83:* 99; *108:* 19
Bloom, Suzanne *172:* 23, 24
Blossom, Dave *34:* 29
Blumenschein, E.L. *YABC 1:* 113, 115
Blumer, Patt *29:* 214
Blundell, Kim *29:* 36
Bluthenthal, Diana Cain *93:* 32; *104:* 106; *177:* 26
Blythe, Benjamin *128:* 7
Blythe, Gary *112:* 52; *181:* 166; *182:* 64; *185:* 7; *186:* 116, 117
Boake, Kathy *176:* 185
Board, Perry *171:* 99
Boardman, Gwenn *12:* 60
Boatwright, Phil *211:* 195
Bober, Richard *125:* 145; *132:* 40
Bobri *30:* 138; *47:* 27
Bock, Vera *1:* 187; *21:* 41
Bock, William Sauts *8:* 7; *14:* 37; *16:* 120; *21:* 141; *36:* 177; *62:* 203
Bodecker, N(iels) M(ogens) *8:* 13; *14:* 2; *17:* 55, 56, 57; *73:* 22, 23, 24
Boehm, Linda *40:* 31
Bogacki, Tomek *138:* 31, 32; *144:* 123; *202:* 13
Bogan, Paulette *197:* 152; *201:* 17
Bogdan, Florentina *107:* 43
Bohdal, Susi *22:* 44; *101:* 20
Bohlen, Nina *58:* 13
Boies, Alex *96:* 53
Bok, Chip *205:* 16
Bolam, Emily *101:* 216; *159:* 12; *205:* 59
Bolian, Polly *3:* 270; *4:* 30; *13:* 77; *29:* 197
Bolle, Frank *87:* 100; *208:* 101
Bollen, Roger *79:* 186; *83:* 16
Bolling, Vickey *114:* 44
Bollinger, Peter *101:* 7; *128:* 198; *172:* 26
Bolognese, Don *2:* 147, 231; *4:* 176; *7:* 146; *17:* 43; *23:* 192; *24:* 50; *34:* 108; *36:* 133; *71:* 24, 25; *103:* 131; *129:* 39, 40
Bolster, Rob *186:* 169
Bolton, A.T. *57:* 158
Bond, Arnold *18:* 116
Bond, Barbara Higgins *21:* 102
Bond, Bruce *52:* 97
Bond, Felicia *38:* 197; *49:* 55, 56; *89:* 170; *90:* 171; *126:* 37
Bond, Higgins *177:* 22, 23; *209:* 175; *220:* 22, 23, 24
Bonn, Pat *43:* 40
Bonner, Hannah *197:* 13, 14
Bonners, Susan *41:* 40; *85:* 36; *94:* 99, 100; *151:* 105, 106
Bono, Mary *184:* 73
Bonsall, Crosby *23:* 6
Boon, Debbie *103:* 6; *144:* 188
Boon, Emilie *86:* 23, 24
Boone, Debbie *165:* 77
Boore, Sara *60:* 73
Bootman, Colin *155:* 13; *159:* 35; *174:* 192
Booth, Franklin *YABC 2:* 76
Booth, George *191:* 13
Booth, Graham *32:* 193; *37:* 41, 42
Borda, Juliette *102:* 188
Bordier, Georgette *16:* 54
Boren, Tinka *27:* 128
Borges, Jose Francisco *119:* 62
Borja, Robert *22:* 48
Born, Adolf *49:* 63
Bornstein, Ruth *14:* 44; *88:* 45, 46; *107:* 30
Borten, Helen *3:* 54; *5:* 24
Bosin, Blackbear *69:* 104
Bossom, Naomi *35:* 48
Bostock, Mike *83:* 221; *114:* 14; *188:* 205
Boston, Peter *19:* 42
Bosustow, Stephen *34:* 202

Boszko, Ron *75:* 47
Bottner, Barbara *14:* 46
Boucher, Joelle *41:* 138
Boulat, Pierre *44:* 40
Boulet, Susan Seddon *50:* 47
Bouma, Paddy *118:* 25; *128:* 16
Bour, Daniele *66:* 145
Bourke-White, Margaret *15:* 286, 287; *57:* 102
Boutavant, Marc *200:* 136
Boutet de Monvel, M. *30:* 61, 62, 63, 65
Bowen, Betsy *105:* 222
Bowen, Richard *42:* 134
Bowen, Ruth *31:* 188
Bower, Ron *29:* 33
Bowers, David *95:* 38; *115:* 20; *127:* 169, 170; *165:* 57; *207:* 11
Bowers, Tim *185:* 35; *201:* 41; *218:* 13
Bowman, Claire *174:* 177
Bowman, Eric *151:* 23
Bowman, Leslie *85:* 203; *105:* 108; *116:* 76; *128:* 234; *182:* 24, 25
Bowman, Peter *146:* 214, 215; *150:* 115
Bowser, Carolyn Ewing *22:* 253
Boxall, Ed *178:* 28
Boyd, Aaron *158:* 242
Boyd, Patti *45:* 31
Boyle, Eleanor Vere *28:* 50, 51
Boynton, Sandra *57:* 13, 14, 15; *107:* 36, 37; *152:* 12, 13, 14
Bozzo, Frank *4:* 154
Brabbs, Derry *55:* 170
Brace, Eric *132:* 193, 194; *152:* 71; *184:* 195; *197:* 6; *201:* 54
Brackers de Hugo, Pierre *115:* 21
Bradford, June *158:* 138
Bradford, Ron *7:* 157
Bradley, David P. *69:* 105
Bradley, Richard D. *26:* 182
Bradley, William *5:* 164
Brady, Irene *4:* 31; *42:* 37; *68:* 191
Bragg, Michael *32:* 78; *46:* 31
Bragg, Ruth Gembicki *77:* 18
Brainerd, John W. *65:* 19
Braithwaite, Althea *23:* 12, 13; *119:* 16
Brak, Syd *146:* 187
Bralds, Braldt *90:* 28; *91:* 151
Bram, Elizabeth *30:* 67
Bramley, Peter *4:* 3
Brandenberg, Aliki *2:* 36, 37; *24:* 222; *35:* 49, 50, 51,52, 53, 54, 56, 57; *75:* 15, 17; *92:* 205; *113:* 18, 19, 20; *157:* 28; *156:* 111
Brandenburg, Alexa *75:* 19
Brandenburg, Jim *47:* 58; *150:* 212
Brandi, Lillian *31:* 158
Brandon, Brumsic, Jr. *9:* 25
Brannen, Sarah S. *202:* 15; *216:* 199
Bransom, Paul *17:* 121; *43:* 44
Braren, Loretta Trezzo *87:* 193
Brassard, France *186:* 22
Braun, Wendy *80:* 17, 18; *213:* 14
Brautigam, Don *115:* 175, 176
Brazell, Derek *75:* 105; *79:* 9
Breathed, Berkeley *86:* 27, 28, 29; *161:* 13, 14
Breckenreid, Julia *192:* 209
Breen, Steve *186:* 23
Brennan, Steve *83:* 230; *101:* 184
Brenner, Fred *22:* 85; *36:* 34; *42:* 34
Brett, Bernard *22:* 54
Brett, Harold M. *26:* 98, 99, 100
Brett, Jan *30:* 135; *42:* 39; *71:* 31, 32; *130:* 23, 24, 25, 26, 27; *171:* 15, 16
Brewer, Paul *106:* 115; *145:* 202
Brewer, Sally King *33:* 44
Brewster, Patience *40:* 68; *45:* 22, 183; *51:* 20; *66:* 144; *89:* 4; *97:* 30, 31; *212:* 99
Brick, John *10:* 15
Brickman, Robin D. *131:* 88; *142:* 150; *155:* 18; *178:* 109; *184:* 32
Bridge, David R. *45:* 28
Bridgman, L.J. *37:* 77
Bridwell, Norman *4:* 37; *138:* 36, 37, 40

Brierley, Louise *91:* 22; *96:* 165; *183:* 51
Briggs, Harry *172:* 187
Briggs, Raymond *10:* 168; *23:* 20, 21; *66:* 29, 31, 32; *131:* 28, 29; *184:* 15, 16
Brigham, Grace A. *37:* 148
Bright, Robert *24:* 55
Brighton, Catherine *107:* 39; *206:* 23
Brinckloe, Julie *13:* 18; *24:* 79, 115; *29:* 35; *63:* 140; *81:* 131
Brion *47:* 116
Brisley, Joyce L. *22:* 57
Brisson, James F. *110:* 60
Brittingham, Geoffrey *88:* 37
Brix-Henker, Silke *81:* 194
Broadway, Hannah *208:* 104
Brock, Charles E. *15:* 97; *19:* 247, 249; *23:* 224, 225; *36:* 88; *42:* 41, 42, 43, 44, 45; *100:* 189; *YABC 1:* 194, 196, 203
Brock, Emma *7:* 21
Brock, Henry Matthew *15:* 81; *16:* 141; *19:* 71; *34:* 115; *40:* 164; *42:* 47, 48, 49; *49:* 66
Brocksopp, Arthur *57:* 157
Broda, Ron *136:* 180; *174:* 123
Brodkin, Gwen *34:* 135
Brodovitch, Alexi *52:* 22
Bromhall, Winifred *5:* 11; *26:* 38
Bromley, Lizzy *159:* 179
Bronson, Linda *150:* 210; *174:* 133; *203:* 16, 17
Brooke, L. Leslie *16:* 181, 182, 183, 186; *17:* 15, 16, 17; *18:* 194
Brooker, Christopher *15:* 251
Brooker, Kyrsten *111:* 94; *140:* 28; *162:* 111; *175:* 108; *186:* 42, 225; *199:* 12; *201:* 30; *219:* 98
Brooks, Erik *166:* 52; *182:* 30
Brooks, Karen Stormer *186:* 110; *220:* 65
Brooks, Maya Itzna *92:* 153
Brooks, Ron *94:* 15; *197:* 188; *212:* 6, 7, 8, 9
Brooks, S.G. *178:* 127
Broomfield, Maurice *40:* 141
Brotman, Adolph E. *5:* 21
Brown, Buck *45:* 48
Brown, Calef *179:* 18; *210:* 206; *217:* 30, 31
Brown, Christopher *62:* 124, 125, 127, 128
Brown, Craig McFarland *73:* 28; *84:* 65
Brown, Dan *61:* 167; *115:* 183, 184; *116:* 28, 29; *193:* 190; *200:* 21, 23
Brown, David *7:* 47; *48:* 52
Brown, Denise *11:* 213
Brown, Don *172:* 29
Brown, Elbrite *195:* 39; *198:* 5
Brown, Ford Madox *48:* 74
Brown, Hunter *191:* 111, 112
Brown, Judith Gwyn *1:* 45; *7:* 5; *8:* 167; *9:* 182, 190; *20:* 16, 17, 18; *23:* 142; *29:* 117; *33:* 97; *36:* 23, 26; *43:* 184; *48:* 201, 223; *49:* 69; *86:* 227; *110:* 188; *153:* 7
Brown, Kathryn *98:* 26
Brown, Lisa *187:* 175
Brown, Laurie Krasny *99:* 30
Brown, Marc (Tolon) *10:* 17, 197; *14:* 263; *51:* 18; *53:* 11, 12, 13, 15, 16, 17; *75:* 58; *80:* 24, 25, 26; *82:* 261; *99:* 29; *145:* 22, 23, 25, 27; *162:* 198
Brown, Marcia *7:* 30; *25:* 203; *47:* 31, 32, 33, 34, 35,36, 37, 38, 39, 40, 42, 43, 44; *YABC 1:* 27
Brown, Margery W. *5:* 32, 33; *10:* 3
Brown, Martin *101:* 43
Brown, Mary Barrett *97:* 74
Brown, Palmer *36:* 40
Brown, Paul *25:* 26; *26:* 107
Brown, Richard *61:* 18; *67:* 30
Brown, Rick *78:* 71; *150:* 154
Brown, Robert S. *85:* 33
Brown, Rod *157:* 142
Brown, Ruth *55:* 165; *86:* 112, 113; *105:* 16, 17, 18; *171:* 178
Brown, Trevor *99:* 160; *139:* 247; *189:* 206

Browne, Anthony *45:* 50, 51, 52; *61:* 21, 22, 23, 24, 25; *105:* 21, 22, 23, 25
Browne, Dik *8:* 212; *67:* 32, 33, 35, 37, 39
Browne, Gordon *16:* 97; *64:* 114, 116, 117, 119, 121
Browne, Hablot K. *15:* 65, 80; *21:* 14, 15, 16, 17, 18, 19,20; *24:* 25
Browne, Jane *165:* 222
Browning, Coleen *4:* 132
Browning, Mary Eleanor *24:* 84
Bruce, Robert *23:* 23
Brude, Dick *48:* 215
Bruel, Nick *166:* 41; *205:* 17, 18
Brule, Al *3:* 135
Brumbeau, Jeff *157:* 29
Bruna, Dick *43:* 48, 49, 50; *76:* 27, 28
Brundage, Frances *19:* 244
Brunhoff, Jean de *24:* 57, 58
Brunhoff, Laurent de *24:* 60; *71:* 35, 36, 37
Brunkus, Denise *84:* 50; *123:* 117; *178:* 209; *193:* 99; *204:* 10, 11, 12; *209:* 202
Brunson, Bob *43:* 135
Bryan, Ashley *31:* 44; *72:* 27, 28, 29; *107:* 92; *116:* 192; *132:* 24; *178:* 33, 34, 35; *208:* 83
Bryant, Laura J. *176:* 36; *183:* 168; *214:* 141
Bryant, Michael *93:* 74
Brychta, Alex *21:* 21
Bryer, Diana *107:* 121
Bryson, Bernarda *3:* 88, 146; *39:* 26; *44:* 185; *131:* 40
Buba, Joy *12:* 83; *30:* 226; *44:* 56
Buchanan, George *166:* 198
Buchanan, Lilian *13:* 16
Buchanan, Rachel *171:* 71
Bucholtz-Ross, Linda *44:* 137
Buchs, Thomas *40:* 38
Buck, Margaret Waring *3:* 30
Buckhardt, Marc *172:* 59
Buckley, Mike *166:* 180
Budwine, Greg *175:* 172
Buehner, Mark *104:* 12, 15; *105:* 160; *119:* 98; *157:* 188; *159:* 39, 40, 43; *192:* 111; *219:* 13, 14, 15, 16; *221:* 17, 18, 19
Buehr, Walter *3:* 31
Buff, Conrad *19:* 52, 53, 54
Buff, Mary *19:* 52, 53
Bull, Charles Livingston *18:* 207; *88:* 175, 176
Bullen, Anne *3:* 166, 167
Buller, Jon *205:* 21
Bullock, Kathleen *77:* 24
Bumgarner-Kirby, Claudia *77:* 194
Burbank, Addison *37:* 43
Burchard, Peter Duncan *3:* 197; *5:* 35; *6:* 158, 218; *143:* 17
Burckhardt, Marc *94:* 48; *110:* 89; *196:* 41; *199:* 116
Burger, Carl *3:* 33; *45:* 160, 162
Burgeson, Marjorie *19:* 31
Burgess, Anne *76:* 252
Burgess, Gelett *32:* 39, 42
Burgess, Mark *157:* 31
Burke, Jim *179:* 19; *185:* 63
Burke, Phillip *95:* 117
Burkert, Nancy Ekholm *18:* 186; *22:* 140; *24:* 62, 63,64, 65; *26:* 53; *29:* 60, 61; *46:* 171; *YABC 1:* 46
Burkhardt, Bruce *142:* 86
Burkhardt, Melissa A. *142:* 86
Burleson, Joe *104:* 35; *172:* 139
Burn, Doris *6:* 172
Burn, Jeffrey *89:* 125; *152:* 132
Burn, Ted
　See Burn, Thomas E.
Burn, Thomas E. *151:* 41
Burnard, Damon *115:* 23
Burnett, Lindy *210:* 59
Burnett, Virgil *44:* 42
Burningham, John *9:* 68; *16:* 60, 61; *59:* 28, 29, 30,31, 32, 33, 35; *111:* 18, 19, 21; *160:* 37
Burns, Howard M. *12:* 173

Burns, Jim *47:* 70; *86:* 32; *91:* 197; *123:* 16
Burns, M.F. *26:* 69
Burns, Raymond *9:* 29
Burns, Robert *24:* 106
Burr, Dan *65:* 28; *108:* 134; *164:* 203; *182:* 68
Burr, Dane *12:* 2
Burra, Edward *YABC 2:* 68
Burrell, Galen *56:* 76
Burri, Rene *41:* 143; *54:* 166
Burridge, Marge Opitz *14:* 42
Burris, Burmah *4:* 81
Burroughs, John Coleman *41:* 64
Burroughs, Studley O. *41:* 65
Burton, Marilee Robin *46:* 33
Burton, Virginia Lee *2:* 43; *44:* 49, 51; *100:* 46, 47; *YABC 1:* 24; *147:* 56
Busoni, Rafaello *1:* 186; *3:* 224; *6:* 126; *14:* 5; *16:* 62, 63
Butchkes, Sidney *50:* 58
Butler, Geoff *94:* 20
Butler, Ralph *116:* 212
Butterfield, Ned *1:* 153; *27:* 128; *79:* 63
Butterworth, Ian *184:* 48, 49
Butterworth, Nick *106:* 43, 44; *149:* 34
Buxton, John *123:* 12
Buzelli, Christopher *105:* 149
Buzonas, Gail *29:* 88
Buzzell, Russ W. *12:* 177
Byard, Carole *39:* 44; *57:* 18, 19, 20; *60:* 60; *61:* 93, 96; *69:* 210; *78:* 246; *79:* 227
Byars, Betsy *46:* 35
Byfield, Barbara Ninde *8:* 18
Byfield, Graham *32:* 29
Bynum, Janie *176:* 50
Byrd, Robert *13:* 218; *33:* 46; *158:* 70; *212:* 100
Byrd, Samuel *123:* 104

C

Cabat, Erni *74:* 38
Cabban, Vanessa *138:* 73; *176:* 39; *185:* 65
Cabrera, Jane *103:* 24; *152:* 27; *182:* 33, 34
Caceres, Ana Palmero *198:* 106
Caddy, Alice *6:* 41
Cady, Harrison *17:* 21, 23; *19:* 57, 58
Caffrey, Aileen *72:* 223; *141:* 154
Cairns, Julia *177:* 37
Caldecott, Randolph *16:* 98, 103; *17:* 32, 33, 36, 38, 39; *26:* 90; *100:* 49, 50; *YABC 2:* 172
Calder, Alexander *18:* 168
Calderón, Gloria *179:* 5
Calderon, W. Frank *25:* 160
Caldwell, Ben *105:* 75; *149:* 60; *195:* 61
Caldwell, Clyde *98:* 100; *116:* 39; *208:* 145
Caldwell, Doreen *23:* 77; *71:* 41
Caldwell, John *46:* 225
Call, Greg *126:* 135; *165:* 49; *182:* 105, 163; *197:* 18, 19; *200:* 159; *209:* 166; *212:* 161
Callahan, Kevin *22:* 42
Callahan, Philip S. *25:* 77
Callan, Jamie *59:* 37
Calvert, Rosemary *218:* 96
Calvin, James *61:* 92
Camburn-Bracalente, Carol A. *118:* 22
Cameron, Chad *190:* 144
Cameron, Julia Margaret *19:* 203
Cameron, Scott *99:* 18
Camm, Martin *140:* 208, 209, 210
Campbell, Ann *11:* 43; *123:* 182; *183:* 68
Campbell, Bill *89:* 39
Campbell, Ken *126:* 143; *205:* 162
Campbell, Robert *55:* 120
Campbell, Rod *51:* 27; *98:* 34
Campbell, Walter M. *YABC 2:* 158
Camps, Luis *28:* 120, 121; *66:* 35
Canga, C.B. *187:* 165
Caniglia, Jeremy *201:* 89

Cann, Helen *124:* 50; *141:* 78; *170:* 138; *179:* 22, 23
Cannell, Jon *196:* 43
Cannon, Janell *78:* 25; *128:* 40
Canright, David *36:* 162
Cantone, AnnaLaura *182:* 146; *196:* 80
Canty, Thomas *85:* 161; *92:* 47; *113:* 192; *134:* 60; *185:* 117
Canyon, Christopher *150:* 44; *151:* 112
Caparo, Antonio Javier *204:* 128; *218:* 88; *220:* 114; *221:* 167
Caporale, Wende *70:* 42
Capp, Al *61:* 28, 30, 31, 40, 41, 43, 44
Cappon, Manuela *154:* 64; *218:* 149
Caras, Peter *36:* 64
Caraway, Caren *57:* 22
Caraway, James *3:* 200, 201
Carbe, Nino *29:* 183
Cares, Linda *67:* 176
Carigiet, Alois *24:* 67
Carle, Eric *4:* 42; *11:* 121; *12:* 29; *65:* 32,33, 34, 36; *73:* 63, 65; *163:* 55, 56
Carling, Amelia Lau *164:* 46
Carlino, Angela *168:* 43; *188:* 20
Carlson, Nancy L. *41:* 116; *56:* 25; *90:* 45; *144:* 48, 50; *213:* 24, 25, 26
Carluccio, Maria *175:* 129; *221:* 119
Carmi, Giora *79:* 35; *149:* 40; *208:* 126
Carpenter, Nancy *76:* 128; *86:* 173; *89:* 171; *131:* 186; *134:* 8; *138:* 215; *153:* 204; *159:* 93; *165:* 232; *211:* 134; *216:* 113
Carr, Archie *37:* 225
Carrick, Donald *5:* 194; *39:* 97; *49:* 70; *53:* 156; *63:* 15, 16, 17, 18, 19, 21; *80:* 131; *86:* 151; *118:* 24
Carrick, Malcolm *28:* 59, 60
Carrick, Paul *118:* 26; *194:* 28
Carrick, Valery *21:* 47
Carrier, Lark *71:* 43
Carroll, Jim *88:* 211; *140:* 177; *153:* 99; *195:* 75
Carroll, Lewis
  See Dodgson, Charles L.
Carroll, Michael *72:* 5
Carroll, Pamela *84:* 68; *128:* 214; *199:* 130
Carroll, Ruth *7:* 41; *10:* 68
Carter, Abby *81:* 32; *97:* 121; *102:* 61; *163:* 139; *164:* 125; *184:* 22, 23; *191:* 85
Carter, Barbara *47:* 167, 169
Carter, David A. *114:* 24, 25; *170:* 42, 43
Carter, Don *124:* 54; *184:* 100; *192:* 43, 44, 45
Carter, Harry *22:* 179
Carter, Helene *15:* 38; *22:* 202, 203; *YABC 2:* 220, 221
Carter, Penny *173:* 91
Cartlidge, Michelle *49:* 65; *96:* 50, 51
Cartwright, Reg *63:* 61, 62; *78:* 26; *143:* 4
Cartwright, Shannon *176:* 81
Carty, Leo *4:* 196; *7:* 163; *58:* 131
Cary *4:* 133; *9:* 32; *20:* 2; *21:* 143
Cary, Page *12:* 41
Casale, Paul *71:* 63; *109:* 122; *136:* 28
Case, Chris *209:* 23
Case, Sandra E. *16:* 2
Caseley, Judith *87:* 36; *159:* 47, 48, 49
Casilla, Robert *78:* 7; *167:* 124; *211:* 41; *212:* 165
Casino, Steve *85:* 193
Cassel, Lili
  See Wronker, Lili Cassel
Cassel-Wronker, Lili
  See Wronker, Lili Cassel
Cassels, Jean *8:* 50; *150:* 119; *173:* 37; *186:* 182
Cassen, Melody *140:* 51
Cassity, Don *104:* 24
Cassler, Carl *75:* 137, 138; *82:* 162
Casson, Hugh *65:* 38, 40, 42, 43
Castellon, Federico *48:* 45, 46, 47, 48
Castle, Jane *4:* 80
Castro, Antonio *84:* 71

Casu, Danny "casroc" *201:* 10
Catalano, Dominic *94:* 79; *163:* 60, 61; *162:* 54
Catalanotto, Peter *63:* 170; *70:* 23; *71:* 182; *72:* 96; *74:* 114; *76:* 194, 195; *77:* 7; *79:* 157; *80:* 28, 67; *83:* 157; *85:* 27; *108:* 11; *113:* 30, 31, 33, 34, 36; *114:* 27, 28, 29; *117:* 53; *124:* 168; *159:* 54, 55; *195:* 19, 20, 21, 22, 24, 174; *200:* 156; *207:* 103; *209:* 184
Catania, Tom *68:* 82
Cather, Carolyn *3:* 83; *15:* 203; *34:* 216
Catlin, George *214:* 172
Catrow, David *117:* 179; *152:* 31, 33; *173:* 24; *206:* 29
Cauley, Lorinda Bryan *44:* 135; *46:* 49
Cayard, Bruce *38:* 67
Cazet, Denys *52:* 27; *99:* 39, 40; *163:* 65, 66; *191:* 25, 27, 28
Ceccoli, Nicoletta *181:* 39; *188:* 99; *199:* 118; *209:* 6
Cecil, Randy *127:* 132, 133; *187:* 16, 17; *191:* 168; *209:* 5
Cellini, Joseph *2:* 73; *3:* 35; *16:* 116; *47:* 103
Cepeda, Joe *90:* 62; *109:* 91; *134:* 172; *159:* 57, 58, 164; *197:* 157; *203:* 69, 95; *215:* 38, 39, 40
Chabrian, Debbi *45:* 55
Chabrian, Deborah *51:* 182; *53:* 124; *63:* 107; *75:* 84; *79:* 85; *82:* 247; *89:* 93; *101:* 197; *212:* 13
Chagnon, Mary *37:* 158
Chalmers, Mary *3:* 145; *13:* 148; *33:* 125; *66:* 214
Chamberlain, Christopher *45:* 57
Chamberlain, Margaret *46:* 51; *106:* 89; *188:* 193; *212:* 16, 17
Chamberlain, Nigel *78:* 140
Chambers, C.E. *17:* 230
Chambers, Dave *12:* 151
Chambers, Jill *134:* 110
Chambers, Mary *4:* 188
Chambliss, Maxie *42:* 186; *56:* 159; *93:* 163, 164; *103:* 178; *186:* 33, 34; *196:* 39
Champlin, Dale *136:* 124
Chan, Harvey *96:* 236; *99:* 153; *143:* 218; *179:* 144; *211:* 219
Chan, Peter *207:* 21; *221:* 39
Chandler, David P. *28:* 62
Chaney, Howard *139:* 27
Chang, Warren *101:* 209
Chapel, Jody *68:* 20
Chapman, C.H. *13:* 83, 85, 87
Chapman, Frederick T. *6:* 27; *44:* 28
Chapman, Gaye *203:* 133
Chapman, Gaynor *32:* 52, 53
Chapman, Jane *145:* 186; *150:* 56; *166:* 220; *174:* 202; *176:* 43, 44; *179:* 131; *202:* 189; *212:* 20, 21, 22; *216:* 123, 225; *221:* 181, 182
Chapman, Lynne *175:* 31; *197:* 25; *208:* 44
Chapman-Crane, Jeff *220:* 101
Chappell, Warren *3:* 172; *21:* 56; *27:* 125
Charles, Donald *30:* 154, 155
Charlip, Remy *4:* 48; *34:* 138; *68:* 53, 54; *119:* 29, 30; *210:* 63, 64
Charlot, Jean *1:* 137, 138; *8:* 23; *14:* 31; *48:* 151; *56:* 21
Charlot, Martin *64:* 72
Charlton, Michael *34:* 50; *37:* 39
Charmatz, Bill *7:* 45
Chartier, Normand *9:* 36; *52:* 49; *66:* 40; *74:* 220; *145:* 169; *168:* 91; *177:* 108
Chase, Lynwood M. *14:* 4
Chast, Roz *97:* 39, 40; *212:* 25
Chastain, Madye Lee *4:* 50
Chateron, Ann *152:* 19
Chatterton, Martin *68:* 102; *152:* 19
Chau, Tungwai *140:* 35
Chauncy, Francis *24:* 158
Chayka, Doug *145:* 97; *177:* 150; *196:* 46; *212:* 58

Chee, Cheng-Khee *79:* 42; *81:* 224; *180:* 245
Chen, Chih-sien *90:* 226
Chen, Tony *6:* 45; *19:* 131; *29:* 126; *34:* 160
Chen, Wendy *221:* 76
Chen, Yong *183:* 34
Cheney, T.A. *11:* 47
Cheng, Andrea *205:* 28
Cheng, Judith *36:* 45; *51:* 16
Chermayeff, Ivan *47:* 53
Cherry, David *93:* 40
Cherry, Lynne *34:* 52; *65:* 184; *87:* 111; *99:* 46, 47
Chesak, Lina *135:* 118
Chess, Victoria *12:* 6; *33:* 42, 48, 49; *40:* 194; *41:* 145; *69:* 80; *72:* 100; *92:* 33, 34; *104:* 167
Chessare, Michele *41:* 50; *56:* 48; *69:* 145
Chesterton, G.K. *27:* 43, 44, 45, 47
Chestnutt, David *47:* 217
Chesworth, Michael *75:* 24, 152; *88:* 136; *94:* 25; *98:* 155; *160:* 42; *207:* 23, 24, 25; *214:* 145
Chetham, Celia *134:* 34
Chetwin, Grace *86:* 40
Cheung, Irving *158:* 96
Chevalier, Christa *35:* 66
Chew, Ruth *7:* 46; *132:* 147
Chewning, Randy *92:* 206
Chichester Clark, Emma *72:* 121; *77:* 212; *78:* 209; *87:* 143; *117:* 37, 39, 40; *144:* 138; *156:* 24, 25; *209:* 26
Chifflart *47:* 113, 127
Child, Lauren *119:* 32; *183:* 30, 31
Chin, Alex *28:* 54
Chitwood, Susan Tanner *163:* 16
Cho, Shinta *8:* 126
Chodos-Irvine, Margaret *52:* 102, 103, 107; *152:* 44
Choi, Yangsook *171:* 134; *173:* 135; *178:* 38, 39, 40
Chollat, Emilie *170:* 203
Chollick, Jay *25:* 175
Choma, Christina *99:* 169
Chomey, Steve *188:* 53
Chorao, Kay *7:* 200, 201; *8:* 25; *11:* 234; *33:* 187; *35:* 239; *69:* 35; *70:* 235; *123:* 174; *193:* 179; *215:* 43, 44, 45, 46
Chorney, Steve *221:* 63
Chow, Frances J. Soo Ping *206:* 36
Chowdhury, Subrata *62:* 130; *162:* 22, 23
Christelow, Eileen *38:* 44; *83:* 198, 199; *90:* 57, 58; *184:* 26
Christensen, Bonnie *93:* 100; *153:* 67; *213:* 29, 30
Christensen, Gardell Dano *1:* 57
Christensen, James C. *140:* 226
Christiana, David *90:* 64; *135:* 13; *171:* 7; *195:* 26, 27
Christiansen, Per *40:* 24
Christie, R. Gregory *116:* 107; *127:* 20, 21; *162:* 179; *164:* 114; *165:* 137; *174:* 157; *179:* 172; *185:* 17, 18, 19; *200:* 2; *204:* 85; *215:* 207; *218:* 57; *220:* 80, 130
Christy, Howard Chandler *17:* 163, 164, 165, 168, 169; *19:* 186, 187; *21:* 22, 23, 24, 25
Christy, Jana *194:* 21
Chronister, Robert *23:* 138; *63:* 27; *69:* 167
Church, Caroline Jayne *179:* 27; *219:* 28, 29
Church, Frederick *YABC 1:* 155
Chute, Marchette *1:* 59
Chwast, Jacqueline *1:* 63; *2:* 275; *6:* 46, 47; *11:* 125; *12:* 202; *14:* 235
Chwast, Seymour *3:* 128, 129; *18:* 43; *27:* 152; *92:* 79; *96:* 56, 57, 58; *146:* 32, 33; *197:* 99
Cieslawksi, Steve *101:* 142; *127:* 116; *158:* 169, 171; *190:* 174; *212:* 85
Cinelli, Lisa *146:* 253
Cirlin, Edgard *2:* 168
Clairin, Georges *53:* 109

Clapp, John *105:* 66; *109:* 58; *126:* 7; *129:* 148; *130:* 165; *195:* 48; *220:* 102
Clark, Brenda *119:* 85; *153:* 55
Clark, David *77:* 164; *134:* 144, 145; *216:* 66, 67
Clark, Emma Chichester
   See Chichester Clark, Emma
Clark, Victoria *35:* 159
Clarke, Greg *169:* 134; *215:* 47, 115
Clarke, Gus *72:* 226; *134:* 31
Clarke, Harry *23:* 172, 173
Clarke, Peter *75:* 102
Claverie, Jean *38:* 46; *88:* 29
Clavis, Philippe Goossens *182:* 167
Clay, Wil *203:* 29
Clayton, Elaine *159:* 60; *209:* 32
Clayton, Robert *9:* 181
Cleary, Brian P. *186:* 37
Cleaver, Elizabeth *8:* 204; *23:* 36
Cleland, T.M. *26:* 92
Clemens, Peter *61:* 125
Clement, Charles *20:* 38
Clement, Gary *186:* 79; *191:* 32
Clement, Janet *182:* 50
Clement, Nathan *200:* 30
Clement, Rod *97:* 42
Clement, Stephen *88:* 3
Clementson, John *84:* 213
Clemesha, David *192:* 49, 50
Cleminson, Kate *221:* 26
Clevin, Jorgen *7:* 50
Clifford, Judy *34:* 163; *45:* 198
Clokey, Art *59:* 44
Clouse, Dennis *187:* 158
Clouse, James *84:* 15
Clouse, Nancy L. *78:* 31; *114:* 90
Clover, Peter *152:* 45
Cneut, Carll *156:* 166; *165:* 67; *197:* 26
Coalson, Glo *9:* 72, 85; *25:* 155; *26:* 42; *35:* 212; *53:* 31; *56:* 154; *94:* 37, 38, 193
Cober, Alan E. *17:* 158; *32:* 77; *49:* 127
Cober-Gentry, Leslie *92:* 111
Cocca-Leffler, Maryann *80:* 46; *136:* 60; *139:* 193; *194:* 31, 33, 34
Cochran, Bobbye *11:* 52
Cochran, Josh *221:* 27
CoConis, Ted *4:* 41; *46:* 41; *51:* 104
Cocozza, Chris *87:* 18; *110:* 173; *111:* 149
Cockroft, Jason *152:* 20
Coerr, Eleanor *1:* 64; *67:* 52
Coes, Peter *35:* 172
Cogancherry, Helen *52:* 143; *69:* 131; *77:* 93; *78:* 220; *109:* 204; *110:* 129; *203:* 92
Coggins, Jack *2:* 69
Cohen, Alix *7:* 53
Cohen, Miriam *155:* 23, 24
Cohen, Nancy R. *165:* 35
Cohen, Santiago *164:* 26; *215:* 52, 199
Cohen, Sheldon *105:* 33, 34; *166:* 46, 47
Cohen, Vincent O. *19:* 243
Cohen, Vivien *11:* 112
Coker, Paul *51:* 172
Colbert, Anthony *15:* 41; *20:* 193
Colby, C.B. *3:* 47
Cole, Babette *58:* 172; *96:* 63, 64; *155:* 29
Cole, Brock *68:* 223; *72:* 36, 37, 38, 192; *127:* 23; *136:* 64, 65; *197:*
Cole, Gwen *87:* 185
Cole, Henry *178:* 120; *181:* 42, 43; *189:* 60; *213:* 35, 36
Cole, Herbert *28:* 104
Cole, Michael *59:* 46
Cole, Olivia H.H. *1:* 134; *3:* 223; *9:* 111; *38:* 104
Cole, Rachael *209:* 39
Colin, Paul *102:* 59; *123:* 118; *126:* 152; *192:* 129
Colley, Jacqui *202:* 20
Collicott, Sharleen *98:* 39; *143:* 29, 30
Collier, Bryan *126:* 54; *151:* 166; *174:* 16, 17, 18; *204:* 18, 19; *208:* 84; *211:* 143

Collier, David *13:* 127
Collier, John *27:* 179; *208:* 154
Collier, Steven *50:* 52
Collier-Morales, Roberta *168:* 61
Collins, Heather *66:* 84; *67:* 68; *81:* 40; *98:* 192, 193; *129:* 95, 96, 98
Collins, Matt *167:* 90
Collins, Ross *140:* 23, 24; *200:* 36, 37; *209:* 54
Colman, Audrey *146:* 161
Colón, Raul *108:* 112; *113:* 5; *117:* 167; *134:* 112; *146:* 23; *159:* 92; *166:* 73; *180:* 107; *186:* 156; *190:* 6; *193:* 24, 205; *202:* 21, 22, 23; *217:* 68; *220:* 126, 157
Colonna, Bernard *21:* 50; *28:* 103; *34:* 140; *43:* 180; *78:* 150
Comport, Sally Wern *117:* 169; *169:* 104; *190:* 42; *207:* 50
Conahan, Carolyn *215:* 17
Conde, J.M. *100:* 120
Condon, Grattan *54:* 85 Condon, Ken *161:* 44; *195:* 28, 29
Cone, Ferne Geller *39:* 49
Cone, J. Morton *39:* 49
Conklin, Paul *43:* 62
Connelly, Gwen *212:* 30
Connelly, James *198:* 12
Connolly, Howard *67:* 88
Connolly, Jerome P. *4:* 128; *28:* 52
Connolly, Peter *47:* 60
Conoly, Walle *110:* 224
Conover, Chris *31:* 52; *40:* 184; *41:* 51; *44:* 79; *213:* 39
Constantin, Pascale *207:* 159
Contreras, Gerry *72:* 9
Converse, James *38:* 70
Conway *62:* 62
Conway, Michael *69:* 12; *81:* 3; *92:* 108
Cook, Ande *188:* 135
Cook, G.R. *29:* 165
Cook, Joel *108:* 160
Cookburn, W.V. *29:* 204
Cooke, Donald E. *2:* 77
Cooke, Tom *52:* 118
Coomaraswamy, A.K. *50:* 100
Coombs, Charles *43:* 65
Coombs, Deborah *139:* 175
Coombs, Patricia *2:* 82; *3:* 52; *22:* 119; *51:* 32, 33, 34, 35, 36, 37, 38, 39, 40, 42, 43
Cooney, Barbara *6:* 16, 17, 50; *12:* 42; *13:* 92; *15:* 145; *16:* 74, 111; *18:* 189; *23:* 38, 89, 93; *32:* 138; *38:* 105; *59:* 48, 49, 51, 52, 53; *74:* 222; *81:* 100; *91:* 25; *96:* 71, 72, 74; *100:* 149; *YABC2:* 10
Cooper, Elisha *157:* 38, 39
Cooper, Floyd *79:* 95; *81:* 45; *84:* 82; *85:* 74; *91:* 118; *96:* 77, 78; *103:* 149; *144:* 54; *145:* 151; *159:* 198; *176:* 133, 134; *187:* 26, 27, 28, 29; *188:* 22; *199:* 175; *219:* 66
Cooper, Heather *50:* 39
Cooper, Helen *102:* 42, 43, 44
Cooper, Mario *24:* 107
Cooper, Marjorie *7:* 112
Cope, Jane *61:* 201; *108* 52
Copeland, Mark *180:* 12
Copelman, Evelyn *8:* 61; *18:* 25
Copley, Heather *30:* 86; *45:* 57
Corace, Jen *208:* 48
Corbett, Grahame *30:* 114; *43:* 67
Corbino, John *19:* 248
Corcos, Lucille *2:* 223; *10:* 27; *34:* 66
Cordell, Matthew *197:* 93; *199:* 20, 21
Córdova, Amy *220:* 194
Corey, Robert *9:* 34
Corlass, Heather *10:* 7
Cornell, James *27:* 60
Cornell, Jeff *11:* 58
Cornell, Laura *94:* 179; *95:* 25
Corr, Christopher *204:* 98
Corral, Ridrigs *212:* 87
Corrigan, Barbara *8:* 37

Corrigan, Patrick *145:* 149
Corwin, Judith Hoffman *10:* 28
Corwin, Oliver *191:* 119
Cory, Fanny Y. *20:* 113; *48:* 29
Cosentino, Ralph *169:* 32
Cosgrove, Margaret *3:* 100; *47:* 63; *82:* 133
Costabel, Eva Deutsch *45:* 66, 67
Costanza, John *58:* 7, 8, 9
Costello, Chris *86:* 78
Costello, David F. *23:* 55
Côté, Geneviéve *184:* 37, 39; *210:* 256; *211:* 151
Cote, Nancy *126:* 139; *156:* 101; *174:* 101; *182:* 53, 54, 55
Cottenden, Jeff *190:* 45
Couch, Greg *94:* 124; *110:* 13; *162:* 31; *168:* 149; *199:* 22; *216:* 144
Councell, Ruth Tietjen *79:* 29
Courtney, Cathy *58:* 69, 144; *59:* 15; *61:* 20, 87
Courtney, R. *35:* 110
Counihan, Claire *133:* 106
Cousineau, Normand *89:* 180; *112:* 76
Cousins, Lucy *172:* 53, 54; *205:* 34, 35
Couture, Christin *41:* 209
Covarrubias, Miguel *35:* 118, 119, 123, 124, 125
Coville, Katherine *32:* 57; *36:* 167; *92:* 38
Covington, Neverne *113:* 87
Cowdrey, Richard *169:* 170; *178:* 205; *204:* 22, 23; *215:* 31
Cowell, Cressida *140:* 39
Cowell, Lucinda *77:* 54
Cowles, Rose *203:* 164, 167
Cox *43:* 93
Cox, Charles *8:* 20
Cox, David *56:* 37; *90:* 63; *119:* 38
Cox, Palmer *24:* 76, 77
Cox, Steve *140:* 96
Coxe, Molly *69:* 44
Coxon, Michele *158:* 80
Crabb, Gordon *70:* 39
Crabtree, Judith *98:* 42
Craft, Kinuko *22:* 182; *36:* 220; *53:* 122, 123, 148,149; *74:* 12; *81:* 129; *86:* 31; *89:* 139; *127:* 27, 28, 29; *132:* 142; *139:* 38
Craig, Daniel *177:* 67; *180:* 11; *185:* 203; *211:* 212
Craig, David *136:* 198; *205:* 37
Craig, Helen *49:* 76; *62:* 70, 71, 72; *69:* 141; *94:* 42, 43, 44; *112:* 53; *135:* 101, 102; *213:* 45, 46, 47, 55, 81, 82
Crane, Alan H. *1:* 217
Crane, H.M. *13:* 111
Crane, Jack *43:* 183
Crane, Jordan *174:* 21
Crane, Walter *18:* 46, 47, 48, 49, 53, 54, 56, 57, 59, 60, 61; *22:* 128; *24:* 210, 217; *100:* 70, 71
Cravath, Lynne Avril *98:* 45; *182:* 58, 59; *216:* 48; *219:* 61; *220:* 124
Crawford, Allen *212:* 181
Crawford, Denise *137:* 213
Crawford, Will *43:* 77
Credle, Ellis *1:* 69
Czekaj, Jef *217:* 44; *218:* 77
Czernecki, Stefan *154:* 104; *178:* 68, 69
Crespi, Francesca *87:* 90
Cressy, Michael *124:* 55; *203:* 132
Crews, Donald *32:* 59, 60; *76:* 42, 43, 44
Crews, Nina *97:* 49
Crichlow, Ernest *74:* 88; *83:* 203
Crilley, Mark *210:* 71
Croft, James *150:* 57
Crofut, Bob *80:* 87; *81:* 47
Crofut, Susan *23:* 61
Croll, Carolyn *80:* 137; *102:* 52
Cross, Peter *56:* 78; *63:* 60, 65
Crossman, David A. *219:* 38
Crowe, Elizabeth *88:* 144
Crowell, Pers *3:* 125

Cruikshank, George *15:* 76, 83; *22:* 74, 75, 76, 77, 78, 79,80, 81, 82, 84, 137; *24:* 22, 23
Crump, Fred H. *11:* 62
Cruz, Ray *6:* 55; *70:* 234; *123:* 173; *172:* 192
Csatari, Joe *44:* 82; *55:* 152; *63:* 25, 28; *102:* 58
Cuetara, Mittie *158:* 85
Cuffari, Richard *4:* 75; *5:* 98; *6:* 56; *7:* 13,84, 153; *8:* 148, 155; *9:* 89; *11:* 19; *12:* 55, 96,114; *15:* 51, 202; *18:* 5; *20:* 139; *21:* 197; *22:* 14, 192; *23:* 15, 106; *25:* 97; *27:* 133; *28:* 196; *29:* 54; *30:* 85; *31:* 35; *36:* 101; *38:* 171; *42:* 97; *44:* 92, 192; *45:* 212, 213; *46:* 36, 198; *50:* 164; *54:* 80, 136, 137, 145; *56:* 17; *60:* 63; *66:* 49, 50; *70:* 41; *71:* 132; *77:* 157; *78:* 58, 149; *79:* 120; *85:* 2, 152
Cugat, Xavier *19:* 120
Cumings, Art *35:* 160
Cummings, Chris *29:* 167
Cummings, Michael *159:* 142
Cummings, Pat *42:* 61; *61:* 99; *69:* 205; *71:* 57,58; *78:* 24, 25; *93:* 75; *107:* 49, 50; *164:* 259; *203:* 45, 46
Cummings, Richard *24:* 119
Cunette, Lou *20:* 93; *22:* 125
Cunningham, Aline *25:* 180
Cunningham, David *11:* 13
Cunningham, Imogene *16:* 122, 127
Cunningham, Kelley *176:* 159
Cupples, Pat *107:* 12; *126:* 109; *182:* 13; *198:* 68; *217:* 21, 22
Curlee, Lynn *98:* 48; *141:* 39; *190:* 48
Currey, Anna *190:* 145; *202:* 130, 132
Curry, John Steuart *2:* 5; *19:* 84; *34:* 36; *144:* 126
Curry, Tom *127:* 131; *185:* 25, 26
Curtis, Bruce *23:* 96; *30:* 88; *36:* 22
Curtis, Neil *167:* 30
Curtis, Stacy *205:* 38
Cusack, Margaret *58:* 49, 50, 51
Cushman, Doug *65:* 57; *101:* 39, 40; *133:* 179; *157:* 45; *186:* 157; *210:* 76, 77
Cutting, Ann *196:* 194
Cyrus, Kurt *132:* 39; *179:* 36, 37
Czechowski, Alicia *95:* 21; *171:* 37
Czernecki, Stefan *117:* 173

D

Dabcovich, Lydia *25:* 105; *40:* 114; *99:* 75, 76
Dacey, Bob *82:* 175; *152:* 65
d'Achille, Gino *127:* 175, 176
Daily, Don *78:* 197; *220:* 154
Dain, Martin J. *35:* 75
Dale, Penny *127:* 224; *151:* 57; *160:* 89; *197:* 75
Dale, Rae *72:* 197
Daley, Joann *50:* 22
Dalton, Anne *40:* 62; *63:* 119
Daly, Deborah M. *74:* 213
Daly, Jim *103:* 60; *150:* 48
Daly, Jude *138:* 118, 119; *213:* 41
Daly, Nicholas *37:* 53; *76:* 48, 49
Daly, Niki *107:* 15; *114:* 38, 39, 40; *164:* 86; *192:* 53; *198:* 26, 27
Daly, Paul *97:* 205
Dalziel, Brothers *33:* 113
D'Amato, Alex *9:* 48; *20:* 25
D'Amato, Janet *9:* 48; *20:* 25; *26:* 118
D'Amico, Steve *170:* 52
Danalis, Johnny *167:* 27
D'Andrea, Domenick *183:* 108
Daniel, Alan *23:* 59; *29:* 110; *76:* 50, 53, 55, 56; *153:* 76 *115:* 74; *134:* 70
Daniel, Lea *76:* 53, 55; *153:* 76
Daniel, Lewis C. *20:* 216
Daniels, Beau *73:* 4
Daniels, Steve *22:* 16
Daniels, Stewart *56:* 12

Dann, Bonnie *31:* 83
Dann, Penny *82:* 128
Danska, Herbert *24:* 219
Danyell, Alice *20:* 27
Darbyshire, Kristen *218:* 41
Dardik, Helen *208:* 200
Darley, F.O.C. *16:* 145; *19:* 79, 86, 88, 185; *21:* 28,36; *35:* 76, 77, 78, 79, 80, 81; *YABC 2:* 175
Darling, Lois *3:* 59; *23:* 30, 31
Darling, Louis *1:* 40, 41; *2:* 63; *3:* 59; *23:* 30,31; *43:* 54, 57, 59; *121:* 53
Darnell, K.L. *210:* 247
Darrow, David R. *84:* 101
Darrow, Whitney, Jr. *13:* 25; *38:* 220, 221
Darwin, Beatrice *43:* 54
Darwin, Len *24:* 82
Dastolfo, Frank *33:* 179
Dauber, Liz *1:* 22; *3:* 266; *30:* 49
Daugherty, James *3:* 66; *8:* 178; *13:* 27, 28, 161; *18:* 101; *19:* 72; *29:* 108; *32:* 156; *42:* 84; *YABC 1:* 256; *2:* 174
d'Aulaire, Edgar Parin *5:* 51; *66:* 53
d'Aulaire, Ingri Parin *5:* 51; *66:* 53
Davalos, Felipe *99:* 197; *159:* 66; *174:* 163
Davenier, Christine *125:* 88; *127:* 32; *128:* 152; *179:* 39, 40; *216:* 84, 85, 86, 87; *218:* 62, 63
Davick, Linda *151:* 124; *208:* 187
David, Jacques-Louis *193:* 22
David, Jonathan *19:* 37
Davidson, Kevin *28:* 154
Davidson, Raymond *32:* 61
Davie, Helen K. *77:* 48, 49
Davies, Andy Robert *205:* 169
Davies, Lottie *214:* 69
Davis, Allen *20:* 11; *22:* 45; *27:* 222; *29:* 157; *41:* 99; *47:* 99; *50:* 84; *52:* 105
Davis, Bette J. *15:* 53; *23:* 95
Davis, Dimitris *45:* 95
Davis, Eleanor *209:* 33
Davis, Hendon *151:* 122
Davis, Jack E. *145:* 139; *175:* 84, 85; *208:* 102; *210:* 81, 82; *213:* 151
Davis, Jim *32:* 63, 64
Davis, Katie *152:* 52, 53, 54; *208:* 52
Davis, Lambert *110:* 23, 24; *176:* 58
Davis, Marguerite *31:* 38; *34:* 69, 70; *100:* 34; *YABC 1:* 126, 230
Davis, Nelle *69:* 191
Davis, Paul *78:* 214
Davis, Rich *206:* 38
Davis, Stuart *211:* 69
Davis, Yvonne LeBrun *94:* 144
Davisson, Virginia H. *44:* 178
DaVolls, Andy *85:* 53
Dawson, Diane *24:* 127; *42:* 126; *52:* 130; *68:* 104
Dawson, Janine *215:* 198
Dawson, Willow *208:* 54; *216:* 119
Day, Alexandra *67:* 59; *97:* 54; *166:* 65; *169:* 40; *197:* 50, 51, 52, 54
Day, Larry *169:* 88; *185:* 59
Day, Rob *94:* 110; *127:* 24; *197:* 32
Dean, Bob *19:* 211
Dean, David *192:* 55
de Angeli, Marguerite *1:* 77; *27:* 62, 65, 66, 67, 69, 70, 72; *100:* 75, 76; *YABC 1:* 166
DeArmond, Dale *70:* 47
Deas, Michael *27:* 219, 221; *30:* 156; *67:* 134; *72:* 24; *75:* 155; *84:* 206; *88:* 124
Deas, Rich *191:* 87; *193:* 10; *212:* 79
deBarros, Jim *196:* 60
Debon, Nicolas *151:* 60; *177:* 46
de Bosschere, Jean *19:* 252; *21:* 4; *186:* 44, 45
De Bruyn, M(onica) G. *13:* 30, 31
Decker, C.B. *172:* 120; *215:* 94
De Cuir, John F. *1:* 28, 29
Deeter, Catherine *74:* 110; *103:* 150; *137:* 50

Degen, Bruce *40:* 227, 229; *57:* 28, 29; *56:* 156; *75:* 229; *76:* 19; *81:* 36, 37; *92:* 26; *93:* 199; *97:* 56, 58, 59; *124:* 40; *147:* 39, 40, 41; *168:* 23; *205:* 45, 46
De Grazia *14:* 59; *39:* 56, 57
DeGrazio, George *88:* 40
deGroat, Diane *9:* 39; *18:* 7; *23:* 123; *28:* 200, 201; *31:* 58, 59; *34:* 151; *41:* 152; *43:* 88; *46:* 40, 200; *49:* 163; *50:* 89; *52:* 30, 34; *54:* 43; *63:* 5; *70:* 136; *71:* 99; *73:* 117,156; *77:* 34; *85:* 48; *86:* 201; *87:* 142; *90:* 72, 73, 143; *95:* 182; *111:* 123; *118:* 160; *126:* 8; *130:* 130; *138:* 93, 94; *169:* 46, 47
de Groot, Lee *6:* 21
Deines, Brian *110:* 139; *220:* 36, 37
DeJohn, Marie *89:* 78
Dekhteryov, B. *61:* 158
de Kiefte, Kees *94:* 107
Delacre, Lulu *36:* 66; *156:* 35; *202:* 10, 53; *209:* 36
Delaney, A. *21:* 78
Delaney, Michael *180:* 16
Delaney, Molly *80:* 43
Delaney, Ned *28:* 68; *56:* 80; *102:* 11
DeLapine, Jim *79:* 21
De La Roche Saint Andre, Anne *75:* 37
de Larrea, Victoria *6:* 119, 204; *29:* 103; *72:* 203; *87:* 199
DeLeon, Melanie *210:* 43
Delessert, Étienne *7:* 140; *46:* 61, 62, 63, 65, 67, 68; *130:* 38, 39, 40, 41, 42; *179:* 46, 47, 48, 49; *YABC 2:* 209
Delezenne, Christine *186:* 126
Del Negro, Janice *196:* 161
Delon, Melanie *216:* 30
DeLorenzo, Christopher *154:* 149
Delulio, John *15:* 54
DeLuna, Tony *88:* 95
Demarest, Chris L. *45:* 68, 69, 70; *73:* 172, 173, 176; *78:* 106; *82:* 48, 49; *89:* 212; *92:* 86; *128:* 57, 58; *175:* 46, 48
De Mejo, Oscar *40:* 67
De Muth, Roger *205:* 184; *221:* 35
Demi *11:* 135; *15:* 245; *66:* 129, 130; *89:* 216; *102:* 66, 67, 68; *210:* 86, 87, 89
Denetsosie, Hoke *13:* 126; *82:* 34
Denise, Christopher *147:* 43, 44; *176:* 101; *193:* 35, 36, 37; *201:* 37
Dennis, Morgan *18:* 68, 69; *64:* 89
Dennis, Wesley *2:* 87; *3:* 111; *11:* 132; *18:* 71, 72, 73, 74; *22:* 9; *24:* 196, 200; *46:* 178; *69:* 94, 96; *129:* 62
Denos, Julia *202:* 26
Denslow, W.W. *16:* 84, 85, 86, 87; *18:* 19, 20, 24; *29:* 211; *100:* 21
Denton, Kady MacDonald *110:* 82; *130:* 70; *181:* 54, 55, 56; *192:* 75
Denton, Phil *220:* 6
Denton, Terry *72:* 163; *174:* 26; *186:* 52; *196:* 83, 84
DePalma, Mary Newell *132:* 114; *139:* 75; *185:* 30, 31; *186:* 121; *213:* 62
dePaola, Tomie *8:* 95; *9:* 93; *11:* 69; *25:* 103; *28:* 157; *29:* 80; *39:* 52, 53; *40:* 226; *46:* 187; *59:* 61, 62, 63, 64, 65, 66, 67, 68, 69, 71, 72, 74; *62:* 19; *108:* 63, 67, 68, 70; *155:* 62, 64, 66; *180:* 105; *200:* 47, 48, 49, 50
Deraney, Michael J. *77:* 35; *78:* 148
deRosa, Dee *70:* 48; *71:* 210; *91:* 78
Dervaux, Isabelle *111:* 117
DeSaix, Deborah Durland *180:* 15; *188:* 24
De Saulles, Tony *119:* 39
de Sève, Peter *146:* 261; *207:* 78; *219:* 42
Deshaprabhu, Meera Dayal *86:* 192
Desimini, Lisa *86:* 68; *94:* 47; *96:* 7; *104:* 107; *125:* 194; *131:* 180; *172:* 56; *216:* 89, 90
de St. Menin, Charles *70:* 17
Detmold, Edward J. *22:* 104, 105, 106, 107; *35:* 120; *64:* 5; *YABC 2:* 203
Detrich, Susan *20:* 133

Deutermann, Diana *77:* 175
DeVelasco, Joseph E. *21:* 51
de Veyrac, Robert *YABC 2:* 19
DeVille, Edward A. *4:* 235
de Visser, John *55:* 119
Devito, Bert *12:* 164
Devlin, Harry *11:* 74; *74:* 63, 65; *136:* 77, 78
Dewan, Ted *108:* 73; *157:* 55; *165:* 129
Dewar, Nick *133:* 122
Dewdney, Anna *184:* 43, 44
Dewey, Ariane *7:* 64; *33:* 195; *35:* 208; *68:* 16,17; *75:* 46; *93:* 91; *94:* 197; *109:* 65, 66, 67; *125:* 2, 3, 4, 5; *127:* 188; *143:* 25; *178:* 17, 19, 74; *188:* 166; *202:* 164
Dewey, Jennifer (Owings) *58:* 54; *64:* 214; *65:* 207; *88:* 169; *103:* 45
Dewey, Kenneth *39:* 62; *51:* 23; *56:* 163
de Zanger, Arie *30:* 40
Diakité, Baba Wagué *174:* 28
Diamond, Donna *21:* 200; *23:* 63; *26:* 142; *35:* 83, 84, 85, 86, 87, 88, 89; *38:* 78; *40:* 147; *44:* 152; *50:* 144; *53:* 126; *69:* 46, 47, 48, 201; *71:* 133; *123:* 19
Dias, Ron *71:* 67
Diaz, David *80:* 213; *96:* 83, 84; *108:* 228; *110:* 29; *149:* 106; *150:* 63; *179:* 160; *184:* 95, 97; *189:* 51, 52, 53; *221:* 86
Dibley, Glin *138:* 83; *141:* 128; *211:* 162; *221:* 61
DiCesare, Joe *70:* 38; *71:* 63, 106; *79:* 214; *93:* 147; *116:* 217; *143:* 111; *166:* 57
Dick, John Henry *8:* 181
Dickens, Frank *34:* 131
Dickey, Robert L. *15:* 279
Dickson, Mora *84:* 21
Didier, Sam *166:* 114
Dietz, James *128:* 223; *193:* 136
di Fate, Vincent *37:* 70; *90:* 11; *93:* 60; *109:* 219, 220
Di Fiori, Lawrence *10:* 51; *12:* 190; *27:* 97; *40:* 219; *93:* 57; *130:* 45
Digby, Desmond *97:* 180
Dignan, James *196:* 143
Di Grazia, Thomas *32:* 66; *35:* 241
Dillard, Annie *10:* 32
Dillard, Sarah *136:* 186; *217:* 53
Dillon, Corinne B. *1:* 139
Dillon, Diane *4:* 104, 167; *6:* 23; *13:* 29; *15:* 99; *26:* 148; *27:* 136, 201; *51:* 29, 48, 51, 52, 53, 54,55, 56, 57, 58, 59, 60, 61, 62; *54:* 155; *56:* 69; *58:* 127,128; *61:* 95; *62:* 27; *64:* 46; *68:* 3; *69:* 209; *74:* 89; *79:* 92; *86:* 89; *92:* 28, 177; *93:* 7, 210; *94:* 239, 240; *97:* 167; *106:* 58, 59,61, 64; *107:* 3; *139:* 246; *167:* 77; *189:* 202; *191:* 191; *194:* 45, 46, 48, 49
Dillon, Leo *4:* 104, 167; *6:* 23; *13:* 29; *15:* 99; *26:* 148; *27:* 136, 201; *51:* 29, 48, 51, 52, 53, 54,55, 56, 57, 58, 59, 60, 61, 62; *54:* 155; *56:* 69; *58:* 127,128; *61:* 95; *62:* 27; *64:* 46; *68:* 3; *69:* 209; *74:* 89; *79:* 92; *86:* 89; *92:* 28, 177; *93:* 7, 210; *94:* 239, 240; *97:* 167; *106:* 58, 59,61, 64; *107:* 3; *139:* 246; *167:* 77; *189:* 202; *191:* 191; *194:* 45, 46, 48, 49
Dillon, Sharon Saseen *59:* 179, 188
DiMaccio, Gerald *121:* 80
DiMaggio, Joe *36:* 22
DiMassi, Gina *169:* 17
Dinan, Carol *25:* 169; *59:* 75
Dines, Glen *7:* 66, 67
Dinesen, Thomas *44:* 37
Dinh, Pham Viet *167:* 184
Dinnerstein, Harvey *42:* 63, 64, 65, 66, 67, 68; *50:* 146
Dinsdale, Mary *10:* 65; *11:* 171
Dinyer, Eric *86:* 148; *109:* 163; *110:* 239; *124:* 11; *150:* 69; *170:* 4; *171:* 30
Dion, Nathalie *170:* 124; *213:* 52
DiRocco, Carl *181:* 23

DiSalvo-Ryan, DyAnne *59:* 77; *62:* 185; *117:* 46; *144:* 64; *150:* 153; *186:* 162
Disney, Walt *28:* 71, 72, 73, 76, 77, 78, 79, 80, 81, 87, 88, 89,90, 91, 94
DiTerlizzi, Tony *105:* 7; *147:* 22; *154:* 31, 32, 33; *214:* 74
Divito, Anna *83:* 159
Dixon, Don *74:* 17; *109:* 196
Dixon, Larry *127:* 125
Dixon, Maynard *20:* 165
Doares, Robert G. *20:* 39
Dob, Bob *205:* 14
Dobias, Frank *22:* 162
Dobrin, Arnold *4:* 68
Dobson, Steven Gaston *102:* 103
Docherty, Thomas *218:* 45, 46
Dockray, Tracy *139:* 77
Docktor, Irv *43:* 70
Dodd, Ed *4:* 69
Dodd, Emma *203:* 57
Dodd, Julie *74:* 73
Dodd, Lynley *35:* 92; *86:* 71; *132:* 45, 46, 47
Dodge, Bill *96:* 36; *118:* 7, 8, 9; *133:* 135
Dodgson, Charles L. *20:* 148; *33:* 146; *YABC 2:* 98
Dodson, Bert *9:* 138; *14:* 195; *42:* 55; *54:* 8; *60:* 49; *101:* 125
Dodson, Liz Brenner *105:* 117; *111:* 15
Dohanos, Stevan *16:* 10
Dolce, J. Ellen *74:* 147; *75:* 41
Dolch, Marguerite P. *50:* 64
Dolesch, Susanne *34:* 49
Dollar, Diane *57:* 32
Dolobowsky, Mena *81:* 54
Dolson, Hildegarde *5:* 57
Domanska, Janina *6:* 66, 67; *YABC 1:* 166
Domi *134:* 113
Dominguez, El *53:* 94
Domjan, Joseph *25:* 93
Domm, Jeffrey C. *84:* 69; *135:* 70
Donahey, William *68:* 209
Donahue, Dorothy *76:* 170
Donahue, Vic *2:* 93; *3:* 190; *9:* 44
Donald, Elizabeth *4:* 18
Donalty, Alison *149:* 195, 196, 197
Donato *85:* 59; *149:* 204; *191:* 19
Donato, Michael A. *200:* 143
Doner, Kim *208:* 57
Doney, Todd L.W. *87:* 12; *93:* 112; *98:* 135; *101:* 57; *104:* 40; *118:* 163; *135:* 162, 163; *151:* 18
Donna, Natalie *9:* 52
Donohue, Dorothy *95:* 2; *132:* 30; *176:* 54, 55; *178:* 77, 78, 79
Dooling, Michael *82:* 19; *105:* 55; *106:* 224; *125:* 135; *171:* 46; *172:* 12; *176:* 120; *197:* 89; *220:* 39, 40
Doran, Ben-Ami *128:* 189
Doran, Colleen *211:* 48
Dore, Gustave *18:* 169, 172, 175; *19:* 93, 94, 95, 96, 97, 98,99, 100, 101, 102, 103, 104, 105; *23:* 188; *25:* 197, 199
Doremus, Robert *6:* 62; *13:* 90; *30:* 95, 96, 97; *38:* 97
Dorfman, Ronald *11:* 128
Doriau *86:* 59; *91:* 152
Dorman, Brandon *197:* 35; *204:* 6; *210:* 104; *212:* 95; *216:* 156
Dormer, Frank W. *200:* 55
Dorros, Arthur *78:* 42, 43; *91:* 28
Doruyter, Karel *165:* 105
dos Santos, Joyce Audy *57:* 187, 189
Doty, Roy *28:* 98; *31:* 32; *32:* 224; *46:* 157; *82:* 71; *142:* 7
Doucet, Bob *132:* 238; *169:* 159
Dougherty, Charles *16:* 204; *18:* 74
Doughty, Rebecca *177:* 174
Doughty, Thomas *118:* 31; *140:* 60
Douglas, Aaron *31:* 103
Douglas, Carole Nelson *73:* 48
Douglas, Goray *13:* 151

Dow, Brian *150:* 92
Dowd, Jason *132:* 51, 52; *164:* 244
Dowd, Vic *3:* 244; *10:* 97
Dowden, Anne Ophelia *7:* 70, 71; *13:* 120
Dowdy, Mrs. Regera *29:* 100
Downard, Barry *202:* 32
Downes, Belinda *180:* 29
Downing, Julie *60:* 140; *81:* 50; *86:* 200; *99:* 129
Doyle, Janet *56:* 31
Doyle, Richard *21:* 31, 32, 33; *23:* 231; *24:* 177; *31:* 87
Draper, Angie *43:* 84
Drath, Bill *26:* 34
Drawson, Blair *17:* 53; *126:* 65
Dray, Matt *177:* 47
Drescher, Henrik *105:* 60, 62, 63; *172:* 72
Drescher, Joan *30:* 100, 101; *35:* 245; *52:* 168; *137:* 52
Dressell, Peggy *186:* 41
Drew, Janet *201:* 177
Drew, Patricia *15:* 100
Dronzek, Laura *199:* 28, 29; *207:* 69
Drummond, Allan *209:* 41
Drummond, V.H. *6:* 70
Drury, Christian Potter *105:* 97; *186:* 224
Dubanevich, Arlene *56:* 44
Dubin, Jill *205:* 56; *217:* 25
Dubois, Claude K. *196:* 2
Dubois, Gerard *182:* 9
DuBurke, Randy *187:* 89
Ducak, Danilo *99:* 130; *108:* 214
Duchesne, Janet *6:* 162; *79:* 8
Duda, Jana *102:* 155; *209:* 134
Dudash, C. Michael *32:* 122; *77:* 134; *82:* 149; *212:* 93, 94
Duer, Douglas *34:* 177
Duewell, Kristina *195:* 76
Duffy, Daniel Mark *76:* 37; *101:* 196; *108:* 147, 148
Duffy, Joseph *38:* 203
Duffy, Pat *28:* 153
Dugan, Karen *181:* 26; *202:* 35
Dugin, Andrej *77:* 60
Dugina, Olga *77:* 60
Duke, Chris *8:* 195; *139:* 164
Duke, Kate *87:* 186; *90:* 78, 79, 80, 81; *192:* 21, 59, 60, 61, 63
Duke, Marion *165:* 87
Dulac, Edmund *19:* 108, 109, 110, 111, 112, 113, 114, 115, 117; *23:* 187; *25:* 152; *YABC 1:* 37; *2:* 147
Dulac, Jean *13:* 64
Dumas, Philippe *52:* 36, 37, 38, 39, 40, 41, 42, 43, 45; *119:* 40, 41, 42
Dunaway, Nancy *108:* 161
Dunbar, James *76:* 63
Dunbar, Polly *181:* 60, 61; *211:* 51, 52, 53; *212:* 42
Duncan, Beverly *72:* 92
Duncan, John *116:* 94
Dunn, H.T. *62:* 196
Dunn, Harvey *34:* 78, 79, 80, 81
Dunn, Iris *5:* 175
Dunn, Phoebe *5:* 175
Dunne, Jeanette *72:* 57, 173, 222
Dunnick, Regan *176:* 51; *178:* 83, 84; *219:* 36
Dunnington, Tom *3:* 36; *18:* 281; *25:* 61; *31:* 159; *35:* 168; *48:* 195; *79:* 144; *82:* 230
Dunn-Ramsey, Marcy *117:* 131
Dunrea, Olivier *59:* 81; *118:* 53, 54; *124:* 43
Duntze, Dorothee *88:* 28; *160:* 76
Dupasquier, Philippe *86:* 75; *104:* 76; *151:* 63
duPont, Lindsay Harper *207:* 39
DuQuette, Keith *90:* 83; *155:* 73, 74
Durand, Delphine *200:* 56
Durham, Sarah *192:* 248
Durney, Ryan *208:* 122
Duroussy, Nathalie *146:* 150
Durrell, Julie *82:* 62; *94:* 62
Dutz *6:* 59

Duvoisin, Roger *2:* 95; *6:* 76, 77; *7:* 197; *28:* 125; *30:* 101, 102, 103, 104, 105, 107; *47:* 205; *84:* 254
Dyer, Dale *141:* 71
Dyer, Jane *75:* 219; *129:* 28; *147:* 49, 50, 51; *168:* 121; *190:* 4; *191:* 57, 59, 60; *203:* 4
Dyer, Sarah *212:* 40
Dypold, Pat *15:* 37

E

E.V.B.
    See Boyle, Eleanor Vere (Gordon)
Eachus, Jennifer *29:* 74; *82:* 201; *164:* 153
Eadie, Bob *63:* 36
Eagle, Bruce *95:* 119
Eagle, Ellen *82:* 121; *89:* 3
Eagle, Jeremy *141:* 71
Eagle, Michael *11:* 86; *20:* 9; *23:* 18; *27:* 122; *28:* 57; *34:* 201; *44:* 189; *73:* 9; *78:* 235; *85:* 43
Earl-Bridges, Michele *159:* 128
Earle, Edwin *56:* 27
Earle, Olive L. *7:* 75
Earle, Vana *27:* 99
Earley, Lori *132:* 2; *186:* 4; *195:* 8
Early, Margaret *72:* 59
East, Jacqueline *218:* 198
East, Stella *131:* 223
Eastman, P.D. *33:* 57
Easton, Reginald *29:* 181
Eaton, Tom *4:* 62; *6:* 64; *22:* 99; *24:* 124
Ebbeler, Jeffrey *193:* 62; *206:* 45
Ebel, Alex *11:* 89
Eberbach, Andrea *192:* 115
Ebert, Len *9:* 191; *44:* 47
Echevarria, Abe *37:* 69
Echo Hawk, Bunky *187:* 192
Eckersley, Maureen *48:* 62
Eckert, Horst *72:* 62
Ede, Janina *33:* 59
Edens, Cooper *49:* 81, 82, 83, 84, 85; *112:* 58
Edens, John *109:* 115
Edgar, Sarah E. *41:* 97
Edgerton, Perky *195:* 144
Edliq, Emily S. *131:* 107
Edrien *11:* 53
Edwards, Freya *45:* 102
Edwards, George Wharton *31:* 155
Edwards, Gunvor *2:* 71; *25:* 47; *32:* 71; *54:* 106
Edwards, Jeanne *29:* 257
Edwards, Linda Strauss *21:* 134; *39:* 123; *49:* 88, 89
Edwards, Michelle *152:* 62, 63
Edwards, Wallace *170:* 55
Egan, Tim *155:* 76, 77, 78
Egge, David *102:* 71
Eggenhofer, Nicholas *2:* 81
Eggleton, Bob *74:* 40; *81:* 190, 191; *105:* 6; *121:* 183; *149:* 203; *166:* 215
Egielski, Richard *11:* 90; *16:* 208; *33:* 236; *38:* 35; *49:* 91, 92, 93, 95, 212, 213, 214, 216; *79:* 122; *106:* 67, 68, 69; *134:* 135; *144:* 244; *163:* 82, 84; *207:* 125
Ehlert, Lois *35:* 97; *69:* 51; *112:* 7; *113:* 208; *128:* 63, 64, 65; *172:* 77, 79, 80; *220:* 43, 44, 45, 46, 47, 48
Ehrlich, Bettina *1:* 83
Eitan, Ora *160:* 165
Eichenberg, Fritz *1:* 79; *9:* 54; *19:* 248; *23:* 170; *24:* 200; *26:* 208; *50:* 67, 68, 69, 70, 71, 72, 73,74, 75, 77, 79, 80, 81; *60:* 165; *100:* 137; *YABC 1:* 104, 105; *2:* 213
Einsel, Naiad *10:* 35; *29:* 136
Einsel, Walter *10:* 37
Einzig, Susan *3:* 77; *43:* 78; *67:* 155; *129:* 154
Eisner, Will *165:* 82, 83

Eitzen, Allan *9:* 56; *12:* 212; *14:* 226; *21:* 194; *38:* 162; *76:* 218
Eldridge, H. *54:* 109
Eldridge, Harold *43:* 83
Elgaard, Greta *19:* 241
Elgin, Kathleen *9:* 188; *39:* 69
Ellacott, S.E. *19:* 118
Elliot, David *192:* 26; *208:* 62, 63
Elliott, Mark *93:* 69; *105:* 108; *107:* 123; *140:* 53; *165:* 189; *173:* 67; *195:* 95; *203:* 67; *210:* 99; *221:* 57, 70
Elliott, Sarah M. *14:* 58
Ellis, Carson *216:* 210
Ellis, Dianne *130:* 208
Ellis, Jan Davey *88:* 50; *115:* 80
Ellis, Richard *130:* 47, 48
Ellison, Chris *196:* 66; *199:* 131; *207:* 193
Ellison, Pauline *55:* 21
Ellwand, David *213:* 60
Elmer, Richard *78:* 5
Elmore, Larry *90:* 8
Elschner, Géraldine *183:* 38
Elwell, Peter *195:* 150
Elwell, Tristan *110:* 39; *121:* 182; *127:* 46; *137:* 144; *141:* 173; *151:* 236; *158:* 264; *167:* 119, 120, 121; *169:* 20; *190:* 12; *202:* 16
Elzbieta *88:* 80, 81
Ember, Kathi *214:* 147
Emberley, Ed *8:* 53; *70:* 53, 54; *146:* 65, 69, 70; *218:* 50
Emberley, Rebecca *218:* 50
Emberley, Michael *34:* 83; *80:* 72; *119:* 47, 48; *147:* 100; *158:* 115; *189:* 62, 64; *203:* 87, 89
Emerling, Dorothy *104:* 27
Emery, Leslie *49:* 187
Emmett, Bruce *49:* 147; *80:* 175; *101:* 206; *220:* 200
Emry-Perrott, Jennifer *61:* 57
Emshwiller, Ed *174:* 45
Endle, Kate *191:* 167; *207:* 41
Engel, Diana *70:* 57
Engle, Mort *38:* 64
Englebert, Victor *8:* 54
English, Mark *101:* 207; *220:* 201
Enik, Ted *142:* 39
Enos, Randall *20:* 183
Enright, Maginel Wright *19:* 240, 243; *39:* 31, 35, 36
Enrique, Romeo *34:* 135
Ensor, Barbara *180:* 30
Epstein, Stephen *50:* 142, 148
Erdogan, Buket *174:* 179
Erdrich, Louise *141:* 62
Erhard, Walter *1:* 152
Erickson, Jim *196:* 190
Erickson, Phoebe *11:* 83; *59:* 85
Erikson, Mel *31:* 69
Eriksson, Eva *63:* 88, 90, 92, 93; *203:* 99; *207:* 44
Ering, Timothy Basil *131:* 100; *176:* 63, 64; *202:* 29; *204:* 8
Erlbruch, Wolf *181:* 66
Ernst, Lisa Campbell *47:* 147; *95:* 47; *154:* 46, 47, 48; *164:* 88; *212:* 45
Esco, Jo *61:* 103
Escourido, Joseph *4:* 81
Escrivá, Viví *119:* 51; *181:* 36
Essakalli, Julie Klear *200:* 58
Este, Kirk *33:* 111
Estep, David *73:* 57
Estes, Eleanor *91:* 66
Estoril, Jean *32:* 27
Estrada, Pau *74:* 76
Estrada, Ric *5:* 52, 146; *13:* 174
Etchemendy, Teje *38:* 68
Etheredges, the *73:* 12
Etienne, Kirk-Albert *145:* 184
Ets, Marie Hall *2:* 102

Ettlinger, Doris *171:* 98; *186:* 106; *197:* 126; *214:* 125
Eulalie *YABC 2:* 315
Evangelista, Theresa M. *213:* 67
Evans, Greg *73:* 54, 55, 56; *143:* 40, 41
Evans, Katherine *5:* 64
Evans, Leslie *144:* 227; *207:* 57; *214:* 88; *221:* 28
Evans, Shane W. *159:* 142; *160:* 190; *168:* 39; *188:* 88; *189:* 66, 67, 68
Everitt, Betsy *151:* 110
Ewart, Claire *76:* 69; *145:* 59, 60
Ewing, Carolyn *66:* 143; *79:* 52
Ewing, Juliana Horatia *16:* 92
Eyolfson, Norman *98:* 154

F

Fabian, Limbert *136:* 114
Facklam, Paul *132:* 62
Falconer, Ian *125:* 66; *179:* 59
Falconer, Pearl *34:* 23
Falkenstern, Lisa *70:* 34; *76:* 133; *78:* 171; *127:* 16; *191:* 151
Falls, C.B. *1:* 19; *38:* 71, 72, 73, 74
Falter, John *40:* 169, 170
Falwell, Cathryn *118:* 77; *137:* 185; *196:* 71, 72
Fancher, Lou *138:* 219; *141:* 64; *144:* 199; *177:* 51; *214:* 95; *221:* 63
Fanelli, Sara *89:* 63; *126:* 69
Faria, Rosana *150:* 143
Faricy, Patrick *185:* 182; *212:* 61
Farooqi, Musharraf Ali *207:* 46
Farmer, Andrew *49:* 102
Farmer, Peter *24:* 108; *38:* 75
Farnsworth, Bill *93:* 189; *116:* 147; *124:* 8; *135:* 52; *146:* 242, 243, 244; *182:* 176; *186:* 31, 83, 84, 85; *191:* 197
Farquharson, Alexander *46:* 75
Farrell, David *40:* 135
Farrell, Russell *196:* 38
Farris, David *74:* 42
Fasolino, Teresa *118:* 145
Fatigati, Evelyn *24:* 112
Fatus, Sophie *182:* 74; *190:* 218
Faul-Jansen, Regina *22:* 117
Faulkner, Jack *6:* 169
Faulkner, Matt *161:* 174; *167:* 75
Fava, Rita *2:* 29
Fax, Elton C. *1:* 101; *4:* 2; *12:* 77; *25:* 107
Fay *43:* 93
Fearnley, Jan *153:* 82, 83; *205:* 63, 64, 65
Fearrington, Ann *146:* 80
Federspiel, Marian *33:* 51
Fedorov, Nickolai Ivanovich *110:* 102
Feelings, Tom *5:* 22; *8:* 56; *12:* 153; *16:* 105; *30:* 196; *49:* 37; *61:* 101; *69:* 56, 57; *93:* 74; *105:* 88
Fehr, Terrence *21:* 87
Feiffer, Jules *3:* 91; *8:* 58; *61:* 66, 67, 70, 74, 76,77, 78; *111:* 47, 48, 49, 50; *132:* 122; *157:* 62; *201:* 48, 49, 50
Feigeles, Neil *41:* 242
Feldman, Elyse *86:* 7
Feller, Gene *33:* 130
Fellows, Muriel H. *10:* 42
Felstead, Cathie *116:* 85
Felts, Shirley *33:* 71; *48:* 59
Fennell, Tracy *171:* 69
Fennelli, Maureen *38:* 181
Fenton, Carroll Lane *5:* 66; *21:* 39
Fenton, Mildred Adams *5:* 66; *21:* 39
Ferguson, Peter *177:* 30, 31; *181:* 154; *197:* 4; *199:* 40; *215:* 104; *221:* 66
Ferguson, Walter W. *34:* 86
Fernandes, Eugenie *77:* 67; *205:* 68
Fernandes, Stanislaw *70:* 28
Fernandez, Fernando *77:* 57

Fernandez, Laura *77:* 153; *101:* 117; *131:* 222; *170:* 119; *175:* 182
Ferrari, Alex *188:* 121
Ferrington, Susan *172:* 22
Fetz, Ingrid *11:* 67; *12:* 52; *16:* 205; *17:* 59; *29:* 105; *30:* 108, 109; *32:* 149; *43:* 142; *56:* 29; *60:* 34; *85:* 48; *87:* 146
Fiammenghi, Gioia *9:* 66; *11:* 44; *12:* 206; *13:* 57, 59; *52:* 126, 129; *66:* 64; *85:* 83; *91:* 161; *166:* 169
Fiedler, Joseph Daniel *96:* 42; *113:* 173; *129:* 164; *146:* 17; *159:* 68; *162:* 104
Field, Rachel *15:* 113
Fielding, David *70:* 124
Fieser, Stephen *152:* 36
Fine, Howard *145:* 159; *159:* 64; *165:* 134; *174:* 129; *181:* 68
Fine, Peter K. *43:* 210
Finger, Helen *42:* 81
Fink, Sam *18:* 119
Finlay, Winifred *23:* 72
Finney, Pat *79:* 215
Fiore, Peter *99:* 196; *125:* 139; *144:* 225; *160:* 169; *180:* 72; *212:* 103
Fiorentino, Al *3:* 240
Firehammer, Karla *174:* 202; *221:* 183
Firmin, Charlotte *29:* 75; *48:* 70
Firmin, Peter *58:* 63, 64, 65, 67, 68, 70, 71
Firth, Barbara *81:* 208; *127:* 218; *179:* 62
Fischel, Lillian *40:* 204
Fischer, Hans *25:* 202
Fischer, Scott M. *207:* 37; *217:* 29
Fischer-Nagel, Andreas *56:* 50
Fischer-Nagel, Heiderose *56:* 50
Fisher, Carolyn *154:* 50
Fisher, Chris *79:* 62; *158:* 248; *188:* 195
Fisher, Cynthia *117:* 45; *137:* 118; *195:* 40
Fisher, Jeffrey *142:* 80
Fisher, Leonard Everett *3:* 6; *4:* 72, 86; *6:* 197; *9:* 59; *16:* 151, 153; *23:* 44; *27:* 134; *29:* 26; *34:* 87, 89, 90, 91, 93, 94, 95, 96; *40:* 206; *50:* 150; *60:* 158; *73:* 68, 70, 71, 72, 73; *176:* 71, 72, 73; *208:* 131; *YABC 2:* 169
Fisher, Lois *20:* 62; *21:* 7
Fisher, Valorie *177:* 55; *214:* 92
Fisk, Nicholas *25:* 112
Fitschen, Marilyn *2:* 20, 21; *20:* 48
Fitz-Maurice, Jeff *175:* 2
Fitzgerald, F.A. *15:* 116; *25:* 86, 87
Fitzgerald, Joanne *157:* 153, 154; *198:* 34, 35
Fitzgerald, Royce *205:* 5
Fitzhugh, Louise *1:* 94; *9:* 163; *45:* 75, 78
Fitzhugh, Susie *11:* 117
Fitzpatrick, Jim *109:* 130
Fitzpatrick, Marie-Louise *125:* 69, 70; *189:* 72, 73
Fitzsimmons, Arthur *14:* 128
Fix, Philippe *26:* 102
Flack, Marjorie *21:* 67; *100:* 93; *YABC 2:* 122
Flagg, James Montgomery *17:* 227
Flavin, Teresa *132:* 115; *186:* 119
Flax, Zeona *2:* 245
Fleetwood, Tony *171:* 51
Fleishman, Seymour *14:* 232; *24:* 87
Fleming, Denise *71:* 179; *81:* 58; *126:* 71, 72, 73; *173:* 52, 53
Fleming, Guy *18:* 41
Flesher, Vivienne *85:* 55
Fletcher, Claire *80:* 106; *157:* 159
Flint, Russ *74:* 80
Floate, Helen *111:* 163
Floca, Brian *155:* 88, 89; *190:* 10, 66, 67
Floethe, Richard *3:* 131; *4:* 90
Floherty, John J., Jr. *5:* 68
Flook, Helen *160:* 81
Flora, James *1:* 96; *30:* 111, 112
Florczak, Robert *166:* 51
Florian, Douglas *19:* 122; *83:* 64, 65; *125:* 71, 72, 74, 76; *128:* 130; *177:* 58, 60
Flory, Jane *22:* 111

Flower, Renee *125:* 109
Floyd, Gareth *1:* 74; *17:* 245; *48:* 63; *62:* 35,36, 37, 39, 40, 41; *74:* 245; *79:* 56
Fluchere, Henri A. *40:* 79
Flynn, Alice *183:* 2
Flynn, Barbara *7:* 31; *9:* 70
Fogarty, Thomas *15:* 89
Foley, Greg *190:* 69
Folger, Joseph *9:* 100
Folkard, Charles *22:* 132; *29:* 128, 257, 258
Foott, Jeff *42:* 202
Forberg, Ati *12:* 71, 205; *14:* 1; *22:* 113; *26:* 22; *48:* 64, 65
Ford, George *24:* 120; *31:* 70, 177; *58:* 126; *81:* 103; *107:* 91; *136:* 100; *194:* 47; *208:* 81; *218:* 56
Ford, Gilbert *199:* 10
Ford, H.J. *16:* 185, 186
Ford, Jason *174:* 119
Ford, Pamela Baldwin *27:* 104
Fordham, John *168:* 160, 161
Foreman, Michael *2:* 110, 111; *67:* 99; *73:* 78, 79, 80,81, 82; *93:* 146; *135:* 55, 56, 57; *184:* 58, 59; *216:* 100, 101, 102, 103
Forrester, Victoria *40:* 83
Forsey, Chris *140:* 210
Fortnum, Peggy *6:* 29; *20:* 179; *24:* 211; *26:* 76, 77, 78; *39:* 78; *58:* 19, 21, 23, 27; *YABC 1:* 148
Fortune, Eric *191:* 52
Foster, Brad W. *34:* 99
Foster, Genevieve *2:* 112
Foster, Gerald L. *7:* 78; *198:* 40
Foster, Jon *146:* 18; *198:* 7
Foster, Laura Louise *6:* 79
Foster, Marian Curtis *23:* 74; *40:* 42
Foster, Sally *58:* 73, 74
Fotheringham, Edwin *219:* 32
Foucher, Adele *47:* 118
Foust, Mitch *168:* 50
Fowler, Jim *184:* 190
Fowler, Mel *36:* 127
Fowler, Richard *87:* 219
Fowles, Shelley *165:* 127; *205:* 72
Fox, Charles Phillip *12:* 84
Fox, Christyan *188:* 36
Fox, Jim *6:* 187
Fox, Nathan *208:* 64
Fox-Davies, Sarah *76:* 150; *182:* 63; *199:* 42, 43
Frace, Charles *15:* 118
Frailey, Joy *72:* 108
Frame, Paul *2:* 45, 145; *9:* 153; *10:* 124; *21:* 71; *23:* 62; *24:* 123; *27:* 106; *31:* 48; *32:* 159; *34:* 195; *38:* 136; *42:* 55; *44:* 139; *60:* 39, 40, 41, 42, 43, 44, 46; *73:* 183
Frampton, David *85:* 72; *102:* 33; *139:* 182; *152:* 37; *189:* 171
Francis, Guy *198:* 164
Francois, Andre *25:* 117
Francoise
　See Seignobosc, Francoise
Frank, Lola Edick *2:* 199
Frank, Mary *4:* 54; *34:* 100
Franke, Phil *45:* 91
Frankel, Alona *66:* 70
Frankel, Julie *40:* 84, 85, 202
Frankenberg, Robert *22:* 116; *30:* 50; *38:* 92, 94, 95; *68:* 111
Frankfeldt, Gwen *84:* 223; *110:* 92
Frankland, David *169:* 137; *182:* 164; *201:* 159
Franklin, Ashton *165:* 144
Franklin, John *24:* 22
Franson, Leanne R. *111:* 57, 58; *151:* 7
Frascino, Edward *9:* 133; *29:* 229; *33:* 190; *48:* 80, 81, 82, 83, 84, 85, 86
Frasconi, Antonio *6:* 80; *27:* 208; *53:* 41, 43, 45, 47,48; *68:* 145; *73:* 226; *131:* 68
Fraser, Betty *2:* 212; *6:* 185; *8:* 103; *31:* 72,73; *43:* 136; *111:* 76

Fraser, Eric *38:* 78; *41:* 149, 151
Fraser, F.A. *22:* 234
Fraser, James *171:* 68
Fraser, Mary Ann *137:* 63; *214:* 98
Frasier, Debra *69:* 60; *112:* 67; *182:* 81, 82, 83
Fraustino, Lisa Rowe *146:* 87
Frazee, Marla *72:* 98; *105:* 79, 80; *151:* 67, 68; *164:* 165; *171:* 190, 191; *187:* 53, 54,55, 56, 143
Frazetta, Frank *41:* 72; *58:* 77, 78, 79, 80, 81, 82, 83
Frazier, Craig *177:* 63; *221:* 47
Freas, John *25:* 207
Fredrickson, Mark *103:* 33
Freeland, Michael J. *118:* 115
Freeman, Don *2:* 15; *13:* 249; *17:* 62, 63, 65, 67, 68; *18:* 243; *20:* 195; *23:* 213, 217; *32:* 155; *55:* 129
Freeman, Irving *67:* 150
Freeman, Laura *144:* 111; *200:* 62, 63
Freeman, Pietri *140:* 223
Freeman, Tom *167:* 118
Freeman, Tor *164:* 93
Fregosi, Claudia *24:* 117
Fremaux, Charlotte Murray *138:* 29; *141:* 95
French, Fiona *6:* 82, 83; *75:* 61; *109:* 170; *132:* 79, 80, 81, 82
French, Martin *163:* 4
French, S. Terrell *216:* 106
Frendak, Rodney *126:* 97, 98
Freschet, Gina *175:* 73
Freynet, Gilbert *72:* 221
Fried, Janice *202:* 121
Frieden, Sarajo *213:* 119
Friedman, Judith *43:* 197; *131:* 221
Friedman, Marvin *19:* 59; *42:* 86
Frinta, Dagmar *36:* 42
Frith, Michael K. *15:* 138; *18:* 120
Fritz, Ronald *46:* 73; *82:* 124
Fromm, Lilo *29:* 85; *40:* 197
Frost, A.B. *17:* 6, 7; *19:* 123, 124, 125, 126, 127, 128, 129,130; *100:* 119; *YABC 1:* 156, 157, 160; *2:* 107
Frost, Helen *183:* 51
Frost, Kristi *118:* 113
Frost, Michael *151:* 209; *209:* 44; *212:* 70
Froud, Brian *150:* 82, 83
Froud, Wendy *151:* 237
Fry, Guy *2:* 224
Fry, Rosalie *3:* 72; *YABC 2:* 180, 181
Fry, Rosalind *21:* 153, 168
Fryer, Elmer *34:* 115
Fuchs, Bernie *110:* 10; *162:* 46
Fuchs, Erich *6:* 84
Fuchshuber, Annegert *43:* 96
Fucile, Tony *221:* 48
Fufuka, Mahiri *32:* 146
Fuge, Charles *144:* 91, 93
Fujikawa, Gyo *39:* 75, 76; *76:* 72, 73, 74
Fulford, Deborah *23:* 159
Fuller, Margaret *25:* 189
Fulweiler, John *93:* 99
Funai, Mamoru *38:* 105
Funfhausen, Christian *196:* 30
Funk, Tom *7:* 17, 99
Furchgott, Terry *29:* 86
Furness, William Henry, Jr. *94:* 18
Furukawa, Mel *25:* 42
Fusari, Erika *164:* 227

G

Gaadt, David *78:* 212; *121:* 166; *201:* 171
Gaadt, George *71:* 9
Gaber, Susan *99:* 33; *115:* 57, 58; *164:* 195; *169:* 61, 62, 63; *185:* 50, 51; *188:* 124
Gaberell, J. *19:* 236
Gable, Brian *195:* 68, 69
Gabler, Mirko *99:* 71; *195:* 32

Gabor, Tim *216:* 61
Gackenbach, Dick *19:* 168; *41:* 81; *48:* 89, 90, 91, 92,93, 94; *54:* 105; *79:* 75, 76, 77
Gad, Victor *87:* 161
Gaetano, Nicholas *23:* 209
Gaffney-Kessell, Walter *94:* 219; *174:* 188
Gag, Flavia *17:* 49, 52
Gag, Wanda *100:* 101, 102; *YABC 1:* 135, 137, 138, 141, 143
Gagnon, Cecile *11:* 77; *58:* 87
Gaillard, Jason *200:* 69; *204:* 74
Gal, Laszlo *14:* 127; *52:* 54, 55, 56; *65:* 142; *68:* 150; *81:* 185; *96:* 104, 105
Gale, Cathy *140:* 22; *143:* 52; *213:* 166
Gall, Chris *176:* 79, 80
Gallagher, Jack *187:* 100
Gallagher, S. Saelig *105:* 154; *198:* 91
Gallagher, Sears *20:* 112 Gallagher-Cole, Mernie *206:* 56
Galloway, Ewing *51:* 154
Galouchka, Annouchka Gravel *95:* 55; *182:* 40
Galster, Robert *1:* 66
Galsworthy, Gay John *35:* 232
Galvez, Daniel *125:* 182
Gamble, Kim *112:* 64, 65; *124:* 77; *183:* 40, 42, 43, 56, 57; *187:* 170
Gammell, Stephen *7:* 48; *13:* 149; *29:* 82; *33:* 209; *41:* 88; *50:* 185, 186, 187; *53:* 51, 52, 53, 54, 55, 56,57, 58; *54:* 24, 25; *56:* 147, 148, 150; *57:* 27, 66; *81:* 62, 63; *87:* 88; *89:* 10; *106:* 223; *126:* 2; *128:* 71, 73, 74, 77; *154:* 34; *211:* 210
Gamper, Ruth *84:* 198
Gampert, John *58:* 94
Ganly, Helen *56:* 56
Gannett, Ruth Chrisman *3:* 74; *18:* 254; *33:* 77, 78
Gannon, Ned *205:* 6
Gantschev, Ivan *45:* 32
Garafano, Marie *73:* 33
Garbot, Dave *131:* 106
Garbutt, Bernard *23:* 68
Garcia *37:* 71
Garcia, Manuel *74:* 145
Garcia-Franco, Rebecca *173:* 46
Gardiner, Lindsey *178:* 128; *186:* 137
Gardner, Earle *45:* 167
Gardner, Joan *40:* 87
Gardner, Joel *40:* 87, 92
Gardner, John *40:* 87
Gardner, Lucy *40:* 87
Gardner, Richard
    See Cummings, Richard
Gardner, Sally *171:* 177; *177:* 66, 68
Gargiulo, Frank *84:* 158
Garland, Michael *36:* 29; *38:* 83; *44:* 168; *48:* 78, 221, 222; *49:* 161; *60:* 139; *71:* 6, 11; *72:* 229; *74:* 142; *89:* 187; *93:* 183; *104:* 110; *131:* 55; *139:* 209; *168:* 56; *208:* 72, 73, 75
Garland, Peggy *60:* 139
Garland, Sarah *62:* 45; *135:* 67, 68; *171:* 118
Garn, Aimee *75:* 47
Garner, Joan *128:* 170
Garneray, Ambroise Louis *59:* 140
Garnett, Eve *3:* 75
Garnett, Gary *39:* 184
Garns, Allen *80:* 125; *84:* 39; *165:* 231; *209:* 44
Garófoli, Viviana *186:* 123
Garraty, Gail *4:* 142; *52:* 106
Garrett, Agnes *46:* 110; *47:* 157

Garrett, Edmund H. *20:* 29
Garrett, Tom *107:* 194; *215:* 179
Garrick, Jacqueline *67:* 42, 43; *77:* 94
Garrison, Barbara *19:* 133; *104:* 146; *109:* 87
Garro, Mark *108:* 131; *128:* 210
Garvey, Robert *98:* 222
Garza, Carmen Lomas *80:* 211; *182:* 86
Garza, Xavier *184:* 64
Gates, Frieda *26:* 80
Gaughan, Jack *26:* 79; *43:* 185
Gaver, Becky *20:* 61
Gavril, David *211:* 196
Gawing, Toby *72:* 52
Gay, Marie-Louise *68:* 76, 77, 78; *102:* 136; *126:* 76, 78, 81, 83; *127:* 55, 56; *179:* 70, 72, 73, 74
Gay, Zhenya *19:* 135, 136
Gaydos, Tim *62:* 201
Gazsi, Ed *80:* 48
Gazso, Gabriel *73:* 85
Geary, Clifford N. *1:* 122; *9:* 104; *51:* 74
Geary, Rick *142:* 44, 46
Gee, Frank *33:* 26
Geehan, Wayne *157:* 181
Geer, Charles *1:* 91; *3:* 179; *4:* 201; *6:* 168; *7:* 96; *9:* 58; *10:* 72; *12:* 127; *39:* 156,157, 158, 159, 160; *42:* 88, 89, 90, 91; *55:* 111, 116
Geerinck, Manuel *173:* 128
Gehm, Charlie *36:* 65; *57:* 117; *62:* 60, 138
Geis, Alissa Imre *189:* 77
Geisel, Theodor Seuss *1:* 104, 105, 106; *28:* 108, 109, 110,111, 112, 113; *75:* 67, 68, 69, 70, 71; *89:* 127, 128; *100:* 106, 107, 108
Geisert, Arthur *92:* 67, 68; *133:* 72, 73, 74; *165:* 97, 98; *171:* 64, 65
Geldart, William *15:* 121; *21:* 202
Genia *4:* 84
Gentry, Cyrille R. *12:* 66
Genzo, John Paul *136:* 74
George, Jean *2:* 113
George, Lindsay Barrett *95:* 57; *155:* 97, 98
Geraghty, Paul *130:* 60, 61
Gerard, Jean Ignace *45:* 80
Gerard, Rolf *27:* 147, 150
Gerber, Mark *61:* 105
Gerber, Mary Jane *112:* 124; *171:* 56
Gerber, Stephanie *71:* 195
Gerdstein, Mordecai *169:* 105
Gergely, Tibor *54:* 15, 16
Geritz, Franz *17:* 135
Gerlach, Geff *42:* 58
Gerrard, Roy *47:* 78; *90:* 96, 97, 98, 99
Gerritsen, Paula *177:* 69; *217:* 166
Gershinowitz, George *36:* 27
Gerstein, Mordicai *31:* 117; *47:* 80, 81, 82, 83, 84, 85, 86; *51:* 173; *69:* 134; *107:* 122; *142:* 49, 52; *165:* 209; *176:* 119; *178:* 95, 97, 99; *215:* 173
Gervase *12:* 27
Geter, Tyrone *146:* 249; *150:* 86
Getz, Arthur *32:* 148
Gévry, Claudine *188:* 47
Gewirtz, Bina *61:* 81
Giancola, Donato *95:* 146; *164:* 226
Gibala-Broxholm, Scott *205:* 76; *219:* 186
Gibbons, Gail *23:* 78; *72:* 77, 78, 79; *82:* 182; *104:* 65; *160:* 99, 100; *201:* 59, 60, 62
Gibbs, Tony *40:* 95
Gibran, Kahlil *32:* 116
Gibson, Barbara Leonard *205:* 77; *212:* 151
Gider, Iskender *81:* 193
Giebfried, Rosemary *170:* 135
Giesen, Rosemary *34:* 192, 193
Giffard, Hannah *83:* 70
Giguere, George *20:* 111
Gilbert, John *19:* 184; *54:* 115; *YABC 2:* 287
Gilbert, W.S. *36:* 83, 85, 96
Gilbert, Yvonne *116:* 70; *128:* 84; *149:* 119; *185:* 69; *192:* 25; *195:* 81

Gilchrist, Jan Spivey *72:* 82, 83, 84, 85, 87; *77:* 90; *105:* 89, 91; *130:* 63, 64; *155:* 105, 107; *182:* 67
Giles, Will *41:* 218
Gili, Phillida *70:* 73
Gill, Margery *4:* 57; *7:* 7; *22:* 122; *25:* 166; *26:* 146, 147
Gillen, Denver *28:* 216
Gillette, Henry J. *23:* 237
Gilliam, Stan *39:* 64, 81
Gillies, Chuck *62:* 31
Gilliland, Jillian *87:* 58
Gillman, Alec *98:* 105
Gilman, Esther *15:* 124
Gilman, Phoebe *104:* 70, 71
Gilpin, Stephen *213:* 68
Ginsberg, Sari *111:* 184
Ginsburg, Max *62:* 59; *68:* 194 Girard, Roge *161:* 30
Girouard, Patrick *155:* 100; *218:* 165
Giovanopoulos, Paul *7:* 104; *60:* 36
Giovine, Sergio *79:* 12; *93:* 118; *139:* 118; *205:* 114
Gist, E.M. *206:* 60
Githens, Elizabeth M. *5:* 47
Gladden, Scott *99:* 108; *103:* 160; *193:* 46, 47
Gladstone, Gary *12:* 89; *13:* 190
Gladstone, Lise *15:* 273
Glanzman, Louis S. *2:* 177; *3:* 182; *36:* 97, 98; *38:* 120, 122; *52:* 141, 144; *71:* 191; *91:* 54, 56
Glaser, Byron *154:* 59, 60
Glaser, Milton *3:* 5; *5:* 156; *11:* 107; *30:* 26; *36:* 112; *54:* 141; *151:* 70
Glass, Andrew *36:* 38; *44:* 133; *48:* 205; *65:* 3; *68:* 43, 45; *90:* 104, 105; *150:* 89
Glass, Marvin *9:* 174
Glasser, Judy *41:* 156; *56:* 140; *69:* 79; *72:* 101
Glattauer, Ned *5:* 84; *13:* 224; *14:* 26
Glauber, Uta *17:* 76
Gleeson, J.M. *YABC 2:* 207
Glegg, Creina *36:* 100
Glienke, Amelie *63:* 150
Gliewe, Unada *3:* 78, 79; *21:* 73; *30:* 220
Gliori, Debi *72:* 91; *138:* 82; *162:* 37; *189:* 79, 81, 82
Glovach, Linda *7:* 105
Gobbato, Imero *3:* 180, 181; *6:* 213; *7:* 58; *9:* 150; *18:* 39; *21:* 167; *39:* 82, 83; *41:* 137, 251; *59:* 177
Goble, Paul *25:* 121; *26:* 86; *33:* 65; *69:* 68, 69; *131:* 79, 80
Goble, Warwick *46:* 78, 79; *194:* 143
Godal, Eric *36:* 93
Godbey, Cory *221:* 154
Godkin, Celia *145:* 84, 86
Godfrey, Michael *17:* 279
Godon, Ingrid *166:* 163; *186:* 99
Goede, Irene *208:* 87
Goembel, Ponder *42:* 124
Goffe, Toni *61:* 83, 84, 85; *89:* 11; *90:* 124; *178:* 118
Goffstein, M.B. *8:* 71; *70:* 75, 76, 77
Golbin, Andre *15:* 125
Gold, Robert *166:* 151, 152
Goldfeder, Cheryl *11:* 191
Goldfinger, Jennifer P. *185:* 71
Goldman, Todd H. *221:* 50, 51
Goldsborough, June *5:* 154, 155; *8:* 92; *14:* 226; *19:* 139; *54:* 165
Goldsmith, Robert *110:* 77
Goldstein, Barry *198:* 147
Goldstein, Leslie *5:* 8; *6:* 60; *10:* 106
Goldstein, Nathan *1:* 175; *2:* 79; *11:* 41, 232; *16:* 55
Goldstrom, Robert *98:* 36; *145:* 51, 52
Golembe, Carla *79:* 80, 81; *136:* 91; *144:* 113; *193:* 53
Golin, Carlo *74:* 112
Gomez, Elena *188:* 122; *191:* 72

Gomez, Elizabeth *127:* 70; *133:* 76
Gomi, Taro *64:* 102; *103:* 74, 76
Gon, Adriano *101:* 112
Gonsalves, Ron *178:* 213; *212:* 196
Gonzalez, Maya Christina *104:* 3; *136:* 92; *215:* 4, 5
Gonzalez, Yolanda *212:* 65
Good, Karen Hillard *212:* 143; *214:* 103
Goodall, John S. *4:* 92, 93; *10:* 132; *66:* 92, 93; *YABC 1:* 198
Goode, Diane *15:* 126; *50:* 183; *52:* 114, 115; *76:* 195; *84:* 94; *99:* 141; *114:* 76, 77, 78; *170:* 99, 101
Goodelman, Aaron *40:* 203
Goodenow, Earle *40:* 97
Goodfellow, Peter *62:* 95; *94:* 202
Goodman, Joan Elizabeth *50:* 86
Goodman, Vivienne *82:* 251; *146:* 181, 182
Goodnow, Patti *117:* 33
Goodrich, Carter *221:* 52, 53
Goodwin, Harold *13:* 74
Goodwin, Philip R. *18:* 206
Goor, Nancy *39:* 85, 86
Goor, Ron *39:* 85, 86
Goossens, Philippe *195:* 71
Gorbachev, Valeri *89:* 96; *112:* 97; *143:* 63, 64; *184:* 66, 67, 68, 101
Gordon, David *216:* 159
Gordon, Gwen *12:* 151
Gordon, Margaret *4:* 147; *5:* 48, 49; *9:* 79
Gordon, Mike *101:* 62, 63, 64
Gordon, Russell *136:* 204; *137:* 214
Gordon, Walter *138:* 9
Gore, Leonid *89:* 51; *94:* 74; *136:* 8; *158:* 117; *166:* 136; *168:* 36; *170:* 107; *181:* 94; *185:* 73
Gorecka-Egan, Erica *18:* 35
Gorey, Edward *1:* 60, 61; *13:* 169; *18:* 192; *20:* 201; *29:* 90, 91, 92, 93, 94, 95, 96, 97, 98, 99, 100; *30:* 129; *32:* 90; *34:* 200, 65: 48; *68:* 24, 25; *69:* 79; *70:* 80, 82, 83, 84; *85:* 136; *127:* 62
Gorsline, Douglas *1:* 98; *6:* 13; *11:* 113; *13:* 104; *15:* 14; *28:* 117, 118; *YABC 1:* 15
Gorton, Julia *108:* 94; *178:* 81, 82
Gosfield, Josh *118:* 165, 166; *149:* 67
Gosner, Kenneth *5:* 135
Gosney, Joy *167:* 142
Gotlieb, Jules *6:* 127
Goto, Scott *115:* 86; *136:* 69; *203:* 77, 78
Gott, Barry *197:* 95; *212:* 102
Gottlieb, Dale *67:* 162; *107:* 16; *149:* 6
Goudey, Ray *97:* 86
Gough, Alan *91:* 57
Gough, Philip *23:* 47; *45:* 90
Gould, Chester *49:* 112, 113, 114, 116, 117, 118
Gould, Jason *151:* 232
Gourbault, Martine *177:* 159
Govern, Elaine R. *26:* 94
Gower, Teri *102:* 184
Gowing, Toby *60:* 25; *63:* 33; *78:* 70, 252; *83:* 228; *86:* 187; *93:* 145; *108:* 133; *110:* 217; *184:* 125
Grabianski *20:* 144
Grabianski, Janusz *39:* 92, 93, 94, 95
Graboff, Abner *35:* 103, 104
Graef, Renée *61:* 188; *72:* 207; *204:* 45; *210:* 249
Grafe, Max *156:* 173; *178:* 237; *192:* 240; *198:* 51
Graham, A.B. *11:* 61
Graham, Bob *101:* 66, 67, 68; *151:* 74, 75; *187:* 65, 67, 68, 70
Graham, Georgia *188:* 3; *190:* 75
Graham, L. *7:* 108
Graham, Margaret Bloy *11:* 120; *18:* 305, 307
Graham, Mark *88:* 208; *159:* 153; *182:* 3
Grahame-Johnstone, Janet *13:* 61
Grahame-Johnstone, Anne *13:* 61
Grainger, Sam *42:* 95

Gralley, Jean *166:* 86
Gramatky, Hardie *1:* 107; *30:* 116, 119, 120, 122, 123
Gran, Julie *168:* 118
Granahan, Julie *84:* 84
GrandPré, Mary *84:* 131; *109:* 199; *118:* 76; *180:* 65; *184:* 70, 71, 180; *192:* 87; *215:* 24
Grandström, Brita *176:* 139
Grandville, J.J. *45:* 81, 82, 83, 84, 85, 86, 87, 88; *47:* 125; *64:* 10
Granger, Paul *39:* 153
Granström, Brita *162:* 35; *167:* 46
Grant, (Alice) Leigh *10:* 52; *15:* 131; *20:* 20; *26:* 119; *48:* 202
Grant, Gordon *17:* 230, 234; *25:* 123, 124, 125, 126; *52:* 69; *YABC 1:* 164
Grant, Melvyn *159:* 186, 187; *170:* 48, 49; *213:* 168, 169
Grant, Michelle *210:* 95
Grant, Renee *77:* 40
Grant, Shirley *109:* 45
Graves, Elizabeth *45:* 101
Graves, Keith *167:* 89; *191:* 74; *216:* 34
Gray, Harold *33:* 87, 88
Gray, Les *82:* 76; *83:* 232
Gray, Reginald *6:* 69
Greco, Tony *184:* 6
Greder, Armin *76:* 235
Green, Ann Canevari *62:* 48
Green, Eileen *6:* 97
Green, Elizabeth Shippen *139:* 109
Green, Jonathan *86:* 135; *105:* 109; *221:* 73
Green, Ken *111:* 68
Green, Michael *32:* 216
Green, Robina *87:* 138
Green, Jonathan *157:* 105
Greene, Jeffrey *117:* 93
Greenaway, Kate *17:* 275; *24:* 180; *26:* 107; *41:* 222, 232; *100:* 115, 116; *YABC 1:* 88, 89; *2:* 131, 133, 136,138, 139, 141
Greenberg, Melanie Hope *72:* 93; *80:* 125; *101:* 174; *133:* 180; *186:* 189; *214:* 105
Greenseid, Diane *178:* 106, 107
Greenstein, Elaine *150:* 100
Greenwald, Sheila *1:* 34; *3:* 99; *8:* 72
Greger, Carol *76:* 86
Gregorian, Joyce Ballou *30:* 125
Gregory, Emilian *177:* 146; *187:* 10
Gregory, Fran *130:* 4; *140:* 93
Gregory, Frank M. *29:* 107
Greiffenhagen, Maurice *16:* 137; *27:* 57; *YABC 2:* 288
Greiner, Robert *6:* 86
Gretter, J. Clemens *31:* 134
Gretz, Susanna *7:* 114
Gretzer, John *1:* 54; *3:* 26; *4:* 162; *7:* 125; *16:* 247; *18:* 117; *28:* 66; *30:* 85, 211; *33:* 235; *56:* 16
Grey, Mini *166:* 90; *192:* 71
Grey Owl *24:* 41
Gri *25:* 90
Grieder, Walter *9:* 84
Griesbach/Martucci *59:* 3
Grifalconi, Ann *2:* 126; *3:* 248; *11:* 18; *13:* 182; *46:* 38; *50:* 145; *66:* 99, 100, 101, 104, 106; *69:* 38; *70:* 64; *87:* 128; *90:* 53; *93:* 49; *128:* 48; *133:* 79, 81; *210:* 111
Griffin, Gillett Good *26:* 96
Griffin, James *30:* 166
Griffin, John Howard *59:* 186
Griffin, Rachel *131:* 23
Griffith, Gershom *94:* 214
Griffiths, Dave *29:* 76
Griffiths, Dean *168:* 180; *169:* 182
Grimly, Gris *186:* 102; *192:* 112; *197:* 86; *219:* 34
Grimsdell, Jeremy *83:* 75
Grimwood, Brian *82:* 89
Gringhuis, Dirk *6:* 98; *9:* 196
Gripe, Harald *2:* 127; *74:* 98
Grisha *3:* 71

Grobler, Piet *201:* 100
Grohmann, Susan *84:* 97
Gropper, William *27:* 93; *37:* 193
Gros *60:* 199
Grose, Helen Mason *YABC 1:* 260; *2:* 150
Grossman, Nancy *24:* 130; *29:* 101
Grossman, Robert *11:* 124; *46:* 39
Groth, John *15:* 79; *21:* 53, 54; *83:* 230
Grover, Lorie Ann *168:* 59
Grubb, Lisa *160:* 116
Grue, Lisa *187:* 193
Gruelle, Johnny *35:* 107
Gschwind, William *11:* 72
Guarnaccia, Steven *201:* 170, 173
Guay-Mitchell, Rebecca *110:* 95, 96; *135:* 240; *180:* 76; *181:* 71, 73; *216:* 77
Guback, Georgia *88:* 102
Gudeon, Karla *212:* 67
Guerguerion, Claudine *105:* 73
Guevara, Susan *97:* 87; *167:* 49; *194:* 54
Guggenheim, Hans *2:* 10; *3:* 37; *8:* 136
Guhathaakurta, Ajanta *183:* 199
Guida, Lisa Chauncy *172:* 188
Guilbeau, Honore *22:* 69
Guillette, Joseph *137:* 37
Guisewite, Cathy *57:* 52, 53, 54, 56, 57
Gukova, Julia *95:* 104; *154:* 103; *168:* 195
Gundersheimer, Karen *35:* 240; *82:* 100
Gunderson, Nick *57:* 120
Gunnella *192:* 144
Gurney, James *76:* 97; *86:* 32
Gurney, John Steven *75:* 39, 82; *110:* 175; *143:* 67, 68; *169:* 172; *217:* 50, 88
Gusman, Annie *38:* 62
Gustafson, Scott *34:* 111; *43:* 40
Gustavson, Adam *104:* 10; *171:* 183; *176:* 87; *197:* 94; *204:* 35; *219:* 187
Guthridge, Bettina *108:* 79; *186:* 92
Guthrie, R. Dale *64:* 143
Guthrie, Robin *20:* 122
Gutierrez, Akemi *172:* 87; *205:* 135
Gutierrez, Alan *136:* 31, 32
Gutierrez, Rudy *97:* 162; *203:* 79; *216:* 158
Gutmann, Bessie Pease *73:* 93, 94
Gwynne, Fred *41:* 94, 95
Gyberg, Bo-Erik *38:* 131

H

Haas, Irene *17:* 77; *87:* 46; *96:* 117
Hack, Konrad *51:* 127
Hader, Berta H. *16:* 126
Hader, Elmer S. *16:* 126
Haeffele, Deborah *76:* 99
Haemer, Alan *62:* 109
Hafner, Marylin *22:* 196, 216; *24:* 44; *30:* 51; *35:* 95; *51:* 25, 160, 164; *86:* 16; *105:* 196; *121:* 93, 94; *149:* 208, 209; *179:* 82, 83, 84, 115; *190:* 200; *201:* 29; *217:* 91
Hagerty, Sean *62:* 181
Hague, Michael *32:* 128; *48:* 98, 99, 100, 101, 103, 105,106, 107, 108, 109, 110; *49:* 121; *51:* 105; *64:* 14, 15; *79:* 134; *80:* 91, 92; *83:* 135; *100:* 241; *102:* 29; *129:* 101, 103, 104; *185:* 80, 81, 82; *215:* 89
Hair, Jonathan *115:* 135
Halas, John *29:* 41, 47, 48
Haldane, Roger *13:* 76; *14:* 202
Hale, Bruce *203:* 83
Hale, Christy *79:* 124; *84:* 200; *114:* 201; *128:* 2, 3; *146:* 203; *158:* 243; *167:* 99; *179:* 87
Hale, Irina *26:* 97
Hale, James Graham *88:* 207
Hale, Kathleen *17:* 79; *66:* 114, 116, 118
Hale, Nathan *210:* 115, 116; *214:* 179
Haley, Amanda *205:* 82, 83
Haley, Gail E. *43:* 102, 103, 104, 105; *78:* 65, 67; *136:* 106, 107
Hall, Amanda *96:* 110

Hall, August N. *217:* 74
Hall, Chuck *30:* 189
Hall, Douglas *15:* 184; *43:* 106, 107; *86:* 100; *87:* 82; *129:* 72
Hall, H. Tom *1:* 227; *30:* 210
Hall, Melanie *116:* 48, 49; *169:* 77, 78; *219:* 170
Hall, Sydney P. *31:* 89
Hall, Tim *164:* 196; *202:* 41
Hall, Vicki *20:* 24
Hallinan, P.K. *39:* 98
Hallman, Tom *98:* 166
Hally, Greg *101:* 200; *151:* 224
Halperin, Wendy Anderson *96:* 151; *125:* 96, 97, 98, 99; *139:* 22; *140:* 84; *200:* 77, 78; *210:* 157; *215:* 65
Halpern, Joan *10:* 25
Halpern, Shari *174:* 172
Halsey, Megan *96:* 172; *114:* 185; *180:* 8; *185:* 85
Halstead, Virginia *125:* 105
Halverson, Janet *49:* 38, 42, 44
Hallensleben, Georg *134:* 5, 6; *172:* 17
Hallett, Mark *220:* 63
Hamanaka, Sheila *71:* 100
Hamann, Brad *78:* 151
Hamann, Sigune *104:* 115
Hamberger, John *6:* 8; *8:* 32; *14:* 79; *34:* 136; *88:* 78
Hamil, Tom *14:* 80; *43:* 163
Hamilton, Bill and Associates *26:* 215
Hamilton, Helen S. *2:* 238
Hamilton, J. *19:* 83, 85, 87
Hamilton, Laurie *116:* 210
Hamilton, Todd Cameron *84:* 15
Hamlin, Janet *97:* 136; *124:* 90; *137:* 157; *182:* 117
Hamlin, Louise *71:* 135
Hammill, Matt *206:* 65
Hammond, Chris *21:* 37
Hammond, Elizabeth *5:* 36, 203
Hampshire, Michael *5:* 187; *7:* 110, 111; *48:* 150; *51:* 129
Hampson, Denman *10:* 155; *15:* 130
Hampton, Blake *41:* 244
Handford, Martin *64:* 105, 106, 107, 109
Handforth, Thomas *42:* 100, 101, 102, 103, 104, 105, 107
Handville, Robert *1:* 89; *38:* 76; *45:* 108, 109
Hane, Roger *17:* 239; *44:* 54
Haney, Elizabeth Mathieu *34:* 84
Hanke, Ted *71:* 10
Hankinson, Phil *181:* 164
Hanley, Catherine *8:* 161
Hann, Jacquie *19:* 144
Hanna, Cheryl *91:* 133
Hanna, Wayne A. *67:* 145
Hannon, Mark *38:* 37
Hanrahan, Kelly-Anne *203:* 142
Hansen, Gaby *159:* 11; *186:* 25
Hansen, Mia *149:* 76
Hanson, Joan *8:* 76; *11:* 139
Hanson, Peter E. *52:* 47; *54:* 99, 100; *73:* 21; *84:* 79; *116:* 144
Hansson, Gunilla *64:* 111, 112
Harbour, Elizabeth *221:* 68
Hardcastle, Nick *121:* 82; *175:* 185
Hardy, David A. *9:* 96; *119:* 74
Hardy, Paul *YABC 2:* 245
Hargis, Wes *219:* 70 Haring, Keith *145:* 65
Harlan, Jerry *3:* 96
Harlin, Greg *89:* 194; *103:* 82; *118:* 161; *121:* 167; *182:* 76; *201:* 172; *215:* 76
Harman, Dominic *206:* 48
Harness, Cheryl *106:* 80; *131:* 87; *178:* 111; *200:* 39
Harnischfeger *18:* 121
Harper, Arthur *YABC 2:* 121
Harper, Betty *126:* 90
Harper, Jamie *174:* 71; *214:* 212
Harper, Piers *79:* 27; *105:* 102; *161:* 67

Harrington, Glenn *82:* 18; *94:* 66, 68; *185:* 118
Harrington, Jack *83:* 162
Harrington, Richard *5:* 81
Harris, Andrew N. *191:* 78
Harris, Jim *127:* 130; *183:* 4
Harris, John *83:* 25
Harris, Nick *86:* 177
Harris, Susan Yard *42:* 121
Harrison, Florence *20:* 150, 152
Harrison, Harry *4:* 103
Harrison, Jack *28:* 149
Harrison, Mark *105:* 157; *165:* 190
Harrison, Ted *56:* 73
Harsh, Fred *72:* 107
Harston, Jerry *105:* 143
Hart, Lewis *98:* 115
Hart, Thomas *181:* 165
Hart, William *13:* 72
Hartland, Jessie *171:* 80, 81; *186:* 165
Hartung, Susan Kathleen *150:* 107, 108; *173:* 106; *175:* 106; *192:* 78; *211:* 19
Hartelius, Margaret *10:* 24
Hartshorn, Ruth *5:* 115; *11:* 129
Harvey, Amanda *145:* 44
Harvey, Bob *48:* 219
Harvey, Gerry *7:* 180
Harvey, Lisa *97:* 21
Harvey, Paul *88:* 74
Harvey, Roland *71:* 88; *123:* 63; *179:* 94; *218:* 94; *219:* 74
Haskamp, Steve *195:* 36
Hassall, Joan *43:* 108, 109
Hassell, Hilton *YABC 1:* 187
Hassett, John *162:* 59
Hasselriis, Else *18:* 87; *YABC 1:* 96
Hastings, Glenn *89:* 183
Hastings, Ian *62:* 67
Hauman, Doris *2:* 184; *29:* 58, 59; *32:* 85, 86, 87
Hauman, George *2:* 184; *29:* 58, 59; *32:* 85, 86, 87
Hausherr, Rosmarie *15:* 29
Hawkes, Kevin *78:* 72; *104:* 198; *105:* 197; *112:* 109; *126:* 87; *144:* 88; *149:* 210; *150:* 110, 135; *156:* 94; *164:* 35; *186:* 18; *190:* 197; *198:* 152; *201:* 70, 71, 72; *220:* 99; *221:* 90, 92, 93
Hawkins, Jacqui *112:* 86; *162:* 64
Hawkinson, John *4:* 109; *7:* 83; *21:* 64
Hawkinson, Lucy *21:* 64
Hawthorne, Mike *140:* 228
Haxton, Elaine *28:* 131
Haydock, Robert *4:* 95
Hayes, Geoffrey *26:* 111; *44:* 133; *91:* 85; *207:* 63
Hayes, Karel *207:* 65
Haynes, Max *72:* 107
Hays, Michael *73:* 207; *83:* 93; *139:* 197; *146:* 202, 250; *202:* 47
Haywood, Carolyn *1:* 112; *29:* 104
Heale, Jonathan *104:* 117
Healy, Daty *12:* 143
Healy, Deborah *58:* 181, 182; *101:* 111
Heap, Sue *102:* 207; *150:* 113, 114; *187:* 84, 85, 87
Hearn, Diane Dawson *79:* 99; *113:* 13; *209:* 71, 72; *211:* 106
Hearon, Dorothy *34:* 69
Heaslip, William *57:* 24, 25
Hechtkopf, H. *11:* 110
Heck, Ed *173:* 81
Hector, Julian *205:* 85
Hedderwick, Mairi *30:* 127; *32:* 47; *36:* 104; *77:* 86; *145:* 91, 93, 95
Heffernan, Phil *146:* 197; *195:* 172; *218:* 123
Hefter, Richard *28:* 170; *31:* 81, 82; *33:* 183
Hehenberger, Shelly *126:* 91
Heigh, James *22:* 98
Heighway, Richard *25:* 160; *64:* 4
Heighway-Bury, Robin *159:* 89

Heine, Helme *67:* 86; *135:* 91, 92
Heinly, John *45:* 113
Hellard, Susan *81:* 21; *204:* 82; *209:* 92
Hellebrand, Nancy *26:* 57
Heller, Linda *46:* 86
Heller, Ruth M. *66:* 125; *77:* 30, 32
Hellmuth, Jim *38:* 164
Helms, Georgeann *33:* 62
Helquist, Brett *142:* 203; *146:* 133, 134; *156:* 10; *173:* 25; *180:* 106; *187:* 90, 91; *193:* 12
Helweg, Hans *41:* 118; *50:* 93; *58:* 22, 26
Hemingway, Edward *212:* 71
Hemphill, Helen *179:* 95
Henba, Bobbie *90:* 195
Henderling, Lisa *214:* 65
Henderson, Dave *73:* 76; *75:* 191, 192, 193, 194; *82:* 4
Henderson, D.F. *216:* 77
Henderson, Douglas *103:* 68
Henderson, Kathy *55:* 32; *155:* 118
Henderson, Keith *35:* 122
Henderson, Meryl *127:* 58, 60; *169:* 81
Hendrix, John *187:* 133; *208:* 106, 107, 108; *216:* 115
Hendry, Linda *80:* 104; *83:* 83; *164:* 216
Hengeveld, Dennis *142:* 86
Henkes, Kevin *43:* 111; *108:* 106, 107, 108
Henneberger, Robert *1:* 42; *2:* 237; *25:* 83
Henriquez, Celeste *103:* 137
Henriquez, Elsa *82:* 260
Henriquez, Emile F. *89:* 88; *211:* 56
Henry, Everett *29:* 191
Henry, Matthew *117:* 58
Henry, Paul *93:* 121; *194:* 125
Henry, Rohan *217:* 77
Henry, Thomas *5:* 102
Hensel *27:* 119
Henshaw, Jacqui *141:* 127
Henstra, Friso *8:* 80; *36:* 70; *40:* 222; *41:* 250; *73:* 100, 101
Henterly, Jamichael *93:* 4
Heo, Yumi *89:* 85, 86; *94:* 89, 90; *146:* 40, 137, 138; *163:* 227; *201:* 192
Hepple, Norman *28:* 198
Herbert, Helen *57:* 70
Herbert, Jennifer *189:* 47
Herbert, Wally *23:* 101
Herbster, Mary Lee *9:* 33
Herder, Edwin *182:* 104
Herge
See Remi, Georges
Hermansen, Pal *133:* 113
Hermanson, Dennis *10:* 55
Hermes, Gertrude *54:* 161
Herr, Margo *57:* 191
Herr, Susan *83:* 163
Herriman, George *140:* 74, 75, 76, 77, 78
Herriman, Lisa *87:* 190
Herring, Michael *121:* 76; *182:* 103
Herrington, Roger *3:* 161
Herscovici, C. *165:* 240
Hescox, Richard *85:* 86; *90:* 30; *139:* 35
Heslop, Mike *38:* 60; *40:* 130
Hess, Lydia J. *85:* 17
Hess, Mark *111:* 146; *113:* 207
Hess, Paul *134:* 47; *166:* 133; *193:* 13
Hess, Richard *42:* 31
Hester, Ronnie *37:* 85
Heuser, Olga J. *121:* 116
Heusser, Sibylle *168:* 195
Heustis, Louise L. *20:* 28
Hewgill, Jody *201:* 90
Hewitson, Jennifer *74:* 119; *124:* 167
Hewitt, Kathryn *80:* 126; *149:* 105; *184:* 93; *196:* 36
Hewitt, Margaret *84:* 112
Heyduck-Huth, Hilde *8:* 82
Heyer, Carol *74:* 122; *130:* 72, 73; *192:* 35; *203:* 78
Heyer, Hermann *20:* 114, 115

Heyer, Marilee *102:* 108
Heyman, Ken *8:* 33; *34:* 113
Heyne, Ulrike *146:* 151
Heywood, Karen *48:* 114
Hickling, P.B. *40:* 165
Hickman, Stephen *85:* 58; *136:* 33; *171:* 128
Hierstein, Judith *56:* 40; *162:* 168; *212:* 72
Higashi, Sandra *154:* 59, 60
Higginbottom, J. Winslow *8:* 170; *29:* 105, 106
Higgins, Chester *101:* 79
Higham, David *50:* 104
Hilb, Nora *176:* 8
Hild, Anja *215:* 194
Hildebrandt, Greg *8:* 191; *55:* 35, 36, 38, 39, 40, 42, 46; *172:* 110
Hildebrandt, Tim *8:* 191; *55:* 44, 45, 46
Hilder, Rowland *19:* 207
Hill, Eric *66:* 127, 128; *133:* 91
Hill, Gregory *35:* 190
Hill, Pat *49:* 120
Hillenbrand, Will *84:* 115; *92:* 76, 80; *93:* 131; *104:* 168; *128:* 137; *145:* 187; *146:* 184; *147:* 105, 106, 107; *152:* 59; *184:* 179; *195:* 34, 180; *196:* 125; *210:* 122, 123, 124; *217:* 62
Hilliard, Richard *183:* 74
Hillier, Matthew *45:* 205
Hillman, Priscilla *48:* 115
Hills, Tad *113:* 4; *137:* 147; *173:* 83; *208:* 199
Himler, Ronald *6:* 114; *7:* 162; *8:* 17, 84, 125; *14:* 76; *19:* 145; *26:* 160; *31:* 43; *38:* 116; *41:* 44, 79; *43:* 52; *45:* 120; *46:* 43; *54:* 44, 83; *58:* 180; *59:* 38; *68:* 146; *69:* 231; *70:* 98; *71:* 177, 178; *77:* 219; *79:* 212; *83:* 62; *89:* 5; *91:* 160; *92:* 91, 92, 93; *94:* 93; *95:* 69, 174, 194; *99:* 99, 112; *113:* 92; *118:* 114; *137:* 73, 74, 77, 167; *163:* 99; *165:* 138; *178:* 9, 220; *183:* 77, 79, 80, 81; *184:* 80, 83; *215:* 151
Himmelman, John *47:* 109; *65:* 87; *94:* 96, 97; *159:* 85; *221:* 79, 80, 81, 82
Hinds, Bill *37:* 127, 130
Hines, Anna Grossnickle *51:* 90; *74:* 124; *95:* 78, 79,80, 81
Hines, Bob *135:* 149, 150
Hirao, Amiko *203:* 98
Hiroko *99:* 61
Hiroshige *25:* 71
Hirsh, Marilyn *7:* 126
Hiscock, Bruce *137:* 80, 81; *204:* 51, 53
Hissey, Jane *103:* 90; *130:* 81
Hitch, Jeff *99:* 206; *128:* 86
Hitz, Demi *11:* 135; *15:* 245; *66:* 129, 130; *152:* 94, 95
Hnizdovsky, Jacques *32:* 96; *76:* 187
Ho, Kwoncjan *15:* 132
Hoban, Lillian *1:* 114; *22:* 157; *26:* 72; *29:* 53; *40:* 105, 107, 195; *41:* 80; *69:* 107, 108; *71:* 98; *77:* 168; *106:* 50; *113:* 86; *136:* 118
Hoban, Tana *22:* 159; *104:* 82, 83, 85
Hobbie, Jocelyn *190:* 78; *196:* 92
Hobbie, Nathaniel *196:* 92
Hobbs, Leigh *166:* 95
Hoberman, Norman *5:* 82
Hobson, Sally *77:* 185
Hockerman, Dennis *39:* 22; *56:* 23
Hodgell, P.C. *42:* 114
Hodges, C. Walter *2:* 139; *11:* 15; *12:* 25; *23:* 34; *25:* 96; *38:* 165; *44:* 197; *45:* 95; *100:* 57; *YABC 2:* 62, 63
Hodges, David *9:* 98
Hodgetts, Victoria *43:* 132
Hofbauer, Imre *2:* 162
Hoff, Syd *9:* 107; *10:* 128; *33:* 94; *72:* 115,116, 117, 118; *138:* 114, 115
Hoffman, Rosekrans *15:* 133; *50:* 219; *63:* 97
Hoffman, Sanford *38:* 208; *76:* 174; *88:* 160, 161; *151:* 156
Hoffmann, Felix *9:* 109
Hoffnung, Gerard *66:* 76, 77

Hofsinde, Robert *21:* 70
Hogan, Inez *2:* 141
Hogan, Jamie *192:* 94; *198:* 177
Hogarth, Burne *41:* 58; *63:* 46, 48, 49, 50, 52, 53, 54, 55,56
Hogarth, Paul *41:* 102, 103, 104; *YABC 1:* 16
Hogarth, William *42:* 33
Hogenbyl, Jan *1:* 35
Hogner, Nils *4:* 122; *25:* 144
Hogrogian, Nonny *3:* 221; *4:* 106, 107; *5:* 166; *7:* 129; *15:* 2; *16:* 176; *20:* 154; *22:* 146; *25:* 217; *27:* 206; *74:* 127, 128, 129, 149, 152; *127:* 99; *YABC 2:* 84, 94
Hokanson, Lars *93:* 111; *172:* 137; *212:* 88
Hokusai *25:* 71
Hol, Colby *126:* 96
Holberg, Richard *2:* 51
Holbrook, Kathy *107:* 114
Holdcroft, Tina *38:* 109
Holden, Caroline *55:* 159
Holder, Heidi *36:* 99; *64:* 9
Holder, Jim *204:* 163
Holder, Jimmy *151:* 224
Holderness, Grizelda *215:* 107
Hole, Stian *204:* 55
Holiday, Henry *YABC 2:* 107
Holl, F. *36:* 91
Holland, Brad *45:* 59, 159
Holland, Gay W. *128:* 105
Holland, Janice *18:* 118
Holland, Marion *6:* 116
Holland, Richard *216:* 109, 124
Holldobler, Turid *26:* 120
Holliday, Keaf *144:* 236
Holling, Holling C. *15:* 136, 137
Hollinger, Deanne *12:* 116
Holm, Sharon Lane *114:* 84; *115:* 52
Holmes, B. *3:* 82
Holmes, Bea *7:* 74; *24:* 156; *31:* 93
Holmes, Dave *54:* 22
Holmes, Lesley *135:* 96
Holmgren, George Ellen *45:* 112
Holmlund, Heather D. *150:* 140
Holt, Norma *44:* 106
Holt, Pater *151:* 188
Holtan, Gene *32:* 192
Holub, Joan *149:* 72
Holyfield, John *149:* 231
Holz, Loretta *17:* 81
Hom, Nancy *79:* 195
Homar, Lorenzo *6:* 2
Homer, Winslow *128:* 8; *YABC 2:* 87
Honey, Elizabeth *112:* 95, 96; *137:* 93, 94
Honeywood, Varnette P. *110:* 68, 70
Hong, Lily Toy *76:* 104
Honigman, Marian *3:* 2
Honore, Paul *42:* 77, 79, 81, 82
Hood, Alun *69:* 145, 218; *72:* 41; *80:* 226; *87:* 4; *95:* 139
Hood, Susan *12:* 43
Hook, Christian *104:* 103
Hook, Frances *26:* 188; *27:* 127
Hook, Jeff *14:* 137; *103:* 105
Hook, Richard *26:* 188
Hooks *63:* 30
Hooper, Hadley *177:* 145
Hoover, Carol A. *21:* 77
Hoover, Russell *12:* 95; *17:* 2; *34:* 156
Hope, James *141:* 116
Hopkins, Chris *99:* 127
Hopkinson, Leigh *202:* 70
Hopman, Philip *178:* 184
Hoppe, Paul *209:* 85
Hoppin, Augustus *34:* 66
Horacek, Judy *211:* 86
Horacek, Petr *163:* 117; *214:* 113
Horder, Margaret *2:* 108; *73:* 75
Horen, Michael *45:* 121
Horne, Daniel *73:* 106; *91:* 153; *109:* 127; *110:* 232; *164:* 176
Horne, Richard *111:* 80

Horowitz, Dave *204:* 58
Horse, Harry *128:* 195; *169:* 86
Horstman, Lisa *219:* 79
Horton, Anthony *211:* 98
Horvat, Laurel *12:* 201
Horvath, David *192:* 95
Horvath, Ferdinand Kusati *24:* 176
Horvath, Maria *57:* 171
Horwitz, Richard *57:* 174
Hotchkiss, De Wolfe *20:* 49
Hough, Charlotte *9:* 112; *13:* 98; *17:* 83; *24:* 195
Houlihan, Ray *11:* 214
House, Caroline *183:* 121
Housman, Laurence *25:* 146, 147
Houston, James *13:* 107; *74:* 132, 134, 135
Hovland, Gary *88:* 172; *171:* 148
Hoyt, Eleanor *158:* 231
How, W.E. *20:* 47
Howard, Alan *16:* 80; *34:* 58; *45:* 114
Howard, Arthur *165:* 111, 112; *190:* 5
Howard, J.N. *15:* 234
Howard, John *33:* 179
Howard, Kim *116:* 71
Howard, Paul *142:* 126, 129; *144:* 187
Howard, Rob *40:* 161
Howarth, Daniel *170:* 34
Howe, John *79:* 101; *80:* 150; *115:* 47; *176:* 106; *207:* 32, 35
Howe, Phillip *79:* 117; *175:* 115
Howe, Stephen *1:* 232
Howell, Karen *119:* 123
Howell, Pat *15:* 139
Howell, Troy *23:* 24; *31:* 61; *36:* 158; *37:* 184; *41:* 76, 235; *48:* 112; *56:* 13; *57:* 3; *59:* 174; *63:* 5; *74:* 46; *89:* 188; *90:* 231; *95:* 97, 98; *99:* 189; *153:* 156, 157, 158; *176:* 104; *199:* 96, 98
Howes, Charles *22:* 17
Hoyt, Ard *145:* 141; *190:* 82; *207:* 148
Hranilovich, Barbara *127:* 51
Hu, Ying-Hwa *116:* 107; *152:* 236; *173:* 171
Huang, Benrei *137:* 55
Huang, Zhong-Yang *117:* 30, 32; *213:* 18
Hubbard, Woodleigh Marx *98:* 67; *115:* 79; *160:* 138; *214:* 120
Hubley, Faith *48:* 120, 121, 125, 130, 131, 132, 134
Hubley, John *48:* 125, 130, 131, 132, 134
Hudak, Michal *143:* 74
Hudnut, Robin *14:* 62
Huerta, Catherine *76:* 178; *77:* 44, 45; *90:* 182; *210:* 202
Huffaker, Sandy *10:* 56
Huffman, Joan *13:* 33
Huffman, Tom *13:* 180; *17:* 212; *21:* 116; *24:* 132; *33:* 154; *38:* 59; *42:* 147
Hughes, Arthur *20:* 148, 149, 150; *33:* 114, 148, 149
Hughes, Darren *95:* 44
Hughes, David *36:* 197
Hughes, Shirley *1:* 20, 21; *7:* 3; *12:* 217; *16:* 163; *29:* 154; *63:* 118; *70:* 102, 103, 104; *73:* 169; *88:* 70; *110:* 118, 119; *159:* 103
Hugo, Victor *47:* 112
Huliska-Beith, Laura *204:* 108; *220:* 137
Hull, Cathy *78:* 29
Hull, Richard *95:* 120; *123:* 175; *172:* 195
Hulsmann, Eva *16:* 166
Hume, Lachie *189:* 93
Hummel, Berta *43:* 137, 138, 139
Hummel, Lisl *29:* 109; *YABC 2:* 333, 334
Humphrey, Henry *16:* 167
Humphreys, Graham *25:* 168
Humphries, Tudor *76:* 66; *80:* 4; *124:* 4, 5
Huneck, Stephen *183:* 88, 89
Hunt, James *2:* 143
Hunt, Jonathan *84:* 120
Hunt, Paul *119:* 104; *129:* 135; *139:* 160; *173:* 112

Hunt, Robert *110:* 206, 235; *147:* 136, 137; *170:* 3; *211:* 76
Hunt, Scott *190:* 143
Hunter, Anne *133:* 190; *178:* 150
Huntington, Amy *180:* 99
Hurd, Clement *2:* 148, 149; *64:* 127, 128, 129, 131, 133, 134,135, 136; *100:* 37, 38
Hurd, Peter *24:* 30, 31,; *YABC 2:* 56
Hurd, Thacher *46:* 88, 89; *94:* 114, 115, 116; *123:* 81, 82, 84; *219:* 82
Hurlimann, Ruth *32:* 99
Hurst, Carol Otis *185:* 92
Hurst, Elise *221:* 98
Hurst, Philip *196:* 79
Hurst, Tracey *192:* 238
Hussar, Michael *114:* 113; *117:* 159
Hustler, Tom *6:* 105
Hutchins, Laurence *55:* 22
Hutchins, Pat *15:* 142; *70:* 106, 107, 108; *178:* 131, 132
Hutchinson, Sascha *95:* 211
Hutchinson, William M. *6:* 3, 138; *46:* 70
Hutchison, Paula *23:* 10
Hutton, Clarke *YABC 2:* 335
Hutton, Kathryn *35:* 155; *89:* 91
Hutton, Warwick *20:* 91
Huyette, Marcia *29:* 188
Hyatt, John *54:* 7
Hyatt, Mitch *178:* 162
Hyde, Maureen *82:* 17; *121:* 145, 146
Hyman, David *117:* 64
Hyman, Miles *210:* 132
Hyman, Trina Schart *1:* 204; *2:* 194; *5:* 153; *6:* 106; *7:* 138, 145; *8:* 22; *10:* 196; *13:* 96; *14:* 114; *15:* 204; *16:* 234; *20:* 82; *22:* 133; *24:* 151; *25:* 79, 82; *26:* 82; *29:* 83; *31:* 37, 39; *34:* 104; *38:* 84, 100, 128; *41:* 49; *43:* 146; *46:* 91, 92, 93, 95, 96, 97, 98, 99, 100, 101, 102, 103, 104, 105,108, 109, 111, 197; *48:* 60, 61; *52:* 32; *60:* 168; *66:* 38; *67:* 214; *72:* 74; *75:* 92; *79:* 57; *82:* 95, 238; *89:* 46; *95:* 91, 92, 93; *100:* 33, 199; *132:* 12; *147:* 33, 35, 36; *167:* 58, 60; *177:* 189, 190; *211:* 188

I

Ibarra, Rosa *147:* 91
Ibatoulline, Bagram *156:* 48; *174:* 33, 82; *202:* 30; *211:* 213
Ichikawa, Satomi *29:* 152; *41:* 52; *47:* 133, 134,135, 136; *78:* 93, 94; *80:* 81; *146:* 143, 145, 146; *208:* 117, 118, 119
Ide, Jacqueline *YABC 1:* 39
Ilsley, Velma *3:* 1; *7:* 55; *12:* 109; *37:* 62; *38:* 184
Imai, Ayano *190:* 85, 86
in den Bosch, Nicole *150:* 204
Inga *1:* 142
Ingman, Bruce *134:* 50; *182:* 91, 92; *214:* 10
Ingpen, Robert *109:* 103, 104; *132:* 138; *137:* 177; *166:* 103; *181:* 140
Ingraham, Erick *21:* 177; *84:* 256; *103:* 66
Inkpen, Mick *99:* 104, 105; *106:* 44
Innerst, Stacy *149:* 104
Innocenti, Roberto *21:* 123; *96:* 122; *159:* 111, 197; *199:* 176
Inoue, Yosuke *24:* 118
Iofin, Michael *97:* 157
Iosa, Ann *63:* 189
Ipcar, Dahlov *1:* 124, 125; *49:* 137, 138, 139, 140, 141, 142,143, 144, 145; *147:* 122, 124, 126
Irvin, Fred *13:* 166; *15:* 143, 144; *27:* 175
Irving, Jay *45:* 72
Irving, Laurence *27:* 50
Isaac, Joanne *21:* 76
Isaacs, Gary *170:* 188

Isadora, Rachel *43:* 159, 160; *54:* 31; *79:* 106, 107,108; *121:* 100, 102; *165:* 116, 117; *204:* 61, 63, 64
Ishmael, Woodi *24:* 111; *31:* 99
Isol *220:* 73
Ives, Ruth *15:* 257
Iwai, Melissa *149:* 233; *183:* 92; *199:* 115
Iwamura, Kazuo *213:* 87

J

Jabar, Cynthia *101:* 201; *210:* 134, 135
Jackness, Andrew *94:* 237
Jackson, Julian *91:* 104, 106
Jackson, Michael *43:* 42
Jackson, Shelley *79:* 71; *99:* 109; *187:* 82
Jacob, Murv *89:* 30
Jacobi, Kathy *62:* 118
Jacobs, Barbara *9:* 136
Jacobs, Lou, Jr. *9:* 136; *15:* 128
Jacobsen, Laura *176:* 98; *177:* 85, 86
Jacobson, Rick *131:* 222; *170:* 119
Jacobus, Tim *79:* 140; *109:* 126; *129:* 180
Jacques, Robin *1:* 70; *2:* 1; *8:* 46; *9:* 20; *15:* 187; *19:* 253; *32:* 102, 103, 104; *43:* 184; *73:* 135; *YABC 1:* 42
Jaeggi, Yoshiko *186:* 184
Jaffee, Al *66:* 131, 132
Jago *216:* 122
Jagr, Miloslav *13:* 197
Jahn-Clough, Lisa *88:* 114; *152:* 104; *193:* 70, 71
Jahnke, Robert *84:* 24
Jainschigg, Nicholas *80:* 64; *91:* 138; *95:* 63; *99:* 25; *108:* 50; *171:* 41
Jakesavic, Nenad *85:* 102
Jakobsen, Kathy *116:* 83
Jakubowski, Charles *14:* 192
Jambor, Louis *YABC 1:* 11
James, Ann *73:* 50; *82:* 113; *158:* 61; *183:* 44
James, Brian *140:* 91
James, Curtis E. *182:* 93
James, Derek *35:* 187; *44:* 91; *61:* 133; *74:* 2; *80:* 57; *86:* 88; *130:* 30; *179:* 29; *218:* 31
James, Gilbert *YABC 1:* 43
James, Gordon C. *195:* 89
James, Harold *2:* 151; *3:* 62; *8:* 79; *29:* 113; *51:* 195; *74:* 90
James, Kennon *126:* 211
James, Robin *50:* 106; *53:* 32, 34, 35
James, Simon *202:* 73, 74
James, Will *19:* 150, 152, 153, 155, 163
Janosch
    See Eckert, Horst
Janovitch, Marilyn *68:* 168
Janovitz, Marilyn *87:* 187; *130:* 198; *194:* 91
Jansons, Inese *48:* 117
Jansson, Alexander *216:* 59
Jansson, Tove *3:* 90; *41:* 106, 108, 109, 110, 111, 113, 114
Jaques, Faith *7:* 11, 132, 133; *21:* 83, 84; *69:* 114,116; *73:* 170
Jaques, Frances Lee *29:* 224
Jarka, Jeff *221:* 94
Jarrett, Clare *201:* 77
Jarrie, Martin *219:* 86
Jauss, Anne Marie *1:* 139; *3:* 34; *10:* 57, 119; *11:* 205; *23:* 194
Jay, Alison *158:* 97, 98; *183:* 126, 127; *196:* 95, 96, 97, 98; *200:* 72, 73, 74; *212:* 39
Jeffers, Oliver *175:* 111; *213:* 89
Jeffers, Susan *17:* 86, 87; *25:* 164, 165; *26:* 112; *50:* 132, 134, 135; *70:* 111, 112, 113; *137:* 107, 108, 109, 110, 111; *202:* 77, 78
Jefferson, Louise E. *4:* 160
Jenkin-Pearce, Susie *78:* 16
Jenkins, Debra Reid *85:* 202; *114:* 89; *173:* 134
Jenkins, Jean *98:* 79, 102

Jenkins, Leonard *157:* 169; *167:* 128; *189:* 96, 97; *190:* 89
Jenkins, Patrick *72:* 126
Jenkins, Steve *124:* 177; *154:* 90, 91, 92, 93; *185:* 194; *188:* 81, 82, 83, 84, 85, 86; *218:* 67, 69, 70, 71, 72
Jenks, Aleta *73:* 117; *124:* 225
Jenkyns, Chris *51:* 97
Jensen, Bruce *95:* 39
Jensinius, Kirsten *56:* 58
Jeram, Anita *89:* 135; *102:* 122, 123; *129:* 112; *154:* 96, 97, 98; *164:* 154; *203:* 123, 124; *219:* 88, 89, 90, 91
Jernigan, E. Wesley *85:* 92
Jerome, Karen A. *72:* 194
Jeruchim, Simon *6:* 173; *15:* 250
Jeschke, Susan *20:* 89; *39:* 161; *41:* 84; *42:* 120
Jessel, Camilla *29:* 115
Jessell, Tim *159:* 3; *177:* 87; *181:* 95; *205:* 4; *213:* 74
Jeyaveeran, Ruth *182:* 100
Jiang, Cheng An *109:* 108
Jiang, Wei *109:* 108
Jimenez, Maria *77:* 158; *93:* 127
Jobling, Curtis *138:* 74
Jocelyn, Marthe *118:* 83; *137:* 219; *163:* 119, 120; *198:* 62
Joerns, Consuelo *38:* 36; *44:* 94
John, Diana *12:* 209
John, Helen I. *215:* 15; *28:* 204
Johns, Elizabeth *127:* 33
Johns, Jasper *61:* 172
Johns, Jeanne *24:* 114
Johnson, Adrian *143:* 50
Johnson, Bruce *9:* 47
Johnson, Cathy *92:* 136; *218:* 112
Johnson, Crockett
    See Leisk, David
Johnson, D. William *23:* 104
Johnson, D.B. *183:* 98, 139
Johnson, David A. *175:* 18; *191:* 91; *218:* 19
Johnson, Gillian *119:* 175; *164:* 217; *215:* 99
Johnson, Harper *1:* 27; *2:* 33; *18:* 302; *19:* 61; *31:* 181; *44:* 46, 50, 95
Johnson, Ingrid *37:* 118
Johnson, James Ralph *1:* 23, 127
Johnson, James David *12:* 195
Johnson, Jane *48:* 136
Johnson, Joel Peter *98:* 18; *128:* 111; *201:* 13; *213:* 189
Johnson, John E. *34:* 133
Johnson, Kevin *72:* 44
Johnson, Kevin Eugene *109:* 215
Johnson, Larry *47:* 56; *123:* 107; *159:* 203
Johnson, Layne *187:* 94; *209:* 63
Johnson, Margaret S. *35:* 131
Johnson, Meredith Merrell *71:* 181; *83:* 158; *89:* 103; *104:* 88
Johnson, Milton *1:* 67; *2:* 71; *26:* 45; *31:* 107; *60:* 112; *68:* 96
Johnson, Pamela *16:* 174; *52:* 145; *62:* 140; *73:* 116; *85:* 64
Johnson, Paul Brett *83:* 95; *132:* 119
Johnson, Stephen T. *80:* 15; *131:* 35; *141:* 96; *145:* 40; *164:* 187; *175:* 32; *189:* 99, 100; *208:* 43
Johnson, Steve *138:* 219; *141:* 64; *144:* 199; *177:* 51; *214:* 95; *221:* 63
Johnson, William R. *38:* 91
Johnson-Petrov, Arden *115:* 206
Johnston, David McCall *50:* 131, 133
Johnston, Lynne *118:* 85, 87, 89; *216:* 127, 128, 131
Johnstone, Anne *8:* 120; *36:* 89
Johnstone, Janet Grahame *8:* 120; *36:* 89
Jonas, Ann *50:* 107, 108, 109; *135:* 113
Jones, Bob *71:* 5; *77:* 199
Jones, Carol *5:* 131; *72:* 185, 186; *153:* 111, 112
Jones, Chuck *53:* 70, 71

Jones, Curtis *211:* 144
Jones, Davy *89:* 176
Jones, Douglas B. *185:* 192; *202:* 82
Jones, Elizabeth Orton *18:* 124, 126, 128, 129
Jones, Harold *14:* 88; *52:* 50
Jones, Holly *127:* 3
Jones, Jeff *41:* 64
Jones, Laurian *25:* 24, 27
Jones, Margaret *74:* 57
Jones, Noah Z. *182:* 37; *203:* 159
Jones, Randy *131:* 104
Jones, Richard *127:* 222
Jones, Robert *25:* 67
Jones, Wilfred *35:* 115; *YABC 1:* 163
Jordan, Charles *89:* 58
Jordan, Jess *158:* 136; *203:* 111
Jordan, Martin George *84:* 127
Jordan, Richard *84:* 36
Jorgenson, Andrea *91:* 111
Jorisch, Stéphane *153:* 56, 193; *177:* 29; *178:* 138, 139; *187:* 23; *211:* 182
Joseph, James *53:* 88
Joudrey, Ken *64:* 145; *78:* 6
Joyce, William *72:* 131, 132, 133, 134; *73:* 227; *145:* 37
Joyner, Jerry *34:* 138
Joyner, Loraine M. *209:* 17
Joysmith, Brenda *210:* 237
Juan, Ana *175:* 38; *179:* 111, 112; *213:* 9
Jucker, Sita *5:* 93
Judge, Lita *192:* 99
Judkis, Jim *37:* 38
Juhasz, Victor *31:* 67
Jullian, Philippe *24:* 206; *25:* 203
Jung, Tom *91:* 217
Junge, Alexandra *183:* 37
Junge, Walter *67:* 150
Jupo, Frank *7:* 148, 149
Jurisch, Stephane *154:* 105
Justice, Martin *34:* 72

K

Kabatova-Taborska, Zdenka *107:* 153
Kachik, John *165:* 230
Kaczman, James *156:* 98
Kadair, Deborah Ousley *184:* 45, 89
Kahl, David *74:* 95; *97:* 35; *109:* 174; *110:* 213; *198:* 15
Kahl, M.P. *37:* 83
Kahl, Virginia *48:* 138
Kahn, Katherine Janus *90:* 135; *211:* 155; *218:* 75, 76; *220:* 89,90
Kakimoo, Kozo *11:* 148
Kalett, Jim *48:* 159, 160, 161
Kalin, Victor *39:* 186
Kalis, Jennifer *207:* 82; *219:* 62
Kalman, Maira *96:* 131, 132; *137:* 115
Kalmenoff, Matthew *22:* 191
Kalow, Gisela *32:* 105
Kamen, Gloria *1:* 41; *9:* 119; *10:* 178; *35:* 157; *78:* 236; *98:* 82
Kaminsky, Jef *102:* 153
Kandell, Alice *35:* 133
Kane, Henry B. *14:* 90; *18:* 219, 220
Kane, Robert *18:* 131
Kanfer, Larry *66:* 141
Kangas, Juli *200:* 88
Kappes, Alfred *28:* 104
Karalus, Bob *41:* 157
Karas, G. Brian *80:* 60; *99:* 179; *115:* 41; *118:* 50; *136:* 168; *145:* 166; *149:* 245; *159:* 65; *171:* 192; *178:* 142, 143; *202:* 38; *209:* 142
Karasz, Ilonka *128:* 163
Karlin, Eugene *10:* 63; *20:* 131
Karlin, Nurit *63:* 78; *103:* 110
Karpinski, Tony *134:* 160
Kasamatsu, Shiro *139:* 155
Kasparavicius, Kestutis *139:* 210

Kassian, Olena *64:* 94
Kastner, Jill *79:* 135; *117:* 84, 85
Kasuya, Masahiro *41:* 206, 207; *51:* 100
Kasza, Keiko *191:* 99, 100, 101, 102, 103
Katona, Robert *21:* 85; *24:* 126
Katz, Avi *199:* 55
Katz, Karen *158:* 123
Kauffer, E. McKnight *33:* 103; *35:* 127; *63:* 67
Kaufman, Angelika *15:* 156
Kaufman, Joe *33:* 119
Kaufman, John *13:* 158
Kaufman, Stuart *62:* 64; *68:* 226; *137:* 44
Kaufmann, John *1:* 174; *4:* 159; *8:* 43, 1; *10:* 102; *18:* 133, 134; *22:* 251
Kaye, Graham *1:* 9; *67:* 7, 8
Kaye, M.M. *62:* 95
Kazalovski, Nata *40:* 205
Keane, Bil *4:* 135
Kearney, David *72:* 47; *121:* 83
Keating, Pamel T. *77:* 37
Keats, Ezra Jack *3:* 18, 105, 257; *14:* 101, 102; *33:* 129; *57:* 79, 80, 82, 83, 84, 87
Keegan, Charles *166:* 211
Keegan, Marcia *9:* 122; *32:* 93
Keeler, Patricia A. *81:* 56; *183:* 102, 103
Keely, Jack *119:* 95
Keely, John *26:* 104; *48:* 214
Keen, Eliot *25:* 213
Keep, Richard C. *170:* 122
Keeping, Charles *9:* 124, 185; *15:* 28, 134; *18:* 115; *44:* 194, 196; *47:* 25; *52:* 3; *54:* 156; *69:* 123, 124; *74:* 56; *155:* 9
Keeter, Susan *168:* 46; *183:* 192
Keith, Eros *4:* 98; *5:* 138; *31:* 29; *43:* 220; *52:* 91, 92, 93, 94; *56:* 64, 66; *60:* 37; *79:* 93
Keleinikov, Andrei *65:* 101, 102
Kelen, Emery *13:* 115
Keller, A.J. *62:* 198
Keller, Arthur I. *26:* 106
Keller, Dick *36:* 123, 125
Keller, Holly *45:* 79; *76:* 118, 119, 120, 121; *108:* 137, 138, 140; *157:* 117, 118, 119; *216:* 136
Keller, Katie *79:* 222; *93:* 108
Keller, Laurie *196:* 105, 106
Keller, Ronald *45:* 208
Kelley, Gary *183:* 105; *216:* 78; *217:* 95, 96, 97
Kelley, Marty *211:* 91
Kelley, True *41:* 114, 115; *42:* 137; *75:* 35; *92:* 104, 105; *124:* 62; *130:* 100, 101; *179:* 120, 121, 122; *192:* 251
Kellogg, Steven *8:* 96; *11:* 207; *14:* 130; *20:* ; *201:* 38 58; *29:* 140, 141; *30:* 35; *41:* 141; *57:* 89, 90, 92,93, 94, 96; *59:* 182; *73:* 141; *77:* 129; *130:* 105, 106; *177:* 94, 95, 96, 97; *199:* 57; *217:* 61; *YABC 1:* 65, 73
Kelly, Billy *158:* 143
Kelly, Geoff *97:* 196; *112:* 25
Kelly, Irene *147:* 134; *210:* 144, 145
Kelly, John *194:* 186
Kelly, Joseph *174:* 94
Kelly, Kathleen M. *71:* 109
Kelly, Laura *89:* 217
Kelly, True *163:* 87
Kelly, Walt *18:* 136, 137, 138, 139, 140, 141, 144, 145, 146, 148, 149
Kemble, E.W. *34:* 75; *44:* 178; *YABC 2:* 54, 59
Kemly, Kathleen *209:* 165
Kemp-Welsh, Lucy *24:* 197; *100:* 214
Kendall, Jane *150:* 105; *186:* 109
Kendall, Peter *152:* 85
Kendrick, Dennis *79:* 213
Kennaway, Adrienne *60:* 55, 56; *171:* 88, 89
Kennedy, Anne *212:* 34
Kennedy, Doug *189:* 104
Kennedy, Paul Edward *6:* 190; *8:* 132; *33:* 120
Kennedy, Richard *3:* 93; *12:* 179; *44:* 193; *100:* 15; *YABC 1:* 57

Kent, Jack *24:* 136; *37:* 37; *40:* 81; *84:* 89; *86:* 150; *88:* 77
Kent, Rockwell *5:* 166; *6:* 129; *20:* 225, 226, 227,229; *59:* 144
Kenyon, Tony *81:* 201; *127:* 74
Kepes, Juliet *13:* 119
Kerins, Anthony *76:* 84
Kerr, Judity *24:* 137
Kerr, Phyllis Forbes *72:* 141
Kessler, Leonard *1:* 108; *7:* 139; *14:* 107, 227; *22:* 101; *44:* 96; *67:* 79; *82:* 123
Kest, Kristin *168:* 99; *173:* 23
Kesteven, Peter *35:* 189
Ketcham, Hank *28:* 140, 141, 142
Kettelkamp, Larry *2:* 164
Key, Alexander *8:* 99
Khalsa, Dayal Kaur *62:* 99
Kiakshuk *8:* 59
Kid, Tom *207:* 54
Kidd, Chip *94:* 23
Kidd, Richard *152:* 110
Kidd, Tom *64:* 199; *81:* 189; *185:* 173
Kiddell-Monroe, Joan *19:* 201; *55:* 59, 60; *87:* 174; *121:* 112
Kidder, Harvey *9:* 105; *80:* 41
Kidwell, Carl *43:* 145
Kieffer, Christa *41:* 89
Kiesler, Kate *110:* 105; *136:* 142
Kiff, Ken *40:* 45
Kilbride, Robert *37:* 100
Kilby, Don *141:* 144
Kim, David *201:* 79; *202:* 97
Kim, Glenn *99:* 82
Kimball, Anton *78:* 114; *119:* 105
Kimball, Yeffe *23:* 116; *37:* 88
Kimber, Murray *171:* 91
Kimmel, Warren *176:* 112
Kincade, Orin *34:* 116
Kindersley, Barnabas *96:* 110
Kindred, Wendy *7:* 151
King, Colin *53:* 3
King, Robin *10:* 164, 165
King, Stephen Michael *141:* 31; *197:* 191; *218:* 81, 82
King, Tara Calahan *139:* 172
King, Tony *39:* 121
Kingman, Dong *16:* 287; *44:* 100, 102, 104
Kingsley, Charles *YABC 2:* 182
Kingston, Julie *147:* 14
Kingston, Maxine Hong *53:* 92
Kinney, Jeff *187:* 97
Kipling, John Lockwood *YABC 2:* 198
Kipling, Rudyard *YABC 2:* 196
Kipniss, Robert *29:* 59
Kirchherr, Astrid *55:* 23
Kirchhoff, Art *28:* 136
Kirk, Daniel *153:* 115, 116, 117; *173:* 101; *196:* 113, 114, 115, 116
Kirk, David *117:* 88, 89; *161:* 97, 98
Kirk, Ruth *5:* 96
Kirk, Steve *170:* 37
Kirk, Tim *32:* 209, 211; *72:* 89; *83:* 49
Kirmse, Marguerite *15:* 283; *18:* 153
Kirsch, Vincent X. *124:* 207
Kirschner, Ruth *22:* 154
Kirwan, Wednesday *198:* 73
Kish, Ely *73:* 119; *79:* 2
Kitamura, Satoshi *62:* 102; *98:* 91; *101:* 147; *138:* 2; *143:* 83, 85, 86; *201:* 83
Kiss, Andrew *168:* 115
Kitchel, JoAnn E. *133:* 32
Kitchen, Bert *70:* 126; *193:* 49
Kittelsen, Theodor *62:* 14
Kiuchi, Tatsuro *114:* 71
Kiwak, Barbara *172:* 135
Klahr, Susan *176:* 196
Klapholz, Mel *13:* 35
Klee, Jutte *209:* 136
Klein, Bill *89:* 105
Klein, Robert *55:* 77
Klein, Suzanna *63:* 104

Kleinman, Zalman *28:* 143
Kleven, Elisa *173:* 96, 97; *217:* 100, 102
Kliban, B. *35:* 137, 138
Kline, Michael *127:* 66
Klise, M. Sarah *180:* 117, 118; *181:* 97; *221:* 100, 102
Knabel, Lonnie *73:* 103; *75:* 187, 228; *194:* 216
Kneen, Maggie *140:* 139; *221:* 104, 105
Knight, Ann *34:* 143
Knight, Christopher *13:* 125
Knight, Hilary *1:* 233; *3:* 21; *15:* 92, 158, 159; *16:* 258, 259, 260; *18:* 235; *19:* 169; *35:* 242; *46:* 167; *52:* 116; *69:* 126, 127; *132:* 129; *YABC 1:* 168, 169, 172
Knorr, Laura *200:* 91
Knorr, Peter *126:* 92, 93
Knotts, Howard *20:* 4; *25:* 170; *36:* 163
Knutson, Barbara *112:* 134; *202:* 108
Knutson, Kimberley *115:* 90
Kobayashi, Ann *39:* 58
Kochalka, James *196:* 120, 121, 122
Kocsis, J.C.
    See Paul, James
Kodman, Stanislawa *201:* 85
Koehler, Hanne Lore *176:* 203
Koehn, Ilse *34:* 198; *79:* 123
Koelsch, Michael *99:* 182; *107:* 164; *109:* 239; *138:* 142; *150:* 94; *176:* 105; *187:* 63; *198:* 63
Koering, Ursula *3:* 28; *4:* 14; *44:* 5; *64:* 140,141; *85:* 46
Koerner, Henry
    See Koerner, W.H.D.
Koerner, W.H.D. *14:* 216; *21:* 88, 89, 90, 91; *23:* 211
Koetsch, Mike *166:* 68
Koffler, Camilla *36:* 113
Kogan, Deborah Ray *161:* 101, 102
Koide, Yasuko *50:* 114
Kolado, Karen *102:* 228
Kolesova, Juliana *217:* 81
Komoda, Kiyo *9:* 128; *13:* 214
Kompaneyets, Marc *169:* 92
Konashevich, Vladimir *61:* 160
Konashevicha, V. *YABC 1:* 26
Konigsburg, E.L. *4:* 138; *48:* 141, 142, 144, 145; *94:* 129, 130; *126:* 129, 130, 131; *194:* 95, 98
Kono, Erin Eitter *177:* 99
Kooiker, Leonie *48:* 148
Koonook, Simon *65:* 157
Koontz, Robin Michal *136:* 155
Koopmans, Loek *101:* 121
Kopelke, Lisa *154:* 107
Kopper, Lisa *72:* 152, 153; *105:* 135, 136
Korach, Mimi *1:* 128, 129; *2:* 52; *4:* 39; *5:* 159; *9:* 129; *10:* 21; *24:* 69
Koren, Edward *5:* 100; *65:* 65, 67
Kosaka, Fumi *164:* 130
Koscielniak, Bruce *99:* 122; *153:* 120, 121, 122
Koshkin, Alexander *92:* 180
Kossin, Sandy *10:* 71; *23:* 105
Kostin, Andrej *26:* 204
Kosturko, Bob *164:* 56
Kotzky, Brian *68:* 184
Kovacevic, Zivojin *13:* 247
Kovalski, Maryann *58:* 120; *84:* 88; *97:* 124, 125, 126; *158:* 3; *186:* 80
Kozjan, Drazen *209:* 99
Krahn, Fernando *2:* 257; *34:* 206; *49:* 152
Krall, Dan *218:* 84, 85
Kramer, Anthony *33:* 81
Kramer, David *96:* 162; *109:* 132; *150:* 220
Kramer, Frank *6:* 121
Krantz, Kathy *35:* 83
Kratter, Paul *139:* 65
Kraus, Robert *13:* 217; *65:* 113; *93:* 93, 94
Krause, Jon *176:* 62
Krauss, Trisha *174:* 10

Kredel, Fritz *6:* 35; *17:* 93, 94, 95, 96; *22:* 147; *24:* 175; *29:* 130; *35:* 77; *YABC 2:* 166, 300
Kreloff, Eliot *189:* 107, 108; *205:* 182
Krementz, Jill *17:* 98; *49:* 41
Krenina, Katya *117:* 106; *125:* 133; *176:* 117; *221:* 107
Kresin, Robert *23:* 19
Krieger, Salem *54:* 164
Kriegler, Lyn *73:* 29
Krinitz, Esther Nisenthal *193:* 196
Krommes, Beth *128:* 141; *149:* 136; *181:* 100, 101; *184:* 105; *188:* 125; *208:* 135; *209:* 185
Krone, Mike *101:* 71
Kronheimer, Ann *135:* 119
Krosoczka, Jarrett J. *155:* 142; *200:* 93, 94
Kruck, Gerald *88:* 181
Krudop, Walter Lyon *199:* 19
Krupinski, Loretta *67:* 104; *102:* 131; *161:* 105, 106
Krupp, Robin Rector *53:* 96, 98
Krush, Beth *1:* 51, 85; *2:* 233; *4:* 115; *9:* 61; *10:* 191; *11:* 196; *18:* 164, 165; *32:* 72; *37:* 203; *43:* 57; *60:* 102, 103, 107, 108, 109
Krush, Joe *2:* 233; *4:* 115; *9:* 61; *10:* 191; *11:* 196; *18:* 164, 165; *32:* 72, 91; *37:* 203; *43:* 57; *60:* 102, 103, 107, 108, 109
Krych, Duane *91:* 43
Krykorka, Vladyana *96:* 147; *143:* 90, 91; *168:* 14
Kubick, Dana *165:* 91; *212:* 104, 105, 212
Kubinyi, Laszlo *4:* 116; *6:* 113; *16:* 118; *17:* 100; *28:* 227; *30:* 172; *49:* 24, 28; *54:* 23; *167:* 149
Kubricht, Mary *73:* 118
Kucharik, Elena *139:* 31
Kuchera, Kathleen *84:* 5
Kuhn, Bob *17:* 91; *35:* 235
Kulikov, Boris *163:* 185; *185:* 23; *205:* 99, 100; *217:* 160
Kulka, Joe *188:* 110
Kukalis, Romas *90:* 27; *139:* 37
Kuklin, Susan *63:* 82, 83, 84
Kunhardt, Dorothy *53:* 101
Kunhardt, Edith *67:* 105, 106
Kunstler, Mort *10:* 73; *32:* 143
Kurchevsky, V. *34:* 61
Kurczok, Belinda *121:* 118
Kurelek, William *8:* 107
Kuriloff, Ron *13:* 19
Kurisu, Jane *160:* 120
Kuskin, Karla *2:* 170; *68:* 115, 116; *111:* 116
Kutzer, Ernst *19:* 249
Kuzma, Steve *57:* 8; *62:* 93
Kuznetsova, Berta *74:* 45
Kvasnosky, Laura McGee *93:* 103; *142:* 83; *182:* 108
Kwas, Susan Estelle *179:* 116; *217:* 90
Kyong, Yunmee *165:* 139

L

LaBlanc, Andre *24:* 146
Laboccetta, Mario *27:* 120
LaBrose, Darcie *157:* 134
Labrosse, Darcia *58:* 88; *108:* 77; *178:* 89
LaCava, Vince *95:* 118
Laceky, Adam *32:* 121
Lacis, Astra *85:* 117
Lacome, Julie *174:* 96, 97
La Croix *YABC 2:* 4
Ladd, London *206:* 50
Ladwig, Tim *98:* 212; *117:* 76; *215:* 32
La Farge, Margaret *47:* 141
LaFave, Kim *64:* 177; *72:* 39; *97:* 146; *99:* 172; *106:* 123; *149:* 126; *196:* 128, 129
Lafontaine, Roger *167:* 158
Lafrance, Marie *197:* 109
Lagarrigue, Jerome *136:* 102; *187:* 81

Laimgruber, Monika *11:* 153
Laio, Jimmy *213:* 57
Laite, Gordon *1:* 130, 131; *8:* 209; *31:* 113; *40:* 63; *46:* 117
Laliberté, Louise-Andrée *169:* 98
LaMarche, Jim *46:* 204; *61:* 56; *94:* 69; *114:* 22; *129:* 163; *162:* 78, 80
Lamb, Jim *10:* 117
Lambase, Barbara *101:* 185; *150:* 221; *166:* 234
Lambert, J.K. *38:* 129; *39:* 24
Lambert, Sally Anne *133:* 191
Lambert, Saul *23:* 112; *33:* 107; *54:* 136
Lambert, Stephen *109:* 33; *174:* 99
Lambo, Don *6:* 156; *35:* 115; *36:* 146
Lamontagne, Jacques *166:* 227
Lamut, Sonja *57:* 193
Lamut, Sonya *85:* 102
Landa, Peter *11:* 95; *13:* 177; *53:* 119
Landau, Jacob *38:* 111
Landis, Joan *104:* 23; *203:* 32
Landon, Lucinda *79:* 31
Landshoff, Ursula *13:* 124
Landström, Lena *146:* 165, 166
Landström, Olof *146:* 166, 168; *170:* 22
Lane, Daniel *112:* 60
Lane, John R. *8:* 145
Lane, John *15:* 176, 177; *30:* 146
Lane, Nancy *166:* 74
Lang, G.D. *48:* 56
Lang, Gary *73:* 75
Lang, Glenna *221:* 113
Lang, Jerry *18:* 295
Langdo, Bryan *186:* 187; *191:* 113, 114, 115
Lange, Dorothea *50:* 141
Langley, Jonathan *162:* 128
Langner, Nola *8:* 110; *42:* 36
Lanino, Deborah *105:* 148
Lantz, Paul *1:* 82, 102; *27:* 88; *34:* 102; *45:* 123
Larkin, Bob *84:* 225
Laroche, Giles *126:* 140; *146:* 81; *221:* 116, 117
LaRochelle, David *171:* 97
Larrecq, John *44:* 108; *68:* 56
Larsen, Suzanne *1:* 13
Larson, Gary *57:* 121, 122, 123, 124, 125, 126, 127
Larsson, Carl *35:* 144, 145, 146, 147, 148, 149, 150, 152, 153, 154
Larsson, Karl *19:* 177
Lartitegui, Ana G. *105:* 167
LaRue, Jenna *167:* 20
La Rue, Michael D. *13:* 215
Lasker, Joe *7:* 186, 187; *14:* 55; *38:* 115; *39:* 47; *83:* 113, 114, 115
Latham, Barbara *16:* 188, 189; *43:* 71
Lathrop, Dorothy *14:* 117, 118, 119; *15:* 109; *16:* 78, 79, 81; *32:* 201, 203; *33:* 112; *YABC 2:* 301
Lattimore, Eleanor Frances *7:* 156
Lauden, Claire *16:* 173
Lauden, George, Jr. *16:* 173
Laune, Paul *2:* 235; *34:* 31
Laure, Jason *49:* 53; *50:* 122
Lauter, Richard *63:* 29; *67:* 111; *77:* 198
Lavallee, Barbara *74:* 157; *92:* 154; *96:* 126; *145:* 193; *166:* 125, 126; *186:* 155; *192:* 172
Lave, Fitz Hugh *59:* 139
Lavis, Stephen *43:* 143; *87:* 137, 164, 165
Layton, Neal *152:* 120, 121; *182:* 65; *187:* 103, 105, 106
Law, Jenny *201:* 31
Lawrason, June *168:* 30
Lawrence, John *25:* 131; *30:* 141; *44:* 198, 200; *214:* 7
Lawrence, Stephen *20:* 195
Lawson, Carol *6:* 38; *42:* 93, 131; *174:* 56; *189:* 89; *209:* 59
Lawson, George *17:* 280

Lawson, Robert 5: 26; 6: 94; 13: 39; 16: 11; 20: 100, 102, 103; 54: 3; 66: 12; 100: 144, 145; YABC 2: 222, 224, 225, 227, 228, 229, 230, 231, 232, 233, 234, 235, 237, 238, 239, 240, 241
Layfield, Kathie 60: 194
Lazare, Jerry 44: 109; 74: 28
Lazarevich, Mila 17: 118
Lazarus, Claire 103: 30
Lazarus, Keo Felker 21: 94
Lazzaro, Victor 11: 126
Lea, Bob 166: 208; 203: 108
Lea, Tom 43: 72, 74
Leacroft, Richard 6: 140
Leaf, Munro 20: 99
Leake, Donald 70: 41
Leander, Patricia 23: 27
Lear, Edward 18: 183, 184, 185
Lear, Rebecca 149: 46
Lebenson, Richard 6: 209; 7: 76; 23: 145; 44: 191; 87: 153
Le Cain, Errol 6: 141; 9: 3; 22: 142; 25: 198; 28: 173; 68: 128, 129; 86: 49
Lechon, Daniel 113: 211
Leder, Dora 129: 172
Ledger, Bill 181: 58
Leduc, Bernard 102: 36
Lee, Alan 62: 25, 28
Lee, Bryce 99: 60; 101: 195; 196: 53
Lee, Chinlun 181: 138; 182: 112
Lee, Declan 191: 20
Lee, Dom 83: 118, 120; 93: 123; 121: 121, 126; 146: 174, 175, 206, 207; 174: 204
Lee, Doris 13: 246; 32: 183; 44: 111
Lee, Hector Viveros 115: 96
Lee, Ho Baek 200: 160
Lee, Huy Voun 217: 106
Lee, Jeanne M. 158: 56
Lee, Jared 93: 200; 157: 229; 215: 113, 191, 192, 193
Lee, Jody 81: 121; 82: 225; 91: 155; 100: 182
Lee, Jody A. 127: 124, 126, 127
  See also Lee, Jody
Lee, Manning de V. 2: 200; 17: 12; 27: 87; 37: 102, 103, 104; YABC 2: 304
Lee, Margaret 213: 179
Lee, Marie G. 138: 157
Lee, Paul 97: 100; 105: 72, 209; 109: 177; 128: 113; 202: 45
Lee, Robert J. 3: 97; 67: 124
Lee, Victor 96: 228; 105: 182; 140: 196; 208: 191
Lee, Virginia 208: 139, 140; 218: 28
Leech, Dorothy 98: 76
Leech, John 15: 59
Leedy, Loreen 84: 142; 128: 144, 145, 146; 175: 125, 126, 127
Leeman, Michael 44: 157
Leeming, Catherine 87: 39
Lees, Harry 6: 112
LeFever, Bill 88: 220, 221
Legenisel 47: 111
Legrand, Edy 18: 89, 93
Lehman, Barbara 73: 123; 170: 130
Lehrman, Rosalie 2: 180
Leichman, Seymour 5: 107
Leick, Bonnie 205: 104
Leighton, Clare 25: 130; 33: 168; 37: 105, 106, 108,109
Leisk, David 1: 140, 141; 11: 54; 30: 137, 142, 143,144
Leister, Brian 89: 45; 106: 37; 114: 67; 149: 236
Leloir, Maurice 18: 77, 80, 83, 99
Lemaître, Pascal 144: 175; 176: 130; 189: 135
Lemieux, Michele 100: 148; 139: 153
Lemke, Horst 14: 98; 38: 117, 118, 119
Lemke, R.W. 42: 162
Lemon, David Gwynne 9: 1
LeMoult, Adolph 82: 116
Lenn, Michael 136: 89

Lennon, John 114: 100
Lennox, Elsie 95: 163; 143: 160
Lenski, Lois 1: 144; 26: 135, 137, 139, 141; 100: 153, 154
Lent, Blair 1: 116, 117; 2: 174; 3: 206, 207; 7: 168, 169; 34: 62; 68: 217; 133: 101; 183: 60
Leonard, David 212: 149
Leonard, Richard 91: 128
Leonard, Tom 207: 95; 219: 55
Leone, Leonard 49: 190
Lerner, Carol 86: 140, 141, 142
Lerner, Judith 116: 138
Lerner, Sharon 11: 157; 22: 56
Leroux-Hugon, Helene 132: 139
Leslie, Cecil 19: 244
Lessac, Frané 80: 182, 207; 96: 182; 202: 58; 209: 104
Lessing, Erich 167: 52; 173: 60
Lester, Alison 50: 124; 90: 147, 148; 129: 130; 218: 91, 93
Lester, Mike 208: 50
Lethcoe, Jason 191: 116, 117
Le Tord, Bijou 49: 156; 95: 112
Leutz, Emanuel 165: 27
Levai, Blaise 39: 130
Levert, Mireille 211: 101
Levin, Ted 12: 148
Levine, David 43: 147, 149, 150, 151, 152; 64: 11
Levine, Joe 71: 88; 219: 74
Levine, Marge 81: 127
Levinson, David 178: 232
Levit, Herschel 24: 223
Levstek, Ljuba 131: 192; 134: 216; 149: 65; 168: 180
Levy, Jessica Ann 19: 225; 39: 191
Levy, Lina 117: 126
Lewin, Betsy 32: 114; 48: 177; 90: 151; 91: 125; 92: 85; 115: 105; 169: 110, 111; 178: 47; 186: 188; 194: 201
Lewin, Ted 4: 77; 8: 168; 20: 110; 21: 99,100; 27: 110; 28: 96, 97; 31: 49; 45: 55; 48: 223; 60: 20, 119, 120; 62: 139; 66: 108; 71: 12; 72: 21; 74: 226; 76: 139, 140; 77: 82; 79: 87; 85: 49, 177; 86: 55; 88: 182; 93: 28, 29; 94: 34, 182, 194; 99: 156; 104: 8; 115: 123; 118: 74; 119: 114, 116; 131: 54; 145: 99; 165: 151; 177: 75; 178: 42; 190: 30; 192: 86; 195: 101, 102; 203: 52
Lewis, Allen 15: 112
Lewis, E.B. 88: 143; 93: 109; 119: 79; 124: 113; 128: 49; 151: 167; 168: 110; 173: 121; 174: 66; 176: 7; 184: 150; 185: 191; 211: 108, 109, 110, 111
Lewis, H.B. 170: 124
Lewis, J. Patrick 162: 83
Lewis, Jan 81: 22
Lewis, Kim 136: 165; 217: 109, 111
Lewis, Richard W. 52: 25
Lewis, Robin Baird 98: 193
Leydon, Rita Floden 21: 101
Li, Xiojun 187: 172
Liao, Jimmy 202: 100
Lichtenheld, Tom 152: 125, 126
Lieblich, Irene 22: 173; 27: 209, 214
Lieder, Rick 108: 197; 199: 58, 59, 60
Lies, Brian 92: 40; 141: 101; 150: 138; 190: 97, 98, 99,
Liese, Charles 4: 222
Liew, Sonny 219: 108
Life, Kay 79: 49
Lifton, Robert Jay 66: 154
Lightburn, Ron 86: 153; 91: 122
Lightfoot, Norman R. 45: 47
Lignell, Lois 37: 114
Lill, Debra 121: 70
Lilly, Charles 8: 73; 20: 127; 48: 53; 72: 9,16; 77: 98; 102: 94
Lilly, Ken 37: 224
Lim, John 43: 153

Limona, Mercedes 51: 183
Lin, Grace 143: 217; 162: 86, 87; 174: 185
Lincoln, Patricia Henderson 27: 27; 78: 127
Lindahn, Ron 84: 17
Lindahn, Val 84: 17
Lindberg, Howard 10: 123; 16: 190
Lindberg, Jeffrey 64: 77; 77: 71; 79: 54; 80: 149; 174: 109; 179: 52
Linden, Seymour 18: 200, 201; 43: 140
Lindenbaum, Pija 144: 143; 183: 113
Linder, Richard 27: 119
Lindman, Maj 43: 154
Lindsay, Norman 67: 114
Lindsay, Vachel 40: 118
Lindstrom, Jack 145: 118
Line, Les 27: 143
Linell
  See Smith, Linell
Lionni, Leo 8: 115; 72: 159, 160, 161
Lipinsky, Lino 2: 156; 22: 175
Lippincott, Gary A. 70: 35; 119: 118; 220: 105, 106, 107
Lippman, Peter 8: 31; 31: 119, 120, 160
Lisi, Victoria 89: 145
Lisker, Emily 169: 114
Lisker, Sonia O. 16: 274; 31: 31; 44: 113, 114
Lisowski, Gabriel 47: 144; 49: 157
Lissim, Simon 17: 138
Little, Ed 89: 145; 151: 53
Little, Harold 16: 72
Little, Mary E. 28: 146
Littlewood, Karen 165: 126; 211: 112
Litty, Julie 111: 63
Litzinger, Rosanne 151: 101; 176: 118; 196: 133, 134, 135; 208: 129; 209: 147
Liu, Lesley 143: 72
Livesly, Lorna 19: 216
Livingston, Susan 95: 22
Liwska, Renata 164: 113; 199: 25, 69; 220: 79
Ljungkvist, Laura 180: 120
Llerena, Carlos Antonio 19: 181
Lloyd, Errol 11: 39; 22: 178
Lloyd, Megan 77: 118; 80: 113; 97: 75; 117: 94, 95; 189: 121, 122; 208: 128; 211: 72
Lloyd, Sam 183: 116, 117
Lo, Beth 165: 154
Lo, Koon-chiu 7: 134
Loates, Glen 63: 76
Lobel, Anita 6: 87; 9: 141; 18: 248; 55: 85,86, 87, 88, 93, 104; 60: 67; 78: 263; 82: 110; 96: 157, 159; 101: 84; 132: 35; 162: 93, 94
Lobel, Arnold 1: 188, 189; 5: 12; 6: 147; 7: 167, 209; 18: 190, 191; 25: 39, 43; 27: 40; 29: 174; 52: 127; 55: 89, 91, 94, 95, 97, 98, 99, 100, 101, 102,103, 105, 106; 60: 18, 31; 66: 181, 183; 75: 57; 82: 246; 136: 146
Lobel, Gillian 190: 21
Locker, Thomas 109: 134
Lodge, Bernard 107: 125, 126; 153: 93
Loeb, Jeph 153: 177
Lodge, Jo 112: 119
Loefgren, Ulf 3: 108
Loescher, Ann 20: 108
Loescher, Gil 20: 108
Loew, David 93: 184; 171: 120; 211: 187
Lofting, Hugh 15: 182, 183; 100: 161, 162
Lofts, Pamela 60: 188
Loh, George 38: 88
Lomberg, Jon 58: 160
Lonette, Reisie 11: 211; 12: 168; 13: 56; 36: 122; 43: 155
Long, Ethan 168: 146; 178: 12; 182: 120, 121; 196: 124
Long, Laurel 162: 135; 190: 11; 203: 113, 114
Long, Loren 99: 176; 172: 65; 182: 78; 188: 114, 115
Long, Melinda 152: 128
Long, Miles 115: 174
Long, Sally 42: 184
Long, Sylvia 74: 168; 132: 63; 179: 134
Longoni, Eduardo 73: 85

Longtemps, Ken *17:* 123; *29:* 221; *69:* 82
Looser, Heinz *YABC 2:* 208
Lopez, Loretta *190:* 100
López, Rafael *197:* 160; *198:* 85
Lopshire, Robert *6:* 149; *21:* 117; *34:* 166; *73:* 13
Lord, John Vernon *21:* 104; *23:* 25; *51:* 22
Lorenz, Albert *40:* 146; *115:* 127
Loretta, Sister Mary *33:* 73
Lorraine, Walter H. *3:* 110; *4:* 123; *16:* 192; *103:* 119
Los, Marek *146:* 22; *193:* 23
Loss, Joan *11:* 163
Louderback, Walt *YABC 1:* 164
Loughridge, Stuart *214:* 131
Louis, Catherine *212:* 186
Lousada, Sandra *40:* 138
Louth, Jack *149:* 252; *151:* 191, 192
Love, Judy *173:* 43; *196:* 40
Lovelock, Brian *214:* 132, 197
Low, Joseph *14:* 124, 125; *18:* 68; *19:* 194; *31:* 166; *80:* 239
Low, William *62:* 175; *80:* 147; *112:* 194; *150:* 202; *169:* 175; *177:* 110; *192:* 27
Lowe, Vicky *177:* 130
Lowenheim, Alfred *13:* 65, 66
Lowenstein, Sallie *116:* 90, 91
Lowitz, Anson *17:* 124; *18:* 215
Lowrey, Jo *8:* 133
Lubach, Vanessa *142:* 152
Lubell, Winifred *1:* 207; *3:* 15; *6:* 151
Lubin, Leonard B. *19:* 224; *36:* 79, 80; *45:* 128, 129,131, 132, 133, 134, 135, 136, 137, 139, 140, 141; *70:* 95; *YABC2:* 96
Lucas, David *208:* 148
Lucht, Irmgard *82:* 145
Ludwig, Helen *33:* 144, 145
Luebs, Robin *212:* 109
Lufkin, Raymond *38:* 138; *44:* 48
Luhrs, Henry *7:* 123; *11:* 120
Lujan, Tonita *82:* 33
Lupo, Dom *4:* 204
Lustig, Loretta *30:* 186; *46:* 134, 135, 136, 137
Lutes, Jason *210:* 163
Luthardt, Kevin *172:* 125, 126; *217:* 2
Luxbacher, Irene *153:* 145; *219:* 112, 113
Luzak, Dennis *52:* 121; *99:* 142
Lydbury, Jane *82:* 98
Lydecker, Laura *21:* 113; *42:* 53
Lynch, Charles *16:* 33
Lynch, Marietta *29:* 137; *30:* 171
Lynch, P.J. *126:* 228; *129:* 110; *132:* 247; *183:* 64; *207:* 184; *213:* 100, 101, 102
Lyne, Alison Davis *188:* 118, 198
Lyon, Carol *102:* 26
Lyon, Elinor *6:* 154
Lyon, Fred *14:* 16
Lyon, Lea *212:* 110
Lyon, Tammie *175:* 170
Lyons, Oren *8:* 193
Lyster, Michael *26:* 41

M

Maas, Dorothy *6:* 175
Maas, Julie *47:* 61
Macaulay, David *46:* 139, 140, 141, 142, 143, 144, 145, 147, 149, 150; *72:* 167, 168, 169; *137:* 129, 130, 131, 132
MacCarthy, Patricia *69:* 141
Macdonald, Alister *21:* 55
Macdonald, Roberta *19:* 237; *52:* 164
MacDonald, Norman *13:* 99
MacDonald, Ross *201:* 103
MacDonald, Suse *54:* 41; *109* 138; *130:* 156; *193:* 106, 107, 109, 110
Mace, Varian *49:* 159
MacEachern, Stephen *206:* 2

Macguire, Robert Reid *18:* 67
Machetanz, Fredrick *34:* 147, 148
MacInnes, Ian *35:* 59
MacIntyre, Elisabeth *17:* 127, 128
Mack, Jeff *161:* 128; *194:* 119, 120; *219:* 67
Mack, Stan *17:* 129; *96:* 33
Mackay, Donald *17:* 60
MacKaye, Arvia *32:* 119
Mackenzie, Robert *204:* 78
Mackenzie, Stuart *73:* 213
MacKenzie, Garry *33:* 159
Mackie, Clare *87:* 134
Mackinlay, Miguel *27:* 22
MacKinstry, Elizabeth *15:* 110; *42:* 139, 140, 141, 142, 143,144, 145
MacLeod, Lee *91:* 167
Maclise, Daniel *YABC 2:* 257
Macnaughton, Tina *182:* 145; *218:* 106, 107
MacRae, Tom *181:* 112
Madden, Don *3:* 112, 113; *4:* 33, 108, 155; *7:* 193; *78:* 12; *YABC 2:* 211
Maddison, Angela Mary *10:* 83
Madsen, Jim *146:* 259; *152:* 237; *184:* 106; *197:* 21; *202:* 103, 104
Maestro, Giulio *8:* 124; *12:* 17; *13:* 108; *25:* 182; *54:* 147; *59:* 114, 115, 116, 117, 118, 121, 123, 124, 125,126, 127; *68:* 37, 38; *106:* 129, 130, 131, 136, 137, 138
Maffia, Daniel *60:* 200
Maggio, Viqui *58:* 136, 181; *74:* 150; *75:* 90; *85:* 159; *90:* 158; *109:* 184; *193:* 113
Magnus, Erica *77:* 123
Magnuson, Diana *28:* 102; *34:* 190; *41:* 175
Magoon, Scott *181:* 104; *217:* 165
Magovern, Peg *103:* 123; *218:* 164
Maguire, Sheila *41:* 100
Magurn, Susan *91:* 30
Mahony, Will *37:* 120
Mahony, Will *85:* 116
Mahood, Kenneth *24:* 141
Mahurin, Matt *164:* 225; *175:* 95; *189:* 37; *196:* 14; *209:* 163
Maik, Henri *9:* 102
Maione, Heather *106:* 5; *178:* 8; *189:* 126, 127; *193:* 58
Maisto, Carol *29:* 87
Maitland, Antony *1:* 100, 176; *8:* 41; *17:* 246; *24:* 46; *25:* 177, 178; *32:* 74; *60:* 65, 195; *67:* 156; *87:* 131; *101:* 110
Majewski, Dawn W. *169:* 95
Mak, Kam *72:* 25; *75:* 43; *87:* 186; *97:* 24; *102:* 154; *149:* 195; *186:* 28; *209:* 132
Makie, Pam *37:* 117
Maktima, Joe *116:* 191
Maland, Nick *99:* 77
Male, Alan *132:* 64
Malone, James Hiram *84:* 161
Malone, Nola Langner *82:* 239
Malone, Peter *191:* 121, 122, 123
Malsberg, Edward *51:* 175
Malvern, Corinne *2:* 13; *34:* 148, 149
Manchess, Gregory *165:* 241; *203:* 119
Mancusi, Stephen *63:* 198, 199
Mandelbaum, Ira *31:* 115
Manders, John *138:* 152, 155; *188:* 171; *190:* 92; *199:* 5; *217:* 52; *219:* 35; *219:* 115, 116, 117
Manet, Edouard *23:* 170
Mangiat, Jeff *173:* 127
Mangurian, David *14:* 133
Manham, Allan *42:* 109; *77:* 180; *80:* 227
Manley, Matt *103:* 167; *117:* 98; *172:* 49; *212:* 207
Manna, Giovanni *178:* 44
Manniche, Lise *31:* 121
Manning, Jane *96:* 203
Manning, Jo *63:* 154
Manning, Lawrence *191:* 153
Manning, Maurie J. *211:* 116
Manning, Mick *176:* 139
Manning, Samuel F. *5:* 75

Mantel, Richard *57:* 73; *63:* 106; *82:* 255
Mantha, John *205:* 164; *217:* 117
Maraja *15:* 86; *YABC 1:* 28; *2:* 115
Marcellino, Fred *20:* 125; *34:* 222; *53:* 125; *58:* 205; *61:* 64, 121, 122; *68:* 154, 156, 157, 158, 159; *72:* 25; *86:* 184; *98:* 181; *118:* 129, 130, 131; *149:* 218; *194:* 7
Marchesi, Stephen *34:* 140; *46:* 72; *50:* 147; *66:* 239; *70:* 33; *73:* 18, 114, 163; *77:* 47, 76,147; *78:* 79; *80:* 30; *81:* 6; *89:* 66; *93:* 21,130; *94:* 94; *97:* 66; *98:* 96; *114:* 115, 116
Marchiori, Carlos *14:* 60
Marciano, John Bemelmans *118:* 133; *167:* 110, 111, 112
Marconi, Guilherme *220:* 143
Marcus, Barry David *139:* 248; *145:* 18
Maren, Julie *199:* 73
Margules, Gabriele *21:* 120
Mariana
  See Foster, Marian Curtis
Mariano, Michael *52:* 108
Marino, Dorothy *6:* 37; *14:* 135
Mario, Heide Stetson *101:* 202
Maris, Ron *71:* 123
Maritz, Nicolaas *85:* 123
Mark, Mona *65:* 105; *68:* 205; *116:* 213
Markham, R.L. *17:* 240
Marklew, Gilly *211:* 118
Marks, Alan *104:* 104; *109:* 182; *164:* 92; *185:* 134; *187:* 120, 121, 122; *218:* 114, 115
Marks, Cara *54:* 9
Marks, Colin *203:* 129
Marokvia, Artur *31:* 122
Marquez, Susan *108:* 121; *219:* 95
Marrella, Maria Pia *62:* 116
Marriott, Pat *30:* 30; *34:* 39; *35:* 164, 165, 166; *44:* 170; *48:* 186, 187, 188, 189, 191, 192, 193; *91:* 92
Mars, W.T. *1:* 161; *3:* 115; *4:* 208, 225; *5:* 92, 105, 186; *8:* 214; *9:* 12; *13:* 121; *27:* 151; *31:* 180; *38:* 102; *48:* 66; *62:* 164, 165; *64:* 62; *68:* 229; *79:* 55
Marschall, Ken *85:* 29
Marsh, Christine *3:* 164
Marsh, James *73:* 137
Marsh, Reginald *17:* 5; *19:* 89; *22:* 90, 96
Marshall, Anthony D. *18:* 216
Marshall, Felicia *170:* 190
Marshall, James *6:* 160; *40:* 221; *42:* 24, 25, 29; *51:* 111, 112, 113, 114, 115, 116, 117, 118, 119, 120, 121; *64:* 13; *75:* 126, 127, 128, 129; *102:* 10, 12; *216:* 26, 28
Marshall, Janet *97:* 154
Marstall, Bob *55:* 145; *84:* 153, 170; *104:* 145; *154:* 166, 167, 168
Martchenko, Michael *50:* 129, 153, 155, 156, 157; *83:* 144,145; *154:* 137, 138, 139
Marten, Ruth *129:* 52
Martin, Brad *199:* 186
Martin, Charles E. *70:* 144
Martin, Courtney A. *214:* 28
Martin, David Stone *24:* 232; *62:* 4
Martin, Fletcher *18:* 213; *23:* 151
Martin, Rene *7:* 144; *42:* 148, 149, 150
Martin, Richard E. *51:* 157; *131:* 203
Martin, Ron *32:* 81
Martin, Stefan *8:* 68; *32:* 124, 126; *56:* 33
Martin, Whitney *166:* 137
Martinez, Ed *58:* 192; *72:* 231; *77:* 33; *80:* 214; *167:* 123
Martinez, John *6:* 113; *118:* 13; *139:* 143
Martinez, Sergio *158:* 190; *220:* 156
Martini, Angela *183:* 161
Martiniere, Stephan *171:* 130
Marton, Jirina *95:* 127, 128; *144:* 145
Martorell, Antonio *84:* 6; *97:* 161
Martucci, Griesbach *52:* 106
Marvin, Frederic *83:* 86
Marx, Robert F. *24:* 143
Marzollo, Jean *190:* 127

Masefield, Judith *19:* 208, 209
Masheris, Robert *78:* 51
Masiello, Ralph *186:* 171; *214:* 134
Mason, George F. *14:* 139
Mason, Robert *84:* 96
Masse, Josée *208:* 45; *217:* 19; *221:* 134
Massey, Barbara *68:* 142
Massie, Diane Redfield *16:* 194
Massie, Kim *31:* 43
Massini, Sarah *213:* 79
Mataya, David *121:* 66
Mathers, Petra *119:* 135; *163:* 104; *176:* 143, 144; *187:* 142; *196:* 101
Mathewuse, James *51:* 143
Mathieu, Joseph *14:* 33; *39:* 206; *43:* 167; *56:* 180; *79:* 126; *94:* 147; *185:* 140
Matje, Martin *169:* 177, 178; *172:* 180
Matsubara, Naoko *12:* 121
Matsuda, Shizu *13:* 167
Matsuoka, Mei *192:* 135; *214:* 84
Matte, L'Enc *22:* 183
Mattelson, Marvin *36:* 50, 51
Mattheson, Jenny *180:* 132
Matthews, Elizabeth *194:* 128
Matthews, F. Leslie *4:* 216
Matthews, Tina *190:* 130
Mattingly, David *71:* 76, 77; *82:* 64; *91:* 216, 217; *109:* 25
Matulay, Laszlo *5:* 18; *43:* 168
Matus, Greta *12:* 142
Maughan, Bill *181:* 31; *211:* 211
Mauldin, Bill *27:* 23
Mauterer, Erin Marie *119:* 5
Mawicke, Tran *9:* 137; *15:* 191; *47:* 100
Mawson, Matt *74:* 115
Max, Peter *45:* 146, 147, 148, 149, 150
Maxie, Betty *40:* 135
Maxwell, John Alan *1:* 148
May, Steve *204:* 30
Mayan, Earl *7:* 193
Maydak, Michael S. *220:* 117
Mayer, Bill *200:* 138
Mayer, Danuta *117:* 103
Mayer, Marianna *32:* 132
Mayer, Mercer *11:* 192; *16:* 195, 196; *20:* 55, 57; *32:* 129, 130, 132, 133, 134; *41:* 144, 248, 252; *58:* 186; *73:* 140, 142, 143; *137:* 137, 138
Mayforth, Hal *166:* 77
Mayhew, James *85:* 121; *138:* 187; *149:* 140; *204:* 81
Mayhew, Richard *3:* 106
Mays, Victor *5:* 127; *8:* 45, 153; *14:* 245; *23:* 50; *34:* 155; *40:* 79; *45:* 158; *54:* 91; *66:* 240
Mazal, Chanan *49:* 104
Maze, Deborah *71:* 83
Mazellan, Ron *75:* 97, 98; *210:* 169
Mazetti, Alan *112:* 72
Mazille, Capucine *96:* 168
Mazza, Adriana Saviozzi *19:* 215
Mazzella, Mary Jo *82:* 165
Mazzetti, Alan *45:* 210
McAfee, Steve *135:* 146; *167:* 176; *191:* 84; *210:* 117; *218:* 34
McAlinden, Paul *112:* 128
McBride, Angus *28:* 49; *103:* 40
McBride, Will *30:* 110
McCaffery, Janet *38:* 145
McCall, Bruce *209:* 119
McCallum, Graham *78:* 78
McCallum, Stephen *141:* 143; *156:* 5; *166:* 228
McCann, Gerald *3:* 50; *4:* 94; *7:* 54; *41:* 121
McCarthy, Dan *174:* 74
McCarthy, Linda *177:* 128; *218:* 104
McCarthy, Meghan *168:* 134; *199:* 74
McCauley, Adam *157:* 36; *184:* 199; *193:* 100; *209:* 122

McCay, Winsor *41:* 124, 126, 128, 129, 130, 131; *134:* 77, 79
McClary, Nelson *1:* 111
McClements, George *196:* 146
McClennan, Connie *210:* 181
McClintock, Barbara *57:* 135; *95:* 130; *146:* 190; *213:* 3, 5, 107, 108
McClintock, Theodore *14:* 141
McCloskey, Robert *1:* 184, 185; *2:* 186, 187; *17:* 209; *39:* 139, 140, 141, 142, 143, 146, 147, 148; *85:* 150, 151; *100:* 172, 173, 174
McClung, Robert *2:* 189; *68:* 166, 167
McClure, Gillian *31:* 132; *150:* 53
McClure, Nikki *218:* 120
McConnel, Jerry *31:* 75, 187
McConnell, Mary *102:* 49
McCord, Kathleen Garry *78:* 236
McCormack, John *66:* 193
McCormick, A.D. *35:* 119
McCormick, Dell J. *19:* 216
McCoy, Glenn *212:* 132
McCrady, Lady *16:* 198; *39:* 127
McCrea, James *3:* 122; *33:* 216
McCrea, Ruth *3:* 122; *27:* 102; *33:* 216
McCue, Lisa *65:* 148, 149; *77:* 54; *80:* 132; *175:* 33; *177:* 133, 135; *212:* 136, 137, 138
McCully, Emily Arnold *2:* 89; *4:* 120, 121, 146, 197; *5:* 2, 129; *7:* 191; *11:* 122; *15:* 210; *33:* 23; *35:* 244; *37:* 122; *39:* 88; *40:* 103; *50:* 30,31, 32, 33, 34, 35, 36, 37; *52:* 89, 90; *57:* 6; *62:* 3; *70:* 195; *86:* 82; *96:* 192; *97:* 93; *110:* 143,144; *117:* 47; *167:* 96; *210:* 175, 176
McCurdy, Michael *13:* 153; *24:* 85; *81:* 160; *82:* 157, 158; *86:* 125; *97:* 92; *117:* 178; *132:* 6; *147:* 159, 160
McCusker, Paul *99:* 19
McDaniel, Jerry *132:* 135
McDaniel, Preston *160:* 206; *170:* 139
McDermott, Beverly Brodsky *11:* 180
McDermott, Gerald *16:* 201; *74:* 174, 175; *163:* 150, 151
McDermott, Mike *96:* 187
McDonald, Jill *13:* 155; *26:* 128
McDonald, Mercedes *169:* 118
McDonald, Ralph J. *5:* 123, 195
McDonnell, Flora *146:* 199, 200
McDonnell, Patrick *179:* 153, 154; *221:* 136, 137, 138
McDonough, Don *10:* 163
McElligott, Matt *196:* 147
McElmurry, Jill *137:* 148; *163:* 141; *202:* 186
McElrath-Eslick, Lori *129:* 145; *142:* 21; *173:* 123; *202:* 194; *204:* 88, 89
McEntee, Dorothy *37:* 124
McEwan, Keith *88:* 116; *165:* 122, 123
McEwen, Katharine *169:* 34
McFall, Christie *12:* 144
McFeely, Daniel *160:* 213
McGaw, Laurie *109:* 243; *143:* 216; *211:* 218
McGee, Barbara *6:* 165
McGee, Marni *163:* 153
McGillvray, Kim *158:* 171; *165:* 213; *186:* 183; *190:* 175
McGinley-Nally, Sharon *131:* 19
McGinnis, Robert *110:* 113; *177:* 80
McGovern, Tara *98:* 171
McGraw, Sheila *83:* 146
McGregor, Barbara *200:* 155
McGregor, Malcolm *23:* 27
McGrory, Anik *193:* 120
McGuire, Robert *204:* 57; *209:* 86
McGuirk, Leslie *152:* 159
McHale, John *138:* 190
McHenry, E.B. *193:* 122
McHugh, Tom *23:* 64
McIntosh, Jon *42:* 56
McKay, Donald *2:* 118; *32:* 157; *45:* 151, 152
McKean, Dave *150:* 71; *174:* 156; *197:* 83, 118
McKeating, Eileen *44:* 58

McKee, David *10:* 48; *21:* 9; *70:* 154, 155; *107:* 139, 140, 141; *134:* 218; *158:* 148, 149, 150, 151
McKee, Diana *109:* 185
McKelvey, Patrick *164:* 141
McKendry, Joe *170:* 136
McKeveny, Tom *164:* 60; *173:* 79
McKie, Roy *7:* 44
McKie, Todd *205:* 181
McKillip, Kathy *30:* 153
McKinney, Ena *26:* 39
McKinnon, James *136:* 75
McKowen, Scott *172:* 63; *202:* 49
McLachlan, Edward *5:* 89
McLaren, Chesley *133:* 53; *213:* 112; *219:* 31
McLaren, Kirsty *123:* 99; *124:* 226
Mclean, Andrew *113:* 117, 118, 120, 121; *172:* 130, 131
Mclean, Janet *172:* 130
McLean, Meg *94:* 196
McLean, Sammis *32:* 197
McLean, Wilson *90:* 29; *113:* 195
McLoughlin, John C. *47:* 149
McLoughlin, Wayne *102:* 230; *134:* 178; *216:* 196
McMahon, Robert *36:* 155; *69:* 169
McManus, Shawn *85:* 71
McMenemy, Sarah *156:* 139 ; *211:* 93
McMillan, Bruce *22:* 184
McMullan, James *40:* 33; *67:* 172; *87:* 142; *99:* 63, 64; *189:* 133; *196:* 51
McMullen, Nigel *146:* 177
McNeely, Tom *162:* 55
McNaught, Harry *12:* 80; *32:* 136
McNaughton, Colin *39:* 149; *40:* 108; *92:* 144, 145, 146; *134:* 104, 106; *211:* 122, 123, 124
McNicholas, Maureen *38:* 148
McNicholas, Shelagh *173:* 61; *191:* 125, 126
McPhail, David *14:* 105; *23:* 135; *37:* 217, 218, 220,221; *47:* 151, 152, 153, 154, 155, 156, 158, 159, 160, 162, 163, 164; *71:* 211; *81:* 139, 140, 142; *86:* 123; *132:* 150; *140:* 129, 131, 132; *183:* 134, 135, 137; *189:* 132; *219:* 121, 122, 123, 124, 125
McPhee, Richard B. *41:* 133
McPheeters, Neal *78:* 132; *86:* 90; *99:* 162; *111:* 141; *142:* 162
McQuade, Jacqueline *124:* 223
McQueen, Lucinda *28:* 149; *41:* 249; *46:* 206; *53:* 103
McQuillan, Mary *153:* 97; *200:* 140
McVay, Tracy *11:* 68
McVicker, Charles *39:* 150
McWilliam, Howard *219:* 135
Mead, Ben Carlton *43:* 75
Meade, Holly *90:* 102; *94:* 101; *149:* 8; *151:* 107
Mecray, John *33:* 62
Meddaugh, Susan *20:* 42; *29:* 143; *41:* 241; *77:* 50; *84:* 173, 174, 175, 176, 177, 178; *125:* 160, 161, 162; *176:* 148, 149, 150, 151
Meehan, Dennis B. *56:* 144
Meents, Len W. *73:* 147, 150
Meers, Tony *99:* 113
Meisel, Paul *98:* 137; *124:* 18; *162:* 180; *179:* 16; *181:* 62; *194:* 154; *221:* 5
Melanson, Luc *149:* 229; *198:* 97, 98; *221:* 166
Melendez, Francisco *72:* 180
Melling, David *202:* 199
Melnychuk, Monika *153:* 65
Melo, Esperança *196:* 90
Melo, John *16:* 285; *58:* 203
Meloni, Maria Teresa *98:* 62
Meltzer, Ericka
   See O'Rourke, Ericka
Menasco, Milton *43:* 85
Menchin, Scott *188:* 129
Mendelson, Steven T. *86:* 154
Mendelssohn, Felix *19:* 170
Mendola, Christopher *88:* 223

Meng, Heinz *13:* 158
Merian, Maria Sibylla *140:* 88
Mero, Lee *34:* 68
Merrell, David *205:* 3
Merrill, Frank T. *16:* 147; *19:* 71; *YABC 1:* 226, 229,273
Merriman, Rachel *98:* 108; *114:* 122; *149:* 142
Merveille, David *200:* 142
Meryman, Hope *27:* 41
Meryweather, Jack *10:* 179
Meseldzija, Petar *168:* 97
Meserve, Jessica *184:* 137; *211:* 127
Messick, Dale *64:* 150, 151, 152
Meth, Harold *24:* 203
Meyer, Herbert *19:* 189
Meyer, Renate *6:* 170
Meyers, Bob *11:* 136
Meyers, Nancy *172:* 124
Meynell, Louis *37:* 76
Micale, Albert *2:* 65; *22:* 185
Miccuci, Charles *82:* 163; *144:* 150
Micich, Paul *164:* 163
Middleton, Jeffrey *177:* 173
Middleton, Joshua *208:* 146; *219:* 24
Middleton-Sandford, Betty *2:* 125
Mieke, Anne *45:* 74
Mighell, Patricia *43:* 134
Miglio, Paige *101:* 203; *151:* 223; *201:* 118, 119; *204:* 162
Mikec, Larry *204:* 125
Mikolaycak, Charles *9:* 144; *12:* 101; *13:* 212; *21:* 121; *22:* 168; *30:* 187; *34:* 103, 150; *37:* 183; *43:* 179; *44:* 90; *46:* 115, 118, 119; *49:* 25; *78:* 121, 122, 205, 207; *81:* 4
Milelli, Pascal *129:* 66; *135:* 153; *187:* 45
Miles, Elizabeth *117:* 77
Miles, Jennifer *17:* 278
Milgrim, David *158:* 157; *187:* 125, 126, 128
Milhous, Katherine *15:* 193; *17:* 51
Millais, John E. *22:* 230, 231
Millar, H.R. *YABC 1:* 194, 195, 203
Millard, C.E. *28:* 186
Millard, Kerry *105:* 124; *204:* 93, 94
Miller, Don *15:* 195; *16:* 71; *20:* 106; *31:* 178
Miller, Edna *29:* 148
Miller, Edward *115:* 64; *183:* 140, 141; *218:* 129, 130, 131
Miller, Frank J. *25:* 94
Miller, Grambs *18:* 38; *23:* 16
Miller, Ian *99:* 128
Miller, Jane *15:* 196
Miller, Marcia *13:* 233
Miller, Marilyn *1:* 87; *31:* 69; *33:* 157
Miller, Mitchell *28:* 183; *34:* 207
Miller, Phil *175:* 150
Miller, Shane *5:* 140
Miller, Virginia *81:* 206
Millman, Isaac *172:* 18
Mills, Elaine *72:* 181
Mills, Judith Christine *130:* 168, 169
Mills, Lauren *92:* 170
Mills, Yaroslava Surmach *35:* 169, 170; *46:* 114
Millsap, Darrel *51:* 102
Milone, Karen *89:* 169
Milord, Susan *147:* 163, 164; *200:* 144
Milton, Debbie *162:* 161
Mims, Ashley *170:* 51
Miner, Julia *98:* 69
Minor, Wendell *39:* 188; *52:* 87; *56:* 171; *58:* 116; *62:* 56; *66:* 109; *74:* 93; *78:* 129; *94:* 67; *117:* 12, 13; *124:* 84, 86; *136:* 121; *164:* 168, 169; *170:* 71; *199:* 79, 80, 81, 82; *217:* 63
Minter, Daniel *176:* 154; *179:* 177
Mirocha, Paul *81:* 133; *192:* 148; *194:* 36
Misako Rocks! *192:* 149, 150
Mitchell, Judith *109:* 117
Mitchell, Mark *91:* 208
Mitchell, Tracy *190:* 15
Mitgutsch, Ali *76:* 161

Mitsuhashi, Yoko *45:* 153
Miyake, Yoshi *38:* 141
Mizumura, Kazue *10:* 143; *18:* 223; *36:* 159
Mochi, Ugo *8:* 122; *38:* 150
Mock, Paul *55:* 83; *123:* 32
Modarressi, Mitra *90:* 236; *126:* 168; *173:* 165, 166; *200:* 147, 148
Modell, Frank *39:* 152
Mogenson, Jan *74:* 183
Mohn, Susan *89:* 224
Mohr, Mark *133:* 201
Mohr, Nicholasa *8:* 139; *113:* 127
Molan, Christine *60:* 177; *84:* 183
Moldon, Peter L. *49:* 168
Molk, Laurel *92:* 150
Mollica, Gene *197:* 11
Momaday, N. Scott *48:* 159
Mombourquette, Paul *112:* 91; *126:* 142
Monk, Julie *165:* 231; *191:* 96
Monks, Lydia *189:* 136, 137
Monroe, Chris *219:* 133
Monroy, Manuel *199:* 192
Montgomery, Lucy *150:* 126
Montgomery, Michael G. *208:* 159
Montgomery-Higham, Amanda *169:* 131
Monteiel, David *201:* 95
Montiel, David *69:* 106; *84:* 145
Montijo, Rhode *193:* 164
Montresor, Beni *2:* 91; *3:* 138; *38:* 152, 153, 154,155, 156, 157, 158, 159, 160; *68:* 63
Montserrat, Pep *128:* 135; *181:* 119; *184:* 53
Moon, Carl *25:* 183, 184, 185
Moon, Eliza *14:* 40
Moon, Ivan *22:* 39; *38:* 140
Moore, Adrienne *67:* 147
Moore, Agnes Kay Randall *43:* 187
Moore, Cyd *117:* 107, 108; *159:* 137, 138; *186:* 148, 149, 151; *203:* 15; *214:* 138, 139
Moore, Gustav *127:* 181, 182; *170:* 162, 163
Moore, Jackie *128:* 79
Moore, Janet *63:* 153
Moore, Margie *176:* 156; *221:* 125
Moore, Mary *29:* 160
Moore, Patrick *184:* 121
Moore, Yvette *101:* 11, 12; *154:* 141
Mora, Giovanni *179:* 127; *184:* 11
Mora, Raul Mina *20:* 41
Moraes, Odilon *102:* 144
Morales, Yuyi *154:* 144
Moran, Rosslyn *111:* 26
Moran, Tom *60:* 100
Mordan, C.B. *193:* 115
Mordvinoff, Nicolas *15:* 179
Moreno, René King *169:* 59; *190:* 133, 209; *212:* 52
Morgan, Barbara *169:* 116
Morgan, Jacqui *58:* 57
Morgan, Mary *114:* 133, 134, 135; *123:* 11; *213:* 115, 116, 117
Morgan, Tom *42:* 157
Morgan, Pierr *173:* 148
Morgenstern, Michael *158:* 7, 57; *171:* 103; *174:* 60
Morice, Dave *93:* 142
Morin, Paul *73:* 132; *79:* 130; *88:* 140; *137:* 143
Moriuchi, Mique *177:* 203
Morozumi, Atsuko *110:* 155; *217:* 126, 127
Morrill, Leslie *18:* 218; *29:* 177; *33:* 84; *38:* 147; *42:* 127; *44:* 93; *48:* 164, 165, 167, 168, 169, 170,171; *49:* 162; *63:* 136, 180; *70:* 72; *71:* 70, 91,92; *72:* 228; *80:* 163, 164, 165; *90:* 121; *121:* 88; *178:* 117
Morrill, Rowena A. *84:* 16; *98:* 163
Morris *47:* 91
Morris, Frank *55:* 133; *60:* 28; *76:* 2
Morris, Harry O. *119:* 138
Morris, Jackie *128:* 194; *144:* 119; *151:* 146; *202:* 126, 127; *204:* 83; *211:* 80; *214:* 163
Morris, Jennifer E. *179:* 157
Morris, Oradel Nolen *128:* 180

Morris, Tony *62:* 146; *70:* 97
Morrison, Bill *42:* 116; *66:* 170; *69:* 40
Morrison, Gordon *87:* 150; *113:* 93; *128:* 181, 182; *183:* 144, 145, 146
Morrison, Frank *169:* 162; *205:* 156
Morrison, Taylor *159:* 144, 145; *187:* 131
Morrow, Gray *2:* 64; *5:* 200; *10:* 103, 114; *14:* 175
Morse, Scott *200:* 149, 150
Morton, Lee Jack *32:* 140
Morton, Marian *3:* 185
Mosberg, Hilary *117:* 195; *118:* 164; *149:* 55
Moser, Barry *56:* 68, 117, 118, 119, 120, 121, 122, 123, 124; *59:* 141; *60:* 160; *79:* 91, 147, 149, 151, 152; *82:* 81; *90:* 118; *91:* 35; *95:* 210; *97:* 91, 93; *102:* 152; *126:* 4; *128:* 175; *133:* 141; *138:* 167, 171, 174; *153:* 205; *174:* 130; *185:* 152, 154; *195:* 163; *204:* 115; *209:* 201
Moser, Cara *90:* 118; *138:* 167
Moses, Grandma *18:* 228
Moses, Will *178:* 170, 171
Moskof, Martin Stephen *27:* 152
Mosley, Francis *57:* 144
Moss, Donald *11:* 184
Moss, Geoffrey *32:* 198
Moss, Marissa *71:* 130; *104:* 127; *163:* 156; *216:* 164, 165, 166
Most, Bernard *48:* 173; *91:* 142, 143; *134:* 120
Mourning, Tuesday *205:* 25; *220:* 68; *221:* 42
Mowll, Joshua *188:* 133
Mowry, Carmen *50:* 62
Moxley, Sheila *96:* 174; *169:* 26; *206:* 16
Moyers, William *21:* 65
Moyler, Alan *36:* 142
Mozley, Charles *9:* 87; *20:* 176, 192, 193; *22:* 228; *25:* 205; *33:* 150; *43:* 170, 171, 172, 173, 174; *YABC2:* 89
Mueller, Hans Alexander *26:* 64; *27:* 52, 53
Mugnaini, Joseph *11:* 35; *27:* 52, 53; *35:* 62
Mujica, Rick *72:* 67; *88:* 95; *111:* 53; *180:* 185; *197:* 70
Mullen, Douglas *180:* 178
Muller, Robin *86:* 161
Muller, Steven *32:* 167
Muller, Jorg *35:* 215; *67:* 138, 139
Mulock, Julie *163:* 112
Mullins, Edward S. *10:* 101
Mullins, Patricia *51:* 68
Multer, Scott *80:* 108
Munari, Bruno *15:* 200
Munch, Edvard *140:* 143
Munowitz, Ken *14:* 148; *72:* 178, 179
Muñoz, Claudio *208:* 161
Munoz, William *42:* 160
Munro, Roxie *58:* 134; *136:* 177; *137:* 218; *184:* 133, 134
Munsinger, Lynn *33:* 161; *46:* 126; *71:* 92; *82:* 80; *89:* 218; *92:* 125; *94:* 157, 158, 159, 160; *98:* 196; *103:* 198; *142:* 143; *145:* 133, 134, 136; *153:* 203; *176:* 162; *177:* 140, 141, 142; *189:* 113, 114, 116, 117; *201:* 42; *221:* 148, 149,150
Munson, Russell *13:* 9
Munster, Sebastian *166:* 107
Munzar, Barbara *149:* 75
Murdocca, Salvatore *73:* 212; *98:* 132; *111:* 168; *157:* 228; *164:* 257
Murphy, Bill *5:* 138; *130:* 170
Murphy, Jill *37:* 142; *70:* 166; *142:* 132, 134
Murphy, Kelly *130:* 212; *143:* 119; *176:* 158; *190:* 135
Murphy, Liz *210:* 183; *212:* 157
Murphy, Mary *196:* 158
Murphy, Tom *192:* 40
Murr, Karl *20:* 62
Murray, Joe *175:* 37
Murray, Ossie *43:* 176
Mussino, Attilio *29:* 131; *100:* 164
Mutchler, Dwight *1:* 25

Myers, Bernice 9: 147; 36: 75; 81: 146, 147, 148
Muth, Jon J. 165: 169; 167: 109; 190: 227; 193: 59
Myers, Christopher 183: 150; 193: 139
Myers, Duane O. 99: 145
Myers, Tim 147: 168
Myers, V.G. 142: 41
Myers, Lou 11: 2

N

Nachreiner, Tom 29: 182
Nacht, Merle 65: 49
Nadler, Ellis 88: 91
Nagle, Shane 180: 223
Nagy, Ian 195: 64
Najaka, Marlies 62: 101
Nakai, Michael 30: 217; 54: 29
Nakata, Hiroe 157: 156; 162: 30; 205: 124, 125
Nakatani, Chiyoko 12: 124
Narahashi, Keiko 77: 188; 82: 213; 115: 142, 143, 144
Nascimbene, Yan 133: 128; 173: 132, 133
Nash, Lesa 87: 135
Nash, Linell 46: 175
Nash, Scott 130: 36; 188: 196
Naso, John 33: 183
Nason, Thomas W. 14: 68
Nasser, Muriel 48: 74
Nast, Thomas 21: 29; 28: 23; 51: 132, 133, 134, 135,136, 137, 138, 139, 141
Nasta, Vincent 78: 185
Natale, Vincent 76: 3; 78: 125; 112: 47; 166: 81; 174: 189; 185: 212; 197: 59; 218: 35
Natchev, Alexi 96: 177
Nathan, Charlott 125: 151
Nathan, Cheryl 150: 104; 186: 112
Natti, Susanna 20: 146; 32: 141, 142; 35: 178; 37: 143; 71: 49; 93: 98; 125: 166, 168; 126: 228; 151: 6; 178: 8; 188: 106
Navarra, Celeste Scala 8: 142
Naylor, Penelope 10: 104
Nazz, James 72: 8
Nebel, M. 45: 154
Neebe, William 7: 93
Needham, Dave 196: 85
Needler, Jerry 12: 93
Neel, Alice 31: 23
Neely, Beth 119: 184
Neely, Keith R. 46: 124
Neff, Leland 78: 74
Negri, Rocco 3: 213; 5: 67; 6: 91, 108; 12: 159
Negrin, Fabian 174: 125; 175: 15
Neidigh, Sherry 128: 53; 204: 101, 102, 103
Neilan, Eujin Kim 180: 241; 200: 151, 152
Neill, John R. 18: 8, 10, 11, 21, 30; 100: 22
Neilsen, Cliff 158: 131; 177: 112, 121; 209: 8; 215: 150
Neilsen, Terese 116: 74
Nelson, Craig 62: 151; 153; 183: 86
Nelson, Gail White 68: 140
Nelson, Jennifer 152: 199; 199: 132
Nelson, Kadir 151: 185; 154: 146, 147; 157: 189, 222; 181: 122, 124; 197: 155; 213: 122, 123, 124
Nelson, S.D. 131: 34; 181: 126, 127
Ness, Evaline 1: 164, 165; 2: 39; 3: 8; 10: 147; 12: 53; 26: 150, 151, 152, 153; 49: 30, 31, 32; 56: 30; 60: 113
Neubecker, Robert 170: 143; 214: 157
Neville, Vera 2: 182
Nevins, Daniel 191: 173
Nevwirth, Allan 79: 168
Newberry, Clare Turlay 1: 170
Newbold, Greg 108: 125; 145: 199; 151: 23; 193: 178; 197: 10; 199: 92, 93

Newfeld, Frank 14: 121; 26: 154
Newland, Gillian 220: 132
Newman, Andy 61: 195: 63
Newman, Ann 43: 90
Newman, Barbara Johansen 191: 137, 138
Newsham, Ian 143: 162
Newsom, Carol 40: 159; 44: 60; 47: 189; 65: 29; 70: 192; 80: 36; 85: 137, 138; 92: 167; 191: 82
Newsom, Tom 49: 149; 71: 13, 62; 75: 156; 91: 113
Newton, Jill 83: 105; 200: 154
Nez, John 218: 136
Ng, Michael 29: 171
Ng, Simon 167: 7
Nguyen, Vincent 189: 49
Nichols, Sandy 219: 103
Nicholson, William 15: 33, 34; 16: 48
Nickens, Bessie 104: 153
Nicklaus, Carol 45: 194; 62: 132, 133
Nickle, John 181: 128
Nickless, Will 16: 139
Nicholas, Corasue 154: 20
Nicolas 17: 130, 132, 133; YABC 2: 215
Niebrugge, Jane 6: 118
Nielsen, Cliff 95: 207, 208; 105: 58; 114: 112; 124: 12; 125: 91, 92; 132: 224; 135: 187; 136: 40; 137: 168; 145: 54; 149: 28; 158: 129; 165: 64, 158; 168: 169; 170: 6; 175: 114, 116; 187: 75, 76; 194: 107; 197: 172; 201: 14; 208: 192; 211: 186; 216: 215; 217: 67
Nielsen, Jon 6: 100; 24: 202
Nielsen, Kay 15: 7; 16: 211, 212, 213, 215, 217; 22: 143; YABC 1: 32, 33
Niemann, Christoph 191: 141
Nikola-Lisa, W. 180: 180
Niland, Deborah 25: 191; 27: 156; 135: 50; 172: 143
Niland, Kilmeny 25: 191; 75: 143
Nino, Alex 59: 145
Ninon 1: 5; 38: 101, 103, 108
Nissen, Rie 44: 35
Nithael, Mark 158: 237
Nivola, Claire A. 78: 126; 140: 147; 208: 164
Nixon, K. 14: 152
Nobati, Eugenia 194: 118
Noble, Louise 61: 170
Noble, Marty 97: 168; 125: 171
Noble, Trinka Hakes 39: 162; 84: 157
Noda, Takayo 168: 143
Noguchi, Yoshie 30: 99
Nolan, Dennis 42: 163; 67: 163; 78: 189; 82: 225; 83: 26; 92: 169, 170; 103: 166; 111: 35; 112: 213; 127: 171; 166: 161; 194: 218
Noll, Sally 82: 171
Nolte, Larry 121: 63, 65
Nones, Eric Jon 61: 111; 76: 38; 77: 177
Noonan, Daniel 100: 224
Noonan, Julia 4: 163; 7: 207; 25: 151; 91: 29; 95: 149
Norcia, Ernie 108: 155; 140: 47
Nordenskjold, Birgitta 2: 208
Noreika, Robert 173: 20; 217: 24
Norling, Beth 149: 153, 154; 209: 77
Norman, Elaine 77: 72, 176; 94: 35; 136: 63; 178: 42
Norman, Mary 36: 138, 147
Norman, Michael 12: 117; 27: 168
Northway, Jennifer 85: 96
Nostlinger, Christiana 162: 131
Novak, Linda 166: 205
Novak, Matt 104: 132, 133; 165: 173, 174; 204: 104, 106
Novelli, Luca 61: 137
Novgorodoff, Danica 215: 133
Nugent, Cynthia 106: 189; 205: 126, 127; 209: 180
Numberman, Neil 220: 133
Numeroff, Laura Joffe 28: 161; 30: 177
Nurse, Chris 164: 91

Nussbaumer, Paul 16: 219; 39: 117
Nutt, Ken 72: 69; 97: 170
Nyce, Helene 19: 219
Nygren, Tord 30: 148; 127: 164

O

Oakley, Graham 8: 112; 30: 164, 165; 84: 188,189, 190, 191, 192
Oakley, Thornton YABC 2: 189
Oberheide, Heide 118: 37
Obligado, Lilian 2: 28, 66, 67; 6: 30; 14: 179; 15: 103; 25: 84; 61: 138, 139, 140, 141, 143
Oblinski, Rafael 190: 139
Obrant, Susan 11: 186
O'Brien, Anne Sibley 53: 116, 117; 155: 115; 213: 127
O'Brien, John 41: 253; 72: 12; 89: 59, 60; 98: 16; 161: 185; 169: 16; 180: 196
O'Brien, Patrick 193: 142, 143, 144
O'Brien, Teresa 87: 89
O'Brien, Tim 93: 25; 136: 94; 164: 57; 169: 57; 173: 55; 175: 86; 184: 192; 191: 134; 193: 137; 210: 159
O'Clair, Dennis 127: 25
O'Connor, George 183: 153
Odell, Carole 35: 47
Odem, Mel 99: 164; 167: 84, 87
O'Donohue, Thomas 40: 89
Oechsli, Kelly 5: 144, 145; 7: 115; 8: 83, 183; 13: 117; 20: 94; 81: 199
Ofer, Avi 208: 143
Offen, Hilda 42: 207
Ogden, Bill 42: 59; 47: 55
Ogg, Oscar 33: 34
Ogle, Nancy Gray 163: 144
Ohi, Ruth 90: 175, 177; 131: 63; 135: 106; 175: 107; 179: 55
Ohlsson, Ib 4: 152; 7: 57; 10: 20; 11: 90; 19: 217; 41: 246; 82: 106; 92: 213
Ohtomo, Yasuo 37: 146; 39: 212, 213
O'Keefe, Jennifer 136: 184
O'Kelley, Mattie Lou 36: 150
Olbinski, Rafal 149: 27; 158: 77; 203: 36
O'Leary, Chris 208: 166
Oleynikov, Igor 202: 134
Oliver, Isaac 171: 182
Oliver, Jenni 23: 121; 35: 112
Oliver, Narelle 152: 192; 197: 129, 130
Oller, Erika 128: 186; 134: 126
Olschewski, Alfred 7: 172
Olsen, Ib Spang 6: 178, 179; 81: 164
Olson, Alan 77: 229
Olson-Brown, Ellen 183: 154
Olugebefola, Ademola 15: 205
O'Malley, Kevin 94: 180; 106: 8; 113: 108; 136: 70; 157: 193; 191: 146; 203: 78; 217: 84
O'Neil, Dan IV 7: 176
O'Neill, Catharine 72: 113; 84: 78; 134: 153
O'Neill, Jean 22: 146
O'Neill, Martin 187: 39; 203: 118
O'Neill, Michael J. 54: 172
O'Neill, Rose 48: 30, 31
O'Neill, Steve 21: 118
Ono, Chiyo 7: 97
Orbaan, Albert 2: 31; 5: 65, 171; 9: 8; 14: 241; 20: 109
Orbach, Ruth 21: 112
Orback, Craig 197: 132
Orfe, Joan 20: 81
Org, Ed 119: 93
Ormai, Stella 72: 129
Ormerod, Jan 55: 124; 70: 170, 171; 90: 39; 132: 172, 173, 174; 147: 98
Ormsby, Virginia H. 11: 187

O'Rourke, Ericka *108:* 216; *117:* 194; *111:* 142; *119:* 194; *137:* 152; *150:* 134; *167:* 64; *172:* 164; *188:* 163; *191:* 172; *201:* 15; *203:* 75; *209:* 130; *219:* 99
O'Rourke, Ericka Meltzer
  See O'Rourke, Ericka
Orozco, Jose Clemente *9:* 177
Orr, Forrest W. *23:* 9
Orr, N. *19:* 70
Ortiz, Vilma *88:* 158
Osborn, Kathy *152:* 232; *199:* 101, 102; *206:* 67
Osborn, Robert *65:* 49
Osborne, Billie Jean *35:* 209
Osmond, Edward *10:* 111
O'Sullivan, Tom *3:* 176; *4:* 55; *78:* 195
Otani, June *124:* 42; *156:* 53
Otis, Rebecca *185:* 92
Ottley, Matt *147:* 221; *171:* 133
Otto, Svend *22:* 130, 141; *67:* 188, 189
Oudry, J.B. *18:* 167
Oughton, Taylor *5:* 23; *104:* 136
Overeng, Johannes *44:* 36
Overlie, George *11:* 156
Owens, Carl *2:* 35; *23:* 521
Owens, Gail *10:* 170; *12:* 157; *19:* 16; *22:* 70; *25:* 81; *28:* 203, 205; *32:* 221, 222; *36:* 132; *46:* 40; *47:* 57; *54:* 66, 67, 68, 69, 70, 71, 72, 73; *71:* 100; *73:* 64; *77:* 157; *80:* 32; *82:* 3; *99:* 226
Owens, Mary Beth *113:* 202, 203; *191:* 148, 149
Owens, Nubia *84:* 74
Oxenbury, Helen *3:* 150, 151; *24:* 81; *68:* 174, 175,176; *81:* 209; *84:* 213, 245; *129:* 56; *149:* 159; *184:* 181
Oz, Robin *88:* 167; *185:* 181

P

Padgett, Jim *12:* 165
Page, Gail *205:* 128
Page, Homer *14:* 145
Page, Mark *162:* 70
Paget, Sidney *24:* 90, 91, 93, 95, 97
Paget, Walter *64:* 122
Paillot, Jim *173:* 89
Pajouhesh, Noushin *160:* 121
Pak *12:* 76
Pak, Yu Cha *86:* 174
Paladino, Lance *134:* 30
Palazzo, Tony *3:* 152, 153
Palecek, Josef *56:* 136; *89:* 158
Palen, Debbie *135:* 88; *195:* 148, 149
Palencar, John Jude *84:* 12, 45; *85:* 87; *92:* 187; *99:* 128; *110:* 204; *150:* 122; *171:* 86; *207:* 36
Palin, Nicki *81:* 201; *89:* 161
Palladini, David *4:* 113; *40:* 176, 177, 178, 179, 181,224, 225; *50:* 138; *78:* 186
Pallarito, Don *43:* 36
Palmer, Carol *158:* 230; *195:* 187
Palmer, Heidi *15:* 207; *29:* 102
Palmer, Jan *42:* 153; *82:* 161
Palmer, Judd *153:* 160, 161
Palmer, Juliette *6:* 89; *15:* 208
Palmer, Kate Salley *104:* 143; *154:* 169
Palmer, Lemuel *17:* 25, 29
Palmisciano, Diane *110:* 62; *162:* 26; *202:* 138, 139
Palmquist, Eric *38:* 133
Pamintuan, Macky *214:* 160
Panesis, Nicholas *3:* 127
Panter, Gary *182:* 191
Panton, Doug *52:* 99
Paparone, Pamela *129:* 174
Papas, William *11:* 223; *50:* 160
Papin, Joseph *26:* 113
Papish, Robin Lloyd *10:* 80

Papp, Robert *198:* 41; *205:* 130; *219:* 53
Paradis, Susan *40:* 216
Paraquin, Charles H. *18:* 166
Pardo DeLange, Alex *179:* 128; *211:* 135, 136
Paris, Peter *31:* 127
Parisi, Elizabeth B. *141:* 82; *164:* 57
Park, Nick *113:* 143
Park, Seho *39:* 110
Park, W.B. *22:* 189
Parker, Ant *82:* 87, 88; *104:* 121
Parker, Lewis *2:* 179
Parker, Nancy Winslow *10:* 113; *22:* 164; *28:* 47, 144; *52:* 7; *69:* 153; *91:* 171, 174; *132:* 175
Parker, Robert *4:* 161; *5:* 74; *9:* 136; *29:* 39
Parker, Robert Andrew *11:* 81; *29:* 186; *39:* 165; *40:* 25; *41:* 78; *42:* 123; *43:* 144; *48:* 182; *54:* 140; *74:* 141; *91:* 24; *111:* 115; *151:* 201; *154:* 156; *200:* 163, 164; *211:* 67
Parker-Rees, Guy *149:* 145; *193:* 149, 150
Parkin, Trevor *140:* 151
Parkins, David *114:* 123; *146:* 176; *176:* 168; *192:* 107; *218:* 139, 140, 141, 148
Parkinson, Kathy *71:* 143; *144:* 234
Parkinson, Keith *70:* 66
Parks, Gordon, Jr. *33:* 228
Parnall, Peter *5:* 137; *16:* 221; *24:* 70; *40:* 78; *51:* 130; *69:* 17, 155; *136:* 22, 23, 24
Parnall, Virginia *40:* 78
Paros, Jennifer *210:* 197
Parow, Lorraine *158:* 127
Parr, Todd *134:* 139, 140; *179:* 163, 164, 165
Parrish, Anne *27:* 159, 160
Parrish, Dillwyn *27:* 159
Parrish, Maxfield *14:* 160, 161, 164, 165; *16:* 109; *18:* 12, 13; *YABC 1:* 149, 152, 267; *2:* 146, 149
Parry, David *26:* 156
Parry, Marian *13:* 176; *19:* 179
Parsons, Garry *197:* 135
Partch, Virgil *45:* 163, 165
Pascal, David *14:* 174
Paschkis, Julie *177:* 153, 154; *220:* 140, 141
Pasquier, J.A. *16:* 91
Pastel, Elyse *201:* 123
Pasternak, Robert *119:* 53
Paterson, Diane *13:* 116; *39:* 163; *59:* 164, 165, 166,167; *72:* 51, 53; *129:* 175; *177:* 156, 157
Paterson, Helen *16:* 93
Patkau, Karen *112:* 123
Paton, Jane *15:* 271; *35:* 176
Patricelli, Leslie *207:* 129
Patrick, John *139:* 190
Patrick, Pamela *90:* 160; *93:* 211; *105:* 12
Patrick, Tom *190:* 103
Patterson, Geoffrey *54:* 75
Patterson, Robert *25:* 118
Patti, Joyce *187:* 145, 146
Patz, Nancy *111:* 40; *154:* 161; *214:* 80
Paul, James *4:* 130; *23:* 161
Paul, Korky *102:* 85
Paull, Grace *24:* 157; *87:* 127
Paulsen, Ruth Wright *79:* 160, 164; *189:* 146
Pavlov, Elena *80:* 49
Payne, Adam S. *135:* 166
Payne, C.F. *145:* 138, 140; *179:* 168
Payne, Joan Balfour *1:* 118
Payne, Tom *170:* 27
Payson, Dale *7:* 34; *9:* 151; *20:* 140; *37:* 22
Payzant, Charles *21:* 147
Peacock, Ralph *64:* 118
Peake, Mervyn *22:* 136, 149; *23:* 162, 163, 164; *YABC2:* 307
Pearson, Larry *38:* 225
Pearson, Tracey Campbell *64:* 163, 164, 167, 168, 169; *118:* 51; *156:* 169, 171, 172; *163:* 140; *219:* 140, 141, 142, 143
Peat, Fern B. *16:* 115
Peck, Anne Merriman *18:* 241; *24:* 155

Peck, Beth *66:* 242; *79:* 166; *80:* 136; *91:* 34; *95:* 9; *101:* 77; *164:* 197; *190:* 170
Peddicord, Jane Ann *199:* 106
Pedersen, Janet *193:* 152; *217:* 57; *218:* 15
Pedersen, Judy *66:* 217; *121:* 36; *172:* 67
Pedersen, Vilhelm *YABC 1:* 40
Pederson, Sharleen *12:* 92
Pedlar, Elaine *161:* 45
Peek, Merle *39:* 168
Peet, Bill *2:* 203; *41:* 159, 160, 161, 162, 163; *78:* 158, 159, 160, 161
Peguero, Adrian *116:* 133
Peguero, Gerard *116:* 133
Pels, Winslow Pinney *55:* 126
Peltier, Leslie C. *13:* 178
Peltzer, Marc *202:* 92
Penberthy, Mark *171:* 78
Pendle, Alexy *7:* 159; *13:* 34; *29:* 161; *33:* 215; *86:* 62
Pendola, Joanne *76:* 203; *81:* 125; *105:* 181; *178:* 152, 153
Pene du Bois, William *4:* 70; *10:* 122; *26:* 61; *27:* 145, 211; *35:* 243; *41:* 216; *68:* 180, 181; *73:* 45
Penfound, David *102:* 185
Pennington, Eunice *27:* 162
Peppe, Mark *28:* 142
Peppe, Rodney *4:* 164, 165; *74:* 187, 188, 189
Pepper, Hubert *64:* 143
Percy, Graham *63:* 2
Pericoli, Matteo *178:* 177
Perini, Ben *173:* 77
Perkins, David *60:* 68
Perkins, Lucy Fitch *72:* 199
Perkins, Lynne Rae *172:* 146; *212:* 153
Perl, Susan *2:* 98; *4:* 231; *5:* 44, 45, 118; *6:* 199; *8:* 137; *12:* 88; *22:* 193; *34:* 54, 55; *52:* 128; *YABC 1:* 176
Perrone, Donna *78:* 166
Perry, Marie Fritz *165:* 180
Perry, Patricia *29:* 137; *30:* 171
Perry, Roger *27:* 163
Perske, Martha *46:* 83; *51:* 108, 147
Persson, Stina *175:* 166
Pesek, Ludek *15:* 237
Petach, Heidi *149:* 166; *200:* 207
Peters, David *72:* 205; *182:* 116
Petersen, Jeff *181:* 95
Petersham, Maud *17:* 108, 147, 148, 149, 150, 151, 152, 153
Petersham, Miska *17:* 108, 147, 148, 149, 150, 151, 152, 153
Peterson, Eric *109:* 125
Peterson, Nisse *99:* 27
Peterson, R.F. *7:* 101
Peterson, Russell *7:* 130
Petie, Haris *2:* 3; *10:* 41, 118; *11:* 227; *12:* 70
Petricic, Dusan *153:* 75, 76, 77; *170:* 12; *172:* 13; *176:* 170; *179:* 56
Petrides, Heidrun *19:* 223
Petrone, Valeria *159:* 160; *171:* 92; *186:* 173; *204:* 49; *216:* 208; *220:* 98
Petrosino, Tamara *177:* 40; *193:* 154, 155
Petruccio, Steven James *67:* 159; *127:* 5
Pettingill, Ondre *64:* 181; *70:* 64
Peyo *40:* 56, 57
Peyton, K.M. *15:* 212
Pfeifer, Herman *15:* 262
Pfister, Marcus *83:* 165, 166, 167; *146:* 152; *150:* 160; *207:* 132, 134, 135, 136
Pfloog, Jan *124:* 60
Pham, LeUyen *160:* 48; *175:* 154, 156; *179:* 149; *201:* 124, 125, 126, 127; *204:* 28; *208:* 206; *217:* 92
Phelan, Matt *182:* 160; *184:* 222; *215:* 140, 141; *221:* 157
Phillipps, J.C. *218:* 142
Phillips, Craig *70:* 151; *207:* 74; *221:* 159
Phillips, Douglas *1:* 19
Phillips, F.D. *6:* 202
Phillips, Louise *133:* 67

Phillips, Matt *184:* 173
Phillips, Thomas *30:* 55
Philpot, Glyn *54:* 46
Phiz
  See Browne, Hablot K.
Piatti, Celestino *16:* 223
Pica, Steve *115:* 181
Picarella, Joseph *13:* 147
Picart, Gabriel *121:* 165; *201:* 169
Pichon, Liz *174:* 139
Pickard, Charles *12:* 38; *18:* 203; *36:* 152
Picken, George A. *23:* 150
Pickens, David *22:* 156
Pickering, Jimmy *195:* 152; *197:* 163
Pienkowski, Jan *6:* 183; *30:* 32; *58:* 140, 141, 142,143, 146, 147; *73:* 3; *87:* 156, 157; *131:* 189
Pieper, Christiane *200:* 168
Pignataro, Anna *163:* 220 *Pile, Emma 218:* 156 *Pileggi, Steve 145:* 122
Pilkey, Dav *68:* 186; *115:* 164, 166; *166:* 173, 174, 175
Pimlott, John *10:* 205
Pincus, Harriet *4:* 186; *8:* 179; *22:* 148; *27:* 164, 165; *66:* 202
Pini, Wendy *89:* 166
Pinkett, Neil *60:* 8
Pinkney, Brian *81:* 184, 185; *94:* 107; *113:* 146, 147; *117:* 121, 166; *132:* 145; *158:* 108, 191; *160:* 189; *200:* 8
Pinkney, Jerry *8:* 218; *10:* 40; *15:* 276; *20:* 66; *24:* 121; *33:* 109; *36:* 222; *38:* 200; *41:* 165, 166, 167, 168, 169, 170, 171, 173, 174; *44:* 198; *48:* 51; *53:* 20; *56:* 61, 68; *58:* 184; *60:* 59; *61:* 91; *71:* 146, 148, 149; *72:* 17; *73:* 149; *74:* 159,192; *75:* 45; *80:* 206; *81:* 44; *85:* 144; *95:* 50; *107:* 158, 159, 160; *108:* 164; *112:* 114, 115; *133:* 58; *195:* 140
Pinkwater, Daniel Manus *8:* 156; *46:* 180, 181, 182, 185, 188, 189, 190; *151:* 161 76: 178, 179, 180; *210:* 203
Pinkwater, Manus
  See Pinkwater, Daniel Manus
Pinkwater, Jill *114:* 160, 161; *158:* 179; *188:* 143, 145, 146
Pinto, Ralph *10:* 131; *45:* 93
Pinto, Sara *200:* 165
Pinon, Mark *74:* 22
Piven, Hanoch *173:* 142
Pistolesi *73:* 211
Pitcairn, Ansel *188:* 10
Pittman, Helena Clare *71:* 151
Pitz, Henry C. *4:* 168; *19:* 165; *35:* 128; *42:* 80; *YABC 2:* 95, 176
Pitzenberger, Lawrence J. *26:* 94
Pitzer, Susanna *181:* 131
Place, François *218:* 42
Plant, Andrew *214:* 166
Player, Stephen *82:* 190
Plecas, Jennifer *84:* 201; *106:* 124; *149:* 168; *205:* 180; *220:* 81
Ploog, Mike *180:* 19
Plowden, David *52:* 135, 136
Plume, Ilse *170:* 149
Plummer, William *32:* 31
Podevin, Jean François *184:* 185
Podwal, Mark *56:* 170, 173; *101:* 154, 155, 157; *149:* 176; *160:* 194
Pogany, Willy *15:* 46, 49; *19:* 222, 256; *25:* 214; *44:* 142, 143, 144, 145, 146, 147, 148
Pohrt, Tom *67:* 116; *104:* 80; *152:* 199; *195:* 154; *199:* 85
Poirson, V.A. *26:* 89
Polacco, Patricia *74:* 195, 196, 197, 198; *123:* 121, 122, 123; *180:* 189, 190, 191, 193, 194; *212:* 168, 170, 171
Polgreen, John *21:* 44
Polhemus, Coleman *210:* 209
Politi, Leo *1:* 178; *4:* 53; *21:* 48; *47:* 173,174, 176, 178, 179, 180, 181
Pollack, Barbara *219:* 60

Pollema-Cahill, Phyllis *123:* 126
Pollen, Samson *64:* 80
Polonsky, Arthur *34:* 168
Polseno, Jo *1:* 53; *3:* 117; *5:* 114; *17:* 154; *20:* 87; *32:* 49; *41:* 245
Pomaska, Anna *117:* 148
Pons, Bernadette *184:* 100
Ponter, James *5:* 204
Poole, Colin *111:* 27
Poortvliet, Rien *6:* 212; *65:* 165, 166, 167
Pope, Kevin *183:* 158
Popp, Wendy *72:* 122; *158:* 68
Poppel, Hans *71:* 154, 155
Porfirio, Guy *76:* 134
Portal, Colette *6:* 186; *11:* 203
Porter, George *7:* 181
Porter, Janice Lee *136:* 175; *164:* 37
Porter, John *113:* 47
Porter, Pat Grant *84:* 112; *125:* 101
Porter, Sue *146:* 246, 247; *213:* 139, 140, 141; *221:* 91
Porter, Walter *124:* 175
Porto, James *221:* 14
Posada, Mia *187:* 151
Posen, Michael *175:* 82
Posthuma, Sieb *150:* 163
Postier, Jim *202:* 140; *204:* 25
Postma, Lidia *79:* 17
Potter, Beatrix *100:* 194, 195; *132:* 179, 180, 181, 182; *YABC 1:* 208, 209, 210, 212, 213
Potter, Giselle *117:* 123; *143:* 44; *144:* 170, 197; *149:* 7; *150:* 165; *187:* 152, 153; *190:* 198; *196:* 152; *200:* 12
Potter, Katherine *104:* 147; *171:* 135; *173:* 136; *217:* 130, 131
Potter, Miriam Clark *3:* 162
Poulin, Stephane *98:* 140, 141
Poullis, Nick *146:* 210
Powell, Constance Buffington *174:* 141
Powell, Gary *151:* 208
Powell, Ivan *67:* 219
Power, Margaret *105:* 122
Powers, Daniel *161:* 173
Powers, Richard M. *1:* 230; *3:* 218; *7:* 194; *26:* 186
Powledge, Fred *37:* 154
Powzyk, Joyce *74:* 214
Poydar, Nancy *96:* 149; *190:* 180, 181, 182
Pracher, Richard *91:* 166
Prachaticka, Marketa *126:* 126
Prange, Beckie *181:* 169
Prap, Lila *177:* 165
Prater, John *103:* 142, 143, 144; *149:* 172
Pratt, Charles *23:* 29
Pratt, Christine Joy *214:* 167
Pratt, George *116:* 208; *212:* 37
Pratt, Pierre *150:* 73; *166:* 183; *168:* 172; *201:* 27; *208:* 171, 172, 173
Prebenna, David *73:* 174
Preiss-Glasser, Robin *123:* 176; *152* 40; *172:* 194
Press, Jenny *116:* 95
Preston, Mark *152:* 162
Pretro, Korinna *91:* 126
Prevost, Mikela *209:* 111
Price, Christine *2:* 247; *3:* 163, 253; *8:* 166
Price, Cynthia *118:* 156
Price, Edward *33:* 34
Price, Garrett *1:* 76; *2:* 42
Price, Hattie Longstreet *17:* 13
Price, Nick *216:* 173; *220:* 7
Price, Norman *YABC 1:* 129
Price, Willard *48:* 184
Priceman, Marjorie *81:* 171; *136:* 169; *156:* 200; *168:* 153, 154; *188:* 45
Priestley, Alice *168:* 33
Priestley, Chris *198:* 144
Primavera, Elise *26:* 95; *58:* 151; *73:* 37; *80:* 79; *86:* 156; *105:* 161; *213:* 157
Primrose, Jean *36:* 109
Prince, Alison *86:* 188, 189

Prince, Leonora E. *7:* 170
Pritchett, Shelley *116:* 148
Prittie, Edwin J. *YABC 1:* 120
Proimos, James *176:* 4; *217:* 132, 133, 134
Proimos, John *173:* 144
Prosmitsky, Jenya *132:* 33
Provensen, Alice *37:* 204, 215, 222; *70:* 176, 177, 178, 180, *71:* 213; *147:* 184; *191:* 190
Provensen, Martin *37:* 204, 215, 222; *70:* 176, 177, 178, 180; *71:* 213; *191:* 190
Pucci, Albert John *44:* 154
Pudlo *8:* 59
Puggaard, Ulla *196:* 25
Pullen, Zachary *211:* 161
Pulver, Harry, Jr. *129:* 159
Pulver, Robin *160:* 4
Punchatz, Don *99:* 57
Purdy, Susan *8:* 162
Pursell, Weimer *55:* 18
Purtscher, Alfons *97:* 6
Puskas, James *5:* 141
Pyk, Jan *7:* 26; *38:* 123
Pyle, Chuck *99:* 149; *191:* 83
Pyle, Howard *16:* 225, 226, 227, 228, 230, 231, 232, 235; *24:* 27; *34:* 124, 125, 127, 128; *59:* 132; *100:* 198

Q

Quackenbush, Robert *4:* 190; *6:* 166; *7:* 175, 178; *9:* 86; *11:* 65, 221; *41:* 154; *43:* 157; *70:* 185, 186; *71:* 137; *85:* 47; *92:* 148; *133:* 154, 164, 169
Qualls, Sean *177:* 167, 168; *193:* 43
Quennell, Marjorie (Courtney) *29:* 163, 164
Quidor, John *19:* 82
Quirk, John *62:* 170
Quirk, Thomas *12:* 81

R

Rackham, Arthur *15:* 32, 78, 214-227; *17:* 105, 115; *18:* 233; *19:* 254; *20:* 151; *22:* 129, 131, 132, 133; *23:* 175; *24:* 161, 181; *26:* 91; *32:* 118; *64:* 18; *100:* 9, 16, 203, 204; *YABC 1:* 25, 45, 55, 147; *2:* 103, 142, 173, 210
Racz, Michael *56:* 134
Raczka, Bob *191:* 155, 156
Radcliffe, Andrew *82:* 215
Rader, Laura *101:* 219; *197:* 147; *203:* 53
Radunsky, Vladimir *177:* 170; *192:* 30
Radzinski, Kandy *212:* 174
Rafilson, Sidney *11:* 172
Raglin, Tim *125:* 24
Raible, Alton *1:* 202, 203; *28:* 193; *35:* 181; *110:* 207
Raine, Patricia *82:* 74; *88:* 154
Ramá, Sue *173:* 45; *185:* 186; *190:* 184
Ramhorst, John *117:* 11
Ramirez, Gladys *177:* 19
Ramirez, Jose *207:* 27
Ramsey, James *16:* 41
Ramsey, Marcy Dunn *82:* 11; *180:* 186
Ramus, Michael *51:* 171
Rand, Paul *6:* 188
Rand, Ted *67:* 9, 10, 121, 123; *74:* 190; *84:* 170; *103:* 170; *112:* 6; *114:* 73; *139:* 168; *143:* 194; *156:* 154; *161:* 9, 10; *200:* 38; *204:* 7
Randazzo, Tony *81:* 98
Randell, William *55:* 54
Rane, Walter *93:* 144; *143:* 109; *184:* 126
Rankin, Joan *163:* 40; *212:* 176
Rankin, Laura *176:* 173, 174; *179:* 150
Ransome, Arthur *22:* 201

Ransome, James E. *74:* 137; *75:* 80; *84:* 181; *94:* 108; *117:* 115; *123:* 128, 129, 130; *158:* 101, 102; *159:* 205; *178:* 188, 189, 190; *216:* 114

Rantz, Don *119:* 184

Rao, Anthony *28:* 126

Raphael, Elaine *23:* 192; *71:* 24, 25

Rappaport, Eva *6:* 190

Raschka, Chris *80:* 187, 189, 190; *97:* 211; *115:* 210; *117:* 151, 152, 153, 154; *143:* 195; *145:* 153; *166:* 190, 191; *170:* 114; *207:* 140, 143, 144, 145; *208:* 82; *220:* 85

Rash, Andy *158:* 178; *162:* 172; *210:* 204; *219:* 145

Raskin, Ellen *2:* 208, 209; *4:* 142; *13:* 183; *22:* 68; *29:* 139; *36:* 134; *38:* 173, 174, 175, 176, 177, 178,179, 180, 181; *60:* 163; *86:* 81

Rathmann, Peggy *93:* 32; *94:* 168; *157:* 212, 214

Ratkus, Tony *77:* 133

Ratzkin, Lawrence *40:* 143

Rau, Margaret *9:* 157

Raverat, Gwen *YABC 1:* 152

Ravid, Joyce *61:* 73

Ravielli, Anthony *1:* 198; *3:* 168; *11:* 143

Ravilious, Robin *77:* 169

Rawlins, Donna *72:* 198; *73:* 15, 129

Rawlins, Janet *76:* 79

Rawlings, Steve *143:* 139; *151:* 54; *208:* 150

Rawlinson, Debbie *75:* 132

Ray, Deborah Kogan *8:* 164; *29:* 238; *50:* 112, 113; *62:* 119; *78:* 191; *203:* 149, 150, 151

Ray, Jane *96:* 166; *97:* 104; *152:* 208; *190:* 221; *196:* 165

Ray, Ralph *2:* 239; *5:* 73

Rayann, Omar *162:* 205; *186:* 29, 30

Rayevsky, Robert *64:* 17; *70:* 173; *80:* 204; *117:* 79; *190:* 187, 188

Raymond, Larry *31:* 108; *97:* 109

Rayner, Hugh *151:* 170

Rayner, Mary *22:* 207; *47:* 140; *72:* 191; *87:* 171, 172; *192:* 104

Rayner, Shoo
See Rayner, Hugh

Raynes, John *71:* 19

Raynor, Dorka *28:* 168

Raynor, Paul *24:* 73

Rayyan, Omar *110:* 222; *112:* 17; *125:* 131

Razzi, James *10:* 127

Read, Alexander D. *20:* 45

Reader, Dennis *71:* 157

Reasoner, Charles *53:* 33, 36, 37

Rebenschied, Shane *203:* 76; *215:* 124

Reczuch, Karen *115:* 132; *145:* 131

Redlich, Ben *163:* 221; *198:* 193

Reddy, Mike *203:* 67

Reed, Joseph *116:* 139

Reed, Lynn Rowe *115:* 173; *171:* 146; *208:* 177; *215:* 144, 145

Reed, Mike *211:* 147; *215:* 131

Reed, Tom *34:* 171

Reeder, Colin *74:* 202; *77:* 113

Rees, Mary *134:* 219

Reese, Bob *60:* 135

Reeve, Philip *171:* 50

Reeves, Eira B. *130:* 173, 174; *141:* 151

Reeves, Rick *181:* 179

Reeves, Rosie *202:* 200

Regan, Dana *117:* 116

Regan, Laura *103:* 198; *153:* 206

Reichert, Renée *169:* 127

Reid, Barbara *82:* 178; *92:* 17; *93:* 169, 170

Reid, Stephen *19:* 213; *22:* 89

Reim, Melanie *104:* 151; *150:* 98

Reinert, Kirk *89:* 138; *195:* 129

Reinertson, Barbara *44:* 150; *62:* 103

Reiniger, Lotte *40:* 185

Reisberg, Mira *119:* 2

Reisch, Jesse *158:* 130

Reiser, Lynn *81:* 175; *138:* 184; *180:* 200

Reiss, John J. *23:* 193

Relf, Douglas *3:* 63

Relyea, C.M. *16:* 29; *31:* 153

Remi, Georges *13:* 184

Remington, Frederic *19:* 188; *41:* 178, 179, 180, 181, 183,184, 185, 186, 187, 188; *62:* 197

Remkiewicz, Frank *67:* 102; *77:* 171; *80:* 130; *113:* 107; *152:* 116; *152:* 211, 212; *157:* 148; *217:* 120, 138, 139, 140, 141

Rendon, Maria *116:* 141; *192:* 134; *134:* 152

Renfro, Ed *79:* 176

Renier, Aaron *202:* 141; *207:* 119

Renlie, Frank *11:* 200

Reschofsky, Jean *7:* 118

Rethi *60:* 181

Rethi, Lili *2:* 153; *36:* 156

Reusswig, William *3:* 267

Revell, Cindy *195:* 93

Rex, Adam *156:* 172; *169:* 91; *186:* 178, 179; *215:* 103

Rex, Michael *157:* 147; *191:* 159, 160; *221:* 124

Rey, H.A. *1:* 182; *26:* 163, 164, 166, 167, 169; *69:* 172, 173, 174, 175; *86:* 195, 196, 197; *100:* 211; *YABC 2:* 17

Rey, Luis V. *201:* 162

Reynolds, Adrian *192:* 159, 160

Reynolds, Doris *5:* 71; *31:* 77

Reynolds, Peter H. *142:* 12; *179:* 175, 176; *202:* 113, 114

Rhead, Louis *31:* 91; *100:* 228

Rhodes, Andrew *38:* 204; *50:* 163; *54:* 76; *61:* 123, 124; *87:* 200

Ribbons, Ian *3:* 10; *37:* 161; *40:* 76

Ricci, Regolo *93:* 22; *164:* 148

Rice, Elizabeth *2:* 53, 214

Rice, Eve *34:* 174, 175; *91:* 172

Rice, James *22:* 210; *93:* 173

Rich, Anna *212:* 180

Rich, Martha *195:* 16

Richards, Chuck *170:* 154

Richards, George *40:* 116, 119, 121; *44:* 179

Richards, Henry *YABC 1:* 228, 231

Richardson, Ernest *2:* 144

Richardson, Frederick *18:* 27, 31

Richardson, John *110:* 88

Richman, Hilda *26:* 132

Richmond, George *24:* 179

Riddell, Chris *114:* 170, 195; *166:* 179; *199:* 164, 166, 167; *218:* 146, 148; *219:* 149, 150, 152, 153

Riddle, Tohby *74:* 204; *151:* 179

Riding, Peter *63:* 195

Rieniets, Judy King *14:* 28

Riger, Bob *2:* 166

Riggio, Anita *73:* 191; *85:* 63; *137:* 184; *172:* 165

Rigano, Giovanni *219:* 45

Riley, Jon *74:* 70

Riley, Kenneth *22:* 230

Riley, Terry *203:* 100

Riley-Webb, Charlotte *153:* 143

Rinaldi, Angelo *165:* 60, 69

Ringgold, Faith *71:* 162; *114:* 173, 174, 176; *187:* 160, 161, 163

Ringi, Kjell *12:* 171

Rios, Tere
See Versace, Marie

Rioux, Jo *215:* 110

Ripper, Charles L. *3:* 175

Ripplinger, Henry *117:* 31

Ritchie, Scot *217:* 145

Ritchie, William *74:* 183

Ritter, John *175:* 14

Ritz, Karen *41:* 117; *72:* 239; *87:* 125; *102:* 7; *106:* 6

Rivas, Victor *209:* 193

Rivers, Ruth *178:* 193

Rivkin, Jay *15:* 230

Rivoche, Paul *45:* 125

Roach, Marilynne *9:* 158

Robbin, Jodi *44:* 156, 159

Robbins, Frank *42:* 167

Robbins, Ken *147:* 191, 192

Robbins, Ruth *52:* 102

Roberts, Cliff *4:* 126

Roberts, David *154:* 4, 6; *191:* 162; *196:* 184; *197:* 105; *210:* 257

Roberts, Doreen *4:* 230; *28:* 105

Roberts, Jim *22:* 166; *23:* 69; *31:* 110

Roberts, Tony *109:* 195, 214

Roberts, W. *22:* 2, 3

Robertson, M.P. *197:* 153

Robins, Arthur *137:* 172; *151:* 225; *204:* 161

Robinson, Aminah Brenda Lynn *86:* 205; *103:* 55; *159:* 175

Robinson, Charles [1870-1937] *17:* 157, 171, 172, 173, 175, 176; *24:* 207; *25:* 204; *YABC 2:* 308, 309, 310, 331

Robinson, Charles *3:* 53; *5:* 14; *6:* 193; *7:* 150; *7:* 183; *8:* 38; *9:* 81; *13:* 188; *14:* 248, 249; *23:* 149; *26:* 115; *27:* 48; *28:* 191; *32:* 28; *35:* 210; *36:* 37; *48:* 96; *52:* 33; *53:* 157; *56:* 15; *62:* 142; *77:* 41; *111:* 148

Robinson, Jerry *3:* 262

Robinson, Joan G. *7:* 184

Robinson, Lolly *90:* 227

Robinson, T.H. *17:* 179, 181, 182, 183; *29:* 254

Robinson, W. Heath *17:* 185, 187, 189, 191, 193, 195, 197, 199, 202; *23:* 167; *25:* 194; *29:* 150; *YABC 2:* 183

Rocco, John *187:* 4; *188:* 151; *208:* 180, 181, 182; *213:* 94

Roche, Christine *41:* 98

Roche, Denis *99:* 184; *180:* 32; *196:* 168

Roche, P.K. *57:* 151, 152

Rocker, Fermin *7:* 34; *13:* 21; *31:* 40; *40:* 190,191

Rocklen, Margot *101:* 181

Rockwell, Anne *5:* 147; *33:* 171, 173; *71:* 166, 167,168; *114:* 183, 184; *194:* 152, 155

Rockwell, Gail *7:* 186

Rockwell, Harlow *33:* 171, 173, 175

Rockwell, Lizzy *114:* 182; *162:* 182; *185:* 189

Rockwell, Norman *23:* 39, 196, 197, 199, 200, 203, 204, 207; *41:* 140, 143; *123:* 47; *YABC 2:* 60

Rockwood, Richard *119:* 75

Rodanas, Kristina *156:* 183, 184; *221:* 127

Rodegast, Roland *43:* 100

Rodgers, Frank *69:* 177

Rodriguez, Albert G. *182:* 50

Rodriguez, Christina *184:* 12

Rodriguez, Edel *204:* 86

Rodriguez, Joel *16:* 65

Rodriguez, Robert *145:* 145; *212:* 33

Rodriguez-Howard, Pauline *177:* 18

Roe, Monika *210:* 94

Roeckelein, Katrina *134:* 223

Roennfeldt, Robert *66:* 243

Roever, J.M. *4:* 119; *26:* 170

Roffey, Maureen *33:* 142, 176, 177

Rogasky, Barbara *46:* 90

Rogé *173:* 160

Rogers, Carol *2:* 262; *6:* 164; *26:* 129

Rogers, Chris M. *150:* 59; *196:* 61

Rogers, Forest *87:* 160; *101:* 76

Rogers, Frances *10:* 130

Rogers, Gregory *104:* 76; *126:* 57; *171:* 26

Rogers, Jacqueline *78:* 249; *80:* 34; *86:* 54; *103:* 70; *115:* 72; *129:* 173; *131:* 57, 225; *143:* 211; *153:* 100; *190:* 186; *203:* 51; *213:* 144, 145, 146; *214:* 142

Rogers, Sherry *191:* 66

Rogers, Walter S. *31:* 135, 138; *67:* 65, 168; *100:* 81

Rogers, William A. *15:* 151, 153, 154; *33:* 35

Rogoff, Barbara *95:* 20

Rohmann, Eric *103:* 152; *198:* 151

Rojankovsky, Feodor *6:* 134, 136; *10:* 183; *21:* 128,129, 130; *25:* 110; *28:* 42; *68:* 120

Rolfsen, Alf *62:* 15
Rolston, Steve *209:* 154
Romain, Trevor *134:* 157
Roman, Barbara J. *103:* 171
Romas *114:* 111; *165:* 63
Romano, Robert *64:* 68
Romero, Alejandro *187:* 185
Roos, Maryn *168:* 198
Root, Barry *80:* 212; *90:* 196; *146:* 78; *156:* 165; *159:* 161; *182:* 18, 172
Root, Kimberly Bulcken *86:* 72; *98:* 21; *108:* 111; *127:* 114; *159:* 162; *176:* 134; *192:* 163
Roper, Bob *65:* 153
Roraback, Robin *111:* 156
Rorer, Abigail *43:* 222; *85:* 155
Rosales, Melodye *80:* 35
Rosamilia, Patricia *36:* 120
Rose, Carl *5:* 62
Rose, David S. *29:* 109; *70:* 120
Rose, Gerald *68:* 200, 201; *86:* 48
Rose, Ted *93:* 178
Rosen, Elizabeth *205:* 137
Rosenbaum, Jonathan *50:* 46
Rosenberg, Amye *74:* 207, 208
Rosenberry, Vera *87:* 22, 26; *144:* 212, 213; *158:* 120; *219:* 163, 164
Rosenblum, Richard *11:* 202; *18:* 18
Rosenstiehl, Agnès *203:* 153
Rosier, Lydia *16:* 236; *20:* 104; *21:* 109; *22:* 125; *30:* 151, 158; *42:* 128; *45:* 214; *77:* 227, 228
Rosing, Jens *85:* 142
Ross
　See Thomson, Ross
Ross, Christine *83:* 172, 173
Ross, Clare Romano *3:* 123; *21:* 45; *48:* 199
Ross, Dave *32:* 152; *57:* 108
Ross, Graham *199:* 4
Ross, Herbert *37:* 78
Ross, John *3:* 123; *21:* 45
Ross, Johnny *32:* 190
Ross, Larry *47:* 168; *60:* 62
Ross, Ruth *109:* 233
Ross, Tony *17:* 204; *56:* 132; *65:* 176, 177, 179; *90:* 123; *123:* 186, 187, 190; *130:* 188, 190, 191, 192; *132:* 242; *174:* 159; *176:* 181, 182, 183; *202:* 198
Rossetti, Dante Gabriel *20:* 151, 153
Rostant, Larry *180:* 221; *194:* 108; *195:* 96; *197:* 12; *207:* 53; *210:* 189
Roth, Arnold *4:* 238; *21:* 133
Roth, Julie Jersild *180:* 206
Roth, Marci *135:* 223
Roth, R.G. *184:* 50
Roth, Rob *105:* 98; *146:* 41
Roth, Robert *176:* 159
Roth, Roger *61:* 128; *190:* 192
Roth, Ruby *216:* 185
Roth, Stephanie *136:* 171, 172
Roth, Susan L. *80:* 38; *93:* 78; *134:* 165, 166; *181:* 145, 146
Rothenberg, Joani Keller *162:* 190, 191
Rothman, Michael *139:* 62; *184:* 34 Rotman, Jeffrey L. *145:* 30
Rotondo, Pat *32:* 158
Roughsey, Dick *35:* 186
Rouille, M. *11:* 96
Rounds, Glen *8:* 173; *9:* 171; *12:* 56; *32:* 194; *40:* 230; *51:* 161, 162, 166; *56:* 149; *70:* 198, 199; *YABC 1:* 1, 2, 3; *112:* 163
Roundtree, Katherine *114:* 88; *168:* 102
Rovetch, Lissa *201:* 164
Rowan, Evadne *52:* 51
Rowe, Eric *111:* 161
Rowe, Gavin *27:* 144; *72:* 47; *88:* 201
Rowe, John *132:* 70, 71; *180:* 126
Rowell, Kenneth *40:* 72
Rowen, Amy *52:* 143
Rowena *116:* 101
Rowland, Andrew *164:* 136
Rowland, Jada *83:* 73

Rowles, Daphne *58:* 24
Roy, Jeroo *27:* 229; *36:* 110
Royo *118:* 32; *144:* 105, 106, 108; *165:* 19; *166:* 166
Rubbino, Salvatore *220:* 147
Rubel, Nicole *18:* 255; *20:* 59; *81:* 66, 67; *95:* 169, 170; *119:* 60; *135:* 177, 179, 180; *169:* 68; *181:* 150
Rubel, Reina *33:* 217
Rud, Borghild *6:* 15
Ruddell, Gary *110:* 238; *116:* 207
Rudolph, Norman Guthrie *17:* 13
Rue, Leonard Lee III *37:* 164
Rueda, Claudia *183:* 170, 171
Ruelle, Karen Gray *126:* 193
Ruff, Donna *50:* 173; *72:* 203; *78:* 49; *80:* 120,121; *93:* 162; *164:* 121
Ruffins, Reynold *10:* 134, 135; *41:* 191, 192, 193, 194, 195, 196; *125:* 187, 188, 189; *162:* 197
Ruhlin, Roger *34:* 44
Rui, Paolo *217:* 115
Ruiz, Art *95:* 154; *110:* 91
Rumford, James *193:* 167
Runnerstroem, Bengt Arne *75:* 161
Ruse, Margaret *24:* 155
Rush, Ken *98:* 74
Rush, Peter *42:* 75
Russell, Charles M. *167:* 171
Russell, E.B. *18:* 177, 182
Russell, Jim *53:* 134
Russell, Natalie *218:* 170, 171
Russell, P. Craig *80:* 196; *146:* 102; *162:* 186
Russo, Marisabina *84:* 51; *106:* 164; *151:* 183; *188:* 153, 154, 155, 156
Russo, Susan *30:* 182; *36:* 144
Russon, Mary *87:* 145
Ruth, Greg *183:* 125
Ruth, Rod *9:* 161
Rutherford, Alexa *110:* 108
Rutherford, Jenny *78:* 5
Rutherford, Meg *25:* 174; *34:* 178, 179; *69:* 73; *72:* 31
Rutland, Jonathan *31:* 126
Ruurs, Margriet *147:* 195
Ruzzier, Sergio *159:* 176, 177; *163:* 184; *210:* 214, 216
Ryan, Amy *188:* 50
Ryan, Will *86:* 134
Ryden, Hope *8:* 176
Rylant, Cynthia *112:* 170, 172
Rymer, Alta M. *34:* 181
Ryniak, Christopher *178:* 11
Rystedt, Rex *49:* 80

S

Saaf, Chuck *49:* 179
Saaf, Donald *101:* 220; *124:* 180
Sabaka, Donna R. *21:* 172
Sabin, Robert *45:* 35; *60:* 30; *99:* 161
Sabuda, Robert *170:* 166, 167, 168
Sacker, Amy *16:* 100
Saelig, S.M. *129:* 73; *173:* 59
Saffioti, Lino *36:* 176; *48:* 60
Saflund, Birgitta *94:* 2
Sagsoorian, Paul *12:* 183; *22:* 154; *33:* 106; *87:* 152
Sahara, Tony *168:* 106; *177:* 181; *178:* 228; *186:* 132; *207:* 89
Sahlberg, Myron *57:* 165
Saidens, Amy *145:* 162; *191:* 131; *210:* 129
Saint Exupery, Antoine de *20:* 157
Saint James, Synthia *152:* 220; *188:* 90; *200:* 7
Sakai, Komako *213:* 148
Saldutti, Denise *39:* 186; *57:* 178
Sale, Morton *YABC 2:* 31
Sale, Tim *153:* 177

Salerno, Steven *150:* 79; *176:* 188; *202:* 39; *216:* 190
Salter, George *72:* 128, 130
Saltzberg, Barney *135:* 184, 185; *194:* 160
Saltzman, David *86:* 209
Salwowski, Mark *71:* 54
Salzman, Yuri *86:* 12
Sambourne, Linley *YABC 2:* 181
Sampson, Katherine *9:* 197
Samson, Anne S. *2:* 216
San Souci, Daniel *40:* 200; *96:* 199, 200; *113:* 171; *157:* 149; *170:* 69; *192:* 167, 168; *220:* 152; *221:* 126
Sancha, Sheila *38:* 185
Sanchez, Enrique O. *155:* 84
Sand, George X. *45:* 182
Sandberg, Lasse *15:* 239, 241
Sanders, Beryl *39:* 173
Sanderson, Ruth *21:* 126; *24:* 53; *28:* 63; *33:* 67; *41:* 48, 198, 199, 200, 201, 202, 203; *43:* 79; *46:* 36,44; *47:* 102; *49:* 58; *62:* 121, 122; *85:* 3; *109:* 207, 208, 209, 210; *172:* 157, 158
Sandia *119:* 74
Sandin, Joan *4:* 36; *6:* 194; *7:* 177; *12:* 145,185; *20:* 43; *21:* 74; *26:* 144; *27:* 142; *28:* 224, 225; *38:* 86; *41:* 46; *42:* 35; *59:* 6; *80:* 136; *94:* 188; *140:* 116; *153:* 179, 180; *197:* 168
Sandland, Reg *39:* 215
Sandoz, Edouard *26:* 45, 47
Sanford, John *66:* 96, 97
Sanger, Amy Wilson *205:* 140
Sankey, Tom *72:* 103
Sano, Kazuhiko *153:* 208; *195:* 171; *203:* 21; *221:* 71
Santat, Dan *188:* 160; *221:* 62
Santiago, Wilfred *210:* 48
Santore, Charles *54:* 139; *200:* 171, 172
Santoro, Christopher *74:* 215
Santos, Jesse J. *99:* 24
Sapieha, Christine *1:* 180
Saport, Linda *123:* 137, 138; *215:* 29
Sara
　See De La Roche Saint Andre, Anne
Sarcone-Roach, Julia *215:* 158
Sardinha, Rick *175:* 151
Sarg, Tony *YABC 2:* 236
Sargent, Claudia *64:* 181
Sargent, Robert *2:* 217
Saris *1:* 33
Sarony *YABC 2:* 170
Saroff, Phyllis V. *202:* 160
Sasaki, Goro *170:* 46
Sasaki, Ellen Joy *216:* 49
Sasek, Miroslav *16:* 239, 240, 241, 242
Sassman, David *9:* 79
Sattler, Jennifer Gordon *218:* 175
Satty *29:* 203, 205
Sauber, Robert *40:* 183; *76:* 256; *78:* 154; *87:* 92
Saunders, Dave *85:* 163, 164, 165
Savadier, Elivia *84:* 50; *145:* 45; *164:* 206
Savage, Naomi *56:* 172
Savage, Steele *10:* 203; *20:* 77; *35:* 28
Savage, Stephen *174:* 182
Savio *76:* 4
Savitt, Sam *8:* 66, 182; *15:* 278; *20:* 96; *24:* 192; *28:* 98
Sawyer, Kem Knapp *84:* 228, 229
Say, Allen *28:* 178; *69:* 182, 183, 232; *110:* 194, 195,196; *161:* 154, 155
Sayles, Elizabeth *82:* 93; *105:* 155; *109:* 116; *180:* 64; *220:* 160, 161
Scabrini, Janet *13:* 191; *44:* 128
Scanlan, Peter *83:* 27; *153:* 165; *187:* 149
Scanlon, Paul *83:* 87
Scannell, Reece *105:* 105
Scarry, Huck *35:* 204, 205

Scarry, Richard 2: 220, 221; 18: 20; 35: 193, 194, 195,196, 197, 198, 199, 200, 201, 202; 75: 165, 167, 168
Schachner, Judith Byron 88: 180; 92: 163; 93: 102; 142: 82; 178: 199, 200; 190: 140
Schade, Susan 205: 21
Schaeffer, Mead 18: 81, 94; 21: 137, 138, 139; 47: 128
Schaffer, Amanda 90: 206
Schanzer, Rosalyn 138: 192, 193
Scharl, Josef 20: 132; 22: 128
Scheel, Lita 11: 230
Scheffler, Axel 180: 23, 24
Scheib, Ida 29: 28
Schermer, Judith 30: 184
Schick, Eleanor 82: 210, 211; 144: 222
Schick, Joel 16: 160; 17: 167; 22: 12; 27: 176; 31: 147, 148; 36: 23; 38: 64; 45: 116, 117; 52: 5, 85; 104: 159
Schields, Gretchen 75: 171, 203
Schindelman, Joseph 1: 74; 4: 101; 12: 49; 26: 51; 40: 146; 56: 158; 73: 40
Schindler, Edith 7: 22
Schindler, S.D. 38: 107; 46: 196; 74: 162; 75: 172, 173; 99: 133; 112: 177; 118: 185, 186; 121: 71; 136: 159; 143: 45; 149: 120; 156: 30; 169: 135; 171: 161, 162, 163; 172: 9; 186: 163; 194: 109; 195: 35; 198: 170, 171, 172
Schlesinger, Bret 7: 77
Schlossberg, Elisabeth 221: 161
Schmid, Eleanore 12: 188; 126: 196, 197
Schmiderer, Dorothy 19: 224
Schmidt, Bill 73: 34; 76: 220, 222, 224
Schmidt, Elizabeth 15: 242
Schmidt, George Paul 132: 122
Schmidt, Karen Lee 54: 12; 71: 174; 92: 56; 94: 190, 191; 127: 103
Schmidt, Lynette 76: 205
Schmitz, Tamara 207: 147
Schneider, Christine M. 171: 165
Schneider, Howie 181: 159
Schneider, Rex 29: 64; 44: 171
Schnurr, Edward 170: 62
Schoberle, Cecile 80: 200; 92: 134; 218: 113
Schoenherr, Ian 32: 83; 173: 41
Schoenherr, John 1: 146, 147, 173; 3: 39, 139; 17: 75; 29: 72; 32: 83; 37: 168, 169, 170; 43: 164, 165; 45: 160, 162; 51: 127; 66: 196, 197, 198; 68: 83; 72: 240; 75: 225; 88: 176
Scholder, Fritz 69: 103
Schomburg, Alex 13: 23
Schongut, Emanuel 4: 102; 15: 186; 47: 218, 219; 52: 147, 148, 149, 150; 185: 27
Schoonover, Frank 17: 107; 19: 81, 190, 233; 22: 88,129; 24: 189; 31: 88; 41: 69; YABC 2: 282, 316
Schories, Pat 164: 210
Schottland, Miriam 22: 172
Schramm, Ulrik 2: 16; 14: 112
Schreiber, Elizabeth Anne 13: 193
Schreiber, Ralph W. 13: 193
Schreiter, Rick 14: 97; 23: 171; 41: 247; 49: 131
Schroades, John 214: 129
Schroeder, Binette 56: 128, 129
Schroeder, E. Peter 12: 112
Schroeder, Ted 11: 160; 15: 189; 30: 91; 34: 43
Schrotter, Gustav 22: 212; 30: 225
Schubert, Dieter 101: 167, 168; 217: 151, 152, 153, 155
Schubert, Ingrid 217: 151, 152, 153, 155
Schubert-Gabrys, Ingrid 101: 167, 168
Schucker, James 31: 163
Schuett, Stacey 72: 137; 208: 204
Schulder, Lili 146: 29
Schulke, Debra 57: 167
Schulke, Flip 57: 167
Schulz, Barbara 167: 24

Schulz, Charles M. 10: 137, 138, 139, 140, 141, 142; 118: 192, 193, 194, 196, 199
Schutzer, Dena 109: 32
Schwark, Mary Beth 51: 155; 72: 175
Schwartz, Amy 47: 191; 82: 100; 83: 178, 179, 180,181; 129: 107; 131: 197, 198; 189: 166, 168
Schwartz, Carol 124: 41; 130: 199
Schwartz, Charles 8: 184
Schwartz, Daniel 46: 37
Schwartz, Joanie 124: 170
Schwartzberg, Joan 3: 208
Schwarz, Viviane 204: 132
Schweitzer, Iris 2: 137; 6: 207
Schweninger, Ann 29: 172; 82: 246; 159: 202; 168: 166; 211: 193
Schwinger, Laurence 84: 44; 91: 61
Scofield, Penrod 61: 107; 62: 160
Scott, Anita Walker 7: 38
Scott, Art 39: 41
Scott, Frances Gruse 38: 43
Scott, Julian 34: 126
Scott, Roszel 33: 238
Scott, Sally 87: 27
Scott, Steve 166: 230, 231; 171: 93
Scott, Trudy 27: 172
Scotton, Rob 214: 183
Scrace, Carolyn 143: 95, 96
Scrambly, Crab 198: 196
Scribner, Joanne 14: 236; 29: 78; 33: 185; 34: 208; 78: 75; 164: 237; 203: 73
Scrofani, Joseph 31: 65; 74: 225
Scroggs, Kirk 187: 169
Seaman, Mary Lott 34: 64
Searle, Ronald 24: 98; 42: 172, 173, 174, 176, 177, 179; 66: 73, 74; 70: 205, 206, 207
Searle, Townley 36: 85
Sebree, Charles 18: 65
Sedacca, Joseph M. 11: 25; 22: 36
Seder, Jason 108: 102
Seeger, Laura Vaccaro 172: 162
Seegmiller, Don 174: 57
Seely, David 164: 173
Seeley, Laura L. 97: 105
Segal, John 178: 202
Segar, E.C. 61: 179, 181
Segur, Adrienne 27: 121
Seibold, J. Otto 83: 188, 190, 191; 149: 212, 214, 215, 216; 196: 177, 179; 215: 204
Seignobosc, Francoise 21: 145, 146
Sejima, Yoshimasa 8: 187
Selig, Sylvie 13: 199
Seltzer, Isadore 6: 18; 133: 59
Seltzer, Meyer 17: 214
Selven, Maniam 144: 133
Selway, Martina 169: 157
Selznick, Brian 79: 192; 104: 25; 117: 175; 126: 156; 134: 171; 158: 76, 78; 169: 70; 171: 172, 173; 191: 106; 192: 130; 197: 158; 203: 35; 205: 92; 210: 219, 220, 221, 222
Sempe, Jean-Jacques 47: 92; YABC 2: 109
Sendak, Maurice 1: 135, 190; 3: 204; 7: 142; 15: 199; 17: 210; 27: 181, 182, 183, 185, 186, 187, 189,190, 191, 192, 193, 194, 195, 197, 198, 199, 203; 28: 181, 182; 32: 108; 33: 148, 149; 35: 238; 44: 180, 181; 45: 97, 99; 46: 174; 73: 225; 91: 10, 11 YABC1: 167; 113: 163, 165, 167, 168; 118: 153; 127: 161
Senders, Marci 180: 79
Sengler, Johanna 18: 256
Senn, Steve 60: 145
Seredy, Kate 1: 192; 14: 20, 21; 17: 210
Sergeant, John 6: 74
Serra, Sebastiá 212: 215
Servello, Joe 10: 144; 24: 139; 40: 91; 70: 130, 131; 146: 159
Seton, Ernest Thompson 18: 260-269, 271
Seuss, Dr.
    See Geisel, Theodor

Severin, John Powers 7: 62
Sewall, Marcia 15: 8; 22: 170; 37: 171, 172, 173; 39: 73; 45: 209; 62: 117; 69: 185, 186; 71: 212; 90: 232; 96: 127; 102: 101; 107: 129; 119: 176, 177, 178, 180
Seward, James 70: 35
Seward, Prudence 16: 243
Sewell, Helen 3: 186; 15: 308; 33: 102; 38: 189, 190, 191, 192
Seymour, Stephen 54: 21
Sfar, Joann 182: 183
Shachat, Andrew 82: 179
Shadbolt, Robert 203: 68
Shahn, Ben 39: 178; 46: 193
Shalansky, Len 38: 167
Shanks, Anne Zane 10: 149
Shannon, David 57: 137; 107: 184; 112: 216; 135: 12; 152: 223, 224, 225; 158: 192; 212: 159, 160, 163
Sharkey, Niamh 213: 152
Sharp, Paul 52: 60
Sharp, William 6: 131; 19: 241; 20: 112; 25: 141
Sharratt, Nick 102: 207, 208; 104: 163; 153: 198; 175: 176; 192: 208; 199: 141, 142, 143, 184, 187, 188
Shaw, Barclay 74: 14, 16; 118: 138
Shaw, Charles 21: 135; 38: 187; 47: 124; 126: 219
Shaw, Charles G. 13: 200
Shaw-Smith, Emma 144: 117
Shea, Edmund 56: 19
Shearer, Ted 43: 193, 194, 195, 196
Sheban, Chris 182: 185; 190: 102, 104; 202: 28; 204: 112, 114; 209: 150; 210: 107; 220: 103
Shecter, Ben 16: 244; 25: 109; 33: 188, 191; 41: 77
Shed, Greg 74: 94; 84: 204; 129: 149, 167: 91; 179: 192
Sheehan, Chris 144: 190; 158: 163
Shefcik, James 48: 221, 222; 60: 141
Shefelman, Karl 58: 168
Shefelman, Tom 204: 137
Shefts, Joelle 48: 210
Shein, Bob 139: 189
Sheinkin, Stephen 204: 139
Shekerjian, Haig 16: 245
Shekerjian, Regina 16: 245; 25: 73
Sheldon, David 184: 174; 185: 204; 211: 189
Shelley, John 186: 223
Shemie, Bonnie 96: 207
Shenton, Edward 45: 187, 188, 189; YABC 1: 218, 219, 221
Shepard, Ernest H. 3: 193; 4: 74; 16: 101; 17: 109; 25: 148; 33: 152, 199, 200, 201, 202, 203, 204, 205, 206,207; 46: 194; 98: 114; 100: 111, 178, 179, 217, 219, 220,221; YABC 1: 148, 153, 174, 176, 180, 181
Shepard, Mary 4: 210; 22: 205; 30: 132, 133; 54: 150, 152, 153, 157, 158; 59: 108, 109, 111; 100: 246
Shepherd, Amanda 198: 14
Shepherd, Irana 171: 112
Sheppard, Kate 195: 176
Shepperson, Rob 96: 153; 177: 163; 178: 204; 197: 34; 205: 108
Sheridan, Brian 196: 193
Sherman, Theresa 27: 167
Sherwan, Earl 3: 196
Shields, Charles 10: 150; 36: 63
Shields, Leonard 13: 83, 85, 87
Shiffman, Lena 139: 167; 168: 136
Shigley, Neil K. 66: 219
Shillabeer, Mary 35: 74
Shilston, Arthur 49: 61; 62: 58
Shimin, Symeon 1: 93; 2: 128, 129; 3: 202; 7: 85; 11: 177; 12: 139; 13: 202, 203; 27: 138; 28: 65; 35: 129; 36: 130; 48: 151; 49: 59; 56: 63, 65, 153
Shimizu, Yuko 215: 197

Shine, Andrea *104:* 165; *128:* 34
Shinn, Everett *16:* 148; *18:* 229; *21:* 149, 150, 151; *24:* 218
Shinn, Florence Scovel *63:* 133, 135
Shore, Robert *27:* 54; *39:* 192, 193; *YABC 2:* 200
Shortall, Leonard *4:* 144; *8:* 196; *10:* 166; *19:* 227, 228, 229, 230; *25:* 78; *28:* 66, 167; *33:* 127; *52:* 125; *73:* 12, 212
Shortt, T.M. *27:* 36
Shpitalnik, Vladimir *83:* 194
Shropshire, Sandy *170:* 191
Shtainments, Leon *32:* 161
Shulevitz, Uri *3:* 198, 199; *17:* 85; *22:* 204; *27:* 212; *28:* 184; *50:* 190, 191, 192, 193, 194, 195, 196,197, 198, 199, 201; *106:* 181, 182, 183; *165:* 203, 205; *166:* 138
Shulman, Dee *180:* 140
Shupe, Bobbi *139:* 80, 81
Shute, A.B. *67:* 196
Shute, Linda *46:* 59; *74:* 118
Siberell, Anne *29:* 193
Sibley, Don *1:* 39; *12:* 196; *31:* 47
Sibthorp, Fletcher *94:* 111, 112
Sidjakov, Nicolas *18:* 274
Siebel, Fritz *3:* 120; *17:* 145
Siebold, J. Otto *158:* 227
Siegel, Hal *74:* 246
Sieger, Ted *189:* 172
Siegl, Helen *12:* 166; *23:* 216; *34:* 185, 186
Silin-Palmer, Pamela *184:* 102
Sill, John *140:* 194; *141:* 157; *221:* 163
Sills, Joyce *5:* 199
Silva, Simon *108:* 122
Silver, Maggie *85:* 210
Silveria, Gordon *96:* 44
Silverstein, Alvin *8:* 189
Silverstein, Shel *33:* 211; *92:* 209, 210
Silverstein, Virginia *8:* 189
Silvey, Joe *135:* 203
Simard, Rémy *95:* 156; *221:* 144
Siminovich, Laura *219:* 172
Simmons, Elly *110:* 2; *127:* 69; *134:* 181
Simon, Eric M. *7:* 82
Simon, Hilda *28:* 189
Simon, Howard *2:* 175; *5:* 132; *19:* 199; *32:* 163, 164, 165
Simont, Marc *2:* 119; *4:* 213; *9:* 168; *13:* 238,240; *14:* 262; *16:* 179; *18:* 221; *26:* 210; *33:* 189, 194; *44:* 132; *58:* 122; *68:* 117; *73:* 204, 205, 206; *74:* 221; *126:* 199, 200; *133:* 195; *164:* 128
Sims, Agnes *54:* 152
Sims, Blanche *44:* 116; *57:* 129; *75:* 179, 180; *77:* 92; *104:* 192; *152:* 117; *156:* 160; *160:* 70; *168:* 174, 175; *198:* 17
Singer, Edith G. *2:* 30
Singer, Gloria *34:* 56; *36:* 43
Singer, Julia *28:* 190
Singh, Jen *178:* 146
Sinquette, Jaclyn *215:* 83
Siomades, Lorianne *134:* 45; *204:* 48; *217:* 157
Simont, Marc *163:* 40
Siracusa, Catherine *68:* 135; *82:* 218
Sís, Peter *67:* 179, 181, 183, 184, 185; *96:* 96, 98; *106:* 193, 194, 195; *149:* 224, 226; *180:* 177; *192:* 180, 182
Sivard, Robert *26:* 124
Sivertson, Liz *116:* 84
Skardinski, Stanley *23:* 144; *32:* 84; *66:* 122; *84:* 108
Slack, Michael *185:* 108; *189:* 173, 174
Slackman, Charles B. *12:* 201
Slade, Christian *193:* 187; *204:* 134
Slade, Paul *61:* 170
Slark, Albert *99:* 212; *205:* 161
Slater, Rod *25:* 167
Slavin, Bill *182:* 14, 15; *196:* 90; *199:* 148, 149, 150; *217:* 20
Sloan, Joseph *16:* 68

Sloane, Eric *21:* 3; *52:* 153, 154, 155, 156, 157, 158, 160
Sloat, Teri *164:* 231
Slobodkin, Louis *1:* 200; *3:* 232; *5:* 168; *13:* 251; *15:* 13, 88; *26:* 173, 174, 175, 176, 178, 179; *60:* 180
Slobodkina, Esphyr *1:* 201
Slonim, David *166:* 167, 168
Small, David *50:* 204, 205; *79:* 44; *95:* 189, 190, 191; *126:* 203, 204; *136:* 119; *143:* 201, 202, 203; *144:* 246; *150:* 5; *161:* 176; *183:* 181, 182, 183, 184; *200:* 211; *212:* 86; *216:* 202, 203, 204
Small, W. *33:* 113
Smalley, Janet *1:* 154
Smath, Jerry *198:* 179, 180
Smedley, William T. *34:* 129
Smee, David *14:* 78; *62:* 30
Smee, Nicola *167:* 156
Smith, A.G., Jr. *35:* 182
Smith, Ali *204:* 68
Smith, Alvin *1:* 31, 229; *13:* 187; *27:* 216; *28:* 226; *48:* 149; *49:* 60
Smith, Andy *188:* 20; *207:* 151
Smith, Anne *194:* 147
Smith, Anne Warren *41:* 212
Smith, Barry *75:* 183
Smith, Brian *200:* 183
Smith, Carl *36:* 41
Smith, Cat Bowman *146:* 39; *164:* 219; *201:* 55, 184
Smith, Craig *97:* 197; *172:* 175; *206:* 40; *215:* 19; *217:* 129; *220:* 145
Smith, Donald A. *178:* 7
Smith, Doris Susan *41:* 139
Smith, Douglas *189:* 159; *213:* 170
Smith, Duane *171:* 152; *208:* 97
Smith, E. Boyd *19:* 70; *22:* 89; *26:* 63; *YABC 1:* 4, 5, 240, 248, 249
Smith, Edward J. *4:* 224
Smith, Elwood H. *157:* 231; *181:* 79; *203:* 160, 161, 162
Smith, Eunice Young *5:* 170
Smith, Gary *113:* 216
Smith, George *102:* 169
Smith, Howard *19:* 196
Smith, J. Gerard *95:* 42
Smith, Jacqueline Bardner *27:* 108; *39:* 197
Smith, Jay J. *61:* 119
Smith, Jeff *93:* 191
Smith, Jessie Willcox *15:* 91; *16:* 95; *18:* 231; *19:* 57, 242; *21:* 29, 156, 157, 158, 159, 160, 161; *34:* 65; *100:* 223; *YABC 1:* 6; *2:* 180, 185, 191, 311, 325
Smith, Jos. A. *52:* 131; *72:* 120; *74:* 151; *84:* 147, 148; *85:* 146; *87:* 96; *94:* 219; *96:* 97; *104:* 33; *108:* 126, 127, 128; *111:* 140; *136:* 145; *181:* 173; *200:* 213; *201:* 94
Smith, Kenneth R. *47:* 182
Smith, Keri *216:* 60
Smith, Kevin Warren *89:* 112
Smith, Kristin *209:* 197
Smith, L.H. *35:* 174
Smith, Lane *76:* 211, 213; *88:* 115; *105:* 202, 203,204, 205; *131:* 207; *160:* 217, 221; *179:* 183, 184, 185, 186; *199:* 122, 123, 124, 126
Smith, Lee *29:* 32
Smith, Linell Nash *2:* 195
Smith, Maggie Kaufman *13:* 205; *35:* 191; *110:* 158; *178:* 226; *190:* 204; *209:* 145
Smith, Mavis *101:* 219
Smith, Moishe *33:* 155
Smith, Philip *44:* 134; *46:* 203
Smith, Ralph Crosby *2:* 267; *49:* 203
Smith, Robert D. *5:* 63
Smith, Sally J. *84:* 55
Smith, Susan Carlton *12:* 208
Smith, Terry *12:* 106; *33:* 158
Smith, Virginia *3:* 157; *33:* 72
Smith, William A. *1:* 36; *10:* 154; *25:* 65
Smith-Moore, J.J. *98:* 147

Smolinski, Dick *84:* 217
Smoljan, Joe *112:* 201
Smollin, Mike *39:* 203
Smyth, Iain *105:* 207
Smyth, M. Jane *12:* 15
Smythe, Fiona *151:* 213
Smythe, Theresa *141:* 37
Snair, Andy *176:* 4
Sneed, Brad *125:* 25; *191:* 175, 176; *211:* 194
Snyder, Andrew A. *30:* 212
Snyder, Jerome *13:* 207; *30:* 173
Snyder, Joel *28:* 163
So, Meilo *162:* 201; *208:* 188
Soentpiet, Chris K. *97:* 208; *110:* 33; *159:* 184; *161:* 10; *163:* 130
Sofia *1:* 62; *5:* 90; *32:* 166; *86:* 43
Sofilas, Mark *93:* 157
Sogabe, Aki *207:* 153; *221:* 110
Sohn, Jiho *182:* 78
Sokol, Bill *37:* 178; *49:* 23
Sokolov, Kirill *34:* 188
Solbert, Ronni *1:* 159; *2:* 232; *5:* 121; *6:* 34; *17:* 249
Solomon, Michael *174:* 115
Solonevich, George *15:* 246; *17:* 47
Soma, Liana *81:* 118
Soman, David *90:* 122; *102:* 126; *140:* 120; *93:* 188; *43:* 89; *200:* 180, 181
Sommer, Robert *12:* 211
Song, Jae *203:* 27
Soo, Kean *201:* 185
Sorel, Edward *4:* 61; *36:* 82; *65:* 191, 193; *126:* 214
Sorensen, Henri *196:* 58
Sorensen, Henrik *62:* 16
Sorensen, Svend Otto *22:* 130, 141; *67:* 188, 189
Sorra, Kristin *155:* 80
Sosa, Hernan *198:* 66
Sostre, Maria *187:* 36
Sotomayor, Antonio *11:* 215
Souhami, Jessica *112:* 128; *176:* 193
Sousa, Natalie C. *209:* 89
Souza, Diana *71:* 139
Sovak, Jan *115:* 190
Sowards, Ben *215:* 62
Soyer, Moses *20:* 177
Spaenkuch, August *16:* 28
Spafford, Suzy *160:* 228
Spain, Valerie *105:* 76
Spain, Sunday Sahara *133:* 204
Spalenka, Greg *149:* 69; *151:* 228; *184:* 195; *191:* 21; *196:* 12; *198:* 181, 182, 201; *208:* 92
Spanfeller, James *1:* 72, 149; *2:* 183; *19:* 230, 231,232; *22:* 66; *36:* 160, 161; *40:* 75; *52:* 166; *76:* 37
Spangler, Brie *212:* 188
Sparks, Mary Walker *15:* 247
Spears, Rick *182:* 187; *220:* 67
Speidel, Sandra *78:* 233; *94:* 178; *134:* 180; *210:* 67
Speirs, John *67:* 178
Spence, Geraldine *21:* 163; *47:* 196
Spence, Jim *38:* 89; *50:* 102
Spencer, Laurie *113:* 12
Spencer, Mark *57:* 170
Spengler, Kenneth J. *146:* 256
Sperling, Andrea *133:* 182
Spiegel, Beth *184:* 203
Spiegel, Doris *29:* 111
Spiegelman, Art *109:* 227
Spier, Jo *10:* 30
Spier, Peter *3:* 155; *4:* 200; *7:* 61; *11:* 78; *38:* 106; *54:* 120, 121, 122, 123, 124, 125, 126, 127, 128, 129, 130,131, 132, 133, 134
Spilka, Arnold *5:* 120; *6:* 204; *8:* 131
Spirin, Gennady *95:* 196, 197; *113:* 172; *128:* 9; *129:* 49; *134:* 210; *153:* 9; *204:* 143, 144, 145; *220:* 153
Spiro, Ruth *208:* 197

Spivak, I. Howard *8:* 10; *13:* 172
Spohn, David *72:* 233
Spohn, Kate *87:* 195; *147:* 201, 202
Spollen, Christopher J. *12:* 214
Spooner, Malcolm *40:* 142
Spoor, Mike *220:* 92
Spowart, Robin *82:* 228; *92:* 149; *133:* 131; *176:* 163; *177:* 183, 184; *217:* 123, 124
Sprague, Kevin *150:* 60; *196:* 62
Spranger, Nina *201:* 199
Sprattler, Rob *12:* 176
Spring, Bob *5:* 60
Spring, Ira *5:* 60
Springer, Harriet *31:* 92
Spudvilas, Anne *110:* 74; *197:* 192; *199:* 154
Spurll, Barbara *78:* 199; *88:* 141, 142; *99:* 215
Spurrier, Steven *28:* 198
Spuvilas, Anne *85:* 114
Spy
    See Ward, Leslie
Squires, Stuart *127:* 74
St. Aubin, Bruno *179:* 54
St. John, J. Allen *41:* 62
Staake, Bob *209:* 168, 169
Stabin, Victor *101:* 131; *164:* 158
Stadler, John *62:* 33; *204:* 149
Stadnyk, Greg *212:* 55
Staffan, Alvin E. *11:* 56; *12:* 187
Stahl, Ben *5:* 181; *12:* 91; *49:* 122; *71:* 128; *87:* 206; *112:* 107
Stair, Gobin *35:* 214
Stallwood, Karen *73:* 126
Stamaty, Mark Alan *12:* 215
Stammen, JoEllen McAllister *113:* 14
Stampnick, Ken *51:* 142
Stanbridge, Joanne *150:* 91
Stanley, Diane *3:* 45; *37:* 180; *80:* 217, 219
Stanley, Sanna *145:* 228
Star, Lindsay *219:* 39
Starcke, Helmut *86:* 217
Stark, Ken *197:* 102
Starr, Branka *73:* 25
Stasiak, Krystyna *49:* 181; *64:* 194
Staub, Leslie *103:* 54
Stauffer, Brian *220:* 123
Staunton, Ted *112:* 192
Stawicki, Matt *164:* 250
Stead, L. *55:* 51, 56
Steadman, Broeck *97:* 185, 186; *99:* 56; *121:* 48; *208:* 190
Steadman, Henry *211:* 130
Steadman, Ralph *32:* 180; *123:* 143, 145
Stearn, Nick *183:* 26
Stearn, Todd *218:* 179
Steckler, June *90:* 178
Steele, Robert Gantt *169:* 174
Steichen, Edward *30:* 79
Steig, William *18:* 275, 276; *70:* 215, 216, 217, 218; *111:* 173, 174, 175, 176, 177
Stein, David Ezra *211:* 168
Stein, Harve *1:* 109
Steinberg, Saul *47:* 193
Steinel, William *23:* 146
Steiner, Charlotte *45:* 196
Steiner, Joan *110:* 219; *199:* 160, 161
Steirnagel, Michael *80:* 56
Stemp, Eric *60:* 184
Stephens, Alice Barber *66:* 208, 209
Stephens, Charles H. *YABC 2:* 279
Stephens, Pam *198:* 69
Stephens, Pat *126:* 110; *128:* 101
Stephens, William M. *21:* 165
Steptoe, Javaka *151:* 203, 204; *190:* 169; *213:* 163, 164
Steptoe, John *8:* 197; *57:* 9; *63:* 158, 159, 160, 161,163, 164, 165, 166, 167; *96:* 4; *105:* 87
Stern, Simon *15:* 249, 250; *17:* 58; *34:* 192, 193
Sterret, Jane *53:* 27
Stetsios, Debbie *165:* 108, 109
Steven, Kat *158:* 237

Stevens, David *62:* 44
Stevens, Helen *189:* 31; *207:* 83
Stevens, Janet *40:* 126; *57:* 10, 11; *80:* 112; *90:* 221, 222; *109:* 156; *130:* 34; *166:* 202; *176:* 53, 116; *193:* 199, 200, 202; *208:* 127; *212:* 182
Stevens, Mary *11:* 193; *13:* 129; *43:* 95
Stevenson, Harvey *66:* 143; *80:* 201, 221; *153:* 60; *191:* 166
Stevenson, James *42:* 182, 183; *51:* 163; *66:* 184; *71:* 185, 187, 188; *78:* 262; *87:* 97; *113:* 182, 183,184, 185; *161:* 182, 183
Stevenson, Sucie *92:* 27; *104:* 194, 195; *112:* 168; *160:* 202; *194:* 172, 173; *195:* 166
Stewart, April Blair *75:* 210
Stewart, Arvis *33:* 98; *36:* 69; *60:* 118; *75:* 91; *127:* 4
Stewart, Charles *2:* 205
Stewart, Joel *151:* 205; *211:* 170, 171
Stieg, William *172:* 58
Stiles, Fran *26:* 85; *78:* 56; *82:* 150
Stillman, Susan *44:* 130; *76:* 83
Stimpson, Tom *49:* 171
Stimson, James *208:* 46
Stinemetz, Morgan *40:* 151
Stinson, Paul *110:* 86
Stirnweis, Shannon *10:* 164
Stites, Joe *86:* 96
Stobbs, William *1:* 48, 49; *3:* 68; *6:* 20; *17:* 117, 217; *24:* 150; *29:* 250; *60:* 179; *87:* 204, 205,206
Stock, Catherine *37:* 55; *65:* 198; *72:* 7; *99:* 225; *114:* 197, 198, 199; *126:* 3; *145:* 161; *161:* 82; *173:* 149; *208:* 210; *214:* 192,194
Stockman, Jack *113:* 24
Stoeke, Janet Morgan *90:* 225; *136:* 196; *202:* 182, 183
Stoerrle, Tom *55:* 147
Stolp, Jaap *49:* 98
Stolp, Todd *89:* 195
Stone, David L. *87:* 154
Stone, David *9:* 173
Stone, David K. *4:* 38; *6:* 124; *9:* 180; *43:* 182; *60:* 70
Stone, Helen V. *6:* 209
Stone, Helen *44:* 121, 122, 126
Stone, Kazuko G. *134:* 43
Stone, Kyle M. *202:* 185
Stone, Phoebe *86:* 212; *134:* 213; *162:* 188; *205:* 145
Stone, Steve *166:* 213; *208:* 185; *220:* 57,58
Stone, Tony *150:* 34, 35
Storms, Patricia *217:* 163
Storrings, Michael *191:* 108; *216:* 217
Stoud, Virginia A. *89:* 31
Stover, Jill *82:* 234
Stower, Adam *217:* 89
Strachan, Bruce *205:* 146
Stratton, Helen *33:* 151
Stratton-Porter, Gene *15:* 254, 259, 263, 264, 268, 269
Straub, Matt *192:* 176
Straub, Phillip *197:* 22
Streano, Vince *20:* 173
Street, Janet Travell *84:* 235
Streeter, Clive *121:* 2
Strickland, Shadra *209:* 179
Stringer, Lauren *129:* 187; *154:* 172, 173; *161:* 127; *183:* 187, 188
Strodl, Daniel *47:* 95
Strogart, Alexander *63:* 139
Stromoski, Rick *111:* 179; *124:* 161, 190
Strong, Joseph D., Jr. *YABC 2:* 330
Stroyer, Poul *13:* 221
Strugnell, Ann *27:* 38
Struzan, Drew *117:* 6
Stubbs, William *73:* 196
Stubis, Talivaldis *5:* 182, 183; *10:* 45; *11:* 9; *18:* 304; *20:* 127
Stubley, Trevor *14:* 43; *22:* 219; *23:* 37; *28:* 61; *87:* 26

Stuck, Marion *104:* 44
Stuecklen, Karl W. *8:* 34, 65; *23:* 103
Stull, Betty *11:* 46
Stutzman, Mark *119:* 99
Stutzmann, Laura *73:* 185
Suarez, Maribel *162:* 208; *200:* 202
Suave, Gordon *209:* 66
Suba, Susanne *4:* 202, 203; *14:* 261; *23:* 134; *29:* 222; *32:* 30
Sue, Majella Lue *209:* 182; *212:* 146
Sueling, Barbara *98:* 185
Sueling, Gwenn *98:* 186
Sugarman, Tracy *3:* 76; *8:* 199; *37:* 181, 182
Sugimoto, Yugo *170:* 144
Sugita, Yutaka *36:* 180, 181
Suh, John *80:* 157
Sullivan, Dorothy *89:* 113
Sullivan, Edmund J. *31:* 86
Sullivan, James F. *19:* 280; *20:* 192
Sully, Tom *104:* 199, 200; *182:* 77
Sumichrast, Jozef *14:* 253; *29:* 168, 213
Sumiko *46:* 57
Summers, Leo *1:* 177; *2:* 273; *13:* 22
Summers, Mark *118:* 144
Summers, Mike *190:* 176
Sutton, Judith *94:* 164
Svarez, Juan *56:* 113
Svendsen, Mark *181:* 176
Svolinsky, Karel *17:* 104
Swain, Carol *172:* 182
Swain, Su Zan Noguchi *21:* 170
Swan, Susan *22:* 220, 221; *37:* 66; *60:* 146; *145:* 205; *181:* 168
Swann, Susan *86:* 55
Swanson, Karl *79:* 65; *89:* 186
Swarner, Kristina *203:* 62; *215:* 184
Swayne, Sam *53:* 143, 145
Swayne, Zoa *53:* 143, 145
Swearingen, Greg *152:* 56; *165:* 135; *173:* 2
Sweat, Lynn *25:* 206; *57:* 176; *73:* 184; *168:* 178
Sweet, Darrell K. *60:* 9; *69:* 86; *74:* 15; *75:* 215; *76:* 130, 131; *81:* 96, 122; *82:* 253; *83:* 11; *84:* 14; *85:* 37; *89:* 140; *90:* 6; *91:* 137,139; *95:* 160, 161; *126:* 25; *185:* 175; *195:* 132
Sweet, Darrell K. *1:* 163; *4:* 136; *164:* 175
Sweet, Melissa *71:* 94; *72:* 172; *111:* 82; *139:* 53, 58; *141:* 88; *142:* 231; *155:* 121; *159:* 121, 122; *172:* 185; *188:* 127; *209:* 81; *211:* 174, 175; *218:* 21
Sweet, Ozzie *31:* 149, 151, 152
Sweetland, Robert *12:* 194
Swiatkowska, Gabi *132:* 43; *175:* 139; *180:* 218; *183:* 176
Swope, Martha *43:* 160; *56:* 86, 87, 89
Sylvada, Peter *154:* 174
Sylvester, Natalie G. *22:* 222
Szafran, Gene *24:* 144
Szasz, Susanne *13:* 55, 226; *14:* 48
Szekeres, Cyndy *2:* 218; *5:* 185; *8:* 85; *11:* 166; *14:* 19; *16:* 57, 159; *26:* 49, 214; *34:* 205; *60:* 150, 151, 152, 153, 154; *73:* 224; *74:* 218; *131:* 213, 215
Szpura, Beata *81:* 68; *119:* 65; *168:* 201
Szuc, Jeff *220:* 188

T

Taback, Simms *40:* 207; *52:* 120; *57:* 34; *80:* 241; *104:* 202, 203; *170:* 176, 177; *205:* 183
Taber, Patricia *75:* 124
Tabor, Nancy Maria Grande *89:* 210; *161:* 188
Taddei, Richard *112:* 13, 14
Tadgell, Nicole *150:* 77; *161:* 20; *177:* 186; *209:* 16; *220:* 190, 191
Tadiello, Ed *133:* 200
Tafuri, Nancy *39:* 210; *75:* 199, 200; *92:* 75; *130:* 215, 216, 217

Tailfeathers, Gerald *86:* 85
Tait, Douglas *12:* 220; *74:* 105, 106
Takabayashi, Mari *113:* 112; *130:* 22; *156:* 169
Takahashi, Hideko *136:* 160; *187:* 6; *209:* 152, 187
Takakjian, Portia *15:* 274
Takashima, Shizuye *13:* 228
Talarczyk, June *4:* 173
Talbott, Hudson *84:* 240; *163:* 100; *212:* 191, 192, 193
Tallarico, Tony *116:* 197
Tallec, Olivier *218:* 4
Tallon, Robert *2:* 228; *43:* 200, 201, 202, 203, 204, 205,206, 207, 209
Tamaki, Jillian *201:* 188
Tamas, Szecsko *29:* 135
Tamburine, Jean *12:* 222
Tanaka, Yoko *215:* 187
Tancredi, Sharon *215:* 127
Tandy, H.R. *13:* 69
Tandy, Russell H. *65:* 9; *100:* 30, 131
Tang, Charles *81:* 202; *90:* 192
Tang, Susan *80:* 174; *108:* 158
Tang, You-shan *63:* 100
Tankersley, Paul *69:* 206; *133:* 219
Tannenbaum, Robert *48:* 181
Tanner, Jane *87:* 13; *97:* 37
Tanner, Tim *72:* 192; *84:* 35
Tanobe, Miyuki *23:* 221
Tarabay, Sharif *110:* 149; *113:* 123; *169:* 83
Tarkington, Booth *17:* 224, 225
Tarlow, Phyllis *61:* 198
Tate, Don *159:* 141, 191; *183:* 69; *186:* 120
Tauss, Herbert *95:* 179
Tauss, Marc *117:* 160; *126:* 155; *178:* 221; *197:* 7
Tavares, Matt *159:* 192, 193; *198:* 188, 189, 190; *199:* 86
Taylor, Ann *41:* 226
Taylor, Dahl *129:* 157
Taylor, Geoff *93:* 156; *197:* 173, 175; *204:* 151, 152
Taylor, Isaac *41:* 228
Taylor, Mike *143:* 99, 100
Teague, Mark *83:* 6; *139:* 241; *170:* 180, 181; *205:* 150, 151
Teale, Edwin Way *7:* 196
Teason, James *1:* 14
Teckentrup, Britta *200:* 191, 192
Teeple, Lyn *33:* 147
Tee-Van, Helen Damrosch *10:* 176; *11:* 182
Teicher, Dick *50:* 211
Teichman, Mary *77:* 220; *124:* 208; *127:* 22; *197:* 33
Temertey, Ludmilla *96:* 232; *104:* 43, 45; *109:* 244
Tempest, Margaret *3:* 237, 238; *88:* 200
Temple, Frances *85:* 185, 186, 187
Temple, Herbert *45:* 201
Templeton, Owen *11:* 77
ten Cate, Marijke *183:* 193
Tenggren, Gustaf *18:* 277, 278, 279; *19:* 15; *28:* 86; *YABC2:* 145
Tennent, Julie *81:* 105
Tenneson, Joyce *153:* 166
Tenney, Gordon *24:* 204
Tenniel, John *74:* 234, 235; *100:* 89; *YABC 2:* 99; *153:* 63
Tepper, Matt *116:* 80
Terkel, Ari *103:* 162
Terry, Michael *180:* 209
Terry, Will *131:* 73; *205:* 155
Teskey, Donald *71:* 51
Tessler, Manya *200:* 193
Thacher, Mary M. *30:* 72
Thackeray, William Makepeace *23:* 224, 228
Thamer, Katie *42:* 187
Tharlet, Eve *146:* 149
Thelwell, Norman *14:* 201
Theobalds, Prue *40:* 23
Theurer, Marilyn Churchill *39:* 195

Thiesing, Lisa *89:* 134; *95:* 202; *156:* 190; *159:* 195
Thiewes, Sam *133:* 114
Thistlethwaite, Miles *12:* 224
Thollander, Earl *11:* 47; *18:* 112; *22:* 224
Thomas, Allan *22:* 13
Thomas, Art *48:* 217
Thomas, Eric *28:* 49
Thomas, Harold *20:* 98
Thomas, Jacqui *125:* 95
Thomas, Jan *197:* 180
Thomas, Mark *42:* 136
Thomas, Martin *14:* 255
Thomas, Middy *177:* 114
Thompson, Arthur *34:* 107
Thompson, Carol *85:* 189; *95:* 75; *102:* 86; *147:* 166; *189:* 179, 180, 181; *190:* 84; *207:* 18
Thompson, Colin *95:* 204
Thompson, Ellen *51:* 88, 151; *60:* 33; *67:* 42; *77:* 148; *78:* 75, 219; *79:* 122, 170; *84:* 219; *85:* 97; *87:* 37; *88:* 192, 194; *89:* 80; *93:* 37; *98:* 59; *132:* 14
Thompson, George W. *22:* 18; *28:* 150; *33:* 135
Thompson, John *58:* 201; *102:* 226; *124:* 154; *128:* 228; *129:* 157; *150:* 49; *185:* 160; *191:* 192
Thompson, Julie *44:* 158
Thompson, Katherine *132:* 146
Thompson, K. Dyble *84:* 6
Thompson, Miles *152:* 77
Thompson, Sharon *74:* 113; *158:* 60; *165:* 87
Thomson, Arline K. *3:* 264
Thomson, Bill *186:* 160
Thomson, Hugh *26:* 88
Thomson, Ross *36:* 179
Thorkelson, Gregg *95:* 183, 184; *98:* 58; *165:* 30, 31
Thorn, Lori *189:* 119
Thornberg, Dan *104:* 125
Thornburgh, Rebecca McKillip *143:* 37
Thorne, Diana *25:* 212
Thornhill, Jan *77:* 213
Thorpe, Peter *58:* 109
Thorvall, Kerstin *13:* 235
Threadgall, Colin *77:* 215
Thurber, James *13:* 239, 242, 243, 245, 248, 249
Thurman, Mark *63:* 173; *168:* 116
Tibbles, Jean-Paul *115:* 200
Tibbles, Paul *45:* 23
Tibo, Gilles *67:* 207; *107:* 199, 201
Tichenor, Tom *14:* 207
Tichnor, Richard *90:* 218
Tiegreen, Alan *36:* 143; *43:* 55, 56, 58; *77:* 200; *94:* 216, 217; *121:* 54, 59
Tierney, Tom *113:* 198, 200, 201
Tildes, Phyllis Limbacher *210:* 240
Tilley, Debbie *102:* 134; *133:* 226; *137:* 101; *159:* 96; *190:* 211, 212; *213:* 51
Tillman, Nancy *211:* 129, 178
Tilney, F.C. *22:* 231
Timbs, Gloria *36:* 90
Timmins, Harry *2:* 171
Timmons, Bonnie *194:* 189
Tinkelman, Murray *12:* 225; *35:* 44
Titherington, Jeanne *39:* 90; *58:* 138; *75:* 79; *135:* 161
Tjader, Ella *209:* 14
Tobin, Nancy *145:* 197
Toddy, Irving *172:* 144
Tokunbo, Dimitrea *181:* 183; *187:* 182, 183
Tolbert, Jeff *128:* 69
Toledo, Francisco *197:* 182; *198:* 199
Toledo, Natalia *197:* 182
Tolford, Joshua *1:* 221
Tolkien, J.R.R. *2:* 243; *32:* 215
Tolman, Marije *195:* 43
Tolmie, Ken *15:* 292
Tomei, Lorna *47:* 168, 171

Tomes, Jacqueline *2:* 117; *12:* 139
Tomes, Margot *1:* 224; *2:* 120, 121; *16:* 207; *18:* 250; *20:* 7; *25:* 62; *27:* 78, 79; *29:* 81, 199; *33:* 82; *36:* 186, 187, 188, 189, 190; *46:* 129; *56:* 71; *58:* 183; *70:* 228; *75:* 73, 75; *80:* 80; *83:* 97; *90:* 205
Tommaso, Rich *200:* 198
Toner, Raymond John *10:* 179
Tong, Gary *66:* 215
Tongier, Stephen *82:* 32
Tooke, Susan *173:* 162
Toothill, Harry *6:* 54; *7:* 49; *25:* 219; *42:* 192
Toothill, Ilse *6:* 54
Topolski, Feliks *44:* 48
Torbert, Floyd James *22:* 226
Torgersen, Don *55:* 157
Torline, Kevin *169:* 171
Tormey, Bertram M. *75:* 3, 4
Torrecilla, Pablo *176:* 207
Torres, Leyla *156:* 199, 201
Torrey, Helen *87:* 41
Torrey, Marjorie *34:* 105
Torrey, Richard *189:* 182; *205:* 24
Toschik, Larry *6:* 102
Totten, Bob *13:* 93
Toy, Julie *128:* 112
Trachok, Cathy *131:* 16
Tracy, Libba *82:* 24
Trago, Keith *158:* 253
Trail, Lee *55:* 157
Trang, To Ngoc *167:* 180
Trang, Winson *89:* 151
Trapani, Iza *116:* 202; *214:* 203
Trapp, Bob *49:* 100; *63:* 145
Treatner, Meryl *95:* 180
Tremain, Ruthven *17:* 238
Tresilian, Stuart *25:* 53; *40:* 212
Trez, Alain *17:* 236
Trezzo, Loretta *86:* 45
Trier, Walter *14:* 96
Trimby, Elisa *47:* 199
Trinkle, Sally *53:* 27
Triplett, Gina *182:* 193; *188:* 100; *198:* 38
Tripp, F.J. *24:* 167
Tripp, Wallace *2:* 48; *7:* 28; *8:* 94; *10:* 54,76; *11:* 92; *31:* 170, 171; *34:* 203; *42:* 57; *60:* 157; *73:* 182
Trivas, Irene *53:* 4; *54:* 168; *82:* 46, 101
Trnka, Jiri *22:* 151; *43:* 212, 213, 214, 215; *YABC 1:* 30, 31
Trondheim, Lewis *182:* 183
Troughton, Joanna *37:* 186; *48:* 72
Troyer, Johannes *3:* 16; *7:* 18
Trudeau, G.B. *35:* 220, 221, 222; *48:* 119, 123, 126, 127,128, 129, 133; *168:* 189
Trueman, Matthew *165:* 208; *183:* 191; *220:* 61
Truesdell, Sue *55:* 142; *108:* 219, 220; *212:* 202; *220:* 78
Tryon, Leslie *84:* 7; *139:* 214; *143:* 10; *181:* 10
Tseng, Jean *72:* 195; *94:* 102; *119:* 126; *151:* 106; *173:* 138, 139; *200:* 158
Tseng, Mou-sien *72:* 195; *94:* 102; *119:* 126; *151:* 106; *173:* 138, 139; *200:* 158
Tsinajinie, Andy *2:* 62
Tsinganos, Jim *180:* 142
Tsugami, Kyuzo *18:* 198, 199
Tucker, Ezra *156:* 31
Tuckwell, Jennifer *17:* 205
Tudor, Bethany *7:* 103
Tudor, Tasha *18:* 227; *20:* 185, 186, 187; *36:* 111; *69:* 196, 198; *100:* 44; *YABC 2:* 46, 314; *160:* 234
Tuerk, Hanne *71:* 201
Tugeau, Jeremy *199:* 170; *203:* 96
Tulloch, Maurice *24:* 79
Tunis, Edwin *1:* 218, 219; *28:* 209, 210, 211, 212
Tunnicliffe, C.F. *62:* 176; *177:* 178, 179; *181*

Turkle, Brinton *1:* 211, 213; *2:* 249; *3:* 226; *11:* 3; *16:* 209; *20:* 22; *50:* 23; *67:* 50; *68:* 65; *79:* 205, 206, 207; *128:* 47; *YABC 1:* 79
Turnbull, Christopher J. *143:* 99, 100
Turner, Gwenda *59:* 195
Turner, Helen *203:* 154
Turska, Krystyna *12:* 103; *31:* 173, 174, 175; *56:* 32,34; *100:* 66
Tusa, Tricia *72:* 242; *111:* 180, 181; *157:* 165; *164:* 186; *189:* 40; *201:* 9; *207:* 163, 164
Tusan, Stan *6:* 58; *22:* 236, 237
Tuschman, Richard *219:* 100
Tworkov, Jack *47:* 207
Tyers, Jenny *89:* 220
Tylden-Wright, Jenny *114:* 119
Tyrol, Adelaide Murphy *103:* 27
Tyrrell, Frances *107:* 204
Tzimoulis, Paul *12:* 104

U

Uchida, Yoshiko *1:* 220
Uderzo *47:* 88
Udovic, David *189:* 185; *195:* 201
Ueno, Noriko *59:* 155
Ugliano, Natascia *196:* 186
Ulm, Robert *17:* 238
Ulrich, George *73:* 15; *75:* 136, 139; *99:* 150
Ulriksen, Mark *101:* 58; *182:* 43; *210:* 243
Unada *84:* 67
  See Gliewe, Unada
Underhill, Liz *53:* 159
Underwood, Beck *192:* 36
Underwood, Clarence *40:* 166
Unger, Jim *67:* 208
Ungerer, Tomi *5:* 188; *9:* 40; *18:* 188; *29:* 175; *33:* 221, 222, 223, 225; *71:* 48; *106:* 209, 210, 211, 212
Unwin, Nora S. *3:* 65, 234, 235; *4:* 237; *44:* 173, 174; *YABC 1:* 59; *2:* 301
Upitis, Alvis *145:* 179
Urban, Helle *149:* 243
Urbanovic, Jackie *86:* 86; *189:* 186, 187
Urberuaga, Emilio *219:* 110, 175
U'ren, Andrea *213:* 177
Uris, Jill *49:* 188, 197
Ursell, Martin *50:* 51
Utpatel, Frank *18:* 114
Utz, Lois *5:* 190

V

Vagin, Vladimir *66:* 10; *142:* 215
Vaillancourt, Francois *107:* 199
Vainio, Pirkko *123:* 157, 158
Valério, Geraldo *180:* 225; *194:* 116
Vallejo, Boris *62:* 130; *72:* 212; *91:* 38; *93:* 61
Van Abbe, S. *16:* 142; *18:* 282; *31:* 90; *YABC 2:* 157, 161
Van Allsburg, Chris *37:* 205, 206; *53:* 161, 162, 163, 165,166, 167, 168, 169, 170, 171; *105:* 215, 216, 217, 218; *156:* 176, 177, 178
Vance, James *65:* 28
Van Der Linde, Henry *99:* 17
van der Meer, Ron *98:* 204, 205
van der Meer, Atie *98:* 204, 205
Vandivert, William *21:* 175
Van Dongen, H.R. *81:* 97
Van Dusen, Chris W. *173:* 169
Vane, Mitch *210:* 160; *218:* 152
Van Everen, Jay *13:* 160; *YABC 1:* 121
Van Fleet, John *165:* 12, 13
Van Frankenhuyzen, Gijsbert *145:* 230; *149:* 164; *184:* 151; *210:* 248
van Genechten, Guido *165:* 226
van Haeringen, Annemarie *193:* 206

Van Horn, William *43:* 218
van Hout, Mies *195:* 191; *207:* 58
van Kampen, Vlasta *194:* 217
van Lawick, Hugo *62:* 76, 79
Van Lieshout, Maria *201:* 196
Van Loon, Hendrik Willem *18:* 285, 289, 291
Van Munching, Paul *83:* 85
van Ommen, Sylvia *186:* 192
Van Patter, Bruce *183:* 195
Van Rynbach, Iris *102:* 192
Van Sciver, Ruth *37:* 162
VanSeveren, Joe *63:* 182
Van Stockum, Hilda *5:* 193
Van Vleet, John *213:* 180
Van Wassenhove, Sue *202:* 193
Van Wely, Babs *16:* 50; *79:* 16
Van Wright, Cornelius *72:* 18; *102:* 208; *116:* 107; *152:* 236; *173:* 170, 171; *199:* 185
Van Zyle, Jon *103:* 125; *160:* 181, 182; *176:* 199, 200; *221:* 128
Vardzigulyants, Ruben *90:* 54
Varga, Judy *29:* 196
Vargo, Kurt *79:* 224
Varley, Susan *61:* 199; *63:* 176, 177; *101:* 148; *134:* 220
Varon, Sara *195:* 208
Vasconcellos, Daniel *80:* 42
Vasiliu, Mircea *2:* 166, 253; *9:* 166; *13:* 58; *68:* 42
Vaughn, Frank *34:* 157
Vavra, Robert *8:* 206
Vawter, Will *17:* 163
Vayas, Diana *71:* 61
Vazquez, Carlos *125:* 184
Veeder, Larry *18:* 4
Velasquez, Eric *45:* 217; *61:* 45; *63:* 110, 111; *88:* 162; *90:* 34, 144; *94:* 213; *107:* 147; *132:* 192; *138:* 213; *159:* 126; *181:* 184; *184:* 96; *191:* 16; *192:* 234; *208:* 37; *214:* 81
Velasquez, Jose A. *63:* 73
Velez, Walter *71:* 75; *91:* 154; *121:* 181; *168:* 49; *207:* 52
Velthuijs, Max *110:* 228, 229
Vendrell, Carme Sole *42:* 205
Venezia, Mike *54:* 17
Venti, Anthony Bacon *124:* 103; *126:* 26
Venturo, Piero *61:* 194, 195
Ver Beck, Frank *18:* 16, 17
Verkaaik, Ben *110:* 209
Verling, John *71:* 27
Verney, John *14:* 225; *75:* 8
Vernon, Ursula *204:* 157
Verrier, Suzanne *5:* 20; *23:* 212
Versace, Marie *2:* 255
Verstraete, Randy *108:* 193
Vess, Charles *215:* 201
Vestal, H.B. *9:* 134; *11:* 101; *27:* 25; *34:* 158
Vestergaard, Hope *190:* 203
Vicatan *59:* 146
Vickrey, Robert *45:* 59, 64
Victor, Joan Berg *30:* 193
Vieceli, Emma *210:* 245
Viereck, Ellen *3:* 242; *14:* 229
Vigna, Judith *15:* 293; *102:* 194, 195, 196, 197
Vila, Laura *207:* 172
Vilato, Gaspar E. *5:* 41
Villiard, Paul *51:* 178
Vimnera, A. *23:* 154
Vincent, Eric *34:* 98
Vincent, Felix *41:* 237
Vincent, Gabrielle *121:* 175
Vip *45:* 164
Viskupic, Gary *83:* 48
Vitale, Stefano *109:* 71, 107; *114:* 219, 220; *123:* 106; *138:* 232; *180:* 228, 229; *212:* 38
Vivas, Julie *51:* 67, 69; *96:* 225; *197:* 190; *199:* 71
Voake, Charlotte *114:* 221, 222; *180:* 232
Vo-Dinh, Mai *16:* 272; *60:* 191
Vogel, Ilse-Margret *14:* 230

Voigt, Erna *35:* 228
Vojnar, Kamil *95:* 31; *114:* 4; *115:* 62; *121:* 90; *124:* 72; *130:* 31; *141:* 81; *146:* 196; *150:* 123; *158:* 5, 6; *158:* 154; *171:* 119, 188; *179:* 15; *180:* 112; *203:* 74
Vojtech, Anna *42:* 190; *108:* 222, 223; *150:* 203; *174:* 173
von Buhler, Cynthia *149:* 237; *162:* 177; *177:* 205; *180:* 77; *185:* 214, 215, 216
von Roehl, Angela *126:* 191
von Schmidt, Eric *8:* 62; *50:* 209, 210
von Schmidt, Harold *30:* 80
Vosburgh, Leonard *1:* 161; *7:* 32; *15:* 295, 296; *23:* 110; *30:* 214; *43:* 181
Voss, Tom *127:* 104
Voter, Thomas W. *19:* 3, 9
Vroman, Tom *10:* 29
Vulliamy, Clara *72:* 65

W

Waber, Bernard *47:* 209, 210, 211, 212, 213, 214; *95:* 215, 216, 217; *156:* 203, 205, 206, 207
Wachenje, Benjamin *194:* 170
Wack, Jeff *95:* 140; *110:* 90
Wagner, John *8:* 200; *52:* 104
Wagner, Ken *2:* 59
Wagner, Michael *211:* 159
Wahman, Wendy *218:* 186
Waide, Jan *29:* 225; *36:* 139
Wainwright, Jerry *14:* 85
Waites, Joan C. *171:* 2
Wakeen, Sandra *47:* 97
Wakiyama, Hanako *171:* 96; *192:* 236; *200:* 16
Waldherr, Kris *81:* 186
Waldman, Bruce *15:* 297; *43:* 178
Waldman, Neil *35:* 141; *50:* 163; *51:* 180; *54:* 78; *77:* 112; *79:* 162; *82:* 174; *84:* 5, 56, 106; *94:* 232, 233, 234; *96:* 41; *111:* 139; *113:* 9; *118:* 30; *142:* 220, 223; *203:* 173, 174
Waldrep, Richard *111:* 147; *198:* 202
Walker, Brian *144:* 128
Walker, Charles *1:* 46; *4:* 59; *5:* 177; *11:* 115; *19:* 45; *34:* 74; *62:* 168; *72:* 218
Walker, Dugald Stewart *15:* 47; *32:* 202; *33:* 112
Walker, Gil *8:* 49; *23:* 132; *34:* 42
Walker, Jeff *55:* 154; *123:* 116
Walker, Jim *10:* 94
Walker, Mort *8:* 213
Walker, Norman *41:* 37; *45:* 58
Walker, Stephen *12:* 229; *21:* 174
Wallace, Beverly Dobrin *19:* 259
Wallace, Cly *87:* 93
Wallace, Ian *53:* 176, 177; *56:* 165, 166; *58:* 4; *98:* 4; *101:* 191; *112:* 124; *141:* 197, 198, 199, 200; *151:* 212; *219:* 180, 182
Wallace, John *105:* 228
Wallace, Nancy Elizabeth *141:* 204; *186:* 195, 197, 199
Wallenta, Adam *123:* 180
Waller, S.E. *24:* 36
Wallner, Alexandra *15:* 120; *156:* 183
Wallner, John C. *9:* 77; *10:* 188; *11:* 28; *14:* 209; *31:* 56, 118; *37:* 64; *51:* 186, 187, 188, 189, 190, 191,192, 193, 194, 195; *52:* 96; *53:* 23, 26; *71:* 99; *73:* 158; *89:* 215; *141:* 9
Wallner, John *162:* 17
Wallower, Lucille *11:* 226
Walotsky, Ron *93:* 87
Walsh, Ellen Stoll *99:* 209; *147:* 219; *194:* 194, 195, 196
Walsh, Rebecca *158:* 193; *217:* 169, 170
Walsh, Vivian *149:* 215; *158:* 227
Walters, Anita *205:* 163
Walters, Audrey *18:* 294
Walther, Tom *31:* 179

Walton, Garry 69: 149
Walton, Tony 11: 164; 24: 209; 153: 8; 177: 73
Waltrip, Lela 9: 195
Waltrip, Mildred 3: 209; 37: 211
Waltrip, Rufus 9: 195
Wan 12: 76
Wan, Shelly 212: 131
Wang, Lin 221: 179
Wang, Shaoli 216: 220
Wang, Suling 191: 183; 213: 194
Warburton, Sarah 154: 187
Wappers, G. 121: 40
Ward, Chad Michael 217: 121
Ward, Fred 52: 19
Ward, Helen 72: 244; 144: 240, 242
Ward, John 42: 191; 96: 54; 97: 110; 123: 105; 124: 71; 173: 66; 221: 55
Ward, Keith 2: 107; 132: 69
Ward, Leslie 34: 126; 36: 87
Ward, Lynd 1: 99, 132, 133, 150; 2: 108, 158, 196, 259; 18: 86; 27: 56; 29: 79, 187, 253, 255; 36: 199,200, 201, 202, 203, 204, 205, 206, 207, 209; 43: 34; 56: 28; 60: 116; 100: 65
Ward, Peter 37: 116
Waring, Geoff 172: 84
Warhola, James 92: 5; 115: 85, 87; 118: 174, 175, 177; 176: 84; 187: 189, 190
Warner, Ben 159: 171
Warner, Peter 14: 87
Warner, Sally 214: 210
Warnes, Tim 175: 159; 202: 188; 216: 224
Warnick, Elsa 113: 223
Warren, Betsy 2: 101
Warren, Jim 85: 81
Warren, Marion Cray 14: 215
Warshaw, Jerry 30: 197, 198; 42: 165
Wasden, Kevin 102: 162
Washington, Nevin 20: 123
Washington, Phyllis 20: 123
Wasserman, Amy L. 92: 110; 209: 95
Waterman, Stan 11: 76
Watkins-Pitchford, D.J. 6: 215, 217
Watling, James 67: 210; 78: 112; 101: 81; 117: 189, 190; 127: 119, 120
Watson, Aldren A. 2: 267; 5: 94; 13: 71; 19: 253; 32: 220; 42: 193, 194, 195, 196, 197, 198, 199, 200, 201; YABC 2: 202
Watson, G. 83: 162
Watson, Gary 19: 147; 36: 68; 41: 122; 47: 139
Watson, J.D. 22: 86
Watson, Jesse Joshua 197: 124; 199: 181; 202: 136
Watson, Karen 11: 26
Watson, Mary 117: 193
Watson, Richard Jesse 62: 188, 189; 211: 201
Watson, Wendy 5: 197; 13: 101; 33: 116; 46: 163; 64: 12; 74: 242, 243; 91: 21; 142: 228; 215: 79
Watt, Mélanie 136: 206; 193: 211
Wattenberg, Jane 174: 200; 185: 46; 187: 108
Watterson, Bill 66: 223, 225, 226
Watts, Bernadette 4: 227; 103: 182, 183
Watts, James 59: 197; 74: 145; 86: 124
Watts, John 37: 149
Watts, Leslie Elizabeth 150: 207; 165: 106; 209: 67
Watts, Stan 116: 205
Weatherby, Mark Alan 77: 141
Webb, Jennifer 110: 79
Webb, Lanny 142: 175
Webb, Sophie 135: 214
Webber, Helen 3: 141
Webber, Irma E. 14: 238
Weber, Erik 56: 19, 20
Weber, Florence 40: 153
Weber, Jill 127: 227, 228; 189: 163; 208: 157; 209: 190, 191; 216: 46
Weber, Roland 61: 204

Weber, Sam 190: 227
Weber, William J. 14: 239
Webster, Jean 17: 241
Weeks, Sarah 162: 39
Wegman, William 78: 243
Wegner, Fritz 14: 250; 20: 189; 44: 165; 86: 62
Weidenear, Reynold H. 21: 122
Weigel, Jeff 170: 193
Weihs, Erika 4: 21; 15: 299; 72: 201; 107: 207, 208
Weil, Lisl 7: 203; 10: 58; 21: 95; 22: 188,217; 33: 193
Weiman, Jon 50: 162, 165; 52: 103; 54: 78, 79, 81; 78: 80; 82: 107; 93: 82; 97: 69; 105: 179; 193: 65
Weiner, Greg 215: 21
Weiner, Sandra 14: 240
Weiner, Scott 55: 27
Weinhaus, Karen Ann 53: 90; 71: 50; 86: 124
Weinman, Brad 197: 20
Weinstock, Robert 204: 165, 166
Weisgard, Leonard 1: 65; 2: 191, 197, 204, 264, 265; 5: 108; 21: 42; 30: 200, 201, 203, 204; 41: 47; 44: 125; 53: 25; 85: 196, 198, 200, 201; 100: 139,207; YABC 2: 13
Weisman, David 173: 47
Weiss, Ellen 44: 202
Weiss, Emil 1: 168; 7: 60
Weiss, Harvey 1: 145, 223; 27: 224, 227; 68: 214; 76: 245, 246, 247
Weiss, Nicki 33: 229
Weissman, Bari 49: 72; 90: 125; 139: 142
Weitzman, David L. 172: 199
Welch, Sheila Kelly 130: 221
Welkes, Allen 68: 218
Wellington, Monica 99: 223; 157: 259, 260, 261
Welliver, Norma 76: 94
Wellner, Fred 127: 53
Wells, Frances 1: 183
Wells, H.G. 20: 194, 200
Wells, Haru 53: 120, 121
Wells, Robert E. 184: 208
Wells, Rosemary 6: 49; 18: 297; 60: 32; 66: 203; 69: 215, 216; 114: 227; 118: 149, 150; 156: 188, 189, 190, 191; 207: 180, 181, 182, 183
Wells, Rufus III 56: 111, 113
Wells, Susan 22: 43
Wendelin, Rudolph 23: 234
Wengenroth, Stow 37: 47
Weninger, Brigitte 189: 192, 194
Werenskiold, Erik 15: 6; 62: 17
Werner, Honi 24: 110; 33: 41; 88: 122
Werth, Kurt 7: 122; 14: 157; 20: 214; 39: 128
Wesson,
West, Harry A. 124: 38
Westcott, Nadine Bernard 68: 46; 84: 49; 86: 133; 106: 199; 111: 78; 113: 111; 130: 224; 139: 54; 158: 256; 194: 199
Westerberg, Christine 29: 226
Westerduin, Anne 105: 229
Westerman, Johanna 162: 206
Weston, Martha 29: 116; 30: 213; 33: 85, 100; 53: 181, 182, 183, 184; 77: 95; 80: 152; 119: 196,197, 198, 199; 127: 189; 133: 196; 209: 199
Wetherbee, Margaret 5: 3
Wexler, Jerome 49: 73; 150: 129
Whalley, Peter 50: 49
Whatley, Bruce 186: 93, 95; 207: 127; 213: 183, 184
Wheatley, Arabelle 11: 231; 16: 276
Wheeler, Cindy 49: 205
Wheeler, Dora 44: 179
Wheelright, Rowland 15: 81; YABC 2: 286
Whelan, Michael 56: 108; 70: 27, 29, 67, 68, 148; 74: 18; 84: 14; 91: 195, 196; 95: 147; 98: 150, 151; 106: 157; 113: 218, 220; 116: 99, 100

Whelan, Patrick 135: 145
Whistler, Rex 16: 75; 30: 207, 208
White, Beth 216: 139
White, Craig 110: 130; 119: 193; 130: 33; 179: 31
White, David Omar 5: 56; 18: 6
White, Joan 83: 225
White, Lee 221: 176
White, Martin 51: 197; 85: 127
Whitear 32: 26
Whitehead, Beck 86: 171
Whitehead, Jenny 221: 16
Whitehead, S.B. 154: 132
Whithorne, H.S. 7: 49
Whitman, Candace 208: 208
Whitney, George Gillett 3: 24
Whitney, Jean 99: 53
Whitson, Paul 102: 161
Whittam, Geoffrey 30: 191
Whyte, Mary 96: 127
Wiberg, Harald 38: 127; 93: 215
Wick, Walter 77: 128
Wickstrom, Sylvie 106: 87; 169: 180; 214: 110
Wickstrom, Thor 200: 205
Widener, Terry 105: 230; 106: 7; 163: 23; 200: 17; 209: 195
Wiese, Kurt 3: 255; 4: 206; 14: 17; 17: 18, 19; 19: 47; 24: 152; 25: 212; 32: 184; 36: 211,213, 214, 215, 216, 217, 218; 45: 161; 100: 92
Wiesner, David 33: 47; 51: 106; 57: 67; 58: 55; 64: 78, 79, 81; 69: 233; 72: 247, 248, 249, 251,252, 253, 254; 83: 134; 104: 31; 117: 197, 199, 200, 202; 139: 223, 224; 151: 51; 181: 189, 190
Wiesner, William 4: 100; 5: 200, 201; 14: 262
Wight, Eric 218: 190
Wiggins, George 6: 133
Wijngaard, Juan 111: 36; 114: 124
Wikkelsoe, Otto 45: 25, 26
Wikland, Ilon 5: 113; 8: 150; 38: 124, 125, 130; 127: 162
Wikler, Madeline 114: 233
Wilbur, C. Keith, M.D. 27: 228
Wilburn, Kathy 53: 102; 68: 234
Wilcox, Cathy 105: 123
Wilcox, J.A.J. 34: 122
Wilcox, Lydia 207: 187
Wilcox, R. Turner 36: 219
Wild, Jocelyn 46: 220, 221, 222; 80: 117
Wilde, George 7: 139
Wildsmith, Brian 16: 281, 282; 18: 170, 171; 66: 25; 69: 224, 225, 227; 77: 103; 83: 218; 124: 214,217, 219
Wildsmith, Mike 140: 229
Wilhelm, Hans 58: 189, 191; 73: 157; 77: 127; 135: 229, 230, 233, 234; 196: 209
Wilkin, Eloise 36: 173; 49: 208, 209, 210
Wilkinson, Barry 50: 213
Wilkinson, Gerald 3: 40
Wilkon, Jozef 31: 183, 184; 71: 206, 207, 209; 133: 222
Wilks, Mike 34: 24; 44: 203
Willems, Mo 154: 245, 246, 247; 180: 236, 237, 239
Willey, Bee 103: 129; 139: 159; 173: 115
Willhoite, Michael A. 71: 214
William, Maria 168: 51
Williams, Berkeley, Jr. 64: 75
Williams, Ferelith Eccles 22: 238
Williams, Garth 1: 197; 2: 49, 270; 4: 205; 15: 198, 302, 304, 307; 16: 34; 18: 283, 298, 299, 300, 301; 29: 177, 178, 179, 232, 233, 241, 242, 243, 244, 245, 248; 40: 106; 66: 229, 230, 231, 233, 234; 71: 192; 73: 218, 219, 220; 78: 261; 100: 251, 252, 255; 136: 117; YABC 2: 15, 16, 19
Williams, J. Scott 48: 28
Williams, Jennifer 102: 201
Williams, Jenny 60: 202; 81: 21; 88: 71

Williams, Kent *180:* 18
Williams, Kit *44:* 206, 207, 208, 209, 211, 212
Williams, Marcia *97:* 214; *159:* 208, 209
Williams, Maureen *12:* 238
Williams, Patrick *14:* 218
Williams, Richard *44:* 93; *72:* 229; *74:* 133; *78:* 155, 237; *91:* 178; *110:* 212; *136:* 201, 202, 203; *152:* 115
Williams, Sam *124:* 222; *153:* 11; *177:* 201, 202; *180:* 34; *212:* 49
Williams, Sophy *135:* 236
Williams, Vera B. *53:* 186, 187, 188, 189; *102:* 201, 202, 203; *210:* 65
Williamson, Alex *177:* 180; *205:* 50
Williamson, Mel *60:* 9
Willingham, Fred *104:* 206; *154:* 157
Willis, Adam *181:* 75; *209:* 11
Willmore, J.T. *54:* 113, 114
Wilsdorf, Anne *180:* 122; *189:* 124; *191:* 195
Wilson, Anne *160:* 114
Wilson, Charles Banks *17:* 92; *43:* 73
Wilson, Connie *113:* 179
Wilson, Dagmar *10:* 47
Wilson, Dawn *67:* 161; *81:* 120; *113:* 158
Wilson, Edward A. *6:* 24; *16:* 149; *20:* 220, 221; *22:* 87; *26:* 67; *38:* 212, 214, 215, 216, 217
Wilson, Forrest *27:* 231
Wilson, Gahan *35:* 234; *41:* 136
Wilson, George *76:* 87
Wilson, Helen Miranda *140:* 61
Wilson, Jack *17:* 139
Wilson, Janet *77:* 154; *96:* 114; *99:* 219, 220; *153:* 64 *106:* 122; *130:* 210; *145:* 178; *173:* 64
Wilson, John *22:* 240
Wilson, Maurice *46:* 224
Wilson, Patten *35:* 61
Wilson, Peggy *15:* 4; *84:* 20
Wilson, Phil *181:* 29
Wilson, Rowland B. *30:* 170
Wilson, Sarah *50:* 215
Wilson, Tom *33:* 232
Wilson, W.N. *22:* 26
Wilson-Max, Ken *170:* 196; *180:* 181
Wilton, Nicholas *103:* 52; *183:* 111
Wilwerding, Walter J. *9:* 202
Wimmer, Mike *63:* 6; *70:* 121; *75:* 186; *76:* 21,22, 23; *91:* 114; *97:* 45, 68; *98:* 28; *107:* 130; *146:* 21; *149:* 47; *173:* 126; *193:* 21, 25; *194:* 204, 205
Winborn, Marsha *78:* 34; *99:* 70; *192:* 20
Winch, John *165:* 233
Winchester, Linda *13:* 231
Wind, Betty *28:* 158
Windham, Kathryn Tucker *14:* 260
Windham, Sophie *184:* 212
Winfield, Alison *115:* 78; *214:* 121
Winfield, Wayne *72:* 23
Wing, Gary *64:* 147
Wing, Ron *50:* 85
Wingerter, Linda S. *132:* 199; *174:* 181; *200:* 196
Winick, Judd *124:* 227, 228, 229
Winn-Lederer, Ilene *202:* 91
Winnick, Karen B. *211:* 207
Winslow, Will *21:* 124
Winstead, Rosie *180:* 243
Winsten, Melanie Willa *41:* 41
Winter, Jeanette *151:* 240, 241, 242; *184:* 215, 217, 218, 219
Winter, Milo *15:* 97; *19:* 221; *21:* 181, 203, 204, 205; *64:* 19; *YABC 2:* 144
Winter, Paula *48:* 227
Winter, Susan *163:* 177; *182:* 201
Winters, Greg *70:* 117
Winters, Nina *62:* 194
Wise, Louis *13:* 68
Wiseman, Ann *31:* 187
Wiseman, B. *4:* 233
Wishnefsky, Phillip *3:* 14

Wiskur, Darrell *5:* 72; *10:* 50; *18:* 246
Wisniewski, David *95:* 220, 221
Wisniewski, Robert *95:* 10; *119:* 192
Witschonke, Alan *153:* 149, 150
Witt, Dick *80:* 244
Wittmann, Patrick *162:* 204
Wittman, Sally *30:* 219
Wittner, Dale *99:* 43
Wittwer, Hala *158:* 267; *195:* 80
Woehr, Lois *12:* 5
Wohlberg, Meg *12:* 100; *14:* 197; *41:* 255
Wohnoutka, Mike *137:* 68; *190:* 199; *195:* 218; *205:* 132; *221:* 6
Wojtowycz, David *167:* 168
Woldin, Beth Weiner *34:* 211
Wolf, Elizabeth *133:* 151; *208:* 175
Wolf, J. *16:* 91
Wolf, Janet *78:* 254
Wolf, Linda *33:* 163
Wolfe, Corey *72:* 213
Wolfe, Frances *216:* 227
Wolfe, Gillian *199:* 193
Wolff, Ashley *50:* 217; *81:* 216; *156:* 216, 217; *170:* 57; *174:* 174; *184:* 72; *203:* 181, 182, 183, 184
Wolff, Glenn *178:* 230
Wolff, Jason *213:* 186
Wolfsgruber, Linda *166:* 61
Wondriska, William *6:* 220
Wong, Janet S. *98:* 225; *152:* 43
Wong, Nicole *174:* 13; *214:* 216; *215:* 25
Wonsetler, John C. *5:* 168
Wood, Audrey *50:* 221, 222, 223; *81:* 219, 221; *198:* 206
Wood, Don *50:* 220, 225, 226, 228, 229; *81:* 218, 220; *139:* 239, 240
Wood, Grant *19:* 198
Wood, Heather *133:* 108
Wood, Ivor *58:* 17
Wood, Jakki *211:* 209
Wood, Muriel *36:* 119; *77:* 167; *171:* 55; *187:* 46
Wood, Myron *6:* 220
Wood, Owen *18:* 187; *64:* 202, 204, 205, 206, 208, 210
Wood, Rob *193:* 48
Wood, Ruth *8:* 11
Woodbridge, Curtis *133:* 138; *204:* 113
Wooding, Sharon L. *66:* 237
Woodruff, Liza *132:* 239; *182:* 46, 204
Woodruff, Thomas *171:* 73
Woods, John, Jr. *109:* 142
Woodson, Jack *10:* 201
Woodson, Jacqueline *94:* 242
Woodward, Alice *26:* 89; *36:* 81
Wool, David *26:* 27
Woolley, Janet *112:* 75
Woolman, Steven *106:* 47; *163:* 73
Wooten, Vernon *23:* 70; *51:* 170
Worboys, Evelyn *1:* 166, 167
Word, Reagan *103:* 204
Wormell, Christopher *154:* 251; *202:* 206
Worth, Jo *34:* 143
Worth, Wendy *4:* 133
Wosmek, Frances *29:* 251
Wrenn, Charles L. *38:* 96; *YABC 1:* 20, 21
Wright, Barbara Mullarney *98:* 161
Wright, Cliff *168:* 203
Wright, Dare *21:* 206
Wright-Frierson, Virginia *58:* 194; *110:* 246
Wright, George *YABC 1:* 268
Wright, Joseph *30:* 160
Wronker, Lili Cassel *3:* 247; *10:* 204; *21:* 10
Wu, Donald *200:* 18
Wummer, Amy *154:* 181; *168:* 150; *176:* 85; *201:* 202, 203; *218:* 154
Wyant, Alexander Helwig *110:* 19
Wyatt, David *97:* 9; *101:* 44; *114:* 194; *140:* 20; *167:* 13; *188:* 48
Wyatt, Stanley *46:* 210
Wyeth, Andrew *13:* 40; *YABC 1:* 133, 134

Wyeth, Jamie *41:* 257
Wyeth, N.C. *13:* 41; *17:* 252, 253, 254, 255, 256, 257, 258, 259, 264, 265, 266, 267, 268; *18:* 181; *19:* 80, 191, 200; *21:* 57, 183; *22:* 91; *23:* 152; *24:* 28, 99; *35:* 61; *41:* 65; *100:* 206; *YABC1:* 133, 223; *2:* 53, 75, 171, 187, 317
Wyman, Cherie R. *91:* 42
Wynne, Patricia J. *210:* 260

X

Xuan, YongSheng *119:* 202, 207, 208; *140:* 36; *187:* 21

Y

Yaccarino, Dan *141:* 208, 209; *147:* 171; *192:* 244, 245; *207:* 168
Yakovetic, Joe *59:* 202; *75:* 85
Yalowitz, Paul *93:* 33; *211:* 92
Yamaguchi, Marianne *85:* 118
Yamasaki, James *167:* 93
Yang, Belle *170:* 198
Yang, Jay *1:* 8; *12:* 239
Yap, Weda *6:* 176
Yaroslava
  See Mills, Yaroslava Surmach
Yashima, Taro *14:* 84
Yates, John *74:* 249, 250
Yates, Kelly *208:* 214
Yayo *178:* 88
Yeatts, Tabatha *215:* 210
Yee, Cora *166:* 233
Yee, Wong Herbert *115:* 216, 217; *172:* 204, 205; *194:* 59
Yelchin, Eugene *204:* 4
Yeo, Brad *135:* 121; *192:* 106
Yerxa, Leo *181:* 195
Yezerski, Thomas F. *162:* 29
Ylla
  See Koffler, Camilla
Yohn, F.C. *23:* 128; *YABC 1:* 269
Yoo, Taeeun *191:* 198
Yorinks, Adrienne *144:* 248; *200:* 214
Yorke, David *80:* 178
Yoshida, Toshi *77:* 231
Yoshikawa, Sachiko *168:* 104; *177:* 28; *181:* 196, 197
Youll, Paul *91:* 218
Youll, Stephen *92:* 227; *118:* 136, 137; *164:* 248; *202:* 92
Young, Amy L. *185:* 218; *190:* 46
Young, Cybéle *167:* 9
Young, Ed *7:* 205; *10:* 206; *40:* 124; *63:* 142; *74:* 250, 251, 252, 253; *75:* 227; *81:* 159; *83:* 98; *94:* 154; *115:* 160; *137:* 162; *YABC 2:* 242; *173:* 174, 175, 176; *205:* 29; *212:* 82; *221:* 72
Young, Mary O'Keefe *77:* 95; *80:* 247; *134:* 214; *140:* 213; *211:* 223, 225
Young, Noela *8:* 221; *89:* 231; *97:* 195
Young, Paul *190:* 222
Young, Selina *153:* 12; *201:* 204, 205
Yum, Hyewon *211:* 228
Yun, Cheng Mung *60:* 143
Yung, Jennifer *220:* 136

Z

Zacharow, Christopher *88:* 98
Zacks, Lewis *10:* 161
Zadig *50:* 58
Zaffo, George *42:* 208

Zagwyn, Deborah Turney *138:* 227
Zahares, Wade *193:* 219
Zaid, Barry *50:* 127; *51:* 201
Zaidenberg, Arthur *34:* 218, 219, 220
Zalben, Jane Breskin *7:* 211; *79:* 230, 231, 233; *170:* 202
Zallinger, Jean *4:* 192; *8:* 8, 129; *14:* 273; *68:* 36; *80:* 254; *115:* 219, 220, 222
Zallinger, Rudolph F. *3:* 245
Zakrajsek, Molly *177:* 146
Zappa, Ahmet *180:* 250
Zebot, George *83:* 214
Zecca, Katherine *207:* 195
Zeck, Gerry *40:* 232
Zeff, Joe *181:* 98; *221:* 101
Zeifert, Harriet *154:* 265, 267
Zeiring, Bob *42:* 130
Zeldich, Arieh *49:* 124; *62:* 120
Zeldis, Malcah *86:* 239; *94:* 198; *146:* 265, 266

Zelinsky, Paul O. *14:* 269; *43:* 56; *49:* 218-223; *53:* 111; *68:* 195; *102:* 219, 222, 221, 222; *154:* 255, 256, 257; *171:* 141; *185:* 96
Zelvin, Diana *72:* 190; *76:* 101; *93:* 207
Zemach, Kaethe *149:* 250
Zemach, Margot *3:* 270; *8:* 201; *21:* 210, 211; *27:* 204, 205, 210; *28:* 185; *49:* 22, 183, 224; *53:* 151; *56:* 146; *70:* 245, 246; *92:* 74
Zeman, Ludmila *153* 212
Zemsky, Jessica *10:* 62
Zepelinsky, Paul *35:* 93
Zerbetz, Evon *127:* 34; *158:* 109
Zezejl, Daniel *197:* 74
Zhang, Ange *101:* 190; *172:* 41
Zhang, Son Nang *163:* 113; *170:* 206
Ziegler, Jack *84:* 134
Zimdars, Berta *129:* 155
Zimet, Jay *147:* 94; *152:* 74; *196:* 75
Zimic, Tricia *72:* 95
Zimmer, Dirk *38:* 195; *49:* 71; *56:* 151; *65:* 214; *84:* 159; *89:* 26; *147:* 224

Zimmer, Tracie Vaughn *169:* 183
Zimmerman, Andrea *192:* 49, 50
Zimmermann, H. Werner *101:* 223; *112:* 197
Zimnik, Reiner *36:* 224
Zingone, Robin *180:* 134
Zinkeisen, Anna *13:* 106
Zinn, David *97:* 97
Zoellick, Scott *33:* 231
Zollars, Jaime *190:* 190
Zonia, Dhimitri *20:* 234, 235
Zorn, Peter A., Jr. *142:* 157
Zudeck, Darryl *58:* 129; *63:* 98; *80:* 52
Zug, Mark *88:* 131; *204:* 169
Zulewski, Tim *164:* 95
Zuma *99:* 36
Zvorykin, Boris *61:* 155
Zweifel, Francis *14:* 274; *28:* 187
Zwerger, Lisbeth *54:* 176, 178; *66:* 246, 247, 248; *130:* 230, 231, 232, 233; *181:* 92; *194:* 224, 225, 226
Zwinger, Herman H. *46:* 227
Zwolak, Paul *67:* 69, 71, 73, 74

Author Index

The following index gives the number of the volume in which an author's biographical sketch, Autobiography Feature, Brief Entry, or Obituary appears.

This index includes references to all entries in the following series, which are also published by The Gale Group.

YABC—*Yesterday's Authors of Books for Children: Facts and Pictures about Authors and Illustrators of Books for Young People from Early Times to 1960*

CLR—*Children's Literature Review: Excerpts from Reviews, Criticism, and Commentary on Books for Children*

SAAS—*Something about the Author Autobiography Series*

A

Aardema, Verna 1911-2000 107
  Obituary 119
  Earlier sketches in SATA :4, 68
  See also CLR 17
  See also SAAS 8
Aaron, Chester 1923- 216
  Autobiography Feature 216
  Earlier sketches in SATA 9, 74
  See also SAAS 12
Aaseng, Nate
  See Aaseng, Nathan
Aaseng, Nathan 1953- 172
  Brief entry 38
  Earlier sketches in SATA 51, 88
  See also CLR 54
  See also SAAS 12
Abadzis, Nick 1965- 193
Abalos, Rafael 1956-
  See Abalos, Rafael
Abalos, Rafael 1956- 197
Abbas, Jailan 1952- 91
Abbey, Lynn
  See Abbey, Marilyn Lorraine
Abbey, Marilyn Lorraine 1948- 156
Abbott, Alice
  See Borland, Kathryn Kilby
  and Speicher, Helen Ross S(mith)
Abbott, Jacob 1803-1879 22
Abbott, Manager Henry
  See Stratemeyer, Edward L.
Abbott, R(obert) Tucker 1919-1995 61
  Obituary 87
Abbott, Sarah
  See Zolotow, Charlotte
Abbott, Tony 1952- 205
  Earlier sketch in SATA 159
Abdelsayed, Cindy 1962- 123
Abdul, Raoul 1929- 12
Abeele, Veronique van den 196
Abel, Raymond 1911- 12
Abell, Kathleen 1938- 9
Abelove, Joan 110
Abels, Harriette S(heffer) 1926- 50
Abercrombie, Barbara 1939- 182
  Earlier sketch in SATA 16
Abercrombie, Barbara Mattes
  See Abercrombie, Barbara

Abercrombie, Lynn
  See Sorrells, Walter
Abernethy, Robert G(ordon) 1927- 5
Abisch, Roslyn Kroop 1927- 9
Abisch, Roz
  See Abisch, Roslyn Kroop
Ablow, Gail 1962- 198
Abodaher, David J. (Naiph) 1919- 17
Abolafia, Yossi 1944-
  See Abulafia, Yossi
Abolivier, Aurelie 219
Abouzeid, Chris 175
Abrahall, Clare Hoskyns
  See Hoskyns-Abrahall, Clare (Constance Drury)
Abrahams, Hilary (Ruth) 1938- 29
Abrahams, Peter 1947- 194
Abrahams, Robert David 1905-1998 4
Abramovitz, Anita (Zeltner Brooks) 1914- 5
Abrams, Joy 1941- 16
Abrams, Lawrence F. 58
  Brief entry 47
Abrashkin, Raymond 1911-1960 50
Abulafia, Yossi 1944- 177
  Brief entry 46
  Earlier sketch in SATA 60
Acampora, Paul 175
Accardo, Anthony 191
Acer, David 206
Achebe, Albert Chinualumogu
  See Achebe, Chinua
Achebe, Chinua 1930- 40
  Brief entry 38
  Earlier sketch in SATA 38
  See also CLR 156
Ackerman, Diane 1948- 102
Ackerman, Eugene (Francis) 1888-1974 10
Ackerman, Karen 1951- 126
Ackerman, Susan Yoder 1945- 92
Ackison, Wendy Wassink 1956- 103
Ackley, Peggy Jo 1955- 58
Ackroyd, Peter 1949- 153
Acorn, John (Harrison) 1958- 79
Acredolo, Linda (Potter) 1947- 159
Acs, Laszlo (Bela) 1931- 42
  Brief entry 32
Acuff, Selma Boyd 1924- 45

Ada, Alma Flor 1938- 181
  Earlier sketches in SATA 43, 84, 143
  See also CLR 62
Adair, Gilbert 1944- 98
Adair, Ian 1942- 53
Adair, Margaret Weeks (?)-1971 10
Adam, Cornel
  See Lengyel, Cornel Adam
Adam, Mark
  See Alexander, Marc
Adam, Robert 1948- 93
Adams, Adrienne 1906- 90
  Earlier sketch in SATA 8
  See also CLR 73
Adams, Andy 1859-1935
  See YABC 1
Adams, Barbara Johnston 1943- 60
Adams, Bruin
  See Ellis, Edward S.
Adams, Captain Bruin
  See Ellis, Edward S.
Adams, Captain J. F. C.
  See Ellis, Edward S.
Adams, Dale
  See Quinn, Elisabeth
Adams, Daniel
  See Nicole, Christopher (Robin)
Adams, Debra
  See Speregen, Devra Newberger
Adams, Diane 1960- 217
Adams, Douglas 1952-2001 116
  Obituary 128
Adams, Douglas Noel
  See Adams, Douglas
Adams, Edith
  See Shine, Deborah
Adams, Florence 1932- 61
Adams, Georgie 1945- 216
Adams, Harriet S(tratemeyer) 1892(?)-1982 .. 1
  Obituary 29
Adams, Harrison
  See Rathborne, St. George (Henry)
  and Stratemeyer, Edward L.
Adams, Hazard 1926- 6
Adams, Hazard Simeon
  See Adams, Hazard
Adams, John Anthony 1944- 67
Adams, Laurie 1941- 33

Adams, Lowell
　See Joseph, James (Herz)
Adams, Nicholas
　See Pine, Nicholas
Adams, Nicholas
　See Smith, Sherwood
Adams, Nicholas
　See Doyle, Debra
　and Macdonald, James D.
Adams, Pam 1919- 112
Adams, Pamela
　See Adams, Pam
Adams, Richard 1920- 69
　Earlier sketch in SATA 7
　See also CLR 121
Adams, Richard George
　See Adams, Richard
Adams, Ruth Joyce 14
Adams, Tricia
　See Kite, Pat
Adams, William Taylor 1822-1897 28
Adam Smith, Janet (Buchanan) 1905-1999 .. 63
Adamson, Gareth 1925-1982(?) 46
　Obituary 30
Adamson, George 1906-1989
　Obituary 63
Adamson, George (Worsley) 1913-2005 30
Adamson, Graham
　See Groom, Arthur William
Adamson, Joy(-Friederike Victoria)
　1910-1980 11
　Obituary 22
Adamson, Wendy Writson 1942- 22
Addasi, Maha 1968- 205
Addison, Kenneth 1949(?)-2005 187
Addison, Kenneth L.
　See Addison, Kenneth
Addona, Angelo F. 1925- 14
Addy, Sharon Hart 1943- 192
　Earlier sketch in SATA 108
Addy, Ted
　See Winterbotham, R(ussell) R(obert)
Adelberg, Doris
　See Orgel, Doris
Adelson, Leone 1908- 11
Adinolfi, JoAnn 176
Adkins, Jan 1944- 210
　Autobiography Feature 210
　Earlier sketches in SATA 8, 69, 144
　See also CLR 77
　See also SAAS 19
Adler, C. S. 1932- 126
　Earlier sketches in SATA 26, 63, 102
　See also CLR 78
　See also SAAS 15
Adler, Carole Schwerdtfeger
　See Adler, C. S.
Adler, David A. 1947- 178
　Earlier sketches in SATA 14, 70, 106, 151
　See also CLR 108
Adler, Irene
　See Penzler, Otto
　and Storr, Catherine (Cole)
Adler, Irving 1913- 29
　Autobiography Feature 164
　Earlier sketch in SATA 1
　See also CLR 27
　See also SAAS 15
Adler, Larry 1939- 36
Adler, Peggy 22
Adler, Ruth 1915-1968 1
Adlerman, Daniel (Ezra) 1963- 163
　Earlier sketch in SATA 96
Adlerman, Kim
　See Adlerman, Kimberly M(arie)
Adlerman, Kimberly M(arie) 1964- 163
　Earlier sketch in SATA 96
Adoff, Arnold 1935- 96
　Earlier sketches in SATA 5, 57
　See also CLR 7
　See also SAAS 15

Adoff, Jaime 163
Adoff, Jaime Levi
　See Adoff, Jaime
Adorjan, Carol (Madden) 1934- 71
　Earlier sketch in SATA 10
Adrian, Frances
　See Polland, Madeleine A(ngela Cahill)
Adrian, Mary
　See Jorgensen, Mary Venn
Adshead, Gladys L(ucy) 1896-1985 3
Aesop 620(?)B.C.-560(?)B.C. 64
　See also CLR 14
Aesop, Abraham
　See Newbery, John
Affabee, Eric
　See Stine, R.L.
Agapida, Fray Antonio
　See Irving, Washington
Agard, John 1949- 138
Agard, Nadema 1948- 18
Agarwal, Deepa 1947- 141
Agee, Jon 1960- 196
　Earlier sketches in SATA 116, 157
Agell, Charlotte 1959- 214
　Earlier sketches in SATA 99, 150
Agent Orange
　See Moseley, James W(illett)
Aghill, Gordon
　See Garrett, Randall
　and Silverberg, Robert
Agle, Nan Hayden 1905- 3
　See also SAAS 10
Agnew, Edith J(osephine) 1897-1988 11
Agonito, Joseph 177
Agonito, Rosemary 1937- 177
Aguilar, David 214
Aguilar, David A.
　See Aguilar, David
Ahern, Margaret McCrohan 1921- 10
Ahl, Anna Maria 1926- 32
Ahlberg, Allan 1938- 214
　Brief entry 35
　Earlier sketches in SATA 68, 120, 165
　See also CLR 18
Ahlberg, Janet 1944-1994 120
　Brief entry 32
　Obituary 83
　Earlier sketch in SATA 68
　See also CLR 18
Aho, Julia Kay
　See Kay, Julia
Aichinger, Helga 1937- 4
Aiken, Clarissa (M.) Lorenz 1899-1992 12
　Obituary 109
Aiken, Conrad 1889-1973 30
　Earlier sketch in SATA 3
Aiken, Conrad Potter
　See Aiken, Conrad
Aiken, Joan (Delano) 1924-2004 73
　Autobiography Feature 109
　Obituary 152
　Earlier sketches in SATA 2, 30
　See also CLR 90
　See also SAAS 1
Aillaud, Cindy Lou 1955- 184
Ainsley, Alix
　See Steiner, Barbara A(nnette)
Ainsworth, Catherine Harris 1910- 56
Ainsworth, Norma 1911-1987 9
Ainsworth, Ruth (Gallard) 1908- 73
　Earlier sketch in SATA 7
Ainsworth, William Harrison 1805-1882 24
Aistrop, Jack 1916- 14
Aitken, Amy 1952- 54
　Brief entry 40
Aitken, Dorothy 1916- 10
Aitmatov, Chingiz 1928-2008 56
Aitmatov, Chingiz Torekulovich
　See Aitmatov, Chingiz
Ajhar, Brian 1957- 220
Akaba, Suekichi 1910- 46

Akers, Floyd
　See Baum, L. Frank
Akib, Jamel 181
Aks, Patricia 1926-1994 68
Alagoa, Ebiegberi Joe 1933- 108
Alain
　See Brustlein, Daniel
Alajalov, Constantin 1900-1987
　Obituary 53
Alalou, Ali 203
Alalou, Elizabeth 203
Alan, David
　See Horsfield, Alan
Alan, Robert
　See Silverstein, Robert Alan
Alarcon, Francisco X. 1954- 215
　Earlier sketch in SATA 104
Alarcon, Francisco Xavier
　See Alarcon, Francisco X.
Alarcon, Karen Beaumont
　See Beaumont, Karen
Albert, Burton 1936- 22
Albert, Louise 1928- 157
Albert, Michael 1966- 202
Albert, Richard E. 1909-1999 82
Albert, Susan Wittig 1940- 107
Alberts, Frances Jacobs 1907-1989 14
Albertson, Susan
　See Wojciechowski, Susan
Albion, Lee Smith 29
Alborough, Jez 1959- 149
　Earlier sketch in SATA 86
Albrecht, Lillie (Vanderveer H.)
　1894-1985 12
Albyn, Carole Lisa 1955- 83
Alchemy, Jack
　See Gershator, David
Alcock, Gudrun 1908- 56
　Brief entry 33
Alcock, Vivien (Dolores) 1924-2003 76
　Brief entry 38
　Obituary 148
　Earlier sketch in SATA 45
　See also CLR 26
Alcorn, John 1935- 31
　Brief entry 30
Alcorn, Stephen 1958- 207
　Earlier sketch in SATA 110
Alcott, Louisa May 1832-1888 100
　See also YABC 1
　See also CLR 109
Alda, Arlene 1933- 205
　Brief entry 36
　Earlier sketches in SATA 44, 106, 158
　See also CLR 93
Alden, Isabella (Macdonald) 1841-1930 115
　See also YABC 2
Alden, Sue
　See Francis, Dorothy
Alderman, Clifford Lindsey 1902-1988 3
Alderson, Sue Ann 1940- 59
　Brief entry 48
Alding, Peter
　See Jeffries, Roderic
Aldis, Dorothy (Keeley) 1896-1966 2
Aldiss, Brian W. 1925- 34
Aldiss, Brian Wilson
　See Aldiss, Brian W.
Aldon, Adair
　See Meigs, Cornelia Lynde
Aldous, Allan (Charles) 1911- 27
Aldrich, Ann
　See Meaker, Marijane
Aldrich, Bess Streeter 1881-1954
　See CLR 70
Aldrich, Thomas (Bailey) 1836-1907 114
　Earlier sketch in SATA 17
Aldridge, (Harold Edward) James 1918- 87
Aldridge, Josephine Haskell 14
Aldridge, Sheila 1974- 192

Aleas, Richard
    See Appelt, Kathi
Alegria, Malin 1974(?)- *190*
Alegria, Ricardo E(nrique) 1921- *6*
Aleksin, Anatolii Georgievich 1924- *36*
Alenov, Lydia 1948- *61*
Alex, Ben (a pseudonym) 1946- *45*
Alex, Marlee (a pseudonym) 1948- *45*
Alexander, Alma 1963- *217*
Alexander, Anna B(arbara Cooke) 1913- *1*
Alexander, Anne
    See Alexander, Anna B(arbara Cooke)
Alexander, Ellen 1938- *91*
Alexander, Frances (Laura) 1888-1979 .... *4*
Alexander, Janet 1907-1994 .... *97*
    Earlier sketch in SATA *1*
Alexander, Jocelyn Anne Arundel 1930- *22*
Alexander, Linda 1935- *2*
Alexander, Lloyd 1924-2007 .... *135*
    Obituary *182*
    Earlier sketches in SATA *3, 49, 81, 129*
    See also CLR *48*
    See also SAAS *19*
Alexander, Lloyd Chudley
    See Alexander, Lloyd
Alexander, Marc 1929- *117*
Alexander, Martha 1920- *136*
    Earlier sketches in SATA *11, 70*
Alexander, Rae Pace
    See Alexander, Raymond Pace
Alexander, Raymond Pace 1898-1974 .... *22*
Alexander, Robert *200*
Alexander, Rod
    See Pellowski, Michael (Joseph)
Alexander, Sally Hobart 1943- *84*
Alexander, Sue 1933-2008 .... *136*
    Obituary *195*
    Earlier sketches in SATA *12, 89*
    See also SAAS *15*
Alexander, Vincent Arthur 1925-1980
    Obituary *23*
Alexeieff, Alexandre A. 1901-1979 .... *14*
Alger, Horatio, Jr.
    See Stratemeyer, Edward L.
Alger, Horatio, Jr. 1832-1899 .... *16*
    See also CLR *87*
Alger, Leclaire (Gowans) 1898-1969 .... *15*
Aliki
    See Brandenberg, Aliki
Alkema, Chester Jay 1932- *12*
Al-Khalili, Jim 1962- *124*
Alkiviades, Alkis 1953- *105*
Alko, Selina 1968- *218*
Alkouatli, Claire *186*
Allaby, John Michael
    See Allaby, Michael
Allaby, Michael 1933- *167*
Allamand, Pascale 1942- *12*
Allan, Mabel Esther 1915-1998 .... *75*
    Earlier sketches in SATA *5, 32*
    See also CLR *43*
    See also SAAS *11*
Allan, Nicholas 1956- *123*
    Earlier sketch in SATA *79*
Allan-Meyer, Kathleen 1918- *51*
    Brief entry *46*
Allard, Harry
    See Allard, Harry G., Jr.
Allard, Harry G.
    See Allard, Harry G., Jr.
Allard, Harry G., Jr. 1928- *216*
    Earlier sketches in SATA *42, 102*
    See also CLR *85*
Allee, Marjorie Hill 1890-1945 .... *17*
Allen, Adam
    See Epstein, Beryl
    and Epstein, Samuel
Allen, Alex B.
    See Heide, Florence Parry
Allen, Allyn
    See Eberle, Irmengarde

Allen, Betsy
    See Harrison, Elizabeth (Allen) Cavanna
Allen, Bob 1961- *76*
Allen, Gertrude E(lizabeth) 1888-1984 .... *9*
Allen, Grace
    See Hogarth, Grace (Weston Allen)
Allen, Jeffrey (Yale) 1948- *42*
Allen, John
    See Perry, Ritchie (John Allen)
Allen, Jonathan 1957- *177*
    Earlier sketch in SATA *131*
Allen, Jonathan Dean
    See Allen, Jonathan
Allen, Joy 1948- *217*
Allen, Judy (Christina) 1941- *124*
    Earlier sketch in SATA *80*
Allen, Kenneth S. 1913-1981 .... *56*
Allen, Leroy 1912- *11*
Allen, Linda 1925- *33*
Allen, Marjorie 1931- *22*
Allen, Maury 1932-2010 .... *26*
Allen, Merritt Parmelee 1892-1954 .... *22*
Allen, Nancy Kelly 1949- *171*
    Earlier sketch in SATA *127*
Allen, Nina (Stroemgren) 1935- *22*
Allen, Pamela (Kay) 1934- *123*
    Earlier sketches in SATA *50, 81*
    See also CLR *44*
Allen, Raul *205*
Allen, Rodney F. 1938-1999 .... *27*
Allen, Roger MacBride 1957- *105*
Allen, Ruth
    See Peterson, Esther (Allen)
Allen, Samuel W(ashington) 1917- *9*
Allen, T. D.
    See Allen, Terril Diener
Allen, Terril Diener 1908- *35*
Allen, Terry D.
    See Allen, Terril Diener
Allen, Thomas B. 1929- *193*
    Earlier sketches in SATA *45, 140*
Allen, Thomas Benton
    See Allen, Thomas B.
Allen, Tom
    See Allen, Thomas B.
Allende, Isabel 1942- *163*
    See also CLR *99*
Allerton, Mary
    See Govan, (Mary) Christine Noble
Alley, Robert W.
    See Alley, R.W.
Alley, R.W. *211*
    Earlier sketch in SATA *169*
Alley, Zoe B. *214*
Alleyn, Ellen
    See Rossetti, Christina
Allington, Richard L(loyd) 1947- *39*
    Brief entry *35*
Allison, Amy 1956- *138*
Allison, Bob *14*
Allison, Diane Worfolk *78*
Allison, Jennifer *173*
Allison, Linda 1948- *43*
Allison, Margaret
    See Klam, Cheryl
Allman, Barbara 1950- *137*
Allmendinger, David F(rederick), Jr. 1938- . *35*
Allred, Alexandra Powe 1965- *144*
Allred, Gordon T(hatcher) 1930- *10*
Allsop, Kenneth 1920-1973 .... *17*
Allsopp, Sophie *188*
Alma, Ann 1946- *201*
Almedingen, E. M.
    See Almedingen, Martha Edith von
Almedingen, Martha Edith von 1898-1971 .... *3*
Almon, Russell
    See Clevenger, William R.
    and Downing, David A(lmon)
Almond, David 1951- *158*
    Earlier sketch in SATA *114*
    See also CLR *85*

Almond, Linda Stevens 1881(?)-1987
    Obituary *50*
Almquist, Don 1929- *11*
Alonzo, Sandra *199*
Alphin, Elaine Marie 1955- *139*
    Autobiography Feature *139*
    Earlier sketches in SATA *80, 130*
Alsenas, Linas 1979- *186*
Alsop, Mary O'Hara 1885-1980 .... *34*
    Obituary *24*
    Earlier sketch in SATA *2*
Alter, Anna 1974- *206*
    Earlier sketch in SATA *135*
Alter, Judith 1938- *101*
    Earlier sketch in SATA *52*
Alter, Judith MacBain
    See Alter, Judith
Alter, Judy
    See Alter, Judith
Alter, Robert Edmond 1925-1965 .... *9*
Alter, Stephen 1956- *187*
Althea
    See Braithwaite, Althea
Altman, Linda Jacobs 1943- *21*
Altman, Suzanne
    See Orgel, Doris
    and Schecter, Ellen
Alton, Steve *169*
Altschuler, Franz 1923- *45*
Altsheler, Joseph A(lexander) 1862-1919
    See YABC *1*
Alvarez, John
    See del Rey, Lester
Alvarez, Joseph A. 1930- *18*
Alvarez, Julia 1950- *129*
al-Windawi, Thura
    See Windawi, Thura al-
Alyer, Philip A.
    See Stratemeyer, Edward L.
Amado, Elisa *193*
Amann, Janet 1951- *79*
Amato, Carol A. 1942- *92*
Amato, Mary 1961- *178*
    Earlier sketch in SATA *140*
Ambrose, Stephen E. 1936-2002 .... *138*
    Earlier sketch in SATA *40*
Ambrose, Stephen Edward
    See Ambrose, Stephen E.
Ambrus, Gyozo Laszlo 1935- *1*
    See also SAAS *4*
Ambrus, Victor G.
    See Ambrus, Gyozo Laszlo
Amend, Bill 1962- *147*
Amerman, Lockhart 1911-1969 .... *3*
Ames, Evelyn 1908-1990 .... *13*
    Obituary *64*
Ames, Gerald 1906-1993 .... *11*
    Obituary *74*
Ames, Lee J(udah) 1921- *151*
    Earlier sketch in SATA *3*
Ames, Mildred 1919-1994 .... *85*
    Earlier sketches in SATA *22, 81*
Amico, Tom 1960(?)- *176*
Amit, Ofra 1966- *205*
Ammon, Richard 1942- *124*
Amon, Aline 1928- *9*
Amory, Jay
    See Lovegrove, James
Amoss, Berthe 1925- *112*
    Earlier sketch in SATA *5*
Amstutz, Andre 1925- *214*
Anastasio, Dina 1941- *94*
    Brief entry *30*
    Earlier sketch in SATA *37*
Anaya, Rudolfo 1937-
    See CLR *129*
Anaya, Rudolfo A.
    See Anaya, Rudolfo
Anaya, Rudolpho Alfonso
    See Anaya, Rudolfo
Anckarsvard, Karin Inez Maria 1915-1969 .... *6*

Ancona, George 1929- 208
  Autobiography Feature 208
  Earlier sketches in SATA *12, 85, 145, 192*
  See also SAAS *18*
Anders, C. J.
  See Bennett, Cherie
Anders, Isabel 1946- 101
Anders, Lou 176
Andersdatter, Karla M. 1938- 34
Andersen, Bethanne 1954- 191
Andersen, Hans Christian 1805-1875 100
  See also YABC *1*
  See also CLR *113*
Andersen, Ted
  See Boyd, Waldo T.
Andersen, Yvonne 1932- 27
Anderson, Bernice G(oudy) 1894-1997 33
Anderson, Bob 1944- 139
  Earlier sketch in SATA *136*
Anderson, Brad 1924- 33
  Brief entry 31
Anderson, Bradley Jay
  See Anderson, Brad
Anderson, Brian 1974- 211
Anderson, C. C.
  See Anderson, Catherine Corley
Anderson, C(larence) W(illiam) 1891-1971 . 11
Anderson, Carolyn Dunn
  See Dunn, Carolyn
Anderson, Catherine C.
  See Anderson, Catherine Corley
Anderson, Catherine Corley 1909-2001 72
Anderson, Clifford
  See Gardner, Richard (M.)
Anderson, Daryl Shon 1963- 93
Anderson, Dave
  See Anderson, David
Anderson, David 1929- 60
Anderson, Derek 1969- 169
Anderson, Eloise Adell 1927- 9
Anderson, George
  See Groom, Arthur William
Anderson, Grace Fox 1932- 43
Anderson, J(ohn) R(ichard) L(ane)
  1911-1981 15
  Obituary 27
Anderson, Jodi Lynn 182
Anderson, John David 197
Anderson, John L. 1905- 2
Anderson, Joy 1928- 1
Anderson, Kevin J. 1962- 117
  Earlier sketch in SATA *74*
Anderson, Kevin James
  See Anderson, Kevin J.
Anderson, Kirsty 1978- 108
Anderson, K.J.
  See Moesta, Rebecca
Anderson, Laurie Halse 1961- 186
  Earlier sketches in SATA *95, 132*
  See also CLR *138*
Anderson, LaVere Francis Shoenfelt
  1907-1998 27
Anderson, Leone Castell 1923- 53
  Brief entry 49
Anderson, Lisa G. 1963- 108
Anderson, Lonzo
  See Anderson, John L.
Anderson, Lucia (Lewis) 1922- 10
Anderson, Madelyn Klein 1926-2005 28
Anderson, Margaret J(ean) 1931- 27
  See also SAAS *8*
Anderson, Marilyn D. 1943- 144
Anderson, Mary 1939- 82
  Earlier sketch in SATA *7*
  See also SAAS *23*
Anderson, Matthew Tobin
  See Anderson, M.T.
Anderson, Mona 1910-2004 40
Anderson, Mrs. Melvin
  See Anderson, Catherine Corley

Anderson, M.T. 1968- 182
  Earlier sketches in SATA *97, 146*
Anderson, Norman Dean 1928- 22
Anderson, Peggy Perry 1953- 179
  Earlier sketch in SATA *84*
Anderson, Poul 1926-2001 90
  Autobiography Feature 106
  Brief entry 39
  See also CLR *58*
Anderson, Poul William
  See Anderson, Poul
Anderson, Rachel 1943- 86
  Earlier sketch in SATA *34*
  See also SAAS *18*
Anderson, Rebecca J.
  See Anderson, R.J.
Anderson, Rebecca M.
  See Moesta, Rebecca
Anderson, Rebecca Moesta
  See Moesta, Rebecca
Anderson, Richard
  See Anderson, J(ohn) R(ichard) L(ane)
Anderson, R.J. 1970(?)- 216
Anderson, Sara 173
Anderson, Scoular 201
Anderson, (Tom) Scoular 138
Anderson, Susan 1952- 90
Anderson, Thomas Scoular
  See Anderson, Scoular
Anderson, W. B.
  See Schultz, James Willard
Anderson, Wayne 1946- 202
  Earlier sketches in SATA *56, 147*
Andersson, Kenneth 1970- 200
Andre, Evelyn M. 1924- 27
Andre, Evelyn Marie
  See Andre, Evelyn M.
Andreasen, Dan 186
Andreassen, Karl
  See Boyd, Waldo T.
Andreassi, K. Robert
  See DeCandido, Keith R.A.
Andree, Louise
  See Coury, Louise Andree
Andrew, Ian 1962- 166
  Earlier sketch in SATA *116*
Andrew, Ian Peter
  See Andrew, Ian
Andrew, Prudence (Hastings) 1924- 87
Andrews, Benny 1930-2006 31
  Obituary 178
Andrews, Eleanor Lattimore
  See Lattimore, Eleanor Frances
Andrews, Elton V.
  See Pohl, Frederik
Andrews, F(rank) Emerson 1902-1978 22
Andrews, J(ames) S(ydney) 1934- 4
Andrews, Jan 1942- 167
  Brief entry 49
  Earlier sketches in SATA *58, 98*
Andrews, Julie 1935- 153
  Earlier sketch in SATA *7*
  See also CLR *85*
Andrews, Laura
  See Coury, Louise Andree
Andrews, Roy Chapman 1884-1960 19
Andrews, Tamra 1959- 129
Andrews, V(irginia) C(leo) 1924(?)-1986
  Obituary 50
Andrews, Wendy
  See Sharmat, Marjorie Weinman
Andrews, William G. 1930- 74
Andrews, William George
  See Andrews, William G.
Andrezel, Pierre
  See Blixen, Karen
Andriani, Renee
  See Williams-Andriani, Renee
Andriola, Alfred J. 1912-1983
  Obituary 34
Andrist, Ralph K. 1914-2004 45

Andronik, Catherine M. 189
Andryszewski, Tricia 1956- 148
  Earlier sketch in SATA *88*
Anelli, Melissa 1979- 215
Angel, Ann 1952- 192
Angel, Carl 178
Angel, Marie 1923- 47
Angeles, Peter A. 1931- 40
Angeletti, Roberta 1964- 124
Angeli, Marguerite (Lofft) de
  See de Angeli, Marguerite (Lofft)
Angell, Judie 1937- 78
  Earlier sketch in SATA *22*
  See also CLR *33*
Angell, Madeline 1919- 18
Angelo, Valenti 1897- 14
Angelou, Maya 1928- 136
  Earlier sketch in SATA *49*
  See also CLR *53*
Angier, Bradford -1997 12
Angle, Kimberly Greene 203
Angle, Paul M(cClelland) 1900-1975
  Obituary 20
Anglund, Joan Walsh 1926- 2
  See also CLR *94*
Ango, Fan D.
  See Longyear, Barry B(rookes)
Angrist, Stanley W(olff) 1933- 4
Anholt, Catherine 1958- 131
  Earlier sketch in SATA *74*
Anholt, Laurence 1959- 141
  Earlier sketch in SATA *74*
Anita
  See Daniel, Anita
Anmar, Frank
  See Nolan, William F.
Annett, Cora
  See Scott, Cora Annett (Pipitone)
Annie-Jo
  See Blanchard, Patricia
  and Suhr, Joanne
Annixter, Jane
  See Sturtzel, Jane Levington
Annixter, Paul
  See Sturtzel, Howard A(llison)
Anno, Mitsumasa 1926- 157
  Earlier sketches in SATA *5, 38, 77*
  See also CLR *122*
Anrooy, Francine Van
  See Van Anrooy, Francine
Ansary, Mir Tamim 1948- 140
Anstey, Caroline 1958- 81
Antell, Will D. 1935- 31
Anthony, Barbara
  See Barber, Antonia
Anthony, C. L.
  See Smith, Dorothy Gladys
Anthony, Edward 1895-1971 21
Anthony, John
  See Beckett, Ronald Brymer
  and Ciardi, John (Anthony)
  and Sabini, John Anthony
Anthony, Joseph Patrick 1964- 103
Anthony, Patricia 1947- 109
Anthony, Piers 1934- 129
  Autobiography Feature 129
  Earlier sketch in SATA *84*
  See also CLR *118*
  See also SAAS *22*
Anthony, Susan C(arol) 1953- 87
Anticaglia, Elizabeth 1939- 12
Antieau, Kim 214
Antilles, Kem
  See Moesta, Rebecca
Antle, Nancy 1955- 102
Antolini, Margaret Fishback 1904-1985
  Obituary 45
Anton, Michael J(ames) 1940- 12
Antonacci, Robert J(oseph) 1916- 45
  Brief entry 37
Anvil, Christopher 1925-2009 102

Anzaldua, Gloria (Evanjelina) 1942-2004
　Obituary *154*
Aoki, Hisako 1942- *45*
Apfel, Necia H(alpern) 1930- *51*
　Brief entry *41*
Aphrodite, J.
　See Livingston, Carole
Apikuni
　See Schultz, James Willard
Apostolina, M. *184*
Apostolina, Michael
　See Apostolina, M.
Apostolou, Christine Hale 1955- *179*
　Earlier sketches in SATA *82, 128*
Appel, Allen (R.) 1945- *115*
Appel, Benjamin 1907-1977 .... *39*
　Obituary *21*
Appel, Martin 1948- *45*
Appel, Martin Eliot
　See Appel, Martin
Appel, Marty
　See Appel, Martin
Appelbaum, Diana Muir Karter 1953- *132*
Appelt, Kathi 1954- *190*
　Earlier sketches in SATA *83, 129*
Apperley, Dawn 1969- *135*
Appiah, Peggy 1921-2006 .... *84*
　Earlier sketch in SATA *15*
　See also SAAS *19*
Apple, Margot *214*
　Brief entry *42*
　Earlier sketches in SATA *64, 152*
Applebaum, Stan 1922- *45*
Applegate, K.A.
　See Applegate, Katherine
Applegate, Katherine 1956- *196*
　Earlier sketches in SATA *109, 162*
　See also CLR *90*
Applegate, Katherine Alice
　See Applegate, Katherine
Appleton, Victor
　See Barrett, Neal, Jr.
　and Doyle, Debra
　and Stratemeyer, Edward L.
　and Vardeman, Robert E.
Appollo 1969- *214*
Appollodorus, Olivier
　See Appollo
Apsler, Alfred 1907-1982 .... *10*
Aragones, Sergio 1937- *48*
　Brief entry *39*
Araujo, Frank P. 1937- *86*
Arbo, Cris 1950- *220*
　Earlier sketch in SATA *103*
Arbuckle, Dorothy Fry 1910-1982
　Obituary *33*
Arbuthnot, May Hill 1884-1969 .... *2*
Archambault, John *163*
　Earlier sketches in SATA *67, 112*
Archambault, Matthew 1968- *219*
Archbold, Rick 1950- *97*
Archer, Colleen Rutherford 1949- *164*
Archer, Frank
　See O'Connor, Richard
Archer, Jules 1915- *85*
　Earlier sketch in SATA *4*
　See also SAAS *5*
Archer, Lily 1981- *193*
Archer, Marion Fuller 1917- *11*
Archer, Nathan
　See Watt-Evans, Lawrence
Archer, Peggy 1947- *199*
Archibald, Joe
　See Archibald, Joseph S(topford)
Archibald, Joseph S(topford) 1898-1986 .... *3*
　Obituary *47*
Ard, William
　See Jakes, John
Ardagh, Philip 1961- *154*
Ardai, Charles 1969- *85*

Arden, Barbi
　See Stoutenburg, Adrien (Pearl)
Arden, William
　See Lynds, Dennis
Ardizzone, Edward (Jeffrey Irving)
　1900-1979 .... *28*
　Obituary *21*
　Earlier sketch in SATA *1*
　See also CLR *3*
Ardley, Neil 1937- *121*
　Earlier sketch in SATA *43*
Ardley, Neil Richard
　See Ardley, Neil
Arehart-Treichel, Joan 1942- *22*
Arena, Felice 1968- *151*
Arenella, Roy 1939- *14*
Argent, Kerry 1960- *138*
Arguelles, Francisco Xavier
　See Stork, Francisco X.
Argueta, Jorge *179*
Arihara, Shino 1973- *201*
Arkin, Alan 1934- *59*
　Brief entry *32*
Arkin, Alan Wolf
　See Arkin, Alan
Arksey, Neil *158*
Arlen, Leslie
　See Nicole, Christopher (Robin)
Arley, Robert
　See Jackson, Mike
Armer, Alberta (Roller) 1904-1986 .... *9*
Armer, Laura Adams 1874-1963 .... *13*
Armistead, John 1941- *130*
Armitage, David 1943- *155*
　Brief entry *38*
　Earlier sketch in SATA *99*
Armitage, Frank
　See Carpenter, John
Armitage, Ronda (Jacqueline) 1943- *155*
　Brief entry *38*
　Earlier sketches in SATA *47, 99*
Armour, Richard (Willard) 1906-1989 .... *14*
　Obituary *61*
Armstrong, Alan 1939- *172*
Armstrong, Alan W.
　See Armstrong, Alan
Armstrong, George D. 1927- *10*
Armstrong, Gerry (Breen) 1929- *10*
Armstrong, Jeannette (C.) 1948- *102*
Armstrong, Jennifer 1961- *165*
　Autobiography Feature *120*
　Earlier sketches in SATA *77, 111*
　See also CLR *66*
　See also SAAS *24*
Armstrong, Louise *43*
　Brief entry *33*
Armstrong, Martin Donisthorpe
　1882-1974 .... *115*
Armstrong, Matthew 1975- *188*
Armstrong, Matthew S.
　See Armstrong, Matthew
Armstrong, Ralph Richard
　See Armstrong, Richard
Armstrong, Richard 1903-1986 .... *11*
Armstrong, William H(oward) 1914-1999 ..... *4*
　Obituary *111*
　See also CLR *117*
　See also SAAS *7*
Armstrong-Ellis, Carey (Fraser) 1956- *145*
Arndt, Ursula (Martha H.) *56*
　Brief entry *39*
Arneson, D(on) J(on) 1935- *37*
Arnett, Caroline
　See Cole, Lois Dwight
Arnett, Jack
　See Goulart, Ron
Arnette, Robert
　See Silverberg, Robert
Arno, Enrico 1913-1981 .... *43*
　Obituary *28*
Arnold, Ann 1953(?)- *207*

Arnold, Caroline 1944- *174*
　Brief entry *34*
　Earlier sketches in SATA *36, 85, 131*
　See also CLR *61*
　See also SAAS *23*
Arnold, Elizabeth 1944- *164*
Arnold, Elliott 1912-1980 .... *5*
　Obituary *22*
Arnold, Emily 1939- *210*
　Autobiography Feature *134*
　Earlier sketches in SATA *5, 50, 76, 110, 134*
　See also CLR *46*
　See also SAAS *7*
Arnold, Gillian Clare
　See Cross, Gillian
Arnold, Katya 1947- *168*
　Earlier sketches in SATA *82, 115*
Arnold, Louise *175*
Arnold, Louise Claire
　See Arnold, Louise
Arnold, Marsha Diane 1948- *147*
　Earlier sketch in SATA *93*
Arnold, Nick 1961- *113*
Arnold, Oren 1900-1980 .... *4*
Arnold, Susan (Riser) 1951- *58*
Arnold, Tedd 1949- *208*
　Earlier sketches in SATA *69, 116, 160*
Arnoldy, Julie
　See Bischoff, Julia Bristol
Arnosky, James Edward 1946- *189*
　Earlier sketches in SATA *70, 118*
　See also CLR *93*
Arnosky, Jim
　See Arnosky, James Edward
Arnott, Kathleen 1914- *20*
Arnov, Boris, Jr. 1926- *12*
Arnow, Harriette (Louisa) Simpson
　1908-1986 .... *42*
　Obituary *47*
Arnsteen, Katy Keck 1934- *68*
Arnstein, Helene S(olomon) 1915- *12*
Arntson, Herbert E(dward) 1911-1982 .... *12*
Aroner, Miriam *82*
Aronin, Ben 1904-1980
　Obituary *25*
Aronson, Marc 1950- *189*
　Autobiography Feature *189*
　Earlier sketches in SATA *126, 175*
Aronson, Marc Henry
　See Aronson, Marc
Aronson, Sarah *196*
Aronson, Virginia 1954- *122*
Arora, Shirley (Lease) 1930- *2*
Arrasmith, Patrick *176*
Arrick, Fran
　See Angell, Judie
Arrigan, Mary 1943- *142*
Arrington, Aileen *183*
Arrington, Stephen L. 1948- *97*
Arrington, Stephen Lee
　See Arrington, Stephen L.
Arrley, Richmond
　See Delany, Samuel R., Jr.
Arrou-Vignod, Jean-Philippe 1958- *218*
Arrowood, (McKendrick Lee) Clinton
　1939- *19*
Arrowsmith, Pat 1930- *59*
Arsenault, Isabelle 1978- *207*
Artell, Mike 1948- *183*
　Earlier sketches in SATA *89, 134*
Arthur, Robert (Andrew) 1909-1969
　See Arthur, Robert, (Jr.)
Arthur, Robert, (Jr.) 1909-1969 .... *118*
Arthur, Ruth M(abel) 1905-1979 .... *26*
　Earlier sketch in SATA *7*
Artis, Vicki Kimmel 1945- *12*
Artzybasheff, Boris (Miklailovich)
　1899-1965 .... *14*
Aruego, Ariane
　See Dewey, Ariane

Aruego, Jose 1932- 178
  Earlier sketches in SATA *6, 68, 125*
  See also CLR *5*
Aruego, Jose Espiritu
  See Aruego, Jose
Arundel, Honor (Morfydd) 1919-1973 .... *4*
  Obituary 24
  See also CLR *35*
Arundel, Jocelyn
  See Alexander, Jocelyn Anne Arundel
Arvey, Michael 1948- 79
Arzoumanian, Alik *177*
Asare, Meshack (Yaw) 1945- *139*
  Earlier sketch in SATA *86*
Asaro, Catherine 1955- 165
  Earlier sketch in SATA *101*
Asaro, Catherine Ann 1955-
  See Asaro, Catherine
Asay, Donna Day 1945- 127
Asbjornsen, Peter Christen 1812-1885 15
  See also CLR *104*
Asch, Frank 1946- 154
  Earlier sketches in SATA *5, 66, 102*
Ash, Jutta 1942- 38
Ashabranner, Brent 1921- 166
  Earlier sketches in SATA *1, 67, 130*
  See also CLR *28*
  See also SAAS *14*
Ashabranner, Brent Kenneth
  See Ashabranner, Brent
Ashbless, William
  See Blaylock, James P.
  and Powers, Tim
Ashby, Gil 1958- 146
Ashby, Gwynneth 1922- 44
Ashby, Ruth 170
Ashby, Yvonne 1955- 121
Ashe, Arthur (Robert, Jr.) 1943-1993 65
  Obituary 87
Ashe, Geoffrey (Thomas) 1923- *17*
  Autobiography Feature 125
Ashe, Mary Ann
  See Lewis, Mary
Asher, Bridget
  See Baggott, Julianna
Asher, Sandra Fenichel
  See Asher, Sandy
Asher, Sandy 1942- 71
  Autobiography Feature 158
  Brief entry 34
  Earlier sketch in SATA *36*
  See also SAAS *13*
Asheron, Sara
  See Moore, Lilian
Ashey, Bella
  See Breinburg, Petronella
Ashford, Daisy
  See Ashford, Margaret Mary
Ashford, Jeffrey
  See Jeffries, Roderic
Ashford, Margaret Mary 1881-1972 .... *10*
Ashland, Monk 1972- 207
Ashley, Bernard (John) 1935- 155
  Brief entry 39
  Earlier sketches in SATA *47, 79*
  See also CLR *4*
Ashley, Elizabeth
  See Salmon, Annie Elizabeth
Ashley, Ray
  See Abrashkin, Raymond
Ashman, Linda 1960- 203
  Earlier sketch in SATA *150*
Ashton, Lorayne
  See Gottfried, Theodore Mark
Ashton, Warren T.
  See Adams, William Taylor
Asimov, Isaac 1920-1992 74
  Earlier sketches in SATA *1, 26*
  See also CLR *79*
Asinof, Eliot 1919-2008 6

Asinof, Eliot Tager
  See Asinof, Eliot
Aska, Warabe
  See Masuda, Takeshi
Asprin, Robert 1946-2008 92
Asprin, Robert L.
  See Asprin, Robert
Asprin, Robert Lynn
  See Asprin, Robert
Asquith, Cynthia Mary Evelyn (Charteris)
  1887-1960 107
Asquith, Ros 153
Astley, Juliet
  See Lofts, Norah (Robinson)
Aston, Dianna Hutts 1964- 176
Aston, James
  See White, T(erence) H(anbury)
Ata, Te 1895-1995 119
Atene, Ann
  See Atene, (Rita) Anna
Atene, (Rita) Anna 1922- 12
Atheling, William, Jr.
  See Blish, James
Atkins, Catherine 160
Atkins, Jeannine 1953- 172
  Earlier sketch in SATA *113*
Atkinson, Allen G. 1953(?)-1987 60
  Brief entry 46
  Obituary 55
Atkinson, Elizabeth 215
Atkinson, M. E.
  See Frankau, Mary Evelyn Atkinson
Atkinson, Margaret Fleming *14*
Atteberry, Kevan J. 186
Attema, Martha 1949- 156
  Earlier sketch in SATA *94*
Atticus
  See Davies, Hunter
  and Fleming, Ian
  and Pawle, Gerald Strachan
  and Wilson, (Thomas) Woodrow
Atwater, Florence (Hasseltine Carroll)
  1896-1979 66
  Earlier sketch in SATA *16*
  See also CLR *19*
Atwater, Montgomery Meigs 1904-1976 15
Atwater, Richard (Tupper) 1892-1948 66
  Brief entry 27
  Earlier sketch in SATA *54*
  See also CLR *19*
Atwater-Rhodes, Amelia 1984- 170
  Earlier sketch in SATA *124*
Atwell, Debby 1953- 150
  Earlier sketch in SATA *87*
Atwood, Ann (Margaret) 1913-1992 7
Atwood, Margaret 1939- 170
  Earlier sketch in SATA *50*
Atwood, Margaret Eleanor
  See Atwood, Margaret
Aubrey, Meg Kelleher 1963- 83
Aubry, Claude B. 1914-1984 29
  Obituary 40
Auch, Herm 173
Auch, Mary Jane 173
  Earlier sketch in SATA *138*
Auch, M.J.
  See Auch, Mary Jane
Auclair, Joan 1960- 68
Auel, Jean 1936- 91
Auel, Jean M.
  See Auel, Jean
Auel, Jean Marie
  See Auel, Jean
Auer, Martin 1951- 77
Augarde, Steve 1950- 210
  Earlier sketches in SATA *25, 159*
Augarde, Steven Andre
  See Augarde, Steve
Augelli, John P(at) 1921- 46
Augustine, Mildred
  See Benson, Mildred

Ault, Phil
  See Ault, Phillip H(alliday)
Ault, Phillip H(alliday) 1914- 23
Ault, Rosalie Sain 1942- 38
Ault, Roz
  See Ault, Rosalie Sain
Aung, (Maung) Htin 1909- 21
Auntie Deb
  See Coury, Louise Andree
Auntie Louise
  See Coury, Louise Andree
Aunt Weedy
  See Alcott, Louisa May
Auseon, Andrew 1976- 217
  Earlier sketch in SATA *166*
Austen, Carrie
  See Bennett, Cherie
Austin, Carrie
  See Seuling, Barbara
Austin, Elizabeth S. 1907-1977 5
Austin, Harry
  See McInerny, Ralph
Austin, Margot 1909(?)-1990 11
  Obituary 66
Austin, Michael 178
Austin, Oliver L(uther), Jr. 1903-1988 7
  Obituary 59
Austin, Patricia 1950- 137
Austin, R. G.
  See Gelman, Rita Golden
  and Lamb, Nancy
Austin, Virginia 1951- 152
  Earlier sketch in SATA *80*
Auteur, Hillary
  See Gottfried, Theodore Mark
Auth, Tony
  See Auth, William Anthony, Jr.
Auth, William Anthony, Jr. 1942- 192
Autry, Gloria Diener
  See Allen, Terril Diener
Auvil, Peggy A 1954- 122
Auvil, Peggy Appleby
  See Auvil, Peggy A
Aveni, Anthony F. 1938- 181
Aveni, Anthony Francis
  See Aveni, Anthony F.
Averbeck, Jim 1963- 201
Averill, Esther (Holden) 1902-1992 28
  Obituary 72
  Earlier sketch in SATA *1*
Avery, A. A.
  See Montgomery, Rutherford George
Avery, Al
  See Montgomery, Rutherford George
Avery, Gillian 1926- 137
  Autobiography Feature 137
  Earlier sketches in SATA *7, 75*
  See also SAAS *6*
Avery, Gillian Elise
  See Avery, Gillian
Avery, Kay 1908- 5
Avery, Lorraine
  See Older, Effin
  and Older, Jules
Avery, Lynn
  See Cole, Lois Dwight
Avi 1937- 190
  Earlier sketches in SATA *14, 71, 108, 156*
  See also CLR *68*
Aviles, Martha 218
Avishai, Susan 1949- 82
Avril, Francois 1961- 191
Avril, Lynne
  See Cravath, Lynne W.
Awdry, Christopher Vere 1940- 67
Awdry, Wilbert Vere 1911-1997 94
  See also CLR *23*
Axelrod, Amy 131
Axelsen, Stephen 1953- 165
Axton, David
  See Koontz, Dean

Ayars, James S(terling) 1898-1986 .... *4*
Aye, A. K.
  See Edwards, Hazel (Eileen)
Ayer, Eleanor H. 1947-1998 .... *121*
  Earlier sketch in SATA *78*
Ayer, Jacqueline 1930- *13*
Ayer, Margaret (?)-1981 .... *15*
Aylesworth, Jim 1943- *213*
  Earlier sketches in SATA *38, 89, 139*
  See also CLR *89*
Aylesworth, Thomas G(ibbons) 1927-1995 .. *88*
  Earlier sketch in SATA *4*
  See also CLR *6*
  See also SAAS *17*
Ayliffe, Alex *190*
Aylward, Marcus
  See Alexander, Marc
Aymar, Brandt 1911- *22*
Ayme, Marcel (Andre) 1902-1967 .... *91*
  See also CLR *25*
Ayres, Becky
  See Hickox, Rebecca (Ayres)
Ayres, Katherine 1947- *187*
Ayres, Pam 1947- *90*
Ayres, Patricia Miller 1923-1985
  Obituary *46*
Aytmatov, Chingiz
  See Aitmatov, Chingiz
Ayto, Russell 1960- *206*
  Earlier sketches in SATA *111, 166*
Azaid
  See Zaidenberg, Arthur
Azar, Penny 1952- *121*
Azarian, Mary 1940- *171*
  Earlier sketch in SATA *112*
Azore, Barbara 1934- *188*

B

Baasansuren, Bolormaa 1982- *216*
Baastad, Babbis Friis
  See Friis-Baastad, Babbis Ellinor
Bab
  See Gilbert, W(illiam) S(chwenck)
Babbis, Eleanor
  See Friis-Baastad, Babbis Ellinor
Babbitt, Lucy Cullyford 1960- *85*
Babbitt, Natalie 1932- *194*
  Earlier sketches in SATA *6, 68, 106*
  See also CLR *141*
  See also SAAS *5*
Babbitt, Natalie Zane Moore
  See Babbitt, Natalie
Babcock, Chris 1963- *83*
Babcock, Dennis 1948- *22*
Babcock, Dennis Arthur
  See Babcock, Dennis
Baber, Carolyn Stonnell 1936- *96*
Baboni, Elena *198*
Baca, Ana 1967- *191*
Baca, Maria 1951- *104*
Bach, Alice (Hendricks) 1942- *93*
  Brief entry *27*
  Earlier sketch in SATA *30*
Bach, Bellamy
  See Windling, Terri
Bach, Mary 1960- *125*
Bach, Richard 1936- *13*
Bach, Richard David
  See Bach, Richard
Bache, Ellyn 1942- *124*
Bachel, Beverly K. 1957- *142*
Bachelet, Gilles 1952- *196*
Bachman, Fred 1949- *12*
Bachman, Richard
  See King, Stephen
Bachrach, Deborah *80*
Backus, James Gilmore 1913-1989
  Obituary *63*

Backus, Jim
  See Backus, James Gilmore
Bacmeister, Rhoda W(arner) 1893-1991 .... *11*
Bacon, Betty
  See Bacon, Elizabeth
Bacon, Elizabeth 1914-2001 .... *3*
  Obituary *131*
Bacon, Joan Chase
  See Bowden, Joan Chase
Bacon, Josephine Dodge (Daskam)
  1876-1961 .... *48*
Bacon, Margaret Frances
  See Bacon, Peggy
Bacon, Margaret Hope 1921- *6*
Bacon, Martha Sherman 1917-1981 .... *18*
  Obituary *27*
  See also CLR *3*
Bacon, Melvin 1950- *93*
Bacon, Melvin L.
  See Bacon, Melvin
Bacon, Peggy 1895-1987 .... *50*
Bacon, R(onald) L(eonard) 1924- *84*
  Earlier sketch in SATA *26*
Baddiel, Ivor 1963- *210*
Baden, Robert 1936- *70*
Baden-Powell, Robert (Stephenson Smyth)
  1857-1941 .... *16*
Badt, Karin L(uisa) 1963- *91*
Bae, Hyun-Joo *186*
Baehr, Kingsley M. 1937- *89*
Baehr, Patricia 1952- *65*
Baehr, Patricia Goehner
  See Baehr, Patricia
Baek, Matthew J. 1971- *202*
Baer, Jill
  See Gilbert, (Agnes) Joan (Sewell)
Baer, Judy 1951- *71*
Baer, Julie 1960- *161*
Baer-Block, Roxanna *172*
Baerg, Harry J(ohn) 1909-1996 .... *12*
Baeten, Lieve 1954- *83*
Bagert, Brod 1947- *191*
  Earlier sketch in SATA *80*
Baggette, Susan K. 1942- *126*
Baggott, Julianna 1969- *197*
Bagnold, Enid 1889-1981 .... *25*
  Earlier sketch in SATA *1*
Baguley, Elizabeth 1959- *199*
Bahlke, Valerie Worth -1994
  See Worth, Valerie
Bahous, Sally 1939- *86*
Bahr, Mary (Madelyn) 1946- *95*
Bahr, Robert 1940- *38*
Bahti, Tom 1926-1972 .... *57*
  Brief entry *31*
Bai, Durga *211*
Baicker-McKee, Carol 1958- *177*
Bailey, Alice Cooper 1890-1978 .... *12*
Bailey, Anne 1958- *71*
Bailey, Bernadine (Freeman) 1901-1995 ...... *14*
Bailey, Carolyn Sherwin 1875-1961 .... *14*
Bailey, Debbie 1954- *123*
Bailey, Donna (Veronica Anne) 1938- *68*
Bailey, Jane H(orton) 1916- *12*
Bailey, John (Robert) 1940- *52*
Bailey, Len *193*
Bailey, Linda 1948- *217*
  Earlier sketches in SATA *107, 182*
Bailey, Maralyn Collins (Harrison) 1941- *12*
Bailey, Matilda
  See Radford, Ruby L(orraine)
Bailey, Maurice Charles 1932- *12*
Bailey, Pearl (Mae) 1918-1990 .... *81*
Bailey, Peter 1946- *194*
Bailey, Ralph Edgar 1893-1982 .... *11*
Bailey, Sheila (Lucas) 1960- *155*
Baillie, Allan 1943- *151*
  Earlier sketch in SATA *87*
  See also CLR *49*
  See also SAAS *21*

Baillie, Allan Stuart
  See Baillie, Allan
Baines, John (David) 1943- *71*
Bains, Larry
  See Sabin, Louis
Baird, Alison 1963- *138*
Baird, Bil 1904-1987 .... *30*
  Obituary *52*
Baird, Thomas (P.) 1923-1990 .... *45*
  Brief entry *39*
  Obituary *64*
Baird, William Britton
  See Baird, Bil
Baity, Elizabeth Chesley 1907-1989 .... *1*
Baiul, Oksana 1977- *108*
Bajoria, Paul 1964- *187*
Bakeless, John (Edwin) 1894-1978 .... *9*
Bakeless, Katherine Little 1895-1992 .... *9*
Baker, Alan 1951- *146*
  Earlier sketches in SATA *22, 93*
Baker, Augusta 1911-1998 .... *3*
Baker, Barbara 1947- *192*
Baker, Betty Lou 1928-1987 .... *73*
  Obituary *54*
  Earlier sketch in SATA *5*
Baker, Carin Greenberg 1959- *79*
Baker, Charlotte 1910- *2*
Baker, Christina
  See Kline, Christina Baker
Baker, Christopher W. 1952- *144*
Baker, Deirdre 1955- *195*
Baker, E.D. *190*
Baker, (Mary) Elizabeth (Gillette) 1923- *7*
Baker, Gayle Cunningham 1950- *39*
Baker, James W. 1924- *65*
  Earlier sketch in SATA *22*
Baker, James W. 1926- *122*
Baker, Janice E(dla) 1941- *22*
Baker, Jeanette *178*
Baker, Jeannie 1950- *156*
  Earlier sketches in SATA *23, 88*
  See also CLR *28*
Baker, Jeffrey J(ohn) W(heeler) 1931- *5*
Baker, Jim
  See Baker, James W.
Baker, Keith 1953- *179*
Baker, Ken 1962- *133*
Baker, Laura Nelson 1911- *3*
Baker, Margaret 1890-1965 .... *4*
Baker, Margaret J(oyce) 1918- *12*
  See also SAAS *8*
Baker, Mary Gladys Steel 1892-1974 .... *12*
Baker, (Robert) Michael (Graham) 1938- *4*
Baker, Nina (Brown) 1888-1957 .... *15*
Baker, Pamela J. 1947- *66*
Baker, Rachel 1904-1978 .... *2*
  Obituary *26*
Baker, Roberta *206*
Baker, Rosalie F. 1945- *166*
Baker, Samm Sinclair 1909-1997 .... *12*
  Obituary *96*
Baker, Sharon Reiss 1962- *207*
Baker, Susan (Catherine) 1942-1991 .... *29*
Balaam
  See Lamb, G(eoffrey) F(rederick)
Balan, Bruce 1959- *113*
Balcavage, Dynise 1965- *137*
Balch, Glenn 1902-1989 .... *3*
  Obituary *83*
  See also SAAS *11*
Baldacci, David 1960- *184*
Baldacci, David G.
  See Baldacci, David
  and Baldacci, David
Balderose, Nancy Ward 1952- *93*
Balderson, Margaret 1935- *151*
Baldini, Michelle *205*
Baldry, Cherith 1947- *167*
  Earlier sketch in SATA *72*
Balducci, Carolyn 1946- *5*

Balducci, Carolyn Feleppa
  See Balducci, Carolyn
Baldwin, Alex
  See Griffin, W. E. B.
Baldwin, Anne Norris 1938- 5
Baldwin, Clara 11
Baldwin, Gordo
  See Baldwin, Gordon C(ortis)
Baldwin, Gordon C(ortis) 1908-1983 12
Baldwin, James 1841-1925 24
Baldwin, James 1924-1987 9
  Obituary 54
Baldwin, Louis 1919- 110
Baldwin, Margaret
  See Weis, Margaret
Baldwin, Stan(ley C.) 1929- 62
  Brief entry 28
Bales, Carol Ann 1940- 57
  Brief entry 29
Balet, Jan (Bernard) 1913- 11
Balgassi, Haemi 1971- 131
Balian, Lorna 1929- 91
  Earlier sketch in SATA 9
Balit, Christina 1961- 212
  Earlier sketches in SATA *102, 159*
Ball, Duncan 1941- 73
Ball, Zachary
  See Janas, Frankie-Lee
  and Masters, Kelly R(ay)
Ballantine, Lesley Frost
  See Frost, Lesley
Ballantyne, R(obert) M(ichael) 1825-1894 ... 24
  See also CLR *137*
Ballard, James G.
  See Ballard, J.G.
Ballard, James Graham
  See Ballard, J.G.
Ballard, Jane
  See Gorman, Carol
Ballard, J.G. 1930-2009 93
  Obituary 203
Ballard, Jim G.
  See Ballard, J.G.
Ballard, John 1945- 110
Ballard, Lowell C(lyne) 1904-1986 12
  Obituary 49
Ballard, (Charles) Martin 1929- 1
Ballard, Mignon F. 1934- 64
  Brief entry 49
Ballard, Mignon Franklin
  See Ballard, Mignon F.
Ballard, Robert D(uane) 1942- 85
  See also CLR *60*
Ballard, Robin 1965- 126
Balliett, Blue 1955- 156
Ballinger, Bryan 1968- 161
Ballouhey, Pierre 1944- 90
Balog, Cyn 221
Balogh, Penelope 1916-1975 1
  Obituary 34
Balouch, Kristen 176
Balow, Tom 1931- 12
Baltazzi, Evan S(erge) 1921- 90
Balterman, Marcia Ridlon 1942- 22
Baltimore, J.
  See Catherall, Arthur
Baltzer, Hans (Adolf) 1900- 40
Balzano, Jeanne (Koppel) 1912- 7
Bambara, Toni Cade 1939-1995 112
Bamfylde, Walter
  See Bevan, Tom
Bamman, Henry A. 1918- 12
Banat, D. R.
  See Bradbury, Ray
Bancroft, Bronwyn 1958- 216
Bancroft, Griffing 1907-1999 6
Bancroft, Laura
  See Baum, L. Frank
Bandel, Betty 1912- 47
Baner, Skulda Vanadis 1897-1964 10
Banerjee, Anjali 174

Banfill, A. Scott 1956- 98
Bang, Betsy 1912- 48
  Brief entry 37
Bang, Garrett
  See Bang, Molly
Bang, Molly 1943- 215
  Earlier sketches in SATA *24, 69, 111, 158*
  See also CLR 8
Bang, Molly Garrett
  See Bang, Molly
Bang-Campbell, Monika 1975(?)- 195
  Earlier sketch in SATA *140*
Banjo, The
  See Paterson, A(ndrew) B(arton)
Banke, Cecile de
  See de Banke, Cecile
Banks, Erin Bennett 1978- 211
Banks, Kate 1960- 200
  Earlier sketches in SATA *134, 172*
Banks, Laura Stockton Voorhees 1908(?)-1980
  Obituary 23
Banks, Lynne Reid
  See Reid Banks, Lynne
Banks, Merry 197
Banks, Michael A. 1951- 101
Banks, Paul 1952- 174
Banks, Sara
  See Harrell, Sara Gordon
Banks, Sara Jeanne Gordon Harrell
  See Harrell, Sara Gordon
Bannatyne-Cugnet, Elizabeth Jo-Anne
  See Bannatyne-Cugnet, Jo
Bannatyne-Cugnet, Jo 1951- 101
Banner, Angela
  See Maddison, Angela Mary
Bannerman, Helen (Brodie Cowan Watson)
  1862(?)-1946 19
  See also CLR *144*
Banning, Evelyn I. 1903-1993 36
Bannon, Laura (?)-1963 6
Bannor, Brett 1959- 143
Banta, Susan 181
Bantock, Nick 1950(?)- 95
Banyai, Istvan 193
Barakat, Ibtisam 1963- 186
Barasch, Lynne 1939- 186
  Earlier sketches in SATA *74, 126*
Barbalet, Margaret 1949- 77
Barbary, James
  See Baumann, Amy Beeching
  and Beeching, Jack
Barbash, Shepard 1957- 84
Barbauld, Anna Laetitia 1743-1825
  See CLR *160*
Barbe, Walter Burke 1926- 45
Barber, Antonia 1932- 163
  Earlier sketch in SATA *29*
Barber, Atiim Kiambu
  See Barber, Tiki
Barber, Lynda
  See Graham-Barber, Lynda
Barber, Lynda Graham
  See Graham-Barber, Lynda
Barber, Richard (William) 1941- 35
Barber, Ronde 1975- 182
Barber, Tiki 1975- 182
Barbera, Joe 1911-2006 51
  Obituary 179
Barbera, Joseph
  See Barbera, Joe
Barbera, Joseph Roland
  See Barbera, Joe
Barberis, Juan C(arlos) 1920- 61
Barbour, Karen 1956- 170
  Earlier sketches in SATA *63, 121*
Barbour, Ralph Henry 1870-1944 16
Barclay, Bill
  See Moorcock, Michael
Barclay, Isabel
  See Dobell, I(sabel) M(arian) B(arclay)

Barclay, William Ewert
  See Moorcock, Michael
Barclay, William Ewert
  See Moorcock, Michael
Bardhan-Quallen, Sudipta 1977- 214
  Earlier sketch in SATA *168*
Bardoe, Cheryl 181
Bare, Arnold Edwin 1920- 16
Bare, Colleen Stanley 32
Bar-el, Dan 199
Barenholtz, Bernard 1914-1989
  Obituary 64
Bargar, Gary W. 1947-1985 63
Barger, Jan 1948- 147
Barish, Matthew 1907-2000 12
Barkan, Joanne 127
  Earlier sketch in SATA *77*
Barker, Albert W. 1900- 8
Barker, Carol (Minturn) 1938- 31
Barker, Cicely Mary 1895-1973 49
  Brief entry 39
  See also CLR *88*
Barker, Melvern 1907-1989 11
Barker, S. Omar 1894-1985 10
Barker, Squire Omar
  See Barker, S. Omar
Barker, Will 1913-1983 8
Barkin, Carol 1944- 52
  Earlier sketch in SATA *42*
Barklem, Jill 1951- 96
  See also CLR *31*
Barkley, Brad 178
Barkley, James Edward 1941- 6
Barks, Carl 1901-2000 37
Barley, Janet Crane 1934- 95
Barlow, Steve 1952- 211
Barnaby, Ralph S(tanton) 1893-1986 9
Barnard, A. M.
  See Alcott, Louisa May
Barnard, Bryn 1956- 169
  Earlier sketch in SATA *115*
Barne, Kitty
  See Barne, Marion Catherine
Barne, Marion Catherine 1883-1957 97
Barneda, David 206
Barner, Bob 1947- 136
  Earlier sketch in SATA *29*
Barnes, Dawn 1957- 175
Barnes, Derrick 191
Barnes, Derrick D.
  See Barnes, Derrick
Barnes, (Frank) Eric Wollencott 1907-1962 . 22
Barnes, Joyce Annette 1958- 85
Barnes, Laura T. 1958- 119
Barnes, Loutricia
  See Barnes-Svarney, Patricia L(ou)
Barnes, Malcolm 1909(?)-1984
  Obituary 41
Barnes, Michael 1934- 55
Barnes-Murphy, Frances 1951- 88
Barnes-Murphy, Rowan 1952- 88
Barnes-Svarney, Patricia L(ou) 1953- 67
Barnet, Nancy 1954- 84
Barnett, Ivan 1947- 70
Barnett, Lincoln (Kinnear) 1909-1979 36
Barnett, Moneta 1922-1976 33
Barnett, Naomi 1927- 40
Barney, Maginel Wright 1881(?)-1966 39
  Brief entry 32
Barnhart, Clarence L(ewis) 1900-1993 48
  Obituary 78
Barnouw, Adriaan Jacob 1877-1968
  Obituary 27
Barnouw, Victor 1915-1989 43
  Brief entry 28
Barnstone, Willis 1927- 20
Barnum, Jay Hyde 1888(?)-1962 20
Barnum, P. T., Jr.
  See Stratemeyer, Edward L.
Barnum, Richard 67
  Earlier sketch in SATA *1*

Barnum, Theodore
  See Stratemeyer, Edward L.
Barnwell, Ysaye M. 1946- 200
Baron, Kathy 1954- 90
Baron, Virginia Olsen 1931- 46
  Brief entry 28
Barr, Donald 1921-2004 20
  Obituary 152
Barr, George 1907-1992 2
Barr, Jene 1922-1985 16
  Obituary 42
Barr, Nevada 1952- 126
  Earlier sketch in SATA *115*
Barragan, Paula 1963- 216
Barrer, Gertrude
  See Barrer-Russell, Gertrude
Barrer-Russell, Gertrude 1921- 27
Barrett, Angela (Jane) 1955- 145
  Earlier sketch in SATA *75*
Barrett, Ethel 87
  Brief entry 44
Barrett, Joyce Durham 1943- 138
Barrett, Judi
  See Barrett, Judith
Barrett, Judith 1941- 204
  Earlier sketch in SATA *26*
  See also CLR *98*
Barrett, Robert T(heodore) 1949- 92
Barrett, Ron 1937- 14
Barrett, Susan (Mary) 1938- 113
Barrett, Tracy 1955- 207
  Earlier sketches in SATA *84, 115, 156*
Barrett, William E(dmund) 1900-1986
  Obituary 49
Barretta, Gene 214
  Earlier sketch in SATA *176*
Barretton, Grandall
  See Garrett, Randall
Barrie, Baronet
  See Barrie, J. M.
Barrie, J. M. 1860-1937 100
  See also YABC *1*
  See also CLR *124*
Barrie, James Matthew
  See Barrie, J. M.
Barringer, William 1940-1996 153
Barrington, Michael
  See Moorcock, Michael
Barris, George 1925- 47
Barrol, Grady
  See Bograd, Larry
Barron, Rex 1951- 84
Barron, T.A. 1952- 192
  Earlier sketches in SATA *83, 126*
  See also CLR *86*
Barron, Thomas Archibald
  See Barron, T.A.
Barron, Tom
  See Barron, T.A.
Barrow, Lloyd H. 1942- 73
Barrows, Annie 1962- 180
Barry, Dan 1958- 177
Barry, Dana (Marie Malloy) 1949- 139
Barry, James P(otvin) 1918- 14
Barry, Katharina Watjen 1936- 4
Barry, Robert 1931- 6
Barry, Robert Everett
  See Barry, Robert
Barry, Scott 1952- 32
Barry, Sheila Anne -2003 91
Barshaw, Ruth McNally 203
Bartell, Susan S. 175
Bartenbach, Jean 1918- 40
Barth, Edna 1914-1980 7
  Obituary 24
Barth, Kelly L. 1964- 152
Barthelme, Donald 1931-1989 7
  Obituary 62
Barth-Grozinger, Inge 1950- 185
Bartholomew, Barbara 1941- 86
  Brief entry 42

Bartholomew, Jean
  See Beatty, Patricia (Robbins)
Bartlett, Alison 153
Bartlett, Philip A. 1
Bartlett, Robert Merrill 1899-1995 12
Bartoletti, Susan Campbell 1958- 173
  Earlier sketches in SATA *88, 129, 135*
Barton, Byron 1930- 126
  Earlier sketches in SATA *9, 90*
Barton, Jill(ian) 1940- 75
Barton, May Hollis 67
  Earlier sketch in SATA *1*
Barton, Pat
  See Arrowsmith, Pat
Bartos-Hoeppner, Barbara 1923- 5
Bartram, Simon 218
  Earlier sketch in SATA *156*
Bartsch, Jochen 1906- 39
Baruch, Dorothy W(alter) 1899-1962 21
Barunga, Albert 1912(?)-1977 120
Baryshnikov, Mikhail 1948- 192
Bas, Rutger
  See Rutgers van der Loeff-Basenau, An(na)
    Maria Margaretha
Base, Graeme 1958- 162
  Earlier sketches in SATA *67, 101*
  See also CLR *22*
Base, Graeme Rowland
  See Base, Graeme
Baseman, Gary 1960- 174
Bash, Barbara 1948- 132
Bashevis, Isaac
  See Singer, Isaac Bashevis
Bashevis, Yitskhok
  See Singer, Isaac Bashevis
Bashista, Adrienne Ehlert 203
Basile, Gloria Vitanza 1929- 180
Baskin, Leonard 1922-2000 120
  Brief entry 27
  Earlier sketch in SATA *30*
Baskin, Nora Raleigh 1961- 189
  Earlier sketch in SATA *129*
Bason, Lillian 1913- 20
Bass, L. G.
  See Geringer, Laura
Bassett, Jeni 1959- 64
  Brief entry 43
Bassett, John Keith
  See Keating, Lawrence A.
Bassett, Lisa 1958- 61
Bassil, Andrea
  See Nilsen, Anna
Bastyra, Judy 108
Basye, Dale E. 205
Bataille, Marion 1963- 209
Bat-Ami, Miriam 1950- 150
  Autobiography Feature 150
  Earlier sketches in SATA *82, 122*
Bate, Lucy 1939-1993 18
Bate, Norman (Arthur) 1916- 5
Bateman, Colin 1962- 172
Bateman, Donna M. 190
Bateman, Teresa 1957- 216
  Earlier sketches in SATA *112, 168*
Bates, Amy June 189
Bates, Barbara S(nedeker) 1919- 12
Bates, Betty
  See Bates, Elizabeth
Bates, Dianne 1948- 147
Bates, Elizabeth 1921- 19
Bates, Ivan 175
Bates, Katharine Lee 1859-1929 113
Bates, Martine
  See Leavitt, Martine
Bateson, Catherine 1960- 197
  Earlier sketch in SATA *157*
Batey, Tom 1946- 52
  Brief entry 41
Bath, Kevin P.
  See Bath, K.P.
Bath, K.P. 1959- 171

Batherman, Muriel
  See Sheldon, Muriel
Batson, Larry 1930- 35
Batt, Tanya Robyn 1970- 131
Battaglia, Aurelius 1910- 50
  Brief entry 33
Batten, H(arry) Mortimer 1888-1958 25
Batten, Mary 1937- 162
  Earlier sketches in SATA *5, 102*
Batterberry, Ariane Ruskin 1935- 13
Batterberry, Michael Carver 1932-2010 32
Battle-Lavert, Gwendolyn 1951- 155
  Earlier sketches in SATA *85, 131*
Battles, (Roxy) Edith 1921- 7
Baudouy, Michel-Aime 1909- 7
Bauer, A.C.E. 201
Bauer, Caroline Feller 1935- 98
  Brief entry 46
  Earlier sketch in SATA *52*
  See also SAAS *24*
Bauer, Fred 1934- 36
Bauer, Helen 1900-1988 2
Bauer, Joan 1951- 160
  Earlier sketch in SATA *117*
Bauer, Jutta 1955- 150
Bauer, Marion Dane 1938- 192
  Autobiography Feature 144
  Earlier sketches in SATA *20, 69, 113, 144*
  See also SAAS *9*
Bauer, Michael Gerard 1955(?)- 167
Bauer, Steven 1948- 125
Bauerschmidt, Marjorie 1926- 15
Baughman, Dorothy 1940- 61
Baum, Allyn Z(elton) 1924-1997 98
  Earlier sketch in SATA *20*
Baum, L. Frank
  See Thompson, Ruth Plumly
Baum, L. Frank 1856-1919 100
  Earlier sketch in SATA *18*
  See also CLR *107*
Baum, Louis 1948- 182
  Brief entry 52
  Earlier sketch in SATA *64*
Baum, Louis F.
  See Baum, L. Frank
Baum, Lyman Frank
  See Baum, L. Frank
Baum, Maxie 188
Baum, Willi 1931- 4
Bauman, Beth Ann 1964- 220
Baumann, Amy Beeching 1922- 10
Baumann, Amy Brown Beeching
  See Baumann, Amy Beeching
Baumann, Hans 1914- 2
  See also CLR *35*
Baumann, Kurt 1935- 21
Baumgartner, Barbara 1939- 86
Baurys, Flo 1938- 122
Baurys, Florence
  See Baurys, Flo
Bausum, Ann 173
Bawden, Nina 1925- 132
  Earlier sketches in SATA *4, 72*
  See also CLR *51*
  See also SAAS *16*
Bawden, Nina Mary Mabey
  See Bawden, Nina
Baxter, Roberta 1952- 219
Baxter, Valerie
  See Meynell, Laurence Walter
Bay, Jeanette Graham 1928- 88
Bayer, Harold
  See Gregg, Andrew K.
Bayer, Jane E. (?)-1985
  Obituary 44
Bayley, Nicola 1949- 129
  Earlier sketches in SATA *41, 69*
Baylor, Byrd 1924- 136
  Earlier sketches in SATA *16, 69*
  See also CLR *3*

Baynes, Pauline 1922-2008 .... *133*
   Obituary *196*
   Earlier sketches in SATA *19, 59*
Baynes, Pauline Diana
   See Baynes, Pauline
Bayoc, Cbabi *186*
Bayrock, Fiona *215*
BB
   See Watkins-Pitchford, Denys James
Beach, Charles
   See Reid, (Thomas) Mayne
Beach, Charles Amory *1*
Beach, Edward L. 1918-2002 .... *12*
   Obituary *140*
Beach, Edward Latimer
   See Beach, Edward L.
Beach, Lisa 1957- *111*
Beach, Lynn
   See Lance, Kathryn
Beach, Stewart T(aft) 1899-1979 .... *23*
Beachcroft, Nina 1931- *18*
Beagle, Peter S. 1939- *130*
   Earlier sketch in SATA *60*
Beagle, Peter Soyer
   See Beagle, Peter S.
Beaglehole, Helen 1946- *117*
Beake, Lesley 1949- *209*
Beale, Fleur *107*
Bealer, Alex W(inkler III) 1921-1980 .... *8*
   Obituary *22*
Beales, Valerie 1915- *74*
Beals, Carleton 1893-1979 .... *12*
Beals, Frank Lee 1881-1972
   Obituary *26*
Beam, Matt 1970- *187*
Beame, Rona 1934- *12*
Beamer, Charles 1942- *43*
Beamer, George Charles, Jr.
   See Beamer, Charles
Bean, Jonathan 1979- *194*
Bean, Normal
   See Burroughs, Edgar Rice
Beaney, Jan
   See Udall, Jan Beaney
Beaney, Jane
   See Udall, Jan Beaney
Bear, Carolyn
   See Rayban, Chloe
Bear, Greg 1951- *105*
   Earlier sketch in SATA *65*
Bear, Gregory Dale
   See Bear, Greg
Bearanger, Marie
   See Messier, Claire
Beard, Charles A(ustin) 1874-1948 .... *18*
Beard, Dan(iel Carter) 1850-1941 .... *22*
Beard, Darleen Bailey 1961- *96*
Bearden, Romare (Howard) 1914(?)-1988 ... *22*
   Obituary *56*
Beardmore, Cedric
   See Beardmore, George
Beardmore, George 1908-1979 .... *20*
Beardshaw, Rosalind 1969- *190*
Beardsley, Martyn R. 1957- *150*
Bearman, Jane (Ruth) 1917- *29*
Bearn, Emily *220*
Beaton, Clare 1947- *220*
   Earlier sketch in SATA *125*
Beatty, Elizabeth
   See Holloway, Teresa (Bragunier)
Beatty, Hetty Burlingame 1907-1971 .... *5*
Beatty, Jerome, Jr. 1918- *5*
Beatty, John (Louis) 1922-1975 .... *6*
   Obituary *25*
Beatty, Patricia (Robbins) 1922-1991 .... *73*
   Obituary *68*
   Earlier sketches in SATA *1, 30*
   See also SAAS *4*
Beaty, Andrea *186*
Beaty, Mary (T.) 1947- *146*
Beaudoin, Sean *210*

Beaumont, Karen 1954- *204*
Beccia, Carlyn *189*
Bechard, Margaret 1953- *164*
   Earlier sketch in SATA *85*
Bechtel, Louise Seaman 1894-1985 .... *4*
   Obituary *43*
Bechtold, Lisze *208*
Beck, Barbara L. 1927- *12*
Beck, Ian 1947- *190*
   Earlier sketch in SATA *138*
   See Beck, Ian Archibald
Beck, Peggy 1949- *171*
Beck, Scott *197*
Becker, Beril 1901-1999 .... *11*
Becker, Bonny *184*
Becker, Deborah Zimmett 1955- *138*
Becker, Helaine 1961- *142*
Becker, John (Leonard) 1901- *12*
Becker, John E(mil) 1942- *148*
Becker, Joyce 1936- *39*
Becker, May Lamberton 1873-1958 .... *33*
Becker, Neesa 1951- *123*
Becker, Shari *174*
Beckerman, Chad W. *198*
Beckett, Sheilah 1913- *33*
Beckhorn, Susan Williams 1953- *189*
Beckles Willson, Robina 1930- *27*
Beckman, Delores 1914-1994 .... *51*
Beckman, Gunnel 1910- *6*
   See also CLR *25*
   See also SAAS *9*
Beckman, Kaj
   See Beckman, Karin
Beckman, Karin 1913- *45*
Beckman, Per (Frithiof) 1913- *45*
Bedard, Michael 1949- *154*
   Earlier sketch in SATA *93*
   See also CLR *35*
Beddor, Frank *194*
Beddows, Eric
   See Nutt, Ken
Bedford, A. N.
   See Watson, Jane Werner
Bedford, Annie North
   See Watson, Jane Werner
Bedford, David *159*
Bedoukian, Kerop 1907-1981 .... *53*
Bee, Jay
   See Brainerd, John W(hiting)
Bee, William *188*
Beebe, B. F.
   See Johnson, B. F.
Beebe, (Charles) William 1877-1962 .... *19*
Beeby, Betty 1923- *25*
Beech, Mark 1971- *191*
Beech, Webb
   See Griffin, W. E. B.
Beecham, Jahnna *161*
Beechcroft, William
   See Hallstead, William F(inn III)
Beeching, Jack 1922- *14*
Beeke, Tiphanie *219*
   Earlier sketch in SATA *163*
Beeler, Janet
   See Shaw, Janet
Beeler, Nelson F(rederick) 1910-1978 .... *13*
Beere, Peter 1951- *97*
Beers, Dorothy Sands 1917- *9*
Beers, Lorna 1897-1989 .... *14*
Beers, V(ictor) Gilbert 1928- *130*
   Earlier sketch in SATA *9*
Beeton, Max
   See Redding, Robert Hull
Begay, Shonto 1954- *137*
Begaye, Lisa Shook
   See Beach, Lisa
Begin, Mary Jane 1963- *82*
Begin-Callanan, Mary Jane
   See Begin, Mary Jane
Begley, Kathleen A. 1948- *21*

Begley, Kathleen Anne
   See Begley, Kathleen A.
Beguine, Anna
   See Saintcrow, Lilith
Beha, Eileen *221*
Beha, Philippe *211*
Behan, Leslie
   See Gottfried, Theodore Mark
Behler, Deborah A. 1947- *145*
Behler, John L. 1943-2006 .... *145*
   Obituary *173*
Behler, John Luther
   See Behler, John L.
Behn, Harry 1898-1973 .... *2*
   Obituary *34*
Behnke, Frances L. *8*
Behr, Joyce 1929- *15*
Behrens, June York 1925- *19*
Behrman, Carol H(elen) 1925- *144*
   Earlier sketch in SATA *14*
Beifuss, John, (Jr.) 1959- *92*
Beil, Karen Magnuson 1950- *221*
   Earlier sketch in SATA *124*
Beiler, Edna 1923- *61*
Beingessner, Laura 1965- *220*
Beinicke, Steve 1956- *69*
Beirne, Barbara 1933- *71*
Beiser, Arthur 1931- *22*
Beiser, Germaine 1931- *11*
Belair, Richard L. 1934- *45*
Belaney, Archibald Stansfeld 1888-1938 .... *24*
   See also CLR *32*
Belasen, Amy 1983- *213*
Belbin, David 1958- *164*
   Earlier sketch in SATA *106*
Belden, Wilanne Schneider 1925- *56*
Belfrage, Sally 1936-1994 .... *65*
   Obituary *79*
Belknap, B. H.
   See Ellis, Edward S.
Belknap, Boynton
   See Ellis, Edward S.
Belknap, Boynton M.D.
   See Ellis, Edward S.
Bell, Anthea 1936- *148*
   Earlier sketch in SATA *88*
Bell, Cathleen Davitt 1971- *203*
Bell, Cece *202*
Bell, Clare (Louise) 1952- *99*
Bell, Corydon Whitten 1894-1980 .... *3*
Bell, David Owen 1949- *99*
Bell, Emerson
   See Stratemeyer, Edward L.
Bell, Emily Mary
   See Cason, Mabel Earp
Bell, Frank
   See Benson, Mildred
Bell, Gertrude (Wood) 1911-1987 .... *12*
Bell, Gina
   See Balzano, Jeanne (Koppel)
Bell, Hilari 1958- *197*
   Earlier sketch in SATA *151*
Bell, Jadrien
   See Golden, Christie
Bell, Janet
   See Clymer, Eleanor
Bell, Janet Cheatham 1937- *127*
Bell, Krista 1950- *215*
   Earlier sketch in SATA *126*
Bell, Krista Anne Blakeney
   See Bell, Krista
Bell, Margaret E(lizabeth) 1898-1990 .... *2*
Bell, Mary Reeves 1946- *88*
Bell, Norman (Edward) 1899- *11*
Bell, Raymond Martin 1907-1999 .... *13*
Bell, Siobhan *177*
Bell, Thelma Harrington 1896-1985 .... *3*
Bell, William 1945- *90*
   See also CLR *91*

Bellairs, John (Anthony) 1938-1991 .... *160*
　Obituary *66*
　Earlier sketches in SATA *2, 68*
　See also CLR *37*
Beller, Susan Provost 1949- *128*
　Earlier sketch in SATA *84*
　See also CLR *106*
Bellingham, Brenda 1931- *99*
　Brief entry *51*
Bello, Rosario de
　See De Bello, Rosario
Belloc, Hilaire 1870-1953 .... *112*
　See also YABC *1*
　See also CLR *102*
Belloc, Joseph Hilaire Pierre Sebastien Rene
　Swanton
　See Belloc, Hilaire
Belloc, Joseph Peter Rene Hilaire
　See Belloc, Hilaire
Belloc, Joseph Pierre Hilaire
　See Belloc, Hilaire
Belloli, Andrea P. A. 1947- *86*
Bell-Rehwoldt, Sheri 1962- *199*
Bellville, Cheryl Walsh 1944- *54*
　Brief entry *49*
Bell-Zano, Gina
　See Balzano, Jeanne (Koppel)
Belpre, Pura 1899-1982 .... *16*
　Obituary *30*
Belting, Natalia Maree 1915-1997 .... *6*
Belton, John Raynor 1931- *22*
Belton, Sandra 1939- *186*
　Earlier sketches in SATA *85, 134*
Belton, Sandra Yvonne
　See Belton, Sandra
Beltran, Alberto 1923- *43*
Beltran-Hernandez, Irene 1945- *74*
Belvedere, Lee
　See Grayland, Valerie (Merle Spanner)
Bemelmans, Ludwig 1898-1962 .... *100*
　Earlier sketch in SATA *15*
　See also CLR *93*
Benander, Carl D. 1941- *74*
Benary, Margot
　See Benary-Isbert, Margot
Benary-Isbert, Margot 1889-1979 .... *2*
　Obituary *21*
　See also CLR *12*
Benasutti, Marion 1908-1992 .... *6*
Benatar, Raquel 1955- *167*
Benchley, Nathaniel (Goddard) 1915-1981 .. *25*
　Obituary *28*
　Earlier sketch in SATA *3*
Benchley, Peter 1940-2006 .... *164*
　Earlier sketches in SATA *3, 89*
Benchley, Peter Bradford
　See Benchley, Peter
Bendall-Brunello, John *185*
Bender, Edna 1941- *92*
Bender, Esther 1942- *88*
Bender, Lucy Ellen 1942- *22*
Bender, Robert 1962- *160*
　Earlier sketch in SATA *79*
Bendick, Jeanne 1919- *135*
　Earlier sketches in SATA *2, 68*
　See also CLR *5*
　See also SAAS *4*
Bendick, Robert L(ouis) 1917- *11*
Benedetto, William R. 1928- *180*
Benedetto, William Ralph
　See Benedetto, William R.
Benedict, Andrew
　See Arthur, Robert, (Jr.)
Benedict, Dorothy Potter 1889-1979 .... *11*
　Obituary *23*
Benedict, Lois Trimble 1902-1967 .... *12*
Benedict, Rex 1920-1995 .... *8*
Benedict, Stewart H(urd) 1924- *26*
Beneduce, Ann Keay *128*
Benet, Laura 1884-1979 .... *3*
　Obituary *23*

Benet, Stephen Vincent 1898-1943
　See YABC *1*
Benet, Sula 1906-1982 .... *21*
　Obituary *33*
Ben-Ezer, Ehud 1936- *122*
Benezra, Barbara (Beardsley) 1921- *10*
Benham, Leslie 1922- *48*
Benham, Lois (Dakin) 1924- *48*
Benham, Mary Lile 1914-1991 .... *55*
Benjamin, E. M. J.
　See Bache, Ellyn
Benjamin, Floella 1949- *206*
Benjamin, Nora
　See Kubie, Nora Gottheil Benjamin
Benjamin, Saragail Katzman 1953- *86*
Benner, Cheryl 1962- *80*
Benner, Judith Ann 1942- *94*
Bennett, Alice
　See Ziner, Florence
Bennett, Cherie 1960- *158*
　Earlier sketch in SATA *97*
Bennett, Dorothea
　See Young, Dorothea Bennett
Bennett, Erin Susanne
　See Banks, Erin Bennett
Bennett, Holly 1957- *181*
Bennett, James (W.) 1942- *153*
　Autobiography Feature *153*
　Earlier sketches in SATA *93, 148*
Bennett, Jay 1912- *87*
　Brief entry *27*
　Earlier sketch in SATA *41*
　See also SAAS *4*
Bennett, Jill (Crawford) 1934- *41*
Bennett, John 1865-1956
　See YABC *1*
Bennett, Penelope (Agnes) 1938- *94*
Bennett, Rachel
　See Hill, Margaret (Ohler)
Bennett, Rainey 1907-1998 .... *15*
　Obituary *111*
Bennett, Richard 1899- *21*
Bennett, Russell H(oradley) 1896- *25*
Bennett, Veronica 1953- *178*
Bennett, William (John) 1943- *102*
Benning, Elizabeth
　See Rice, Bebe Faas
Benny, Mike 1964- *203*
Benson, Elizabeth P(olk) 1924- *65*
Benson, Kathleen 1947- *183*
　Earlier sketches in SATA *62, 111*
Benson, Linda M(aria) 1959- *84*
Benson, Mildred 1905-2002 .... *100*
　Obituary *135*
　Earlier sketches in SATA *1, 65, 67*
Benson, Mildred Augustine Wirt
　See Benson, Mildred
Benson, Mildred Wirt
　See Benson, Mildred
Benson, Millie
　See Benson, Mildred
Benson, Patrick 1956- *147*
Benson, Sally 1900-1972 .... *35*
　Obituary *27*
　Earlier sketch in SATA *1*
Bentley, Judith (McBride) 1945- *89*
　Earlier sketch in SATA *40*
Bentley, Karen
　See Taschek, Karen
Bentley, Nancy (L.) 1946- *78*
Bentley, Nicolas Clerihew 1907-1978
　Obituary *24*
Bentley, Phyllis Eleanor 1894-1977 .... *6*
　Obituary *25*
Bentley, Roy 1947- *46*
Bentley, William (George) 1916- *84*
Bently, Peter 1960- *221*
Benton, Jim 1963- *172*
ben Uzair, Salem
　See Horne, Richard Henry Hengist

Ben-Zvi, Rebeccca Tova
　See O'Connell, Rebecca
Bercaw, Edna Coe 1961- *124*
Berck, Judith 1960- *75*
Berelson, Howard 1940- *5*
Berends, Polly Berrien 1939- *50*
　Brief entry *38*
Berenstain, Jan 1923- *135*
　Earlier sketches in SATA *12, 64, 129*
　See also CLR *150*
　See also SAAS *20*
Berenstain, Janice
　See Berenstain, Jan
Berenstain, Michael 1951- *220*
　Earlier sketch in SATA *45*
Berenstain, Mike
　See Berenstain, Michael
Berenstain, Stan 1923-2005 .... *135*
　Obituary *169*
　Earlier sketches in SATA *12, 64, 129*
　See also CLR *150*
　See also SAAS *20*
Berenstain, Stanley
　See Berenstain, Stan
Berenzy, Alix 1957- *168*
　Earlier sketch in SATA *65*
Beresford, Elisabeth 1928-2010 .... *141*
　Earlier sketches in SATA *25, 86*
　See also SAAS *20*
Berg, Adriane G(ilda) 1948- *152*
Berg, Dave
　See Berg, David
Berg, David 1920-2002 .... *27*
　Obituary *137*
Berg, Elizabeth 1948- *104*
Berg, Jean Horton 1913-1995 .... *6*
Berg, Joan
　See Victor, Joan Berg
Berg, Ron 1952- *48*
Bergaust, Erik 1925-1978 .... *20*
Bergel, Colin J. 1963- *137*
Bergen, Joyce 1949- *95*
Berger, Barbara (Helen) 1945- *77*
Berger, Carin *185*
Berger, Gilda 1935- *88*
　Brief entry *42*
Berger, Joe 1970- *221*
Berger, Josef 1903-1971 .... *36*
Berger, Lou 1950- *213*
Berger, Melvin H. 1927- *158*
　Autobiography Feature *124*
　Earlier sketches in SATA *5, 88*
　See also CLR *32*
　See also SAAS *2*
Berger, Phil 1942-2001 .... *62*
Berger, Samantha 1969- *140*
Berger, Samantha Allison
　See Berger, Samantha
Berger, Terry 1933- *8*
Bergey, Alyce 1934- *45*
Bergey, Alyce Mae
　See Bergey, Alyce
Bergin, Mark 1961- *160*
　Earlier sketch in SATA *114*
Berglin, Ruth Marie 1970- *181*
Bergman, Donna 1934- *73*
Bergman, Mara 1956- *196*
Bergman, Tamar 1939- *95*
Bergren, Lisa T.
　See Bergren, Lisa Tawn
Bergren, Lisa Tawn *200*
Bergsma, Jody Lynn *163*
Bergstein, Rita M. *211*
Bergum, Constance R. 1952- *208*
　Earlier sketch in SATA *121*
Berk, Ari *208*
Berkebile, Fred D(onovan) 1900-1978
　Obituary *26*
Berkeley, Jon 1962- *204*
Berkes, Marianne *217*
　Earlier sketch in SATA *173*

Berkey, Barry Robert 1935- *24*
Berkowitz, Freda Pastor 1908-1994 .... *12*
Berkus, Clara Widess 1909- *78*
Berlan, Kathryn Hook 1946- *78*
Berlfein, Judy Reiss 1958- *79*
Berlin, Eric 1968- *195*
Berliner, Don 1930- *33*
Berliner, Franz 1930- *13*
Berlitz, Charles (L. Frambach) 1914-2003 ... *32*
   Obituary *151*
Berman, Linda 1948- *38*
Berman, Paul (Lawrence) 1949- *66*
Berman, Rachel 1946- *217*
Berna, Paul 1910-1994 .... *15*
   Obituary *78*
   See also CLR *19*
Bernadette
   See Watts, (Anna) Bernadette
Bernard, Bruce 1928-2000 .... *78*
   Obituary *124*
Bernard, George I. 1949- *39*
Bernard, Jacqueline (de Sieyes) 1921-1983 ... *8*
   Obituary *45*
Bernard, Patricia 1942- *181*
   Earlier sketch in SATA *106*
Bernard, Trish
   See Bernard, Patricia
Bernardin, James (B.) 1966- *112*
Bernardo, Anilu *184*
Bernards, Neal 1963- *71*
Bernasconi, Pablo 1973- *183*
Bernays, Anne 1930- *32*
Berner, Rotraut Susanne 1948- *214*
Bernhard, Durga T. 1961- *80*
Bernhard, Emery 1950- *80*
Bernheimer, Kate *201*
Bernier-Grand, Carmen T. 1947- *202*
Bernstein, Daryl (Evan) 1976- *81*
Bernstein, Joanne E(ckstein) 1943- *15*
Bernstein, Jonathan *217*
Bernstein, Margery 1933- *114*
Bernstein, Nina 1949- *180*
Bernstein, Theodore M(enline) 1904-1979 ... *12*
   Obituary *27*
Berrien, Edith Heal
   See Heal, Edith
Berrill, Jacquelyn (Batsel) 1905- *12*
Berrington, John
   See Brownjohn, Alan
Berry, B. J.
   See Berry, Barbara J.
Berry, Barbara J. 1937- *7*
Berry, Erick
   See Best, (Evangel) Allena Champlin
Berry, Holly 1957- *210*
Berry, James 1924- *110*
   Earlier sketch in SATA *67*
   See also CLR *143*
Berry, Jane Cobb 1915(?)-1979
   Obituary *22*
Berry, Joy 1944- *58*
   Brief entry *46*
Berry, Joy Wilt
   See Berry, Joy
Berry, Julie 1974- *218*
Berry, Lynne *190*
Berry, William D(avid) 1926- *14*
Bersani, Shennen 1961- *164*
Berson, Harold 1926- *4*
Bertagna, Julie 1962- *151*
Bertholf, Bret *189*
Bertin, Charles-Francois
   See Berlitz, Charles (L. Frambach)
Bertolet, Paul
   See McLaughlin, Frank
Berton, Pierre (Francis de Marigny)
   1920-2004 .... *99*
   Obituary *158*
Bertrand, Cecile 1953- *76*
Bertrand, Diane Gonzales 1956- *177*
   Earlier sketch in SATA *106*

Bertrand, Lynne 1963- *164*
   Earlier sketch in SATA *81*
Beskow, Elsa (Maartman) 1874-1953 .... *20*
   See also CLR *17*
Bess, Clayton
   See Locke, Robert
Besson, Luc 1959- *199*
Best, (Evangel) Allena Champlin 1892-1974 . *2*
   Obituary *25*
Best, Cari 1951- *200*
   Earlier sketches in SATA *107, 149*
Best, (Oswald) Herbert 1894-1980 .... *2*
Bestall, A(lfred) E(dmeades) 1892-1986 ...... *97*
   Obituary *48*
Betancourt, Jeanne 1941- *148*
   Brief entry *43*
   Earlier sketches in SATA *55, 96*
Beth, Mary
   See Miller, Mary Beth
Bethancourt, T. Ernesto
   See Paisley, Tom
Bethel, Dell 1929- *52*
Bethell, Jean (Frankenberry) 1922- *8*
Bethers, Ray 1902-1973 .... *6*
Bethke, Bruce Raymond 1955- *114*
Bethlen, T.D.
   See Silverberg, Robert
Bethune, J. G.
   See Ellis, Edward S.
Bethune, J. H.
   See Ellis, Edward S.
Betteridge, Anne
   See Potter, Margaret
Betteridge, Deirdre *214*
Bettina
   See Ehrlich, Bettina Bauer
Bettmann, Otto Ludwig 1903-1998 .... *46*
Bettoli, Delana *187*
Betts, James
   See Haynes, Betsy
Betz, Eva Kelly 1897-1968 .... *10*
Bevan, Tom 1868-1930(?)
   See YABC *2*
Bevis, Mary 1939- *202*
Bewick, Thomas 1753-1828 .... *16*
Beyer, Audrey White 1916- *9*
Beyer, Paul J. III 1950- *74*
Beynon, John
   See Harris, John (Wyndham Parkes Lucas)
   Beynon
Bezencon, Jacqueline (Buxcel) 1924- *48*
Bhatia, Jamunadevi 1919- *48*
Bhatia, June
   See Bhatia, Jamunadevi
Bial, Morrison David 1917- *62*
Bial, Raymond 1948- *165*
   Earlier sketches in SATA *76, 116*
Biala
   See Brustlein, Janice Tworkov
Biale, Rachel 1952- *99*
Bialk, Elisa
   See Krautter, Elisa (Bialk)
Bianchi, John 1947- *91*
Bianchi, Robert S(teven) 1943- *92*
Bianco, Margery
   See Bianco, Margery Williams
Bianco, Margery Williams 1881-1944 .... *15*
   See also CLR *146*
Bianco, Pamela 1906- *28*
Bibby, Violet 1908-1996 .... *24*
Bible, Charles 1937- *13*
Bibo, Bobette
   See Gugliotta, Bobette
Bice, Clare 1909-1976 .... *22*
Bickerstaff, Isaac
   See Swift, Jonathan
Bidner, Jenni 1963- *193*
Biedrzycki, David 1955- *219*

Biegel, Paul 1925- *79*
   Earlier sketch in SATA *16*
   See also CLR *27*
   See also SAAS *18*
Biemiller, Carl L(udwig), Jr.) 1912-1979 ..... *40*
   Obituary *21*
Bienenfeld, Florence L(ucille) 1929- *39*
Bierhorst, John (William) 1936- *149*
   Autobiography Feature *149*
   Earlier sketches in SATA *6, 91*
   See also SAAS *10*
Biggar, Joan R. 1936- *120*
Biggar, Joan Rawlins
   See Biggar, Joan R.
Biggle, Lloyd, Jr. 1923-2002 .... *65*
Biggs, Brian 1968- *192*
Bilal, Abdel W(ahab) 1970- *92*
Bilbrough, Norman 1941- *111*
Bildner, Phil *173*
Bileck, Marvin 1920- *40*
Bilibin, Ivan (Iakolevich) 1876-1942 .... *61*
Bill, Alfred Hoyt 1879-1964 .... *44*
Billam, Rosemary 1952- *61*
Billings, Charlene W(interer) 1941- *41*
Billingsley, Franny 1954- *132*
Billington, Elizabeth T(hain) *50*
   Brief entry *43*
Billout, Guy (Rene) 1941- *144*
   Earlier sketch in SATA *10*
   See also CLR *33*
Bilson, Geoffrey 1938-1987 .... *99*
Binch, Caroline (Lesley) 1947- *140*
   Earlier sketch in SATA *81*
Bing, Christopher (H.) *126*
Bingham, Caroline 1962- *158*
Bingham, Jane M. 1941- *163*
Bingham, Jane Marie
   See Bingham, Jane M.
Bingham, Janet 1959- *200*
Bingham, Kelly 1967- *207*
Bingham, Sam 1944- *96*
Bingham, Samuel A.
   See Bingham, Sam
Bingley, Margaret (Jane Kirby) 1947- *72*
Binkley, Anne
   See Rand, Ann (Binkley)
Binzen, Bill
   See Binzen, William
Binzen, William *24*
Birch, David (W.) 1913-1996 .... *89*
Birch, Reginald B(athurst) 1856-1943 .... *19*
Birchman, David 1949- *72*
Birchmore, Daniel A. 1951- *92*
Bird, Carmel 1940- *124*
Bird, E(lzy) J(ay) 1911- *58*
Birdsall, Jeanne 1952(?)- *170*
Birdseye, Tom 1951- *148*
   Earlier sketches in SATA *66, 98*
Birenbaum, Barbara 1941- *65*
Birmingham, Christian 1970- *220*
Birmingham, Lloyd P(aul) 1924- *83*
   Earlier sketch in SATA *12*
Birmingham, Ruth
   See Sorrells, Walter
Birney, Betty G. 1947- *169*
   Earlier sketch in SATA *98*
Biro, B.
   See Biro, B. S.
Biro, B. S. 1921- *1*
   See also CLR *28*
   See also SAAS *13*
Biro, Val
   See Biro, B. S.
Bischoff, Julia Bristol 1899-1970 .... *12*
Bishop, Bonnie 1943- *37*
Bishop, Claire Huchet 1899(?)-1993 .... *14*
   Obituary *74*
   See also CLR *80*
Bishop, Courtney
   See Ruemmler, John D(avid)
Bishop, Curtis (Kent) 1912-1967 .... *6*

Author Index

Bishop, Elizabeth 1911-1979
  Obituary 24
Bishop, Gavin 1946- 216
  Earlier sketches in SATA 97, 144
Bishop, Kathleen Wong 1954- 120
Bishop, Kathy
  See Bishop, Kathleen Wong
Bishop, Nic 1955- 161
  Earlier sketch in SATA 107
Bisset, Donald 1910-1995 86
  Earlier sketch in SATA 7
Bisson, Terry 1942- 99
Bisson, Terry Ballantine
  See Bisson, Terry
Bitter, Gary G(len) 1940- 22
Bixby, William (Courtney) 1920-1986 6
  Obituary 47
Bjoerk, Christina 1938- 99
  Earlier sketch in SATA 67
  See also CLR 22
Bjork, Christina
  See Bjoerk, Christina
Bjorklund, Lorence F. 1913-1978 35
  Brief entry 32
Bjorkman, Steve 163
Blabey, Aaron 1975(?)- 214
Black, Algernon David 1900-1993 12
  Obituary 76
Black, Holly 1971- 210
  Earlier sketch in SATA 147
Black, Irma Simonton 1906-1972 2
  Obituary 25
Black, Kat 217
Black, Katherine
  See Black, Kat
Black, Mansell
  See Trevor, Elleston
Black, MaryAnn
  See Easley, MaryAnn
Black, Susan Adams 1953- 40
Blackall, Bernie 1956- 126
Blackall, Sophie 182
Blackburn, Claire
  See Altman, Linda Jacobs
Blackburn, John(ny) Brewton 1952- 15
Blackburn, Joyce Knight 1920- 29
Blacker, Terence 1948- 194
Blacker, Tina
  See Louise, Tina
Blackett, Veronica Heath 1927- 12
Blackie, Jean Cutler 1943- 79
Blacklin, Malcolm
  See Chambers, Aidan
Blacklock, Dyan 1951- 112
Blackman, Malorie 1962- 196
  Earlier sketches in SATA 83, 128
Blackton, Peter
  See Wilson, Lionel
Blackwood, Alan 1932- 70
Blackwood, Freya 199
Blackwood, Gary
  See Blackwood, Gary L.
Blackwood, Gary L. 1945- 169
  Earlier sketches in SATA 72, 118
Blade, Alexander
  See Garrett, Randall
  and Hamilton, Edmond
  and Silverberg, Robert
Blades, Ann (Sager) 1947- 69
  Earlier sketch in SATA 16
  See also CLR 15
Bladow, Suzanne Wilson 1937- 14
Blaine, Chris
  See Gardner, Craig Shaw
Blaine, John
  See Goodwin, Harold L(eland)
Blaine, Marge
  See Blaine, Margery Kay
Blaine, Margery Kay 1937- 11
Blair, Alison
  See Lerangis, Peter

Blair, Anne Denton 1914-1993 46
Blair, David Nelson 1954- 80
Blair, Eric
  See Orwell, George
Blair, Jay 1953- 45
Blair, Lucile
  See Yeakley, Marjory Hall
Blair, Margaret Whitman 1951- 124
Blair, Mary 1911-1978 195
Blair, Pauline Hunter
  See Clarke, Pauline
Blair, Ruth Van Ness 1912-1999 12
Blair, Shannon
  See Kaye, Marilyn
Blair, Walter 1900-1992 12
  Obituary 72
Blaisdell, Bob
  See Blaisdell, Robert
Blaisdell, Robert 1959- 105
Blake, Bronwyn 1940- 149
Blake, Francis 198
Blake, Jon 1954- 171
  Earlier sketch in SATA 78
Blake, Olive
  See Supraner, Robyn
Blake, Quentin 1932- 211
  Earlier sketches in SATA 9, 52, 96, 125
  See also CLR 31
Blake, Robert 1949- 42
Blake, Robert J. 160
Blake, Walker E.
  See Griffin, W. E. B.
Blake, William 1757-1827 30
  See also CLR 52
Blakely, Gloria 1950- 139
Blakely, Roger K. 1922- 82
Blakeney, Jay D.
  See Chester, Deborah
Blakeslee, Lys 1985- 218
Blakey, Nancy 1955- 94
Blanc, Esther S. 1913-1997 66
Blanc, Mel 1908-1989
  Obituary 64
Blanchard, Patricia 125
Blanchet, M(uriel) Wylie 1891-1961 106
Blanco, Richard L(idio) 1926- 63
Bland, E.
  See Nesbit, E.
Bland, Edith Nesbit
  See Nesbit, E.
Bland, Fabian
  See Nesbit, E.
Blane, Gertrude
  See Blumenthal, Gertrude
Blank, Clarissa Mabel 1915-1965 62
Blankenship, LeeAnn 1944- 181
Blassingame, Wyatt Rainey 1909-1985 34
  Obituary 41
  Earlier sketch in SATA 1
Blatchford, Claire H. 1944- 94
Blauer, Ettagale 1940- 49
Bleck, Linda 207
Bledsoe, Glen L. 1951- 108
Bledsoe, Glen Leonard
  See Bledsoe, Glen L.
Bledsoe, Karen E. 1962- 167
  Earlier sketch in SATA 108
Bledsoe, Karen Elizabeth
  See Bledsoe, Karen E.
Bledsoe, Lucy Jane 1957- 162
  Earlier sketch in SATA 97
Bleeker, Sonia
  See Zim, Sonia Bleeker
Blegen, Daniel M. 1950- 92
Blegvad, Erik 1923- 132
  Earlier sketches in SATA 14, 66
Blegvad, Lenore 1926- 176
  Earlier sketches in SATA 14, 66
Bley, Anette 1967- 188
Blish, James 1921-1975 66

Blish, James Benjamin
  See Blish, James
Blishen, Edward (William) 1920-1996 66
  Obituary 93
  Earlier sketch in SATA 8
Bliss, Corinne Demas 1947- 203
  Earlier sketches in SATA 37, 131
Bliss, Frederick
  See Card, Orson Scott
Bliss, Gillian
  See Paton Walsh, Jill
Bliss, Harry 1964- 196
  Earlier sketch in SATA 156
Bliss, Reginald
  See Wells, H. G.
Bliss, Ronald G(ene) 1942- 12
Blitt, Barry 187
Bliven, Bruce, Jr. 1916-2002 2
Blixen, Karen 1885-1962 44
Blizzard, Gladys S. (?)-1992 79
Blobaum, Cindy 1966- 123
Bloch, Lucienne 1909-1999 10
Bloch, Marie Halun 1910-1998 6
  See also SAAS 9
Bloch, Robert (Albert) 1917-1994 12
  Obituary 82
Bloch, Serge 1956- 213
Blochman, Lawrence G(oldtree)
  1900-1975 22
Block, Francesca Lia 1962- 213
  Earlier sketches in SATA 80, 116, 158
  See also CLR 116
  See also SAAS 21
Block, Irvin 1917- 12
Blomgren, Jennifer (Alice) 1954- 136
Blonder, Terry Joyce
  See Golson, Terry
Blood, Charles Lewis 1929- 28
Bloom, Barbara Lee 1943- 146
Bloom, Freddy 1914-2000 37
  Obituary 121
Bloom, Lloyd 1947- 108
  Brief entry 43
Bloom, Suzanne 1950- 172
Bloomfield, Michaela 1966- 70
Bloor, Edward 1950- 201
  Earlier sketches in SATA 98, 155
Bloor, Edward William
  See Bloor, Edward
Blos, Joan W. 1928- 153
  Autobiography Feature 153
  Brief entry 27
  Earlier sketches in SATA 33, 69, 109
  See also CLR 18
  See also SAAS 11
Blos, Joan Winsor
  See Blos, Joan W.
Blough, Glenn O(rlando) 1907-1995 1
Blue, Rose 1931- 166
  Autobiography Feature 117
  Earlier sketches in SATA 5, 91, 93
  See also SAAS 24
Blue, Zachary
  See Stine, R.L.
Bluemle, Elizabeth 209
Bluggage, Oranthy
  See Alcott, Louisa May
Blumberg, Leda 1956- 59
Blumberg, Rhoda 1917- 123
  Earlier sketches in SATA 35, 70
  See also CLR 21
Blume, Judy 1938- 195
  Earlier sketches in SATA 2, 31, 79, 142
  See also CLR 69
Blume, Judy Sussman
  See Blume, Judy
Blume, Lesley M.M. 1975- 180
Blumenthal, Deborah 204
  Earlier sketch in SATA 161
Blumenthal, Gertrude 1907-1971
  Obituary 27

Blumenthal, Shirley 1943- 46
Blutig, Eduard
  See Gorey, Edward (St. John)
Bly, Janet 1945- 43
Bly, Janet Chester
  See Bly, Janet
Bly, Stephen A(rthur) 1944- 116
  Earlier sketch in SATA 43
Blyler, Allison Lee 1966- 74
Blythe, Gary 1959- 185
Blyton, Carey 1932-2002 9
  Obituary 138
Blyton, Enid 1897-1968 25
  See also CLR 31
Blyton, Enid Mary
  See Blyton, Enid
Bo, Ben
  See Richardson, V.A.
Boardman, Fon Wyman, Jr. 1911-2000 6
Boardman, Gwenn R.
  See Petersen, Gwenn Boardman
Boase, Wendy 1944-1999 28
  Obituary 110
Boatner, Mark Mayo III 1921- 29
Bobbe, Dorothie de Bear 1905-1975 1
  Obituary 25
Bober, Natalie S. 1930- 134
  Earlier sketch in SATA 87
  See also SAAS 23
Bobette, Bibo
  See Gugliotta, Bobette
Bobri, Vladimir V. 1898-1986 47
  Brief entry 32
Bobritsky, Vladimir
  See Bobri, Vladimir V.
Bochak, Grayce 1956- 76
Bock, Hal
  See Bock, Harold I.
Bock, Harold I. 1939- 10
Bock, William Sauts Netamux'we 1939- 14
Bodanis, David 179
Bode, Janet 1943-1999 96
  Obituary 118
  Earlier sketch in SATA 60
Bode, N.E.
  See Baggott, Julianna
Bodecker, N(iels) M(ogens) 1922-1988 73
  Obituary 54
  Earlier sketch in SATA 8
Bodeen, S. A. 1965- 158
  Earlier sketch in SATA 114
Boden, Hilda
  See Bodenham, Hilda Morris
Bodenham, Hilda Morris 1901- 13
Bodett, Thomas Edward 1955- 70
Bodett, Tom
  See Bodett, Thomas Edward
Bodie, Idella F(allaw) 1925- 89
  Earlier sketch in SATA 12
Bodker, Cecil
  See Bodker, Cecil
Bodker, Cecil 1927- 133
  Earlier sketch in SATA 14
  See also CLR 23
Bodsworth, (Charles) Fred(erick) 1918- 27
Boeckman, Charles 1920- 12
Boegehold, Betty (Doyle) 1913-1985
  Obituary 42
Boelts, Maribeth 1964- 200
  Earlier sketches in SATA 78, 163
Boerst, William J. 1939- 170
  Earlier sketch in SATA 121
Boesch, Mark J(oseph) 1917- 12
Boesen, Victor 1908- 16
Bogacki, Tomek 1950- 214
  Earlier sketch in SATA 138
Bogaerts, Gert 1965- 80
Bogan, Paulette 1960- 201
  Earlier sketch in SATA 129
Bogart, Jo Ellen 1945- 92
  See also CLR 59

Boggs, Ralph Steele 1901-1994 7
Bograd, Larry 1953- 89
  Earlier sketch in SATA 33
  See also SAAS 21
Bogue, Gary 1938- 195
Bogue, Gary L.
  See Bogue, Gary
Bohdal, Susi 1951- 101
  Earlier sketch in SATA 22
Bohlen, Nina 1931- 58
Bohlmeijer, Arno 1956- 94
Bohner, Charles (Henry) 1927- 62
Bohnhoff, Maya Kaathryn 1954- 88
Boie, Kirsten 1950- 221
Boiger, Alexandra 178
Boissard, Janine 1932- 59
Bojunga, Lygia
  See Nunes, Lygia Bojunga
Bojunga-Nunes, Lygia
  See Nunes, Lygia Bojunga
Bok, Arthur
  See Bok, Chip
Bok, Chip 1952- 205
Bolam, Emily 1969- 206
Boland, Janice 98
Bolden, Tonya 1959- 188
  Earlier sketches in SATA 79, 138
Bolden, Tonya Wilyce
  See Bolden, Tonya
Boles, Paul Darcy 1916-1984 9
  Obituary 38
Bolian, Polly 1925- 4
Bollen, Roger 1941(?)- 83
  Brief entry 29
Bolliger, Max 1929- 7
Bollinger, Max 1929- 167
Bollinger, Peter 172
Bolognese, Don(ald Alan) 1934- 129
  Earlier sketches in SATA 24, 71
Bolognese, Elaine 1933- 23
Bolotin, Norman (Phillip) 1951- 93
Bolton, Carole 1926- 6
Bolton, Elizabeth
  See St. John, Nicole
Bolton, Evelyn
  See Bunting, Eve
Bonar, Veronica
  See Bailey, Donna (Veronica Anne)
Bond, B. J.
  See Heneghan, James
Bond, Bruce 1939- 61
Bond, Felicia 1954- 219
  Earlier sketches in SATA 49, 126
Bond, Gladys Baker 1912- 14
Bond, Higgins 1951- 220
  Earlier sketches in SATA 83, 177
Bond, J. Harvey
  See Winterbotham, R(ussell) R(obert)
Bond, (Thomas) Michael 1926- 157
  Earlier sketches in SATA 6, 58
  See also CLR 95
  See also SAAS 3
Bond, Nancy 1945- 159
  Autobiography Feature 159
  Earlier sketches in SATA 22, 82
  See also CLR 11
  See also SAAS 13
Bond, Nancy Barbara
  See Bond, Nancy
Bond, Rebecca 1972- 214
  Earlier sketch in SATA 130
Bond, Ruskin 1934- 87
  Earlier sketch in SATA 14
Bondie, J. D.
  See Cunningham, Chet
Bondoux, Anne-Laure 1971- 175
Bone, Ian 1956- 158
  Earlier sketch in SATA 117
Bonehill, Captain Ralph
  See Stratemeyer, Edward L.

Bonestell, Chesley 1888-1986
  Obituary 48
Bonham, Barbara Thomas 1926- 7
Bonham, Frank 1914-1989 49
  Obituary 62
  Earlier sketch in SATA 1
  See also SAAS 3
Boniface, William 1963- 182
  Earlier sketch in SATA 102
Bonino, Louise
  See Williams, Louise Bonino
Bonk, John J. 189
Bonn, Pat
  See Bonn, Patricia Carolyn
Bonn, Patricia Carolyn 1948- 43
Bonner, Hannah 197
Bonner, Mary Graham 1890-1974 19
Bonner, Mike 1951- 121
Bonners, Susan 1947- 85
  Brief entry 48
Bonnett-Rampersaud, Louise 173
Bonning, Tony 1948- 169
Bonsall, Crosby Barbara (Newell)
  1921-1995 23
  Obituary 84
Bonsall, Joseph S. 1948- 119
Bonsignore, Joan 1959- 140
Bontemps, Arna 1902-1973 44
  Obituary 24
  Earlier sketch in SATA 2
  See also CLR 6
Bontemps, Arnaud Wendell
  See Bontemps, Arna
Bonzon, Paul-Jacques 1908-1978 22
Boock, Paula 1964- 134
Booher, Dianna Daniels 1948- 33
Book, Rick 1949- 119
Book, Rita
  See Holub, Joan
Bookman, Charlotte
  See Zolotow, Charlotte
Boon, Debbie 1960- 103
Boon, Emilie (Laetitia) 1958- 86
Boone, Charles Eugene
  See Boone, Pat
Boone, Pat 1934- 7
Booraem, Ellen 211
Boorman, Linda 1940- 46
Boorman, Linda Kay
  See Boorman, Linda
Boorstin, Daniel J(oseph) 1914-2004 52
Boos, Ben 1971- 206
Booth, Coe 187
Booth, Ernest Sheldon 1915-1984 43
Booth, George 1926- 191
Booth, Graham (Charles) 1935- 37
Bootman, Colin 159
Borden, Louise 1949- 190
  Autobiography Feature 141
  Earlier sketches in SATA 68, 104, 141
Bordier, Georgette 1924- 16
Borgman, James
  See Borgman, Jim
Borgman, James Mark
  See Borgman, Jim
Borgman, Jim 1954- 122
Borgo, Lacy Finn 1972- 194
Boring, Mel 1939- 168
  Earlier sketch in SATA 35
Borja, Corinne 1929- 22
Borja, Robert 1923- 22
Borland, Hal
  See Borland, Harold Glen
Borland, Harold Glen 1900-1978 5
  Obituary 24
Borland, Kathryn Kilby 1916- 16
Borlenghi, Patricia 1951- 79
Born, Adolf 1930- 49
Bornstein, Ruth Lercher
  See Bornstein-Lercher, Ruth

Bornstein-Lercher, Ruth 1927- 88
  Autobiography Feature 107
  Earlier sketch in SATA 14
Borris, Albert 221
Borski, Lucia Merecka 18
Borten, Helen Jacobson 1930- 5
Bortolotti, Dan 1969- 157
Borton, Elizabeth
  See Trevino, Elizabeth B(orton) de
Borton, Lady 1942- 98
Borton de Trevino, Elizabeth
  See Trevino, Elizabeth B(orton) de
Bortstein, Larry 1942-2010 16
Bortz, Alfred B(enjamin) 1944- 139
  Earlier sketch in SATA 74
Bortz, Fred
  See Bortz, Alfred B(enjamin)
Bosch, Pseudonymous 199
Bosco, Jack
  See Holliday, Joseph
Bose, Mitali
  See Perkins, Mitali
Boshell, Gordon 1908-1991 15
Boshinski, Blanche 1922- 10
Bosman, Paul 1929- 107
Bosse, Malcolm (Joseph, Jr.) 1926-2002 136
  Earlier sketch in SATA 35
Bosserman, Charles Phillip
  See Bosserman, Phillip
Bosserman, Phillip 1931- 84
Bossley, Michele Martin 1969- 219
Bossom, Naomi 1933- 35
Bostock, Mike 1962- 114
Boston, L(ucy) M(aria Wood) 1892-1990 19
  Obituary 64
  See also CLR 3
Bostrom, Kathleen (Susan) Long 1954- 139
Bostrom, Kathy
  See Bostrom, Kathleen (Susan) Long
Boswell, Addie 208
Boswell, Addie Kay
  See Boswell, Addie
Bosworth, J. Allan 1925- 19
Bothwell, Jean (?)-1977 2
Botkin, B(enjamin) A(lbert) 1901-1975 40
Botsford, Ward 1927-2004 66
Botting, Douglas (Scott) 1934- 43
Bottner, Barbara 1943- 170
  Autobiography Feature 121
  Earlier sketches in SATA 14, 93
  See also SAAS 26
Bottone, Frank G., Jr. 1969- 141
Bouchard, David 1952- 213
  Earlier sketch in SATA 117
Boucher, (Clarence) Carter 1954- 129
Boudelang, Bob
  See Pell, Ed(ward)
Boughton, Richard 1954- 75
Boulet, Susan Seddon 1941- 50
Boulle, Pierre (Francois Marie-Louis)
  1912-1994 22
  Obituary 78
Boulton, Jane 1921- 91
Bouma, Paddy 1947- 128
Bour, Daniele 1939- 62
Bourbonniere, Sylvie 1966- 182
Bourdon, David 1934-1998 46
Bourgeois, Paulette 1951- 153
Bourne, Lesley
  See Marshall, Evelyn
Bourne, Miriam Anne 1931-1989 16
  Obituary 63
Boutavant, Marc 1970- 200
Boutet de Monvel, (Louis) M(aurice)
  1850(?)-1913 30
  See also CLR 32
Bouwman, Heather M.
  See Bouwman, H.M.
Bouwman, H.M. 209

Bova, Ben 1932- 133
  Earlier sketches in SATA 6, 68
  See also CLR 96
Bova, Benjamin William
  See Bova, Ben
Bovaird, Anne E(lizabeth) 1960- 90
Bow, Patricia 1946- 168
Bowden, Joan Chase 1925- 51
  Brief entry 38
Bowe, Julie 1962- 194
Bowen, Alexandria Russell 97
Bowen, Andy Russell
  See Bowen, Alexandria Russell
Bowen, Anne 1952- 202
  Earlier sketch in SATA 170
Bowen, Betty Morgan
  See West, Betty
Bowen, Catherine (Shober) Drinker
  1897-1973 7
Bowen, David
  See Bowen, Joshua David
Bowen, Fred 1953- 136
Bowen, Joshua David 1930- 22
Bowen, Rhys
  See Quin-Harkin, Janet
Bowen, Robert Sydney 1900-1977 52
  Obituary 21
Bowermaster, Jon 1954- 135
  Earlier sketch in SATA 77
Bowers, Terrell L. 1945- 101
Bowers, Terry
  See Bowers, Terrell L.
Bowers, Tim 218
  Earlier sketch in SATA 185
Bowie, C. W.
  See Old, Wendie C(orbin)
  and Wirths, Claudine (Turner) G(ibson)
Bowie, Jim
  See Norwood, Victor G(eorge) C(harles)
  and Stratemeyer, Edward L.
Bowkett, Stephen 1953- 67
Bowler, Jan Brett
  See Brett, Jan
Bowler, Tim 1953- 209
  Earlier sketch in SATA 149
Bowman, Catherine
  See Smith, Cat Bowman
Bowman, Crystal 1951- 105
Bowman, James Cloyd 1880-1961 23
Bowman, John S(tewart) 1931- 16
Bowman, Kathleen (Gill) 1942- 52
  Brief entry 40
Bowman, Leslie
  See Bowman, Leslie W.
Bowman, Leslie W. 182
Bowsher, Melodie 195
Boxall, Ed 178
Boyce, Frank Cottrell 182
Boyce, George A(rthur) 1898- 19
Boyd, Candy Dawson 1946- 72
  See also CLR 50
Boyd, Pauline
  See Schock, Pauline
Boyd, Selma
  See Acuff, Selma Boyd
Boyd, Waldo T. 1918- 18
Boyden, Linda 1948- 143
Boyer, Allen B. 1963- 153
Boyer, Robert E(rnst) 1929- 22
Boyes, Vivien 1952- 106
Boyes, Vivien Elizabeth
  See Boyes, Vivien
Boyle, Ann (Peters) 1916- 10
Boyle, Eleanor Vere (Gordon) 1825-1916 28
Boyle, Robert H. 1928- 65
Boylston, Helen Dore 1895-1984 23
  Obituary 39
Boyne, John 1971- 181

Boynton, Sandra (Keith) 1953- 152
  Brief entry 38
  Earlier sketches in SATA 57, 107
  See also CLR 105
Boz
  See Dickens, Charles
Braasch, Gary 201
Bracken, Charles
  See Pellowski, Michael (Joseph)
Brackers de Hugo, Pierre 1960- 115
Brackett, Dolli Tingle 1911-1993 137
Brackett, Virginia 1950- 166
  Earlier sketch in SATA 121
Brackett, Virginia Roberts Meredith
  See Brackett, Virginia
Bradbury, Bianca (Ryley) 1908-1982 56
  Earlier sketch in SATA 3
Bradbury, Edward P.
  See Moorcock, Michael
Bradbury, Ray 1920- 123
  Earlier sketches in SATA 11, 64
Bradbury, Ray Douglas
  See Bradbury, Ray
Bradby, Marie 161
Bradfield, Carl 1942- 91
Bradford, Ann (Liddell) 1917- 56
  Brief entry 38
Bradford, Barbara Taylor 1933- 66
Bradford, Chris 1974- 215
Bradford, Karleen 1936- 96
  Earlier sketch in SATA 48
Bradford, Lois J(ean) 1936- 36
Bradford, Richard (Roark) 1932-2002 59
  Obituary 135
Bradley, Duane
  See Sanborn, Duane
Bradley, Kimberly Brubaker 1967- 179
Bradley, Marion Zimmer 1930-1999 139
  Obituary 116
  Earlier sketch in SATA 90
  See also CLR 158
Bradley, Timothy J. 193
Bradley, Virginia 1912- 23
Bradley, Will
  See Strickland, Brad
Bradman, Tony 1954- 152
  Earlier sketch in SATA 81
Bradshaw, Gillian (Joan) 1949- 118
Bradshaw, Gillian 1956- 127
Bradshaw, Gillian Marucha
  See Bradshaw, Gillian
Bradstreet, T. J.
  See Thesman, Jean
Brady, Esther Wood 1905-1987 31
  Obituary 53
Brady, Irene 1943- 4
Brady, Kimberley S. 1953- 101
Brady, Kimberley Smith
  See Brady, Kimberley S.
Brady, Lillian 1902- 28
Bragdon, Elspeth MacDuffie 1897-1980 6
Bragdon, Lillian Jacot 24
Brager, Bruce L. 1949- 146
Bragg, Mabel Caroline 1870-1945 24
Bragg, Michael 1948- 46
Bragg, Ruth Gembicki 1943- 77
Brahm, Sumishta 1954- 58
Brailsford, Frances
  See Wosmek, Frances
Brainerd, John W(hiting) 1918- 65
Braithwaite, Althea 1940- 23
  Autobiography Feature 119
  See also SAAS 24
Bram, Elizabeth 1948- 30
Brancato, Robin F. 1936- 97
  See also CLR 32
  See also SAAS 9
Brancato, Robin Fidler
  See Brancato, Robin F.
Branch, Muriel Miller 1943- 152
  Earlier sketch in SATA 94

Brand, Christianna
  See Lewis, Mary
Brand, Rebecca
  See Charnas, Suzy McKee
Brande, Robin 194
Brandel, Marc 1919- 71
Brandenberg, Alexa (Demetria) 1966- 97
Brandenberg, Aliki 1929- 157
  Earlier sketches in SATA 2, 35, 75, 113
  See also CLR 71
Brandenberg, Franz 1932- 75
  Earlier sketches in SATA 8, 35
Brandenburg, Jim 1945- 87
Brandhorst, Carl T(heodore) 1898-1988 23
Brandis, Marianne 1938- 149
  Earlier sketches in SATA 59, 96
Brandon, Brumsic, Jr. 1927- 9
Brandon, Curt
  See Bishop, Curtis (Kent)
Brandreth, Gyles 1948- 28
Brandreth, Gyles Daubeney
  See Brandreth, Gyles
Brandt, Catharine 1905-1997 40
Brandt, Keith
  See Sabin, Louis
Brandt, Sue R(eading) 1916- 59
Branfield, John (Charles) 1931- 11
Branford, Henrietta 1946-1999 106
Branley, Franklyn M(ansfield) 1915-2002 .. 136
  Earlier sketches in SATA 4, 68
  See also CLR 13
  See also SAAS 16
Brannen, Sarah S. 202
Branscum, Robbie (Tilley) 1937-1997 72
  Obituary 96
  Earlier sketch in SATA 23
  See also SAAS 17
Bransom, (John) Paul 1885-1979 43
Brashares, Ann 1967- 188
  Earlier sketch in SATA 145
  See also CLR 113
Brassard, France 1963- 186
Braswell, E.J.
  See Lynn, Tracy
Braswell, Elizabeth J.
  See Lynn, Tracy
Braswell, Liz
  See Lynn, Tracy
Bratton, Helen 1899-1986 4
Bratun, Katy 1950- 160
  Earlier sketch in SATA 83
Braude, Michael 1936- 23
Braun, Lilian Jackson 1916(?)- 109
Brautigan, Richard 1935-1984 56
Brautigan, Richard Gary
  See Brautigan, Richard
Bray, Libba 203
  Earlier sketch in SATA 159
Bray, Martha E.
  See Bray, Libba
Braymer, Marjorie Elizabeth 1911-1988 6
Brazil, Angela 1869(?)-1947
  See CLR 157
Breathed, Berke 1957- 161
  Earlier sketch in SATA 86
Breathed, Berkeley
  See Breathed, Berke
Breathed, Guy Berkeley
  See Breathed, Berke
Brecht, Edith 1895-1975 6
  Obituary 25
Breck, Vivian
  See Breckenfeld, Vivian Gurney
Breckenfeld, Vivian Gurney 1895-1992 1
Breda, Tjalmar
  See DeJong, David C(ornel)
Bredeson, Carmen 1944- 163
  Earlier sketch in SATA 98
Breen, M.E. 216
Breen, Molly
  See Breen, M.E.

Breen, Steve 1970- 186
Breinburg, Petronella 1927- 11
  See also CLR 31
Breisky, William J(ohn) 1928- 22
Brenaman, Miriam 172
Brennan, Caitlin
  See Tarr, Judith
Brennan, Gale (Patrick) 1927- 64
  Brief entry 53
Brennan, Herbie 1940- 214
  Autobiography Feature 214
  Earlier sketches in SATA 140, 183
Brennan, J. H.
  See Brennan, Herbie
Brennan, James Herbert
  See Brennan, Herbie
Brennan, Jan
  See Brennan, Herbie
Brennan, Joseph Lomas 1903-2000 6
Brennan, Linda Crotta 1952- 130
Brennan, Sarah Rees 1983- 221
Brennan, Tim
  See Conroy, John Wesley
Brennan-Nelson, Denise 203
Brenner, Anita 1905-1974 56
Brenner, Barbara (Johnes) 1925- 124
  Earlier sketches in SATA 4, 42, 76
  See also SAAS 14
Brenner, Fred 1920- 36
  Brief entry 34
Brent, Hope 1935(?)-1984
  Obituary 39
Brent, Stuart 1912-2010 14
Breskin, Jane
  See Zalben, Jane Breskin
Breslin, Theresa 128
  Autobiography Feature 128
  Earlier sketch in SATA 70
Breslow, Maurice 1935- 72
Breslow, Maurice A
  See Breslow, Maurice
Breslow, Susan 1951- 69
Brett, Bernard 1925- 22
Brett, Grace N(eff) 1900-1975 23
Brett, Jan 1949- 171
  Earlier sketches in SATA 42, 71, 130
  See also CLR 27
Brett, Jan Churchill
  See Brett, Jan
Brett Bowler, Jan
  See Brett, Jan
Brewer, Heather 1973- 196
Brewer, James D. 1951- 108
Brewer, Sally King 1947- 33
Brewster, Benjamin
  See Folsom, Franklin (Brewster)
Brewster, Hugh 1950- 191
  Earlier sketch in SATA 95
Brewster, Patience 1952- 97
Brewton, John E(dmund) 1898-1982 5
Breznak, Irene 218
Brian, Janeen (Paulette) 1948- 141
Briant, Ed 218
  Earlier sketch in SATA 180
Brick, John 1922-1973 10
Brickman, Robin D. 1954- 155
Bride, Nadja
  See Nobisso, Josephine
Bridgers, Sue Ellen 1942- 90
  Autobiography Feature 109
  Earlier sketch in SATA 22
  See also CLR 18
  See also SAAS 1
Bridges, Laurie
  See Bruck, Lorraine
Bridges, Ruby (Nell) 1954- 131
Bridges, William (Andrew) 1901-1984 5
Bridwell, Norman (Ray) 1928- 138
  Earlier sketches in SATA 4, 68
  See also CLR 96
Brier, Howard M(axwell) 1903-1969 8

Brierley, (Louise) 1958- 59
Briggs, Katharine Mary 1898-1980 101
  Obituary 25
Briggs, Peter 1921-1975 39
  Obituary 31
Briggs, Raymond 1934- 184
  Earlier sketches in SATA 23, 66, 131
  See also CLR 10
Briggs, Raymond Redvers
  See Briggs, Raymond
Bright, Paul 1949- 182
Bright, Robert Sr.) 1902-1988 63
  Obituary 60
  Earlier sketch in SATA 24
Bright, Robert Douglas
  See Bright, Robert Sr.)
Bright, Sarah
  See Shine, Deborah
Brightfield, Richard 1927- 65
  Brief entry 53
Brightfield, Rick
  See Brightfield, Richard
Brighton, Catherine 1943- 206
  Earlier sketches in SATA 65, 107
Brill, Marlene Targ 1945- 124
  Earlier sketch in SATA 77
Brimberg, Stanlee 1947- 9
Brimner, Larry Dane 1949- 170
  Autobiography Feature 112
  Earlier sketch in SATA 79
Brin, David 1950- 65
Brin, Ruth Firestone 1921- 22
Brinckloe, Julie 1950- 13
Brinckloe, Julie Lorraine
  See Brinckloe, Julie
Brindel, June (Rachuy) 1919- 7
Brindle, Max
  See Fleischman, Sid
Brindze, Ruth 1903-1984 23
Brink, Carol Ryrie 1895-1981 100
  Obituary 27
  Earlier sketches in SATA 1, 31
  See also CLR 149
Brinsmead, H. F(ay)
  See Brinsmead, H(esba) F(ay)
Brinsmead, H. F.
  See Brinsmead, H(esba) F(ay)
Brinsmead, H(esba) F(ay) 1922- 78
  Earlier sketch in SATA 18
  See also CLR 47
  See also SAAS 5
Briquebec, John
  See Rowland-Entwistle, (Arthur) Theodore
  (Henry)
Brisbane, Henry R.
  See Ellis, Edward S.
Brisco, P. A.
  See Matthews, Patricia
Brisco, Patty
  See Matthews, Patricia
  and Matthews, Clayton (Hartley)
Briscoe, Jill (Pauline) 1935- 56
  Brief entry 47
Brisley, Joyce Lankester 1896-1978 22
  Obituary 84
Brissenden, Connie
  See Brissenden, Constance
Brissenden, Constance 1947- 150
Brisson, Pat 1951- 177
  Autobiography Feature 133
  Earlier sketches in SATA 67, 128, 133
Britt, Albert 1874-1969
  Obituary 28
Britt, Dell 1934- 1
Brittain, Bill
  See Brittain, William
Brittain, C. Dale 1948- 82
Brittain, William 1930- 76
  Earlier sketch in SATA 36
  See also SAAS 7
Brittingham, Geoffrey (Hugh) 1959- 76

Brittney, L. 209
Britton, Kate
  See Stegeman, Janet Allais
Britton, Louisa
  See McGuire, Leslie (Sarah)
Britton, Rick 1952- 82
Bro, Margueritte (Harmon) 1894-1977 19
  Obituary 27
Broach, Elise 1963- 173
Broadhead, Helen Cross 1913- 25
Broadway, Hannah 208
Brochmann, Elizabeth 1938- 41
Brock, Betty (Carter) 1923-2003 4
  Obituary 150
Brock, C(harles) E(dmund) 1870-1938 42
  Brief entry 32
Brock, Delia
  See Ephron, Delia
Brock, Emma L(illian) 1886-1974 8
Brock, H(enry) M(atthew) 1875-1960 42
Brockett, Eleanor Hall 1913-1967 10
Brockman, C(hristian) Frank 1902-1985 26
Brockmeier, Kevin 1972- 176
Broda, Ron 1954- 209
Broderick, Dorothy M. 1929- 5
Brodeur, Ruth Wallace
  See Wallace-Brodeur, Ruth
Brodie, Sally
  See Cavin, Ruth (Brodie)
Brodsky, Beverly
  See McDermott, Beverly Brodsky
Brody, Wendy
  See Staub, Wendy Corsi
Broekel, Rainer Lothar
  See Broekel, Ray
Broekel, Ray 1923- 38
Broekstra, Lorette 1964- 189
  Earlier sketch in SATA *124*
Brogden, Sherryl
  See Jordan, Sherryl
Broger, Achim
  See Broger, Achim
Broger, Achim 1944- 31
Broida, Marian 154
Brokamp, Marilyn 1920- 10
Broman, Fred
  See Moseley, James W(illett)
Bromhall, Winifred 26
Brommer, Gerald F(rederick) 1927- 28
Brondfield, Jerome 1913-1998 22
Brondfield, Jerry
  See Brondfield, Jerome
Bronner, Stephen Eric 1949- 101
Bronowski, Jacob 1908-1974 55
Bronson, Alice
  See Watkins, Dawn L.
Bronson, Linda 203
Bronson, Lynn
  See Lampman, Evelyn Sibley
Bronson, Wilfrid Swancourt 1894-1985
  Obituary 43
Brook, Judith (Penelope) 1926- 59
  Brief entry 51
Brook, Judy
  See Brook, Judith (Penelope)
Brooke, L(eonard) Leslie 1862-1940 17
  See also CLR *20*
Brooke, William J. 1946- 139
Brooke-Haven, P.
  See Wodehouse, P. G.
Brooker, Kyrsten 199
Brookins, Dana 1931- 28
Brooks, Anita
  See Abramovitz, Anita (Zeltner Brooks)
Brooks, Bill 1939- 59
Brooks, Bruce 1950- 112
  Brief entry 53
  Earlier sketch in SATA *72*
  See also CLR *25*
Brooks, Caryl 1924- 84

Brooks, Charlotte K(endrick) 1918-1998 24
  Obituary 112
Brooks, Erik 1972- 182
  Earlier sketch in SATA *152*
Brooks, George
  See Baum, L. Frank
Brooks, Gwendolyn 1917-2000 6
  Obituary 123
  See also CLR *27*
Brooks, Gwendolyn Elizabeth
  See Brooks, Gwendolyn
Brooks, Jerome 1931- 23
Brooks, Kevin 1959- 197
  Earlier sketch in SATA *150*
Brooks, Kevin M.
  See Brooks, Kevin
Brooks, Laurie 209
Brooks, Lester 1924- 7
Brooks, Martha 1944- 134
  Autobiography Feature 134
  Earlier sketches in SATA *68, 121*
Brooks, Maurice (Graham) 1900- 45
Brooks, Polly Schoyer 1912- 12
Brooks, Ron 1948- 212
  Brief entry 33
  Earlier sketch in SATA *94*
Brooks, Ronald George
  See Brooks, Ron
Brooks, Terry 1944- 60
Brooks, Walter R(ollin) 1886-1958 17
Brooks-Hill, Helen (Mason) 1908-1994 59
Broome, Errol 1937- 158
  Earlier sketch in SATA *105*
Brophy, Nannette 1963- 73
Brosnan, James Patrick 1929- 14
Brosnan, Jim
  See Brosnan, James Patrick
Brostoff, Anita 1931- 132
Brothers Grimm
  See Grimm, Jacob Ludwig Karl
  and Grimm, Wilhelm Karl
Brothers Hildebrandt, The
  See Hildebrandt, Greg
  and Hildebrandt, Tim
Broun, Emily
  See Sterne, Emma Gelders
Brouwer, S. W.
  See Brouwer, Sigmund (W.)
Brouwer, Sigmund (W.) 1959- 109
Brow, Thea 1934- 60
Brower, Millicent 8
Brower, Pauline 1929- 22
Browin, Frances Williams 1898-1986 5
Brown, Alexis
  See Baumann, Amy Beeching
Brown, Anne Ensign 1937- 61
Brown, Beverly Swerdlow 97
Brown, Bill
  See Brown, William L(ouis)
Brown, Billye Walker
  See Cutchen, Billye Walker
Brown, Bob
  See Brown, Robert Joseph
Brown, Buck 1936- 45
Brown, Calef 217
  Earlier sketch in SATA *179*
Brown, Cassie 1919-1986 55
Brown, Charlotte Lewis 181
Brown, Conrad 1922- 31
Brown, Craig McFarland 1947- 73
Brown, David
  See Brown, David A(lan)
  and Myller, Rolf
Brown, Dee 1908-2002 110
  Obituary 141
  Earlier sketch in SATA *5*
Brown, Dee Alexander
  See Brown, Dee
Brown, Don 1949- 200
  Earlier sketch in SATA *172*
Brown, Drew T. III 1955- 83

Brown, Drollene P. 1939- 53
Brown, Elbrite 198
Brown, Eleanor Frances 1908-1987 3
Brown, Elizabeth Ferguson 1937- 153
Brown, Elizabeth M(yers) 1915- 43
Brown, Fern G. 1918- 34
Brown, (Robert) Fletch 1923- 42
Brown, Fornan 1901-1996 71
  Obituary 88
Brown, George Earl 1883-1964 11
Brown, George Mackay 1921-1996 35
Brown, Irene Bennett 1932- 3
Brown, Irving
  See Adams, William Taylor
Brown, Ivor (John Carnegie) 1891-1974 5
  Obituary 26
Brown, Jane Clark 1930- 81
Brown, Janet Mitsui 87
Brown, Jo 1964- 170
Brown, Joanne 1933- 147
Brown, Joe David 1915-1976 44
Brown, Joseph E(dward) 1929- 59
  Brief entry 51
Brown, Judith Gwyn 1933- 20
Brown, Kathryn 1955- 168
  Earlier sketch in SATA *98*
Brown, Kathy
  See Brown, Kathryn
Brown, Ken (James) 129
Brown, Kevin 1960- 101
Brown, Laurene Krasny 1945- 99
  Earlier sketch in SATA *54*
Brown, Laurie Krasny
  See Brown, Laurene Krasny
Brown, Lloyd Arnold 1907-1966 36
Brown, Mahlon A.
  See Ellis, Edward S.
Brown, Marc (Tolon) 1946- 145
  Earlier sketches in SATA *10, 53, 80*
  See also CLR *29*
Brown, Marcia (Joan) 1918- 47
  Earlier sketch in SATA *7*
  See also CLR *12*
Brown, Margaret Wise 1910-1952 100
  See also YABC *2*
  See also CLR *107*
Brown, Margery (Wheeler) 78
  Earlier sketch in SATA *5*
Brown, Marion Marsh 1908-2001 6
Brown, Myra Berry 1918- 6
Brown, Palmer 1919- 36
Brown, Pamela (Beatrice) 1924-1989 5
  Obituary 61
Brown, Paul 1942- 221
Brown, Peter 1979- 178
Brown, Rachel W.N. 1947- 203
Brown, Reeve Lindbergh
  See Lindbergh, Reeve
Brown, Richard E. 1946- 61
Brown, Robert Joseph 1907-1989 14
Brown, Roderick (Langmere) Haig-
  See Haig-Brown, Roderick (Langmere)
Brown, Rosalie
  See Moore, Rosalie (Gertrude)
Brown, Roswell
  See Webb, Jean Francis (III)
Brown, Roy (Frederick) 1921-1982 51
  Obituary 39
Brown, Ruth 1941- 170
  Earlier sketch in SATA *105*
Brown, Scott 1971- 134
Brown, Sue Ellen 1954- 81
Brown, Tricia 1954- 114
Brown, Vinson 1912-1991 19
Brown, Walter R(eed) 1929- 19
Brown, Will
  See Ainsworth, William Harrison
Brown, William L(ouis) 1910-1964 5

Browne, Anthony 1946- *163*
  Brief entry *44*
  Earlier sketches in SATA *45, 61, 105*
  See also CLR *156*
Browne, Anthony Edward Tudor
  See Browne, Anthony
Browne, Dik
  See Browne, Richard Arthur Allen
Browne, Hablot Knight 1815-1882 .... *21*
Browne, Matthew
  See Rands, William Brighty
Browne, Nicki M.
  See Browne, N.M.
Browne, Nicky Matthews
  See Browne, N.M.
Browne, N.M. 1960- *167*
Browne, Richard Arthur Allen 1917-1989 ... *67*
  Brief entry *38*
Browne, Vee F. 1956- *214*
  Earlier sketch in SATA *90*
Browning, Robert 1812-1889
  See YABC *1*
  See also CLR *97*
Brownjohn, Alan 1931- *6*
Brownlee, Walter 1930- *62*
Brownlie, Betty 1946- *159*
Brownlow, Kevin 1938- *65*
Brownlow, Mike *183*
Brownridge, William R(oy) 1932- *94*
Broyles, Anne 1953- *201*
Bruce, Dorita Fairlie 1885-1970
  Obituary *27*
Bruce, (William) Harry 1934- *77*
Bruce, Mary 1927- *1*
Bruchac, Joseph III
  See Bruchac, Joseph
Bruchac, Joseph 1942- *176*
  Autobiography Feature *176*
  Earlier sketches in SATA *42, 89, 131*
  See also CLR *46*
Bruchac, Margaret M.
  See Bruchac, Marge
Bruchac, Marge *181*
Bruck, Lorraine 1921- *55*
  Brief entry *46*
Bruel, Nick *205*
  Earlier sketch in SATA *166*
Bruel, Robert O. 1929-2002 .... *189*
Bruemmer, Fred 1929- *47*
Brugman, Alyssa (F.) 1974- *152*
Brumbeau, Jeff 1955- *157*
Bruna, Dick 1927- *76*
  Brief entry *30*
  Earlier sketch in SATA *43*
  See also CLR *7*
Brunhoff, Jean de 1899-1937 .... *24*
  See also CLR *116*
Brunhoff, Laurent de 1925- *150*
  Earlier sketches in SATA *24, 71*
  See also CLR *116*
Brunkus, Denise *204*
Bruno, Elsa Knight 1935-2009 .... *221*
Brunskill, Elizabeth Ann Flatt
  See Flatt, Lizann
Brush, Karen A(lexandra) 1960- *85*
Brussel-Smith, Bernard 1914- *58*
Brust, Steven 1955- *121*
  Earlier sketch in SATA *86*
Brust, Steven Karl Zoltan
  See Brust, Steven
Brustlein, Daniel 1904- *40*
Brustlein, Janice Tworkov -2000 .... *40*
  Obituary *126*
Brutschy, Jennifer 1960- *84*
Bryan, Ashley 1923- *178*
  Earlier sketches in SATA *31, 72, 132*
  See also CLR *66*
Bryan, Ashley F.
  See Bryan, Ashley
Bryan, Dorothy M. 1896(?)-1984
  Obituary *39*

Bryan, Jennifer *190*
Bryan, Sean *192*
Bryant, Bernice (Morgan) 1908-1976 .... *11*
Bryant, Jen 1960- *218*
  Earlier sketches in SATA *94, 175*
Bryant, Jennifer
  See Bryant, Jen
Bryant, Jennifer Fisher
  See Bryant, Jen
Bryant, Laura J. *176*
Brychta, Alex 1956- *21*
Brynie, Faith H. 1946- *113*
Brynie, Faith Hickman
  See Brynie, Faith H.
Bryson, Bernarda 1903-2004 .... *9*
Buba, Joy Flinsch 1904- *44*
Buchan, Bryan 1945- *36*
Buchan, John 1875-1940
  See YABC *2*
Buchan, Stuart 1942-1987
  Obituary *54*
Buchanan, Debby 1952- *82*
Buchanan, Deborah Leevonne
  See Buchanan, Debby
Buchanan, Jane 1956- *160*
Buchanan, Paul 1959- *116*
Buchanan, Sue 1939- *139*
Buchheimer, Naomi Barnett
  See Barnett, Naomi
Buchignani, Walter 1965- *84*
Buchmann, Stephen L. *194*
Buchwald, Art 1925-2007 .... *10*
Buchwald, Arthur
  See Buchwald, Art
Buchwald, Emilie 1935- *7*
Buck, Gisela 1941- *101*
Buck, Lewis 1925- *18*
Buck, Margaret Waring 1905-1997 .... *3*
Buck, Nola
  See Godwin, Laura
Buck, Pearl S. 1892-1973 .... *25*
  Earlier sketch in SATA *1*
Buck, Pearl Sydenstricker
  See Buck, Pearl S.
Buck, Siegfried 1941- *101*
Buckalew, Clare B.
  See Dunkle, Clare B.
Buckeridge, Anthony (Malcolm)
  1912-2004 .... *85*
  Earlier sketch in SATA *6*
Buckholtz, Eileen (Garber) 1949- *54*
  Brief entry *47*
Buckingham, Royce 1966- *210*
Buckingham, Royce Scott
  See Buckingham, Royce
Buckler, Ernest 1908-1984 .... *47*
Buckless, Andrea K. 1968- *117*
Buckley, Helen E(lizabeth) 1918- *90*
  Earlier sketch in SATA *2*
Buckley, James, Jr. 1963- *166*
  Earlier sketch in SATA *114*
Buckley, Michael *177*
Buckley, Susan *184*
Buckley, Susan Washburn
  See Buckley, Susan
Buckley-Archer, Linda *185*
Buckmaster, Henrietta
  See Stephens, Henrietta Henkle
Bucks, Brad
  See Holub, Joan
Budd, E. S.
  See Sirimarco, Elizabeth
Budd, Lillian (Peterson) 1897-1989 .... *7*
Budhos, Marina *173*
Buehler, Stephanie Jona 1956- *83*
Buehner, Caralyn 1963- *219*
  Earlier sketches in SATA *104, 159*
Buehner, Mark 1959- *221*
  Earlier sketches in SATA *104, 159*
Buehr, Walter Franklin 1897-1971 .... *3*

Buell, Ellen Lewis
  See Cash, Ellen Lewis Buell
Buell, Janet 1952- *185*
  Earlier sketch in SATA *106*
Buergel, Paul-Hermann H. 1949- *83*
Buettner, Dan 1960- *95*
Buff, Conrad 1886-1975 .... *19*
Buff, Mary (E. Marsh) 1890-1970 .... *19*
Buffett, Jimmy 1946- *110*
  Earlier sketch in SATA *76*
Buffie, Margaret 1945- *161*
  Earlier sketches in SATA *71, 107*
  See also CLR *39*
Bugbee, Emma 1888(?)-1981
  Obituary *29*
Bugni, Alice 1951- *122*
Buhhos, Marina Tamar
  See Budhos, Marina
Bujold, Lois McMaster 1949- *136*
Bulfinch, Thomas 1796-1867 .... *35*
Bulion, Leslie 1958- *209*
  Earlier sketch in SATA *161*
Bull, Angela (Mary) 1936- *45*
Bull, Emma 1954- *190*
  Autobiography Feature *103*
  Earlier sketch in SATA *99*
Bull, Norman John 1916- *41*
Bull, Peter (Cecil) 1912-1984
  Obituary *39*
Bull, Schuyler M. 1974- *138*
Bulla, Clyde R. 1914-2007 .... *139*
  Obituary *182*
  Earlier sketches in SATA *2, 41, 91*
  See also SAAS *6*
Bullard, Lisa 1961- *142*
Buller, Jon *205*
Bullock, Kathleen (Mary) 1946- *77*
Bullock, Robert (D.) 1947- *92*
Bulpin, (Barbara) Vicki *92*
Bulwer-Lytton, Edward 1803-1873 .... *23*
Bulwer-Lytton, Edward George Earle Lytton
  See Bulwer-Lytton, Edward
Bumstead, Kathleen Mary 1918-1987 .... *53*
Bundles, A'Lelia Perry 1952- *76*
Bunge, Daniela 1973- *207*
Bunin, Catherine 1967- *30*
Bunin, Sherry 1925- *30*
Bunkers, Suzanne L. 1950- *136*
Bunting, A.E.
  See Bunting, Eve
Bunting, Anne Evelyn
  See Bunting, Eve
Bunting, Eve 1928- *196*
  Earlier sketches in SATA *18, 64, 110, 158*
  See also CLR *82*
Bunting, Glenn (Davison) 1957- *22*
Bunyan, John 1628-1688
  See CLR *124*
Bupp, Walter
  See Garrett, Randall
Burack, Sylvia K. 1916-2003 .... *35*
  Obituary *143*
Burbank, Addison (Buswell) 1895-1961 ...... *37*
Burch, Joann J(ohansen) *75*
Burch, Robert J(oseph) 1925- *74*
  Earlier sketch in SATA *1*
  See also CLR *63*
Burchard, Peter Duncan 1921- *143*
  Earlier sketches in SATA *5, 74*
  See also SAAS *13*
Burchard, S. H.
  See Burchard, Sue
Burchard, Sue 1937- *22*
Burchardt, Nellie 1921- *7*
Burckhardt, Marc 1962- *196*
Burdett, Lois *117*
Burdick, Eugene (Leonard) 1918-1965 ...... *22*
Burford, Eleanor
  See Hibbert, Eleanor Alice Burford
Burg, Ann E. 1954- *217*
Burg, Shana 1968- *204*

Burgan, Michael 1960- 167
  Earlier sketch in SATA *118*
Burger, Carl 1888-1967 9
Burgess, Ann Marie
  See Gerson, Noel Bertram
Burgess, Barbara Hood 1926- 69
Burgess, Em
  See Burgess, Mary Wyche
Burgess, (Frank) Gelett 1866-1951 32
  Brief entry 30
Burgess, Mark 157
Burgess, Mary Wyche 1916- 18
Burgess, Melvin 1954- 198
  Earlier sketches in SATA *96, 146*
Burgess, Michael
  See Gerson, Noel Bertram
Burgess, Robert F(orrest) 1927- 4
Burgess, Starling
  See Tudor, Tasha
Burgess, Thornton Waldo 1874-1965 17
Burgess, Trevor
  See Trevor, Elleston
Burgwyn, Mebane Holoman 1914-1992 7
Burke, David 1927- 46
Burke, Diana G.
  See Gallagher, Diana G.
Burke, Diana Gallagher
  See Gallagher, Diana G.
Burke, Dianne O'Quinn 1940- 89
Burke, Janine 1952- 139
Burke, Jim 1973- 179
Burke, John
  See O'Connor, Richard
Burke, Katie 1953- 168
Burke, Patrick 1958- 114
Burke, Ralph
  See Garrett, Randall
  and Silverberg, Robert
Burkert, Nancy Ekholm 1933- 24
  See also SAAS *14*
Burkett, D. Brent 194
Burke-Weiner, Kimberly 1962- 95
Burks, Brian 1955- 95
Burland, Brian (Berkeley) 1931- 34
Burland, C. A.
  See Burland, Cottie (Arthur)
Burland, Cottie (Arthur) 1905-1983 5
Burleigh, Robert 1936- 193
  Earlier sketches in SATA *55, 98, 146*
Burlingame, (William) Roger 1889-1967 2
Burman, Alice Caddy 1896(?)-1977
  Obituary 24
Burman, Ben Lucien 1896-1984 6
  Obituary 40
Burn, Doris 1923- 1
Burn, Ted
  See Burn, Thomas E.
Burn, Thomas E. 1940- 150
Burnard, Damon 1963- 115
Burnett, Constance Buel 1893-1975 36
Burnett, Frances Eliza Hodgson
  See Burnett, Frances Hodgson
Burnett, Frances Hodgson 1849-1924 100
  See also YABC *2*
  See also CLR *122*
Burnett, Lindy 210
Burnett Bossi, Lisa 193
Burney, Anton
  See Hopkins, (Hector) Kenneth
Burnford, Sheila (Philip Cochrane Every)
  1918-1984 3
  Obituary 38
  See also CLR *2*
Burnham, Gretchen
  See Sprague, Gretchen
Burnham, Nicole 1970- 161
Burnham, Niki
  See Burnham, Nicole
Burnham, Sophy 1936- 65

Burningham, John 1936- 160
  Earlier sketches in SATA *16, 59, 111*
  See also CLR *9*
Burningham, Robin Yoko
  See Racoma, Robin Yoko
Burningham, Sarah O'Leary 216
Burns, Diane L. 1950- 81
  See also SAAS *24*
Burns, Eloise Wilkin
  See Wilkin, Eloise
Burns, Florence M. 1905-1988 61
Burns, Khephra 1950- 92
Burns, Loree Griffin 193
Burns, Marilyn 1941- 96
  Brief entry 33
Burns, Olive Ann 1924-1990 65
Burns, Paul C. 5
Burns, Ray
  See Burns, Raymond (Howard)
Burns, Raymond (Howard) 1924- 9
Burns, Theresa 1961- 84
Burns, William A. 1909-1999 5
Burr, Dan 1951- 65
Burr, Dan 1960- 219
Burr, Lonnie 1943- 47
Burrell, Roy E(ric) C(harles) 1923- 72
Burroughs, Edgar Rice 1875-1950 41
  See also CLR *157*
Burroughs, Jean Mitchell 1908- 28
Burroughs, Polly 1925- 2
Burroway, Janet 1936- 23
Burroway, Janet Gay
  See Burroway, Janet
Burstein, Chaya M(alamud) 1923- 64
Burstein, Fred 1950- 83
Burstein, John 1949- 54
  Brief entry 40
Burstein, Stanley M.
  See Burstein, Stanley Mayer
Burstein, Stanley Mayer 1941- 175
Bursztynski, Sue 1953- 114
Burt, Jesse Clifton 1921-1976 46
  Obituary 20
Burt, Olive Woolley 1894-1981 4
Burtinshaw, Julie 185
Burton, Gennett 1945- 95
Burton, Hester (Wood-Hill) 1913-2000 74
  Earlier sketch in SATA *7*
  See also CLR *1*
  See also SAAS *8*
Burton, Leslie
  See McGuire, Leslie (Sarah)
Burton, Marilee Robin 1950- 82
  Earlier sketch in SATA *46*
Burton, Maurice 1898-1992 23
Burton, Rebecca 1970- 183
Burton, Robert (Wellesley) 1941- 22
Burton, Virginia Lee 1909-1968 100
  Earlier sketch in SATA *2*
  See also CLR *11*
Burton, William H(enry) 1890-1964 11
Busby, Ailie 192
Busby, Cylin 1970- 118
Busby, Edith (A. Lake) (?)-1964
  Obituary 29
Busby, John 1942- 209
Buscaglia, (Felice) Leo(nardo) 1924-1998 ... 65
Buscaglia, Leo F.
  See Buscaglia, (Felice) Leo(nardo)
Busch, Phyllis S. 1909- 30
Bush, Anne Kelleher
  See Kelleher, Anne
Bush, Catherine 1961- 128
Bush, Jenna 1981- 208
Bush, Laura 1946- 208
Bushmiller, Ernest Paul 1905-1982 31
Bushmiller, Ernie
  See Bushmiller, Ernest Paul
Bushnell, Jack 1952- 86
Busoni, Rafaello 1900-1962 16

Buss, Helen M.
  See Clarke, Margaret
Busse, Sarah Martin 194
Busselle, Rebecca 1941- 80
Bustard, Anne 1951- 173
Butcher, Kristin 1951- 140
Butenko, Bohdan 1931- 90
Butler, Beverly Kathleen 1932- 7
Butler, Bill
  See Butler, William Vivian
  and Butler, Ernest Alton
  and Butler, William Huxford
Butler, Charles 1963- 175
  Earlier sketch in SATA *121*
Butler, Charles Cadman
  See Butler, Charles
Butler, Dori Hillestad 1965- 207
  Earlier sketch in SATA *164*
Butler, Dorothy 1925- 73
Butler, Geoff 1945- 94
Butler, M. Christina 1934- 170
  Earlier sketch in SATA *72*
Butler, Octavia 1947-2006 84
  See also CLR *65*
Butler, Octavia E.
  See Butler, Octavia
Butler, Octavia Estelle
  See Butler, Octavia
Butler, Vivian
  See Butler, William Vivian
Butler, William
  See Butler, William Vivian
Butler, William Vivian 1927-1987 79
Butterfield, Moira 1960- 219
Butters, Dorothy Gilman
  See Gilman, Dorothy
Butterworth, Emma Macalik 1928- 43
Butterworth, Nick 1946- 149
  Earlier sketch in SATA *106*
Butterworth, Oliver 1915-1990 1
  Obituary 66
Butterworth, W. E.
  See Griffin, W. E. B.
Butterworth, William E.
  See Griffin, W. E. B.
Butterworth, William Edmund III
  See Griffin, W. E. B.
Butts, Ed 1951- 177
Butts, Edward P.
  See Butts, Ed
Butts, Ellen R. 1942- 93
Butts, Ellen Rubinstein
  See Butts, Ellen R.
Butzer, C. M. 1974- 212
Buxton, Ralph
  See Silverstein, Alvin
  and Silverstein, Virginia B.
Buzzeo, Toni 1951- 215
  Earlier sketch in SATA *135*
Byalick, Marcia 1947- 141
  Earlier sketch in SATA *97*
Byard, Carole (Marie) 1941- 57
Byars, Betsy 1928- 163
  Autobiography Feature 108
  Earlier sketches in SATA *4, 46, 80*
  See also CLR *72*
  See also SAAS *1*
Byars, Betsy Cromer
  See Byars, Betsy
Byfield, Barbara Ninde 1930- 8
Byman, Jeremy 1944- 129
Bynum, Janie 133
Byrd, Elizabeth 1912-1989 34
Byrd, Nicole
  See Zach, Cheryl (Byrd)
Byrd, Robert (John) 1942- 158
  Earlier sketches in SATA *33, 112*
Byrd, Tim 1964- 216
Byrne, Gayle 218
Byrne, Mary Gregg 1951- 162

C

C. 3. 3.
  See Wilde, Oscar
C. E. M.
  See Mastrangelo, Charles E(lmer)
Cabaniss, J(ames) Allen 1911-1997 5
Cabat, Erni 1914- 74
Cabban, Vanessa 1971- 176
Cable, Mary 1920- 9
Cabot, Meg 1967- 217
  Earlier sketches in SATA *127, 175*
  See also CLR *85*
Cabot, Meggin
  See Cabot, Meg
Cabot, Meggin Patricia
  See Cabot, Meg
Cabot, Patricia
  See Cabot, Meg
Cabral, O. M.
  See Cabral, Olga
Cabral, Olga 1909- 46
Cabrera, Cozbi A. 1963- 177
Cabrera, Jane 1968- 182
  Earlier sketches in SATA *103, 152*
Cabrera, Marcela 1966- 90
Caddy, Alice
  See Burman, Alice Caddy
Cade, Toni
  See Bambara, Toni Cade
Cadmus and Harmonia
  See Buchan, John
Cadnum, Michael 1949- 165
  Earlier sketches in SATA *87, 121*
  See also CLR *78*
Caduto, Michael J. 1955- 103
Cadwallader, Sharon 1936- 7
Cady, (Walter) Harrison 1877(?)-1970 19
Caffey, Donna (J.) 1954- 110
Cagle, Malcolm W(infield) 1918- 32
Cahn, Rhoda 1922- 37
Cahn, William 1912-1976 37
Cain, Arthur H(omer) 1913-1981 3
Cain, Christopher
  See Fleming, Thomas
Cain, Sheridan 1952- 186
Caine, Geoffrey
  See Walker, Robert W.
Caines, Jeannette (Franklin) 1938- 78
  Brief entry 43
  See also CLR *24*
Cairns, Trevor 1922- 14
Calabro, Marian 1954- 79
Caldecott, Moyra 1927- 22
Caldecott, Randolph (J.) 1846-1886 100
  Earlier sketch in SATA *17*
  See also CLR *110*
Calder, Charlotte 1952- 125
Calder, David 1932-1997 105
Calder, Lyn
  See Calmenson, Stephanie
Calder, Marie D(onais) 1948- 96
Calderone-Stewart, Lisa
  See Calderone-Stewart, Lisa-Marie
Calderone-Stewart, Lisa-Marie 1958- 123
Caldwell, Doreen (Mary) 1942- 71
Caldwell, John C(ope) 1913-1984 7
Caletti, Deb 1963- 221
  Earlier sketch in SATA *171*
Calhoun, B. B. 1961- 98
Calhoun, Chad
  See Barrett, Neal, Jr.
  and Cunningham, Chet
  and Goulart, Ron
Calhoun, Dia 1959- 183
  Earlier sketch in SATA *129*
Calhoun, Mary
  See Wilkins, Mary Huiskamp
Calhoun, T.B.
  See Bisson, Terry
Cali, Davide 1972- 190

Calif, Ruth 1922- 67
Calkins, Franklin
  See Stratemeyer, Edward L.
Call, Greg 197
Call, Hughie Florence 1890-1969 1
Callahan, Dorothy M. 1934- 39
  Brief entry 35
Callahan, Dorothy Monahan
  See Callahan, Dorothy M.
Callahan, Philip Serna 1923- 25
Callan, Jamie 1954- 59
Callan, Jim 1951- 181
Callaway, Bernice (Anne) 1923- 48
Callaway, Kathy 1943- 36
Callen, Larry
  See Callen, Lawrence Willard, Jr.
Callen, Lawrence Willard, Jr. 1927- 19
Calley, Karin 1965- 92
Calmenson, Stephanie 1952- 211
  Brief entry 37
  Earlier sketches in SATA *51, 84, 139*
Calonita, Jen 216
Calvert, Elinor H.
  See Lasell, Elinor H.
Calvert, John
  See Leaf, (Wilbur) Munro
Calvert, Pam 1966- 205
Calvert, Patricia 1931- 132
  Earlier sketches in SATA *45, 69*
  See also SAAS *17*
Camburn, Carol A.
  See Camburn-Bracalente, Carol A.
Camburn-Bracalente, Carol A. 1962- 118
Cameron, Ann 1943- 129
  Earlier sketches in SATA *27, 89*
  See also SAAS *20*
Cameron, Edna M. 1905-1999 3
Cameron, Eleanor (Frances) 1912-1996 25
  Obituary 93
  Earlier sketch in SATA *1*
  See also CLR *72*
  See also SAAS *10*
Cameron, Elizabeth
  See Nowell, Elizabeth Cameron
Cameron, Elizabeth Jane 1910-1976 32
  Obituary 30
Cameron, Ian
  See Payne, Donald Gordon
Cameron, M(alcolm) G(ordon) Graham
  See Graham-Cameron, M(alcolm) G(ordon)
Cameron, M. Graham
  See Graham-Cameron, M(alcolm) G(ordon)
Cameron, Mike Graham
  See Graham-Cameron, M(alcolm) G(ordon)
Cameron, Natalie Russell
  See Russell, Natalie
Cameron, Polly 1928- 2
Cameron, Scott 1962- 84
Camp, Charles L. 1893-1975
  Obituary 31
Camp, Lindsay 1957- 133
Camp, Madeleine L'Engle
  See L'Engle, Madeleine
Camp, Walter (Chauncey) 1859-1925
  See YABC *1*
Campbell, (Elizabeth) Andrea 1963- 50
Campbell, Ann R. 1925- 11
Campbell, Bill 1960- 89
Campbell, Bruce
  See Epstein, Samuel
Campbell, Camilla 1905-1992 26
Campbell, Carole R. 1939- 125
Campbell, Hope 1925- 20
Campbell, Hugh 1930- 90
Campbell, Jane
  See Edwards, Jane Campbell
Campbell, Julie
  See Tatham, Julie Campbell
Campbell, Patricia J(ean) 1930- 45
Campbell, Patty
  See Campbell, Patricia J(ean)

Campbell, Peter A. 1948- 99
Campbell, R. W.
  See Campbell, Rosemae Wells
Campbell, Robin
  See Strachan, Ian
Campbell, Rod 1945- 98
  Brief entry 44
  Earlier sketch in SATA *51*
Campbell, Rosemae Wells 1909- 1
Campbell, Sarah C. 1966- 207
Camper, Cathy 1956- 170
Campion, Nardi Reeder 1917-2007 22
Campling, Elizabeth 1948- 53
Campoy, F. Isabel 1946- 181
  Earlier sketch in SATA *143*
Camps, Luis 1928- 66
Canales, Viola 1957- 141
Candell, Victor 1903-1977
  Obituary 24
Canfield, Dorothea F.
  See Fisher, Dorothy (Frances) Canfield
Canfield, Dorothea Frances
  See Fisher, Dorothy (Frances) Canfield
Canfield, Dorothy
  See Fisher, Dorothy (Frances) Canfield
Canfield, Jack 1944- 164
Canfield, Jane White 1897-1984 32
  Obituary 38
Canfield, Muriel 1935- 94
Canga, C.B. 1976- 216
Canga, Chris
  See Canga, C.B.
Caniff, Milton 1907-1988
  Obituary 58
Caniff, Milton Arthur Paul
  See Caniff, Milton
Cann, Helen 1969- 179
  Earlier sketch in SATA *124*
Cann, Kate 1954- 152
  Earlier sketch in SATA *103*
Cannan, Joanna
  See Pullein-Thompson, Joanna Maxwell
Cannell, Jon 196
Cannell, Jonathan C.
  See Cannell, Jon
Cannon, A.E. 202
  Earlier sketches in SATA *93, 163*
Cannon, Ann Edwards
  See Cannon, A.E.
Cannon, Bettie (Waddell) 1922- 59
Cannon, Curt
  See Hunter, Evan
Cannon, Eileen E(mily) 1948- 119
Cannon, Frank
  See Mayhar, Ardath
Cannon, Janell 1957- 128
  Earlier sketch in SATA *78*
  See also CLR *120*
Cannon, Marian G. 1923- 85
Cannon, Taffy
  See Cannon, Eileen E(mily)
Cantone, AnnaLaura 182
Cantrell, Julie 1973- 217
Canusi, Jose
  See Barker, S. Omar
Canyon, Christopher 1966- 150
  Earlier sketch in SATA *104*
Caparo, Antonio
  See Caparo, Antonio Javier
Caparo, Antonio Javier 205
Capek, Michael 1947- 142
  Earlier sketch in SATA *96*
Capes, Bernard (Edward Joseph)
  1854-1918 116
Caple, Kathy 193
Caple, Laurie 1958- 201
Caplin, Alfred Gerald 1909-1979 61
  Obituary 21
Caponigro, John Paul 1965- 84
Capote, Truman 1924-1984 91

Capp, Al
    See Caplin, Alfred Gerald
Cappel, Constance 1936- 22
Cappetta, Cynthia 1949- *125*
Cappo, Nan Willard 1955- *143*
Capps, Benjamin (Franklin) 1922- 9
Cappy Dick
    See Cleveland, George
Captain Kangaroo
    See Keeshan, Robert J.
Captain Wheeler
    See Ellis, Edward S.
Captain Young of Yale
    See Stratemeyer, Edward L.
Capucilli, Alyssa Satin 1957- *203*
    Earlier sketches in SATA *115, 163*
Capucine
    See Mazille, Capucine
Carafoli, Marci
    See Balterman, Marcia Ridlon
Caraher, Kim(berley Elizabeth) 1961- *105*
Caraker, Mary 1929- 74
Caras, Roger A(ndrew) 1928-2001 .... *12*
    Obituary *127*
Caravantes, Peggy 1935- *140*
Caraway, Caren 1939- 57
Carbone, Elisa 1954- *173*
    Earlier sketches in SATA *81, 137*
Carbone, Elisa Lynn
    See Carbone, Elisa
Carbonnier, Jeanne 1894-1974 3
    Obituary 34
Card, Orson Scott 1951- *127*
    Earlier sketch in SATA *83*
    See also CLR *116*
Care, Felicity
    See Coury, Louise Andree
Carew, Jan 1925- 51
    Brief entry 40
Carew, Jan Rynveld
    See Carew, Jan
Carey, Benedict 1960- *219*
Carey, Bonnie
    See Marshall, Bonnie C.
Carey, Charles W., Jr. 1951- *170*
Carey, Ernestine Gilbreth 1908-2006 2
    Obituary *177*
Carey, Janet Lee 1954(?)- *185*
Carey, Lisa *110*
Carey, M. V.
    See Carey, Mary V(irginia)
Carey, Mary V(irginia) 1925-1994 44
    Brief entry 39
Carey, Peter 1943- 94
Carey, Peter Philip
    See Carey, Peter
Carey, Valerie Scho 1949- 60
Carheden, Goorel Kristina
    See Naaslund, Goorel Kristina
Carigiet, Alois 1902-1985 24
    Obituary 47
    See also CLR *38*
Carini, Edward 1923- 9
Carkeet, David 1946- 75
Carle, Eric 1929- *163*
    Earlier sketches in SATA *4, 65, 120*
    See also CLR *72*
    See also SAAS *6*
Carleton, Captain L. C.
    See Ellis, Edward S.
Carleton, Captain Latham C.
    See Ellis, Edward S.
Carleton, Latham C.
    See Ellis, Edward S.
Carley, V(an Ness) Royal 1906-1976
    Obituary 20
Carling, Amelia Lau 1949- *164*
    Earlier sketch in SATA *119*
Carlisle, Carolyn
    See Hawes, Louise

Carlisle, Clark
    See Holding, James (Clark Carlisle, Jr.)
Carlisle, Olga Andreyev 1930- 35
Carlock, Miriam
    See Eyerly, Jeannette
Carls, Claudia 1978- *198*
Carlsen, G(eorge) Robert 1917- 30
Carlsen, Ruth C(hristoffer) 1918- 2
Carlson, Bernice Wells 1910- 8
Carlson, Christopher C. *202*
Carlson, Dale (Bick) 1935- *1*
Carlson, Daniel (Bick) 1960- 27
Carlson, Kirsten 1968- *192*
Carlson, Kirsten M.
    See Carlson, Kirsten
Carlson, Laurie 1952- *173*
    Earlier sketch in SATA *101*
Carlson, Laurie Winn
    See Carlson, Laurie
Carlson, Melody 1956- *171*
    Earlier sketch in SATA *113*
Carlson, Nancy 1953- *213*
    Brief entry 45
    Earlier sketches in SATA *56, 90, 144*
Carlson, Nancy L.
    See Carlson, Nancy
Carlson, Natalie Savage 1906-1997 68
    Earlier sketch in SATA *2*
    See also SAAS *4*
Carlson, Susan Johnston 1953- 88
Carlson, Vada F. 1897- 16
Carlstrom, Nancy White 1948- *215*
    Brief entry 48
    Earlier sketches in SATA *53, 92, 156*
Carlton, Keith
    See Robertson, Keith (Carlton)
Carlton, Susan 1960- *195*
Carlyon, Richard 55
Carman, Patrick 1966- *197*
    Earlier sketch in SATA *161*
Carmer, Carl (Lamson) 1893-1976 37
    Obituary 30
Carmer, Elizabeth Black 1904- 24
Carmi, Giora 1944- *149*
    Earlier sketch in SATA *79*
Carmichael, Carrie
    See Carmichael, Harriet
Carmichael, Clay *218*
Carmichael, Harriet 40
Carmody, Isobelle 1958- *191*
    Earlier sketch in SATA *161*
Carmody, Isobelle Jane
    See Carmody, Isobelle
Carney, Elizabeth 1981- *199*
Carney, Jeff 1962- *196*
Carney, Mary Lou 1949- *170*
Carol, Bill J.
    See Knott, William C(ecil, Jr.)
Caron, Romi
    See Caron-Kyselkova', Romana
Caron-Kyselkova', Romana 1967- 94
Caroselli, Remus F(rancis) 1916- 36
Carpelan, Bo 1926- 8
Carpelan, Bo Gustaf Bertelsson
    See Carpelan, Bo
Carpenter, (John) Allan 1917- 81
    Earlier sketch in SATA *3*
Carpenter, Angelica Shirley 1945- *153*
    Earlier sketch in SATA *71*
Carpenter, Frances 1890-1972 3
    Obituary 27
Carpenter, John 1948- 58
Carpenter, John Howard
    See Carpenter, John
Carpenter, Johnny
    See Carpenter, John
Carpenter, Nancy *215*
Carpenter, Nancy Sippel
    See Carpenter, Nancy
Carpenter, Patricia (Healy Evans) 1920- *11*

Carr, Glyn
    See Styles, (Frank) Showell
Carr, Harriett H(elen) 1899-1977 3
Carr, Jan 1953- *132*
    Earlier sketch in SATA *89*
Carr, M. J.
    See Carr, Jan
Carr, Mary Jane 1899-1988 2
    Obituary 55
Carr, Philippa
    See Hibbert, Eleanor Alice Burford
Carr, Roger Vaughan 1937- 95
Carrel, Annette Felder 1929- 90
Carrick, Carol (Hatfield) 1935- *118*
    Earlier sketches in SATA *7, 63*
    See also SAAS *18*
Carrick, Donald (F.) 1929-1989 63
    Earlier sketch in SATA *7*
Carrick, Malcolm 1945- 28
Carrick, Paul 1972- *194*
Carrier, Lark 1947- 71
    Brief entry 50
Carrier, Roch 1937- *166*
    Earlier sketch in SATA *105*
Carrighar, Sally 1898-1985 24
Carrillo, Patricia S.
    See Carrillo, P.S.
Carrillo, P.S. *209*
Carrington, G. A.
    See Cunningham, Chet
Carrington, Marsha Gray 1954- *168*
    Earlier sketch in SATA *111*
Carris, Joan 1938- *182*
    Brief entry 42
    Earlier sketch in SATA *44*
Carris, Joan Davenport
    See Carris, Joan
Carroll, Curt
    See Bishop, Curtis (Kent)
Carroll, Elizabeth
    See Barkin, Carol
    and James, Elizabeth
Carroll, Jaye
    See Carroll, Michael
Carroll, Jenny
    See Cabot, Meg
Carroll, (Archer) Latrobe 1894-1996 7
Carroll, Laura
    See Parr, Lucy
Carroll, Lewis 1832-1898 .... *100*
    See also YABC *2*
    See also CLR *108*
Carroll, Michael 1966- *203*
Carroll, Raymond 1924- 86
    Brief entry 47
Carruth, Hayden 1921-2008 47
    Obituary *197*
Carryl, Charles E. 1841-1920 .... *114*
Carryl, Charles Edward
    See Carryl, Charles E.
Carse, Robert 1902-1971 5
Carson, J(ohn) Franklin 1920-1981 .... *1*
    Obituary *107*
Carson, Mary Kay 1964- *200*
    Earlier sketch in SATA *150*
Carson, Rachel 1907-1964 23
Carson, Rachel Louise
    See Carson, Rachel
Carson, Rosalind
    See Chittenden, Margaret
Carson, S. M.
    See Gorsline, (Sally) Marie
Carson, William C. 1928- *154*
Carter, Abby *184*
Carter, Alden R 1947- *137*
    Earlier sketch in SATA *67*
    See also CLR *22*
    See also SAAS *18*
Carter, Alden Richardson
    See Carter, Alden R
Carter, Andy 1948- *134*

Carter, Angela 1940-1992 .... *66*
  Obituary *70*
Carter, Angela Olive
  See Carter, Angela
Carter, Anne Laurel 1953- *209*
  Earlier sketch in SATA *135*
Carter, Asa Earl
  See Carter, Forrest
Carter, Avis Murton
  See Allen, Kenneth S.
Carter, Bruce
  See Hough, Richard (Alexander)
Carter, Carol S(hadis) 1948- *124*
Carter, David A. 1957- *170*
  Earlier sketch in SATA *114*
Carter, Don 1958- *192*
  Earlier sketch in SATA *124*
Carter, Dorothy Sharp 1921- *8*
Carter, Forrest 1927(?)-1979 .... *32*
Carter, Helene 1887-1960 .... *15*
Carter, (William) Hodding, Jr. 1907-1972 ...... *2*
  Obituary *27*
Carter, James Earl, Jr.
  See Carter, Jimmy
Carter, Jimmy 1924- *79*
Carter, Katharine J(ones) 1905-1984 .... *2*
Carter, Lin(wood Vrooman) 1930-1988 .... *91*
Carter, Mike 1936- *138*
Carter, Nick
  See Avallone, Michael (Angelo, Jr.)
  and Ballard, (Willis) Todhunter
  and Crider, Bill
  and Cassiday, Bruce (Bingham)
  and Chastain, Thomas
  and Dey, Frederic (Merrill) Van Rensselaer
  and Garside, Jack
  and Hayes, Ralph E(ugene)
  and Henderson, M(arilyn) R(uth)
  and Lynds, Dennis
  and Lynds, Gayle (Hallenbeck)
  and Randisi, Robert J.
  and Rasof, Henry
  and Stratemeyer, Edward L.
  and Smith, Martin Cruz
  and Swain, Dwight V(reeland)
  and Vardeman, Robert E.
  and Wallmann, Jeffrey M(iner)
  and White, Lionel
Carter, Peter 1929- *57*
Carter, Phyllis Ann
  See Eberle, Irmengarde
Carter, Samuel (Thomson) III 1904-1988 .... *37*
  Obituary *60*
Carter, William E. 1926-1983 .... *1*
  Obituary *35*
Cartlidge, Michelle 1950- *96*
  Brief entry *37*
  Earlier sketch in SATA *49*
Cartner, William Carruthers 1910- *11*
Cartwright, Ann 1940- *78*
Cartwright, Reg(inald Ainsley) 1938- *64*
Cartwright, Sally 1923- *9*
Carusone, Al 1949- *89*
Carvell, Marlene *172*
Carver, John
  See Gardner, Richard (M.)
Carwell, L'Ann
  See McKissack, Patricia C.
Cary
  See Cary, Louis F(avreau)
Cary, Barbara Knapp 1912(?)-1975
  Obituary *31*
Cary, Kate 1967(?)- *174*
Cary, Louis F(avreau) 1915- *9*
Caryl, Jean
  See Kaplan, Jean Caryl Korn
Casanova, Mary 1957- *186*
  Earlier sketches in SATA *94, 136*
Cascone, A.G.
  See Cascone, Annette
  and Cascone, Gina

Cascone, Annette 1960- *103*
Cascone, Gina 1955- *103*
Case, Chris 1976- *209*
Case, Marshal T(aylor) 1941- *9*
Case, Michael
  See Howard, Robert West
Caseley, Judith 1951- *159*
  Brief entry *53*
  Earlier sketch in SATA *87*
Casewit, Curtis W(erner) 1922-2002 ... *4*
Casey, Barbara (Louise) 1944- *147*
  Earlier sketch in SATA *79*
Casey, Brigid 1950- *9*
Casey, Tina 1959- *141*
Cash, Ellen Lewis Buell 1905-1989
  Obituary *64*
Cash, John Carter 1970- *218*
Cash, Megan Montague *160*
Cashore, Kristin 1976(?)- *206*
Casilla, Robert 1959- *211*
  Earlier sketches in SATA *75, 146*
Cason, Mabel Earp 1892-1965 .... *10*
Cass, Joan E(velyn) *1*
Cass-Beggs, Barbara 1904- *62*
Cassedy, Patrice (Rinaldo) 1953- *149*
Cassedy, Sylvia 1930-1989 .... *77*
  Obituary *61*
  Earlier sketch in SATA *27*
  See also CLR *26*
Cassel, Lili
  See Wronker, Lili Cassel
Cassels, Jean *173*
Cassidy, Anne 1952- *166*
Cassidy, Anne Josephine
  See Cassidy, Anne
Cassidy, Cathy 1962- *183*
Casson, Hugh Maxwell 1910-1999 .... *65*
  Obituary *115*
Cassutt, Michael 1954- *78*
Cassutt, Michael Joseph
  See Cassutt, Michael
Castaldi, Elicia *194*
Castaldo, Nancy Fusco 1962- *151*
  Earlier sketch in SATA *93*
Castaneda, Omar S. 1954- *71*
Castell, Megan
  See Williams, Jeanne
Castellanos, Jane Mollie Robinson
  1913-2001 .... *9*
Castellon, Federico 1914-1971 .... *48*
Castellucci, Cecil 1969- *176*
Castillo, Edmund L. 1924-2005 .... *1*
  Obituary *167*
Castillo, Lauren *195*
Castle, Lee
  See Ogan, George F.
  and Ogan, Margaret E. (Nettles)
Castle, Paul
  See Howard, Vernon (Linwood)
Castle, Robert
  See Hamilton, Edmond
Castrovilla, Selene 1966- *186*
Caswell, Brian 1954- *171*
  Earlier sketch in SATA *97*
Caswell, Helen (Rayburn) 1923- *12*
Catalano, Dominic 1956- *163*
  Earlier sketch in SATA *76*
Catalano, Grace (A.) 1961- *99*
Catalanotto, Peter 1959- *195*
  Autobiography Feature *113*
  Earlier sketches in SATA *70, 114, 159*
  See also CLR *68*
  See also SAAS *25*
Catanese, P. W. 1961- *179*
Cate, Annette LeBlanc *196*
Cate, Dick
  See Cate, Richard Edward Nelson
Cate, Richard Edward Nelson 1932- *28*
Cather, Willa 1873-1947 .... *30*
  See also CLR *98*

Catherall, Arthur 1906-1980 .... *74*
  Earlier sketches in SATA *3, 4*
Cathon, Laura E(lizabeth) 1908-1991 .... *27*
Catlett, Elizabeth 1919(?)- *82*
Catlin, Wynelle 1930- *13*
Catlow, Nikalas
  See Catlow, Niki
Catlow, Niki 1975- *193*
Cato, Heather *105*
Cato, Sheila *114*
Catran, Ken 1944- *190*
Catrow, David
  See Catrow, David J. III
Catrow, David J. III *206*
  Earlier sketch in SATA *152*
Catt, Louis
  See French, Vivian
Cattell, James 1954- *123*
Catton, (Charles) Bruce 1899-1978 .... *2*
  Obituary *24*
Catz, Max
  See Glaser, Milton
Caudell, Marian 1930- *52*
Caudill, Rebecca 1899-1985 .... *1*
  Obituary *44*
Cauley, Lorinda Bryan 1951- *46*
  Brief entry *43*
Caulfield, Peggy F. 1926-1987
  Obituary *53*
Cauman, Samuel 1910-1971 .... *48*
Causley, Charles (Stanley) 1917-2003 .... *66*
  Obituary *149*
  Earlier sketch in SATA *3*
  See also CLR *30*
Cavallaro, Ann (Abelson) 1918- *62*
Cavallo, Diana 1931- *7*
Cavanagh, Helen (Carol) 1939- *98*
  Brief entry *37*
  Earlier sketch in SATA *48*
Cavanah, Frances 1899-1982 .... *31*
  Earlier sketch in SATA *1*
Cavanna, Betty
  See Harrison, Elizabeth (Allen) Cavanna
Cavanna, Elizabeth
  See Harrison, Elizabeth (Allen) Cavanna
Cave, Kathryn 1948- *123*
  Earlier sketch in SATA *76*
Cavendish, Peter
  See Horler, Sydney
Caveney, Philip 1951- *219*
Caveney, Philip Richard
  See Caveney, Philip
Cavin, Ruth (Brodie) 1918- *38*
Cavoukian, Raffi 1948- *68*
Cawley, Winifred 1915- *13*
Cazeau, Charles J(ay) 1931- *65*
Cazet, Denys 1938- *191*
  Brief entry *41*
  Earlier sketches in SATA *52, 99, 163*
Cazzola, Gus 1934- *73*
Cebulash, Mel 1937- *91*
  Earlier sketch in SATA *10*
Ceccoli, Nicoletta *181*
Cecil, Randy 1968- *187*
Cecka, Melanie *199*
Ceder, Georgiana Dorcas -1985 .... *10*
Celenza, Anna Harwell *133*
Celestino, Martha Laing
  See Laing, Martha
Cepeda, Joe *215*
  Earlier sketch in SATA *159*
Cerf, Bennett (Alfred) 1898-1971 .... *7*
Cerf, Christopher (Bennett) 1941- *2*
Cermak, Martin
  See Duchacek, Ivo D(uka)
Cerullo, Mary M. 1949- *145*
  Earlier sketch in SATA *86*
Cervon, Jacqueline
  See Moussard, Jacqueline
Cetin, Frank Stanley 1921- *2*
Chabon, Michael 1963- *145*

Chabrian, Deborah
  See Chabrian, Deborah L.
Chabrian, Deborah L. 212
Chaconas, D.J.
  See Chaconas, Dori
Chaconas, Dori 1938- 208
  Earlier sketches in SATA *145, 175*
Chaconas, Doris J.
  See Chaconas, Dori
Chadwick, Lester 67
  Earlier sketch in SATA *1*
Chaffee, Allen 3
Chaffin, Lillie D(orton) 1925- 4
Chaikin, Miriam 1924- 152
  Earlier sketches in SATA *24, 102*
Chall, Marsha Wilson 150
Challand, Helen J(ean) 1921- 64
Challans, Mary
  See Renault, Mary
Chalmers, Mary (Eileen) 1927- 6
  See also SAAS *14*
Chamberlain, Barbara A.
  See Azore, Barbara
Chamberlain, Margaret 1954- 212
  Earlier sketch in SATA *46*
Chamberlin, Kate 1945- 105
Chamberlin, Mary 1960- 177
Chamberlin, Rich 177
Chamberlin, Richard
  See Chamberlin, Rich
Chambers, Aidan 1934- 171
  Earlier sketches in SATA *1, 69, 108*
  See also CLR *151*
  See also SAAS *12*
Chambers, Bradford 1922-1984
  Obituary 39
Chambers, Catherine E.
  See St. John, Nicole
Chambers, John W. 1933- 57
  Brief entry 46
Chambers, Kate
  See St. John, Nicole
Chambers, Margaret Ada Eastwood 1911- 2
Chambers, Peggy
  See Chambers, Margaret Ada Eastwood
Chambers, Robert W(illiam) 1865-1933 107
Chambliss, Maxie 186
Chan, Gillian 1954- 147
  Earlier sketch in SATA *102*
Chan, Peter 1980(?)- 207
Chance, James T.
  See Carpenter, John
Chance, John T.
  See Carpenter, John
Chance, Stephen
  See Turner, Philip (William)
Chandler, Caroline A(ugusta) 1906-1979 22
  Obituary 24
Chandler, David P. 1933- 28
Chandler, David Porter
  See Chandler, David P.
Chandler, Edna Walker 1908-1982 11
  Obituary 31
Chandler, Jennifer
  See Westwood, Jennifer
Chandler, Karen 1959- 122
Chandler, Linda S(mith) 1929- 39
Chandler, Pauline 175
Chandler, Robert 1953- 40
Chandler, Ruth Forbes 1894-1978 2
  Obituary 26
Chandonnet, Ann F. 1943- 92
Chaney, Jill 1932- 87
Chang, Chih-Wei 1966- 111
Chang, Cindy 1968- 90
Chang, Margaret 1941- 71
Chang, Margaret Scrogin
  See Chang, Margaret
Chang, Raymond 1939- 142
  Earlier sketches in SATA *71, 142 PEN*
Chanin, Michael 1952- 84

Channel, A. R.
  See Catherall, Arthur
Chapian, Marie 1938- 29
Chapin, Alene Olsen Dalton 1915(?)-1986
  Obituary 47
Chapin, Tom 1945- 83
Chapman, Allen 67
  Earlier sketch in SATA *1*
Chapman, Cheryl O(rth) 1948- 80
Chapman, (Constance) Elizabeth (Mann)
  1919- 10
Chapman, Gaye 1970- 200
Chapman, Gaye Coralie
  See Chapman, Gaye
Chapman, Gaynor 1935- 32
Chapman, Gillian 1955- 120
Chapman, Jane 1970- 212
  Earlier sketches in SATA *122, 176*
Chapman, Jean 104
  Earlier sketch in SATA *34*
  See also CLR *65*
Chapman, John Stanton Higham 1891-1972
  Obituary 27
Chapman, Lee
  See Bradley, Marion Zimmer
Chapman, Lynne 1960- 197
Chapman, Lynne F(erguson) 1963- 150
  Earlier sketch in SATA *94*
Chapman, Maristan
  See Chapman, John Stanton Higham
Chapman, Vera (Ivy May) 1898-1996 33
Chapman, Walker
  See Silverberg, Robert
Chappell, Audrey 1954- 72
Chappell, Crissa-Jean 198
Chappell, Warren 1904-1991 68
  Obituary 67
  Earlier sketch in SATA *6*
  See also SAAS *10*
Chapra, Mimi 182
Charbonneau, Eileen 1951- 118
  Earlier sketch in SATA *84*
Charbonnet, Gabrielle 1961- 81
Chardiet, Bernice 1927(?)- 27
Chardiet, Bernice Kroll
  See Chardiet, Bernice
Charest, Emily MacLachlan 198
Charles, Donald
  See Meighan, Donald Charles
Charles, Louis
  See Stratemeyer, Edward L.
Charles, Nicholas
  See Kuskin, Karla
Charles, Nicholas J.
  See Kuskin, Karla
Charles, Norma 153
Charles, Veronika Martenova 182
Charlip, Remy 1929- 119
  Earlier sketches in SATA *4, 68*
  See also CLR *8*
Charlot, Jean 1898-1979 8
  Obituary 31
Charlot, Martin 1944- 64
Charlot, Martin Day
  See Charlot, Martin
Charlton, Michael (Alan) 1923- 34
Charlton-Trujillo, e.E. 189
Charmatz, Bill 1925-2005 7
Charnas, Suzy McKee 1939- 110
  Earlier sketch in SATA *61*
Charosh, Mannis 1906- 5
Chartier, Normand L. 1945- 66
Chase, Alice
  See McHargue, Georgess
Chase, Alyssa 1965- 92
Chase, Andra 1942- 91
Chase, Emily
  See Aks, Patricia
  and Garwood, Julie
  and Sachs, Judith
  and White, Carol

Chase, Mary (Coyle) 1907-1981 17
  Obituary 29
Chase, Mary Ellen 1887-1973 10
Chase, Paula 214
Chase, Richard 1904-1988 64
  Obituary 56
Chase, Samantha
  See Glick, Ruth (Burtnick)
Chast, Roz 1954- 212
  Earlier sketch in SATA *97*
Chastain, Madye Lee 1908-1989 4
Chataway, Carol 1955- 140
Chatterjee, Debjani 1952- 83
Chauncy, Nan(cen Beryl Masterman)
  1900-1970 6
  See also CLR *6*
Chaundler, Christine 1887-1972 1
  Obituary 25
Chayka, Doug 196
Chbosky, Stephen 1972- 164
Cheaney, Janie B.
  See Cheaney, J.B.
Cheaney, J.B. 1950- 188
Chee, Cheng-Khee 1934- 79
Cheese, Chloe 1952- 118
Chekhonte, Antosha
  See Chekhov, Anton
Chekhov, Anton 1860-1904 90
Chekhov, Anton Pavlovich
  See Chekhov, Anton
Chelushkin, Kirill 1968- 186
Chen, Anthony 1929- 6
Chen, Chih-Yuan 1975- 216
  Earlier sketch in SATA *155*
Chen, Ju-Hong 1941- 78
Chen, Pauline 1966- 202
Chen, Sara
  See Odgers, Sally Farrell
Chen, Tony
  See Chen, Anthony
Chen, Yong 1963- 183
Chen, Yuan-tsung 1932- 65
Chen, Zhiyuan
  See Chen, Chih-Yuan
Chenault, Nell
  See Smith, Linell Nash
Chen Chih-Yuan
  See Chen, Chih-Yuan
Chenery, Janet (Dai) 1923- 25
Cheney, Cora 1916-1999 3
  Obituary 110
Cheney, Glenn (Alan) 1951- 99
Cheney, Lynne V. 1941- 152
Cheney, Lynne Vincent
  See Cheney, Lynne V.
Cheney, Ted
  See Cheney, Theodore Albert
Cheney, Theodore A. Rees
  See Cheney, Theodore Albert
Cheney, Theodore Albert 1928- 11
Cheng, Andrea 1957- 205
  Earlier sketches in SATA *128, 172*
Cheng, Christopher 1959- 173
  Earlier sketch in SATA *106*
Cheng, Judith 1955- 36
Cheng, Shan
  See Jiang, Cheng An
Cheripko, Jan 1951- 155
  Earlier sketch in SATA *83*
Chermayeff, Ivan 1932- 47
Chernenko, Dan
  See Turtledove, Harry
Chernoff, Dorothy A.
  See Ernst, (Lyman) John
Chernoff, Goldie Taub 1909- 10
Cherry, Carolyn Janice
  See Cherryh, C.J.
Cherry, Lynne 1952- 99
  Earlier sketch in SATA *34*
Cherryh, C.J. 1942- 172
  Earlier sketch in SATA *93*

Cherryholmes, Anne
  See Price, Olive
Cheshire, Simon *172*
Chesler, Bernice 1932-2002 .... *59*
Chess, Victoria (Dickerson) 1939- *92*
  Earlier sketch in SATA *33*
Chessa, Francesca *191*
Chester, Deborah 1957- *85*
Chester, Kate
  See Guccione, Leslie Davis
Chesterton, G. K. 1874-1936 .... *27*
Chesterton, Gilbert Keith
  See Chesterton, G. K.
Chesworth, Michael *207*
  Earlier sketch in SATA *160*
Chetin, Helen 1922- *6*
Chetwin, Grace *86*
  Brief entry *50*
Chevalier, Christa 1937- *35*
Chevalier, Tracy 1962- *128*
Chew, Ruth 1920-2010 .... *7*
Chichester Clark, Emma 1955- *209*
  Earlier sketches in SATA *117, 156, 69*
Chidsey, Donald Barr 1902-1981 .... *3*
  Obituary *27*
Chiefari, Janet D. 1942- *58*
Chien, Catia *193*
Chien-min, Lin
  See Rumford, James
Child, L. Maria
  See Child, Lydia Maria
Child, Lauren 1965- *183*
  Earlier sketches in SATA *119, 160*
Child, Lincoln 1957- *113*
Child, Lincoln B.
  See Child, Lincoln
Child, Lydia Maria 1802-1880 .... *67*
Child, Mrs.
  See Child, Lydia Maria
Child, Philip 1898-1978 .... *47*
Children's Shepherd, The
  See Westphal, Arnold Carl
Childress, Alice 1920-1994 .... *81*
  Earlier sketches in SATA *7, 48*
  See also CLR *14*
Childs, H(alla) Fay (Cochrane) 1890-1971 .... *1*
  Obituary *25*
Chilton, Charles (Frederick William)
  1917- *102*
Chima, Cinda Williams *192*
Chimaera
  See Farjeon, Eleanor
Chin, Jason 1978- *218*
Chin, Richard (M.) 1946- *52*
Chinery, Michael 1938- *26*
Chin-Lee, Cynthia 1958- *102*
Chin-Lee D., Cynthia
  See Chin-Lee, Cynthia
Chippendale, Lisa A. *158*
Chipperfield, Joseph Eugene 1912-1980(?) .. *87*
  Earlier sketch in SATA *2*
Chisholm, P. F.
  See Finney, Patricia
Chislett, Gail (Elaine) 1948- *58*
Chittenden, Elizabeth F. 1903-1999 .... *9*
Chittenden, Margaret 1935- *28*
Chittum, Ida 1918- *7*
Chitwood, Suzanne Tanner 1958- *160*
Chmielarz, Sharon Lee 1940- *72*
Choate, Judith (Newkirk) 1940- *30*
Chocolate, Debbi 1954- *96*
Chocolate, Deborah M. Newton
  See Chocolate, Debbi
Chodos-Irvine, Margaret *211*
  Earlier sketch in SATA *152*
Choi, Sook Nyul 1937- *73*
  Autobiography Feature *126*
  See also CLR *53*
Choi, Yangsook *178*
Choldenko, Gennifer 1957- *182*
  Earlier sketch in SATA *135*

Chorao, Kay 1936- *215*
Chorao, (Ann Mc)Kay (Sproat) 1936- *162*
  Earlier sketch in SATA *8, 69*
Choron, Sandra (Zena Samelson) 1950- *146*
Choung, Eun-hee *199*
Chown, Marcus 1959- *137*
Choyce, Lesley 1951- *165*
  Earlier sketch in SATA *94*
Choyce, Lesley Willis
  See Choyce, Lesley
Chrisman, Arthur Bowie 1889-1953 .... *124*
  See also YABC *1*
Christelow, Eileen 1943- *184*
  Autobiography Feature *120*
  Brief entry *35*
  Earlier sketches in SATA *38, 90*
Christensen, Bonnie 1951- *213*
  Earlier sketches in SATA *110, 157*
Christensen, Gardell Dano 1907-1991 .... *1*
Christensen, Laurie
  See Steding, Laurie
Christesen, Barbara 1940- *40*
Christgau, Alice Erickson 1902-1977 .... *13*
Christian, Mary Blount 1933- *9*
Christiana, David *195*
Christie, Agatha 1890-1976 .... *36*
Christie, Agatha Mary Clarissa
  See Christie, Agatha
Christie, Ann Philippa
  See Pearce, Philippa
Christie, Gregory
  See Christie, R. Gregory
Christie, Philippa
  See Pearce, Philippa
Christie, R. Gregory 1971- *185*
  Earlier sketch in SATA *127*
Christopher, John
  See Youd, Samuel
Christopher, Louise
  See Hale, Arlene
Christopher, Matt(hew Frederick)
  1917-1997 .... *80*
  Obituary *99*
  Earlier sketches in SATA *2, 47*
  See also CLR *119*
  See also SAAS *9*
Christopher, Milbourne 1914(?)-1984 .... *46*
Christy, Howard Chandler 1873-1952 .... *21*
Chrustowski, Rick *176*
Chrystie, Frances N(icholson) 1904-1986 .... *60*
Chu, Daniel 1933- *11*
Chukovsky, Kornei (Ivanovich) 1882-1969 . *34*
  Earlier sketch in SATA *5*
Church, Caroline Jayne *219*
  Earlier sketch in SATA *179*
Church, Richard 1893-1972 .... *3*
Churchill, E(lmer) Richard 1937- *11*
Churchill, Elizabeth
  See Hough, Richard (Alexander)
Chute, B(eatrice) J(oy) 1913-1987 .... *2*
  Obituary *53*
Chute, Marchette (Gaylord) 1909-1994 .... *1*
Chwast, Jacqueline 1932- *6*
Chwast, Seymour 1931- *146*
  Earlier sketches in SATA *18, 96*
Ciardi, John (Anthony) 1916-1986 .... *65*
  Obituary *46*
  Earlier sketch in SATA *1*
  See also CLR *19*
  See also SAAS *26*
Ciccone, Madonna Louise Veronica
  See Madonna
Ciddor, Anna 1957- *213*
Ciment, James D. 1958- *140*
Cirrone, Dorian *182*
Cisneros, Sandra 1954-
  See CLR *123*
Citra, Becky 1954- *137*
Citrin, Michael 1965(?)- *183*
Claflin, Willy 1944- *208*
Clair, Andree *19*

Clampett, Bob 1914(?)-1985 .... *44*
  Obituary *38*
Clampett, Robert
  See Clampett, Bob
Clapp, John 1968- *109*
Clapp, Patricia 1912- *74*
  Earlier sketch in SATA *4*
  See also SAAS *4*
Clare, Ellen
  See Sinclair, Olga
Clare, Helen
  See Clarke, Pauline
Claremont, Chris 1950- *87*
Claremont, Christopher Simon
  See Claremont, Chris
Clark, Ann Nolan 1896-1995 .... *82*
  Obituary *87*
  Earlier sketch in SATA *4*
  See also CLR *16*
  See also SAAS *16*
Clark, Champ 1923-2002 .... *47*
Clark, Christopher (Anthony) Stuart
  See Stuart-Clark, Christopher (Anthony)
Clark, Clara Gillow 1951- *154*
  Earlier sketch in SATA *84*
Clark, David
  See Hardcastle, Michael
Clark, David Allen
  See Ernst, (Lyman) John
Clark, Emma Chichester
  See Chichester Clark, Emma
Clark, Frank J(ames) 1922- *18*
Clark, Garel
  See Garelick, May
Clark, Halsey
  See Deming, Richard
Clark, Joan
  See Benson, Mildred
Clark, Joan 1934- *182*
  Earlier sketches in SATA *59, 96*
Clark, Leonard 1905-1981 .... *30*
  Obituary *29*
Clark, M. R.
  See Clark, Mavis Thorpe
Clark, Margaret (D.) 1943- *126*
Clark, Margaret Goff 1913- *82*
  Earlier sketch in SATA *8*
Clark, Mary Higgins 1929- *46*
Clark, Mavis Thorpe 1909-1999 .... *74*
  Earlier sketch in SATA *8*
  See also CLR *30*
  See also SAAS *5*
Clark, Merle
  See Gessner, Lynne
Clark, Patricia Denise 1921- *117*
Clark, Patricia Finrow 1929- *11*
Clark, Ronald Harry 1904-1999 .... *193*
Clark, Ronald William 1916-1987 .... *2*
  Obituary *52*
Clark, Sherryl 1956- *149*
Clark, Van D(eusen) 1909-1974 .... *2*
Clark, Virginia
  See Gray, Patricia (Clark)
Clark, Walter Van Tilburg 1909-1971 .... *8*
Clarke, Arthur
  See Clarke, Arthur C.
Clarke, Arthur C. 1917-2008 .... *115*
  Obituary *191*
  Earlier sketches in SATA *13, 70*
  See also CLR *119*
Clarke, Arthur Charles
  See Clarke, Arthur C.
Clarke, Clorinda 1917- *7*
Clarke, Elizabeth L. 1934- *103*
Clarke, Greg 1959- *215*
Clarke, Gus 1948- *134*
Clarke, J.
  See Clarke, Judith
Clarke, James Hall
  See Rowland-Entwistle, (Arthur) Theodore
  (Henry)

Clarke, Joan B. 1921- 42
  Brief entry 27
Clarke, John
  See Laklan, Carli
  and Sontup, Dan(iel)
Clarke, Judith 1943- 164
  Earlier sketches in SATA *75, 110*
  See also CLR *61*
Clarke, Julia 1950- 138
Clarke, Kenneth 1957- 107
Clarke, Lea
  See Rowland-Entwistle, (Arthur) Theodore
  (Henry)
Clarke, Margaret 1941-
  See CLR *99*
Clarke, Mary Stetson 1911-1994 5
Clarke, Michael
  See Newlon, (Frank) Clarke
Clarke, Pauline 1921- 131
  Earlier sketch in SATA *3*
  See also CLR *28*
Clarkson, E(dith) Margaret 1915- 37
Clarkson, Ewan 1929- 9
Claudia, Susan
  See Goulart, Ron
  and Johnston, William
Claverie, Jean 1946- 38
Clay, Patrice 1947- 47
Clay, Wil 203
Clayman, Deborah Paula
  See Da Costa, Deborah
Claypool, Jane
  See Miner, Jane Claypool
Clayton, Elaine 1961- 209
  Earlier sketches in SATA *94, 159*
Clayton, Lawrence (Otto, Jr.) 1945- 75
Clayton, Sally Pomme 218
Clayton, Sandra 1951- 110
Cle, Troy 202
Clea, Super
  See Hantman, Clea
Cleary, Beverly 1916- 121
  Earlier sketches in SATA *2, 43, 79*
  See also CLR *72*
  See also SAAS *20*
Cleary, Beverly Atlee Bunn
  See Cleary, Beverly
Cleary, Brian P. 1959- 186
  Earlier sketches in SATA *93, 132*
Cleaver, Bill
  See Cleaver, William J.
Cleaver, Carole 1934- 6
Cleaver, Elizabeth (Ann Mrazik)
  1939-1985 23
  Obituary 43
  See also CLR *13*
Cleaver, Hylton Reginald 1891-1961 49
Cleaver, Vera 1919-1993 76
  Earlier sketch in SATA *22*
  See also CLR *6*
Cleaver, Vera Allen
  See Cleaver, Vera
Cleaver, William J. 1920-1981 22
  Obituary 27
  See also CLR *6*
Cleishbotham, Jebediah
  See Scott, Sir Walter
Cleland, Mabel
  See Widdemer, Mabel Cleland
Clem, Margaret H(ollingsworth) 1923- 90
Clemens, James
  See Rollins, James
Clemens, Samuel
  See Twain, Mark
Clemens, Samuel Langhorne
  See Twain, Mark
Clemens, Virginia Phelps 1941- 35
Clement, Gary 191
Clement, Janet 182
Clement, Nathan 1966- 200
Clement, Priscilla Ferguson 1942- 171

Clement, Rod 97
Clement-Moore, Rosemary 188
Clements, Andrew 1949- 203
  Earlier sketches in SATA *104, 158*
Clements, Bruce 1931- 178
  Earlier sketches in SATA *27, 94*
Clemesha, David 192
Cleminson, Katie 221
Clemons, Elizabeth
  See Nowell, Elizabeth Cameron
Clerk, N. W.
  See Lewis, C. S.
Cleveland, Bob
  See Cleveland, George
Cleveland, George 1903(?)-1985
  Obituary 43
Cleveland-Peck, Patricia 80
Cleven, Cathrine
  See Cleven, Kathryn Seward
Cleven, Kathryn Seward 2
Clevenger, William R. 1954- 84
Clevenger, William Russell
  See Clevenger, William R.
Clevin, Joergen 1920- 7
Clevin, Jorgen
  See Clevin, Joergen
Clewes, Dorothy (Mary) 1907-2003 86
  Obituary 138
  Earlier sketch in SATA *1*
Clifford, David
  See Rosenberg, Eth Clifford
Clifford, Eth
  See Rosenberg, Eth Clifford
Clifford, Harold B(urton) 1893-1988 10
Clifford, Margaret Cort 1929- 1
Clifford, Martin
  See Hamilton, Charles (Harold St. John)
Clifford, Mary Louise Beneway 1926- 23
Clifford, Peggy
  See Clifford, Margaret Cort
Clifford, Rachel Mark
  See Lewis, Brenda Ralph
Clifton, Lucille 1936-2010 128
  Earlier sketches in SATA *20, 69*
  See also CLR *5*
Clifton, Thelma Lucille
  See Clifton, Lucille
Climo, Shirley 1928- 166
  Autobiography Feature 110
  Brief entry 35
  Earlier sketches in SATA *39, 77*
  See also CLR *69*
Cline-Ransome, Lesa 201
Clinton, Catherine 1952- 203
Clinton, Cathryn 1957- 136
Clinton, Dirk
  See Silverberg, Robert
Clinton, Jon
  See Prince, J(ack) H(arvey)
Clippinger, Carol 193
Clish, (Lee) Marian 1946- 43
Clive, Clifford
  See Hamilton, Charles (Harold St. John)
Clokey, Art 1921- 59
Cloudsley-Thompson, J(ohn) L(eonard)
  1921- 19
Clouse, Nancy L. 1938- 78
Clover, Peter 1952- 215
  Earlier sketch in SATA *152*
Clutha, Janet Paterson Frame
  See Frame, Janet
Clymer, Eleanor 1906-2001 85
  Obituary 126
  Earlier sketch in SATA *9*
  See also SAAS *17*
Clyne, Patricia (Edwards) 31
Cneut, Carll 1969- 197
Coalson, Glo 1946- 94
  Earlier sketch in SATA *26*
Coates, Anna 1958- 73
Coates, Belle 1896-1986 2

Coates, Ruth Allison 1915- 11
Coats, Alice M(argaret) 1905-1976 11
Coatsworth, Elizabeth (Jane) 1893-1986 100
  Obituary 49
  Earlier sketches in SATA *2, 56*
  See also CLR *2*
Cobalt, Martin
  See Mayne, William
Cobb, Jane
  See Berry, Jane Cobb
Cobb, Mary 1931- 88
Cobb, Vicki 1938- 136
  Autobiography Feature 136
  Earlier sketches in SATA *8, 69, 131*
  See also CLR *2*
  See also SAAS *6*
Cobbett, Richard
  See Pluckrose, Henry (Arthur)
Cober, Alan E(dwin) 1935-1998 7
  Obituary 101
Cobham, Sir Alan
  See Hamilton, Charles (Harold St. John)
Coburn, Jake 1978- 155
Cocagnac, Augustin Maurice(-Jean) 1924- 7
Cocca-Leffler, Maryann 1958- 194
  Earlier sketches in SATA *80, 136*
Cochran, Bill 187
Cochran, Bobbye A. 1949- 11
Cochran, Josh 221
Cochran, Thomas 1955- 198
Cochrane, Hamilton E.
  See Cochrane, Mick
Cochrane, Mick 1956- 215
Cockcroft, Jason 217
Cockett, Mary 3
Cocks, Peter 204
Cocovini, Abby 202
Coddell, Esme Raji
  See Codell, Esme Raji
Codell, Esme Raji 1968- 160
Cody, C. S.
  See Waller, Leslie
Cody, Jess
  See Cunningham, Chet
Coe, Anne (E.) 1949- 95
Coe, Douglas
  See Epstein, Beryl
  and Epstein, Samuel
Coe, Lloyd 1899(?)-1976
  Obituary 30
Coen, Rena Neumann 1925- 20
Coerr, Eleanor (Beatrice) 1922- 67
  Earlier sketch in SATA *1*
Cofer, Judith Ortiz 1952- 164
  Earlier sketch in SATA *110*
Coffelt, Nancy 1961- 189
Coffey, Brian
  See Koontz, Dean
Coffin, Geoffrey
  See Mason, F(rancis) van Wyck
Coffin, M. T.
  See Stanley, George Edward
Coffman, Ramon Peyton 1896-1989 4
Cogan, Karen 1954- 125
Coggins, Jack (Banham) 1911-2006 2
Cohen, Barbara 1932-1992 77
  Obituary 74
  Earlier sketch in SATA *10*
  See also SAAS *7*
Cohen, Daniel (E.) 1936- 70
  Earlier sketch in SATA *8*
  See also CLR *43*
  See also SAAS *4*
Cohen, Deborah Bodin 1968- 180
Cohen, Jan Barger
  See Barger, Jan
Cohen, Jene Barr
  See Barr, Jene
Cohen, Joan Lebold 1932- 4
Cohen, Judith Love 1933- 78

Cohen, Miriam 1926-1955 .... *155*
  Earlier sketches in SATA *29, 106*
  See also SAAS *11*
Cohen, Nora *75*
Cohen, Paul 1945- *58*
Cohen, Paul S.
  See Cohen, Paul
Cohen, Peter Zachary 1931- *150*
  Earlier sketch in SATA *4*
Cohen, Robert Carl 1930- *8*
Cohen, Santiago 1954- *215*
Cohen, Sholom 1951- *94*
Cohn, Angelo 1914-1997 .... *19*
Cohn, Diana *194*
Cohn, Rachel 1968- *161*
Coit, Margaret Louise 1922-2003 .... *2*
  Obituary *142*
Colasanti, Susane 1973- *214*
Colato Lainez, Rene 1970- *176*
Colbert, Anthony 1934-2007 .... *15*
Colbert, Nancy A. 1936- *139*
Colby, C(arroll) B(urleigh) 1904-1977 .... *35*
  Earlier sketch in SATA *3*
Colby, Jean Poindexter 1909-1993 .... *23*
Cole, Annette
  See Steiner, Barbara A(nnette)
Cole, Babette 1949- *155*
  Earlier sketches in SATA *61, 96*
Cole, Betsy 1940- *83*
Cole, Brock 1938- *200*
  Earlier sketches in SATA *72, 136*
  See also CLR *18*
Cole, Davis
  See Elting, Mary
Cole, Hannah 1954- *74*
Cole, Henry 1955- *213*
  Earlier sketch in SATA *181*
Cole, Jack -1974
  See Stewart, John
Cole, Jackson
  See Curry, Thomas Albert
  and Germano, Peter B.
  and Heckelmann, Charles N(ewman)
  and Newton, D(wight) B(ennett)
  and Schisgall, Oscar
Cole, Jennifer
  See Zach, Cheryl (Byrd)
Cole, Joanna 1944- *168*
  Brief entry *37*
  Earlier sketches in SATA *49, 81, 120*
  See also CLR *40*
Cole, Lois Dwight 1903-1979 .... *10*
  Obituary *26*
Cole, Michael 1947- *59*
Cole, Samantha
  See Cole, Stephen
Cole, Sheila 1939- *171*
  Earlier sketches in SATA *24, 95*
Cole, Sheila R.
  See Cole, Sheila
Cole, Sheila Rotenberg
  See Cole, Sheila
Cole, Stephen 1971- *161*
Cole, William (Rossa) 1919-2000 .... *71*
  Earlier sketch in SATA *9*
  See also SAAS *9*
Coleman, Andrew
  See Pine, Nicholas
Coleman, Clare
  See Bell, Clare (Louise)
  and Easton, M(alcolm) Coleman
Coleman, Janet Wyman *184*
Coleman, Loren 1947- *164*
Coleman, Loren Elwood, Jr.
  See Coleman, Loren
Coleman, Mary Ann 1928- *83*
Coleman, Michael
  See Jones, Allan Frewin
Coleman, Michael 1946- *199*
  Autobiography Feature *133*
  Earlier sketches in SATA *108, 133*

Coleman, Rowan *187*
Coleman, William L(eRoy) 1938- *49*
  Brief entry *34*
Coleman, Wim 1926- *212*
Coles, Robert (Martin) 1929- *23*
Colfer, Eoin 1965- *197*
  Earlier sketch in SATA *148*
  See also CLR *112*
Colin, Ann
  See Ure, Jean
Collard, Sneed B. III 1959- *184*
  Earlier sketches in SATA *84, 139*
Colledge, Anne 1939- *142*
Colley, Jacqui 1965- *202*
Collicott, Sharleen 1937- *143*
  Earlier sketch in SATA *98*
Collier, Bryan *204*
  Earlier sketches in SATA *126, 174*
Collier, Christopher 1930- *70*
  Earlier sketch in SATA *16*
  See also CLR *126*
Collier, Ethel 1903-1999 .... *22*
Collier, James Lincoln 1928- *166*
  Earlier sketches in SATA *8, 70*
  See also CLR *126*
  See also SAAS *21*
Collier, Jane
  See Collier, Zena
Collier, Kristi *182*
Collier, Steven 1942- *61*
Collier, Zena 1926- *23*
Collings, Gillian 1939- *102*
Collington, Peter 1948- *99*
  Earlier sketch in SATA *59*
Collins, Ace 1953- *82*
Collins, Andrew J.
  See Collins, Ace
Collins, B. R. 1981- *214*
Collins, David R(aymond) 1940-2001 .... *121*
  Earlier sketch in SATA *7*
Collins, Heather 1946- *81*
Collins, Hunt
  See Hunter, Evan
Collins, Michael
  See Lynds, Dennis
Collins, Michael 1930- *58*
Collins, Pat Lowery 1932- *217*
  Earlier sketches in SATA *31, 151*
Collins, Paul 1954- *126*
Collins, Ross 1972- *200*
Collins, Ruth Philpott 1890-1975
  Obituary *30*
Collins, Suzanne *180*
Collins, Yvonne *194*
Collinson, A. S.
  See Collinson, Alan S.
Collinson, Alan S. 1934- *80*
Collinson, Roger (Alfred) 1936- *133*
Collison, Linda 1953- *185*
Collodi, Carlo 1826-1890 .... *100*
  Earlier sketch in SATA *29*
  See also CLR *120*
Colloms, Brenda 1919- *40*
Colman, Hila 1909-2008 .... *53*
  Earlier sketch in SATA *1*
  See also SAAS *14*
Colman, Morris 1899(?)-1981
  Obituary *25*
Colman, Penny (Morgan) 1944- *160*
  Autobiography Feature *160*
  Earlier sketches in SATA *77, 114*
Colman, Warren (David) 1944- *67*
Coloma, Cindy
  See Martinusen-Coloma, Cindy
Colombo, John Robert 1936- *50*
Colon, Raul *156*
Colon, Raul 1952- *202*
Colonius, Lillian 1911-1992 .... *3*
Colorado, Antonio J.
  See Colorado (Capella), Antonio J(ulio)

Colorado (Capella), Antonio J(ulio)
  1903-1994 .... *23*
  Obituary *79*
Colquhoun, Glenn 1964- *165*
Colston, Fifi E. 1960- *150*
Colt, Martin
  See Epstein, Beryl
  and Epstein, Samuel
Colum, Padraic 1881-1972 .... *15*
  See also CLR *36*
Columbus, Chris 1959- *97*
Columbus, Christopher
  See Columbus, Chris
Columella
  See Moore, Clement Clarke
Colver, Anne 1908- *7*
Colvin, James
  See Moorcock, Michael
Colwell, Eileen (Hilda) 1904-2002 .... *2*
Colwyn, Stewart
  See Pepper, Frank S.
Coman, Carolyn 1951- *197*
  Earlier sketch in SATA *127*
Combs, Lisa M.
  See McCourt, Lisa
Combs, Robert
  See Murray, John
Comfort, Jane Levington
  See Sturtzel, Jane Levington
Comfort, Mildred Houghton 1886-1976 .... *3*
Comins, Ethel M(ae) *11*
Comins, Jeremy 1933- *28*
Commager, Henry Steele 1902-1998 .... *23*
  Obituary *102*
Comora, Madeleine *190*
Compere, Mickie
  See Davidson, Margaret
Compestine, Ying Chang 1963- *187*
  Earlier sketch in SATA *140*
Comport, Sally Wern *190*
Compton, Patricia A. 1936- *75*
Comte, The Great
  See Hawkesworth, Eric
Comus
  See Ballantyne, R(obert) M(ichael)
Comyns, Nance
  See Comyns-Toohey, Nantz
Comyns-Toohey, Nantz 1956- *86*
Conahan, Carolyn
  See Conahan, Carolyn Digby
Conahan, Carolyn Digby 1961- *216*
Conan Doyle, Arthur
  See Doyle, Sir Arthur Conan
Condie, Ally *204*
Condie, Allyson B.
  See Condie, Ally
Condit, Martha Olson 1913- *28*
Condon, Bill 1949- *142*
Condon, Judith *83*
Condon, Ken *195*
Condy, Roy 1942- *96*
Cone, Ferne Geller 1921- *39*
Cone, Molly (Lamken) 1918- *151*
  Autobiography Feature *151*
  Earlier sketches in SATA *1, 28, 115*
  See also SAAS *11*
Cone, Patrick 1954- *89*
Coney, Michael G. 1932-2005 .... *61*
  Obituary *170*
Coney, Michael Greatrex
  See Coney, Michael G.
Coney, Mike
  See Coney, Michael G.
Conford, Ellen 1942- *162*
  Earlier sketches in SATA *6, 68, 110*
  See also CLR *71*
Conger, Lesley
  See Suttles, Shirley (Smith)
Conklin, Gladys Plemon 1903- *2*

Conklin, Paul S. 1929(?)-2003 .... *43*
    Brief entry *33*
    Obituary *147*
Conkling, Hilda 1910-1986 .... *23*
Conlan, Kathleen Elizabeth 1950- *145*
Conlan, Kathy
    See Conlan, Kathleen Elizabeth
Conley, Robyn 1963- *125*
Conley-Weaver, Robyn
    See Conley, Robyn
Conlon-McKenna, Marita 1956- *71*
Conly, Jane Leslie 1948- *164*
    Earlier sketches in SATA *80, 112*
Conly, Robert Leslie 1918(?)-1973 .... *23*
    See also CLR *2*
Connell, Kirk
    See Chapman, John Stanton Higham
Connell, Tom *206*
Connelly, Gwen 1952- *212*
Connelly, Marc(us Cook) 1890-1980
    Obituary *25*
Connolly, Jerome P(atrick) 1931- *8*
Connolly, Pat 1943- *74*
Connolly, Peter 1935- *105*
    Earlier sketch in SATA *47*
Conover, Chris 1950- *213*
    Earlier sketch in SATA *31*
Conquest, Owen
    See Hamilton, Charles (Harold St. John)
Conrad, Joseph 1857-1924 .... *27*
Conrad, Pam 1947-1996 .... *133*
    Brief entry *49*
    Obituary *90*
    Earlier sketches in SATA *52, 80*
    See also CLR *18*
    See also SAAS *19*
Conroy, Jack
    See Conroy, John Wesley
Conroy, John Wesley 1899-1990 .... *19*
    Obituary *65*
Conroy, Robert
    See Goldston, Robert (Conroy)
Constable, Kate 1966- *172*
Constant, Alberta Wilson 1908-1981 .... *22*
    Obituary *28*
Constantin, Pascale *185*
Conway, Celeste *210*
Conway, David 1970- *213*
Conway, Diana C. 1943- *91*
Conway, Diana Cohen
    See Conway, Diana C.
Conway, Gordon
    See Hamilton, Charles (Harold St. John)
Cook, Ande *192*
Cook, Bernadine 1924- *11*
Cook, Fred J(ames) 1911-2003 .... *2*
    Obituary *145*
Cook, Glen 1944- *171*
    Earlier sketch in SATA *108*
Cook, Glen Charles
    See Cook, Glen
Cook, Hugh 1956- *85*
Cook, Hugh, Walter Gilbert
    See Cook, Hugh
Cook, Jean Thor 1930- *94*
Cook, Joel 1934- *79*
Cook, Joseph Jay 1924- *8*
Cook, Lisa Broadie *157*
Cook, Lyn
    See Waddell, Evelyn Margaret
Cook, Roy
    See Silverberg, Robert
Cook, Sally *207*
Cook, Trish *175*
Cooke, Ann
    See Cole, Joanna
Cooke, Arthur
    See Lowndes, Robert A(ugustine) W(ard)
Cooke, Barbara
    See Alexander, Anna B(arbara Cooke)
Cooke, David Coxe 1917- *2*

Cooke, Donald Ewin 1916-1985 .... *2*
    Obituary *45*
Cooke, Frank E. 1920- *87*
Cooke, Jean (Isobel Esther) 1929- *74*
Cooke, John Estes
    See Baum, L. Frank
Cooke, Trish 1962- *129*
Cookson, Catherine (McMullen) 1906-1998 .. *9*
    Obituary *116*
Cooley, Beth *210*
Cooley, Elizabeth
    See Cooley, Beth
Cooley, Regina Francoise 1940- *177*
Coolidge, Olivia E(nsor) 1908- *26*
    Earlier sketch in SATA *1*
Cooling, Wendy *169*
    Earlier sketch in SATA *111*
Coombs, Charles I(ra) 1914-1994 .... *43*
    Earlier sketch in SATA *3*
    See also SAAS *15*
Coombs, Chick
    See Coombs, Charles I(ra)
Coombs, Jonathan *204*
Coombs, Kate *190*
Coombs, Patricia 1926- *51*
    Earlier sketch in SATA *3*
    See also SAAS *22*
Cooney, Barbara 1917-2000 .... *96*
    Obituary *123*
    Earlier sketches in SATA *6, 59*
    See also CLR *23*
Cooney, Caroline B. 1947- *218*
    Brief entry *41*
    Earlier sketches in SATA *48, 80, 113, 130,*
    179
Cooney, Doug *181*
Cooney, Nancy Evans 1932- *42*
Coontz, Otto 1946- *33*
Cooper, Ann (Catharine) 1939- *104*
Cooper, Dutch
    See Kuyper, Sjoerd
Cooper, Elisha 1971- *157*
    Earlier sketch in SATA *99*
Cooper, Elizabeth Keyser -1992 .... *47*
Cooper, Floyd *187*
    Earlier sketches in SATA *96, 144*
    See also CLR *60*
Cooper, Gordon 1932- *23*
Cooper, Helen 1963- *169*
    Earlier sketch in SATA *102*
Cooper, Henry S. F., Jr. 1933- *65*
Cooper, Henry Spotswood Fenimore, Jr.
    See Cooper, Henry S. F., Jr.
Cooper, Ilene 1948- *145*
    Earlier sketches in SATA *66, 97*
Cooper, James Fenimore 1789-1851 .... *19*
    See also CLR *105*
Cooper, John R. *1*
Cooper, Kay 1941- *11*
Cooper, Lee Pelham 1926- *5*
Cooper, Lester (Irving) 1919-1985 .... *32*
    Obituary *43*
Cooper, Lettice (Ulpha) 1897-1994 .... *35*
    Obituary *82*
Cooper, Louise 1952-2009 .... *152*
Cooper, M.E.
    See Davis, Maggie S.
Cooper, M.E.
    See Lerangis, Peter
Cooper, Melrose
    See Kroll, Virginia L.
Cooper, Michael L. 1950- *181*
    Earlier sketches in SATA *79, 117*
Cooper, Patrick 1949- *134*
Cooper, Susan 1935- *151*
    Earlier sketches in SATA *4, 64, 104*
    See also CLR *67*
    See also SAAS *6*
Cooper, Susan Mary
    See Cooper, Susan
Cope, Jane U(rsula) 1949- *108*

Copeland, Helen 1920- *4*
Copeland, Mark 1956- *180*
Copeland, Paul W. *23*
Coplans, Peta 1951- *84*
Copley (Diana) Heather Pickering 1918- *45*
Coppard, A(lfred) E(dgar) 1878-1957
    See YABC *1*
Copper, Melinda 1952- *172*
Copper, Melinda McConnaughey
    See Copper, Melinda
Corace, Jen *208*
Coralie
    See Anderson, Catherine Corley
Corbett, Grahame *43*
    Brief entry *36*
Corbett, Scott 1913- *42*
    Earlier sketch in SATA *2*
    See also CLR *1*
    See also SAAS *2*
Corbett, Sue *174*
Corbett, W(illiam) J(esse) 1938- *102*
    Brief entry *44*
    Earlier sketch in SATA *50*
    See also CLR *19*
Corbin, Sabra Lee
    See Malvern, Gladys
Corbin, William
    See McGraw, William Corbin
Corbman, Marjorie 1987- *179*
Corby, Dan
    See Catherall, Arthur
Corcoran, Barbara (Asenath) 1911-2003 ...... *77*
    Autobiography Feature *125*
    Earlier sketch in SATA *3*
    See also CLR *50*
    See also SAAS *20*
Corcos, Lucille 1908-1973 .... *10*
Cordell, Alexander
    See Graber, Alexander
Cordell, Matthew 1975- *199*
Corder, Zizou
    See Young, Louisa
Corella, Joseph
    See Odgers, Sally Farrell
Coren, Alan 1938-2007 .... *32*
    Obituary *187*
Corey, Dorothy *23*
Corey, Shana 1974- *219*
    Earlier sketch in SATA *133*
Corfe, Thomas Howell 1928- *27*
Corfe, Tom
    See Corfe, Thomas Howell
Corfield, Robin Bell 1952- *74*
Corke, Estelle 1969- *220*
Corlett, William 1938-2005 .... *46*
    Brief entry *39*
Cormack, M(argaret) Grant 1913- *11*
Cormack, Maribelle B. 1902-1984 .... *39*
Cormier, Robert 1925-2000 .... *83*
    Obituary *122*
    Earlier sketches in SATA *10, 45*
    See also CLR *55*
Cormier, Robert Edmund
    See Cormier, Robert
Cornelius, Carol 1942- *40*
Cornelius, Kay 1933- *157*
Cornell, J.
    See Cornell, Jeffrey
Cornell, James (Clayton, Jr.) 1938- *27*
Cornell, Jean Gay 1920- *23*
Cornell, Jeffrey 1945- *11*
Cornell, Laura *189*
Cornish, D.M. 1972- *185*
Cornish, Sam(uel James) 1935- *23*
Cornwall, Nellie
    See Sloggett, Nellie
Cornwell, Autumn *195*
Corr, Christopher 1955- *189*
Correy, Lee
    See Stine, G(eorge) Harry
Corrick, James A. 1945- *76*

Corrigan, (Helen) Adeline 1909- 23
Corrigan, Barbara 1922- 8
Corrigan, Eireann 1977- 163
Corrin, Sara 1918- 86
   Brief entry 48
Corrin, Stephen 86
   Brief entry 48
Corsi, Wendy
   See Staub, Wendy Corsi
Cort, M. C.
   See Clifford, Margaret Cort
Cort, Margaret
   See Clifford, Margaret Cort
Corwin, Judith H(offman) 1946- 10
Corwin, Oliver
   See Corwin, Oliver J.
Corwin, Oliver J. 206
Cory, Rowena
   See Lindquist, Rowena Cory
Cosby, Bill 1937- 110
   Earlier sketch in SATA 66
Cosby, William Henry, Jr.
   See Cosby, Bill
   and Cosby, Bill
Cosentino, Ralph 169
Cosgrave, John O'Hara II 1908-1968
   Obituary 21
Cosgrove, Margaret (Leota) 1926- 47
Cosgrove, Stephen E(dward) 1945- 53
   Brief entry 40
Coskey, Evelyn 1932- 7
Cosner, Shaaron 1940- 43
Cossi, Olga 1921- 216
   Earlier sketches in SATA 67, 102
Costabel, Eva Deutsch 1924- 45
Costabel-Deutsch, Eva
   See Costabel, Eva Deutsch
Coste, Marion 1938- 183
Costello, David 174
Costello, David F(rancis) 1904-1990 23
Cte, Genevieve 1964- 184
Cote, Nancy 1952- 182
Cott, Jonathan 1942- 23
Cottam, Clarence 1899-1974 25
Cotten, Cynthia 188
Cottin, Menena 1950- 213
Cottle, Joan 1960- 135
Cottler, Joseph 1899-1996 22
Cottonwood, Joe 1947- 92
Cottrell, Leonard 1913-1974 24
Cottringer, Anne 1952- 150
   Earlier sketch in SATA 97
Couch, Greg 199
Coulman, Valerie 1969- 161
Couloumbis, Audrey 173
Counsel, June 1926- 70
Countryman, The
   See Whitlock, Ralph
Courlander, Harold 1908-1996 6
   Obituary 88
Coursen, Valerie 1965(?)- 102
Courtis, Stuart Appleton 1874-1969
   Obituary 29
Courtland, Tyler
   See Stevens, Serita
Courtney, Dayle
   See Goldsmith, Howard
Coury, Louise Andree 1895(?)-1983
   Obituary 34
Cousins, Linda 1946- 90
Cousins, Lucy 1964- 205
   Earlier sketch in SATA 172
Cousins, Margaret 1905-1996 2
   Obituary 92
Cousteau, Jacques 1910-1997 98
   Earlier sketch in SATA 38
Cousteau, Jacques-Yves
   See Cousteau, Jacques
Couture, Christin 1951- 73
Couvillon, Jacques 195
Covert, Ralph 1968- 197

Coville, Bruce 1950- 216
   Autobiography Feature 155
   Earlier sketches in SATA 32, 77, 118, 155
Covington, Dennis 109
Covington, Linda
   See Windsor, Linda
Cowan, Catherine 121
Cowan, Rebecca M.
   See Moesta, Rebecca
Cowan, Rebecca Moesta
   See Moesta, Rebecca
Coward, Fiona 1963- 178
Cowdrey, Richard 1959- 204
Cowell, Cressida 1966- 140
Cowen, Eve
   See Werner, Herma
Cowen, Ida 1898-1993 64
Cowie, Leonard W(allace) 1919- 4
Cowles, Kathleen
   See Krull, Kathleen
Cowley, Cassia Joy
   See Cowley, Joy
Cowley, Joy 1936- 164
   Autobiography Feature 118
   Earlier sketches in SATA 4, 90
   See also CLR 55
   See also SAAS 26
Cowley, Marjorie 1925- 111
Cox, (Christopher) Barry 1931- 62
Cox, Clinton 1934- 108
   Earlier sketch in SATA 74
Cox, David 1933- 56
Cox, David Dundas
   See Cox, David
Cox, Donald William 1921- 23
Cox, Jack
   See Cox, John Roberts
Cox, John Roberts 1915-1981 9
Cox, Judy 1954- 198
   Earlier sketches in SATA 117, 160
Cox, Marion Monroe 1898-1983
   Obituary 34
Cox, Palmer 1840-1924 24
   See also CLR 24
Cox, Vic 1942- 88
Cox, Vicki 1945- 158
Cox, Victoria 1945- 44
Cox, Wallace 1924-1973 25
Cox, Wally
   See Cox, Wallace
Cox, William R(obert) 1901-1988 46
   Brief entry 31
   Obituary 57
Coxe, Molly 1959- 101
   Earlier sketch in SATA 69
Coxon, Michele 1950- 158
   Earlier sketch in SATA 76
Coy, Harold 1902-1986 3
Coy, John 1958- 171
   Earlier sketch in SATA 120
Craats, Rennay 1973- 131
Crabtree, Judith 1928- 98
   Earlier sketch in SATA 63
Crabtree, Julie 1970- 214
Cracker, Edward E.B.
   See Odgers, Sally Farrell
Craft, Elizabeth 1971(?)- 204
Craft, K. Y.
   See Craft, Kinuko Y.
Craft, Kinuko Y. 1940- 127
   Earlier sketch in SATA 65
Craft, Kinuko Yamabe
   See Craft, Kinuko Y.
Craft, Ruth 1935- 87
   Brief entry 31
Craig, A. A.
   See Anderson, Poul
Craig, Alisa
   See MacLeod, Charlotte (Matilda)
Craig, David
   See James, Bill

Craig, Helen 1934- 213
   Earlier sketches in SATA 46, 49, 94
Craig, Joe 1979- 198
Craig, Joe Alexander
   See Craig, Joe
Craig, John Eland
   See Chipperfield, Joseph Eugene
Craig, John Ernest 1921- 23
Craig, Kit
   See Reed, Kit
Craig, M. F.
   See Craig, Mary (Francis) Shura
Craig, M. Jean 17
Craig, M. S.
   See Craig, Mary (Francis) Shura
Craig, Margaret (Maze) 1911-1964 9
Craig, Mary
   See Craig, Mary (Francis) Shura
Craig, Mary Shura
   See Craig, Mary (Francis) Shura
Craig, Mary (Francis) Shura 1923-1991 86
   Obituary 65
   Earlier sketch in SATA 6
   See also SAAS 7
Craig, Ruth 1922- 95
Craik, Mrs.
   See Craik, Dinah Maria (Mulock)
Craik, Dinah Maria (Mulock) 1826-1887 34
Crandall, Court 1965- 175
Crandell, Rachel 1943- 152
Crane, Barbara (Joyce) 1934- 31
Crane, Caroline 1930- 11
Crane, Jordan 1973- 174
Crane, M. A.
   See Wartski, Maureen (Ann Crane)
Crane, Royston Campbell 1901-1977
   Obituary 22
Crane, Stephen 1871-1900
   See YABC 2
   See also CLR 132
Crane, Stephen Townley
   See Crane, Stephen
Crane, Walter 1845-1915 100
   Earlier sketch in SATA 18
   See also CLR 56
Crane, William D(wight) 1892-1976 1
Cranfield, Ingrid 1945- 74
Cranshaw, Stanley
   See Fisher, Dorothy (Frances) Canfield
Crary, Elizabeth (Ann) 1942- 99
   Brief entry 43
Crary, Margaret (Coleman) 1906-1986 9
Craste, Marc 201
Cravath, Lynne Avril
   See Cravath, Lynne W.
Cravath, Lynne W. 1951- 182
   Earlier sketches in SATA 98, 148
Craven, Thomas 1889-1969 22
Crawford, Brent 1975- 220
Crawford, Charles P. 1945- 28
Crawford, Deborah 1922- 6
Crawford, John E(dmund) 1904-1971 3
Crawford, K(aren) Michael 1959- 155
Crawford, Mel 1925- 44
   Brief entry 33
Crawford, Phyllis 1899- 3
Crawley, Dave 177
Cray, Roberta
   See Emerson, Ru
Crayder, Dorothy 7
Crayder, Teresa
   See Colman, Hila
Crayon, Geoffrey
   See Irving, Washington
Craz, Albert G. 1926- 24
Crebbin, June 1938- 169
   Earlier sketch in SATA 80
Crecy, Jeanne
   See Williams, Jeanne
Credle, Ellis 1902-1998 1

Creech, Sharon 1945- *172*
　Earlier sketches in SATA *94, 139*
　See also CLR *89*
Creeden, Sharon 1938- *91*
Creel, Ann Howard 1953- *187*
Creighton, (Mary) Helen 1899-1989
　Obituary *64*
Creighton, Jill 1949- *96*
Crelin, Bob 1959(?)- *221*
Crenson, Victoria 1952- *159*
　Earlier sketch in SATA *88*
Cresp, Gael 1954- *119*
Crespo, George 1962- *82*
Cresswell, Helen 1934-2005 .... *79*
　Obituary *168*
　Earlier sketches in SATA *1, 48*
　See also CLR *18*
　See also SAAS *20*
Cressy, Michael 1955- *124*
Cressy, Mike
　See Cressy, Michael
Cretan, Gladys (Yessayan) 1921- *2*
Cretzmeyer, Stacy (Megan) 1959- *124*
Crew, Gary 1947- *163*
　Earlier sketches in SATA *75, 110*
　See also CLR *42*
Crew, Helen (Cecilia) Coale 1866-1941
　See YABC *2*
Crew, Linda (Jean) 1951- *137*
　Earlier sketch in SATA *71*
Crews, Donald 1938- *76*
　Brief entry *30*
　Earlier sketch in SATA *32*
　See also CLR *7*
Crews, Nina 1963- *158*
　Earlier sketch in SATA *97*
Crichton, John Michael
　See Crichton, Michael
Crichton, Michael 1942-2008 .... *88*
　Obituary *199*
　Earlier sketch in SATA *9*
Crider, Allen Billy
　See Crider, Bill
Crider, Bill 1941- *99*
Crilley, Mark 1966- *210*
　Autobiography Feature *148*
　Earlier sketches in SATA *120, 148*
Crimi, Carolyn 1959- *219*
　Earlier sketch in SATA *176*
Cripps, Enid Margaret
　See Appiah, Peggy
Crisler, Curtis L. *188*
Crisman, Ruth 1914- *73*
Crisp, Marta Marie
　See Crisp, Marty
Crisp, Marty 1947- *128*
Crispin, A(nn) C(arol) 1950- *86*
Crist, James J. 1961- *168*
Cristall, Barbara *79*
Crist-Evans, Craig 1954- *153*
Crocker, Carter *193*
Crocker, Nancy 1956- *185*
Crofford, Emily (Ardell) 1927- *61*
Crofut, William E. III 1934- *23*
Croggon, Alison 1962- *194*
Croll, Carolyn 1945- *102*
　Brief entry *52*
　Earlier sketch in SATA *56*
Croman, Dorothy Young
　See Rosenberg, Dorothy
Cromie, Alice Hamilton 1914-2000 .... *24*
Cromie, William J(oseph) 1930- *4*
Crompton, Anne Eliot 1930- *73*
　Earlier sketch in SATA *23*
Crompton, Richmal
　See Lamburn, Richmal Crompton
Cronbach, Abraham 1882-1965 .... *11*
Crone, Ruth 1919-2003 .... *4*
Cronin, A(rchibald) J(oseph) 1896-1981 ...... *47*
　Obituary *25*
Cronin, Doreen (A.) *125*

Cronin, Doreen 1966(?)- *178*
　See also CLR *136*
Cronin, Doreen A.
　See Cronin, Doreen
Crook, Beverly Courtney *38*
　Brief entry *35*
Crook, Connie Brummel 1930- *168*
　Earlier sketch in SATA *98*
Crook, Constance
　See Crook, Connie Brummel
Crosby, Alexander L. 1906-1980 .... *2*
　Obituary *23*
Crosby, Harry C.
　See Anvil, Christopher
Crosby, Margaret
　See Rathmann, Peggy
Crosher, G. R. *14*
Cross, Gilbert B. 1939- *60*
　Brief entry *51*
Cross, Gillian 1945- *178*
　Autobiography Feature *178*
　Earlier sketches in SATA *38, 71, 110, 165*
　See also CLR *28*
Cross, Gillian Clare
　See Cross, Gillian
Cross, Helen Reeder
　See Broadhead, Helen Cross
Cross, Peter 1951- *95*
Cross, Sarah *216*
Cross, Shauna 1976(?)- *196*
Cross, Tom 1954- *146*
Cross, Verda 1914- *75*
Cross, Wilbur Lucius III 1918- *2*
Crossland, Caroline 1964- *83*
Crossley-Holland, Kevin 1941- *165*
　Earlier sketches in SATA *5, 74, 120*
　See also CLR *84*
　See also SAAS *20*
Crossley-Holland, Kevin John William
　See Crossley-Holland, Kevin
Crossman, David A. 1951- *219*
Crouch, Karen Hillard
　See Good, Karen Hillard
Crouch, Marcus 1913-1996 .... *4*
Crout, George C(lement) 1917- *11*
Crow, Donna Fletcher 1941- *40*
Crow, Francis Luther
　See Luther, Frank
Crow, Kristyn *208*
Crowe, Andrew *111*
Crowe, Carole 1943- *204*
Crowe, Chris *206*
Crowe, Ellie *203*
Crowe, John
　See Lynds, Dennis
Crowe, (Bettina) Peter Lum 1911- *6*
Crowell, Grace Noll 1877-1969 .... *34*
Crowell, Pers 1910-1990 .... *2*
Crowell, Robert Leland 1909-2001 .... *63*
Crowfield, Christopher
　See Stowe, Harriet Beecher
Crowley, Arthur 1945- *38*
Crowley, Arthur McBlair
　See Crowley, Arthur
Crowley, John 1942- *140*
　Earlier sketch in SATA *65*
Crowley, Suzanne 1963- *196*
Crowley, Suzanne Carlisle
　See Crowley, Suzanne
Crownfield, Gertrude 1867-1945
　See YABC *1*
Crowther, James Gerald 1899-1983 .... *14*
Crowther, Kitty 1970- *220*
Crowther, Robert 1948- *163*
Cruikshank, George 1792-1878 .... *22*
　See also CLR *63*
Cruise, Robin 1951- *179*
Crum, Shutta *192*
　Earlier sketch in SATA *134*
Crummel, Susan Stevens 1949- *176*
　Earlier sketch in SATA *130*

Crump, Fred H., Jr. 1931- *76*
　Earlier sketch in SATA *11*
Crump, J(ames) Irving 1887-1979 .... *57*
　Obituary *21*
Crump, William D(rake) 1949- *138*
Crunden, Reginald
　See Cleaver, Hylton Reginald
Crunk, T.
　See Crunk, Tony
Crunk, Tony 1956- *130*
Crutcher, Chris 1946- *196*
　Earlier sketches in SATA *52, 99, 153*
　See also CLR *159*
Crutcher, Christopher C.
　See Crutcher, Chris
Cruz, Ray(mond) 1933- *6*
Cruz Martinez, Alejandro (?)-1987 .... *74*
Crystal, Billy 1947- *154*
Crystal, William
　See Crystal, Billy
Ctvrtek, Vaclav 1911-1976
　Obituary *27*
Cuate, Melodie A. *219*
Cuetara, Mittie 1957- *158*
　Earlier sketch in SATA *106*
Cuffari, Richard 1925-1978 .... *66*
　Obituary *25*
　Earlier sketch in SATA *6*
Cuffe-Perez, Mary 1946- *199*
Cullen, Countee 1903-1946 .... *18*
Cullen, Lynn *190*
Culliford, Pierre 1928-1992 .... *40*
　Obituary *74*
Cullinan, Bernice E(llinger) 1926- *135*
Culp, Louanna McNary 1901-1965 .... *2*
Culper, Felix
　See McCaughrean, Geraldine
Cumbaa, Stephen 1947- *72*
Cumming, Peter 1951- *168*
Cumming, Primrose Amy 1915- *24*
Cumming, Robert 1945- *65*
Cummings, Betty Sue 1918- *15*
　See also SAAS *9*
Cummings, John Michael 1963(?)- *216*
Cummings, Mary 1951- *185*
Cummings, Parke 1902-1987 .... *2*
　Obituary *53*
Cummings, Pat 1950- *203*
　Earlier sketches in SATA *42, 71, 107*
　See also CLR *48*
　See also SAAS *13*
Cummings, Phil 1957- *123*
　Earlier sketch in SATA *74*
Cummings, Priscilla 1951- *170*
　Earlier sketch in SATA *129*
Cummings, Richard
　See Gardner, Richard (M.)
Cummins, Julie *200*
Cummins, Maria Susanna 1827-1866
　See YABC *1*
Cumpiano, Ina *207*
Cuneo, Mary Louise -2001 .... *85*
Cunliffe, John Arthur 1933- *86*
　Earlier sketch in SATA *11*
Cunliffe, Marcus (Falkner) 1922-1990 .... *37*
　Obituary *66*
Cunnane, Kelly *175*
Cunningham, Bob
　See May, Julian
Cunningham, Captain Frank
　See Glick, Carl (Cannon)
Cunningham, Cathy
　See Cunningham, Chet
Cunningham, Chet 1928- *23*
Cunningham, Dale S(peers) 1932- *11*
Cunningham, Dru *91*
Cunningham, E. V.
　See Fast, Howard
Cunningham, Julia (Woolfolk) 1916- *132*
　Earlier sketches in SATA *1, 26*
　See also SAAS *2*

Cunningham, Lawrence J. 1943- 125
Cunningham, Virginia
   See Holmgren, Virginia C(unningham)
Cunxin, Li 1961- 220
Curiae, Amicus
   See Fuller, Edmund (Maybank)
Curie, Eve 1904-2007 1
   Obituary 188
Curlee, Lynn 1947- 190
   Earlier sketches in SATA 98, 141
Curley, Daniel 1918-1988 23
   Obituary 61
Curley, Marianne 1959- 175
   Earlier sketch in SATA 131
Currey, Anna 194
Currie, Robin 1948- 120
Currie, Stephen 1960- 132
   Earlier sketch in SATA 82
Curry, Ann (Gabrielle) 1934- 72
Curry, Jane L(ouise) 1932- 138
   Autobiography Feature 138
   Earlier sketches in SATA 1, 52, 90
   See also CLR 31
   See also SAAS 6
Curry, Peggy Simson 1911-1987 8
   Obituary 50
Curry, Tom 185
Curtis, Bruce (Richard) 1944- 30
Curtis, Chara M(ahar) 1950- 78
Curtis, Christopher Paul 1953- 187
   Earlier sketches in SATA 93, 140
   See also CLR 68
Curtis, Gavin 1965- 107
Curtis, Jamie Lee 1958- 144
   Earlier sketch in SATA 95
   See also CLR 88
Curtis, Jennifer Keats 185
Curtis, Marci 160
Curtis, Munzee
   See Caseley, Judith
Curtis, Neil 1950-2006 202
Curtis, Patricia 1921- 101
   Earlier sketch in SATA 23
Curtis, Peter
   See Lofts, Norah (Robinson)
Curtis, Philip (Delacourt) 1920- 62
Curtis, Richard 1937- 29
Curtis, Richard Alan
   See Curtis, Richard
Curtis, Richard Hale
   See Deming, Richard
   and Levinson, Leonard
   and Rothweiler, Paul Roger
Curtis, Stacy 205
Curtis, Wade
   See Pournelle, Jerry
Curtiss, A(rlene) B. 1934- 90
Cusack, Margaret 1945- 58
Cushman, Doug 1953- 210
   Earlier sketches in SATA 65, 101, 157
Cushman, Jerome 2
Cushman, Karen 1941- 147
   Earlier sketch in SATA 89
   See also CLR 55
Cusick, Richie Tankersley 1952- 140
   Earlier sketch in SATA 67
Cutbill, Andy 1972- 201
Cutchen, Billye Walker 1930- 15
Cutchins, Judy 1947- 59
Cutler, Daniel S. 1951- 78
Cutler, Daniel Solomon
   See Cutler, Daniel S.
Cutler, Ebbitt 1923- 9
Cutler, Ivor 1923-2006 24
   Obituary 174
Cutler, Jane 1936- 162
   Earlier sketches in SATA 75, 118
Cutler, May Ebbitt
   See Cutler, Ebbitt
Cutler, Samuel
   See Folsom, Franklin (Brewster)

Cutlip, Kimbra L(eigh-Ann) 1964- 128
Cutrate, Joe
   See Spiegelman, Art
Cutt, W(illiam) Towrie 1898-1981 16
   Obituary 85
Cuyler, Margery 1948- 195
   Earlier sketches in SATA 39, 99, 156
Cuyler, Margery Stuyvesant
   See Cuyler, Margery
Cuyler, Stephen
   See Bates, Barbara S(nedeker)
Cyrus, Kurt 1954- 179
   Earlier sketch in SATA 132
Czajkowski, James
   See Rollins, James
Czekaj, Jef 1969- 217
Czernecki, Stefan 1946- 178

D

Dabba Smith, Frank 174
Dabcovich, Lydia 99
   Brief entry 47
   Earlier sketch in SATA 58
Dace, Dolores B(oelens) 1929- 89
Da Costa, Deborah 193
Daddo, Andrew 1967- 198
Dadey, Debbie 1959- 217
   Earlier sketches in SATA 73, 136
Dahl, Borghild (Margarethe) 1890-1984 7
   Obituary 37
Dahl, Roald 1916-1990 73
   Obituary 65
   Earlier sketches in SATA 1, 26
   See also CLR 111
Dahlberg, Maurine F. 1951- 171
Dahlstedt, Marden (Stewart) 1921-1983 8
   Obituary 110
Dahme, Joanne 206
Dain, Martin J. 1924-2000 35
Dakos, Kalli 1950- 115
   Earlier sketch in SATA 80
Dale, Anna 1971- 170
Dale, Gary
   See Reece, Colleen L.
Dale, George E.
   See Asimov, Isaac
Dale, Jack
   See Holliday, Joseph
Dale, Kim 1957- 123
Dale, Margaret J(essy) Miller 1911- 39
Dale, Mitzi
   See Hemstock, Gillian
Dale, Norman
   See Denny, Norman (George)
Dale, Penny 1954- 151
   Earlier sketch in SATA 70
Daley, Michael J. 170
Dalgliesh, Alice 1893-1979 17
   Obituary 21
   See also CLR 62
Dalkey, Kara 1953- 132
Dalkey, Kara Mia
   See Dalkey, Kara
Dallas, Ruth 1919- 86
Dalmas, John
   See Jones, John R(obert)
Dalton, Alene
   See Chapin, Alene Olsen Dalton
Dalton, Annie 1948- 140
   Earlier sketch in SATA 40
Dalton, Kit
   See Cunningham, Chet
Dalton, Pamela
   See Johnson, Pamela
Dalton, Sean
   See Chester, Deborah
Dalton, Sheila 1949- 108
D'Aluisio, Faith 1957- 205

Daly, James 217
Daly, Jim
   See Stratemeyer, Edward L.
Daly, Jude 1951- 177
Daly, Kathleen N(orah) 124
   Brief entry 37
Daly, Maureen 1921-2006 129
   Obituary 176
   Earlier sketch in SATA 2
   See also CLR 96
   See also SAAS 1
Daly, Nicholas
   See Daly, Niki
Daly, Niki 1946- 198
   Earlier sketches in SATA 37, 76, 114, 164
   See also CLR 41
   See also SAAS 21
D'Amato, Alex 1919- 20
D'Amato, Janet (Potter) 1925- 9
Damerow, Gail 1944- 83
Damerow, Gail Jane
   See Damerow, Gail
D'Amico, Carmela 170
D'Amico, Steve 170
Damrell, Liz 1956- 77
Damrosch, Helen
   See Tee-Van, Helen Damrosch
Dana, Barbara 1940- 218
   Earlier sketch in SATA 22
Dana, Richard Henry, Jr. 1815-1882 26
Danachair, Caoimhin O
   See Danaher, Kevin
Danaher, Kevin 1913-2002 22
Danakas, John 1963- 94
Dandi
   See Mackall, Dandi Daley
D'Andrea, Kate
   See Steiner, Barbara A(nnette)
Dangerfield, Balfour
   See McCloskey, (John) Robert
Daniel, Alan 1939- 76
   Brief entry 53
Daniel, Anita 1893(?)-1978 23
   Obituary 24
Daniel, Anne
   See Steiner, Barbara A(nnette)
Daniel, Becky 1947- 56
Daniel, Claire 1949- 164
Daniel, Colin
   See Windsor, Patricia
Daniel, Hawthorne 1890- 8
Daniel, (Donna) Lee 1944- 76
Daniel, Rebecca
   See Daniel, Becky
Daniels, Guy 1919-1989 11
   Obituary 62
Daniels, Kit
   See Diver, Lucienne
Daniels, Lucy
   See Oldfield, Jenny
Daniels, Max
   See Gellis, Roberta
Daniels, Olga
   See Sinclair, Olga
Daniels, Patricia 1955- 93
Daniels, Zoe
   See Laux, Constance
Dank, Gloria Rand 1955- 56
   Brief entry 46
Dank, Leonard D(ewey) 1929- 44
Dank, Milton 1920- 31
Dann, Max 1955- 62
Danneberg, Julie 1958- 173
Dantz, William R.
   See Philbrick, Rodman
Danzig, Dianne 213
Danziger, Paula 1944-2004 149
   Brief entry 30
   Obituary 155
   Earlier sketches in SATA 36, 63, 102
   See also CLR 20

Darby, Gene Kegley
  See Darby, Jean (Kegley)
Darby, J. N.
  See Govan, (Mary) Christine Noble
Darby, Jean (Kegley) 1921- 68
Darby, Patricia (Paulsen) 14
Darby, Ray(mond) 1912-1982 7
Darbyshire, Kristen 218
d'Arcy, Willard
  See Cox, William R(obert)
Dare, Geena
  See McNicoll, Sylvia (Marilyn)
D'arge, Mackie 218
Darian, Shea 1959- 97
Daringer, Helen Fern 1892-1986 1
Darke, Marjorie 1929- 87
  Earlier sketch in SATA 16
Darley, F(elix) O(ctavius) C(arr)
  1822-1888 35
Darling, David J. 1953- 60
  Brief entry 44
Darling, Kathy
  See Darling, Mary Kathleen
Darling, Lois (MacIntyre) 1917-1989 3
  Obituary 64
Darling, Louis, (Jr.) 1916-1970 3
  Obituary 23
Darling, Mary Kathleen 1943- 124
  Earlier sketches in SATA 9, 79
Darling, Sandra Louise Woodward
  See Day, Alexandra
Darnell, K(athryn) L(ynne) 1955- 150
Darroll, Sally
  See Odgers, Sally Farrell
Darrow, Sharon 181
Darrow, Whitney, (Jr.) 1909-1999 13
  Obituary 115
Darwin, Len
  See Darwin, Leonard
Darwin, Leonard 1916- 24
Dasent, Sir George Webbe 1817-1896 62
  Brief entry 29
Dash, Joan 1925- 142
Daskam, Josephine Dodge
  See Bacon, Josephine Dodge (Daskam)
D'ath, Justin 1953- 174
  Earlier sketch in SATA 106
Dauer, Rosamond 1934- 23
Daugherty, Charles Michael 1914- 16
Daugherty, James (Henry) 1889-1974 13
  See also CLR 78
Daugherty, Richard D(eo) 1922- 35
Daugherty, Sonia Medwedeff (?)-1971
  Obituary 27
d'Aulaire, Edgar Parin 1898-1986 66
  Obituary 47
  Earlier sketch in SATA 5
  See also CLR 21
d'Aulaire, Ingri 1904-1980 66
  Obituary 24
  Earlier sketch in SATA 5
  See also CLR 21
d'Aulaire, Ingri Mortenson Parin
  See d'Aulaire, Ingri
Dave, Dave
  See Berg, David
Daveluy, Paule Cloutier 1919- 11
Davenier, Christine 1961- 216
  Earlier sketches in SATA 127, 179
Davenport, John 1960- 156
Daves, Michael 1938- 40
David, A. R.
  See David, A(nn) Rosalie
David, A(nn) Rosalie 1946- 103
David, Jonathan
  See Ames, Lee J(udah)
David, Lawrence 1963- 165
  Earlier sketch in SATA 111
David, Peter 1956- 72
David, Peter Allen
  See David, Peter

David, Rosalie
  See David, A(nn) Rosalie
Davidson, Alice Joyce 1932- 54
  Brief entry 45
Davidson, Basil 1914-2010 13
Davidson, (Marie) Diane 1924- 91
Davidson, Hugh
  See Hamilton, Edmond
Davidson, Jessica 1915-1986 5
Davidson, Judith 1953- 40
Davidson, Lionel 1922-2009 87
Davidson, Margaret 1936- 5
Davidson, Marion
  See Garis, Howard R.
Davidson, Mary R. 1885-1973 9
Davidson, Mary S. 1940- 61
Davidson, Mickie
  See Davidson, Margaret
Davidson, Nicole
  See Jensen, Kathryn
Davidson, R.
  See Davidson, Raymond
Davidson, Raymond 1926- 32
Davidson, Rosalie 1921- 23
Davie, Helen K(ay) 1952- 148
  Earlier sketch in SATA 77
Davies, Andrew (Wynford) 1936- 27
Davies, Andy Robert 200
Davies, Bettilu D(onna) 1942- 33
Davies, Hunter 1936- 55
  Brief entry 45
Davies, Jacqueline 1962- 186
  Earlier sketch in SATA 155
Davies, Joan 1934- 50
  Brief entry 47
Davies, Nicola 1958- 182
  Earlier sketches in SATA 99, 150
Davies, Peter J(oseph) 1937- 52
Davies, Sumiko 1942- 46
Davis, (A.) Aubrey 1949- 153
Davis, Barbara Steincrohn
  See Davis, Maggie S.
Davis, Bette J. 1923- 15
Davis, Burke 1913- 4
Davis, Christopher 1928- 6
Davis, D(elbert) Dwight 1908-1965 33
Davis, Daniel S(heldon) 1936- 12
Davis, David R. 1948- 106
Davis, Donald 1944- 169
  Earlier sketch in SATA 93
Davis, Donald D.
  See Davis, Donald
Davis, Eleanor 1983(?)- 209
Davis, Emma
  See Davis, Maggie S.
Davis, Gibbs 1953- 102
  Brief entry 41
  Earlier sketch in SATA 46
Davis, Grania 1943- 88
  Brief entry 50
Davis, H(arold) L(enoir) 1896-1960 114
Davis, Heather 1970- 221
Davis, Hubert J(ackson) 1904-1997 31
Davis, Jack E. 210
Davis, Jacky 204
Davis, James Robert 1945- 32
Davis, Jenny 1953- 74
Davis, Jim
  See Davis, James Robert
Davis, Julia 1900(?)-1993 6
  Obituary 75
Davis, Karen (Elizabeth) 1944- 109
Davis, Katie 1959(?)- 208
  Earlier sketch in SATA 152
Davis, Lambert 176
Davis, Leslie
  See Guccione, Leslie Davis
Davis, Louise Littleton 1921- 25
Davis, Maggie S. 1943- 57
Davis, Marguerite 1889- 34
Davis, Mary L(ee) 1935- 9

Davis, Mary Octavia 1901-1976 6
Davis, Nelle 1958- 73
Davis, Ossie 1917-2005 81
  See also CLR 56
Davis, Paxton 1925-1994 16
Davis, Rich 1958- 206
Davis, Robert 1881-1949
  See YABC 1
Davis, Robin W(orks) 1962- 87
Davis, Russell Gerard 1922- 3
Davis, Tanita S. 212
Davis, Tim(othy N.) 1957- 94
Davis, Verne Theodore 1889-1973 6
Davis, Yvonne 1927- 115
Davol, Marguerite W. 1928- 146
  Earlier sketch in SATA 82
DaVolls, Andy (P.) 1967- 85
DaVolls, Linda 1966- 85
Davys, Sarah
  See Manning, Rosemary
Dawes, Claiborne 1935- 111
Dawson, Arthur L. 207
Dawson, Elmer A. 67
  Earlier sketch in SATA 1
Dawson, Imogen (Zoe) 1948- 126
  Earlier sketch in SATA 90
Dawson, Janine 1957- 196
Dawson, Mary 1919- 11
Dawson, Willow 1975- 208
Day, A(rthur) Grove 1904-1994 59
Day, Alexandra 1941- 197
  Autobiography Feature 197
  Earlier sketches in SATA 67, 97, 169
  See also CLR 22
  See also SAAS 19
Day, Beth (Feagles) 1924- 33
Day, Donna
  See Asay, Donna Day
Day, Edward C. 1932- 72
Day, Jon 1936(?)- 79
Day, Karen 187
Day, Larry 1956- 181
Day, Nancy 1953- 140
Day, Nancy Raines 1951- 148
  Earlier sketch in SATA 93
Day, Shirley 1962- 94
Day, Thomas 1748-1789
  See YABC 1
Day, Trevor 1955- 124
Dazey, Agnes J(ohnston) 2
Dazey, Frank M. 2
Deacon, Alexis 1978- 139
Deacon, Eileen
  See Geipel, Eileen
Deacon, Richard
  See McCormick, (George) Donald (King)
Deadman, Ronald 1919-1988(?)
  Obituary 56
Deak, Erzsi 1959- 152
Dean, Anabel 1915- 12
Dean, Carolee 1962- 148
Dean, Claire 215
Dean, David 1976- 192
Dean, Karen Strickler 1923- 49
Dean, Ruth (Brigham) 1947- 145
Dean, Zoey
  See Bennett, Cherie
de Angeli, Marguerite (Lofft) 1889-1987 ... 100
  Obituary 51
  Earlier sketches in SATA 1, 27
  See also CLR 1
Deans, Karen 195
Deans, Sis Boulos 1955- 136
  Earlier sketch in SATA 78
DeArmand, Frances Ullmann 1904(?)-1984 . 10
  Obituary 38
DeArmond, Dale 1914- 70
DeArmond, Dale Burlison
  See DeArmond, Dale

Deary, Terry 1946- *171*
  Brief entry *41*
  Earlier sketches in SATA *51, 101*
Deaver, Julie Reece 1953- *68*
de Banke, Cecile 1889-1965 .... *11*
De Bello, Rosario 1923- *89*
Debon, Nicolas *186*
  Earlier sketch in SATA *151*
de Bono, Edward 1933- *66*
de Brissac, Malcolm
  See Dickinson, Peter
de Brunhoff, Jean
  See Brunhoff, Jean de
De Brunhoff, Laurent
  See Brunhoff, Laurent de
De Bruyn, Monica G. 1952- *13*
De Bruyn, Monica Jean Grembowicz
  See De Bruyn, Monica G.
DeBry, Roger K. 1942- *91*
de Camp, Catherine Crook 1907-2000 .... *83*
  Earlier sketch in SATA *12*
de Camp, L. Sprague 1907-2000 .... *83*
  Earlier sketch in SATA *9*
de Camp, Lyon Sprague
  See de Camp, L. Sprague
DeCandido, Keith R.A. *112*
Dechausay, Sonia E. *94*
Decker, C.B. *172*
Decker, Cynthia B.
  See Decker, C.B.
Decker, Duane 1910-1964 .... *5*
Decker, Timothy 1974- *197*
DeClements, Barthe 1920- *131*
  Earlier sketches in SATA *35, 71*
  See also CLR 23
DeClements, Barthe Faith
  See DeClements, Barthe
de Clercq Zubli, Rita la Fontaine 1929- *199*
de Conte, Sieur Louis
  See Twain, Mark
Dedman, Stephen *108*
Dee, Barbara 1958- *220*
Dee, Catherine 1964- *138*
Dee, Ruby
  See Wallace, Ruby Ann
Deeble, Jason 1979- *221*
Deedy, Carmen Agra 1960- *196*
Deedy, John 1923- *24*
Deegan, Paul Joseph 1937- *48*
  Brief entry *38*
Deem, James M. 1950- *191*
  Autobiography Feature *191*
  Earlier sketches in SATA *75, 134*
Deem, James Morgan
  See Deem, James M.
Deeter, Catherine 1947- *137*
DeFelice, Cynthia 1951- *165*
  Earlier sketches in SATA *79, 121*
DeFelice, Cynthia C.
  See DeFelice, Cynthia
Defoe, Daniel 1660(?)-1731 .... *22*
  See also CLR 61
de Fombelle, Timothee
  See Fombelle, Timothee de
DeFord, Deborah H. *123*
deFrance, Anthony
  See DiFranco, Anthony (Mario)
Degen, Bruce 1945- *205*
  Brief entry *47*
  Earlier sketches in SATA *57, 97, 147*
DeGering, Etta (Belle) Fowler 1898-1996 ..... *7*
De Goldi, Kate 1959- *123*
De Goldi, Kathleen Domenica
  See De Goldi, Kate
de Goursac, Olivier 1959- *184*
De Grazia, Ettore 1909-1982 .... *39*
De Grazia, Ted
  See De Grazia, Ettore
deGroat, Diane 1947- *169*
  Earlier sketches in SATA *31, 90*

deGros, J. H.
  See Villiard, Paul
de Grummond, Lena Young *62*
  Earlier sketch in SATA *6*
de Hamel, Joan Littledale 1924- *86*
De Haven, Tom 1949- *72*
de Hugo, Pierre
  See Brackers de Hugo, Pierre
Deines, Brian 1955- *220*
Deiss, Joseph Jay 1915- *12*
de Jenkins, Lyll Becerra 1925-1997 ... *102*
DeJong, David C(ornel) 1905-1967 .... *10*
de Jong, Dola
  See de Jong, Dorothea Rosalie
de Jong, Dorothea Rosalie 1911-2003 ... *7*
  Obituary *149*
DeJong, Meindert 1906-1991 .... *2*
  Obituary *68*
  See also CLR 73
DeJonge, Joanne E. 1943- *56*
Deka, Connie
  See Laux, Constance
de Kay, Ormonde (Jr.) 1923-1998 ...... *7*
  Obituary *106*
DeKeyser, Stacy 1959- *214*
de Kiriline, Louise
  See Lawrence, Louise de Kiriline
Dekker, Carl
  See Laffin, John (Alfred Charles)
  and Lynds, Dennis
deKruif, Paul (Henry) 1890-1971 .... *50*
  Earlier sketch in SATA *5*
Delacre, Lulu 1957- *209*
  Earlier sketches in SATA *36, 156*
DeLaCroix, Alice 1940- *195*
  Earlier sketch in SATA *75*
de la Cruz, Melissa 1971- *179*
De la Garza, Phyllis 1942- *169*
De Lage, Ida 1918- *11*
de la Mare, Walter (John) 1873-1956 .... *16*
  See also CLR 148
Delaney, Harry 1932- *3*
Delaney, Joseph 1945- *172*
Delaney, M.C.
  See Delaney, Michael
Delaney, Michael 1955- *180*
  Earlier sketch in SATA *96*
Delaney, Michael Clark
  See Delaney, Michael
Delaney, Ned 1951- *28*
Delaney, Thomas Nicholas III
  See Delaney, Ned
DeLange, Alex Pardo
  See Pardo DeLange, Alex
Delano, Hugh 1933- *20*
Delano, Marfe Ferguson *215*
Delany, Samuel R., Jr. 1942- *92*
Delany, Samuel Ray
  See Delany, Samuel R., Jr.
de la Pena, Matt *205*
De La Ramee, Marie Louise 1839-1908 ... *20*
de la Roche, Mazo 1879-1961 .... *64*
De La Roche Saint Andre, Anne 1950- *75*
de Las Casas, Dianne 1970- *221*
Delaune, (Jewel) Lynn (de Grummond) *7*
DeLaurentis, Louise Budde 1920- *12*
del Barco, Lucy Salamanca 1900(?)-1989
  Obituary *64*
Delderfield, Eric R(aymond) 1909-1995 ...... *14*
Delderfield, Ronald Frederick 1912-1972 .... *20*
DeLeeuw, Adele (Louise) 1899-1988 .... *30*
  Obituary *56*
  Earlier sketch in SATA *1*
De Leon, Nephtali 1945- *97*
Delessert, Etienne 1941- *179*
  Brief entry *27*
  Earlier sketches in SATA *46, 130*
  See also CLR 81
Delgado, James P. 1958- *122*
de Lint, Charles 1951- *207*
  Earlier sketches in SATA *115, 157*

de Lint, Charles Henri Diederick Hofsmit
  See de Lint, Charles
Delmar, Roy
  See Wexler, Jerome (LeRoy)
Del Negro, Janice M. *197*
Deloria, Vine, Jr. 1933-2005 .... *21*
  Obituary *171*
Deloria, Vine Victor, Jr.
  See Deloria, Vine, Jr.
del Rey, Lester 1915-1993 .... *22*
  Obituary *76*
Delrio, Martin
  See Doyle, Debra
  and Macdonald, James D.
Delton, Judy 1931-2001 .... *77*
  Obituary *130*
  Earlier sketch in SATA *14*
  See also SAAS 9
Delulio, John 1938- *15*
Delving, Michael
  See Williams, Jay
de Marcken, Gail *186*
Demarest, Chris L. 1951- *175*
  Brief entry *44*
  Earlier sketches in SATA *45, 82, 128*
Demarest, Christopher Lynn
  See Demarest, Chris L.
Demarest, Doug
  See Barker, Will
De Mari, Silvana 1953- *193*
Demas, Corinne
  See Bliss, Corinne Demas
Demas, Vida 1927- *9*
Dematons, Charlotte 1957- *203*
DeMatteis, J.M. 1953- *180*
DeMatteis, John Marc
  See DeMatteis, J.M.
De Mejo, Oscar 1911-1992 .... *40*
Demers, Dominique 1956- *177*
de Messieres, Nicole 1930- *39*
Demi 1942- *210*
  Earlier sketches in SATA *11, 66, 102, 152*
  See also CLR 58
Demijohn, Thom
  See Disch, Thomas M.
  and Sladek, John
Deming, Richard 1915-1983 .... *24*
Deming, Sarah *191*
de Monfreid, Dorothee 1973- *189*
Demuth, Patricia Brennan 1948- *84*
  Brief entry *51*
De Muth, Roger 1948- *221*
Dendinger, Roger E. 1952- *158*
Denenberg, Barry 1940- *175*
Dengler, Marianna (Herron) 1935- *103*
Dengler, Sandy 1939- *54*
  Brief entry *40*
Denim, Sue
  See Pilkey, Dav
Denise, Anika *210*
Denise, Christopher 1968- *193*
  Earlier sketch in SATA *147*
Denman, K.L. 1957- *186*
Denmark, Harrison
  See Zelazny, Roger
Dennard, Deborah 1953- *136*
  Earlier sketch in SATA *78*
Denney, Diana 1910-2000 .... *25*
  Obituary *120*
Dennis, Morgan 1891(?)-1960 .... *18*
Dennis, Wesley 1903-1966 .... *18*
Denniston, Elinore 1900-1978
  Obituary *24*
Denny, Norman (George) 1901-1982 .... *43*
Denos, Julia *202*
Denslow, Sharon Phillips 1947- *142*
  Earlier sketch in SATA *68*
Denslow, W(illiam) W(allace) 1856-1915 .... *16*
  See also CLR 15
Dent, Grace 1973- *187*

Denton, Kady MacDonald *181*
    Earlier sketches in SATA *66, 110*
    See also CLR *71*
Denton, Terry 1950- *186*
Denver, Walt
    See Redding, Robert Hull
    and Sherman, Jory (Tecumseh)
Denzel, Justin F(rancis) 1917-1999 .... *46*
    Brief entry *38*
Denzer, Ann Wiseman
    See Wiseman, Ann (Sayre)
DePalma, Mary Newell 1961- *185*
    Earlier sketch in SATA *139*
De Palma, Toni *199*
dePaola, Thomas Anthony 1934- *200*
    Earlier sketches in SATA *11, 59, 108, 155*
    See also CLR *81*
    See also SAAS *15*
dePaola, Tomie
    See dePaola, Thomas Anthony
deParrie, Paul 1949- *74*
DePauw, Linda Grant 1940- *24*
DeRan, David 1946- *76*
Derby, Ken 1956- *181*
Derby, Kenneth R.
    See Derby, Ken
Derby, Pat 1942- *172*
Derby, Sally 1934- *189*
    Earlier sketches in SATA *89, 132*
de Regniers, Beatrice Schenk (Freedman)
    1914-2000 .... *68*
    Obituary *123*
    Earlier sketch in SATA *2*
    See also SAAS *6*
Dereske, Jo 1947- *72*
Deriso, Christine Hurley 1961- *210*
Derleth, August (William) 1909-1971 .... *5*
Derman, Martha (Winn) *74*
Derman, Sarah Audrey 1915- *11*
DeRoberts, Lyndon
    See Silverstein, Robert Alan
de Roo, Anne Louise 1931-1997 .... *84*
    Earlier sketch in SATA *25*
    See also CLR *63*
deRosa, Dee *70*
Derrick, Lionel
    See Cunningham, Chet
Derrickson, Jim 1959- *141*
Derry Down Derry
    See Lear, Edward
Dervaux, Isabelle 1961- *106*
Derwent, Lavinia *14*
Desai, Anita 1937- *126*
    Earlier sketch in SATA *63*
DeSaix, Deborah Durland *188*
De Saulles, Tony 1958- *119*
Desbarats, Peter 1933- *39*
de Selincourt, Aubrey 1894-1962 .... *14*
de Seve, Peter 1958- *219*
de Seve, Randall *198*
Deshpande, Chris 1950- *69*
Desimini, Lisa 1964- *216*
    Earlier sketches in SATA *86, 148*
Desjarlais, John 1953- *71*
Desjarlais, John J.
    See Desjarlais, John
Desmoinaux, Christel 1967- *149*
    Earlier sketch in SATA *103*
Desmond, Adrian 1947- *51*
Desmond, Adrian J.
    See Desmond, Adrian
Desmond, Adrian John
    See Desmond, Adrian
Desmond, Alice Curtis 1897-1990 .... *8*
Desnoettes, Caroline *183*
DeSpain, Pleasant 1943- *87*
Desputeaux, Helene 1959- *95*
Dessen, Sarah 1970- *172*
    Earlier sketch in SATA *120*
Detine, Padre
    See Olsen, Ib Spang

de Trevino, Elizabeth B.
    See Trevino, Elizabeth B(orton) de
de Trevino, Elizabeth Borton
    See Trevino, Elizabeth B(orton) de
Detwiler, Susan Dill 1956- *58*
Deuker, Carl 1950- *196*
    Earlier sketches in SATA *82, 150*
Deutsch, Babette 1895-1982 .... *1*
    Obituary *33*
Deutsch, Eva Costabel
    See Costabel, Eva Deutsch
Deutsch, Helen 1906-1992 .... *76*
Deutsch, Kurt
    See Singer, Kurt D.
De Valera, Sinead 1879(?)-1975
    Obituary *30*
Devaney, John 1926-1994 .... *12*
de Varennes, Monique 1947- *168*
de Varona, Frank J. 1943- *83*
Devereux, Frederick L(eonard), Jr.
    1914-1993 .... *9*
Devi, Nila
    See Woody, Regina Jones
deVinck, Christopher 1951- *85*
DeVita, James *195*
DeVito, Cara 1956- *80*
Devlin, Dorothy Wende
    See Devlin, Wende
Devlin, Harry 1918-2001 .... *136*
    Earlier sketches in SATA *11, 74*
Devlin, Wende 1918-2002 .... *74*
    Earlier sketch in SATA *11*
Devon, Paddie 1953- *92*
Devons, Sonia 1974- *72*
Devorah-Leah *111*
de Vos, Gail 1949- *122*
DeVries, Douglas 1933- *122*
De Waard, E(lliott) John 1935- *7*
Dewan, Ted 1961- *157*
    Earlier sketch in SATA *108*
Dewdney, Anna *184*
Dewdney, Selwyn (Hanington) 1909-1979 ... *64*
DeWeese, Gene
    See DeWeese, Thomas Eugene
DeWeese, Jean
    See DeWeese, Thomas Eugene
DeWeese, Thomas Eugene 1934- *46*
    Brief entry *45*
Dewey, Ariane 1937- *178*
    Earlier sketches in SATA *7, 109*
Dewey, Jennifer (Owings) 1941- *103*
    Brief entry *48*
    Earlier sketch in SATA *58*
Dewey, Kenneth Francis 1940- *39*
Dewin, Howie
    See Howie, Betsy
De Wire, Elinor 1953- *180*
deWit, Dorothy (May Knowles) 1916-1980 . *39*
    Obituary *28*
Dexter, Alison 1966- *125*
Dexter, John
    See Bradley, Marion Zimmer
Deyneka, Anita 1943- *24*
Deyrup, Astrith Johnson 1923- *24*
Dezern, Chad *201*
Dhami, Narinder 1958- *152*
Dhondy, Farrukh 1944- *152*
    Earlier sketch in SATA *65*
    See also CLR *41*
Diakite, Baba Wague 1961- *174*
Diakite, Penda 1993(?)- *174*
Diamond, Arthur 1957- *76*
Diamond, Donna 1950- *69*
    Brief entry *30*
    Earlier sketch in SATA *35*
Diamond, Petra
    See Sachs, Judith
Diamond, Rebecca
    See Sachs, Judith
Dias, Earl Joseph 1916- *41*
Dias, Ron 1937- *71*

Diaz, David 1959(?)- *189*
    Earlier sketches in SATA *96, 150*
    See also CLR *65*
Dibley, Glin *188*
DiCamillo, Kate 1964- *202*
    Earlier sketches in SATA *121, 163*
    See also CLR *117*
Di Certo, J(oseph) J(ohn) 1933- *60*
DiCianni, Ron 1952- *107*
Dick, Trella Lamson 1889-1974 .... *9*
Dickens, Charles 1812-1870 .... *15*
    See also CLR *95*
Dickens, Charles John Huffam
    See Dickens, Charles
Dickens, Frank
    See Huline-Dickens, Frank William
Dickens, Monica (Enid) 1915-1992 .... *4*
    Obituary *74*
Dickerson, Roy Ernest 1886-1965
    Obituary *26*
Dickinson, Emily 1830-1886 .... *29*
Dickinson, Emily Elizabeth
    See Dickinson, Emily
Dickinson, Mary 1949- *48*
    Brief entry *41*
Dickinson, Mary-Anne
    See Rodda, Emily
Dickinson, Peter 1927- *150*
    Earlier sketches in SATA *5, 62, 95*
    See also CLR *125*
Dickinson, Peter Malcolm de Brissac
    See Dickinson, Peter
Dickinson, Susan 1931- *8*
Dickinson, Terence 1943- *102*
Dickinson, W(illiam) Croft 1897-1963 .... *13*
Dickson, Gordon R. 1923-2001 .... *77*
Dickson, Gordon Rupert
    See Dickson, Gordon R.
Dickson, Helen
    See Reynolds, Helen Mary Greenwood Camp-
    bell
Dickson, Naida 1916- *8*
Diehn, Gwen 1943- *80*
Dierssen, Andreas 1962- *190*
Diesen, Deborah 1967- *200*
Dieterich, Michele M. 1962- *78*
Dietz, David H(enry) 1897-1984 .... *10*
    Obituary *41*
Dietz, Lew 1907-1997 .... *11*
    Obituary *95*
Diffily, Deborah *159*
Di Fiori, Larry
    See Di Fiori, Lawrence
Di Fiori, Lawrence 1934- *130*
DiFranco, Anthony (Mario) 1945- *42*
Digby, Anne 1935- *72*
Digges, Jeremiah
    See Berger, Josef
Digman, Kristina 1959- *176*
D'Ignazio, Fred 1949- *39*
    Brief entry *35*
D'Ignazio, Frederick
    See D'Ignazio, Fred
Di Grazia, Thomas (?)-1983 .... *32*
Dijkstra, Lida 1961- *195*
Dikty, Julian May
    See May, Julian
Dillard, Annie 1945- *140*
    Earlier sketch in SATA *10*
Dillard, Kristine 1964- *113*
Dillard, Polly Hargis 1916- *24*
Dillard, Sarah 1961- *217*
Diller, Harriett 1953- *78*
Dillon, Anna
    See Scott, Michael
Dillon, Barbara 1927- *44*
    Brief entry *39*
Dillon, Diane 1933- *194*
    Earlier sketches in SATA *15, 51, 106*
    See also CLR *44*

Dillon, Diane Claire
  See Dillon, Diane
Dillon, Eilis 1920-1994 74
  Autobiography Feature 105
  Obituary 83
  Earlier sketch in SATA 2
  See also CLR 26
Dillon, Jana (a pseudonym) 1952- 117
Dillon, Leo 1933- 194
  Earlier sketches in SATA 15, 51, 106
  See also CLR 44
Dillon, Sharon Saseen
  See Saseen, Sharon (Dillon)
Dils, Tracey E. 1958- 83
Dilson, Jesse 1914-1988 24
Dinan, Carolyn 59
  Brief entry 47
Dines, Carol 1956- 175
Dines, (Harry) Glen 1925-1996 7
Dinesen, Isak
  See Blixen, Karen
Dinessi, Alex
  See Schembri, Jim
Dinneen, Betty 1929- 61
Dinnerstein, Harvey 1928- 42
Dinsdale, Tim(othy Kay) 1924-1987 11
Dion, Nathalie 1964- 213
Dionne, Erin 1975- 217
Diop, Birago (Ismael) 1906-1989
  Obituary 64
Diouf, Sylviane A. 168
Diouf, Sylviane Anna
  See Diouf, Sylviane A.
DiPucchio, Kelly 204
  Earlier sketch in SATA 159
Dirk
  See Gringhuis, Richard H.
Dirks, Wilhelmina 1916- 59
Dirks, Willy
  See Dirks, Wilhelmina
Dirtmeister
  See Tomecek, Steve
DiSalvo, DyAnne 1960- 144
  Earlier sketch in SATA 59
DiSalvo-Ryan, DyAnne
  See DiSalvo, DyAnne
Disch, Thomas M. 1940-2008 92
  Obituary 195
  See also CLR 18
  See also SAAS 15
Disch, Thomas Michael
  See Disch, Thomas M.
Disch, Tom
  See Disch, Thomas M.
Disher, Garry 1949- 125
  Earlier sketch in SATA 81
Disney, Walt(er Elias) 1901-1966 28
  Brief entry 27
Ditchfield, Christin 1973- 189
DiTerlizzi, Tony 1969- 214
  Earlier sketch in SATA 154
DiTerlooney, Tiny
  See DiTerlizzi, Tony
Divakaruni, Chitra Banerjee 1956- 160
Di Valentin, Maria (Amelia) Messuri
  1911-1985 7
Diver, Lucienne 1971- 218
Divine, Arthur Durham 1904-1987
  Obituary 52
Divine, David
  See Divine, Arthur Durham
Dixon, Ann 1954- 212
  Earlier sketches in SATA 77, 127
Dixon, Ann Renee
  See Dixon, Ann
Dixon, Dougal 1947- 190
  Earlier sketches in SATA 45, 127

Dixon, Franklin W.
  See Barrett, Neal, Jr.
  and Goulart, Ron
  and Lantz, Francess L(in)
  and Lerangis, Peter
  and McFarlane, Leslie
  and Stanley, George Edward
  and Stratemeyer, Edward L.
Dixon, Jeanne 1936- 31
Dixon, Paige
  See Corcoran, Barbara (Asenath)
Dixon, Peter L(ee) 1931- 6
Dixon, Rachel 1952- 74
Djoleto, (Solomon Alexander) Amu 1929- ... 80
d'lacey, Chris 1949- 165
Doak, Annie
  See Dillard, Annie
Doane, Pelagie 1906-1966 7
Dob, Bob 207
Dobell, I(sabel) M(arian) B(arclay)
  1909-1998 11
Dobie, J(ames) Frank 1888-1964 43
Dobkin, Alexander 1908-1975
  Obituary 30
Dobler, Lavinia G. 1910- 6
Dobrin, Arnold 1928- 4
Dobson, Jill 1969- 140
Dobson, Julia 1941- 48
Dobson, Mary 1954- 117
DoCampo, Valeria 1976- 217
Docherty, James
  See Docherty, Jimmy
Docherty, Jimmy 1976- 204
Docherty, Thomas 1955- 218
Dockery, Wallene T. 1941- 27
Dockray, Tracy 1962- 139
Dockrey, Karen 1955- 103
Doctor, Bernard
  See Doctor, Bernard Aquina
Doctor, Bernard Aquina 1950- 81
Doctor X
  See Nourse, Alan E(dward)
Dodd, Ed(ward Benton) 1902-1991 4
  Obituary 68
Dodd, Emma 1969- 203
Dodd, Lynley (Stuart) 1941- 132
  Earlier sketches in SATA 35, 86
  See also CLR 62
Dodd, Marty 1921- 142
Dodd, Quentin 1972- 137
Dodds, Bill 1952- 78
Dodds, Dayle Ann 1952- 201
  Earlier sketches in SATA 75, 150
Doder, Josh 1968- 187
Dodge, Bertha S(anford) 1902-1995 8
Dodge, Fremont
  See Grimes, Lee
Dodge, Gil
  See Hano, Arnold
Dodge, Mary (Elizabeth) Mapes
  1831(?)-1905 100
  Earlier sketch in SATA 21
  See also CLR 62
Dodgson, Charles Lutwidge
  See Carroll, Lewis
Dodson, Kenneth MacKenzie 1907-1999 11
Dodson, Susan 1941- 50
  Brief entry 40
Doerrfeld, Cori 1964- 214
Dogar, Sharon 1962- 211
Dogyear, Drew
  See Gorey, Edward (St. John)
Doherty, Berlie 1943- 111
  Earlier sketch in SATA 72
  See also CLR 21
  See also SAAS 16
Doherty, Charles Hugh 1913- 6
Doherty, Craig A. 1951- 169
  Earlier sketch in SATA 83
Doherty, Katherine M(ann) 1951- 83
Doherty, Kieran 1945- 164

Dokas, Dara 1968- 216
Dokey, Cameron 1956- 97
Dolan, Edward F(rancis), Jr. 1924- 94
  Brief entry 31
  Earlier sketch in SATA 45
Dolan, Ellen M(eara) 1929-1998 88
Dolan, Sean J. 1958- 74
Dolce, J. Ellen 1948- 75
Dolch, Edward William 1889-1961 50
Dolch, Marguerite Pierce 1891-1978 50
Dollar, Diane (Hills) 1933- 57
Dolson, Hildegarde
  See Lockridge, Hildegarde (Dolson)
Domanska, Janina 1913(?)-1995 68
  Obituary 84
  Earlier sketch in SATA 6
  See also CLR 40
  See also SAAS 18
Dominguez, Angel 1953- 76
Dominguez, Angela N. 1982- 219
Domino, John
  See Averill, Esther (Holden)
Domjan, Joseph (Spiri) 1907-1992 25
Domm, Jeffrey C. 1958- 84
Donahue, Dorothy 178
Donald, Rhonda Lucas 1962- 147
Donalds, Gordon
  See Shirreffs, Gordon D(onald)
Donaldson, Bryna
  See Stevens, Bryna
Donaldson, Gordon 1913-1993 64
  Obituary 76
Donaldson, Joan 1953- 78
Donaldson, Julia 1948- 180
  Earlier sketches in SATA 82, 132
Donaldson, Stephen R. 1947- 121
Donaldson, Stephen Reeder
  See Donaldson, Stephen R.
Doner, Kim 1955- 208
  Earlier sketch in SATA 91
Doney, Todd L. W. 1959- 104
Dong-Sung, Kim 1970- 195
Dong-Sung Kim
  See Dong-Sung, Kim
Donkin, Andrew 219
Donkin, Nance (Clare) 1915- 95
Donna, Natalie 1934-1979 9
Donnelly, Elfie 1950-
  See CLR 104
Donnelly, Jennifer 1963- 154
Donnelly, Matt 1972- 148
Donnio, Sylviane 188
Donofrio, Beverly 1950- 209
Donoghue, Emma 1969- 101
Donohue, Moira Rose 1954- 201
Donoughue, Carol 1935- 139
Donovan, Frank (Robert) 1906-1975
  Obituary 30
Donovan, Gail 1962- 217
Donovan, John 1928-1992 72
  Brief entry 29
  See also CLR 3
Donovan, Mary Lee 1961- 86
Donovan, William
  See Berkebile, Fred D(onovan)
Donze, Mary Terese 1911- 89
Doob, Leonard W(illiam) 1909-2000 8
Doodler, Todd H.
  See Goldman, Todd Harris
Dooley, Norah 1953- 74
Dooling, Michael 1958- 220
  Earlier sketch in SATA 105
Dor, Ana
  See Ceder, Georgiana Dorcas
Doran, Colleen 1963- 211
Dore, (Louis Christophe Paul) Gustave
  1832-1883 19
Doremus, Robert 1913- 30
Doren, Marion (Walker) 1928- 57
Dorenkamp, Michelle 1957- 89
Dorflinger, Carolyn 1953- 91

Dorfman, Joaquin 1979- *180*
Dorfman, Joaquin Emiliano
　See Dorfman, Joaquin
Dorian, Edith M(cEwen) 1900-1983 .... *5*
Dorian, Harry
　See Hamilton, Charles (Harold St. John)
Dorian, Marguerite *7*
Dorin, Patrick C(arberry) 1939- *59*
　Brief entry *52*
Dorman, Brandon *194*
Dorman, Michael 1932- *7*
Dorman, N. B. 1927- *39*
Dormer, Frank W. *200*
Dorris, Michael 1945-1997 .... *75*
　Obituary *94*
　See also CLR *58*
Dorris, Michael A.
　See Dorris, Michael
Dorris, Michael Anthony
　See Dorris, Michael
Dorritt, Susan
　See Schlein, Miriam
Dorros, Alex 1991- *194*
Dorros, Arthur 1950- *168*
　Earlier sketches in SATA *78, 122*
　See also CLR *42*
　See also SAAS *20*
Dorros, Arthur M.
　See Dorros, Arthur
Dorson, Richard M(ercer) 1916-1981 .... *30*
Doss, Helen (Grigsby) 1918- *20*
Doss, Margot Patterson *6*
dos Santos, Joyce Audy 1949- *57*
　Brief entry *42*
Dothers, Anne
　See Chess, Victoria (Dickerson)
Dotlich, Rebecca Kai 1951- *182*
Dottig
　See Grider, Dorothy
Dotts, Maryann J. 1933- *35*
Doty, Jean Slaughter 1929- *28*
Doty, Roy 1922- *28*
Doubtfire, Dianne (Abrams) 1918- *29*
Doucet, Sharon Arms 1951- *144*
　Autobiography Feature *144*
　Earlier sketch in SATA *125*
Dougherty, Charles 1922- *18*
Dougherty, Terri (L.) 1964- *146*
Doughty, Rebecca 1955- *174*
Douglas, Blaise 1960- *101*
Douglas, Carole Nelson 1944- *73*
Douglas, Garry
　See Kilworth, Garry
Douglas, James McM.
　See Griffin, W. E. B.
Douglas, Kathryn
　See Ewing, Kathryn
Douglas, Leonard
　See Bradbury, Ray
Douglas, Lola
　See Zeises, Lara M.
Douglas, Marjory Stoneman 1890-1998 .... *10*
Douglas, Michael
　See Crichton, Michael
Douglas, Michael
　See Bright, Robert Sr.)
Douglas, Shirley Stewart
　See Tepper, Sheri S.
Douglass, Barbara 1930- *40*
Douglass, Frederick 1817(?)-1895 .... *29*
Douglass, Keith
　See Cunningham, Chet
Douty, Esther M(orris) 1909-1978 .... *8*
　Obituary *23*
Dow, Emily R. 1904-1987 .... *10*
Dow, Vicki
　See McVey, Vicki
Dowd, John David 1945- *78*
Dowd, Siobhan 1960-2007 .... *204*
Dowdell, Dorothy (Florence) Karns 1910- ... *12*

Dowden, Anne Ophelia Todd 1907-2007 .... *7*
　Obituary *180*
　See also SAAS *10*
Dowdey, Landon Gerald 1923- *11*
Dowdy, Mrs. Regera
　See Gorey, Edward (St. John)
Dowell, Frances O'Roark 1964- *205*
　Earlier sketch in SATA *157*
Dower, Laura 1967- *185*
Dowling, Terry 1947- *101*
Downard, Barry 1956- *202*
Downer, Ann 1960- *155*
Downer, Marion 1892(?)-1971 .... *25*
Downes, Belinda 1962- *180*
Downey, Fairfax D(avis) 1893-1990 .... *3*
　Obituary *66*
Downey, Lisa *214*
Downey, Lynn 1961- *185*
Downham, Jenny 1964- *192*
Downie, John 1931- *87*
Downie, Mary Alice 1934- *171*
　Earlier sketches in SATA *13, 87*
Downie, Mary Alice Dawe
　See Downie, Mary Alice
Downing, David A(lmon) 1958- *84*
Downing, Johnette *184*
Downing, Julie 1956- *148*
　Earlier sketch in SATA *81*
Downing, Paula E. 1951- *80*
Downing, Warwick
　See Downing, Wick
Downing, Wick 1931- *138*
Dowswell, Paul 1957- *184*
Doyle, A. Conan
　See Doyle, Sir Arthur Conan
Doyle, Sir Arthur Conan 1859-1930 .... *24*
　See also CLR *106*
Doyle, Brian 1935- *156*
　Earlier sketches in SATA *67, 104*
　See also CLR *22*
　See also SAAS *16*
Doyle, Charlotte 1937- *178*
　Earlier sketch in SATA *94*
Doyle, Charlotte Lackner
　See Doyle, Charlotte
Doyle, Conan
　See Doyle, Sir Arthur Conan
Doyle, Debra 1952- *165*
　Earlier sketch in SATA *105*
Doyle, Donovan
　See Boegehold, Betty (Doyle)
Doyle, John
　See Graves, Robert
Doyle, Malachy 1954- *165*
　Earlier sketch in SATA *120*
　See also CLR *83*
Doyle, Richard 1824-1883 .... *21*
Doyle, Sir A. Conan
　See Doyle, Sir Arthur Conan
Dr. A
　See Asimov, Isaac
　and Silverstein, Alvin
　and Silverstein, Virginia B.
Dr. Alphabet
　See Morice, Dave
Dr. Fred
　See Bortz, Alfred B(enjamin)
Dr. Laura
　See Schlessinger, Laura (Catherine)
Dr. Seuss 1904-1991 .... *100*
　Obituary *67*
　Earlier sketches in SATA *1, 28, 75*
　See also CLR *100*
Dr. Zed
　See Penrose, Gordon
Drabble, Margaret 1939- *48*
Drackett, Phil(ip Arthur) 1922- *53*
Draco, F.
　See Davis, Julia
Dracup, Angela 1943- *74*
Dragisic, Patricia *116*

Dragonwagon, Crescent 1952- *186*
　Autobiography Feature *186*
　Earlier sketches in SATA *11, 41, 75, 133*
　See also SAAS *14*
Drake, David 1945- *85*
Drake, David Allen
　See Drake, David
Drake, Frank
　See Hamilton, Charles (Harold St. John)
Drake, Jane 1954- *82*
Drake, Salamanda
　See Barlow, Steve
Drakeford, Dale B 1952- *113*
Drakeford, Dale Benjamin
　See Drakeford, Dale B
Draper, Hastings
　See Jeffries, Roderic
Draper, Sharon
　See Draper, Sharon M.
Draper, Sharon M. 1948- *195*
　Autobiography Feature *146*
　Earlier sketches in SATA *98, 146*
　See also CLR *57*
Draper, Sharon Mills
　See Draper, Sharon M.
Drapier, M. B.
　See Swift, Jonathan
Drawson, Blair 1943- *126*
　Earlier sketch in SATA *17*
Dray, Matt 1967- *177*
Dray, Matthew Frederick
　See Dray, Matt
Dresang, Eliza (Carolyn Timberlake) 1941- . *19*
Drescher, Henrik 1955- *172*
　Earlier sketches in SATA *67, 105*
　See also CLR *20*
Drescher, Joan E(lizabeth) 1939- *137*
　Earlier sketch in SATA *30*
Dressen-McQueen, Stacey *191*
Dreves, Veronica R. 1927-1986
　Obituary *50*
Drew, Patricia 1938- *15*
Drew, Patricia Mary
　See Drew, Patricia
Drewery, Mary 1918- *6*
Drewery, Melanie 1970- *165*
Drewry, Henry N(athaniel) 1924- *138*
Dreyer, Ellen *177*
Drial, J. E.
　See Laird, Jean E(louise)
Drimmer, Frederick 1916-2000 .... *60*
　Obituary *124*
Driskill, J. Lawrence 1920- *90*
Driskill, Larry
　See Driskill, J. Lawrence
Driving Hawk, Virginia
　See Sneve, Virginia Driving Hawk
Dron, Laura
　See Matthews, L. S.
Dronzek, Laura *199*
Drucker, Malka 1945- *214*
　Brief entry *29*
　Earlier sketches in SATA *39, 111*
Drucker, Olga Levy 1927- *79*
Druitt, Tobias
　See Purkiss, Diane
Drummond, Allan 1957- *209*
Drummond, Karona 1965- *220*
Drummond, V(iolet) H(ilda) 1911-2000 .... *6*
Drummond, Walter
　See Silverberg, Robert
Drury, Clare Marie
　See Hoskyns-Abrahall, Clare (Constance Drury)
Drury, Roger W(olcott) 1914-1996 .... *15*
Druse, Eleanor
　See King, Stephen
Dryden, Pamela
　See St. John, Nicole
D.T., Hughes
　See Hughes, Dean

Duane, Diane (Elizabeth) 1952- *145*
  Brief entry *46*
  Earlier sketches in SATA *58, 95*
Dubanevich, Arlene 1950- 56
Dubelaar, Thea 1947- 60
Dubin, Jill 205
du Blane, Daphne
  See Groom, Arthur William
Duble, Kathleen Benner 1958- *164*
Dubois, Claude K. 1960- 196
DuBois, Rochelle Holt 1946- 41
Du Bois, Shirley Graham 1907(?)-1977 24
  See Graham, Shirley
Du Bois, W. E. B. 1868-1963 42
Du Bois, William Edward Burghardt
  See Du Bois, W. E. B.
du Bois, William Pene
  See Pene du Bois, William (Sherman)
Duboise, Novella 1911-1999 88
Dubosarsky, Ursula 1961- *193*
  Earlier sketches in SATA *107, 147*
DuBose, LaRocque (Russ) 1926- 2
Dubrovin, Vivian 1931- *139*
  Earlier sketch in SATA *65*
DuBurke, Randy 172
Ducey, Jean Sparks 1915- 93
Duchacek, Ivo D(uka) 1913-1988
  Obituary 55
Du Chaillu, Paul (Belloni) 1835(?)-1903 26
Ducharme, Dede Fox
  See Ducharme, Lilian Fox
Ducharme, Lilian Fox 1950- 122
Ducornet, Erica 1943- 7
Ducornet, Rikki
  See Ducornet, Erica
Duddle, Jonny 1971(?)- 219
Duden, Jane 1947- 136
Duder, Tessa 1940- 117
  Earlier sketch in SATA *80*
  See also CLR *43*
  See also SAAS *23*
Dudley, Helen
  See Hope Simpson, Jacynth
Dudley, Martha Ward 1909(?)-1985
  Obituary 45
Dudley, Nancy
  See Cole, Lois Dwight
Dudley, Robert
  See Baldwin, James
Dudley, Ruth H(ubbell) 1905-2001 11
Dudley-Smith, T.
  See Trevor, Elleston
Due, Linnea A. 1948- 64
Dueck, Adele 1955- 97
Dueland, Joy V(ivian) 27
Duerr, Gisela 1968- 89
Duey, Kathleen 1950- 199
  Earlier sketch in SATA *132*
Dufault, Joseph Ernest Nephtali
  See James, Will(iam Roderick)
Duff, Annis (James) 1904(?)-1986
  Obituary 49
Duff, Maggie
  See Duff, Margaret K(app)
Duff, Margaret K(app) 1916-2003 37
  Obituary 144
Duffey, Betsy (Byars) 1953- 131
  Earlier sketch in SATA *80*
Duffie, Charles 1960- 144
Duffield, Katy S. 1961- 147
Duffy, Carol Ann 1955- 165
  Earlier sketch in SATA *95*
Duffy Stone, Heather 217
Dugan, Jack
  See Griffin, W. E. B.
Dugan, John Kevin
  See Griffin, W. E. B.
Dugan, Karen 202
Dugan, Karen M.
  See Dugan, Karen
Dugan, Michael (Gray) 1947- 15

Duggan, Alfred Leo 1903-1964 25
Duggan, Maurice 1922-1974 40
  Obituary 30
Duggan, Maurice Noel
  See Duggan, Maurice
Dugger, Elizabeth L.
  See Kanell, Beth
Duggleby, John 1952- 94
Dugin, Andrej 1955- 77
Dugina, Olga 1964- 77
du Jardin, Rosamond Neal 1902-1963 2
Duka, Ivo
  See Duchacek, Ivo D(uka)
Duke, Kate 1956- 192
  Earlier sketches in SATA *90, 148*
  See also CLR *51*
Duke, Will
  See Gault, William Campbell
Dulac, Edmund 1882-1953 19
Dumas, Alexandre (pere) 1802-1870 18
  See also CLR *134*
Dumas, Jacqueline 1946- 55
Dumas, Philippe 1940- 119
  Earlier sketch in SATA *52*
du Maurier, Daphne 1907-1989 27
  Obituary 60
Dumbleton, Mike 1948- 206
  Earlier sketches in SATA *73, 124*
Dunbar, Fiona 1961- 167
Dunbar, Joyce 1944- 213
  Earlier sketches in SATA *76, 112, 162*
Dunbar, Paul Laurence 1872-1906 34
Dunbar, Polly 1980(?)- 211
  Earlier sketch in SATA *181*
Dunbar, Robert E(verett) 1926- 32
Duncan, Alexandra
  See Moore, Ishbel (Lindsay)
Duncan, Alice Faye 1967- 168
  Earlier sketch in SATA *95*
Duncan, Gregory
  See McClintock, Marshall
Duncan, Jane
  See Cameron, Elizabeth Jane
Duncan, Julia K.
  See Benson, Mildred
Duncan, Lois 1934- 219
  Autobiography Feature 141
  Earlier sketches in SATA *1, 36, 75, 133, 141*
  See also CLR *129*
  See also SAAS *2*
Duncan, Norman 1871-1916
  See YABC *1*
Duncan, Terence
  See Nolan, William F.
Duncombe, Frances (Riker) 1900-1994 25
  Obituary 82
Dungy, Anthony
  See Dungy, Tony
Dungy, Tony 1955- 206
Dunham, Montrew 1919- 162
Dunham, Montrew Goetz
  See Dunham, Montrew
Dunkle, Clare B. 1964- 155
Dunlap, Julie 1958- 84
Dunleavy, Deborah 1951- 133
Dunlop, Agnes M. R. (?)-1982 87
Dunlop, Eileen (Rhona) 1938- 76
  Earlier sketch in SATA *24*
  See also SAAS *12*
Dunmore, Helen 1952- 201
Dunn, Anne M. 1940- 107
Dunn, Carolyn 1965- 208
Dunn, Harvey T(homas) 1884-1952 34
Dunn, Herb
  See Gutman, Dan
Dunn, John M. (III) 1949- 93
Dunn, Judy
  See Spangenberg, Judith Dunn
Dunn, Mary Lois 1930- 6
Dunnahoo, Terry Janson 1927- 7
Dunne, Jeanette 1952- 72

Dunne, Kathleen 1933- 126
Dunne, Marie
  See Clark, Ann Nolan
Dunne, Mary Collins 1914- 11
Dunne, Mary Jo
  See Dunne, Mary Collins
Dunnett, Kaitlyn
  See Emerson, Kathy Lynn
Dunnett, Margaret (Rosalind) 1909-1977 42
Dunnick, Regan 178
Dunphy, Madeleine 1962- 219
Dunrea, Olivier 1953- 160
  Brief entry 46
  Earlier sketches in SATA *59, 118*
Dunrea, Olivier Jean-Paul Dominique
  See Dunrea, Olivier
Dunstan Muller, Rachel 221
Dunton, Dorothy 1912- 92
Dupasquier, Philippe 1955- 151
  Earlier sketch in SATA *86*
duPont, Lindsay 207
duPont, Lindsay Harper
  See duPont, Lindsay
DuPrau, Jeanne 1944- 215
  Earlier sketch in SATA *144*
Dupuy, T(revor) N(evitt) 1916-1995 4
  Obituary 86
DuQuette, Keith 1960- 155
  Earlier sketch in SATA *90*
Duran, Gloria 1924- 171
Duran, Gloria Bradley
  See Duran, Gloria
Duranceau, Suzanne 1952- 162
Durand, Delphine 1971- 200
Durand, Hallie 1964(?)- 216
Durango, Julia 1967- 215
  Earlier sketch in SATA *173*
Durant, Alan 1958- 214
  Earlier sketches in SATA *121, 165*
Durant, John 1902- 27
Durbin, William 1951- 174
  Earlier sketch in SATA *143*
Durell, Ann 1930- 66
Durkee, Sarah 173
Durney, Ryan 205
Durrant, Lynda 1954- 212
  Earlier sketches in SATA *96, 148*
Durrant, Sabine 210
Durrell, Gerald (Malcolm) 1925-1995 8
  Obituary 84
Durrell, Julie 1955- 94
Durrett, Deanne 1940- 144
  Earlier sketch in SATA *92*
Durst, Sarah Beth 1974- 203
Du Soe, Robert C. 1892-1958
  See YABC *2*
Dussling, Jennifer 1970- 143
  Earlier sketch in SATA *96*
DuTemple, Lesley A. 1952- 113
Dutton, Sandra 191
Dutz
  See Davis, Mary Octavia
Duval, Katherine
  See James, Elizabeth
Duval, Kathy 1946- 181
Duvall, Aimee
  See Thurlo, Aimee
  and Thurlo, David
Duvall, Evelyn Millis 1906- 9
Duvall, Jill D. 1932- 102
Duvall, Jill Donovan
  See Duvall, Jill D.
Duvoisin, Roger (Antoine) 1904-1980 30
  Obituary 23
  Earlier sketch in SATA *2*
  See also CLR *23*
Dwiggins, Don(ald J.) 1913-1988 4
  Obituary 60
Dwight, Allan
  See Cole, Lois Dwight

Dwyer, Deanna
  See Koontz, Dean
Dwyer, K.R.
  See Koontz, Dean
Dyck, Peter J. 1914- 75
Dyer, Alan 1953- 218
Dyer, James (Frederick) 1934- 37
Dyer, Jane 191
  Earlier sketch in SATA *147*
Dyer, Sarah 1978- 212
Dyer, Sarah L.
  See Dyer, Sarah
Dyess, John (Foster) 1939- 76
Dygard, Thomas J. 1931-1996 97
  Obituary 92
  Earlier sketch in SATA *24*
  See also SAAS *15*
Dyke, John 1935- 35

E

E. V. L.
  See Lucas, E(dward) V(errall)
Eagar, Frances (Elisabeth Stuart)
  1940-1978 11
  Obituary 55
Eager, Edward (McMaken) 1911-1964 17
  See also CLR *43*
Eager, George 1921- 56
Eager, George B.
  See Eager, George
Eagle, Ellen 1953- 61
Eagle, Kin
  See Adlerman, Daniel (Ezra)
  and Adlerman, Kimberly M(arie)
Eagle, Mike 1942- 11
Earle, Olive L(ydia) 1888-1982 7
Earle, William
  See Johns, W(illiam) E(arle)
Earls, Nick 1963- 156
  Earlier sketch in SATA *95*
Early, Jack
  See Scoppettone, Sandra
Early, Jon
  See Johns, W(illiam) E(arle)
Early, Margaret 1951- 72
Earnshaw, Brian 1929- 17
Earnshaw, Micky 1939- 88
Earnshaw, Spencer Wright
  See Earnshaw, Micky
Easley, MaryAnn 94
Eason, Alethea 1957- 197
Eastman, Charles A(lexander) 1858-1939
  See YABC *1*
Eastman, P(hilip) D(ey) 1909-1986 33
  Obituary 46
Easton, Kelly 1960- 192
  Earlier sketch in SATA *141*
Eastwick, Ivy (Ethel) O(live) 3
Eaton, Anne T(haxter) 1881-1971 32
Eaton, Anthony 1971- 167
Eaton, George L.
  See Verral, Charles Spain
Eaton, Janet
  See Givens, Janet E(aton)
Eaton, Jeanette 1886-1968 24
Eaton, Maxwell III 1981- 199
Eaton, Tom 1940- 22
Ebbeler, Jeff
  See Ebbeler, Jeffrey
Ebbeler, Jeffrey 1974- 206
Ebel, Alex 1927- 11
Eber, Dorothy (Margaret) Harley 1930- 27
Eberhart, Sheri S.
  See Tepper, Sheri S.
Eberle, Irmengarde 1898-1979 2
  Obituary 23
Eble, Diane 1956- 74
Eboch, Chris 113

Eccles Williams, Ferelith 1920- 22
Echeverria-Bis, Olivia 217
Echeverria Gyorkos, Charmaine 216
Echlin, Kim 1955- 166
Eckblad, Edith Berven 1923- 23
Ecke, Wolfgang 1927-1983
  Obituary 37
Eckert, Allan W. 1931- 91
  Brief entry 27
  Earlier sketch in SATA *29*
  See also SAAS *21*
Eckert, Horst 1931- 72
  Earlier sketch in SATA *8*
  See also CLR *26*
Ecklar, Julia (Marie) 1964- 112
Eddings, David 1931-2009 91
Eddings, David Carroll
  See Eddings, David
Ede, Janina 1937- 33
Edell, Celeste 12
Edelman, Lily (Judith) 1915-1981 22
Edelson, Edward 1932- 51
Edens, Cooper 1945- 166
  Earlier sketches in SATA *49, 112*
Edens, (Bishop) David 1926- 39
Edey, Maitland A(rmstrong) 1910-1992 25
  Obituary 71
Edgerton, Perky 196
Edgeworth, Maria 1768-1849 21
  See also CLR *153*
Edgson, Alison 211
Edgy, Wardore
  See Gorey, Edward (St. John)
Edison, Theodore
  See Stratemeyer, Edward L.
Edler, Tim(othy) 1948- 56
Edmiston, Jim 1948- 80
Edmonds, I(vy) G(ordon) 1917- 8
Edmonds, Walter D(umaux) 1903-1998 27
  Obituary 99
  Earlier sketch in SATA *1*
  See also SAAS *4*
Edmund, Sean
  See Pringle, Laurence
Edsall, Marian (Stickney) 1920- 8
Edwards, Al
  See Nourse, Alan E(dward)
Edwards, Anne 1927- 35
Edwards, Audrey 1947- 52
  Brief entry 31
Edwards, Becky (Jane) 1966- 125
Edwards, Bertram
  See Edwards, Herbert Charles
Edwards, Bronwen Elizabeth
  See Rose, Wendy
Edwards, Cecile Pepin 1916- 25
Edwards, David 1962- 198
Edwards, Dorothy 1914-1982 88
  Obituary 31
  Earlier sketch in SATA *4*
Edwards, F. E.
  See Nolan, William F.
Edwards, Frank B. 1952- 93
Edwards, Gunvor 32
Edwards, Harvey 1929- 5
Edwards, Hazel (Eileen) 1945- 135
Edwards, Herbert Charles 1912- 12
Edwards, Jane Campbell 1932- 10
Edwards, Julia
  See Stratemeyer, Edward L.
Edwards, Julie
  See Andrews, Julie
Edwards, Julie Andrews
  See Andrews, Julie
Edwards, June
  See Bhatia, Jamunadevi
Edwards, Linda Strauss 1948- 49
  Brief entry 42
Edwards, Margaret (Alexander) 1902-1988
  Obituary 56

Edwards, Michelle 1955- 152
  Earlier sketch in SATA *70*
Edwards, Monica le Doux Newton
  1912-1998 12
Edwards, Olwen
  See Gater, Dilys
Edwards, Page (Lawrence, Jr.) 1941-1999 ... 59
Edwards, Pamela Duncan 189
Edwards, R. T.
  See Goulart, Ron
Edwards, Sally (Cary) 1929- 7
Edwards, Samuel
  See Gerson, Noel Bertram
Edwards, Wallace 1957(?)- 170
Eeckhout, Emmanuelle 1976- 208
Egan, E. W. 1922- 35
Egan, Edward Welstead
  See Egan, E. W.
Egan, Kerry 175
Egan, Lorraine Hopping 1960- 134
  Earlier sketch in SATA *91*
Egan, Tim 1957- 191
  Earlier sketches in SATA *89, 155*
Egermeier, Elsie E(milie) 1890-1986 65
Eggenberger, David 1918- 6
Eggleston, Edward 1837-1902 27
Egielski, Richard 1952- 220
  Earlier sketches in SATA *11, 49, 106, 163*
Egypt, Ophelia Settle 1903-1984 16
  Obituary 38
Ehlert, Lois 1934- 172
  Earlier sketches in SATA *35, 69, 128*
  See also CLR *28*
Ehlert, Lois Jane
  See Ehlert, Lois
Ehling, Katalin Olah 1941- 93
Ehrenberg, Pamela 1972- 219
Ehrenfreund, Norbert 1921- 86
Ehrenhaft, Daniel 1970- 185
Ehrenhaft, Daniel Parker
  See Ehrenhaft, Daniel
Ehrhardt, Karen 1963- 184
Ehrlich, Amy 1942- 217
  Earlier sketches in SATA *25, 65, 96, 132*
Ehrlich, Bettina Bauer 1903-1985 1
Ehrlich, Fred 205
Ehrlich, Fred M.D.
  See Ehrlich, Fred
Ehrlich, H. M.
  See Ziefert, Harriet
Eichenberg, Fritz 1901-1990 50
  Earlier sketch in SATA *9*
Eichler, Margrit 1942- 35
Eichner, James A. 1927- 4
Eidson, Thomas 1944- 112
Eifert, Virginia (Louise) S(nider) 1911-1966 . 2
Eige, (Elizabeth) Lillian 1915- 65
Eiken, J. Melia 1967- 125
Einhorn, Edward 1970- 204
Einsel, Naiad 10
Einsel, Walter 1926- 10
Einzig, Susan 1922- 43
Eiseman, Alberta 1925- 15
Eisenberg, Azriel (Louis) 1903-1985 12
Eisenberg, Lisa 1949- 155
  Brief entry 50
  Earlier sketch in SATA *57*
Eisenberg, Phyllis Rose 1924- 41
Eisner, Vivienne
  See Margolis, Vivienne
Eisner, Will 1917-2005 165
  Earlier sketch in SATA *31*
Eisner, William Erwin
  See Eisner, Will
Eitzen, Allan 1928- 9
Eitzen, Ruth (Carper) 1924- 9
Ekwensi, C. O. D.
  See Ekwensi, Cyprian
Ekwensi, Cyprian 1921-2007 66
Ekwensi, Cyprian Odiatu Duaka
  See Ekwensi, Cyprian

Elam, Richard M(ace, Jr.) 1920- 9
Elborn, Andrew
  See Clements, Andrew
  and Clements, Andrew
Elboz, Stephen 1956- 152
Eldin, Peter 1939- 154
Eldon, Kathy 1946- 107
Eldridge, Marion 199
Eley, Robin 219
Elfman, Blossom 1925- 8
Elgin, Kathleen 1923- 39
Elia
  See Lamb, Charles
Eliot, A. D.
  See Jewett, Sarah Orne
Eliot, Alice
  See Jewett, Sarah Orne
Eliot, Anne
  See Cole, Lois Dwight
Eliot, Dan
  See Silverberg, Robert
Elish, Dan 1960- 204
  Earlier sketches in SATA *68, 129*
Elisha, Ron 1951- 104
Elisofon, Eliot 1911-1973
  Obituary 21
Elkeles, Simone 1970- 187
Elkin, Benjamin 1911-1995 3
Elkins, Dov Peretz 1937- 5
Ellacott, S(amuel) E(rnest) 1911- 19
Elleman, Barbara 1934- 147
Ellen, Jaye
  See Nixon, Joan Lowery
Eller, Scott
  See Holinger, William (Jacques)
  and Shepard, Jim
Ellery, Amanda 216
Ellestad, Myrvin
  See Ellestad, Myrvin H.
Ellestad, Myrvin H. 1921- 120
Elliot, Bruce
  See Field, Edward
Elliot, David 1952- 208
  Earlier sketch in SATA *122*
Elliott, Bruce
  See Field, Edward
Elliott, David 1947- 201
  Earlier sketch in SATA *163*
Elliott, Don
  See Silverberg, Robert
Elliott, Elizabeth Shippen Green
  See Green, Elizabeth Shippen
Elliott, Janice 1931-1995 119
Elliott, Joey
  See Houk, Randy
Elliott, Laura Malone 1957- 197
Elliott, L.M.
  See Elliott, Laura Malone
Elliott, Louise 111
Elliott, Mark 1949- 210
Elliott, Odette 1939- 75
Elliott, Patricia 1946- 176
Elliott, Sarah M(cCarn) 1930- 14
Elliott, (Robert) Scott 1970- 153
Elliott, William
  See Bradbury, Ray
Elliott, Zetta 206
Ellis, (Mary) Amabel (Nassau Strachey)
  Williams
  See Williams-Ellis, (Mary) Amabel (Nassau
  Strachey)
Ellis, Ann Dee 210
Ellis, Anyon
  See Rowland-Entwistle, (Arthur) Theodore
  (Henry)
Ellis, Carson 1975- 190
Ellis, Carson Friedman
  See Ellis, Carson
Ellis, Deborah 1960- 187
  Earlier sketch in SATA *129*

Ellis, E. S.
  See Ellis, Edward S.
Ellis, Edward S. 1840-1916
  See YABC *1*
Ellis, Edward Sylvester
  See Ellis, Edward S.
Ellis, Ella Thorp 1928- 127
  Earlier sketch in SATA *7*
  See also SAAS *9*
Ellis, Harry Bearse 1921-2004 9
Ellis, Herbert
  See Wilson, Lionel
Ellis, Mel(vin Richard) 1912-1984 7
  Obituary 39
Ellis, Richard 1938- 130
Ellis, Sarah 1952- 179
  Earlier sketches in SATA *68, 131*
  See also CLR *42*
Ellison, Chris 196
Ellison, Elizabeth Stow 1970- 209
Ellison, Emily 114
Ellison, Lucile Watkins 1907(?)-1979 50
  Obituary 22
Ellison, Virginia H(owell) 1910- 4
Ellsberg, Edward 1891-1983 7
Ellsworth, Loretta 1954- 199
Ellsworth, Mary Ellen (Tressel) 1940- 146
Ellwand, David 1965(?)- 213
Elmer, Robert 1958- 154
  Earlier sketch in SATA *99*
Elmore, (Carolyn) Patricia 1933- 38
  Brief entry 35
El-Moslimany, Ann P(axton) 1937- 90
Elschner, Geraldine 1954- 183
Elspeth
  See Bragdon, Elspeth MacDuffie
Elster, Jean Alicia 1953- 150
Elting, Mary 1906- 88
  Earlier sketch in SATA *2*
  See also SAAS *20*
Elvgren, Jennifer Riesmeyer 179
Elwart, Joan Potter 1927- 2
Elwell, Peter 220
Elwood, Ann 1931- 55
  Brief entry 52
Elwood, Roger 1943-2007 58
Ely, Lesley 212
Elya, Susan Middleton 1955- 202
  Earlier sketches in SATA *106, 159*
Elzbieta 88
Ember, Kathi 190
Emberley, Barbara A. 1932- 146
  Earlier sketches in SATA *8, 70*
  See also CLR *5*
Emberley, Barbara Anne
  See Emberley, Barbara A.
Emberley, Ed 1931- 146
  Earlier sketches in SATA *8, 70*
  See also CLR *81*
Emberley, Edward Randolph
  See Emberley, Ed
Emberley, Michael 1960- 189
  Earlier sketches in SATA *34, 80, 119*
Emberley, Rebecca 1958- 218
Embry, Margaret Jacob 1919-1975 5
Emecheta, Buchi 1944- 66
  See also CLR *158*
Emecheta, Florence Onye Buchi
  See Emecheta, Buchi
Emerson, Alice B.
  See Benson, Mildred
Emerson, Kathy Lynn 1947- 63
Emerson, Kevin 209
Emerson, Ru 1944- 107
  Earlier sketch in SATA *70*
Emerson, Sally 1952- 111
Emerson, William K(eith) 1925- 25
Emert, Phyllis R. 1947- 93
Emert, Phyllis Raybin
  See Emert, Phyllis R.

Emery, Anne (McGuigan) 1907- 33
  Earlier sketch in SATA *1*
Emmens, Carol Ann 1944- 39
Emmett, Jonathan 1965- 188
  Earlier sketch in SATA *138*
Emmons, Della (Florence) Gould 1890-1983
  Obituary 39
Emory, Jerry 1957- 96
Emrich, Duncan (Black Macdonald)
  1908-1970(?) 11
Emshwiller, Carol 1921- 174
  Autobiography Feature 174
Emshwiller, Carol Fries
  See Emshwiller, Carol
Emslie, M. L.
  See Simpson, Myrtle L(illias)
Ende, Michael (Andreas Helmuth)
  1929-1995 130
  Brief entry 42
  Obituary 86
  Earlier sketch in SATA *61*
  See also CLR *138*
Enderle, Dotti 1954- 203
  Earlier sketch in SATA *145*
Enderle, Judith (Ann) Ross 1941- 89
  Autobiography Feature 114
  Earlier sketch in SATA *38*
  See also SAAS *26*
Endle, Kate 207
Enell, Trinka (Gochenour) 1951- 79
Enfield, Carrie
  See Smith, Susan Vernon
Engdahl, Sylvia Louise 1933- 4
  Autobiography Feature 122
  See also CLR *2*
  See also SAAS *5*
Engel, Diana 1947- 70
Engelbreit, Mary 1952- 169
Engelhart, Margaret S. 1924- 59
Engelmann, Kim (V.) 1959- 87
England, George Allan 1877-1936 102
Englart, Mindi Rose 1965- 146
Engle, Eloise
  See Paananen, Eloise (Katherine)
Engle, Margarita 1951- 193
Englebert, Victor 1933- 8
English, James W(ilson) 1915- 37
English, Karen 202
Engstrom, Elizabeth 1951- 110
Enright, D(ennis) J(oseph) 1920-2002 25
  Obituary 140
Enright, Dominique 194
Enright, Elizabeth (Wright) 1909-1968 9
  See also CLR *4*
Ensor, Barbara 180
Ensor, Robert (T.) 1922- 93
Enthoven, Sam 1974- 187
Entwistle, (Arthur) Theodore (Henry) Rowland
  See Rowland-Entwistle, (Arthur) Theodore
  (Henry)
Enys, Sarah L.
  See Sloggett, Nellie
Epanya, Christian A(rthur Kingue) 1956- 91
Ephraim, Shelly S(chonebaum) 1952- 97
Ephron, Delia 1944- 197
  Brief entry 50
  Earlier sketch in SATA *65*
Epler, Doris M. 1928- 73
Epp, Margaret A(gnes) 1913- 20
Eppenstein, Louise (Kohn) 1892-1987
  Obituary 54
Epple, Anne Orth 1927- 20
Epstein, Anne Merrick 1931- 20
Epstein, Beryl 1910- 31
  Earlier sketch in SATA *1*
  See also CLR *26*
  See also SAAS *17*
Epstein, Beryl M. Williams
  See Epstein, Beryl
Epstein, Perle S(herry) 1938- 27
Epstein, Rachel S. 1941- 102

Epstein, Samuel 1909-2000 .... *31*
  Earlier sketch in SATA *1*
  See also CLR *26*
  See also SAAS *17*
Erdman, Loula Grace 1905(?)-1976 .... *1*
Erdoes, Richard 1912- *33*
  Brief entry *28*
Erdogan, Buket *187*
Erdrich, Karen Louise
  See Erdrich, Louise
Erdrich, Louise 1954- *141*
  Earlier sketch in SATA *94*
Erickson, Betty J. 1923- *97*
Erickson, Betty Jean
  See Erickson, Betty J.
Erickson, John R. 1943- *136*
  Earlier sketch in SATA *70*
Erickson, Jon 1948- *141*
Erickson, Phoebe *59*
Erickson, Russell E(verett) 1932- *27*
Erickson, Sabra Rollins 1912-1995 .... *35*
Erickson, Walter
  See Fast, Howard
Ericson, Walter
  See Fast, Howard
Ericsson, Jennifer A. *170*
Erikson, Mel 1937- *31*
Eriksson, Eva 1949- *207*
Ering, Timothy Basil *176*
Erlanger, Baba
  See Trahey, Jane
Erlbach, Arlene 1948- *160*
  Earlier sketches in SATA *78, 115*
Erlbruch, Wolf 1948- *181*
Erlich, Lillian (Feldman) 1910-1983 .... *10*
Erlings, Fridrik 1962- *196*
Erlingsson, Fri****rik
  See Erlings, Fridrik
Ermatinger, James W. 1959- *170*
Ernest, William
  See Berkebile, Fred D(onovan)
Ernst, (Lyman) John 1940- *39*
Ernst, Kathleen
  See Ernst, Kathleen A.
Ernst, Kathleen A. 1959- *162*
Ernst, Kathryn (Fitzgerald) 1942- *25*
Ernst, Lisa Campbell 1957- *212*
  Brief entry *44*
  Earlier sketches in SATA *55, 95, 154*
Erskine, Kathryn *193*
Ervin, Janet Halliday 1923- *4*
Erwin, Will
  See Eisner, Will
Esbaum, Jill *213*
  Earlier sketch in SATA *174*
Esbensen, Barbara J(uster) 1925-1996 .... *97*
  Brief entry *53*
  Earlier sketch in SATA *62*
Eschbacher, Roger *160*
Eschmeyer, R. E. 1898-1989 .... *29*
Escriva, Vivi *182*
Eseki, Bruno
  See Mphahlele, Es'kia
Esekie, Bruno
  See Mphahlele, Es'kia
Eshmeyer, Reinhart Ernst
  See Eschmeyer, R. E.
Eskridge, Ann E. 1949- *84*
Espeland, Pamela (Lee) 1951- *128*
  Brief entry *38*
  Earlier sketch in SATA *52*
Espinosa, Laura *203*
Espinosa, Leo *203*
Espriella, Don Manuel Alvarez
  See Southey, Robert
Espy, Willard R(ichardson) 1910-1999 .... *38*
  Obituary *113*
Essakalli, Julie Klear *200*
Essrig, Harry 1912- *66*
Estep, Irene Compton *5*
Esterl, Arnica 1933- *77*

Estes, Eleanor (Ruth) 1906-1988 .... *91*
  Obituary *56*
  Earlier sketch in SATA *7*
  See also CLR *70*
Estoril, Jean
  See Allan, Mabel Esther
Estrada, Pau 1961- *200*
  Earlier sketch in SATA *74*
Etchemendy, Nancy 1952- *166*
  Earlier sketch in SATA *38*
Etchemendy, Nancy Elise Howell
  See Etchemendy, Nancy
Etchison, Birdie L(ee) 1937- *38*
Etchison, Craig 1945- *133*
Etherington, Frank 1945- *58*
Eton, Robert
  See Meynell, Laurence Walter
Ets, Marie Hall 1893-1984 .... *2*
  See also CLR *33*
Ettlinger, Doris 1950- *173*
Eunson, (John) Dale 1904-2002 .... *5*
  Obituary *132*
Evan, Frances Y. 1951- *167*
Evanoff, Vlad 1916- *59*
Evans, Cambria 1981- *178*
Evans, Douglas 1953- *144*
  Earlier sketch in SATA *93*
Evans, Eva (Knox) 1905-1998 .... *27*
Evans, Freddi Williams 1957- *211*
  Earlier sketch in SATA *134*
Evans, Greg 1947- *143*
  Earlier sketch in SATA *73*
Evans, Hubert Reginald 1892-1986 .... *118*
  Obituary *48*
Evans, Katherine (Floyd) 1901-1964 .... *5*
Evans, Larry
  See Evans, Laurence Chubb
Evans, Laurence Chubb 1939- *88*
Evans, Lawrence Watt
  See Watt-Evans, Lawrence
Evans, Leslie 1953- *214*
Evans, Lezlie *180*
Evans, Mari 1923- *10*
Evans, Mark *19*
Evans, Nancy 1950- *65*
Evans, Nate *201*
Evans, Patricia Healy
  See Carpenter, Patricia (Healy Evans)
Evans, (Alice) Pearl 1927- *83*
Evans, Shane W. *189*
Evans, Shirlee 1931- *58*
Evans, Tabor
  See Cameron, Lou
  and Knott, William C(ecil, Jr.)
  and Wallmann, Jeffrey M(iner)
  and Whittington, Harry (Benjamin)
Evarts, Esther
  See Benson, Sally
Evarts, Hal G., (Jr.) 1915-1989 .... *6*
Everett, Gail
  See Hale, Arlene
Evernden, Margery 1916- *5*
Eversole, Robyn 1971- *74*
Eversole, Robyn H.
  See Eversole, Robyn
Eversole, Robyn Harbert
  See Eversole, Robyn
Evslin, Bernard 1922-1993 .... *83*
  Brief entry *28*
  Obituary *77*
  Earlier sketch in SATA *45*
Ewart, Claire 1958- *145*
  Earlier sketch in SATA *76*
Ewart, Franzeska G. 1950- *205*
Ewen, David 1907-1985 .... *4*
  Obituary *47*
Ewing, Juliana (Horatia Gatty) 1841-1885 ... *16*
  See also CLR *78*
Ewing, Kathryn 1921- *20*

Eyerly, Jeannette 1908-2008 .... *86*
  Obituary *196*
  Earlier sketch in SATA *4*
  See also SAAS *10*
Eyerly, Jeannette Hyde
  See Eyerly, Jeannette
Eyre, Dorothy
  See McGuire, Leslie (Sarah)
Eyre, Frank 1910-1988
  Obituary *62*
Eyre, Katherine Wigmore 1901-1970 .... *26*
Ezzell, Marilyn 1937- *42*
  Brief entry *38*

F

Fabe, Maxene 1943- *15*
Faber, Doris (Greenberg) 1924- *78*
  Earlier sketch in SATA *3*
Faber, Harold 1919-2010 .... *5*
Fabre, Jean Henri (Casimir) 1823-1915 .... *22*
Fabry, Glenn 1961- *205*
Facklam, Margaret
  See Thomas, Peggy
Facklam, Margery (Metz) 1927- *132*
  Earlier sketches in SATA *20, 85*
Fadden, David Kanietakeron *196*
Fadiman, Clifton (Paul) 1904-1999 .... *11*
  Obituary *115*
Fagan, Cary 1957- *186*
Fagan, Deva *220*
Fahs, Sophia Blanche Lyon 1876-1978 ...... *102*
Failing, Barbara Larmon *182*
Fain, Sarah 1971- *204*
Fair, David 1952- *96*
Fair, Sylvia 1933- *13*
Fairfax-Lucy, Brian (Fulke Cameron-Ramsay)
  1898-1974 .... *6*
  Obituary *26*
Fairfield, Flora
  See Alcott, Louisa May
Fairlie, Gerard 1899-1983
  Obituary *34*
Fairman, Joan A(lexandra) 1935- *10*
Faithfull, Gail 1936- *8*
Falcone, L(ucy) M. 1951- *155*
Falconer, Ian 1959- *179*
  Earlier sketch in SATA *125*
  See also CLR *146*
Falconer, James
  See Kirkup, James
Falconer, Lee N.
  See May, Julian
Falkner, Brian 1962- *206*
Falkner, Leonard 1900-1977 .... *12*
Fall, Andrew
  See Arthur, Robert, (Jr.)
Fall, Thomas
  See Snow, Donald Clifford
Faller, Regis 1968- *187*
Falls, C(harles) B(uckles) 1874-1960 .... *38*
  Brief entry *27*
Falstein, Louis 1909-1995 .... *37*
Falwell, Cathryn 1952- *196*
Fancher, Lou 1960- *177*
Fanelli, Sara 1969- *126*
  Earlier sketch in SATA *89*
Fanning, Leonard M(ulliken) 1888-1967 .... *5*
Fantaskey, Beth 1965- *217*
Faralla, Dana 1909- *9*
Faralla, Dorothy W.
  See Faralla, Dana
Farb, Peter 1929-1980 .... *12*
  Obituary *22*
Farber, Norma 1909-1984 .... *75*
  Obituary *38*
  Earlier sketch in SATA *25*
Fardell, John 1967- *195*

Fardell, John William
  See Fardell, John
Faria, Rosana *213*
Farish, Terry 1947- *146*
  Earlier sketch in SATA *82*
Farjeon, (Eve) Annabel 1919-2004 .... *11*
  Obituary *153*
Farjeon, Eleanor 1881-1965 .... *2*
  See also CLR *34*
Farley, Carol (J.) 1936- *137*
  Earlier sketch in SATA *4*
Farley, Terri *165*
Farley, Walter (Lorimer) 1915-1989 .... *132*
  Earlier sketches in SATA *2, 43*
Farlow, James O(rville, Jr.) 1951- *75*
Farmer, Jacqueline *210*
Farmer, Nancy 1941- *161*
  Earlier sketches in SATA *79, 117*
Farmer, Patti 1948- *79*
Farmer, Penelope (Jane) 1939- *105*
  Brief entry *39*
  Earlier sketch in SATA *40*
  See also CLR *8*
  See also SAAS *22*
Farmer, Peter 1950- *38*
Farmer, Philip Jose
  See Farmer, Philip Jose
Farmer, Philip Jose 1918-2009 .... *93*
  Obituary *201*
Farmer, Philipe Jos
  See Farmer, Philip Jose
Farnham, Burt
  See Clifford, Harold B(urton)
Farnsworth, Bill 1958- *186*
  Earlier sketches in SATA *84, 135*
Farooqi, Musharraf Ali 1968- *207*
Farquhar, Margaret C(utting) 1905-1988 ...... *13*
Farquharson, Alexander 1944- *46*
Farquharson, Martha
  See Finley, Martha
Farr, Diana *82*
  Earlier sketch in SATA *3*
Farr, Finis (King) 1904-1982 .... *10*
Farr, Richard 1960- *209*
Farrar, Jill
  See Morris, Jill
Farrar, Susan Clement 1917- *33*
Farrell, Ben
  See Cebulash, Mel
Farrell, John 1951- *204*
Farrell, Patrick
  See Odgers, Sally Farrell
Farrell, Sally
  See Odgers, Sally Farrell
Farrer, Vashti *167*
Farrington, Benjamin 1891-1974
  Obituary *20*
Farrington, S(elwyn) Kip, Jr. 1904-1983 ...... *20*
Farris, Christine King 1927- *206*
Farshtey, Greg(ory T.) 1965- *148*
Farthing, Alison 1936- *45*
  Brief entry *36*
Farthing-Knight, Catherine 1933- *92*
Fassler, Joan (Grace) 1931- *11*
Fast, Howard 1914-2003 .... *7*
  Autobiography Feature *107*
Fast, Howard Melvin
  See Fast, Howard
Fasulo, Michael 1963- *83*
Fatchen, Max 1920- *84*
  Earlier sketch in SATA *20*
  See also SAAS *20*
Fate, Marilyn
  See Collins, Paul
Father Goose
  See Ghigna, Charles
Fatigati, Evelyn 1948- *24*
Fatigati, Frances Evelyn
  See Fatigati, Evelyn
Fatio, Louise 1904-1993 .... *6*
Fatus, Sophie 1957- *182*

Faulhaber, Martha 1926- *7*
Faulkner, Anne Irvin 1906- *23*
Faulkner, Frank
  See Ellis, Edward S.
Faulkner, Nancy
  See Faulkner, Anne Irvin
Faulknor, Cliff(ord Vernon) 1913- *86*
Favole, Robert J(ames) 1950- *125*
Fax, Elton Clay 1909-1993 .... *25*
Faxon, Lavinia
  See Russ, Lavinia (Faxon)
Feagles, Anita M.
  See Feagles, Anita MacRae
Feagles, Anita MacRae 1927- *9*
Feagles, Elizabeth
  See Day, Beth (Feagles)
Feague, Mildred H. 1915- *14*
Fearnley, Jan 1965- *205*
  Earlier sketch in SATA *153*
Fearrington, Ann (Peyton) 1945- *146*
Fecher, Constance
  See Heaven, Constance (Christina)
Feder, Chris Welles 1938- *81*
Feder, Harriet K. 1928- *73*
Feder, Paula (Kurzband) 1935- *26*
Federici, Debbie 1965- *175*
Federici, Debbie Tanner
  See Federici, Debbie
Feelings, Muriel 1938- *16*
  See also CLR *5*
  See also SAAS *8*
Feelings, Muriel Lavita Grey
  See Feelings, Muriel
Feelings, Thomas 1933-2003 .... *69*
  Obituary *148*
  Earlier sketch in SATA *8*
  See also CLR *58*
  See also SAAS *19*
Feelings, Tom
  See Feelings, Thomas
Fehler, Gene 1940- *201*
  Earlier sketch in SATA *74*
Fehrenbach, T(heodore) R(eed, Jr.) 1925- *33*
Feiffer, Jules 1929- *201*
  Earlier sketches in SATA *8, 61, 111, 157*
Feiffer, Jules Ralph
  See Feiffer, Jules
Feiffer, Kate 1964- *206*
  Earlier sketch in SATA *170*
Feig, Barbara Krane 1937- *34*
Feig, Paul *221*
Feikema, Feike
  See Manfred, Frederick (Feikema)
Feil, Hila 1942- *12*
Feilen, John
  See May, Julian
Feinberg, Barbara Jane 1938- *123*
  Earlier sketch in SATA *58*
Feinberg, Barbara Silberdick
  See Feinberg, Barbara Jane
Feinstein, John 1956- *195*
  Earlier sketch in SATA *163*
Feldman, Anne (Rodgers) 1939- *19*
Feldman, Elane *79*
Feldman, Eve B. *221*
Feldman, Jody *200*
Felin, M. Sindy *194*
Felix
  See Vincent, Felix
Fell, Derek 1939- *167*
Fell, Derek John
  See Fell, Derek
Fellowes, Julian 1950- *198*
Fellows, Muriel H. *10*
Fellows, Stan 1957- *177*
Fellows, Stanley
  See Fellows, Stan
Felsen, Henry Gregor 1916-1995 .... *1*
  See also SAAS *2*
Felstead, Cathie 1954- *192*
Feltenstein, Arlene 1934- *119*

Feltenstine, Arlene H.
  See Feltenstein, Arlene
Felton, Harold William 1902-1991 .... *1*
Felton, Ronald Oliver 1909- *3*
Felts, Shirley 1934- *33*
Felts, Susannah 1973- *214*
Fenderson, Lewis H., Jr. 1907-1983 .... *47*
  Obituary *37*
Fenner, Carol (Elizabeth) 1929-2002 .... *89*
  Obituary *132*
  Earlier sketch in SATA *7*
  See also SAAS *24*
Fenner, Phyllis R(eid) 1899-1982 .... *1*
  Obituary *29*
Fensham, Elizabeth *169*
Fenten, Barbara D(oris) 1935- *26*
Fenten, D(onald) X. 1932- *4*
Fenton, Carroll Lane 1900-1969 .... *5*
Fenton, Edward 1917-1995 .... *7*
  Obituary *89*
Fenton, Joe *213*
Fenton, Mildred Adams 1899-1995 .... *21*
Fenwick, Patti
  See Grider, Dorothy
Feravolo, Rocco Vincent 1922- *10*
Ferber, Brenda A. 1967- *184*
Ferber, Edna 1887-1968 .... *7*
Fergus, Charles *114*
Ferguson, Alane 1957- *182*
  Earlier sketch in SATA *85*
Ferguson, Bob
  See Ferguson, Robert Bruce
Ferguson, Cecil 1931- *45*
Ferguson, Peter 1968- *199*
Ferguson, Robert Bruce 1927-2001 .... *13*
Ferguson, Sarah 1959- *180*
  Earlier sketches in SATA *66, 110*
Ferguson, Sarah Margaret
  See Ferguson, Sarah
Ferguson, Walter (W.) 1930- *34*
Fergusson, Erna 1888-1964 .... *5*
Fermi, Laura 1907-1977 .... *6*
  Obituary *28*
Fern, Eugene A. 1919-1987 .... *10*
  Obituary *54*
Fern, Tracey E. *202*
Fernandes, Eugenie 1943- *205*
  Earlier sketches in SATA *77, 139*
Fernandez, Laura 1960- *171*
Ferraiolo, Jack D. *208*
Ferrari, Maria *123*
Ferreiro, Carmen 1958- *158*
Ferrell, Nancy Warren 1932- *70*
Ferri, Giuliano 1965- *197*
Ferrier, Lucy
  See Penzler, Otto
Ferris, Helen Josephine 1890-1969 .... *21*
Ferris, James Cody
  See McFarlane, Leslie
Ferris, Jean 1939- *202*
  Brief entry *50*
  Earlier sketches in SATA *56, 105, 149*
Ferris, Jeri Chase 1937- *84*
Ferry, Charles 1927- *92*
  Earlier sketch in SATA *43*
  See also CLR *34*
  See also SAAS *20*
Fetz, Ingrid 1915- *30*
Feydy, Anne Lindbergh
  See Sapieyevski, Anne Lindbergh
Fiammenghi, Gioia 1929- *66*
  Earlier sketch in SATA *9*
Fiarotta, Noel
  See Ficarotta, Noel
Fiarotta, Phyllis
  See Ficarotta, Phyllis
Ficarotta, Noel 1944- *15*
Ficarotta, Phyllis 1942- *15*
Fichter, George S. 1922-1993 .... *7*
Ficocelli, Elizabeth *189*

Fidler, Kathleen (Annie) 1899-1980 87
    Obituary 45
    Earlier sketch in SATA 3
Fiedler, Jean(nette Feldman) 4
Fiedler, Joseph Daniel 159
Fiedler, Lisa 185
Field, Dorothy 1944- 97
Field, Edward 1924- 109
    Earlier sketch in SATA 8
Field, Elinor Whitney 1889-1980
    Obituary 28
Field, Eugene 1850-1895 16
Field, Gans T.
    See Wellman, Manly Wade
Field, James 1959- 113
Field, Peter
    See Drago, Harry Sinclair
    and Dresser, Davis
    and Mann, E(dward) B(everly)
Field, Rachel (Lyman) 1894-1942 15
    See also CLR 21
Fielding, Kate
    See Oldfield, Jenny
Fields, Bryan W. 1958(?)- 188
Fields, Lisa 1984(?)- 216
Fields, Terri 1948- 191
Fields, T.S.
    See Fields, Terri
Fienberg, Anna 1956- 183
    Earlier sketch in SATA 112
Fiery, Ann
    See Barrows, Annie
Fife, Dale (Odile Hollerbach) 1901- 18
Fighter Pilot, A
    See Johnston, H(ugh) A(nthony) S(tephen)
Figler, Jeanie 1949- 123
Figley, Marty Rhodes 1948- 158
    Earlier sketch in SATA 88
Figueredo, D(anilo) H. 1951- 155
Figueroa, Pablo 1938- 9
Fijan, Carol 1918- 12
Filderman, Diane E(lizabeth) 1959- 87
Files, Meg 1946- 107
Fillmore, Parker H(oysted) 1878-1944
    See YABC 1
Filstrup, Chris
    See Filstrup, E(dward) Christian
Filstrup, E(dward) Christian 1942- 43
Filstrup, Janie
    See Merrill, Jane
Finbarr, Desmond
    See Zobel Nolan, Allia
Finchler, Judy 1943- 93
Finder, Martin
    See Salzmann, Siegmund
Findlay, Jamieson 1958- 169
Findon, Joanne 1957- 161
Fine, Anne 1947- 197
    Earlier sketches in SATA 29, 72, 111, 160
    See also CLR 25
    See also SAAS 15
Fine, Edith Hope 169
Fine, Howard 1961- 181
Fine, Jane
    See Ziefert, Harriet
Finger, Charles J(oseph) 1869(?)-1941 42
Fink, William B(ertrand) 1916- 22
Finke, Blythe Foote 1922- 26
Finkel, George (Irvine) 1909-1975 8
Finkelstein, Norman H. 1941- 220
    Earlier sketches in SATA 73, 137
Finkelstein, Norman Henry
    See Finkelstein, Norman H.
Finlay, Alice Sullivan 1946- 82
Finlay, Winifred Lindsay Crawford
    (McKissack) 1910-1989 23
Finlayson, Ann 1925- 8
Finley, Martha 1828-1909 43
    See also CLR 148
Finley, Mary Peace 1942- 83
Finn, Mary 208

Finney, Jack 1911-1995 109
Finney, Patricia 1958- 163
Finney, Shan 1944- 65
Finney, Walter Braden
    See Finney, Jack
Firer, Ben Zion
    See Firer, Benzion
Firer, Benzion 1914- 64
Fireside, Bryna J. 1932- 73
Firmin, Charlotte 1954- 29
Firmin, Peter 1928- 58
    Earlier sketch in SATA 15
Firth, Barbara 179
Fischbach, Julius 1894-1988 10
Fischer, John
    See Fluke, Joanne
Fischer, R.J.
    See Fluke, Joanne
Fischer, Scott M. 1971- 195
Fischer-Nagel, Andreas 1951- 56
Fischer-Nagel, Heiderose 1956- 56
Fischler, Shirley (Walton) 66
Fischler, Stan(ley I.) 66
    Brief entry 36
Fischtrom, Harvey 1933-1974 3
Fishback, Margaret
    See Antolini, Margaret Fishback
Fishbone, Greg R. 195
Fisher, Aileen (Lucia) 1906-2002 73
    Obituary 143
    Earlier sketches in SATA 1, 25
    See also CLR 49
Fisher, Barbara 1940- 44
    Brief entry 34
Fisher, Carolyn 1968- 154
Fisher, Catherine 1957- 155
Fisher, Chris 1958- 80
Fisher, Clavin C(argill) 1912- 24
Fisher, Cynthia 195
Fisher, Dorothy (Frances) Canfield 1879-1958
    See YABC 1
    See also CLR 71
Fisher, Gary L. 1949- 86
Fisher, John 1909-1996 15
Fisher, John Oswald Hamilton
    See Fisher, John
Fisher, Laura Harrison 1934- 5
Fisher, Leonard Everett 1924- 176
    Autobiography Feature 122
    Earlier sketches in SATA 4, 34, 73, 120
    See also CLR 18
    See also SAAS 1
Fisher, Lois I. 1948- 38
    Brief entry 35
Fisher, Margery (Turner) 1913-1992 20
    Obituary 74
Fisher, Marshall Jon 1963- 113
Fisher, Nikki
    See Strachan, Ian
Fisher, Robert (Tempest) 1943- 47
Fisher, Suzanne
    See Staples, Suzanne Fisher
Fisher, Valorie 214
    Earlier sketch in SATA 177
Fishman, Cathy Goldberg 1951- 106
Fisk, Nicholas
    See Higginbottom, David
Fisk, Pauline 1948- 160
    Earlier sketch in SATA 66
Fiske, Tarleton
    See Bloch, Robert (Albert)
Fisscher, Catharina G. M. 1958- 142
Fisscher, Tiny
    See Fisscher, Catharina G. M.
Fitch, Clarke
    See Sinclair, Upton
Fitch, John IV
    See Cormier, Robert
Fitch, Sheree 1956- 178
    Earlier sketch in SATA 108
Fitschen, Dale 1937- 20

Fitzalan, Roger
    See Trevor, Elleston
Fitzgerald, Captain Hugh
    See Baum, L. Frank
FitzGerald, Cathleen 1932-1987
    Obituary 50
Fitzgerald, Dawn 175
Fitzgerald, Edward Earl 1919-2001 20
Fitzgerald, F(rancis) A(nthony) 1940- 15
Fitzgerald, Joanne 1956- 198
Fitzgerald, John D(ennis) 1907(?)-1988 20
    Obituary 56
    See also CLR 1
Fitzgerald, Merni Ingrassia 1955- 53
Fitzgibbon, Terry 1948- 121
Fitzhardinge, Joan Margaret 1912- 73
    Earlier sketch in SATA 2
    See also CLR 5
    See also SAAS 3
Fitzhugh, Louise (Perkins) 1928-1974 45
    Obituary 24
    Earlier sketch in SATA 1
    See also CLR 72
Fitzhugh, Percy Keese 1876-1950 65
Fitzmaurice, Kathryn 217
Fitzpatrick, Marie-Louise 1962- 189
    Earlier sketch in SATA 125
FitzRalph, Matthew
    See McInerny, Ralph
Fitz-Randolph, Jane (Currens) 1915- 51
Fitzsimons, Cecilia 1952- 97
Fitzsimons, Cecilia A.L.
    See Fitzsimons, Cecilia
Flack, Marjorie 1897-1958 100
    See also YABC 2
    See also CLR 28
Flack, Naomi John White -1999 40
    Brief entry 35
Flake, Sharon G. 166
Flanagan, John 1944- 180
Flanagan, John Anthony
    See Flanagan, John
Flannery, Kate
    See De Goldi, Kate
Flatt, Lizann 1966- 88
Fleagle, Gail S(hatto) 1940- 117
Fleetwood, Jenni 1947- 80
Fleischer, Jane
    See Oppenheim, Joanne
Fleischhauer-Hardt, Helga 1936- 30
Fleischman, Albert Sidney
    See Fleischman, Sid
Fleischman, John 1948- 145
Fleischman, Paul 1952- 156
    Brief entry 32
    Earlier sketches in SATA 39, 72, 110
    See also CLR 66
    See also SAAS 20
Fleischman, Sid 1920-2010 185
    Earlier sketches in SATA 8, 59, 96, 148
    See also CLR 15
Fleischner, Jennifer 1956- 188
    Earlier sketch in SATA 93
Fleisher, Paul 1948- 132
    Earlier sketch in SATA 81
Fleisher, Robbin 1951-1977 52
    Brief entry 49
Fleishman, Seymour 1918- 66
    Brief entry 32
Fleming, A. A.
    See Arthur, Robert, (Jr.)
Fleming, Alice Mulcahey 1928- 9
Fleming, Candace 1962- 190
    Earlier sketches in SATA 94, 143
Fleming, Denise 1950- 173
    Earlier sketches in SATA 81, 126
Fleming, Elizabeth P. 1888-1985
    Obituary 48
Fleming, Ian 1908-1964 9
Fleming, Ian Lancaster
    See Fleming, Ian

Fleming, Ronald Lee 1941- 56
Fleming, Sally
　See Walker, Sally M.
Fleming, Stuart
　See Knight, Damon (Francis)
Fleming, Susan 1932- 32
Fleming, Thomas 1927- 8
Fleming, Thomas James
　See Fleming, Thomas
Fleming, Virginia (Edwards) 1923- 84
Flesch, Y.
　See Flesch, Yolande
Flesch, Yolande 1950- 55
Flesch, Yolande Catarina
　See Flesch, Yolande
Fletcher, Charlie 220
Fletcher, Charlie May Hogue 1897-1977 3
Fletcher, Colin 1922-2007 28
Fletcher, Dirk
　See Cunningham, Chet
Fletcher, George U.
　See Pratt, (Murray) Fletcher
Fletcher, Helen Jill 1910- 13
Fletcher, Ralph 1953- 195
　Earlier sketches in SATA *105, 149*
　See also CLR *104*
Fletcher, Ralph J.
　See Fletcher, Ralph
Fletcher, Richard E. 1917(?)-1983
　Obituary 34
Fletcher, Rick
　See Fletcher, Richard E.
Fletcher, Susan 1951- 181
　Earlier sketches in SATA *70, 110*
Fletcher, Susan Clemens
　See Fletcher, Susan
Fleur, Paul
　See Pohl, Frederik
Flexner, James Thomas 1908-2003 9
Flinn, Alex 1966- 198
　Earlier sketch in SATA *159*
Flint, Helen 1952- 102
Flint, Russ 1944- 74
Flitner, David, Jr. 1949- 7
Flitner, David Perkins
　See Flitner, David, Jr.
Floca, Brian 190
　Earlier sketch in SATA *155*
Floethe, Louise Lee 1913-1988 4
Floethe, Richard 1901-1998 4
Floherty, John Joseph 1882-1964 25
Flood, Bo
　See Flood, Nancy Bo
Flood, Nancy Bo 1945- 130
Flood, Pansie Hart 1964- 140
Flood, William 1942- 129
Flooglebuckle, Al
　See Spiegelman, Art
Flora, James (Royer) 1914-1998 30
　Obituary 103
　Earlier sketch in SATA *1*
　See also SAAS *6*
Flores-Galbis, Enrique 1952- 186
Florian, Douglas 1950- 177
　Earlier sketches in SATA *19, 83, 125*
Flory, Jane Trescott 1917- 22
Flournoy, Valerie 1952- 95
Flournoy, Valerie Rose
　See Flournoy, Valerie
Flowerdew, Phyllis -1994 33
Flowers, Pam 1946- 136
Flowers, Sarah 1952- 98
Floyd, Gareth 1940- 62
　Brief entry 31
Fluchere, Henri 1914-1991 40
Fluke, Joanne 1943- 88
Flutsztejn-Gruda, Ilona 1930- 170
Flynn, Barbara 1928- 9
Flynn, Jackson
　See Bensen, Donald R.
　and Shirreffs, Gordon D(onald)

Flynn, Nicholas
　See Odgers, Sally Farrell
Flynn, Pat 1968- 214
Flynn, Patrick
　See Flynn, Pat
Flynn, Rachel 1953- 171
　Earlier sketch in SATA *109*
Flynn, Warren (G.) 1950- 154
Fodor, R. V. 1944- 25
Fodor, Ronald Victor
　See Fodor, R. V.
Fogelin, Adrian 1951- 175
　Earlier sketch in SATA *129*
Foley, (Anna) Bernice Williams 1902-1987 . 28
Foley, Greg E. 1969- 190
Foley, June 1944- 44
Foley, (Mary) Louise Munro 1933- 106
　Brief entry 40
　Earlier sketch in SATA *54*
Foley, Rae
　See Denniston, Elinore
Folke, Will
　See Bloch, Robert (Albert)
Follett, Helen Thomas 1884(?)-1970
　Obituary 27
Folsom, Franklin (Brewster) 1907-1995 5
　Obituary 88
Folsom, Michael (Brewster) 1938-1990 40
　Obituary 88
Fombelle, Timothee de 1973- 218
Fontenot, Mary Alice 1910-2003 91
　Obituary 209
　Earlier sketch in SATA *34*
Fontes, Justine 172
Fontes, Ron 1952- 183
Foon, Dennis 1951- 119
Fooner, Michael 22
Foote, Timothy (Gilson) 1926- 52
Forberg, Ati
　See Forberg, Beate Gropius
Forberg, Beate Gropius 1925- 22
Forbes, Anna 1954- 101
Forbes, Bryan 1926- 37
Forbes, Cabot L.
　See Hoyt, Edwin P(almer), Jr.
Forbes, Esther 1891-1967 100
　Earlier sketch in SATA *2*
　See also CLR *147*
Forbes, Graham B. 1
Forbes, Kathryn
　See McLean, Kathryn (Anderson)
Forbes, Robert
　See Arthur, Robert, (Jr.)
Ford, Albert Lee
　See Stratemeyer, Edward L.
Ford, Barbara 56
　Brief entry 34
Ford, Bernette 212
Ford, Bernette G.
　See Ford, Bernette
Ford, B.G.
　See Ford, Bernette
Ford, Brian J(ohn) 1939- 49
Ford, Carolyn 1938- 98
Ford, Carolyn Mott
　See Ford, Carolyn
Ford, Christine 1953- 176
Ford, David
　See Baldacci, David
　and Baldacci, David
Ford, David B.
　See Baldacci, David
Ford, David Baldacci
　See Baldacci, David
Ford, Elbur
　See Hibbert, Eleanor Alice Burford
Ford, Ellen 1949- 89
Ford, George (Jr.) 31
Ford, Hilary
　See Youd, Samuel

Ford, Hildegarde
　See Morrison, Velma Ford
Ford, Jerome W. 1949- 78
Ford, Jerry
　See Ford, Jerome W.
Ford, John C. 1971- 221
Ford, Juwanda G(ertrude) 1967- 102
Ford, Marcia
　See Radford, Ruby L(orraine)
Ford, Nancy K(effer) 1906-1961
　Obituary 29
Ford, Peter 1936- 59
Ford, S. M.
　See Uhlig, Susan
Forde, Catherine 1961- 170
Foreman, Mark 199
Foreman, Michael 1938- 216
　Earlier sketches in SATA *2, 73, 129, 135, 184*
　See also CLR *32*
　See also SAAS *21*
Foreman, Wilmoth 1939- 153
Forest, Antonia 1915-2003 29
　Obituary 149
Forest, Dial
　See Gault, William Campbell
Forest, Heather 1948- 185
　Earlier sketch in SATA *120*
Forester, C. S. 1899-1966 13
Forester, Cecil Scott
　See Forester, C. S.
Forester, Victoria 214
Forman, Brenda 1936- 4
Forman, James
　See Forman, James D.
Forman, James D. 1932-2009 70
　Earlier sketch in SATA *8*
Forman, James Douglas
　See Forman, James D.
Forman, Mark L.
　See Forman, M.L.
Forman, M.L. 1964- 215
Forman, Ruth 1970- 186
Forrest, Elizabeth
　See Salsitz, Rhondi Vilott
Forrest, Mary
　See Pausacker, Jenny
Forrest, Sybil
　See Markun, Patricia Maloney
Forrestal, Elaine 1941- 165
　Earlier sketch in SATA *117*
Forrester, Frank H. 1919(?)-1986
　Obituary 52
Forrester, Helen
　See Bhatia, Jamunadevi
Forrester, Jade
　See Pausacker, Jenny
Forrester, Marian
　See Schachtel, Roger
Forrester, Sandra 1949- 166
　Earlier sketch in SATA *90*
Forrester, Victoria 1940- 40
　Brief entry 35
Forsee, (Frances) Aylesa -1986 1
Forsey, Chris 1950- 59
Forshay-Lunsford, Cin 1965- 60
Forster, E. M. 1879-1970 57
Forster, Edward Morgan
　See Forster, E. M.
Forsyth, Kate 1966- 154
Fort, Paul
　See Stockton, Francis Richard
Forte, Maurizio 1961- 110
Fortey, Richard 1946- 109
Fortey, Richard A.
　See Fortey, Richard
Fortey, Richard Alan
　See Fortey, Richard
Forth, Melissa D(eal) 96
Fortnum, Peggy
　See Nuttall-Smith, Margaret Emily Noel
Fortune, Eric 182

Forward, Robert L(ull) 1932-2002 82
Foster, Alan Dean 1946- 70
Foster, Brad W. 1955- 34
Foster, Doris Van Liew 1899-1993 10
Foster, E(lizabeth) C(onnell) 1902- 9
Foster, Elizabeth 1902- 12
Foster, Elizabeth 1905-1963 10
Foster, F. Blanche 1919- 11
Foster, G(eorge) Allen 1907-1969 26
Foster, Genevieve (Stump) 1893-1979 2
    Obituary 23
    See also CLR 7
Foster, Gerald L. 198
Foster, Hal
    See Foster, Harold
Foster, Harold 1892-1982 31
Foster, Jeanne
    See Williams, Jeanne
Foster, John
    See Foster, John L(ouis)
    and Furcolo, Foster
Foster, John (Thomas) 1925- 8
Foster, John L(ouis) 1941- 102
Foster, Juliana 196
Foster, Laura Louise (James) 1918- 6
Foster, Leila Merrell 1929- 73
Foster, Lynne 1937- 74
Foster, Margaret Lesser 1899(?)-1979
    Obituary 21
Foster, Marian Curtis 1909-1978 23
Foster, Mark 1961- 197
Foster, Sally 58
Fotheringham, Edwin 201
Foulds, E. V.
    See Foulds, Elfrida Vipont
Foulds, Elfrida Vipont 1902-1992 52
Fountas, Angela Jane 180
Fourie, Corlia 1944- 91
Fourth Brother, The
    See Aung, (Maung) Htin
Fowke, Edith (Margaret) 1913-1996 14
Fowles, John 1926-2005 22
    Obituary 171
Fowles, John Robert
    See Fowles, John
Fowles, Shelley 1956- 205
Fox, Aileen 1907-2005 58
    Obituary 170
Fox, Aileen Mary
    See Fox, Aileen
Fox, Annie 1950- 175
Fox, Charles Philip 1913-2003 12
    Obituary 150
Fox, Christyan 188
Fox, Diane 188
Fox, Eleanor
    See St. John, Wylly Folk
Fox, Fontaine Talbot, Jr. 1884-1964
    Obituary 23
Fox, Fred 1903(?)-1981
    Obituary 27
Fox, Freeman
    See Hamilton, Charles (Harold St. John)
Fox, Geoffrey 1941- 73
Fox, Grace
    See Anderson, Grace Fox
Fox, Helen 1962- 181
Fox, Larry 30
Fox, Lorraine 1922-1976 27
    Earlier sketch in SATA 11
Fox, Louisa
    See Kroll, Virginia L.
Fox, Mary Virginia 1919- 152
    Brief entry 39
    Earlier sketches in SATA 44, 88
Fox, Mem 1946- 211
    Earlier sketches in SATA 51, 103, 155
    See also CLR 80
Fox, Merrion Frances
    See Fox, Mem
Fox, Michael W(ilson) 1937- 15

Fox, Norma Diane
    See Mazer, Norma Fox
Fox, Paula 1923- 167
    Earlier sketches in SATA 17, 60, 120
    See also CLR 96
Fox, Robert J. 1927- 33
Fox, Robert Joseph
    See Fox, Robert J.
Fox-Davies, Sarah 1956- 199
Foyt, Victoria .... 187.
Fradin, Dennis
    See Fradin, Dennis Brindell
Fradin, Dennis Brindell 1945- 185
    Earlier sketches in SATA 29, 90, 135
Fradin, Judith Bloom 1945- 185
    Earlier sketches in SATA 90, 152
Frailey, Paige (Menefee) 1965- 82
Frame, Janet 1924-2004 119
Frame, Paul 1913-1994 60
    Brief entry 33
    Obituary 83
Frances, Miss
    See Horwich, Frances R(appaport)
Franchere, Ruth 18
Francis, Charles
    See Holme, Bryan
Francis, Dee
    See Haas, Dorothy F.
Francis, Dorothy 1926- 127
    Earlier sketch in SATA 10
Francis, Dorothy B.
    See Francis, Dorothy
Francis, Dorothy Brenner
    See Francis, Dorothy
Francis, Jaye
    See Pausacker, Jenny
Francis, Pamela (Mary) 1926- 11
Franck, Eddie
    See Cooke, Frank E.
Franco, Betsy 188
    Earlier sketch in SATA 150
Franco, Eloise (Bauder) 1910- 62
Franco, Johan (Henri Gustave) 1908-1988 ... 62
Franco, Marjorie 38
Francois, Andre 1915-2005 25
Francoise
    See Seignobosc, Francoise
Frank, Anne 1929-1945 87
    Brief entry 42
    See also CLR 101
Frank, Annelies Marie
    See Frank, Anne
Frank, Daniel B. 1956- 55
Frank, Emily R.
    See Frank, E.R.
Frank, E.R. 1967- 157
Frank, Helene
    See Vautier, Ghislaine
Frank, Hillary 1976- 148
Frank, John 199
Frank, Josette 1893-1989 10
    Obituary 63
Frank, Lucy 1947- 166
    Earlier sketch in SATA 94
Frank, Mary 1933- 34
Frank, R., Jr.
    See Ross, Frank (Xavier), Jr.
Frankau, Mary Evelyn Atkinson 1899-1974 .. 4
Frankel, Alona 1937- 66
Frankel, Bernice 9
Frankel, Edward 1910- 44
Frankel, Ellen 1951- 78
Frankel, Julie 1947- 40
    Brief entry 34
Frankenberg, Robert 1911- 22
Frankland, David 207
Franklin, Cheryl J. 1955- 70
Franklin, Harold 1926- 13
Franklin, Kristine L. 1958- 124
    Earlier sketch in SATA 80

Franklin, Lance
    See Lantz, Francess L(in)
Franklin, Madeleine
    See L'Engle, Madeleine
Franklin, Madeleine L'Engle
    See L'Engle, Madeleine
Franklin, Madeleine L'Engle Camp
    See L'Engle, Madeleine
Franklin, Max
    See Deming, Richard
Franklin, Steve
    See Stevens, Franklin
Franson, Leanne R. 1963- 111
Franson, Scott E. 1966- 192
Franzen, Nils-Olof 1916- 10
Frascino, Edward 48
    Brief entry 33
    See also SAAS 9
Frasconi, Antonio 1919- 131
    Earlier sketches in SATA 6, 53
    See also SAAS 11
Fraser, Betty
    See Fraser, Elizabeth Marr
Fraser, Elizabeth Marr 1928- 31
Fraser, Eric (George) 1902-1983 38
Fraser, Mary Ann 1959- 214
    Earlier sketches in SATA 76, 137
    See also SAAS 23
Fraser, Wynnette (McFaddin) 1925- 90
Frasier, Debra 1953- 182
    Earlier sketches in SATA 69, 112
Fraustino, Lisa Rowe 1961- 146
    Autobiography Feature 146
    Earlier sketch in SATA 84
Frazee, Marla 1958- 187
    Earlier sketches in SATA 105, 151
Frazer, Megan 1977- 221
Frazetta, Frank 1928-2010 58
Frazier, Craig 1955- 221
    Earlier sketch in SATA 177
Frazier, Neta (Osborn) Lohnes 1890-1990 7
Frazier, Sundee T. 1968- 198
Frazier, Sundee Tucker
    See Frazier, Sundee T.
Frederic, Mike
    See Cox, William R(obert)
Frederick, Heather Vogel 207
Fredericks, Anthony D. 1947- 113
Freed, Alvyn M. 1913-1993 22
Freedman, Benedict 1919- 27
Freedman, Claire 185
Freedman, Deborah 1960- 191
Freedman, Jeff 1953- 90
Freedman, Nancy 1920-2010 27
Freedman, Russell 1929- 175
    Earlier sketches in SATA 16, 71, 123
    See also CLR 71
Freedman, Russell Bruce
    See Freedman, Russell
Freeman, Barbara C. 1906-1999 28
Freeman, Barbara Constance
    See Freeman, Barbara C.
Freeman, Bill
    See Freeman, William Bradford
Freeman, Don 1908-1978 17
    See also CLR 90
Freeman, Ira Maximilian 1905-1987 21
Freeman, Kimberley
    See Wilkins, Kim
Freeman, Laura 200
Freeman, Lucy (Greenbaum) 1916-2004 24
Freeman, Mae 1907-1985 25
Freeman, Mae Blacker
    See Freeman, Mae
Freeman, Marcia S. 1937- 102
Freeman, Marcia Sheehan
    See Freeman, Marcia S.
Freeman, Martha 1956- 201
    Earlier sketches in SATA 101, 152
Freeman, Nancy 1932- 61

Freeman, Peter J.
See Calvert, Patricia
Freeman, Sarah (Caroline) 1940- 66
Freeman, Tor 1977- 164
Freeman, VicToria
See Freeman, Tor
Freeman, William Bradford 1938- 58
Brief entry 48
Fregosi, Claudia (Anne Marie) 1946- 24
Freitas, Donna 1972- 205
French, Allen 1870-1946
See YABC 1
French, Dorothy Kayser 1926- 5
French, Fiona 1944- 132
Earlier sketches in SATA 6, 75
See also CLR 37
See also SAAS 21
French, Jackie 186
Autobiography Feature 139
Earlier sketches in SATA 108, 139
See French, Jackie Anne
and French, Jacqueline Anne
French, Kathryn
See Mosesson, Gloria R(ubin)
French, Martin 176
French, Michael 1944- 49
Brief entry 38
French, Paul
See Asimov, Isaac
French, S. Terrell 216
French, Simon 1957- 147
Earlier sketch in SATA 86
French, Vivian 209
Earlier sketch in SATA 165
Frenette, Liza 126
Freschet, Gina 1960- 175
Earlier sketch in SATA 139
Frewer, Glyn (M.) 1931- 11
Frey, Darcy 98
Freymann, Saxton 1958(?)- 178
Freymann-Weyr, Garret 1965- 145
Freymann-Weyr, Rhoda Garret Michaela
See Freymann-Weyr, Garret
Frick, C. H.
See Irwin, Constance (H.) Frick
Frick, Constance
See Irwin, Constance (H.) Frick
Fricke, Aaron 1962- 89
Fridell, Ron 1943- 124
Fried, Janice 197
Friedlander, Joanne K(ohn) 1930- 9
Friedman, Aimee 1979- 189
Friedman, D. Dina 1957- 180
Friedman, Debra 1955- 150
Friedman, Estelle (Ehrenwald) 1920- 7
Friedman, Frieda 1905- 43
Friedman, Ina R(osen) 1926- 136
Brief entry 41
Earlier sketch in SATA 49
Friedman, Jerrold David
See Gerrold, David
Friedman, Judi 1935- 59
Friedman, Laurie 1964- 219
Earlier sketches in SATA 138, 179
Friedman, Marvin 1930- 42
Brief entry 33
Friedman, Robin 1968- 219
Earlier sketch in SATA 162
Friedmann, Stan 1953- 80
Friedrich, Otto (Alva) 1929-1995 33
Friedrich, Priscilla 1927- 39
Friend, Catherine 1957(?)- 194
Friend, David Michael 1975- 195
Friend, Natasha 1972- 184
Friendlich, Dick
See Friendlich, Richard J.
Friendlich, Richard J. 1909- 11
Friermood, Elisabeth Hamilton 1903-1992 5
Friesen, Bernice (Sarah Anne) 1966- 105
Friesen, Gayle 1960- 200
Earlier sketch in SATA 109

Friesen, Jonathan 1967(?)- 206
Friesner, Esther 1951- 207
Earlier sketches in SATA 71, 168
Friesner, Esther M.
See Friesner, Esther
Friis-Baastad, Babbis Ellinor 1921-1970 7
Frimmer, Steven 1928- 31
Frischmuth, Barbara 1941- 114
Friskey, Margaret (Richards) 1901-1995 5
Fritts, Mary Bahr
See Bahr, Mary (Madelyn)
Fritz, Jean (Guttery) 1915- 163
Autobiography Feature 122
Earlier sketches in SATA 1, 29, 72, 119
See also CLR 96
See also SAAS 2
Froehlich, Margaret W(alden) 1930- 56
Frois, Jeanne 1953- 73
Froissart, Jean 1338(?)-1410(?) 28
Froman, Elizabeth Hull 1920-1975 10
Froman, Robert (Winslow) 1917- 8
Fromm, Lilo 1928- 29
Frommer, Harvey 1937- 41
Frost, A(rthur) B(urdett) 1851-1928 19
Frost, Elizabeth
See Frost-Knappman, Elizabeth
Frost, Erica
See Supraner, Robyn
Frost, Helen 1949- 194
Autobiography Feature 194
Earlier sketches in SATA 157, 183
Frost, Helen Marie
See Frost, Helen
Frost, Lesley 1899-1983 14
Obituary 34
Frost, Robert 1874-1963 14
See also CLR 67
Frost, Robert Lee
See Frost, Robert
Frost, Shelley 1960- 138
Frost-Knappman, Elizabeth 1943- 179
Froud, Brian 1947- 150
Fry, Annette R(iley) 89
Fry, Christopher 1907-2005 66
Fry, Edward Bernard 1925- 35
Fry, Rosalie Kingsmill 1911-1992 3
See also SAAS 11
Fry, Virginia Lynn 1952- 95
Frye, Sally
See Moore, Elaine
Fuchs, Bernie 1932- 162
Earlier sketch in SATA 95
Fuchs, Erich 1916- 6
Fuchshuber, Annegert 1940- 43
Fucile, Tony 221
Fuerst, Jeffrey B. 1956- 143
Fuertes, Gloria 1918-1998 115
Fuge, Charles 1966- 144
Earlier sketch in SATA 74
Fujikawa, Gyo 1908-1998 76
Brief entry 30
Obituary 110
Earlier sketch in SATA 39
See also CLR 25
See also SAAS 16
Fujita, Tamao 1905-1999 7
Fujiwara, Kim 1957- 81
Fujiwara, Michiko 1946- 15
Fuka, Vladimir 1926-1977
Obituary 27
Fulcher, Jennifer
See Westwood, Jennifer
Fuller, Catherine Leuthold 1916- 9
Fuller, Edmund (Maybank) 1914- 21
Fuller, Iola
See McCoy, Iola Fuller
Fuller, John G(rant, Jr.) 1913-1990 65
Fuller, Kathleen
See Gottfried, Theodore Mark
Fuller, Lois Hamilton 1915- 11
Fuller, Margaret 1810-1850 25

Fuller, Maud
See Petersham, Maud
Fuller, Roy (Broadbent) 1912-1991 87
Fuller, Sarah Margaret
See Fuller, Margaret
Fults, John Lee 1932- 33
Funk, Thompson 1911- 7
Funk, Tom
See Funk, Thompson
Funke, Cornelia 1958- 209
Earlier sketches in SATA 154, 174
See also CLR 145
Funke, Cornelia Caroline
See Funke, Cornelia
Funke, Lewis 1912-1992 11
Fuqua, Jonathon Scott 1966- 141
Furbee, Mary R.
See Furbee, Mary Rodd
Furbee, Mary Rodd 1954- 138
Furchgott, Terry 1948- 29
Furlong, Monica (Mavis) 1930-2003 86
Obituary 142
Furlonger, Patricia
See Wrightson, Patricia
Furman, Gertrude Lerner Kerman 1909- 21
Furniss, Tim 1948- 49
Furrow, Robert 1985- 172
Furukawa, Toshi 1924- 24
Fusillo, Archimede 1962- 137
Futcher, Jane P. 1947- 76
Futehali, Zahida
See Whitaker, Zai
Fyleman, Rose (Amy) 1877-1957 21
Fyson, Jenny Grace
See Fyson, J.G.
Fyson, J.G. 1904-1998 42

G

Gaan, Margaret 1914- 65
Gaber, Susan 1956- 169
Earlier sketch in SATA 115
Gaberman, Judie Angell
See Angell, Judie
Gabhart, Ann
See Gabhart, Ann H.
Gabhart, Ann H. 1947- 75
Gable, Brian 1949- 195
Gabler, Mirko 1951- 77
Gabriel, Adriana
See Rojany, Lisa
Gabrys, Ingrid Schubert
See Schubert-Gabrys, Ingrid
Gackenbach, Dick 1927- 79
Brief entry 30
Earlier sketch in SATA 48
Gadd, Jeremy 1949- 116
Gaddis, Vincent H. 1913-1997 35
Gadler, Steve J. 1905-1985 36
Gaeddert, Lou Ann (Bigge) 1931- 103
Earlier sketch in SATA 20
Gaeddert, Louann
See Gaeddert, Lou Ann (Bigge)
Gaer, Joseph 1897-1969 118
Gaer, Yossef
See Gaer, Joseph
Gaetz, Dayle Campbell 1947- 138
Gaffney, Timothy R. 1951- 170
Earlier sketch in SATA 69
Gaffron, Norma 1931- 97
Gaffron, Norma Bondeson
See Gaffron, Norma
Gag, Flavia 1907-1979
Obituary 24
Gag, Wanda (Hazel) 1893-1946 100
See also YABC 1
See also CLR 150
Gage, Brian 162

Gage, Wilson
  See Steele, Mary Q(uintard Govan)
Gagliano, Eugene M. 1946- *150*
Gagliardo, Ruth Garver 1895(?)-1980
  Obituary *22*
Gagnon, Cecile 1936- *58*
Gaillard, Jason 1965- *200*
Gaiman, Neil 1960- *197*
  Earlier sketches in SATA *85, 146*
  See also CLR *109*
Gaiman, Neil Richard
  See Gaiman, Neil
Gainer, Cindy 1962- *74*
Gaines, Ernest J. 1933- *86*
  See also CLR *62*
Gaines, Ernest James
  See Gaines, Ernest J.
Gaither, Gloria 1942- *127*
Gal, Laszlo 1933- *96*
  Brief entry *32*
  Earlier sketch in SATA *52*
  See also CLR *61*
Galbraith, Ben 1980- *200*
Galbraith, Kathryn O. 1945- *219*
  Earlier sketch in SATA *85*
Galbraith, Kathryn Osebold
  See Galbraith, Kathryn O.
Galdone, Paul 1907(?)-1986 .... *66*
  Obituary *49*
  Earlier sketch in SATA *17*
  See also CLR *16*
Galindo, Claudia 1979- *203*
Galinsky, Ellen 1942- *23*
Gall, Chris 1961- *176*
Gallagher, Diana G. 1946- *153*
Gallagher, Lurlene Nora
  See McDaniel, Lurlene
Gallagher-Cole, Mernie 1958- *206*
Gallant, Roy A(rthur) 1924- *110*
  Earlier sketches in SATA *4, 68*
  See also CLR *30*
Gallardo, Evelyn 1948- *78*
Gallaz, Christophe 1948- *162*
  See also CLR *126*
Gallego Garcia, Laura 1977- *173*
Gallico, Paul 1897-1976 .... *13*
Gallico, Paul William
  See Gallico, Paul
Gallo, Donald R. 1938- *112*
  Autobiography Feature *104*
Gallo, Donald Robert
  See Gallo, Donald R.
Galloway, Owateka (S.) 1981- *121*
Galloway, Priscilla 1930- *112*
  Earlier sketch in SATA *66*
Gallup, Joan 1957- *128*
Galouchko, Annouchka Gravel 1960- *95*
Galt, Thomas Franklin, Jr. 1908-1989 .... *5*
Galt, Tom
  See Galt, Thomas Franklin, Jr.
Galvin, Matthew R. 1950- *93*
Galvin, Matthew Reppert
  See Galvin, Matthew R.
Gamble, Kim 1952- *183*
  Earlier sketches in SATA *81, 124*
Gambrell, Jamey *82*
Gamerman, Martha 1941- *15*
Gammell, Stephen 1943- *128*
  Earlier sketches in SATA *53, 81*
  See also CLR *83*
Ganly, Helen (Mary) 1940- *56*
Gannett, Ruth Chrisman (Arens)
  1896-1979 .... *33*
Gannett, Ruth Stiles 1923- *3*
Gannij, Joan *208*
Gannij, Joan Levine
  See Gannij, Joan
Gannon, Ned 1974- *205*
Gannon, Robert Haines 1931- *8*
Gano, Lila 1949- *76*

Gans, Roma 1894-1996 .... *45*
  Obituary *93*
Gant, Matthew
  See Hano, Arnold
Gantner, Susan (Verble) 1939- *63*
Gantos, Jack 1951- *169*
  Earlier sketches in SATA *20, 81, 119*
  See also CLR *85*
Gantos, John Bryan, Jr.
  See Gantos, Jack
Ganz, Yaffa 1938- *61*
  Brief entry *52*
Garafano, Marie 1942- *84*
Garant, Andre J. 1968- *123*
Garbe, Ruth Moore
  See Moore, Ruth (Ellen)
Garber, Esther
  See Lee, Tanith
Garcia, Cristina 1958- *208*
Garcia, Emma 1969- *198*
Garcia, Yolanda P. 1952- *113*
Garcia, Yolanda Pacheco
  See Garcia, Yolanda P.
Gard, Janice
  See Latham, Jean Lee
Gard, Joyce
  See Reeves, Joyce
Gard, Robert Edward 1910-1992 .... *18*
  Obituary *74*
Gard, (Sanford) Wayne 1899-1986
  Obituary *49*
Gardam, Jane 1928- *130*
  Brief entry *28*
  Earlier sketches in SATA *39, 76*
  See also CLR *12*
  See also SAAS *9*
Gardam, Jane Mary
  See Gardam, Jane
Gardella, Tricia 1944- *96*
Garden, Nancy 1938- *147*
  Autobiography Feature *147*
  Earlier sketches in SATA *12, 77, 114*
  See also CLR *51*
  See also SAAS *8*
Gardiner, John Reynolds 1944-2006 .... *64*
  Obituary *174*
Gardiner, Lindsey 1971- *144*
Gardner, Craig Shaw 1949- *99*
Gardner, Dic
  See Gardner, Richard (M.)
Gardner, Graham *159*
Gardner, Hugh 1910-1986
  Obituary *49*
Gardner, Jane Mylum 1946- *83*
Gardner, Jeanne LeMonnier 1925- *5*
Gardner, John, Jr. 1933-1982 .... *40*
  Obituary *31*
Gardner, John Champlin, Jr.
  See Gardner, John, Jr.
Gardner, John E(dward) 1917- *192*
Gardner, Lyn *192*
Gardner, Martin 1914-2010 .... *142*
  Earlier sketch in SATA *16*
Gardner, Miriam
  See Bradley, Marion Zimmer
Gardner, Richard (M.) 1931- *24*
Gardner, Richard A(lan) 1931-2003 .... *13*
  Obituary *144*
Gardner, Sally *177*
Gardner, Sandra 1940- *70*
Gardner, Scot 1968- *143*
Gardner, Sheldon 1934- *33*
Gardner, Ted
  See Gardner, Theodore Roosevelt II
Gardner, Theodore Roosevelt
  See Gardner, Theodore Roosevelt II
Gardner, Theodore Roosevelt II 1934- *84*
Garelick, May 1910-1989 .... *19*
Garfield, James B. 1881-1984 .... *6*
  Obituary *38*

Garfield, Leon 1921-1996 .... *76*
  Obituary *90*
  Earlier sketches in SATA *1, 32*
  See also CLR *21*
Garfinkle, Debra L.
  See Garfinkle, D.L.
Garfinkle, D.L. *187*
Garis, Howard R. 1873-1962 .... *13*
Garis, Howard Roger
  See Garis, Howard R.
Garland, Mark 1953- *79*
Garland, Mark A.
  See Garland, Mark
Garland, Michael 1952- *208*
  Earlier sketch in SATA *168*
Garland, Sarah 1944- *135*
  Earlier sketch in SATA *62*
Garland, Sherry 1948- *145*
  Autobiography Feature *145*
  Earlier sketches in SATA *73, 114*
Garner, Alan 1934- *69*
  Autobiography Feature *108*
  Earlier sketch in SATA *18*
  See also CLR *130*
Garner, David 1958- *78*
Garner, Eleanor Ramrath 1930- *122*
Garner, James Finn 1960(?)- *92*
Garnet, A. H.
  See Slote, Alfred
Garnett, Eve C. R. 1900-1991 .... *3*
  Obituary *70*
Garofoli, Viviana 1970- *186*
Garou, Louis P.
  See Bowkett, Stephen
Garraty, John A. 1920-2007 .... *23*
  Obituary *189*
Garraty, John Arthur
  See Garraty, John A.
Garren, Devorah-Leah
  See Devorah-Leah
Garret, Maxwell R. 1917- *39*
Garretson, Victoria Diane
  See Cox, Victoria
Garrett, Helen 1895- *21*
Garrett, Randall 1927-1987 .... *180*
Garrett, Richard 1920- *82*
Garrigue, Sheila 1931- *21*
Garrison, Barbara 1931- *163*
  Earlier sketch in SATA *19*
Garrison, Frederick
  See Sinclair, Upton
Garrison, Mary 1952- *146*
Garrison, Peter
  See Gardner, Craig Shaw
Garrison, Webb B(lack) 1919-2000 .... *25*
Garrity, Jennifer Johnson 1961- *124*
Garrity, Linda K. 1947- *128*
Garsee, Jeannine *199*
Garst, Doris Shannon 1894-1981 .... *1*
Garst, Shannon
  See Garst, Doris Shannon
Garth, Will
  See Hamilton, Edmond
  and Kuttner, Henry
Garthwaite, Marion H(ook) 1893-1981 .... *7*
Garton, Malinda D(ean) (?)-1976
  Obituary *26*
Garvie, Maureen 1944- *175*
Garvie, Maureen McCallum
  See Garvie, Maureen
Garza, Carmen Lomas 1948- *182*
Garza, Xavier *184*
Gascoigne, Bamber 1935- *62*
Gaskins, Pearl Fuyo 1957- *134*
Gasperini, Jim 1952- *54*
  Brief entry *49*
Gater, Dilys 1944- *41*
Gates, Doris 1901-1987 .... *34*
  Obituary *54*
  Earlier sketch in SATA *1*
  See also SAAS *1*

Gates, Frieda 1933- 26
Gates, Susan 1950- 153
Gates, Viola R. 1931- 101
Gathorne-Hardy, Jonathan G. 1933- 124
  Earlier sketch in SATA 26
Gatti, Anne 1952- 103
Gatty, Juliana Horatia
  See Ewing, Juliana (Horatia Gatty)
Gauch, Patricia Lee 1934- 80
  Earlier sketch in SATA 26
  See also CLR 56
  See also SAAS 21
Gaudasinska, Elzbieta 1943- 190
Gaul, Randy 1959- 63
Gault, Clare 1925- 36
Gault, Frank 1926-1982 36
  Brief entry 30
Gault, William Campbell 1910-1995 8
Gauthier, Gail 1953- 203
  Earlier sketches in SATA 118, 160
Gaver, Becky
  See Gaver, Rebecca
Gaver, Rebecca 1952- 20
Gavin, Jamila 1941- 125
  Earlier sketch in SATA 96
Gay, Amelia
  See Hogarth, Grace (Weston Allen)
Gay, Francis
  See Gee, H(erbert) L(eslie)
Gay, Kathlyn 1930- 144
  Earlier sketch in SATA 9
Gay, Marie-Louise 1952- 179
  Earlier sketches in SATA 68, 126
  See also CLR 27
  See also SAAS 21
Gay, Michel 1947- 162
Gay, Zhenya 1906-1978 19
Gaze, Gillian
  See Barklem, Jill
Gear, Kathleen M. O'Neal
  See Gear, Kathleen O'Neal
Gear, Kathleen O'Neal 1954- 166
  Earlier sketch in SATA 71
Gear, W. Michael 1955- 166
  Earlier sketch in SATA 71
Geary, Rick 1946- 142
Geason, Susan 1946- 122
Gedalof, Robin
  See McGrath, Robin
Gedge, Pauline (Alice) 1945- 101
Gee, H(erbert) L(eslie) 1901-1977
  Obituary 26
Gee, Maurice 1931- 101
  Earlier sketch in SATA 46
  See also CLR 56
Gee, Maurice Gough
  See Gee, Maurice
Geehan, Wayne (E.) 1947- 107
Geer, Charles 1922- 42
  Brief entry 32
Geeslin, Campbell 1925- 163
  Earlier sketch in SATA 107
Gehman, Mary W. 1923- 86
Gehr, Mary 1910(?)-1997 32
  Obituary 99
Geipel, Eileen 1932- 30
Geis, Alissa Imre 1976- 189
Geis, Darlene Stern 1918(?)-1999 7
  Obituary 111
Geisel, Helen 1898-1967 26
Geisel, Theodor Seuss
  See Dr. Seuss
Geisert, Arthur 1941- 171
  Brief entry 52
  Earlier sketches in SATA 56, 92, 133
  See also CLR 87
  See also SAAS 23
Geisert, Arthur Frederick
  See Geisert, Arthur
Geisert, Bonnie 1942- 165
  Earlier sketch in SATA 92

Geist, Ken 191
Gelber, Lisa 210
Geldart, William 1936- 15
Gelinas, Paul J. 1904-1996 10
Gellis, Roberta 1927- 128
Gellis, Roberta Leah Jacobs
  See Gellis, Roberta
Gellman, Marc 112
Gelman, Amy 1961- 72
Gelman, Jan 1963- 58
Gelman, Rita Golden 1937- 131
  Brief entry 51
  Earlier sketch in SATA 84
Gelman, Steve 1934- 3
Gemignani, Tony 1973- 220
Gemming, Elizabeth 1932- 11
Gendel, Evelyn W. 1916(?)-1977
  Obituary 27
Gennaro, Joseph F., Jr. 1924- 53
Gennaro, Joseph Francis, Jr.
  See Gennaro, Joseph F., Jr.
Gentieu, Penny 204
Gentile, Petrina 1969- 91
Gentle, Mary 1956- 48
Gentleman, David (William) 1930- 7
Gentry, Marita 215
Geoghegan, Adrienne 1962- 143
George, Barbara
  See Katz, Bobbi
George, Emily
  See Katz, Bobbi
George, Gail
  See Katz, Bobbi
George, Jean
  See George, Jean Craighead
George, Jean C.
  See George, Jean Craighead
George, Jean Craighead 1919- 170
  Earlier sketches in SATA 2, 68, 124
  See also CLR 136
George, Jessica Day 1976- 210
George, John L(othar) 1916- 2
George, Kristine O'Connell 1954- 156
  Earlier sketch in SATA 110
George, Lindsay Barrett 1952- 206
  Earlier sketches in SATA 95, 155
George, S. C. 1898- 11
George, Sally
  See Orr, Wendy
George, Sidney Charles
  See George, S. C.
George, Twig C. 1950- 114
George, W(illiam) Lloyd 1900(?)-1975
  Obituary 30
Georgiou, Constantine 1927- 7
Georgiou, Theo
  See Odgers, Sally Farrell
Geraghty, Paul 1959- 130
Gerard, Jean Ignace Isidore 1803-1847 45
Geras, Adele 1944- 180
  Autobiography Feature 180
  Earlier sketches in SATA 23, 87, 129, 173
  See also SAAS 21
Geras, Adele Daphne Weston
  See Geras, Adele
Gerber, Carole 1947- 207
Gerber, Linda 213
Gerber, Merrill Joan 1938- 170
  Autobiography Feature 170
  Earlier sketches in SATA 64, 127
Gerber, Perren 1933- 104
Gerberg, Mort 1931- 64
Gergely, Tibor 1900-1978 54
  Obituary 20
Geringer, Laura 1948- 164
  Earlier sketches in SATA 29, 94
Gerler, William R(obert) 1917-1996 47
Gerrard, Jean 1933- 51

Gerrard, Roy 1935-1997 90
  Brief entry 45
  Obituary 99
  Earlier sketch in SATA 47
  See also CLR 23
Gerritsen, Paula 1956- 177
Gerrold, David 1944- 144
  Earlier sketch in SATA 66
Gershator, David 1937- 180
Gershator, Phillis 1942- 188
  Earlier sketches in SATA 90, 158
Gershon, Dann 1955- 187
Gershon, Gina 1962- 187
Gerson, Corinne 1927- 37
Gerson, Mary-Joan 136
  Earlier sketch in SATA 79
Gerson, Noel Bertram 1914-1988 22
  Obituary 60
Gerstein, Mordicai 1935- 178
  Brief entry 36
  Earlier sketches in SATA 47, 81, 142
  See also CLR 102
Gertridge, Allison 1967- 132
Gervais, Bernadette 1959- 80
Gervay, Susanne 183
Gesner, Clark 1938-2002 40
  Obituary 143
Gessner, Lynne 1919- 16
Geter, Tyrone 150
Getz, David 1957- 91
Getzinger, Donna 1968- 128
Geus, Mireille 1964- 207
Gevirtz, Eliezer 1950- 49
Gevry, Claudine 188
Gewe, Raddory
  See Gorey, Edward (St. John)
Ghan, Linda (R.) 1947- 77
Ghent, Natale 1962- 148
Gherman, Beverly 1934- 123
  Earlier sketch in SATA 68
Ghigna, Charles 1946- 153
  Earlier sketch in SATA 108
Giacobbe, Beppe 1953- 174
Giambastiani, Kurt R. A. 1958- 141
Giannini, Enzo 1946- 68
Gibala-Broxholm, Scott 1959(?)- 205
Gibbons, Alan 1953- 198
  Earlier sketch in SATA 124
Gibbons, Faye 1938- 103
  Earlier sketch in SATA 65
Gibbons, Gail 1944- 201
  Earlier sketches in SATA 23, 72, 104, 160
  See also CLR 8
  See also SAAS 12
Gibbons, Gail Gretchen
  See Gibbons, Gail
Gibbons, Kaye 1960- 117
Gibbs, Adrea 1960- 126
Gibbs, Alonzo (Lawrence) 1915-1992 5
Gibbs, (Cecilia) May 1877-1969
  Obituary 27
Gibbs, Tony
  See Gibbs, Wolcott, Jr.
Gibbs, Wolcott, Jr. 1935- 40
Giblin, James Cross 1933- 197
  Earlier sketches in SATA 33, 75, 122
  See also CLR 29
  See also SAAS 12
Gibson, Andrew (William) 1949- 72
Gibson, Barbara L. 205
Gibson, Barbara Leonard
  See Gibson, Barbara L.
Gibson, Betty 1911- 75
Gibson, Jo
  See Fluke, Joanne
Gibson, Josephine
  See Hine, Sesyle Joslin
  and Hine, Al(fred Blakelee)
Gibson, Sarah P. 1962- 211
Gibson, William 1914-2008 66
  Obituary 199

Gibson, William Ford
　See Gibson, William
Gidal, Nachum
　See Gidal, Tim Nachum
Gidal, Sonia (Epstein) 1922- 2
Gidal, Tim Nachum 1909-1996 2
Gidalewitsch, Nachum
　See Gidal, Tim Nachum
Gideon, Melanie 1963- 175
Giegling, John A(llan) 1935- 17
Gifaldi, David 1950- 209
　Earlier sketch in SATA 76
Giff, Patricia Reilly 1935- 203
　Earlier sketches in SATA 33, 70, 121, 160
Giffard, Hannah 1962- 83
Gifford, Clive 1966- 198
Gifford, Griselda 1931- 171
　Earlier sketch in SATA 42
Gifford, Kerri 1961- 91
Gifford, Peggy 1952- 191
Gilbert, Ann
　See Taylor, Ann
Gilbert, Anne Yvonne 1951- 185
Gilbert, Barbara Snow 1954- 97
Gilbert, Catherine
　See Murdock, Catherine Gilbert
Gilbert, Frances
　See Collings, Gillian
Gilbert, Harriett 1948- 30
Gilbert, (Agnes) Joan (Sewell) 1931- 10
Gilbert, John (Raphael) 1926- 36
Gilbert, Nan
　See Gilbertson, Mildred Geiger
Gilbert, Roby Goodale 1966- 90
Gilbert, Ruth Gallard Ainsworth
　See Ainsworth, Ruth (Gallard)
Gilbert, Sara (Dulaney) 1943- 82
　Earlier sketch in SATA 11
Gilbert, Sheri L. 157
Gilbert, Suzie 1956- 97
Gilbert, W(illiam) S(chwenck) 1836-1911 ... 36
Gilbert, Yvonne
　See Gilbert, Anne Yvonne
Gilbertson, Mildred Geiger 1908-1988 2
Gilbreath, Alice 1921- 12
Gilbreth, Frank B., Jr. 1911-2001 2
Gilbreth, Frank Bunker
　See Gilbreth, Frank B., Jr.
Gilchrist, Jan Spivey 1949- 130
　Earlier sketch in SATA 72
Gilden, Mel 1947- 97
Giles, Gail 196
　Earlier sketch in SATA 152
Gilfond, Henry 2
Gilge, Jeanette 1924- 22
Gili, Phillida 1944- 70
Gill, Derek (Lewis Theodore) 1919-1997 9
Gill, Margery Jean 1925- 22
Gill, Shelley 176
Gill, Stephen 1932- 63
Gillespie, Carol Ann 1951- 158
Gillett, Mary (Bledsoe) 7
Gillette, Henry Sampson 1915- 14
Gillette, J. Lynett 1946- 103
Gillette, Jan Lynett
　See Gillette, J. Lynett
Gilley, Jeremy 1969- 174
Gillham, Bill
　See Gillham, W(illiam) E(dwin) C(harles)
Gillham, W(illiam) E(dwin) C(harles)
　1936- 42
Gilliam, Stan 1946- 39
　Brief entry 35
Gilliland, Alexis A. 1931- 72
Gilliland, Alexis Arnaldus
　See Gilliland, Alexis A.
Gilliland, (Cleburne) Hap 1918- 92
Gilliland, Judith Heide 180
Gillmor, Don 1954- 127
Gilman, Dorothy 1923- 5
Gilman, Esther 1925- 15

Gilman, Laura Anne 178
Gilman, Phoebe 1940-2002 104
　Obituary 141
　Earlier sketch in SATA 58
Gilmore, Iris 1900-1982 22
Gilmore, Kate 1931- 87
Gilmore, Mary (Jean Cameron) 1865-1962 . 49
Gilmore, Rachna 1953- 209
Gilmore, Susan 1954- 59
Gilpin, Stephen 213
　Earlier sketch in SATA 177
Gilroy, Beryl (Agatha) 1924- 80
Gilson, Barbara
　See Gilson, Charles James Louis
Gilson, Charles James Louis 1878-1943
　See YABC 2
Gilson, Jamie 1933- 176
　Brief entry 34
　Earlier sketches in SATA 37, 91
Gimpel, Carolyn
　See Hart, Carolyn
Ginsburg, Mirra 1909-2000 92
　Earlier sketch in SATA 6
　See also CLR 45
Giovanni, Nikki 1943- 208
　Earlier sketches in SATA 24, 107
　See also CLR 73
Giovanni, Yolanda Cornelia
　See Giovanni, Nikki
Giovanni, Yolanda Cornelia
　See Giovanni, Nikki
Giovanni, Yolande Cornelia, Jr.
　See Giovanni, Nikki
Giovanopoulos, Paul (Arthur) 1939- 7
Gipson, Billie
　See Letts, Billie
Gipson, Fred(erick Benjamin) 1908-1973 2
　Obituary 24
Girard, Linda (Walvoord) 1942- 41
Giraudon, David 1975- 215
Girion, Barbara 1937- 78
　Earlier sketch in SATA 26
　See also SAAS 14
Girl, Nerdy
　See Castellucci, Cecil
Girouard, Patrick 1957- 155
Girzone, Joseph F. 1930- 76
Girzone, Joseph Francis
　See Girzone, Joseph F.
Gise, Joanne
　See Mattern, Joanne
Gist, E.M. 206
Gittings, Jo (Grenville) Manton 1919- 3
Gittings, Robert (William Victor) 1911-1992 . 6
　Obituary 70
Givens, Janet E(aton) 1932- 60
Givner, Joan 1936- 171
Givner, Joan Mary
　See Givner, Joan
Gladstone, Eve
　See Werner, Herma
Gladstone, Gary 1935- 12
Gladstone, M(yron) J. 1923- 37
Glanville, Brian (Lester) 1931- 42
Glanzman, Louis S. 1922- 36
Glaser, Byron 1954- 154
Glaser, Dianne E(lizabeth) 1937- 50
　Brief entry 31
Glaser, Isabel Joshlin 1929- 94
Glaser, Milton 1929- 151
　Earlier sketch in SATA 11
Glaser, Shirley 151
Glaspell, Susan 1882(?)-1948
　See YABC 2
Glass, Andrew 1949- 150
　Brief entry 46
　Earlier sketch in SATA 90
Glass, Linzi 175
Glass, Linzi Alex
　See Glass, Linzi

Glasscock, Amnesia
　See Steinbeck, John
Glassman, Bruce 1961- 76
Glatt, Lisa 1963- 217
Glauber, Uta (Heil) 1936- 17
Glazer, Thomas (Zachariah) 1914-2003 9
Glazer, Tom
　See Glazer, Thomas (Zachariah)
Gleasner, Diana (Cottle) 1936- 29
Gleason, Judith 1929- 24
Gleason, Katherine (A.) 1960- 104
Gleeson, Libby 1950- 142
　Autobiography Feature 142
　Earlier sketches in SATA 82, 118
Gleiter, Jan 1947- 111
Gleitzman, Morris 1953- 156
　Earlier sketch in SATA 88
　See also CLR 88
Glen, Maggie 1944- 88
Glendinning, Richard 1917-1988 24
Glendinning, Sally
　See Glendinning, Sara W(ilson)
Glendinning, Sara W(ilson) 1913-1993 24
Glenn, John W. 195
Glenn, Mel 1943- 93
　Brief entry 45
　Earlier sketch in SATA 51
　See also CLR 51
Glenn, Patricia Brown 1953- 86
Glenn, Sharlee 159
Glenn, Sharlee Mullins
　See Glenn, Sharlee
Glennon, Karen M. 1946- 85
Gles, Margaret Breitmaier 1940- 22
Glick, Carl (Cannon) 1890-1971 14
Glick, Ruth (Burtnick) 1942- 125
Glick, Virginia Kirkus 1893-1980
　Obituary 23
Gliewe, Unada (Grace) 1927- 3
Glimmerveen, Ulco 1958- 85
Glines, Carroll V(ane), Jr. 1920- 19
Gliori, Debi 1959- 189
　Earlier sketches in SATA 72, 138
Globe, Leah Ain 1900- 41
Glori Ann
　See Blakely, Gloria
Glovach, Linda 1947- 105
　Earlier sketch in SATA 7
Glover, Denis (James Matthews) 1912-1980 . 7
Glubok, Shirley (Astor) 146
　Autobiography Feature 146
　Earlier sketches in SATA 6, 68
　See also CLR 1
　See also SAAS 7
Gluck, Felix 1923-1981
　Obituary 25
Glyman, Caroline A. 1967- 103
Glynne-Jones, William 1907-1977 11
Gobbato, Imero 1923- 39
Gobbletree, Richard
　See Quackenbush, Robert M(ead)
Goble, Dorothy 26
Goble, Paul 1933- 131
　Earlier sketches in SATA 25, 69
　See also CLR 21
Goble, Warwick (?)-1943 46
Godden, (Margaret) Rumer 1907-1998 36
　Obituary 109
　Earlier sketch in SATA 3
　See also CLR 20
　See also SAAS 12
Gode, Alexander
　See Gode von Aesch, Alexander (Gottfried
　Friedrich)
Gode von Aesch, Alexander (Gottfried
　Friedrich) 1906-1970 14
Godfrey, Jane
　See Bowden, Joan Chase
Godfrey, Martyn
　See Godfrey, Martyn N.
　and Godfrey, Martyn N.

Godfrey, Martyn N. 1949-2000 95
See also CLR 57
Godfrey, William
See Youd, Samuel
Godkin, Celia 1948- 145
Earlier sketch in SATA 66
Godkin, Celia Marilyn
See Godkin, Celia
Godon, Ingrid 1958- 186
Godwin, Laura 1956- 179
Godwin, Sam
See Pirotta, Saviour
Godwin, Sarah Massini
See Massini, Sarah
Goede, Irene 1966- 208
Goedecke, Christopher (John) 1951- 81
Goekler, Susan
See Wooley, Susan Frelick
Goembel, Ponder 204
Goertzen, Glenda 172
Goettel, Elinor 1930- 12
Goetz, Delia 1898-1996 22
Obituary 91
Goffe, Toni 1936- 61
Goffstein, Brooke
See Goffstein, Marilyn Brooke
Goffstein, M. B.
See Goffstein, Marilyn Brooke
Goffstein, Marilyn Brooke 1940- 70
Earlier sketch in SATA 8
See also CLR 3
Goforth, Ellen
See Francis, Dorothy
Gogol, Sara 1948-2004 80
Goh, Chan Hon 1969- 145
Going, Kelly L.
See Going, K.L.
Going, Kelly Louise
See Going, K.L.
Going, K.L. 199
Earlier sketch in SATA 156
Golann, Cecil Paige 1921-1995 11
Golbin, Andree 1923- 15
Gold, Alison Leslie 1945- 104
Gold, August 1955- 215
Gold, Bernice 150
Gold, Phyllis
See Goldberg, Phyllis
Gold, Robert S(tanley) 1924- 63
Gold, Sharlya 9
Gold, Susan
See Gold, Susan Dudley
Gold, Susan Dudley 1949- 147
Goldbach, Veronica 1980- 220
Goldberg, Grace 1956- 78
Goldberg, Herbert S. 1926- 25
Goldberg, Jacob 1943- 94
Goldberg, Jake
See Goldberg, Jacob
Goldberg, Myla 1972(?)- 210
Goldberg, Phyllis 1941- 21
Goldberg, Stan J. 1939- 26
Goldberg, Susan 1948- 71
Goldberg, Whoopi 1955- 119
Goldberger, Judith M. 1948- 80
Goldblatt, Stacey 1969(?)- 191
Golden, Christie 1963- 167
Earlier sketch in SATA 116
Goldentyer, Debra 1960- 84
Goldfeder, Cheryl
See Pahz, Cheryl Suzanne
Goldfeder, James
See Pahz, James Alon
Goldfeder, Jim
See Pahz, James Alon
Goldfinger, Jennifer P. 1963- 185
Goldfrank, Helen Colodny 1912- 6
Goldin, Augusta 1906-1999 13

Goldin, Barbara Diamond 1946- 129
Autobiography Feature 129
Earlier sketch in SATA 92
See also SAAS 26
Goldin, David 1963- 101
Golding, Julia 1969- 188
Golding, Theresa Martin 1960- 150
Golding, William 1911-1993
See CLR 130
Golding, William Gerald
See Golding, William
Goldman, Alex J. 1917- 65
Goldman, E. M. 1943- 103
Goldman, Eleanor Maureen
See Goldman, E. M.
Goldman, Elizabeth 1949- 90
Goldman, Judy 1955- 212
Goldman, Steven 1964- 207
Goldman, Todd Harris 221
Goldring, Ann 1937- 149
Goldsborough, June 1923- 19
Goldschmidt, Judy 202
Goldsmith, Connie 1945- 147
Goldsmith, Howard 1943- 108
Earlier sketch in SATA 24
Goldsmith, John Herman Thorburn 1903-1987
Obituary 52
Goldsmith, Oliver 1730(?)-1774 26
Goldsmith, Ruth M. 1919- 62
Goldstein, Nathan 1927- 47
Goldstein, Philip 1910-1997 23
Goldston, Robert (Conroy) 1927- 6
Goldstone, Bruce 183
Goldstone, Lawrence A.
See Treat, Lawrence
Goldszmit, Henryk 1878-1942 65
See also CLR 152
Golembe, Carla 1951- 79
Golenbock, Peter 1946- 99
Goll, Reinhold W(eimar) 1897-1993 26
Gollub, Matthew 1960- 134
Earlier sketch in SATA 83
Golson, Terry 213
Golson, Terry Blonder
See Golson, Terry
Gomes, Filomena 1965- 183
Gomez, Elena 191
Gomez, Elizabeth 133
Gomez-Freer, Elizabeth
See Gomez, Elizabeth
Gomi, Taro 1945- 103
Earlier sketch in SATA 64
See also CLR 57
Gondosch, Linda 1944- 58
Gonsalves, Rob 1959- 209
Gonyea, Mark 194
Gonzalez, Catherine Troxell 1917-2000 87
Gonzalez, Christina
See Gonzalez, Maya Christina
Gonzalez, Gloria 1940- 23
Gonzalez, Julie 1958- 174
Gonzalez, Julie Sehers
See Gonzalez, Julie
Gonzalez, Lucia M. 1957- 202
Gonzalez, Maya
See Gonzalez, Maya Christina
Gonzalez, Maya Christina 1964- 175
Earlier sketch in SATA 115
Gonzalez, Rigoberto 1970- 147
Goobie, Beth 1959- 128
Good, Alice 1950- 73
Good, Clare
See Romano, Clare
Good, Karen Hillard 214
Goodall, Daphne Machin
See Machin Goodall, Daphne (Edith)
Goodall, Jane 1934- 111
Goodall, John S(trickland) 1908-1996 66
Obituary 91
Earlier sketch in SATA 4
See also CLR 25

Goodbody, Slim
See Burstein, John
Goode, Diane 1949- 170
Earlier sketches in SATA 15, 84, 114
Goode, Diane Capuozzo
See Goode, Diane
Goode, Stephen Ray 1943- 55
Brief entry 40
Goodenow, Earle 1913- 40
Goodhart, Pippa 1958- 196
Earlier sketch in SATA 153
Goodhue, Thomas W. 1949- 143
Goodin, Sallie (Brown) 1953- 74
Goodman, Alison 1966- 111
Goodman, Deborah Lerme 1956- 50
Brief entry 49
Goodman, Elaine 1930- 9
Goodman, Emily 217
Goodman, Joan Elizabeth 1950- 162
Earlier sketches in SATA 50, 94
Goodman, Susan E. 1952- 181
Goodman, Walter 1927-2002 9
Goodman Koz, Paula 211
Goodrich, Carter 1959(?)- 221
Goodrich, Samuel Griswold 1793-1860 23
Goodsell, Jane Neuberger 1921(?)-1988
Obituary 56
Goodweather, Hartley
See King, Thomas
GoodWeather, Hartley
See King, Thomas
Goodwin, Hal
See Goodwin, Harold L(eland)
Goodwin, Harold L(eland) 1914-1990 51
Obituary 65
Earlier sketch in SATA 13
Goodwin, William 1943- 117
Goor, Nancy (Ruth Miller) 1944- 39
Brief entry 34
Goor, Ron(ald Stephen) 1940- 39
Brief entry 34
Goossen, Agnes
See Epp, Margaret A(gnes)
Goossens, Philippe 1963- 195
Gootman, Marilyn E. 1944- 179
Gopnik, Adam 1956- 171
Gorbachev, Valeri 1944- 184
Autobiography Feature 143
Earlier sketches in SATA 98, 143
Gordion, Mark
See Turtledove, Harry
Gordon, Ad
See Hano, Arnold
Gordon, Amy 1949- 197
Earlier sketches in SATA 115, 156
Gordon, Bernard Ludwig 1931-2010 27
Gordon, Colonel H. R.
See Ellis, Edward S.
Gordon, David
See Garrett, Randall
Gordon, Donald
See Payne, Donald Gordon
Gordon, Dorothy 1893-1970 20
Gordon, Esther S(aranga) 1935- 10
Gordon, Frederick 1
Gordon, Gaelyn 1939-1997
See CLR 75
Gordon, Garrett
See Garrett, Randall
Gordon, Gary
See Edmonds, I(vy) G(ordon)
Gordon, Hal
See Goodwin, Harold L(eland)
Gordon, Jeffie Ross
See Enderle, Judith (Ann) Ross
and Gordon, Stephanie Jacob
Gordon, John
See Gesner, Clark
Gordon, John (William) 1925- 84
Gordon, Lew
See Baldwin, Gordon C(ortis)

Gordon, Margaret (Anna) 1939- 9
Gordon, Mike 1948- 101
Gordon, Mildred 1912-1979
　Obituary 24
Gordon, Selma
　See Lanes, Selma G.
Gordon, Sheila 1927- 88
　See also CLR 27
Gordon, Shirley 1921- 48
　Brief entry 41
Gordon, Sol 1923- 11
Gordon, Stephanie Jacob 1940- 89
　Autobiography Feature 114
　Earlier sketch in SATA *64*
　See also SAAS 26
Gordon, Stewart
　See Shirreffs, Gordon D(onald)
Gordons, The
　See Gordon, Mildred
　and Gordon, Gordon
Gore, Leonid 185
Gorelick, Molly C(hernow) 1920-2003 9
　Obituary 153
Gorey, Edward (St. John) 1925-2000 70
　Brief entry 27
　Obituary 118
　Earlier sketch in SATA *29*
　See also CLR 36
Gorham, Charles Orson 1868-1936 36
Gorham, Michael
　See Folsom, Franklin (Brewster)
Gorman, Carol 187
　Earlier sketch in SATA *150*
Gorman, Jacqueline Laks 1955- 148
Gorman, Mike 206
Gormley, Beatrice 1942- 202
　Brief entry 35
　Earlier sketches in SATA *39, 127*
Gorog, Judith (Katharine Allen) 1938- 75
　Earlier sketch in SATA *39*
Gorrell, Gena K. 1946- 170
Gorsline, Douglas (Warner) 1913-1985 11
　Obituary 43
Gorsline, (Sally) Marie 1928- 28
Gorsline, S. M.
　See Gorsline, (Sally) Marie
Gorton, Julia 218
Gorton, Kaitlyn
　See Emerson, Kathy Lynn
Gorton, Kathy Lynn
　See Emerson, Kathy Lynn
Goryan, Sirak
　See Saroyan, William
Goschke, Julia 1973- 208
Goscinny, Rene 1926-1977 47
　Brief entry 39
　See also CLR 37
Goss, Clay(ton E.) 1946- 82
Goss, Gary 1947- 124
Goss, Mini 1963- 186
Goto, Scott 203
Gott, Barry 197
Gottesman, S. D.
　See Kornbluth, C(yril) M.
　and Lowndes, Robert A(ugustine) W(ard)
　and Pohl, Frederik
Gottfried, Ted
　See Gottfried, Theodore Mark
Gottfried, Theodore Mark 1928- 150
　Earlier sketch in SATA *85*
Gottlieb, Gerald 1923- 7
Gottlieb, William P. 1917-2006 24
Gottlieb, William Paul
　See Gottlieb, William P.
Goudey, Alice E(dwards) 1898-1993 20
Goudge, Eileen 1950- 88
Goudge, Elizabeth (de Beauchamp)
　1900-1984 2
　Obituary 38
　See also CLR 94

Gough, Catherine
　See Mulgan, Catherine
Gough, Philip 1908-1986 45
Gough, Sue 1940- 106
Goulart, Ron 1933- 67
　Earlier sketch in SATA *1*
Goulart, Ronald Joseph
　See Goulart, Ron
Gould, Alberta 1945- 96
Gould, Chester 1900-1985 49
　Obituary 43
Gould, Jean R(osalind) 1909-1993 11
　Obituary 77
Gould, Lilian 6
Gould, Marilyn 1928- 76
　Earlier sketch in SATA *15*
Gould, Robert 154
Gould, Steven 1955- 95
Gould, Steven Charles
　See Gould, Steven
Gourley, Catherine 1950- 190
　Earlier sketch in SATA *95*
Gourse, Leslie 1939-2004 89
Govan, (Mary) Christine Noble 1898-1985 ... 9
Gove, Doris 1944- 72
Govenar, Alan 1952- 189
Govenar, Alan Bruce
　See Govenar, Alan
Govern, Elaine 1939- 26
Gowen, L. Kris 1968- 156
Graaf, Peter
　See Youd, Samuel
Graber, Alexander 1914-1997 98
　Earlier sketch in SATA *7*
Graber, George Alexander
　See Graber, Alexander
Graber, Janet 1942- 170
Graber, Richard (Fredrick) 1927- 26
Grabiński, Janusz 1928-1976 39
　Obituary 30
Graboff, Abner 1919-1986 35
Grace, Fran(ces Jane) 45
Grace, N.B.
　See Harper, Suzanne
Grace, Theresa
　See Mattern, Joanne
Gracza, Margaret Young 1928- 56
Graduate of Oxford, A
　See Ruskin, John
Grady, Denise 1952- 189
Graeber, Charlotte Towner 106
　Brief entry 44
　Earlier sketch in SATA *56*
Graef, Renee 1956- 204
Graeme, Roderic
　See Jeffries, Roderic
Graf, Michael
　See Graf, Mike
Graf, Mike 1960- 164
Grafe, Max 198
Graff, Lisa 1981- 188
Graff, Polly Anne Colver
　See Colver, Anne
Graff, (S.) Stewart 1908- 9
Graham, Ada 1931- 11
Graham, Alastair 1945- 74
Graham, Arthur Kennon
　See Harrison, David L.
Graham, Bob 1942- 187
　Earlier sketches in SATA *63, 101, 151*
　See also CLR 31
Graham, Brenda Knight 1942- 32
Graham, Charlotte
　See Bowden, Joan Chase
Graham, Eleanor 1896-1984 18
　Obituary 38
Graham, Ennis
　See Molesworth, Mary Louisa
Graham, Frank, Jr. 1925- 11
Graham, Georgia 1959- 190
Graham, Ian 1953- 112

Graham, John 1926-2007 11
Graham, Kennon
　See Harrison, David L.
Graham, Larry
　See Graham, Lawrence
Graham, Lawrence 1962- 63
Graham, Lawrence Otis
　See Graham, Lawrence
Graham, Linda
　See Graham-Barber, Lynda
Graham, Lorenz (Bell) 1902-1989 74
　Obituary 63
　Earlier sketch in SATA *2*
　See also CLR 10
　See also SAAS 5
Graham, Margaret Bloy 1920- 11
Graham, Robin Lee 1949- 7
Graham, Shirley 1896(?)-1977
　See Du Bois, Shirley Graham
Graham-Barber, Lynda 1944- 159
　Earlier sketch in SATA *42*
Graham-Cameron, M.
　See Graham-Cameron, M(alcolm) G(ordon)
Graham-Cameron, M(alcolm) G(ordon)
　1931- 53
　Brief entry 45
Graham-Cameron, Mike
　See Graham-Cameron, M(alcolm) G(ordon)
Grahame, Kenneth 1859-1932 100
　See also YABC 1
　See also CLR 135
Gralley, Jean 166
Gramatky, Hardie 1907-1979 30
　Obituary 23
　Earlier sketch in SATA *1*
　See also CLR 22
Grambling, Lois G. 1927- 206
　Earlier sketches in SATA *71, 148*
Grambo, Rebecca L(ynn) 1963- 109
Grammer, June Amos 1927- 58
Grand, Samuel 1912-1988 42
Grandits, John 1949- 192
GrandPre, Mary 1954- 184
Grandville, J. J.
　See Gerard, Jean Ignace Isidore
Grandville, Jean Ignace Isidore Gerard
　See Gerard, Jean Ignace Isidore
Granfield, Linda 1950- 160
　Earlier sketch in SATA *96*
Grange, Peter
　See Nicole, Christopher (Robin)
Granger, Margaret Jane 1925(?)-1977
　Obituary 27
Granger, Michele 1949- 88
Granger, Peggy
　See Granger, Margaret Jane
Granowsky, Alvin 1936- 101
Granstaff, Bill 1925- 10
Granstrom, Brita 1969- 167
　Earlier sketch in SATA *111*
Grant, Bruce 1893-1977 5
　Obituary 25
Grant, Cynthia D. 1950- 147
　Earlier sketches in SATA *33, 77*
Grant, Eva 1907-1996 7
Grant, Evva H. 1913-1977
　Obituary 27
Grant, Gordon 1875-1962 25
Grant, Gwen(doline Ellen) 1940- 47
Grant, Judyann Ackerman 211
Grant, Katie M.
　See Grant, K.M.
Grant, K.M. 175
Grant, (Alice) Leigh 1947- 10
Grant, Matthew G.
　See May, Julian
Grant, Maxwell
　See Gibson, Walter B(rown)
　and Lynds, Dennis
Grant, Melvyn 183
Grant, Myrna (Lois) 1934- 21

Grant, Neil 1938- *154*
    Earlier sketch in SATA *14*
Grant, Nicholas
    See Nicole, Christopher (Robin)
Grant, Richard 1948- *80*
Grant, Skeeter
    See Spiegelman, Art
Grater, Michael 1923- *57*
Gratz, Alan 1972- *212*
Gravel, Fern
    See Hall, James Norman
Gravelle, Karen 1942- *166*
    Earlier sketch in SATA *78*
Graves, Charles Parlin 1911-1972 .... *4*
Graves, Keith *191*
    Earlier sketch in SATA *156*
Graves, Robert 1895-1985 .... *45*
Graves, Robert von Ranke
    See Graves, Robert
Graves, Valerie
    See Bradley, Marion Zimmer
Gravett, Emily 1972(?)- *189*
Gray, Betsy
    See Poole, Gray Johnson
Gray, Caroline
    See Nicole, Christopher (Robin)
Gray, Claudia *213*
Gray, Dianne E. *183*
Gray, Elizabeth Janet
    See Vining, Elizabeth Gray
Gray, Genevieve S(tuck) 1920-1995 .... *4*
Gray, Harold (Lincoln) 1894-1968 .... *33*
    Brief entry *32*
Gray, Jenny
    See Gray, Genevieve S(tuck)
Gray, John Lee
    See Jakes, John
Gray, Judith A. 1949- *93*
Gray, Judith Anne
    See Gray, Judith A.
Gray, Keith *151*
Gray, Kes 1960- *153*
Gray, Les 1929- *82*
Gray, Libba Moore 1937- *83*
Gray, Luli 1945- *149*
    Earlier sketch in SATA *90*
Gray, Marian
    See Pierce, Edith Gray
Gray, Nicholas Stuart 1922-1981 .... *4*
    Obituary *27*
Gray, Nigel 1941- *104*
    Earlier sketch in SATA *33*
Gray, (Lucy) Noel (Clervaux) 1898-1983 .... *47*
Gray, Patricia (Clark) *7*
Gray, Patsey
    See Gray, Patricia (Clark)
Gray, Rita *184*
Graydon, Shari 1958- *158*
Grayland, V. Merle
    See Grayland, Valerie (Merle Spanner)
Grayland, Valerie (Merle Spanner) *7*
Grayson, Devin (Kalile) 1970- *119*
Grayson, Kristine
    See Rusch, Kristine Kathryn
Grayson, Paul 1946- *79*
Graystone, Lynn
    See Brennan, Joseph Lomas
Great Comte, The
    See Hawkesworth, Eric
Greaves, Margaret 1914-1995 .... *87*
    Earlier sketch in SATA *7*
Greaves, Nick 1955- *77*
Gree, Alain 1936- *28*
Green, Adam
    See Weisgard, Leonard (Joseph)
Green, Anne Canevari 1943- *62*
Green, Brian
    See Card, Orson Scott
Green, Cliff(ord) 1934- *126*
Green, Connie Jordan 1938- *80*

Green, D.
    See Casewit, Curtis W(erner)
Green, Elizabeth Shippen 1871-1954 .... *139*
Green, Hannah
    See Greenberg, Joanne (Goldenberg)
Green, Jane 1937- *9*
Green, Jessica *211*
Green, John 1977(?)- *170*
Green, Mary Moore 1906- *11*
Green, Morton 1937- *8*
Green, Norma B(erger) 1925- *11*
Green, Phyllis 1932- *20*
Green, Roger (Gilbert) Lancelyn 1918-1987 . *2*
    Obituary *53*
Green, (James Le)Roy 1948- *89*
Green, Sheila Ellen 1934- *148*
    Earlier sketches in SATA *8, 87*
Green, Timothy 1953- *91*
Greenaway, Kate 1846-1901 .... *100*
    See also YABC *2*
    See also CLR *111*
Greenbank, Anthony Hunt 1933- *39*
Greenberg, David 1954- *171*
Greenberg, David T.
    See Greenberg, David
Greenberg, Harvey R. 1935- *5*
Greenberg, Jan 1942- *211*
    Earlier sketches in SATA *61, 125*
Greenberg, Joanne (Goldenberg) 1932- *25*
Greenberg, Melanie Hope 1954- *214*
    Earlier sketch in SATA *72*
Greenberg, Polly 1932- *52*
    Brief entry *43*
Greenblat, Rodney Alan 1960- *106*
Greenburg, Dan 1936- *175*
    Earlier sketch in SATA *102*
Greene, Bette 1934- *161*
    Earlier sketches in SATA *8, 102*
    See also CLR *140*
    See also SAAS *16*
Greene, Carla 1916- *67*
    Earlier sketch in SATA *1*
Greene, Carol *102*
    Brief entry *44*
    Earlier sketch in SATA *66*
Greene, Constance C(larke) 1924- *72*
    Earlier sketch in SATA *11*
    See also CLR *62*
    See also SAAS *11*
Greene, Edgar
    See Papademetriou, Lisa
Greene, Ellin 1927- *23*
Greene, Graham 1904-1991 .... *20*
Greene, Graham Henry
    See Greene, Graham
Greene, Jacqueline Dembar 1946- *212*
    Earlier sketches in SATA *76, 131*
Greene, Laura Offenhartz 1935- *38*
Greene, Meg
    See Malvasi, Meg Greene
Greene, Michele 1962- *178*
Greene, Michele Dominguez
    See Greene, Michele
Greene, Rhonda Gowler 1955- *160*
    Earlier sketch in SATA *101*
Greene, Stephanie 1950- *221*
    Earlier sketches in SATA *127, 173*
Greene, Wade 1933- *11*
Greene, Yvonne
    See Flesch, Yolande
Greenfeld, Howard (Scheinman) 1928- *140*
    Earlier sketch in SATA *19*
Greenfeld, Josh(ua Joseph) 1928- *62*
Greenfield, Eloise 1929- *155*
    Earlier sketches in SATA *19, 61, 105*
    See also CLR *38*
    See also SAAS *16*
Greenhaus, Thelma Nurenberg 1903-1984
    Obituary *45*
Greenhut, Josh
    See Mercer, Sienna

Greening, Hamilton
    See Hamilton, Charles (Harold St. John)
Greenlaw, M. Jean 1941- *107*
Greenleaf, Barbara Kaye 1942- *6*
Greenleaf, Peter 1910-1997 .... *33*
Greenlee, Sharon 1935- *77*
Greeno, Gayle 1949- *81*
Greenseid, Diane 1948- *178*
    Earlier sketch in SATA *93*
Greenspun, Adele Aron 1938- *142*
    Earlier sketch in SATA *76*
Greenstein, Elaine 1959- *150*
    Earlier sketch in SATA *82*
Greenwald, Sheila
    See Green, Sheila Ellen
Greenwood, Barbara 1940- *129*
    Earlier sketch in SATA *90*
Greenwood, Mark 1958- *202*
Greenwood, Pamela D. 1944- *115*
Greer, Richard
    See Garrett, Randall
    and Silverberg, Robert
Gregg, Andrew K. 1929- *81*
Gregg, Charles T(hornton) 1927- *65*
Gregg, Walter H(arold) 1919- *20*
Gregor, Arthur 1923- *36*
Gregor, Lee
    See Pohl, Frederik
Gregori, Leon 1919- *15*
Gregorian, Joyce Ballou 1946-1991 .... *30*
    Obituary *83*
Gregorich, Barbara 1943- *184*
    Earlier sketch in SATA *66*
Gregorowski, Christopher 1940- *30*
Gregory, Diana (Jean) 1933- *49*
    Brief entry *42*
Gregory, Harry
    See Gottfried, Theodore Mark
Gregory, Jean
    See Ure, Jean
Gregory, Kristiana 1951- *212*
    Earlier sketches in SATA *74, 136*
Gregory, Nan 1944- *192*
    Earlier sketch in SATA *148*
Gregory, Philippa 1954- *122*
Gregory, Stephen
    See Penzler, Otto
Gregory, Valiska 1940- *82*
Greif, Jean-Jacques 1944- *195*
Greisman, Joan Ruth 1937- *31*
Grendon, Stephen
    See Derleth, August (William)
Grenville, Pelham
    See Wodehouse, P. G.
Gretz, Susanna 1937- *7*
Gretzer, John *18*
Grewdead, Roy
    See Gorey, Edward (St. John)
Grey, Carol
    See Lowndes, Robert A(ugustine) W(ard)
Grey, Christopher *191*
Grey, Christopher Peter
    See Grey, Christopher
Grey, Jerry 1926- *11*
Grey, Mini *205*
    Earlier sketch in SATA *166*
Greybeard the Pirate
    See Macintosh, Brownie
Grey Owl
    See Belaney, Archibald Stansfeld
Gri
    See Denney, Diana
Gribbin, John 1946- *159*
Gribbin, John R.
    See Gribbin, John
Grice, Frederick 1910-1983 .... *6*
Grider, Dorothy 1915- *31*
Gridley, Marion E(leanor) 1906-1974 .... *35*
    Obituary *26*
Grieco-Tiso, Pina 1954- *108*
Grieder, Walter 1924- *9*

Griego, Tony A. 1955- 77
Griese, Arnold A(lfred) 1921- 9
Griessman, Annette 1962- 170
  Earlier sketch in SATA *116*
Grieve, James 1934- 146
Grifalconi, Ann 1929- 210
  Earlier sketches in SATA *2, 66, 133*
  See also CLR *35*
  See also SAAS *16*
Griffin, Adele 1970- 195
  Earlier sketches in SATA *105, 153*
Griffin, Elizabeth May 1985- 89
Griffin, Gillett Good 1928- 26
Griffin, Judith Berry 34
Griffin, Kitty 1951- 137
Griffin, Peni R. 1961- 193
  Earlier sketches in SATA *67, 99*
Griffin, Steven A. 1953- 89
Griffin, Steven Arthur
  See Griffin, Steven A.
Griffin, W. E. B. 1929- 5
Griffith, Connie 1946- 89
Griffith, Gershom 1960- 85
Griffith, Helen V. 1934- 87
  Autobiography Feature 107
  Earlier sketch in SATA *39*
Griffith, Helen Virginia
  See Griffith, Helen V.
Griffith, Jeannette
  See Eyerly, Jeannette
Griffith, Saul 1974- 200
Griffiths, Andy 1961- 196
  Earlier sketch in SATA *152*
Griffiths, G(ordon) D(ouglas) 1910-1973
  Obituary 20
Griffiths, Helen 1939- 86
  Earlier sketch in SATA *5*
  See also CLR *75*
  See also SAAS *5*
Grigson, Jane (McIntire) 1928-1990 63
Grimes, Lee 1920- 68
Grimes, Nikki 1950- 218
  Earlier sketches in SATA *93, 136, 174*
  See also CLR *42*
Grimly, Gris 186
Grimm, Jacob Ludwig Karl 1785-1863 22
  See also CLR *112*
Grimm, Wilhelm Karl 1786-1859 22
  See also CLR *112*
Grimm, William C(arey) 1907-1992 14
Grimm and Grim
  See Grimm, Jacob Ludwig Karl
  and Grimm, Wilhelm Karl
Grimm Brothers
  See Grimm, Jacob Ludwig Karl
  and Grimm, Wilhelm Karl
Grimsdell, Jeremy 1942- 83
Grimshaw, Nigel (Gilroy) 1925- 23
Grimsley, Gordon
  See Groom, Arthur William
Grindley, Jane Sally
  See Grindley, Sally
Grindley, Sally 1953- 148
Gringhuis, Dirk
  See Gringhuis, Richard H.
Gringhuis, Richard H. 1918-1974 6
  Obituary 25
Grinnell, David
  See Wollheim, Donald A(llen)
Grinnell, George Bird 1849-1938 16
Grinspoon, David
  See Grinspoon, David H.
Grinspoon, David H. 1959- 156
Grinspoon, David Harry
  See Grinspoon, David H.
Gripe, Maria 1923- 74
  Earlier sketch in SATA *2*
  See also CLR *5*
Gripe, Maria Kristina
  See Gripe, Maria
Grobler, Piet 1959- 201

Groch, Judith (Goldstein) 1929- 25
Grode, Redway
  See Gorey, Edward (St. John)
Groener, Carl
  See Lowndes, Robert A(ugustine) W(ard)
Groening, Matt 1954- 116
  Earlier sketch in SATA *81*
Grohmann, Susan 1948- 84
Grohskopf, Bernice 7
Grol, Lini R(icharda) 1913- 9
Grollman, Earl A. 1925- 22
Groom, Arthur William 1898-1964 10
Grooms, Duffy 1964- 169
Gross, Alan 1947- 54
  Brief entry 43
Gross, Ernie 1913- 67
Gross, Philip 1952- 164
  Earlier sketch in SATA *84*
Gross, Philip John
  See Gross, Philip
Gross, Ruth Belov 1929- 33
Gross, Sarah Chokla 1906-1976 9
  Obituary 26
Grosser, Morton 1931- 74
Grosser, Vicky 1958- 83
Grossman, Bill 1948- 126
  Earlier sketch in SATA *72*
Grossman, Nancy 1940- 29
Grossman, Patricia 1951- 73
Grossman, Robert 1940- 11
Grossmann-Hensel, Katharina 1973- 219
Grote, JoAnn A. 1951- 113
Groten, Dallas 1951- 64
Groth, John (August) 1908-1988 21
  Obituary 56
Groth-Fleming, Candace
  See Fleming, Candace
Grove, Vicki 1948- 151
  Autobiography Feature 151
  Earlier sketch in SATA *122*
Grover, Lorie Ann 1964- 168
Grover, Wayne 1934- 69
Groves, Georgina
  See Symons, (Dorothy) Geraldine
Groves, Maketa 1950- 107
Groves, Seli 77
Grubb, Lisa 160
Gruber, Michael 1940- 173
Gruber, Terry (deRoy) 1953- 66
Gruelle, John 1880-1938 35
  Brief entry 32
  See also CLR *34*
Gruelle, Johnny
  See Gruelle, John
Gruenberg, Sidonie Matsner 1881-1974 2
  Obituary 27
Gruhzit-Hoyt, Olga (Margaret) 1922- 127
  Earlier sketch in SATA *16*
Grummer, Arnold E(dward) 1923- 49
Grunewalt, Pine
  See Kunhardt, Edith
Grunwell, Jeanne Marie 1971- 147
Grupper, Jonathan 137
Gryski, Camilla 1948- 72
Guarino, Dagmar
  See Guarino, Deborah
Guarino, Deborah 1954- 68
Guay, Georgette (Marie Jeanne) 1952- 54
Guay, Rebecca 209
Guay-Mitchell, Rebecca
  See Guay, Rebecca
Guback, Georgia 88
Guccione, Leslie Davis 1946- 111
  Earlier sketch in SATA *72*
Guck, Dorothy 1913-2002 27
Gudeon, Karla 212
Guerny, Gene
  See Gurney, Gene
Guest, Elissa Haden 1953- 218
  Earlier sketch in SATA *125*
Guest, Jacqueline 1952- 135

Guevara, Susan 167
  Earlier sketch in SATA *97*
Gugler, Laurel Dee 95
Gugliotta, Bobette 1918-1994 7
Guianan, Eve 1965- 102
Guiberson, Brenda Z. 1946- 211
  Earlier sketches in SATA *71, 124*
Guibert, Emmanuel 1964- 181
Guile, Melanie 1949- 152
  Earlier sketch in SATA *104*
Guillaume, Jeanette G. Flierl 1899-1990 8
Guillot, Rene 1900-1969 7
  See also CLR *22*
Guisewite, Cathy 1950- 57
Guisewite, Cathy Lee
  See Guisewite, Cathy
Gulbis, Stephen 1959- 142
Gulley, Judie 1942- 58
Gump, P. Q.
  See Card, Orson Scott
Gundrey, Elizabeth 1924- 23
Gunn, James E. 1923- 35
Gunn, James Edwin
  See Gunn, James E.
Gunn, Robin Jones 1955- 84
Gunnella 1956- 197
Gunning, Monica Olwen 1930- 161
Gunston, Bill
  See Gunston, William Tudor
Gunston, William Tudor 1927- 9
Gunterman, Bertha Lisette 1886(?)-1975
  Obituary 27
Gunther, John 1901-1970
Guravich, Dan 1918- 74
Gurko, Leo 1914- 9
Gurko, Miriam 1910(?)-1988 9
  Obituary 58
Gurney, Gene 1924- 65
Gurney, James 1958- 120
  Earlier sketch in SATA *76*
Gurney, John Steven 1962- 143
  Earlier sketch in SATA *75*
Gustafson, Sarah R.
  See Riedman, Sarah R(egal)
Gustafson, Scott 1956- 34
Gustavson, Adam 1974- 214
  Earlier sketch in SATA *176*
Guthrie, A(lfred) B(ertram), Jr. 1901-1991 .. 62
  Obituary 67
Guthrie, Anne 1890-1979 28
Guthrie, Donna W. 1946- 105
  Earlier sketch in SATA *63*
Gutierrez, Akemi 172
Gutierrez, Rudy 203
Gutman, Bill 128
  Brief entry 43
  Earlier sketch in SATA *67*
Gutman, Dan 1955- 221
  Earlier sketches in SATA *77, 139, 188*
Gutman, Naham 1899(?)-1981
  Obituary 25
Gutmann, Bessie Pease 1876-1960 73
Guy, Geoffrey 1942- 153
Guy, Ginger Foglesong 1954- 171
Guy, Rosa 1925- 122
  Earlier sketches in SATA *14, 62*
  See also CLR *137*
Guy, Rosa Cuthbert
  See Guy, Rosa
Guy, Susan 1948- 149
Guymer, (Wilhelmina) Mary 1909- 50
Guzman, Lila 1952- 168
Guzman, Rick 1957- 168
Gwaltney, Doris 1932- 181
Gwynne, Fred(erick Hubbard) 1926-1993 41
  Brief entry 27
  Obituary 75
Gwynne, Oscar A.
  See Ellis, Edward S.
Gwynne, Oswald A.
  See Ellis, Edward S.

Gyorkos, Charmaine Echeverria
See Echeverria Gyorkos, Charmaine

H

Haab, Sherri 1964- *169*
Earlier sketch in SATA *91*
Haar, Jaap ter
See ter Haar, Jaap
Haarsma, P.J. *183*
Haas, Carolyn Buhai 1926- *43*
Haas, Dan 1957- *105*
Haas, Dorothy F. *46*
Brief entry *43*
See also SAAS *17*
Haas, Irene 1929- *96*
Earlier sketch in SATA *17*
Haas, James E. 1943- *40*
Haas, James Edward
See Haas, James E.
Haas, Jessie 1959- *215*
Haas, (Katherine) Jessie 1959- *135*
Autobiography Feature *135*
Earlier sketch in SATA *98*
Haas, Merle S. 1896(?)-1985
Obituary *41*
Habenstreit, Barbara 1937- *5*
Haber, Karen 1955- *78*
Haber, Louis 1910-1988 .... *12*
Hacker, Randi 1951- *185*
Hacker, Randi Dawn
See Hacker, Randi
Hackett, John Winthrop 1910-1997 .... *65*
Hacks, Peter 1928-2003
Obituary *151*
Haddix, Margaret Peterson 1964- *187*
Earlier sketches in SATA *94, 125*
Haddon, Mark 1962- *155*
Hader, Berta (Hoerner) 1891(?)-1976 .... *16*
Hader, Elmer (Stanley) 1889-1973 .... *16*
Hadithi, Mwenye
See Hobson, Bruce
Hadley, Franklin
See Winterbotham, R(ussell) R(obert)
Hadley, Lee 1934-1995 .... *89*
Brief entry *38*
Obituary *86*
Earlier sketch in SATA *47*
See also CLR *40*
See also SAAS *14*
Haeffele, Deborah 1954- *76*
Haenel, Wolfram 1956- *89*
See also CLR *64*
Hafner, Marylin 1925- *179*
Earlier sketches in SATA *7, 121*
Haft, Erin
See Ehrenhaft, Daniel
Hager, Alan 1940- *176*
Hager, Alice Rogers 1894-1969
Obituary *26*
Hager, Betty 1923- *89*
Hager, Jenna Bush
See Bush, Jenna
Hager, Sarah *171*
Hager, Thomas 1953- *119*
Hager, Tom
See Hager, Thomas
Hagerup, Klaus 1946- *186*
Haggard, H(enry) Rider 1856-1925 .... *16*
Haggerty, James J(oseph) 1920- *5*
Hagon, Priscilla
See Allan, Mabel Esther
Hague, Kathleen 1949- *49*
Brief entry *45*
Hague, Michael 1948- *185*
Brief entry *32*
Earlier sketches in SATA *48, 80, 129*
Hague, Michael R.
See Hague, Michael

Hague, Susan Kathleen
See Hague, Kathleen
Hahn, Emily 1905-1997 .... *3*
Obituary *96*
Hahn, Hannelore *8*
Hahn, James (Sage) 1947- *9*
Hahn, Lynn 1949- *9*
Hahn, Mary Downing 1937- *208*
Autobiography Feature *157*
Brief entry *44*
Earlier sketches in SATA *50, 81, 138, 157*
See also SAAS *12*
Hahn, Michael T. 1953- *92*
Hahn, Mona Lynn
See Hahn, Lynn
Haig, Matt 1975- *221*
Haig-Brown, Roderick (Langmere)
1908-1976 .... *12*
See also CLR *31*
Haight, Anne Lyon 1895-1977
Obituary *30*
Haight, Rip
See Carpenter, John
Haight, Sandy 1949- *79*
Haij, Vera
See Jansson, Tove (Marika)
Hailstone, Ruth *219*
Haines, Gail Kay 1943- *11*
Haines, Margaret Ann Beck
See Beck, Peggy
Haining, Peter 1940-2007 .... *14*
Obituary *188*
Haining, Peter Alexander
See Haining, Peter
Hains, Harriet
See Watson, Carol
Hajdusiewicz, Babs Bell *163*
Hakim, Joy 1931- *173*
Earlier sketch in SATA *83*
Halacy, D. S., Jr. 1919-2002 .... *36*
See also SAAS *8*
Halacy, Dan
See Halacy, D. S., Jr.
Halam, Ann
See Jones, Gwyneth A.
Haldane, Roger John 1945- *13*
Hale, Arlene 1924-1982 .... *49*
Hale, Bruce 1957- *203*
Earlier sketch in SATA *123*
Hale, Christy
See Apostolou, Christine Hale
Hale, Edward Everett 1822-1909 .... *16*
Hale, Glenn
See Walker, Robert W.
Hale, Helen
See Mulcahy, Lucille Burnett
Hale, Irina 1932- *26*
Hale, Kathleen 1898-2000 .... *66*
Obituary *121*
Earlier sketch in SATA *17*
Hale, Linda (Howe) 1929- *6*
Hale, Lucretia P.
See Hale, Lucretia Peabody
Hale, Lucretia Peabody 1820-1900 .... *26*
See also CLR *105*
Hale, Marian *194*
Hale, Nancy 1908-1988 .... *31*
Obituary *57*
Hale, Nathan 1976- *210*
Hale, Shannon *200*
Earlier sketch in SATA *158*
Haley, Amanda *205*
Haley, Gail E(inhart) 1939- *161*
Autobiography Feature *161*
Brief entry *28*
Earlier sketches in SATA *43, 78, 136*
See also CLR *21*
See also SAAS *13*
Haley, Neale *52*
Halfmann, Janet 1944- *208*

Hall, Adam
See Trevor, Elleston
Hall, Adele 1910- *7*
Hall, Anna Gertrude 1882-1967 .... *8*
Hall, August *207*
Hall, Barbara 1961- *68*
Hall, Becky 1950- *186*
Hall, Beverly B. 1918- *95*
Hall, Borden
See Yates, Raymond F(rancis)
Hall, Brian P(atrick) 1935- *31*
Hall, Cameron
See del Rey, Lester
Hall, Caryl
See Hansen, Caryl (Hall)
Hall, Donald 1928- *97*
Earlier sketch in SATA *23*
Hall, Donald Andrew, Jr.
See Hall, Donald
Hall, Douglas 1931- *43*
Hall, Elizabeth 1929- *77*
Hall, Elvajean 1910-1984 .... *6*
Hall, Francie 1940- *166*
Hall, James Norman 1887-1951 .... *21*
Hall, Jesse
See Boesen, Victor
Hall, Katy
See McMullan, Kate
Hall, Kirsten Marie 1974- *67*
Hall, Lynn 1937- *79*
Earlier sketches in SATA *2, 47*
See also SAAS *4*
Hall, Malcolm 1945- *7*
Hall, Marcellus *203*
Hall, Marjory
See Yeakley, Marjory Hall
Hall, Melanie W. 1949- *169*
Earlier sketches in SATA *78, 116*
Hall, Patricia 1940- *136*
Hall, Rosalys Haskell 1914- *7*
Hall, Willis 1929-2005 .... *66*
Hallard, Peter
See Catherall, Arthur
Hallas, Richard
See Knight, Eric
Hall-Clarke, James
See Rowland-Entwistle, (Arthur) Theodore
(Henry)
Hallensleben, Georg 1958- *173*
Haller, Dorcas Woodbury 1946- *46*
Hallett, Mark 1947- *220*
Earlier sketch in SATA *83*
Halliburton, Richard 1900-1939(?) *81*
Halliburton, Warren J. 1924- *19*
Halliday, Brett
See Dresser, Davis
and Johnson, (Walter) Ryerson
and Terrall, Robert
Halliday, William R(oss) 1926- *52*
Hallin, Emily Watson 1916-1995 .... *6*
Hallinan, P. K. 1944- *39*
Brief entry *37*
Hallinan, Patrick Kenneth
See Hallinan, P. K.
Hallman, Ruth 1929- *43*
Brief entry *28*
Hallowell, Tommy
See Hill, Thomas
Hall-Quest, (Edna) Olga W(ilbourne)
1899-1986 .... *11*
Obituary *47*
Halls, Kelly Milner 1957- *220*
Earlier sketch in SATA *131*
Hallstead, William F(inn III) 1924- *11*
Hallward, Michael 1889-1982 .... *12*
Halperin, Michael *156*
Halperin, Wendy Anderson 1952- *200*
Earlier sketches in SATA *80, 125*
Halpern, Julie 1975- *198*
Halpin, Brendan 1968- *193*
Halpin, Marlene 1927- *88*

Halse, Laurie Beth
See Anderson, Laurie Halse
Halsell, Grace (Eleanor) 1923-2000 .... *13*
Halsey, Megan *185*
Halsted, Anna Roosevelt 1906-1975
Obituary *30*
Halter, Jon C(harles) 1941- *22*
Halverson, Deborah *202*
Halvorson, Adeline *218*
Halvorson, Marilyn 1948- *123*
Hamalian, Leo 1920- *41*
Hamberger, John 1934- *14*
Hamblin, Dora Jane 1920- *36*
Hambly, Barbara 1951- *108*
Hambly, Barbara Joan
See Hambly, Barbara
Hamer, Martyn
See Eldin, Peter
Hamerstrom, Frances 1907-1998 .... *24*
Hamil, Thomas Arthur 1928- *14*
Hamill, Ethel
See Webb, Jean Francis (III)
Hamilton, (John) Alan 1943- *66*
Hamilton, Alice
See Cromie, Alice Hamilton
Hamilton, Anita 1919- *92*
Hamilton, Buzz
See Hemming, Roy G.
Hamilton, Carol (Jean Barber) 1935- *94*
Hamilton, Charles (Harold St. John)
1876-1961 .... *13*
Hamilton, Charles 1913-1996 .... *65*
Obituary *93*
Hamilton, Clive
See Lewis, C. S.
Hamilton, Dorothy (Drumm) 1906-1983 ...... *12*
Obituary *35*
Hamilton, Edith 1867-1963 .... *20*
Hamilton, Edmond 1904-1977 .... *118*
Hamilton, (Muriel) Elizabeth (Mollie)
1906- *23*
Hamilton, Emma Walton 1962- *177*
Hamilton, Franklin
See Silverberg, Robert
Hamilton, Gail
See Corcoran, Barbara (Asenath)
and Dodge, Mary Abigail
Hamilton, Kersten 1958- *204*
Earlier sketch in SATA *134*
Hamilton, K.R.
See Hamilton, Kersten
Hamilton, Martha 1953- *183*
Earlier sketch in SATA *123*
Hamilton, Mary (E.) 1927- *55*
Hamilton, Mollie
See Kaye, M.M.
Hamilton, Morse 1943-1998 .... *101*
Earlier sketch in SATA *35*
Hamilton, Peter F. 1960- *109*
Hamilton, Priscilla
See Gellis, Roberta
Hamilton, Ralph
See Stratemeyer, Edward L.
Hamilton, Virginia 1936-2002 .... *123*
Obituary *132*
Earlier sketches in SATA *4, 56, 79*
See also CLR *127*
Hamilton, Virginia Esther
See Hamilton, Virginia
Hamilton-Paterson, James 1941- *82*
Hamlet, Ova
See Lupoff, Richard A(llen)
Hamley, D. C.
See Hamley, Dennis
Hamley, Dennis 1935- *69*
Earlier sketch in SATA *39*
See also CLR *47*
See also SAAS *22*
Hamley, Dennis C.
See Hamley, Dennis
Hamlin, Peter J. 1970- *84*

Hamm, Diane Johnston 1949- *78*
Hammer, Charles 1934- *58*
Hammer, Richard 1928- *6*
Hammerman, Gay M(orenus) 1926- *9*
Hammill, Matt 1982- *206*
Hammond, Andrew 1970- *181*
Hammond, Ralph
See Hammond Innes, Ralph
Hammond, Winifred G(raham) 1899-1992 ... *29*
Obituary *107*
Hammond Innes, Ralph 1913-1998 .... *116*
Hammontree, Marie (Gertrude) 1913- *13*
Hample, Zack 1977- *161*
Hampshire, Joyce Gregorian
See Gregorian, Joyce Ballou
Hampshire, Susan 1942- *98*
Hampson, (Richard) Denman 1929- *15*
Hampson, Frank 1918(?)-1985
Obituary *46*
Hampton, Wilborn 1940- *196*
Earlier sketch in SATA *156*
Hamre, Leif 1914- *5*
Hamsa, Bobbie 1944- *52*
Brief entry *38*
Han, Jenny 1981- *175*
Han, Lu
See Stickler, Soma Han
Han, Soma
See Stickler, Soma Han
Han, Suzanne Crowder 1953- *89*
Hancock, Mary A. 1923- *31*
Hancock, Sibyl 1940- *9*
Hand, Elizabeth 1957- *167*
Earlier sketch in SATA *118*
See also CLR *22*
Handford, Martin (John) 1956- *64*
Handforth, Thomas (Schofield) 1897-1948 .. *42*
Handler, Daniel
See Snicket, Lemony
Handville, Robert (Tompkins) 1924- *45*
Hane, Roger 1940-1974
Obituary *20*
Hanel, Wolfram
See Haenel, Wolfram
Haney, Lynn 1941- *23*
Hanff, Helene 1916-1997 .... *97*
Earlier sketch in SATA *11*
Hanft, Josh 1956- *197*
Hanft, Joshua E.
See Hanft, Josh
Hanley, Boniface Francis 1924- *65*
Hanlon, Emily 1945- *15*
Hann, Jacquie 1951- *19*
Hann, Judith 1942- *77*
Hanna, Bill
See Hanna, William (Denby)
Hanna, Cheryl 1951- *84*
Hanna, Dan *200*
Hanna, Jack (Bushnell) 1947- *74*
Hanna, Nell(ie L.) 1908- *55*
Hanna, Paul R(obert) 1902-1988 .... *9*
Hanna, William (Denby) 1910-2001 .... *51*
Obituary *126*
Hannam, Charles 1925- *50*
Hannan, Peter 1954- *187*
Hannigan, Katherine *170*
Hannon, Ezra
See Hunter, Evan
Hann-Syme, Marguerite *127*
Hano, Arnold 1922- *12*
Hano, Renee Roth
See Roth-Hano, Renee
Hanover, Terri
See Huff, Tanya
Hansen, Ann Larkin 1958- *96*
Hansen, Brooks 1965- *104*
Hansen, Caryl (Hall) 1929- *39*
Hansen, Ian V. 1929- *113*
Hansen, Jennifer 1972- *156*

Hansen, Joyce 1942- *172*
Autobiography Feature *172*
Brief entry *39*
Earlier sketches in SATA *46, 101*
See also CLR *21*
See also SAAS *15*
Hansen, Joyce Viola
See Hansen, Joyce
Hansen, Mark Victor *112*
Hansen, Ron 1947- *56*
Hansen, Ronald Thomas
See Hansen, Ron
Hanser, Richard (Frederick) 1909-1981 .... *13*
Hanson, Joan 1938- *8*
Hanson, Joseph E. 1894(?)-1971
Obituary *27*
Hanson, Mary Elizabeth *188*
Hanson, Warren 1949- *155*
Hansson, Gunilla 1939- *64*
Hantman, Clea *200*
Harald, Eric
See Boesen, Victor
Harazin, S. A. *210*
Harbour, Elizabeth 1968- *221*
Harcourt, Ellen Knowles 1890(?)-1984
Obituary *36*
Hard, Charlotte (Ann) 1969- *98*
Hardcastle, Michael 1933- *216*
Brief entry *38*
Earlier sketch in SATA *47*
Harding, Lee 1937- *32*
Brief entry *31*
Hardinge, Frances 1973- *210*
Hardt, Helga Fleischhauer
See Fleischhauer-Hardt, Helga
Hardwick, Richard Holmes, Jr. 1923- *12*
Hardy, Alice Dale *67*
Earlier sketch in SATA *1*
Hardy, David A(ndrews) 1936- *9*
Hardy, Jon 1958- *53*
Hardy, LeAnne 1951- *154*
Hardy, Stuart
See Schisgall, Oscar
Hare, Norma Q(uarles) 1924- *46*
Brief entry *41*
Harel, Nira 1936- *154*
Harford, Henry
See Hudson, W(illiam) H(enry)
Hargis, Wes *219*
Hargrave, Leonie
See Disch, Thomas M.
Hargreaves, (Charles) Roger 1935-1988
Obituary *56*
Hargrove, James 1947- *57*
Brief entry *50*
Hargrove, Jim
See Hargrove, James
Harik, Elsa
See Marston, Elsa
Harik, Elsa M.
See Marston, Elsa
Harik, Elsa Marston
See Marston, Elsa
Hariton, Anca I. 1955- *79*
Hark, Mildred
See McQueen, Mildred Hark
Harkaway, Hal
See Stratemeyer, Edward L.
Harkins, Philip 1912-1997 .... *6*
Obituary *129*
Harlan, Elizabeth 1945- *41*
Brief entry *35*
Harlan, Glen
See Cebulash, Mel
Harlan, Judith 1949- *135*
Earlier sketch in SATA *74*
See also CLR *81*
Harland, Richard 1947- *152*
Harlee, J. V.
See Leese, Jennifer L.B.

Harler, Ann
See Van Steenwyk, Elizabeth (Ann)
Harley, Avis *183*
Harley, Bill 1954- *208*
Earlier sketch in SATA *87*
Harlow, Joan Hiatt 1932- *157*
Harman, Fred 1902(?)-1982
Obituary *30*
Harman, Hugh 1903-1982
Obituary *33*
Harmelink, Barbara (Mary) *9*
Harmer, Mabel 1894-1992 .... *45*
Harmon, Dan
See Harmon, Daniel E(lton)
Harmon, Daniel E(lton) 1949- *157*
Harmon, Margaret 1906- *20*
Harmon, Michael 1969- *189*
Harmon, Michael B.
See Harmon, Michael
Harmon, William (Ruth) 1938- *65*
Harnan, Terry 1920- *12*
Harness, Cheryl 1951- *178*
Earlier sketch in SATA *131*
Harnett, Cynthia (Mary) 1893-1981 .... *5*
Obituary *32*
Harper, Anita 1943- *41*
Harper, Betty 1946- *126*
Harper, Charise
See Harper, Charise Mericle
Harper, Charise Mericle *179*
Harper, Elaine
See Hallin, Emily Watson
Harper, Ellen
See Noble, Marty
Harper, Jamie *174*
Harper, Jessica 1949- *148*
Harper, Jo 1932- *169*
Earlier sketch in SATA *97*
Harper, Lee *201*
Harper, Mary Wood
See Dixon, Jeanne
Harper, Piers 1966- *161*
Earlier sketch in SATA *105*
Harper, Suzanne *194*
Harper, Wilhelmina 1884-1973 .... *4*
Obituary *26*
Harrah, Madge 1931- *154*
Harrah, Michael 1940- *41*
Harrah, Monique
See Harrah, Madge
Harrar, George E. 1949- *124*
Harrell, Beatrice Orcutt 1943- *93*
Harrell, Janice 1945- *70*
Harrell, Sara Gordon 1940- *26*
Harrell, Sara Jeanne Gordon
See Harrell, Sara Gordon
Harries, Joan 1922- *39*
Harrill, Ronald 1950- *90*
Harrington, Denis J(ames) 1932- *88*
Harrington, Evelyn Davis 1911- *5*
Harrington, Janice N. 1956- *187*
Harrington, Lyn
See Harrington, Evelyn Davis
Harris, Alan 1944- *71*
Harris, Aurand 1915-1996 .... *37*
Obituary *91*
Harris, Bob
See Harris, Robert J.
Harris, Carol Flynn 1933- *135*
Harris, Catherine
See Ainsworth, Catherine Harris
Harris, Christie
See Harris, Christie (Lucy) Irwin
Harris, Christie (Lucy) Irwin 1907-2002 ...... *74*
Autobiography Feature *116*
Earlier sketch in SATA *6*
See also CLR *47*
See also SAAS *10*
Harris, Christine 1955- *105*
Harris, Colver
See Colver, Anne

Harris, David 1942- *118*
Harris, David William
See Harris, David
Harris, Dorothy Joan 1931- *153*
Earlier sketch in SATA *13*
Harris, Geraldine 1951- *54*
Harris, Geraldine Rachel
See Harris, Geraldine
Harris, Jacqueline L. 1929- *62*
Harris, Janet 1932-1979 .... *4*
Obituary *23*
Harris, Jesse
See Standiford, Natalie
Harris, Joan 1946- *146*
Harris, Joe 1928- *201*
Harris, Joel Chandler 1848-1908 .... *100*
See also YABC *1*
See also CLR *128*
Harris, John (Wyndham Parkes Lucas) Beynon
1903-1969 .... *118*
Harris, Johnson
See Harris, John (Wyndham Parkes Lucas)
Beynon
Harris, Jonathan 1921-1997 .... *52*
Harris, Larry Vincent 1939- *59*
Harris, Lavinia
See St. John, Nicole
Harris, Leon A., Jr. 1926-2000 .... *4*
Harris, Lois V. *199*
Harris, Lorle K(empe) 1912-2001 .... *22*
Harris, Marilyn
See Springer, Marilyn Harris
Harris, Mark Jonathan 1941- *84*
Earlier sketch in SATA *32*
Harris, Mary K(athleen) 1905-1966 .... *119*
Harris, Robert J. 1955- *195*
Harris, Robie H. 1940- *203*
Brief entry *53*
Earlier sketches in SATA *90, 147*
Harris, Robin
See Shine, Deborah
Harris, Rosemary (Jeanne) *82*
Earlier sketch in SATA *4*
See also CLR *30*
See also SAAS *7*
Harris, Ruth Elwin 1935- *164*
Harris, Sherwood 1932-2009 .... *25*
Harris, Steven Michael 1957- *55*
Harris, Trudy 1949- *191*
Earlier sketch in SATA *128*
Harris-Filderman, Diane
See Filderman, Diane E(lizabeth)
Harrison, C(hester) William 1913-1994 .... *35*
Harrison, Carol
See Harrison, Carol Thompson
Harrison, Carol Thompson *113*
Harrison, David L. 1937- *186*
Earlier sketches in SATA *26, 92, 150*
Harrison, Deloris 1938- *9*
Harrison, Edward Hardy 1926- *56*
Harrison, Elizabeth (Allen) Cavanna
1909-2001 .... *30*
Earlier sketch in SATA *1*
See also SAAS *4*
Harrison, Harry 1925- *4*
Harrison, Harry Max
See Harrison, Harry
Harrison, Mette Ivie 1970- *202*
Earlier sketch in SATA *149*
Harrison, Michael 1939- *106*
Harrison, Molly (Hodgett) 1909-2002 .... *41*
Harrison, Sarah 1946- *63*
Harrison, Ted
See Harrison, Edward Hardy
Harsh, Fred (T.) 1925- *72*
Harshaw, Ruth H(etzel) 1890-1968 .... *27*
Harshman, Marc 1950- *109*
Earlier sketch in SATA *71*
Hart, Alexandra 1939- *14*
Hart, Alison
See Leonhardt, Alice

Hart, Bruce 1938-2006 .... *57*
Brief entry *39*
Hart, Carole 1943- *57*
Brief entry *39*
Hart, Carolyn 1936- *74*
Hart, Carolyn G.
See Hart, Carolyn
Hart, Carolyn Gimpel
See Hart, Carolyn
Hart, Jan Siegel 1940- *79*
Hart, Joyce 1954- *148*
Hart, Karen *185*
Hart, Lenore *171*
Hart, Philip S. 1944- *180*
Hart, Virginia 1949- *83*
Harte, Bret 1836(?)-1902 .... *26*
Harte, Francis Brett
See Harte, Bret
Harter, Debbie 1963- *107*
Hartfield, Claire 1957- *147*
Hartinger, Brent 1964- *217*
Earlier sketches in SATA *145, 174*
Hartland, Jessie *171*
Hartley, Ellen (Raphael) 1915-1980 .... *23*
Hartley, Fred Allan III 1953- *41*
Hartley, William B(rown) 1913-1980 .... *23*
Hartling, Peter
See Hartling, Peter
Hartling, Peter 1933- *66*
See also CLR *29*
Hartman, Cassie *202*
Hartman, Dan 1955- *202*
Hartman, Evert 1937- *38*
Brief entry *35*
Hartman, Jane E. 1928- *47*
Hartman, Jane Evangeline
See Hartman, Jane E.
Hartman, Louis F(rancis) 1901-1970 .... *22*
Hartman, Rachel *174*
Hartman, Victoria 1942- *91*
Hartnett, Sonya 1968- *176*
Earlier sketches in SATA *93, 130*
Hartry, Nancy *219*
Hartshorn, Ruth M. 1928- *11*
Hartung, Susan Kathleen *192*
Earlier sketch in SATA *150*
Hartwig, Manfred 1950- *81*
Harvey, Brett 1936- *61*
Harvey, Edith 1908(?)-1972
Obituary *27*
Harvey, Gill *189*
Harvey, Karen D. 1935- *88*
Harvey, Roland 1945- *219*
Earlier sketches in SATA *71, 123, 179*
Harvey-Fitzhenry, Alyxandra 1974- *189*
Harwick, B. L.
See Keller, Beverly L(ou)
Harwin, Brian
See Henderson, LeGrand
Harwood, Pearl Augusta (Bragdon)
1903-1998 .... *9*
Haseley, Dennis 1950- *221*
Brief entry *44*
Earlier sketches in SATA *57, 105, 157*
Hashmi, Kerri 1955- *108*
Haskell, Arnold L(ionel) 1903-1981(?) *6*
Haskins, James
See Haskins, James S.
Haskins, James S. 1941-2005 .... *132*
Autobiography Feature *132*
Earlier sketches in SATA *9, 69, 105*
See also CLR *39*
See also SAAS *4*
Haskins, Jim
See Haskins, James S.
Hasler, Eveline 1933- *181*
Hasler, Joan 1931- *28*
Hass, Robert 1941- *94*
Hassall, Joan 1906-1988 .... *43*
Obituary *56*
Hassett, Ann 1958- *162*

Hassett, John *162*
Hassler, Jon 1933-2008 .... *19*
  Obituary *191*
Hassler, Jon Francis
  See Hassler, Jon
Hastings, Beverly
  See Barkin, Carol
  and James, Elizabeth
Hastings, Graham
  See Jeffries, Roderic
Hastings, Ian 1912- *62*
Hastings, Victor
  See Disch, Thomas M.
Haszard, Patricia Moyes 1923-2000 .... *63*
Hatch, Lynda S. 1950- *90*
Hathaway, Barbara *164*
Hathorn, Elizabeth
  See Hathorn, Elizabeth Helen
Hathorn, Elizabeth Helen 1943- *156*
  Autobiography Feature *156*
  Earlier sketches in SATA *74, 120*
Hathorn, Libby 1943-
  See Hathorn, Elizabeth Helen
Hatkoff, Craig 1954- *192*
Hatlo, Jimmy 1898-1963
  Obituary *23*
Hatton, Caroline 1957- *205*
Hauff, Wilhelm 1802-1827
  See CLR *155*
Haugaard, Erik Christian 1923- *68*
  Earlier sketch in SATA *4*
  See also CLR *11*
  See also SAAS *12*
Haugaard, Kay *117*
Haugen, Hayley Mitchell 1968- *172*
Haugen, Tormod 1945- *66*
Hauman, Doris 1898-1984 .... *32*
Hauman, George 1890-1961 .... *32*
Hauptly, Denis J. 1945- *57*
Hauptly, Denis James
  See Hauptly, Denis J.
Hauser, Jill Frankel 1950- *127*
Hauser, Margaret L(ouise) 1909- *10*
Hausherr, Rosmarie 1943- *86*
Hausman, Gerald 1945- *180*
  Earlier sketches in SATA *13, 90, 132*
  See also CLR *89*
Hausman, Gerry
  See Hausman, Gerald
Hauth, Katherine B. 1940- *99*
Hautman, Pete 1952- *173*
  Earlier sketches in SATA *82, 128*
Hautman, Peter Murray
  See Hautman, Pete
Hautzig, Deborah 1956- *106*
  Earlier sketch in SATA *31*
Hautzig, Esther Rudomin 1930-2009 .... *148*
  Earlier sketches in SATA *4, 68*
  See also CLR *22*
  See also SAAS *15*
Havel, Geoff 1955- *152*
Havel, Jennifer
  See Havill, Juanita
Havelin, Kate 1961- *143*
Haven, Paul 1971(?)- *213*
Havighurst, Walter (Edwin) 1901-1994 .... *1*
  Obituary *79*
Haviland, Virginia 1911-1988 .... *6*
  Obituary *54*
Havill, Juanita 1949- *155*
  Earlier sketch in SATA *74*
Hawes, Judy 1913- *4*
Hawes, Louise 1943- *180*
  Earlier sketch in SATA *60*
Hawke, Rosanne 1953- *165*
  Earlier sketch in SATA *124*
Hawke, Rosanne Joy
  See Hawke, Rosanne
Hawkes, Kevin 1959- *201*
  Earlier sketches in SATA *78, 150*
Hawkes, Nigel 1943- *119*

Hawkesworth, Eric 1921- *13*
Hawking, Lucy 1969- *197*
Hawkins, Arthur 1903-1985 .... *19*
Hawkins, Colin 1945- *162*
  Earlier sketch in SATA *112*
Hawkins, Jacqui *162*
  Earlier sketch in SATA *112*
Hawkins, Jimmy 1941- *188*
Hawkins, Laura 1951- *74*
Hawkins, (Helena Ann) Quail 1905-2002 ...... *6*
  Obituary *141*
Hawkinson, John (Samuel) 1912-1994 .... *4*
Hawkinson, Lucy (Ozone) 1924-1971 .... *21*
Hawks, Robert 1961- *85*
Hawley, Mabel C. *67*
  Earlier sketch in SATA *1*
Haworth, Danette *207*
Haworth-Attard, Barbara 1953- *215*
Hawthorne, Captain R. M.
  See Ellis, Edward S.
Hawthorne, Nathaniel 1804-1864
  See YABC *2*
  See also CLR *103*
Hay, Jeff T. *154*
Hay, John 1915- *13*
Hay, Samantha *213*
Hay, Timothy
  See Brown, Margaret Wise
Hayashi, Leslie Ann 1954- *115*
Hayashi, Nancy 1939- *186*
  Earlier sketch in SATA *80*
Haycak, Cara 1961- *180*
Haycock, Kate 1962- *77*
Haycraft, Howard 1905-1991 .... *6*
  Obituary *70*
Haycraft, Molly Costain 1911- *6*
Hayden, Gwendolen Lampshire 1904- *35*
Hayden, Robert
  See Hayden, Robert Earl
Hayden, Robert C(arter), Jr. 1937- *47*
  Brief entry *28*
Hayden, Robert E.
  See Hayden, Robert Earl
Hayden, Robert Earl 1913-1980 .... *19*
  Obituary *26*
Hayden, Torey L. 1951- *163*
  Earlier sketch in SATA *65*
Hayden, Torey Lynn
  See Hayden, Torey L.
Hayes, Carlton J(oseph) H(untley)
  1882-1964 .... *11*
Hayes, Daniel 1952- *109*
  Earlier sketch in SATA *73*
Hayes, Geoffrey 1947- *207*
  Earlier sketches in SATA *26, 91*
Hayes, Joe 1945- *131*
  Earlier sketch in SATA *88*
Hayes, John F. 1904-1980 .... *11*
Hayes, Karel 1949- *207*
Hayes, Rosemary *158*
Hayes, Sarah 1945- *208*
Hayes, Sheila 1937- *51*
  Brief entry *50*
Hayes, Will *7*
Hayes, William D(imitt) 1913-1976 .... *8*
Haynes, Betsy 1937- *94*
  Brief entry *37*
  Earlier sketch in SATA *48*
  See also CLR *90*
Haynes, David 1955- *97*
Haynes, Linda
  See Swinford, Betty (June Wells)
Haynes, Mary 1938- *65*
Haynes, Max 1956- *72*
Hays, Anna Jane *214*
Hays, H(offmann) R(eynolds) 1904-1980 .... *26*
Hays, Thomas A.
  See Hays, Tony
Hays, Thomas Anthony
  See Hays, Tony
Hays, Tony 1957- *84*

Hays, Wilma Pitchford 1909- *28*
  Earlier sketch in SATA *1*
  See also CLR *59*
  See also SAAS *3*
Hayward, Linda 1943- *185*
  Brief entry *39*
  Earlier sketch in SATA *101*
Haywood, Carolyn 1898-1990 .... *75*
  Obituary *64*
  Earlier sketches in SATA *1, 29*
  See also CLR *22*
Hazelaar, Cor *217*
Hazell, Rebecca (Eileen) 1947- *141*
Hazen, Barbara Shook 1930- *178*
  Earlier sketches in SATA *27, 90*
Hazen, Lynn E. *202*
Head, Gay
  See Hauser, Margaret L(ouise)
Head, Tom 1978- *167*
Headley, Elizabeth
  See Harrison, Elizabeth (Allen) Cavanna
Headley, Justina Chen 1968- *176*
Headstrom, (Birger) Richard 1902-1985 .... *8*
Heady, Eleanor B(utler) 1917-1979 .... *8*
Heagy, William D. 1964- *76*
Heal, Edith 1903-1995 .... *7*
Heal, Gillian 1934- *89*
Heale, Jay (Jeremy Peter Wingfield) 1937- .. *84*
Healey, Brooks
  See Albert, Burton
Healey, Larry 1927- *44*
  Brief entry *42*
Heap, Sue 1954- *187*
  Earlier sketch in SATA *150*
Heaps, Willard A(llison) 1908-1987 .... *26*
Hearn, Diane Dawson 1952- *209*
  Earlier sketch in SATA *79*
Hearn, Emily
  See Valleau, Emily
Hearn, Julie 1958- *212*
  Earlier sketch in SATA *152*
Hearn, Lian
  See Rubinstein, Gillian
Hearn, Sneed
  See Gregg, Andrew K.
Hearne, Betsy 1942- *146*
  Earlier sketches in SATA *38, 95*
Heath, Charles D(ickinson) 1941- *46*
Heath, Veronica
  See Blackett, Veronica Heath
Heaven, Constance (Christina) 1911- *7*
Hebert-Collins, Sheila 1948- *111*
Hecht, George J(oseph) 1895-1980
  Obituary *22*
Hecht, Henri Joseph 1922- *9*
Hechtkopf, Henryk 1910- *17*
Heck, Bessie (Mildred) Holland 1911-1995 . *26*
Heck, Ed 1963- *173*
Heckert, Connie K(aye Delp) 1948- *82*
Hector, Julian *205*
Hedderwick, Mairi 1939- *145*
  Earlier sketches in SATA *30, 77*
Hedges, Sid(ney) G(eorge) 1897-1974 .... *28*
Hedrick, Irene Hope 1920- *175*
Heelan, Jamee Riggio 1965- *146*
Heerboth, Sharon
  See Leon, Sharon
Heffernan, John 1949- *168*
  Earlier sketch in SATA *121*
Heffron, Dorris 1944- *68*
Hefter, Richard 1942- *31*
Hegamin, Tonya C. 1975- *209*
Hegarty, Reginald Beaton 1906-1973 .... *10*
Hehenberger, Shelly 1968- *126*
Heidbreder, Robert 1947- *196*
  Earlier sketch in SATA *130*
Heidbreder, Robert K.
  See Heidbreder, Robert

Heide, Florence Parry 1919- *192*
Earlier sketches in SATA *32, 69, 118*
See also CLR 60
See also SAAS 6
Heiderstadt, Dorothy 1907-2001 .... *6*
Heidi Louise
See Erdrich, Louise
Heidler, David S(tephen) 1955- *132*
Heidler, Jeanne T. 1956- *132*
Heilbroner, Joan Knapp 1922- *63*
Heilbrun, Lois Hussey 1922(?)-1987
Obituary *54*
Heiligman, Deborah 1958- *193*
Earlier sketches in SATA *90, 144*
Heilman, Joan Rattner *50*
Heimann, Rolf 1940- *164*
Earlier sketch in SATA *120*
Hein, Lucille Eleanor 1915-1994 .... *20*
Heine, Helme 1941- *135*
Earlier sketch in SATA *67*
See also CLR 18
Heinlein, Robert A. 1907-1988 .... *69*
Obituary *56*
Earlier sketch in SATA *9*
See also CLR 75
Heinlein, Robert Anson
See Heinlein, Robert A.
Heins, Ethel L(eah) 1918-1997 .... *101*
Heins, Paul 1909- *13*
Heintze, Carl 1922- *26*
Heinz, Bill
See Heinz, W. C.
Heinz, Brian J. 1946- *181*
Earlier sketch in SATA *95*
Heinz, Brian James
See Heinz, Brian J.
Heinz, W. C. 1915-2008 .... *26*
Heinz, Wilfred Charles
See Heinz, W. C.
Heinzen, Mildred
See Masters, Mildred
Heisel, Sharon E(laine) 1941- *125*
Earlier sketch in SATA *84*
Heitzmann, William Ray 1948- *73*
Heitzmann, Wm. Ray
See Heitzmann, William Ray
Helakoski, Leslie *178*
Helberg, Shirley Adelaide Holden 1919- ... *138*
Helfer, Andrew *187*
Helfer, Ralph 1937- *177*
Helfman, Elizabeth S(eaver) 1911-2001 .... *3*
Helfman, Harry Carmozin 1910-1995 .... *3*
Helgerson, Joseph 1950- *181*
Hellard, Susan *182*
Hellberg, Hans-Eric 1927- *38*
Heller, Linda 1944- *46*
Brief entry *40*
Heller, Mike
See Hano, Arnold
Heller, Ruth M. 1924- *112*
Earlier sketch in SATA *66*
Hellman, Hal
See Hellman, Harold
Hellman, Harold 1927- *4*
Helman, Andrea (Jean) 1946- *160*
Earlier sketch in SATA *107*
Helmer, Diana Star 1962- *86*
Helmer, Marilyn *160*
Earlier sketch in SATA *112*
Helps, Racey 1913-1971 .... *2*
Obituary *25*
Helquist, Brett *187*
Earlier sketch in SATA *146*
Helweg, Hans H. 1917- *50*
Brief entry *33*
Helyar, Jane Penelope Josephine 1933- *5*
Autobiography Feature *138*
See also SAAS 2
Hemingway, Edward 1969(?)- *212*
Hemmant, Lynette 1938- *69*

Hemming, Roy G. 1928-1995 .... *11*
Obituary *86*
Hemphill, Helen 1955- *179*
Hemphill, Kris (Harrison) 1963- *118*
Hemphill, Martha Locke 1904-1973 .... *37*
Hemphill, Michael *220*
Hemphill, Stephanie *190*
Hemstock, Gillian 1956- *173*
Henba, Bobbie 1926- *87*
Henbest, Nigel 1951- *55*
Brief entry *52*
Henderley, Brooks *1*
Henderson, Aileen Kilgore 1921- *178*
Henderson, Aileen Mary
See Fox, Aileen
Henderson, Gordon 1950- *53*
Henderson, Kathy 1949- *155*
Brief entry *53*
Earlier sketches in SATA *55, 95*
Henderson, Lauren 1966- *201*
Henderson, LeGrand 1901-1965 .... *9*
Henderson, Nancy Wallace 1916- *22*
Henderson, Zenna (Chlarson) 1917-1983 .... *5*
Hendrickson, Walter Brookfield, Jr. 1936- *9*
Hendrix, John 1976- *208*
Hendry, Diana 1941- *213*
Earlier sketches in SATA *68, 106*
Hendry, Frances Mary 1941- *171*
Earlier sketch in SATA *110*
Hendry, Linda (Gail) 1961- *83*
Heneghan, James 1930- *160*
Earlier sketches in SATA *53, 97*
Henkes, Kevin 1960- *207*
Earlier sketches in SATA *43, 76, 108, 154*
See also CLR 108
Henn, Astrid *214*
Hennessy, Barbara G.
See Hennessy, B.G.
Hennessy, Barbara Gulbrandsen
See Hennessy, B.G.
Hennessy, B.G. 1951- *175*
Hennesy, Carolyn 1962- *221*
Henney, Carolee Wells 1928- *102*
Henriod, Lorraine 1925- *26*
Henriquez, Emile F. 1937- *170*
Earlier sketch in SATA *89*
Henry, April 1959- *174*
Henry, Ernest 1948- *107*
Henry, Joanne Landers 1927- *6*
Henry, Maeve 1960- *75*
Henry, Marguerite 1902-1997 .... *100*
Obituary *99*
See also CLR 4
See also SAAS 7
Henry, Marie H. 1935- *65*
Henry, Marilyn 1939- *117*
Henry, Marion
See del Rey, Lester
Henry, O. 1862-1910
See YABC 2
Henry, Oliver
See Henry, O.
Henry, Rohan *217*
Henry, T. E.
See Rowland-Entwistle, (Arthur) Theodore
(Henry)
Henschel, Elizabeth Georgie *56*
Henson, Heather *206*
Henson, James Maury
See Henson, Jim
Henson, Jim 1936-1990 .... *43*
Obituary *65*
Henstra, Friso 1928- *73*
Earlier sketch in SATA *8*
See also SAAS 14
Hentoff, Nat(han Irving) 1925- *133*
Brief entry *27*
Earlier sketches in SATA *42, 69*
See also CLR 52
Henty, G(eorge) A(lfred) 1832-1902 .... *64*
See also CLR 76

Heo, Yumi 1964- *206*
Earlier sketches in SATA *94, 146*
Hepler, Heather *177*
Herald, Kathleen
See Peyton, Kathleen Wendy
Herb, Angela M. 1970- *92*
Herbert, Cecil
See Hamilton, Charles (Harold St. John)
Herbert, Don 1917-2007 .... *2*
Obituary *184*
Herbert, Donald Jeffrey
See Herbert, Don
Herbert, Frank 1920-1986 .... *37*
Obituary *47*
Earlier sketch in SATA *9*
Herbert, Frank Patrick
See Herbert, Frank
Herbert, Helen (Jean) 1947- *57*
Herbert, Janis 1956- *139*
Herbert, Wally 1934-2007 .... *23*
Herbert, Walter William
See Herbert, Wally
Herbst, Judith 1947- *74*
Herda, D.J. 1948- *80*
Herge
See Remi, Georges
Heritage, Martin
See Horler, Sydney
Herkimer, L(awrence) R(ussell) 1925(?)- *42*
Herlihy, Dirlie Anne 1935- *73*
Herlong, Madaline
See Herlong, M.H.
Herlong, M.H. *211*
Herman, Charlotte 1937- *203*
Earlier sketches in SATA *20, 99*
Hermanson, Dennis (Everett) 1947- *10*
Hermes, Jules 1962- *92*
Hermes, Patricia 1936- *191*
Earlier sketches in SATA *31, 78, 141*
Hermes, Patricia Mary
See Hermes, Patricia
Hernandez, Natalie Nelson 1929- *123*
Herndon, Ernest *91*
Herold, Ann Bixby 1937- *72*
Herrera, Juan Felipe 1948- *127*
Herrick, Steven 1958- *209*
Earlier sketches in SATA *103, 156*
Herriman, George (Joseph) 1880-1944 .... *140*
Herriot, James 1916-1995 .... *135*
Brief entry *44*
Earlier sketch in SATA *86*
See also CLR 80
Herrmanns, Ralph 1933- *11*
Herrold, Tracey
See Dils, Tracey E.
Herron, Carolivia 1947- *203*
Herron, Edward A(lbert) 1912- *4*
Herschler, Mildred Barger *130*
Hersey, John 1914-1993 .... *25*
Obituary *76*
Hersey, John Richard
See Hersey, John
Hershberger, Priscilla (Gorman) 1951- *81*
Hershenhorn, Esther 1945- *151*
Hershey, Kathleen M. 1934- *80*
Hershey, Mary *173*
Hershey, Mary L.
See Hershey, Mary
Hersom, Kathleen 1911- *73*
Hertz, Grete Janus 1915- *23*
Herxheimer, Sophie 1963- *220*
Herzig, Alison Cragin 1935- *87*
Herzog, Brad 1968- *131*
Heslewood, Juliet 1951- *82*
Hess, Lilo 1916- *4*
Hess, Paul 1961- *134*
Hesse, Hermann 1877-1962 .... *50*

Hesse, Karen 1952- *215*
　Autobiography Feature *113*
　Earlier sketches in SATA *74, 103, 158*
　See also CLR *141*
　See also SAAS *25*
Hest, Amy 1950- *193*
　Earlier sketches in SATA *55, 82, 129*
Heuer, Karsten 1968(?)- *202*
Heuer, Kenneth John 1927- *44*
Heuman, William 1912-1971 .... *21*
Heuston, Kimberley 1960- *167*
Heuston, Kimberley Burton
　See Heuston, Kimberley
Hewes, Agnes Danforth 1874-1963 .... *35*
Hewett, Anita 1918-1989 .... *13*
Hewett, Joan 1930- *140*
　Earlier sketch in SATA *81*
Hewett, Richard 1929- *81*
Hewitson, Jennifer 1961- *97*
Hewitt, Margaret 1961- *84*
Hewitt, Sally 1949- *127*
Hext, Harrington
　See Phillpotts, Eden
Hey, Nigel S(tewart) 1936- *20*
Heyduck-Huth, Hilde 1929- *8*
Heyer, Carol 1950- *130*
　Earlier sketch in SATA *74*
Heyer, Marilee 1942- *102*
　Earlier sketch in SATA *64*
Heyerdahl, Thor 1914-2002 .... *52*
　Earlier sketch in SATA *2*
Heyes, (Nancy) Eileen 1956- *150*
　Earlier sketch in SATA *80*
Heyliger, William 1884-1955
　See YABC *1*
Heyman, Ken(neth Louis) 1930- *114*
　Earlier sketch in SATA *34*
Heyward, (Edwin) DuBose 1885-1940 .... *21*
Heywood, Karen 1946- *48*
Hezlep, William (Earl) 1936- *88*
Hiaasen, Carl 1953- *208*
Hibbert, Arthur Raymond
　See Hibbert, Christopher
Hibbert, Christopher 1924-2008 .... *4*
　Obituary *201*
Hibbert, Eleanor Alice Burford 1906-1993 ..... *2*
　Obituary *74*
Hickman, Estella (Lee) 1942- *111*
Hickman, Janet 1940- *127*
　Earlier sketch in SATA *12*
Hickman, Martha Whitmore 1925- *26*
Hickman, Pamela 1958- *186*
　Earlier sketch in SATA *128*
Hickock, Will
　See Harrison, C(hester) William
Hickok, Lorena A. 1893-1968 .... *20*
Hickox, Rebecca (Ayres) *116*
Hicks, Barbara Jean 1953- *165*
Hicks, Betty *191*
Hicks, Clifford B. 1920- *50*
Hicks, Eleanor B.
　See Coerr, Eleanor (Beatrice)
Hicks, Harvey
　See Stratemeyer, Edward L.
Hicks, Peter 1952- *111*
Hicyilmaz, Gaye 1947- *157*
　Earlier sketch in SATA *77*
Hieatt, Constance B(artlett) 1928- *4*
Hiebert, Ray Eldon 1932- *13*
Hierstein, Judith *212*
Hierstein, Judy
　See Hierstein, Judith
Higdon, Hal 1931- *4*
Higginbottom, David 1923- *87*
　Earlier sketch in SATA *25*
Higginbottom, J(effrey) Winslow 1945- *29*
Higgins, F.E. *219*
Higgins, Fiona
　See Higgins, F.E.
Higgins, Joanna 1945- *125*
Higgins, Simon (Richard) 1958- *105*

Higginsen, Vy *79*
High, Linda Oatman 1958- *188*
　Autobiography Feature *188*
　Earlier sketches in SATA *94, 145*
High, Philip E. 1914- *119*
High, Philip Empson
　See High, Philip E.
Higham, David 1949- *50*
Higham, David Michael
　See Higham, David
Higham, Jon Atlas
　See Higham, Jonathan Huw
Higham, Jonathan Huw 1960- *59*
Highet, Helen
　See MacInnes, Helen (Clark)
Hightman, Jason 1971(?)- *189*
Hightman, J.P.
　See Hightman, Jason
Hightower, Florence Cole 1916-1981 .... *4*
　Obituary *27*
Highwater, Jamake (Mamake)
　1942(?)-2001 .... *69*
　Brief entry *30*
　Earlier sketch in SATA *32*
　See also CLR *17*
Hilb, Nora 1953- *178*
Hildebrandt, Greg 1939- *172*
　Brief entry *33*
　Earlier sketch in SATA *55*
Hildebrandt, Tim 1939-2006 .... *55*
　Brief entry *33*
Hildebrandt, Timothy
　See Hildebrandt, Tim
Hildebrandts, The
　See Hildebrandt, Greg
　and Hildebrandt, Tim
Hilder, Rowland 1905-1993 .... *36*
　Obituary *77*
Hildick, E. W.
　See Hildick, Wallace
Hildick, Wallace 1925-2001 .... *68*
　Earlier sketch in SATA *2*
　See also SAAS *6*
Hilgartner, Beth 1957- *58*
Hill, Alexis
　See Craig, Mary (Francis) Shura
　and Glick, Ruth (Burtnick)
Hill, Anthony R. 1942- *164*
　Earlier sketch in SATA *91*
Hill, Anthony Robert
　See Hill, Anthony R.
Hill, David 1942- *152*
　Earlier sketch in SATA *103*
Hill, Donna (Marie) 1921- *124*
　Earlier sketch in SATA *24*
Hill, Douglas 1935-2007 .... *78*
　Earlier sketch in SATA *39*
Hill, Douglas Arthur
　See Hill, Douglas
Hill, Elizabeth Starr 1925- *143*
　Earlier sketch in SATA *24*
Hill, Eric 1927- *133*
　Brief entry *53*
　Earlier sketch in SATA *66*
　See also CLR *13*
Hill, Gordon
　See Eldin, Peter
Hill, Grace Brooks *67*
　Earlier sketch in SATA *1*
Hill, Grace Livingston 1865-1947
　See YABC *2*
Hill, Helen M(orey) 1915- *27*
Hill, John
　See Koontz, Dean
Hill, Johnson
　See Kunhardt, Edith
Hill, Judy I. R.
　See Roberts, Judy I.
Hill, Kathleen Louise 1917- *4*
Hill, Kay
　See Hill, Kathleen Louise

Hill, Kirkpatrick 1938- *188*
　Earlier sketches in SATA *72, 126*
Hill, Laban
　See Hill, Laban Carrick
Hill, Laban Carrick *170*
Hill, Lee Sullivan 1958- *96*
Hill, Lorna 1902-1991 .... *12*
Hill, Margaret (Ohler) 1915- *36*
Hill, Meg
　See Hill, Margaret (Ohler)
Hill, Meredith
　See Craig, Mary (Francis) Shura
Hill, Monica
　See Watson, Jane Werner
Hill, Pamela Smith 1954- *112*
Hill, Ralph Nading 1917-1987 .... *65*
Hill, Robert W(hite) 1919-1982 .... *12*
　Obituary *31*
Hill, Ruth A.
　See Viguers, Ruth Hill
Hill, Ruth Livingston
　See Munce, Ruth Hill
Hill, Stuart 1958- *186*
Hill, Susan 1942- *183*
Hill, Susan Elizabeth
　See Hill, Susan
Hill, Susanna Leonard 1965- *193*
Hill, Thomas 1960- *82*
Hillcourt, William 1900-1992 .... *27*
Hillenbrand, Will 1960- *210*
　Earlier sketches in SATA *84, 147*
Hiller, Ilo (Ann) 1938- *59*
Hillerman, Anthony Grove
　See Hillerman, Tony
Hillerman, Tony 1925-2008 .... *6*
　Obituary *198*
Hillert, Margaret 1920- *91*
　Earlier sketch in SATA *8*
Hilliard, Richard *183*
Hillman, Ben 1957- *202*
Hillman, Elizabeth 1942- *75*
Hillman, John 1952- *120*
Hillman, Martin
　See Hill, Douglas
Hillman, Priscilla 1940- *48*
　Brief entry *39*
Hillman, Shane *200*
Hills, C.A.R. 1955- *39*
Hills, Charles Albert Reis
　See Hills, C.A.R.
Hills, Tad *173*
Hilton, Irene Pothus -1979 .... *7*
Hilton, James 1900-1954 .... *34*
Hilton, Margaret Lynette 1946- *105*
　Earlier sketch in SATA *68*
　See also CLR *25*
　See also SAAS *21*
Hilton, Nette
　See Hilton, Margaret Lynette
Hilton, Ralph 1907-1982 .... *8*
Hilton, Suzanne 1922- *4*
Hilton-Bruce, Anne
　See Hilton, Margaret Lynette
Him, George 1937-1982
　Obituary *30*
Himelblau, Linda -2005 .... *179*
Himelstein, Shmuel 1940- *83*
Himler, Ann 1946- *8*
Himler, Ronald 1937- *183*
　Earlier sketches in SATA *6, 92, 137*
Himler, Ronald Norbert
　See Himler, Ronald
Himmelman, John 1959- *221*
　Earlier sketches in SATA *47, 94, 159*
Himmelman, John C.
　See Himmelman, John
Hinckley, Helen
　See Jones, Helen Hinckley
Hind, Dolores (Ellen) 1931- *53*
　Brief entry *49*

Hindin, Nathan
    See Bloch, Robert (Albert)
Hindley, Judy 1940- *179*
    Earlier sketch in SATA *120*
Hinds, P. Mignon *98*
Hinds, Patricia Mignon
    See Hinds, P. Mignon
Hine, Sesyle Joslin 1929- *2*
Hines, Anna Grossnickle 1946- *209*
    Brief entry *45*
    Earlier sketches in SATA *51, 95, 141*
    See also SAAS *16*
Hines, Gary (Roger) 1944- *136*
    Earlier sketch in SATA *74*
Hinman, Bonnie 1950- *216*
Hinojosa, Maria (de Lourdes) 1961- *88*
Hinton, Nigel 1941- *166*
Hinton, S. E. 1950- *160*
    Earlier sketches in SATA *19, 58, 115*
    See also CLR *23*
Hinton, Sam 1917-2009 .... *43*
Hinton, Susan Eloise
    See Hinton, S. E.
Hintz, Martin 1945- *128*
    Brief entry *39*
    Earlier sketch in SATA *47*
Hintz, Stephen V. 1975- *129*
Hippopotamus, Eugene H.
    See Kraus, (Herman) Robert
Hirano, Cathy 1957- *68*
Hirao, Amiko *203*
Hirsch, Karen 1941- *61*
Hirsch, Odo *157*
    Earlier sketch in SATA *111*
Hirsch, Phil 1926- *35*
Hirsch, S. Carl 1913-1990 .... *2*
    See also SAAS *7*
Hirschfelder, Arlene B. 1943- *138*
    Earlier sketch in SATA *80*
Hirschi, Ron 1948- *192*
    Earlier sketches in SATA *56, 95*
Hirschmann, Linda (Ann) 1941- *40*
Hirsh, Marilyn 1944-1988 .... *7*
    Obituary *58*
Hirshberg, Al(bert Simon) 1909-1973 .... *38*
Hiscock, Bruce 1940- *204*
    Earlier sketches in SATA *57, 137*
Hiser, Constance 1950- *71*
Hiser, Iona Seibert -1998 .... *4*
Hislop, Julia Rose Catherine 1962- *74*
Hissey, Jane 1952- *130*
    Autobiography Feature *130*
    Earlier sketches in SATA *58, 103*
Hissey, Jane Elizabeth
    See Hissey, Jane
Hitchcock, Alfred (Joseph) 1899-1980 .... *27*
    Obituary *24*
Hite, Sid 1954- *175*
    Earlier sketches in SATA *75, 136*
Hitte, Kathryn 1919- *16*
Hitz, Demi
    See Demi
Hitzeroth, Deborah L. 1961- *78*
Hnizdovsky, Jacques 1915- *32*
Ho, Louise *185*
Ho, Minfong 1951- *151*
    Earlier sketches in SATA *15, 94*
    See also CLR *28*
Hoagland, Edward (Morley) 1932- *51*
Hoare, Robert J(ohn) 1921-1975 .... *38*
Hoban, Julia *217*
Hoban, Lillian 1925-1998 .... *69*
    Obituary *104*
    Earlier sketch in SATA *22*
    See also CLR *67*
Hoban, Russell 1925- *136*
    Earlier sketches in SATA *1, 40, 78*
    See also CLR *139*
Hoban, Russell Conwell
    See Hoban, Russell

Hoban, Tana 1917(?)-2006 .... *104*
    Obituary *173*
    Earlier sketches in SATA *22, 70*
    See also CLR *76*
    See also SAAS *12*
Hobart, Lois (Elaine) *7*
Hobbie, Holly 1944- *178*
    See also CLR *88*
Hobbie, Jocelyn *190*
Hobbie, Nathaniel *196*
Hobbs, Leigh 1953- *166*
Hobbs, Valerie 1941- *193*
    Autobiography Feature *145*
    Earlier sketches in SATA *93, 145*
    See also CLR *148*
Hobbs, Will 1947- *177*
    Autobiography Feature *127*
    Earlier sketches in SATA *72, 110*
    See also CLR *59*
Hobbs, William Carl
    See Hobbs, Will
Hoberman, Mary Ann 1930- *158*
    Earlier sketches in SATA *5, 72, 111*
    See also CLR *22*
    See also SAAS *18*
Hobson, Bruce 1950- *62*
Hobson, Burton (Harold) 1933- *28*
Hobson, Laura Z(ametkin) 1900-1986 .... *52*
Hobson, Sally 1967- *172*
    Earlier sketch in SATA *84*
Hoce, Charley E. *174*
Hochman, David *202*
Hochschild, Arlie Russell 1940- *11*
Hockaby, Stephen
    See Mitchell, Gladys (Maude Winifred)
Hockenberry, Hope
    See Newell, Hope Hockenberry
Hodge, Deborah 1954- *163*
    Earlier sketch in SATA *122*
Hodge, P. W.
    See Hodge, Paul W(illiam)
Hodge, Paul W(illiam) 1934- *12*
Hodgell, P(atricia) C(hristine) 1951- *42*
Hodges, C. Walter 1909-2004 .... *2*
    Obituary *158*
Hodges, Carl G. 1902-1964 .... *10*
Hodges, Cyril Walter
    See Hodges, C. Walter
Hodges, Elizabeth Jamison *1*
Hodges, Margaret 1911-2005 .... *167*
    Obituary *172*
    Earlier sketches in SATA *1, 33, 75, 117*
    See also SAAS *9*
Hodges, Margaret Moore
    See Hodges, Margaret
Hodgetts, Blake Christopher 1967- *43*
Hodgkins, Fran 1964- *199*
Hodgkinson, Leigh 1975- *202*
Hodgman, Ann 1956- *198*
Hodgson, Harriet (W.) 1935- *84*
Hoehne, Marcia 1951- *89*
Hoellwarth, Cathryn Clinton
    See Clinton, Cathryn
Hoestlandt, Jo 1948- *221*
    Earlier sketch in SATA *94*
Hoestlandt, Jocelyne
    See Hoestlandt, Jo
Hoexter, Corinne K. 1927- *6*
Hoeye, Michael 1947- *136*
Hoff, Carol 1900-1979 .... *11*
Hoff, Mary (King) 1956- *157*
    Earlier sketch in SATA *74*
Hoff, Syd(ney) 1912-2004 .... *138*
    Obituary *154*
    Earlier sketches in SATA *9, 72*
    See also CLR *83*
    See also SAAS *4*
Hoffman, Edwin D. *49*
Hoffman, Elizabeth P(arkinson) 1921-2003
    Obituary *153*

Hoffman, Mary 1945- *211*
    Earlier sketches in SATA *59, 97, 144*
    See also SAAS *24*
Hoffman, Mat 1972- *150*
Hoffman, Nina Kiriki 1955- *160*
Hoffman, Phyllis M. 1944- *4*
Hoffman, Phyllis Miriam
    See Hoffman, Phyllis M.
Hoffman, Rosekrans 1926- *15*
Hoffmann, E(rnst) T(heodor) A(madeus)
    1776-1822 .... *27*
    See also CLR *133*
Hoffmann, Felix 1911-1975 .... *9*
Hoffmann, Heinrich 1809-1894
    See CLR *122*
Hoffmann, Margaret Jones 1910- *48*
Hoffmann, Peggy
    See Hoffmann, Margaret Jones
Hofher, Catherine Baxley 1954- *130*
Hofher, Cathy
    See Hofher, Catherine Baxley
Hofmeyr, Dianne (Louise) *138*
Hofsepian, Sylvia A. 1932- *74*
Hofsinde, Robert 1902-1973 .... *21*
Hogan, Bernice Harris 1929- *12*
Hogan, Inez 1895-1973 .... *2*
Hogan, James P. 1941-2010 .... *81*
Hogan, James Patrick
    See Hogan, James P.
Hogan, Jamie *192*
Hogan, Linda 1947- *132*
Hogan, Mary 1957- *210*
Hogarth, Burne 1911-1996 .... *89*
    Earlier sketch in SATA *63*
Hogarth, Grace (Weston Allen) 1905-1995 .. *91*
Hogarth, Jr.
    See Kent, Rockwell
Hogarth, (Arthur) Paul 1917-2001 .... *41*
Hogg, Garry 1902-1976 .... *2*
Hogg, Gary 1957- *172*
    Earlier sketch in SATA *105*
Hogner, Dorothy Childs *4*
Hogner, Nils 1893-1970 .... *25*
Hogrogian, Nonny 1932- *74*
    Autobiography Feature *127*
    Earlier sketch in SATA *7*
    See also CLR *95*
    See also SAAS *1*
Hoh, Diane 1937- *102*
    Brief entry *48*
    Earlier sketch in SATA *52*
Hoke, Helen
    See Watts, Helen L. Hoke
Hoke, Helen L.
    See Watts, Helen L. Hoke
Hoke, John 1925- *7*
Hoke, John Lindsay
    See Hoke, John
Hokenson, Terry 1948- *193*
Hol, Coby 1943- *126*
Holabird, Katharine 1948- *213*
    Earlier sketches in SATA *62, 135*
Holaday, Bobbie 1922- *153*
Holbeach, Henry
    See Rands, William Brighty
Holberg, Ruth L(angland) 1889-1984 .... *1*
Holbrook, Kathy 1963- *107*
Holbrook, Peter
    See Glick, Carl (Cannon)
Holbrook, Sabra
    See Erickson, Sabra Rollins
Holbrook, Sara *131*
Holbrook, Stewart Hall 1893-1964 .... *2*
Holcomb, Jerry (Leona) Kimble 1927- *113*
Holcomb, Nan
    See McPhee, Norma H.
Holden, Elizabeth Rhoda
    See Lawrence, Louise
Holding, James (Clark Carlisle, Jr.)
    1907-1997 .... *3*
Hole, Stian 1969- *204*

Holeman, Linda 1949- *136*
    Autobiography Feature *136*
    Earlier sketch in SATA *102*
Holinger, William (Jacques) 1944- *90*
Holisher, Desider 1901-1972 .... *6*
Holl, Adelaide Hinkle 1910- *8*
Holl, Kristi
    See Holl, Kristi D.
Holl, Kristi D. 1951- *51*
Holl, Kristi Diane
    See Holl, Kristi D.
Holland, Gay W. 1941- *128*
Holland, Isabelle (Christian) 1920-2002 .... *70*
    Autobiography Feature *103*
    Obituary *132*
    Earlier sketch in SATA *8*
    See also CLR *57*
Holland, Janice 1913-1962 .... *18*
Holland, John L(ewis) 1919- *20*
Holland, Joyce
    See Morice, Dave
Holland, Julia 1954- *106*
Holland, Lynda (H.) 1959- *77*
Holland, Lys
    See Gater, Dilys
Holland, Marion 1908-1989 .... *6*
    Obituary *61*
Holland, Richard 1976- *216*
Holland, Trish *221*
Hollander, John 1929- *13*
Hollander, Nicole 1940(?)- *101*
Hollander, Paul
    See Silverberg, Robert
Hollander, Phyllis 1928- *39*
Hollander, Zander 1923- *63*
Holldobler, Turid 1939- *26*
Holliday, Joe
    See Holliday, Joseph
Holliday, Joseph 1910- *11*
Holling, Holling C(lancy) 1900-1973 .... *15*
    Obituary *26*
    See also CLR *50*
Hollingsworth, Alvin C(arl) 1930- *39*
Hollingsworth, Mary 1947- *166*
    Earlier sketch in SATA *91*
Holloway, Teresa (Bragunier) 1906- *26*
Hollyer, Belinda *204*
Holm, (Else) Anne (Lise) 1922-1998 .... *1*
    See also CLR *75*
    See also SAAS *7*
Holm, Jennifer L. 1968(?)- *183*
    Earlier sketches in SATA *120, 163*
Holm, Matthew 1974- *174*
Holm, Sharon Lane 1955- *114*
    Earlier sketch in SATA *78*
Holman, Felice 1919- *82*
    Earlier sketch in SATA *7*
    See also SAAS *17*
Holm and Hamel
    See Holm, Jennifer L.
Holmberg, Bo R. 1945- *203*
Holme, Bryan 1913-1990 .... *26*
    Obituary *66*
Holmes, Barbara Ware 1945- *127*
    Earlier sketch in SATA *65*
Holmes, Elizabeth 1957- *191*
Holmes, Elizabeth Ann
    See Holmes, Elizabeth
Holmes, John
    See Souster, (Holmes) Raymond
Holmes, Marjorie (Rose) 1910-2002 .... *43*
Holmes, Martha 1961- *72*
Holmes, Mary Tavener 1954- *199*
Holmes, Mary Z(astrow) 1943- *80*
Holmes, Oliver Wendell 1809-1894 .... *34*
Holmes, Peggy 1898- *60*
Holmes, Raymond
    See Souster, (Holmes) Raymond
Holmes, Rick
    See Hardwick, Richard Holmes, Jr.
Holmes, Sara Lewis *186*

Holmgren, Helen Jean 1930- *45*
Holmgren, Sister George Ellen
    See Holmgren, Helen Jean
Holmgren, Virginia C(unningham) 1909- *26*
Holmquist, Eve 1921- *11*
Holt, K.A.
    See Roy, Kari Anne
Holt, Kimberly Willis 1960- *179*
    Earlier sketch in SATA *122*
Holt, Margaret 1937- *4*
Holt, Margaret Van Vechten (Saunders)
    1899-1963 .... *32*
Holt, Michael (Paul) 1929- *13*
Holt, Rackham
    See Holt, Margaret Van Vechten (Saunders)
Holt, Rochelle L.
    See DuBois, Rochelle Holt
Holt, Stephen
    See Thompson, Harlan
Holt, Victoria
    See Hibbert, Eleanor Alice Burford
Holtei, Christa 1953- *214*
Holton, Leonard
    See Wibberley, Leonard
Holtz, Thomas R., Jr. 1965- *203*
Holtze, Sally Holmes 1952- *64*
Holtzman, Jerome 1926-2008 .... *57*
    Obituary *194*
Holub, Joan 1956- *149*
    Earlier sketch in SATA *99*
Holub, Josef 1926- *175*
Holubitsky, Katherine 1955- *165*
    Earlier sketch in SATA *121*
Holyer, Erna Maria 1925- *22*
Holyer, Ernie
    See Holyer, Erna Maria
Holz, Loretta 1943- *17*
Holz, Loretta Marie
    See Holz, Loretta
Homel, David 1952- *97*
Homze, Alma C. 1932- *17*
Honey, Elizabeth 1947- *137*
    Autobiography Feature *137*
    Earlier sketch in SATA *112*
Honeycutt, Natalie 1945- *97*
Hong, Lily Toy 1958- *76*
Hong, Maxine Ting Ting
    See Kingston, Maxine Hong
Honig, Donald 1931- *18*
Honig, Donald Martin
    See Honig, Donald
Honness, Elizabeth H. 1904- *2*
Hoobler, Dorothy 1941- *161*
    Earlier sketches in SATA *28, 109*
Hoobler, Thomas *161*
    Earlier sketches in SATA *28, 109*
Hood, Joseph F. 1925- *4*
Hood, Robert E. 1926- *21*
Hood, Sarah
    See Killough, (Karen) Lee
Hook, Brendan 1963- *105*
Hook, Frances 1912-1983 .... *27*
Hook, Geoffrey R(aynor) 1928- *103*
Hook, Jeff
    See Hook, Geoffrey R(aynor)
Hook, Martha 1936- *27*
Hooker, Richard
    See Heinz, W. C.
Hooker, Ruth 1920-1998 .... *21*
hooks, bell 1952(?)- *170*
    Earlier sketch in SATA *115*
Hooks, William H(arris) 1921- *94*
    Earlier sketch in SATA *16*
Hoon, Patricia Easterly 1954- *90*
Hooper, Byrd
    See St. Clair, Byrd Hooper
Hooper, Mary 1948- *205*
    Earlier sketch in SATA *160*
Hooper, Maureen Brett 1927- *76*
Hooper, Meredith 1939- *159*
    Earlier sketches in SATA *28, 101*

Hooper, Meredith Jean
    See Hooper, Meredith
Hooper, Patricia 1941- *95*
Hoopes, Lyn Littlefield 1953- *49*
    Brief entry *44*
Hoopes, Ned E(dward) 1932- *21*
Hoopes, Roy 1922-2009 .... *11*
Hoose, Phillip 1947- *215*
    Earlier sketch in SATA *137*
Hoover, H(elen) M(ary) 1935- *132*
    Brief entry *33*
    Earlier sketches in SATA *44, 83*
    See also SAAS *8*
Hoover, Helen (Drusilla Blackburn)
    1910-1984 .... *12*
    Obituary *39*
Hope, Christopher 1944- *62*
Hope, Christopher David Tully
    See Hope, Christopher
Hope, Laura Lee
    See Goulart, Ron
    and Stanley, George Edward
Hope Simpson, Jacynth 1930- *12*
Hopf, Alice (Martha) L(ightner) 1904-1988 ... *5*
    Obituary *55*
Hopkins, A. T.
    See Turngren, Annette
Hopkins, C. M.
    See Hopkins, Cathy
Hopkins, Cathy 1953- *165*
Hopkins, Cathy M.
    See Hopkins, Cathy
Hopkins, Clark 1895-1976
    Obituary *34*
Hopkins, Ellen 1955- *128*
Hopkins, Ellen L.
    See Hopkins, Ellen
Hopkins, Jackie
    See Hopkins, Jackie Mims
Hopkins, Jackie Mims 1952- *178*
    Earlier sketch in SATA *92*
Hopkins, Joseph G(erard) E(dward) 1909- ... *11*
Hopkins, (Hector) Kenneth 1914-1988
    Obituary *58*
Hopkins, Lee Bennett 1938- *215*
    Earlier sketches in SATA *3, 68, 125, 168*
    See also CLR *44*
    See also SAAS *4*
Hopkins, Lyman
    See Folsom, Franklin (Brewster)
Hopkins, Marjorie 1911-1999 .... *9*
Hopkins, Mary R(ice) 1956- *97*
Hopkinson, Amanda 1948- *84*
Hopkinson, Deborah 1952- *216*
    Autobiography Feature *180*
    Earlier sketches in SATA *76, 108, 159, 180*
    See also CLR *118*
Hopman, Philip 1961- *177*
Hoppe, Joanne 1932- *42*
Hoppe, Matthias 1952- *76*
Hoppe, Paul *209*
Hopper, Nancy J. 1937- *38*
    Brief entry *35*
Hopping, Lorraine Jean
    See Egan, Lorraine Hopping
Horacek, Judy 1961- *211*
Horaek, Petr *214*
    Earlier sketch in SATA *163*
Horenstein, Henry 1947- *108*
Horgan, Paul (George Vincent O'Shaughnessy)
    1903-1995 .... *13*
    Obituary *84*
Horlak, E.E.
    See Tepper, Sheri S.
Horler, Sydney 1888-1954 .... *102*
Horn, Sandra Ann 1944- *154*
Hornblow, Arthur, Jr. 1893-1976 .... *15*
Hornblow, Leonora 1920-2005 .... *18*
    Obituary *171*
Hornblow, Leonora Schinasi
    See Hornblow, Leonora

Horne, Constance 1927- *149*
Horne, Richard 1960-2007 .... *169*
　Obituary *180*
　Earlier sketch in SATA *111*
Horne, Richard Henry Hengist
　1802(?)-1884 .... *29*
Horner, Althea (Jane) 1926- *36*
Horner, Dave 1934- *12*
Horner, Jack 1946- *106*
Horner, John R.
　See Horner, Jack
Horner, John Robert
　See Horner, Jack
Hornik, Laurie Miller *159*
Horniman, Joanne 1951- *167*
　Earlier sketch in SATA *98*
Hornos, Axel 1907-1994 .... *20*
Hornstein, Reuben Aaron 1912- *64*
Horowitz, Anthony 1955- *195*
　Earlier sketch in SATA *137*
Horowitz, Dave 1970- *204*
　Earlier sketch in SATA *172*
Horowitz, Ruth 1957- *136*
Horrocks, Anita 1958- *169*
Horse, Harry
　See Horne, Richard
Horsfield, Alan 1939- *153*
Horstman, Lisa 1964- *219*
Hort, Lenny *179*
Horton, James O. 1943- *173*
Horton, James Oliver
　See Horton, James O.
Horton, Joan *217*
Horton, Madelyn (Stacey) 1962- *77*
Horvath, Betty 1927- *4*
Horvath, David 1972(?)- *192*
Horvath, Polly 1957- *194*
　Earlier sketches in SATA *85, 140*
　See also CLR *90*
Horwich, Frances R(appaport) 1908-2001 .... *11*
　Obituary *130*
Horwitz, Elinor Lander *45*
　Brief entry *33*
Horwood, William 1944- *85*
Hosford, Dorothy (Grant) 1900-1952 .... *22*
Hosford, Jessie 1892-1990 .... *5*
Hoshi, Shin'ichi 1926- *101*
Hoshino, Felicia 1968- *189*
Hoskyns-Abrahall, Clare (Constance
　Drury) *13*
Hosler, Danamarie 1978- *184*
Hossack, Sylvia 1939- *83*
Hossack, Sylvie Adams
　See Hossack, Sylvia
Hosseini, Khaled 1965- *156*
Hossell, Karen Price
　See Price, Karen
Hosta, Dar *192*
Hostetler, Marian 1932- *91*
Houck, Carter 1924- *22*
Hough, Charlotte 1924-2008 .... *9*
　Obituary *202*
Hough, Helen Charlotte
　See Hough, Charlotte
Hough, Judy Taylor 1932- *63*
　Brief entry *51*
　Earlier sketch in SATA *56*
Hough, Richard (Alexander) 1922-1999 ...... *17*
Houghton, Eric 1930- *7*
Houk, Randy 1944- *97*
Houlehen, Robert J. 1918- *18*
Houlton, Peggy Mann 1925(?)-1990 .... *6*
Household, Geoffrey 1900-1988 .... *14*
　Obituary *59*
Housman, Laurence 1865-1959 .... *25*
Houston, Dick 1943- *74*
Houston, Gloria *138*
　Autobiography Feature *138*
　Earlier sketch in SATA *81*

Houston, James A(rchibald) 1921-2005 .... *74*
　Obituary *163*
　Earlier sketch in SATA *13*
　See also CLR *3*
　See also SAAS *17*
Houston, James D. 1933-2009 .... *78*
　Obituary *203*
Houston, James Dudley
　See Houston, James D.
Houston, James Dudley
　See Houston, James D.
Houston, Jeanne Toyo Wakatsuki
　See Houston, Jeanne Wakatsuki
Houston, Jeanne Wakatsuki 1934- *168*
　Autobiography Feature *168*
　Earlier sketch in SATA *78*
Houston, Juanita C. 1921- *129*
Houton, Kathleen
　See Kilgore, Kathleen
Houts, Amy F. *164*
Houts, Michelle *219*
Hovey, Kate *158*
Howard, Alan 1922- *45*
Howard, Alyssa
　See Buckholtz, Eileen (Garber)
　and Glick, Ruth (Burtnick)
　and Titchener, Louise
Howard, Arthur 1948- *212*
　Earlier sketch in SATA *165*
Howard, Arthur Charles
　See Howard, Arthur
Howard, Elizabeth Fitzgerald 1927- *119*
　Earlier sketch in SATA *74*
Howard, Ellen 1943- *184*
　Earlier sketches in SATA *67, 99*
Howard, Jane R(uble) 1924- *87*
Howard, Norman Barry 1949- *90*
Howard, P. M.
　See Howard, Pauline Rodriguez
Howard, Paul 1967- *190*
　Earlier sketch in SATA *118*
Howard, Pauline Rodriguez 1951- *124*
Howard, Prosper
　See Hamilton, Charles (Harold St. John)
Howard, Robert West 1908-1988 .... *5*
Howard, Todd 1964- *135*
Howard, Tristan
　See Currie, Stephen
Howard, Vernon (Linwood) 1918-1992 .... *40*
　Obituary *73*
Howard, Warren F.
　See Pohl, Frederik
Howarth, Daniel *188*
Howarth, David (Armine) 1912-1991 .... *6*
　Obituary *68*
Howarth, Lesley 1952- *94*
Howe, Deborah 1946-1978 .... *29*
Howe, James 1946- *161*
　Earlier sketches in SATA *29, 71, 111*
　See also CLR *9*
Howe, John F. 1957- *79*
Howe, Norma 1930- *126*
Howe, Peter 1942- *214*
Howell, Pat 1947- *15*
Howell, S.
　See Styles, (Frank) Showell
Howell, Simmone 1971- *214*
Howell, Virginia
　See Ellison, Virginia H(owell)
Howes, Barbara 1914-1996 .... *5*
Howie, Betsy 1962- *215*
Howie, Diana 1945- *122*
Howie, Diana Melson
　See Howie, Diana
Howker, Janni 1957- *72*
　Brief entry *46*
　See also CLR *14*
　See also SAAS *13*
Howland, Ethan 1963- *131*
Hoy, Linda 1946- *65*

Hoy, Nina
　See Roth, Arthur J(oseph)
Hoyle, Geoffrey 1942- *18*
Hoyt, Ard *190*
Hoyt, Edwin P(almer), Jr. 1923- *28*
Hoyt, Erich 1950- *140*
　Earlier sketch in SATA *65*
Hoyt, Olga
　See Gruhzit-Hoyt, Olga (Margaret)
Hrdlitschka, Shelley 1956- *167*
　Earlier sketch in SATA *111*
Hrdlitschka, Shelley Joanne
　See Hrdlitschka, Shelley
Hromic, Alma A.
　See Alexander, Alma
Htin Aung, U.
　See Aung, (Maung) Htin
Hu, Ying-Hwa *173*
Huang, Benrei 1959- *86*
Hubalek, Linda K. 1954- *111*
Hubbard, Crystal *209*
Hubbard, Margaret Ann
　See Priley, Margaret (Ann) Hubbard
Hubbard, Michelle Calabro 1953- *122*
Hubbard, Patricia 1945- *124*
Hubbard, Woodleigh Marx *160*
　Earlier sketch in SATA *98*
Hubbell, Patricia 1928- *186*
　Earlier sketches in SATA *8, 132*
Hubery, Julia *195*
Hubley, Faith Elliot 1924-2001 .... *48*
　Obituary *133*
Hubley, John 1914-1977 .... *48*
　Obituary *24*
Huck, Charlotte S. 1922- *136*
　Earlier sketch in SATA *82*
Hucke, Johannes 1966- *218*
Hudak, Michal 1956- *143*
Hudson, Cheryl Willis 1948- *160*
　Earlier sketch in SATA *81*
Hudson, Jan 1954-1990 .... *77*
　See also CLR *40*
Hudson, Jeffery
　See Crichton, Michael
Hudson, Jeffrey
　See Crichton, Michael
Hudson, (Margaret) Kirsty 1947- *32*
Hudson, Margaret
　See Shuter, Jane (Margaret)
Hudson, W(illiam) H(enry) 1841-1922 .... *35*
Hudson, Wade 1946- *162*
　Earlier sketch in SATA *74*
Huelsmann, Eva 1928- *16*
Huerlimann, Bettina 1909-1983 .... *39*
　Obituary *34*
Huerlimann, Ruth 1939- *32*
　Brief entry *31*
Huff, Barbara A. 1929- *67*
Huff, Tanya 1957- *171*
　Earlier sketch in SATA *85*
Huff, Tanya Sue
　See Huff, Tanya
Huff, T.S.
　See Huff, Tanya
Huff, Vivian 1948- *59*
Huffaker, Sandy 1943- *10*
Huffman, Tom *24*
Huggins, Nathan Irvin 1927-1989 .... *63*
Huggins, Peter 1951- *178*
Hughes, Carol 1955- *217*
　Earlier sketch in SATA *108*
Hughes, Dean 1943- *139*
　Earlier sketches in SATA *33, 77*
　See also CLR *76*
Hughes, Eden
　See Griffin, W. E. B.
Hughes, Edward James
　See Hughes, Ted
Hughes, James Langston
　See Hughes, Langston

Hughes, Langston 1902-1967 .... *33*
  Earlier sketch in SATA *4*
  See also CLR *17*
Hughes, Libby *71*
Hughes, Matilda
  See MacLeod, Charlotte (Matilda)
Hughes, Monica 1925-2003 .... *162*
  Earlier sketches in SATA *15, 70, 119*
  See also CLR *60*
  See also SAAS *11*
Hughes, Monica Ince
  See Hughes, Monica
Hughes, Pat *197*
Hughes, Richard (Arthur Warren)
  1900-1976 .... *8*
  Obituary *25*
Hughes, Sara
  See Saunders, Susan
Hughes, Shirley 1927- *159*
  Earlier sketches in SATA *16, 70, 110*
  See also CLR *15*
Hughes, Susan 1960- *216*
Hughes, Ted 1930-1998 .... *49*
  Brief entry *27*
  Obituary *107*
  See also CLR *131*
Hughes, Thomas 1822-1896 .... *31*
  See also CLR *160*
Hughes, Virginia
  See Campbell, Hope
Hughes, Walter (Llewellyn) 1910-1993 .... *26*
Hughey, Roberta 1942- *61*
Hugo, Pierre Brackers de
  See Brackers de Hugo, Pierre
Hugo, Victor 1802-1885 .... *47*
Hugo, Victor Marie
  See Hugo, Victor
Huline-Dickens, Frank William 1931- *34*
Huling, Jan *172*
Huliska-Beith, Laura *175*
Hull, Eleanor (Means) 1913- *21*
Hull, Eric Traviss
  See Harnan, Terry
Hull, H. Braxton
  See Jacobs, Helen Hull
Hull, Jesse Redding
  See Hull, Jessie Redding
Hull, Jessie Redding 1932- *51*
Hull, Katharine 1921-1977 .... *23*
Hull, Lise (E.) 1954- *148*
Hull, Maureen 1949- *142*
Hulme, Joy N. 1922- *161*
  Earlier sketches in SATA *74, 112*
Hults, Dorothy Niebrugge 1898-2000 .... *6*
Humble, Richard 1945- *60*
Hume, Lachie *189*
Hume, Lotta Carswell *7*
Hume, Ruth Fox 1922-1980 .... *26*
  Obituary *22*
Hume, Stephen Eaton 1947- *136*
Hummel, Berta 1909-1946 .... *43*
Hummel, Sister Maria Innocentia
  See Hummel, Berta
Hummon, Marcus 1960- *213*
Humphrey, Carol Sue 1956- *167*
Humphrey, Henry (III) 1930- *16*
Humphrey, Kate
  See Forsyth, Kate
Humphrey, Sandra McLeod 1936- *95*
Humphreys, Martha 1943- *71*
Humphreys, Susan L.
  See Lowell, Susan
Hundal, Nancy 1957- *128*
Huneck, Stephen 1949- *183*
  Earlier sketch in SATA *129*
Hungerford, Hesba Fay
  See Brinsmead, H(esba) F(ay)
Hungerford, Pixie
  See Brinsmead, H(esba) F(ay)
Hunkin, Tim 1950- *53*

Hunkin, Timothy Mark Trelawney
  See Hunkin, Tim
Hunt, Angela Elwell 1957- *159*
  Earlier sketch in SATA *75*
Hunt, Bernice 1920- *4*
Hunt, Charlotte Dumaresq
  See Demi
Hunt, Francesca
  See Holland, Isabelle (Christian)
Hunt, Irene 1907-2001 .... *91*
  Earlier sketch in SATA *2*
  See also CLR *1*
Hunt, Janie Louise 1963- *102*
Hunt, Jonathan 1966- *84*
Hunt, Joyce 1927- *31*
Hunt, Linda 1940- *39*
Hunt, Lisa B(ehnke) 1967- *84*
Hunt, Mabel Leigh 1892-1971 .... *1*
  Obituary *26*
Hunt, Morton M(agill) 1920- *22*
Hunt, Nigel
  See Greenbank, Anthony Hunt
Hunt, Peter (Leonard) 1945- *76*
Hunter, Anne B. 1966- *118*
Hunter, Bernice Thurman 1922-2002 .... *85*
  Brief entry *45*
Hunter, Bobbi Dooley 1945- *89*
Hunter, Captain Marcy
  See Ellis, Edward S.
Hunter, Chris
  See Fluke, Joanne
Hunter, Clingham M.D.
  See Adams, William Taylor
Hunter, Edith Fisher 1919- *31*
Hunter, Erin
  See Cary, Kate
Hunter, Evan 1926-2005 .... *25*
  Obituary *167*
Hunter, George E.
  See Ellis, Edward S.
Hunter, Hilda 1921- *7*
Hunter, Jana
  See Hunter, Jana Novotny
Hunter, Jana Novotny *190*
Hunter, Jim 1939- *65*
Hunter, Kristin
  See Lattany, Kristin Hunter
Hunter, Leigh
  See Etchison, Birdie L(ee)
Hunter, Lieutenant Ned
  See Ellis, Edward S.
Hunter, Mel 1927-2004 .... *39*
Hunter, Mollie 1922- *139*
  Autobiography Feature *139*
  Earlier sketches in SATA *2, 54, 106*
  See also CLR *25*
  See also SAAS *7*
Hunter, Ned
  See Ellis, Edward S.
Hunter, Norman (George Lorimer)
  1899-1995 .... *84*
  Earlier sketch in SATA *26*
Hunter, Ryan Ann
  See Greenwood, Pamela D.
  and Macalaster, Elizabeth G.
Hunter, Sara Hoagland 1954- *98*
Hunter Blair, Pauline
  See Clarke, Pauline
Huntington, Amy 1956- *180*
  Earlier sketch in SATA *138*
Huntington, Geoffrey *145*
Huntington, Harriet E(lizabeth) 1909- *1*
Huntsberry, William E(mery) 1916- *5*
Hurd, Clement (G.) 1908-1988 .... *64*
  Obituary *54*
  Earlier sketch in SATA *2*
  See also CLR *49*

Hurd, Edith Thacher 1910-1997 .... *64*
  Obituary *95*
  Earlier sketch in SATA *2*
  See also CLR *49*
  See also SAAS *13*
Hurd, John Thacher
  See Hurd, Thacher
Hurd, Thacher 1949- *219*
  Autobiography Feature *123*
  Brief entry *45*
  Earlier sketches in SATA *46, 94*
Hurley, Jo
  See Dower, Laura
Hurley, Tonya *207*
Hurlimann, Bettina
  See Huerlimann, Bettina
Hurlimann, Ruth
  See Huerlimann, Ruth
Hurmence, Belinda 1921- *77*
  See also CLR *25*
  See also SAAS *20*
Hurst, Carol Otis 1933-2007 .... *185*
  Earlier sketch in SATA *130*
Hurt-Newton, Tania 1968- *84*
Hurwin, Davida Wills 1950- *180*
Hurwitz, Johanna 1937- *175*
  Earlier sketches in SATA *20, 71, 113*
  See also SAAS *18*
Hurwood, Bernhardt J. 1926-1987 .... *12*
  Obituary *50*
Husain, Shahrukh 1950- *108*
Huser, Glen 1943- *151*
Hutchens, Paul 1902-1977 .... *31*
Hutchins, Carleen M.
  See Hutchins, Carleen Maley
Hutchins, Carleen Maley 1911-2009 .... *9*
  Obituary *206*
Hutchins, Hazel J. 1952- *175*
  Brief entry *51*
  Earlier sketches in SATA *81, 135*
  See also SAAS *24*
Hutchins, Pat 1942- *178*
  Earlier sketches in SATA *15, 70, 111*
  See also CLR *20*
  See also SAAS *16*
Hutchins, Ross Elliott 1906- *4*
Hutchison, Linda 1942- *152*
Huthmacher, J. Joseph 1929- *5*
Hutto, Nelson (Allen) 1904-1985 .... *20*
Hutton, Kathryn 1915- *89*
Hutton, Sam
  See Jones, Allan Frewin
Hutton, Warwick 1939-1994 .... *20*
  Obituary *83*
  See also SAAS *17*
Huxley, Aldous 1894-1963 .... *63*
  See also CLR *151*
Huxley, Aldous Leonard
  See Huxley, Aldous
Huxley, Elspeth (Josceline Grant)
  1907-1997 .... *62*
  Obituary *95*
Hyde, Catherine R.
  See Hyde, Catherine Ryan
Hyde, Catherine Ryan 1955- *141*
Hyde, Dayton O(gden) *9*
Hyde, Hawk
  See Hyde, Dayton O(gden)
Hyde, Jeannette
  See Eyerly, Jeannette
Hyde, Margaret O. 1917- *139*
  Earlier sketches in SATA *1, 42, 76*
  See also CLR *23*
  See also SAAS *8*
Hyde, Margaret Oldroyd
  See Hyde, Margaret O.
Hyde, Shelley
  See Reed, Kit
Hyde, Wayne Frederick 1922- *7*
Hylander, Clarence J(ohn) 1897-1964 .... *7*
Hyman, Miles 1962- *210*

Hyman, Paula Chase
  See Chase, Paula
Hyman, Robin 1931- 12
Hyman, Robin Phiilip
  See Hyman, Robin
Hyman, Trina Schart 1939-2004 95
  Obituary 158
  Earlier sketches in SATA 7, 46
  See also CLR 50
Hymes, Lucia M(anley) 1907-1998 7
Hyndman, Jane Andrews Lee 1912-1978 46
  Obituary 23
  Earlier sketch in SATA 1
Hyndman, Robert Utley 1906-1973 18
Hynes, Pat 98

I

Iannone, Jeanne
  See Balzano, Jeanne (Koppel)
Ibatoulline, Bagram 1965(?)- 174
Ibbitson, John Perrie 1955- 102
Ibbotson, Eva 1925-2010 221
  Earlier sketches in SATA 13, 103, 156
Ibbotson, M. C(hristine) 1930- 5
Icenoggle, Jodi 1967- 168
Icenoggle, Jodi O.
  See Icenoggle, Jodi
Ichikawa, Satomi 1949- 208
  Brief entry 36
  Earlier sketches in SATA 47, 78, 146
  See also CLR 62
Iggulden, Hal 1972- 196
Ignoffo, Matthew 1945- 92
Igus, Toyomi 1953- 112
  Earlier sketch in SATA 76
Ihimaera, Witi (Tame) 1944- 148
Ikeda, Daisaku 1928- 77
Ilowite, Sheldon A. 1931- 27
Ilsey, Dent
  See Chapman, John Stanton Higham
Ilsley, Dent
  See Chapman, John Stanton Higham
Ilsley, Velma (Elizabeth) 1918- 12
Imai, Ayano 1980- 190
Imai, Miko 1963- 90
Imershein, Betsy 1953- 62
Immel, Mary Blair 1930- 28
Immell, Myra H. 1941- 92
Impey, Rose 1947- 152
  Earlier sketch in SATA 69
Ingelow, Jean 1820-1897 33
Ingermanson, Randall 1958- 134
Ingermanson, Randy
  See Ingermanson, Randall
Ingersoll, Norman 1928- 79
Ingham, Colonel Frederic
  See Hale, Edward Everett
Ingman, Bruce 1963- 182
  Earlier sketch in SATA 134
Ingman, Nicholas 1948- 52
Ingold, Jeanette 128
Ingpen, Robert 1936- 166
  Earlier sketch in SATA 109
Ingpen, Robert Roger
  See Ingpen, Robert
Ingraham, Erick 1950- 145
Ingraham, Leonard W(illiam) 1913-2003 4
Ingram, Scott 1948- 167
  Earlier sketch in SATA 92
Ingram, W. Scott
  See Ingram, Scott
Ingrams, Doreen 1906-1997 97
  Earlier sketch in SATA 20
Ingrid, Charles
  See Salsitz, Rhondi Vilott
Ingves, Gunilla 1939- 101
Ingves, Gunilla Anna Maria Folkesdotter
  See Ingves, Gunilla

Inkpen, Mick 1952- 154
  Earlier sketch in SATA 99
Innes, (Ralph) Hammond
  See Hammond Innes, Ralph
Innes, Ralph Hammond
  See Hammond Innes, Ralph
Innes, Stephanie 220
Innocenti, Roberto 1940- 159
  Earlier sketch in SATA 96
  See also CLR 126
Innocenti and Gallaz
  See Gallaz, Christophe
  and Innocenti, Roberto
Inns, Chris 212
Inyart, Gene
  See Namovicz, Gene Inyart
Ionesco, Eugene 1909-1994 7
  Obituary 79
Ipcar, Dahlov (Zorach) 1917- 147
  Autobiography Feature 147
  Earlier sketches in SATA 1, 49
  See also SAAS 8
Ireland, Karin 151
  Earlier sketch in SATA 101
Ironside, Jetske 1940- 60
Irvin, Fred 1914- 15
Irvine, Georgeanne 1955- 72
Irvine, Joan 1951- 80
Irving, Alexander
  See Hume, Ruth Fox
Irving, Robert
  See Adler, Irving
Irving, Washington 1783-1859
  See YABC 2
  See also CLR 97
Irwin, Ann(abelle Bowen) 1915-1998 89
  Brief entry 38
  Obituary 106
  Earlier sketch in SATA 44
  See also CLR 40
  See also SAAS 14
Irwin, Constance (H.) Frick 1913-1995 6
Irwin, Hadley
  See Hadley, Lee
  and Irwin, Ann(abelle Bowen)
Irwin, Keith Gordon 1885-1964 11
Isaac, Joanne 1934- 21
Isaacs, Anne 1949- 185
  Earlier sketch in SATA 90
Isaacs, Jacob
  See Kranzler, George G(ershon)
Isaacson, Philip M(arshal) 1924- 87
Isadora, Rachel 1953(?)- 204
  Brief entry 32
  Earlier sketches in SATA 54, 79, 121, 165
  See also CLR 7
Isbell, Rebecca T(emple) 1942- 125
Isham, Charlotte H(ickock) 1912- 21
Ishida, Jui 176
Ish-Kishor, Judith 1892-1972 11
Ish-Kishor, Sulamith 1896-1977 17
Ishmael, Woodi 1914-1995 31
  Obituary 109
Isle, Sue 1963- 105
Isol 1972- 220
Israel, Elaine 1945- 12
Israel, Marion Louise 1882-1973
  Obituary 26
Iterson, S(iny) R(ose) Van
  See Van Iterson, S(iny) R(ose)
Ivanko, John D. 1966- 111
Ivanko, John Duane
  See Ivanko, John D.
Iversen, Jeremy 1980(?)- 174
Iversen, Jeremy Watt
  See Iversen, Jeremy
Iverson, Carol (L.) 1941- 145
Iverson, Diane 1950- 122
Iverson, Eric G.
  See Turtledove, Harry
Ivery, Martha M. 1948- 124

Ives, David 1951- 173
Ives, Morgan
  See Bradley, Marion Zimmer
Ives, Penny 1956- 215
Iwai, Melissa 183
Iwamatsu, Jun Atsushi 1908-1994 81
  Earlier sketch in SATA 14
  See also CLR 4
Iwamura, Kazuo 1939- 213
Iwasaki (Matsumoto), Chihiro 1918-1974
  See CLR 18
Iyengar, Malathi Michelle 1954- 220

J

Jabar, Cynthia 210
Jablonski, Carla 184
Jac, Lee
  See Morton, Lee Jack, Jr.
Jacka, Martin 1943- 72
Jackson, Alison 1953- 160
  Earlier sketches in SATA 73, 108
Jackson, Anne 1896(?)-1984
  Obituary 37
Jackson, Barry
  See Jackson, Barry E.
Jackson, Barry E. 200
Jackson, C(aary) Paul 1902-1991 6
Jackson, Caary
  See Jackson, C(aary) Paul
Jackson, Charlotte E. (Cobden) 1903(?)-1989
  Obituary 62
Jackson, Dave
  See Jackson, J. David
Jackson, Donna M. 1959- 206
Jackson, Ellen 1943- 214
  Earlier sketches in SATA 75, 115, 167
Jackson, Ellen B.
  See Jackson, Ellen
Jackson, Garnet Nelson 1944- 87
Jackson, Geoffrey (Holt Seymour) 1915-1987
  Obituary 53
Jackson, Gina
  See Fluke, Joanne
Jackson, Guida M. 1930- 71
Jackson, J. David 1944- 91
Jackson, Jacqueline 1928- 65
Jackson, Jacqueline Dougan
  See Jackson, Jacqueline
Jackson, Jesse 1908-1983 29
  Obituary 48
  Earlier sketch in SATA 2
  See also CLR 28
Jackson, Marjorie 1928- 127
Jackson, Melanie 1956- 141
Jackson, Mike 1946- 91
Jackson, Neta J. 1944- 91
Jackson, O. B.
  See Jackson, C(aary) Paul
Jackson, Rob 1961- 176
Jackson, Robert B(lake) 1926- 8
Jackson, Robert Bradley
  See Jackson, Rob
Jackson, Sally
  See Kellogg, Jean (Defrees)
Jackson, Shirley 1919-1965 2
Jackson, Woody 1948- 92
Jackson Issa, Kai 205
Jacob, Helen Pierce 1927- 21
Jacobin
  See Bisson, Terry
Jacobs, Deborah Lynn 187
Jacobs, Flora Gill 1918-2006 5
  Obituary 178
Jacobs, Francine 1935- 150
  Brief entry 42
  Earlier sketch in SATA 43
Jacobs, Frank 1929- 30
Jacobs, Helen Hull 1908-1997 12

Jacobs, Joseph 1854-1916 .... *25*
Jacobs, Judy 1952- *69*
Jacobs, Laurie A. 1956- *89*
Jacobs, Leah
   See Gellis, Roberta
Jacobs, Lee
   See Stone, Tanya Lee
Jacobs, Leland Blair 1907-1992 .... *20*
   Obituary *71*
Jacobs, Linda
   See Altman, Linda Jacobs
Jacobs, Lou(is), Jr. 1921- *2*
Jacobs, Shannon K. 1947- *77*
Jacobs, Susan
   See Quinn, Susan
Jacobs, William Jay 1933- *89*
   Earlier sketch in SATA *28*
Jacobsen, Laura *177*
Jacobson, Daniel 1923- *12*
Jacobson, Jennifer
   See Jacobson, Jennifer Richard
Jacobson, Jennifer Richard 1958- *170*
Jacobson, Morris K(arl) 1906- *21*
Jacobson, Rick *170*
Jacopetti, Alexandra
   See Hart, Alexandra
Jacques, Brian 1939- *176*
   Earlier sketches in SATA *62, 95, 138*
   See also CLR *21*
Jacques, Robin 1920-1995 .... *32*
   Brief entry *30*
   Obituary *86*
   See also SAAS *5*
Jaekel, Susan M. 1948- *89*
Jaffe, Michele *179*
Jaffe, Michele Sharon
   See Jaffe, Michele
Jaffee, Al(lan) 1921- *66*
   Earlier sketch in SATA *37*
Jagendorf, Moritz (Adolf) 1888-1981 .... *2*
   Obituary *24*
Jago 1979- *216*
Jahn, Joseph Michael
   See Jahn, Michael
Jahn, Michael 1943- *28*
Jahn, Mike
   See Jahn, Michael
Jahn-Clough, Lisa 1967- *193*
   Earlier sketches in SATA *88, 152*
Jahsmann, Allan Hart 1916- *28*
Jakes, John 1932- *62*
Jakes, John William
   See Jakes, John
James, Andrew
   See Kirkup, James
James, Ann 1952- *168*
   Earlier sketches in SATA *82, 117*
James, Betsy *183*
James, Bill 1929- *205*
James, B.J.
   See James, Brian
James, Brian 1976- *212*
   Earlier sketch in SATA *140*
James, Bronte
   See Nash, Renea Denise
James, Captain Lew
   See Stratemeyer, Edward L.
James, Charlie 1961- *185*
James, Curtis E. *182*
James, Dynely
   See Mayne, William
James, Edwin
   See Gunn, James E.
James, Elizabeth 1942- *97*
   Earlier sketches in SATA *39, 45, 52*
James, Emily
   See Standiford, Natalie
James, Gordon C. 1973- *195*
James, Harry Clebourne 1896-1978 .... *11*
James, J. Alison 1962- *146*
   Earlier sketch in SATA *83*

James, Josephine
   See Sterne, Emma Gelders
James, Mary
   See Meaker, Marijane
James, Matt *201*
James, Philip
   See del Rey, Lester
   and Moorcock, Michael
James, Robin 1953- *50*
James, Robin Irene
   See James, Robin
James, Simon 1961- *202*
James, T. F.
   See Fleming, Thomas
James, Tegan
   See Odgers, Sally Farrell
James, Will(iam Roderick) 1892-1942 .... *19*
Jameson, W. C. 1942- *93*
Jamieson, Ian R.
   See Goulart, Ron
Jamieson, Victoria *218*
Jamiolkowski, Raymond M. 1953- *81*
Jane, Mary Childs 1909- *6*
Jane, Pamela *158*
Janeczko, Paul B(ryan) 1945- *155*
   Earlier sketches in SATA *53, 98*
   See also CLR *47*
   See also SAAS *18*
Janes, Edward C. 1908-1984 .... *25*
Janes, Edward Clarence
   See Janes, Edward C.
Janes, J(oseph) Robert 1935- *148*
   Brief entry *50*
   Earlier sketch in SATA *101*
Janeway, Elizabeth (Hall) 1913-2005 .... *19*
Janger, Kathleen N. 1940- *66*
Jango-Cohen, Judith 1955- *208*
Janice
   See Brustlein, Janice Tworkov
Janisch, Heinz 1960- *181*
Janosch
   See Eckert, Horst
Janover, Caroline (Davis) 1943- *141*
   Earlier sketch in SATA *89*
Janovitz, Marilyn *194*
Jansen, Jared
   See Cebulash, Mel
Janson, Dora Jane (Heineberg) 1916- *31*
Janson, H(orst) W(oldemar) 1913-1982 .... *9*
Jansson, Tove (Marika) 1914-2001 .... *41*
   Earlier sketch in SATA *3*
   See also CLR *125*
Janus, Grete
   See Hertz, Grete Janus
Jaques, Faith 1923-1997 .... *97*
   Earlier sketches in SATA *21, 69*
Jaquith, Priscilla 1908- *51*
Jaramillo, Mari-Luci 1928- *139*
Jarka, Jeff *221*
Jarman, Julia 1946- *198*
   Earlier sketch in SATA *133*
Jarman, Rosemary Hawley 1935- *7*
Jarrell, Mary Von Schrader 1914- *35*
Jarrell, Randall 1914-1965 .... *7*
   See also CLR *111*
Jarrett, Clare 1952- *201*
Jarrett, Roxanne
   See Werner, Herma
Jarrie, Martin 1953- *219*
Jarrow, Gail 1952- *185*
   Earlier sketch in SATA *84*
Jarvis, E.K.
   See Ellison, Harlan
   and Silverberg, Robert
Jarvis, Robin 1963- *181*
Jaskol, Julie 1958- *127*
Jasner, W. K.
   See Watson, Jane Werner
Jassem, Kate
   See Oppenheim, Joanne

Jauss, Anne Marie 1902(?)-1991 .... *10*
   Obituary *69*
Javernick, Ellen 1938- *217*
   Earlier sketch in SATA *89*
Javins, Marie 1966- *212*
Jay, Alison *196*
Jayne, Lieutenant R. H.
   See Ellis, Edward S.
Jaynes, Clare
   See Mayer, Jane Rothschild
Jeake, Samuel, Jr.
   See Aiken, Conrad
Jean-Bart, Leslie 1954- *121*
Jeapes, Ben 1965- *174*
Jecan, Gavriel 1962- *200*
Jefferds, Vincent H(arris) 1916- *59*
   Brief entry *49*
Jefferies, (John) Richard 1848-1887 .... *16*
Jeffers, Dawn *189*
Jeffers, Oliver 1977- *213*
   Earlier sketch in SATA *175*
Jeffers, Susan 1942- *202*
   Earlier sketches in SATA *17, 70, 129, 137*
   See also CLR *30*
Jefferson, Sarah
   See Farjeon, (Eve) Annabel
Jeffries, Roderic 1926- *4*
Jeffries, Roderic Graeme
   See Jeffries, Roderic
Jenkin-Pearce, Susie 1943- *80*
Jenkins, A. M. 1961- *174*
Jenkins, Amanda McRaney
   See Jenkins, A. M.
Jenkins, Debra Reid
   See Reid Jenkins, Debra
Jenkins, Emily 1967- *174*
   Earlier sketch in SATA *144*
Jenkins, Jean *98*
Jenkins, Jerry B. 1949- *149*
Jenkins, Jerry Bruce
   See Jenkins, Jerry B.
Jenkins, Leonard *189*
Jenkins, Marie M(agdalen) 1909- *7*
Jenkins, Martin 1959- *216*
Jenkins, M.D.
   See Jenkins, Martin
Jenkins, Patrick 1955- *72*
Jenkins, Steve 1952- *218*
   Earlier sketches in SATA *154, 188*
Jenkins, William A(twell) 1922-1998 .... *9*
Jenkyns, Chris 1924- *51*
Jennewein, James *215*
Jennewein, Jim
   See Jennewein, James
Jennings, Christopher S. 1971(?)- *201*
Jennings, Coleman A(lonzo) 1933- *64*
Jennings, C.S.
   See Jennings, Christopher S.
Jennings, Dana Andrew 1957- *93*
Jennings, Elizabeth (Joan) 1926-2001 .... *66*
Jennings, Gary 1928-1999 .... *9*
   Obituary *117*
Jennings, Gary Gayne
   See Jennings, Gary
Jennings, Linda 1937- *211*
Jennings, Linda M.
   See Jennings, Linda
Jennings, Patrick 1962- *205*
   Earlier sketches in SATA *96, 160*
Jennings, Paul 1943- *165*
   Earlier sketch in SATA *88*
   See also CLR *40*
Jennings, Richard W. 1945- *185*
   Earlier sketch in SATA *136*
Jennings, Robert
   See Hamilton, Charles (Harold St. John)
Jennings, S. M.
   See Meyer, Jerome Sydney
Jennings, Sharon 1954- *95*
Jennings, Sharon Elizabeth
   See Jennings, Sharon

Jennison, C. S.
  See Starbird, Kaye
Jennison, Keith Warren 1911-1995 .... *14*
Jensen, Kathryn 1949- *81*
Jensen, Kristine Mary 1961- *78*
Jensen, Niels 1927- *25*
Jensen, Vickie (Dee) 1946- *81*
Jensen, Virginia Allen 1927- *8*
Jenson-Elliott, Cynthia L(ouise) 1962- *143*
Jeram, Anita 1965- *219*
  Earlier sketches in SATA *71, 102, 154*
Jerman, Jerry 1949- *89*
Jernigan, E. Wesley 1940- *85*
Jernigan, Gisela (Evelyn) 1948- *85*
Jeschke, Susan 1942- *42*
  Brief entry *27*
Jessel, Camilla (Ruth) 1937- *143*
  Earlier sketch in SATA *29*
Jessell, Tim *177*
Jessey, Cornelia
  See Sussman, Cornelia Silver
Jewel
  See Kilcher, Jewel
Jewell, Nancy 1940- *109*
  Brief entry *41*
Jewett, Eleanore Myers 1890-1967 .... *5*
Jewett, Sarah Orne 1849-1909 .... *15*
Jewett, Theodora Sarah Orne
  See Jewett, Sarah Orne
Jezard, Alison 1919- *57*
  Brief entry *34*
Jiang, Cheng An 1943- *109*
Jiang, Ji-li 1954- *101*
Jiang, Zheng An
  See Jiang, Cheng An
Jiler, John 1946- *42*
  Brief entry *35*
Jimenez, Francisco 1943- *219*
  Earlier sketch in SATA *108*
Jinks, Catherine 1963- *207*
  Earlier sketches in SATA *94, 155*
Jobb, Jamie 1945- *29*
Jobling, Curtis *131*
Jocelyn, Ann Henning 1948- *92*
Jocelyn, Marthe 1956- *198*
  Earlier sketches in SATA *118, 163*
Joerns, Consuelo *44*
  Brief entry *33*
Joey D
  See Macaulay, Teresa
Johansen, Krista V.
  See Johansen, K.V.
Johansen, K.V. 1968- *186*
Johansen, K.V. 1968- *186*
  Earlier sketch in SATA *129*
Johansson, Philip *163*
John, Antony 1972- *206*
John, Joyce *59*
Johns, Avery
  See Cousins, Margaret
Johns, Elizabeth 1943- *88*
Johns, Janetta
  See Quin-Harkin, Janet
Johns, Linda 1945- *173*
Johns, W(illiam) E(arle) 1893-1968 .... *55*
Johns, Captain W. E.
  See Johns, W(illiam) E(arle)
Johnson, A.
  See Johnson, Annabell
Johnson, A. E.
  See Johnson, Annabell
  and Johnson, Edgar (Raymond)
Johnson, Angela 1961- *188*
  Earlier sketches in SATA *69, 102, 150*
  See also CLR *33*
Johnson, Annabel
  See Johnson, Annabell
Johnson, Annabell 1921- *72*
  Earlier sketch in SATA *2*
Johnson, Art 1946- *123*
Johnson, B. F. 1920- *1*

Johnson, Benjamin F., of Boone
  See Riley, James Whitcomb
Johnson, Bettye 1858-1919
  See Rogers, Bettye
Johnson, Caryn
  See Goldberg, Whoopi
Johnson, Caryn E.
  See Goldberg, Whoopi
Johnson, Caryn Elaine
  See Goldberg, Whoopi
Johnson, Charles R. 1925- *11*
Johnson, Charlotte Buel
  See von Wodtke, Charlotte Buel Johnson
Johnson, Chuck
  See Johnson, Charles R.
Johnson, Crockett
  See Leisk, David (Johnson)
Johnson, D(ana) William 1945- *23*
Johnson, Daniel Shahid 1954- *73*
Johnson, David
  See Johnson, David A.
Johnson, David A. 1951- *191*
Johnson, D.B. 1944- *183*
  Earlier sketch in SATA *146*
Johnson, Dianne 1960- *130*
Johnson, Dinah
  See Johnson, Dianne
Johnson, Dolores 1949- *69*
Johnson, Donald B.
  See Johnson, D.B.
Johnson, Dorothy M(arie) 1905-1984 .... *6*
  Obituary *40*
Johnson, E(ugene) Harper *44*
Johnson, Edgar (Raymond) 1912-1990 .... *72*
  Earlier sketch in SATA *2*
Johnson, Eleanor Murdock 1892-1987
  Obituary *54*
Johnson, Elizabeth 1911-1984 .... *7*
  Obituary *39*
Johnson, Eric W(arner) 1918-1994 ....
  Obituary *82*
  Earlier sketch in SATA *8*
Johnson, Evelyne 1922- *20*
Johnson, Fred 19(?)-1982 .... *63*
Johnson, Gaylord 1884-1972 .... *7*
Johnson, Gerald White 1890-1980 .... *19*
  Obituary *28*
Johnson, Gillian 1963- *215*
Johnson, Harper
  See Johnson, E(ugene) Harper
Johnson, Harriett 1908-1987
  Obituary *53*
Johnson, James Ralph 1922- *1*
Johnson, James Weldon 1871-1938 .... *31*
  See also CLR *32*
Johnson, Jane 1951- *48*
Johnson, Joan J. 1942- *59*
Johnson, John E(mil) 1929- *34*
Johnson, Johnny 1901-1995
  See Johnson, (Walter) Ryerson
Johnson, Kathleen Jeffrie 1950- *186*
Johnson, La Verne B(ravo) 1925- *13*
Johnson, Layne *187*
Johnson, Lee Kaiser 1962- *78*
Johnson, Lissa H(alls) 1955- *65*
Johnson, Lois Smith 1894-1993 .... *6*
Johnson, Lois Walfrid 1936- *130*
  Earlier sketches in SATA *22, 91*
Johnson, Margaret S(weet) 1893-1964 .... *35*
Johnson, Marguerite Annie
  See Angelou, Maya
Johnson, Mary Frances K. 1929(?)-1979
  Obituary *27*
Johnson, Maud Battle 1918(?)-1985
  Obituary *46*
Johnson, Maureen 1973- *200*
Johnson, Meredith Merrell 1952- *104*
Johnson, Milton 1932- *31*
Johnson, Neil 1954- *135*
  Earlier sketch in SATA *73*
Johnson, Pamela 1949- *71*

Johnson, Patricia Polin 1956- *84*
Johnson, Paul Brett 1947- *132*
  Earlier sketch in SATA *83*
Johnson, Rebecca L. 1956- *147*
  Earlier sketch in SATA *67*
Johnson, Rick L. 1954- *79*
Johnson, (Walter) Ryerson 1901-1995 .... *10*
  Obituary *106*
Johnson, Scott 1952- *119*
  Earlier sketch in SATA *76*
Johnson, Sherrie 1948- *87*
Johnson, Shirley K(ing) 1927- *10*
Johnson, Siddie Joe 1905-1977
  Obituary *20*
Johnson, Spencer 1938- *145*
  Brief entry *38*
Johnson, Stacie
  See Myers, Walter Dean
Johnson, Stephen T. 1964- *189*
  Earlier sketches in SATA *84, 141*
Johnson, Steve 1960- *177*
Johnson, Sue Kaiser 1963- *78*
Johnson, Sylvia A. *166*
  Brief entry *52*
  Earlier sketch in SATA *104*
Johnson, William R. *38*
Johnson, William Weber 1909-1992 .... *7*
Johnson-Feelings, Dianne
  See Johnson, Dianne
Johnston, Agnes Christine
  See Dazey, Agnes J(ohnston)
Johnston, Annie Fellows 1863-1931 .... *37*
Johnston, Dorothy Grunbock 1915-1979 ...... *54*
Johnston, Ginny 1946- *60*
Johnston, H(ugh) A(nthony) S(tephen)
  1913-1967 .... *14*
Johnston, Janet 1944- *71*
Johnston, Jeffry W. *188*
Johnston, Johanna 1914(?)-1982 .... *12*
  Obituary *33*
Johnston, Julie 1941- *110*
  Autobiography Feature *128*
  Earlier sketch in SATA *78*
  See also CLR *41*
  See also SAAS *24*
Johnston, Lynn 1947- *216*
  Earlier sketch in SATA *118*
Johnston, Lynn Beverley
  See Johnston, Lynn
Johnston, Mark *194*
Johnston, Norma
  See St. John, Nicole
Johnston, Portia
  See Takakjian, Portia
Johnston, Susan Taylor 1942- *180*
  Earlier sketches in SATA *8, 83, 128*
Johnston, Tim(othy Patrick) 1962- *146*
Johnston, Tony
  See Johnston, Susan Taylor
Joinson, Carla *160*
Jolin, Paula *186*
Jolivet, Joelle 1965- *221*
Jonas, Ann 1932- *135*
  Brief entry *42*
  Earlier sketch in SATA *50*
  See also CLR *74*
Jonell, Lynne 1956- *196*
  Earlier sketch in SATA *109*
Jones, Adrienne 1915-2000 .... *82*
  Earlier sketch in SATA *7*
  See also SAAS *10*
Jones, Allan Frewin 1954- *204*
Jones, Annabel
  See Lewis, Mary
Jones, Betty Millsaps 1940- *54*
Jones, Carol 1942- *153*
  Earlier sketch in SATA *79*
Jones, Carrie 1971- *191*
Jones, Charles M.
  See Jones, Chuck

Jones, Charlotte Foltz 1945- 122
  Earlier sketch in SATA 77
Jones, Chuck 1912-2002 53
  Obituary 133
Jones, Constance 112
Jones, Constance A.
  See Jones, Constance
Jones, David 1956- 202
Jones, Diana Wynne 1934- 160
  Earlier sketches in SATA 9, 70, 108
  See also CLR 120
  See also SAAS 7
Jones, Douglas B. 202
Jones, Douglas C(lyde) 1924-1998 52
Jones, Elizabeth McDavid 155
Jones, Elizabeth Orton 1910-2005 18
  Obituary 164
Jones, Evan 1915-1996 3
Jones, Frewin
  See Jones, Allan Frewin
Jones, Geraldine
  See McCaughrean, Geraldine
Jones, Gillingham
  See Hamilton, Charles (Harold St. John)
Jones, Gwyneth A. 1952- 159
Jones, Gwyneth Ann
  See Jones, Gwyneth A.
Jones, Harold 1904-1992 14
  Obituary 72
Jones, Helen Hinckley 1903-1991 26
Jones, Helen L(ouise) 1903-1973
  Obituary 22
Jones, Hettie 1934- 42
  Brief entry 27
Jones, Hortense P. 1918- 9
Jones, J. Sydney 1948- 101
Jones, Jasmine
  See Papademetriou, Lisa
Jones, Jennifer (Berry) 1947- 90
Jones, Jessie Mae Orton 1887(?)-1983
  Obituary 37
Jones, John R(obert) 1926- 76
Jones, Jon Sydney
  See Jones, J. Sydney
Jones, Judith
  See James, Bill
Jones, Kimberly K. 1957- 187
Jones, Marcia Thornton 1958- 217
  Earlier sketches in SATA 73, 115
Jones, Martha T(annery) 1931- 130
Jones, Mary Alice 1898(?)-1980 6
Jones, McClure 34
Jones, Noah Z. 182
Jones, Patrick 1961- 210
  Earlier sketch in SATA 136
Jones, Penelope 1938- 31
Jones, Rebecca C(astaldi) 1947- 99
  Earlier sketch in SATA 33
Jones, Robin D(orothy) 1959- 80
Jones, Sanford W.
  See Thorn, John
Jones, Sylvie 185
Jones, Sylvie Michelle
  See Jones, Sylvie
Jones, Terence Graham Parry 1942- 127
  Brief entry 51
  Earlier sketch in SATA 67
Jones, Terry
  See Jones, Terence Graham Parry
Jones, Tim Wynne
  See Wynne-Jones, Tim
Jones, Traci L. 186
Jones, V. M. 1958- 147
Jones, Veda Boyd 1948- 119
Jones, Victoria Mary
  See Jones, V. M.
Jones, Volcano
  See Mitchell, Adrian
Jones, Weyman (B.) 1928- 4
  See also SAAS 11

Jones, William Glynne
  See Glynne-Jones, William
Jonk, Clarence 1906-1987 10
Jonsberg, Barry 1951- 168
Joos, Francoise 1956- 78
Joos, Frederic 1953- 78
Joosse, Barbara 1949- 220
  Earlier sketches in SATA 52, 96, 164
Joosse, Barbara M.
  See Joosse, Barbara
Joosse, Barbara Monnot
  See Joosse, Barbara
Jordan, Alexis Hill
  See Glick, Ruth (Burtnick)
  and Titchener, Louise
Jordan, Anne Devereaux 1943- 80
Jordan, Chris
  See Philbrick, Rodman
Jordan, Deloris 191
Jordan, Devin 221
Jordan, Don
  See Howard, Vernon (Linwood)
Jordan, Hope Dahle 1905-1995 15
Jordan, Jael (Michal) 1949- 30
Jordan, June 1936-2002 136
  Earlier sketch in SATA 4
  See also CLR 10
Jordan, June Meyer
  See Jordan, June
Jordan, Lee
  See Scholefield, Alan
Jordan, Martin George 1944- 84
Jordan, Robert 1948-2007 95
Jordan, Robert K.
  See Jordan, Robert
Jordan, Rosa 1939- 191
Jordan, Roslyn M. 189
Jordan, Sherryl 1949- 122
  Earlier sketch in SATA 71
  See also SAAS 23
Jordan, Shirley 1930- 154
Jordan, Tanis 1946- 84
Jorgensen, Ivar
  See Ellison, Harlan
  and Garrett, Randall
Jorgensen, Mary Venn -1995 36
Jorgensen, Norman 1954- 157
Jorgenson, Ivar
  See Silverberg, Robert
Jorisch, Stephane 178
Joseph, Anne
  See Coates, Anna
Joseph, James (Herz) 1924- 53
Joseph, Joan 1939- 34
Joseph, Joseph M(aron) 1903-1979 22
Joseph, Patrick
  See O'Malley, Kevin
Josephs, Rebecca
  See Talbot, Toby
Josephson, Judith Pinkerton 1943- 198
Josh
  See Twain, Mark
Joshua, Peter
  See Stone, Peter
Joslin, Mary 1953- 176
Joslin, Sesyle
  See Hine, Sesyle Joslin
Joubert, Beverly 1957- 204
Joubert, Dereck 204
Journet, Mireille
  See Marokvia, Mireille
Joyce, Bill
  See Joyce, William
Joyce, J(ames) Avery 1902-1987 11
  Obituary 50
Joyce, Peter 1937- 127
Joyce, William 1957- 118
  Brief entry 46
  Earlier sketch in SATA 72
  See also CLR 26
Joyner, Jerry 1938- 34

Juan, Ana 1961- 179
Jubb, Sophie 210
Jubert, Herve 185
Juby, Susan 1969- 202
  Earlier sketch in SATA 156
Jucker, Sita 1921- 5
Judah, Aaron 1923- 118
Judd, Cyril
  See Kornbluth, C(yril) M.
  and Merril, Judith
  and Pohl, Frederik
Judd, Denis (O'Nan) 1938- 33
Judd, Frances K.
  See Benson, Mildred
Jude, Conny 81
Judge, Lita 192
Judson, Clara Ingram 1879-1960 38
  Brief entry 27
Judy, Stephen
  See Tchudi, Stephen N.
Judy, Stephen N.
  See Tchudi, Stephen N.
Juhasz, Victor 1954- 177
Jukes, Mavis 1947- 219
  Brief entry 43
  Earlier sketches in SATA 72, 111
  See also SAAS 12
Jules, Jacqueline 1956- 218
  Earlier sketches in SATA 148, 183
Julesberg, Elizabeth Rider Montgomery
  1902-1985 34
  Obituary 41
  Earlier sketch in SATA 3
Julian, Jane
  See Wiseman, David
Jumpp, Hugo
  See MacPeek, Walter G.
Junco, Martha Aviles
  See Aviles, Martha
Jungman, Ann 165
Jupo, Frank J. 1904-1981 7
Jurmain, Suzanne 1945- 169
  Earlier sketch in SATA 72
Jurmain, Suzanne Tripp
  See Jurmain, Suzanne
Juster, Norton 1929- 220
  Earlier sketches in SATA 3, 132
  See also CLR 112
Justus, May 1898-1989 1
  Obituary 106
Juvenilia
  See Taylor, Ann

K

Kaaberbol, Lene
  See Kaaberbol, Lene
Kaaberbol, Lene 1960- 159
Kabdebo, Tamas
  See Kabdebo, Thomas
Kabdebo, Thomas 1934- 10
Kabibble, Osh
  See Jobb, Jamie
Kacer, Kathy 1954- 184
  Earlier sketch in SATA 142
Kaczman, James 156
Kadair, Deborah Ousley 184
Kadefors, Sara 1965- 218
Kadesch, Robert R(udstone) 1922- 31
Kadohata, Cynthia 1956(?)- 180
  Earlier sketch in SATA 155
  See also CLR 121
Kadohata, Cynthia L.
  See Kadohata, Cynthia
Kaempfert, Wade
  See del Rey, Lester
Kaestner, Erich 1899-1974 14
  See also CLR 153
Kahl, Jonathan (D.) 1959- 77

Kahl, M(arvin) P(hilip) 1934- *37*
Kahl, Virginia (Caroline) 1919-2004 .... *48*
  Brief entry *38*
  Obituary *158*
Kahn, Joan 1914-1994 .... *48*
  Obituary *82*
Kahn, Katherine Janus 1942- *220*
  Earlier sketches in SATA *90, 167*
Kahn, Peggy
  See Katz, Bobbi
Kahn, Roger 1927- *37*
Kahukiwa, Robyn 1940- *134*
Kains, Josephine
  See Goulart, Ron
Kaizuki, Kiyonori 1950- *72*
Kajikawa, Kimiko *212*
Kakimoto, Kozo 1915- *11*
Kalashnikoff, Nicholas 1888-1961 .... *16*
Kalb, Jonah 1926- *23*
Kalbacken, Joan 1925- *96*
Kalechofsky, Roberta 1931- *92*
Kaler, James Otis 1848-1912 .... *15*
Kalis, Jennifer *207*
Kalish, Claire M. 1947- *92*
Kallen, Stuart A. 1955- *126*
  Earlier sketch in SATA *86*
Kallen, Stuart Arnold
  See Kallen, Stuart A.
Kallevig, Christine Petrell 1955- *164*
Kalman, Bobbie 1947- *63*
Kalman, Maira 1949- *137*
  Earlier sketch in SATA *96*
  See also CLR *32*
Kalnay, Francis 1899-1992 .... *7*
Kaloustian, Rosanne 1955- *93*
Kalow, Gisela 1946- *32*
Kalstein, Dave *175*
Kamara, Mariatu *214*
Kamen, Gloria 1923- *98*
  Earlier sketch in SATA *9*
Kamerman, Sylvia E.
  See Burack, Sylvia K.
Kamm, Josephine (Hart) 1905-1989 .... *24*
Kammerman, Sylvia K.
  See Burack, Sylvia K.
Kandel, Michael 1941- *93*
Kandell, Alice S. 1938- *35*
Kane, Bob 1916-1998 .... *120*
Kane, Henry Bugbee 1902-1971 .... *14*
Kane, Kim 1973(?)- *221*
Kane, L. A.
  See Mannetti, Lisa
Kane, Robert W. 1910- *18*
Kane, Wilson
  See Bloch, Robert (Albert)
Kanefield, Teri 1960- *135*
Kanell, Beth *215*
Kaner, Etta 1947- *198*
  Earlier sketch in SATA *126*
Kanetzke, Howard W(illiam) 1932- *38*
Kangas, Juli 1958- *200*
Kann, Elizabeth *180*
Kann, Victoria *180*
Kanninen, Barbara *196*
Kanninen, Barbara J.
  See Kanninen, Barbara
Kanoza, Muriel Canfield
  See Canfield, Muriel
Kantner, Seth 1965- *179*
Kanzawa, Toshiko
  See Furukawa, Toshi
Kanzler, John 1963- *188*
Kaplan, Andrew 1960- *78*
Kaplan, Anne Bernays
  See Bernays, Anne
Kaplan, Bess 1927- *22*
Kaplan, Boche 1926- *24*
Kaplan, Elizabeth 1956- *83*
Kaplan, Elizabeth A.
  See Kaplan, Elizabeth
Kaplan, Irma 1900- *10*

Kaplan, Jean Caryl Korn 1926- *10*
Kaplow, Robert 1954- *70*
Karageorge, Michael
  See Anderson, Poul
Karas, G. Brian 1957- *178*
Karas, George Brian
  See Karas, G. Brian
Karasz, Ilonka 1896-1981
  Obituary *29*
Karen, Ruth 1922-1987 .... *9*
  Obituary *54*
Kark, Nina Mary
  See Bawden, Nina
Karl, Herb 1938- *73*
Karl, Jean E(dna) 1927-2000 .... *122*
  Earlier sketch in SATA *34*
  See also SAAS *10*
Karlin, Bernie 1927- *68*
Karlin, Eugene 1918- *10*
Karlin, Nurit *103*
  Earlier sketch in SATA *63*
Karlins, Mark 1947- *219*
Karnes, Frances A. 1937- *110*
Karp, Naomi J. 1926- *16*
Karpinski, J. Rick
  See Karpinski, John Eric
Karpinski, John Eric 1952- *81*
Karpinski, Rick
  See Karpinski, John Eric
Karr, Kathleen 1946- *212*
  Earlier sketches in SATA *82, 127*
Karr, Phyllis Ann 1944- *119*
Karwoski, Gail 1949- *127*
Karwoski, Gail Langer
  See Karwoski, Gail
Kashiwagi, Isami 1925- *10*
Kaslik, Ibi
  See Kaslik, Ibolya Emma
Kaslik, Ibolya Emma 1973- *185*
Kassem, Lou 1931- *62*
  Brief entry *51*
Kastel, Warren
  See Silverberg, Robert
Kastner, Erich
  See Kaestner, Erich
Kastner, Jill (Marie) 1964- *117*
  Earlier sketch in SATA *70*
Kasuya, Masahiro 1937- *51*
Kasza, Keiko 1951- *191*
  Earlier sketch in SATA *124*
Kataphusin
  See Ruskin, John
Katchen, Carole 1944- *9*
Katcher, Brian 1975- *203*
Kathryn
  See Searle, Kathryn Adrienne
Kato, Aya 1982- *202*
Katona, Robert 1949- *21*
Katsarakis, Joan Harries
  See Harries, Joan
Katz, Alan *185*
Katz, Avi 1949- *199*
Katz, Avner 1939- *103*
Katz, Bobbi 1933- *217*
  Earlier sketches in SATA *12, 179*
Katz, Fred(eric Phillip) 1938- *6*
Katz, Jane B(resler) 1934- *33*
Katz, Karen 1947- *195*
  Earlier sketch in SATA *158*
Katz, Marjorie P.
  See Weiser, Marjorie P(hillis) K(atz)
Katz, Susan 1941- *156*
Katz, Welwyn Wilton 1948- *96*
  Autobiography Feature *118*
  Earlier sketch in SATA *62*
  See also CLR *45*
Katz, William 1940- *98*
Katz, William Loren 1927- *13*
Kaufman, Bel *57*
Kaufman, Jeff 1955- *84*
Kaufman, Joe 1911-2001 .... *33*

Kaufman, Joseph
  See Kaufman, Joe
Kaufman, Mervyn D. 1932- *4*
Kaufmann, Angelika 1935- *15*
Kaufmann, John 1931- *18*
Kaula, Edna Mason 1906-1987 .... *13*
Kaur Khalsa, Dayal
  See Khalsa, Dayal Kaur
Kavaler, Lucy 1930- *23*
Kavanagh, Jack 1920- *85*
Kavanagh, P(atrick) J(oseph Gregory)
  1931- *122*
Kavanaugh, Ian
  See Webb, Jean Francis (III)
Kay, Alan N. 1965- *144*
Kay, Elizabeth 1949- *165*
Kay, Guy Gavriel 1954- *167*
  Earlier sketch in SATA *121*
Kay, Helen
  See Goldfrank, Helen Colodny
Kay, Jackie 1961- *165*
  Earlier sketch in SATA *97*
Kay, Jacqueline Margaret
  See Kay, Jackie
Kay, Julia *205*
Kay, Mara *13*
Kay, Verla 1946- *210*
  Earlier sketch in SATA *120*
Kaye, Danny 1913-1987
  Obituary *50*
Kaye, Geraldine (Hughesdon) 1925- *85*
  Earlier sketch in SATA *10*
Kaye, Judy
  See Baer, Judy
Kaye, Marilyn 1949- *110*
  Earlier sketch in SATA *56*
Kaye, Mary Margaret
  See Kaye, M.M.
Kaye, M.M. 1908-2004 .... *62*
  Obituary *152*
Kaye, Mollie
  See Kaye, M.M.
Kaye, Peggy 1948- *143*
Keach, James P. 1950- *125*
Keams, Geri 1951- *117*
Keane, Bil 1922- *4*
Keane, Dave 1965- *216*
Keaney, Brian 1954- *188*
  Earlier sketch in SATA *106*
Kearney, Meg 1964- *178*
Kearny, Jillian
  See Goulart, Ron
Keating, Bern
  See Keating, Leo Bernard
Keating, Frank 1944- *143*
Keating, Lawrence A. 1903-1966 .... *23*
Keating, Leo Bernard 1915- *10*
Keats, Emma 1899(?)-1979(?) *68*
Keats, Ezra Jack 1916-1983 .... *57*
  Obituary *34*
  Earlier sketch in SATA *14*
  See also CLR *35*
Keefer, Catherine
  See Ogan, George F.
  and Ogan, Margaret E. (Nettles)
Keefer, Janice Kulyk
  See Kulyk Keefer, Janice
Keegan, Marcia 1943- *104*
  Earlier sketch in SATA *9*
Keehn, Sally M. 1947- *165*
  Earlier sketch in SATA *87*
Keel, Frank
  See Keeler, Ronald F(ranklin)
Keeler, Patricia *183*
Keeler, Patricia A.
  See Keeler, Patricia
Keeler, Ronald F(ranklin) 1913-1983 .... *47*
Keely, Jack 1951- *119*
Keen, Martin L. 1913-1992 .... *4*
Keenan, Sheila 1953- *95*
Keene, Ann T. 1940- *86*

Keene, Ann Todd
  See Keene, Ann T.
Keene, Carolyn
  See Benson, Mildred
  and Goulart, Ron
  and Lerangis, Peter
  and McFarlane, Leslie
  and Stanley, George Edward
  and Stratemeyer, Edward L.
Keens-Douglas, Richardo 1953- *154*
  Earlier sketch in SATA *95*
Keep, Linda Lowery
  See Lowery, Linda
Keep, Richard 1949- *170*
Keep, Richard Cleminson
  See Keep, Richard
Keeping, Charles (William James)
  1924-1988 .... *69*
  Obituary *56*
  Earlier sketch in SATA *9*
  See also CLR *34*
Keeshan, Robert J. 1927-2004 .... *32*
  Obituary *151*
Kehlenbeck, Angela 1959- *186*
Kehret, Peg 1936- *212*
  Autobiography Feature *149*
  Earlier sketches in SATA *73, 108, 149*
Keillor, Garrison 1942- *58*
Keillor, Gary Edward
  See Keillor, Garrison
Keir, Christine
  See Pullein-Thompson, Christine
Keiser, Paige *220*
Keister, Douglas 1948- *88*
Keith, Doug 1952- *81*
Keith, Eros 1942- *52*
Keith, Hal 1934- *36*
Keith, Harold (Verne) 1903-1998 .... *74*
  Earlier sketch in SATA *2*
Keith, Robert
  See Applebaum, Stan
Keleinikov, Andrei 1924- *65*
Kelemen, Julie 1959- *78*
Kelen, Emery 1896-1978 .... *13*
  Obituary *26*
Kelleam, Joseph E(veridge) 1913-1975 .... *31*
Kelleher, Anne 1959- *97*
Kelleher, Annette 1950- *122*
Kelleher, Daria Valerian 1955- *79*
Kelleher, Victor (Michael Kitchener)
  1939- *129*
  Brief entry *52*
  Earlier sketch in SATA *75*
  See also CLR *36*
Keller, Beverly L(ou) *91*
  Earlier sketch in SATA *13*
Keller, Charles 1942- *82*
  Earlier sketch in SATA *8*
Keller, Debra 1958- *94*
Keller, Dick 1923- *36*
Keller, Emily *96*
Keller, Gail Faithfull
  See Faithfull, Gail
Keller, Holly 1942- *216*
  Brief entry *42*
  Earlier sketches in SATA *76, 108, 157*
  See also CLR *45*
Keller, Irene (Barron) 1927-2002 .... *36*
  Obituary *139*
Keller, Laurie 1961(?)- *196*
Kelley, Ann 1941- *217*
Kelley, Ellen A. *185*
Kelley, Ellen Chavez
  See Kelley, Ellen A.
Kelley, Gary 1945- *217*
  Earlier sketch in SATA *183*
Kelley, Leo P(atrick) 1928- *32*
  Brief entry *31*
Kelley, Marty 1971- *211*
Kelley, Patrick (G.) 1963- *129*
Kelley, Patte 1947- *93*

Kelley, True 1946- *179*
Kelley, True (Adelaide) 1946- *130*
  Brief entry *39*
  Earlier sketches in SATA *41, 92*
Kelley, True Adelaide
  See Kelley, True
Kellin, Sally Moffet 1932- *9*
Kelling, Furn L. 1914-2000 .... *37*
Kellogg, Gene
  See Kellogg, Jean (Defrees)
Kellogg, Jean (Defrees) 1916-1978 .... *10*
Kellogg, Steven 1941- *177*
  Earlier sketches in SATA *8, 57, 130*
  See also CLR *6*
Kellogg, Steven Castle
  See Kellogg, Steven
Kellow, Kathleen
  See Hibbert, Eleanor Alice Burford
Kelly, C. M. O.
  See Gibbs, (Cecilia) May
Kelly, Clint 1950- *140*
Kelly, Eric P(hilbrook) 1884-1960
  See YABC *1*
Kelly, Fiona
  See Coleman, Michael
  and Hendry, Frances Mary
  and Jones, Allan Frewin
  and Oldfield, Jenny
  and Welford, Sue
Kelly, Irene 1957- *210*
  Earlier sketch in SATA *147*
Kelly, Jacqueline *216*
Kelly, Jeff
  See Kelly, Jeffrey
Kelly, Jeffrey 1946- *65*
Kelly, Joanne (W.) 1934- *87*
Kelly, Kate 1958- *91*
Kelly, Kathleen M. 1964- *71*
Kelly, Katy 1955- *215*
  Earlier sketch in SATA *169*
Kelly, Lauren
  See Oates, Joyce Carol
Kelly, Laurene 1954- *123*
Kelly, Martha Rose 1914-1983 .... *37*
Kelly, Marty
  See Kelly, Martha Rose
Kelly, Mij *166*
Kelly, Ralph
  See Geis, Darlene Stern
Kelly, Regina Z(immerman) 1898-1986 .... *5*
Kelly, Rosalie (Ruth) *43*
Kelly, Tom 1961- *191*
Kelly, Walt(er Crawford) 1913-1973 .... *18*
Kelsey, Alice Geer 1896-1982 .... *1*
Kelsey, Elin 1961- *159*
Kelsey, Marybeth *216*
Kemly, Kathleen 1958- *197*
Kemnitz, Thomas Milton, Jr. 1984- *152*
Kemnitz, Tom, Jr.
  See Kemnitz, Thomas Milton, Jr.
Kemp, Gene 1926- *75*
  Earlier sketch in SATA *25*
  See also CLR *29*
Kempner, Mary Jean 1913-1969 .... *10*
Kempter, Christa 1945- *187*
Kempton, Jean Welch 1914- *10*
Kenah, Katharine 1949- *182*
Kenda, Margaret 1942- *71*
Kendall, Carol (Seeger) 1917- *74*
  Earlier sketch in SATA *11*
  See also SAAS *7*
Kendall, Gideon 1966- *215*
Kendall, Katherine
  See Applegate, Katherine
Kendall, Lace
  See Stoutenburg, Adrien (Pearl)
Kendall, Martha E. *87*
Kendall, Russ 1957- *83*
Kenealy, James P. 1927- *52*
  Brief entry *29*

Kenealy, Jim
  See Kenealy, James P.
Kennaway, Adrienne 1945- *171*
  Earlier sketch in SATA *60*
Kennedy, Anne 1955- *198*
Kennedy, Anne Vittur
  See Kennedy, Anne
Kennedy, Brendan 1970- *57*
Kennedy, Dana Forrest 1917- *74*
Kennedy, Dorothy M(intzlaff) 1931- *53*
Kennedy, Doug 1963- *189*
  Earlier sketch in SATA *122*
Kennedy, Frances 1937- *192*
Kennedy, James *214*
Kennedy, John F. 1917-1963 .... *11*
Kennedy, John Fitzgerald
  See Kennedy, John F.
Kennedy, Joseph Charles
  See Kennedy, X. J.
Kennedy, Kim *189*
Kennedy, Marlane 1962- *210*
Kennedy, Pamela (J.) 1946- *87*
Kennedy, Paul E(dward) 1929- *113*
  Earlier sketch in SATA *33*
Kennedy, Richard (Pitt) 1910-1989
  Obituary *60*
Kennedy, (Jerome) Richard 1932- *22*
Kennedy, Robert 1938- *63*
Kennedy, T.A. 1953- *42*
  Brief entry *35*
Kennedy, Teresa
  See Kennedy, T.A.
Kennedy, Teresa A.
  See Kennedy, T.A.
Kennedy, William 1928- *57*
Kennedy, William Joseph
  See Kennedy, William
Kennedy, X. J. 1929- *130*
  Autobiography Feature *130*
  Earlier sketches in SATA *14, 86*
  See also CLR *27*
  See also SAAS *22*
Kennell, Ruth Epperson 1893-1977 .... *6*
  Obituary *25*
Kennemore, Tim 1957- *220*
  Earlier sketch in SATA *133*
Kennen, Ally *190*
Kennett, David 1959- *206*
  Earlier sketch in SATA *121*
Kennison, Ruth *202*
Kenny, Ellsworth Newcomb 1909-1971
  Obituary *26*
Kenny, Herbert Andrew 1912-2002 .... *13*
Kenny, Jude
  See Daly, Jude
Kenny, Kathryn
  See Bowden, Joan Chase
  and Krull, Kathleen
  and Sanderlin, Owenita (Harrah)
  and Stack, Nicolete Meredith
Kenny, Kevin
  See Krull, Kathleen
Kensinger, George
  See Fichter, George S.
Kensington, Kathryn Wesley
  See Rusch, Kristine Kathryn
Kent, Alexander
  See Reeman, Douglas Edward
Kent, David
  See Lambert, David
Kent, Deborah Ann 1948- *155*
  Brief entry *41*
  Earlier sketches in SATA *47, 104*
Kent, Jack
  See Kent, John Wellington
Kent, John Wellington 1920-1985 .... *24*
  Obituary *45*
Kent, Lisa 1942- *90*
Kent, Mallory
  See Lowndes, Robert A(ugustine) W(ard)
Kent, Margaret 1894- *2*

Kent, Rockwell 1882-1971 6
Kent, Rose *188*
Kent, Sherman 1903-1986 20
Obituary *47*
Kenward, Jean 1920- *42*
Kenworthy, Leonard S. 1912-1991 6
Kenyon, Karen (Smith) 1938- *145*
Kenyon, Kate
See Adorjan, Carol (Madden)
and Ransom, Candice F.
Kenyon, Ley 1913-1990 6
Keown, Elizabeth *78*
Kepes, Juliet A(ppleby) 1919-1999 .... *13*
Kephart, Beth 1960- *196*
Kerby, Mona 1951- 202
Earlier sketch in SATA 75
Kerigan, Florence 1896-1984 .... *12*
Kerley, Barbara 1960- *191*
Earlier sketch in SATA 138
Kerman, Gertrude
See Furman, Gertrude Lerner Kerman
Kerns, Thelma 1929- *116*
Kerr, Anne Louise
See Mackey, Weezie Kerr
Kerr, Bob 1951- *120*
Kerr, Jessica 1901-1991 .... *13*
Kerr, (Anne-)Judith 1923-1970 24
Kerr, M. E.
See Meaker, Marijane
Kerr, P.B.
See Kerr, Philip
Kerr, Philip 1956- *168*
Kerr, Phyllis Forbes 1942- *72*
Kerr, Tom 1950- *77*
Kerrin, Jessica Scott *174*
Kerry, Frances
See Kerigan, Florence
Kerry, Lois
See Duncan, Lois
Kershen, (L.) Michael 1982- *82*
Kerven, Rosalind 1954- *83*
Ker Wilson, Barbara 1929- *121*
Earlier sketches in SATA 20, 70
See also SAAS 18
Kerz, Anna 1947- 220
Keselman, Gabriela 1953- *128*
Kesey, Ken 1935-2001 66
Obituary *131*
Kesey, Ken Elton
See Kesey, Ken
Kesler, Jay 1935- *65*
Kessel, Joyce Karen 1937- *41*
Kessler, Cristina *190*
Kessler, Ethel 1922- *44*
Brief entry *37*
Kessler, Leonard P. 1921- *14*
Kessler, Liz 1966- 206
Kest, Kristin 1967- *168*
Earlier sketch in SATA 118
Kesteven, G. R.
See Crosher, G. R.
Ketcham, Hank
See Ketcham, Henry King
Ketcham, Henry King 1920-2001 28
Brief entry *27*
Obituary *128*
Ketcham, Sallie 1963- *124*
Ketchum, Liza 1946- *132*
Earlier sketch in SATA 78
Ketner, Mary Grace 1946- *75*
Kettelkamp, Larry (Dale) 1933- 2
See also SAAS 3
Ketteman, Helen 1945- *167*
Earlier sketches in SATA 73, 115
Kettle, Peter
See Glover, Denis (James Matthews)
Kevles, Bettyann Holtzmann 1938- 23
Key, Alexander (Hill) 1904-1979 8
Obituary *23*
Key, Samuel M.
See de Lint, Charles

Key, Watt 1970- *189*
Keyes, Daniel 1927- *37*
Keyes, Diane 207
Keyes, Fenton 1915-1999 .... *34*
Keyes, Greg 1963- *116*
Keyes, J. Gregory
See Keyes, Greg
Keyser, Marcia 1933- *42*
Keyser, Sarah
See McGuire, Leslie (Sarah)
Khalid, Mohamed Nor
See Lat
Khalsa, Dayal Kaur 1943-1989 62
See also CLR 30
Khan, Hena 214
Khan, Rukhsana 1962- *165*
Earlier sketch in SATA 118
Khanshendel, Chiron
See Rose, Wendy
Kheirabadi, Masoud 1951- *158*
Khemir, Sabiha *87*
Kherdian, David 1931- *74*
Autobiography Feature *125*
Earlier sketch in SATA 16
See also CLR 24
Khing, T.T. 1933- *192*
Kibbe, Pat (Hosley) *60*
Kidd, Diana 1933-2000 .... *150*
Kidd, Richard 1952-2008 .... *152*
Obituary *194*
Kidd, Ronald 1948- *173*
Earlier sketches in SATA 42, 92
Kiddell, John 1922- 3
Kiddell-Monroe, Joan 1908-1972 55
Kidwell, Carl 1910- *43*
Kiefer, Irene 1926- *21*
Kiefer, Kathleen Balmes 1957- *142*
Kiepper, Shirley Morgan 1933- *10*
Kierstead, Vera M.
See Kierstead-Farber, Vera M.
Kierstead-Farber, Vera M. 1913- *121*
Kierstead-Farber, Vera May
See Kierstead-Farber, Vera M.
Kiesel, Stanley 1925- *35*
Kiesler, Kate (A.) 1971- *152*
Earlier sketch in SATA 90
Kihn, Greg 1952- *110*
Kikukawa, Cecily H(arder) 1919- *44*
Brief entry *35*
Kilcher, Jewel 1974- *109*
Kile, Joan 1935- *78*
Kilgore, Kathleen 1946- *42*
Kilian, Crawford 1941- *35*
Killdeer, John
See Mayhar, Ardath
Killien, Christi 1956- *73*
Killilea, Marie (Lyons) 1913-1991 2
Killingback, Julia 1944- *63*
Killough, (Karen) Lee 1942- *64*
Kilpatrick, Don 206
Kilreon, Beth
See Walker, Barbara (Jeanne) K(erlin)
Kilworth, Garry 1941- 216
Earlier sketch in SATA 94
Kilworth, Garry D.
See Kilworth, Garry
Kilworth, Garry Douglas
See Kilworth, Garry
Kim, David 1977- 201
Kim, Helen 1899-1970 .... *98*
Kim, Joung Un 1970- 205
Kimball, Gayle 1943- *90*
Kimball, Violet T(ew) 1932- *126*
Kimball, Yeffe 1914-1978 .... *37*
Kimber, Murray 1964- *171*
Kimble, Warren *176*
Kimbrough, Emily 1899-1989 2
Obituary *59*
Kimeldorf, Martin 1948- *121*
Kimeldorf, Martin R.
See Kimeldorf, Martin

Kimenye, Barbara 1940(?)- *121*
Kimmel, Elizabeth Cody 209
Earlier sketch in SATA 170
Kimmel, Eric A. 1946- 208
Earlier sketches in SATA 13, 80, 125, 176
Kimmel, Margaret Mary 1938- 43
Brief entry *33*
Kimmelman, Burt 1947- *180*
Kimmelman, Leslie 1958- 211
Earlier sketches in SATA 85, 156
Kincaid, Jamaica 1949-
See CLR 63
Kincher, Jonni 1949- *79*
Kindl, Patrice 1951- *128*
Earlier sketch in SATA 82
See also CLR 132
Kindred, Wendy (Good) 1937- 7
Kinerk, Robert *199*
Kines, Pat Decker 1937- *12*
King, Adam
See Hoare, Robert J(ohn)
King, Alison
See Martini, Teri
King, (Maria) Anna 1964- *72*
King, A.S. 1970- 217
King, Billie Jean 1943- *12*
King, Christine
See Farris, Christine King
King, Christopher (L.) 1945- *84*
King, (David) Clive 1924- *144*
Earlier sketch in SATA 28
King, Colin 1943- *76*
King, Cynthia 1925- 7
King, Daniel (John) 1963- *130*
King, Daren 1972- *197*
King, Elizabeth 1953- *83*
King, Frank O. 1883-1969
Obituary *22*
King, Frank R. 1904-1999 .... *127*
King, Jane
See Currie, Stephen
King, Jeanette (Margaret) 1959- *105*
King, Larry L. 1929- *66*
King, Laurie R. 1952- *88*
King, Marian 1900(?)-1986 23
Obituary *47*
King, Martin Luther, Jr. 1929-1968 .... *14*
King, Mary Ellen 1958- *93*
King, Paul
See Drackett, Phil(ip Arthur)
King, Paula
See Downing, Paula E.
King, Stephen 1947- *161*
Earlier sketches in SATA 9, 55
See also CLR 124
King, Stephen Edwin
See King, Stephen
King, Stephen Michael 218
Earlier sketch in SATA 157
King, Steve
See King, Stephen
King, Thomas 1943- *96*
King, Thomas Hunt
See King, Thomas
King, Tony 1947- *39*
King, Willie Christine
See Farris, Christine King
Kingfisher, Rupert 209
Kingman, Dong (Moy Shu) 1911-2000 44
Kingman, Lee
See Natti, Lee
Kingsland, Leslie William 1912- *13*
Kingsley, Charles 1819-1875
See YABC 2
See also CLR 77
Kingsley, Emily Perl 1940- *33*
Kingsley, Kaza *193*
King-Smith, Dick 1922- *192*
Brief entry *38*
Earlier sketches in SATA 47, 80, 135
See also CLR 40

Kingston, Maxine Hong 1940- 53
Kingston, Maxine Ting Ting Hong
See Kingston, Maxine Hong
Kinney, C. Cle(land) 1915- 6
Kinney, Harrison 1921- 13
Kinney, Jean Stout 1912- 12
Kinney, Jeff 1971- 187
Kinsey, Elizabeth
See Clymer, Eleanor
Kinsey, Helen 1948- 82
Kinsey-Warnock, Natalie 1956- 167
Earlier sketches in SATA 71, 116
Kinzel, Dorothy 1950- 57
Kinzel, Dottie
See Kinzel, Dorothy
Kipling, Joseph Rudyard
See Kipling, Rudyard
Kipling, Rudyard 1865-1936 100
See also YABC 2
See also CLR 65
Kippax, Frank
See Needle, Jan
Kirby, David 1944- 78
Kirby, David K.
See Kirby, David
Kirby, David Kirk
See Kirby, David
Kirby, Margaret
See Bingley, Margaret (Jane Kirby)
Kirby, Pamela F. 1952- 220
Kirby, Susan E. 1949- 62
Kirk, Connie Ann 1957- 167
Kirk, Daniel 1952- 196
Earlier sketches in SATA 107, 153
Kirk, David 1955- 161
Earlier sketch in SATA 117
Kirk, Heather 1949- 166
Kirk, Ruth (Kratz) 1925- 5
Kirkham, Dinah
See Card, Orson Scott
Kirkland, Will
See Hale, Arlene
Kirkpatrick, Katherine (Anne) 1964- 113
Kirkup, James 1918-2009 12
Kirkus, Virginia
See Glick, Virginia Kirkus
Kirkwood, Kathryn
See Fluke, Joanne
Kirsch, Vincent X. 211
Kirshenbaum, Binnie 79
Kirshner, David S. 1958- 123
Kirtland, G. B.
See Hine, Sesyle Joslin
and Hine, Al(fred Blakelee)
Kirwan, Wednesday 198
Kish, Eleanor M(ary) 1924- 73
Kish, Ely
See Kish, Eleanor M(ary)
Kishida, Eriko 1929- 12
Kisinger, Grace Gelvin (Maze) 1913-1965 .. 10
Kissel, Richard 209
Kissin, Eva H. 1923- 10
Kissinger, Rosemary K.
See Updyke, Rosemary K.
Kistler, John M. 1967- 160
Kitamura, Satoshi 1956- 201
Earlier sketches in SATA 62, 98, 143
See also CLR 60
Kitchen, Bert
See Kitchen, Herbert Thomas
Kitchen, Herbert Thomas 1940- 70
Kite, L. Patricia
See Kite, Pat
Kite, Pat 1940- 78
Kitt, Tamara
See de Regniers, Beatrice Schenk (Freedman)
Kittinger, Jo S(usenbach) 1955- 148
Earlier sketch in SATA 96
Kituomba
See Odaga, Asenath (Bole)
Kitzinger, Sheila 1929- 57

Kiwak, Barbara 1966- 103
Kjelgaard, James Arthur 1910-1959 17
See also CLR 81
Kjelgaard, Jim
See Kjelgaard, James Arthur
Kjelle, Marylou Morano 1954- 146
Klages, Ellen 1954- 196
Klagsbrun, Francine (Lifton) 36
Klaits, Barrie 1944- 52
Klam, Cheryl 191
Klaperman, Gilbert 1921- 33
Klaperman, Libby Mindlin 1921-1982 33
Obituary 31
Klass, David 1960- 207
Earlier sketches in SATA 88, 142
Klass, Morton 1927-2001 11
Klass, Sheila Solomon 1927- 219
Autobiography Feature 126
Earlier sketches in SATA 45, 99
See also SAAS 26
Klause, Annette Curtis 1953- 175
Earlier sketch in SATA 79
See also CLR 104
Klaveness, Jan O'Donnell 1939- 86
Kleberger, Ilse 1921- 5
Kleeberg, Irene (Flitner) Cumming 1932- 65
Klein, Aaron E. 1930-1998 45
Brief entry 28
Klein, Bill 1945- 89
Klein, David 1919-2001 59
Klein, Frederick C. 1938- 154
Klein, Gerda Weissmann 1924- 44
Klein, H(erbert) Arthur 8
Klein, James 1932- 115
Klein, Leonore (Glotzer) 1916- 6
Klein, Lisa 1958- 211
Klein, Lisa M.
See Klein, Lisa
Klein, Mina C(ooper) 1906-1979 8
Klein, Norma 1938-1989 57
Earlier sketch in SATA 7
See also CLR 19
See also SAAS 1
Klein, Rachel S. 1953- 105
Klein, Robin 1936- 164
Brief entry 45
Earlier sketches in SATA 55, 80
See also CLR 21
Klemin, Diana 65
Klemm, Barry 1945- 104
Klemm, Edward G., Jr. 1910-2001 30
Klemm, Roberta K(ohnhorst) 1884-1975 30
Kleven, Elisa 1958- 217
Earlier sketches in SATA 76, 173
See also CLR 85
Klevin, Jill Ross 1935- 39
Brief entry 38
Kliban, B(ernard) 1935-1990 35
Obituary 66
Klier, Kimberly Wagner 208
Klimo, Kate 214
Klimowicz, Barbara 1927- 10
Kline, Christina Baker 1964- 101
Kline, James
See Klein, James
Kline, Jim
See Kline, Jim
Kline, Lisa Williams 1954- 143
Kline, Suzy 1943- 193
Autobiography Feature 193
Brief entry 48
Earlier sketches in SATA 67, 99, 152
Kliros, Thea 1935- 106
Klise, Kate 221
Earlier sketch in SATA 181
Klise, M. Sarah 1961- 180
Earlier sketch in SATA 128
Klots, Alexander Barrett 1903-1989
Obituary 62
Klug, Ron(ald) 1939- 31

Knaak, Richard A. 1961- 166
Earlier sketch in SATA 86
Knaak, Richard Allen
See Knaak, Richard A.
Knapman, Timothy 200
Knapp, Edward
See Kunhardt, Edith
Knapp, Ron 1952- 34
Knebel, Fletcher 1911-1993 36
Obituary 75
Kneeland, Linda Clarke 1947- 94
Kneen, Maggie 1957- 221
Knickerbocker, Diedrich
See Irving, Washington
Knifesmith
See Cutler, Ivor
Knigge, Robert (R.) 1921(?)-1987 50
Knight, Anne (Katherine) 1946- 34
Knight, Brenda 112
Knight, Christopher G. 1943- 96
Knight, Damon (Francis) 1922-2002 9
Obituary 139
Knight, David C(arpenter) 1925-1984 14
See also CLR 38
Knight, Eric 1897-1943 18
Knight, Eric Mowbray
See Knight, Eric
Knight, Francis Edgar 1905- 14
Knight, Frank
See Knight, Francis Edgar
Knight, Hilary 1926- 132
Earlier sketches in SATA 15, 69
Knight, Joan
See Knight, Joan (MacPhail)
Knight, Joan (MacPhail) 159
Earlier sketch in SATA 82
Knight, Kathryn Lasky
See Lasky, Kathryn
Knight, Mallory T.
See Hurwood, Bernhardt J.
Knight, Ruth Adams 1898-1974
Obituary 20
Knight, Theodore O. 1946- 77
Knobloch, Dorothea 1951- 88
Knoepfle, John (Ignatius) 1923- 66
Knorr, Laura 1971- 200
Knott, Bill
See Knott, William C(ecil, Jr.)
Knott, William C(ecil, Jr.) 1927- 3
Knotts, Howard (Clayton, Jr.) 1922- 25
Knowles, Anne 1933- 37
Knowles, Jo 1970- 197
Knowles, Johanna Beth
See Knowles, Jo
Knowles, John 1926-2001 89
Obituary 134
Earlier sketch in SATA 8
See also CLR 98
Knox, Calvin M.
See Silverberg, Robert
Knox, (Mary) Eleanor Jessie 1909-2000 59
Earlier sketch in SATA 30
Knox, Elizabeth 1959- 176
Knox, Elizabeth Fiona
See Knox, Elizabeth
Knox, James
See Brittain, William
Knox, Jolyne 1937- 76
Knudsen, James 1950- 42
Knudsen, Michelle 1974- 220
Earlier sketch in SATA 171
Knudson, Mike 1965- 209
Knudson, R. R.
See Knudson, Rozanne
Knudson, Richard L(ewis) 1930- 34
Knudson, Rozanne 1932-2008 79
Earlier sketch in SATA 7
See also SAAS 18
Knutson, Barbara 1959-2005 166
Knutson, Kimberley 115

Knye, Cassandra
See Disch, Thomas M.
Kobayashi, Masako Matsuno 1935- 6
Kober, Shahar 1979- 213
Koch, Dorothy Clarke 1924- 6
Koch, Kenneth 1925-2002 65
Koch, Kenneth Jay
See Koch, Kenneth
Koch, Phyllis (Mae) McCallum 1911- 10
Kochalka, James 1967- 196
Kocsis, J. C.
See Paul, James
Koda-Callan, Elizabeth 1944- 140
Earlier sketch in SATA 67
Kodman, Stanislawa 201
Koehler, Phoebe 1955- 85
Koehler-Pentacoff, Elizabeth 1957- 160
Earlier sketch in SATA 96
Koehn, Ilse
See Van Zwienen, Ilse Charlotte Koehn
Koeller, Carol 192
Koenig, Viviane 1950- 80
Koering, Ursula 1921-1976 64
Koerner, W(illiam) H(enry) D(avid)
1878-1938 21
Koertge, Ron 1940- 209
Earlier sketches in SATA 53, 92, 131
Koestler-Grack, Rachel A. 1973- 156
Koff, Richard Myram 1926- 62
Koffinke, Carol 1949- 82
Kogan, Deborah
See Kogan Ray, Deborah
Kogan Ray, Deborah 1940- 203
Earlier sketches in SATA 8, 50, 161
Kogawa, Joy 1935- 99
Kogawa, Joy Nozomi
See Kogawa, Joy
Kogler, Jennie
See Kogler, Jennifer Anne
Kogler, Jennifer Anne 1982(?)- 174
Kohara, Kazuno 207
Kohl, Herbert 1937- 47
Kohl, Herbert R.
See Kohl, Herbert
Kohl, MaryAnn F(aubion) 1947- 144
Earlier sketch in SATA 74
Kohler, Julilly H(ouse) 1908-1976
Obituary 20
Kohn, Bernice
See Hunt, Bernice
Kohn, Rita (T.) 1933- 89
Kohner, Frederick 1905-1986 10
Obituary 48
Koide, Tan 1938-1986 50
Koike, Kay 1940- 72
Koja, Kathe 1960- 199
Earlier sketch in SATA 155
Koja, Stephan 198
Kolar, Bob 1960(?)- 206
Kolb, Larry J. 1953- 175
Kolba, St. Tamara 22
Kolibalova, Marketa
See Kolibalova, Marketa
Kolibalova, Marketa 1953- 126
Koller, Jackie French 1948- 157
Earlier sketches in SATA 72, 109
See also CLR 68
Kolodny, Nancy J. 1946- 76
Kolosov, Jacqueline 1967- 199
Komaiko, Leah 1954- 164
Earlier sketch in SATA 97
Komisar, Lucy 1942- 9
Komoda, Beverly 1939- 25
Komoda, Kiyo 1937- 9
Kompaneyets, Marc 1974- 169
Komroff, Manuel 1890-1974 2
Obituary 20
Konigsberg, Bill 1970- 207
Konigsburg, E.L. 1930- 194
Earlier sketches in SATA 4, 48, 94, 126
See also CLR 81

Konigsburg, Elaine Lobl
See Konigsburg, E.L.
Koning, Hans 1921-2007 5
Obituary 182
Koningsberger, Hans
See Koning, Hans
Konkle, Janet Everest 1917- 12
Kono, Erin Eitter 1973- 177
Konrad, Marla Stewart 218
Konzak, Burt 1946- 151
Koob, Theodora (J. Foth) 1918- 23
Kooiker, Leonie
See Kooyker-Romijn, Johanna Maria
Koons, James
See Pernu, Dennis
Koontz, Dean 1945- 165
Earlier sketch in SATA 92
Koontz, Dean R.
See Koontz, Dean
Koontz, Dean Ray
See Koontz, Dean
Koontz, Robin Michal 1954- 136
Earlier sketch in SATA 70
Kooyker, Leonie
See Kooyker-Romijn, Johanna Maria
Kooyker-Romijn, Johanna Maria 1927- 48
Kooyker-Romyn, Johanna Maria
See Kooyker-Romijn, Johanna Maria
Kopelke, Lisa 1963- 154
Kopper, Lisa 1950- 105
Brief entry 51
Kopper, Lisa Esther
See Kopper, Lisa
Koppes, Steven N. 1957- 169
Koppes, Steven Nelson
See Koppes, Steven N.
Korach, Mimi 1922- 9
Koralek, Jenny 1934- 215
Earlier sketches in SATA 71, 140
Korczak, Janusz
See Goldszmit, Henryk
Koren, Edward (Benjamin) 1935- 148
Earlier sketch in SATA 5
Koren, Edward 1935- 206
Korinets, Iurii Iosifovich
See Korinetz, Yuri (Iosifovich)
Korinetz, Yuri (Iosifovich) 1923- 9
See also CLR 4
Korman, Bernice 1937- 78
Korman, Gordon 1963- 167
Brief entry 41
Earlier sketches in SATA 49, 81, 119
See also CLR 25
Korman, Gordon Richard
See Korman, Gordon
Korman, Justine 1958- 70
Kornblatt, Marc 1954- 147
Earlier sketch in SATA 84
Kornprobst, Jacques 1937- 177
Korte, Gene J. 1950- 74
Korthues, Barbara 1971- 203
Korty, Carol 1937- 15
Koscielniak, Bruce 1947- 153
Earlier sketches in SATA 67, 99
Koshin, Alexander (A.) 1952- 86
Kositsky, Lynne 1947- 158
Koskenmaki, Rosalie
See Maggio, Rosalie
Koss, Amy Goldman 1954- 158
Earlier sketch in SATA 115
Kossin, Sandy (Sanford) 1926- 10
Kossman, Nina 1959- 84
Kostecki-Shaw, Jenny Sue 203
Kostick, Conor 1964- 186
Kotzwinkle, William 1938- 146
Earlier sketches in SATA 24, 70
See also CLR 6
Kouhi, Elizabeth 1917- 54
Brief entry 49
Kouts, Anne 1945- 8
Koutsky, Jan Dale 1955- 146

Kovacs, Deborah 1954- 132
Earlier sketch in SATA 79
Kovalski, Maryann 1951- 175
Earlier sketches in SATA 58, 97
See also CLR 34
See also SAAS 21
Kowalski, Kathiann M. 1955- 151
Earlier sketch in SATA 96
Koz, Paula G.
See Goodman Koz, Paula
Kozjan, Drazen 209
Kraft, Betsy Harvey 1937- 157
Kraft, Erik P. 193
Krahn, Fernando 1935- 49
Brief entry 31
See also CLR 3
Krakauer, Hoong Yee Lee 1955- 86
Krakauer, Jon 1954- 108
Krall, Dan 1970- 218
Kramer, George
See Heuman, William
Kramer, Nora 1896(?)-1984 26
Obituary 39
Kramer, Remi (Thomas) 1935- 90
Krantz, Hazel (Newman) 12
Kranzler, George G(ershon) 1916- 28
Kranzler, Gershon
See Kranzler, George G(ershon)
Krasilovsky, Phyllis 1926- 38
Earlier sketch in SATA 1
See also CLR 83
See also SAAS 5
Krasne, Betty
See Levine, Betty K(rasne)
Krasner, Steven 1953- 154
Krasno, Rena 1923- 104
Kratman, Tom 175
Kraus, Joanna Halpert 1937- 87
Kraus, (Herman) Robert 1925-2001 93
Obituary 130
Earlier sketches in SATA 4, 65
See also SAAS 11
Krauss, Ruth 1911-1993 30
Obituary 75
Earlier sketch in SATA 1
See also CLR 42
Krauss, Ruth Ida
See Krauss, Ruth
Krautter, Elisa (Bialk) 1912(?)-1990 1
Obituary 65
Krautwurst, Terry 1946- 79
Kray, Robert Clement 1930- 82
Krech, Bob 1956- 185
Krech, Robert
See Krech, Bob
Kredel, Fritz 1900-1973 17
Kreikemeier, Gregory Scott 1965- 85
Kreloff, Elliot 189
Krementz, Jill 1940- 134
Earlier sketches in SATA 17, 71
See also CLR 5
See also SAAS 8
Kremer, Marcie
See Sorenson, Margo
Krenina, Katya 1968- 221
Earlier sketch in SATA 101
Krensky, Stephen 1953- 188
Brief entry 41
Earlier sketches in SATA 47, 93, 136
Krensky, Stephen Alan
See Krensky, Stephen
Kresh, Paul 1919-1997 61
Obituary 94
Kress, Nancy 1948- 147
Autobiography Feature 147
Earlier sketch in SATA 85
Kricher, John C. 1944- 113
Krieger, Melanie 96
Krinitz, Esther Nisenthal 1927-2001 194
Kripke, Dorothy Karp 30

Krisher, Trudy 1946- *160*
  Earlier sketch in SATA *86*
Krisher, Trudy B.
  See Krisher, Trudy
Krishnaswami, Uma 1956- *182*
  Earlier sketch in SATA *144*
Kristiansen, Teddy 1964- *210*
Kristiansen, Teddy H.
  See Kristiansen, Teddy
Kristof, Jane 1932- *8*
Kroeber, Theodora (Kracaw) 1897-1979 .... *1*
Kroeger, Mary Kay 1950- *92*
Krohn, Katherine E(lizabeth) 1961- *125*
  Earlier sketch in SATA *84*
Kroll, Francis Lynde 1904-1973 .... *10*
Kroll, Steven 1941- *212*
  Autobiography Feature *135*
  Earlier sketches in SATA *19, 66, 125, 135*
  See also SAAS *7*
Kroll, Virginia L. 1948- *168*
  Earlier sketches in SATA *76, 114*
Kroll, Virginia Louisa
  See Kroll, Virginia L.
Kromhout, Rindert 1958- *189*
Krommes, Beth 1956- *208*
  Earlier sketches in SATA *128, 181*
Kronenwetter, Michael 1943- *62*
Kroniuk, Lisa
  See Berton, Pierre (Francis de Marigny)
Kropp, Paul 1948- *38*
  Brief entry *34*
  See also CLR *96*
Kropp, Paul Stephan
  See Kropp, Paul
Krosoczka, Jarrett J. 1977- *200*
  Earlier sketch in SATA *155*
Krovatin, Christopher 1985- *171*
Krudop, Walter
  See Krudop, Walter Lyon
Krudop, Walter Lyon 1966- *210*
Kruess, James
  See Kruss, James
Kruglik, Gerald *187*
Krull, Kathleen 1952- *184*
  Autobiography Feature *106*
  Brief entry *39*
  Earlier sketches in SATA *52, 80, 149*
  See also CLR *44*
Krumgold, Joseph (Quincy) 1908-1980 .... *48*
  Obituary *23*
  Earlier sketch in SATA *1*
Krupinski, Loretta 1940- *161*
  Earlier sketches in SATA *67, 102*
Krupnick, Karen 1947- *89*
Krupp, E. C. 1944- *123*
  Earlier sketch in SATA *53*
Krupp, Edwin Charles
  See Krupp, E. C.
Krupp, Robin Rector 1946- *53*
Krush, Beth 1918- *18*
Krush, Joe 1918-
  See Krush, Joseph P.
Krush, Joseph P. 1918- *18*
Kruss, James 1926-1997 .... *8*
  See also CLR *9*
Kruusval, Catarina 1951- *201*
Krykorka, Vladyana 1945- *96*
Krystoforski, Andrej 1943- *196*
Kubick, Dana *212*
Kubie, Eleanor Gottheil
  See Kubie, Nora Gottheil Benjamin
Kubie, Nora Benjamin
  See Kubie, Nora Gottheil Benjamin
Kubie, Nora Gottheil Benjamin 1899-1988 . *39*
  Obituary *59*
Kubinyi, Laszlo 1937- *94*
  Earlier sketch in SATA *17*
Kudlinski, Kathleen V. 1950- *213*
  Earlier sketch in SATA *150*
Kuehnert, Stephanie 1979- *205*
Kuenstler, Morton 1927- *10*

Kuh, Charlotte 1892(?)-1985
  Obituary *43*
Kuharski, Janice 1947- *128*
Kuhn, Dwight *199*
Kuijer, Guus 1942- *179*
Kujoth, Jean Spealman 1935-1975
  Obituary *30*
Kuklin, Susan 1941- *163*
  Earlier sketches in SATA *63, 95*
  See also CLR *51*
Kulikov, Boris 1966- *205*
  Earlier sketch in SATA *170*
Kulka, Joe *188*
Kulling, Monica 1952- *89*
Kullman, Harry 1919-1982 .... *35*
Kulyk Keefer, Janice 1952- *132*
Kumin, Maxine 1925- *12*
Kumin, Maxine Winokur
  See Kumin, Maxine
Kunhardt, Dorothy (Meserve) 1901-1979 .... *53*
  Obituary *22*
Kunhardt, Edith 1937- *67*
Kunjufu, Jawanza 1953- *73*
Kunstler, Morton
  See Kuenstler, Morton
Kuntz, J(ohn) L. 1947- *91*
Kuntz, Jerry 1956- *133*
Kupferberg, Herbert 1918-2001 .... *19*
Kuratomi, Chizuko 1939- *12*
  See also CLR *32*
Kurczok, Belinda 1978- *121*
Kurelek, William 1927-1977 .... *8*
  Obituary *27*
  See also CLR *2*
Kurian, George 1928- *65*
Kurjian, Judi(th M.) 1944- *127*
Kurland, Gerald 1942- *13*
Kurland, Michael 1938- *118*
  Earlier sketch in SATA *48*
Kurland, Michael Joseph
  See Kurland, Michael
Kuroi, Ken 1947- *120*
Kurokawa, Mitsuhiro 1954- *88*
Kurten, Bjorn (Olof) 1924-1988 .... *64*
Kurtz, Jane 1952- *139*
  Earlier sketch in SATA *91*
  See also CLR *123*
Kurtz, Katherine 1944- *182*
  Earlier sketches in SATA *76, 126*
Kurtz, Katherine Irene
  See Kurtz, Katherine
Kurz, Rudolf 1952- *95*
Kushner, Donn (J.) 1927- *52*
  See also CLR *55*
Kushner, Ellen 1955- *202*
  Earlier sketch in SATA *98*
Kushner, Ellen Ruth
  See Kushner, Ellen
Kushner, Jill Menkes 1951- *62*
Kushner, Lawrence 1943- *169*
  Earlier sketch in SATA *83*
Kushner, Tony 1956- *160*
Kuskin, Karla 1932-2009 .... *164*
  Obituary *206*
  Earlier sketches in SATA *2, 68, 111*
  See also CLR *4*
  See also SAAS *3*
Kuskin, Karla Seidman
  See Kuskin, Karla
Kusugak, Michael 1948- *143*
Kusugak, Michael Arvaarluk
  See Kusugak, Michael
Kutner, Merrily 1948- *196*
Kuttner, Paul 1922- *18*
Kuyper, Sjoerd 1952- *177*
Kuzma, Kay 1941- *39*
Kvale, Velma R(uth) 1898-1979 .... *8*
Kvasnosky, Laura McGee 1951- *182*
  Earlier sketches in SATA *93, 142*
Kwasney, Michelle D. 1960- *162*

Kyle, Benjamin
  See Gottfried, Theodore Mark
Kyle, Elisabeth
  See Dunlop, Agnes M. R.
Kyte, Kathy S. 1946- *50*
  Brief entry *44*

L

L., Barry
  See Longyear, Barry B(rookes)
L., Tommy
  See Lorkowski, Thomas V(incent)
Labatt, Mary 1944- *215*
Labouisse, Eve Curie
  See Curie, Eve
Labouisse, Eve Denise
  See Curie, Eve
Lace, William W. 1942- *126*
Lacey, Joshua
  See Doder, Josh
Lachenmeyer, Nathaniel 1969- *221*
Lachner, Dorothea
  See Knobloch, Dorothea
Lachtman, Ofelia Dumas 1919- *179*
Lackey, Mercedes
  See Lackey, Mercedes R.
Lackey, Mercedes R. 1950- *127*
  Earlier sketch in SATA *81*
Lackey, Mercedes Ritchie
  See Lackey, Mercedes R.
Lacoe, Addie *78*
Lacombe, Benjamin 1982- *198*
Lacome, Julie 1961- *174*
  Earlier sketch in SATA *80*
Lacy, Leslie Alexander 1937- *6*
Ladd, Cheryl (Jean) 1951- *113*
Ladd, London 1972(?)- *206*
Ladd, Louise 1943- *97*
Ladd, Veronica
  See Miner, Jane Claypool
Laden, Nina 1962- *148*
  Earlier sketch in SATA *85*
Lader, Lawrence 1919-2006 .... *6*
  Obituary *178*
LaDoux, Rita C. 1951- *74*
Lady, A
  See Taylor, Ann
Lady Mears
  See Tempest, Margaret Mary
Lady of Quality, A
  See Bagnold, Enid
La Farge, Oliver 1901-1963 .... *19*
La Farge, Oliver Hazard Perry
  See La Farge, Oliver
La Farge, Phyllis *14*
LaFave, Kim *196*
LaFaye, A. 1970- *220*
  Earlier sketches in SATA *105, 156*
LaFaye, Alexandria R.T.
  See LaFaye, A.
LaFevers, R.L. *191*
LaFevers, Robin L.
  See LaFevers, R.L.
Laffin, John (Alfred Charles) 1922- *31*
LaFleur, Suzanne 1983- *221*
LaFontaine, Bruce 1948- *176*
  Earlier sketch in SATA *114*
La Fontaine, Jean de 1621-1695 .... *18*
Lafrance, Marie 1955- *197*
Lager, Claude
  See Lapp, Christiane (Germain)
Lager, Marilyn 1939- *52*
Lagercrantz, Rose (Elsa) 1947- *39*
Lagerloef, Selma
  See Lagerlof, Selma
Lagerlof, Selma 1858-1940 .... *15*
  See also CLR *7*
Laguna, Sofie 1968- *158*

LaHaye, Tim 1926- *149*
LaHaye, Timothy F.
    See LaHaye, Tim
Laidlaw, Rob *205*
Laiken, Deirdre S. 1948- *48*
    Brief entry *40*
Laiken, Deirdre Susan
    See Laiken, Deirdre S.
Laimgruber, Monika 1946- *11*
Lain, Anna
    See Lamb, Nancy
Laing, Alexander (Kinnan) 1903-1976 .... *117*
Laing, Martha 1951- *39*
Laird, Christa 1944- *108*
    Autobiography Feature *120*
    See also SAAS 26
Laird, Elizabeth 1943- *159*
    Earlier sketches in SATA *77, 114*
    See also CLR 65
Laird, Elizabeth Mary Risk
    See Laird, Elizabeth
Laird, Jean E(louise) 1930- *38*
Laite, Gordon 1925- *31*
Lake, Harriet
    See Taylor, Paula (Wright)
Lakeman, Victoria
    See Forester, Victoria
Lakin, Patricia 1944- *190*
Laklan, Carli 1907-1988 .... *5*
Laliberte, Louise-Andree 1958- *169*
Lalicki, Barbara *61*
Lalicki, Tom 1949- *186*
Lally, Soinbhe 1945- *119*
LaMarche, Jim *162*
Lamb, Albert *187*
Lamb, Beatrice Pitney 1904-1997 .... *21*
Lamb, Charles 1775-1834 .... *17*
Lamb, Elizabeth Searle 1917- *31*
Lamb, G(eoffrey) F(rederick) *10*
Lamb, Harold (Albert) 1892-1962 .... *53*
Lamb, Lynton (Harold) 1907-1977 .... *10*
Lamb, Mary Ann 1764-1847 .... *17*
Lamb, Nancy 1939- *80*
Lamb, Robert (Boyden) 1941- *13*
Lamba, Marie *195*
Lambert, David 1932- *84*
    Brief entry *49*
Lambert, David Compton
    See Lambert, David
Lambert, Janet 1895(?)-1973 .... *25*
Lambert, Martha L. *113*
Lambert, Saul 1928- *23*
Lambert, Stephen *174*
Lamburn, Richmal Crompton 1890-1969 .... *5*
Lamensdorf, Len 1930- *120*
Lamensdorf, Leonard
    See Lamensdorf, Len
Laminack, Lester L. 1956- *163*
    Earlier sketch in SATA *120*
Lammle, Leslie 1965- *213*
Lamont, Priscilla *200*
Lamorisse, Albert (Emmanuel) 1922-1970 ... *23*
Lampert, Emily 1951- *52*
    Brief entry *49*
Lamplugh, Lois 1921- *17*
Lampman, Evelyn Sibley 1907-1980 .... *87*
    Obituary *23*
    Earlier sketch in SATA *4*
Lamprey, Louise 1869-1951
    See YABC 2
Lampton, Chris
    See Lampton, Christopher F.
Lampton, Christopher
    See Lampton, Christopher F.
Lampton, Christopher F. *67*
    Brief entry *47*
Lamstein, Sarah 1943- *174*
    Earlier sketch in SATA *126*
Lamstein, Sarah Marwil
    See Lamstein, Sarah

Lanagan, Margo 1960- *201*
    Earlier sketch in SATA *163*
Lancaster, Bruce 1896-1963 .... *9*
Lancaster, Matthew 1973(?)-1983
    Obituary *45*
Lance, Kathryn 1943- *76*
Land, Barbara (Neblett) 1923- *16*
Land, Jane
    See Borland, Kathryn Kilby
    and Speicher, Helen Ross S(mith)
Land, Myrick (Ebben) 1922-1998 .... *15*
Land, Ross
    See Borland, Kathryn Kilby
    and Speicher, Helen Ross S(mith)
Landa, Norbert 1952- *218*
Landau, Elaine 1948- *141*
    Earlier sketches in SATA *10, 94*
Landau, Jacob 1917- *38*
Landeck, Beatrice 1904-1978 .... *15*
Landin, Les 1923- *2*
Landis, J(ames) D(avid) 1942- *60*
    Brief entry *52*
Landis, James D.
    See Landis, J(ames) D(avid)
Landis, Jill Marie 1948- *101*
Landman, Tanya *207*
Landmann, Bimba 1968- *176*
Landon, Dena 1978(?)- *168*
Landon, Lucinda 1950- *56*
    Brief entry *51*
Landon, Margaret (Dorothea Mortenson)
    1903-1993 .... *50*
Landowne, Youme 1970- *211*
Landry, Leo *202*
Landshoff, Ursula 1908-1989 .... *13*
Landstrom, Lena 1943- *206*
    Earlier sketch in SATA *146*
Landstrom, Olof 1943- *146*
Landy, Derek 1974- *210*
Lane, Alison Hoffman *215*
Lane, Carolyn 1926-1993 .... *10*
Lane, Connie
    See Laux, Constance
Lane, Dakota 1959- *166*
    Earlier sketch in SATA *105*
Lane, Jerry
    See Martin, Patricia Miles
Lane, John (Richard) 1932- *15*
Lane, Leena *199*
Lane, Margaret 1907-1994 .... *65*
    Brief entry *38*
    Obituary *79*
Lane, Rose Wilder 1887-1968 .... *29*
    Brief entry *28*
Lanes, Selma G. 1929- *3*
Lanes, Selma Gordon
    See Lanes, Selma G.
Lanfredi, Judy 1964- *83*
Lang, Andrew 1844-1912 .... *16*
    See also CLR *101*
Lang, Aubrey *169*
Lang, Glenna 1951- *221*
Lang, Lang 1982- *208*
Lang, Paul 1948- *83*
Lang, Susan S. 1950- *68*
Lang, T.T.
    See Taylor, Theodore
Langart, Darrell T.
    See Garrett, Randall
Langdo, Bryan 1973- *191*
    Earlier sketch in SATA *138*
Lange, John
    See Crichton, Michael
Lange, Karen E. *190*
Lange, Suzanne 1945- *5*
Langley, Andrew 1949- *166*
    Earlier sketch in SATA *104*
Langley, Charles P(itman) III 1949- *103*
Langley, Jonathan 1952- *122*
Langley, Noel 1911-1980
    Obituary *25*

Langley, Wanda *173*
Langner, Nola
    See Malone, Nola Langner
Langone, John (Michael) 1929- *46*
    Brief entry *38*
Langreuter, Jutta 1944- *122*
Langrish, Katherine *177*
Langsen, Richard C. 1953- *95*
Langstaff, John 1920-2005 .... *68*
    Obituary *172*
    Earlier sketch in SATA *6*
    See also CLR *3*
Langstaff, John Meredith
    See Langstaff, John
Langstaff, Launcelot
    See Irving, Washington
Langston, Laura 1958- *186*
Langton, Jane 1922- *200*
    Autobiography Feature *140*
    Earlier sketches in SATA *3, 68, 129, 140*
    See also CLR *33*
    See also SAAS *5*
Lanier, Sidney 1842-1881 .... *18*
Lanier, Sterling E. 1927-2007 .... *109*
Lanier, Sterling Edmund
    See Lanier, Sterling E.
Lanino, Deborah 1964- *123*
Lankford, Mary D. 1932- *112*
    Earlier sketch in SATA *77*
Lannin, Joanne 1951- *121*
Lannin, Joanne A.
    See Lannin, Joanne
Lansdale, Joe R. 1951- *116*
Lansdale, Joe Richard
    See Lansdale, Joe R.
Lansing, Alfred 1921-1975 .... *35*
Lansing, Karen E. 1954- *71*
Lansky, Vicki 1942- *177*
Lanthier, Jennifer 1964- *204*
Lantier-Sampon, Patricia 1952- *92*
Lantz, Fran
    See Lantz, Francess L(in)
Lantz, Francess L(in) 1952-2004 .... *153*
    Autobiography Feature *153*
    Obituary *159*
    Earlier sketches in SATA *63, 109*
Lantz, Paul 1908- *45*
Lantz, Walter 1900-1994 .... *37*
    Obituary *79*
Lanza, Barbara 1945- *101*
Lapp, Christiane (Germain) 1948- *74*
Lappin, Peter 1911-1999 .... *32*
Larbalestier, Justine *178*
Lardy, Philippe 1963- *168*
LaReau, Jenna *181*
LaReau, Kara *181*
Larios, Julie 1949- *178*
Larios, Julie Hofstrand
    See Larios, Julie
Larkin, Amy
    See Burns, Olive Ann
Larkin, Maia
    See Wojciechowska, Maia (Teresa)
Larkspur, Penelope
    See Wyatt, Valerie
Laroche, Giles 1956- *221*
    Earlier sketches in SATA *71, 126*
LaRochelle, David 1960- *171*
    Earlier sketch in SATA *115*
Larom, Henry V. 1903(?)-1975
    Obituary *30*
LaRose, Linda *125*
Larrabee, Lisa 1947- *84*
Larrecq, John M(aurice) 1926-1980 .... *44*
    Obituary *25*
Larrick (Crosby), Nancy 1910-2004 .... *4*
Larsen, Anita 1942- *78*
Larsen, Egon 1904- *14*
Larsen, Rebecca 1944- *54*
Larson, Eve
    See St. John, Wylly Folk

Larson, Gary 1950- 57
Larson, Hope 1982- 205
Larson, Ingrid D(ana) 1965- 92
Larson, Jean Russell 1930- 121
Larson, Kirby 1954- 181
　Earlier sketch in SATA 96
Larson, Norita D. 1944- 29
Larson, Norita Dittberner
　See Larson, Norita D.
Larson, William H. 1938- 10
Larsson, Carl (Olof) 1853-1919 35
LaSalle, Charles A.
　See Ellis, Edward S.
LaSalle, Charles E.
　See Ellis, Edward S.
Lasell, Elinor H. 1929- 19
Lasell, Fen H.
　See Lasell, Elinor H.
Lasenby, Jack 1931- 172
　Earlier sketches in SATA 65, 103
Laser, Michael 1954- 117
Lash, Joseph P. 1909-1987 43
Lasher, Faith B. 1921- 12
Lasker, David 1950- 38
Lasker, Joe
　See Lasker, Joseph Leon
Lasker, Joseph Leon 1919- 83
　Earlier sketch in SATA 9
　See also SAAS 17
Laski, Marghanita 1915-1988 55
Laskin, Pamela L. 1954- 75
Lasky, Kathryn 1944- 210
　Earlier sketches in SATA 13, 69, 112, 157
　See also CLR 140
Lasky Knight, Kathryn
　See Lasky, Kathryn
Lass, Bonnie 131
Lassalle, C. E.
　See Ellis, Edward S.
Lassiter, Mary
　See Hoffman, Mary
Lassiter, Rhiannon 1977- 157
Lat 1951- 196
Latham, Barbara 1896- 16
Latham, Frank B(rown) 1910-2000 6
Latham, Jean Lee 1902-1995 68
　Earlier sketch in SATA 2
　See also CLR 50
Latham, Mavis
　See Clark, Mavis Thorpe
Latham, Philip
　See Richardson, Robert S(hirley)
Lathrop, Dorothy P(ulis) 1891-1980 14
　Obituary 24
Lathrop, Francis
　See Leiber, Fritz (Reuter, Jr.)
Latimer, Jim 1943- 80
Latta, Rich
　See Latta, Richard
Latta, Richard 1946- 113
Latta, Sara L. 1960- 174
Lattany, Kristin
　See Lattany, Kristin Hunter
Lattany, Kristin (Eggleston) Hunter 1931- . 154
　Autobiography Feature 154
　Earlier sketch in SATA 132
Lattany, Kristin Hunter 1931-2008 132
　Earlier sketch in SATA 12
　See also CLR 3
　See also SAAS 10
Lattimore, Eleanor Frances 1904-1986 7
　Obituary 48
Lattin, Ann
　See Cole, Lois Dwight
Lauber, Patricia (Grace) 1924- 138
　Earlier sketches in SATA 1, 33, 75
　See also CLR 16
Laugesen, Malene 207
Laugesen, Malene Reynolds
　See Laugesen, Malene
Laugesen, Mary E(akin) 1906-1995 5

Laughbaum, Steve 1945- 12
Laughlin, Florence Young 1910-2001 3
Laughlin, Rosemary 1941- 123
Launder, Sally 206
Laure, Ettagale
　See Blauer, Ettagale
Laure, Jason 1940- 50
　Brief entry 44
Laurence, Ester Hauser 1935- 7
Laurence, Jean Margaret Wemyss
　See Laurence, Margaret
Laurence, Margaret 1926-1987
　Obituary 50
Laurie, Rona 1916- 55
Laurie, Victoria 218
Laurin, Anne
　See McLaurin, Anne
Lauritzen, Jonreed 1902-1979 13
Lauscher, Hermann
　See Hesse, Hermann
Lauture, Denize 1946- 86
Laux, Connie
　See Laux, Constance
Laux, Constance 1952- 97
Laux, Dorothy 1920- 49
Lavallee, Barbara 1941- 166
　Earlier sketch in SATA 74
Lavender, David (Sievert) 1910-2003 97
　Obituary 145
　Earlier sketch in SATA 64
Lavender, William D. 1921- 143
Laverne, Christine 175
Lavert, Gwendolyn Battle 1951-
　See Battle-Lavert, Gwendolyn
Laverty, Donald
　See Blish, James
　and Knight, Damon (Francis)
Lavigne, Louis-Dominique 107
Lavine, David 1928- 31
Lavine, Sigmund Arnold 1908-1986 82
　Earlier sketch in SATA 3
　See also CLR 35
Lavond, Paul Dennis
　See Kornbluth, C(yril) M.
　and Lowndes, Robert A(ugustine) W(ard)
　and Pohl, Frederik
Lawford, Paula Jane 1960- 57
　Brief entry 53
Lawhead, Stephen R. 1950- 109
Lawhead, Steve
　See Lawhead, Stephen R.
Lawlor, Laurie 1953- 137
　Earlier sketch in SATA 80
Lawlor, William
　See Lawlor, William T.
Lawlor, William T. 1951- 183
Lawrence, Ann (Margaret) 1942-1987 41
　Obituary 54
Lawrence, Caroline 1954- 203
Lawrence, Iain 1955- 183
　Earlier sketch in SATA 135
Lawrence, J. T.
　See Rowland-Entwistle, (Arthur) Theodore
　(Henry)
Lawrence, Jerome 1915-2004 65
Lawrence, John 1933- 30
Lawrence, Josephine 1890(?)-1978
　Obituary 24
Lawrence, Louise 1943- 119
　Earlier sketches in SATA 38, 78
Lawrence, Louise de Kiriline 1894-1992 13
Lawrence, Lynn
　See Garland, Sherry
Lawrence, Margery H. 1889-1969 120
Lawrence, Michael 1943- 132
Lawrence, Mildred Elwood 1907-1997 3
Lawrence, R(onald) D(ouglas) 1921- 55
Lawrinson, Julia 1969- 141
Lawson, Amy
　See Gordon, Amy
Lawson, Carol (Antell) 1946- 42

Lawson, Don(ald Elmer) 1917-1990 9
Lawson, Joan 1906- 55
Lawson, Julie 1947- 126
　Earlier sketch in SATA 79
　See also CLR 89
Lawson, Marion Tubbs 1896-1994 22
Lawson, Robert 1892-1957 100
　See also YABC 2
　See also CLR 73
Lawton, Clive A. 1951- 145
Laxdal, Vivienne 1962- 112
Laybourn, Emma 193
Laycock, George (Edwin) 1921- 5
Layne, Laura
　See Knott, William C(ecil, Jr.)
Layne, Steven L. 171
Layson, Annelex Hofstra 1938(?)- 211
Layton, Neal 1971- 187
　Earlier sketch in SATA 152
Layton, Neal Andrew
　See Layton, Neal
Lazare, Gerald John 1927- 44
Lazare, Jerry
　See Lazare, Gerald John
Lazarevich, Mila 1942- 17
Lazarus, Keo Felker 1913-1993 21
　Obituary 129
Lea, Alec 1907- 19
Lea, Bob 1952- 203
Lea, Joan
　See Neufeld, John (Arthur)
Leach, Maria 1892-1977 39
　Brief entry 28
Leacock, Elspeth 1946- 131
Leacroft, Helen (Mabel Beal) 1919- 6
Leacroft, Richard (Vallance Becher) 1914- 6
Leaf, Margaret P. 1909(?)-1988
　Obituary 55
Leaf, (Wilbur) Munro 1905-1976 20
　See also CLR 25
Leaf, VaDonna Jean 1929- 26
Leah, Devorah
　See Devorah-Leah
Leakey, Richard E(rskine Frere) 1944- 42
Leal, Ann Haywood 216
Leander, Ed
　See Richelson, Geraldine
Lear, Edward 1812-1888 100
　Earlier sketch in SATA 18
　See also CLR 75
Lears, Laurie 1955- 127
Leasor, James 1923-2007 54
Leasor, Thomas James
　See Leasor, James
Leavitt, Jerome E(dward) 1916- 23
Leavitt, Martine 1953- 170
LeBar, Mary E(velyn) 1910-1982 35
LeBlanc, Annette M. 1965- 68
LeBlanc, L(ee) 1913- 54
LeBox, Annette 1943- 145
Lebrun, Claude 1929- 66
Le Cain, Errol (John) 1941-1989 68
　Obituary 60
　Earlier sketch in SATA 6
Lechner, Jack 201
Lechner, John 1966- 200
Lecourt, Nancy (Hoyt) 1951- 73
Ledbetter, Suzann 1953- 119
Leder, Jane Mersky 1945- 61
　Brief entry 51
Lederer, Muriel 1929- 48
Lederer, William J. 1912-2009 62
Lederer, William Julius
　See Lederer, William J.
Lee, Amanda
　See Baggett, Nancy
　and Buckholtz, Eileen (Garber)
　and Glick, Ruth (Burtnick)
Lee, Benjamin 1921- 27
Lee, Betsy 1949- 37

Lee, Carol
    See Fletcher, Helen Jill
Lee, Carol Ann 1969- 185
Lee, Chinlun 182
Lee, Cora
    See Anderson, Catherine Corley
Lee, Dennis (Beynon) 1939- 102
    Earlier sketch in SATA 14
    See also CLR 3
Lee, Dom 1959- 146
    Autobiography Feature 121
    Earlier sketch in SATA 83
    See also SAAS 26
Lee, Doris Emrick 1905-1983 44
    Obituary 35
Lee, Edward
    See Lee, J. Edward
Lee, Elizabeth Rogers 1940- 90
Lee, Harper 1926- 11
Lee, Hector Viveros 1962- 115
Lee, Howard N.
    See Goulart, Ron
Lee, Huy Voun 1969- 217
    Earlier sketch in SATA 129
Lee, Insu 213
Lee, J. Edward 1953- 130
Lee, Jared 1943- 215
Lee, Jared D.
    See Lee, Jared
Lee, Jeanne M. 1943- 138
Lee, John R(obert) 1923-1976 27
Lee, Jordan
    See Scholefield, Alan
Lee, Joseph Edward
    See Lee, J. Edward
Lee, Julian
    See Latham, Jean Lee
Lee, Linda
    See Eyerly, Jeannette
Lee, Liz
    See Lee, Elizabeth Rogers
Lee, Lucy
    See Talbot, Charlene Joy
Lee, Lyn 1953- 128
Lee, Manning de Villeneuve 1894-1980 37
    Obituary 22
Lee, Marian
    See Clish, (Lee) Marian
Lee, Marie G. 1964- 178
    Earlier sketches in SATA 81, 130
Lee, Marie Myung-Ok
    See Lee, Marie G.
Lee, Mary Price 1934- 82
    Earlier sketch in SATA 8
Lee, Mildred
    See Scudder, Mildred Lee
Lee, Nelle Harper
    See Lee, Harper
Lee, Richard S. 1927- 82
Lee, Robert C. 1931- 20
Lee, Robert Edwin 1918-1994 65
    Obituary 82
Lee, Robert J. 1921- 10
Lee, Roy
    See Hopkins, Clark
Lee, Sally 1943- 67
Lee, Suzy 193
Lee, Tammie
    See Townsend, Thomas L.
Lee, Tanith 1947- 185
    Earlier sketches in SATA 8, 88, 134
Lee, Virginia 1976- 208
Leech, Ben
    See Bowkett, Stephen
Leeds, Contance 188
Leedy, Loreen 1959- 175
    Brief entry 50
    Earlier sketches in SATA 54, 84, 128
Leedy, Loreen Janelle
    See Leedy, Loreen
Lee-Hostetler, Jeri 1940- 63

Leekley, Thomas B(riggs) 1910-2001 23
Leeming, Jo Ann
    See Leeming, Joseph
Leeming, Joseph 1897-1968 26
Leemis, Ralph B. 1954- 72
Leese, Jennifer L.B. 1970- 163
Leeson, Muriel 1920- 54
Leeson, R. A.
    See Leeson, Robert (Arthur)
Leeson, Robert (Arthur) 1928- 76
    Earlier sketch in SATA 42
Lee Tae-Jun 1904-1956(?) 194
Lee-Tai, Amy 1964- 189
Leffland, Ella 1931- 65
Leffler, Silke 197
Lefler, Irene (Whitney) 1917- 12
LeFrak, Karen 182
Le Gallienne, Eva 1899-1991 9
    Obituary 68
Legg, Gerald 1947- 143
Legg, Sarah Martha Ross Bruggeman (?)-1982
    Obituary 40
LeGrand
    See Henderson, LeGrand
Le Guin, Ursula K. 1929- 194
    Earlier sketches in SATA 4, 52, 99, 149
    See also CLR 91
Le Guin, Ursula Kroeber
    See Le Guin, Ursula K.
Legum, Colin 1919-2003 10
Lehman, Barbara 1963- 170
    Earlier sketch in SATA 115
Lehman, Bob 91
Lehman, Elaine 91
Lehmann, Debra Lynn
    See Vanasse, Deb
Lehn, Cornelia 1920- 46
Lehne, Judith Logan 1947- 93
Lehr, Delores 1920- 10
Lehr, Norma 1930- 71
Leiber, Fritz (Reuter, Jr.) 1910-1992 45
    Obituary 73
Leibold, Jay 1957- 57
    Brief entry 52
Leichman, Seymour 1933- 5
Leick, Bonnie 205
Leigh, Nila K. 1981- 81
Leigh, Tom 1947- 46
Leigh-Pemberton, John 1911-1997 35
Leighton, Clare (Veronica Hope)
    1899-1989 37
Leighton, Margaret (Carver) 1896-1987 1
    Obituary 52
Leijten, Aileen 216
Leiner, Al(an) 1938- 83
Leiner, Katherine 1949- 93
Leipold, L. Edmond 1902-1983 16
Leisk, David (Johnson) 1906-1975 30
    Obituary 26
    Earlier sketch in SATA 1
    See also CLR 98
Leister, Mary 1917- 29
Leitch, Patricia 1933- 98
    Earlier sketch in SATA 11
Leitner, Isabella 1924- 86
Lekich, John 202
Leland, Bob 1956- 92
Leland, Robert E.
    See Leland, Bob
Lematre, Pascal 1967- 176
Lember, Barbara Hirsch 1941- 92
LeMieux, A.C. 1954- 125
    Earlier sketch in SATA 90
LeMieux, Anne
    See LeMieux, A.C.
LeMieux, Anne Connelly
    See LeMieux, A.C.
Lemieux, Michele 1955- 139
Lemke, Horst 1922- 38
Lemna, Don 1936- 216
Lenain, Thierry 1959- 201

Lenanton, Carola Mary Anima Oman
    See Oman, Carola (Mary Anima)
Lenard, Alexander 1910-1972
    Obituary 21
Lendroth, Susan 207
L'Engle, Madeleine 1918-2007 128
    Obituary 186
    Earlier sketches in SATA 1, 27, 75
    See also CLR 57
    See also SAAS 15
L'Engle, Madeleine Camp Franklin
    See L'Engle, Madeleine
Lengyel, Cornel Adam 1915- 27
Lengyel, Emil 1895-1985 3
    Obituary 42
Lennon, John 1940-1980 114
Lennon, John Ono
    See Lennon, John
Leno, Jay 1950- 154
LeNoir, Janice 1941- 89
Lens, Sidney 1912-1986 13
    Obituary 48
Lenski, Lois 1893-1974 100
    Earlier sketches in SATA 1, 26
    See also CLR 26
Lent, Blair 1930-2009 133
    Obituary 200
    Earlier sketch in SATA 2
Lent, Henry Bolles 1901-1973 17
Lent, John 1948- 108
Leodhas, Sorche Nic
    See Alger, Leclaire (Gowans)
Leokum, Arkady 1916(?)- 45
Leon, Carol Boyd 212
Leon, Sharon 1959- 79
Leonard, Alison 1944- 70
Leonard, Anna
    See Gilman, Laura Anne
Leonard, Constance (Brink) 1923- 42
    Brief entry 40
Leonard, Dutch
    See Leonard, Elmore
Leonard, Elmore 1925- 163
Leonard, Elmore John, Jr.
    See Leonard, Elmore
Leonard, Jonathan N(orton) 1903-1975 36
Leonard, Laura 1923- 75
Leonard, Tom 1955- 207
Leonetti, Mike 1958- 202
Leong, Gor Yun
    See Ellison, Virginia H(owell)
Leonhard, Herb 217
Leonhardt, Alice 1950- 152
Lerangis, Peter 1955- 171
    Earlier sketch in SATA 72
Lerman, Josh 215
Lerner, Aaron 1920-2007 35
    Obituary 179
Lerner, Aaron Bunsen
    See Lerner, Aaron
Lerner, Carol 1927- 86
    Earlier sketch in SATA 33
    See also CLR 34
    See also SAAS 12
Lerner, Gerda 1920- 65
Lerner, Harriet 1944- 101
Lerner, Marguerite Rush 1924-1987 11
    Obituary 51
Lerner, Sharon (Ruth) 1938-1982 11
    Obituary 29
Leroe, Ellen 1949- 99
    Brief entry 51
    Earlier sketch in SATA 61
Leroe, Ellen W.
    See Leroe, Ellen
Leroe, Ellen Whitney
    See Leroe, Ellen
Leroux, Gaston 1868-1927 65
Leroux-Hugon, Helene 1955- 132
LeRoy, Gen 52
    Brief entry 36

Lerrigo, Marion Olive 1898-1968
    Obituary 29
LeShan, Eda J(oan) 1922-2002 21
    See also CLR 6
LeSieg, Theo.
    See Dr. Seuss
Lesinski, Jeanne M. 1960- 120
Leslie, Robert Franklin 1911-1990 7
Leslie, Roger 1961- 168
Leslie, Roger James
    See Leslie, Roger
Leslie, Sarah
    See McGuire, Leslie (Sarah)
LeSourd, Catherine
    See Marshall, (Sarah) Catherine (Wood)
Lessac, Frane
    See Lessac, Frane
Lessac, Frane 1954- 209
    Earlier sketches in SATA 61, 148
Lessem, Dino Don
    See Lessem, Don
Lessem, Don 1951- 182
    Earlier sketches in SATA 97, 155
Lesser, Margaret 1899(?)-1979
    Obituary 22
Lesser, Rika 1953- 53
Lester, Alison 1952- 218
    Earlier sketches in SATA 50, 90, 129
Lester, Helen 1936- 189
    Earlier sketches in SATA 46, 92, 145
Lester, Julius 1939- 157
    Earlier sketches in SATA 12, 74, 112
    See also CLR 143
Lester, Julius Bernard
    See Lester, Julius
Lester, Mike 1955- 206
    Earlier sketch in SATA 131
Le Sueur, Meridel 1900-1996 6
Leszczynski, Diana 211
Lethcoe, Jason 191
Le Tord, Bijou 1945- 95
    Earlier sketch in SATA 49
Letts, Billie 1938- 121
Letts, Elizabeth
    See Alalou, Elizabeth
Leuck, Laura 1962- 192
    Earlier sketches in SATA 85, 146
Leutscher, Alfred (George) 1913- 23
Levai, Blaise 1919- 39
Levchuk, Lisa 215
Levenkron, Steven 1941- 86
Leverich, Kathleen 1948- 103
LeVert, John 1946- 55
Levert, Mireille 1956- 211
LeVert, William John
    See LeVert, John
Levete, Sarah 1961- 153
Levin, Betty 1927- 201
    Earlier sketches in SATA 19, 84, 137
    See also SAAS 11
Levin, Ira 1929-2007 66
    Obituary 187
Levin, Ira Marvin
    See Levin, Ira
Levin, Marcia Obrasky 1918- 13
Levin, Meyer 1905-1981 21
    Obituary 27
Levin, Miriam (Ramsfelder) 1962- 97
Levine, Abby 1943- 54
    Brief entry 52
Levine, Anna 212
Levine, Betty K(rasne) 1933- 66
Levine, David 1926-2009 43
    Brief entry 35
Levine, Edna S(imon) 35
Levine, Ellen 1939- 190
Levine, Evan 1962- 77
    Earlier sketch in SATA 74
Levine, Gail Carson 1947- 195
    Earlier sketches in SATA 98, 161
    See also CLR 85

Levine, I(srael) E. 1923-2003 12
    Obituary 146
Levine, Joan Goldman 11
Levine, Joseph 1910- 33
Levine, Kristin 1974- 213
Levine, Marge 1934- 81
Levine, Rhoda 14
Levine, Sarah 1970- 57
Levine, Shar 1953- 131
Levine-Freidus, Gail
    See Provost, Gail Levine
Levinson, Nancy Smiler 1938- 211
    Earlier sketches in SATA 33, 80, 140
Levinson, Riki 99
    Brief entry 49
    Earlier sketch in SATA 52
Levithan, David 1972- 166
Levitin, Sonia 1934- 192
    Autobiography Feature 131
    Earlier sketches in SATA 4, 68, 119, 131
    See also CLR 53
    See also SAAS 2
Levitt, Sidney (Mark) 1947- 68
Levon, O. U.
    See Kesey, Ken
Levoy, Myron 1930- 49
    Brief entry 37
Levy, Barrie 112
Levy, Constance 1931- 140
    Earlier sketch in SATA 73
    See also SAAS 22
Levy, Elizabeth 1942- 169
    Earlier sketches in SATA 31, 69, 107
    See also SAAS 18
Levy, Janice 172
Levy, Marilyn 1937- 67
Levy, Nathan 1945- 63
Levy, Robert 1945- 82
Lewees, John
    See Stockton, Francis Richard
Lewin, Betsy 1937- 169
    Autobiography Feature 115
    Earlier sketches in SATA 32, 90
Lewin, Hugh 1939- 72
    Brief entry 40
    See also CLR 9
Lewin, Ted 1935- 195
    Autobiography Feature 115
    Earlier sketches in SATA 21, 76, 119, 165
Lewis, Alice C. 1936- 46
Lewis, Alice Hudson 1895(?)-1971
    Obituary 29
Lewis, Amanda 1955- 80
Lewis, Anthony 1927- 27
Lewis, Anthony 1966- 120
Lewis, Barbara A. 1943- 73
Lewis, Beverly 1949- 80
Lewis, Brenda Ralph 1932- 72
Lewis, Brian 1963- 128
Lewis, C. S. 1898-1963 100
    Earlier sketch in SATA 13
    See also CLR 109
Lewis, Claudia (Louise) 1907-2001 5
Lewis, Clive Staples
    See Lewis, C. S.
Lewis, Cynthia Copeland 1960- 111
Lewis, E. M. 123
    Earlier sketch in SATA 20
Lewis, Earl Bradley
    See Lewis, E.B.
Lewis, E.B. 1956- 211
    Earlier sketches in SATA 93, 124, 168
Lewis, Elizabeth Foreman 1892-1958 121
    See also YABC 2
Lewis, Francine
    See Wells, Helen
Lewis, Harry Sinclair
    See Lewis, Sinclair
Lewis, Hilda (Winifred) 1896-1974
    Obituary 20

Lewis, J. Patrick 1942- 205
    Earlier sketches in SATA 69, 104, 162
Lewis, Jack P(earl) 1919- 65
Lewis, Jean 1924- 61
Lewis, Jon Samuel
    See Lewis, J.S.
Lewis, Joseph Anthony
    See Lewis, Anthony
Lewis, J.S. 1972- 203
Lewis, Julinda
    See Lewis-Ferguson, Julinda
Lewis, Kevin 173
Lewis, Kim 1951- 217
    Earlier sketches in SATA 84, 136
Lewis, Linda (Joy) 1946- 67
Lewis, Lucia Z.
    See Anderson, Lucia (Lewis)
Lewis, Marjorie 1929- 40
    Brief entry 35
Lewis, Mary 1907(?)-1988 64
    Obituary 56
Lewis, Mervyn
    See Frewer, Glyn (M.)
Lewis, Michael
    See Untermeyer, Louis
Lewis, Naomi 1911-2009 144
    Earlier sketch in SATA 76
Lewis, Paeony 1960- 173
Lewis, Paul
    See Gerson, Noel Bertram
Lewis, Richard 1935- 3
Lewis, Richard 1956- 209
Lewis, Rob 1962- 72
Lewis, Roger
    See Zarchy, Harry
Lewis, Rose 209
Lewis, Rose A.
    See Lewis, Rose
Lewis, Shannon
    See Llywelyn, Morgan
Lewis, Shari 1934-1998 35
    Brief entry 30
    Obituary 104
Lewis, Sylvan R.
    See Aronson, Virginia
Lewis, Thomas P(arker) 1936- 27
Lewis, Wendy A. 1966- 150
Lewis-Ferguson, Julinda 1955- 85
Lewison, Wendy Cheyette 177
Lewiton, Mina 1904-1970 2
Lew-Vriethoff, Joanne 186
Lexau, Joan M. 130
    Earlier sketches in SATA 1, 36
Ley, Willy 1906-1969 2
Leydon, Rita (Floden) 1949- 21
Leyland, Eric (Arthur) 1911- 37
L'Hommedieu, Dorothy Keasley 1885-1961
    Obituary 29
Li, Xiao Jun 1952- 86
Liao, Jimmy 1958- 202
Liatsos, Sandra Olson 1942- 103
Libby, Alisa M. 189
Libby, Barbara M. 153
Libby, Bill
    See Libby, William M.
Libby, William M. 1927-1984 5
    Obituary 39
Liberty, Gene 1924- 3
Lichtenheld, Tom 208
    Earlier sketch in SATA 152
Lichtman, Wendy 1946- 193
Liddell, Kenneth 1912-1975 63
Lidz, Jane 120
Lieberman, E(dwin) James 1934- 62
Liebers, Arthur 1913-1984 12
Lieblich, Irene 1923- 22
Liers, Emil E(rnest) 1890-1975 37
Lies, Brian 1963- 190
    Earlier sketch in SATA 131
Lieshout, Elle van
    See van Lieshout, Elle

Liestman, Vicki 1961- *72*
Lietz, Gerald S. 1918- *11*
Liew, Sonny 1974- *219*
Life, Kay (Guinn) 1930- *83*
Lifton, Betty Jean 1926-2010 .... *118*
  Earlier sketch in SATA *6*
Lifton, Robert Jay 1926- *66*
Lightburn, Ron 1954- *91*
Lightburn, Sandra 1955- *91*
Lightner, A. M.
  See Hopf, Alice (Martha) L(ightner)
Lightner, Alice
  See Hopf, Alice (Martha) L(ightner)
Lignell, Lois 1911- *37*
Liles, Maurine Walpole 1935- *81*
Lillegard, Dee *184*
Lilley, Stephen R. 1950- *97*
Lilley, Stephen Ray
  See Lilley, Stephen R.
Lillington, Kenneth (James) 1916-1998 .... *39*
Lilly, Nate *182*
Lilly, Ray
  See Curtis, Richard
Lim, John 1932- *43*
Liman, Ellen (Fogelson) 1936- *22*
Limb, Sue 1946- *203*
  Earlier sketch in SATA *158*
Limburg, Peter R(ichard) 1929- *13*
Lin, Grace 1974- *198*
  Earlier sketches in SATA *111, 162*
Lincoln, C(harles) Eric 1924-2000 .... *5*
Lincoln, Christopher 1952- *208*
Lincoln, Hazel *187*
Lincoln, James
  See Bates, Katharine Lee
Lindbergh, Anne
  See Sapieyevski, Anne Lindbergh
Lindbergh, Anne Morrow 1906-2001 .... *33*
  Obituary *125*
Lindbergh, Anne Spencer Morrow
  See Lindbergh, Anne Morrow
Lindbergh, Charles A(ugustus, Jr.)
  1902-1974 .... *33*
Lindbergh, Reeve 1945- *163*
  Earlier sketch in SATA *116*
Lindblom, Steven (Winther) 1946- *94*
  Brief entry *39*
  Earlier sketch in SATA *42*
Linde, Gunnel 1924- *5*
Lindenbaum, Pija 1955- *183*
  Earlier sketches in SATA *77, 144*
Lindgren, Astrid (Anna Emilia Ericsson)
  1907-2002 .... *38*
  Obituary *128*
  Earlier sketch in SATA *2*
  See also CLR *119*
Lindgren, Barbro 1937- *207*
  Brief entry *46*
  Earlier sketches in SATA *63, 120*
  See also CLR *86*
Lindman, Maj (Jan) 1886-1972 .... *43*
Lindo, Elvira 1962- *219*
Lindop, Edmund 1925- *5*
Lindquist, Jennie Dorothea 1899-1977 .... *13*
Lindquist, Rowena Cory 1958- *98*
Lindquist, Willis 1908-1988 .... *20*
Lindsay, Nicholas Vachel
  See Lindsay, Vachel
Lindsay, Norman Alfred William
  1879-1969 .... *67*
  See also CLR *8*
Lindsay, Vachel 1879-1931 .... *40*
Lindsey, Kathleen D(orothy) 1949- *153*
Line, David
  See Davidson, Lionel
Line, Les 1935-2010 .... *27*
Lines, Kathleen Mary 1902-1988
  Obituary *61*
Linfield, Esther *40*

Lingard, Joan (Amelia) 1932- *130*
  Autobiography Feature *130*
  Earlier sketches in SATA *8, 74, 114*
  See also CLR *89*
  See also SAAS *5*
Link, Martin 1934- *28*
Linn, Margot
  See Ziefert, Harriet
Linnea, Sharon 1956- *82*
Lion, Melissa 1976- *176*
Lionni, Leo(nard) 1910-1999 .... *72*
  Obituary *118*
  Earlier sketch in SATA *8*
  See also CLR *71*
Lipinsky de Orlov, Lino S. 1908- *22*
Lipkind, William 1904-1974 .... *15*
Lipman, David 1931-2008 .... *21*
Lipman, Matthew 1923- *14*
Lipp, Frederick *204*
Lippincott, Bertram 1898(?)-1985
  Obituary *42*
Lippincott, Gary A. 1953- *220*
  Earlier sketches in SATA *73, 119*
Lippincott, Joseph W(harton) 1887-1976 ..... *17*
Lippincott, Sarah Lee 1920- *22*
Lippman, Peter J. 1936- *31*
Lipsyte, Robert 1938- *198*
  Earlier sketches in SATA *5, 68, 113, 161*
  See also CLR *76*
Lipsyte, Robert Michael
  See Lipsyte, Robert
Lisandrelli, Elaine Slivinski 1951- *94*
Lisker, Sonia O. 1933- *44*
Lisle, Holly 1960- *208*
  Earlier sketch in SATA *98*
Lisle, Janet Taylor 1947- *150*
  Brief entry *47*
  Earlier sketches in SATA *59, 96*
  See also SAAS *14*
Lisle, Rebecca *162*
Lisle, Seward D.
  See Ellis, Edward S.
Lisowski, Gabriel 1946- *47*
  Brief entry *31*
Liss, Howard 1922-1995 .... *4*
  Obituary *84*
Lissiat, Amy
  See Thompson, Colin
Lisson, Deborah 1941- *110*
  Earlier sketch in SATA *71*
List, Ilka Katherine 1935- *6*
Liston, Robert A. 1927- *5*
Litchfield, Ada B(assett) 1916-1999 .... *5*
Litchfield, Jo 1973- *116*
Lithgow, John 1945- *145*
Lithgow, John Arthur
  See Lithgow, John
Litowinsky, Olga 1936- *26*
Litowinsky, Olga Jean
  See Litowinsky, Olga
Littke, Lael J. 1929- *140*
  Earlier sketches in SATA *51, 83*
Little, A. Edward
  See Klein, Aaron E.
Little, Douglas 1942- *96*
Little, (Flora) Jean 1932- *149*
  Earlier sketches in SATA *2, 68, 106*
  See also CLR *4*
  See also SAAS *17*
Little, Lessie Jones 1906-1986 .... *60*
  Obituary *50*
Little, Mary E. 1912-1999 .... *28*
Littlechild, George 1958- *85*
Littledale, Freya (Lota) 1929-1992 .... *74*
  Earlier sketch in SATA *2*
Littlefield, Bill 1948- *83*
Littlefield, Holly 1963- *97*
Littlesugar, Amy 1953- *176*
  Earlier sketch in SATA *122*
Littleton, Mark R. 1950- *142*
  Earlier sketch in SATA *89*

Littlewood, Karin *211*
Littman, Sarah Darer *221*
  Earlier sketch in SATA *175*
Litty, Julie 1971- *181*
Litzinger, Rosanne 1948- *196*
Liu, Cynthea *221*
Lively, Penelope 1933- *164*
  Earlier sketches in SATA *7, 60, 101*
  See also CLR *159*
Lively, Penelope Margaret
  See Lively, Penelope
Liverakos, L. A.
  See Gilman, Laura Anne
Liversidge, (Henry) Douglas 1913- *8*
Livesey, Claire (Warner) 1927- *127*
Livingston, Carole 1941- *42*
Livingston, (M.) Irene 1932- *150*
Livingston, Myra Cohn 1926-1996 .... *68*
  Obituary *92*
  Earlier sketch in SATA *5*
  See also CLR *7*
  See also SAAS *1*
Livingston, Richard R(oland) 1922- *8*
Livo, Norma J. 1929- *76*
Liwska, Renata *199*
Ljungkvist, Laura *180*
Llerena Aguirre, Carlos 1952- *19*
Llerena Aguirre, Carlos Antonio
  See Llerena Aguirre, Carlos
Llewellyn, Claire 1954- *196*
  Earlier sketches in SATA *77, 143*
Llewellyn, Grace 1964- *110*
Llewellyn, Richard
  See Llewellyn Lloyd, Richard Dafydd Vivian
Llewellyn, Sam 1948- *185*
  Earlier sketch in SATA *95*
Llewellyn Lloyd, Richard Dafydd Vivian
  1906-1983 .... *11*
  Obituary *37*
Llewelyn, T. Harcourt
  See Hamilton, Charles (Harold St. John)
Lloyd, Alan
  See Lloyd, A.R.
Lloyd, Alan Richard
  See Lloyd, A.R.
Lloyd, A.R. 1927- *168*
  Earlier sketch in SATA *97*
Lloyd, David
  See Lloyd, David T.
Lloyd, David T. 1954- *167*
Lloyd, E. James
  See James, Elizabeth
Lloyd, Errol 1943- *22*
Lloyd, Hugh
  See Fitzhugh, Percy Keese
Lloyd, James
  See James, Elizabeth
Lloyd, Megan 1958- *189*
  Earlier sketches in SATA *77, 117*
Lloyd, Norman 1909-1980
  Obituary *23*
Lloyd, (Mary) Norris 1908-1993 .... *10*
  Obituary *75*
Lloyd, Saci 1967- *220*
Lloyd, Sam *183*
Lloyd-Jones, Sally 1960- *179*
Lloyd Webber, Andrew 1948- *56*
Llywelyn, Morgan 1937- *109*
Lo, Ginnie *165*
Lo, Virginia M.
  See Lo, Ginnie
Lobato, Jose Bento Monteiro 1882-1948 ... *114*
Lobel, Anita (Kempler) 1934- *162*
  Earlier sketches in SATA *6, 55, 96*
Lobel, Arnold (Stark) 1933-1987 .... *55*
  Obituary *54*
  Earlier sketch in SATA *6*
  See also CLR *5*
Lobel, Gillian *181*
Lobsenz, Amelia *12*
Lobsenz, Norman M(itchell) 1919- *6*

Lochak, Michele 1936- *39*
Lochlons, Colin
  See Jackson, C(aary) Paul
Locke, Clinton W. *1*
Locke, Elsie (Violet) 1912-2001 .... *87*
Locke, Gary 1963- *197*
Locke, Lucie 1904-1989 .... *10*
Locke, Robert 1944- *63*
  See also CLR *39*
Locker, Thomas 1937- *109*
  Earlier sketch in SATA *59*
  See also CLR *14*
Lockhart, E.
  See Jenkins, Emily
Lockridge, Hildegarde (Dolson)
  1908-1981 .... *121*
  Earlier sketch in SATA *5*
Lockwood, Mary
  See Spelman, Mary
Lodge, Bernard 1933- *215*
  Earlier sketches in SATA *33, 107*
Lodge, Jo 1966- *173*
  Earlier sketch in SATA *112*
Loeb, Jeffrey 1946- *57*
Loeb, Robert H., Jr. 1917- *21*
Loefgren, Ulf 1931- *3*
Loehfelm, Bill 1969- *153*
Loehr, Mallory *184*
Loehr, Patrick 1968(?)- *194*
Loeper, John J(oseph) 1929- *118*
  Earlier sketch in SATA *10*
Loescher, Ann Dull 1942- *20*
Loescher, Gil 1945- *20*
Loescher, Gilburt Damian
  See Loescher, Gil
Loewer, Jean Jenkins
  See Jenkins, Jean
Loewer, (Henry) Peter 1934- *98*
LoFaro, Jerry 1959- *77*
Lofo
  See Heimann, Rolf
Lofthouse, Liz *199*
Lofting, Hugh (John) 1886-1947 .... *100*
  Earlier sketch in SATA *15*
  See also CLR *143*
Lofts, Norah (Robinson) 1904-1983 .... *8*
  Obituary *36*
Logan, Jake
  See Knott, William C(ecil, Jr.)
  and Krepps, Robert W(ilson)
  and Pearl, Jacques Bain
  and Riefe, Alan
  and Rifkin, Shepard
  and Smith, Martin Cruz
Logan, Mark
  See Nicole, Christopher (Robin)
Logan, Rochelle 1954- *169*
Logsted, Greg *221*
Logston, Anne 1962- *112*
Logue, Christopher 1926- *23*
Logue, Mary 1952- *161*
  Earlier sketch in SATA *112*
Logue, Mary Louise
  See Logue, Mary
Loh, Morag 1935- *73*
Lohans, Alison 1949- *101*
Loizeaux, William *185*
Loken, Newton Clayton 1919- *26*
Lomas, Steve
  See Brennan, Joseph Lomas
Lomask, Milton (Nachman) 1909-1991 .... *20*
Lombard, Jenny *178*
Lombino, Salvatore
  See Hunter, Evan
LoMonaco, Palmyra 1932- *102*
London, Jack 1876-1916 .... *18*
  See also CLR *108*
London, Jane
  See Geis, Darlene Stern
London, John Griffith
  See London, Jack

London, Jonathan 1947- *221*
  Earlier sketches in SATA *74, 113, 157*
Lonergan, (Pauline) Joy (MacLean) 1909- ... *10*
Lonette, Reisie (Dominee) 1924- *43*
Long, Cathryn J. 1946- *89*
Long, Earlene (Roberta) 1938- *50*
Long, Emmett
  See Leonard, Elmore
Long, Ethan 1968(?)- *182*
Long, Helen Beecher *1*
Long, Judith Elaine 1953- *20*
Long, Judy
  See Long, Judith Elaine
Long, Kim 1949- *69*
Long, Laura Mooney 1892-1967
  Obituary *29*
Long, Laurel *203*
Long, Loren 1966(?)- *188*
  Earlier sketch in SATA *151*
Long, Melinda 1960- *152*
Long, Sylvia 1948- *179*
  Earlier sketch in SATA *120*
Longbeard, Frederick
  See Longyear, Barry B(rookes)
Longfellow, Henry Wadsworth 1807-1882 ... *19*
  See also CLR *99*
Longfellow, Layne 1937- *102*
Longfellow, Layne A.
  See Longfellow, Layne
Longman, Harold S. 1919- *5*
Longsworth, Polly 1933- *28*
Longtemps, Kenneth 1933- *17*
Longway, A. Hugh
  See Lang, Andrew
Longyear, Barry B(rookes) 1942- *117*
Look, Lenore *180*
Loomans, Diane 1955- *90*
Loomis, Christine *160*
  Earlier sketch in SATA *113*
Loomis, Jennifer A. 1942- *101*
Loomis, Robert D. *5*
Lopez, Angelo (Cayas) 1967- *83*
Lopez, Barry 1945- *67*
Lopez, Barry Holstun
  See Lopez, Barry
Lopez, Jack 1950- *178*
Lopez, Loretta 1963- *190*
Lopez, Lorraine 1956- *181*
Lopez, Lorraine M.
  See Lopez, Lorraine
Lopez, Rafael 1961(?)- *198*
Lopshire, Robert M(artin) 1927- *6*
Loraine, Connie
  See Reece, Colleen L.
Lorbiecki, Marybeth 1959- *172*
  Earlier sketch in SATA *121*
Lord, Athena V. 1932- *39*
Lord, Beman 1924-1991 .... *5*
  Obituary *69*
Lord, Bette Bao 1938- *58*
  See also CLR *151*
Lord, Cynthia *182*
Lord, Doreen Mildred Douglas
  See Lord, Douglas
Lord, Douglas 1904-1992 .... *12*
Lord, Janet *204*
Lord, John Vernon 1939- *21*
Lord, Michele *201*
Lord, Nancy
  See Titus, Eve
Lord, Patricia C. 1927-1988
  Obituary *58*
Lord, Walter 1917-2002 .... *3*
Lorde, Diana
  See Reno, Dawn E(laine)
Lorenz, Albert 1941- *115*
Lorenzini, Carlo
  See Collodi, Carlo
Lorey, Dean 1967- *193*
Lorimer, Janet 1941- *60*
Loring, Emilie (Baker) 1864(?)-1951 .... *51*

Lorkowski, Thomas V(incent) 1950- *92*
Lorkowski, Tom
  See Lorkowski, Thomas V(incent)
Lorraine, Walter (Henry) 1929- *16*
Lorrimer, Claire
  See Clark, Patricia Denise
Loss, Joan 1933- *11*
Lothrop, Harriet Mulford Stone 1844-1924 . *20*
Lottridge, Celia Barker 1936- *157*
  Earlier sketch in SATA *112*
LoTurco, Laura 1963- *84*
Lotz, Wolfgang 1912-1981 .... *65*
Loughridge, Stuart 1978- *214*
Louie, Ai-Ling 1949- *40*
  Brief entry *34*
Louis, Catherine 1963- *186*
Louis, Pat
  See Francis, Dorothy
Louisburgh, Sheila Burnford
  See Burnford, Sheila (Philip Cochrane Every)
Louise, Anita
  See Riggio, Anita
Louise, Tina 1934- *191*
Lourie, Helen
  See Storr, Catherine (Cole)
Lourie, Peter 1952- *183*
  Earlier sketches in SATA *82, 142*
Lourie, Peter King
  See Lourie, Peter
Love, Ann 1947- *168*
  Earlier sketch in SATA *79*
Love, D. Anne 1949- *180*
  Earlier sketches in SATA *96, 145*
Love, Douglas 1967- *92*
Love, Judith Dufour
  See Love, Judy
Love, Judy *188*
Love, Katherine (Isabel) 1907- *3*
Love, Kathleen Ann
  See Love, Ann
Love, Sandra (Weller) 1940- *26*
Lovegrove, James 1965- *216*
Lovegrove, J.M.H.
  See Lovegrove, James
Lovejoy, Jack 1937- *116*
Lovelace, Delos Wheeler 1894-1967 .... *7*
Lovelace, Maud Hart 1892-1980 .... *2*
  Obituary *23*
Lovell, Ingraham
  See Bacon, Josephine Dodge (Daskam)
Lovelock, Brian 1956- *214*
Loverseed, Amanda (Jane) 1965- *75*
Lovett, Margaret (Rose) 1915- *22*
Low, Alice 1926- *156*
  Earlier sketches in SATA *11, 76*
Low, Elizabeth Hammond 1898-1991 .... *5*
Low, Joseph 1911-2007 .... *14*
Low, Penelope Margaret
  See Lively, Penelope
Low, William *177*
Lowe, Helen 1961- *206*
Lowe, Jay, Jr.
  See Loeper, John J(oseph)
Lowell, Pamela *187*
Lowell, Susan 1950- *206*
  Earlier sketches in SATA *81, 127*
Lowenstein, Dyno 1914-1996 .... *6*
Lowenstein, Sallie 1949- *116*
Lowery, Linda 1949- *151*
  Earlier sketch in SATA *74*
Lowitz, Anson C. 1901(?)-1978 .... *18*
Lowitz, Sadyebeth Heath 1901-1969 .... *17*
Lowndes, Robert A(ugustine) W(ard)
  1916-1998 .... *117*
Lowrey, Janette Sebring 1892-1986 .... *43*
Lowry, Lois 1937- *177*
  Autobiography Feature *127*
  Earlier sketches in SATA *23, 70, 111*
  See also CLR *72*
  See also SAAS *3*

Lowry, Lois Hammersberg
  See Lowry, Lois
Lowry, Peter 1953- 7
Lowther, George F. 1913-1975
  Obituary 30
Loyie, Larry 1933- 150
Lozansky, Edward D. 1941- 62
Lozier, Herbert 1915- 26
Lubar, David 1954- 190
  Earlier sketch in SATA 133
Lubell, Cecil 1912-2000 6
Lubell, Winifred (A. Milius) 1914- 6
Lubin, Leonard
  See Lubin, Leonard B.
Lubin, Leonard B. 1943-1994 45
  Brief entry 37
Lubka, S. Ruth 1948- 154
Lubner, Susan 185
Luby, Thia 1954- 124
Lucado, Max (Lee) 1955- 104
Lucas, Cedric 1962- 101
Lucas, David 1966- 208
Lucas, E(dward) V(errall) 1868-1938 20
Lucas, Eileen 1956- 113
  Earlier sketch in SATA 76
Lucas, George 1944- 56
Lucas, Jerry 1940- 33
Lucas, Margeaux 186
Lucas, Victoria
  See Plath, Sylvia
Lucashenko, Melissa 1967- 104
Luccarelli, Vincent 1923- 90
Luce, Celia (Geneva Larsen) 1914- 38
Luce, Willard (Ray) 1914-1990 38
Lucht, Irmgard 1937- 82
Lucke, Deb 202
Luckett, Dave 1951- 220
  Earlier sketches in SATA 106, 167
Luckhardt, Mildred Corell 1898-1990 5
Ludden, Allen (Ellsworth) 1918(?)-1981
  Obituary 27
Ludel, Jacqueline 1945- 64
Ludlow, Geoffrey
  See Meynell, Laurence Walter
Ludlum, Mabel Cleland
  See Widdemer, Mabel Cleland
Ludwig, Helen 33
Ludwig, Lyndell 1923- 63
Ludwig, Trudy 1959- 209
  Earlier sketch in SATA 166
Luebs, Robin 1949- 212
Lueders, Edward (George) 1923- 14
Luenn, Nancy 1954- 79
  Earlier sketch in SATA 51
Lufkin, Raymond H. 1897- 38
Lugard, Flora Louisa Shaw 1852-1929 21
Luger, Harriett Mandelay 1914- 23
Luhrmann, Winifred B(ruce) 1934- 11
Luis, Earlene W. 1929- 11
Lujan, Jorge 201
Luke, Pauline 178
Luke, Pauline R.
  See Luke, Pauline
Lum, Peter
  See Crowe, (Bettina) Peter Lum
Lumry, Amanda (R.) 159
Lund, Deb 157
Lund, Doris Herold 1919- 12
Lunde, Darrin 202
Lundebrek, Amy 1975- 213
Lung, Chang
  See Jordan, Robert
Lunge-Larsen, Lise 1955- 184
  Earlier sketch in SATA 138
Lunn, Carolyn (Kowalczyk) 1960- 67
Lunn, Janet (Louise Swoboda) 1928- 110
  Earlier sketches in SATA 4, 68
  See also CLR 18
  See also SAAS 12
Lunsford, Cin Forshay
  See Forshay-Lunsford, Cin

Lupica, Michael
  See Lupica, Mike
Lupica, Michael Thomas
  See Lupica, Mike
Lupica, Mike 1952- 177
Lupoff, Dick
  See Lupoff, Richard A(llen)
Lupoff, Richard A(llen) 1935- 60
Lurie, Alison 1926- 112
  Earlier sketch in SATA 46
Lurie, Morris 1938- 72
Lussert, Anneliese 1929- 101
Lusted, Marcia Amidon 1962- 143
Lustig, Arnost 1926- 56
Lustig, Loretta 1944- 46
Lutes, Jason 1967- 210
Luthardt, Kevin 1973- 172
Luther, Frank 1905-1980
  Obituary 25
Luther, Rebekah (Lyn) S(tiles) 1960- 90
Luttmann, Gail
  See Damerow, Gail
Luttrell, Guy L. 1938- 22
Luttrell, Ida (Alleene) 1934- 91
  Brief entry 35
  Earlier sketch in SATA 40
Luttrell, William (J. III) 1954- 149
Lutz, John 1939- 180
Lutz, John Thomas
  See Lutz, John
Lutz, Norma Jean 1943- 122
Lutzeier, Elizabeth 1952- 72
Lutzker, Edythe 1904-1991 5
Luxbacher, Irene 1970- 219
  Earlier sketch in SATA 153
Luzadder, Patrick 1954- 89
Luzzati, Emanuele 1921-2007 7
Luzzatto, Paola Caboara 1938- 38
Ly, Many 1977- 208
Lybbert, Tyler 1970- 88
Lydon, Michael 1942- 11
Lyfick, Warren
  See Reeves, Lawrence F.
Lyle, Katie Letcher 1938- 8
Lynch, Chris 1962- 209
  Earlier sketches in SATA 95, 131, 171
  See also CLR 58
Lynch, Janet Nichols 1952- 221
Lynch, Jay 1945- 204
Lynch, Lorenzo 1932- 7
Lynch, Marietta 1947- 29
Lynch, Patricia (Nora) 1898-1972 9
Lynch, Patrick James
  See Lynch, P.J.
Lynch, P.J. 1962- 213
  Earlier sketches in SATA 79, 122
Lynds, Dennis 1924-2005 47
  Brief entry 37
Lyne, Alison Davis 188
Lyngseth, Joan
  See Davies, Joan
Lynn, Elizabeth A(nne) 1946- 99
Lynn, Mary
  See Brokamp, Marilyn
Lynn, Patricia
  See Watts, Mabel Pizzey
Lynn, Tracy 175
Lyon, Elinor 1921-2008 6
  Obituary 192
Lyon, Elinor Bruce
  See Lyon, Elinor
Lyon, George Ella 1949- 207
  Autobiography Feature 148
  Earlier sketches in SATA 68, 119, 148
Lyon, Lea 1945- 212
Lyon, Lyman R.
  See de Camp, L. Sprague
Lyons, Dorothy M(arawee) 1907-1997 3
Lyons, Grant 1941- 30
Lyons, Marcus
  See Blish, James

Lyons, Mary E. 1947- 195
  Autobiography Feature 195
  Earlier sketches in SATA 93, 142
Lyons, Mary Evelyn
  See Lyons, Mary E.
Lystad, Mary (Hanemann) 1928- 11
Lytle, Elizabeth Stewart 1949- 79
Lytle, Robert A. 1944- 119
Lyttle, Richard B(ard) 1927- 23
Lytton, Deborah 1966- 218
Lytton, Edward G.E.L. Bulwer-Lytton Baron
  See Bulwer-Lytton, Edward
Lytton of Knebworth, Baron
  See Bulwer-Lytton, Edward

                    M

Ma, Wenhai 1954- 84
Maar, Leonard (Frank, Jr.) 1927- 30
Maartens, Maretha 1945- 73
Maas, Selve -1997 14
Maass, Robert 195
Mabie, Grace
  See Mattern, Joanne
Mac
  See MacManus, Seumas
  and Maccari, Ruggero
Macalaster, Elizabeth G. 1951- 115
MacAlister, Katie 159
MacAlister, V. A.
  See McKernan, Victoria
MacAllan, Andrew
  See Leasor, James
MacAodhagain, Eamon
  See Egan, E. W.
MacArthur-Onslow, Annette Rosemary
  1933- 26
Macaulay, David (Alexander) 1946- 137
  Brief entry 27
  Earlier sketches in SATA 46, 72
  See also CLR 14
Macaulay, Teresa 1947- 95
Macauley, Theresa E.
  See Macaulay, Teresa
Macavinta, Courtney 176
MacBeth, George (Mann) 1932-1992 4
  Obituary 70
MacBride, Roger Lea 1929-1995 85
MacCarter, Don 1944- 91
MacClintock, Dorcas 1932- 8
MacCready, Robin Merrow 1959(?)- 190
MacCullough, Carolyn 174
MacDonald, Alan 1958- 192
MacDonald, Amy 1951- 156
  Autobiography Feature 156
  Earlier sketches in SATA 76, 136
MacDonald, Anne Elizabeth Campbell Bard
  -1958
  See MacDonald, Betty
MacDonald, Anne Louise 1955- 217
MacDonald, Anson
  See Heinlein, Robert A.
MacDonald, Betty 1908-1958
  See YABC 1
Macdonald, Blackie
  See Emrich, Duncan (Black Macdonald)
Macdonald, Caroline 1948- 86
  Obituary 111
  See also CLR 60
Macdonald, Dwight 1906-1982 29
  Obituary 33
MacDonald, George 1824-1905 100
  Earlier sketch in SATA 33
  See also CLR 67
MacDonald, Golden
  See Brown, Margaret Wise
Macdonald, Guy 195
Macdonald, James D. 1954- 67
  Earlier sketches in SATA 81, 114, 165, 1

Macdonald, Marcia
　See Hill, Grace Livingston
MacDonald, Margaret Read 1940- *194*
　Earlier sketches in SATA *94, 164*
Macdonald, Marianne 1934- *113*
Macdonald, Mary
　See Gifford, Griselda
Macdonald, Maryann 1947- *189*
　Earlier sketch in SATA *72*
MacDonald, Ross 1957- *201*
Macdonald, Shelagh 1937- *25*
MacDonald, Suse 1940- *193*
　Brief entry *52*
　Earlier sketches in SATA *54, 109*
Macdonald, Wendy *217*
Macdonald, Wendy M.
　See Macdonald, Wendy
Macdonald, Zillah K(atherine) 1885-1979 ... *11*
MacDonnell, Megan
　See Stevens, Serita
MacDougal, John
　See Blish, James
Mace, Elisabeth 1933- *27*
Mace, Varian 1938- *49*
MacEachern, Stephen *206*
MacEwen, Gwendolyn (Margaret)
　1941-1987 .... *50*
　Obituary *55*
Macfarlan, Allan A. 1892-1982 .... *35*
MacFarlane, Iris 1922- *11*
MacGill-Callahan, Sheila 1926-2000 .... *78*
MacGregor, Carol Lynn *153*
MacGregor, Ellen 1906-1954 .... *39*
　Brief entry *27*
MacGregor-Hastie, Roy (Alasdhair Niall)
　1929- *3*
MacGrory, Yvonne 1948- *142*
Machado, Ana Maria 1941- *150*
MacHale, D.J. 1956- *175*
MacHale, Donald James
　See MacHale, D.J.
Machetanz, Frederick 1908- *34*
Machin, Sue
　See Williams, Sue
Machin Goodall, Daphne (Edith) *37*
Macht, Norm
　See Macht, Norman L.
Macht, Norman L. 1929- *122*
Macht, Norman Lee
　See Macht, Norman L.
Macht, Norman Lee
　See Macht, Norman L.
MacInnes, Helen (Clark) 1907-1985 .... *22*
　Obituary *44*
Macintosh, Brownie 1950- *98*
MacIntyre, Elisabeth 1916- *17*
MacIntyre, Rod
　See MacIntyre, R.P.
MacIntyre, R.P. 1947- *203*
MacIntyre, R.P. 1947- *203*
MacIntyre, Wendy 1947- *196*
Mack, Jeff *194*
Mack, L.V.
　See Kimmelman, Burt
Mack, Stan(ley) *17*
Mack, Todd *168*
Mack, Tracy 1968- *183*
　Earlier sketch in SATA *128*
Mackall, Dandi D.
　See Mackall, Dandi Daley
Mackall, Dandi Daley 1949- *218*
　Earlier sketches in SATA *118, 177, 182*
Mackay, Claire 1930- *97*
　Autobiography Feature *124*
　Earlier sketch in SATA *40*
　See also CLR *43*
Mackay, Constance D'Arcy (?)-1966 .... *125*
Mackay, Donald 1914-2005 .... *81*
　Obituary *173*
Mackay, Donald Alexander
　See Mackay, Donald

MacKaye, Percy (Wallace) 1875-1956 .... *32*
Mackel, Kathryn 1950- *162*
Mackel, Kathy
　See Mackel, Kathryn
MacKellar, William 1914- *4*
Macken, JoAnn Early 1953- *201*
Macken, Walter 1915-1967 .... *36*
Mackenzie, Anna 1963- *212*
MacKenzie, Jill (Kelly) 1947- *75*
Mackenzie, Robert 1974- *204*
Mackey, Ernan
　See McInerny, Ralph
Mackey, Weezie Kerr *188*
Mackie, Maron
　See McNeely, Jeannette
Mackin, Edward
　See McInerny, Ralph
MacKinnon, Bernie 1957- *69*
MacKinnon Groomer, Vera 1915- *57*
MacKinstry, Elizabeth 1879-1956 .... *42*
Mackler, Carolyn 1973- *156*
MacLachlan, Emily
　See Charest, Emily MacLachlan
MacLachlan, Patricia 1938- *168*
　Brief entry *42*
　Earlier sketches in SATA *62, 107*
　See also CLR *14*
MacLane, Jack
　See Crider, Bill
MacLean, Alistair 1922(?)-1987 .... *23*
　Obituary *50*
MacLean, Alistair Stuart
　See MacLean, Alistair
Maclean, Art
　See Shirreffs, Gordon D(onald)
MacLean, Christine Kole 1962- *177*
MacLean, Glynne 1964- *150*
MacLean, Jill 1941- *211*
MacLeod, Beatrice 1910- *162*
　Earlier sketch in SATA *10*
MacLeod, Beatrice Beach
　See MacLeod, Beatrice
MacLeod, Charlotte (Matilda) 1922-2005 .... *28*
　Obituary *160*
MacLeod, Doug 1959- *201*
　Earlier sketch in SATA *60*
MacLeod, Elizabeth *184*
　Earlier sketch in SATA *158*
MacLeod, Ellen Jane (Anderson) 1916- *14*
MacManus, James
　See MacManus, Seumas
MacManus, Seumas 1869-1960 .... *25*
MacMaster, Eve (Ruth) B(owers) 1942- *46*
MacMillan, Annabelle
　See Quick, Annabelle
MacMillan, Dianne M(arie) 1943- *125*
　Earlier sketch in SATA *84*
Macnaughton, Tina *218*
　Earlier sketch in SATA *182*
Macneill, Janet
　See McNeely, Jeannette
MacPeek, Walter G. 1902-1973 .... *4*
　Obituary *25*
MacPhail, Catherine 1946- *197*
　Earlier sketch in SATA *130*
MacPherson, Margaret 1908-2001 .... *9*
　See also SAAS *4*
MacPherson, Thomas George 1915-1976
　Obituary *30*
MacPherson, Winnie 1930- *107*
MacRae, Tom 1980- *181*
Macrae, Travis
　See Feagles, Anita MacRae
MacRaois, Cormac 1944- *72*
Macumber, Mari
　See Sandoz, Mari(e Susette)
Macy, Sue 1954- *134*
　Earlier sketch in SATA *88*
Madaras, Lynda 1947- *151*
Madden, Don 1927- *3*
Madden, Kerry 1961- *168*

Madden-Lunsford, Kerry
　See Madden, Kerry
Maddern, Eric 1950- *166*
Maddigan, Beth 1967- *174*
Maddison, Angela Mary 1923- *10*
　See also CLR *24*
Maddock, Reginald (Bertram) 1912-1994 .... *15*
Madenski, Melissa (Ann) 1949- *77*
Madian, Jon 1941- *9*
Madison, Alan *182*
Madison, Arnold 1937- *6*
Madison, Bennett *220*
Madison, Winifred *5*
Madonna 1958- *149*
Madsen, Gunnar *171*
Madsen, Jim 1964- *202*
Madsen, Ross Martin 1946- *82*
Madsen, Susan A. 1954- *90*
Madsen, Susan Arrington
　See Madsen, Susan A.
Maehlqvist, Stefan 1943- *30*
Maestro, Betsy (Crippen) 1944- *106*
　Brief entry *30*
　Earlier sketch in SATA *59*
　See also CLR *45*
Maestro, Giulio 1942- *106*
　Earlier sketches in SATA *8, 59*
　See also CLR *45*
Maeterlinck, Maurice 1862-1949 .... *66*
Magee, Doug 1947- *78*
Magee, Wes 1939- *64*
Maggio, Rosalie 1943- *69*
Magid, Ken(neth Marshall) *65*
Magnus, Erica 1946- *77*
Magoon, Kekla 1980- *213*
Magoon, Scott *182*
Magorian, James 1942- *92*
　Earlier sketch in SATA *32*
Magorian, Michelle 1947- *128*
　Earlier sketch in SATA *67*
Magorian, Michelle Jane
　See Magorian, Michelle
Magovern, Peg *103*
Magsamen, Sandra 1959- *213*
Maguire, Anne
　See Nearing, Penny
Maguire, Gregory 1954- *200*
　Autobiography Feature *200*
　Earlier sketches in SATA *28, 84, 129*
　See also SAAS *22*
Maguire, Gregory Peter
　See Maguire, Gregory
Maguire, Jack 1920-2000 .... *74*
Maguire, Jesse
　See Smith, Sherwood
Maguire, Jessie
　See Smith, Sherwood
Maher, Ramona 1934- *13*
Mahlqvist, Stefan
　See Maehlqvist, Stefan
Mahon, Julia C(unha) 1916- *11*
Mahony, Elizabeth Winthrop
　See Winthrop, Elizabeth
Mahood, Kenneth 1930- *24*
Mahy, Margaret 1936- *171*
　Earlier sketches in SATA *14, 69, 119*
　See also CLR *155*
Mahy, Margaret May
　See Mahy, Margaret
Maiden, Cecil (Edward) 1902-1981 .... *52*
Maidoff, Ilka
　See List, Ilka Katherine
Maifair, Linda Lee 1947- *83*
Maik, Henri
　See Hecht, Henri Joseph
Maillu, David G(ian) 1939- *111*
Maine, Trevor
　See Catherall, Arthur
Mains, Randolph P. 1946- *80*
Maione, Heather *189*
Maiorano, Robert 1946- *43*

Maisner, Heather 1947- 89
Maison, Della
    See Katz, Bobbi
Maitland, Antony Jasper 1935- 25
Maitland, Barbara 102
Mai-Wyss, Tatjana 1972- 187
Maizels, Jennie 210
Major, Kevin (Gerald) 1949- 134
    Earlier sketches in SATA *32, 82*
    See also CLR *11*
Majure, Janet 1954- 96
Makhijani, Pooja 188
Makie, Pam 1943- 37
Makowski, Silk
    See Sullivan, Silky
Makowski, Silvia Ann
    See Sullivan, Silky
Malam, John 1957- 152
    Earlier sketch in SATA *89*
Maland, Nick 195
Malcolm, Dan
    See Silverberg, Robert
Malcolm, Jahnna N.
    See Beecham, Jahnna
Malcolmson, Anne
    See von Storch, Anne B.
Malcolmson, David 1899-1978 6
Maletta, Dr. Arlene
    See Feltenstein, Arlene
Maley, Carleen
    See Hutchins, Carleen Maley
Mali, Jane Lawrence 1937-1995 51
    Brief entry 44
    Obituary 86
Malkin, Nina 1959(?)- 179
Mallett, Jerry J. 1939- 76
Malley, Gemma 198
Malley, G.R.
    See Malley, Gemma
Mallory, Kenneth 1945- 185
    Earlier sketch in SATA *128*
Mallowan, Agatha Christie
    See Christie, Agatha
Malmberg, Carl 1904-1979 9
Malmgren, Dallin 1949- 65
Malo, John W. 1911-2000 4
Malone, James Hiram 1930- 84
Malone, Nola Langner 1930-2003 8
    Obituary 151
Malone, Patricia 1932- 155
Malone, Peter 1953- 191
Maloney, Pat
    See Markun, Patricia Maloney
Malory, Sir Thomas 1410(?)-1471(?) 59
    Brief entry 33
Maltese, Michael 1909(?)-1981
    Obituary 24
Malvasi, Meg Greene 143
Malvern, Corinne 1905-1956 34
Malvern, Gladys (?)-1962 23
Mama G.
    See Davis, Grania
Mammano, Julie 1962- 202
    Earlier sketch in SATA *107*
Mamonova, Tatyana 1943- 93
Manchel, Frank 1935- 10
Manchess, Gregory 1955- 203
Manchester, William (Raymond)
    1922-2004 65
Mandabach, Brian 1962(?)- 197
Mandel, Brett H. 1969- 108
Mandel, Peter 1957- 87
Mandel, Sally (Elizabeth) 1944- 64
Mandell, Muriel (Hortense Levin) 1921- 63
Manders, John 1957- 219
    Earlier sketch in SATA *175*
Manes, Stephen 1949- 99
    Brief entry 40
    Earlier sketch in SATA *42*
Manfred, Frederick (Feikema) 1912-1994 30
Mangin, Marie France 1940- 59

Mangione, Gerlando 1909-1998 6
    Obituary 104
Mangione, Jerre
    See Mangione, Gerlando
Mango, Karin N. 1936- 52
Mangurian, David 1938- 14
Mania, Cathy 1950- 102
Mania, Robert 1952- 102
Mania, Robert C., Jr.
    See Mania, Robert
Maniatty, Taramesha 1978- 92
Maniscalco, Joseph 1926- 10
Manley, Deborah 1932- 28
Manley, Seon 1921- 15
    See also CLR *3*
    See also SAAS *2*
Mann, Elizabeth 1948- 153
Mann, Josephine
    See Pullein-Thompson, Josephine (Mary
        Wedderburn)
Mann, Kenny 1946- 91
Mann, Pamela 1946- 91
Mann, Patrick
    See Waller, Leslie
Mann, Peggy
    See Houlton, Peggy Mann
Mannetti, Lisa 1953- 57
    Brief entry 51
Mannheim, Grete (Salomon) 1909-1986 10
Manniche, Lise 1943- 31
Manning, Jane K. 185
Manning, Maurie
    See Manning, Maurie J.
Manning, Maurie J. 211
Manning, Maurie Jo
    See Manning, Maurie J.
Manning, Mick 1959- 176
Manning, Rosemary 1911-1988 10
Manning, Sarra 162
Manning-Sanders, Ruth (Vernon)
    1895(?)-1988 73
    Obituary 57
    Earlier sketch in SATA *15*
Mannion, Diane
    See Paterson, Diane
Mannis, Celeste Davidson 173
Mannon, Warwick
    See Hopkins, (Hector) Kenneth
Manos, Helen 199
Mansir, A. Richard 1932- 170
Manson, Ainslie Kertland 1938- 115
Manson, Beverlie 1945- 57
    Brief entry 44
Mantchev, Lisa 221
Mantha, John 1960- 217
Manthorpe, Helen 1958- 122
Mantinband, Gerda (B.) 1917- 74
Manton, Jo
    See Gittings, Jo (Grenville) Manton
Manuel, Lynn 1948- 179
    Earlier sketch in SATA *99*
Manushkin, Fran 1942- 205
    Earlier sketches in SATA *7, 54, 93, 166*
Manushkin, Frances
    See Manushkin, Fran
Man Without a Spleen, A
    See Chekhov, Anton
Many, Paul 1947- 210
Many, Paul A.
    See Many, Paul
Manzano, Sonia 1950- 167
Mapes, Mary A.
    See Ellison, Virginia H(owell)
Maple, Marilyn 1931- 80
Mappin, Strephyn 1956- 109
Mara, Barney
    See Roth, Arthur J(oseph)
Mara, Jeanette
    See Cebulash, Mel
Mara, Rachna
    See Gilmore, Rachna

Marais, Josef 1905-1978
    Obituary 24
Marasmus, Seymour
    See Rivoli, Mario
Marbach, Ethel
    See Pochocki, Ethel (Frances)
Marcal, Annette B.
    See Callaway, Bernice (Anne)
Marcelino
    See Agnew, Edith J(osephine)
Marcellino, Fred 1939-2001 118
    Obituary 127
    Earlier sketch in SATA *68*
March, Carl
    See Fleischman, Sid
Marchant, Bessie 1862-1941
    See YABC *2*
Marchant, Catherine
    See Cookson, Catherine (McMullen)
Marcher, Marion Walden 1890-1987 10
Marchesi, Stephen 1951- 114
Marchesi, Steve
    See Marchesi, Stephen
    and Older, Effin
    and Older, Jules
Marchetta, Melina 1965- 170
Marciano, John Bemelmans 1970- 167
    Earlier sketch in SATA *118*
    See also CLR *93*
Marco, Lou
    See Gottfried, Theodore Mark
Marcus, Leonard S. 1950- 187
    Earlier sketch in SATA *133*
Marcus, Paul 1953- 82
Marcus, Rebecca B(rian) 1907- 9
Marcuse, Aida E. 1934- 89
Marek, Margot L. 1934(?)-1987
    Obituary 54
Maren, Julie 1970- 199
Margaret, Karla
    See Andersdatter, Karla M.
Margolin, Harriet
    See Ziefert, Harriet
Margolis, Jeffrey A. 1948- 108
Margolis, Leslie 187
Margolis, Richard J(ules) 1929-1991 86
    Obituary 67
    Earlier sketch in SATA *4*
Margolis, Vivienne 1922- 46
Mariana
    See Foster, Marian Curtis
Marie, Geraldine 1949- 61
Mariner, Scott
    See Pohl, Frederik
Marino, Dorothy Bronson 1912- 14
Marino, Jan 1936- 114
Marino, Nan 216
Marino, Nick
    See Deming, Richard
Marino, Peter 1960- 179
Mario, Anna
    See Odgers, Sally Farrell
Marion, Henry
    See del Rey, Lester
Maris, Ron 71
    Brief entry 45
Mark, Jan 1943-2006 164
    Obituary 173
    Earlier sketches in SATA *22, 69, 114*
    See also CLR *11*
Mark, Janet Marjorie
    See Mark, Jan
Mark, Joan T. 1937- 122
Mark, Pauline (Dahlin) 1913-1997 14
Mark, Polly
    See Mark, Pauline (Dahlin)
Mark, Ted
    See Gottfried, Theodore Mark
Markel, Michelle 169
Marker, Sherry 1941- 76
Markert, Jennifer 1965- 83

Markert, Jenny
　See Markert, Jennifer
Markey, Kevin 1965- 215
Markham, Lynne 1947- 102
Markham, Marion M. 1929- 60
Markham, Wendy
　See Staub, Wendy Corsi
Markins, W. S.
　See Jenkins, Marie M(agdalen)
Markle, Sandra 1946- 218
　Brief entry 41
　Earlier sketches in SATA 57, 92, 148, 185
Markle, Sandra L.
　See Markle, Sandra
Marklew, Gilly 211
Marko, Katherine D(olores) 28
Markoosie
　See Patsauq, Markoosie
Marks, Alan 1957- 187
　Earlier sketches in SATA 77, 151
Marks, Burton 1930- 47
　Brief entry 43
Marks, Graham 158
Marks, Hannah K.
　See Trivelpiece, Laurel
Marks, J.
　See Highwater, Jamake (Mamake)
Marks, J(ames) M(acdonald) 1921- 13
Marks, Laurie J. 1957- 68
Marks, Margaret L. 1911(?)-1980
　Obituary 23
Marks, Mickey Klar -1986 12
Marks, Peter
　See Smith, Robert Kimmel
Marks, Rita 1938- 47
Marks, Stan(ley) 14
Marks-Highwater, J.
　See Highwater, Jamake (Mamake)
Markun, Patricia Maloney 1924- 15
Markusen, Bruce (Stanley Rodriguez)
　1965- 141
Marley, Louise 1952- 173
　Earlier sketch in SATA 120
Marlin, Hilda
　See Van Stockum, Hilda
Marlow, Layne 204
Marlow, Max
　See Nicole, Christopher (Robin)
Marlow, Susan K. 1953- 178
Marlowe, Amy Bell 67
　Earlier sketch in SATA 1
Marlowe, Jack
　See Deary, Terry
Marlowe, Tess
　See Glick, Ruth (Burtnick)
Marney, Dean 1952- 90
Marokvia, Artur 1909- 31
Marokvia, Mireille 1908-2008 5
　Obituary 197
Marokvia, Mireille Journet
　See Marokvia, Mireille
Marol, Jean-Claude 1946- 125
Marr, John S(tuart) 1940- 48
Marr, Melissa 1972- 189
Marric, J. J.
　See Butler, William Vivian
　and Creasey, John
Marrin, Albert 1936- 193
　Brief entry 43
　Earlier sketches in SATA 53, 90, 126
　See also CLR 53
Marriott, Alice Lee 1910-1992 31
　Obituary 71
Marriott, Janice 1946- 134
Marriott, Pat(ricia) 1920- 35
Marriott, Zoe 1982- 216
Marriott, Zoe Davina
　See Marriott, Zoe
Marroquin, Patricio
　See Markun, Patricia Maloney

Mars, W. T.
　See Mars, Witold Tadeusz J.
Mars, Witold Tadeusz J. 1912-1985 3
Marsden, Carolyn 1950- 212
　Autobiography Feature 212
　Earlier sketches in SATA 140, 175
Marsden, John 1950- 146
　Earlier sketches in SATA 66, 97
　See also CLR 34
　See also SAAS 22
Marsh, Carole 1946- 127
Marsh, Dave 1950- 66
Marsh, J. E.
　See Marshall, Evelyn
Marsh, James 1946- 73
Marsh, Jean
　See Marshall, Evelyn
Marsh, Joan F. 1923- 83
Marsh, Katherine 1974- 220
Marsh, Paul
　See Hopkins, (Hector) Kenneth
Marsh, Valerie 1954- 89
Marshall, Anthony D(ryden) 1924- 18
Marshall, Bonnie C. 1941- 141
　Earlier sketch in SATA 18
Marshall, Bridget M(ary) 1974- 103
Marshall, (Sarah) Catherine (Wood)
　1914-1983 2
　Obituary 34
Marshall, Douglas
　See McClintock, Marshall
Marshall, Edmund
　See Hopkins, (Hector) Kenneth
Marshall, Edward
　See Marshall, James
Marshall, Evelyn 1897-1991 11
Marshall, Felicity 1950- 116
Marshall, Garry 1934- 60
Marshall, H. H.
　See Jahn, Michael
Marshall, James 1942-1992 75
　Earlier sketches in SATA 6, 51
　See also CLR 21
Marshall, James Edward
　See Marshall, James
Marshall, James Vance
　See Payne, Donald Gordon
Marshall, Janet (Perry) 1938- 97
Marshall, Jeff
　See Laycock, George (Edwin)
Marshall, Kim
　See Marshall, Michael (Kimbrough)
Marshall, Michael (Kimbrough) 1948- 37
Marshall, Percy
　See Young, Percy M(arshall)
Marshall, S(amuel) L(yman) A(twood)
　1900-1977 21
Marsoli, Lisa Ann 1958- 101
　Brief entry 53
Marsten, Richard
　See Hunter, Evan
Marston, Elsa 1933- 156
Marston, Hope Irvin 1935- 127
　Earlier sketch in SATA 31
Marszalek, John F. 1939- 167
Marszalek, John Francis, Jr.
　See Marszalek, John F.
Marszalek, John Francis 1939-
　See Marszalek, John F.
Martchenko, Michael 1942- 154
　Earlier sketches in SATA 50, 95
Martel, Aimee
　See Thurlo, Aimee
　and Thurlo, David
Martel, Suzanne 1924- 99
Martignoni, Margaret E. 1908(?)-1974
　Obituary 27
Martin, Ann M. 1955- 192
　Brief entry 41
　Earlier sketches in SATA 44, 70, 126
　See also CLR 32

Martin, Bill, Jr. 1916-2004 145
　Brief entry 40
　Earlier sketches in SATA 40, 67
　See also CLR 97
Martin, Charles E(lmer)
　See Mastrangelo, Charles E(lmer)
Martin, Christopher
　See Hoyt, Edwin P(almer), Jr.
Martin, C.K. Kelly 207
Martin, Claire 1933- 76
Martin, Courtney Autumn 1984- 205
Martin, David Stone 1913-1992 39
Martin, Del 1921-2008 47
Martin, Donald
　See Honig, Donald
Martin, Dorothy
　See Martin, Del
Martin, Dorothy L.
　See Martin, Del
Martin, Eugene 1
Martin, Eva M. 1939- 65
Martin, Frances M(cEntee) 1906-1998 36
Martin, Francesca 1947- 101
Martin, Fred 1948- 119
Martin, Fredric
　See Christopher, Matt(hew Frederick)
Martin, George Raymond Richard
　See Martin, George R.R.
Martin, George R.R. 1948- 118
Martin, J(ohn) P(ercival) 1880(?)-1966 15
Martin, Jacqueline Briggs 1945- 188
　Earlier sketches in SATA 98, 149
Martin, Jane Read 1957- 84
Martin, Jeremy
　See Levin, Marcia Obrasky
Martin, Les
　See Schulman, L(ester) M(artin)
Martin, Linda 1961- 82
Martin, Lynne 1923- 21
Martin, Marcia
　See Levin, Marcia Obrasky
Martin, Marvin 1926- 126
Martin, Melanie
　See Pellowski, Michael (Joseph)
Martin, Nancy
　See Salmon, Annie Elizabeth
Martin, Patricia 200
Martin, Patricia A.
　See Martin, Patricia
Martin, Patricia Miles 1899-1986 43
　Obituary 48
　Earlier sketch in SATA 1
Martin, Peter
　See Chaundler, Christine
Martin, Rafe 1946- 175
Martin, Rene 1891-1977 42
　Obituary 20
Martin, Rupert (Claude) 1905- 31
Martin, S. R.
　See Mappin, Strephyn
Martin, Stefan 1936- 32
Martin, Vicky
　See Storey, Victoria Carolyn
Martin, Webber
　See Silverberg, Robert
Martin, Wendy
　See Martini, Teri
Martin, William Ivan, Jr.
　See Martin, Bill, Jr.
Martineau, Diane 1940- 178
Martineau, Harriet 1802-1876
　See YABC 2
Martinet, Jeanne 1958- 80
Martinez, Agnes 167
Martinez, Arturo O. 1933- 192
Martinez, Claudia Guadalupe 1978- 214
Martinez, Ed(ward) 1954- 98
Martinez, Elizabeth Coonrod 1954- 85
Martinez, Victor 1954- 95
Martini, Teri 1930- 3

Martini, Therese
  See Martini, Teri
Martino, Alfred C. 1964- *174*
Martinson, Janis
  See Herbert, Janis
Martinusen, Cindy
  See Martinusen-Coloma, Cindy
Martinusen, Cindy McCormick
  See Martinusen-Coloma, Cindy
Martinusen-Coloma, Cindy 1970- *218*
Marton, Jirina 1946- *144*
  Earlier sketch in SATA *95*
Marton, Pierre
  See Stone, Peter
Martson, Del
  See Lupoff, Richard A(llen)
Martyr, Paula (Jane)
  See Lawford, Paula Jane
Maruki, Toshi 1912-2000 .... *112*
  See also CLR *19*
Marvin, Isabel R(idout) 1924- *84*
Marx, Patricia Windschill
  See Marx, Trish
Marx, Robert F(rank) 1936- *24*
Marx, Trish 1948- *202*
  Earlier sketches in SATA *112, 160*
Marzani, Carl (Aldo) 1912-1994 .... *12*
Marzollo, Jean 1942- *190*
  Autobiography Feature *190*
  Earlier sketches in SATA *29, 77, 130*
  See also SAAS *15*
Masefield, John (Edward) 1878-1967 .... *19*
Masiello, Ralph 1961- *214*
Masoff, Joy 1951- *118*
Mason, Adrienne 1962- *163*
Mason, Cherie *170*
Mason, Edwin A. 1905-1979
  Obituary *32*
Mason, Ernst
  See Pohl, Frederik
Mason, F(rancis) van Wyck 1901-1978 .... *3*
  Obituary *26*
Mason, Frank W.
  See Mason, F(rancis) van Wyck
Mason, George Frederick 1904-2000 .... *14*
Mason, Miriam E(vangeline) 1900-1973 .... *2*
  Obituary *26*
Mason, Prue *195*
Mason, Simon 1962- *178*
Mason, Tally
  See Derleth, August (William)
Mason, Van Wyck
  See Mason, F(rancis) van Wyck
Mass, Wendy 1967- *196*
  Earlier sketch in SATA *158*
Mass, William
  See Gibson, William
Masse, Josee *221*
Masselman, George 1897-1971 .... *19*
Massey, Misty *212*
Massie, Dianne Redfield 1938- *125*
  Earlier sketch in SATA *16*
Massie, Elizabeth *108*
Massini, Sarah *213*
Masson, Sophie 1959- *179*
  Earlier sketch in SATA *133*
Masters, Anthony (Richard) 1940-2003 ...... *112*
  Obituary *145*
Masters, Kelly R(ay) 1897-1987 .... *3*
Masters, Mildred 1932- *42*
Masters, William
  See Cousins, Margaret
Masters, Zeke
  See Bensen, Donald R.
  and Goulart, Ron
Mastrangelo, Charles E(lmer) 1910-1995 ..... *70*
  Earlier sketch in SATA *69*
Masuda, Takeshi 1944- *56*

Matas, Carol 1949- *194*
  Autobiography Feature *112*
  Earlier sketch in SATA *93*
  See also CLR *52*
Matchette, Katharine E. 1941- *38*
Math, Irwin 1940- *42*
Mathabane, Mark 1960- *123*
Mather, Kirtley F(letcher) 1888-1978 .... *65*
Mathers, Petra 1945- *176*
  Earlier sketch in SATA *119*
  See also CLR *76*
Matheson, Richard (Christian) 1953- *119*
Matheson, Shirlee Smith 1942- *155*
Mathews, Eleanor
  See Mathews, Ellie
Mathews, Ellie 1946(?)- *193*
Mathews, Janet 1914-1992 .... *41*
Mathews, Judith
  See Goldberger, Judith M.
Mathews, Louise
  See Tooke, Louise Mathews
Mathiesen, Egon 1907-1976
  Obituary *28*
Mathieu, Joe 1949- *185*
  Brief entry *36*
  Earlier sketches in SATA *43, 94*
Mathieu, Joseph P.
  See Mathieu, Joe
Mathis, Sharon Bell 1937- *58*
  Earlier sketch in SATA *7*
  See also CLR *147*
  See also SAAS *3*
Matlin, Marlee 1965- *181*
Matlin, Marlee Beth
  See Matlin, Marlee
Matloff, Gregory 1945- *73*
Matott, Justin 1961- *109*
Matranga, Frances Carfi 1922- *78*
Matray, James I. 1948- *161*
Matray, James Irving
  See Matray, James I.
Matson, Emerson N(els) 1926- *12*
Matsui, Tadashi 1926- *8*
Matsuno, Masako
  See Kobayashi, Masako Matsuno
Matsuoka, Mei 1981- *192*
Matte, (Encarnacion) L'Enc 1936- *22*
Mattern, Joanne 1963- *122*
Mattheson, Jenny *180*
Matthew, James
  See Barrie, J. M.
Matthews, Aline
  See De Wire, Elinor
Matthews, Andrew 1948- *138*
Matthews, Caitlin 1952- *122*
Matthews, Cecily 1945- *221*
Matthews, Downs 1925- *71*
Matthews, Elizabeth 1978- *194*
Matthews, Ellen
  See Bache, Ellyn
Matthews, Ellen 1950- *28*
Matthews, Harold Downs
  See Matthews, Downs
Matthews, Jacklyn Meek
  See Meek, Jacklyn O'Hanlon
Matthews, John (Kentigern) 1948- *116*
Matthews, L. S. *183*
Matthews, Laura S.
  See Matthews, L. S.
Matthews, Liz
  See Pellowski, Michael (Joseph)
Matthews, Morgan
  See Pellowski, Michael (Joseph)
Matthews, Nicola
  See Browne, N.M.
Matthews, Patricia 1927-2006 .... *28*
Matthews, Patricia Anne
  See Matthews, Patricia
Matthews, Tina 1961- *190*
Matthews, Tom L.
  See Lalicki, Tom

Matthews, William Henry III 1919- *45*
  Brief entry *28*
Matthiessen, Peter 1927- *27*
Mattingley, Christobel (Rosemary) 1931- *85*
  Earlier sketch in SATA *37*
  See also CLR *24*
  See also SAAS *18*
Matulay, Laszlo 1912- *43*
Matus, Greta 1938- *12*
Matzigkeit, Philip *220*
Maugham, W. S.
  See Maugham, W. Somerset
Maugham, W. Somerset 1874-1965 .... *54*
Maugham, William S.
  See Maugham, W. Somerset
Maugham, William Somerset
  See Maugham, W. Somerset
Maurer, Diane Philippoff
  See Maurer-Mathison, Diane V(ogel)
Maurer, Diane Vogel
  See Maurer-Mathison, Diane V(ogel)
Maurer-Mathison, Diane V(ogel) 1944- *89*
Mauser, Pat Rhoads
  See McCord, Patricia
Mauser, Patricia Rhoads
  See McCord, Patricia
Maves, Mary Carolyn 1916- *10*
Maves, Paul B(enjamin) 1913-1994 .... *10*
Mavor, Salley 1955- *125*
Mawicke, Tran 1911- *15*
Max 1906-1989
  See Diop, Birago (Ismael)
Max, Peter 1939- *45*
Maxon, Anne
  See Best, (Evangel) Allena Champlin
Maxwell, Arthur S. 1896-1970 .... *11*
Maxwell, B.E. 1957- *211*
Maxwell, Bruce E.
  See Maxwell, B.E.
Maxwell, Edith 1923- *7*
Maxwell, Gavin 1914-1969 .... *65*
Maxwell, Katie
  See MacAlister, Katie
Maxwell, William (Keepers, Jr.) 1908-2000
  Obituary *128*
Maxwell-Hyslop, Miranda 1968- *154*
May, Charles Paul 1920- *4*
May, Elaine Tyler 1947- *120*
May, J. C.
  See May, Julian
May, Julian 1931- *11*
May, Robert Lewis 1905-1976
  Obituary *27*
May, Robert Stephen 1929-1996 .... *46*
May, Robin
  See May, Robert Stephen
Mayall, Beth *171*
Mayberry, Florence V(irginia) Wilson *10*
Maybury, Richard J. 1946- *72*
Maybury, Rick
  See Maybury, Richard J.
Maydak, Michael S. 1952- *220*
Mayer, Agatha
  See Maher, Ramona
Mayer, Albert Ignatius, Jr. 1906-1994
  Obituary *29*
Mayer, Ann M(argaret) 1938- *14*
Mayer, Bill *200*
Mayer, Danuta 1958- *117*
Mayer, Hannelore Valencak 1929- *42*
Mayer, Jane Rothschild 1903-2001 .... *38*
Mayer, Marianna 1945- *132*
  Earlier sketches in SATA *32, 83*
Mayer, Mercer 1943- *137*
  Earlier sketches in SATA *16, 32, 73, 129*
  See also CLR *11*
Mayerson, Charlotte Leon *36*
Mayerson, Evelyn Wilde 1935- *55*
Mayfield, Katherine 1958- *118*
Mayfield, Sue 1963- *146*
  Earlier sketch in SATA *72*

Mayhar, Ardath 1930- 38
Mayhew, James 1964- 204
  Earlier sketches in SATA *85, 149*
Maynard, Olga 1920- 40
Mayne, William 1928-2010 122
  Earlier sketches in SATA *6, 68*
  See also CLR *123*
  See also SAAS *11*
Mayne, William James Carter
  See Mayne, William
Maynes, J. O. Rocky, Jr.
  See Maynes, J. Oscar, Jr.
Maynes, J. Oscar, Jr. 1929- 38
Mayo, Gretchen Will 1936- 163
  Earlier sketch in SATA *84*
Mayo, Margaret 1935- 165
  Earlier sketches in SATA *38, 96*
Mayo, Margaret Mary
  See Mayo, Margaret
Mayr, Diane 1949- 197
Mays, Lucinda L(a Bella) 1924- 49
Mays, (Lewis) Victor (Jr.) 1927- 5
Mazellan, Ron 210
Mazer, Anne 1953- 192
  Earlier sketches in SATA *67, 105*
Mazer, Harry 1925- 167
  Earlier sketches in SATA *31, 67, 105*
  See also CLR *16*
  See also SAAS *11*
Mazer, Norma Fox 1931-2009 198
  Earlier sketches in SATA *24, 67, 105, 168*
  See also CLR *23*
  See also SAAS *1*
Mazille, Capucine 1953- 96
Mazza, Adriana 1928- 19
Mazzio, Joann 1926- 74
Mbugua, Kioi Wa 1962- 83
McAfee, Carol 1955- 81
McAllister, Amanda
  See Dowdell, Dorothy (Florence) Karns
  and Hager, Jean
  and Meaker, Eloise
McAllister, Angela 182
McAllister, Margaret I. 1956- 169
  Earlier sketch in SATA *117*
McAllister, M.I.
  See McAllister, Margaret I.
McArdle, Paula 1971- 198
McArthur, Nancy 96
McAvoy, Jim 1972- 142
McBain, Ed
  See Hunter, Evan
McBain, Georgina 189
McBratney, Sam 1943- 203
  Earlier sketches in SATA *89, 164*
  See also CLR *44*
McBrier, Michael
  See Older, Effin
  and Older, Jules
McCafferty, Jim 1954- 84
McCaffery, Janet 1936- 38
McCaffrey, Anne 1926- 152
  Autobiography Feature 152
  Earlier sketches in SATA *8, 70, 116*
  See also CLR *130*
  See also SAAS *11*
McCaffrey, Anne Inez
  See McCaffrey, Anne
McCaffrey, Mary
  See Szudek, Agnes S(usan) P(hilomena)
McCain, Becky Ray 1954- 138
McCain, Murray (David, Jr.) 1926-1981 7
  Obituary 29
McCall, Bruce 1935(?)- 209
McCall, Edith (Sansom) 1911- 6
McCall, Virginia Nielsen 1909-2000 13
McCall, Wendell
  See Pearson, Ridley
McCall Smith, Alexander
  See Smith, Alexander McCall

McCallum, Phyllis
  See Koch, Phyllis (Mae) McCallum
McCallum, Stephen 1960- 91
McCampbell, Darlene Z. 1942- 83
McCann, Edson
  See del Rey, Lester
  and Pohl, Frederik
McCann, Gerald 1916- 41
McCann, Helen 1948- 75
McCannon, Dindga 41
McCants, William D. 1961- 82
McCarter, Neely Dixon 1929- 47
McCarthy, Agnes 1933- 4
McCarthy, Colin (John) 1951- 77
McCarthy, Mary 1951- 203
McCarthy, Meghan 199
  Earlier sketch in SATA *168*
McCarthy, Ralph F. 1950- 139
McCarthy-Tucker, Sherri N. 1958- 83
McCarty, Peter 1966- 182
McCarty, Rega Kramer 1904-1986 10
McCaslin, Nellie 1914-2005 12
McCaughrean, Geraldine 1951- 173
  Earlier sketches in SATA *87, 139*
  See also CLR *38*
McCaughren, Tom 1936- 75
McCauley, Adam 1965- 209
  Earlier sketch in SATA *128*
McCay, (Zenas) Winsor 1869-1934 134
  Earlier sketch in SATA *41*
McClafferty, Carla Killough 1958- 137
McClary, Jane Stevenson 1919-1990
  Obituary 64
McCleery, Patsy R. 1925- 133
  Earlier sketch in SATA *88*
McClelland, Susan 214
McClements, George 196
McClintock, Barbara 1955- 213
  Earlier sketches in SATA *57, 95, 146*
McClintock, Marshall 1906-1967 3
McClintock, May Garelick
  See Garelick, May
McClintock, Mike
  See McClintock, Marshall
McClintock, Norah 178
McClintock, Theodore 1902-1971 14
McClinton, Leon 1933- 11
McCloskey, Kevin 1951- 79
McCloskey, (John) Robert 1914-2003 100
  Obituary 146
  Earlier sketches in SATA *2, 39*
  See also CLR *7*
McCloy, James F(loyd) 1941- 59
McClung, Robert M(arshall) 1916- 135
  Earlier sketches in SATA *2, 68*
  See also CLR *11*
  See also SAAS *15*
McClure, Gillian Mary 1948- 31
McClure, Nikki 218
McColley, Kevin 1961- 80
  See also SAAS *23*
McConduit, Denise Walter 1950- 89
McConnell, James Douglas Rutherford
  1915-1988 40
  Obituary 56
McCord, Anne 1942- 41
McCord, David (Thompson Watson)
  1897-1997 18
  Obituary 96
  See also CLR *9*
McCord, Jean 1924- 34
McCord, Pat Mauser
  See McCord, Patricia
McCord, Patricia 1943- 159
  Earlier sketch in SATA *37*
McCord, Patricia Sue Rhoads Mauser
  See McCord, Patricia
McCormack, Caren McNelly 217
McCormick, Brooks
  See Adams, William Taylor
McCormick, Dell J. 1892-1949 19

McCormick, (George) Donald (King)
  1911-1998 14
McCormick, Edith (Joan) 1934- 30
McCormick, Kimberly A. 1960- 153
McCormick, Patricia 1956- 181
  Earlier sketch in SATA *128*
McCourt, Edward (Alexander) 1907-1972
  Obituary 28
McCourt, Lisa 1964- 214
  Earlier sketches in SATA *117, 159*
McCourt, Malachy 1931- 126
McCoy, Glenn 1965- 212
McCoy, Iola Fuller 3
McCoy, J(oseph) J(erome) 1917- 8
McCoy, Karen Kawamoto 1953- 82
McCoy, Lois (Rich) 1941- 38
McCrady, Lady 1951- 16
McCrea, James (Craig, Jr.) 1920- 3
McCrea, Ruth (Pirman) 1921- 3
McCreigh, James
  See Pohl, Frederik
McCrumb, Sharyn 1948- 109
McCue, Lisa 1959- 212
  Earlier sketches in SATA *65, 177*
McCue, Lisa Emiline
  See McCue, Lisa
McCullen, Andrew
  See Arthur, Robert, (Jr.)
McCullers, Carson 1917-1967 27
McCullers, Lula Carson Smith
  See McCullers, Carson
McCulloch, Derek (Ivor Breashur) 1897-1967
  Obituary 29
McCulloch, John Tyler
  See Burroughs, Edgar Rice
McCulloch, Sarah
  See Ure, Jean
McCullough, David 1933- 62
McCullough, David Gaub
  See McCullough, David
McCullough, Frances Monson 1938- 8
McCullough, Sharon Pierce 1943- 131
McCully, Emily Arnold
  See Arnold, Emily
McCune, Dan
  See Haas, Dorothy F.
McCunn, Ruthanne Lum 1946- 63
McCurdy, Michael (Charles) 1942- 147
  Earlier sketches in SATA *13, 82*
McCusker, Paul 1958- 220
McCutcheon, Elsie (Mary Jackson) 1937- ... 60
McCutcheon, John 1952- 97
McDaniel, Becky Bring 1953- 61
McDaniel, Lurlene 1944- 218
  Earlier sketches in SATA *71, 146*
McDaniels, Pellom III 1968- 121
McDaniels, Preston 1952- 192
McDearmon, Kay 20
McDermott, Beverly Brodsky 1941- 11
McDermott, Eleni 156
McDermott, Gerald (Edward) 1941- 163
  Earlier sketches in SATA *16, 74*
  See also CLR *9*
McDermott, Michael 1962- 76
McDevitt, Jack 1935- 155
  Earlier sketch in SATA *94*
McDevitt, John Charles
  See McDevitt, Jack
McDole, Carol
  See Farley, Carol (J.)
McDonald, Collin 1943- 79
McDonald, Gerald D(oan) 1905-1970 3
McDonald, Jamie
  See Heide, Florence Parry
McDonald, Janet 1953-2007 204
  Earlier sketch in SATA *148*
McDonald, Jill (Masefield) 1927-1982 13
  Obituary 29
McDonald, Joyce 1946- 164
  Earlier sketch in SATA *101*
McDonald, Lucile Saunders 1898-1992 10

McDonald, Mary Ann 1956- 84
McDonald, Megan 1958- 202
  Autobiography Feature 151
  Earlier sketches in SATA 67, 99, 148, 151
  See also CLR 94
McDonald, Meme 1954- 112
McDonald, Mercedes 1956- 169
  Earlier sketch in SATA 97
McDonald, Rae A. 1952- 201
McDonell, Chris 1960- 138
McDonnell, Christine 1949- 115
  Earlier sketch in SATA 34
McDonnell, Flora (Mary) 1963- 146
  Earlier sketch in SATA 90
McDonnell, Kathleen 1947- 186
McDonnell, Lois Eddy 1914-2001 10
McDonnell, Patrick 1956- 221
  Earlier sketch in SATA 179
McDonough, Yona Zeldis 1957- 73
McDowell, Marilyn Taylor 217
McElligott, Matt 1968- 196
  Earlier sketch in SATA 135
McElligott, Matthew
  See McElligott, Matt
McElmeel, Sharron L. 1942- 128
McElmurry, Jill 198
  Earlier sketch in SATA 159
McElrath, William N. 1932- 65
McElrath-Eslick, Lori 1960- 204
  Earlier sketch in SATA 96
McEntee, Dorothy (Layng) 1902- 37
McEvoy, Anne 214
McEwen, Katherine 183
McEwen, Robert (Lindley) 1926-1980
  Obituary 23
McFadden, Kevin Christopher
  See Pike, Christopher
McFall, Christie 1918- 12
McFall, Gardner 1952- 183
McFarlan, Donald M(aitland) 1915- 59
McFarland, Henry "Hammer"
  See McFarland, Henry O.
McFarland, Henry O. 1934- 143
McFarland, Kenton D(ean) 1920- 11
McFarland, Martha
  See Smith-Ankrom, M. E.
McFarlane, Leslie 1902-1977 100
  Earlier sketches in SATA 31, 1, 65, 67
  See also CLR 118
McFarlane, Leslie Charles
  See McFarlane, Leslie
McFarlane, Peter 1940- 95
McFarlane, Peter William
  See McFarlane, Peter
McFarlane, Sheryl P. 1954- 86
McFarlane, Todd 1961- 117
McGaw, Jessie Brewer 1913-1997 10
McGee, Barbara 1943- 6
McGee, Marni 163
McGhee, Alison 1960- 196
McGhee, Alison R.
  See McGhee, Alison
McGhee, Holly M.
  See Durand, Hallie
McGiffin, (Lewis) Lee (Shaffer) 1908-1978 ... 1
McGill, Alice 159
McGill, Marci
  See Balterman, Marcia Ridlon
McGill, Marci Ridlon
  See Balterman, Marcia Ridlon
McGill, Ormond 1913- 92
McGinley, Jerry 1948- 116
McGinley, Phyllis 1905-1978 44
  Obituary 24
  Earlier sketch in SATA 2
McGinnis, Lila S(prague) 1924- 44
McGinty, Alice B. 1963- 202
  Earlier sketch in SATA 134
McGivern, Justin 1985- 129
McGivern, Maureen Daly
  See Daly, Maureen

McGivern, Maureen Patricia Daly
  See Daly, Maureen
McGough, Elizabeth (Hemmes) 1934- 33
McGovern, Ann 1930- 132
  Earlier sketches in SATA 8, 69, 70
  See also CLR 50
  See also SAAS 17
McGowen, Thomas E. 1927- 109
  Earlier sketch in SATA 2
McGowen, Tom
  See McGowen, Thomas E.
McGrady, Mike 1933- 6
McGrath, Barbara Barbieri 1953- 169
  Earlier sketch in SATA 108
McGrath, Robin 1949- 121
McGrath, Thomas (Matthew) 1916-1990 41
  Obituary 66
McGraw, Eloise Jarvis 1915-2000 67
  Obituary 123
  Earlier sketch in SATA 1
  See also SAAS 6
McGraw, William Corbin 1916-1999 3
McGreal, Elizabeth
  See Yates, Elizabeth
McGregor, Barbara 1959- 82
McGregor, Craig 1933- 8
McGregor, Iona 1929- 25
McGrory, Anik 193
McGuffey, Alexander Hamilton 1816-1896 . 60
McGuigan, Mary Ann 1949- 106
McGuire, Edna 1899- 13
McGuire, Leslie (Sarah) 1945- 94
  Brief entry 45
  Earlier sketch in SATA 52
McGuire, Robert 187
McGuirk, Leslie (A.) 1960- 152
McGurk, Slater
  See Roth, Arthur J(oseph)
McHargue, Georgess 1941- 77
  Earlier sketch in SATA 4
  See also CLR 2
  See also SAAS 5
McHenry, E.B. 1963(?)- 193
McHugh, (Berit) Elisabet 1941- 55
  Brief entry 44
McIlvaine, Jane
  See McClary, Jane Stevenson
McIlwraith, Maureen Mollie Hunter
  See Hunter, Mollie
McInerney, Judith W(hitelock) 1945- 49
  Brief entry 46
McInerny, Ralph 1929-2010 93
McInerny, Ralph Matthew
  See McInerny, Ralph
McKaughan, Larry (Scott) 1941- 75
McKay, Donald 1895- 45
McKay, Hilary 1959- 208
  Earlier sketches in SATA 92, 145
  See also SAAS 23
McKay, Hilary Jane
  See McKay, Hilary
McKay, Lawrence, Jr. 1948- 114
McKay, Robert W. 1921- 15
McKay, Sharon E. 1954- 165
McKay, Simon
  See Nicole, Christopher (Robin)
McKean, Dave 1963- 197
McKean, David Jeff
  See McKean, Dave
McKeating, Eileen 1957- 81
McKee, David (John) 1935- 158
  Earlier sketches in SATA 70, 107
  See also CLR 38
McKee, Tim 1970- 111
McKeever, Marcia
  See Laird, Jean E(louise)
McKellar, Danica 1975- 213
McKelvey, Carole A. 1942- 78
McKelvy, Charles 1950- 124
McKendrick, Melveena (Christine) 1941- 55
McKendry, Joe 1972- 170

McKenna, Colleen O'Shaughnessy 1948- .. 136
  Earlier sketch in SATA 76
McKenzie, Dorothy Clayton 1910-1981
  Obituary 28
McKenzie, Ellen Kindt 1928- 80
McKernan, Victoria 1957- 171
McKie, Robin 112
McKillip, Patricia A. 1948- 174
  Earlier sketches in SATA 30, 80, 126
McKillip, Patricia Anne
  See McKillip, Patricia A.
McKim, Audrey Margaret 1909-1999 47
McKimmie, Chris 194
McKinley, Jennifer Carolyn Robin
  See McKinley, Robin
McKinley, Robin 1952- 195
  Brief entry 32
  Earlier sketches in SATA 50, 89, 130
  See also CLR 127
McKinney, Barbara Shaw 1951- 116
McKinney, Nadine 1938- 91
McKinty, Adrian 186
McKissack, Fredrick L. 1939- 162
  Brief entry 53
  Earlier sketches in SATA 73, 117
  See also CLR 55
McKissack, Fredrick Lemuel
  See McKissack, Fredrick L.
McKissack, Patricia C. 1944- 195
  Earlier sketches in SATA 51, 73, 117, 162
  See also CLR 129
McKissack, Patricia L'Ann Carwell
  See McKissack, Patricia C.
McKissack and McKissack
  See McKissack, Fredrick L.
  and McKissack, Patricia C.
McKown, Robin (?)-1976 6
McKy, Katie 1956- 184
McLaren, Chesley 213
McLaren, Clemence 1938- 158
  Earlier sketch in SATA 105
McLaughlin, Frank 1934- 73
McLaughlin, Lauren 209
McLaurin, Anne 1953- 27
McLean, Andrew 1946- 172
  Earlier sketch in SATA 113
McLean, J. Sloan
  See Gillette, Virginia M(ary)
  and Wunsch, Josephine (McLean)
McLean, Jacqueline
  See Kolosov, Jacqueline
McLean, Janet 1946- 113
McLean, Kathryn (Anderson) 1909-1966 9
McLean, Virginia Overton 1946- 90
McLean-Carr, Carol 1948- 122
McLeish, Kenneth 1940-1997 35
McLenighan, Valjean 1947- 46
  Brief entry 40
McLennan, Connie 171
McLennan, Will
  See Wisler, G(ary) Clifton
McLeod, Bob 1951- 173
McLeod, Chum 1955- 95
McLeod, Emilie Warren 1926-1982 23
  Obituary 31
McLeod, Kirsty
  See Hudson, (Margaret) Kirsty
McLeod, Margaret Vail
  See Holloway, Teresa (Bragunier)
McLerran, Alice 1933- 137
  Earlier sketch in SATA 68
McLimans, David 1949- 182
McLoughlin, John C. 1949- 47
McMahon, Bob 1956- 208
McManus, Patrick F. 1933- 46
McManus, Patrick Francis
  See McManus, Patrick F.
McMeekin, Clark
  See McMeekin, Isabel McLennan
McMeekin, Isabel McLennan 1895-1973 3
McMenemy, Sarah 1965- 156

McMillan, Bruce 1947- *192*
  Earlier sketches in SATA *22, 70, 129*
  See also CLR *47*
McMillan, Naomi
  See Grimes, Nikki
McMorey, James L.
  See Moyer, Terry J.
McMorrow, Annalisa 1969- *104*
McMullan, Jim 1934- *150*
  Earlier sketch in SATA *87*
McMullan, K. H.
  See McMullan, Kate
McMullan, Kate 1947- *189*
  Brief entry *48*
  Earlier sketches in SATA *52, 87, 132*
McMullan, Kate Hall
  See McMullan, Kate
McMullan, Margaret 1960- *203*
McMurtrey, Martin A(loysias) 1921- *21*
McNabb, Linda 1963- *147*
McNair, Kate *3*
McNair, Sylvia 1924-2002 .... *74*
McNamara, Margaret C(raig) 1915-1981
  Obituary *24*
McNaught, Harry *32*
McNaughton, Colin 1951- *211*
  Earlier sketches in SATA *39, 92, 134*
  See also CLR *54*
McNaughton, Janet 1953- *162*
  Earlier sketch in SATA *110*
McNeal, Laura *194*
McNeal, Tom *194*
McNeely, Jeannette 1918- *25*
McNeer, May (Yonge) 1902-1994 .... *81*
  Earlier sketch in SATA *1*
McNeese, Tim 1953- *139*
McNeill, Janet
  See Alexander, Janet
McNicholas, Shelagh *191*
McNickle, D'Arcy 1904-1977
  Obituary *22*
McNickle, William D'Arcy
  See McNickle, D'Arcy
McNicoll, Sylvia (Marilyn) 1954- *113*
  See also CLR *99*
McNulty, Faith 1918-2005 .... *168*
  Earlier sketches in SATA *12, 84, 139*
McPhail, David 1940- *219*
  Brief entry *32*
  Earlier sketches in SATA *47, 81, 140, 183*
McPhail, David M.
  See McPhail, David
McPhail, David Michael
  See McPhail, David
McPhee, Norma H. 1928- *95*
McPhee, Peter 1957- *214*
McPhee, Richard B(yron) 1934- *41*
McPherson, James M. 1936- *141*
  Earlier sketch in SATA *16*
McPherson, James Munro
  See McPherson, James M.
McQueen, Lucinda 1950- *58*
  Brief entry *48*
McQueen, Mildred Hark 1908-1978 .... *12*
McQuillan, Mary *200*
McRae, Russell (William) 1934- *63*
McShean, Gordon 1936- *41*
Mc Swigan, Marie 1907-1962 .... *24*
McTavish, Sandy
  See Eyerly, Jeannette
McVeity, Jen *148*
McVey, Vicki 1946- *80*
McVicker, Charles (Taggart) 1930- *39*
McVicker, Chuck
  See McVicker, Charles (Taggart)
McVoy, Terra Elan *220*
McWhirter, A(lan) Ross 1925-1975 .... *37*
  Obituary *31*
McWhirter, Norris (Dewar) 1925-2004 .... *37*
McWilliam, Howard 1977- *219*
McWilliams, Karen 1943- *65*

Mdurvwa, Hajara E. 1962- *92*
Meacham, Margaret 1952- *203*
  Earlier sketch in SATA *95*
Meachum, Virginia 1918- *133*
  Earlier sketch in SATA *87*
Mead, Alice 1952- *146*
  Earlier sketch in SATA *94*
Mead, Margaret 1901-1978
  Obituary *20*
Mead, Russell (M., Jr.) 1935- *10*
Mead, Stella (?)-1981
  Obituary *27*
Meade, Ellen
  See Roddick, Ellen
Meade, Holly *207*
Meade, Marion 1934- *127*
  Earlier sketch in SATA *23*
Meader, Stephen W(arren) 1892-1977 .... *1*
Meadmore, Susan
  See Sallis, Susan (Diana)
Meadow, Charles T(roub) 1929- *23*
Meadowcroft, Enid LaMonte
  See Wright, Enid Meadowcroft (LaMonte)
Meadows, Graham (W.) 1934- *161*
Meadows, Michelle *202*
Meaker, M. J.
  See Meaker, Marijane
Meaker, Marijane 1927- *160*
  Autobiography Feature *111*
  Earlier sketches in SATA *20, 61, 99*
  See also CLR *29*
  See also SAAS *1*
Meaker, Marijane Agnes
  See Meaker, Marijane
Means, Florence Crannell 1891-1980 .... *1*
  Obituary *25*
  See also CLR *56*
Mearian, Judy Frank 1936- *49*
Mebus, Scott 1974- *216*
Mecca, Judy Truesdell 1955- *127*
Mechling, Lauren 1978(?)- *194*
Mechling, Lauren 1978(?)- *194*
Mechner, Jordan 1964- *205*
Medary, Marjorie 1890-1980 .... *14*
Meddaugh, Susan 1944- *176*
  Earlier sketches in SATA *29, 84, 125*
Medearis, Angela Shelf 1956- *123*
  Earlier sketch in SATA *72*
Medearis, Mary 1915- *5*
Medina, Jane 1953- *167*
  Earlier sketch in SATA *122*
Medina, Meg 1963- *212*
Medina, Nico 1982- *193*
Medlicott, Mary 1946- *88*
Mee, Charles L., Jr. 1938- *72*
  Earlier sketch in SATA *8*
Meehan, Kierin *218*
Meehl, Brian *204*
Meek, Jacklyn O'Hanlon 1933- *51*
  Brief entry *34*
Meek, S(terner St.) P(aul) 1894-1972
  Obituary *28*
Meeker, Clare Hodgson 1952- *96*
Meeker, Oden 1919(?)-1976 .... *14*
Meeker, Richard
  See Brown, Fornan
Meeks, Esther MacBain *1*
Meggs, Libby Phillips 1943- *130*
Mehdevi, Alexander (Sinclair) 1947- *7*
Mehdevi, Anne (Marie) Sinclair 1947- *8*
Meidell, Sherry 1951- *73*
Meier, Minta 1906- *55*
Meighan, Donald Charles 1929- *30*
Meigs, Cornelia Lynde 1884-1973 .... *6*
  See also CLR *55*
Meilach, Dona Z(weigoron) 1926- *34*
Meilman, Philip W(arren) 1951- *79*
Meinstereifel, Ronald L. 1960- *134*
Meisel, Paul *184*
Meister, Cari *204*
Melanson, Luc *198*

Melcher, Daniel 1912-1985
  Obituary *43*
Melcher, Frederic Gershom 1879-1963
  Obituary *22*
Melcher, Marguerite Fellows 1879-1969 ...... *10*
Meldrum, Christina *206*
Melendez, Francisco 1964- *72*
Melhuish, Eva *199*
Melin, Grace Hathaway 1892-1973 .... *10*
Mellersh, H(arold) E(dward) L(eslie)
  1897- *10*
Melling, David *186*
Melmed, Laura Krauss *212*
Melmoth, Sebastian
  See Wilde, Oscar
Melnikoff, Pamela (Rita) *97*
Meltzer, Amy 1968- *202*
Meltzer, Milton 1915-2009 .... *201*
  Autobiography Feature *124*
  Earlier sketches in SATA *1, 50, 80, 128*
  See also CLR *13*
  See also SAAS *1*
Melville, Anne
  See Potter, Margaret
Melville, Herman 1819-1891 .... *59*
Melwood, Mary
  See Lewis, E. M.
Melzack, Ronald 1929- *5*
Memling, Carl 1918-1969 .... *6*
Menchin, Scott *188*
Mendel, Jo
  See Bond, Gladys Baker
  and Gilbertson, Mildred Geiger
Mendelson, Steven T. 1958-1995 .... *86*
Mendelson-Stevens, Serita Deborah
  See Stevens, Serita
Mendes, Valerie 1939- *157*
Mendez, Raymond A. 1947- *66*
Mendez, Simon 1975- *215*
Mendonca, Susan
  See Smith, Susan Vernon
Mendoza, George 1934- *41*
  Brief entry *39*
  See also SAAS *7*
Menendez, Shirley (C.) 1937- *146*
Meng, Cece *194*
Meng, Heinz (Karl) 1924- *13*
Mennen, Ingrid 1954- *85*
Menotti, Gian Carlo 1911-2007 .... *29*
  Obituary *180*
Menuhin, Sir Yehudi 1916-1999 .... *40*
  Obituary *113*
Menville, Douglas 1935- *64*
Menzel, Barbara Jean 1946- *63*
Menzel, Peter 1948- *207*
Mercati, Cynthia *164*
Mercati, Cynthia J.
  See Mercati, Cynthia
Mercer, Charles (Edward) 1917-1988 .... *16*
  Obituary *61*
Mercer, Jessie *21*
Mercer, Sienna *192*
Meredith, Arnold
  See Hopkins, (Hector) Kenneth
Meredith, David William
  See Miers, Earl Schenck
Meringoff, Laurene Krasny
  See Brown, Laurene Krasny
Meriwether, Louise 1923- *52*
  Brief entry *31*
Merlin, Arthur
  See Blish, James
Merlin, Christina
  See Heaven, Constance (Christina)
Merriam, Eve 1916-1992 .... *73*
  Earlier sketches in SATA *3, 40*
  See also CLR *14*
Merrill, Jane 1946- *42*
Merrill, Jane Merrill
  See Merrill, Jane

Merrill, Jean (Fairbanks) 1923- 82
  Earlier sketch in SATA *1*
  See also CLR *52*
Merrill, Phil
  See Merrill, Jane
Merriman, Alex
  See Silverberg, Robert
Merriman, Rachel 1971- 149
  Earlier sketch in SATA *98*
Merrit, Elizabeth
  See Goudge, Eileen
Merski, Patricia K.
  See Merski, P.K.
Merski, P.K. 172
Mertz, Barbara
  See Peters, Elizabeth
Mertz, Barbara Gross
  See Peters, Elizabeth
Merveille, David 200
Merz, Jennifer J. 196
Meschel, Susan V. 1936- 83
Meserve, Jessica 211
Messenger, Charles (Rynd Milles) 1942- 59
Messick, Dale 1906-2005 64
  Brief entry 48
Messier, Claire 1956- 103
Messieres, Nicole de
  See de Messieres, Nicole
Messinger, Carla 198
Messmer, Otto 1892(?)-1983 37
Mesta, Gabriel
  See Moesta, Rebecca
Metaxas, Eric 1963- 211
Metcalf, Doris H(unter) 91
Metcalf, Suzanne
  See Baum, L. Frank
Metos, Thomas H(arry) 1932- 37
Metter, Bert(ram Milton) 1927- 56
Metzenthen, David 1958- 167
  Earlier sketch in SATA *106*
Meunier, Brian 1954- 195
Meyer, Barbara 1939- 77
Meyer, Carolyn 1935- 142
  Autobiography Feature 142
  Earlier sketches in SATA *9, 70, 118*
  See also SAAS *9*
Meyer, Carolyn Mae
  See Meyer, Carolyn
Meyer, Edith Patterson 1895-1993 5
Meyer, F(ranklyn) E(dward) 1932- 9
Meyer, Jean Shepherd 11
Meyer, Jerome Sydney 1895-1975 3
  Obituary 25
Meyer, June
  See Jordan, June
Meyer, Kerstin 1966- 190
Meyer, L.A. 1942- 221
  Earlier sketches in SATA *12, 144*
Meyer, Louis A.
  See Meyer, L.A.
Meyer, Renate 1930- 6
Meyer, Stephenie 1973- 193
  See also CLR *142*
Meyer, Susan E. 1940- 64
Meyerhoff, Jenny 1972- 208
Meyers, Susan 1942- 164
  Earlier sketches in SATA *19, 108*
Meynell, Laurence Walter 1899-1989
  Obituary 61
Meynier, Yvonne (Pollet) 1908- 14
Mezey, Robert 1935- 33
Micale, Albert 1913- 22
Michael, James
  See Scagnetti, Jack
Michael, Jan 1947- 216
Michael, Livi 1960- 172
Michael, Manfred
  See Winterfeld, Henry
Michael, Olivia
  See Michael, Livi
Michaelis, Antonia 1979- 215

Michaels, Barbara
  See Peters, Elizabeth
Michaels, Jamie 195
Michaels, Joanne Louise
  See Teitelbaum, Michael
Michaels, Kristin
  See Williams, Jeanne
Michaels, Molly
  See Untermeyer, Louis
Michaels, Neal
  See Teitelbaum, Michael
Michaels, Rune 194
Michaels, Ski
  See Pellowski, Michael (Joseph)
Michaels, Steve 1955- 71
Michaels, William M. 1917- 77
Michalak, Jamie 1973- 217
Michel, Anna 1943- 49
  Brief entry 40
Michel, Francois 1948- 82
Michelin, Linda 183
Michelson, Richard 198
  Earlier sketch in SATA *173*
Micich, Paul 74
Mickelson, Scott 1963- 213
Micklish, Rita 1931- 12
Micklos, John, Jr. 1956- 173
  Earlier sketch in SATA *129*
Micklos J., John, Jr. 1956-
  See Micklos, John, Jr.
Micucci, Charles (Patrick, Jr.) 1959- 144
  Earlier sketch in SATA *82*
Middleton, Haydn 1955- 152
  Earlier sketch in SATA *85*
Miers, Earl Schenck 1910-1972 1
  Obituary 26
Migdale, Lawrence 1951- 89
Miglio, Paige 1966- 201
Mikaelsen, Ben 1952- 173
  Earlier sketches in SATA *73, 107*
Mikaelsen, Benjamin John
  See Mikaelsen, Ben
Miklowitz, Gloria D. 1927- 129
  Earlier sketches in SATA *4, 68*
  See also SAAS *17*
Mikolaycak, Charles 1937-1993 78
  Obituary 75
  Earlier sketch in SATA *9*
  See also SAAS *4*
Mild, Warren (Paul) 1922- 41
Milelli, Pascal 1965- 135
Miles, Betty 1928- 78
  Earlier sketch in SATA *8*
  See also SAAS *9*
Miles, Miska
  See Martin, Patricia Miles
Miles, (Mary) Patricia 1930- 29
Miles, Patricia A.
  See Martin, Patricia Miles
Miles, Victoria 1966- 188
Milgrim, David 187
  Earlier sketch in SATA *158*
Milgrom, Harry 1912-1978 25
Milhous, Katherine 1894-1977 15
Milich, Zoran 174
Milios, Rita 1949- 79
Militant
  See Sandburg, Carl
Millais, Raoul 1901- 77
Millar, Barbara F. 1924- 12
Millar, Margaret (Ellis Sturm) 1915-1994 61
  Obituary 79
Millard, Glenda 203
Millard, Kerry 204
Millbank, Captain H. R.
  See Ellis, Edward S.
Millen, C(ynthia) M. 1955- 114
Miller, Albert G(riffith) 1905-1982 12
  Obituary 31
Miller, Alice Ann 1958- 150
Miller, Alice P(atricia McCarthy) 22

Miller, Allan 1978- 216
Miller, Christopher 1976- 215
Miller, Debbie 1951- 160
  Earlier sketch in SATA *103*
Miller, Debbie S.
  See Miller, Debbie
Miller, Deborah Uchill 1944- 61
Miller, Don 1923- 15
Miller, Doris R.
  See Mosesson, Gloria R(ubin)
Miller, Eddie
  See Miller, Edward
Miller, Edna Anita 1920- 29
Miller, Edward 1905-1974 8
Miller, Edward 1964- 218
  Earlier sketch in SATA *183*
Miller, Elizabeth 1933- 41
Miller, Ellanita 1957- 87
Miller, Eugene 1925- 33
Miller, Frances A. 1937- 52
  Brief entry 46
Miller, Heather Lynn 1971- 214
Miller, Helen M(arkley) -1984 5
Miller, Helen Topping 1884-1960
  Obituary 29
Miller, Jane (Judith) 1925-1989 15
Miller, Jewel 1956- 73
Miller, John
  See Samachson, Joseph
Miller, Judi 117
Miller, Karen 1949- 210
Miller, Karen Hokanson
  See Miller, Karen
Miller, Kate 1948- 193
Miller, Kirsten 1973- 185
Miller, Louise (Rolfe) 1940- 76
Miller, M. L. 85
Miller, Madge 1918- 63
Miller, Margaret J.
  See Dale, Margaret J(essy) Miller
Miller, Marilyn (Jean) 1925- 33
Miller, Marvin 65
Miller, Mary
  See Northcott, (William) Cecil
Miller, Mary Beth 1942- 9
Miller, Mary Beth 1964- 185
Miller, Maryann 1943- 73
Miller, Natalie 1917-1976 35
Miller, Pat 1951- 214
Miller, Robert H. 1944- 91
Miller, Ron 1947- 185
Miller, Ruth White
  See White, Ruth
Miller, Sandra
  See Miller, Sandy
Miller, Sandra Peden
  See Miller, Sandy
Miller, Sandy 1948- 41
  Brief entry 35
Miller, Sarah 1969- 175
Miller, Virginia
  See Austin, Virginia
Miller, William R. 1959- 116
Miller Brothers
  See Miller, Allan
Milligan, Bryce 1953- 170
Milligan, Spike
  See Milligan, Terence Alan
Milligan, Terence Alan 1918-2002 29
  Obituary 134
  See also CLR *92*
Millington, Ada
  See Deyneka, Anita
Millman, Isaac 1933- 140
Mills, Adam
  See Stanley, George Edward
Mills, Claudia 1954- 191
  Brief entry 41
  Earlier sketches in SATA *44, 89, 145*
Mills, Elaine (Rosemary) 1941- 72
Mills, G. Riley 196

Mills, Joyce C. 1944- *102*
Mills, Judith Christine 1956- *130*
Mills, Yaroslava Surmach 1925- *35*
Millspaugh, Ben P. 1936- *77*
Millstead, Thomas E. *30*
Millward, Gwen *202*
Milne, A. A. 1882-1956 .... *100*
    See also YABC *1*
    See also CLR *108*
Milne, Alan Alexander
    See Milne, A. A.
Milne, Lorus J. *5*
    See also CLR *22*
    See also SAAS *18*
Milne, Margery *5*
    See also CLR *22*
    See also SAAS *18*
Milne, Terry
    See Milne, Theresa Ann
Milne, Theresa Ann 1964- *84*
Milnes, Irma McDonough 1924- *101*
Milonas, Rolf
    See Myller, Rolf
Milone, Karen
    See Dugan, Karen
Milone-Dugan, Karen
    See Dugan, Karen
Milord, Susan 1954- *200*
    Earlier sketches in SATA *74, 147*
Milotte, Alfred G(eorge) 1904-1989 .... *11*
    Obituary *62*
Milstein, Linda 1954- *80*
Milton, Ann *134*
Milton, Hilary (Herbert) 1920- *23*
Milton, John R(onald) 1924- *24*
Milton, Joyce 1946- *101*
    Brief entry *41*
    Earlier sketch in SATA *52*
Milusich, Janice *216*
Milverton, Charles A.
    See Penzler, Otto
Milway, Alex 1978- *215*
Milway, Katie Smith 1960- *203*
Minahan, John A. 1956- *92*
Minar, Barbra (Goodyear) 1940- *79*
Minard, Rosemary 1939- *63*
Minarik, Else Holmelund 1920- *127*
    Earlier sketch in SATA *15*
    See also CLR *33*
Miner, Jane Claypool 1933- *103*
    Brief entry *37*
    Earlier sketch in SATA *38*
Miner, Lewis S. 1909-1971 .... *11*
Mines, Jeanette 1948- *61*
Mines, Jeanette Marie
    See Mines, Jeanette
Minier, Nelson
    See Stoutenburg, Adrien (Pearl)
Minnitt, Ronda Jacqueline
    See Armitage, David
Minor, Wendell 1944- *199*
    Earlier sketches in SATA *78, 109, 164*
Minter, Daniel 1961- *176*
Mintonye, Grace *4*
Miranda, Anne 1954- *109*
    Earlier sketch in SATA *71*
Miranda, Inaki 1983(?)- *207*
Mirocha, Paul *192*
Mirsky, Jeannette 1903-1987 .... *8*
    Obituary *51*
Mirsky, Reba Paeff 1902-1966 .... *1*
Misako Rocks! *192*
Misenta, Marisol
    See Innes, Stephanie
Mishica, Clare 1960- *91*
Miskovits, Christine 1939- *10*
Miss Frances
    See Horwich, Frances R(appaport)
Miss Read
    See Saint, Dora Jessie

Mister Rogers
    See Rogers, Fred McFeely
Mitchard, Jacquelyn 1956- *219*
    Earlier sketches in SATA *98, 168*
Mitchell, Adrian 1932-2008 .... *166*
    Obituary *200*
    Earlier sketch in SATA *104*
Mitchell, Allison
    See Griffin, W. E. B.
Mitchell, Betty Jo
    See Mitchell, B.J.
Mitchell, B.J. 1931- *120*
Mitchell, Clyde
    See Ellison, Harlan
    and Silverberg, Robert
Mitchell, Cynthia 1922- *29*
Mitchell, (Sibyl) Elyne (Keith) 1913- *10*
Mitchell, Gladys (Maude Winifred)
    1901-1983 .... *46*
    Obituary *35*
Mitchell, Jay
    See Roberson, Jennifer
Mitchell, Joyce Slayton 1933- *142*
    Brief entry *43*
    Earlier sketch in SATA *46*
Mitchell, K. L.
    See Lamb, Elizabeth Searle
Mitchell, Kathy 1948- *59*
Mitchell, Lori 1961- *128*
Mitchell, Margaree King 1953- *84*
Mitchell, Marianne 1947- *145*
Mitchell, Rhonda *89*
Mitchell, Saundra 1974(?)- *217*
Mitchell, Stephen 1943- *199*
Mitchell, Susan
    See Mitchell, Susan K.
Mitchell, Susan K. 1972- *210*
Mitchell, Todd 1974- *191*
Mitchell, Yvonne 1925-1979
    Obituary *24*
Mitchelson, Mitch
    See Mitchelson, Peter Richard
Mitchelson, Peter Richard 1950- *104*
Mitchison, Naomi (Margaret Haldane)
    1897-1999 .... *24*
    Obituary *112*
Mitchnik, Helen 1901-1982 .... *41*
    Brief entry *35*
Mitchum, Hank
    See Knott, William C(ecil, Jr.)
    and Murray, Stuart A. P.
    and Newton, D(wight) B(ennett)
    and Sherman, Jory (Tecumseh)
Mitgutsch, Ali 1935- *76*
Mitsuhashi, Yoko *45*
    Brief entry *33*
Mitton, Jacqueline 1948- *162*
    Earlier sketches in SATA *66, 115*
Mitton, Simon 1946- *66*
Mitton, Tony 1951- *203*
    Earlier sketches in SATA *104, 149*
Miura, Taro 1968- *181*
Mizner, Elizabeth Howard 1907- *27*
Mizumura, Kazue *18*
Mlynowski, Sarah 1977(?)- *180*
Mobin-Uddin, Asma *216*
    Earlier sketch in SATA *172*
Mobley, Joe A. 1945- *91*
Moche, Dinah (Rachel) L(evine) 1936- *44*
    Brief entry *40*
Mochi, Ugo (A.) 1889-1977 .... *38*
Mochizuki, Ken 1954- *146*
    Earlier sketch in SATA *81*
    See also SAAS *22*
Modarressi, Mitra 1967- *200*
    Earlier sketch in SATA *126*
Modell, Frank B. 1917- *39*
    Brief entry *36*
Modesitt, Jeanne 1953- *217*
    Earlier sketches in SATA *92, 143*

Modesitt, L.E., Jr. 1943- *164*
    Earlier sketch in SATA *91*
Modesitt, Leland Exton, Jr.
    See Modesitt, L.E., Jr.
Modrell, Dolores 1933- *72*
Moe, Barbara 1937- *20*
Moe, Jorgen (Ingebretsen) 1813-1882
    See CLR *104*
Moed-Kass, Pnina *169*
Moerbeek, Kees 1955- *98*
Moeri, Louise 1924- *93*
    Earlier sketch in SATA *24*
    See also SAAS *10*
Moesta, Rebecca 1956- *182*
Moffett, Jami 1952- *84*
Moffett, Mark W. 1957(?)- *203*
Moffett, Martha (Leatherwood) 1934- *8*
Mogensen, Suzanne A(ncher) 1946- *129*
Mohammed, Khadra *197*
Mohn, Peter B(urnet) 1934- *28*
Mohn, Viola Kohl 1914- *8*
Mohr, Nicholasa 1938- *97*
    Autobiography Feature *113*
    Earlier sketch in SATA *8*
    See also CLR *22*
    See also SAAS *8*
Mok, Esther 1953- *93*
Molan, Christine 1943- *84*
Molarsky, Osmond 1909- *16*
Moldon, Peter L(eonard) 1937- *49*
Mole, John 1941- *103*
    Earlier sketch in SATA *36*
    See also CLR *61*
Molesworth, Mary Louisa 1839-1921 .... *98*
Molin, Charles
    See Mayne, William
Molina, Silvia 1946- *97*
Molk, Laurel 1957- *162*
    Earlier sketch in SATA *92*
Mollel, Tololwa M. 1952- *88*
Molloy, Anne Baker 1907-1999 .... *32*
Molloy, Michael (John) 1940- *162*
Molloy, Paul (George) 1924- *5*
Moloney, James 1954- *202*
    Autobiography Feature *144*
    Earlier sketches in SATA *94, 144*
Molski, Carol *215*
Momaday, N. Scott 1934- *48*
    Brief entry *30*
Momaday, Navarre Scott
    See Momaday, N. Scott
Monaco, Octavia 1963- *169*
Monagle, Bernie 1957- *121*
Moncure, Jane Belk 1926- *23*
Monjo, F(erdinand) N(icholas III)
    1924-1978 .... *16*
    See also CLR *2*
Monk, Isabell 1952- *136*
Monks, Lydia *189*
Monroe, Chris 1962- *219*
Monroe, Christine
    See Monroe, Chris
Monroe, Lyle
    See Heinlein, Robert A.
Monroe, Marion
    See Cox, Marion Monroe
Monroy, Manuel 1970- *196*
Monsell, Helen Albee 1895-1971 .... *24*
Monson-Burton, Marianne 1975- *139*
Montana, Bob 1920-1975
    Obituary *21*
Montanari, Eva 1977- *209*
Montecalvo, Janet *177*
Montenegro, Laura Nyman 1953- *95*
Montero, Gloria 1933- *109*
Montes, Marisa 1951- *144*
Montgomerie, Norah (Mary) 1913- *26*
Montgomery, Constance
    See Cappel, Constance
Montgomery, Elizabeth
    See Julesberg, Elizabeth Rider Montgomery

Montgomery, Elizabeth Rider
   See Julesberg, Elizabeth Rider Montgomery
Montgomery, Hugh (Edward) 1962- *146*
Montgomery, L. M. 1874-1942 .... *100*
   See also YABC *1*
   See also CLR *145*
Montgomery, Lucy Maud
   See Montgomery, L. M.
Montgomery, Michael G. 1952- *208*
Montgomery, Raymond A. (Jr.) 1936- *39*
Montgomery, Rutherford George 1894-1985 . *3*
Montgomery, Sy 1958- *184*
   Autobiography Feature *132*
   Earlier sketches in SATA *114, 132*
Montgomery, Vivian *36*
Monthei, Betty *179*
Montijo, Rhode *179*
Montileaux, Donald F. 1948- *183*
Montpetit, Charles 1958- *101*
Montresor, Beni 1926-2001 .... *38*
   Earlier sketch in SATA *3*
   See also SAAS *4*
Montserrat, Pep *181*
Monty Python
   See Chapman, Graham
   and Cleese, John (Marwood)
   and Gilliam, Terry
   and Idle, Eric
   and Jones, Terence Graham Parry
   and Palin, Michael
Moodie, Craig 1956- *172*
Moodie, Fiona 1952- *133*
Moody, Minerva
   See Alcott, Louisa May
Moody, Ralph Owen 1898-1982 .... *1*
Moon, Carl 1879(?)-1948 .... *25*
Moon, Grace (Purdie) 1877(?)-1947 .... *25*
Moon, Lily
   See Warnes, Tim
Moon, Nicola 1952- *147*
   Earlier sketch in SATA *96*
Moon, Pat 1946- *113*
Moon, Sheila 1910-1991 .... *5*
   Obituary *114*
Moon, Sheila Elizabeth
   See Moon, Sheila
Mooney, Bel 1946- *95*
Mooney, Bill 1936- *122*
Mooney, Elizabeth C(omstock) 1918-1986
   Obituary *48*
Mooney, William
   See Mooney, Bill
Moor, Emily
   See Deming, Richard
Moorcock, Michael 1939- *166*
   Earlier sketch in SATA *93*
Moorcock, Michael John
   See Moorcock, Michael
Moorcock, Michael John
   See Moorcock, Michael
Moore, Anne Carroll 1871-1961 .... *13*
Moore, Cheri
   See Ladd, Cheryl (Jean)
Moore, Clement Clarke 1779-1863 .... *18*
Moore, Cyd 1957- *186*
   Earlier sketches in SATA *83, 133*
Moore, Don W. 1905(?)-1986
   Obituary *48*
Moore, Elaine 1944- *86*
Moore, Eva 1942- *103*
   Earlier sketch in SATA *20*
Moore, Ishbel (Lindsay) 1954- *140*
Moore, Jack (William) 1941- *46*
   Brief entry *32*
Moore, Janet Gaylord 1905-1992 .... *18*
Moore, Jim 1946- *42*
Moore, John Travers 1908- *12*
Moore, Lilian 1909-2004 .... *137*
   Obituary *155*
   Earlier sketch in SATA *52*
   See also CLR *15*

Moore, Liz
   See Moore, M. Elizabeth
Moore, M. Elizabeth 1959- *156*
Moore, Margaret R(umberger) 1903- *12*
Moore, Margie *176*
Moore, Marianne 1887-1972 .... *20*
Moore, Marianne Craig
   See Moore, Marianne
Moore, Patrick (Alfred Caldwell) 1923- *49*
   Brief entry *39*
   See also SAAS *8*
Moore, Patrick 1959- *184*
Moore, Perry *193*
Moore, Peter 1963- *175*
Moore, Peter G.
   See Moore, Peter
Moore, Raina 1970- *212*
Moore, Ray (S.) 1905(?)-1984
   Obituary *37*
Moore, Regina
   See Dunne, Mary Collins
Moore, Rosalie (Gertrude) 1910-2001 .... *9*
Moore, Ruth (Ellen) 1908-1989 .... *23*
Moore, Ruth Nulton 1923- *38*
Moore, S(arah) E. *23*
Moore, Sarah Margaret
   See Hodges, Margaret
Moore, Stephanie Perry 1969(?)- *214*
Moore, Tara 1950- *61*
Moore, Yvette 1958- *154*
   Earlier sketches in SATA *69, 70*
Moores, Dick
   See Moores, Richard (Arnold)
Moores, Richard (Arnold) 1909-1986
   Obituary *48*
Mooser, Stephen 1941- *75*
   Earlier sketch in SATA *28*
Mora, Francisco X(avier) 1952- *90*
Mora, Pat 1942- *186*
   Earlier sketches in SATA *92, 134*
   See also CLR *58*
Mora, Patricia
   See Mora, Pat
Morais, Flavio *207*
Morales, Yuyi *180*
   Earlier sketch in SATA *154*
Moran, Tom 1943- *60*
Moranville, Sharelle Byars *196*
   Earlier sketch in SATA *152*
Moray Williams, Ursula 1911-2006 .... *3*
   Obituary *177*
   See also SAAS *9*
Mordecai, Martin *220*
Morden, Simon 1966(?)- *211*
Mordvinoff, Nicolas 1911-1973 .... *17*
More, Caroline
   See Cone, Molly (Lamken)
   and Strachan, Margaret Pitcairn
Moreau, Jean-Pierre
   See Jarrie, Martin
Moreno, Rene King *190*
Moreton, Andrew Esq.
   See Defoe, Daniel
Morey, Charles
   See Fletcher, Helen Jill
Morey, Walt(er Nelson) 1907-1992 .... *51*
   Obituary *70*
   Earlier sketch in SATA *3*
   See also SAAS *9*
Morgan, Alfred P(owell) 1889-1972 .... *33*
Morgan, Alison (Mary) 1930- *85*
   Earlier sketch in SATA *30*
Morgan, Anne 1954- *121*
Morgan, Christopher 1956- *199*
Morgan, Clay 1950- *198*
Morgan, Douglas
   See Macdonald, James D.
Morgan, Ellen
   See Bumstead, Kathleen Mary
Morgan, Geoffrey 1916- *46*

Morgan, Helen (Gertrude Louise)
   1921-1990 .... *29*
Morgan, Jane
   See Cooper, James Fenimore
   and Franklin, Jane (Morgan)
   and Moren, Sally M(oore)
Morgan, Lenore H. 1908-1976 .... *8*
Morgan, Mary 1957- *213*
   Earlier sketches in SATA *81, 114*
Morgan, McKayla
   See Basile, Gloria Vitanza
Morgan, Michaela
   See Basile, Gloria Vitanza
Morgan, Nicola 1961- *161*
Morgan, Nina 1953- *110*
Morgan, Pierr 1952- *122*
   Earlier sketch in SATA *77*
Morgan, Robin (Evonne) 1941- *80*
Morgan, Roxanne
   See Gentle, Mary
Morgan, Sarah (Nicola) 1959- *68*
Morgan, Shirley
   See Kiepper, Shirley Morgan
Morgan, Stacy T(owle) 1959- *104*
Morgan, Stevie
   See Davies, Nicola
Morgan, Tom 1942- *42*
Morgan, Wendy
   See Staub, Wendy Corsi
Morgan-Vanroyen, Mary
   See Morgan, Mary
Morgenstern, Susie Hoch 1945- *133*
Mori, Hana 1909-1990(?) *88*
Mori, Kyoko 1957- *122*
   Autobiography Feature *126*
   See also CLR *64*
   See also SAAS *26*
Moriarty, Jaclyn 1968- *162*
Moriarty, William J. 1930- *127*
Morice, Dave 1946- *93*
Morin, Isobel V. 1928- *110*
Morine, Hoder
   See Conroy, John Wesley
Morley, Taia *199*
Morley, Wilfred Owen
   See Lowndes, Robert A(ugustine) W(ard)
Morningstar, Mildred (Whaley) 1912-1997 .. *61*
   Obituary *114*
Morozumi, Atsuko *217*
   Earlier sketch in SATA *110*
Morpurgo, Michael 1943- *184*
   Earlier sketches in SATA *93, 143*
   See also CLR *51*
Morrah, Dave
   See Morrah, David Wardlaw, Jr.
Morrah, David Wardlaw, Jr. 1914-1991 .... *10*
Morreale-de la Garza, Phyllis
   See De la Garza, Phyllis
Morressy, John 1930-2006 .... *23*
Morrill, Leslie H(olt) 1934-2003 .... *48*
   Brief entry *33*
   Obituary *148*
   See also SAAS *22*
Morris, Carla *210*
Morris, Carla D.
   See Morris, Carla
Morris, Chris(topher Crosby) 1946- *66*
Morris, Deborah 1956- *91*
Morris, Desmond 1928- *14*
Morris, Desmond John
   See Morris, Desmond
Morris, Don 1954- *83*
Morris, Gerald 1963- *207*
   Earlier sketches in SATA *107, 150*
Morris, Gerald Paul
   See Morris, Gerald
Morris, Gilbert (Leslie) 1929- *104*
Morris, Jackie *202*
   Earlier sketch in SATA *151*
Morris, Janet (Ellen) 1946- *66*

Morris, Jay
  See Tatham, Julie Campbell
Morris, (Margaret) Jean 1924- 98
Morris, Jeffrey
  See Morris, Jeffrey Brandon
Morris, Jeffrey B.
  See Morris, Jeffrey Brandon
Morris, Jeffrey Brandon 1941- 92
Morris, Jennifer E. 1969- 179
Morris, Jill 1936- 165
  Earlier sketch in SATA *119*
Morris, Juddi 85
Morris, Judy K. 1936- 61
Morris, Oradel Nolen 128
Morris, Robert A(da) 1933- 7
Morris, William 1913-1994 29
Morrison, Angela 218
Morrison, Bill 1935- 66
  Brief entry 37
Morrison, Chloe Anthony Wofford
  See Morrison, Toni
Morrison, Dorothy Nafus 29
Morrison, Frank 1971- 185
Morrison, Gordon 1944- 183
  Earlier sketches in SATA *87, 128*
Morrison, Joan 1922- 65
Morrison, Lillian 1917- 108
  Earlier sketch in SATA *3*
Morrison, Lucile Phillips 1896- 17
Morrison, Martha A. 1948- 77
Morrison, Meighan 1966- 90
Morrison, P.R. 196
Morrison, Richard
  See Lowndes, Robert A(ugustine) W(ard)
Morrison, Robert
  See Lowndes, Robert A(ugustine) W(ard)
Morrison, Roberta
  See Webb, Jean Francis (III)
Morrison, Susan Dudley
  See Gold, Susan Dudley
Morrison, Taylor 1971- 187
  Earlier sketches in SATA *95, 159*
Morrison, Toni 1931- 144
  Earlier sketch in SATA *57*
  See also CLR *99*
Morrison, Velma Ford 1909- 21
Morrison, Wilbur Howard 1915- 64
Morrison, William
  See Samachson, Joseph
Morriss, James E(dward) 1932- 8
Morrissey, Dean 183
Morrow, Barbara Olenyik 1952- 167
Morrow, Betty
  See Bacon, Elizabeth
Morrow, Sue Anne 1966- 218
Morse, C. Scott
  See Morse, Scott
Morse, Carol
  See Yeakley, Marjory Hall
Morse, C.S.
  See Morse, Scott
Morse, Dorothy B(ayley) 1906-1979
  Obituary 24
Morse, Flo 1921- 30
Morse, Scott 1973- 200
Morse, Tony 1953- 129
Mort, Vivian
  See Cromie, Alice Hamilton
Mortensen, Denise Dowling 179
Mortensen, Lori 1955- 221
Mortimer, Anne 1958- 206
  Earlier sketch in SATA *116*
Mortimer, Mary H.
  See Coury, Louise Andree
Morton, Alexandra (Hubbard) 1957- 144
Morton, Anthony
  See Arthur, Robert, (Jr.)
Morton, Christine
  See Morton-Shaw, Christine
Morton, Jane 1931- 50
Morton, Joseph C. 1932- 156

Morton, Lee Jack, Jr. 1928- 32
Morton, Miriam 1918(?)-1985 9
  Obituary 46
Morton-Shaw, Christine 1957- 211
Mosatche, Harriet 1949- 122
Mosatche, Harriet S.
  See Mosatche, Harriet
Moscow, Alvin 1925- 3
Mosel, Arlene (Tichy) 1921-1996 7
Moseley, James W(illett) 1931- 139
Moseng, Elisabeth 1967- 90
Moser, Barry 1940- 185
  Earlier sketches in SATA *56, 79, 138*
  See also CLR *49*
  See also SAAS *15*
Moser, Don(ald Bruce) 1932- 31
Moser, Laura 194
Moser, Lisa 192
Moses, Sheila P. 1961- 168
Moses, Will 1956- 178
  Earlier sketch in SATA *120*
Mosesson, Gloria R(ubin) 24
Mosher, Richard 1949- 120
Moskin, Marietta D(unston) 1928- 23
Moskof, Martin Stephen 1930- 27
Mosley, Francis 1957- 57
Moss, Don(ald) 1920- 11
Moss, Elaine (Dora) 1924- 57
  Brief entry 31
Moss, Jeff(rey) 1942-1998 73
  Obituary 106
Moss, Marissa 1959- 216
  Earlier sketches in SATA *71, 104, 163*
  See also CLR *134*
Moss, Miriam 1955- 202
  Earlier sketches in SATA *76, 140*
Moss, Thylias 1954- 108
Moss, Thylias Rebecca Brasier
  See Moss, Thylias
Most, Bernard 1937- 134
  Brief entry 40
  Earlier sketches in SATA *48, 91*
Mosz, Gosia 1972- 194
Mott, Evelyn Clarke 1962- 133
  Earlier sketch in SATA *75*
Motz, Lloyd 1909-2004 20
Mould, Chris 205
Mould, Edwin
  See Whitlock, Ralph
Moulton, Mark Kimball 212
Mouly, Francoise 155
Mountain, Robert
  See Montgomery, Raymond A. (Jr.)
Mountfield, David
  See Grant, Neil
Mourlevat, Jean-Claude 1952- 187
Mourning, Tuesday 206
Moussard, Jacqueline 1924- 24
Mowat, Claire 1933- 123
Mowat, Claire Angel Wheeler
  See Mowat, Claire
Mowat, Farley 1921- 55
  Earlier sketch in SATA *3*
  See also CLR *20*
Mowat, Farley McGill
  See Mowat, Farley
Mowll, Joshua 1970(?)- 188
Mowry, Jess 1960- 131
  Autobiography Feature 131
  Earlier sketch in SATA *109*
  See also CLR *65*
Moxley, Sheila 1966- 96
Moyer, Terry J. 1937- 94
Moyes, Patricia
  See Haszard, Patricia Moyes
Moyler, Alan (Frank Powell) 1926- 36
Mozelle, Shirley 179
Mozley, Charles 1915- 43
  Brief entry 32
Mphahlele, Es'kia 1919-2008 119
  Obituary 198

Mphahlele, Ezekiel
  See Mphahlele, Es'kia
Mphahlele, Zeke
  See Mphahlele, Es'kia
Mr. McGillicuddy
  See Abisch, Roslyn Kroop
Mr. Sniff
  See Abisch, Roslyn Kroop
Mr. Tivil
  See Lorkowski, Thomas V(incent)
Mr. Wizard
  See Herbert, Don
Mraz, David 1947- 219
Mrs. Fairstar
  See Horne, Richard Henry Hengist
Muchamore, Robert 1972- 175
Muchmore, Jo Ann 1937- 103
Mude, O.
  See Gorey, Edward (St. John)
Mudgeon, Apeman
  See Mitchell, Adrian
Mueller, Jorg 1942- 67
  See also CLR *43*
Mueller, Miranda R. 201
Mueller, Virginia 1924- 28
Muggs
  See Watkins, Lois
Muir, Diana
  See Appelbaum, Diana Muir Karter
Muir, Frank (Herbert) 1920-1998 30
Muir, Helen 1937- 65
Muirhead, Margaret 220
Mukerji, Dhan Gopal 1890-1936 40
  See also CLR *10*
Mulcahy, Lucille Burnett 12
Mulford, Philippa G. 1948- 112
  Earlier sketch in SATA *43*
Mulford, Philippa Greene
  See Mulford, Philippa G.
Mulgan, Catherine 1931- 24
Mulila, Vigad G.
  See Maillu, David G(ian)
Mull, Brandon 1974- 190
Mullen, Michael 1937- 122
Muller, Billex
  See Ellis, Edward S.
Muller, Birte 1973- 214
Muller, Jorg
  See Mueller, Jorg
Muller, (Lester) Robin 1953- 86
Mullin, Caryl Cude 1969- 130
Mullins, Edward S(wift) 1922- 10
Mullins, Hilary 1962- 84
Mulock, Dinah Maria
  See Craik, Dinah Maria (Mulock)
Mulvihill, William Patrick 1923- 8
Mumford, Ruth
  See Dallas, Ruth
Mumy, Bill 1954- 112
Mun
  See Leaf, (Wilbur) Munro
Munari, Bruno 1907-1998 15
  See also CLR *9*
Munce, Ruth Hill 1898- 12
Mundy, Simon 1954- 64
Mundy, Simon Andrew James Hainault
  See Mundy, Simon
Munger, Nancy 170
Munowitz, Ken 1935-1977 14
Munoz, Claudio 208
Munoz, William 1949- 92
  Earlier sketch in SATA *42*
Munro, Alice 1931- 29
Munro, Alice Anne
  See Munro, Alice
Munro, Eleanor 1928- 37
Munro, Roxie 1945- 184
  Earlier sketches in SATA *58, 136*
Munsch, Bob
  See Munsch, Robert (Norman)

Munsch, Robert (Norman) 1945- *120*
　Brief entry *48*
　Earlier sketches in SATA *50, 83*
　See also CLR *19*
Munsinger, Lynn 1951- *221*
　Earlier sketches in SATA *33, 94, 177*
Munson, Derek 1970- *139*
Munson, R. W.
　See Karl, Jean E(dna)
Munson-Benson, Tunie 1946- *15*
Munsterberg, Peggy 1921- *102*
Muntean, Michaela *182*
Munthe, Nelly 1947- *53*
Munves, James (Albert) 1922- *30*
Munzer, Martha E. 1899-1999 .... *4*
Murawski, Darlyne A. *193*
Murch, Mel
　See Manes, Stephen
Murdoch, David H(amilton) 1937- *96*
Murdoch, Patricia 1957- *192*
Murdock, Catherine Gilbert *185*
Murhall, J(acqueline) J(ane) 1964- *143*
Murphy, Barbara Beasley 1933- *130*
　Earlier sketch in SATA *5*
Murphy, Claire Rudolf 1951- *137*
　Earlier sketch in SATA *76*
Murphy, E(mmett) Jefferson 1926- *4*
Murphy, Elizabeth Ann Maureen
　See Murphy, Liz
Murphy, Jill 1949- *214*
　Earlier sketches in SATA *37, 70, 142*
　See also CLR *39*
Murphy, Jill Frances
　See Murphy, Jill
Murphy, Jim 1947- *185*
　Brief entry *32*
　Earlier sketches in SATA *37, 77, 124*
　See also CLR *53*
Murphy, Joseph E., Jr. 1930- *65*
Murphy, Kelly 1977- *190*
　Earlier sketch in SATA *143*
Murphy, Liz 1964- *210*
Murphy, Louise 1943- *155*
Murphy, Mary 1961- *196*
Murphy, Pat
　See Murphy, E(mmett) Jefferson
Murphy, Patricia J. 1963- *132*
Murphy, Rita *180*
Murphy, Robert (William) 1902-1971 .... *10*
Murphy, Shirley Rousseau 1928- *126*
　Earlier sketches in SATA *36, 71*
　See also SAAS *18*
Murphy, Stuart J. 1942- *157*
　Earlier sketch in SATA *115*
Murphy, Thomas Basil, Jr. 1935- *191*
Murphy, Tim
　See Murphy, Jim
Murphy, Tom
　See Murphy, Thomas Basil, Jr.
Murray, John 1923- *39*
Murray, Kirsty 1960- *165*
　Earlier sketch in SATA *108*
Murray, Marguerite 1917- *63*
Murray, Marian *5*
Murray, Martine 1965- *125*
Murray, (Judith) Michele (Freedman)
　1933-1974 .... *7*
Murray, Ossie 1938- *43*
Murray, Peter
　See Hautman, Pete
Murrow, Liza Ketchum
　See Ketchum, Liza
Musgrave, Florence 1902-1999 .... *3*
Musgrove, Margaret W(ynkoop) 1943- *124*
　Earlier sketch in SATA *26*
Musgrove, Marianne *207*
Mussey, Virginia Howell
　See Ellison, Virginia H(owell)
Mussey, Virginia T.H.
　See Ellison, Virginia H(owell)
Mussi, Sarah *206*

Mutel, Cornelia F. 1947- *74*
Muth, Jon J. *206*
　Earlier sketch in SATA *165*
Mutz
　See Kuenstler, Morton
Mwangi, Meja 1948- *174*
My Brother's Brother
　See Chekhov, Anton
Myers, Anna *220*
　Earlier sketch in SATA *160*
Myers, Arthur 1917- *91*
　Earlier sketch in SATA *35*
Myers, Bernice *81*
　Earlier sketch in SATA *9*
Myers, Caroline Elizabeth Clark
　1887-1980 .... *28*
Myers, Christopher 1975- *183*
　See also CLR *97*
Myers, Edward 1950- *172*
　Earlier sketch in SATA *96*
Myers, Elisabeth P(erkins) 1918- *36*
Myers, (Mary) Hortense (Powner)
　1913-1987 .... *10*
Myers, Jack 1913-2006 .... *83*
　Obituary *178*
Myers, Jack Edgar
　See Myers, Jack
Myers, Lou 1915-2005 .... *81*
　Obituary *171*
Myers, Louis
　See Myers, Lou
Myers, R.E. 1924- *119*
Myers, Robert Eugene
　See Myers, R.E.
Myers, Tim 1953- *176*
　Earlier sketch in SATA *147*
Myers, Timothy Joseph
　See Myers, Tim
Myers, Walter Dean 1937- *193*
　Brief entry *27*
　Earlier sketches in SATA *41, 71, 109, 157*
　See also CLR *110*
　See also SAAS *2*
Myers, Walter M.
　See Myers, Walter Dean
Myller, Rolf 1926-2006 .... *27*
　Obituary *175*
Myra, Harold L(awrence) 1939- *46*
　Brief entry *42*
Myracle, Lauren 1969- *204*
　Earlier sketch in SATA *162*
Myrus, Donald (Richard) 1927- *23*
Mysterious Traveler, The
　See Arthur, Robert, (Jr.)

N

Na, An *149*
Naaslund, Goorel Kristina 1940- *170*
Nadel, Laurie 1948- *74*
Naden, Corinne J. 1930- *166*
　Earlier sketch in SATA *79*
Nadimi, Suzan *188*
Nagda, Ann Whitehead *199*
Nagel, Andreas Fischer
　See Fischer-Nagel, Andreas
Nagel, Heiderose Fischer
　See Fischer-Nagel, Heiderose
Nagle, Shane *176*
Nahoko, Uehashi
　See Uehashi, Nahoko
Naidoo, Beverley 1943- *180*
　Earlier sketches in SATA *63, 135*
　See also CLR *29*
Nails, Jennifer *213*
Nakae, Noriko 1940- *59*
Nakata, Hiroe *205*

Nakatani, Chiyoko 1930-1981 .... *55*
　Brief entry *40*
　See also CLR *30*
Nally, Susan W. 1947- *90*
Namioka, Lensey 1929- *157*
　Autobiography Feature *116*
　Earlier sketches in SATA *27, 89*
　See also CLR *48*
　See also SAAS *24*
Namovicz, Gene Inyart 1927- *6*
Nance, Andrew *210*
Nanji, Shenaaz 1954- *204*
　Earlier sketch in SATA *131*
Nanogak Agnes 1925- *61*
Napier, Mark
　See Laffin, John (Alfred Charles)
Napoli, Donna Jo 1948- *190*
　Earlier sketches in SATA *92, 137*
　See also CLR *51*
　See also SAAS *23*
Napp, Daniel 1974- *204*
Narahashi, Keiko 1959- *115*
　Earlier sketch in SATA *79*
Narayan, R. K. 1906-2001 .... *62*
Narayan, Rasipuram Krishnaswami
　See Narayan, R. K.
Nascimbene, Yan 1949- *173*
　Earlier sketch in SATA *133*
Nash, Bruce M(itchell) 1947- *34*
Nash, Fredric Ogden
　See Nash, Ogden
Nash, Linell
　See Smith, Linell Nash
Nash, Mary (Hughes) 1925- *41*
Nash, Ogden 1902-1971 .... *46*
　Earlier sketch in SATA *2*
Nash, Renea Denise 1963- *81*
Nast, Elsa Ruth
　See Watson, Jane Werner
Nast, Thomas 1840-1902 .... *51*
　Brief entry *33*
Nastick, Sharon 1954- *41*
Natale, Vince *196*
Natarajan, Srividya *187*
Nathan, Adele (Gutman) 1900(?)-1986
　Obituary *48*
Nathan, Amy *155*
　Earlier sketch in SATA *104*
Nathan, Dorothy (Goldeen) (?)-1966 .... *15*
Nathan, Robert (Gruntal) 1894-1985 .... *6*
　Obituary *43*
Nathanson, Laura Walther 1941- *57*
Natti, Lee 1919- *67*
　Earlier sketch in SATA *1*
　See also SAAS *3*
Natti, Susanna 1948- *125*
　Earlier sketch in SATA *32*
Nau, Thomas *186*
Naughtie, Eleanor
　See Updale, Eleanor
Naughton, Bill
　See Naughton, William John (Francis)
Naughton, James Franklin 1957- *85*
Naughton, Jim
　See Naughton, James Franklin
Naughton, William John (Francis)
　1910-1992 .... *86*
Navarra, John Gabriel 1927- *8*
Naylor, Penelope 1941- *10*
Naylor, Phyllis 1933-
　See Naylor, Phyllis Reynolds
Naylor, Phyllis Reynolds 1933- *209*
　Autobiography Feature *152*
　See also CLR *135*
　See also SAAS *10*
Nazarian, Nikki
　See Nichols, Cecilia Fawn
Nazaroff, Alexander I(vanovich) 1898-1981 .. *4*
Nazoa, Aquiles 1920-1976 .... *198*
Neal, Harry Edward 1906-1993 .... *5*
　Obituary *76*

Neal, Michael
 See Teitelbaum, Michael
Nearing, Penny 1916- 47
 Brief entry 42
Nebel, Gustave E. 45
 Brief entry 33
Nebel, Mimouca
 See Nebel, Gustave E.
Nee, Kay Bonner 10
Needham, Kate 1962- 95
Needle, Jan 1943- 98
 Earlier sketch in SATA 30
 See also CLR 43
 See also SAAS 23
Needleman, Jacob 1934- 6
Neel, David 1960- 82
Neel, Preston 1959- 93
Neff, Henry H. 1973- 221
Negri, Rocco 1932- 12
Negrin, Fabian 1963- 189
Neidigh, Sherry 1956- 204
Neier, Aryeh 1937- 59
Neigoff, Anne 13
Neigoff, Mike 1920- 13
Neilan, Eujin Kim 1969- 200
Neilson, Frances Fullerton (Jones)
 1910-2001 14
Neimark, Anne E. 1935- 145
 Earlier sketch in SATA 4
Neimark, Paul G. 1934- 80
 Brief entry 37
Neitzel, Shirley 1941- 134
 Earlier sketch in SATA 77
Nell
 See Hanna, Nell(ie L.)
Nelscott, Kris
 See Rusch, Kristine Kathryn
Nelson, Blake 1960- 177
Nelson, Catherine Chadwick 1926- 87
Nelson, Cordner 1918-2009 54
 Brief entry 29
Nelson, Cordner Bruce
 See Nelson, Cordner
Nelson, D.A. 1970- 215
Nelson, Dawn Ann
 See Nelson, D.A.
Nelson, Drew 1952- 77
Nelson, Esther L. 1928- 13
Nelson, Jim A.
 See Stotter, Mike
Nelson, Julie L. 1970- 117
Nelson, Kadir 213
 Earlier sketches in SATA 154, 181
Nelson, Kris
 See Rusch, Kristine Kathryn
Nelson, Lawrence E(rnest) 1928-1977
 Obituary 28
Nelson, Marilyn 1946- 60
 Autobiography Feature 180
Nelson, Mary Carroll 1929- 23
Nelson, O. Terry 1941- 62
Nelson, Peter 1953- 73
Nelson, Peter N.
 See Nelson, Peter
Nelson, R. A. 197
Nelson, Richard K(ing) 1941- 65
Nelson, Robin Laura 1971- 141
Nelson, Roy Paul 1923- 59
Nelson, S.D. 181
Nelson, Sharlene (P.) 1933- 96
Nelson, Suzanne 1976- 184
Nelson, Ted (W.) 1931- 96
Nelson, Theresa 1948- 143
 Autobiography Feature 143
 Earlier sketch in SATA 79
Nelson, Vaunda Micheaux 1953- 220
Nemeth, Sally 187
Neri, G. 197
Neri, Greg
 See Neri, G.

Neri, Gregory
 See Neri, G.
Nerlove, Miriam 1959- 53
 Brief entry 49
Nesbit, E. 1858-1924 100
 See also YABC 1
 See also CLR 70
Nesbit, Edith
 See Nesbit, E.
Nesbit, Troy
 See Folsom, Franklin (Brewster)
Nespojohn, Katherine V(eronica) 1912-1975 . 7
Ness, Evaline (Michelow) 1911-1986 26
 Obituary 49
 Earlier sketch in SATA 1
 See also CLR 6
 See also SAAS 1
Ness, Patrick 1971- 207
Nestor, Larry 1940- 149
Nestor, William P(rodromos) 1947- 49
Nethery, Mary 93
Neubecker, Robert 214
 Earlier sketch in SATA 170
Neuberger, Julia (Babette Sarah) 1950- 142
 Earlier sketch in SATA 78
Neufeld, John (Arthur) 1938- 131
 Autobiography Feature 131
 Earlier sketches in SATA 6, 81
 See also CLR 52
 See also SAAS 3
Neuhaus, David 1958- 83
Neumeyer, Peter F(lorian) 1929- 13
Neurath, Marie (Reidemeister) 1898-1986 1
Neuschwander, Cindy 1953- 157
 Earlier sketch in SATA 107
Neusner, Jacob 1932- 38
Neville, Charles
 See Bodsworth, (Charles) Fred(erick)
Neville, Emily Cheney 1919- 1
 See also SAAS 2
Neville, Mary
 See Woodrich, Mary Neville
Nevins, Albert (Francis) J(erome)
 1915-1997 20
Nevius, Carol 1955- 186
Newberger, Devra
 See Speregen, Devra Newberger
Newberry, Clare Turlay 1903-1970 1
 Obituary 26
Newbery, John 1713-1767 20
 See also CLR 147
Newbery, Linda 1952- 184
 Earlier sketch in SATA 142
Newbigging, Martha 198
Newbold, Greg 199
Newcomb, Ellsworth
 See Kenny, Ellsworth Newcomb
Newcombe, Eugene A. 1923-1990 45
 Brief entry 33
Newcombe, Jack
 See Newcombe, Eugene A.
Newcome, Robert 1955- 91
Newcome, Zita 1959- 88
Newell, Crosby
 See Bonsall, Crosby Barbara (Newell)
Newell, Edythe W(eatherford) 1910-1989 11
Newell, Hope Hockenberry 1896-1965 24
Newfeld, Frank 1928- 26
Newgarden, Mark 1959- 194
Newland, Gillian 220
Newlon, (Frank) Clarke 1905(?)-1982 6
 Obituary 33
Newman, Barbara Johansen 191
Newman, C.J.
 See Newman, Coleman J.
Newman, Coleman J. 1935- 82
Newman, Daisy 1904-1994 27
 Obituary 78
Newman, Gerald 1939- 46
 Brief entry 42

Newman, Jerry
 See Newman, Coleman J.
Newman, Leslea 1955- 134
 Earlier sketches in SATA 71, 128
Newman, Margaret
 See Potter, Margaret
Newman, Marjorie 146
Newman, Matthew (Harrison) 1955- 56
Newman, Nanette 1934- 162
Newman, Robert (Howard) 1909-1988 87
 Obituary 60
 Earlier sketch in SATA 4
Newman, Shirlee P(etkin) 144
 Earlier sketches in SATA 10, 90
Newsom, Carol 1948- 92
 Earlier sketch in SATA 40
Newsom, Tom 1944- 80
Newth, Mette 1942- 140
Newton, David E(dward) 1933- 67
Newton, James R(obert) 1935- 23
Newton, Jill 1964- 200
Newton, Robert 1965- 191
Newton, Suzanne 1936- 77
 Earlier sketch in SATA 5
Newton, Vanessa
 See Newton, Vanessa Brantley
Newton, Vanessa Brantley 1962(?)- 206
Ney, John 1923- 43
 Brief entry 33
Nez, John 218
 Earlier sketch in SATA 155
Nez, John Abbott
 See Nez, John
Ng, Franklin 82
Nguyen, Vincent 187
Nichol, B(arrie) P(hillip) 1944-1988 66
Nicholas, Louise D.
 See Watkins, Dawn L.
Nicholls, Judith (Ann) 1941- 61
Nicholls, Sally 1983- 209
Nichols, Cecilia Fawn 1906-1987 12
Nichols, Grace 1950- 164
 Earlier sketch in SATA 98
Nichols, Janet (Louise) 1952- 67
Nichols, Judy 1947- 124
Nichols, Leigh
 See Koontz, Dean
Nichols, Michael 1952- 215
Nichols, Nick
 See Nichols, Michael
Nichols, Paul
 See Hawks, Robert
Nichols, Peter
 See Youd, Samuel
Nichols, (Joanna) Ruth 1948- 15
 See also CLR 149
Nichols, Travis 206
Nicholson, C. R.
 See Nicole, Christopher (Robin)
Nicholson, Christina
 See Nicole, Christopher (Robin)
Nicholson, Joyce Thorpe 1919- 35
Nicholson, Lois P. 1949- 88
Nicholson, Robin
 See Nicole, Christopher (Robin)
Nicholson, William 180
Nicholson, William 1872-1949
 See CLR 76
Nickel, Barbara 1966- 188
Nickell, Joe 1944- 167
 Earlier sketch in SATA 73
Nickelsburg, Janet 1893-1983 11
Nickerson, Betty 1922- 14
Nickerson, Elizabeth
 See Nickerson, Betty
Nickl, Barbara (Elisabeth) 1939- 56
Nicklaus, Carol 62
 Brief entry 33
Nickle, John 181
Nickless, Will 1902-1979(?) 66

Nic Leodhas, Sorche
  See Alger, Leclaire (Gowans)
Nicol, Ann
  See Turnbull, Ann
Nicolas
  See Mordvinoff, Nicolas
Nicolay, Helen 1866-1954
  See YABC *1*
Nicole, Christopher (Robin) 1930- 5
Nicoll, Helen 1937- 87
Nicolson, Cynthia Pratt 1949- 141
Ni Dhuibhne, Eilis 1954- 91
Niehaus, Paddy Bouma
  See Bouma, Paddy
Nields, Nerissa 1967- 166
Nielsen, Kay (Rasmus) 1886-1957 16
  See also CLR *16*
Nielsen, Laura F. 1960- 93
Nielsen, Laura Farnsworth
  See Nielsen, Laura F.
Nielsen, Nancy J. 1951- 77
Nielsen, Susin 1964- 195
Nielsen, Virginia
  See McCall, Virginia Nielsen
Nielsen-Fernlund, Susin
  See Nielsen, Susin
Niemann, Christoph 1970- 191
Nieuwsma, Milton J(ohn) 1941- 142
Nightingale, Sandy 1953- 76
Nikolajeva, Maria 1952- 127
Nikola-Lisa, W. 1951- 180
  Earlier sketch in SATA *71*
Niland, Deborah 1951- 172
  Earlier sketch in SATA *27*
Niland, Kilmeny 75
Nilsen, Anna 1948- 174
  Earlier sketch in SATA *96*
Nilsson, Eleanor 1939- 117
  Earlier sketch in SATA *81*
  See also SAAS *23*
Nilsson, Per 1954- 159
Nimmo, Jenny 1944- 144
  Earlier sketch in SATA *87*
  See also CLR *44*
Nishimura, Kae 196
Niven, Larry 1938- 171
  Earlier sketch in SATA *95*
Niven, Laurence Van Cott
  See Niven, Larry
Niven, Laurence VanCott
  See Niven, Larry
Nivola, Claire A. 1947- 208
  Earlier sketches in SATA *84, 140*
Nix, Garth 1963- 210
  Earlier sketches in SATA *97, 143*
  See also CLR *68*
Nixon, Hershell Howard 1923- 42
Nixon, Joan Lowery 1927-2003 115
  Obituary 146
  Earlier sketches in SATA *8, 44, 78*
  See also CLR *24*
  See also SAAS *9*
Nixon, K.
  See Nixon, Kathleen Irene (Blundell)
Nixon, Kathleen Irene (Blundell)
  1894-1988(?) 14
  Obituary 59
Nobati, Eugenia 1968- 201
Nobisso, Josephine 1953- 121
  Earlier sketch in SATA *78*
Noble, Iris (Davis) 1922-1986 5
  Obituary 49
Noble, Marty 1947- 125
  Earlier sketch in SATA *97*
Noble, Trinka Hakes 1944- 197
  Brief entry 37
  Earlier sketch in SATA *123*
Nobleman, Marc Tyler 1972- 203
Noda, Takayo 1961- 168
Nodelman, Perry 1942- 101

Nodset, Joan L.
  See Lexau, Joan M.
Noel Hume, Ivor 1927- 65
Noestlinger, Christine
  See Nostlinger, Christine
Noguere, Suzanne 1947- 34
Nolan, Dennis 1945- 166
  Brief entry 34
  Earlier sketches in SATA *42, 92*
Nolan, Han 1956- 157
  Earlier sketch in SATA *109*
Nolan, Janet 1956- 191
  Earlier sketch in SATA *145*
Nolan, Jeannette Covert 1897-1974 2
  Obituary 27
Nolan, Lucy 215
Nolan, Paul T(homas) 1919- 48
Nolan, William F. 1928- 88
  Brief entry 28
Nolan, William Francis
  See Nolan, William F.
Nolen, Jerdine 1953- 157
  Earlier sketch in SATA *105*
Noll, Amanda 219
Noll, Sally 1946- 82
Noonan, Brandon 1979- 184
Noonan, Diana 1960- 146
Noonan, Julia 1946- 148
  Earlier sketches in SATA *4, 95*
Norac, Carl 1960- 166
Norcross, John
  See Conroy, John Wesley
Nordan, Robert W(arren) 1934-2004 133
Nordhoff, Charles Bernard 1887-1947 23
Nordlicht, Lillian 29
Nordstrom, Ursula 1910-1988 3
  Obituary 57
Nordtvedt, Matilda 1926- 67
Norling, Beth 1969- 149
Norman, Charles 1904-1996 38
  Obituary 92
Norman, Howard
  See Norman, Howard A.
Norman, Howard A. 1949- 81
Norman, James
  See Schmidt, James Norman
Norman, Jay
  See Arthur, Robert, (Jr.)
Norman, Lilith 1927- 120
  Earlier sketch in SATA *86*
Norman, Mary 1931- 36
Norman, Steve
  See Pashko, Stanley
Norment, Lisa 1966- 91
Norris, Gunilla Brodde 1939- 20
North, Andrew
  See Norton, Andre
North, Anthony
  See Koontz, Dean
North, Captain George
  See Stevenson, Robert Louis
North, Captain George
  See Stevenson, Robert Louis
North, Howard
  See Trevor, Elleston
North, Joan 1920- 16
North, Milou
  See Erdrich, Louise
North, Robert
  See Withers, Carl A.
North, Sara
  See Bonham, Barbara Thomas
  and Hager, Jean
North, Sherry 201
North, Sterling 1906-1974 45
  Obituary 26
  Earlier sketch in SATA *1*
Northcott, (William) Cecil 1902-1987
  Obituary 55
Northeast, Brenda V(ictoria) 1948- 106
Northmore, Elizabeth Florence 1906-1974 . 122

Norton, Alice Mary
  See Norton, Andre
Norton, Andre 1912-2005 91
  Earlier sketches in SATA *1, 43*
  See also CLR *50*
Norton, Browning
  See Norton, Frank R. B(rowning)
Norton, Frank R. B(rowning) 1909-1989 10
Norton, Mary 1903-1992 60
  Obituary 72
  Earlier sketch in SATA *18*
  See also CLR *140*
Nosredna, Trebor
  See Anderson, Bob
Nostlinger, Christine 1936- 162
  Brief entry 37
  Earlier sketch in SATA *64*
  See also CLR *12*
Nourse, Alan E(dward) 1928-1992 48
  See also CLR *33*
Novak, Matt 1962- 204
  Brief entry 52
  Earlier sketches in SATA *60, 104, 165*
Novelli, Luca 1947- 61
Novgorodoff, Danica 1982(?)- 215
Nowell, Elizabeth Cameron 12
Noyes, Deborah 1965- 194
  Earlier sketch in SATA *145*
Nugent, Cynthia 1954- 205
Nugent, Nicholas 1949- 73
Numberman, Neil 1981(?)- 220
Numeroff, Laura 1953- 206
  Earlier sketches in SATA *28, 90, 142*
  See also CLR *85*
Numeroff Joffe, Laura
  See Numeroff, Laura
Nunes, Lygia Bojunga 1932- 154
  Earlier sketch in SATA *75*
Nunn, Laura (Donna) Silverstein 1968- 124
Nurenberg, Thelma
  See Greenhaus, Thelma Nurenberg
Nurnberg, Maxwell 1897-1984 27
  Obituary 41
Nussbaumer, Paul (Edmund) 1934- 16
Nutt, Ken 1951- 163
  Earlier sketch in SATA *97*
Nuttall-Smith, Margaret Emily Noel 1919- .. 26
Nuygen, Mathieu 1967- 80
Nuzum, K. A. 195
Nuzum, Kathy A.
  See Nuzum, K. A.
Nyberg, (Everett Wayne) Morgan 1944- 87
Nyce, (Nellie) Helene von Strecker
  1885-1969 19
Nyce, Vera 1862-1925 19
Nye, Naomi Shihab 1952- 198
  Earlier sketches in SATA *86, 147*
  See also CLR *59*
Nye, Robert 1939- 6
Nyeu, Tao 206
Nyikos, Stacy A. 1969- 164
Nystrom, Carolyn 1940- 130
  Earlier sketch in SATA *67*

O

O. Henry
  See Henry, O.
Oakes, Elizabeth H. 1964- 132
Oakes, Vanya 1909-1983 6
  Obituary 37
Oakley, Don(ald G.) 1927- 8
Oakley, Graham 1929- 84
  Earlier sketch in SATA *30*
  See also CLR *7*
Oakley, Helen (McKelvey) 1906- 10
Oaks, J. Adams 220
Oana, Katherine 1929- 53
  Brief entry 37

Oates, Eddie H. 1943- *88*
Oates, Joyce Carol 1938- *159*
Oates, Stephen B(aery) 1936- *59*
Obed, Ellen Bryan 1944- *74*
Oberle, Joseph 1958- *69*
Oberman, Sheldon 1949-2004 .... *85*
   Autobiography Feature *114*
   Obituary *153*
   See also CLR *54*
   See also SAAS *26*
Obligado, Lilian (Isabel) 1931- *61*
   Brief entry *45*
Obrant, Susan 1946- *11*
O'Brian, E.G.
   See Clarke, Arthur C.
O'Brien, Anne Sibley 1952- *213*
   Brief entry *48*
   Earlier sketches in SATA *53, 80*
O'Brien, E.G.
   See Clarke, Arthur C.
O'Brien, Esse Forrester 1895(?)-1975
   Obituary *30*
O'Brien, Patrick 1960- *193*
O'Brien, Robert C.
   See Conly, Robert Leslie
O'Brien, Thomas C. 1938-2010 .... *29*
O'Brien, Thomas Clement
   See O'Brien, Thomas C.
O'Callaghan, Julie 1954- *113*
O'Callahan, Jay 1938- *88*
O'Carroll, Ryan
   See Markun, Patricia Maloney
Ochiltree, Dianne 1953- *117*
Ockham, Joan Price
   See Price, Joan
O'Connell, Margaret F(orster) 1935-1977 .... *30*
   Obituary *30*
O'Connell, Peg
   See Ahern, Margaret McCrohan
O'Connell, Rebecca 1968- *212*
   Earlier sketch in SATA *130*
O'Connor, Barbara 1950- *193*
   Earlier sketch in SATA *154*
O'Connor, Francine M(arie) 1930- *90*
O'Connor, Genevieve A. 1914- *75*
O'Connor, George *183*
O'Connor, Ian 1965- *188*
O'Connor, Jane 1947- *186*
   Brief entry *47*
   Earlier sketches in SATA *59, 103, 150*
O'Connor, Karen 1938- *89*
   Earlier sketch in SATA *34*
O'Connor, Patrick
   See Wibberley, Leonard
O'Connor, Richard 1915-1975
   Obituary *21*
O'Conor, Jane 1958- *78*
Odaga, Asenath (Bole) 1937- *130*
   Earlier sketch in SATA *67*
   See also SAAS *19*
O Danachair, Caoimhin
   See Danaher, Kevin
Odanaka, Barbara *159*
O'Daniel, Janet 1921- *24*
O'Day, Cathy
   See Crane, Barbara (Joyce)
O'Dell, Scott 1898-1989 .... *134*
   Earlier sketches in SATA *12, 60*
   See also CLR *126*
Odenwald, Robert P(aul) 1899-1965 .... *11*
Odgers, Sally
   See Odgers, Sally Farrell
Odgers, Sally Farrell 1957- *139*
   Earlier sketch in SATA *72*
Odone, Jamison 1980- *209*
O'Donnell, Dick
   See Lupoff, Richard A(llen)
   and Thompson, Don(ald Arthur)
O'Donnell, Liam 1970- *209*
Odriozola, Elena *186*
Oechsli, Kelly 1918-1999 .... *5*

Oesterle, Virginia Rorby
   See Rorby, Ginny
Ofek, Uriel 1926- *36*
   See also CLR *28*
Ofer, Avi 1975- *207*
Offenbacher, Ami 1958- *91*
Offill, Jenny 1968- *211*
Offit, Sidney 1928- *10*
Ofosu-Appiah, L(awrence) H(enry) 1920- ... *13*
Ogan, George F. 1912-1983 .... *13*
Ogan, M. G.
   See Ogan, George F.
   and Ogan, Margaret E. (Nettles)
Ogan, Margaret E. (Nettles) 1923-1979 .... *13*
Ogburn, Charlton (Jr.) 1911-1998 .... *3*
   Obituary *109*
Ogburn, Jacqueline K. *162*
Ogilvie, Elisabeth May 1917-2006 .... *40*
   Brief entry *29*
   Obituary *176*
Ogilvy, Gavin
   See Barrie, J. M.
Ogilvy, Ian 1943- *177*
Ogilvy, Ian Raymond
   See Ogilvy, Ian
Ogle, Lucille Edith 1904-1988
   Obituary *59*
Ogletree, Charles J. 1952- *175*
O'Green, Jennifer
   See Roberson, Jennifer
O'Green, Jennifer Roberson
   See Roberson, Jennifer
O'Hagan, Caroline 1946- *38*
O'Hanlon, Jacklyn
   See Meek, Jacklyn O'Hanlon
O'Hara, Elizabeth
   See Ni Dhuibhne, Eilis
O'Hara, Kenneth
   See Morris, (Margaret) Jean
O'Hara, Mary
   See Alsop, Mary O'Hara
O'Hara (Alsop), Mary
   See Alsop, Mary O'Hara
O'Hare, Jeff(rey A.) 1958- *105*
Ohi, Ruth 1964- *95*
Ohiyesa
   See Eastman, Charles A(lexander)
Ohlsson, Ib 1935- *7*
Ohmi, Ayano 1959- *115*
Ohtomo, Yasuo 1946- *37*
o huigin, sean 1942- *138*
   See also CLR *75*
Oiseau
   See Moseley, James W(illett)
Oke, Janette 1935- *97*
O'Keefe, Susan Heyboer *176*
   Earlier sketch in SATA *133*
O'Keeffe, Frank 1938- *99*
O'Kelley, Mattie Lou 1908-1997 .... *97*
   Earlier sketch in SATA *36*
Okimoto, Jean Davies 1942- *103*
   Earlier sketch in SATA *34*
Okomfo, Amasewa
   See Cousins, Linda
olafsdottir, Gudrun Elin
   See Gunnella
Olaleye, Isaac O. 1941- *96*
   See also SAAS *23*
Olcott, Frances Jenkins 1872(?)-1963 .... *19*
Old, Wendie C(orbin) 1943- *154*
Old Boy
   See Hughes, Thomas
Oldenburg, E(gbert) William 1936-1974 ...... *35*
Older, Effin 1942- *114*
Older, Jules 1940- *156*
   Earlier sketch in SATA *114*
Oldfield, Jenny 1949- *140*
Oldfield, Margaret J(ean) 1932- *56*
Oldfield, Pamela 1931- *86*
Oldham, June *70*
Oldham, Mary 1944- *65*

Olds, Elizabeth 1896-1991 .... *3*
   Obituary *66*
Olds, Helen Diehl 1895-1981 .... *9*
   Obituary *25*
Oldstyle, Jonathan
   See Irving, Washington
O'Leary, Brian (Todd) 1940- *6*
O'Leary, Chris *208*
O'Leary, Patsy B. 1937- *97*
O'Leary, Patsy Baker
   See O'Leary, Patsy B.
Oleynikov, Igor 1953- *202*
Oliphant, B.J.
   See Tepper, Sheri S.
Oliver, Burton
   See Burt, Olive Woolley
Oliver, Chad
   See Oliver, Symmes C.
Oliver, John Edward 1933- *21*
Oliver, Lin *202*
Oliver, Marilyn Tower 1935- *89*
Oliver, Mark 1960- *214*
Oliver, Narelle 1960- *197*
   Earlier sketch in SATA *152*
Oliver, Shirley (Louise Dawkins) 1958- *74*
Oliver, Symmes C. 1928-1993 .... *101*
Oliviero, Jamie 1950- *84*
Olmsted, Lorena Ann 1890-1989 .... *13*
Olney, Ross R. 1929- *13*
Olschewski, Alfred (Erich) 1920- *7*
Olsen, Barbara *148*
Olsen, Carol 1945- *89*
Olsen, Ib Spang 1921- *81*
   Earlier sketch in SATA *6*
Olsen, Violet (Mae) 1922-1991 .... *58*
Olson, Arielle North 1932- *67*
Olson, David J. 1974- *198*
Olson, Gene 1922- *32*
Olson, Gretchen *187*
Olson, Helen Kronberg *48*
Olson, Kay Melchisedech 1948- *175*
Olson, Marianne
   See Mitchell, Marianne
Olson-Brown, Ellen 1967- *183*
Olten, Manuela 1970- *197*
Olugebefola, Ademole 1941- *15*
Oluonye, Mary N(kechi) 1955- *111*
Om
   See Gorey, Edward (St. John)
O'Malley, Donough *208*
O'Malley, Kevin 1961- *191*
   Earlier sketch in SATA *157*
Oman, Carola (Mary Anima) 1897-1978 ..... *35*
O'Mara, Carmel 1965- *166*
O'Mara-Horwitz, Carmel
   See O'Mara, Carmel
O'Meara, Walter (Andrew) 1897-1989 .... *65*
Ommanney, F(rancis) D(ownes) 1903-1980 . *23*
O Mude
   See Gorey, Edward (St. John)
Oneal, Elizabeth 1934- *82*
   Earlier sketch in SATA *30*
   See also CLR *13*
O'Neal, Katherine Pebley 1957- *204*
O'Neal, Reagan
   See Jordan, Robert
O'Neal, Regan
   See Jordan, Robert
Oneal, Zibby
   See Oneal, Elizabeth
O'neill, Alexis 1949- *220*
O'Neill, Amanda 1951- *111*
O'Neill, Catharine *203*
O'Neill, Gerard K(itchen) 1927-1992 .... *65*
O'Neill, Judith (Beatrice) 1930- *34*
O'Neill, Mary L(e Duc) 1908(?)-1990 .... *2*
   Obituary *64*
O'Neill, Reagan
   See Jordan, Robert
Onslow, Annette Rosemary MacArthur
   See MacArthur-Onslow, Annette Rosemary

Onslow, John 1906-1985
    Obituary *47*
Onyefulu, Ifeoma 1959- *157*
    Earlier sketches in SATA *81, 115*
Opie, Iona (Margaret Balfour) 1923- *118*
    Earlier sketches in SATA *3, 63*
    See also SAAS 6
Opie, Peter (Mason) 1918-1982 .... *118*
    Obituary *28*
    Earlier sketches in SATA *3, 63*
Oppel, Kenneth 1967- *199*
    Earlier sketches in SATA *99, 153*
Oppel, Kenneth Kerry
    See Oppel, Kenneth
Oppenheim, Joanne 1934- *174*
    Earlier sketches in SATA *5, 82, 136*
Oppenheim, Shulamith Levey 1928- *177*
Oppenheimer, Joan L(etson) 1925- *28*
Oppong, Joseph Ransford 1953- *160*
Optic, Oliver
    See Adams, William Taylor
    and Stratemeyer, Edward L.
Oram, Hiawyn 1946- *101*
    Earlier sketch in SATA *56*
Orbach, Ruth Gary 1941- *21*
Orback, Craig *197*
Orczy, Emma
    See Orczy, Baroness Emmuska
Orczy, Emma Magdalena Rosalia Maria Josefa
    See Orczy, Baroness Emmuska
Orczy, Emmuska
    See Orczy, Baroness Emmuska
Orczy, Baroness Emmuska 1865-1947 .... *40*
Orde, A.J.
    See Tepper, Sheri S.
O'Reilly, Jackson
    See Jordan, Robert
Orenstein, Denise Gosliner 1950- *157*
Orgad, Dorit 1936- *199*
Orgel, Doris 1929- *148*
    Earlier sketches in SATA *7, 85*
    See also CLR 48
    See also SAAS 19
Orgill, Roxane *198*
Oriolo, Joe
    See Oriolo, Joseph D.
Oriolo, Joseph D. 1913-1985
    Obituary *46*
Orlean, Susan 1955- *209*
Orleans, Ilo 1897-1962 .... *10*
Orlev, Uri 1931- *135*
    Earlier sketch in SATA *58*
    See also CLR 30
    See also SAAS 19
Ormai, Stella *57*
    Brief entry *48*
Ormerod, Jan 1946- *210*
    Brief entry *44*
    Earlier sketches in SATA *55, 70, 132*
    See also CLR 20
Ormerod, Janette Louise
    See Ormerod, Jan
Ormes, Jackie
    See Ormes, Zelda J.
Ormes, Zelda J. 1914-1986
    Obituary *47*
Ormondroyd, Edward 1925- *14*
Ormsby, Virginia H(aire) 1906-1990 .... *11*
Orona-Ramirez, Kristy 1964- *189*
Orozco, Jose-Luis 1948- *179*
Orr, Katherine S(helley) 1950- *72*
Orr, Wendy 1953- *206*
    Earlier sketches in SATA *90, 141*
Orris
    See Ingelow, Jean
Orth, Richard
    See Gardner, Richard (M.)
Ortiz Cofer, Judith
    See Cofer, Judith Ortiz
Orwell, George 1903-1950 .... *29*
    See also CLR 68

Orwin, Joanna 1944- *141*
Os, Eric van
    See van Os, Erik
Osborn, Elinor 1939- *145*
Osborn, Jacob 1981(?)- *215*
Osborn, Kathy 1955(?)- *199*
Osborn, Lois D(orothy) 1915- *61*
Osborne, Charles 1927- *59*
Osborne, Chester G(orham) 1915-1987 .... *11*
Osborne, David
    See Silverberg, Robert
Osborne, George
    See Silverberg, Robert
Osborne, Leone Neal 1914-1996 .... *2*
Osborne, Linda Barrett 1949- *215*
Osborne, Mary Pope 1949- *144*
    Earlier sketches in SATA *41, 55, 98*
    See also CLR 88
Osceola
    See Blixen, Karen
Osgood, William E(dward) 1926- *37*
O'Shaughnessy, Darren
    See Shan, Darren
O'Shaughnessy, Ellen Cassels 1937- *78*
O'shaughnessy, Tam 1951- *221*
O'Shea, Catherine Patricia Shiels
    See O'Shea, Pat
O'Shea, Pat 1931-2007 .... *87*
    See also CLR 18
Osmond, Edward 1900- *10*
Ossoli, Sarah Margaret
    See Fuller, Margaret
Ostendorf, (Arthur) Lloyd, (Jr.) 1921-2000 .. *65*
    Obituary *125*
Osterweil, Adam 1972- *217*
Ostow, Micol 1976- *170*
Otfinoski, Steven 1949- *116*
    Earlier sketch in SATA *56*
Otis, James
    See Kaler, James Otis
O'Toole, Thomas 1941- *71*
O'Trigger, Sir Lucius
    See Horne, Richard Henry Hengist
Otten, Charlotte
    See Otten, Charlotte F.
Otten, Charlotte F. 1926- *98*
Otten, Charlotte Fennema
    See Otten, Charlotte F.
Ottley, Matt 1962- *171*
    Earlier sketch in SATA *102*
Ottley, Reginald Leslie 1909-1985 .... *26*
    See also CLR 16
Otto, Margaret Glover 1909-1976
    Obituary *30*
Otto, Svend
    See Soerensen, Svend Otto
Ouellet, Debbie 1954- *219*
Oughton, Jerrie (Preston) 1937- *131*
    Earlier sketch in SATA *76*
Oughton, (William) Taylor 1925- *104*
Ouida
    See De La Ramee, Marie Louise
Ousley, Odille 1896-1976 .... *10*
Outcalt, Todd 1960- *123*
Overmyer, James E. 1946- *88*
Overton, Jenny (Margaret Mary) 1942- *52*
    Brief entry *36*
Owen, Ann
    See Qualey, Marsha
Owen, Annie 1949- *75*
Owen, Caroline Dale
    See Snedeker, Caroline Dale (Parke)
Owen, Clifford
    See Hamilton, Charles (Harold St. John)
Owen, Dilys
    See Gater, Dilys
Owen, (Benjamin) Evan 1918-1984 .... *38*
Owen, (John) Gareth 1936-2002 .... *162*
    Earlier sketch in SATA *83*
    See also CLR 31
    See also SAAS 14

Owen, James A. *185*
Owens, Bryant 1968- *116*
Owens, Dana Elaine
    See Queen Latifah
Owens, Gail 1939- *54*
Owens, Mary Beth *191*
Owens, Thomas S(heldon) 1960- *86*
Owens, Tom
    See Owens, Thomas S(heldon)
Oxenbury, Helen 1938- *149*
    Earlier sketches in SATA *3, 68*
    See also CLR 70
Oxendine, Bess Holland 1933- *90*
Oz, Frank (Richard) 1944- *60*
Ozer, Jerome S. 1927- *59*

P

Paananen, Eloise (Katherine) 1923-1993 .... *9*
Pace, Lorenzo 1943- *131*
Pace, Mildred Mastin 1907- *46*
    Brief entry *29*
Pachter, Hedwig (?)-1988 .... *63*
Pack, Janet 1952- *77*
Pack, Robert 1929- *118*
Packard, Edward 1931- *148*
    Earlier sketches in SATA *47, 90*
Packer, Kenneth L. 1946- *116*
Packer, Vin
    See Meaker, Marijane
Pad, Peter
    See Stratemeyer, Edward L.
Page, Eileen
    See Heal, Edith
Page, Eleanor
    See Coerr, Eleanor (Beatrice)
Page, Gail 1950- *205*
Page, Jake 1936- *81*
Page, James Keena, Jr.
    See Page, Jake
Page, Lou Williams 1912-1997 .... *38*
Page, Mary
    See Heal, Edith
Page, Robin 1943- *154*
Pagliarulo, Antonio 1977(?)- *212*
Pagnucci, Susan 1944- *90*
Pahlen, Kurt 1907-2003
    Obituary *147*
Pahz, Cheryl
    See Pahz, Cheryl Suzanne
Pahz, Cheryl Suzanne 1949- *11*
Pahz, James Alon 1943- *11*
Paice, Margaret 1920- *10*
Paige, Harry W(orthington) 1922- *41*
    Brief entry *35*
Paige, Richard
    See Koontz, Dean
Paige, Robin
    See Albert, Susan Wittig
Paine, Penelope Colville 1946- *87*
Paine, Roberta M. 1925- *13*
Paisley, Tom 1932- *11*
    See also CLR 3
Palatini, Margie *207*
    Earlier sketches in SATA *134, 174*
Palazzo, Anthony D.
    See Palazzo, Tony
Palazzo, Tony 1905-1970 .... *3*
Palder, Edward L. 1922- *5*
Palecek, Josef 1932- *56*
Palecek, Libuse 1937- *89*
Palen, Debbie *195*
Palin, Michael 1943- *67*
Palin, Michael Edward
    See Palin, Michael
Palladini, David (Mario) 1946- *40*
    Brief entry *32*
Pallas, Norvin 1918-1983 .... *23*

Pallister, John C(lare) 1891-1980
  Obituary 26
Pallotta, Gerard Larry
  See Pallotta, Jerry
Pallotta, Jerry 1953- 186
Pallotta-Chiarolli, Maria 1960- 117
Palmer, Bernard (Alvin) 1914-1998 26
Palmer, C. Everard 1930- 14
Palmer, (Ruth) Candida 1926- 11
Palmer, Cyril Everard
  See Palmer, C. Everard
Palmer, Don
  See Benson, Mildred
Palmer, Hap 1942- 68
Palmer, Heidi 1948- 15
Palmer, Helen Marion
  See Geisel, Helen
Palmer, Jessica 1953- 120
Palmer, Judd 1972- 153
Palmer, Juliette 1930- 15
Palmer, Kate Salley 1946- 97
Palmer, Maria
  See Strachan, Ian
Palmer, Maria
  See Brennan, Herbie
Palmer, Robin 1909-2000 43
Palmero Caceres, Ana 198
Palmisciano, Diane 202
Paltrowitz, Donna 1950- 61
  Brief entry 50
Paltrowitz, Donna Milman
  See Paltrowitz, Donna
Paltrowitz, Stuart 1946- 61
  Brief entry 50
Pamela, Todd 1950- 124
Pamintuan, Macky 214
  Earlier sketch in SATA *178*
Panagopoulos, Janie Lynn 149
Panati, Charles 1943- 65
Panchyk, Richard 1970- 138
Panetta, George 1915-1969 15
Panetta, Joseph N. 1953- 96
Pang, YaWen Ariel 206
Panik, Sharon 1952- 82
Panowski, Eileen Thompson 1920- 49
Pansy
  See Alden, Isabella (Macdonald)
Pantell, Dora (Fuchs) 39
Panter, Carol 1936- 9
Paolini, Christopher 1983- 157
  See also CLR *102*
Papademetriou, Lisa 175
Paparone, Pam 185
Paparone, Pamela
  See Paparone, Pam
Papas, Bill
  See Papas, William
Papas, William 1927-2000 50
Papashvily, George 1898-1978 17
Papashvily, Helen (Waite) 1906-1996 17
Pape, D. L.
  See Pape, Donna (Lugg)
Pape, Donna (Lugg) 1930- 82
  Earlier sketch in SATA *2*
Paperny, Myra (Green) 1932- 51
  Brief entry 33
Papp, Robert 1967- 205
Paradis, Adrian A(lexis) 1912- 67
  Earlier sketch in SATA *1*
  See also SAAS *8*
Paradis, Marjorie Bartholomew
  1886(?)-1970 17
Paradiz, Valerie 1963- 176
Paratore, Coleen
  See Paratore, Coleen Murtagh
Paratore, Coleen Murtagh 1958- 200
Pardo DeLange, Alex 211
Parenteau, Shirley 1935- 199
  Brief entry 40
  Earlier sketch in SATA *47*

Parish, Margaret 1927-1988 73
  Obituary 59
  Earlier sketch in SATA *17*
  See also CLR *22*
Parish, Margaret Holt
  See Holt, Margaret
Parish, Peggy
  See Parish, Margaret
Park, Barbara 1947- 123
  Brief entry 35
  Earlier sketches in SATA *40, 78*
  See also CLR *34*
Park, Bill
  See Park, W(illiam) B(ryan)
Park, Frances 1955- 171
Park, Ginger 173
Park, Janie Jaehyun 150
Park, Jordan
  See Kornbluth, C(yril) M.
  and Pohl, Frederik
Park, Linda Sue 1960- 200
  Earlier sketches in SATA *127, 173*
  See also CLR *84*
Park, Nick 1958- 113
Park, (Rosina) Ruth (Lucia) 1923(?)- 93
  Earlier sketch in SATA *25*
  See also CLR *51*
Park, W(illiam) B(ryan) 1936- 22
Parke, Marilyn 1928- 82
Parker, Barbara Keevil 1938- 157
Parker, Daniel
  See Ehrenhaft, Daniel
Parker, Elinor Milnor 1906- 3
Parker, Julie F. 1961- 92
Parker, Kim 1963- 174
Parker, Kristy 1957- 59
Parker, Lois M(ay) 1912-1996 30
Parker, Margot M. 1937- 52
Parker, Marjorie Blain 1960- 205
  Earlier sketch in SATA *145*
Parker, Mary Jessie 1948- 71
Parker, Nancy Winslow 1930- 132
  Earlier sketches in SATA *10, 69*
  See also SAAS *20*
Parker, Richard 1915-1990 14
Parker, Robert
  See Boyd, Waldo T.
  and Parker, Robert Andrew
Parker, Robert Andrew 1927- 200
Parker, Steve 1954- 213
Parker, Tom S. 215
Parker, Toni Trent 1947-2005 142
  Obituary 169
Parker-Rees, Guy 193
Parker-Rock, Michelle 214
Parkes, Lucas
  See Harris, John (Wyndham Parkes Lucas)
  Beynon
Parkhill, John
  See Cox, William R(obert)
Parkins, David 1955- 218
  Earlier sketch in SATA *176*
Parkinson, Curtis 219
Parkinson, Ethelyn M(inerva) 1906-1999 11
Parkinson, Kathryn N. 1954- 71
Parkinson, Kathy
  See Parkinson, Kathryn N.
Parkinson, Siobhan
  See Parkinson, Siobhan
Parkinson, Siobhan 1954- 178
Parks, Deborah A. 1948- 133
  Earlier sketch in SATA *91*
Parks, Edd Winfield 1906-1968 10
Parks, Gordon 1912-2006 108
  Obituary 175
  Earlier sketch in SATA *8*
Parks, Gordon Roger Alexander
  See Parks, Gordon
Parks, Peggy J. 1951- 143
Parks, PJ
  See Parks, Peggy J.

Parks, Rosa 1913-2005 83
  Obituary 169
Parks, Rosa Louise Lee
  See Parks, Rosa
Parks, Van Dyke 1943- 62
Parley, Peter
  See Goodrich, Samuel Griswold
Parlin, John
  See Graves, Charles Parlin
Parme, Fabrice 1966- 191
Parnall, Peter 1936- 69
  Earlier sketch in SATA *16*
  See also SAAS *11*
Paros, Jennifer 210
Parotti, Phillip (Elliott) 1941- 109
Parr, Ann 1943- 144
Parr, Danny
  See Parr, Ann
Parr, Letitia (Evelyn) 1906-1985(?) 37
Parr, Lucy 1924- 10
Parr, Todd 179
  Earlier sketch in SATA *134*
Parrish, Anne 1888-1957 27
Parrish, Mary
  See Cousins, Margaret
Parrish, Maxfield
  See Parrish, (Frederick) Maxfield
Parrish, (Frederick) Maxfield 1870-1966 14
Parry, Marian 1924- 13
Parry, Rosanne 212
Parson Lot
  See Kingsley, Charles
Parsons, Alexandra 1947- 92
Parsons, Ellen
  See Dragonwagon, Crescent
Parsons, Garry 197
Parsons, Martin 1951- 116
Parsons, Martin Leslie
  See Parsons, Martin
Parsons, Tom
  See MacPherson, Thomas George
Parsons-Yazzi, Evangeline 172
Partch, Virgil Franklin II 1916-1984 39
  Obituary 39
Parton, Dolly 1946- 94
Parton, Dolly Rebecca
  See Parton, Dolly
Partridge, Benjamin W., Jr. 1915-2005 28
  Obituary 163
Partridge, Benjamin Waring, Jr.
  See Partridge, Benjamin W., Jr.
Partridge, Cora Cheney
  See Cheney, Cora
Partridge, Elizabeth 216
  Earlier sketch in SATA *134*
Partridge, Jenny (Lilian) 1947- 52
  Brief entry 37
Pasachoff, Naomi 1947- 147
Pascal, David 1918- 14
Pascal, Francine 1938- 143
  Brief entry 37
  Earlier sketches in SATA *51, 80*
  See also CLR *25*
Paschal, Nancy
  See Trotter, Grace V(iolet)
Paschkis, Julie 1957- 220
  Earlier sketch in SATA *177*
Pascudniak, Pascal
  See Lupoff, Richard A(llen)
Pashko, Stanley 1913-1982 29
Passailaigue, Thomas E.
  See Paisley, Tom
Pastel, Elyse 201
Pateman, Robert 1954- 84
Patent, Dorothy Hinshaw 1940- 162
  Autobiography Feature 162
  Earlier sketches in SATA *22, 69, 120*
  See also CLR *19*
  See also SAAS *13*
Paterson, A(ndrew) B(arton) 1864-1941 97

Paterson, Banjo
  See Paterson, A(ndrew) B(arton)
Paterson, Diane 1946- 177
  Brief entry 33
  Earlier sketch in SATA 59
Paterson, John (Barstow) 1932- 114
Paterson, Katherine 1932- 204
  Earlier sketches in SATA *13, 53, 92, 133*
  See also CLR *127*
Paterson, Katherine Womeldorf
  See Paterson, Katherine
Patience, John 1949- 90
Patneaude, David 1944- 159
  Earlier sketch in SATA 85
Paton, Alan 1903-1988 11
  Obituary 56
Paton, Alan Stewart
  See Paton, Alan
Paton, Jane (Elizabeth) 1934- 35
Paton, Priscilla 1952- 98
Paton Walsh, Gillian
  See Paton Walsh, Jill
Paton Walsh, Jill 1937- 190
  Autobiography Feature 190
  Earlier sketches in SATA *4, 72, 109*
  See also CLR *128*
  See also SAAS *3*
Patricelli, Leslie 207
Patrick, Susan
  See Clark, Patricia Denise
Patron, Susan 1948- 182
  Earlier sketch in SATA 76
Patsauq, Markoosie 1942-
  See CLR *23*
Patschke, Steve 1955- 125
Patten, Brian 1946- 152
  Earlier sketch in SATA 29
Patterson, Charles 1935- 59
Patterson, Geoffrey 1943- 54
  Brief entry 44
Patterson, James 1947- 197
  Earlier sketch in SATA *164*
Patterson, James B.
  See Patterson, James
Patterson, Lillie G. -1999 88
  Earlier sketch in SATA *14*
Patterson, Nancy Ruth 1944- 148
  Earlier sketch in SATA 72
Pattison, Darcy (S.) 1954- 126
  Earlier sketch in SATA 72
Pattou, Edith 164
Patz (Blaustein), Nancy 154
Paul, Aileen 1917- 12
Paul, Alison 196
Paul, Ann Whitford 1941- 209
  Earlier sketch in SATA *76, 110, 168*
Paul, David (Tyler) 1934-1988
  Obituary 56
Paul, Dominique 1973- 184
Paul, Elizabeth
  See Crow, Donna Fletcher
Paul, Hamish Vigne Christie 1951- 151
  See also CLR *87*
Paul, James 1936- 23
Paul, Korky
  See Paul, Hamish Vigne Christie
Paul, Robert
  See Roberts, John G(aither)
Paul, Tessa 1944- 103
Pauley, Kimberly 1973- 208
Pauli, Hertha (Ernestine) 1909-1973 3
  Obituary 26
Paull, Grace A. 1898- 24
Paulsen, Gary 1939- 189
  Earlier sketches in SATA *22, 50, 54, 79, 111,
  158*
  See also CLR *82*
Paulson, Jack
  See Jackson, C(aary) Paul
Pauquet, Gina Ruck
  See Ruck-Pauquet, Gina

Pausacker, Jenny 1948- 72
  See also SAAS *23*
Pausewang, Gudrun 1928- 165
  Earlier sketch in SATA *104*
Pavel, Frances 1907- 10
Paver, Michelle 215
  Earlier sketch in SATA *170*
Paxton
  See Barr, Nevada
Paxton, Thomas R. 1937- 70
Paxton, Tom
  See Paxton, Thomas R.
Paye, Won-Ldy 185
Payne, Alan
  See Jakes, John
Payne, Bernal C., Jr. 1941- 60
Payne, C. Douglas
  See Payne, C.D.
Payne, C.D. 1949- 133
Payne, C.F. 1956- 179
Payne, Chris Fox
  See Payne, C.F.
Payne, Donald Gordon 1924- 37
Payne, Emmy
  See West, Emily Govan
Payne, Nina 135
Payne, Rachel Ann
  See Jakes, John
Payson, Dale 1943- 9
Payzant, Charles 18
Paz, A.
  See Pahz, James Alon
Paz, Natalia Toledo
  See Toledo, Natalia
Paz, Zan
  See Pahz, Cheryl Suzanne
Peace, Mary
  See Finley, Mary Peace
Peacock, Louise 210
Peacock, Shane 1957- 192
Peake, Mervyn 1911-1968 23
Peale, Norman Vincent 1898-1993 20
  Obituary 78
Pearce, Ann Philippa
  See Pearce, Philippa
Pearce, Emily Smith 1975- 199
Pearce, Jacqueline 1962- 146
Pearce, Margaret 104
Pearce, Philippa 1920-2006 129
  Obituary 179
  Earlier sketches in SATA *1, 67*
  See also CLR *9*
Peare, Catherine Owens 1911- 9
Pearle, Ida 207
Pearsall, Shelley 1966- 190
Pearson, Gayle 1947- 119
  Earlier sketch in SATA 53
Pearson, Jean Mary
  See Gardam, Jane
Pearson, Kit 1947- 77
  Autobiography Feature 117
  See also CLR *26*
Pearson, Mary E. 1955- 211
  Earlier sketch in SATA *134*
Pearson, Ridley 1953- 182
Pearson, Susan 1946- 166
  Brief entry 27
  Earlier sketches in SATA *39, 91*
Pearson, Tracey Campbell 1956- 219
  Earlier sketches in SATA *64, 155*
Pease, (Clarence) Howard 1894-1974 2
  Obituary 25
Peavy, Linda 1943- 54
Peck, Anne Merriman 1884-1976 18
Peck, Beth 1957- 190
  Earlier sketch in SATA 79
Peck, Jan 159
Peck, Jeanie J. 1967- 147
Peck, Marshall III 1951- 92

Peck, Richard 1934- 190
  Autobiography Feature 110
  Earlier sketches in SATA *18, 55, 97, 110, 158*
  See also CLR *142*
  See also SAAS *2*
Peck, Richard Wayne
  See Peck, Richard
Peck, Robert Newton 1928- 156
  Autobiography Feature 108
  Earlier sketches in SATA *21, 62, 111*
  See also CLR *45*
  See also SAAS *1*
Peck, Sylvia 1953- 133
Peck-Whiting, Jeanie J.
  See Peck, Jeanie J.
Peddicord, Jane Ann 199
Pedersen, Janet 193
Pederson, Sharleen
  See Collicott, Sharleen
Pedler, Caroline 197
Peebles, Anne
  See Galloway, Priscilla
Peek, Merle 1938- 39
Peel, John 1954- 79
Peel, Norman Lemon
  See Hirsch, Phil
Peeples, Edwin A(ugustus, Jr.) 1915-1994 6
Peers, Judi 1956- 119
Peers, Judith May West
  See Peers, Judi
Peet, Bill
  See Peet, William Bartlett
Peet, Creighton B. 1899-1977 30
Peet, Mal 171
Peet, Malcolm
  See Peet, Mal
Peet, William Bartlett 1915-2002 78
  Obituary 137
  Earlier sketches in SATA *2, 41*
  See also CLR *12*
Peguero, Leone 116
Pelaez, Jill 1924- 12
Pelham, David 1938- 70
Pelikan, Judy 1941- 219
Pell, Ed(ward) 1950- 157
Pelletier, Andrew T. 195
Pelletier, Andrew Thomas
  See Pelletier, Andrew T.
Pellowski, Anne 1933- 20
Pellowski, Michael (Joseph) 1949- 151
  Brief entry 48
  Earlier sketch in SATA 88
Pellowski, Michael Morgan
  See Pellowski, Michael (Joseph)
Pelta, Kathy 1928- 18
Peltier, Leslie C(opus) 1900-1980 13
Pemberton, Bonnie 191
Pemberton, John Leigh
  See Leigh-Pemberton, John
Pembury, Bill
  See Groom, Arthur William
Pemsteen, Hans
  See Manes, Stephen
Pendennis, Arthur Esquir
  See Thackeray, William Makepeace
Pender, Lydia Podger 1907- 61
Pendery, Rosemary (Schmitz) 7
Pendle, Alexy 1943- 29
Pendle, George 1906-1977
  Obituary 28
Pendleton, Don
  See Cunningham, Chet
  and Garside, Jack
  and Jagninski, Tom
  and Krauzer, Steven M(ark)
  and Obstfeld, Raymond
Pendleton, Thomas 1965- 206
Pendziwol, Jean E. 1965- 177

Pene du Bois, William (Sherman)
  1916-1993 .... *68*
  Obituary *74*
  Earlier sketch in SATA *4*
  See also CLR *1*
Penn, Audrey 1947- *212*
Penn, Audrey 1950- *22*
Penn, Ruth Bonn
  See Rosenberg, Eth Clifford
Pennac, Daniel 1944- *155*
Pennage, E. M.
  See Finkel, George (Irvine)
Penner, Fred 1946- *169*
  Earlier sketch in SATA *67*
Penner, Frederick Ralph Cornelius
  See Penner, Fred
Penney, Grace Jackson 1904-2000 .... *35*
Penney, Ian 1960- *76*
Penney, Sue 1957- *152*
  Earlier sketch in SATA *102*
Pennington, Eunice 1923- *27*
Pennington, Lillian Boyer 1904-2003 .... *45*
Pennypacker, Sara 1951- *187*
Penrose, Gordon 1925- *66*
Penson, Mary E. 1917- *78*
Penzler, Otto 1942- *38*
Pepe, Phil 1935- *20*
Pepe, Philip
  See Pepe, Phil
Peppe, Rodney (Darrell) 1934- *74*
  Earlier sketch in SATA *4*
  See also SAAS *10*
Pepper, Frank S. 1910-1988
  Obituary *61*
Percy, Charles Henry
  See Smith, Dorothy Gladys
Percy, Rachel 1930- *63*
Perdrizet, Marie-Pierre 1952- *79*
Perenyi, Constance 1954- *93*
Perenyi, Constance Marie
  See Perenyi, Constance
Perera, Hilda 1926- *105*
Perera, Thomas Biddle 1938- *13*
Peretti, Frank E. 1951- *141*
  Earlier sketch in SATA *80*
Perez, L. King 1940- *199*
Perez, Lana
  See Perez, Marlene
Perez, Lucia Angela 1973- *182*
Perez, Marlene *170*
Pericoli, Matteo 1968- *178*
Perkins, Al(bert Rogers) 1904-1975 .... *30*
Perkins, Lucy Fitch 1865-1937 .... *72*
Perkins, Lynne Rae 1956- *212*
  Earlier sketches in SATA *131, 172*
Perkins, (Richard) Marlin 1905-1986 .... *21*
  Obituary *48*
Perkins, Mitali 1963- *188*
  Earlier sketch in SATA *88*
Perks, Anne-Marie 1955- *122*
Perl, Erica S. *188*
Perl, Lila *72*
  Earlier sketch in SATA *6*
Perl, Susan 1922-1983 .... *22*
  Obituary *34*
Perlman, Rhea 1948- *183*
Perlmutter, O(scar) William 1920-1975 .... *8*
Pernu, Dennis 1970- *87*
Perrault, Charles 1628-1703 .... *25*
  See also CLR *134*
Perret, Delphine 1980- *190*
Perret, Gene (Richard) 1937- *76*
Perriman, Cole
  See Perrin, Pat
Perriman, Cole
  See Coleman, Wim
Perrin, Pat *212*
Perrine, Mary 1913-1976 .... *2*
Perrins, Lesley 1953- *56*
Perrow, Angeli 1954- *121*

Perry, Andrea 1956- *190*
  Earlier sketch in SATA *148*
Perry, Barbara Fisher
  See Fisher, Barbara
Perry, Elizabeth 1959- *174*
Perry, Elizabeth Goodwin
  See Perry, Elizabeth
Perry, Marie Fritz *165*
Perry, Patricia 1949- *30*
Perry, Phyllis J(ean) 1933- *152*
  Earlier sketches in SATA *60, 101*
Perry, Ritchie (John Allen) 1942- *105*
Perry, Roger 1933- *27*
Perry, Steve(n Carl) 1947- *76*
Pershall, Mary K. 1951- *172*
  Earlier sketch in SATA *70*
Pershing, Marie
  See Schultz, Pearle Henriksen
Perske, Robert 1927- *57*
Persun, Morgan Reed
  See Watkins, Dawn L.
Perversi, Margaret *213*
Petach, Heidi *149*
Peter
  See Stratemeyer, Edward L.
Peters, Alexander
  See Hollander, Zander
Peters, Andrew Fusek 1965- *169*
  Earlier sketch in SATA *107*
Peters, Bernadette 1948- *212*
Peters, Caroline
  See Betz, Eva Kelly
Peters, David
  See David, Peter
Peters, Elizabeth 1927- *49*
Peters, Emma
  See Price, Karen
Peters, Gabriel
  See Matott, Justin
Peters, Julie Anne 1952- *197*
  Earlier sketches in SATA *82, 128*
Peters, Linda
  See Catherall, Arthur
Peters, Lisa Westberg 1951- *161*
  Earlier sketches in SATA *74, 115*
Peters, Patricia 1953- *84*
Peters, Russell M. 1929- *78*
Peters, S. H.
  See Henry, O.
  and Proffitt, Nicholas
Petersen, David 1946- *109*
  Earlier sketch in SATA *62*
Petersen, Gwenn Boardman 1924- *12*
Petersen, P(eter) J(ames) 1941- *118*
  Brief entry *43*
  Earlier sketches in SATA *48, 83*
Petersen, Palle 1943- *85*
Petersham, Maud 1890-1971 .... *17*
  See also CLR *24*
Petersham, Maud Sylvia Fuller
  See Petersham, Maud
Petersham, Miska 1888-1960 .... *17*
  See also CLR *24*
Peterson, Cris 1952- *174*
  Earlier sketches in SATA *84, 145*
Peterson, Dawn 1934- *86*
Peterson, Esther (Allen) 1934- *35*
Peterson, Hans 1922- *8*
Peterson, Harold L(eslie) 1922-1978 .... *8*
Peterson, Helen Stone 1910- *8*
Peterson, Jean Sunde 1941- *108*
Peterson, Jeanne Whitehouse 1939- *159*
  Earlier sketch in SATA *29*
Peterson, Kathleen B. 1951- *119*
Peterson, Lorraine 1940- *56*
  Brief entry *44*
Peterson, Mary *215*
Peterson, Shelley 1952- *146*
Peterson, Will
  See Cocks, Peter

Petie, Haris
  See Petty, Roberta
Petricic, Dusan 1946- *176*
Petrides, Heidrun 1944- *19*
Petrie, Catherine 1947- *52*
  Brief entry *41*
Petrone, Valeria *186*
Petrosino, Tamara *193*
Petroski, Catherine (Ann Groom) 1939- *48*
Petrovich, Michael B(oro) 1922- *40*
Petrovskaya, Kyra
  See Wayne, Kyra Petrovskaya
Petruccio, Steven James 1961- *67*
Petrucha, Stefan 1959- *213*
Petry, Ann 1908-1997 .... *5*
  Obituary *94*
  See also CLR *12*
Petry, Ann Lane
  See Petry, Ann
Pettit, Jayne 1932- *108*
Petty, J.T. 1977- *189*
Petty, Kate 1951-2007 .... *204*
Petty, Roberta 1915- *10*
Pevsner, Stella *131*
  Earlier sketches in SATA *8, 77*
  See also SAAS *14*
Peyo
  See Culliford, Pierre
Peyton, K. M.
  See Peyton, Kathleen Wendy
Peyton, Kathleen Wendy 1929- *157*
  Earlier sketches in SATA *15, 62*
  See also CLR *3*
  See also SAAS *17*
Pfanner, (Anne) Louise 1955- *68*
Pfeffer, Susan Beth 1948- *180*
  Earlier sketches in SATA *4, 83*
  See also CLR *11*
  See also SAAS *17*
Pfeffer, Wendy 1929- *204*
  Earlier sketches in SATA *78, 142*
Pfeiffer, Janet (B.) 1949- *96*
Pfister, Marcus *207*
  Earlier sketches in SATA *83, 150*
  See also CLR *42*
Pfitsch, Patricia Curtis 1948- *148*
Pfitzenmaier, Audrey 1959- *220*
Pflieger, Pat 1955- *84*
Pham, LeUyen 1973- *201*
  Earlier sketch in SATA *175*
Phelan, Mary Kay 1914- *3*
Phelan, Matt 1970- *215*
  Earlier sketch in SATA *172*
Phelan, Terry Wolfe 1941- *56*
Phelps, Ethel Johnston 1914-1984 .... *35*
Philbrick, Rodman 1951- *163*
Philbrick, W. Rodman
  See Philbrick, Rodman
Philbrick, W.R.
  See Philbrick, Rodman
Philbrook, Clem(ent E.) 1917- *24*
Phillipps, J.C. *218*
Phillipps, Julie Christine
  See Phillipps, J.C.
Phillips, Aileen Paul
  See Paul, Aileen
Phillips, Betty Lou
  See Phillips, Elizabeth Louise
Phillips, Bob 1940- *95*
Phillips, Douglas A. 1949- *161*
Phillips, Elizabeth Louise *58*
  Brief entry *48*
Phillips, Irv(ing W.) 1905-2000 .... *11*
  Obituary *125*
Phillips, Jack
  See Sandburg, Carl
Phillips, Leon
  See Gerson, Noel Bertram
Phillips, Loretta (Hosey) 1893-1987 .... *10*
Phillips, Louis 1942- *102*
  Earlier sketch in SATA *8*

Phillips, Mark
  See Garrett, Randall
  and Janifer, Laurence M(ark)
Phillips, Mary Geisler 1881-1964 .... *10*
Phillips, Michael
  See Nolan, William F.
Phillips, (Woodward) Prentice 1894-1981 .... *10*
Phillpotts, Eden 1862-1960 .... *24*
Phin
  See Thayer, Ernest Lawrence
Phipson, Joan
  See Fitzhardinge, Joan Margaret
Phiz
  See Browne, Hablot Knight
Phleger, Fred B. 1909-1993 .... *34*
Phleger, Marjorie Temple 1908(?)-1986 .... *1*
  Obituary *47*
Piaget, Jean 1896-1980
  Obituary *23*
Piatti, Celestino 1922- *16*
Picard, Barbara Leonie 1917- *89*
  Earlier sketch in SATA *2*
  See also SAAS *10*
Pichon, Liz *174*
Pickard, Charles 1932- *36*
Pickering, James Sayre 1897-1969 .... *36*
  Obituary *28*
Pickering, Jimmy *195*
Pickering, Robert B. 1950- *93*
Pielichaty, Helena 1955- *142*
Pienkowski, Jan (Michal) 1936- *131*
  Earlier sketches in SATA *6, 58*
  See also CLR *6*
Pierce, Edith Gray 1893-1977 .... *45*
Pierce, Katherine
  See St. John, Wylly Folk
Pierce, Meredith Ann 1958- *127*
  Brief entry *48*
  Earlier sketch in SATA *67*
  See also CLR *20*
Pierce, Ruth (Ireland) 1936- *5*
Pierce, Sharon
  See McCullough, Sharon Pierce
Pierce, Tamora 1954- *187*
  Brief entry *49*
  Earlier sketches in SATA *51, 96, 153*
Pierce, Terry *178*
Pierik, Robert 1921- *13*
Piernas-Davenport, Gail *199*
Piers, Robert
  See Anthony, Piers
Pig, Edward
  See Gorey, Edward (St. John)
Pike, Aprilynne *218*
Pike, Bob
  See Pike, Robert W.
Pike, Christopher 1954(?)- *156*
  Earlier sketch in SATA *68*
  See also CLR *29*
Pike, Deborah 1951- *89*
Pike, E(dgar) Royston 1896-1980 .... *22*
  Obituary *56*
Pike, R. William 1956- *92*
Pike, Robert
  See Pike, Robert W.
Pike, Robert W. 1931- *102*
Pike, Robert Wilson
  See Pike, Robert W.
Pilarski, Laura 1926- *13*
Pilgrim, Anne
  See Allan, Mabel Esther
Pilkey, Dav 1966- *166*
  Earlier sketches in SATA *68, 115*
  See also CLR *160*
Pilkey, David Murray, Jr.
  See Pilkey, Dav
Pilkington, Francis Meredyth 1907-1993 ...... *4*
Pilkington, Roger (Windle) 1915-2003 .... *10*
  Obituary *144*
Pilutti, Deb *208*
Pin, Isabel 1975- *183*

Pinchot, David 1914(?)-1983
  Obituary *34*
Pincus, Harriet 1938- *27*
Pinczes, Elinor J(ane) 1940- *81*
Pine, Nicholas 1951- *91*
Pine, Tillie S(chloss) 1896-1999 .... *13*
Pini, Richard (Alan) 1950- *89*
Pini, Wendy 1951- *89*
Pinkerton, Kathrene Sutherland (Gedney)
  1887-1967
  Obituary *26*
Pinkett, Jada
  See Smith, Jada Pinkett
Pinkney, Andrea Davis 1963- *160*
  Earlier sketch in SATA *113*
Pinkney, Brian 1961- *206*
  Earlier sketches in SATA *74, 148*
  See also CLR *54*
Pinkney, Gloria Jean 1941- *212*
  Earlier sketch in SATA *85*
Pinkney, J. Brian
  See Pinkney, Brian
Pinkney, Jerry 1939- *198*
  Autobiography Feature *198*
  Brief entry *32*
  Earlier sketches in SATA *41, 71, 107, 151*
  See also CLR *43*
  See also SAAS *12*
Pinkney, John *97*
Pinkney, Sandra L. *193*
  Earlier sketch in SATA *128*
Pinkwater, D. Manus
  See Pinkwater, Daniel
Pinkwater, Daniel 1941- *210*
  Earlier sketches in SATA *8, 46, 76, 114, 158*
  See also CLR *4*
  See also SAAS *3*
Pinkwater, Daniel M.
  See Pinkwater, Daniel
Pinkwater, Daniel Manus
  See Pinkwater, Daniel
Pinkwater, Jill *188*
Pinkwater, Manus
  See Pinkwater, Daniel
Pinner, Joma
  See Werner, Herma
Pinto, Sara *200*
Pioneer
  See Yates, Raymond F(rancis)
Piowaty, Kim Kennelly 1957- *49*
Piper, Roger
  See Fisher, John
Pirner, Connie White 1955- *72*
Piro, Richard 1934- *7*
Pirot, Alison Lohans
  See Lohans, Alison
Pirotta, Saviour *184*
Pirsig, Robert M(aynard) 1928- *39*
Pita
  See Rendon, Maria
Pitcher, C.
  See Pitcher, Caroline
Pitcher, Caroline 1948- *214*
  Earlier sketch in SATA *128*
Pitcher, Caroline Nell
  See Pitcher, Caroline
Pitman, (Isaac) James 1901-1985
  Obituary *46*
Pitre, Felix 1949- *84*
Pitrone, Jean Maddern 1920- *4*
Pittman, Helena Clare 1945- *71*
Pitz, Henry C(larence) 1895-1976 .... *4*
  Obituary *24*
Pitzer, Susanna 1958- *181*
Piven, Hanoch 1963- *173*
Pixley, Marcella *194*
Pizer, Vernon 1918- *21*
Place, Marian T(empleton) 1910- *3*
Place, Robin (Mary) 1926- *71*
Plaidy, Jean
  See Hibbert, Eleanor Alice Burford

Plain, Belva 1919-2010 .... *62*
Plaine, Alfred R. 1898(?)-1981
  Obituary *29*
Plant, Andrew *214*
Plath, Sylvia 1932-1963 .... *96*
Platt, Chris 1959- *185*
Platt, Kin 1911- *86*
  Earlier sketch in SATA *21*
  See also SAAS *17*
Platt, Randall 1948- *95*
Platt, Randall Beth
  See Platt, Randall
Platt, Richard 1953- *218*
  Earlier sketches in SATA *120, 166*
Playfellow, Robin
  See Ellis, Edward S.
Playsted, James
  See Wood, James Playsted
Plecas, Jennifer 1966- *149*
  Earlier sketch in SATA *84*
Plimpton, George 1927-2003 .... *10*
  Obituary *150*
Plimpton, George Ames
  See Plimpton, George
Plomer, William Charles Franklin
  1903-1973 .... *24*
Plotz, Helen Ratnoff 1913-2000 .... *38*
Plourde, Lynn 1955- *218*
  Earlier sketches in SATA *122, 168*
Plowden, David 1932- *52*
Plowden, Martha Ward 1948- *98*
Plowhead, Ruth Gipson 1877-1967 .... *43*
Plowman, Stephanie 1922- *6*
Pluckrose, Henry (Arthur) 1931- *141*
  Earlier sketch in SATA *13*
Plum, J.
  See Wodehouse, P. G.
Plum, Jennifer
  See Kurland, Michael
Plumb, Charles P. 1900(?)-1982
  Obituary *29*
Plume, Ilse *170*
  Brief entry *43*
Plumme, Don E.
  See Katz, Bobbi
Plummer, Margaret 1911- *2*
Plum-Ucci, Carol *184*
Pochocki, Ethel (Frances) 1925- *76*
Podendorf, Illa (E.) 1903(?)-1983 .... *18*
  Obituary *35*
Podwal, Mark 1945- *160*
  Earlier sketch in SATA *101*
Podwal, Mark H.
  See Podwal, Mark
Poe, Edgar Allan 1809-1849 .... *23*
Poe, Ty (Christopher) 1975- *94*
Pogany, William Andrew 1882-1955 .... *44*
  Brief entry *30*
Pogany, Willy
  See Pogany, William Andrew
Pohl, Frederik 1919- *24*
Pohlmann, Lillian (Grenfell) 1902-1997 .... *11*
Pohrt, Tom 1953- *195*
  Earlier sketches in SATA *67, 152*
Pointon, Robert
  See Rooke, Daphne
Points, Larry G. 1945- *177*
  Earlier sketch in SATA *133*
Points, Larry Gene
  See Points, Larry G.
Pokeberry, P.J.
  See Mitchell, B.J.
POLA
  See Watson, Pauline
Polacco, Patricia 1944- *212*
  Earlier sketches in SATA *74, 123, 180*
  See also CLR *40*
Polacco, Patricia Ann
  See Polacco, Patricia
Polak, Monique 1960- *178*
Polatnick, Florence T. 1923- *5*

Polcovar, Jane 1948- *211*
Polder, Markus
  See Kruss, James
Polese, Carolyn 1947- *58*
Polese, James 1914- *87*
Polette, Nancy (Jane) 1930- *42*
Polhamus, Jean Burt 1928- *21*
Polhemus, Coleman *210*
Policoff, Stephen Phillip 1948- *77*
Polikoff, Barbara G. 1929- *162*
  Earlier sketch in SATA *77*
Polikoff, Barbara Garland
  See Polikoff, Barbara G.
Polisar, Barry Louis 1954- *134*
  Earlier sketch in SATA *77*
Politi, Leo 1908-1996 .... *47*
  Obituary *88*
  Earlier sketch in SATA *1*
  See also CLR *29*
Polking, Kirk 1925- *5*
Pollack, Jill S. 1963- *88*
Pollack, Merrill S. 1924-1988
  Obituary *55*
Polland, Barbara K(ay) 1939- *44*
Polland, Madeleine A(ngela Cahill) 1918- ... *68*
  Earlier sketch in SATA *6*
  See also SAAS *8*
Pollema-Cahill, Phyllis 1958- *123*
Pollock, Bruce 1945- *46*
Pollock, Mary
  See Blyton, Enid
Pollock, Penny 1935- *137*
  Brief entry *42*
  Earlier sketch in SATA *44*
Pollowitz, Melinda Kilborn 1944- *26*
Polner, Murray 1928- *64*
Polonsky, Arthur 1925- *34*
Polseno, Jo *17*
Pomaska, Anna 1946- *117*
Pomerantz, Charlotte 1930- *177*
  Earlier sketches in SATA *20, 80*
Pomeroy, Pete
  See Roth, Arthur J(oseph)
Pon, Cindy 1973- *216*
Pond, Alonzo W(illiam) 1894-1986 .... *5*
Pontiflet, Ted 1932- *32*
Poole, Gray Johnson 1906- *1*
Poole, Josephine
  See Helyar, Jane Penelope Josephine
Poole, (Jane Penelope) Josephine
  See Helyar, Jane Penelope Josephine
Poole, Lynn 1910-1969 .... *1*
Poole, Peggy 1925- *39*
Poortvliet, Rien 1932- *65*
  Brief entry *37*
Pope, Elizabeth Marie 1917-1992 .... *38*
  Brief entry *36*
Pope, Kevin 1958- *183*
Popescu, Christine
  See Pullein-Thompson, Christine
Poploff, Michelle 1956- *67*
Popp, K. Wendy *91*
Poppel, Hans 1942- *71*
Porfirio, Guy 1958- *197*
Portal, Colette 1936- *6*
Porte, Barbara Ann 1943- *152*
  Brief entry *45*
  Earlier sketches in SATA *57, 93*
Porter, A(nthony) P(eyton) 1945- *68*
Porter, Connie (Rose) 1959(?)- *129*
  Earlier sketch in SATA *81*
Porter, Donald Clayton
  See Gerson, Noel Bertram
Porter, Eleanor H(odgman) 1868-1920
  See CLR *110*
Porter, Gene Stratton
  See Stratton-Porter, Gene
Porter, Janice Lee 1953- *108*
  Earlier sketch in SATA *68*
Porter, Katherine Anne 1890-1980 .... *39*
  Obituary *23*

Porter, Kathryn
  See Swinford, Betty (June Wells)
Porter, Pamela 1956- *193*
Porter, Sheena 1935- *24*
  See also SAAS *10*
Porter, Sue
  See Limb, Sue
Porter, Sue 1951- *213*
  Earlier sketch in SATA *76*
Porter, Tracey *191*
Porter, William Sydney
  See Henry, O.
Portis, Antoinette *189*
Porto, Tony 1960- *153*
Portteus, Eleanora Marie Manthei (?)-1983
  Obituary *36*
Posada, Mia *187*
Posell, Elsa Z(eigerman) -1995 .... *3*
Posesorski, Sherie *216*
Posten, Margaret L(ois) 1915- *10*
Postgate, Daniel 1964- *216*
Posthuma, Sieb 1960- *150*
Postier, Jim 1965- *202*
Potok, Chaim 1929-2002 .... *106*
  Obituary *134*
  Earlier sketch in SATA *33*
  See also CLR *92*
Potok, Herbert Harold
  See Potok, Chaim
Potok, Herman Harold
  See Potok, Chaim
Potter, Alicia *216*
Potter, Beatrix 1866-1943 .... *132*
  Earlier sketch in SATA *100*
  See also YABC *1*
  See also CLR *73*
Potter, Ellen 1973- *218*
Potter, Giselle *187*
  Earlier sketch in SATA *150*
Potter, Helen Beatrix
  See Potter, Beatrix
Potter, Katherine *217*
Potter, Margaret 1926-1998 .... *21*
  Obituary *104*
Potter, Marian 1915- *9*
Potter, Miriam Clark 1886-1965 .... *3*
Poulin, Stephane 1961- *98*
  See also CLR *28*
Poulton, Kimberly 1957(?)- *136*
Pournelle, Jerry 1933- *161*
  Earlier sketches in SATA *26, 91*
Pournelle, Jerry Eugene
  See Pournelle, Jerry
Povelite, Kay 1955- *102*
Pow, Tom 1950- *163*
Powe-Allred, Alexandra
  See Allred, Alexandra Powe
Powell, A. M.
  See Morgan, Alfred P(owell)
Powell, Consie *174*
Powell, E. Sandy 1947- *72*
Powell, E.S.
  See Powell, E. Sandy
Powell, Pamela 1960- *78*
Powell, Patricia Hruby 1951- *136*
Powell, Randy 1956- *118*
Powell, Richard Stillman
  See Barbour, Ralph Henry
Powell, Robert (Stephenson Smyth) Baden
  See Baden-Powell, Robert (Stephenson Smyth)
Powell, Stephanie 1953- *93*
Power, Margaret (M.) 1945- *125*
  Earlier sketch in SATA *75*
Powers, Anne
  See Schwartz, Anne Powers
Powers, Bill 1931- *52*
  Brief entry *31*
Powers, Daniel 1959- *164*
Powers, J. L. *195*

Powers, Jessica
  See Powers, J. L.
Powers, Jessica Lynn
  See Powers, J. L.
Powers, Margaret
  See Heal, Edith
Powers, Tim 1952- *107*
Powers, Timothy Thomas
  See Powers, Tim
Powledge, Fred 1935- *37*
Poydar, Nancy *190*
Poynter, Margaret 1927- *27*
Prachaticka, Marketa
  See Kolibalova, Marketa
Prachatika, Marketa
  See Kolibalova, Marketa
Prager, Arthur *44*
Prager, Ellen J. 1962- *136*
Prange, Beckie *172*
Prap, Lila 1955- *177*
Praprotnik-Zupancic, Lilijana
  See Prap, Lila
Pratchett, Terence David John
  See Pratchett, Terry
Pratchett, Terry 1948- *185*
  Earlier sketches in SATA *82, 139*
  See also CLR *64*
Prater, John 1947- *149*
  Earlier sketches in SATA *72, 103*
Prato, Rodica *184*
Pratt, Christine Joy *214*
Pratt, (Murray) Fletcher 1897-1956 .... *102*
Pratt, Kristin Joy 1976- *87*
Pratt, Pierre 1962- *208*
  Earlier sketches in SATA *95, 166*
Preiss, Byron 1953-2005 .... *166*
  Brief entry *42*
  Earlier sketch in SATA *47*
Preiss, Byron Cary
  See Preiss, Byron
Preller, James 1961- *209*
  Earlier sketch in SATA *88*
Prelutsky, Jack 1940- *171*
  Earlier sketches in SATA *22, 66, 118*
  See also CLR *115*
Prentice, Amy
  See Kaler, James Otis
Prescott, Casey
  See Morris, Chris(topher Crosby)
Presnall, Judith (Ann) Janda 1943- *96*
Pressler, Mirjam 1940- *155*
Preston, Douglas 1956- *113*
Preston, Edna Mitchell *40*
Preston, Lillian Elvira 1918- *47*
Preus, Margi *209*
Preussler, Otfried 1923- *24*
Prevert, Jacques 1900-1977
  Obituary *30*
Prevert, Jacques Henri Marie
  See Prevert, Jacques
Prevost, Guillaume 1964- *192*
Prevost, Mikela *203*
Price, Beverley Joan 1931- *98*
Price, Charlie *187*
Price, Christine (Hilda) 1928-1980 .... *3*
  Obituary *23*
Price, Garrett 1896-1979
  Obituary *22*
Price, Jennifer
  See Hoover, Helen (Drusilla Blackburn)
Price, Joan 1931- *124*
Price, Jonathan (Reeve) 1941- *46*
Price, Karen 1957- *125*
Price, Kathy Z. 1957- *172*
Price, Lucie Locke
  See Locke, Lucie
Price, Olive 1903-1991 .... *8*
Price, Susan 1955- *128*
  Earlier sketches in SATA *25, 85*
Price, Willard 1887-1983 .... *48*
  Brief entry *38*

Price-Groff, Claire 127
Priceman, Marjorie 1958- 168
  Earlier sketches in SATA *81, 120*
Prichard, Katharine Susannah 1883-1969 66
Prideaux, Tom 1908-1993 37
  Obituary 76
Priestley, Alice 1962- 95
Priestley, Chris 1958- 198
Priestley, Lee (Shore) 1904-1999 27
Priestly, Doug 1954- 122
Priestly, Douglas Michael
  See Priestly, Doug
Prieto, Mariana Beeching 1912-1999 8
Priley, Margaret (Ann) Hubbard 1909-1992
  Obituary 130
Primavera, Elise 1954- 185
  Brief entry 48
  Earlier sketches in SATA *58, 109*
Prime, Derek (James) 1931- 34
Prince, Alison (Mary) 1931- 86
  Earlier sketch in SATA *28*
Prince, April Jones 1975- 180
Prince, J(ack) H(arvey) 1908- 17
Prince, Joshua 188
Prince, Maggie 102
Prineas, Sarah 204
Pringle, Eric 138
Pringle, Laurence 1935- 201
  Autobiography Feature 201
  Earlier sketches in SATA *4, 68, 104, 154*
  See also CLR *57*
  See also SAAS *6*
Pringle, Laurence Patrick
  See Pringle, Laurence
Prinz, Yvonne 1960- 175
Prior, Natalie Jane 1963- 106
Pritchett, Elaine H(illyer) 1920- 36
Pritchett, Laura 1971- 178
Pritchett, Laura Rose
  See Pritchett, Laura
Pritts, Kim Derek 1953- 83
Prochazkova, Iva 1953- 68
Proctor, Everitt
  See Montgomery, Rutherford George
Proeysen, Alf 1914-1970 67
  See also CLR *24*
Professor Scribbler
  See Hollingsworth, Mary
Proimos, James 1955- 217
  Earlier sketch in SATA *173*
Prose, Francine 1947- 198
  Earlier sketches in SATA *101, 149*
Prosek, James 1975- 216
Protopopescu, Orel 186
Protopopescu, Orel Odinov
  See Protopopescu, Orel
Provensen, Alice 1918- 147
  Earlier sketches in SATA *9, 70*
  See also CLR *11*
Provensen, Martin 1916-1987 70
  Obituary 51
  Earlier sketch in SATA *9*
  See also CLR *11*
Provensen, Martin Elias
  See Provensen, Martin
Provenzo, Eugene (F., Jr.) 1949- 142
  Earlier sketch in SATA *78*
Provist, d'Alain 1906-1989
  See Diop, Birago (Ismael)
Provost, Gail Levine 1944- 65
Provost, Gary (Richard) 1944-1995 66
Proysen, Alf
  See Proeysen, Alf
Pruett, Candace (J.) 1968- 157
Pryor, Bonnie H. 1942- 69
Pryor, Boori (Monty) 1950- 112
Pryor, Helen Brenton 1897-1972 4
Pryor, Michael 1957- 153
Pucci, Albert John 1920- 44
Pudney, John (Sleigh) 1909-1977 24
Pugh, Ellen (Tiffany) 1920- 7

Pullein-Thompson, Christine 1925-2005 82
  Obituary 172
  Earlier sketch in SATA *3*
Pullein-Thompson, Diana
  See Farr, Diana
Pullein-Thompson, Joanna Maxwell
  1898-1961 82
Pullein-Thompson, Josephine (Mary
  Wedderburn) 82
  Earlier sketch in SATA *3*
Pullen, Zachary 189
Pullman, Philip 1946- 198
  Earlier sketches in SATA *65, 103, 150*
  See also CLR *84*
  See also SAAS *17*
Pullman, Philip Nicholas
  See Pullman, Philip
Pulver, Harry, Jr. 1960- 129
Pulver, Robin 1945- 208
  Earlier sketches in SATA *76, 133*
Puner, Helen W(alker) 1915-1989 37
  Obituary 63
Purdy, Carol 1943- 120
  Earlier sketch in SATA *66*
Purdy, Susan G(old) 1939- 8
Purkiss, Diane 1961- 194
Purmell, Ann 1953- 206
  Earlier sketch in SATA *147*
Purnell, Idella 1901-1982 120
Purscell, Phyllis 1934- 7
Purtill, Richard L. 1931- 53
Pushker, Gloria 1927- 162
  Earlier sketch in SATA *75*
Pushker, Gloria Teles
  See Pushker, Gloria
Pushkin, Aleksandr Sergeevich
  See Pushkin, Alexander
Pushkin, Alexander 1799-1837 61
Putnam, Alice 1916- 61
Putnam, Arthur Lee
  See Alger, Horatio, Jr.
Putnam, Peter B(rock) 1920-1998 30
  Obituary 106
Puttapipat, Niroot 199
Puttock, Simon 178
Puvilland, Alex 205
Puvilland, Alexandre
  See Puvilland, Alex
Puybaret, Eric 1976- 195
Pyle, Howard 1853-1911 100
  Earlier sketch in SATA *16*
  See also CLR *117*
Pyle, Katharine 1863-1938 66
Pyne, Mable Mandeville 1903-1969 9
Pyrnelle, Louise-Clarke 1850-1907 114

Q

Quackenbush, Robert M(ead) 1929- 133
  Autobiography Feature 133
  Earlier sketches in SATA *7, 70*
  See also CLR *122*
  See also SAAS *7*
Qualey, Marsha 1953- 124
  Earlier sketch in SATA *79*
Qualls, Sean 177
Quammen, David 1948- 7
Quark, Jason
  See Eldin, Peter
Quarles, Benjamin 1904-1996 12
Quarles, Benjamin Arthur
  See Quarles, Benjamin
Quatermass, Martin
  See Carpenter, John
Quattlebaum, Mary 1958- 185
  Earlier sketches in SATA *88, 134*
Quay, Emma 173
  Earlier sketch in SATA *119*

Queen, Ellery
  See Deming, Richard
  and Dannay, Frederic
  and Davidson, Avram (James)
  and Fairman, Paul W.
  and Flora, Fletcher
  and Holding, James (Clark Carlisle, Jr.)
  and Hoch, Edward D.
  and Kane, Henry
  and Lee, Manfred B.
  and Marlowe, Stephen
  and Powell, (Oval) Talmage
  and Sheldon, Walter J(ames)
  and Sturgeon, Theodore (Hamilton)
  and Tracy, Don(ald Fiske)
  and Vance, Jack
Queen Latifah 1970- 185
Quennell, Marjorie Courtney 1884-1972 29
Quentin
  See Sheldon, David
Quentin, Brad
  See Bisson, Terry
Quest, (Edna) Olga W(ilbourne) Hall
  See Hall-Quest, (Edna) Olga W(ilbourne)
Quick, Annabelle 1922-1986 2
Quigg, Jane (Hulda) (?)-1986
  Obituary 49
Quigley, Sarah 1976- 220
Quill, Monica
  See McInerny, Ralph
Quin-Harkin, Janet 1941- 165
  Earlier sketches in SATA *18, 90, 119*
Quin-Harkin, Janet Elizabeth
  See Quin-Harkin, Janet
Quinlan, Susan E. 1954- 88
Quinlan, Susan Elizabeth
  See Quinlan, Susan E.
Quinn, Elisabeth 1881-1962 22
Quinn, Pat 1947- 130
Quinn, Patrick 1950- 73
Quinn, Rob 1972- 138
Quinn, Susan 1940- 30
Quinn, Susan Taft
  See Quinn, Susan
Quinn, Theodora K.
  See Kroeber, Theodora (Kracaw)
Quinn, Vernon
  See Quinn, Elisabeth
Quirk, Anne (E.) 1956- 99
Quixley, Jim 1931- 56
Quyth, Gabriel
  See Jennings, Gary

R

Ra, Carol F. 1939- 76
Raab, Evelyn 1951- 129
Rabb, Margo 1972- 188
Rabb, M.E.
  See Rabb, Margo
Rabe, Berniece (Louise) 1928- 148
  Autobiography Feature 148
  Earlier sketches in SATA *7, 77*
  See also SAAS *10*
Rabe, Olive H(anson) (?)-1968 13
Rabin, Staton 1958- 162
  Earlier sketch in SATA *84*
Rabinowich, Ellen 1946- 29
Rabinowitz, Sandy 1954- 52
  Brief entry 39
Rachlin, Carol K(ing) 1919- 64
Rachlin, Harvey 1951- 47
Rachlin, Harvey Brant
  See Rachlin, Harvey
Rachlin, Nahid 64
Rachlis, Eugene (Jacob) 1920-1986
  Obituary 50

Rackham, Arthur 1867-1939 .... *100*
  Earlier sketch in SATA *15*
  See also CLR *57*
Racoma, Robin Yoko 1953- *207*
Raczka, Bob 1963- *191*
  Earlier sketch in SATA *163*
Radencich, Marguerite C. 1952-1998 .... *79*
Rader, Laura *197*
Radford, Ruby L(orraine) 1891-1971 .... *6*
Radin, Ruth Yaffe 1938- *107*
  Brief entry *52*
  Earlier sketch in SATA *56*
Radlauer, David 1952- *28*
Radlauer, Edward 1921- *15*
Radlauer, Ruth Shaw 1926- *98*
  Earlier sketch in SATA *15*
Radley, Gail 1951- *112*
  Earlier sketch in SATA *25*
Radunsky, Vladimir *177*
Radzinski, Kandy 1948- *212*
Rae, Gwynedd 1892-1977 .... *37*
Raebeck, Lois 1921- *5*
Rael, Elsa Okon 1927-
  See CLR *84*
Raffi
  See Cavoukian, Raffi
Raftery, Gerald (Bransfield) 1905-1986 .... *11*
Ragan-Reid, Gale 1956- *90*
Rahaman, Vashanti 1953- *98*
Rahn, Joan Elma 1929- *27*
Rai, Bali 1971- *152*
Raible, Alton (Robert) 1918- *35*
Raiff, Stan 1930- *11*
Raines, Shirley C(arol) 1945- *128*
Rainey, W. B.
  See Blassingame, Wyatt Rainey
Rake, Jody 1961- *157*
Rallison, Janette 1966- *183*
Ralston, Jan
  See Dunlop, Agnes M. R.
Rama, Sue *190*
Ramal, Walter
  See de la Mare, Walter (John)
Ramanujan, A(ttipat) K(rishnaswami)
  1929-1993 .... *86*
Rame, David
  See Divine, Arthur Durham
Ramirez, Jose 1967- *198*
Ramirez, Orlando L. 1972- *194*
Ramos, Jorge 1958- *205*
Ramstad, Ralph L. 1919- *115*
Ramthun, Bonnie *214*
Rana, Indi
  See Rana, Indira Higham
Rana, Indira Higham 1944- *82*
Rana, J.
  See Bhatia, Jamunadevi
Ranadive, Gail 1944- *10*
Rand, Ann (Binkley) *30*
Rand, Gloria 1925- *156*
  Earlier sketch in SATA *101*
Rand, Paul 1914-1996 .... *6*
Randall, Carrie
  See Ransom, Candice F.
Randall, David 1972- *167*
Randall, Florence Engel 1917-1997 .... *5*
Randall, Janet
  See Young, Janet Randall
  and Young, Robert W(illiam)
Randall, Robert
  See Garrett, Randall
  and Silverberg, Robert
Randall, Ruth (Elaine) Painter 1892-1971 ..... *3*
Randell, Beverley
  See Price, Beverley Joan
Randle, Kristen D. 1952- *92*
  Autobiography Feature *119*
  See also SAAS *24*
Randle, Kristen Downey
  See Randle, Kristen D.

Randolph, Boynton M.D.
  See Ellis, Edward S.
Randolph, Ellen
  See Rawn, Melanie
Randolph, Geoffrey
  See Ellis, Edward S.
Randolph, J. H.
  See Ellis, Edward S.
Randolph, Lieutenant J. H.
  See Ellis, Edward S.
Rands, William Brighty 1823-1882 .... *17*
Raney, Ken 1953- *74*
Rankin, Joan 1940- *212*
  Earlier sketches in SATA *88, 148*
Rankin, Laura 1953(?)- *176*
Ranney, Agnes V. 1916-1985 .... *6*
Ransom, Candice F. 1952- *183*
  Brief entry *49*
  Earlier sketches in SATA *52, 89, 135*
Ransom, Jeanie Franz 1957- *187*
Ransome, Arthur (Michell) 1884-1967 .... *22*
  See also CLR *8*
Ransome, James E. 1961- *178*
  Earlier sketches in SATA *76, 123*
  See also CLR *86*
Rant, Tol E.
  See Longyear, Barry B(rookes)
Rao, Rohitash *218*
Raphael, Elaine
  See Bolognese, Elaine
Raposo, Joseph Guilherme 1938-1989
  Obituary *61*
Rapp, Adam 1968- *148*
Rappaport, Doreen *211*
  Earlier sketch in SATA *151*
Rappaport, Eva 1924- *6*
Rappoport, Ken 1935- *167*
  Earlier sketch in SATA *89*
Rarick, Carrie 1911-2002 .... *41*
Raschka, Chris 1959- *207*
  Earlier sketches in SATA *80, 117, 166*
Raschka, Christopher
  See Raschka, Chris
Rascol, Sabina I. *159*
Rash, Andy 1969- *219*
  Earlier sketch in SATA *162*
Raskin, Edith Lefkowitz 1908-1987 .... *9*
Raskin, Ellen 1928-1984 .... *139*
  Earlier sketches in SATA *2, 38*
  See also CLR *12*
Raskin, Joseph 1897-1982 .... *12*
  Obituary *29*
Rathjen, Carl Henry 1909-1984 .... *11*
Rathmann, Peggy 1953- *157*
  Earlier sketch in SATA *94*
  See also CLR *77*
Ratliff, Thomas M. 1948- *118*
Ratner, Sue Lynn
  See Alexander, Sue
Rattigan, Jama Kim 1951- *99*
Ratto, Linda Lee 1952- *79*
Rattray, Simon
  See Trevor, Elleston
Ratz de Tagyos, Paul 1958- *198*
  Earlier sketch in SATA *76*
Rau, Dana Meachen 1971- *218*
  Earlier sketches in SATA *94, 167*
Rau, Margaret 1913- *168*
  Earlier sketch in SATA *9*
  See also CLR *8*
Rauch, Mabel Thompson 1888-1972
  Obituary *26*
Raucher, Herman 1928- *8*
Raude, Karina *199*
Rauh, Sherry
  See North, Sherry
Raum, Elizabeth 1949- *155*
Raven, Margot Theis *184*
RavenWolf, Silver 1956- *155*
Ravielli, Anthony 1916-1997 .... *3*
  Obituary *95*

Ravilious, Robin 1944- *77*
Ravishankar, Anushka 1961- *200*
Rawding, F(rederick) W(illiam) 1930- *55*
Rawlings, Marjorie Kinnan 1896-1953 ...... *100*
  See also YABC *1*
  See also CLR *63*
Rawlins, Donna 1956- *206*
Rawlinson, Julia *212*
  Earlier sketch in SATA *175*
Rawls, (Woodrow) Wilson 1913-1984 .... *22*
  See also CLR *81*
Rawlyk, George Alexander 1935- *64*
Rawn, Melanie 1954- *98*
Rawn, Melanie Robin
  See Rawn, Melanie
Rawson, Katherine 1955- *190*
Ray, Carl 1943-1978 .... *63*
Ray, Deborah
  See Kogan Ray, Deborah
Ray, Delia 1963- *179*
  Earlier sketch in SATA *70*
Ray, Irene
  See Sutton, Margaret Beebe
Ray, Jane 1960- *196*
  Earlier sketches in SATA *72, 152*
Ray, JoAnne 1935- *9*
Ray, Mary (Eva Pedder) 1932- *127*
  Earlier sketch in SATA *2*
Ray, Mary Lyn 1946- *154*
  Earlier sketch in SATA *90*
Rayban, Chloe 1944- *167*
Rayevsky, Robert 1955- *190*
  Earlier sketch in SATA *81*
Raymond, James Crossley 1917-1981
  Obituary *29*
Raymond, Robert
  See Alter, Robert Edmond
Rayner, Catherine *204*
Rayner, Hugh *151*
Rayner, Mary 1933- *87*
  Earlier sketch in SATA *22*
  See also CLR *41*
Rayner, Shoo
  See Rayner, Hugh
Rayner, William 1929- *55*
  Brief entry *36*
Raynor, Dorka *28*
Raynor, Gemma 1985- *216*
Rayson, Steven 1932- *30*
Rayyan, Omar 1968- *216*
Razzell, Arthur (George) 1925- *11*
Razzell, Mary (Catherine) 1930- *102*
Razzi, James 1931- *10*
Read, Elfreida 1920- *2*
Read, Nicholas 1956- *146*
Read, Piers Paul 1941- *21*
Reade, Deborah 1949- *69*
Reader, Dennis 1929- *71*
Reading, Richard P(atrick) 1962- *161*
Readman, Jo 1958- *89*
Ready, Kirk L(ewis) 1943- *39*
Reaney, James 1926-2008 .... *43*
Reaney, James Crerar
  See Reaney, James
Reardon, Joyce
  See Pearson, Ridley
Reaver, Chap 1935-1993 .... *69*
  Obituary *77*
Reaver, Herbert R.
  See Reaver, Chap
Reaves, J. Michael
  See Reaves, (James) Michael
Reaves, (James) Michael 1950- *99*
Reber, Deborah *189*
Recorvits, Helen *191*
Redding, Robert Hull 1919- *2*
Redekopp, Elsa *61*
Redlich, Ben 1977- *181*
Redsand, Anna 1948- *184*
Redway, Ralph
  See Hamilton, Charles (Harold St. John)

Redway, Ridley
  See Hamilton, Charles (Harold St. John)
Reece, Colleen L. 1935- *116*
Reece, Gabrielle 1970- *108*
Reed, Betty Jane 1921- *4*
Reed, Dallas
  See Pendleton, Thomas
Reed, E.
  See Evans, Mari
Reed, Gwendolyn E(lizabeth) 1932- *21*
Reed, Kit 1932- *184*
  Autobiography Feature *184*
  Earlier sketches in SATA *34, 116*
Reed, Lynn Rowe *215*
  Earlier sketch in SATA *171*
Reed, Mike 1951- *211*
Reed, Neil 1961- *99*
Reed, Talbot Baines 1852-1893
  See CLR *76*
Reed, Thomas (James) 1947- *34*
Reed, William Maxwell 1871-1962 .... *15*
Reeder, Carolyn 1937- *97*
  Earlier sketch in SATA *66*
  See also CLR *69*
Reeder, Colin (Dawson) 1938- *74*
Reeder, Colonel Red
  See Reeder, Russell P(otter), Jr.
Reeder, Russell P(otter), Jr. 1902-1998 .... *4*
  Obituary *101*
Reeder, Stephanie Owen 1951- *102*
Reed-Jones, Carol 1955- *112*
Reef, Catherine 1951- *189*
  Earlier sketches in SATA *73, 128*
Reekie, Jocelyn (Margaret) 1947- *145*
Reeman, Douglas Edward 1924- *63*
  Brief entry *28*
Rees, Celia 1949- *124*
Rees, David (Bartlett) 1936-1993 .... *69*
  Obituary *76*
  Earlier sketch in SATA *36*
  See also SAAS *5*
Rees, Douglas 1947- *169*
Rees, Ennis (Samuel, Jr.) 1925- *3*
Rees, (George) Leslie (Clarence)
  1905-2000 .... *105*
  Obituary *135*
Reese, Bob
  See Reese, Robert A.
Reese, Carolyn Johnson 1938- *64*
Reese, Della 1931(?)- *114*
Reese, Lyn
  See Reese, Carolyn Johnson
Reese, Robert A. 1938- *60*
  Brief entry *53*
Reese, (John) Terence 1913-1996 .... *59*
Reeve, Joel
  See Cox, William R(obert)
Reeve, Kirk 1934- *117*
Reeve, Philip *201*
  Earlier sketch in SATA *170*
Reeve, Rosie *188*
  Earlier sketch in SATA *186*
Reeves, Faye Couch 1953- *76*
Reeves, James
  See Reeves, John Morris
Reeves, Jeni 1947- *111*
Reeves, John Morris 1909-1978 .... *87*
  Earlier sketch in SATA *15*
Reeves, Joyce 1911- *17*
Reeves, Lawrence F. 1926- *29*
Reeves, Ruth Ellen
  See Ranney, Agnes V.
Regan, Dian Curtis 1950- *149*
  Autobiography Feature *149*
  Earlier sketches in SATA *75, 133*
Regehr, Lydia 1903-1991 .... *37*
Reger, James P. 1952- *106*
Reggiani, Renee 1925- *18*
Rehm, Karl M. 1935- *72*
Reibstein, Mark *211*

Reich, Ali
  See Katz, Bobbi
Reich, Susanna 1954- *214*
  Earlier sketch in SATA *113*
Reiche, Dietlof 1941- *159*
Reichert, Edwin C(lark) 1909-1988
  Obituary *57*
Reichert, Mickey Zucker
  See Reichert, Miriam Zucker
Reichert, Miriam Zucker 1962- *85*
Reichert, Renee *172*
Reichhold, Jane(t E.) 1937- *147*
Reid, Alastair 1926- *46*
Reid, Barbara 1922- *21*
Reid, Barbara (Jane) 1957- *93*
  See also CLR *64*
Reid, Desmond
  See Moorcock, Michael
  and McNeilly, Wilfred (Glassford)
Reid, Eugenie Chazal 1924- *12*
Reid, John Calvin *21*
Reid, (Thomas) Mayne 1818-1883 .... *24*
Reid, Meta Mayne 1905-1991 .... *58*
  Brief entry *36*
Reid, Robin (Nicole) 1969- *145*
Reid Banks, Lynne 1929- *165*
  Earlier sketches in SATA *22, 75, 111*
  See also CLR *86*
Reider, Katja 1960- *126*
Reid Jenkins, Debra 1955- *87*
Reiff, Stephanie Ann 1948- *47*
  Brief entry *28*
Reig, June 1933- *30*
Reigot, Betty Polisar 1924- *55*
  Brief entry *41*
Reilly, Joan *195*
Reim, Melanie (K.) 1956- *104*
Reinach, Jacquelyn (Krasne) 1930-2000 ...... *28*
Reiner, Carl 1922- *151*
Reiner, William B(uck) 1910-1976 .... *46*
  Obituary *30*
Reinfeld, Fred 1910-1964 .... *3*
Reinhardt, Dana 1971- *175*
Reinhart, Matthew 1971- *197*
  Earlier sketch in SATA *161*
Reiniger, Lotte 1899-1981 .... *40*
  Obituary *33*
Reinsma, Carol 1949- *91*
Reinstedt, Randall A. 1935- *101*
Reinstedt, Randy
  See Reinstedt, Randall A.
Reisberg, Mira 1955- *82*
Reisberg, Veg
  See Reisberg, Mira
Reiser, Lynn 1944- *180*
  Earlier sketches in SATA *81, 138*
Reiser, Lynn Whisnant
  See Reiser, Lynn
Reisgies, Teresa (Maria) 1966- *74*
Reiss, Johanna 1929(?)- *18*
  See also CLR *19*
Reiss, Johanna de Leeuw
  See Reiss, Johanna
Reiss, John J. *23*
Reiss, Kathryn 1957- *144*
  Earlier sketch in SATA *76*
Reit, Seymour Victory 1918-2001 .... *21*
  Obituary *133*
Reit, Sy
  See Reit, Seymour Victory
Relf, Patricia 1954- *134*
  Earlier sketch in SATA *71*
Remark, Erich Paul
  See Remarque, Erich Maria
Remarque, Erich Maria 1898-1970
  See CLR *159*
Remi, Georges 1907-1983 .... *13*
  Obituary *32*
  See also CLR *114*
Remington, Frederic S(ackrider)
  1861-1909 .... *41*

Remkiewicz, Frank 1939- *217*
  Earlier sketches in SATA *77, 152*
Rempt, Fiona 1973- *198*
Remy, Georges
  See Remi, Georges
Renaud, Anne 1957- *211*
Renaud, Bernadette 1945- *66*
Renault, Mary 1905-1983 .... *23*
  Obituary *36*
Rendell, Joan *28*
Rendina, Laura (Jones) Cooper 1902- *10*
Rendon, Marcie R. 1952- *97*
Rendon, Maria 1965- *116*
Renee, Janina 1956- *140*
Renfro, Ed 1924- *79*
Renick, Marion (Lewis) 1905-1983 .... *1*
Renier, Aaron 1977- *202*
Renken, Aleda 1907- *27*
Renlie, Frank H. 1936- *11*
Rennert, Richard Scott 1956- *67*
Rennison, Louise 1951- *149*
Reno, Dawn E(laine) 1953- *130*
Rensie, Willis
  See Eisner, Will
Renton, Cam
  See Armstrong, Richard
Renvoize, Jean *5*
Resau, Laura 1973- *190*
Resciniti, Angelo G. 1952- *75*
Resnick, Michael David
  See Resnick, Mike
Resnick, Mike 1942- *159*
  Earlier sketches in SATA *38, 106*
Resnick, Seymour 1920- *23*
Retla, Robert
  See Alter, Robert Edmond
Rettig, Liz *199*
Rettstatt, Chris
  See Ashland, Monk
Reuter, Bjarne (B.) 1950- *142*
  Earlier sketch in SATA *68*
Reuter, Carol (Joan) 1931- *2*
Revena
  See Wright, Betty Ren
Revsbech, Vicki
  See Liestman, Vicki
Rex, Adam *186*
Rex, Michael *191*
Rey, H. A. 1898-1977 .... *100*
  Earlier sketches in SATA *1, 26, 69*
  See also CLR *93*
Rey, Hans Augusto
  See Rey, H. A.
Rey, Luis V. 1955- *201*
Rey, Margret 1906-1996 .... *86*
  Obituary *93*
  Earlier sketch in SATA *26*
  See also CLR *93*
Rey, Margret Elisabeth
  See Rey, Margret
Reyher, Becky
  See Reyher, Rebecca Hourwich
Reyher, Rebecca Hourwich 1897-1987 .... *18*
  Obituary *50*
Reynold, Ann
  See Bernardo, Anilu
Reynolds, Aaron 1970- *197*
Reynolds, Adrian 1963- *192*
Reynolds, C. Buck 1957- *107*
Reynolds, Dickson
  See Reynolds, Helen Mary Greenwood Campbell
Reynolds, Helen Mary Greenwood Campbell
  1884-1969
  Obituary *26*
Reynolds, Jan 1956- *180*
Reynolds, John
  See Whitlock, Ralph
Reynolds, Madge
  See Whitlock, Ralph

Reynolds, Malvina 1900-1978 .... *44*
  Obituary *24*
Reynolds, Marilyn 1935- *121*
  See also SAAS 23
Reynolds, Marilyn M.
  See Reynolds, Marilyn
Reynolds, Marilynn 1940- *141*
  Earlier sketch in SATA 80
Reynolds, Pamela 1923- *34*
Reynolds, Peter H. 1961- *128*
Reynolds, Peter J. 1961- *179*
Reynolds, Susan *179*
Rhine, Richard
  See Silverstein, Alvin
    and Silverstein, Virginia B.
Rhoades, Diane 1952- *90*
Rhodes, Bennie (Loran) 1927- *35*
Rhodes, Donna McKee 1962- *87*
Rhodes, Frank Harold Trevor 1926- *37*
Rhue, Morton
  See Strasser, Todd
Rhyne, Nancy 1926- *66*
Rhynes, Martha E. 1939- *141*
Ribbons, Ian 1924- *37*
  Brief entry *30*
  See also SAAS 3
Ricciuti, Edward R(aphael) 1938- *10*
Rice, Alice (Caldwell) Hegan 1870-1942 ..... *63*
Rice, Bebe Faas 1932- *89*
Rice, Charles D(uane) 1910-1971
  Obituary *27*
Rice, Dale R. 1948- *42*
Rice, Dale Richard
  See Rice, Dale R.
Rice, Dick
  See Rice, R. Hugh
Rice, Earle (Wilmont), Jr. 1928- *151*
  Earlier sketch in SATA 92
Rice, Edward 1918-2001 .... *47*
  Brief entry *42*
Rice, Elizabeth 1913-1976 .... *2*
Rice, Eve 1951- *91*
  Earlier sketch in SATA 34
Rice, Eve Hart
  See Rice, Eve
Rice, Inez 1907- *13*
Rice, James 1934- *93*
  Earlier sketch in SATA 22
Rice, John F. 1958- *82*
Rice, R. Hugh 1929- *115*
Rice, Richard H.
  See Rice, R. Hugh
Rich, Anna 1956- *212*
Rich, Barbara
  See Graves, Robert
Rich, Elaine Sommers 1926- *6*
Rich, Josephine Bouchard 1912- *10*
Rich, Louise Dickinson 1903-1991 .... *54*
  Obituary *67*
Rich, Naomi *217*
Richard, Adrienne 1921- *5*
  See also SAAS 9
Richard, James Robert
  See Bowen, Robert Sydney
Richards, Chuck 1957- *170*
Richards, Frank
  See Hamilton, Charles (Harold St. John)
Richards, Hilda
  See Hamilton, Charles (Harold St. John)
Richards, Jackie 1925- *102*
Richards, Jean 1940- *135*
Richards, Justin *169*
Richards, Kay
  See Baker, Susan (Catherine)
Richards, Laura E(lizabeth Howe) 1850-1943
  See YABC 1
  See also CLR 54
Richards, Leigh
  See King, Laurie R.
Richards, Marlee
  See Brill, Marlene Targ

Richards, Norman 1932- *48*
Richards, R(onald) C(harles) W(illiam)
    1923- *59*
  Brief entry *43*
Richards, Walter Alden (Jr.) 1907-1988
  Obituary *56*
Richardson, Andrew (William) 1986- *120*
Richardson, Carol 1932- *58*
Richardson, Frank Howard 1882-1970
  Obituary *27*
Richardson, Grace Lee
  See Dickson, Naida
Richardson, Jean (Mary) *59*
Richardson, Judith Benet 1941- *77*
Richardson, Nigel 1957- *187*
Richardson, Robert S(hirley) 1902-1981 .... *8*
Richardson, Sandy 1949- *116*
Richardson, V.A. *189*
Richardson, Willis 1889-1977 .... *60*
Richelson, Geraldine 1922- *29*
Richemont, Enid 1940- *82*
Richler, Mordecai 1931-2001 .... *98*
  Brief entry *27*
  Earlier sketch in SATA 44
  See also CLR 17
Richman, Sophia 1941- *142*
Rich-McCoy, Lois
  See McCoy, Lois (Rich)
Richmond, Robin 1951- *75*
Richoux, Pat(ricia) 1927- *7*
Richter, Alice 1941- *30*
Richter, Conrad (Michael) 1890-1968 .... *3*
Richter, Hans Peter 1925-1993 .... *6*
  See also CLR 21
  See also SAAS 11
Richter, Jutta 1955- *184*
Rickard, Graham 1949- *71*
Rico, Don(ato) 1917-1985
  Obituary *43*
Riddell, Chris 1962- *219*
  Earlier sketches in SATA 114, 166
Riddell, Christopher Barry
  See Riddell, Chris
Riddell, Edwina 1955- *82*
Ridden, Brian 1934- *123*
  See Ridden, Brian John
Riddle, Tohby 1965- *151*
  Earlier sketch in SATA 74
Riddleburger, Sam *202*
Riddles, Libby 1956- *140*
Ride, Sally 1951- *219*
Ride, Sally Kristen
  See Ride, Sally
Rideout, Sandy *194*
Ridge, Antonia (Florence) (?)-1981 .... *7*
  Obituary *27*
Ridge, Martin 1923-2003 .... *43*
Ridley, Philip *171*
  Earlier sketch in SATA 88
Ridlon, Marci
  See Balterman, Marcia Ridlon
Riedman, Sarah R(egal) 1902-1995 .... *1*
Riehecky, Janet 1953- *164*
Ries, Lori *185*
Riesenberg, Felix, Jr. 1913-1962 .... *23*
Rieu, E(mile) V(ictor) 1887-1972 .... *46*
  Obituary *26*
Riffenburgh, Beau 1955- *175*
Rigg, Sharon
  See Creech, Sharon
Riggenbach, Holly
  See Black, Holly
Riggio, Anita 1952- *148*
  Earlier sketch in SATA 73
Riggs, Shannon *190*
Riggs, Sidney Noyes 1892-1975
  Obituary *28*
Riggs, Stephanie 1964- *138*
Riglietti, Serena 1969- *189*
Rigney, James Oliver, Jr.
  See Jordan, Robert

Rikhoff, Jean 1928- *9*
Rikki
  See Ducornet, Erica
Riley, James A. 1939- *97*
Riley, James Whitcomb 1849-1916 .... *17*
Riley, Jocelyn 1949- *60*
  Brief entry *50*
Riley, Jocelyn Carol
  See Riley, Jocelyn
Riley, Linda Capus 1950- *85*
Riley, Martin 1948- *81*
Rimbauer, Steven
  See Pearson, Ridley
Rimes, (Margaret) LeAnn 1982- *154*
Rinaldi, Ann 1934- *202*
  Brief entry *50*
  Earlier sketches in SATA 51, 78, 117, 161
  See also CLR 46
Rinard, Judith E(llen) 1947- *140*
  Earlier sketch in SATA 44
Rinck, Maranke 1976- *214*
Rinder, Lenore 1949- *92*
Ring, Elizabeth 1920- *79*
Ringdahl, Mark
  See Longyear, Barry B(rookes)
Ringgold, Faith 1930- *187*
  Earlier sketches in SATA 71, 114
  See also CLR 30
Ringi, Kjell (Arne Soerensen) 1939- *12*
Rinkoff, Barbara Jean (Rich) 1923-1975 .... *4*
  Obituary *27*
Rinn, Miriam 1946- *127*
Riordan, James 1936- *95*
Riordan, Rick *208*
  Earlier sketch in SATA 174
Rios, Tere
  See Versace, Marie Teresa Rios
Ripken, Cal, Jr. 1960- *215*
  Earlier sketch in SATA 114
Ripken, Calvin Edward, Jr.
  See Ripken, Cal, Jr.
Ripley, Catherine 1957- *82*
Ripley, Elizabeth Blake 1906-1969 .... *5*
Ripper, Charles L(ewis) 1929- *3*
Ripper, Chuck
  See Ripper, Charles L(ewis)
Rippin, Sally *220*
Riq
  See Atwater, Richard (Tupper)
Rish, David 1955- *110*
Riskind, Mary 1944- *60*
Rissinger, Matt 1956- *93*
Rissman, Art
  See Sussman, Susan
Rissman, Susan
  See Sussman, Susan
Ritchie, Barbara Gibbons *14*
Ritchie, Scot 1954- *217*
Ritter, Felix
  See Kruss, James
Ritter, John H. 1951- *215*
  Earlier sketches in SATA 129, 137
Ritter, Lawrence S(tanley) 1922-2004 .... *58*
  Obituary *152*
Ritthaler, Shelly 1955- *91*
Ritts, Paul 1920(?)-1980
  Obituary *25*
Ritz, Karen 1957- *202*
  Earlier sketch in SATA 80
Rivera, Geraldo (Miguel) 1943- *54*
  Brief entry *28*
Rivers, Elfrida
  See Bradley, Marion Zimmer
Rivers, Karen 1970- *131*
Riverside, John
  See Heinlein, Robert A.
Rivkin, Ann 1920- *41*
Rivoli, Mario 1943- *10*
Roach, Marilynne K. 1946- *9*
Roach, Marilynne Kathleen
  See Roach, Marilynne K.

Roach, Portia
See Takakjian, Portia
Robb, Don 1937- 194
Robb, Laura 1937- 95
Robberecht, Thierry 1960- 182
Robbins, Frank 1917-1994(?) 42
Brief entry 32
Robbins, Jacqui 221
Robbins, Ken 1945- 219
Brief entry 53
Earlier sketches in SATA 94, 147
Robbins, Raleigh
See Hamilton, Charles (Harold St. John)
Robbins, Ruth 1917(?)- 14
Robbins, Tony
See Pashko, Stanley
Robbins, Wayne
See Cox, William R(obert)
Robel, S. L.
See Fraustino, Lisa Rowe
Roberson, Jennifer 1953- 72
Roberson, John R(oyster) 1930- 53
Robert, Adrian
See St. John, Nicole
Roberts, Bethany 202
Earlier sketch in SATA 133
Roberts, Bruce (Stuart) 1930- 47
Brief entry 39
Roberts, Charles G(eorge) D(ouglas)
1860-1943 88
Brief entry 29
See also CLR 33
Roberts, David
See Cox, John Roberts
Roberts, David 1970- 191
Roberts, Diane 1937- 184
Roberts, Elizabeth 1944- 80
Roberts, Elizabeth Madox 1886-1941 33
Brief entry 27
See also CLR 100
Roberts, Jim
See Bates, Barbara S(nedeker)
Roberts, Jody 218
Roberts, John G(aither) 1913-1993 27
Roberts, Judy I. 1957- 93
Roberts, Katherine 1962- 152
Roberts, M. L.
See Mattern, Joanne
Roberts, Marion 1966- 212
Roberts, Nancy Correll 1924- 52
Brief entry 28
Roberts, Priscilla 1955- 184
Roberts, Terence
See Sanderson, Ivan T(erence)
Roberts, Willo Davis 1928-2004 150
Autobiography Feature 150
Obituary 160
Earlier sketches in SATA 21, 70, 133
See also CLR 95
See also SAAS 8
Robertson, Barbara (Anne) 1931- 12
Robertson, Don 1929-1999 8
Obituary 113
Robertson, Dorothy Lewis 1912- 12
Robertson, Ellis
See Ellison, Harlan
and Silverberg, Robert
Robertson, James I., Jr. 1930- 182
Robertson, James Irvin
See Robertson, James I., Jr.
Robertson, Janet (E.) 1935- 68
Robertson, Jennifer Sinclair 1942-1998 12
Robertson, Jenny
See Robertson, Jennifer Sinclair
Robertson, Keith (Carlton) 1914-1991 85
Obituary 69
Earlier sketch in SATA 1
See also SAAS 15
Robertson, Mark
See Robertson, M.P.
Robertson, M.P. 1965- 197

Robertson, Stephen
See Walker, Robert W.
Robertus, Polly M. 1948- 212
Earlier sketch in SATA 73
Robeson, Kenneth
See Dent, Lester
and Goulart, Ron
Robeson, Kenneth
See Johnson, (Walter) Ryerson
Robinet, Harriette Gillem 1931- 104
Earlier sketch in SATA 27
See also CLR 64
Robins, Deri 1958- 166
Earlier sketch in SATA 117
Robins, Patricia
See Clark, Patricia Denise
Robins, Rollo, Jr.
See Ellis, Edward S.
Robins, Seelin
See Ellis, Edward S.
Robinson, Adjai 1932- 8
Robinson, Aminah Brenda Lynn 1940- 159
Earlier sketch in SATA 77
Robinson, Barbara (Webb) 1927- 84
Earlier sketch in SATA 8
Robinson, C(harles) A(lexander), Jr.
1900-1965 36
Robinson, Charles 1870-1937 17
Robinson, Charles 1931- 6
Robinson, Dorothy W. 1929- 54
Robinson, Elizabeth Keeler 1959- 204
Robinson, Eve
See Tanselle, Eve
Robinson, Glen 1953- 92
Robinson, Glendal P.
See Robinson, Glen
Robinson, Jan M. 1933- 6
Robinson, Jean O. 1934- 7
Robinson, Joan (Mary) G(ale Thomas)
1910-1988 7
Robinson, Kim Stanley 1952- 109
Robinson, Lee 1948- 110
Robinson, Lloyd
See Silverberg, Robert
Robinson, Lynda S(uzanne) 1951- 107
Robinson, Marileta 1942- 32
Robinson, Maudie Millian Oller 1914- 11
Robinson, Maurice R(ichard) 1895-1982
Obituary 29
Robinson, Nancy K(onheim) 1942-1994 91
Brief entry 31
Obituary 79
Earlier sketch in SATA 32
Robinson, Ray 1920- 23
Robinson, Raymond Kenneth
See Robinson, Ray
Robinson, Shari
See McGuire, Leslie (Sarah)
Robinson, Sharon 1950- 197
Earlier sketch in SATA 162
Robinson, Spider 1948- 118
Robinson, Sue
See Robinson, Susan Maria
Robinson, Susan Maria 1955- 105
Robinson, Susan Patricia
See Gates, Susan
Robinson, Suzanne
See Robinson, Lynda S(uzanne)
Robinson, T(homas) H(eath) 1869-1950 17
Robinson, Tim 1963- 205
Robinson, (Wanda) Veronica 1926- 30
Robinson, W(illiam) Heath 1872-1944 17
Robison, Bonnie 1924- 12
Robison, Nancy L(ouise) 1934- 32
Robles, Harold E. 1948- 87
Robottom, John 1934- 7
Robson, Eric 1939- 82
Roca, Francois 1971- 200
Rocco, John 1967- 188

Roche, A. K.
See Abisch, Roslyn Kroop
and Kaplan, Boche
Roche, Denis 1967- 196
Earlier sketch in SATA 99
Roche, Denis Mary
See Roche, Denis
Roche, Luane 1937- 170
Roche, P(atricia) K. 1935- 57
Brief entry 34
Roche, Terry
See Poole, Peggy
Rochman, Hazel 1938- 105
Rock, Lois
See Joslin, Mary
Rock, Maxine 1940- 108
Rocker, Fermin 1907- 40
Rocklin, Joanne 1946- 134
Earlier sketch in SATA 86
Rockwell, Anne F. 1934- 194
Earlier sketches in SATA 33, 71, 114, 162
See also SAAS 19
Rockwell, Anne Foote
See Rockwell, Anne F.
Rockwell, Bart
See Pellowski, Michael (Joseph)
Rockwell, Harlow 1910-1988 33
Obituary 56
Rockwell, Lizzy 1961- 185
Rockwell, Norman (Percevel) 1894-1978 23
Rockwell, Thomas 1933- 70
Earlier sketch in SATA 7
See also CLR 6
Rockwood, Joyce 1947- 39
Rockwood, Roy
See McFarlane, Leslie
and Stratemeyer, Edward L.
Rodanas, Kristina 1952- 155
Rodari, Gianni 1920-1980
See CLR 24
Rodd, Kathleen Tennant
See Rodd, Kylie Tennant
Rodd, Kylie Tennant 1912-1988 57
Obituary 55
Earlier sketch in SATA 6
Rodda, Emily 1948- 146
Earlier sketch in SATA 97
See also CLR 32
Roddenberry, Eugene Wesley 1921-1991 45
Obituary 69
Roddenberry, Gene
See Roddenberry, Eugene Wesley
Roddick, Ellen 1936- 5
Roddie, Shen 153
Roddy, Lee 1921- 57
Rodenas, Paula 73
Rodgers, Frank 1944- 69
Rodgers, Mary 1931- 130
Earlier sketch in SATA 8
See also CLR 20
Rodman, Emerson
See Ellis, Edward S.
Rodman, Eric
See Silverberg, Robert
Rodman, Maia
See Wojciechowska, Maia (Teresa)
Rodman, Mary Ann 185
Rodman, (Cary) Selden 1909-2002 9
Rodowsky, Colby 1932- 164
Earlier sketches in SATA 21, 77, 120
See also SAAS 22
Rodowsky, Colby F.
See Rodowsky, Colby
Rodriguez, Alejo 1941- 83
Rodriguez, Alex 1975- 189
Rodriguez, Christina 1981- 177
Rodriguez, Edel 1971- 196
Rodriguez, Luis J. 1954- 125
Rodriguez, Rachel 180
Rodriguez, Rachel Victoria
See Rodriguez, Rachel

Roeder, Virginia Marsh 1926- *98*
Roehrig, Catharine H. 1949- *67*
Roennfeldt, Robert 1953- *78*
Roessel-Waugh, C. C.
    See Waugh, Carol-Lynn Rossel
    and Waugh, Charles G(ordon)
Roets, Lois F. 1937- *91*
Roever, J(oan) M(arilyn) 1935- *26*
Rofes, Eric 1954-2006 .... *52*
Rofes, Eric Edward 1954-2006
    See Rofes, Eric
Roffey, Maureen 1936- *33*
Rogak, Lisa 1962- *80*
Rogak, Lisa Angowski
    See Rogak, Lisa
Rogan, S. Jones *199*
Rogan, Sally Jones
    See Rogan, S. Jones
Rogasky, Barbara 1933- *144*
    Earlier sketch in SATA *86*
Rogers, (Thomas) Alan (Stinchcombe)
    1937- *81*
    Earlier sketch in SATA *2*
Rogers, Bettye 1858-1919 .... *103*
Rogers, Cindy 1950- *89*
Rogers, Emma 1951- *74*
Rogers, Frances 1888-1974 .... *10*
Rogers, Fred McFeely 1928-2003 .... *33*
    Obituary *138*
Rogers, Gregory 1957- *211*
Rogers, Hal
    See Sirimarco, Elizabeth
Rogers, Jacqueline 1958- *213*
Rogers, Jean 1919- *55*
    Brief entry *47*
Rogers, Matilda 1894-1976 .... *5*
    Obituary *34*
Rogers, Pamela 1927- *9*
Rogers, Paul 1950- *98*
    Earlier sketch in SATA *54*
Rogers, Robert
    See Hamilton, Charles (Harold St. John)
Rogers, Sherry *193*
Rogers, W(illiam) G(arland) 1896-1978 .... *23*
Rohan, M. S.
    See Rohan, Michael Scott
Rohan, Michael Scott 1951- *98*
Rohan, Mike Scott
    See Rohan, Michael Scott
Rohmann, Eric 1957- *171*
    See also CLR *100*
Rohmer, Harriet 1938- *56*
Rohrer, Doug 1962- *89*
Rojan
    See Rojankovsky, Feodor (Stepanovich)
Rojankovsky, Feodor (Stepanovich)
    1891-1970 .... *21*
Rojany, Lisa *94*
Rokeby-Thomas, Anna E(lma) 1911- *15*
Roland, Albert 1925-2002 .... *11*
Roland, Mary
    See Lewis, Mary
Roleff, Tamara L. 1959- *143*
Rolerson, Darrell A(llen) 1946- *8*
Roll, Winifred 1909-1998 .... *6*
Rollins, Charlemae Hill 1897-1979 .... *3*
    Obituary *26*
Rollins, James 1961- *216*
Rollock, Barbara T(herese) 1924- *64*
Rolston, Steve 1978- *209*
Romack, Janice Reed
    See LeNoir, Janice
Romain, Trevor *134*
Romanenko, Vitaliy 1962- *101*
Romano, Christy
    See Romano, Christy Carlson
Romano, Christy Carlson 1984- *210*
Romano, Clare 1922- *111*
    Earlier sketch in SATA *48*
Romano, Louis G. 1921- *35*
Romano, Melora A. 1966- *118*

Romano, Ray 1957- *170*
Romano, Raymond
    See Romano, Ray
Romijn, Johanna Maria Kooyker
    See Kooyker-Romijn, Johanna Maria
Romyn, Johanna Maria Kooyker
    See Kooyker-Romijn, Johanna Maria
Rong, Yu 1970- *174*
Rongen, Bjoern 1906- *10*
Rongen, Bjorn
    See Rongen, Bjoern
Ronson, Mark
    See Alexander, Marc
Rood, Ronald (N.) 1920- *12*
Rook, Sebastian
    See Jeapes, Ben
Rooke, Daphne 1914-2009 .... *12*
Rooke, Daphne Marie
    See Rooke, Daphne
Rooney, Ronnie 1970- *212*
Roop, Connie 1951- *167*
    Brief entry *49*
    Earlier sketches in SATA *54, 116*
Roop, Constance Betzer
    See Roop, Connie
Roop, Peter 1951- *167*
    Brief entry *49*
    Earlier sketches in SATA *54, 116*
Roop, Peter G.
    See Roop, Peter
Roop, Peter Geiger
    See Roop, Peter
Roos, Stephen 1945- *128*
    Brief entry *41*
    Earlier sketches in SATA *47, 77*
Roosa, Karen 1961- *218*
Roose-Evans, James 1927- *65*
Roosevelt, Eleanor 1884-1962 .... *50*
Root, Barry *182*
Root, Betty *84*
Root, Kimberly Bulcken *192*
Root, Phyllis 1949- *184*
    Brief entry *48*
    Earlier sketches in SATA *55, 94, 145*
Root, Shelton L., Jr. 1923-1986
    Obituary *51*
Roper, Laura (Newbold) Wood 1911-2003 .. *34*
    Obituary *150*
Roper, Robert 1946- *142*
    Earlier sketch in SATA *78*
Roraback, Robin (Ellan) 1964- *111*
Rorby, Ginny 1944- *94*
Rorer, Abigail 1949- *85*
Rosaler, Maxine *208*
Rosamel, Godeleine de 1968- *151*
Roscoe, D(onald) T(homas) 1934- *42*
Rose, Anne *8*
Rose, Deborah Lee 1955- *185*
    Earlier sketches in SATA *71, 124*
Rose, Elizabeth (Jane Pretty) 1933- *68*
    Brief entry *28*
Rose, Florella
    See Carlson, Vada F.
Rose, Gerald (Hembdon Seymour) 1935- *68*
    Brief entry *30*
Rose, Malcolm 1953- *168*
    Earlier sketch in SATA *107*
Rose, Nancy A.
    See Sweetland, Nancy A(nn)
Rose, Ted 1940- *93*
Rose, Wendy 1948- *12*
Rosen, Elizabeth 1961- *205*
Rosen, Lillian (Diamond) 1928- *63*
Rosen, Marvin 1933- *161*
Rosen, Michael 1946- *181*
    Brief entry *40*
    Earlier sketches in SATA *48, 84, 137*
    See also CLR *45*
Rosen, Michael J. 1954- *199*
    Earlier sketch in SATA *86*

Rosen, Michael Wayne
    See Rosen, Michael
Rosen, Sidney 1916- *1*
Rosen, Winifred 1943- *8*
Rosenbaum, Maurice 1907-1987 .... *6*
Rosenberg, Amye 1950- *74*
Rosenberg, Dorothy 1906- *40*
Rosenberg, Eth Clifford 1915- *92*
    See also SAAS *22*
Rosenberg, Jane 1949- *58*
Rosenberg, Liz 1958- *129*
    Earlier sketch in SATA *75*
Rosenberg, Maxine B(erta) 1939- *93*
    Brief entry *47*
    Earlier sketch in SATA *55*
Rosenberg, Nancy (Sherman) 1931- *4*
Rosenberg, Sharon 1942- *8*
Rosenberry, Vera 1948- *219*
    Earlier sketches in SATA *83, 144*
Rosenblatt, Arthur
    See Rosenblatt, Arthur S.
Rosenblatt, Arthur S. 1938- *68*
    Brief entry *45*
Rosenblatt, Lily 1956- *90*
Rosenbloom, Joseph 1928- *21*
Rosenblum, Richard 1928- *11*
Rosenburg, John M. 1918- *6*
Rosenfeld, Dina 1962- *99*
Rosenstiehl, Agnes 1941- *203*
Rosenthal, Amy Krouse 1965- *177*
Rosenthal, Betsy R. 1957- *178*
Rosenthal, Harold 1914-1999 .... *35*
Rosenthal, M(acha) L(ouis) 1917-1996 .... *59*
Rosenthal, Marc 1949- *193*
Rosenthal, Mark A(lan) 1946- *64*
Rosing, Norbert 1953- *196*
Rosman, Steven M 1956- *81*
Rosman, Steven Michael
    See Rosman, Steven M
Rosoff, Meg 1956- *209*
    Earlier sketch in SATA *160*
Ross, Alan
    See Warwick, Alan R(oss)
Ross, Christine 1950- *172*
    Earlier sketch in SATA *83*
Ross, Clare
    See Romano, Clare
Ross, Dana Fuller
    See Cockrell, Amanda
    and Gerson, Noel Bertram
Ross, Dave
    See Ross, David
Ross, David 1896-1975 .... *49*
    Obituary *20*
Ross, David 1949- *133*
    Earlier sketch in SATA *32*
Ross, Deborah J.
    See Wheeler, Deborah
Ross, Diana
    See Denney, Diana
Ross, Edward S(hearman) 1915- *85*
Ross, Eileen 1950- *115*
Ross, Frank (Xavier), Jr. 1914- *28*
Ross, Jane 1961- *79*
Ross, John 1921- *45*
Ross, Judy 1942- *54*
Ross, Katharine Reynolds
    See Ross, Kathy
Ross, Kathy 1948- *169*
    Earlier sketch in SATA *89*
Ross, Kent 1956- *91*
Ross, Lillian Hammer 1925- *72*
Ross, Michael Elsohn 1952- *170*
    Earlier sketches in SATA *80, 127*
Ross, Pat(ricia Kienzle) 1943- *53*
    Brief entry *48*
Ross, Ramon R(oyal) 1930- *62*
Ross, Stewart 1947- *134*
    Earlier sketch in SATA *92*
    See also SAAS *23*
Ross, Tom 1958- *84*

Ross, Tony 1938- 176
  Earlier sketches in SATA 17, 65, 130
Ross, Wilda 1915- 51
  Brief entry 39
Rossel, Seymour 1945- 28
Rossell, Judith 1953- 187
Rossel-Waugh, C. C.
  See Waugh, Carol-Lynn Rossel
Rossetti, Christina 1830-1894 20
  See also CLR 115
Rossetti, Christina Georgina
  See Rossetti, Christina
Rossi, Joyce 1943- 116
Rossotti, Hazel Swaine 1930- 95
Rostkowski, Margaret I. 1945- 59
Roth, Arnold 1929- 21
Roth, Arthur J(oseph) 1925-1993 43
  Brief entry 28
  Obituary 75
  See also SAAS 11
Roth, David 1940- 36
Roth, Julie Jersild 180
Roth, Matthue 1978(?)- 174
Roth, Roger 190
Roth, Ruby 1983(?)- 216
Roth, Stephanie 202
Roth, Susan L. 181
  Earlier sketch in SATA 134
Rothberg, Abraham 1922- 59
Roth-Hano, Renee 1931- 85
Rothkopf, Carol Z. 1929- 4
Rothman, Joel 1938- 7
Rotner, Shelley 1951- 169
  Earlier sketch in SATA 76
Rottman, S.L. 1970- 157
  Earlier sketch in SATA 106
Rottman, Susan Lynn
  See Rottman, S.L.
Roueche, Berton 1911-1994 28
Roughsey, Dick 1921(?)-1985 35
  See also CLR 41
Roughsey, Goobalathaldin
  See Roughsey, Dick
Rounds, Glen (Harold) 1906-2002 112
  Obituary 141
  Earlier sketches in SATA 8, 70
Rourke, Constance Mayfield 1885-1941
  See YABC 1
Rouss, Sylvia 211
Rovetch, Gerda 1925(?)- 202
Rovetch, L. Bob
  See Rovetch, Lissa
Rovetch, Lissa 201
Rowan, Deirdre
  See Williams, Jeanne
Rowe, Jennifer
  See Rodda, Emily
Rowe, John A. 1949- 198
  Earlier sketch in SATA 146
Rowe, Viola Carson 1903-1969
  Obituary 26
Rowh, Mark 1952- 90
Rowland, Florence Wightman 1900-1997 8
  Obituary 108
Rowland-Entwistle, (Arthur) Theodore (Henry)
  1925- 94
  Earlier sketch in SATA 31
Rowling, J.K. 1965- 174
  Earlier sketch in SATA 109
  See also CLR 112
Rowling, Joanne Kathleen
  See Rowling, J.K.
Rowsome, Frank (Howard), Jr. 1914-1983 .. 36
Roy, Gabrielle 1909-1983 104
Roy, Jacqueline 1954- 74
Roy, James 1968- 218
Roy, Jennifer
  See Roy, Jennifer Rozines
Roy, Jennifer Rozines 1967- 178
Roy, Jessie Hailstalk 1895-1986
  Obituary 51

Roy, Kari Anne 1977(?)- 221
Roy, Liam
  See Scarry, Patricia (Murphy)
Roy, Ron(ald) 1940- 110
  Brief entry 35
  Earlier sketch in SATA 40
Roybal, Laura 1956- 85
Roybal, Laura Husby
  See Roybal, Laura
Royds, Caroline 1953- 55
Royston, Angela 1945- 169
  Earlier sketch in SATA 120
Rozakis, Laurie E. 1952- 84
Rozen, Anna 1960- 206
Rubbino, Salvatore 1970- 220
Rubel, Nicole 1953- 181
  Earlier sketches in SATA 18, 95, 135
Rubin, Eva Johanna 1925- 38
Rubin, Susan Goldman 1939- 182
  Earlier sketches in SATA 84, 132
Rubin, Vicky 1964- 193
Rubinetti, Donald 1947- 92
Rubinstein, Gillian 1942- 158
  Autobiography Feature 116
  Earlier sketches in SATA 68, 105
  See also CLR 35
  See also SAAS 25
Rubinstein, Gillian Margaret
  See Rubinstein, Gillian
Rubinstein, Patricia -2003
  See Forest, Antonia
Rubinstein, Patricia Giulia Caulfield Kate
  See Forest, Antonia
Rubinstein, Robert E(dward) 1943- 49
Rublowsky, John M(artin) 1928- 62
Rubright, Lynn 1936- 171
Ruby, Laura 181
  Earlier sketch in SATA 155
Ruby, Lois 1942- 184
  Autobiography Feature 105
  Brief entry 34
  Earlier sketches in SATA 35, 95
Ruby, Lois F.
  See Ruby, Lois
Ruchlis, Hy(man) 1913-1992 3
  Obituary 72
Ruckdeschel, Liz 214
Rucker, Mike 1940- 91
Ruckman, Ivy 1931- 93
  Earlier sketch in SATA 37
Ruck-Pauquet, Gina 1931- 40
  Brief entry 37
Ruddell, Deborah 1949- 210
Ruditis, Paul 190
Rudley, Stephen 1946- 30
Rudolph, Marguerita 1908- 21
Rudomin, Esther
  See Hautzig, Esther Rudomin
Rue, Leonard Lee III 1926- 142
  Earlier sketch in SATA 37
Rueda, Claudia 183
Ruedi, Norma Paul
  See Ainsworth, Norma
Ruelle, Karen Gray 1957- 209
  Earlier sketches in SATA 84, 126
Ruemmler, John D(avid) 1948- 78
Ruepp, Krista 1947- 143
Ruffell, Ann 1941- 30
Ruffins, Reynold 1930- 125
  Earlier sketch in SATA 41
Rugg, Jim 206
Rugoff, Milton 1913- 30
Ruhen, Olaf 1911-1989 17
Rui, Paolo 1962- 217
Rukeyser, Muriel 1913-1980
  Obituary 22
Rumbaut, Hendle 1949- 84
Rumford, James 1948- 193
  Earlier sketch in SATA 116
Rumsey, Marian (Barritt) 1928- 16

Rumstuckle, Cornelius
  See Brennan, Herbie
Runholt, Susan 216
Runnerstroem, Bengt Arne 1944- 75
Runyan, John
  See Palmer, Bernard (Alvin)
Runyon, Brent 217
Runyon, Catherine 1947- 62
Ruoff, A. LaVonne Brown 1930- 76
Rupp, Rebecca 185
Rusch, Elizabeth 1966- 198
Rusch, Kris
  See Rusch, Kristine Kathryn
Rusch, Kristine Kathryn 1960- 113
Rush, Alison 1951- 41
Rush, Peter 1937- 32
Rushdie, Ahmed Salman
  See Rushdie, Salman
Rushdie, Salman 1947-
  See CLR 125
Rushford, Patricia H(elen) 1943- 134
Rushmore, Helen 1898-1994 3
Rushmore, Robert (William) 1926-1986 8
  Obituary 49
Ruskin, Ariane
  See Batterberry, Ariane Ruskin
Ruskin, John 1819-1900 24
Russ, Lavinia (Faxon) 1904-1992 74
Russell, Charlotte
  See Rathjen, Carl Henry
Russell, Ching Yeung 1946- 107
Russell, Don(ald Bert) 1899-1986
  Obituary 47
Russell, Franklin (Alexander) 1926- 11
Russell, Gertrude Barrer
  See Barrer-Russell, Gertrude
Russell, Helen Ross 1915- 8
Russell, James 1933- 53
Russell, Jim
  See Russell, James
Russell, Joan Plummer 1930- 139
Russell, Natalie 1972- 218
Russell, P(hilip) Craig 1951- 162
  Earlier sketch in SATA 80
Russell, Patrick
  See Sammis, John
Russell, Paul (Gary) 1942- 57
Russell, Sarah
  See Laski, Marghanita
Russell, Sharman Apt 1954- 123
Russell, Solveig Paulson 1904-1985 3
Russo, Marisabina 1950- 188
  Earlier sketches in SATA 106, 151
Russo, Monica J. 1950- 83
Russo, Susan 1947- 30
Russon, Penni 1974- 179
Rutgers van der Loeff, An
  See Rutgers van der Loeff-Basenau, An(na)
  Maria Margaretha
Rutgers van der Loeff-Basenau, An(na) Maria
  Margaretha 1910- 22
Ruth, Rod 1912-1987 9
Rutherford, Douglas
  See McConnell, James Douglas Rutherford
Rutherford, Meg 1932- 34
Ruthin, Margaret
  See Catherall, Arthur
Rutkoski, Marie 1977- 219
Rutledge, Jill Zimmerman 1951- 155
Rutz, Viola Larkin 1932- 12
Ruurs, Margriet 1952- 215
  Earlier sketches in SATA 97, 147
Ruzicka, Rudolph 1883-1978
  Obituary 24
Ruzzier, Sergio 1966- 210
  Earlier sketch in SATA 159
, Ryan
  See Ryan, John
Ryan, Betsy
  See Ryan, Elizabeth (Anne)
Ryan, Cheli Duran 20

Ryan, Darlene 1958- *176*
Ryan, Elizabeth (Anne) 1943- *30*
Ryan, Jeanette
　See Mines, Jeanette
Ryan, John 1921-2009 .... *22*
Ryan, Margaret 1950- *166*
　Earlier sketch in SATA *78*
Ryan, Mary E. 1953- *61*
Ryan, Mary Elizabeth
　See Ryan, Mary E.
Ryan, Pam Munoz 1951- *197*
　Earlier sketch in SATA *134*
Ryan, Patrick 1957- *138*
Ryan, Peter (Charles) 1939- *15*
Ryan-Lush, Geraldine 1949- *89*
Rybakov, Anatoli (Naumovich) 1911-1998 .. *79*
　Obituary *108*
Rybakov, Anatolii (Naumovich)
　See Rybakov, Anatoli (Naumovich)
Rybolt, Thomas R. 1954- *62*
Rybolt, Thomas Roy
　See Rybolt, Thomas R.
Rybolt, Tom
　See Rybolt, Thomas R.
Rydberg, Ernest E(mil) 1901-1993 .... *21*
Rydberg, Lou(isa Hampton) 1908- *27*
Rydell, Katy 1942- *91*
Rydell, Wendell
　See Rydell, Wendy
Rydell, Wendy *4*
Ryden, Hope *91*
　Earlier sketch in SATA *8*
Ryder, Joanne (Rose) 1946- *163*
　Brief entry *34*
　Earlier sketches in SATA *65, 122*
　See also CLR *37*
Ryder, Pamela
　See Lamb, Nancy
Rye, Anthony
　See Youd, Samuel
Rylant, Cynthia 1954- *195*
　Brief entry *44*
　Earlier sketches in SATA *50, 76, 112, 160*
　See also CLR *86*
　See also SAAS *13*
Rymer, Alta May 1925- *34*
Rymond, Lynda Gene *199*

S

S. L. C.
　See Twain, Mark
S., Svend Otto
　See Soerensen, Svend Otto
Saaf, Donald W(illiam) 1961- *124*
Saal, Jocelyn
　See Sachs, Judith
Sabbeth, Carol (Landstrom) 1957- *125*
Saberhagen, Fred 1930-2007 .... *89*
　Obituary *184*
　Earlier sketch in SATA *37*
Saberhagen, Fred T.
　See Saberhagen, Fred
Saberhagen, Fred Thomas
　See Saberhagen, Fred
Saberhagen, Frederick Thomas
　See Saberhagen, Fred
Sabin, Edwin L(egrand) 1870-1952
　See YABC *2*
Sabin, Francene *27*
Sabin, Lou
　See Sabin, Louis
Sabin, Louis 1930- *27*
Sabre, Dirk
　See Laffin, John (Alfred Charles)
Sabuda, Robert (James) 1965- *120*
　Earlier sketch in SATA *81*
Sabuda, Robert 1965- *170*

Sabuda, Robert James
　See Sabuda, Robert
Sachar, Louis 1954- *154*
　Brief entry *50*
　Earlier sketches in SATA *63, 104*
　See also CLR *79*
Sachs, Elizabeth-Ann 1946- *48*
Sachs, Judith 1947- *52*
　Brief entry *51*
Sachs, Marilyn 1927- *164*
　Autobiography Feature *110*
　Earlier sketches in SATA *3, 68*
　See also CLR *2*
　See also SAAS *2*
Sachs, Marilyn Stickle
　See Sachs, Marilyn
Sackett, S(amuel) J(ohn) 1928- *12*
Sackson, Sid 1920- *16*
Sacre, Antonio 1968- *152*
Saddler, Allen
　See Richards, R(onald) C(harles) W(illiam)
Saddler, K. Allen
　See Richards, R(onald) C(harles) W(illiam)
Sadie, Stanley 1930-2005 .... *14*
Sadie, Stanley John
　See Sadie, Stanley
Sadiq, Nazneen
　See Sheikh, Nazneen
Sadler, Catherine Edwards 1952- *60*
　Brief entry *45*
Sadler, Marilyn (June) 1950- *79*
Sadler, Mark
　See Lynds, Dennis
Saffer, Barbara *144*
Sagan, Carl 1934-1996 .... *58*
　Obituary *94*
Sagan, Carl Edward
　See Sagan, Carl
Sage, Angie 1952- *197*
Sage, Juniper
　See Brown, Margaret Wise
　and Hurd, Edith Thacher
Sagsoorian, Paul 1923- *12*
Said, S.F. 1967- *174*
Saidman, Anne 1952- *75*
Saint, Dora Jessie 1913- *10*
St. Anthony, Jane *175*
St. Antoine, Sara L. 1966- *84*
St. Clair, Byrd Hooper 1905-1976
　Obituary *28*
St. Crow, Lili
　See Saintcrow, Lilith
Saintcrow, Lilith 1976- *221*
Saint-Exupery, Antoine de 1900-1944 .... *20*
　See also CLR *142*
Saint-Exupery, Antoine Jean Baptiste Marie
　Roger de
　See Saint-Exupery, Antoine de
St. George, Judith 1931- *161*
　Earlier sketches in SATA *13, 99*
　See also CLR *57*
　See also SAAS *12*
St. George, Judith Alexander
　See St. George, Judith
St. James, Blakely
　See Gottfried, Theodore Mark
　and Platt, Charles
St. James, Blakely
　See Griffin, W. E. B.
St. James, Sierra
　See Rallison, Janette
Saint James, Synthia 1949- *152*
　Earlier sketch in SATA *84*
St. John, Lauren 1966- *214*
St. John, Nicole *143*
　Autobiography Feature *143*
　Earlier sketches in SATA *29, 89*
　See also CLR *46*
　See also SAAS *7*
St. John, Patricia Mary 1919-1993
　Obituary *79*

St. John, Philip
　See del Rey, Lester
St. John, Wylly Folk 1908-1985 .... *10*
　Obituary *45*
St. Max, E. S.
　See Ellis, Edward S.
St. Meyer, Ned
　See Stratemeyer, Edward L.
St. Mox, E. A.
　See Ellis, Edward S.
St. Myer, Ned
　See Stratemeyer, Edward L.
St. Tamara
　See Kolba, St. Tamara
Saito, Michiko
　See Fujiwara, Michiko
Sakai, Komako 1966- *213*
Sakaki, Ichiro 1969- *192*
Sakamoto, Miki *198*
Sakers, Don 1958- *72*
Sakharnov, S.
　See Sakharnov, Svyatoslav
Sakharnov, Svyatoslav 1923- *65*
Sakharnov, Svyatoslav Vladimirovich
　See Sakharnov, Svyatoslav
Saksena, Kate *148*
Sakurai, Gail 1952- *153*
　Earlier sketch in SATA *87*
Salamanca, Lucy
　See del Barco, Lucy Salamanca
Salas, Laura Purdie 1966- *216*
Salassi, Otto R(ussell) 1939-1993 .... *38*
　Obituary *77*
Salat, Cristina *82*
Saldana, Rene, Jr. *186*
Saldutti, Denise 1953- *39*
Sale, Tim 1956- *153*
Salem, Kay 1952- *92*
Salerno, Steven *176*
Salinger, J.D. 1919-2010 .... *67*
　See also CLR *18*
Salinger, Jerome David
　See Salinger, J.D.
Salisbury, Graham 1944- *195*
　Earlier sketches in SATA *76, 108, 161*
Salisbury, Joyce E(llen) 1944- *138*
Salkey, (Felix) Andrew (Alexander)
　1928-1995 .... *118*
　Earlier sketch in SATA *35*
Salley, Coleen *166*
Sallis, Susan (Diana) 1929- *55*
Salmieri, Daniel 1983- *208*
Salmon, Annie Elizabeth 1899- *13*
Salmon, Dena K. 1959(?)- *219*
Salonen, Roxane Beauclair 1968- *184*
Salsi, Lynn 1947- *130*
Salsitz, R. A. V.
　See Salsitz, Rhondi Vilott
Salsitz, Rhondi Vilott *115*
Salten, Felix
　See Salzmann, Siegmund
Salter, Cedric
　See Knight, Francis Edgar
Salter, Sydney *220*
Saltman, Judith 1947- *64*
Saltzberg, Barney 1955- *194*
　Earlier sketch in SATA *135*
Saltzman, David (Charles Laertes)
　1967-1990 .... *86*
Salvadori, Mario (George) 1907-1997 .... *97*
　Earlier sketch in SATA *40*
Salwood, F.K.
　See Kilworth, Garry
Salzer, L. E.
　See Wilson, Lionel
Salzman, Marian 1959- *77*
Salzmann, Siegmund 1869-1945 .... *25*
Samachson, Dorothy (Mirkin) 1914-1997 ...... *3*
Samachson, Joseph 1906-1980 .... *3*
　Obituary *52*
Sammis, John 1942- *4*

Sampson, Emma (Keats) Speed 1868-1947 . *68*
Sampson, Fay (Elizabeth) 1935- *151*
  Brief entry *40*
  Earlier sketch in SATA *42*
Sampson, Michael 1952- *143*
  Earlier sketch in SATA *95*
Samson, Anne S(tringer) 1933- *2*
Samson, Joan 1937-1976 .... *13*
Samson, Suzanne M. 1959- *91*
Samuels, Barbara *199*
Samuels, Charles 1902-1982 .... *12*
Samuels, Cynthia K(alish) 1946- *79*
Samuels, Gertrude 1910(?)-2003 .... *17*
  Obituary *147*
Sanborn, Duane 1914-1996 .... *38*
Sancha, Sheila 1924- *38*
Sanchez, Alex 1957- *151*
Sanchez, Anita 1956- *209*
Sanchez, Sonia 1934- *136*
  Earlier sketch in SATA *22*
  See also CLR *18*
Sanchez-Silva, Jose Maria 1911- *132*
  Earlier sketch in SATA *16*
  See also CLR *12*
Sand, George X. *45*
Sandak, Cass R(obert) 1950-2001 .... *51*
  Brief entry *37*
Sandberg, (Karin) Inger 1930- *15*
Sandberg, Karl C. 1931- *35*
Sandberg, Lasse (E. M.) 1924- *15*
Sandburg, Carl 1878-1967 .... *8*
  See also CLR *67*
Sandburg, Carl August
  See Sandburg, Carl
Sandburg, Charles
  See Sandburg, Carl
Sandburg, Charles A.
  See Sandburg, Carl
Sandburg, Helga 1918- *3*
  See also SAAS *10*
Sandell, Lisa Ann 1977- *175*
Sandemose, Iben 1950- *211*
Sander, Heather L. 1947- *157*
Sanderlin, George 1915- *4*
Sanderlin, Owenita (Harrah) 1916- *11*
Sanders, Betty Jane
  See Monthei, Betty
Sanders, Nancy I. 1960- *141*
  Earlier sketch in SATA *90*
Sanders, Scott Russell 1945- *109*
  Earlier sketch in SATA *56*
Sanders, Winston P.
  See Anderson, Poul
Sanderson, Irma 1912- *66*
Sanderson, Ivan T(erence) 1911-1973 .... *6*
Sanderson, Margaret Love
  See Keats, Emma
  and Sampson, Emma (Keats) Speed
Sanderson, Ruth 1951- *172*
  Earlier sketches in SATA *41, 109*
Sanderson, Ruth L.
  See Sanderson, Ruth
Sanders-Wells, Linda *220*
Sand-Eveland, Cyndi *211*
Sandin, Joan 1942- *197*
  Earlier sketches in SATA *12, 94, 153*
Sandison, Janet
  See Cameron, Elizabeth Jane
Sandler, Martin W. *216*
  Earlier sketch in SATA *160*
Sandom, J. Gregory
  See Welsh, T.K.
Sandom, J.G.
  See Welsh, T.K.
Sandoz, Mari(e Susette) 1900-1966 .... *5*
Sanford, Agnes (White) 1897-1976 .... *61*
Sanford, Doris 1937- *69*
Sanford, Rose
  See Simmonds, Posy
Sanger, Amy Wilson 1967- *205*
Sanger, Marjorie Bartlett 1920- *8*

San Jose, Christine 1929- *167*
Sankey, Alice (Ann-Susan) 1910- *27*
San Souci, Daniel *192*
  Earlier sketch in SATA *96*
San Souci, Robert D. 1946- *220*
  Earlier sketches in SATA *40, 81, 117, 158*
  See also CLR *43*
Santamaria, Benjamin 1955- *184*
Santat, Dan *188*
Santesson, Hans Stefan 1914(?)-1975
  Obituary *30*
Santiago, Esmeralda 1948- *129*
Santopolo, Jill *214*
Santore, Charles 1935- *200*
Santoro, C.
  See Santoro, Christopher
Santoro, Christopher *218*
Santos, Helen
  See Griffiths, Helen
Santrey, Louis
  See Sabin, Louis
Santucci, Barbara 1948- *130*
Sapergia, Barbara 1943- *181*
Sapet, Kerrily 1972- *214*
Sapieyevski, Anne Lindbergh 1940-1993 ..... *81*
  Brief entry *32*
  Earlier sketches in SATA *35, 78*
Saport, Linda 1954- *123*
Sapp, Allen 1929- *151*
Sarac, Roger
  See Caras, Roger A(ndrew)
Sarah, Duchess of York
  See Ferguson, Sarah
Sarasin, Jennifer
  See Sachs, Judith
Sarcone-Roach, Julia *215*
Sardinha, Rick *192*
Sarg, Anthony Frederick
  See Sarg, Tony
Sarg, Tony 1882-1942
  See YABC *1*
Sargent, Pamela 1948- *78*
  Earlier sketch in SATA *29*
Sargent, Robert 1933- *2*
Sargent, Sarah 1937- *44*
  Brief entry *41*
Sargent, Shirley 1927-2004 .... *11*
Sarnoff, Jane 1937- *10*
Saroff, Phyllis V. *202*
Saroyan, William 1908-1981 .... *23*
  Obituary *24*
Sarton, Eleanor May
  See Sarton, May
Sarton, May 1912-1995 .... *36*
  Obituary *86*
Sasaki, Chris *182*
Sasaki, Ellen Joy *206*
Saseen, Sharon (Dillon) 1949- *59*
Sasek, Miroslav 1916-1980 .... *16*
  Obituary *23*
  See also CLR *4*
Sasso, Sandy Eisenberg 1947- *162*
  Earlier sketches in SATA *86, 116*
Sathre, Vivian 1952- *133*
  Earlier sketch in SATA *79*
Satterfield, Charles
  See del Rey, Lester
  and Pohl, Frederik
Sattgast, L. J.
  See Sattgast, Linda J.
Sattgast, Linda J. 1953- *91*
Sattler, Helen Roney 1921-1992 .... *74*
  Earlier sketch in SATA *4*
  See also CLR *24*
Sattler, Jennifer
  See Sattler, Jennifer Gordon
Sattler, Jennifer Gordon *218*
Sauer, Julia Lina 1891-1983 .... *32*
  Obituary *36*
Sauerwein, Leigh 1944- *155*

Saul, Carol P. 1947- *117*
  Earlier sketch in SATA *78*
Saul, John III
  See Saul, John
Saul, John 1942- *98*
Saul, John W.
  See Saul, John
Saul, John W. III
  See Saul, John
Saul, John Woodruff III
  See Saul, John
Saul, (Ellen) Wendy 1946- *42*
Saulnier, Karen Luczak 1940- *80*
Saunders, Caleb
  See Heinlein, Robert A.
Saunders, Dave 1939- *85*
Saunders, Julie 1939- *85*
Saunders, (William) Keith 1910-1994 .... *12*
Saunders, Rubie (Agnes) 1929- *21*
Saunders, Steven
  See Jones, Allan Frewin
Saunders, Susan 1945- *96*
  Brief entry *41*
  Earlier sketch in SATA *46*
Saunders-Smith, Gail 1952- *169*
Sauvain, Philip Arthur 1933- *111*
Savadier, Elivia 1950- *164*
  Earlier sketch in SATA *79*
Savage, Alan
  See Nicole, Christopher (Robin)
Savage, Blake
  See Goodwin, Harold L(eland)
Savage, Candace 1949- *142*
Savage, Deborah 1955- *76*
Savage, Jeff 1961- *97*
Savage, Katharine James 1905-1989
  Obituary *61*
Savage, Stephen 1965- *194*
Savage, Thomas 1915-2003
  Obituary *147*
Savageau, Cheryl 1950- *96*
Savery, Constance (Winifred) 1897-1999 .... *1*
Saville, Andrew
  See Taylor, Andrew
Saville, (Leonard) Malcolm 1901-1982 .... *23*
  Obituary *31*
Saviozzi, Adriana
  See Mazza, Adriana
Savitt, Sam 1917-2000 .... *8*
  Obituary *126*
Savitz, Harriet May 1933-2008 .... *72*
  Earlier sketch in SATA *5*
  See also SAAS *26*
Sawicki, Mary 1950- *90*
Sawyer, (Frederick) Don(ald) 1947- *72*
Sawyer, Kem Knapp 1953- *84*
Sawyer, Robert J. 1960- *149*
  Earlier sketch in SATA *81*
Sawyer, Robert James
  See Sawyer, Robert J.
Sawyer, Ruth 1880-1970 .... *17*
  See also CLR *36*
Saxby, H.M.
  See Saxby, (Henry) Maurice
Saxby, (Henry) Maurice 1924- *71*
Saxon, Andrew
  See Arthur, Robert, (Jr.)
Saxon, Antonia
  See Sachs, Judith
Say, Allen 1937- *161*
  Earlier sketches in SATA *28, 69, 110*
  See also CLR *135*
Sayers, Frances Clarke 1897-1989 .... *3*
  Obituary *62*
Sayles, Elizabeth 1956- *220*
  Earlier sketches in SATA *108, 163*
Saylor-Marchant, Linda 1963- *82*
Sayre, April Pulley 1966- *191*
  Earlier sketches in SATA *88, 131*
Sazer, Nina 1949- *13*
Scabrini, Janet 1953- *13*

Scagell, Robin 1946- *107*
Scagnetti, Jack 1924- 7
Scaletta, Kurtis 1968- *215*
Scamander, Newt
  See Rowling, J.K.
Scamell, Ragnhild 1940- *180*
  Earlier sketch in SATA 77
Scanlon, Marion Stephany *11*
Scannel, John Vernon
  See Scannell, Vernon
Scannell, Vernon 1922-2007 59
  Obituary *188*
Scarborough, Elizabeth
  See Scarborough, Elizabeth Ann
Scarborough, Elizabeth Ann 1947- *171*
  Earlier sketch in SATA 98
Scarf, Maggi
  See Scarf, Maggie
Scarf, Maggie 1932- 5
Scariano, Margaret M. 1924- 86
Scarlett, Susan
  See Streatfeild, Noel
Scarry, Huck
  See Scarry, Richard McClure, Jr.
Scarry, Patricia (Murphy) 1924- 2
Scarry, Patsy
  See Scarry, Patricia (Murphy)
Scarry, Richard (McClure) 1919-1994 75
  Obituary 90
  Earlier sketches in SATA 2, 35
  See also CLR 41
Scarry, Richard McClure, Jr. 1953- 35
Schachner, Judith Byron 1951- *178*
  Earlier sketch in SATA 88
Schachner, Judy
  See Schachner, Judith Byron
Schachtel, Roger 1949- 38
Schachtel, Roger Bernard
  See Schachtel, Roger
Schade, Susan *189*
Schaedler, Sally *116*
Schaefer, Carole Lexa *173*
Schaefer, Jack (Warner) 1907-1991 66
  Obituary 65
  Earlier sketch in SATA 3
Schaefer, Lola M. 1950- *183*
  Earlier sketches in SATA 91, 144
Schaeffer, Mead 1898- 21
Schaeffer, Susan Fromberg 1941- 22
Schaer, Brigitte 1958- *112*
Schaller, George
  See Schaller, George B.
Schaller, George B. 1933- 30
Schaller, George Beals
  See Schaller, George B.
Schanzer, Rosalyn (Good) 1942- *138*
  Earlier sketch in SATA 77
Schatell, Brian 66
  Brief entry 47
Schechter, Betty (Goodstein) 1921- 5
Schechter, Simone
  See Elkeles, Simone
Schecter, Ellen 1944- 85
Scheeder, Louis 1946- *141*
Scheer, Julian (Weisel) 1926-2001 8
Scheffer, Victor B(lanchard) 1906- 6
Scheffler, Axel 1957- *180*
Scheffler, Ursel 1938- 81
Scheffrin-Falk, Gladys 1928- 76
Scheidl, Gerda Marie 1913- 85
Scheier, Michael 1943- 40
  Brief entry 36
Schell, Mildred 1922- 41
Schell, Orville (Hickok) 1940- 10
Scheller, Melanie 1953- 77
Schellie, Don 1932- 29
Schembri, Jim 1962- *124*
Schembri, Pamela 1969- *195*
Schemm, Mildred Walker 1905-1998 21
  Obituary *103*

Schenker, Dona 1947- *133*
  Earlier sketch in SATA 68
Scher, Paula 1948- 47
Scherer, Jeffrey *194*
Scherf, Margaret 1908-1979 10
Schermer, Judith (Denise) 1941- 30
Schertle, Alice 1941- *192*
  Earlier sketches in SATA 36, 90, 145
Schick, Alice 1946- 27
Schick, Eleanor 1942- *144*
  Earlier sketches in SATA 9, 82
Schick, Joel 1945- 31
  Brief entry 30
Schields, Gretchen 1948- 75
Schiff, Ken(neth Roy) 1942- 7
Schiller, Andrew 1919- 21
Schiller, Barbara (Heyman) 1928- 21
Schiller, Pamela (Byrne) *127*
Schindel, John 1955- *213*
  Earlier sketches in SATA 77, 115
Schindelman, Joseph 1923- 67
  Brief entry 32
Schindler, S.D. 1952- *198*
  Brief entry 50
  Earlier sketches in SATA 75, 118, 171
Schindler, Steven D.
  See Schindler, S.D.
Schinto, Jeanne 1951- 93
Schisgall, Oscar 1901-1984 12
  Obituary 38
Schlaepfer, Gloria G. 1931- *154*
Schlee, Ann 1934- 44
  Brief entry 36
Schleichert, Elizabeth 1945- 77
Schlein, Miriam 1926-2004 .... *130*
  Obituary *159*
  Earlier sketches in SATA 2, 87
  See also CLR 41
Schlesinger, Arthur M., Jr. 1917-2007 61
  Obituary *181*
  See Schlesinger, Arthur Meier
Schlesinger, Arthur Meier 1888-1965
Schlessinger, Laura (Catherine) 1947- *160*
  Earlier sketch in SATA 110
Schlitz, Laura Amy *184*
Schloat, G. Warren, Jr. 1914-2000 4
Schlossberg, Elisabeth *221*
Schmatz, Pat *197*
Schmid, Eleonore 1939- *126*
  Earlier sketches in SATA 12, 84
Schmid, Susan Maupin *208*
Schmiderer, Dorothy 1940- 19
Schmidt, Annie M. G. 1911-1995 67
  Obituary 91
  See also CLR 22
Schmidt, C.A. *196*
Schmidt, Diane 1953- 70
Schmidt, Elizabeth 1915- 15
Schmidt, Gary D. 1957- *193*
  Earlier sketches in SATA 93, 135
Schmidt, James Norman 1912-1983 21
Schmidt, Karen Lee 1953- *185*
  Earlier sketch in SATA 94
Schmidt, Lynette 1952- 76
Schmitz, Tamara *207*
Schneider, Antonie 1954- *167*
  Earlier sketch in SATA 89
Schneider, Christine M. 1972(?)- *171*
  Earlier sketch in SATA 120
Schneider, Dick
  See Schneider, Richard H.
Schneider, Elisa
  See Kleven, Elisa
Schneider, Herman 1905-2003 7
  Obituary *148*
Schneider, Howie -2007 .... *181*
Schneider, Josh 1980- *196*
Schneider, Laurie
  See Adams, Laurie
Schneider, Nina 1913-2007 2
  Obituary *186*

Schneider, Nina Zimet
  See Schneider, Nina
Schneider, Rex 1937- 44
Schneider, Richard H. 1922- *171*
Schneider, Richard Henry
  See Schneider, Richard H.
Schneider, Robyn 1986- *187*
Schnirel, James R. 1931- 14
Schnitter, Jane T. 1958- 88
Schnitzlein, Danny *134*
Schnur, Steven 1952- *144*
  Earlier sketch in SATA 95
Schnurre, Wolfdietrich 1920-1989
  Obituary 63
Schoberle, Cecile 1949- 80
Schock, Pauline 1928- 45
Schoell, William 1951- *160*
Schoen, Barbara (Taylor) 1924-1993 13
Schoenherr, Ian *177*
Schoenherr, John 1935-2010 66
  Earlier sketch in SATA 37
  See also SAAS 13
Schoenherr, John Carl
  See Schoenherr, John
Schofield, Sandy
  See Rusch, Kristine Kathryn
Scholastica, Sister Mary
  See Jenkins, Marie M(agdalen)
Scholefield, A. T.
  See Scholefield, Alan
Scholefield, Alan 1931- 66
Scholefield, Edmund O.
  See Griffin, W. E. B.
Scholey, Arthur 1932- 28
Scholz, Jackson Volney 1897-1986
  Obituary 49
Schone, Virginia 22
Schongut, Emanuel 1936- *184*
  Brief entry 36
  Earlier sketch in SATA 52
Schoonover, Frank (Earle) 1877-1972 24
Schoor, Gene 1921- 3
Schories, Pat 1952- *164*
  Earlier sketch in SATA 116
Schorr, Melissa 1972- *194*
Schorr, Melissa Robin
  See Schorr, Melissa
Schott, Jane A. 1946- *172*
Schotter, Roni *190*
  Earlier sketches in SATA 105, 149
Schraff, Anne E(laine) 1939- 92
  Earlier sketch in SATA 27
Schram, Penninah 1934- *219*
  Earlier sketch in SATA 119
Schrank, Joseph 1900-1984
  Obituary 38
Schrecengost, Maity 1938- *118*
Schrecengost, S. Maitland
  See Schrecengost, Maity
Schreck, Karen
  See Schreck, Karen Halvorsen
Schreck, Karen Halvorsen 1962- *185*
Schrecker, Judie 1954- 90
Schreiber, Elizabeth Anne (Ferguson)
  1947- 13
Schreiber, Ralph W(alter) 1942- 13
Schreiner, Samuel A(gnew), Jr. 1921- 70
Schroades, John *214*
Schroeder, Alan 1961- 98
  Earlier sketch in SATA 66
Schroeder, Binette
  See Nickl, Barbara (Elisabeth)
Schroeder, Russell (K.) 1943- *146*
Schroeder, Ted 1931(?)-1973
  Obituary 20
Schubert, Dieter 1947- *217*
  Earlier sketches in SATA 62, 101
Schubert, Ingrid 1953- *217*
Schubert, Leda 1950(?)- *181*
Schubert-Gabrys, Ingrid 1953- *101*
  Earlier sketch in SATA 62

Schuelein-Steel, Danielle
    See Steel, Danielle
Schuelein-Steel, Danielle Fernande
    See Steel, Danielle
Schuerger, Michele R. 110
Schuett, Stacey 1960- 168
    Earlier sketch in SATA 75
Schulke, Flip Phelps Graeme 1930- 57
Schulman, Arlene 1961- 105
Schulman, Janet 1933- 208
    Earlier sketches in SATA 22, 137
Schulman, L(ester) M(artin) 1934- 13
Schulte, Elaine L(ouise) 1934- 36
Schultz, Betty K(epka) 1932- 125
Schultz, Gwendolyn 21
Schultz, James Willard 1859-1947
    See YABC 1
Schultz, Pearle Henriksen 1918- 21
Schulz, Charles M. 1922-2000 10
    Obituary 118
Schulz, Charles Monroe
    See Schulz, Charles M.
Schumacher, Julie 1958- 191
Schumaker, Ward 1943- 96
Schuman, Michael A. 1953- 134
    Earlier sketch in SATA 85
Schur, Maxine
    See Schur, Maxine Rose
Schur, Maxine Rose 1948- 135
    Autobiography Feature 135
    Brief entry 49
    Earlier sketches in SATA 53, 98
Schurfranz, Vivian 1925- 13
Schutzer, A. I. 1922- 13
Schuyler, Pamela R. 1948- 30
Schwabach, Karen 185
Schwager, Tina 1964- 110
Schwandt, Stephen (William) 1947- 61
Schwark, Mary Beth 1954- 51
Schwartz, Alvin 1927-1992 56
    Obituary 71
    Earlier sketch in SATA 4
    See also CLR 89
Schwartz, Amy 1954- 189
    Brief entry 41
    Earlier sketches in SATA 47, 83, 131
    See also CLR 25
    See also SAAS 18
Schwartz, Anne Powers 1913-1987 10
Schwartz, Carol 1954- 77
Schwartz, Charles W(alsh) 1914- 8
Schwartz, David M. 1951- 110
    Earlier sketch in SATA 59
Schwartz, David Martin
    See Schwartz, David M.
Schwartz, Elizabeth Reeder 1912- 8
Schwartz, Ellen 1949- 117
Schwartz, Jerome L.
    See Lawrence, Jerome
Schwartz, Joanne 1960- 220
Schwartz, Joel L. 1940- 54
    Brief entry 51
Schwartz, Joyce R. 1950- 93
Schwartz, Julius 1907-2004 45
Schwartz, Perry 1942- 75
Schwartz, Sheila (Ruth) 1929- 27
Schwartz, Stephen (Lawrence) 1948- 19
Schwartz, Virginia Frances 1950- 184
    Earlier sketch in SATA 131
Schwarz, Silvia Tessa Viviane
    See Schwarz, Viviane
Schwarz, Viviane 1977- 204
Schwarz, (Silvia Tessa) Viviane 1977- 141
Schweitzer, Byrd Baylor
    See Baylor, Byrd
Schweitzer, Iris 59
    Brief entry 36
Schweninger, Ann 1951- 168
    Earlier sketches in SATA 29, 98
Schwerin, Doris H(alpern) 1922- 64
Schy, Yael 197

Scieszka, Jon 1954- 199
    Earlier sketches in SATA 68, 105, 160
    See also CLR 107
Scillian, Devin 199
    Earlier sketch in SATA 128
Scioscia, Mary (Hershey) 1926- 63
Sciurba, Katie 1957- 196
Scofield, Penrod 1933- 62
    Obituary 78
Scoggin, Margaret C(lara) 1905-1968 47
    Brief entry 28
Scoltock, Jack 1942- 141
    Earlier sketch in SATA 72
Scoppettone, Sandra 1936- 92
    Earlier sketch in SATA 9
Scot, Michael
    See Rohan, Michael Scott
Scot-Bernard, P.
    See Bernard, Patricia
Scotland, Jay
    See Jakes, John
Scott, Alastair
    See Allen, Kenneth S.
Scott, Ann Herbert 1926- 140
    Autobiography Feature 140
    Brief entry 29
    Earlier sketches in SATA 56, 94
Scott, Bill
    See Scott, William N(eville)
Scott, Bill 1920(?)-1985
    Obituary 46
Scott, Cora Annett (Pipitone) 1931- 11
Scott, Dan
    See Barker, S. Omar
Scott, Elaine 1940- 198
    Earlier sketches in SATA 36, 90, 164
Scott, Elizabeth 1972- 194
Scott, Jack Denton 1915-1995 83
    Earlier sketch in SATA 31
    See also CLR 20
    See also SAAS 14
Scott, Jane (Harrington) 1931- 55
Scott, Jessica
    See De Wire, Elinor
Scott, John 1912-1976 14
Scott, John Anthony 1916- 23
Scott, John M(artin) 1913- 12
Scott, Mary
    See Mattern, Joanne
Scott, Melissa 1960- 109
Scott, Michael 1959- 211
Scott, Michael Peter
    See Scott, Michael
Scott, Mike
    See Scott, Michael
Scott, Richard
    See Rennert, Richard Scott
Scott, Roney
    See Gault, William Campbell
Scott, Sally 1909-1978 43
Scott, Sally 1948- 44
Scott, Sally Elisabeth
    See Scott, Sally
Scott, W. N.
    See Scott, William N(eville)
Scott, Sir Walter 1771-1832
    See YABC 2
    See also CLR 154
Scott, Warwick
    See Trevor, Elleston
Scott, William N(eville) 1923- 87
Scotti, Anna
    See Coates, Anna
Scotton, Rob 1960- 214
    Earlier sketch in SATA 177
Scribner, Charles, Jr. 1921-1995 13
    Obituary 87
Scribner, Joanne L. 1949- 33
Scribner, Kimball 1917- 63
Scrimger, Richard 1957- 164
    Earlier sketch in SATA 119

Scrimsher, Lila Gravatt 1897-1974
    Obituary 28
Scroder, Walter K. 1928- 82
Scroggs, Kirk 187
Scruggs, Sandy 1961- 89
Scudder, Brooke 1959- 154
Scudder, Mildred Lee 1908- 6
    See also SAAS 12
Scull, Marie-Louise 1943-1993 77
Scuro, Vincent 1951- 21
Seabrooke, Brenda 1941- 148
    Earlier sketches in SATA 30, 88
Seaman, Augusta Huiell 1879-1950 31
Seamands, Ruth 1916- 9
Searcy, Margaret Zehmer 1926- 54
    Brief entry 39
Searight, Mary W(illiams) 1918- 17
Searle, Kathryn Adrienne 1942- 10
Searle, Ronald (William Fordham) 1920- 70
    Earlier sketch in SATA 42
Sears, Stephen W. 1932- 4
Seaskull, Cecil
    See Castellucci, Cecil
Sebastian, Lee
    See Silverberg, Robert
Sebestyen, Igen
    See Sebestyen, Ouida
Sebestyen, Ouida 1924- 140
    Earlier sketch in SATA 39
    See also CLR 17
    See also SAAS 10
Sebrey, Mary Ann 1951- 62
Sechrist, Elizabeth Hough 1903-1991 2
Sederman, Marty 211
Sedges, John
    See Buck, Pearl S.
Sedgwick, Marcus 1968- 197
    Earlier sketch in SATA 160
Seed, Cecile Eugenie 1930- 86
    Earlier sketch in SATA 8
    See also CLR 76
Seed, Jenny
    See Seed, Cecile Eugenie
Seed, Sheila Turner 1937(?)-1979
    Obituary 23
Seeger, Elizabeth 1889-1973
    Obituary 20
Seeger, Laura Vaccaro 200
    Earlier sketch in SATA 172
Seeger, Pete 1919- 139
    Earlier sketch in SATA 13
Seeger, Peter R.
    See Seeger, Pete
Seeley, Laura L. 1958- 71
Seever, R.
    See Reeves, Lawrence F.
Sefozo, Mary 1925- 82
Sefton, Catherine
    See Waddell, Martin
Segal, John 178
Segal, Joyce 1940- 35
Segal, Lore 1928- 163
    Earlier sketches in SATA 4, 66
    See also SAAS 11
Segal, Lore Groszmann
    See Segal, Lore
Segar, E(lzie) C(risler) 1894-1938 61
Segovia, Andres 1893(?)-1987
    Obituary 52
Seguin, Marilyn W(eymouth) 1951- 91
Seguin-Fontes, Marthe 1924- 109
Seibold, J. Otto 1960- 196
    Earlier sketches in SATA 83, 149
    See also SAAS 22
Seidel, Ross 95
Seidelman, James Edward 1926- 6
Seiden, Art(hur) 107
    Brief entry 42
Seidensticker, John 1944- 200
Seidler, Ann (G.) 1925- 131

Seidler, Tor 1952- *149*
   Brief entry *46*
   Earlier sketches in SATA *52, 98*
Seidman, Karla
   See Kuskin, Karla
Seidman, Laurence Ivan 1925- *15*
Seigel, Kalman 1917-1998 .... *12*
   Obituary *103*
Seignobosc, Francoise 1897-1961 .... *21*
Seinfeld, Jerry 1954- *146*
Seitz, Jacqueline 1931- *50*
Seixas, Judith S. 1922- *17*
Sejima, Yoshimasa 1913- *8*
Selberg, Ingrid (Maria) 1950- *68*
Selden, George
   See Thompson, George Selden
Selden, Neil R(oy) 1931- *61*
Self, Margaret Cabell 1902-1996 .... *24*
Selfors, Suzanne 1963- *193*
Selick, Henry 1952- *183*
Selig, Sylvie 1942- *13*
Selkirk, Jane
   See Chapman, John Stanton Higham
Sellers, Naomi
   See Flack, Naomi John White
Sellier, Marie 1953- *212*
Selman, LaRue W. 1927- *55*
Selsam, Millicent E(llis) 1912-1996 .... *29*
   Obituary *92*
   Earlier sketch in SATA *1*
   See also CLR *1*
Seltzer, Meyer 1932- *17*
Seltzer, Richard 1946- *41*
Seltzer, Richard Warren, Jr.
   See Seltzer, Richard
Selvadurai, Shyam 1965(?)- *171*
Selway, Martina 1940- *169*
   Earlier sketch in SATA *74*
Selzer, Adam 1980- *192*
Selznick, Brian 1966- *210*
   Earlier sketches in SATA *79, 117, 171*
Semel, Nava 1954- *107*
Semloh
   See Holmes, Peggy
Sendak, Jack 1924(?)-1995 .... *28*
Sendak, Maurice 1928- *165*
   Earlier sketches in SATA *1, 27, 113*
   See also CLR *131*
Sendak, Maurice Bernard
   See Sendak, Maurice
Sender, Ruth M(insky) 1926- *62*
Sengler, Johanna 1924- *18*
Senisi, Ellen B. 1951- *116*
Senisi, Ellen Babinec
   See Senisi, Ellen B.
Senn, J(oyce) A(nn) 1941- *115*
Senn, Steve 1950- *60*
   Brief entry *48*
Sensel, Joni 1962- *204*
Serafini, Frank *201*
Serage, Nancy 1924- *10*
Seredy, Kate 1899-1975 .... *1*
   Obituary *24*
   See also CLR *10*
Serfozo, Mary 1925- *194*
Seroff, Victor I(ilyitch) 1902-1979 .... *12*
   Obituary *26*
Serra, Sebastia 1966- *202*
Serraillier, Ian (Lucien) 1912-1994 .... *73*
   Obituary *83*
   Earlier sketch in SATA *1*
   See also CLR *2*
   See also SAAS *3*
Serros, Michele *175*
Serros, Michele M.
   See Serros, Michele
Servello, Joe 1932- *10*
Service, Pamela F. 1945- *64*
Service, Robert
   See Service, Robert W.
Service, Robert W. 1874(?)-1958 .... *20*

Serwadda, W(illiam) Moses 1931- *27*
Serwer-Bernstein, Blanche L(uria)
   1910-1997 .... *10*
Sescoe, Vincent E. 1938- *123*
Seskin, Steve 1953- *211*
Seth, Mary
   See Lexau, Joan M.
Seton, Anya 1904(?)-1990 .... *3*
   Obituary *66*
Seton, Ernest (Evan) Thompson 1860-1946 . *18*
   See also CLR *59*
Seton-Thompson, Ernest
   See Seton, Ernest (Evan) Thompson
Seuling, Barbara 1937- *220*
   Autobiography Feature *220*
   Earlier sketches in SATA *10, 98, 145, 193*
   See also SAAS *24*
Seuss, Dr.
   See Dr. Seuss
Severn, Bill
   See Severn, William Irving
Severn, David
   See Unwin, David S.
Severn, William Irving 1914- *1*
Sewall, Marcia 1935- *119*
   Earlier sketches in SATA *37, 69*
Seward, Prudence 1926- *16*
Sewell, Anna 1820-1878 .... *100*
   Earlier sketch in SATA *24*
   See also CLR *17*
Sewell, Helen (Moore) 1896-1957 .... *38*
Sexton, Anne 1928-1974 .... *10*
Sexton, Anne Harvey
   See Sexton, Anne
Seymour, Alta Halverson *10*
Seymour, Jane 1951- *139*
Seymour, Tres 1966- *164*
   Earlier sketch in SATA *82*
Sfar, Joann 1971- *182*
Shachtman, Tom 1942- *49*
Shackleton, C.C.
   See Aldiss, Brian W.
Shader, Rachel
   See Sofer, Barbara
Shadow, Jak
   See Sutherland, Jon
Shadyland, Sal
   See Cooper, Louise
Shafer, Audrey *183*
Shafer, Robert E(ugene) 1925- *9*
Shaffer, Terea 1968- *79*
Shahan, Sherry 1949- *216*
   Earlier sketches in SATA *92, 134*
Shahn, Ben(jamin) 1898-1969
   Obituary *21*
Shahn, Bernarda Bryson
   See Bryson, Bernarda
Shaik, Fatima *114*
Shalant, Phyllis 1949- *150*
Shan, Darren 1972- *199*
   Earlier sketches in SATA *129, 168*
Shan, D.B.
   See Shan, Darren
Shanahan, Lisa *199*
Shanberg, Karen
   See Shragg, Karen (I.)
Shane, Harold Gray 1914-1993 .... *36*
   Obituary *76*
Shange, Ntozake 1948- *157*
Shanks, Ann Zane (Kushner) *10*
Shannon, David 1959- *152*
   Earlier sketch in SATA *107*
   See also CLR *87*
Shannon, George 1952- *202*
   Earlier sketches in SATA *35, 94, 143*
Shannon, George William Bones
   See Shannon, George
Shannon, Jacqueline *63*
Shannon, Margaret
   See Silverwood, Margaret Shannon
Shannon, Monica 1905(?)-1965 .... *28*

Shannon, Terry
   See Mercer, Jessie
Shannon, Terry Miller 1951- *148*
Shapiro, Irwin 1911-1981 .... *32*
Shapiro, Jody Fickes 1940- *193*
Shapiro, Karen Jo 1964- *186*
Shapiro, Michelle 1961- *196*
Shapiro, Milton J. 1926- *32*
Shapiro, Tricia
   See Andryszewski, Tricia
Shapiro, Zachary 1970- *213*
Shapp, Charles M(orris) 1906-1989
   Obituary *61*
Shapp, Martha Glauber 1910- *3*
Sharenow, Robert *193*
Sharfman, Amalie *14*
Sharkey, Niamh *213*
Sharma, Partap 1939- *15*
Sharma, Rashmi
   See Singh, Rashmi Sharma
Sharman, Alison
   See Leonard, Alison
Sharmat, Marjorie Weinman 1928- *133*
   Earlier sketches in SATA *4, 33, 74*
Sharmat, Mitchell 1927- *127*
   Earlier sketch in SATA *33*
Sharp, Anne Wallace 1947- *144*
Sharp, Luke
   See Alkiviades, Alkis
Sharp, Margery 1905-1991 .... *29*
   Obituary *67*
   Earlier sketch in SATA *1*
   See also CLR *27*
Sharp, Zerna A. 1889-1981
   Obituary *27*
Sharpe, Jon
   See Duncan, Alice
   and Knott, William C(ecil, Jr.)
   and Messman, Jon
Sharpe, Mitchell R(aymond) 1924- *12*
Sharpe, Susan 1946- *71*
Sharratt, Nick 1962- *199*
   Earlier sketches in SATA *104, 153*
Shasha, Mark 1961- *80*
Shattuck, Roger 1923-2005 .... *64*
   Obituary *174*
Shattuck, Roger Whitney
   See Shattuck, Roger
Shaw, Arnold 1909-1989 .... *4*
   Obituary *63*
Shaw, Carolyn V. 1934- *91*
Shaw, Charles (Green) 1892-1974 .... *13*
Shaw, Evelyn S. 1927- *28*
Shaw, Flora Louisa
   See Lugard, Flora Louisa Shaw
Shaw, Janet 1937- *146*
   Earlier sketch in SATA *61*
   See also CLR *96*
Shaw, Janet Beeler
   See Shaw, Janet
Shaw, Lisa
   See Rogak, Lisa
Shaw, Margret 1940- *68*
Shaw, Mary 1965- *180*
Shaw, Nancy 1946- *162*
   Earlier sketch in SATA *71*
Shaw, Ray *7*
Shaw, Richard 1923- *12*
Shawn, Frank S.
   See Goulart, Ron
Shay, Art
   See Shay, Arthur
Shay, Arthur 1922- *4*
Shay, Lacey
   See Shebar, Sharon Sigmond
Shea, Bob *188*
Shea, George 1940- *54*
   Brief entry *42*
Shea, Pegi Deitz 1960- *172*
   Earlier sketches in SATA *77, 137*
Shearer, Alex 1949- *204*

Shearer, John 1947- 43
   Brief entry 27
   See also CLR 34
Shearer, Ted 1919- 43
Shearing, Leonie 1972- 184
Sheban, Chris 182
Shebar, Sharon Sigmond 1945- 36
Shecter, Ben 1935- 16
Shedd, Warner 1934- 147
   Earlier sketch in SATA 87
Sheedy, Alexandra Elizabeth 1962- 39
   Earlier sketch in SATA 19
Sheehan, Ethna 1908-2000 9
Sheehan, Patty 1945- 77
Sheehan, Sean 1951- 154
   Earlier sketch in SATA 86
Sheen, Barbara 1949- 143
Shefelman, Janice 1930- 205
   Earlier sketches in SATA 58, 129
Shefelman, Janice Jordan
   See Shefelman, Janice
Shefelman, Tom 1927- 204
   Earlier sketch in SATA 58
Sheffer, H. R.
   See Abels, Harriette S(heffer)
Sheffield, Charles 1935-2002 109
Sheffield, Janet N. 1926- 26
Sheikh, Nazneen 1944- 101
Sheinkin, Steve 1968- 204
Sheinmel, Courtney 1977- 211
Shekerjian, Regina Tor 16
Shelby, Anne 1948- 85
   Autobiography Feature 121
   See also SAAS 26
Sheldon, Ann
   See Antle, Nancy
Sheldon, Ann 67
   Earlier sketch in SATA 1
Sheldon, Aure 1917-1976 12
Sheldon, David 185
Sheldon, Deyan 181
Sheldon, John
   See Bloch, Robert (Albert)
Sheldon, Muriel 1926- 45
   Brief entry 39
Shell, Barry 1951- 176
Shelley, Frances
   See Wees, Frances Shelley
Shelley, John 1959- 202
Shelley, Mary
   See Shelley, Mary Wollstonecraft
Shelley, Mary Wollstonecraft 1797-1851 29
   See also CLR 133
Shelton, William Roy 1919-1995 5
   Obituary 129
Shemie, Bonnie (Jean Brenner) 1949- 96
Shemin, Margaretha (Hoeneveld) 1928- 4
Shen, Michele 1953- 173
Shenker, Michele
   See Shen, Michele
Shenton, Edward 1895-1977 45
Shepard, Aaron 1950- 187
   Earlier sketches in SATA 75, 113
Shepard, Ernest Howard 1879-1976 100
   Obituary 24
   Earlier sketches in SATA 3, 33
   See also CLR 27
Shepard, James R.
   See Shepard, Jim
Shepard, Jim 1956- 164
   Earlier sketch in SATA 90
Shepard, Mary
   See Knox, (Mary) Eleanor Jessie
Shephard, Esther 1891-1975 5
   Obituary 26
Shepherd, Amanda 201
Shepherd, Donna Walsh
   See Walsh Shepherd, Donna
Shepherd, Elizabeth 4
Shepherd, Irana 173

Shepherd, Roni
   See Shepherd, Irana
Sheppard, Kate 195
Shepperson, Rob 178
Sherburne, Zoa (Lillian Morin) 1912-1995 3
   See also SAAS 18
Sherk-Savage, Candace
   See Savage, Candace
Sherlock, Patti 71
Sherman, D(enis) R(onald) 1934- 48
   Brief entry 29
Sherman, Diane (Finn) 1928- 12
Sherman, Elizabeth
   See Friskey, Margaret (Richards)
Sherman, Harold (Morrow) 1898-1987 37
   Obituary 137
Sherman, Josepha 163
   Earlier sketch in SATA 75
Sherman, Michael
   See Lowndes, Robert A(ugustine) W(ard)
Sherman, Nancy
   See Rosenberg, Nancy (Sherman)
Sherman, Pat 174
Sherman, Peter Michael
   See Lowndes, Robert A(ugustine) W(ard)
Sherrard, Valerie (Anne) 1957- 141
Sherrod, Jane
   See Singer, Jane Sherrod
Sherry, Clifford J. 1943- 84
Sherry, (Dulcie) Sylvia 1932- 122
   Earlier sketch in SATA 8
Sherwan, Earl 1917- 3
Sherwood, Jonathan
   See London, Jonathan
Sheth, Kashmira 186
Shetterly, Will 1955- 78
   Autobiography Feature 106
Shetterly, William Howard
   See Shetterly, Will
Shiefman, Vicky 1942- 22
Shields, Brenda Desmond (Armstrong)
   1914- 37
Shields, Carol Diggory 174
Shields, Charles 1944- 10
Shields, Gillian 203
Shiels, Barbara
   See Adams, Barbara Johnston
Shiffman, Lena 1957- 101
Shiina, Makoto 1944- 83
Shimin, Symeon 1902-1984 13
Shimko, Bonnie 1941- 191
Shine, Andrea 1955- 104
Shine, Deborah 1932- 71
Shinn, Everett 1876-1953 21
Shinn, Sharon 1957- 164
   Earlier sketch in SATA 110
Shippen, Katherine B(inney) 1892-1980 1
   Obituary 23
   See also CLR 36
Shippey, T. A. 1943- 143
Shippey, Thomas Alan
   See Shippey, T. A.
Shipton, Eric Earle 1907-1977 10
Shipton, Jonathan 1948- 215
Shipton, Paul 1963- 196
Shiraz, Yasmin 173
Shirer, William L(awrence) 1904-1993 45
   Obituary 78
Shirley, Debra 203
Shirley, Gayle C 1955- 96
Shirley, Gayle Corbett
   See Shirley, Gayle C
Shirley, Jean 1919- 70
Shirreffs, Gordon D(onald) 1914-1996 11
Shirts, Morris A(lpine) 1922- 63
Shlichta, Joe 1968- 84
Shmurak, Carole B. 1944- 118
Sholokhov, Mikhail 1905-1984
   Obituary 36
Sholokhov, Mikhail Aleksandrovich
   See Sholokhov, Mikhail

Shore, Diane Z. 215
   Earlier sketch in SATA 179
Shore, Diane ZuHone
   See Shore, Diane Z.
Shore, June Lewis 30
Shore, Nancy 1960- 124
Shore, Robert 1924- 39
Short, Michael 1937- 65
Short, Roger
   See Arkin, Alan
Shortall, Leonard W. 19
Shortt, Tim(othy Donald) 1961- 96
Shotwell, Louisa Rossiter 1902-1993 3
Shoulders, Michael 1954- 216
Shoup, Barbara 1947- 156
   Earlier sketch in SATA 86
   See also SAAS 24
Shoveller, Herb 184
Showalter, Jean B(reckinridge) 12
Showell, Ellen Harvey 1934- 33
Showers, Paul C. 1910-1999 92
   Obituary 114
   Earlier sketch in SATA 21
   See also CLR 6
   See also SAAS 7
Shpakow, Tanya 1959(?)- 94
Shpitalnik, Vladimir 1964- 83
Shragg, Karen (I.) 1954- 142
Shreeve, Elizabeth 1956- 156
Shreve, Susan
   See Shreve, Susan Richards
Shreve, Susan Richards 1939- 152
   Brief entry 41
   Earlier sketches in SATA 46, 95
Shriver, Jean Adair 1932- 75
Shriver, Maria 1955- 134
Shriver, Maria Owings
   See Shriver, Maria
Shrode, Mary
   See Hollingsworth, Mary
Shtainmets, Leon 32
Shub, Elizabeth 1915(?)-2004 5
Shuken, Julia 1948- 84
Shulevitz, Uri 1935- 165
   Earlier sketches in SATA 3, 50, 106
   See also CLR 61
Shulman, Alix Kates 1932- 7
Shulman, Dee 1957- 146
Shulman, Irving 1913-1995 13
Shulman, Lisa 202
Shulman, Mark 1962- 184
Shulman, Max 1919-1988
   Obituary 59
Shulman, Milton 1913-2004
   Obituary 154
Shulman, Neil B(arnett) 1945- 89
Shumsky, Zena
   See Collier, Zena
Shura, Mary Francis
   See Craig, Mary (Francis) Shura
Shusterman, Neal 1962- 201
   Autobiography Feature 140
   Earlier sketches in SATA 85, 121, 140
Shuter, Jane (Margaret) 1955- 151
   Earlier sketch in SATA 90
Shuttlesworth, Dorothy Edwards 3
Shwartz, Susan (Martha) 1949- 94
Shyer, Christopher 1961- 98
Shyer, Marlene Fanta 13
Siberell, Anne 29
Sibley, Don 1922- 12
Siburt, Ruth 1951- 121
Siculan, Daniel 1922- 12
Siddon, Barbara
   See Bradford, Barbara Taylor
Sidgwick, Ethel 1877-1970 116
Sidjakov, Nicolas 1924- 18
Sidman, Joyce 1956- 181
   Earlier sketch in SATA 145
Sidney, Frank
   See Warwick, Alan R(oss)

Sidney, Margaret
    See Lothrop, Harriet Mulford Stone
Siebert, Diane 1948- *189*
Siegal, Aranka 1930- *88*
    Brief entry *37*
Siegel, Beatrice *36*
Siegel, Helen
    See Siegl, Helen
Siegel, Robert 1939- *39*
Siegel, Robert Harold
    See Siegel, Robert
Siegel, Siena Cherson 1967(?)- *185*
Siegelson, Kim L. 1962- *114*
Sieger, Ted 1958- *189*
Siegl, Helen 1924- *34*
Siepmann, Mary Aline
    See Wesley, Mary (Aline)
Sierra, Judy 1945- *195*
    Earlier sketches in SATA *104, 162*
Sieswerda, Paul L. 1942- *147*
Sievert, Terri
    See Dougherty, Terri (L.)
Sigsawa, Keiichi 1972- *211*
Silas
    See McCay, (Zenas) Winsor
Silcock, Sara Lesley 1947- *12*
Silin-Palmer, Pamela *184*
Sill, Cathryn 1953- *221*
    Earlier sketches in SATA *74, 141*
Sill, John 1947- *140*
    Earlier sketch in SATA *74*
Sillitoe, Alan 1928-2010 .... *61*
Sills, Leslie (Elka) 1948- *129*
Silly, E. S.
    See Kraus, (Herman) Robert
Silsbe, Brenda 1953- *73*
Silva, Joseph
    See Goulart, Ron
Silver, Jago
    See Jago
Silver, Maggie *216*
Silver, Ruth
    See Chew, Ruth
Silverberg, Robert 1935- *91*
    Autobiography Feature *104*
    Earlier sketch in SATA *13*
    See also CLR *59*
Silverman, Erica 1955- *165*
    Earlier sketches in SATA *78, 112*
Silverman, Janis L. 1946- *127*
Silverman, Mel(vin Frank) 1931-1966 .... *9*
Silverman, Robin L. 1954- *96*
Silverman, Robin Landew
    See Silverman, Robin L.
Silverstein, Alvin 1933- *124*
    Earlier sketches in SATA *8, 69*
    See also CLR *25*
Silverstein, Herma 1945- *106*
Silverstein, Robert Alan 1959- *124*
    Earlier sketch in SATA *77*
Silverstein, Shel 1932-1999 .... *92*
    Brief entry *27*
    Obituary *116*
    Earlier sketch in SATA *33*
    See also CLR *96*
Silverstein, Sheldon Allan
    See Silverstein, Shel
Silverstein, Virginia B. 1937- *124*
    Earlier sketches in SATA *8, 69*
    See also CLR *25*
Silverstein, Virginia Barbara Opshelor
    See Silverstein, Virginia B.
Silverthorne, Elizabeth 1930- *35*
Silverwood, Margaret Shannon 1966- *137*
    Earlier sketch in SATA *83*
Silvey, Diane F. 1946- *135*
Sim, David 1953- *162*
Sim, Dorrith M. 1931- *96*
Simak, Clifford D(onald) 1904-1988
    Obituary *56*
Simard, Remy 1959- *168*

Siminovich, Lorena 1976(?)- *219*
Simmie, Lois (Ann) 1932- *106*
Simmonds, Posy 1945- *130*
    See also CLR *23*
Simmonds, Rosemary Elizabeth
    See Simmonds, Posy
Simmons, Andra 1939- *141*
Simmons, Elly 1955- *134*
Simmons, Michael 1970- *185*
Simms, Laura 1947- *117*
Simner, Janni Lee *113*
Simon, Charlie May
    See Fletcher, Charlie May Hogue
Simon, Francesca 1955- *111*
Simon, Gabriel 1972- *118*
Simon, Hilda Rita 1921- *28*
    See also CLR *39*
Simon, Howard 1903-1979 .... *32*
    Obituary *21*
Simon, Joe
    See Simon, Joseph H.
Simon, Joseph H. 1913- *7*
Simon, Martin P(aul William) 1903-1969 .... *12*
Simon, Mina Lewiton
    See Lewiton, Mina
Simon, Norma (Feldstein) 1927- *129*
    Earlier sketches in SATA *3, 68*
Simon, Seymour 1931- *202*
    Earlier sketches in SATA *4, 73, 138*
    See also CLR *63*
Simon, Shirley (Schwartz) 1921- *11*
Simon, Solomon 1895-1970 .... *40*
Simonetta, Linda 1948- *14*
Simonetta, Sam 1936- *14*
Simons, Barbara B(rooks) 1934- *41*
Simont, Marc 1915- *126*
    Earlier sketches in SATA *9, 73*
Simpson, Colin 1908-1983 .... *14*
Simpson, Harriette
    See Arnow, Harriette (Louisa) Simpson
Simpson, Jacynth Hope
    See Hope Simpson, Jacynth
Simpson, Lesley 1963- *150*
Simpson, Margaret 1943- *128*
Simpson, Myrtle L(illias) 1931- *14*
Sims, Blanche *168*
    Earlier sketch in SATA *75*
Sims, Blanche L.
    See Sims, Blanche
Simundsson, Elva 1950- *63*
Sinclair, Clover
    See Gater, Dilys
Sinclair, Emil
    See Hesse, Hermann
Sinclair, Jeff 1958- *77*
Sinclair, Olga 1923- *121*
Sinclair, Rose
    See Smith, Susan Vernon
Sinclair, Upton 1878-1968 .... *9*
Sinclair, Upton Beall
    See Sinclair, Upton
Singer, A.L.
    See Lerangis, Peter
Singer, Arthur 1917-1990 .... *64*
Singer, Isaac
    See Singer, Isaac Bashevis
Singer, Isaac Bashevis 1904-1991 .... *27*
    Obituary *68*
    Earlier sketch in SATA *3*
    See also CLR *1*
Singer, Jane Sherrod 1917-1985 .... *4*
    Obituary *42*
Singer, Julia 1917- *28*
Singer, Kurt D. 1911-2005 .... *38*
    Obituary *172*
Singer, Marilyn 1948- *201*
    Autobiography Feature *158*
    Brief entry *38*
    Earlier sketches in SATA *48, 80, 125, 158*
    See also CLR *48*
    See also SAAS *13*

Singer, Muff 1942-2005 .... *104*
    Obituary *160*
Singer, Nicky 1956- *194*
Singer, Susan (Mahler) 1941- *9*
Singh, Rashmi Sharma 1952- *90*
Singleton, Linda Joy 1957- *166*
    Earlier sketch in SATA *88*
Singleton, L.J.
    See Singleton, Linda Joy
Singleton, Sarah 1966- *214*
Sinykin, Sheri
    See Sinykin, Sheri Cooper
Sinykin, Sheri Cooper 1950- *142*
    Autobiography Feature *142*
    Earlier sketches in SATA *72, 133*
Sinykin, Sheril Terri Cooper
    See Sinykin, Sheri Cooper
Siomades, Lorianne *217*
Sipiera, Paul P., (Jr.) 1948- *144*
    Earlier sketch in SATA *89*
Siracusa, Catherine (Jane) 1947- *82*
Sirett, Dawn (Karen) 1966- *88*
Sirimarco, Elizabeth 1966- *158*
Sirof, Harriet 1930- *94*
    Earlier sketch in SATA *37*
Sirois, Allen L. 1950- *76*
Sirvaitis (Chernyaev), Karen (Ann) 1961- ... *79*
Sis, Peter 1949- *192*
    Earlier sketch in SATA *149*
    See also CLR *110*
Sisson, Rosemary Anne 1923- *11*
Sister Mary Terese
    See Donze, Mary Terese
Sita, Lisa 1962- *87*
Sitarski, Anita *200*
Sitomer, Alan Lawrence *174*
Sitomer, Harry 1903-1985 .... *31*
Sitomer, Mindel 1903-1987 .... *31*
Sittenfeld, Curtis 1975(?)- *164*
Sive, Helen R(obinson) 1951- *30*
Sivulich, Sandra (Jeanne) Stroner 1941- *9*
Siy, Alexandra *193*
Skarmeta, Antonio 1940- *57*
Skeers, Linda 1958- *207*
Skelly, James R(ichard) 1927- *17*
Skelton, Matthew 1971- *185*
Skinner, Constance Lindsay 1877-1939
    See YABC *1*
Skinner, Cornelia Otis 1901-1979 .... *2*
Skipper, G. C. 1939- *46*
    Brief entry *38*
Sklansky, Amy E(dgar) 1971- *145*
Sklansky, Amy E. 1971- *204*
Skofield, James *95*
    Brief entry *44*
Skold, Betty Westrom 1923- *41*
Skorpen, Liesel Moak 1935- *3*
Skott, Maria
    See Nikolajeva, Maria
Skrypuch, Marsha Forchuk 1954- *134*
Skultety, Nancy Laney 1960- *175*
Skurzynski, Gloria 1930- *145*
    Autobiography Feature *145*
    Earlier sketches in SATA *8, 74, 122*
    See also SAAS *9*
Skurzynski, Gloria Joan
    See Skurzynski, Gloria
Skutch, Robert 1925- *89*
Skye, Maggie
    See Werner, Herma
Skye, Obert *200*
    Earlier sketch in SATA *170*
Slack, Michael 1969- *189*
Slackman, Charles B. 1934- *12*
Slade, Arthur G. 1967- *221*
    Earlier sketches in SATA *106, 149*
Slade, Arthur Gregory
    See Slade, Arthur G.
Slade, Christian 1974- *193*
Slade, Richard 1910-1971 .... *9*
Slangerup, Erik Jon 1969- *130*

Slate, Joseph 1928- *174*
　Earlier sketches in SATA *38, 122*
Slate, Joseph Frank
　See Slate, Joseph
Slater, Dashka 1963- *179*
Slater, David Michael 1970- *212*
Slater, Ray
　See Lansdale, Joe R.
Slaughter, Hope 1940- *84*
Slaughter, Jean
　See Doty, Jean Slaughter
Slaughter, Tom 1955- *152*
Slavicek, Louise Chipley 1956- *144*
Slavin, Bill 1959- *199*
　Earlier sketches in SATA *76, 148*
Slaymaker, Melissa Eskridge 1958- *158*
Slayton, Fran Cannon *221*
Sleator, William 1945- *208*
　Earlier sketches in SATA *3, 68, 118, 161*
　See also CLR *128*
Sleator, William Warner III
　See Sleator, William
Slegers, Liesbet 1975- *154*
Sleigh, Barbara 1906-1982 .... *86*
　Obituary *30*
　Earlier sketch in SATA *3*
Slepian, Jan 1921- *85*
　Brief entry *45*
　Earlier sketch in SATA *51*
　See also SAAS *8*
Slepian, Janice B.
　See Slepian, Jan
Slicer, Margaret O. 1920- *4*
Slier, Debby
　See Shine, Deborah
Sloan, Brian 1966- *172*
Sloan, Carolyn 1937- *116*
　Earlier sketch in SATA *58*
Sloan, Glenna 1930- *120*
Sloan, Glenna Davis
　See Sloan, Glenna
Sloane, Eric 1910(?)-1985 .... *52*
　Obituary *42*
Sloane, Todd 1955- *88*
Sloat, Teri 1948- *164*
　Earlier sketches in SATA *70, 106*
Slobodkin, Florence Gersh 1905-1994 .... *5*
　Obituary *107*
Slobodkin, Louis 1903-1975 .... *26*
　Earlier sketch in SATA *1*
Slobodkina, Esphyr 1908-2002 .... *1*
　Obituary *135*
　See also SAAS *8*
Sloggett, Nellie 1851-1923 .... *44*
Slonim, David 1966- *207*
Sloss, Lesley Lord 1965- *72*
Slote, Alfred 1926- *72*
　Earlier sketch in SATA *8*
　See also CLR *4*
　See also SAAS *21*
Slote, Elizabeth 1956- *80*
Small, Charlie
　See Ward, Nick
Small, David 1945- *216*
　Brief entry *46*
　Earlier sketches in SATA *50, 95, 126, 183*
　See also CLR *53*
Small, Ernest
　See Lent, Blair
Small, Mary 1932- *165*
Small, Terry 1942- *75*
Smallcomb, Pam 1954- *159*
Smallman, Steve *197*
Smalls, Irene
　See Smalls-Hector, Irene
Smalls-Hector, Irene 1950- *146*
　Earlier sketch in SATA *73*
　See also CLR *103*
Smallwood, Norah (Evelyn) 1910(?)-1984
　Obituary *41*
Smaridge, Norah (Antoinette) 1903-1994 ...... *6*

Smath, Jerry 1933- *198*
Smee, Nicola 1948- *167*
　Earlier sketch in SATA *76*
Smiley, Virginia Kester 1923- *2*
Smit, Noelle 1972- *199*
Smith, Alexander McCall 1948- *179*
　Earlier sketch in SATA *73*
Smith, Andrew 1959- *209*
Smith, Andrew Anselmo
　See Smith, Andrew
Smith, Andy J. 1975- *207*
Smith, Anne Warren 1938- *41*
　Brief entry *34*
Smith, Barry (Edward Jervis) 1943- *75*
Smith, Beatrice S(chillinger) *12*
Smith, Betsy Covington 1937- *55*
　Earlier sketch in SATA *43*
Smith, Betty (Wehner) 1904-1972 .... *6*
Smith, Bradford 1909-1964 .... *5*
Smith, Brenda 1946- *82*
Smith, C. Pritchard
　See Hoyt, Edwin P(almer), Jr.
Smith, Caesar
　See Trevor, Elleston
Smith, Cat Bowman 1939- *201*
Smith, Charles R., Jr. 1969- *203*
　Earlier sketch in SATA *159*
Smith, Craig 1955- *172*
　Earlier sketches in SATA *81, 117*
Smith, Cynthia Leitich 1967- *215*
　Earlier sketch in SATA *152*
Smith, D. James 1955- *176*
Smith, Danna *216*
Smith, Danna Kessimakis
　See Smith, Danna
Smith, Datus C(lifford), Jr. 1907-1999 .... *13*
　Obituary *116*
Smith, Debra 1955- *89*
Smith, Derek 1943- *141*
Smith, Dick King
　See King-Smith, Dick
Smith, D.J.
　See Smith, D. James
Smith, Dodie
　See Smith, Dorothy Gladys
Smith, Doris Buchanan 1934-2002 .... *75*
　Obituary *140*
　Earlier sketch in SATA *28*
　See also SAAS *10*
Smith, Dorothy Gladys 1896-1990 .... *82*
　Obituary *65*
Smith, Dorothy Stafford 1905- *6*
Smith, Duane 1974- *202*
Smith, E(lmer) Boyd 1860-1943
　See YABC *1*
Smith, E(dric) Brooks 1917- *40*
Smith, Elwood H. 1941- *203*
Smith, Emily Wing 1980- *215*
Smith, Emma 1923- *52*
　Brief entry *36*
Smith, (Katherine) Eunice (Young)
　1902-1993 .... *5*
Smith, Frances C(hristine) 1904-1986 .... *3*
Smith, Gary R. 1932- *14*
Smith, Geof 1969- *102*
Smith, George Harmon 1920- *5*
Smith, Gordon 1951- *184*
Smith, Greg Leitich *152*
Smith, H(arry) Allen 1907-1976
　Obituary *20*
Smith, Helene 1937- *142*
Smith, Hope Anita *202*
Smith, Howard E(verett), Jr. 1927- *12*
Smith, Hugh L(etcher) 1921-1968 .... *5*
Smith, Imogene Henderson 1922- *12*
Smith, Jacqueline B. 1937- *39*
Smith, Jada Pinkett 1971- *161*
Smith, James Noel 1950- *193*
Smith, Janet (Buchanan) Adam
　See Adam Smith, Janet (Buchanan)

Smith, Janice Lee 1949- *155*
　Earlier sketch in SATA *54*
Smith, Jean
　See Smith, Frances C(hristine)
Smith, Jean Pajot 1945- *10*
Smith, Jeff 1958- *161*
　Earlier sketch in SATA *93*
Smith, Jeff Allen
　See Smith, Jeff
Smith, Jenny 1963- *90*
Smith, Jessie
　See Kunhardt, Edith
Smith, Jessie Willcox 1863-1935 .... *21*
　See also CLR *59*
Smith, Joan (Mary) 1933- *54*
　Brief entry *46*
Smith, Johnston
　See Crane, Stephen
Smith, Jos A. 1936- *181*
　Earlier sketches in SATA *73, 120*
Smith, Joseph Arthur
　See Smith, Jos A.
Smith, Judie R. 1936- *80*
Smith, Kirsten 1970- *210*
Smith, Lafayette
　See Higdon, Hal
Smith, Lane 1959- *179*
　Earlier sketches in SATA *76, 131*
　See also CLR *47*
Smith, Lee
　See Albion, Lee Smith
Smith, Lendon H(oward) 1921- *64*
Smith, Lillian H(elena) 1887-1983
　Obituary *32*
Smith, Linda 1949- *177*
Smith, Linell Nash 1932- *2*
Smith, Lucia B. 1943- *30*
Smith, Maggie 1965- *190*
Smith, Margaret Emily Noel Nuttall
　See Nuttall-Smith, Margaret Emily Noel
Smith, Marion Hagens 1913- *12*
Smith, Marion Jaques 1899-1987 .... *13*
Smith, Mary Ellen *10*
Smith, Marya 1945- *78*
Smith, Mike
　See Smith, Mary Ellen
Smith, Nancy Covert 1935- *12*
Smith, Norman F. 1920- *70*
　Earlier sketch in SATA *5*
Smith, Patricia Clark 1943- *96*
Smith, Pauline C.
　See Arthur, Robert, (Jr.)
Smith, Pauline C(oggeshall) 1908-1994 .... *27*
Smith, Philip Warren 1936- *46*
Smith, R. Alexander McCall
　See Smith, Alexander McCall
Smith, Rebecca 1946- *123*
Smith, Robert Kimmel 1930- *77*
　Earlier sketch in SATA *12*
Smith, Robert Paul 1915-1977 .... *52*
　Obituary *30*
Smith, Roland 1951- *193*
　Earlier sketches in SATA *115, 161*
Smith, Rosamond
　See Oates, Joyce Carol
Smith, Ruth Leslie 1902- *2*
Smith, Samantha 1972-1985
　Obituary *45*
Smith, Sandra Lee 1945- *75*
Smith, Sarah Stafford
　See Smith, Dorothy Stafford
Smith, Sharon 1947- *82*
Smith, Sherri L. 1971- *156*
Smith, Sherwood 1951- *206*
　Autobiography Feature *206*
　Earlier sketches in SATA *82, 140*
Smith, Shirley Raines
　See Raines, Shirley C(arol)
Smith, Susan Carlton 1923- *12*
Smith, Susan Mathias 1950- *43*
　Brief entry *35*

Smith, Susan Vernon 1950- *48*
   Brief entry *45*
Smith, Tim(othy R.) 1945- *151*
Smith, Ursula 1934- *54*
Smith, Vian (Crocker) 1920-1969 .... *11*
Smith, Wanda VanHoy 1926- *65*
Smith, Ward
   See Goldsmith, Howard
Smith, William A. 1918- *10*
Smith, William Jay 1918- *154*
   Autobiography Feature *154*
   Earlier sketches in SATA *2, 68*
   See also SAAS *22*
Smith, Winsome 1935- *45*
Smith, Z.Z.
   See Westheimer, David
Smith-Ankrom, M. E. 1942- *130*
Smith-Griswold, Wendy 1955- *88*
Smith-Rex, Susan J. 1950- *94*
Smithsen, Richard
   See Pellowski, Michael (Joseph)
Smithson, Ryan 1985- *216*
Smits, Teo
   See Smits, Theodore R(ichard)
Smits, Theodore R(ichard) 1905-1996 .... *45*
   Brief entry *28*
Smolinski, Dick 1932- *86*
Smothers, Ethel Footman 1944- *149*
   Earlier sketch in SATA *76*
Smucker, Anna Egan 1948- *209*
Smucker, Barbara 1915-2003 .... *130*
   Earlier sketches in SATA *29, 76*
   See also CLR *10*
   See also SAAS *11*
Smucker, Barbara Claassen
   See Smucker, Barbara
Smyth, Iain 1959- *105*
Snedeker, Caroline Dale (Parke) 1871-1956
   See YABC *2*
Sneed, Brad *191*
Sneider, Marian 1932-2005 .... *197*
Snell, Nigel (Edward Creagh) 1936- *57*
   Brief entry *40*
Snellgrove, L(aurence) E(rnest) 1928- *53*
Snelling, Dennis (Wayne) 1958- *84*
Sneve, Virginia Driving Hawk 1933- *95*
   Earlier sketch in SATA *8*
   See also CLR *2*
Snicket, Lemony 1970- *215*
   Earlier sketches in SATA *126, 187*
   See also CLR *79*
Sniegoski, Thomas E. *195*
Sniegoski, Tom
   See Sniegoski, Thomas E.
Snodgrass, Mary Ellen 1944- *75*
Snodgrass, Quentin Curtius
   See Twain, Mark
Snodgrass, Thomas Jefferson
   See Twain, Mark
Snook, Barbara (Lillian) 1913-1976 .... *34*
Snow, Alan 1959- *190*
Snow, Carol 1965- *208*
Snow, Donald Clifford 1917-1979 .... *16*
Snow, Dorothea J(ohnston) 1909- *9*
Snow, Richard F(olger) 1947- *52*
   Brief entry *37*
Snyder, Anne 1922-2001 .... *4*
   Obituary *125*
Snyder, Bernadette McCarver 1930- *97*
Snyder, Carol 1941- *35*
Snyder, Gerald S(eymour) 1933- *48*
   Brief entry *34*
Snyder, Jerome 1916-1976
   Obituary *20*
Snyder, Laurel 1974- *209*
Snyder, Midori 1954- *106*
Snyder, Paul A. 1946- *125*

Snyder, Zilpha Keatley 1927- *163*
   Autobiography Feature *163*
   Earlier sketches in SATA *1, 28, 75, 110*
   See also CLR *121*
   See also SAAS *2*
Snyderman, Reuven K. 1922- *5*
So, Meilo *162*
Sobel, June 1950- *149*
Soble, Jennie
   See Cavin, Ruth (Brodie)
Sobol, Donald J. 1924- *132*
   Earlier sketches in SATA *1, 31, 73*
   See also CLR *4*
Sobol, Harriet Langsam 1936- *47*
   Brief entry *34*
Sobol, Richard *211*
Sobol, Rose 1931- *76*
Sobott-Mogwe, Gaele 1956- *97*
Soderlind, Arthur E(dwin) 1920- *14*
Soentpiet, Chris K. 1970- *159*
   Earlier sketch in SATA *97*
Soerensen, Svend Otto 1916- *67*
Sofer, Barbara 1949- *109*
Sofer, Rachel
   See Sofer, Barbara
Softly, Barbara Frewin 1924- *12*
Sogabe, Aki *207*
Soglow, Otto 1900-1975
   Obituary *30*
Sohl, Frederic J(ohn) 1916- *10*
Sohr, Daniel 1973- *190*
Sokol, Bill
   See Sokol, William
Sokol, William 1923- *37*
Sokolov, Kirill 1930- *34*
Solbert, Romaine G. 1925- *2*
Solbert, Ronni
   See Solbert, Romaine G.
Solheim, James *133*
Solomon, Heather M. *188*
Solomon, Joan 1930- *51*
   Brief entry *40*
Solomons, Ikey Esquir
   See Thackeray, William Makepeace
Solonevich, George 1915-2003 .... *15*
Solot, Mary Lynn 1939- *12*
Soman, David 1965- *200*
Somerlott, Robert 1928-2001 .... *62*
Somers, Kevin *205*
Somervill, Barbara A(nn) 1948- *140*
Sommer, Angela
   See Sommer-Bodenburg, Angela
Sommer, Carl 1930- *175*
   Earlier sketch in SATA *126*
Sommer, Elyse 1929- *7*
Sommer, Robert 1929- *12*
Sommer-Bodenburg, Angela 1948- *113*
   Earlier sketch in SATA *63*
Sommerdorf, Norma 1926- *131*
Sommerdorf, Norma Jean
   See Sommerdorf, Norma
Sommerfelt, Aimee 1892-1975 .... *5*
Son, John *160*
Sones, Sonya *131*
Sonneborn, Ruth (Cantor) 1899-1974 .... *4*
   Obituary *27*
Sonnenblick, Jordan 1969- *185*
   See also CLR *144*
Sonnenmark, Laura A. 1958- *73*
Soo, Kean *201*
Sopko, Eugen 1949- *58*
Sorel, Edward 1929- *126*
   Brief entry *37*
   Earlier sketch in SATA *65*
Sorensen, Henri 1950- *115*
   Earlier sketch in SATA *77*
Sorensen, Svend Otto
   See Soerensen, Svend Otto
Sorensen, Virginia 1912-1991 .... *2*
   Obituary *72*
   See also SAAS *15*

Sorenson, Jane 1926- *63*
Sorenson, Margo 1946- *96*
Sorley Walker, Kathrine *41*
Sorra, Kristin *185*
Sorrells, Walter *177*
Sorrentino, Joseph N. 1937- *6*
Sortor, June Elizabeth 1939- *12*
Sortor, Toni
   See Sortor, June Elizabeth
Sosa, Hernan 1977- *203*
Soskin, V. H.
   See Ellison, Virginia H(owell)
Soto, Gary 1952- *174*
   Earlier sketches in SATA *80, 120*
   See also CLR *38*
Sotomayor, Antonio 1902-1985 .... *11*
Souci, Robert D. San
   See San Souci, Robert D.
Soudley, Henry
   See Wood, James Playsted
Souhami, Jessica *176*
Soule, Gardner (Bosworth) 1913-2000 .... *14*
Soule, Jean Conder 1919- *10*
Souster, (Holmes) Raymond 1921- *63*
South, Sheri Cobb 1959- *82*
Southall, Ivan 1921-2008 .... *134*
   Autobiography Feature *134*
   Earlier sketches in SATA *3, 68*
   See also CLR *2*
   See also SAAS *3*
Southall, Ivan Francis
   See Southall, Ivan
Southey, Robert 1774-1843 .... *54*
Southgate, Vera *54*
Souza, Janet
   See Tashjian, Janet
Sovak, Jan 1953- *115*
Sowden, Celeste
   See Walters, Celeste
Sowter, Nita *69*
Spafford, Suzy 1945- *160*
Spagnoli, Cathy 1950- *134*
   Earlier sketch in SATA *79*
Spain, Sahara Sunday 1991- *133*
Spain, Susan Rosson *185*
Spalding, Andrea 1944- *150*
   Earlier sketch in SATA *101*
Spalenka, Greg 1958- *198*
Spanfeller, James J. 1930- *19*
   See also SAAS *8*
Spanfeller, Jim
   See Spanfeller, James J.
Spangenberg, Judith Dunn 1942- *5*
Spangler, Brie *212*
Spanyol, Jessica 1965- *206*
   Earlier sketch in SATA *137*
Spar, Jerome 1918- *10*
Sparks, Barbara 1942- *78*
Sparks, Beatrice (Mathews) 1918- *44*
   Brief entry *28*
   See also CLR *139*
Sparks, Mary W. 1920- *15*
Spaulding, Douglas
   See Bradbury, Ray
Spaulding, Leonard
   See Bradbury, Ray
Spaulding, Norma *107*
Speare, Elizabeth George 1908-1994 .... *62*
   Obituary *83*
   Earlier sketch in SATA *5*
   See also CLR *8*
Spearing, Judith (Mary Harlow) 1922- *9*
Spears, Rick *182*
Speck, Katie *196*
Speck, Nancy 1959- *104*
Specking, Inez 1890-1960(?) *11*
Speed, Nell
   See Keats, Emma
   and Sampson, Emma (Keats) Speed
Speed, Nell (Ewing) 1878-1913 .... *68*
Speer, Bonnie Stahlman 1929- *113*

Speer-Lyon, Tammie L. 1965- 89
Speicher, Helen Ross S(mith) 1915- 8
Speir, Nancy 1958- 210
Earlier sketch in SATA 81
Spellman, John W(illard) 1934- 14
Spellman, Roger G.
See Cox, William R(obert)
Spelman, Cornelia Maude 1946- 144
Earlier sketch in SATA 96
Spelman, Mary 1934- 28
Spelvin, George
See Lerangis, Peter
and Phillips, David Atlee
Spence, Cynthia
See Eble, Diane
Spence, Eleanor (Rachel) 1928- 21
See also CLR 26
Spence, Geraldine 1931- 47
Spencer, Ann 1918- 10
Spencer, Britt 206
Spencer, Cornelia
See Yaukey, Grace S(ydenstricker)
Spencer, Donald D(ean) 1931- 41
Spencer, Elizabeth 1921- 14
Spencer, Leonard G.
See Garrett, Randall
and Silverberg, Robert
Spencer, William 1922- 9
Spencer, Zane A(nn) 1935- 35
Sper, Emily 1957- 142
Speregen, Devra Newberger 1964- 84
Sperling, Dan(iel Lee) 1949- 65
Sperry, Armstrong W. 1897-1976 1
Obituary 27
Sperry, Raymond
See Garis, Howard R.
Sperry, Raymond, Jr. 1
Spetter, Jung-Hee 1969- 134
Spicer, Dorothy Gladys -1975 32
Spiegel, Beth 184
Spiegelman, Art 1948- 158
Earlier sketch in SATA 109
Spiegelman, Judith M. 5
Spielberg, Steven 1947- 32
Spier, Peter (Edward) 1927- 54
Earlier sketch in SATA 4
See also CLR 5
Spilhaus, Athelstan (Frederick) 1911-1998 .. 13
Obituary 102
Spilka, Arnold 1917- 6
Spillane, Frank Morrison
See Spillane, Mickey
Spillane, Mickey 1918-2006 66
Obituary 176
Spinelli, Eileen 1942- 186
Earlier sketches in SATA 38, 101, 150
Spinelli, Jerry 1941- 195
Earlier sketches in SATA 39, 71, 110, 158
See also CLR 82
Spink, Reginald (William) 1905-1994 11
Spinka, Penina Keen 1945- 72
Spinner, Stephanie 1943- 132
Earlier sketches in SATA 38, 91
Spinossimus
See White, William, Jr.
Spiotta-DiMare, Loren 173
Spires, Ashley 1978- 183
Spires, Elizabeth 1952- 215
Earlier sketches in SATA 71, 111
Spiridellis, Gregg 1971(?)- 199
Spirin, Gennadii
See Spirin, Gennady
Spirin, Gennadij
See Spirin, Gennady
Spirin, Gennady 1948- 204
Earlier sketches in SATA 95, 134
See also CLR 88
Spiro, Ruth 208
Spivak, Dawnine 101
Spizman, Robyn Freedman 194
Spohn, David 1948- 72

Spohn, Kate 1962- 147
Earlier sketch in SATA 87
Spollen, Christopher 1952- 12
Spooner, Michael (Tim) 1954- 92
Spoor, Mike 218
Spowart, Robin 1947- 177
Earlier sketch in SATA 82
Spradlin, Michael P. 204
Sprague, Gretchen 1926-2003 27
Spranger, Nina 1969- 203
Sprengel, Artie
See Lerangis, Peter
Sprigge, Elizabeth (Miriam Squire)
1900-1974 10
Spring, (Robert) Howard 1889-1965 28
Springer, Margaret 1941- 78
Springer, Marilyn Harris 1931- 47
Springer, Nancy 1948- 172
Earlier sketches in SATA 65, 110
Springstubb, Tricia 1950- 78
Brief entry 40
Earlier sketch in SATA 46
Spudvilas, Anne 1951- 199
Earlier sketch in SATA 94
Spurll, Barbara 1952- 78
Spurr, Elizabeth 172
Spykman, E(lizabeth) C(hoate) 1896-1965 .. 10
See also CLR 35
Spyri, Johanna (Heusser) 1827-1901 100
Earlier sketch in SATA 19
See also CLR 115
Squires, Janet 215
Squires, Phil
See Barker, S. Omar
Srba, Lynne 98
Sreenivasan, Jyotsna 1964- 101
S-Ringi, Kjell
See Ringi, Kjell (Arne Soerensen)
Staake, Bob 1957- 209
Stacey, Cherylyn 1945- 96
Stacy, Donald
See Pohl, Frederik
Stadler, John 204
Stadtler, Bea 1921- 17
Stafford, Jean 1915-1979
Obituary 22
Stafford, Liliana 1950- 141
Stafford, Paul 1966- 116
Stahl, Ben(jamin) 1910-1987 5
Obituary 54
Stahl, Hilda 1938-1993 48
Obituary 77
Stahler, David, Jr. 218
Earlier sketch in SATA 162
Staines, Bill 1949- 213
Stainton, Sue 187
Stair, Gobin (John) 1912- 35
Stalder, Valerie 27
Stamaty, Mark Alan 1947- 12
Stambler, Irwin 1924- 5
Stampler, Ann Redisch 209
Standiford, Natalie 1961- 169
Earlier sketch in SATA 81
Stanek, Lou Willett 1931- 63
Stang, Judit 1921-1977 29
Stang, Judy
See Stang, Judit
Stangl, (Mary) Jean 1928- 67
Stanhope, Eric
See Hamilton, Charles (Harold St. John)
Stankevich, Boris 1928- 2
Stanley, Diane 1943- 213
Brief entry 32
Earlier sketches in SATA 37, 80, 115, 164
See also CLR 46
See also SAAS 15
Stanley, George Edward 1942- 67
Earlier sketches in SATA 53, 111, 157, 1
Stanley, Jerry 1941- 127
Earlier sketch in SATA 79

Stanley, Mandy 165
Stanley, Robert
See Hamilton, Charles (Harold St. John)
Stanley, Sanna 1962- 145
Stanli, Sue
See Meilach, Dona Z(weigoron)
Stanstead, John
See Groom, Arthur William
Stanton, Karen 1960- 190
Stanton, Schuyler
See Baum, L. Frank
Staples, Suzanne Fisher 1945- 207
Earlier sketches in SATA 70, 105, 151
See also CLR 137
Stapleton, Marjorie (Winifred) 1932- 28
Stapp, Arthur D(onald) 1906-1972 4
Starbird, Kaye 1916- 6
See also CLR 60
Stark, Evan 1942- 78
Stark, James
See Goldston, Robert (Conroy)
Stark, Ken 1943- 199
Stark, Ulf 1944- 124
Starke, Ruth (Elaine) 1946- 129
Starkey, Marion L(ena) 1901-1991 13
Starr, Ward
See Manes, Stephen
Starret, William
See McClintock, Marshall
Starr Taylor, Bridget 1959- 99
Stasiak, Krystyna 49
Staub, Frank 1949- 116
Staub, Frank Jacob
See Staub, Frank
Staub, Wendy Corsi 1964- 114
Stauffacher, Sue 1961- 199
Earlier sketch in SATA 155
Stauffer, Don
See Berkebile, Fred D(onovan)
Staunton, Schuyler
See Baum, L. Frank
Staunton, Ted 1956- 167
Earlier sketch in SATA 112
Stead, Judy 210
Stead, Rebecca 1968(?)- 188
Steadman, Ralph 1936- 123
Earlier sketch in SATA 32
Steadman, Ralph Idris
See Steadman, Ralph
Stearman, Kaye 1951- 118
Stearn, Ted 1961- 218
Stearns, Monroe (Mather) 1913-1987 5
Obituary 55
Steckler, Arthur 1921-1985 65
Steding, Laurie 1953- 119
Steel, Danielle 1947- 66
Steel, Danielle Fernande
See Steel, Danielle
Steele, Addison II
See Lupoff, Richard A(llen)
Steele, Alexander 1958- 116
Steele, Henry Maxwell
See Steele, Max
Steele, Mary 1930- 94
Steele, Mary Q(uintard Govan) 1922-1992 .. 51
Obituary 72
Earlier sketch in SATA 3
Steele, Max 1922-2005 168
Earlier sketch in SATA 10
Steele, Philip 1948- 140
Earlier sketch in SATA 81
Steele, William O(wen) 1917-1979 51
Obituary 27
Earlier sketch in SATA 1
Steelhammer, Ilona 1952- 98
Steelsmith, Shari 1962- 72
Stefanik, Alfred T. 1939- 55
Steffanson, Con
See Cassiday, Bruce (Bingham)
and Goulart, Ron

Steffens, Bradley 1955- *166*
  Earlier sketch in SATA 77
Steffensmeier, Alexander 1977- *195*
Stegeman, Janet Allais 1923- *49*
  Brief entry *49*
Steggall, Susan 1967- *182*
Steig, William 1907-2003 .... *111*
  Obituary *149*
  Earlier sketches in SATA 18, 70
  See also CLR 103
Steig, William H.
  See Steig, William
Stein, David Ezra *211*
  Earlier sketch in SATA 180
Stein, Janet 1955- *218*
Stein, M(eyer) L(ewis) 1920- *6*
Stein, Mathilde 1969- *195*
Stein, Mini *2*
Stein, R(ichard) Conrad 1937- *154*
  Earlier sketches in SATA 31, 82
Stein, Wendy 1951- *77*
Steinbeck, John 1902-1968 .... *9*
Steinbeck, John Ernst
  See Steinbeck, John
Steinberg, Alfred 1917-1995 .... *9*
Steinberg, David 1962- *200*
Steinberg, D.J.
  See Steinberg, David
Steinberg, Fannie 1899-1990 .... *43*
Steinberg, Fred J. 1933- *4*
Steinberg, Phillip Orso 1921- *34*
Steinberg, Rafael (Mark) 1927- *45*
Steinberg, Saul 1914-1999 .... *67*
Steincrohn, Maggie
  See Davis, Maggie S.
Steiner, Barbara A(nnette) 1934- *83*
  Earlier sketch in SATA 13
  See also SAAS 13
Steiner, Charlotte 1900-1981 .... *45*
Steiner, George 1929- *62*
Steiner, Joan *199*
  Earlier sketch in SATA 110
Steiner, Jorg
  See Steiner, Jorg
Steiner, Jorg 1930- *35*
Steiner, K. Leslie
  See Delany, Samuel R., Jr.
Steiner, Stan(ley) 1925-1987 .... *14*
  Obituary *50*
Steins, Richard 1942- *79*
Stem, Jacqueline 1931- *110*
Stemple, Heidi E.Y. 1966- *214*
Stemple, Jason *179*
Steneman, Shep 1945- *132*
Stengel, Joyce A. 1938- *158*
Stephanie, Gordon
  See Gordon, Stephanie Jacob
Stephens, Alice Barber 1858-1932 .... *66*
Stephens, Casey
  See Wagner, Sharon B.
Stephens, Henrietta Henkle 1909-1993 .... *6*
Stephens, J.B.
  See Lynn, Tracy
Stephens, Mary Jo 1935- *8*
Stephens, Rebecca 1961- *141*
Stephens, Reed
  See Donaldson, Stephen R.
Stephens, Suzanne
  See Kirby, Susan E.
Stephens, William M(cLain) 1925- *21*
Stephensen, A. M.
  See Manes, Stephen
Stephenson, Lynda 1941- *179*
Stephenson, Lynda A.
  See Stephenson, Lynda
Stepp, Ann 1935- *29*
Stepto, Michele 1946- *61*
Steptoe, Javaka 1971- *213*
  Earlier sketch in SATA 151

Steptoe, John (Lewis) 1950-1989 .... *63*
  Earlier sketch in SATA 8
  See also CLR 12
Sterling, Brett
  See Bradbury, Ray
  and Hamilton, Edmond
  and Samachson, Joseph
Sterling, Dorothy 1913-2008 .... *83*
  Autobiography Feature *127*
  Obituary *200*
  Earlier sketch in SATA 1
  See also CLR 1
  See also SAAS 2
Sterling, Helen
  See Watts, Helen L. Hoke
Sterling, Philip 1907-1989 .... *8*
  Obituary *63*
Sterling, Shirley (Anne) 1948- *101*
Stern, Ellen Norman 1927- *26*
Stern, Judith M. 1951- *75*
Stern, Madeleine
  See Stern, Madeleine B.
Stern, Madeleine B. 1912-2007 .... *14*
Stern, Madeleine Bettina
  See Stern, Madeleine B.
Stern, Maggie 1953- *156*
Stern, Philip Van Doren 1900-1984 .... *13*
  Obituary *39*
Stern, Simon 1943- *15*
Sterne, Emma Gelders 1894- *6*
Steurt, Marjorie Rankin 1888-1978 .... *10*
Stevens, April 1963- *208*
Stevens, Bryna 1924- *65*
Stevens, Carla M(cBride) 1928- *13*
Stevens, Chambers 1968- *128*
Stevens, Diane 1939- *94*
Stevens, Franklin 1933- *6*
Stevens, Greg
  See Cook, Glen
Stevens, Gwendolyn 1944- *33*
Stevens, Helen *209*
Stevens, Jan Romero 1953- *95*
Stevens, Janet 1953- *193*
  Earlier sketches in SATA 90, 148
Stevens, Kathleen 1936- *49*
Stevens, Leonard A. 1920- *67*
Stevens, Lucile Vernon 1899-1994 .... *59*
Stevens, Margaret Dean
  See Aldrich, Bess Streeter
Stevens, Patricia Bunning 1931- *27*
Stevens, Peter
  See Geis, Darlene Stern
Stevens, Serita 1949- *70*
Stevens, Serita Deborah
  See Stevens, Serita
Stevens, Serita Mendelson
  See Stevens, Serita
Stevens, Shira
  See Stevens, Serita
Stevenson, Anna (M.) 1905- *12*
Stevenson, Augusta 1869(?)-1976 .... *2*
  Obituary *26*
Stevenson, Burton Egbert 1872-1962 .... *25*
Stevenson, Drew 1947- *60*
Stevenson, Emma *207*
Stevenson, Harvey 1960- *148*
  Earlier sketch in SATA 80
Stevenson, James 1929- *195*
  Brief entry *34*
  Earlier sketches in SATA 42, 71, 113, 161
  See also CLR 17
Stevenson, Janet 1913- *8*
Stevenson, Robert Louis 1850-1894 .... *100*
  See also YABC 2
  See also CLR 107
Stevenson, Robert Louis Balfour
  See Stevenson, Robert Louis
Stevenson, Sucie
  See Stevenson, Sucie
Stevenson, Sucie 1956- *194*
  Earlier sketch in SATA 104

Stewart, A(gnes) C(harlotte) *15*
Stewart, Amber *181*
Stewart, Chantal 1945- *173*
  Earlier sketch in SATA 121
Stewart, Charles
  See Zurhorst, Charles (Stewart, Jr.)
Stewart, Eleanor
  See Porter, Eleanor H(odgman)
Stewart, Elisabeth J(ane) 1927- *93*
Stewart, Elizabeth Laing 1907- *6*
Stewart, Gail B. 1949- *141*
Stewart, George Rippey 1895-1980 .... *3*
  Obituary *23*
Stewart, Jennifer J. 1960- *128*
Stewart, Jennifer Jenkins
  See Stewart, Jennifer J.
Stewart, Joel *211*
  Earlier sketch in SATA 151
Stewart, John 1920- *14*
Stewart, Mary (Florence Elinor) 1916- *12*
Stewart, Mary Rainbow
  See Stewart, Mary (Florence Elinor)
Stewart, Melissa 1968- *209*
  Earlier sketches in SATA 111, 167
Stewart, Paul 1955- *199*
  Earlier sketches in SATA 114, 163
Stewart, Robert Neil 1891-1972 .... *7*
Stewart, Sarah *143*
Stewart, Scott
  See Zaffo, George J.
Stewart, Trenton Lee 1970- *216*
Stewart, W(alter) P. 1924- *53*
Stewart, Whitney 1959- *167*
  Earlier sketch in SATA 92
Stewig, John Warren 1937- *162*
  Earlier sketches in SATA 26, 110
Stickler, Soma Han 1942- *128*
Stidworthy, John 1943- *63*
Stiegemeyer, Julie *180*
Stier, Catherine *198*
Stiles, Martha Bennett *108*
  Earlier sketch in SATA 6
Still, James 1906-2001 .... *29*
  Obituary *127*
Stille, Darlene R. 1942- *170*
  Earlier sketch in SATA 126
Stille, Darlene Ruth
  See Stille, Darlene R.
Stillerman, Marci *104*
Stillerman, Robbie 1947- *12*
Stilley, Frank 1918- *29*
Stilton, Geronimo *158*
Stimpson, Gerald
  See Mitchell, Adrian
Stimson, James 1964- *213*
Stine, Catherine *165*
Stine, G(eorge) Harry 1928-1997 .... *136*
  Earlier sketch in SATA 10
Stine, Jovial Bob
  See Stine, R.L.
Stine, R.L. 1943- *194*
  Earlier sketches in SATA 31, 76, 129
  See also CLR 111
Stine, Robert Lawrence
  See Stine, R.L.
Stinetorf, Louise (Allender) 1900-1992 .... *10*
Stinson, Kathy 1952- *98*
Stirling, Arthur
  See Sinclair, Upton
Stirling, Ian 1941- *77*
Stirling, Nora B(romley) 1900-1997 .... *3*
Stirnweis, Shannon 1931- *10*
Stobbs, William 1914-2000 .... *17*
  Obituary *120*
Stock, Carolmarie 1951- *75*
Stock, Catherine 1952- *214*
  Earlier sketches in SATA 65, 114, 158
Stockdale, Susan 1954- *206*
  Earlier sketch in SATA 98
Stockham, Peter (Alan) 1928- *57*

Stockton, Francis Richard 1834-1902 .... *44*
  Brief entry *32*
Stockton, Frank R.
  See Stockton, Francis Richard
Stockwell-Moniz, Marc J. 1954- *164*
Stoddard, Edward G. 1923- *10*
Stoddard, Hope 1900-1987 .... *6*
Stoddard, Sandol 1927- *98*
  Earlier sketch in SATA *14*
Stoehr, Shelley 1969- *107*
Stoeke, Janet Morgan 1957- *202*
  Earlier sketches in SATA *90, 136*
Stohner, Anu 1952- *179*
Stoiko, Michael 1919- *14*
Stojic, Manya 1967- *156*
Stoker, Abraham
  See Stoker, Bram
Stoker, Bram 1847-1912 .... *29*
Stokes, Cedric
  See Beardmore, George
Stokes, Jack (Tilden) 1923- *13*
Stokes, Olivia Pearl 1916- *32*
Stolarz, Laurie Faria *203*
Stolz, Mary 1920-2006 .... *133*
  Obituary *180*
  Earlier sketches in SATA *10, 71*
  See also SAAS *3*
Stolz, Mary Slattery
  See Stolz, Mary
Stone, Alan
  See Svenson, Andrew E(dward)
Stone, David K(arl) 1922- *9*
Stone, David Lee 1978- *166*
Stone, Eugenia 1879-1971 .... *7*
Stone, Gene
  See Stone, Eugenia
Stone, Helen V(irginia) *6*
Stone, Idella Purnell
  See Purnell, Idella
Stone, Ikey
  See Purnell, Idella
Stone, Irving 1903-1989 .... *3*
  Obituary *64*
Stone, Jeff *178*
Stone, Jon 1931-1997 .... *39*
  Obituary *95*
Stone, Josephine Rector
  See Dixon, Jeanne
Stone, Kyle M. 1972- *202*
Stone, Lesley
  See Trevor, Elleston
Stone, Peter 1930-2003 .... *65*
  Obituary *143*
Stone, Phoebe *205*
  Earlier sketch in SATA *134*
Stone, Raymond *1*
Stone, Rosetta
  See Dr. Seuss
Stone, Tanya Lee 1965- *217*
  Earlier sketch in SATA *182*
Stonehouse, Bernard 1926- *140*
  Earlier sketches in SATA *13, 80*
Stones, (Cyril) Anthony 1934- *72*
Stong, Phil(ip Duffield) 1899-1957 .... *32*
Stoops, Erik D(aniel) 1966- *142*
  Earlier sketch in SATA *78*
Stoppelmoore, Cheryl Jean
  See Ladd, Cheryl (Jean)
Stops, Sue 1936- *86*
Storace, Patricia *193*
Storad, Conrad J. 1957- *119*
Storey, Margaret 1926- *9*
Storey, Victoria Carolyn 1945- *16*
Stork, Francisco
  See Stork, Francisco X.
Stork, Francisco X. 1953- *210*
Storme, Peter
  See Stern, Philip Van Doren
Storms, Patricia 1963- *217*

Storr, Catherine (Cole) 1913-2001 .... *87*
  Obituary *122*
  Earlier sketch in SATA *9*
Story, Josephine
  See Loring, Emilie (Baker)
Stotko, Mary-Ann 1960- *154*
Stott, Ann *219*
Stott, Dorothy (M.) 1958- *99*
  Earlier sketch in SATA *67*
Stott, Dot
  See Stott, Dorothy (M.)
Stotter, Mike 1957- *108*
Stout, William 1949- *132*
Stoutenburg, Adrien (Pearl) 1916-1982 .... *3*
Stoutland, Allison 1963- *130*
Stover, Allan C(arl) 1938- *14*
Stover, Jill (Griffin) 1958- *82*
Stover, Marjorie Filley 1914- *9*
Stowe, Harriet Beecher 1811-1896
  See YABC *1*
  See also CLR *131*
Stowe, Harriet Elizabeth Beecher
  See Stowe, Harriet Beecher
Stowe, Leland 1899-1994 .... *60*
  Obituary *78*
Stowe, Rosetta
  See Ogan, George F.
  and Ogan, Margaret E. (Nettles)
Stower, Adam *195*
Strachan, Bruce 1959- *205*
Strachan, Ian 1938- *85*
Strachan, Linda *167*
Strachan, Margaret Pitcairn 1908-1998 .... *14*
Strahinich, H. C.
  See Strahinich, Helen C.
Strahinich, Helen C. 1949- *78*
Strait, Treva Adams 1909-2002 .... *35*
Strand, Mark 1934- *41*
Strange, Philippa
  See Coury, Louise Andree
Stranger, Joyce
  See Wilson, Joyce M.
Strangis, Joel 1948- *124*
Strannigan, Shawn 1956- *93*
Strannigan, Shawn Alyne
  See Strannigan, Shawn
Strasser, Todd 1950- *215*
  Earlier sketches in SATA *41, 45, 71, 107, 153*
  See also CLR *11*
Stratemeyer, Edward L. 1862-1930 .... *100*
  Earlier sketches in SATA *1, 67*
  See Adams, Harrison
Stratford, Philip 1927- *47*
Stratton, Allan 1951- *178*
Stratton, J. M.
  See Whitlock, Ralph
Stratton, Thomas
  See Coulson, Robert S(tratton)
  and DeWeese, Thomas Eugene
Stratton-Porter, Gene 1863-1924 .... *15*
  See also CLR *87*
Strauss, Gwen 1963- *77*
Strauss, Joyce 1936- *53*
Strauss, Linda Leopold 1942- *127*
Strauss, Susan (Elizabeth) 1954- *75*
Strayer, E. Ward
  See Stratemeyer, Edward L.
Streano, Vince(nt Catello) 1945- *20*
Streatfeild, Mary Noel
  See Streatfeild, Noel
Streatfeild, Noel 1897(?)-1986 .... *20*
  Obituary *48*
  See also CLR *83*
Street, Janet Travell 1959- *84*
Street, Julia Montgomery 1898-1993 .... *11*
Streissguth, Thomas 1958- *116*
Strelkoff, Tatiana 1957- *89*
Stren, Patti 1949- *88*
  Brief entry *41*
  See also CLR *5*

Strete, Craig Kee 1950- *96*
  Earlier sketch in SATA *44*
Stretton, Barbara (Humphrey) 1936- *43*
  Brief entry *35*
Strickland, Brad 1947- *200*
  Earlier sketches in SATA *83, 137, 142*
Strickland, Craig (A.) 1956- *102*
Strickland, Dorothy S(alley) 1933- *89*
Strickland, Michael R. 1965- *144*
  Earlier sketch in SATA *83*
Strickland, Shadra *209*
Strickland, Tessa *173*
Strickland, William Bradley
  See Strickland, Brad
Striegel, Jana 1955- *140*
Striegel-Wilson, Jana
  See Striegel, Jana
Striker, Lee
  See Clark, Margaret (D.)
Striker, Susan 1942- *63*
Stringer, Lauren 1957- *183*
  Earlier sketch in SATA *129*
Stroeyer, Poul 1923- *13*
Stromoski, Rick 1958- *111*
Strong, Charles
  See Epstein, Beryl
  and Epstein, Samuel
Strong, David
  See McGuire, Leslie (Sarah)
Strong, Jeremy 1949- *175*
  Earlier sketches in SATA *36, 105*
Strong, J.J.
  See Strong, Jeremy
Strong, Pat
  See Hough, Richard (Alexander)
Strong, Stacie 1965- *74*
Stroud, Bettye 1939- *165*
  Earlier sketch in SATA *96*
Stroud, Jonathan 1970- *213*
  Earlier sketches in SATA *102, 159*
  See also CLR *134*
Stroyer, Poul
  See Stroeyer, Poul
Strug, Kerri 1977- *108*
Stryer, Andrea Stenn 1938- *192*
Stryker, Daniel
  See Morris, Chris(topher Crosby)
  and Stump, Jane Barr
Stuart, David
  See Hoyt, Edwin P(almer), Jr.
Stuart, Derek
  See Foster, John L(ouis)
Stuart, Forbes 1924- *13*
Stuart, Ian
  See MacLean, Alistair
Stuart, Jesse (Hilton) 1906-1984 .... *2*
  Obituary *36*
Stuart, Ruth McEnery 1849(?)-1917 .... *116*
Stuart, Sheila
  See Baker, Mary Gladys Steel
Stuart-Clark, Christopher (Anthony) 1940- .. *32*
Stubis, Talivaldis 1926- *5*
Stubley, Trevor (Hugh) 1932- *22*
Stuchner, Joan Betty *209*
Stucky, Naomi R. 1922- *72*
Stucley, Elizabeth
  See Northmore, Elizabeth Florence
Stultifer, Morton
  See Curtis, Richard
Sture-Vasa, Mary
  See Alsop, Mary O'Hara
Sturges, Philemon *174*
Sturtevant, Katherine 1950- *180*
  Earlier sketch in SATA *130*
Sturton, Hugh
  See Johnston, H(ugh) A(nthony) S(tephen)
Sturtzel, Howard A(llison) 1894-1985 .... *1*
Sturtzel, Jane Levington 1903-1996 .... *1*
Stutley, D(oris) J(ean) 1959- *142*
Stutson, Caroline 1940- *104*

Stuve-Bodeen, Stephanie
　　See Bodeen, S. A.
Stux, Erica 1929- 140
Styles, (Frank) Showell 1908- 10
Stynes, Barbara White 133
Suarez, Maribel 1952- 201
Suba, Susanne 4
Suber, Melissa 213
Subond, Valerie
　　See Grayland, Valerie (Merle Spanner)
Sudbery, Rodie 1943- 42
Sudyka, Diana 208
Sue, Majella Lue 209
Suen, Anastasia 1956(?)- 157
Sufrin, Mark 1925- 76
Sugarman, Joan G. 1917- 64
Sugarman, Tracy 1921- 37
Sugita, Yutaka 1930- 36
Suhl, Yuri (Menachem) 1908-1986 8
　　Obituary 50
　　See also CLR 2
　　See also SAAS 1
Suhr, Joanne 129
Suid, Murray 1942- 27
Sullivan, Edward T. 206
Sullivan, George (Edward) 1927- 147
　　Earlier sketches in SATA 4, 89
Sullivan, Jacqueline Levering 203
Sullivan, Jody
　　See Rake, Jody
Sullivan, Kathryn A. 1954- 141
Sullivan, Mary Ann 1954- 63
Sullivan, Mary W(ilson) 1907- 13
Sullivan, Pat
　　See Messmer, Otto
Sullivan, Paul 1939- 106
Sullivan, Sarah G. 1953- 179
Sullivan, Silky 1940- 101
Sullivan, Sue
　　See Sullivan, Susan E.
Sullivan, Susan E. 1962- 123
Sullivan, Thomas Joseph, Jr. 1947- 16
Sullivan, Tom
　　See Sullivan, Thomas Joseph, Jr.
Sully, Tom 1959- 104
Sumichrast, Jozef 1948- 29
Sumiko
　　See Davies, Sumiko
Summerforest, Ivy B.
　　See Kirkup, James
Summers, Barbara 1944- 182
Summers, Cassia Joy
　　See Cowley, Joy
Summers, James L(evingston) 1910-1973 57
　　Brief entry 28
Summertree, Katonah
　　See Windsor, Patricia
Summy, Barrie 208
Sun, Chyng Feng 1959- 90
Sunderlin, Sylvia (S.) 1911-1997 28
　　Obituary 99
Sung, Betty Lee 26
Supeene, Shelagh Lynne 1952- 153
Supplee, Suzanne 204
Supraner, Robyn 1930- 101
　　Earlier sketch in SATA 20
Supree, Burt(on) 1941-1992 73
Surface, Mary Hall 1958- 126
Surge, Frank 1931- 13
Susac, Andrew 1929- 5
Susi, Geraldine Lee 1942- 98
Sussman, Cornelia Silver 1914-1999 59
Sussman, Irving 1908-1996 59
Sussman, Michael 1953- 217
Sussman, Michael B.
　　See Sussman, Michael
Sussman, Susan 1942- 48
Sutcliff, Rosemary 1920-1992 78
　　Obituary 73
　　Earlier sketches in SATA 6, 44
　　See also CLR 138

Sutcliffe, Jane 1957- 138
Sutherland, Colleen 1944- 79
Sutherland, Efua (Theodora Morgue)
　　1924-1996 25
Sutherland, Jon 1958- 167
Sutherland, Jonathan D.
　　See Sutherland, Jon
Sutherland, Jonathan David
　　See Sutherland, Jon
Sutherland, Margaret 1941- 15
Sutherland, Zena Bailey 1915-2002 37
　　Obituary 137
Suttles, Shirley (Smith) 1922- 21
Sutton, Ann (Livesay) 1923- 31
Sutton, Eve(lyn Mary) 1906-1992 26
Sutton, Felix 1910(?)-1973 31
Sutton, Jane 1950- 52
　　Brief entry 43
Sutton, Larry M(atthew) 1931- 29
Sutton, Margaret Beebe 1903-2001 1
　　Obituary 131
Sutton, Myron Daniel 1925- 31
Sutton, Roger 1956- 93
Sutton, Sally 1973- 214
Suzanne, Jamie
　　See Hawes, Louise
　　and Lantz, Francess L(in)
　　and Singleton, Linda Joy
　　and Zach, Cheryl (Byrd)
Suzuki, David 1936- 138
Suzuki, David Takayoshi
　　See Suzuki, David
Svendsen, Mark 1962- 181
　　Earlier sketch in SATA 120
Svendsen, Mark Nestor
　　See Svendsen, Mark
Svenson, Andrew E(dward) 1910-1975 2
　　Obituary 26
Swaab, Neil 1978- 191
Swaim, Jessica 1950- 202
Swain, Carol 1962- 172
Swain, Gwenyth 1961- 134
　　Earlier sketch in SATA 84
Swain, Ruth
　　See Swain, Ruth Freeman
Swain, Ruth Freeman 1951- 161
　　Earlier sketch in SATA 119
Swain, Su Zan (Noguchi) 1916- 21
Swallow, Pamela Curtis 178
Swamp, Jake 1941- 98
Swan, Susan 1944- 108
　　Earlier sketch in SATA 22
Swann, Brian (Stanley Frank) 1940- 116
Swann, E.L.
　　See Lasky, Kathryn
Swann, Ruth Rice 1920- 84
Swanson, Diane 1944- 203
Swanson, Helen M(cKendry) 1919- 94
Swanson, June 1931- 76
Swanson, Susan Marie 209
Swanson, Wayne 1942- 167
Swarner, Kristina 1965- 215
Swarthout, Glendon (Fred) 1918-1992 26
Swarthout, Kathryn 1919- 7
Swayne, Sam(uel F.) 1907- 53
Swayne, Zoa (Lourana) 1905- 53
Sweat, Lynn 1934- 168
　　Earlier sketch in SATA 57
Swede, George 1940- 67
Sweeney, James B(artholomew) 1910-1999 . 21
Sweeney, Joyce 1955- 167
　　Earlier sketches in SATA 65, 68, 108
Sweeney, Joyce Kay
　　See Sweeney, Joyce
Sweeney, Karen O'Connor
　　See O'Connor, Karen
Sweeney, Matthew (Gerard) 1952- 156
Sweet, Melissa 1956- 211
　　Earlier sketch in SATA 172
Sweet, Sarah C.
　　See Jewett, Sarah Orne

Sweetland, Nancy A(nn) 1934- 48
Swenson, Allan A(rmstrong) 1933- 21
Swenson, May 1919-1989 15
Swentzell, Rina 1939- 79
Swiatkowska, Gabi 1971(?)- 180
Swift, Bryan
　　See Knott, William C(ecil, Jr.)
Swift, David
　　See Kaufmann, John
Swift, Hildegarde Hoyt 1890(?)-1977
　　Obituary 20
Swift, Jonathan 1667-1745 19
　　See also CLR 53
Swift, Merlin
　　See Leeming, Joseph
Swiger, Elinor Porter 1927- 8
Swinburne, Laurence (Joseph) 1924- 9
Swinburne, Stephen R. 1952- 188
　　Earlier sketch in SATA 150
Swinburne, Steve
　　See Swinburne, Stephen R.
Swindells, Robert (Edward) 1939- 150
　　Brief entry 34
　　Earlier sketches in SATA 50, 80
　　See also SAAS 14
Swinford, Betty (June Wells) 1927- 58
Swinford, Bob
　　See Swinford, Betty (June Wells)
Swithen, John
　　See King, Stephen
Switzer, Ellen 1923- 48
Swope, Sam 156
Swope, Samuel
　　See Swope, Sam
Sybesma, Jetske
　　See Ironside, Jetske
Sydney, Frank
　　See Warwick, Alan R(oss)
Sydor, Colleen 1960- 207
Sykes, Julie 1963- 202
Sylvada, Peter 1964- 202
Sylvester, Natalie G(abry) 1922- 22
Syme, (Neville) Ronald 1913-1992 87
　　Earlier sketch in SATA 2
Symes, R. F. 77
Symes, Ruth Louise 1962- 179
Symons, (Dorothy) Geraldine 1909- 33
Symons, Stuart
　　See Stanley, George Edward
Symynkywicz, Jeffrey B. 1954- 87
Symynkywicz, Jeffrey Bruce
　　See Symynkywicz, Jeffrey B.
Synge, (Phyllis) Ursula 1930- 9
Sypher, Lucy Johnston 1907- 7
Szasz, Suzanne (Shorr) 1915-1997 13
　　Obituary 99
Szekeres, Cyndy 1933- 157
　　Autobiography Feature 157
　　Earlier sketches in SATA 5, 60, 131
　　See also SAAS 13
Szekessy, Tanja 98
Szpura, Beata 1961- 93
Szuc, Jeff 1975- 220
Szudek, Agnes S(usan) P(hilomena) 57
　　Brief entry 49
Szulc, Tad 1926-2001 26
Szydlow, Jarl
　　See Szydlowski, Mary Vigliante
Szydlowski, Mary Vigliante 1946- 94
Szymanski, Lois 1957- 91

T

Taback, Simms 1932- 170
　　Brief entry 36
　　Earlier sketches in SATA 40, 104
　　See also CLR 100
Taber, Gladys (Bagg) 1899-1980
　　Obituary 22

Tabor, Nancy Maria Grande 1949- *161*
  Earlier sketch in SATA *89*
Tabrah, Ruth Milander 1921- *14*
Tacang, Brian *213*
Tackach, James 1953- *123*
Tackach, James M.
  See Tackach, James
Tadgell, Nicole 1969- *220*
  Earlier sketch in SATA *177*
Tafolla, Carmen 1951- *220*
Tafolla, Mary Carmen
  See Tafolla, Carmen
Tafuri, Nancy 1946- *192*
  Autobiography Feature *192*
  Earlier sketches in SATA *39, 75, 130*
  See also CLR *74*
  See also SAAS *14*
Tagg, Christine Elizabeth 1962- *138*
Tagliaferro, Linda *173*
Taha, Karen T(erry) 1942- *156*
  Earlier sketch in SATA *71*
Tai, Sharon O. 1963- *153*
Tait, Douglas 1944- *12*
Takabayashi, Mari 1960- *156*
  Earlier sketch in SATA *115*
Takahashi, Hideko *209*
Takahashi, Rumiko 1957- *163*
Takakjian, Portia 1930- *15*
Takashima, Misako
  See Misako Rocks!
Takashima, Shizuye 1928- *13*
Takayama, Sandi 1962- *106*
Takeda, Pete(r M.) 1964- *148*
Tal, Eve 1947- *176*
Talbert, Marc (Alan) 1953- *154*
  Autobiography Feature *154*
  Earlier sketches in SATA *68, 99*
Talbot, Charlene Joy 1928- *10*
Talbot, Toby 1928- *14*
Talbott, Hudson 1949- *212*
  Earlier sketches in SATA *84, 131*
Taliaferro, Dorothy L.
  See Martin, Del
Talifero, Gerald 1950- *75*
Talker, T.
  See Rands, William Brighty
Tallarico, Tony 1933- *116*
Tallcott, Emogene *10*
Tallec, Olivier 1970- *197*
Tallis, Robyn
  See Smith, Sherwood
Tallon, Robert 1939- *43*
  Brief entry *28*
Talmadge, Marian *14*
Tamaki, Jillian 1980- *201*
Tamar, Erika 1934- *150*
  Earlier sketches in SATA *62, 101*
Tamarin, Alfred H. 1913-1980 .... *13*
Tamburine, Jean 1930- *12*
Tames, Richard (Lawrence) 1946- *102*
  Earlier sketch in SATA *67*
Tamminga, Frederick W(illiam) 1934- *66*
Tammuz, Benjamin 1919-1989
  Obituary *63*
Tan, Amy 1952- *75*
Tan, Amy Ruth
  See Tan, Amy
Tan, Shaun 1974- *198*
Tanaka, Beatrice 1932- *76*
Tanaka, Shelley *214*
  Earlier sketch in SATA *136*
Tanaka, Yoko 1947- *215*
Tang, Charles 1948- *81*
Tang, Greg *172*
Tang, You-Shan 1946- *53*
Tania B.
  See Blixen, Karen
Tankard, Jeremy 1973- *191*
Tannen, Mary 1943- *37*
Tannenbaum, Beulah Goldstein 1916- *3*
Tannenbaum, D(onald) Leb 1948- *42*

Tanner, Jane 1946- *74*
Tanner, Louise S(tickney) 1922-2000 .... *9*
Tanobe, Miyuki 1937- *23*
Tanselle, Eve 1933- *125*
Tapio, Pat Decker
  See Kines, Pat Decker
Tapp, Kathy Kennedy 1949- *88*
  Brief entry *50*
Tarbescu, Edith 1939- *107*
Tarkington, (Newton) Booth 1869-1946 .... *17*
Tarpley, Natasha A(nastasia) 1971- *147*
Tarr, Judith 1955- *149*
  Earlier sketch in SATA *64*
Tarry, Ellen 1906- *16*
  See also CLR *26*
  See also SAAS *16*
Tarshis, Jerome 1936- *9*
Tarshis, Lauren *187*
Tarsky, Sue 1946- *41*
Taschek, Karen 1956- *185*
Tashjian, Janet 1956- *151*
  Earlier sketch in SATA *102*
Tashjian, Virginia A. 1921-2008 .... *3*
Tasker, James 1908- *9*
Tate, Don(ald E.) *159*
Tate, Eleanora E. 1948- *191*
  Earlier sketches in SATA *38, 94*
  See also CLR *37*
Tate, Eleanora Elaine
  See Tate, Eleanora E.
Tate, Ellalice
  See Hibbert, Eleanor Alice Burford
Tate, Joan 1922- *86*
  Earlier sketch in SATA *9*
  See also SAAS *20*
Tate, Mary Anne
  See Hale, Arlene
Tate, Nikki *134*
Tate, Richard
  See Masters, Anthony (Richard)
Tate, Suzanne 1930- *91*
Tatham, Betty *142*
Tatham, Campbell
  See Elting, Mary
Tatham, Julie
  See Tatham, Julie Campbell
Tatham, Julie Campbell 1908-1999 .... *80*
Tavares, Matt *198*
  Earlier sketch in SATA *159*
Tavares, Victor 1971- *176*
Taves, Isabella 1915- *27*
Tayleur, Karen 1961- *213*
Taylor, Alastair 1959- *130*
Taylor, Andrew 1951- *70*
Taylor, Andrew John Robert
  See Taylor, Andrew
Taylor, Ann 1782-1866 .... *41*
  Brief entry *35*
Taylor, Audilee Boyd 1931- *59*
Taylor, Barbara J. 1927- *10*
Taylor, Ben
  See Strachan, Ian
Taylor, Brooke *205*
Taylor, Carl 1937-2010 .... *14*
Taylor, Cheryl Munro 1957- *96*
Taylor, Cora (Lorraine) 1936- *103*
  Earlier sketch in SATA *64*
  See also CLR *63*
Taylor, Dave 1948- *78*
Taylor, David
  See Taylor, Dave
Taylor, David 1900-1965 .... *10*
Taylor, Debbie A. 1955- *169*
Taylor, Eleanor 1969- *206*
Taylor, Elizabeth 1912-1975 .... *13*
Taylor, Florance Walton *9*
Taylor, Florence M(arian Tompkins)
  1892-1983 .... *9*
Taylor, Gage 1942-2000 .... *87*
Taylor, Geoff 1946- *204*

Taylor, G.P. 1958(?)- *216*
  Earlier sketch in SATA *156*
Taylor, Graham Peter
  See Taylor, G.P.
Taylor, Greg 1951- *221*
Taylor, Herb(ert Norman, Jr.) 1942-1987 ..... *22*
  Obituary *54*
Taylor, J. David
  See Taylor, Dave
Taylor, Jane 1783-1824 .... *41*
  Brief entry *35*
Taylor, Jerry D(uncan) 1938- *47*
Taylor, John Robert
  See Taylor, Andrew
Taylor, Judy
  See Hough, Judy Taylor
Taylor, Kenneth N. 1917-2005 .... *26*
Taylor, Kenneth Nathaniel
  See Taylor, Kenneth N.
Taylor, Kim *180*
Taylor, L(ester) B(arbour), Jr. 1932- *27*
Taylor, Lois Dwight Cole
  See Cole, Lois Dwight
Taylor, Louise Todd 1939- *47*
Taylor, Margaret 1950- *106*
Taylor, Mark 1927- *32*
  Brief entry *28*
Taylor, Mildred D. 1943- *135*
  See also CLR *144*
  See also SAAS *5*
Taylor, Mildred Delois
  See Taylor, Mildred D.
Taylor, Paula (Wright) 1942- *48*
  Brief entry *33*
Taylor, Peter Lane *210*
Taylor, Robert Lewis 1912-1998 .... *10*
Taylor, Sean 1965- *192*
Taylor, Sydney (Brenner) 1904(?)-1978 .... *28*
  Obituary *26*
  Earlier sketch in SATA *1*
Taylor, Theodore 1921-2006 .... *128*
  Obituary *177*
  Earlier sketches in SATA *5, 54, 83*
  See also CLR *30*
  See also SAAS *4*
Taylor, William 1938- *164*
  Earlier sketches in SATA *78, 113*
  See also CLR *63*
Taylor-Butler, Christine 1959- *218*
Tazewell, Charles 1900-1972 .... *74*
Tchana, Katrin
  See Tchana, Katrin Hyman
Tchana, Katrin H.
  See Tchana, Katrin Hyman
Tchana, Katrin Hyman 1963- *177*
  Earlier sketch in SATA *125*
Tchekhov, Anton
  See Chekhov, Anton
Tchen, Richard *120*
Tchudi, Stephen N. 1942- *55*
Teague, Bob
  See Teague, Robert
Teague, Mark 1963- *205*
  Earlier sketches in SATA *68, 99, 170*
Teague, Mark Christopher
  See Teague, Mark
Teague, Robert 1929- *32*
  Brief entry *31*
Teal, Val 1902-1997 .... *10*
  Obituary *114*
Teal, Valentine M.
  See Teal, Val
Teale, Edwin Way 1899-1980 .... *7*
  Obituary *25*
Teasdale, Sara 1884-1933 .... *32*
Tebbel, John (William) 1912-2004 .... *26*
Teckentrup, Britta 1969- *200*
Tedesco, P.R.
  See Naylor, Phyllis Reynolds
Teensma, Lynne Bertrand
  See Bertrand, Lynne

Tee-Van, Helen Damrosch 1893-1976 .... *10*
　Obituary *27*
Tegner, Bruce 1928- *62*
Teitelbaum, Michael 1953- *116*
　Earlier sketch in SATA *59*
Tejima
　See Tejima, Keizaburo
Tejima, Keizaburo 1931- *139*
　See also CLR *20*
Telander, Todd (G.) 1967- *88*
Teleki, Geza 1943- *45*
Telemaque, Eleanor Wong 1934- *43*
Telescope, Tom
　See Newbery, John
Tellis, Annabel 1967- *191*
Temkin, Sara Anne Schlossberg 1913-1996 . *26*
Temko, Florence *13*
Tempest, Margaret Mary 1892-1982
　Obituary *33*
Templar, Maurice
　See Groom, Arthur William
Temple, Arthur
　See Northcott, (William) Cecil
Temple, Charles 1947- *79*
Temple, Frances (Nolting) 1945-1995 .... *85*
Temple, Herbert 1919- *45*
Temple, Paul
　See McConnell, James Douglas Rutherford
Temple, William F(rederick) 1914-1989 .... *107*
Tenggren, Gustaf 1896-1970 .... *18*
　Obituary *26*
Tennant, Kylie
　See Rodd, Kylie Tennant
Tennant, Veronica 1947- *36*
Tenneshaw, S.M.
　See Beaumont, Charles
　and Garrett, Randall
　and Silverberg, Robert
Tenniel, John 1820-1914 .... *74*
　Brief entry *27*
　See also CLR *146*
Tepper, Sheri S. 1929- *113*
Terada, Alice M. 1928- *90*
Terban, Marvin 1940- *54*
　Brief entry *45*
Teresi, Judith M.
　See Goldberger, Judith M.
ter Haar, Jaap 1922- *6*
　See also CLR *15*
Terhune, Albert Payson 1872-1942 .... *15*
Terkel, Susan N(eiburg) 1948- *103*
　Earlier sketch in SATA *59*
Terlouw, Jan (Cornelis) 1931- *30*
Terrazzini, Daniela Jaglenka *218*
Terrell, John Upton 1900-1988
　Obituary *60*
Terrill, Beth *198*
Terrill, Elizabeth
　See Terrill, Beth
Terris, Susan 1937- *77*
　Earlier sketch in SATA *3*
Terry, Luther L(eonidas) 1911-1985 .... *11*
　Obituary *42*
Terry, Margaret
　See Dunnahoo, Terry Janson
Terry, Walter 1913-1982 .... *14*
Terry, Will 1966- *205*
Terzian, James P. 1915- *14*
Tessendorf, K(enneth) C(harles) 1925-2003 . *75*
　Obituary *142*
Tessler, Manya *200*
Tessler, Stephanie Gordon
　See Gordon, Stephanie Jacob
Testa, Dom *208*
Tester, Sylvia Root 1939- *64*
　Brief entry *37*
Tether, (Cynthia) Graham 1950- *46*
　Brief entry *36*
Tetzner, Lisa 1894-1963 .... *169*
Thach, James Otis 1969- *195*
Thacher, Mary McGrath 1933- *9*

Thackeray, William Makepeace 1811-1863 .. *23*
Thaler, Michael C.
　See Thaler, Mike
Thaler, Mike 1936- *215*
　Brief entry *47*
　Earlier sketches in SATA *56, 93*
Thaler, Shmuel 1958- *126*
　Earlier sketch in SATA *72*
Thamer, Katie 1955- *42*
Thane, Elswyth 1900-1984(?) *32*
Tharp, Louise (Marshall) Hall 1898-1992 ..... *3*
　Obituary *129*
Tharp, Tim 1957- *189*
Thayer, Ernest Lawrence 1863-1940 .... *60*
Thayer, Jane
　See Woolley, Catherine
Thayer, Marjorie 1908-1992 .... *74*
　Brief entry *37*
Thayer, Peter
　See Wyler, Rose
Thelwell, Norman 1923-2004 .... *14*
Themerson, Stefan 1910-1988 .... *65*
Thermes, Jennifer 1966- *155*
Theroux, Paul 1941- *109*
　Earlier sketch in SATA *44*
Theroux, Paul Edward
　See Theroux, Paul
Thesman, Jean *124*
　Earlier sketch in SATA *74*
The Tjong-Khing
　See Khing, T.T.
Thieda, Shirley Ann 1943- *13*
Thiele, Colin 1920-2006 .... *125*
　Earlier sketches in SATA *14, 72*
　See also CLR *27*
　See also SAAS *2*
Thiele, Colin Milton
　See Thiele, Colin
Thiesing, Lisa 1958- *159*
　Earlier sketch in SATA *95*
Thimmesh, Catherine *189*
Thiry, Joan (Marie) 1926- *45*
Thistlethwaite, Miles 1945- *12*
Thollander, Earl 1922- *22*
Thomas, Abigail 1941- *112*
Thomas, Andrea
　See Hill, Margaret (Ohler)
Thomas, Art(hur Lawrence) 1952- *48*
　Brief entry *38*
Thomas, Carroll
　See Ratliff, Thomas M.
　and Shmurak, Carole B.
Thomas, Dylan 1914-1953 .... *60*
Thomas, Dylan Marlais
　See Thomas, Dylan
Thomas, Egbert S.
　See Ellis, Edward S.
Thomas, Estelle Webb 1899-1982 .... *26*
Thomas, Frances 1943- *171*
　Earlier sketch in SATA *92*
Thomas, Garen *213*
Thomas, H. C.
　See Keating, Lawrence A.
Thomas, Ianthe 1951- *139*
　Brief entry *42*
　See also CLR *8*
Thomas, J. F.
　See Fleming, Thomas
Thomas, Jan 1958- *197*
Thomas, Jane Resh 1936- *171*
　Earlier sketches in SATA *38, 90*
Thomas, Jerry D. 1959- *91*
Thomas, Joan Gale
　See Robinson, Joan (Mary) G(ale Thomas)
Thomas, Joyce Carol 1938- *210*
　Autobiography Feature *137*
　Earlier sketches in SATA *40, 78, 123, 137*
　See also CLR *19*
　See also SAAS *7*

Thomas, Lee
　See Floren, Lee
　and Pendleton, Thomas
Thomas, Lowell Jackson, Jr. 1923- *15*
Thomas, Margaret
　See Thomas, Peggy
Thomas, Meredith 1963- *119*
Thomas, Michael
　See Wilks, Michael Thomas
Thomas, Middy 1931- *191*
Thomas, Patricia 1934- *199*
　Earlier sketch in SATA *51*
Thomas, Peggy *174*
Thomas, Rob 1965- *97*
Thomas, Scott 1959- *147*
Thomas, Velma Maia 1955- *171*
Thomas, Vernon (Arthur) 1934- *56*
Thomas, Victoria
　See DeWeese, Thomas Eugene
　and Kugi, Constance Todd
Thomasma, Kenneth R. 1930- *90*
Thomason, Mark *215*
Thomassie, Tynia 1959- *92*
Thompson, Brenda 1935- *34*
Thompson, Carol 1951- *189*
　Earlier sketch in SATA *85*
Thompson, China
　See Lewis, Mary
Thompson, Colin 1942- *198*
　Earlier sketches in SATA *95, 163*
Thompson, David H(ugh) 1941- *17*
Thompson, Eileen
　See Panowski, Eileen Thompson
Thompson, George Selden 1929-1989 .... *73*
　Obituary *63*
　Earlier sketch in SATA *4*
　See also CLR *8*
Thompson, Harlan 1894-1987 .... *10*
　Obituary *53*
Thompson, Hilary 1943- *56*
　Brief entry *49*
Thompson, Joanna Maxwell Pullein
　See Pullein-Thompson, Joanna Maxwell
Thompson, Julian F(rancis) 1927- *155*
　Brief entry *40*
　Earlier sketches in SATA *55, 99*
　See also CLR *24*
　See also SAAS *13*
Thompson, K(athryn Carolyn) Dyble
　1952- *82*
Thompson, Kate 1956- *204*
Thompson, Kay 1912(?)-1998 .... *16*
　See also CLR *22*
Thompson, Lauren 1962- *200*
　Earlier sketches in SATA *132, 174*
Thompson, Lauren Stevens
　See Thompson, Lauren
Thompson, Megan Lloyd
　See Lloyd, Megan
Thompson, Richard 1951- *184*
Thompson, Ruth Plumly 1891-1976 .... *66*
Thompson, Sharon 1952- *119*
Thompson, Sharon Elaine
　See Thompson, Sharon
Thompson, Stith 1885-1976 .... *57*
　Obituary *20*
Thompson, Vivian L(aubach) 1911- *3*
Thomson, Bill 1963- *187*
Thomson, Celia
　See Lynn, Tracy
Thomson, David (Robert Alexander)
　1914-1988 .... *40*
　Obituary *55*
Thomson, Melissa 1979- *205*
Thomson, Pat 1939- *122*
　Earlier sketch in SATA *77*
Thomson, Peggy 1922- *31*
Thomson, Sarah L. *212*
　Earlier sketch in SATA *178*
Thon, Melanie Rae 1957- *132*
Thong, Roseanne *174*

Thorburn, John
    See Goldsmith, John Herman Thorburn
Thorn, John 1947- 59
Thorndyke, Helen Louise
    See Benson, Mildred
Thorne, Ian
    See May, Julian
Thorne, Jean Wright
    See May, Julian
Thornhill, Jan 1955- 148
    Earlier sketch in SATA 77
Thornton, Hall
    See Silverberg, Robert
Thornton, W. B.
    See Burgess, Thornton Waldo
Thornton, Yvonne S. 1947- 96
Thornton, Yvonne Shirley
    See Thornton, Yvonne S.
Thorpe, E(ustace) G(eorge) 1916- 21
Thorpe, J. K.
    See Nathanson, Laura Walther
Thorvall, Kerstin 1925- 13
Thorvall-Falk, Kerstin
    See Thorvall, Kerstin
Thrasher, Crystal (Faye) 1921- 27
Threadgall, Colin 1941- 77
Three Little Pigs
    See Lantz, Francess L(in)
Thum, Gladys 1920- 26
Thum, Marcella 28
    Earlier sketch in SATA 3
Thundercloud, Katherine
    See Witt, Shirley Hill
Thurber, James 1894-1961 13
Thurber, James Grover
    See Thurber, James
Thurlo, Aimee 161
Thurlo, David 161
Thurman, Judith 1946- 33
Thurman, Mark (Gordon Ian) 1948- 63
Thwaite, Ann (Barbara Harrop) 1932- 14
Tibbetts, Peggy 127
Tibbles, Jean-Paul 1958- 115
Tibo, Gilles 1951- 107
    Earlier sketch in SATA 67
Tiburzi, Bonnie 1948- 65
Ticheburn, Cheviot
    See Ainsworth, William Harrison
Tichenor, Tom 1923-1992 14
Tichnor, Richard 1959- 90
Tichy, William 1924- 31
Tickle, Jack
    See Chapman, Jane
Tiegreen, Alan F. 1935- 94
    Brief entry 36
Tierney, Frank M. 1930- 54
Tierney, Tom 1928- 113
Tiffault, Benette W. 1955- 77
Tildes, Phyllis Limbacher 1945- 210
Tiller, Ruth L. 1949- 83
Tilley, Debbie 190
Tillman, Nancy 211
Tilly, Nancy 1935- 62
Tilton, Madonna Elaine 1929- 41
Tilton, Rafael
    See Tilton, Madonna Elaine
Timberlake, Amy 156
Timberlake, Carolyn
    See Dresang, Eliza (Carolyn Timberlake)
Timmers, Leo 1970- 190
Timmins, William F(rederick) 10
Tinbergen, Niko(laas) 1907-1988
    Obituary 60
Tincknell, Cathy 194
Tiner, John Hudson 1944- 32
Tingle, Dolli (?)-
    See Brackett, Dolli Tingle
Tingle, Rebecca 174
Tingle, Tim 208
Tingum, Janice 1958- 91
Tinkelman, Murray 1933- 12

Tinkham, Kelly A. 188
Tinkle, (Julien) Lon 1906-1980 36
Tinling, Marion (Rose) 1904- 140
Tipene, Tim 1972- 141
Tippett, James S(terling) 1885-1958 66
Tirone Smith, Mary-Ann 1944- 143
Titlebaum, Ellen 195
Titler, Dale M(ilton) 1926- 35
    Brief entry 28
Titmarsh, Michael Angelo
    See Thackeray, William Makepeace
Titus, Eve 1922- 2
Tjia, Sherwin 1975- 204
Tjong Khing, The 1933- 76
Tobias, Katherine
    See Gottfried, Theodore Mark
Tobias, Tobi 1938- 82
    Earlier sketch in SATA 5
    See also CLR 4
Tocci, C. Lee 1958- 220
Tocci, Cynthia Lee
    See Tocci, C. Lee
Todd, Anne Ophelia
    See Dowden, Anne Ophelia Todd
Todd, Barbara 1961- 173
Todd, Barbara K(eith) 1917- 10
Todd, Chuck 195
Todd, H(erbert) E(atton) 1908-1988 84
    Earlier sketch in SATA 11
Todd, Loreto 1942- 30
Todd, Pamela 212
Todd, Peter
    See Hamilton, Charles (Harold St. John)
Toews, Miriam 1964- 165
Tofel, Richard J. 1957- 140
Toft, Kim Michelle 1960- 170
Tokunbo, Dimitrea 187
Tolan, Stephanie S. 1942- 142
    Earlier sketches in SATA 38, 78
Toland, John (Willard) 1912-2004 38
Tolbert, Steve 1944- 143
Toledo, Francisco 1940- 198
Toledo, Natalia 1967- 197
Tolkien, J. R. R. 1892-1973 100
    Obituary 24
    Earlier sketches in SATA 2, 32
    See also CLR 152
Tolkien, John Ronald Reuel
    See Tolkien, J. R. R.
Toll, Emily
    See Cannon, Eileen E(mily)
Toll, Nelly S. 1935- 78
Tolland, W. R.
    See Heitzmann, William Ray
Tolles, Martha 1921- 76
    Earlier sketch in SATA 8
Tolliver, Ruby C(hangos) 1922- 110
    Brief entry 41
    Earlier sketch in SATA 55
Tolmie, Kenneth Donald 1941- 15
Tolstoi, Lev
    See Tolstoy, Leo
Tolstoy, Leo 1828-1910 26
Tolstoy, Count Leo
    See Tolstoy, Leo
Tolstoy, Leo Nikolaevich
    See Tolstoy, Leo
Tomalin, Ruth 29
Tomaselli, Rosa
    See Pausacker, Jenny
Tomecek, Steve 172
Tomes, Margot (Ladd) 1917-1991 70
    Brief entry 27
    Obituary 69
    Earlier sketch in SATA 36
Tomey, Ingrid 1943- 77
Tomfool
    See Farjeon, Eleanor
Tomic, Tomislav 1977- 202
Tomkins, Jasper
    See Batey, Tom

Tomline, F. Latour
    See Gilbert, W(illiam) S(chwenck)
Tomlinson, Heather 192
Tomlinson, Jill 1931-1976 3
    Obituary 24
Tomlinson, Reginald R(obert) 1885-1979(?)
    Obituary 27
Tomlinson, Theresa 1946- 165
    Earlier sketch in SATA 103
    See also CLR 60
Tommaso, Rich 1970(?)- 200
Tompert, Ann 1918- 139
    Earlier sketches in SATA 14, 89
Tompkins, Troy
    See Cle, Troy
Toner, Raymond John 1908-1986 10
Tong, Gary S. 1942- 66
Tong, Paul 188
Took, Belladonna
    See Chapman, Vera (Ivy May)
Tooke, Louise Mathews 1950- 38
Tooke, Susan 173
Toonder, Martin
    See Groom, Arthur William
Toothaker, Roy Eugene 1928- 18
Tooze, Ruth (Anderson) 1892-1972 4
Topaz, Ksenia 212
Topek, Susan Remick 1955- 78
Topping, Audrey R(onning) 1928- 14
Tor, Regina
    See Shekerjian, Regina Tor
Torbert, Floyd James 1922- 22
Torgersen, Don Arthur 1934- 55
    Brief entry 41
Torley, Luke
    See Blish, James
Torrecilla, Pablo 1967- 206
Torres, Andres Segovia
    See Segovia, Andres
Torres, Daniel 1958- 102
Torres, John A. 1965- 163
    Earlier sketch in SATA 94
Torres, John Albert
    See Torres, John A.
Torres, Laura 1967- 146
    Earlier sketch in SATA 87
Torres, Leyla 1960- 155
Torrey, Rich
    See Torrey, Richard
Torrey, Richard 189
Torrie, Malcolm
    See Mitchell, Gladys (Maude Winifred)
Toten, Teresa 1955- 99
Totham, Mary
    See Breinburg, Petronella
Touponce, William F. 1948- 114
Tournier, Michel 1924- 23
Tournier, Michel Edouard
    See Tournier, Michel
Towle, Wendy 1963- 79
Towne, Mary
    See Spelman, Mary
Townley, Rod
    See Townley, Roderick
Townley, Roderick 1942- 177
Townsend, Brad W. 1962- 91
Townsend, John Rowe 1922- 132
    Autobiography Feature 132
    Earlier sketches in SATA 4, 68
    See also CLR 2
    See also SAAS 2
Townsend, Michael 1981- 194
Townsend, Sue 1946- 93
    Brief entry 48
    Earlier sketch in SATA 55
Townsend, Susan Lilian
    See Townsend, Sue
Townsend, Thomas L. 1944- 59
Townsend, Tom
    See Townsend, Thomas L.
Townsend, Wendy 1962- 201

Townson, Hazel *134*
Toye, William Eldred 1926- *8*
Traherne, Michael
  See Watkins-Pitchford, Denys James
Trahey, Jane 1923-2000 .... *36*
  Obituary *120*
Trapani, Iza 1954- *214*
  Earlier sketches in SATA *80, 116*
Trapp, Maria Augusta von
  See von Trapp, Maria Augusta
Travers, P(amela) L(yndon) 1899-1996 ...... *100*
  Obituary *90*
  Earlier sketches in SATA *4, 54*
  See also CLR *93*
  See also SAAS *2*
Travis, Lucille *133*
  Earlier sketch in SATA *88*
Treadgold, Mary 1910- *49*
Trease, (Robert) Geoffrey 1909-1998 .... *60*
  Obituary *101*
  Earlier sketch in SATA *2*
  See also CLR *42*
  See also SAAS *6*
Treat, Lawrence 1903-1998 .... *59*
Tredez, Alain 1926- *17*
Tredez, Denise 1930- *50*
Treece, Henry 1912-1966 .... *2*
  See also CLR *2*
Tregarthen, Enys
  See Sloggett, Nellie
Tregaskis, Richard 1916-1973 .... *3*
  Obituary *26*
Treherne, Katie Thamer 1955- *76*
Trell, Max 1900-1996 .... *14*
  Obituary *108*
Tremain, Ruthven 1922- *17*
Trembath, Don 1963- *168*
  Earlier sketch in SATA *96*
Tremens, Del
  See MacDonald, Amy
Trent, Robbie 1894-1988 .... *26*
Trent, Timothy
  See Malmberg, Carl
Treseder, Terry Walton 1956- *68*
Tresilian, (Cecil) Stuart 1891-(?) *40*
Tresselt, Alvin 1916-2000 .... *7*
  See also CLR *30*
Trevino, Elizabeth B(orton) de 1904- *29*
  Earlier sketch in SATA *1*
  See also SAAS *5*
Trevor, Elleston 1920-1995 .... *28*
Trevor, Frances
  See Teasdale, Sara
Trevor, Glen
  See Hilton, James
Trevor, (Lucy) Meriol 1919-2000 .... *113*
  Obituary *122*
  Earlier sketch in SATA *10*
Trewellard, J.M. *195*
Trewellard, Juliet
  See Trewellard, J.M.
Trez, Alain
  See Tredez, Alain
Trez, Denise
  See Tredez, Denise
Trezise, Percy 1923-
  See CLR *41*
Trezise, Percy James
  See Trezise, Percy
Triggs, Tony D. 1946- *70*
Trimble, Marshall I(ra) 1939- *93*
Trimby, Elisa 1948- *47*
  Brief entry *40*
Tring, A. Stephen
  See Meynell, Laurence Walter
Tripp, Eleanor B(aldwin) 1936- *4*
Tripp, Janet 1942- *108*
Tripp, Jenny *188*
Tripp, John
  See Moore, John Travers
Tripp, Nathaniel 1944- *101*

Tripp, Paul 1916-2002 .... *8*
  Obituary *139*
Tripp, Valerie 1951- *168*
  Earlier sketch in SATA *78*
Tripp, Wallace (Whitney) 1940- *31*
Trivelpiece, Laurel 1926- *56*
  Brief entry *46*
Trivett, Daphne Harwood 1940- *22*
Trivizas, Eugene 1946- *84*
Trnka, Jiri 1912-1969 .... *43*
  Brief entry *32*
Trollope, Anthony 1815-1882 .... *22*
Trost, Lucille W(ood) 1938- *149*
  Earlier sketch in SATA *12*
Trott, Betty 1933- *91*
Trotter, Deborah W. *184*
Trotter, Grace V(iolet) 1900-1991 .... *10*
Trottier, Maxine 1950- *175*
  Earlier sketch in SATA *131*
Troughton, Joanna (Margaret) 1947- *37*
Trout, Kilgore
  See Farmer, Philip Jose
Trout, Richard E. *123*
Trudeau, Garretson Beekman
  See Trudeau, G.B.
Trudeau, Garry
  See Trudeau, G.B.
Trudeau, Garry B.
  See Trudeau, G.B.
Trudeau, G.B. 1948- *168*
  Earlier sketch in SATA *35*
Trueit, Trudi
  See Trueit, Trudi Strain
Trueit, Trudi Strain 1963- *179*
Trueman, Matthew *183*
Trueman, Terry 1947- *178*
  Earlier sketch in SATA *132*
Truesdell, Judy
  See Mecca, Judy Truesdell
Truesdell, Sue
  See Truesdell, Susan G.
Truesdell, Susan G. *212*
  Brief entry *45*
  Earlier sketch in SATA *108*
Trumbauer, Lisa (Trutkoff) 1963- *149*
Truss, Jan 1925- *35*
Truss, Lynne 1955(?)- *194*
Tryon, Leslie *194*
  Earlier sketch in SATA *139*
Tubb, Jonathan N. 1951- *78*
Tubb, Kristin O'Donnell 1971- *209*
Tubby, I. M.
  See Kraus, (Herman) Robert
Tucker, Allan James
  See James, Bill
Tucker, Caroline
  See Nolan, Jeannette Covert
Tucker, James
  See James, Bill
Tudor, Edward
  See Browne, Anthony
Tudor, Tasha 1915-2008 .... *160*
  Obituary *205*
  Earlier sketches in SATA *20, 69*
  See also CLR *13*
Tuerk, Hanne 1951- *71*
Tugeau, Jeremy *199*
Tulloch, Richard 1949- *180*
  Earlier sketch in SATA *76*
Tulloch, Richard George
  See Tulloch, Richard
Tulloch, Shirley *169*
Tully, John (Kimberley) 1923- *14*
Tumanov, Vladimir A. 1961- *138*
Tung, Angela 1972- *109*
Tunis, Edwin (Burdett) 1897-1973 .... *28*
  Obituary *24*
  Earlier sketch in SATA *1*
  See also CLR *2*
Tunis, John R(oberts) 1889-1975 .... *37*
  Brief entry *30*

Tunnell, Michael
  See Tunnell, Michael O.
Tunnell, Michael O. 1950- *157*
  Earlier sketch in SATA *103*
Tunnell, Michael O'Grady
  See Tunnell, Michael O.
Tunnicliffe, C(harles) F(rederick)
  1901-1979 .... *62*
Turck, Mary C. 1950- *144*
Turk, Hanne
  See Tuerk, Hanne
Turk, Ruth 1917- *82*
Turkle, Brinton 1915- *79*
  Earlier sketch in SATA *2*
Turlington, Bayly 1919-1977 .... *5*
  Obituary *52*
Turnbull, Agnes Sligh 1888-1982 .... *14*
Turnbull, Ann 1943- *160*
  Earlier sketch in SATA *18*
Turnbull, Ann Christine
  See Turnbull, Ann
Turner, Alice K. 1940- *10*
Turner, Ann 1945- *188*
  Autobiography Feature *188*
  Earlier sketches in SATA *14, 77, 113, 178*
Turner, Ann Warren
  See Turner, Ann
Turner, Bonnie 1932- *75*
Turner, Elizabeth 1774-1846
  See YABC *2*
Turner, Glennette Tilley 1933- *183*
  Earlier sketch in SATA *71*
Turner, Josie
  See Crawford, Phyllis
Turner, Megan Whalen 1965- *174*
  Earlier sketch in SATA *94*
Turner, Pamela S. 1957- *211*
Turner, Philip (William) 1925- *83*
  Earlier sketch in SATA *11*
  See also CLR *89*
  See also SAAS *6*
Turner, Robyn 1947- *77*
Turner, Sheila R.
  See Seed, Sheila Turner
Turngren, Annette 1902(?)-1980
  Obituary *23*
Turngren, Ellen (?)-1964 .... *3*
Turska, Krystyna (Zofia) 1933- *31*
  Brief entry *27*
Turteltaub, H. N.
  See Turtledove, Harry
Turtledove, Harry 1949- *166*
  Earlier sketch in SATA *116*
Turtledove, Harry Norman
  See Turtledove, Harry
Tusa, Tricia 1960- *207*
  Earlier sketches in SATA *72, 111*
Tusiani, Joseph 1924- *45*
Twain, Mark 1835-1910 .... *100*
  See also YABC *2*
  See also CLR *156*
Tweit, Susan J 1956- *94*
Tweit, Susan Joan
  See Tweit, Susan J
Tweton, D. Jerome 1933- *48*
Twinem, Neecy 1958- *92*
Twohill, Maggie
  See Angell, Judie
Tworkov, Jack 1900-1982 .... *47*
  Obituary *31*
Tyche
  See Papademetriou, Lisa
Tyers, Jenny 1969- *89*
Tyers, Kathy 1952- *82*
Tyler, Anne 1941- *173*
  Earlier sketches in SATA *7, 90*
Tyler, Linda
  See Tyler, Linda W(agner)
Tyler, Linda W(agner) 1952- *65*
Tyler, Vicki 1952- *64*

Tyne, Joel
  See Schembri, Jim
Tyrrell, Frances 1959- *107*

U

Ubell, Earl 1926-2007 .... *4*
  Obituary *182*
Uchida, Yoshiko 1921-1992 .... *53*
  Obituary *72*
  Earlier sketch in SATA *1*
  See also CLR *56*
  See also SAAS *1*
Udall, Jan Beaney 1938- *10*
Uden, (Bernard Gilbert) Grant 1910- *26*
Uderzo, Albert 1927-
  See CLR *37*
Udovic, David 1950- *189*
Udry, Janice May 1928- *152*
  Earlier sketch in SATA *4*
Uegaki, Chieri 1969- *211*
  Earlier sketch in SATA *153*
Uehashi, Nahoko 1962- *215*
Ueno, Noriko
  See Nakae, Noriko
Ugliano, Natascia *196*
Uhlberg, Myron *174*
Uhlig, Richard 1970- *195*
Uhlig, Susan 1955- *129*
Ulam, S(tanislaw) M(arcin) 1909-1984 .... *51*
Ullman, Barb Bentler *210*
Ullman, James Ramsey 1907-1971 .... *7*
Ulm, Robert 1934-1977 .... *17*
Ulmer, Louise 1943- *53*
Ulmer, Wendy K. 1950- *201*
Ulrich, Maureen 1958- *206*
Ulriksen, Mark 1957- *210*
Ulyatt, Kenneth 1920- *14*
Umansky, Kaye 1946- *188*
  Earlier sketch in SATA *158*
Unada
  See Gliewe, Unada (Grace)
Uncle Carter
  See Boucher, (Clarence) Carter
Uncle Eric
  See Maybury, Richard J.
Uncle Gus
  See Rey, H. A.
Uncle Mac
  See McCulloch, Derek (Ivor Breashur)
Uncle Ray
  See Coffman, Ramon Peyton
Uncle Shelby
  See Silverstein, Shel
Underhill, Alice Mertie (Waterman)
  1900-1971 .... *10*
Underhill, Liz 1948- *53*
  Brief entry *49*
Underwood, Deborah 1962- *206*
Unger, Harlow G. 1931- *75*
Unger, Harlow Giles
  See Unger, Harlow G.
Unger, Jim 1937- *67*
Ungerer, (Jean) Thomas 1931- *106*
  Earlier sketches in SATA *5, 33*
  See also CLR *77*
Ungerer, Tomi 1931-
  See Ungerer, (Jean) Thomas
Unkelbach, Kurt 1913-1992 .... *4*
Unnerstad, Edith (Totterman) 1900-1982 .... *3*
  See also CLR *36*
Unobagha, Uzo *139*
Unrau, Ruth 1922- *9*
Unstead, R(obert) J(ohn) 1915-1988 .... *12*
  Obituary *56*
Unsworth, Walt(er) 1928- *4*
Untermeyer, Bryna Ivens 1909-1985 .... *61*

Untermeyer, Louis 1885-1977 .... *37*
  Obituary *26*
  Earlier sketch in SATA *2*
Unwin, David S. 1918-2010 .... *14*
Unwin, David Storr
  See Unwin, David S.
Unwin, Nora S(picer) 1907-1982 .... *3*
  Obituary *49*
Unzner, Christa 1958- *141*
  Earlier sketch in SATA *80*
Unzner-Fischer, Christa
  See Unzner, Christa
Updale, Eleanor 1953- *175*
Updyke, Rosemary K. 1924- *103*
Upitis, Alvis *109*
Urbain, Cat 1956- *211*
Urbain, Catherine
  See Urbain, Cat
Urban, Helle (Denise) 1957- *149*
Urban, Linda *199*
Urbanovic, Jackie *189*
Urberuaga, Emilio 1954- *219*
Urbigkit, Cat 1965- *196*
Urdahl, Catherine *215*
Ure, Jean 1943- *192*
  Autobiography Feature *192*
  Earlier sketches in SATA *48, 78, 129*
  See also CLR *34*
  See also SAAS *14*
U'Ren, Andrea 1968- *213*
  Earlier sketch in SATA *142*
Uris, Leon 1924-2003 .... *49*
  Obituary *146*
Uris, Leon Marcus
  See Uris, Leon
Ursu, Anne *177*
Ury, Allen B. 1954- *98*
Uschan, Michael V. 1948- *129*
Usher, Margo Scegge
  See McHargue, Georgess
Usher, Mark David
  See Usher, M.D.
Usher, M.D. 1966- *221*
Uslan, Michael E. 1951- *169*
Uston, Ken(neth Senzo) 1935-1987 .... *65*
Uttley, Alice Jane 1884-1976 .... *88*
  Obituary *26*
  Earlier sketch in SATA *3*
Uttley, Alison
  See Uttley, Alice Jane
Utz, Lois (Marie) 1932-1986 .... *5*
  Obituary *50*

V

Vaeth, J. Gordon 1921- *17*
Vaeth, Joseph Gordon
  See Vaeth, J. Gordon
Vagin, Vladimir (Vasilevich) 1937- *142*
Vail, Rachel 1966- *201*
  Earlier sketches in SATA *94, 163*
Vainio, Pirkko 1957- *123*
  Earlier sketch in SATA *76*
Valen, Nanine 1950- *21*
Valencak, Hannelore
  See Mayer, Hannelore Valencak
Valens, Amy 1946- *70*
Valens, E(vans) G(ladstone), Jr. 1920-1992 ... *1*
Valentine, Johnny *72*
Valerio, Geraldo 1970- *180*
Valgardson, W. D. 1939- *151*
  Earlier sketch in SATA *101*
Valgardson, William Dempsey
  See Valgardson, W. D.
Valleau, Emily 1925- *51*
Vamos, Samantha R. *215*
Van Abbe, Salaman 1883-1955 .... *18*

Van Allsburg, Chris 1949- *156*
  Earlier sketches in SATA *37, 53, 105*
  See also CLR *113*
Van Anrooy, Francine 1924- *2*
Van Anrooy, Frans
  See Van Anrooy, Francine
Vanasse, Deb 1957- *170*
Van Buren, David *203*
Vance, Cynthia *207*
Vance, Eleanor Graham 1908-1985 .... *11*
Vance, Gerald
  See Garrett, Randall
  and Silverberg, Robert
Vance, Marguerite 1889-1965 .... *29*
Vance-Abrams, Cynthia
  See Vance, Cynthia
VanCleave, Janice 1942- *116*
  Autobiography Feature *123*
  Earlier sketch in SATA *75*
Vandenburg, Mary Lou 1943- *17*
Vander Boom, Mae M. *14*
Vander-Els, Betty 1936- *63*
van der Heide, Iris 1970- *183*
van der Linde, Laurel 1952- *78*
van der Linden, Martijn 1979- *214*
van der Meer, Ron 1945- *98*
van de Ruit, John 1975- *199*
Van der Veer, Judy 1912-1982 .... *4*
  Obituary *33*
Vanderwal, Andrew H. 1956- *219*
Vanderwerff, Corrine 1939- *117*
Vander Zee, Ruth *199*
  Earlier sketch in SATA *159*
Vande Velde, Vivian 1951- *211*
  Earlier sketches in SATA *62, 95, 141*
  See also CLR *145*
Vandivert, Rita (Andre) 1905-1986 .... *21*
Van Draanen, Wendelin *207*
  Earlier sketch in SATA *122*
Van Dusen, Chris *173*
Van Duyn, Janet 1910- *18*
Van Dyne, Edith
  See Baum, L. Frank
  and Sampson, Emma (Keats) Speed
  and van Zantwijk, Rudolf (Alexander
    Marinus)
Vane, Mitch
  See Vane, Mitchelle
Vane, Mitchelle *176*
van Frankenhuyzen, Gijsbert 1951- *132*
Van Genechten, Guido 1957- *165*
van Haeringen, Annemarie *193*
Van Hook, Beverly 1941- *99*
Van Hook, Beverly H.
  See Van Hook, Beverly
Van Hook, Beverly Hennen
  See Van Hook, Beverly
Van Horn, William 1939- *43*
van Hout, Mies 1962- *178*
Van Iterson, S(iny) R(ose) *26*
Van Kampen, Vlasta 1943- *163*
  Earlier sketch in SATA *54*
Van Laan, Nancy 1939- *214*
  Earlier sketch in SATA *105*
van Lawick-Goodall, Jane
  See Goodall, Jane
Van Leeuwen, Jean 1937- *211*
  Autobiography Feature *141*
  Earlier sketches in SATA *6, 82, 132, 141*
  See also SAAS *8*
van Lhin, Erik
  See del Rey, Lester
van Lieshout, Elle 1963- *217*
van Lieshout, Maria *201*
Van Loon, Hendrik Willem 1882-1944 .... *18*
van Ommen, Sylvia 1978- *186*
VanOosting, James 1951- *170*
Van Orden, M(erton) D(ick) 1921- *4*
van Os, Erik 1963- *217*
Van Patter, Bruce *183*
Van Reek, Wouter *204*

Van Rensselaer, Alexander (Taylor Mason)
    1892-1962 .... *14*
Van Riper, Guernsey, Jr. 1909-1995 .... *3*
van Rossum, Heleen 1962- *174*
Van Rynbach, Iris 1952- *102*
Vansant, Rhonda Joy Edwards 1950- *92*
Van Steenwyk, Elizabeth (Ann) 1928- *89*
    Earlier sketch in SATA *34*
Van Stockum, Hilda 1908-2006 .... *5*
    Obituary *179*
van Straaten, Harmen 1961- *218*
    Earlier sketch in SATA *195*
Van Tuyl, Barbara 1940- *11*
van Vogt, A(lfred) E(lton) 1912-2000 .... *14*
    Obituary *124*
Van Wassenhove, Sue 1951- *202*
Van Woerkom, Dorothy (O'Brien)
    1924-1996 .... *21*
Van Wormer, Joe
    See Van Wormer, Joseph Edward
Van Wormer, Joseph Edward 1913-1998 ...... *35*
Van Wright, Cornelius *173*
Van Zwienen, Ilse Charlotte Koehn
    1929-1991 .... *34*
    Brief entry *28*
    Obituary *67*
Van Zyle, Jon 1942- *176*
    Earlier sketch in SATA *84*
Varela, Barry *180*
Varga, Judy
    See Stang, Judit
Varley, Dimitry V. 1906-1984 .... *10*
Varley, Susan 1961- *134*
    Earlier sketch in SATA *63*
Varon, Sara *195*
Vasileva, Tatiana
    See Wassiljewa, Tatjana
Vasiliev, Valery 1949- *80*
Vasilieva, Tatiana
    See Wassiljewa, Tatjana
Vasiliu, Mircea 1920- *2*
Vass, George 1927- *57*
    Brief entry *31*
Vaughan, Carter A.
    See Gerson, Noel Bertram
Vaughan, Harold Cecil 1923- *14*
Vaughan, Marcia (K.) 1951- *159*
    Earlier sketches in SATA *60, 95*
Vaughan, Richard 1947- *87*
Vaughan, Sam(uel) 1928- *14*
Vaughn, Ruth 1935- *14*
Vaught, Susan 1965- *195*
Vaupel, Robin *198*
Vautier, Ghislaine 1932- *53*
Vavra, Robert James 1935- *8*
Vecsey, George Spencer 1939- *9*
Vedral, Joyce L(auretta) 1943- *65*
Vega, Denise *216*
    Earlier sketch in SATA *174*
Vega, Denise B.
    See Vega, Denise
Vega, Diego
    See Adkins, Jan
Veglahn, Nancy (Crary) 1937- *5*
Vejjajiva, Jane 1963- *189*
Velasquez, Eric *192*
Velasquez, Gloria 1949- *113*
Velasquez, Gloria 1949-
    See Velasquez, Gloria
Velthuijs, Max 1923-2005 .... *110*
    Obituary *160*
    Earlier sketch in SATA *53*
Venable, Alan (Hudson) 1944- *8*
Venezia, Mike 1945- *150*
Ventura, Anthony
    See Pellowski, Michael (Joseph)
Ventura, Piero (Luigi) 1937- *61*
    Brief entry *43*
    See also CLR *16*
Vequin, Capini
    See Quinn, Elisabeth

Verba, Joan Marie 1953- *78*
Verboven, Agnes 1951- *103*
verDorn, Bethea (Stewart) 1952- *76*
Vere, Ed *197*
Verissimo, Erico (Lopes) 1905-1975 .... *113*
Verne, Jules 1828-1905 .... *21*
    See also CLR *88*
Verne, Jules Gabriel
    See Verne, Jules
Verner, Gerald 1897(?)-1980
    Obituary *25*
Verney, John 1913-1993 .... *14*
    Obituary *75*
Verniero, Joan C. 1949- *181*
Vernon, (Elda) Louise A(nderson) 1914- *14*
Vernon, Rosemary
    See Smith, Susan Vernon
Vernon, Ursula *204*
Vernor, D.
    See Casewit, Curtis W(erner)
Verr, Harry Coe
    See Kunhardt, Edith
Verral, Charles Spain 1904-1990 .... *11*
    Obituary *65*
Verrillo, Erica 1953- *199*
Verrillo, Erica F.
    See Verrillo, Erica
Verrone, Robert J. 1935(?)-1984
    Obituary *39*
Versace, Marie Teresa Rios 1917- *2*
Vertreace, Martha M(odena) 1945- *78*
Vesey, A(manda) 1939- *62*
Vesey, Mark (David) 1958- *123*
Vesey, Paul
    See Allen, Samuel W(ashington)
Vess, Charles 1951- *215*
Vestergaard, Hope *178*
Vestly, Anne-Cath(arina) 1920- *14*
    See also CLR *99*
Vevers, (Henry) Gwynne 1916-1988 .... *45*
    Obituary *57*
Viator, Vacuus
    See Hughes, Thomas
Viau, Nancy *208*
Vicar, Henry
    See Felsen, Henry Gregor
Vick, Helen Hughes 1950- *88*
Vicker, Angus
    See Felsen, Henry Gregor
Vickers, Sheena 1960- *94*
Vickery, Kate
    See Kennedy, T.A.
Victor, Edward 1914- *3*
Victor, Joan Berg 1942- *30*
Vidrine, Beverly Barras 1938- *188*
    Earlier sketch in SATA *103*
Vieceli, Emma 1979- *210*
Viereck, Ellen K. 1928- *14*
Viereck, Phillip 1925- *3*
Viertel, Janet 1915- *10*
Vigliante, Mary
    See Szydlowski, Mary Vigliante
Vigna, Judith 1936- *102*
    Earlier sketch in SATA *15*
Viguers, Ruth Hill 1903-1971 .... *6*
Vila, Laura *207*
Vilela, Fernando 1973- *216*
Villareal, Ray *187*
Villasenor, Edmund
    See Villasenor, Victor E.
Villasenor, Edmundo
    See Villasenor, Victor E.
Villasenor, Victor
    See Villasenor, Victor E.
Villasenor, Victor E. 1940- *171*
Villasenor, Victor Edmundo
    See Villasenor, Victor E.
Villiard, Paul 1910-1974 .... *51*
    Obituary *20*
Villiers, Alan (John) 1903-1982 .... *10*

Vilott, Rhondi
    See Salsitz, Rhondi Vilott
Vincent, Amy
    See Gray, Claudia
Vincent, Eric Douglas 1953- *40*
Vincent, Erin 1969- *188*
Vincent, Felix 1946- *41*
Vincent, Gabrielle 1928-2000 .... *121*
    Earlier sketch in SATA *61*
    See also CLR *13*
Vincent, Mary Keith
    See St. John, Wylly Folk
Vincent, William R.
    See Heitzmann, William Ray
Vinegar, Tom
    See Gregg, Andrew K.
Vinest, Shaw
    See Longyear, Barry B(rookes)
Vinge, Joan (Carol) D(ennison) 1948- *113*
    Earlier sketch in SATA *36*
Vining, Elizabeth Gray 1902-1999 .... *6*
    Obituary *117*
Vinson, Kathryn 1911-1995 .... *21*
Vinton, Iris 1906(?)-1988 .... *24*
    Obituary *55*
Viola, Herman J(oseph) 1938- *126*
Viorst, Judith 1931- *172*
    Earlier sketches in SATA *7, 70, 123*
    See also CLR *90*
Vip
    See Partch, Virgil Franklin II
Vipont, Charles
    See Foulds, Elfrida Vipont
Vipont, Elfrida
    See Foulds, Elfrida Vipont
Viramontes, Helena Maria 1954-
    See CLR *285*
Viscott, David S(teven) 1938-1996 .... *65*
Visser, W(illem) F(rederik) H(endrik)
    1900-1968 .... *10*
Vitale, Stefano 1958- *180*
    Earlier sketch in SATA *114*
Vivas, Julie 1947- *96*
Vivelo, Jackie 1943- *63*
Vivelo, Jacqueline J.
    See Vivelo, Jackie
Vivelo, Jacqueline Jean
    See Vivelo, Jackie
Vivian, Siobhan 1979(?)- *215*
Vizzini, Ned 1981- *179*
    Earlier sketch in SATA *125*
Vlahos, Olivia 1924- *31*
Vlasic, Bob
    See Hirsch, Phil
Voake, Charlotte *180*
    Earlier sketch in SATA *114*
Voake, Steve 1961- *178*
Vo-Dinh, Mai 1933- *16*
Vogel, Carole Garbuny 1951- *105*
    Earlier sketch in SATA *70*
Vogel, Ilse-Margret 1918- *14*
Vogel, John H., Jr. 1950- *18*
Vogt, Esther Loewen 1915-1999 .... *14*
Vogt, Gregory L. *94*
Vogt, Marie Bollinger 1921- *45*
Vohwinkel, Astrid 1969- *207*
Voight, Virginia Frances 1909-1989 .... *8*
Voigt, Cynthia 1942- *160*
    Brief entry *33*
    Earlier sketches in SATA *48, 79, 116*
    See also CLR *141*
Voigt, Erna 1925- *35*
Voigt-Rother, Erna
    See Voigt, Erna
Vojtech, Anna 1946- *108*
    Earlier sketch in SATA *42*
Vollstadt, Elizabeth Weiss 1942- *121*
Volponi, Paul *175*
Volting, Dr. R.E.
    See Lerangis, Peter
Von Ahnen, Katherine 1922- *93*

von Buhler, Cynthia 185
Vondra, J. Gert
    See Vondra, Josef
Vondra, Josef 1941- 121
Vondra, Josef Gert
    See Vondra, Josef
Von Gunden, Kenneth 1946- 113
Von Hagen, Victor Wolfgang 1908-1985 29
von Klopp, Vahrah
    See Malvern, Gladys
von Schmidt, Eric 1931-2007 50
    Brief entry 36
    Obituary 181
von Storch, Anne B. 1910- 1
von Trapp, Maria Augusta 1905-1987 16
von Wodtke, Charlotte Buel Johnson
    1918-1982 46
von Ziegesar, Cecily 1970- 161
Vos, Ida 1931-2006 121
    Earlier sketch in SATA 69
    See also CLR 85
Vosburgh, Leonard (W.) 1912- 15
Votaw, Carol 1961- 201
Voyle, Mary
    See Manning, Rosemary
Vrettos, Adrienne Maria 187
Vriens, Jacques 1946- 151
Vugteveen, Verna Aardema
    See Aardema, Verna
Vulture, Elizabeth T.
    See Gilbert, Suzie
Vuong, Lynette Dyer 1938- 110
    Earlier sketch in SATA 60

W

Waas, Uli
    See Waas-Pommer, Ulrike
Waas-Pommer, Ulrike 1949- 85
Waber, Bernard 1924- 155
    Brief entry 40
    Earlier sketches in SATA 47, 95
    See also CLR 55
Wachtel, Shirley Russak 1951- 88
Wachter, Oralee (Roberts) 1935- 61
    Brief entry 51
Waddell, Evelyn Margaret 1918- 10
Waddell, Martin 1941- 129
    Autobiography Feature 129
    Earlier sketches in SATA 43, 81, 127
    See also CLR 31
    See also SAAS 15
Waddy, Lawrence 1912-2010 91
Waddy, Lawrence Heber
    See Waddy, Lawrence
Wade, Mary Dodson 1930- 151
    Earlier sketch in SATA 79
Wade, Suzanne
    See Kirby, Susan E.
Wade, Theodore E., Jr. 1936- 37
Wademan, Peter John 1946- 122
Wademan, Spike
    See Wademan, Peter John
Wadsworth, Ginger 1945- 157
    Earlier sketch in SATA 103
Wagenheim, Kal 1935- 21
Wagner, Michele R. 1975- 157
Wagner, Sharon B. 1936- 4
Wagoner, David (Russell) 1926- 14
Wahl, Jan (Boyer) 1933- 132
    Earlier sketches in SATA 2, 34, 73
    See also SAAS 3
Wahl, Mats 1945- 186
Wahman, Wendy 218
Waide, Jan 1952- 29
Wainscott, John Milton 1910-1981 53
Wainwright, Debra 218
Wainwright, Richard M. 1935- 91

Wainwright, Ruth
    See Symes, Ruth Louise
Wait, Lea 1946- 137
Waite, Judy 174
Waite, Judy Bernard
    See Bernard, Patricia
Waite, Michael
    See Waite, Michael P.
Waite, Michael P. 1960- 101
Waite, P(eter) B(usby) 1922- 64
Waites, Joan C. 187
Waitley, Douglas 1927- 30
Wakefield, Jean L.
    See Laird, Jean E(louise)
Wakin, Daniel (Joseph) 1961- 84
Wakin, Edward 1927- 37
Wakiyama, Hanako 1966- 192
Walck, Henry Z. 1908(?)-1984
    Obituary 40
Walden, Amelia Elizabeth 3
Walden, Mark 188
Waldherr, Kris 1963- 76
Waldman, Bruce 1949- 15
Waldman, Neil 1947- 203
    Earlier sketches in SATA 51, 94, 142
Waldrep, Richard 198
Waldron, Ann Wood 1924-2010 16
Waldron, Kathleen Cook 176
Wales, Dirk 1931- 205
Walgren, Judy 1963- 118
Walker, Addison
    See Walker, (Addison) Mort
Walker, Alice 1944- 31
Walker, Alice Malsenior
    See Walker, Alice
Walker, Barbara (Jeanne) K(erlin) 1921- 80
    Earlier sketch in SATA 4
Walker, Barbara M(uhs) 1928- 57
Walker, (James) Braz(elton) 1934-1983 45
Walker, David 1965- 197
Walker, David G(ordon) 1926- 60
Walker, David Harry 1911-1992 8
    Obituary 71
Walker, Diana 1925- 9
Walker, Diane Marie Catherine
    See Walker, Kate
Walker, Dick
    See Pellowski, Michael (Joseph)
Walker, Frank 1931-2000 36
Walker, Holly Beth
    See Bond, Gladys Baker
Walker, Kate 1950- 165
    Earlier sketch in SATA 82
Walker, Kathrine Sorley
    See Sorley Walker, Kathrine
Walker, Lou Ann 1952- 66
    Brief entry 53
Walker, Louise Jean 1891-1976
    Obituary 35
Walker, Mary Alexander 1927- 61
Walker, Mildred
    See Schemm, Mildred Walker
Walker, (Addison) Mort 1923- 8
Walker, Pamela 1948- 142
    Earlier sketch in SATA 24
Walker, Paul Robert 1953- 154
Walker, Robert W. 1948- 66
Walker, Sally M. 1954- 221
    Earlier sketch in SATA 135
Walker, Stephen J. 1951- 12
Walker-Blondell, Becky 1951- 89
Wallace, Barbara Brooks 1922- 136
    Earlier sketches in SATA 4, 78
    See also CLR 150
    See also SAAS 17
Wallace, Beverly Dobrin 1921- 19
Wallace, Bill 1947- 169
    Brief entry 47
    Earlier sketches in SATA 53, 101
Wallace, Carol 1948- 218

Wallace, Daisy
    See Cuyler, Margery
Wallace, Ian 1950- 219
    Earlier sketches in SATA 53, 56, 141
    See also CLR 37
Wallace, John 1966- 155
    Earlier sketch in SATA 105
Wallace, John A(dam) 1915-2004 3
    Obituary 155
Wallace, Karen 1951- 188
    Earlier sketches in SATA 83, 139
Wallace, Nancy Elizabeth 1948- 186
    Earlier sketch in SATA 141
Wallace, Nigel
    See Hamilton, Charles (Harold St. John)
Wallace, Paula S. 153
Wallace, Rich 1957- 196
    Earlier sketches in SATA 117, 158
Wallace, Robert 1932-1999 47
    Brief entry 37
Wallace, Ruby Ann 1923(?)- 77
Wallace, William Keith
    See Wallace, Bill
Wallace-Brodeur, Ruth 1941- 169
    Brief entry 41
    Earlier sketches in SATA 51, 88
Wallenta, Adam 1974- 123
Waller, Leslie 1923-2007 20
Walley, Byron
    See Card, Orson Scott
Wallis, Diz 1949- 77
Wallis, G. McDonald
    See Campbell, Hope
Wallner, Alexandra 1946- 156
    Brief entry 41
    Earlier sketches in SATA 51, 98
Wallner, John C. 1945- 133
    Earlier sketches in SATA 10, 51
Wallower, Lucille 11
Walrod, Amy 1973(?)- 182
Walsh, Ann 1942- 176
    Earlier sketch in SATA 62
Walsh, Ellen Stoll 1942- 194
    Earlier sketches in SATA 49, 99, 147
Walsh, George Johnston 1889-1981 53
Walsh, Gillian Paton
    See Paton Walsh, Jill
Walsh, Jill Paton
    See Paton Walsh, Jill
Walsh, Joanna 1970- 182
Walsh, Lawrence 1942- 170
Walsh, Marissa 1972- 195
Walsh, Mary Caswell 1949- 118
Walsh, Mitzy
    See Walsh, Marissa
Walsh, Rebecca 217
Walsh, Suella 170
Walsh, V. L.
    See Walsh, Vivian
Walsh, Vivian 1960- 120
Walsh Shepherd, Donna 1948- 78
Walter, Frances V. 1923- 71
Walter, Mildred Pitts 1922- 133
    Brief entry 45
    Earlier sketch in SATA 69
    See also CLR 61
    See also SAAS 12
Walter, Villiam Christian
    See Andersen, Hans Christian
Walter, Virginia
    See Walter, Virginia A.
Walter, Virginia A. 134
Walters, Audrey 1929- 18
Walters, Celeste 1938- 126
Walters, Eric 1957- 205
    Earlier sketches in SATA 99, 155
Walters, Eric Robert
    See Walters, Eric
Walters, Gregory 1964- 213
Walters, Helen B. (?)-1987
    Obituary 50

Walters, Hugh
    See Hughes, Walter (Llewellyn)
Walther, Thomas A. 1950- *31*
Walther, Tom
    See Walther, Thomas A.
Waltner, Elma 1912-1987 .... *40*
Waltner, Willard H. 1909- *40*
Walton, Darwin McBeth 1926- *119*
Walton, Fiona L. M. 1959- *89*
Walton, Richard J. 1928- *4*
Walton, Rick 1957- *204*
    Earlier sketches in SATA *101, 151*
Waltrip, Lela (Kingston) 1904-1995 .... *9*
Waltrip, Mildred 1911- *37*
Waltrip, Rufus (Charles) 1898-1988 .... *9*
Walworth, Nancy Zinsser 1917- *14*
Wang, Gabrielle *212*
Wang, Lin 1973- *221*
Wang, Shaoli *216*
Wangerin, Walter, Jr. 1944- *98*
    Brief entry *37*
    Earlier sketch in SATA *45*
Waniek, Marilyn Nelson 1946-
    See Nelson, Marilyn
Wannamaker, Bruce
    See Moncure, Jane Belk
Warbler, J. M.
    See Cocagnac, Augustin Maurice(-Jean)
Warburg, Sandol Stoddard
    See Stoddard, Sandol
Warburton, Tom 1968(?)- *218*
Ward, David 1967- *213*
Ward, E. D.
    See Gorey, Edward (St. John)
    and Lucas, E(dward) V(errall)
Ward, Ed
    See Stratemeyer, Edward L.
Ward, Helen 1962- *206*
    Earlier sketches in SATA *72, 144*
Ward, Jay 1920-1989
    Obituary *63*
Ward, Jennifer 1963- *146*
Ward, John (Stanton) 1917- *42*
Ward, Jonas
    See Ard, William
    and Cox, William R(obert)
    and Garfield, Brian (Francis Wynne)
Ward, Lynd (Kendall) 1905-1985 .... *36*
    Obituary *42*
    Earlier sketch in SATA *2*
Ward, Martha (Eads) *5*
Ward, Melanie
    See Curtis, Richard
    and Lynch, Marilyn
Ward, Nicholas John
    See Ward, Nick
Ward, Nick 1955- *190*
Ward, Tom
    See Stratemeyer, Edward L.
Wardell, Dean
    See Prince, J(ack) H(arvey)
Wardlaw, Lee 1955- *115*
    Earlier sketch in SATA *79*
Ware, Cheryl 1963- *101*
Ware, Chris 1967- *140*
Ware, Leon (Vernon) 1909-1976 .... *4*
Wargin, Kathy-jo 1964- *210*
    Earlier sketch in SATA *145*
Warhola, James 1955- *187*
Warner, Frank A. *67*
    Earlier sketch in SATA *1*
Warner, Gertrude Chandler 1890-1979 .... *9*
    Obituary *73*
Warner, J(ohn) F. 1929- *75*
Warner, Lucille Schulberg *30*
Warner, Matt
    See Fichter, George S.
Warner, Oliver (Martin Wilson) 1903-1976 . *29*
Warner, Sally 1946- *214*
    Earlier sketch in SATA *131*
Warner, Sunny (B.) 1931- *108*

Warnes, Tim 1971- *216*
    Earlier sketches in SATA *116, 166*
Warnes, Timothy
    See Warnes, Tim
Warnick, Elsa 1942- *113*
Warren, Andrea 1946- *98*
Warren, Betsy
    See Warren, Elizabeth Avery
Warren, Billy
    See Warren, William Stephen
Warren, Cathy 1951- *62*
    Brief entry *46*
Warren, Elizabeth
    See Supraner, Robyn
Warren, Elizabeth Avery 1916- *46*
    Brief entry *38*
Warren, Jackie M. 1953- *135*
Warren, Joshua P(aul) 1976- *107*
Warren, Joyce W(illiams) 1935- *18*
Warren, Mary Phraner 1929- *10*
Warren, Robert Penn 1905-1989 .... *46*
    Obituary *63*
Warren, Scott S. 1957- *79*
Warren, William Stephen 1882-1968 .... *9*
Warrick, Patricia Scott 1925- *35*
Warriner, John 1907(?)-1987
    Obituary *53*
Warsh
    See Warshaw, Jerry
Warshaw, Jerry 1929- *30*
Warshaw, Mary 1931- *89*
Warshofsky, Fred 1931- *24*
Warshofsky, Isaac
    See Singer, Isaac Bashevis
Wartski, Maureen (Ann Crane) 1940- *50*
    Brief entry *37*
Warwick, Alan R(oss) 1900-1973 .... *42*
Wa-sha-quon-asin
    See Belaney, Archibald Stansfeld
Wa-Sha-Quon-Asin
    See Belaney, Archibald Stansfeld
Washburn, Bradford 1910-2007 .... *38*
    Obituary *181*
Washburn, Henry Bradford, Jr.
    See Washburn, Bradford
Washburn, Jan(ice) 1926- *63*
Washburn, Lucia *193*
Washburne, Carolyn Kott 1944- *86*
Washburne, Heluiz Chandler 1892-1970 ...... *10*
    Obituary *26*
Washington, Booker T. 1856-1915 .... *28*
Washington, Donna L. 1967- *159*
    Earlier sketch in SATA *98*
Wasserman, Robin 1978- *207*
Wasserstein, Wendy 1950-2006 .... *94*
    Obituary *174*
Wassiljewa, Tatjana 1928- *106*
Watanabe, Etsuko 1968- *219*
Watanabe, Shigeo 1928- *131*
    Brief entry *32*
    Earlier sketch in SATA *39*
    See also CLR *8*
Waters, John F(rederick) 1930- *4*
Waters, Summer
    See Sykes, Julie
Waters, Tony 1958- *75*
Waterton, Betty 1923- *99*
    Brief entry *34*
    Earlier sketch in SATA *37*
Waterton, Betty Marie
    See Waterton, Betty
Watkins, Dawn L. *126*
Watkins, Gloria Jean
    See hooks, bell
Watkins, Lis
    See Watkins, Liselotte
Watkins, Liselotte 1971- *215*
Watkins, Lois 1930- *88*
Watkins, Peter 1934- *66*
Watkins, Yoko Kawashima 1933- *93*

Watkins-Pitchford, Denys James
    1905-1990 .... *87*
    Obituary *66*
    Earlier sketch in SATA *6*
    See also SAAS *4*
Watling, James 1933- *117*
    Earlier sketch in SATA *67*
Watson, Aldren A(uld) 1917- *42*
    Brief entry *36*
Watson, Amy Zakrzewski 1965- *76*
Watson, B. S.
    See Teitelbaum, Michael
Watson, Carol 1949- *78*
Watson, C.G. *193*
Watson, Clyde 1947- *68*
    Earlier sketch in SATA *5*
    See also CLR *3*
Watson, Helen Orr 1892-1978
    Obituary *24*
Watson, James 1936- *106*
    Earlier sketch in SATA *10*
Watson, Jane Werner 1915- *54*
    Earlier sketch in SATA *3*
Watson, Jesse Joshua *199*
Watson, John H.
    See Farmer, Philip Jose
Watson, Mary 1953- *117*
Watson, N. Cameron 1955- *81*
Watson, Nancy Dingman *32*
Watson, Pauline 1925- *14*
Watson, Richard F.
    See Silverberg, Robert
Watson, Richard Jesse 1951- *211*
    Earlier sketch in SATA *62*
Watson, Sally (Lou) 1924- *3*
Watson, Sasha *211*
Watson, Wendy (McLeod) 1942- *142*
    Earlier sketches in SATA *5, 74*
Watson Taylor, Elizabeth 1915- *41*
Watt, Melanie 1975- *193*
    Earlier sketch in SATA *136*
Watt, Thomas 1935- *4*
Wattenberg, Jane *174*
Watterson, Bill 1958- *66*
Watt-Evans, Lawrence 1954- *121*
Watts, (Anna) Bernadette 1942- *103*
    Earlier sketch in SATA *4*
Watts, Ephraim
    See Horne, Richard Henry Hengist
Watts, Franklin (Mowry) 1904-1978 .... *46*
    Obituary *21*
Watts, Helen L. Hoke 1903-1990
    Obituary *65*
Watts, Irene N(aemi) 1931- *111*
    Earlier sketch in SATA *56*
Watts, Isaac 1674-1748 .... *52*
Watts, James K(ennedy) M(offitt) 1955- *59*
Watts, Jeri Hanel 1957- *170*
Watts, Julia 1969- *103*
Watts, Leander 1956- *146*
Watts, Leslie Elizabeth 1961- *168*
Watts, Mabel Pizzey 1906-1994 .... *11*
Watts, Nigel 1957-1999 .... *121*
Waugh, C. C. Roessel
    See Waugh, Carol-Lynn Rossel
    and Waugh, Charles G(ordon)
Waugh, Carol-Lynn Rossel 1947- *41*
Waugh, Dorothy -1996 .... *11*
Waugh, Sylvia 1935- *169*
Waugh, Virginia
    See Sorensen, Virginia
Wax, Wendy A. 1963- *219*
    Earlier sketches in SATA *73, 163*
Wayland, April Halprin 1954- *143*
    Earlier sketch in SATA *78*
    See also SAAS *26*
Wayland, Patrick
    See O'Connor, Richard
Wayne, (Anne) Jenifer 1917-1982 .... *32*
Wayne, Kyra Petrovskaya 1918- *8*

Wayne, Richard
  See Decker, Duane
Wayshak, Deborah Noyes
  See Noyes, Deborah
Waystaff, Simon
  See Swift, Jonathan
Weales, Gerald (Clifford) 1925- *11*
Weary, Ogdred
  See Gorey, Edward (St. John)
Weatherford, Carole Boston 1956- *181*
  Earlier sketch in SATA *138*
Weatherill, Cat *203*
Weatherly, Lee 1967- *192*
Weatherly, Myra 1926- *130*
Weatherly, Myra S.
  See Weatherly, Myra
Weaver, Brian M.
  See Numberman, Neil
Weaver, Harriett E. 1908-1993 .... *65*
Weaver, John L. 1949- *42*
Weaver, Robyn
  See Conley, Robyn
Weaver, Robyn M.
  See Conley, Robyn
Weaver, Tess *197*
Weaver, Ward
  See Mason, F(rancis) van Wyck
Weaver, Will 1950- *217*
  Earlier sketches in SATA *88, 109, 161*
Weaver, William Weller
  See Weaver, Will
Weaver-Gelzer, Charlotte 1950- *79*
Webb, Christopher
  See Wibberley, Leonard
Webb, Jacqueline
  See Pearce, Margaret
Webb, Jacquelyn
  See Pearce, Margaret
  and Pearce, Margaret
Webb, Jean Francis (III) 1910-1991 .... *35*
Webb, Kaye 1914- *60*
Webb, Lois Sinaiko 1922- *82*
Webb, Margot 1934- *67*
Webb, Sharon 1936-2010 .... *41*
Webb, Sophie 1958- *135*
Webber, Andrew Lloyd
  See Lloyd Webber, Andrew
Webber, Desiree Morrison 1956- *170*
Webber, Irma E(leanor Schmidt)
  1904-1995 .... *14*
Weber, Alfons 1921- *8*
Weber, Bruce 1942- *120*
  Earlier sketch in SATA *73*
Weber, Debora 1955- *58*
Weber, EdNah New Rider 1919(?)- *168*
Weber, Elka 1968- *219*
Weber, Jill 1950- *209*
  Earlier sketch in SATA *127*
Weber, Judith E(ichler) 1938- *64*
Weber, Ken(neth J.) 1940- *90*
Weber, Lenora Mattingly 1895-1971 .... *2*
  Obituary *26*
Weber, Lisa K. *217*
Weber, Lori 1959- *220*
Weber, Michael 1945- *87*
Weber, Sandra 1961- *158*
Weber, William J(ohn) 1927- *14*
Webster, Alice Jane Chandler 1876-1916 ..... *17*
Webster, David 1930- *11*
Webster, Frank V. *67*
  Earlier sketch in SATA *1*
Webster, Gary
  See Garrison, Webb B(lack)
Webster, James 1925-1981 .... *17*
  Obituary *27*
Webster, Jean
  See Webster, Alice Jane Chandler
Wechsler, Doug *189*
Wechsler, Herman J. 1904-1976
  Obituary *20*

Wechter, Nell (Carolyn) Wise 1913-1989 .. *127*
  Earlier sketch in SATA *60*
Weck, Thomas L. 1942- *62*
Wedd, Kate
  See Gregory, Philippa
Weddle, Ethel Harshbarger 1897-1996 .... *11*
Wedekind, Annie *204*
Weeks, Sarah *194*
  Earlier sketch in SATA *158*
Weems, David B(urnola) 1922- *80*
Wees, Frances Shelley 1902-1982 .... *58*
Weevers, Peter 1944- *59*
Wegen, Ronald 1946-1985 .... *99*
Wegman, William (George) 1943- *135*
  Earlier sketches in SATA *78, 129*
Wegner, Fritz 1924- *20*
Weidhorn, Manfred 1931- *60*
Weidt, Maryann N. 1944- *85*
Weigel, Jeff 1958- *170*
Weigelt, Udo 1960- *201*
  Earlier sketch in SATA *168*
Weihs, Erika 1917- *107*
  Earlier sketch in SATA *15*
Weik, Mary Hays 1898(?)-1979 .... *3*
  Obituary *23*
Weil, Ann Yezner 1908-1969 .... *9*
Weil, Lisl 1910- *7*
Weilerstein, Sadie Rose 1894-1993 .... *3*
  Obituary *75*
Weill, Cynthia 1959- *167*
Wein, Elizabeth E. 1964- *151*
  Earlier sketch in SATA *82*
Wein, Elizabeth Eve
  See Wein, Elizabeth E.
Wein, Hallie
  See Zobel Nolan, Allia
Weinberg, Larry
  See Weinberg, Lawrence (E.)
Weinberg, Lawrence (E.) *92*
  Brief entry *48*
Weinberger, Tanya 1939- *84*
Weiner, Sandra 1922- *14*
Weingarten, Lynn *217*
Weingarten, Violet (Brown) 1915-1976 .... *3*
  Obituary *27*
Weingartner, Charles 1922- *5*
Weinheimer, Beckie 1958- *186*
Weinstein, Bruce 1960- *220*
Weinstein, Bruce M.
  See Weinstein, Bruce
Weinstein, Ellen Slusky 1959- *200*
Weinstein, Muriel Harris *215*
Weinstein, Nina 1951- *73*
Weinstock, Robert 1967- *204*
Weir, Bob 1947- *76*
Weir, Diana (R.) Loiewski 1958- *111*
Weir, Joan S(herman) 1928- *99*
Weir, LaVada *2*
Weir, Rosemary (Green) 1905-1994 .... *21*
Weir, Wendy 1949- *76*
Weis, Margaret 1948- *164*
  Earlier sketches in SATA *38, 92*
Weisberger, Bernard A(llen) 1922- *21*
Weisburd, Stefi 1957- *202*
Weiser, Marjorie P(hillis) K(atz) 1934- *33*
Weisgard, Leonard (Joseph) 1916-2000 ...... *85*
  Obituary *122*
  Earlier sketches in SATA *2, 30*
  See also SAAS *19*
Weiss, Adelle 1920- *18*
Weiss, Ann E(dwards) 1943- *69*
  Earlier sketch in SATA *30*
  See also SAAS *13*
Weiss, Edna
  See Barth, Edna
Weiss, Ellen 1953- *44*
Weiss, Harvey 1922- *76*
  Earlier sketches in SATA *1, 27*
  See also CLR *4*
  See also SAAS *19*
Weiss, Jaqueline Shachter 1926- *65*

Weiss, Malcolm E. 1928- *3*
Weiss, Margaret Edith
  See Weis, Margaret
Weiss, Miriam
  See Schlein, Miriam
Weiss, Mitch 1951- *183*
  Earlier sketch in SATA *123*
Weiss, Nicki 1954- *86*
  Earlier sketch in SATA *33*
Weiss, Renee Karol 1923- *5*
Weissberger, Ela 1930- *181*
Weissberger, Ela Stein
  See Weissberger, Ela
Weissenborn, Hellmuth 1898-1982
  Obituary *31*
Weissman, Elissa Brent *217*
Weitzman, David L. 1936- *172*
  Earlier sketch in SATA *122*
Wekesser, Carol A. 1963- *76*
Welber, Robert *26*
Welch, Amanda (Jane) 1945- *75*
Welch, D'Alte Aldridge 1907-1970
  Obituary *27*
Welch, Holly *206*
Welch, Jean-Louise
  See Kempton, Jean Welch
Welch, Pauline
  See Bodenham, Hilda Morris
Welch, Ronald
  See Felton, Ronald Oliver
Welch, Sheila Kelly 1945- *130*
Welch, Willy 1952- *93*
Weldin, Frauke 1969- *188*
Welford, Sue 1942- *75*
Weller, George 1907-2002 .... *31*
  Obituary *140*
Weller, George Anthony
  See Weller, George
Welling, Peter J. 1947- *135*
Wellington, Monica 1957- *157*
  Earlier sketches in SATA *67, 99*
Wellman, Alice 1900-1984 .... *51*
  Brief entry *36*
Wellman, Manly Wade 1903-1986 .... *6*
  Obituary *47*
Wellman, Paul I. 1898-1966 .... *3*
Wellman, Paul Iselin
  See Wellman, Paul I.
Wellman, Sam 1939- *122*
Wellman, Samuel
  See Wellman, Sam
Wells, H. G. 1866-1946 .... *20*
  See also CLR *133*
Wells, Helen
  See Campbell, Hope
Wells, Helen 1910-1986 .... *49*
  Earlier sketch in SATA *2*
Wells, Herbert George
  See Wells, H. G.
Wells, J. Wellington
  See de Camp, L. Sprague
Wells, June
  See Swinford, Betty (June Wells)
Wells, Robert
  See Welsch, Roger L(ee)
Wells, Robert E. *184*
Wells, Rosemary 1943- *207*
  Earlier sketches in SATA *18, 69, 114, 156*
  See also CLR *69*
  See also SAAS *1*
Wells, Susan (Mary) 1951- *78*
Wels, Byron G(erald) 1924-1993 .... *9*
Welsbacher, Anne 1955- *89*
Welsch, Roger L(ee) 1936- *82*
Welsh, David
  See Hills, C.A.R.
Welsh, Mary Flynn 1910(?)-1984
  Obituary *38*
Welsh, T.K. 1956- *184*
Weltner, Linda R(iverly) 1938- *38*

Welton, Jude 1955- *143*
Earlier sketch in SATA *79*
Welty, S. F.
See Welty, Susan F.
Welty, Susan F. 1905- *9*
Wemmlinger, Raymond *190*
Wendelin, Rudolph 1910-2000 .... *23*
Weninger, Brigitte 1960- *189*
Wentworth, Robert
See Hamilton, Edmond
Werlin, Nancy 1961- *161*
Earlier sketches in SATA *87, 119*
Werner, Elsa Jane
See Watson, Jane Werner
Werner, Herma 1926- *47*
Brief entry *41*
Werner, Jane
See Watson, Jane Werner
Werner, K.
See Casewit, Curtis W(erner)
Wersba, Barbara 1932- *58*
Autobiography Feature *103*
Earlier sketch in SATA *1*
See also CLR *78*
See also SAAS *2*
Werstein, Irving 1914(?)-1971 .... *14*
Werth, Kurt 1896-1983 .... *20*
Wesley, Alison
See Barnes, Michael
Wesley, Kathryn
See Rusch, Kristine Kathryn
Wesley, Mary (Aline) 1912-2002 .... *66*
Wesley, Valerie Wilson 1947- *168*
Earlier sketch in SATA *106*
West, Andrew
See Arthur, Robert, (Jr.)
West, Anna 1938- *40*
West, Barbara
See Price, Olive
West, Betty 1921- *11*
West, Bruce 1951- *63*
West, C. P.
See Wodehouse, P. G.
West, Dorothy
See Benson, Mildred
West, Emily Govan 1919- *38*
West, Emmy
See West, Emily Govan
West, James
See Withers, Carl A.
West, Jerry
See Svenson, Andrew E(dward)
West, (Mary) Jessamyn 1902-1984
Obituary *37*
West, John
See Arthur, Robert, (Jr.)
West, Owen
See Koontz, Dean
West, Ward
See Borland, Harold Glen
Westall, Robert (Atkinson) 1929-1993 .... *69*
Obituary *75*
Earlier sketch in SATA *23*
See also CLR *13*
See also SAAS *2*
Westaway, Jane 1948- *121*
Westcott, Nadine Bernard 1949- *130*
Westera, Marleen 1962- *187*
Westerberg, Christine 1950- *29*
Westerduin, Anne 1945- *105*
Westerfeld, Scott 1963- *161*
Westervelt, Virginia Veeder 1914-2005 .... *10*
Westheimer, David 1917-2005 .... *14*
Obituary *170*
Westheimer, David Kaplan
See Westheimer, David
Westmacott, Mary
See Christie, Agatha
Westman, Barbara *70*
Westman, Paul (Wendell) 1956- *39*
Westmoreland, William C. 1914-2005 .... *63*

Westmoreland, William Childs
See Westmoreland, William C.
Weston, Allen
See Hogarth, Grace (Weston Allen)
and Norton, Andre
Weston, Carol 1956- *135*
Weston, Carrie *190*
Weston, John (Harrison) 1932- *21*
Weston, Martha 1947- *119*
Earlier sketch in SATA *53*
Weston, Robert Paul *209*
Westphal, Arnold Carl 1897- *57*
Westrup, Hugh *102*
Westwood, Jennifer 1940-2008 .... *10*
Obituary *192*
Wexler, Jerome (LeRoy) 1923- *14*
Weyland, Jack 1940- *81*
Weyn, Suzanne 1955- *220*
Earlier sketches in SATA *63, 101, 164*
Weyr, Garret
See Freymann-Weyr, Garret
Wezyk, Joanna 1966- *82*
Whaley, Joyce Irene 1923- *61*
Whalin, W. Terry 1953- *93*
Wharf, Michael
See Weller, George
Wharmby, Margot *63*
Wharton, Edith 1862-1937
See CLR *136*
Wharton, Edith Newbold Jones
See Wharton, Edith
Whatley, Bruce 1954- *213*
Earlier sketch in SATA *177*
Wheatley, Arabelle 1921- *16*
Wheatley, Nadia 1949- *147*
Wheeler, Cindy 1955- *49*
Brief entry *40*
Wheeler, Deborah 1947- *83*
Wheeler, Janet D. *1*
Wheeler, Jill C. 1964- *136*
Earlier sketch in SATA *86*
Wheeler, Jody 1952- *148*
Earlier sketch in SATA *84*
Wheeler, Lisa 1963- *200*
Earlier sketch in SATA *162*
Wheeler, Opal 1898- *23*
Whelan, Elizabeth M(urphy) 1943- *14*
Whelan, Gloria 1923- *178*
Earlier sketches in SATA *85, 128*
See also CLR *90*
Whelan, Gloria Ann
See Whelan, Gloria
Whipple, A(ddison) B(eecher) C(olvin)
1918- *64*
Whipple, Cal
See Whipple, A(ddison) B(eecher) C(olvin)
Whisp, Kennilworthy
See Rowling, J.K.
Whistler, Reginald John 1905-1944 .... *30*
Whistler, Rex
See Whistler, Reginald John
Whitaker, Zai *183*
Whitcher, Susan (Godsil) 1952- *96*
Whitcomb, Jon 1906-1988 .... *10*
Obituary *56*
Whitcomb, Laura 1958- *214*
Earlier sketch in SATA *171*
White, Anne Terry 1896-1980 .... *2*
White, Bessie (Felstiner) 1892(?)-1986
Obituary *50*
White, Carolyn 1948- *130*
White, Dale
See Place, Marian T(empleton)
White, Dori 1919- *10*
White, E. B. 1899-1985 .... *100*
Obituary *44*
Earlier sketches in SATA *2, 29*
See also CLR *107*
White, Eliza Orne 1856-1947
See YABC *2*

White, Elwyn Brooks
See White, E. B.
White, Florence M(eiman) 1910- *14*
White, Laurence B(arton), Jr. 1935- *10*
White, Lee *176*
White, Martin 1943- *51*
White, Nancy 1942- *126*
White, Ramy Allison *67*
Earlier sketch in SATA *1*
White, Robb 1909-1990 .... *83*
Earlier sketch in SATA *1*
See also CLR *3*
See also SAAS *1*
White, Ruth 1942- *186*
Autobiography Feature *186*
Earlier sketches in SATA *39, 117, 165*
White, Ruth C.
See White, Ruth
White, T(erence) H(anbury) 1906-1964 .... *12*
See also CLR *139*
White, Tekla N. 1934- *115*
White, Timothy (Thomas Anthony)
1952-2002 .... *60*
White, Tom 1923- *148*
White, William, Jr. 1934- *16*
Whitehead, Don(ald) F. 1908-1981 .... *4*
Whitehead, Jenny 1964- *191*
Whitehead, Kathy 1957- *176*
Whitehouse, Arch
See Whitehouse, Arthur George Joseph
Whitehouse, Arthur George Joseph
1895-1979 .... *14*
Obituary *23*
Whitehouse, Elizabeth S(cott) 1893-1968 .... *35*
Whitehouse, Jeanne
See Peterson, Jeanne Whitehouse
Whitelaw, Nancy 1933- *166*
Earlier sketch in SATA *76*
Whitesel, Cheryl Aylward *162*
Whiting, Sue 1960- *205*
Whiting, Susan Allana
See Whiting, Sue
Whitinger, R. D.
See Place, Marian T(empleton)
Whitley, Mary Ann
See Sebrey, Mary Ann
Whitley, Peggy 1938- *140*
Whitlock, Pamela 1921(?)-1982
Obituary *31*
Whitlock, Ralph 1914-1995 .... *35*
Whitman, Alice
See Marker, Sherry
Whitman, Candace 1958- *208*
Whitman, Sylvia (Choate) 1961- *135*
Earlier sketch in SATA *85*
Whitman, Walt 1819-1892 .... *20*
Whitman, Walter
See Whitman, Walt
Whitmore, Arvella 1922- *125*
Whitmore, Benette 1955- *203*
Whitney, Alex(andra) 1922- *14*
Whitney, David C(harles) 1921- *48*
Brief entry *29*
Whitney, Kim Ablon *162*
Whitney, Phyllis A. 1903-2008 .... *30*
Obituary *189*
Earlier sketch in SATA *1*
See also CLR *59*
Whitney, Phyllis Ayame
See Whitney, Phyllis A.
Whitney, Sharon 1937- *63*
Whitney, Thomas P. 1917-2007 .... *25*
Obituary *189*
Whitney, Thomas Porter
See Whitney, Thomas P.
Whittington, Mary K(athrine) 1941- *75*
Whitworth, John 1945- *123*
Whybrow, Ian *202*
Earlier sketch in SATA *132*
Whyte, Mal(colm Kenneth, Jr.) 1933- *62*

Whyte, Mary 1953- *148*
  Earlier sketch in SATA *94*
Whyte, Ron 1942(?)-1989
  Obituary *63*
Whytock, Cherry *177*
Wiater, Stanley 1953- *84*
Wibbelsman, Charles J(oseph) 1945- *59*
Wibberley, Leonard 1915-1983 .... *45*
  Obituary *36*
  Earlier sketch in SATA *2*
  See also CLR *3*
Wibberley, Leonard Patrick O'Connor
  See Wibberley, Leonard
Wiberg, Harald (Albin) 1908- *93*
  Brief entry *40*
Wick, Walter 1953- *148*
Wickberg, Susan
  See Rottman, S.L.
Wickens, Elaine *86*
Wicker, Ireene 1905(?)-1987
  Obituary *55*
Wickstrom, Sylvie 1960- *169*
Wickstrom, Thor 1960- *200*
Widdemer, Mabel Cleland 1902-1964 .... *5*
Widener, Terry 1950- *209*
  Earlier sketch in SATA *105*
Widerberg, Siv 1931- *10*
Wiebe, Rudy 1934- *156*
Wiebe, Rudy Henry
  See Wiebe, Rudy
Wieler, Diana (Jean) 1961- *109*
Wiener, Lori 1956- *84*
Wier, Ester (Alberti) 1910-2000 .... *3*
Wiese, Kurt 1887-1974 .... *36*
  Obituary *24*
  Earlier sketch in SATA *3*
  See also CLR *86*
Wiesel, Elie 1928- *56*
Wiesel, Eliezer
  See Wiesel, Elie
Wiesner, David 1956- *181*
  Earlier sketches in SATA *72, 117, 139*
  See also CLR *84*
Wiesner, Portia
  See Takakjian, Portia
Wiesner, William 1899-1984 .... *5*
Wiggers, Raymond 1952- *82*
Wiggin, Eric E. 1939- *167*
  Earlier sketch in SATA *88*
Wiggin, Eric Ellsworth 1939-
  See Wiggin, Eric E.
Wiggin (Riggs), Kate Douglas (Smith)
  1856-1923
  See YABC *1*
  See also CLR *52*
Wiggins, VeraLee (Chesnut) 1928-1995 .... *89*
Wight, Eric 1974- *218*
Wight, James Alfred
  See Herriot, James
Wignell, Edel 1936- *69*
Wijnberg, Ellen *85*
Wikland, Ilon 1930- *93*
  Brief entry *32*
Wikler, Madeline 1943- *114*
Wilber, Donald N(ewton) 1907-1997 .... *35*
Wilbur, C. Keith 1923- *27*
Wilbur, Frances 1921- *107*
Wilbur, Helen L. 1948- *204*
Wilbur, Richard 1921- *108*
  Earlier sketch in SATA *9*
Wilbur, Richard Purdy
  See Wilbur, Richard
Wilburn, Kathy 1948- *68*
Wilcox, Charlotte 1948- *72*
Wilcox, Leah 1975(?)- *207*
Wilcox, R(uth) Turner 1888-1970 .... *36*
Wilcox, Roger
  See Collins, Paul
Wild, Jocelyn 1941- *46*
Wild, Kate 1954- *192*

Wild, Margaret 1948- *197*
  Earlier sketch in SATA *151*
Wild, Robin (Evans) 1936- *46*
Wild, Robyn 1947- *117*
Wilde, D. Gunther
  See Hurwood, Bernhardt J.
Wilde, Oscar 1854(?)-1900 .... *24*
  See also CLR *114*
Wilde, Oscar Fingal O'Flahertie Willis
  See Wilde, Oscar
Wilder, Buck
  See Smith, Tim(othy R.)
Wilder, Laura Elizabeth Ingalls
  See Wilder, Laura Ingalls
Wilder, Laura Ingalls 1867-1957 .... *100*
  Earlier sketches in SATA *15, 29*
  See also CLR *111*
Wildsmith, Brian 1930- *124*
  Earlier sketches in SATA *16, 69*
  See also CLR *52*
  See also SAAS *5*
Wiles, Deborah *171*
Wilhelm, Doug 1952- *190*
Wilhelm, Hans 1945- *196*
  Autobiography Feature *196*
  Earlier sketches in SATA *58, 135*
  See also CLR *46*
  See also SAAS *21*
Wilkie, Katharine E(lliott) 1904-1980 .... *31*
Wilkin, Eloise 1904-1987 .... *49*
  Obituary *54*
Wilkins, Frances 1923- *14*
Wilkins, Kim *147*
Wilkins, Marilyn (Ruth) 1926- *30*
Wilkins, Marne
  See Wilkins, Marilyn (Ruth)
Wilkins, Mary Huiskamp 1926- *2*
  See also CLR *42*
Wilkins, Mary Huiskamp Calhoun
  See Wilkins, Mary Huiskamp
Wilkins, Rose *180*
Wilkinson, (Thomas) Barry 1923- *50*
  Brief entry *32*
Wilkinson, Beth 1925- *80*
Wilkinson, Brenda 1946- *91*
  Earlier sketch in SATA *14*
  See also CLR *20*
Wilkinson, (John) Burke 1913-2000 .... *4*
Wilkinson, Carole 1950- *210*
Wilkinson, Sylvia 1940- *56*
  Brief entry *39*
Wilkon, Jozef 1930- *133*
  Earlier sketches in SATA *31, 71*
Wilkowski, Sue *193*
Wilks, Michael Thomas 1947- *44*
Wilks, Mike
  See Wilks, Michael Thomas
Will
  See Lipkind, William
Willard, Barbara (Mary) 1909-1994 .... *74*
  Earlier sketch in SATA *17*
  See also CLR *2*
  See also SAAS *5*
Willard, Elizabeth Kimmel
  See Kimmel, Elizabeth Cody
Willard, Mildred Wilds 1911-1978 .... *14*
Willard, Nancy 1936- *191*
  Brief entry *30*
  Earlier sketches in SATA *37, 71, 127*
  See also CLR *5*
Willcox, Isobel 1907-1996 .... *42*
Willems, Mo *180*
  Earlier sketch in SATA *154*
  See also CLR *114*
Willett, Edward 1959- *115*
Willett, Edward C.
  See Willett, Edward
Willey, Bee *184*
Willey, Margaret 1950- *86*
Willey, Robert
  See Ley, Willy

Willhoite, Michael A. 1946- *71*
William, Kate
  See Armstrong, Jennifer
Williams, Alex 1969- *209*
Williams, Arlene *171*
Williams, Barbara 1925- *107*
  Earlier sketch in SATA *11*
  See also CLR *48*
  See also SAAS *16*
Williams, Barbara 1937- *62*
Williams, Beryl
  See Epstein, Beryl
Williams, Brian (Peter) 1943- *54*
Williams, Carol Lynch 1959- *212*
  Earlier sketch in SATA *110*
Williams, Charles
  See Collier, James Lincoln
Williams, Clyde C. 1881-1974 .... *8*
  Obituary *27*
Williams, Coe
  See Harrison, C(hester) William
Williams, Colleen Madonna Flood 1963- .. *156*
Williams, Cynthia G. 1958- *123*
Williams, Dar 1967- *168*
Williams, Donna Reilly 1945- *83*
Williams, Dorothy
  See Williams, Marcia
Williams, Dorothy Snowden
  See Williams, Dar
Williams, Eric (Ernest) 1911-1983 .... *14*
  Obituary *38*
Williams, Ferelith Eccles
  See Eccles Williams, Ferelith
Williams, Frances B.
  See Browin, Frances Williams
Williams, Garth (Montgomery) 1912-1996 .. *66*
  Obituary *90*
  Earlier sketch in SATA *18*
  See also CLR *57*
  See also SAAS *7*
Williams, Guy R(ichard) 1920- *11*
Williams, Hawley
  See Heyliger, William
Williams, Helen 1948- *77*
Williams, J. R.
  See Williams, Jeanne
Williams, J. Walker
  See Wodehouse, P. G.
Williams, Jay 1914-1978 .... *41*
  Obituary *24*
  Earlier sketch in SATA *3*
  See also CLR *8*
Williams, Jeanne 1930- *5*
Williams, Jenny 1939- *60*
Williams, Karen Lynn 1952- *99*
  Earlier sketch in SATA *66*
Williams, Kit 1946(?)- *44*
  See also CLR *4*
Williams, L. E.
  See Williams, Laura E.
Williams, Laura E.
  See Williams, Laura Ellen
Williams, Laura Ellen *180*
Williams, Leslie 1941- *42*
Williams, Linda 1948- *59*
Williams, Louise Bonino 1904(?)-1984
  Obituary *39*
Williams, Lynn
  See Hale, Arlene
Williams, Marcia 1945- *159*
  Earlier sketches in SATA *71, 97*
Williams, Marcia Dorothy
  See Williams, Marcia
Williams, Margery
  See Bianco, Margery Williams
Williams, Mark
  See Arthur, Robert, (Jr.)
Williams, Mark London 1959- *140*
Williams, Maureen 1951- *12*
Williams, Michael
  See St. John, Wylly Folk

Williams, Patrick J.
  See Griffin, W. E. B.
Williams, Paulette Linda
  See Shange, Ntozake
Williams, Pete
  See Faulknor, Cliff(ord Vernon)
Williams, S. P.
  See Hart, Virginia
Williams, Sam 177
  Earlier sketch in SATA *124*
Williams, Selma R(uth) 1925- 14
Williams, Sherley Anne 1944-1999 78
  Obituary 116
Williams, Sheron 1955- 77
Williams, Shirley
  See Williams, Sherley Anne
Williams, Slim
  See Williams, Clyde C.
Williams, Sophy 1965- 135
Williams, Sue 1948-2007 208
Williams, Susan
  See Beckhorn, Susan Williams
Williams, Suzanne
  See Williams, Suzanne Morgan
Williams, Suzanne 1953- 202
  Earlier sketch in SATA *71*
Williams, Suzanne M.
  See Williams, Suzanne Morgan
Williams, Suzanne Morgan 1949- 207
Williams, Ursula Moray
  See Moray Williams, Ursula
Williams, Vera B(aker) 1927- 102
  Brief entry 33
  Earlier sketch in SATA *53*
  See also CLR *9*
Williams-Andriani, Renee 1963- 98
Williams-Ellis, (Mary) Amabel (Nassau
  Strachey) 1894-1984 29
  Obituary 41
Williams-Garcia, Rita 1957- 160
  Earlier sketch in SATA *98*
  See also CLR *36*
Williamson, Gwyneth 1965- 109
Williamson, Henry (William) 1895-1977 37
  Obituary 30
Williamson, Joanne S(mall) 1926- 122
  Earlier sketch in SATA *3*
Williamson, Kate T. 1979- 215
Williamson, Melanie 196
Willis, Charles
  See Clarke, Arthur C.
Willis, Connie 1945- 110
  See also CLR *66*
Willis, Cynthia Chapman 215
Willis, Jeanne 1959- 195
  Earlier sketches in SATA *61, 123*
Willis, Jeanne Mary
  See Willis, Jeanne
Willis, Meredith Sue 1946- 101
Willis, Nancy Carol 1952- 139
  Earlier sketch in SATA *93*
Willis, Paul J. 1955- 113
Willms, Russ 95
Willoughby, Lee Davis
  See Avallone, Michael (Angelo, Jr.)
  and Brandner, Gary (Phil)
  and Deming, Richard
  and DeAndrea, William L(ouis)
  and Laymon, Richard (Carl)
  and Streib, Dan(iel Thomas)
  and Toombs, John
  and Webb, Jean Francis (III)
Willson, Robina Beckles
  See Beckles Willson, Robina
Wilma, Dana
  See Faralla, Dana
Wilsdorf, Anne 1954- 191
Wilson, April 80
Wilson, Barbara Ker
  See Ker Wilson, Barbara
Wilson, Beth P(ierre) 8

Wilson, Budge 1927- 55
  Brief entry 51
Wilson, Carletta 1951- 81
Wilson, Carter 1941- 6
Wilson, Charles Morrow 1905-1977 30
Wilson, Christopher B. 1910(?)-1985
  Obituary 46
Wilson, Darryl B(abe) 1939- 90
Wilson, Diane Lee 172
Wilson, Dirk
  See Pohl, Frederik
Wilson, Dorothy Clarke 1904-2003 16
Wilson, Edward A(rthur) 1886-1970 38
Wilson, Ellen (Janet Cameron) (?)-1976 9
  Obituary 26
Wilson, Eric (H.) 1940- 34
  Brief entry 32
Wilson, Erica 51
Wilson, Forrest 1918- 27
Wilson, Gahan 1930- 35
  Brief entry 27
Wilson, Gina 1943- 85
  Brief entry 34
  Earlier sketch in SATA *36*
Wilson, (Leslie) Granville 1912- 14
Wilson, Hazel (Hutchins) 1898-1992 3
  Obituary 73
Wilson, J(erry) M. 1964- 121
Wilson, Jacqueline 1945- 199
  Brief entry 52
  Earlier sketches in SATA *61, 102, 153*
Wilson, John 1922- 22
Wilson, John 1951- 182
Wilson, John Alexander
  See Wilson, John
Wilson, Johnniece Marshall 1944- 75
Wilson, Jonathan 1950- 181
Wilson, Joyce M. 84
  Earlier sketch in SATA *21*
  See also SAAS *24*
Wilson, Karma 221
  Earlier sketch in SATA *174*
Wilson, Leslie 1952- 166
Wilson, Linda Miller 1936- 116
Wilson, Lionel 1924-2003 33
  Brief entry 31
  Obituary 144
Wilson, Marjorie
  See Wilson, Budge
Wilson, Martin 1973- 205
Wilson, Maurice (Charles John) 1914- 46
Wilson, Nancy Hope 1947- 138
  Earlier sketch in SATA *81*
Wilson, Nathan D.
  See Wilson, N.D.
Wilson, N.D. 1978- 194
Wilson, Nick
  See Ellis, Edward S.
Wilson, Phil 1948- 181
Wilson, Ron(ald William) 1941- 38
Wilson, Sarah 1934- 208
  Earlier sketches in SATA *50, 142*
Wilson, Tom 1931- 33
  Brief entry 30
Wilson, Troy 1970- 169
Wilson, Walt(er N.) 1939- 14
Wilson-Max, Ken 1965- 170
  Earlier sketch in SATA *93*
Wilton, Elizabeth 1937- 14
Wilton, Hal
  See Pepper, Frank S.
Wilwerding, Walter Joseph 1891-1966 9
Wimmer, Mike 1961- 194
  Earlier sketch in SATA *70*
Winborn, Marsha (Lynn) 1947- 75
Winch, John 1944- 165
  Earlier sketch in SATA *117*
Winchester, James H(ugh) 1917-1985 30
  Obituary 45
Winchester, Stanley
  See Youd, Samuel

Windawi, Thura al- 1983(?)- 165
Winders, Gertrude Hecker -1987 3
Windham, Basil
  See Wodehouse, P. G.
Windham, Kathryn T(ucker) 1918- 14
Windham, Sophie 184
Windling, Terri 1958- 151
Windrow, Martin
  See Windrow, Martin Clive
Windrow, Martin C.
  See Windrow, Martin Clive
Windrow, Martin Clive 1944- 68
Windsor, Claire
  See Hamerstrom, Frances
Windsor, Linda 1950- 124
Windsor, Patricia 1938- 78
  Earlier sketch in SATA *30*
  See also SAAS *19*
Wineman-Marcus, Irene 1952- 81
Winer, Yvonne 1934- 120
Winerip, Michael 175
Winfield, Arthur M.
  See Stratemeyer, Edward L.
Winfield, Edna
  See Stratemeyer, Edward L.
Winfield, Julia
  See Armstrong, Jennifer
Wing, Natasha 1960- 200
  Earlier sketch in SATA *82*
Wingerter, Linda S. 1973(?)- 207
Winget, Susan 211
Winick, Judd 1970- 124
Winks, Robin William 1930-2003 61
Winn, Alison
  See Wharmby, Margot
Winn, Chris 1952- 42
Winn, Janet Bruce 1928- 43
Winn, Marie 1936(?)- 38
Winnick, Karen B. 1946- 211
Winnick, Karen B(eth) B(inkoff) 1946- 51
Winn-Lederer, Ilene 198
Winslow, Barbara 1947- 91
Winstead, Rosie 180
Winston, Clara 1921-1983 54
  Obituary 39
Winston, Richard 1917-1979 54
Winston, Sherri 1964(?)- 201
Winter, Janet 1926- 126
Winter, Jeanette 1939- 184
  Earlier sketch in SATA *151*
Winter, Jonah 1962- 179
Winter, Milo (Kendall) 1888-1956 21
Winter, Paula Cecelia 1929- 48
Winter, R. R.
  See Winterbotham, R(ussell) R(obert)
Winter, Susan 182
Winterbotham, R(ussell) R(obert)
  1904-1971 10
Winterbotham, Russ
  See Winterbotham, R(ussell) R(obert)
Winterfeld, Henry 1901-1990 55
Winters, J. C.
  See Cross, Gilbert B.
Winters, Jon
  See Cross, Gilbert B.
Winters, Katherine
  See Winters, Kay
Winters, Kay 1936- 153
  Earlier sketch in SATA *103*
Winters, Nina 1944- 62
Winters, Paul A. 1965- 106
Winterson, Jeanette 1959- 190
Winterton, Gayle
  See Adams, William Taylor
Winthrop, Elizabeth 1948- 164
  Autobiography Feature 116
  Earlier sketches in SATA *8, 76*
  See also CLR *89*
Winton, Ian (Kenneth) 1960- 76
Winton, Tim 1960- 98

Wintz-Litty, Julie
  See Litty, Julie
Wirt, Ann
  See Benson, Mildred
Wirt, Mildred A.
  See Benson, Mildred
Wirtenberg, Patricia Z. 1932-2007 .... *10*
Wirtenberg, Patricia Zarrella
  See Wirtenberg, Patricia Z.
Wirth, Beverly 1938- *63*
Wirths, Claudine (Turner) G(ibson)
  1926-2000 .... *104*
  Earlier sketch in SATA *64*
Wise, Bill 1958- *191*
Wise, Lenny
  See Wise, Leonard
Wise, Leonard 1940- *167*
Wise, Leonard A.
  See Wise, Leonard
Wise, Leonard Allan
  See Wise, Leonard
Wise, William 1923- *163*
  Earlier sketch in SATA *4*
Wise, Winifred E. *2*
Wiseman, Ann (Sayre) 1926- *31*
Wiseman, B(ernard) 1922-1995 .... *4*
Wiseman, David 1916- *43*
  Brief entry *40*
Wiseman, Eva 1947- *210*
Wishinsky, Frieda 1948- *166*
  Earlier sketches in SATA *70, 112*
Wisler, G(ary) Clifton 1950- *103*
  Brief entry *46*
  Earlier sketch in SATA *58*
Wismer, Donald (Richard) 1946- *59*
Wisner, Bill
  See Wisner, William L.
Wisner, William L. 1914(?)-1983 .... *42*
Wisnewski, David 1953-2002
  See Wisniewski, David
Wisniewski, David 1953-2002 .... *95*
  Obituary *139*
  See also CLR *51*
Wister, Owen 1860-1938 .... *62*
Witham, (Phillip) Ross 1917- *37*
Withers, Carl A. 1900-1970 .... *14*
Withers, Pam 1956- *182*
Withrow, Sarah 1966- *199*
  Earlier sketch in SATA *124*
Witt, Dick 1948- *80*
Witt, Shirley Hill 1934- *17*
Wittanen, Etolin 1907- *55*
Wittels, Harriet Joan 1938- *31*
Wittig, Susan
  See Albert, Susan Wittig
Wittlinger, Ellen 1948- *189*
  Autobiography Feature *128*
  Earlier sketches in SATA *83, 122*
Wittman, Sally (Anne Christensen) 1941- *30*
Witty, Paul 1898-1976 .... *50*
  Obituary *30*
Wodehouse, P. G. 1881-1975 .... *22*
Wodehouse, Pelham Grenville
  See Wodehouse, P. G.
Wodge, Dreary
  See Gorey, Edward (St. John)
Woelfle, Gretchen 1945- *145*
Wohlberg, Meg 1905-1990 .... *41*
  Obituary *66*
Wohlrabe, Raymond A. 1900-1977 .... *4*
Wohnoutka, Mike *195*
Wojciechowska, Maia (Teresa) 1927-2002 ... *83*
  Autobiography Feature *104*
  Obituary *134*
  Earlier sketches in SATA *1, 28*
  See also CLR *1*
  See also SAAS *1*
Wojciechowski, Susan *126*
  Earlier sketch in SATA *78*
Wojnarowski, Adrian 1970- *190*
Wojtusik, Elizabeth *208*

Wolcott, Patty 1929- *14*
Wold, Allen L. 1943- *64*
Wold, Jo Anne 1938- *30*
Woldin, Beth Weiner 1955- *34*
Wolf, Allan 1963- *192*
Wolf, Bernard 1930- *102*
  Brief entry *37*
Wolf, Erica (Van Varick) 1978- *156*
Wolf, Gita 1956- *101*
Wolf, J. M.
  See Wolf, Joan M.
Wolf, Janet 1957- *78*
Wolf, Joan M. 1966- *193*
Wolf, Sallie 1950- *205*
  Earlier sketch in SATA *80*
Wolfe, Art 1952- *76*
Wolfe, Burton H. 1932- *5*
Wolfe, Frances *216*
Wolfe, Gene 1931- *165*
  Earlier sketch in SATA *118*
Wolfe, Gene Rodman
  See Wolfe, Gene
Wolfe, Gillian *199*
Wolfe, Louis 1905-1985 .... *8*
  Obituary *133*
Wolfe, Rinna (Evelyn) 1925- *38*
Wolfenden, George
  See Beardmore, George
Wolfer, Dianne 1961- *167*
  Autobiography Feature *117*
  Earlier sketch in SATA *104*
Wolff, Alexander (Nikolaus) 1957- *137*
  Earlier sketch in SATA *63*
Wolff, Ashley 1956- *203*
  Earlier sketches in SATA *50, 81, 155*
Wolff, Diane 1945- *27*
Wolff, Ferida 1946- *164*
  Earlier sketch in SATA *79*
Wolff, Jason 1972- *213*
Wolff, Jennifer Ashley
  See Wolff, Ashley
Wolff, Nancy *202*
Wolff, Robert Jay 1905-1977 .... *10*
Wolff, Sonia
  See Levitin, Sonia
Wolff, Virginia Euwer 1937- *137*
  Earlier sketch in SATA *78*
  See also CLR *62*
Wolfman, Judy 1933- *138*
Wolfson, Evelyn 1937- *62*
Wolitzer, Hilma 1930- *31*
Wolkoff, Judie (Edwards) *93*
  Brief entry *37*
Wolkstein, Diane 1942- *138*
  Earlier sketches in SATA *7, 82*
Wollheim, Donald A(llen) 1914-1990
  Obituary *69*
Wolny, P.
  See Janeczko, Paul B(ryan)
Wolters, Richard A. 1920-1993 .... *35*
Wondriska, William 1931- *6*
Wong, Jade Snow 1922-2006 .... *112*
  Obituary *175*
Wong, Janet S. 1962- *210*
  Earlier sketches in SATA *98, 148*
  See also CLR *94*
Wong, Nicole *214*
Woo, Howie 1974- *207*
Wood, Addie Robinson
  See Wiggin, Eric E.
Wood, Anne (Savage) 1937- *64*
Wood, Audrey *198*
  Brief entry *44*
  Earlier sketches in SATA *50, 81, 139*
  See also CLR *26*
Wood, Catherine
  See Etchison, Birdie L(ee)
Wood, David 1944- *212*
  Earlier sketch in SATA *87*

Wood, Don 1945- *50*
  Brief entry *44*
  See also CLR *26*
Wood, Douglas 1951- *180*
  Earlier sketches in SATA *81, 132*
Wood, Douglas Eric
  See Wood, Douglas
Wood, Edgar A(llardyce) 1907-1998 .... *14*
Wood, Esther
  See Brady, Esther Wood
Wood, Frances Elizabeth *34*
Wood, Frances M. 1951- *97*
Wood, Jacqueline
  See Wood, Jakki
Wood, Jakki 1957- *211*
Wood, James Playsted 1905- *1*
Wood, Jenny 1955- *88*
Wood, John Norris 1930- *85*
Wood, June Rae 1946- *120*
  Earlier sketch in SATA *79*
  See also CLR *82*
Wood, Kerry
  See Wood, Edgar A(llardyce)
Wood, Kim Marie *134*
Wood, Laura N.
  See Roper, Laura (Newbold) Wood
Wood, Linda C(arol) 1945- *59*
Wood, Marcia 1956- *80*
Wood, Marcia Mae
  See Wood, Marcia
Wood, Nancy
  See Wood, Nancy C.
Wood, Nancy C. 1936- *178*
  Earlier sketch in SATA *6*
Wood, Nuria
  See Nobisso, Josephine
Wood, Owen 1929- *64*
Wood, Phyllis Anderson 1923- *33*
  Brief entry *30*
Wood, Richard 1949- *110*
Wood, Tim(othy William Russell) 1946- *88*
Wood, Wallace 1927-1981
  Obituary *33*
Woodard, Carol 1929- *14*
Woodburn, John Henry 1914- *11*
Woodbury, David Oakes 1896-1981 .... *62*
Woodford, Peggy 1937- *25*
Woodhouse, Barbara (Blackburn)
  1910-1988 .... *63*
Woodhull, Ann Love *194*
Wooding, Chris 1977- *166*
Wooding, Sharon
  See Wooding, Sharon L(ouise)
Wooding, Sharon L(ouise) 1943- *66*
Woodman, Allen 1954- *76*
Woodrich, Mary Neville 1915- *2*
Woodruff, Elvira 1951- *211*
  Earlier sketches in SATA *70, 106, 162*
Woodruff, Joan Leslie 1953- *104*
Woodruff, Liza 1971(?)- *182*
Woodruff, Marian
  See Goudge, Eileen
Woodruff, Noah 1977- *86*
Woods, George A(llan) 1926-1988 .... *30*
  Obituary *57*
Woods, Geraldine 1948- *111*
  Brief entry *42*
  Earlier sketch in SATA *56*
Woods, Harold 1945- *56*
  Brief entry *42*
Woods, Lawrence
  See Lowndes, Robert A(ugustine) W(ard)
Woods, Margaret 1921- *2*
Woods, Nat
  See Stratemeyer, Edward L.
Woods, Titania
  See Weatherly, Lee
Woodson, Jack
  See Woodson, John Waddie Jr.

Woodson, Jacqueline 1964- *189*
  Earlier sketches in SATA *94, 139*
  See also CLR *49*
Woodson, Jacqueline Amanda
  See Woodson, Jacqueline
Woodson, John Waddie Jr. 1913- *10*
Woodtor, Dee
  See Woodtor, Delores Parmer
Woodtor, Dee Parmer 1945(?)-2002
  See Woodtor, Delores Parmer
Woodtor, Delores Parmer 1945-2002 .... *93*
Wood-Trost, Lucille
  See Trost, Lucille W(ood)
Woodward, (Landon) Cleveland 1900-1986 . *10*
  Obituary *48*
Woodworth, Chris 1957- *168*
Woodworth, Viki 1952- *127*
Woody, Regina Jones 1894-1983 .... *3*
Woodyadd, Charlotte
  See Hough, Charlotte
Woog, Adam 1953- *125*
  Earlier sketch in SATA *84*
Wooldridge, Connie Nordhielm 1950- *143*
  Earlier sketch in SATA *92*
Wooldridge, Frosty 1947- *140*
Wooldridge, Rhoda 1906-1988 .... *22*
Wooley, Susan Frelick 1945- *113*
Woolf, Paula 1950- *104*
Woolfe, Angela 1976- *169*
Woolley, Catherine 1904-2005 .... *3*
  Obituary *166*
Woolman, Steven 1969-2004 .... *163*
  Earlier sketch in SATA *90*
Woolsey, Janette 1904-1989 .... *3*
  Obituary *131*
Worcester, Donald E(mmet) 1915- *18*
Word, Reagan 1944- *103*
Work, Virginia 1946- *57*
  Brief entry *45*
Worline, Bonnie Bess 1914- *14*
Wormell, Christopher 1955- *154*
  Earlier sketch in SATA *103*
Wormell, Mary 1959- *96*
Wormser, Richard 1933- *106*
  Autobiography Feature *118*
  See also SAAS *26*
Wormser, Sophie 1897-1979 .... *22*
Worth, Richard
  See Wiggin, Eric E.
Worth, Richard 1945- *59*
  Brief entry *46*
Worth, Valerie 1933-1994 .... *81*
  Earlier sketches in SATA *8, 70*
  See also CLR *21*
Worthington, Leonie 1956- *200*
Wortis, Avi
  See Avi
Wortis, Edward Irving
  See Avi
Wosmek, Frances 1917- *29*
Woychuk, Denis 1953- *71*
Wrede, Patricia C(ollins) 1953- *146*
  Earlier sketch in SATA *67*
Wriggins, Sally Hovey 1922- *17*
Wright, Alexandra 1979- *103*
Wright, Betty Ren 1927- *109*
  Brief entry *48*
  Earlier sketch in SATA *63*
Wright, Cliff 1963- *168*
  Earlier sketch in SATA *76*
Wright, Courtni
  See Wright, Courtni C(rump)
Wright, Courtni C(rump) 1950- *84*
Wright, Courtni Crump
  See Wright, Courtni C(rump)
Wright, Dare 1914(?)-2001 .... *21*
  Obituary *124*
Wright, David K. 1943- *112*
  Earlier sketch in SATA *73*
Wright, Elinor
  See Lyon, Elinor

Wright, Enid Meadowcroft (LaMonte)
  1898-1966 .... *3*
Wright, Esmond 1915-2003 .... *10*
Wright, Frances Fitzpatrick 1897-1982 .... *10*
Wright, J. B.
  See Barkan, Joanne
Wright, Johanna *220*
Wright, Judith 1915-2000 .... *14*
  Obituary *121*
Wright, Judith Arundell
  See Wright, Judith
Wright, Katrina
  See Gater, Dilys
Wright, Kenneth
  See del Rey, Lester
Wright, Kit 1944- *87*
Wright, Leslie B(ailey) 1959- *91*
Wright, Michael 1954- *198*
Wright, Nancy Means *38*
Wright, R(obert) H(amilton) 1906- *6*
Wright, Rachel *220*
  Earlier sketch in SATA *134*
Wright, Susan Kimmel 1950- *97*
Wrightfrierson
  See Wright-Frierson, Virginia (Marguerite)
Wright-Frierson, Virginia (Marguerite)
  1949- *110*
  Earlier sketch in SATA *58*
Wrightson, Alice Patricia
  See Wrightson, Patricia
Wrightson, Patricia 1921-2010 .... *112*
  Obituary *215*
  Earlier sketches in SATA *8, 66*
  See also CLR *154*
  See also SAAS *4*
Wroble, Lisa A. 1963- *134*
Wrongo, I.B.
  See Katz, Alan
Wronker, Lili
  See Wronker, Lili Cassel
Wronker, Lili Cassel 1924- *10*
Wryde, Dogear
  See Gorey, Edward (St. John)
Wu, Donald *212*
Wu, Elizabeth
  See Wu, Liz
Wu, Liz *184*
Wu, Norbert 1961- *155*
  Earlier sketch in SATA *101*
Wulf, Linda Press *205*
Wulffson, Don 1943- *155*
  Earlier sketches in SATA *32, 88*
Wulffson, Don L.
  See Wulffson, Don
Wummer, Amy 1955- *201*
Wunderli, Stephen 1958- *79*
Wunsch, Josephine (McLean) 1914- *64*
Wunsch, Marjory 1942- *220*
  Earlier sketch in SATA *82*
Wuorio, Eva-Lis 1918- *34*
  Brief entry *28*
Wurts, Janny 1953- *98*
Wyatt, B. D.
  See Robinson, Spider
Wyatt, David 1968- *185*
Wyatt, Jane
  See Bradbury, Bianca (Ryley)
Wyatt, Melissa 1963- *177*
Wyatt, Valerie *209*
Wyeth, Betsy James 1921- *41*
Wyeth, N(ewell) C(onvers) 1882-1945 .... *17*
  See also CLR *106*
Wyler, Rose 1909-2000 .... *18*
  Obituary *121*
Wylie, Betty Jane *48*
Wylie, Laura
  See Matthews, Patricia
Wylie, Laurie
  See Matthews, Patricia
Wyllie, Stephen *86*
Wyman, Andrea *75*

Wyman, Carolyn 1956- *83*
Wymer, Norman (George) 1911- *25*
Wynard, Talbot
  See Hamilton, Charles (Harold St. John)
Wyndham, John
  See Harris, John (Wyndham Parkes Lucas)
  Beynon
Wyndham, Lee
  See Hyndman, Jane Andrews Lee
Wyndham, Robert
  See Hyndman, Robert Utley
Wynne, Patricia J. *210*
Wynne-Jones, Tim 1948- *186*
  Autobiography Feature *136*
  Earlier sketches in SATA *67, 96, 136*
  See also CLR *58*
Wynne-Jones, Timothy
  See Wynne-Jones, Tim
Wynter, Edward (John) 1914- *14*
Wynyard, Talbot
  See Hamilton, Charles (Harold St. John)
Wyss, Johann David Von 1743-1818 .... *29*
  Brief entry *27*
  See also CLR *92*
Wyss, Thelma Hatch 1934- *202*
  Earlier sketches in SATA *10, 140*

X

Xavier, Father
  See Hurwood, Bernhardt J.
Xuan, YongSheng 1952- *116*
  Autobiography Feature *119*

Y

Yaccarino, Dan *192*
  Earlier sketch in SATA *141*
Yadin, (Rav-Aloof) Yigael 1917-1984 .... *55*
Yaffe, Alan
  See Yorinks, Arthur
Yagher, Kevin 1962- *143*
Yakovetic, (Joseph Sandy) 1952- *59*
Yakovetic, Joe
  See Yakovetic, (Joseph Sandy)
Yamada, Utako 1963- *188*
Yamaguchi, Marianne (Illenberger) 1936- *7*
Yamaka, Sara 1978- *92*
Yamanaka, Lois-Ann 1961- *166*
Yamasaki, Katie *206*
Yancey, Diane 1951- *138*
  Earlier sketch in SATA *81*
Yancey, Richard *193*
Yancey, Rick
  See Yancey, Richard
Yang, Belle 1960- *170*
Yang, James 1960- *190*
Yang, Jay 1941- *12*
Yang, Mingyi 1943- *72*
Yarbrough, Camille 1938- *79*
  See also CLR *29*
Yarbrough, Ira 1910(?)-1983
  Obituary *35*
Yaroslava
  See Mills, Yaroslava Surmach
Yarrow, Peter 1938- *195*
Yashima, Taro
  See Iwamatsu, Jun Atsushi
Yates, Elizabeth 1905-2001 .... *68*
  Obituary *128*
  Earlier sketch in SATA *4*
  See also SAAS *6*
Yates, Janelle K(aye) 1957- *77*
Yates, John 1939- *74*
Yates, Kelly 1971- *208*
Yates, Louise 1983(?)- *218*
Yates, Philip 1956- *212*
  Earlier sketches in SATA *92, 149*

Yates, Raymond F(rancis) 1895-1966 .... *31*
Yaukey, Grace S(ydenstricker) 1899-1994 ... *80*
  Earlier sketch in SATA *5*
Yazzie, Johnson 1946- *205*
Ye, Ting-xing 1952- *106*
Yeahpau, Thomas M. 1975- *187*
Yeakley, Marjory Hall 1908- *21*
Yeatman, Linda 1938- *42*
Yeatts, Tabatha 1970- *215*
Yee, Brenda Shannon *133*
Yee, Lisa 1959- *218*
  Earlier sketch in SATA *160*
Yee, Paul 1956- *211*
  Earlier sketches in SATA *67, 96, 143*
  See also CLR *44*
Yee, Tammy *206*
Yee, Wong Herbert 1953- *172*
  Earlier sketches in SATA *78, 115*
Yeh, Chun-Chan 1914- *79*
Ye Junjian
  See Yeh, Chun-Chan
Yelchin, Eugene 1956- *196*
Yenawine, Philip 1942- *85*
Yensid, Retlaw
  See Disney, Walt(er Elias)
Yeo, Wilma (Lethem) 1918-1994 .... *81*
  Earlier sketch in SATA *24*
Yeoman, John 1934- *80*
  Earlier sketch in SATA *28*
  See also CLR *46*
Yep, Kathleen S. *203*
Yep, Laurence 1948- *213*
  Earlier sketches in SATA *7, 69, 123, 176*
  See also CLR *132*
Yep, Laurence Michael
  See Yep, Laurence
Yepsen, Roger B(ennet), Jr. 1947- *59*
Yerian, Cameron John *21*
Yerian, Margaret A. *21*
Yerxa, Leo 1947- *181*
Yetska
  See Ironside, Jetske
Yezerski, Thomas F. 1969- *190*
Yin *194*
Ylvisaker, Anne 1965(?)- *172*
Yoder, Carolyn P. 1953- *149*
Yoder, Carolyn Patricia
  See Yoder, Carolyn P.
Yoder, Dorothy Meenen 1921- *96*
Yoder, Dot
  See Yoder, Dorothy Meenen
Yoder, Walter D. 1933- *88*
Yohalem, Eve *219*
Yolen, Jane 1939- *194*
  Autobiography Feature *111*
  Earlier sketches in SATA *4, 40, 75, 112, 158*
  See also CLR *149*
  See also SAAS *1*
Yolen, Jane Hyatt
  See Yolen, Jane
Yonezu, Yusuke *196*
Yonge, Charlotte 1823-1901 .... *17*
Yonge, Charlotte Mary
  See Yonge, Charlotte
Yoo, Paula 1969(?)- *174*
Yoo, Taeeun *191*
Yoon, Salina 1972- *204*
Yorinks, Adrienne 1956- *171*
Yorinks, Arthur 1953- *200*
  Earlier sketches in SATA *33, 49, 85, 144*
  See also CLR *20*
York, Alison
  See Nicole, Christopher (Robin)
York, Andrew
  See Nicole, Christopher (Robin)
York, Carol Beach 1928- *77*
  Earlier sketch in SATA *6*
York, Rebecca
  See Buckholtz, Eileen (Garber)
  and Glick, Ruth (Burtnick)

York, Simon
  See Heinlein, Robert A.
Yoshida, Toshi 1911- *77*
Yoshikawa, Sachiko *181*
Yost, Edna 1889-1971
  Obituary *26*
Youd, C. S.
  See Youd, Samuel
Youd, Samuel 1922- *135*
  Brief entry *30*
  Earlier sketch in SATA *47*
  See also CLR *2*
  See also SAAS *6*
Youme
  See Landowne, Youme
Young, Amy L. *185*
Young, Anne Mortimer
  See Mortimer, Anne
Young, Bob
  See Young, Robert W(illiam)
  and Young, James Robert
Young, Carol 1945- *102*
Young, Catherine
  See Olds, Helen Diehl
Young, Clarence
  See Garis, Howard R.
  and Stratemeyer, Edward L.
Young, Collier
  See Bloch, Robert (Albert)
Young, Dan 1952- *126*
Young, Dianne 1959- *88*
Young, Dorothea Bennett 1924- *31*
Young, Ed 1931- *211*
  Earlier sketches in SATA *10, 74, 122, 173*
  See also CLR *27*
Young, Ed Tse-chun
  See Young, Ed
Young, Edward
  See Reinfeld, Fred
Young, E.L. 1973- *219*
Young, Elaine L.
  See Schulte, Elaine L(ouise)
Young, Emma L.
  See Young, E.L.
Young, James
  See Graham, Ian
Young, Jan
  See Young, Janet Randall
Young, Janet 1957- *188*
Young, Janet Randall 1919-1994 .... *3*
Young, Janet Ruth
  See Young, Janet
Young, Jeff C. 1948- *132*
Young, John
  See Macintosh, Brownie
Young, Judy 1956- *207*
  Earlier sketch in SATA *155*
Young, Judy (Elaine) Dockrey 1949- *72*
Young, Karen Romano 1959- *168*
  Earlier sketch in SATA *116*
Young, Ken 1956- *86*
Young, Lois Horton 1911-1981 .... *26*
Young, Louisa *161*
Young, Louise B. 1919- *64*
Young, Margaret B. 1922-2009 .... *2*
Young, Margaret Buckner
  See Young, Margaret B.
Young, Mary 1940- *89*
Young, Miriam 1913-1974 .... *7*
Young, Noela 1930- *89*
Young, (Rodney Lee) Patrick (Jr.) 1937- *22*
Young, Percy M(arshall) 1912-2004 .... *31*
  Obituary *154*
Young, Richard Alan 1946- *72*
Young, Robert W(illiam) 1916-1969 .... *3*
Young, Ross B. 1955- *150*
Young, Ruth 1946- *67*
Young, Sara
  See Pennypacker, Sara
Young, Scott A. 1918-2005 .... *5*

Young, Scott Alexander
  See Young, Scott A.
Young, Selina 1971-2006 .... *201*
Young, Vivien
  See Gater, Dilys
Younger, Barbara 1954- *108*
Youngs, Betty 1934-1985 .... *53*
  Obituary *42*
Younkin, Paula 1942- *77*
Yount, Lisa (Ann) 1944- *124*
  Earlier sketch in SATA *74*
Yourgrau, Barry *179*
Yuditskaya, Tatyana 1964- *75*
Yum, Hyewon *211*
Yumoto, Kazumi 1959- *153*

Z

Zach, Cheryl (Byrd) 1947- *98*
  Brief entry *51*
  Earlier sketch in SATA *58*
  See also SAAS *24*
Zacharias, Gary L. 1946- *153*
Zaffo, George J. (?)-1984 .... *42*
Zagarenski, Pamela 1969(?)- *183*
Zagwyn, Deborah Turney 1953- *138*
  Earlier sketch in SATA *78*
Zahares, Wade *193*
Zahn, Timothy 1951- *156*
  Earlier sketch in SATA *91*
Zaid, Barry 1938- *51*
Zaidenberg, Arthur 1908(?)-1990 .... *34*
  Obituary *66*
Zalben, Jane Breskin 1950- *170*
  Earlier sketches in SATA *7, 79, 120*
  See also CLR *84*
Zallinger, Jean (Day) 1918- *115*
  Earlier sketches in SATA *14, 80*
Zallinger, Peter Franz 1943- *49*
Zambreno, Mary Frances 1954- *140*
  Earlier sketch in SATA *75*
Zanderbergen, George
  See May, Julian
Zappa, Ahmet 1974- *180*
Zappa, Ahmet Emuukha Rodan
  See Zappa, Ahmet
Zappler, Lisbeth 1930- *10*
Zarchy, Harry 1912-1987 .... *34*
Zarin, Cynthia 1959- *192*
  Earlier sketch in SATA *108*
Zaring, Jane (Thomas) 1936- *40*
Zarins, Joyce Audy
  See dos Santos, Joyce Audy
Zaslavsky, Claudia 1917- *36*
Zaugg, Sandra L. 1938- *118*
Zaugg, Sandy
  See Zaugg, Sandra L.
Zaunders, Bo 1939- *137*
Zawadzki, Marek 1958- *97*
Zebra, A.
  See Scoltock, Jack
Zebrowski, George 1945- *67*
Zebrowski, George T.
  See Zebrowski, George
Zecca, Katherine *207*
Zeck, Gerald Anthony 1939- *40*
Zeck, Gerry
  See Zeck, Gerald Anthony
Zed, Dr.
  See Penrose, Gordon
Zei, Alki 1925- *24*
  See also CLR *6*
Zeier, Joan T(heresa) 1931- *81*
Zeinert, Karen 1942-2002 .... *137*
  Earlier sketch in SATA *79*
Zeises, Lara M. 1976- *184*
  Earlier sketch in SATA *145*
Zelazny, Roger 1937-1995 .... *57*
  Brief entry *39*

Zelazny, Roger Joseph
   See Zelazny, Roger
Zeldis, Malcah 1931- 146
   Earlier sketch in SATA *86*
Zelinsky, Paul O. 1953- 154
   Brief entry *33*
   Earlier sketches in SATA *49, 102*
   See also CLR *55*
Zellan, Audrey Penn
   See Penn, Audrey
Zemach, Harve
   See Fischtrom, Harvey
Zemach, Kaethe 1958- 149
   Brief entry *39*
   Earlier sketch in SATA *49*
Zemach, Margot 1931-1989 .... *70*
   Obituary *59*
   Earlier sketch in SATA *21*
Zemach-Bersin, Kaethe
   See Zemach, Kaethe
Zeman, Ludmila 1947- 153
Zepeda, Gwendolyn 1971- 206
Zephaniah, Benjamin 1958- 189
   Earlier sketches in SATA *86, 140*
Zephaniah, Benjamin Obadiah Iqbal
   See Zephaniah, Benjamin
Zephaniah, Benjamin Pbadiah Iqubal
   See Zephaniah, Benjamin
Zerman, Melvyn Bernard 1930-2010 .... *46*
Zettner, Pat 1940- *70*
Zevin, Gabrielle 176
Zhang, Christopher Zhong-Yuan 1954- *91*
Zhang, Song Nan 1942- 170
   Earlier sketch in SATA *85*
Ziefert, Harriet 1941- 205
   Earlier sketches in SATA *101, 154*
Ziegler, Jack (Denmore) 1942- *60*
Ziemienski, Dennis (Theodore) 1947- *10*
Ziliox, Marc
   See Fichter, George S.
Zillah
   See Macdonald, Zillah K(atherine)
Zim, Herbert S(pencer) 1909-1994 .... *30*
   Obituary *85*
   Earlier sketch in SATA *1*
   See also CLR *2*
   See also SAAS *2*

Zim, Sonia Bleeker 1909-1971 .... *2*
   Obituary *26*
Zima, Gordon 1920- *90*
Zimelman, Nathan 1921- *65*
   Brief entry *37*
Zimmer, Dirk 1943- 147
   Earlier sketch in SATA *65*
Zimmer, Tracie Vaughn 169
Zimmerman, Andrea 1950- 192
   Earlier sketch in SATA *123*
Zimmerman, Andrea Griffing
   See Zimmerman, Andrea
Zimmerman, H. Werner 1951- 101
Zimmerman, Heinz Werner
   See Zimmerman, H. Werner
Zimmerman, Naoma 1914-2004 .... *10*
Zimmermann, Arnold E. 1909- *58*
Zimmermann, Karl 1943- 211
Zimmermann, Karl R.
   See Zimmermann, Karl
Zimmett, Debbie
   See Becker, Deborah Zimmett
Zimmy
   See Stratemeyer, Edward L.
Zimnik, Reiner 1930- *36*
   See also CLR *3*
Zindel, Bonnie 1943- *34*
Zindel, Lizabeth 187
Zindel, Paul 1936-2003 102
   Obituary 142
   Earlier sketches in SATA *16, 58*
   See also CLR *85*
Ziner, Feenie
   See Ziner, Florence
Ziner, Florence 1921- *5*
Zingara, Professor
   See Leeming, Joseph
Zinger, Yitskhok
   See Singer, Isaac Bashevis
Zink, Michelle 1969- 220
Zion, Eugene 1913-1975 .... *18*
Zion, Gene
   See Zion, Eugene
Zobel, Allia
   See Zobel Nolan, Allia
Zobel Nolan, Allia 218
Zoehfeld, Kathleen Weidner 1954- 193

Zohorsky, Janet R. 1958- 148
Zolkower, Edie Stoltz 171
Zolkowski, Cathy (A.) 1969- 121
Zollars, Jaime 191
Zolotow, Charlotte 1915- 138
   Earlier sketches in SATA *1, 35, 78*
   See also CLR 77
Zolotow, Charlotte Gertrude Shapiro
   See Zolotow, Charlotte
Zolotow, Ellen
   See Dragonwagon, Crescent
Zonderman, Jon 1957- *92*
Zonia, Dhimitri 1921- *20*
Zonta, Pat 1951- 143
Zubrowski, Bernard 1939- *90*
   Earlier sketch in SATA *35*
Zubrowski, Bernie
   See Zubrowski, Bernard
Zucker, Miriam S.
   See Reichert, Miriam Zucker
Zuckerman, Amy 217
Zuckerman, Linda 190
Zudeck, Darryl 1961- *61*
Zug, Mark 204
Zupa, G. Anthony
   See Zeck, Gerald Anthony
Zupancic, Lilijana Praprotnik
   See Prap, Lila
Zurbo, Matt(hew) 1967- *98*
Zurhorst, Charles (Stewart, Jr.) 1913-1989 .. *12*
Zurlo, Tony 1941- 145
Zuromskis, Diane
   See Stanley, Diane
Zuromskis, Diane Stanley
   See Stanley, Diane
Zusak, Markus 1975- 149
Zwahlen, Diana 1947- *88*
Zweifel, Frances W. 1931- *14*
Zwerger, Lisbeth 1954- 194
   Earlier sketches in SATA *66, 130*
   See also CLR *46*
   See also SAAS *13*
Zwinger, Ann (H.) 1925- *46*
Zymet, Cathy Alter 1965- 121